OCCASIONAL PUBLICATIONS
OF THE
NAVY RECORDS SOCIETY

Vol. 1

THE COMMISSIONED SEA OFFICERS OF THE ROYAL NAVY 1660–1815

THE NAVY RECORDS SOCIETY was established in 1893 for the purpose of printing unpublished manuscripts and rare works of naval interest. The Society is open to all who are interested in naval history, and any person wishing to become a member should apply to the Hon. Secretary, c/o Barclays de Zoete Wedd Limited, Ground Floor, Minster House, 12 Arthur Street, London EC4R 9BJ. The annual subscription is £15, which entitles the member to receive one free copy of each work issued by the Society in that year, and to buy earlier issues at much reduced prices.

SUBSCRIPTIONS and orders for back volumes should be sent to the Membership Secretary, 5 Goodwood Close, Midhurst, West Sussex GU29 9JG.

THE COMMISSIONED SEA OFFICERS OF THE ROYAL NAVY 1660–1815

Edited by

David Syrett, Ph.D., F.R. Hist. S.
Professor of History, Queens College, City University of New York

R.L. DiNardo, Ph.D.
Assistant Professor of History, Saint Peter's College

PUBLISHED BY SCOLAR PRESS
FOR THE NAVY RECORDS SOCIETY
1994

Published by
SCOLAR PRESS
Gower House
Croft Road
Aldershot
Hants GU11 3HR
England

Ashgate Publishing Company
Old Post Road
Brookfield
Vermont 05036
USA

Revised and enlarged version of the unpublished listing typed and printed by the Admiralty in 1954

British Library Cataloguing in Publication Data

Commissioned Sea Officers of the Royal Navy, 1660–1815.
I. Syrett, David II. DiNardo, R. L.
III. Series
359. 332

ISBN 1 85928 122 2

Typeset in 10 point Times by Raven Typesetters, Chester
Printed and bound in Great Britain by Bookcraft Ltd, Midsomer Norton.

Contents

Introduction

In updating and revising a work of this nature, a series of issues had to be addressed. First, how much revision did the original work require? How much additional information should be included? Finally, which of the sources used in updating the work could be trusted, and which were suspect? Hopefully this introduction will answer these questions, and give the reader a better idea as to exactly what we have done.

A work of this size was bound to contain errors and omissions, no matter how meticulous the original compiler of the list, Mr. David Bonner-Smith, was in assembling the original list. A few examples will suffice to illustrate this. In the original list, Robert Sansum is listed as dying on 3 January 1665. In fact, he was killed at the battle of Lowestoft on 3 June 1665. In addition, we found many officers who were omitted from the original list, in particular officers who were commissioned during the War of the Spanish Succession. The original list was also incomplete in many ways, in that the death dates of many officers were not included, nor were the subsequent careers of officers initially commissioned during the French Revolutionary and Napoleonic Wars. Thus, the list was clearly in need of updating and revision.

The most drastic difference between this version and the original list is the amount of information added. In addition to the naval ranks as listed in the original, some naval administrative positions have been added. Aside from naval ranks, naval officers, especially those of flag rank or destined for flag rank, were sometimes awarded commissions as colonels or generals in the Royal Marines as sinecures, until the practice was discontinued under Queen Victoria in 1839. During the seventeenth century and right up through the War of the Spanish Succession, naval officers could also hold army ranks, which have also been included. We have also indicated when officers were placed on half-pay, although this applies mainly to officers commissioned in the latter stages of Napoleonic Wars. The dates of superannuated or retired ranks are included as well. During the eighteenth and early nineteenth centuries the term 'superannuated' was used, while 'retired' was used later. For purposes of simplicity, we have made 1825 the dividing line. Officers who retired before 1825 are superannuated, while the term 'retired' is used for all officers who retired during or after 1825. It should be pointed out that when officers were retired with the rank of commander, most retired commanders were placed on the junior list of retired commanders, and then eventually promoted to the list of senior retired commanders. In these cases only the initial date of retirement is provided.

Some of these officers also served in Parliament. Their dates of service are recorded, as well as the constituency they represented. Service in the Irish Parliament is also noted. Finally, we have included honours and titles, such as knighthoods (including foreign knighthoods), baronetcies and peerages, and whether they were created or inherited.

We have also tried to give as much information as possible as to how these men died. This would involve including details as to who was killed in action, drowned, murdered, killed in a duel, executed (including the charge whenever possible), or committed suicide.

Before we go on to discuss the sources used in updating the list, a word must be included on dates. Prior to 1752, the old-style Julian calendar was used in England, as opposed to the new-style Gregorian, which was used in most of Europe. As this is a work of British history, we have used the old-style dating as far as has been possible. Thus, in this work, the date of the battle of Lowestoft is 3 June 1665, not 13 June 1665, while the Four Day Battle is 1–4 June 1666, not 11–14 June 1666. With this calendar, however, we will start the new year on 1 January, not 25 March. Thus, a date in the *London Gazette* given as 21 February 1742/3, would simply be given here as 21 February 1743. After 1752, of course, all dates are in the new style.

The updating of this work involved the use of a number of sources. Each one of these had strengths and weaknesses. The most basic sources used were biographical dictionaries. The most well-known of these would be the *Dictionary of National Biography*.[1] This is useful but limited, in that it covers only figures in naval history who could be considered 'famous.' Also, all of the entries for naval figures in the *Dictionary of National Biography* were written by Sir John Laughton, which was something of a weakness, in that some individuals are dealt with in far more detail than others.

Surprisingly enough , the *Dictionary of American Biography*[2] proved somewhat useful, especially in providing information on some officers who became pirates, especially after the end of the War of the Spanish Succession. The *Dictionary of Canadian Biography*[3] and the *Dictionary of Australian Biography*[4] provided information on figures involved in Canadian and Australian history.

Perhaps the two most useful biographical dictionaries in revising the work were the biographical dictionaries done by John Marshall[5] during the 1820s and by William O'Byrne[6] in the 1840s. These dictionaries were primary sources for tracing the careers of officers commissioned during the French Revolutionary and Napoleonic Wars. An incomplete second edition of O'Byrne was published in 1861, but it was not consulted.

The revision and updating of this list was also greatly aided by the recent profusion of biographical studies. The massive *History of Parliament* series proved very useful. In particular, the volumes by Basil Henning[7] covering the period 1660–1690, were important as information on seventeenth century figures is hard to come by. The eighteenth century was covered by the volumes done by Sir Lewis Namier and John Brooke,[8] and Romney Sedgwick.[9] Thorne's[10] three volumes brought it up into the early nineteenth century.

The next major series of sources were primary sources. These would include journals, letters, diaries and dispatches. These in particular were invaluable for the seventeenth century. The collected volumes of the Navy Records Society contain a multitude of sources. Information on the Second Dutch War was provided by the *Rupert-Monck Letter Book*,[11] especially the Four Days Battle and the St. James Day battle. *The Journal of Edward Montague, First Earl of Sandwich*[12] produced the list of captains killed at the battle of Bergen, 2 August 1665. The Third Dutch War was covered by the Navy Records Society volume *Journals and Narratives of the Third Dutch War.*[13] This volume contains the journals of Richard Haddock, Sir John Narbrough, and Sir Edward Spragg, as well as many others. *The Diary of Sir Thomas Allin*[14] covers both the Second and Third Dutch Wars. Some information was provided by *The Diary of Samuel Pepys.*[15] For the eighteenth century and the French Revolutionary and Napoleonic periods, only a few Navy Records Society volumes were used, including *The Saumarez Papers*,[16] which dealt with British activities in the Baltic during the Napoleonic Wars. The New-York Historical Society's edition of *Letter Books and Order Book of Admiral Lord Rodney*[17] covers the campaign which culminated in the battle of the Saints on 12 April 1782.

The single most utilized primary source for this work throughout the period 1665–1815 and even later is the *London Gazette*. The *London Gazette*, the official newspaper of the British government, was established initially as the *Oxford Gazette*. Its great importance to us lay in the fact that it printed commanders' dispatches. This was important for tracking down officers killed in action during this period. The *London Gazette* was also useful because as the promotion of flag officers became regularized, the promotion lists were published in it. These were helpful in tracing the careers of officers after 1815. The bestowing of knighthoods and baronetcies was also published. We used the *London Gazette* as a source until 1850. The year 1850 was used as a stopping point because by that time it yielded diminishing returns.

Another set of sources is lists. One such list is *The Trafalgar Roll*[18] which lists all those officers who were present at the battle of Trafalgar, including whether they were killed or wounded in the battle. Charles Dalton's *English Army Lists and Commission Registers 1661–1714*[19] was an important source due to the peculiarities of military service during the later Stuart period. Two volumes of the Institute of Historical Research's *Office-Holders in Modern Britain* series are important for *Admiralty Officials*[20] and *Navy Board Officials*[21]. These contain lists of the holders of administrative positions between 1660 and 1870. And the Navy Records Society's *Queen Anne's Navy*[22] gives some useful information, especially relating to those who were Commissioners of Dockyards and on the Victualling Board during the War of the Spanish Succession.

Two secondary histories were also consulted for this work. By far the more important of the two was *The History of the Royal Navy*, a six volume work by one of the pioneers of the 'new' naval history, Sir William Laird Clowes.[23] Clowes' history covered the entire period encompassed in our work in depth. Aside from a number of useful lists of flag officers, Clowes provided a great deal of information on the fate of officers during the period, especially with regard to those killed in battle or, more commonly, drowned in shipwrecks or storms. For the period of the French Revolutionary and Napoleonic Wars, *The History of the Royal Navy* by William James[24] was also consulted. Although much more suspect in terms of accuracy as compared to Clowes, James was useful in that he covered in detail a number of minor ship actions not dealt with by Clowes or published in the *London Gazette*.

The most information for this new edition of *Commissioned Sea Officers* came from lists of annotations, corrections and additions to the original work made in the National Maritime Museum and Public Record Office. The staff of the Public Record Office extensively annotated with additions and corrections their copies of the original *Commissioned Sea Officers*. At the National Maritime Museum, C.G. Pitcairn-Jones also added extensive information to his copy of the list, while Commander William May, A.W.H. Pearsall, and others at the National Maritime Museum also made lists of corrections and additions to *Commissioned Sea Officers*. The collective efforts of the staffs of the National Maritime Museum and the Public Record Office provided the bulk of the data used in the updating of *Commissioned Sea Officers*.

Finally, since much of the revision consists of finding out when officers died, two sets of obituaries were used. For the eighteenth century, we used the lists of obituaries compiled by William Musgrave, published as part of the *Publications of the Harleian Society.*[25] The other obituaries used were those in the *London Times*. We used this source until 1850, when it too became subject to the law of diminishing returns.

As might be assumed from the preceding pages, in updating the work we were confronted by a veritable blizzard of data. How could conflicting data be judged? Which sources were more reliable, and which were suspect? Basically, the major criterion was completeness of information. If one of the sources provided only a year, while another gave a complete date, then the second source was used. Sources which included additional information, such as noting if an officer was killed in action, drowned or executed, always took precedence.

Naturally, some sources were considered more reliable than others. For us, perhaps the most reliable source was the *London Gazette*, as the material there was based on official dispatches. Certainly the next best materials overall were the various lists of annotations and corrections, with the material produced by Pitcairn-Jones, others at the National Maritime Museum and the Public Record Office, being especially valuable for its comprehensive nature. The works by Marshall and O'Byrne were useful, but were limited in that they applied to only a relatively small number of officers out of the total. In many cases the sources contained the same information, so the source listed would be the one being used at the time. In other cases, where sources provided conflicting data with no certainty, sheer guesswork was used. The two least reliable sources were probably Musgrave and James. These sources were used only when nothing else or nothing more detailed was available.

We have retained the format of the original edition of *Commissioned Sea Officers*. That is, an alphabetical listing of entries in two columns running down the left hand side of the page and then continuing down the right hand side of the page. We have also reprinted the original edition's introductory sections 'NOTES ON SOURCES', 'NOTES ON DATES', 'HISTORY OF THE LIST', and 'SCOPE AND NATURE OF THE LIST'. But we have altered the format and contents of the introductory section 'ABBREVIATIONS USED IN THE LIST'. All new material which we have added to the original listing is shown by parenthesis which appear to the right of a particular line of an entry. Within the parenthesis appears an abbreviation which denotes the source from which this new information was obtained. For example:

ADAMSON, John	
T	
L	6 July 1811
CR	7 Mar 1853 (PRO)
d	25 Sept 1874 (NMM)

This shows that John Adamson was commissioned a lieutenant on 6 July 1811, and this information was in the original listing of *Commissioned Sea Officers*. Adamson was also promoted to commander on 7 March 1853 and died on 25 September 1874. The information on his promotion to commander, as is shown by the abbreviation within the parenthesis, was obtained from the annotated copy of *Commissioned Sea Officers* at the Public Record Office and the date of his death is from one of the lists of corrections and additions to *Commissioned Sea Officers* at the National Maritime Museum. The T in the entry shows that Adamson was present at the Battle of Trafalgar. This is the only new information which is not denoted by an abbreviation within parenthesis.

A project of this magnitude could not have been accomplished without the assistance of a number of people and institutions in the United Kingdom and the United States.

Our special thanks go to Kathleen Williams and Carol Bilous. Without their assistance this project would not have been completed.

Many other people also helped us in many ways. In America we would like to thank Scott Rosenthal, Mary Hansen and Judy Salwen; Marie Capps of the United States Military Academy Library; Joe Little of the Computer Science Department of Saint Peter's College; Ruth Liss, Mary Ann Conti, Arlene Diamond and Genie Pagano of Queens College, CUNY; the staffs of the New-York Historical Society and Yale University libraries.

In Britain we would like to thank the staffs of the Institute of Historical Research of the University of London, the Public Record Office, and the National Maritime Museum. We also wish to express our appreciation to P.G.W. Annis,

Royal Artillery Institution; Roger Knight and Roger Morriss of the National Maritime Museum; and A.W.H. Pearsall.

We are wholly responsible for any sins of omission and commission in this volume.

D.S.
R.L.D.

NOTES

1. *The Dictionary of National Biography* (London: Humphry Milford for the Oxford University Press, 1920–1922).
2. *Dictionary of American Biography* (New York: Charles Scribner's Son, 1928–1936).
3. *Dictionary of Canadian Biography* (Toronto: University of Toronto Press, 1960–1991).
4. *Dictionary of Australian Biography* (Sydney: Angus and Robertson, 1949).
5. John Marshall, *Royal Navy Biography* (London: Longmans, 1823).
6. William Richard O'Byrne, *A Naval Biographical Dictionary* (London: Murray, 1849).
7. Basil Duke Henning, *History of Parliament: The House of Commons, 1660–1690* (London: Secker and Warburg, 1983).
8. Sir Lewis Namier and John Brooke, *The History of Parliament: The House of Commons 1754–1790* (London: HMSO, 1964).
9. Romney Sedgwick, *The History of Parliament: The House of Commons, 1715–1754* (London: HMSO, 1970).
10. R.G. Thorne, *The History of Parliament: The House of Commons, 1790–1820* (London: Secker & Warburg, 1986).
11. J.R. Powell and E.T. Timings, eds., *The Rupert and Monck Letter Book, 1666* (London: The Navy Records Society, 1969).
12. R.C. Anderson, ed., *The Journal of Edward Montague, First Earl of Sandwich* (London: The Navy Records Society, 1928).
13. R.C. Anderson, ed., *Journals and Narratives of the Third Dutch War* (London: The Navy Records Society, 1946).
14. R.C. Anderson, ed., *The Journals of Sir Thomas Allin, 1660–1678* 2 Vols. (London: The Navy Records Society, 1939–1940).
15. Robert Latham and William Matthews, eds., *The Diary of Samuel Pepys: A New and Complete Transcription* 11 Vols. (London: 1970).
16. A.N. Ryan, *The Saumarez Papers: The Baltic 1808–12* (London: The Navy Records Society, 1968).
17. Collections of the New-York Historical Society for the Year 1932, *Letter Books and Order-Book of George, Lord Rodney, 1780–1782* (New York: New-York Historical Society, 1932).
18. Robert H. Mackenzie, *The Trafalgar Roll* (London: Allen, 1913).
19. Charles Dalton, *English Army Lists and Commission Registers, 1661–1714* (London: Eyre and Spottiswoode: reprinted London: Francis Edwards, 1960).
20. John C. Scainty, *Admiralty Officials, 1660–1870* (London: Athlone Press for University of London, Institute of Historical Research, 1975).
21. J.M. Collinge, *Navy Board Officials, 1660–1832* (London: Athlone Press for University of London, Institute of Historical Research, 1978).
22. R.D. Merriman, ed., *Queen Anne's Navy* (London: The Navy Records Society, 1961).
23. Sir William Laird Clowes, *The Royal Navy, A History From the Earliest Times to the Present* 6 Vols, (London: Low, Marston, 1897–1903).
24. William James, *The Naval History of Great Britain, 1793–1827,* 6 Vols. (London: Macmillan, 1937).
25. Sir William Musgrave, comp., *A Obituary of the Nobility, Gentry, etc. of England, Scotland and Ireland Prior to 1800* Sir George J. Armytage (ed.) (London: Harleian Society, 1899–1901).

Abbreviations

The Original Abbreviations

L	Lieutenant
CR	Commander
CA	Captain
RAB	Rear Admiral of the Blue
RAW	Rear Admiral of the White
RAR	Rear Admiral of the Red
RAD	Rear Admiral of Detached Squadron
VAB	Vice Admiral of the Blue
VAW	Vice Admiral of the White
VAR	Vice Admiral of the Red
VAD	Vice Admiral of Detached Squadron
AB	Admiral of the Blue
AW	Admiral of the White
AR	Admiral of the Red
AD	Admiral of Detached Squadron
AF	Admiral of the Fleet
SUP	Superannuated
Ret	Retired
d	died

Additional Abbreviations

Army and Marine Ranks

E	Ensign
L	Lieutenant
CA	Captain
M	Major
LC	Lieutenant Colonel
C	Colonel
MG	Major General
LG	Lieutenant General
H	Horse
F	Foot
GG	Governor of a Garrison
DGG	Deputy Governor of a Garrison
MR	Marine Regiment
FMR	First Marine Regiment
SMR	Second Marine Regiment
RM	Royal Marines

During the seventeenth century, sea officers also held ranks in the army or marines. In the case of officers with army commissions, the name of the regiment is mentioned. Since regiments were normally named for the commanding colonel, in cases where an officer was commissioned as colonel of a cavalry or infantry regiment, the name of the regiment is omitted as redundant. During the seventeenth century, the British maintained on permanent establishment a Marine Regiment, or a First and Second Marine Regiments. If an officer received a commission in a provisional marine regiment, the name of the regiment is included.

Naval Administrative Positions

COM AD	Commissioner of the Admiralty
COM N	Commissioner of the Navy
COM E	Extra Commissioner of the Navy
COM V	Commissioner of the Victualling Board
COMM	Commissioner of a Dockyard
CONT	Controller of the Navy
FSL	First Sea Lord
FLA	First Lord of the Admiralty
MCLHA	Member of Council of Lord High Admiral
GGH	Governor of Greenwich Hospital
LGH	Lieutenant Governor of Greenwich Hospital
TGH	Treasurer of Greenwich Hospital

Wherever possible, the full dates of an officer's tenure in an administrative position are included. Where an officer became commissioner of a dockyard, the name of the dockyard is included.

Civil Posts

MP	Member of Parliament
IMP	Member of Irish Parliament

In all cases, the name of the seat held is mentioned.

Awards and Honours

CB	Companion of the Bath
Kt	Knight of the Bath
KCB	Knight Commander of the Bath
GCB	Grand Cross of the Bath
GCMG	Grand Cross of the Military Garter
KH	Knight of Hanover
KCH	Knight Commander of Hanover
Kt (Country)	Foreign Knighthood
Bt	Baronet
EP	English Peerage
IP	Irish Peerage
Cre	Created
Inh	Inherited

Miscellaneous Abbreviations

KLB	King's Letter Boy
T	Present at the battle of Trafalgar
KIA	Killed-in-Action
e	executed

Wherever possible, in cases where an officer was executed, we have tried to include the charge for which he was executed.

Abbreviation of Sources

Biographical Dictionaries

DNB	*Dictionary of National Biography*
DAB	*Dictionary of American Biography*
DCB	*Dictionary of Canadian Biography*
DUB	*Dictionary of Australian Biography*
MB	*Royal Naval Biography* (Marshall)
OB	*Naval Biographical Dictionary* (O'Byrne)
MPH	*The House of Commons* (Henning)
MPS	*The House of Commons* (Sedgwick)
MPN	*The House of Commons* (Namier)
MPT	*The House of Commons* (Thorne)

Lists and Annotated Editions

HBC	*Handbook of British Chronology*
AL	*Army Lists*
EAD	*English Army Lists and Commission Registers 1661–1714*
NMM	National Maritime Museum
PRO	Public Record Office
PJP	Pitcairn-Jones Papers
PMM	Pearsall-May Microfilm
DDA	David Davies Addenda
AO	*Admiralty Officials*
NBO	*Navy Board Officials*
TR	*Trafalgar Roll*
QAN	*Queen Anne's Navy*
LTE	*Lawrence Trading Estate*

Primary Sources

LG	*London Gazette*
ESP	*Sandwich Papers*
PD	*Diary of Samuel Pepys*
FVT	*Torrington Papers*
NJ	*Narbrough's Journal*
SJ	*Spragg's Journal*
LJ	*Legge's Journal*
AJ	*Allin's Journal*
RM	*Rupert-Monck Letter Book*
SPB	*Saumarez Papers*
TBM	*Thomas Byam Martin Papers*
RLB	*Rodney's Letter Book*
WE	*Walker Expedition*

Obituaries

M	*Musgrave's Obituaries*
LT	*London Times*

Secondary Sources

JH	*Naval History of Great Britain* (James)
CH	*The Royal Navy* (Clowes)

Introductory Notes to the first listing

NOTE ON SOURCES

The principal sources from which this List is compiled are:–

			Reference* Letter(s)
I	Pepys's *Flag Officer*	Printed in *The Pepysian Mss* N.R.S. Vol. 26, 1904.	P.
II	Pepys's *Sea Officer* List, 1660–1688		
III	*House of Commons Journal*	2 Feb. 1698/9.	C.
IV	Admiralty '*Entitlement to Half Pay*' List, 18th Apr. 1700 Printed in *The Sergison Papers*, N.R.S. Vol. 89, 1949.		S.
V	'*Sea Officers*' Lists, 1717–1815		S.O.
VI	Chamberlayne's *Present State of Great Britain*. Various years between 1726 and 1748.		Ch.
VII	Rear Admiral *Hardy's* List, 1783.		H.
VIII	*Steel's* Lists, 1780–1815.		St.
IX	*Official Navy Lists*, 1814, 1815.		O.

* These reference letters are used in the present List only where there is a conflict of evidence over a date.

NOTE ON DATES

The decision to include Sources I and II above – the Pepysian Lists – has led to an apparent anomaly. In Pepys's day the terms 'Lieutenant', 'Captain', 'Admiral', etc. – now names of ranks – were not used at all in that sense. They were simply the names of 'posts', or 'appointments'. Thus in his lists many entries of this nature occur:–

Person	*Office*	*Ship*	*Date*
Boone, John	Captain	Wildboar Fireship	1666
	2nd Lieutenant	Warspight	1673

John Boone was not, of course, 'a captain' in the modern sense of 'rank' in 1666: nor was he 'demoted' in 1673 to 'a lieutenant' in rank. All that happened was that, in 1666, he had been given the 'post of Captain of the *Wildboar Fireship*', and, in 1673, the 'post of 2nd Lieutenant in the *Warspight*'. In fact the very idea of 'Rank' was unknown.

On the other hand, it is possible, in dealing with the names which occur in all the other Sources (III to IX), to arrange them in true 'ranks' – i.e., according to the modern method. Indeed, Sources III and IV were themselves instrumental in bringing in the idea, their principal object being to establish an order of seniority among officers who had held commands as Lieutenants and Captains: and the operative formula, in both III and IV, is 'With dates of their first Commission' i.e. their seniority in their rank.

Above 90 per cent of all the names in the whole List here presented can be dealt with in the modern, and natural, manner, which is to set out the various titles in the chronological order in which they occurred: viz. Lieutenant, Commander, Captain, etc. In the interests of uniformity, it has been decided to record the titles from the Pepysian lists in the same order as the rest, i.e. Lieutenant first, and the highest title reached last. But here is the apparent anomaly, for the entry cited above will now read:–

Boone, John

L	1673
CA	1666

HISTORY OF THE LIST

The original idea of such a List was conceived by the late Mr. David Bonner-Smith, Admiralty Librarian up to 1950. He began the work many years ago, transcribing into special notebooks the lists which he found in Sources III, V, VI and IX noted above. It was an immense and wearisome task, and he had finally used, and more or less filled, thirteen large notebooks. These formed the basis of the present work.

On his death, soon after retirement, the notebooks were forwarded by his widow to the Professor of History and English, R.N. College, Greenwich, who, in collaboration with the National Maritime Museum, especially the Keeper of Prints there, undertook to complete the work. This involved, first, the insertion into the 'Bonner-Smith' lists of all new names discoverable from Sources I, II, IV, VII and VIII: and, second, the making of an alphabetical Card Index of all the names now known. This latter step was necessary because, up till then, the names had been arranged in ranks and chronological seniority, not alphabetically. Under that arrangement, all Lieutenants figured in one set of Ms notebooks, all Commanders in another, and all Captains in a third etc. Thus, for instance, the name 'Horatio Nelson' appeared some eight times, and in several different notebooks. These steps were accomplished by the willing help of many volunteers, mainly from the R.N. College and the National Maritime Museum.

When this stage was completed, each card contained all the information known about the promotion-career of each officer, and the cards were in alphabetical order. The last process was the transcription of the contents of the cards into a continuous Alphabetical List. This work was done by a typist supplied by the Admiralty at the National Maritime Museum, under the supervision of the Keeper of Prints there. The reduplication was then undertaken by the Admiralty.

SCOPE AND NATURE OF THE LIST

The inclusion of the Pepys Lists carries the record back to 1660. At the other end, the List stops at 1815. There is no insuperable reason why it should not, ultimately, be extended forwards, from 1815 to the present day. The task, indeed, though long, and productive of a volume of somewhat unwieldy bulk, would be a great deal easier than that already undertaken here. Nor is the need for this later part so urgent.

The choice of 1815 as a finishing-date was not accidental. From 1814 the Admiralty began to produce its own official 'By Authority' Navy List. This publication from its inception, printed *two* lists – not only a Rank and a Seniority one, but also an Alphabetical List, arranged under ranks. It follows from this that:–

(1) All the necessary material for the continuation of the present List could be extracted from one series of volumes – the Official Lists.

(2) These, though not all exactly common, are far less rare, and much more readily available, than most of the earlier unofficial ones, and on the whole much more accurate.

(3) As all the Official 'By Authority' Lists include alphabetical lists, the search in them for any individual officer is a much simpler matter than it is in the earlier lists, in almost all of which – Source V is an exception – the names are arranged in rank and seniority only.

In fine, if the whole task of drawing up an Alphabetical List of Commissioned Officers from 1660 to the present day be divided into two halves, the natural point of division is 1815. And the present List is intended to deal with the first – and the harder – of the two halves only.

No claim is made, even so, that the present List contains the names of all officers commissioned up to 1815, nor that the dates of their promotions are in all cases accurate. For a great variety of reasons which only those who have worked on it would appreciate, perfection in either of these respects is hardly attainable: not at least without many more years of work, Indeed there is not, and probably never will be, a point at which it could be said, 'The List is without error, and complete'.

For this reason it is a difficult problem of policy to decide at what moment the List should be made available to potential users: whether to present it now, with all its known imperfections, or to hold it up until some of them are eradicated. The former alternative has been chosen, mainly on the grounds that more users will lead to the swifter discovery of more errors and omissions, and so hasten the process of improvement. The whole List, therefore, should be regarded, not as a finished article, but as a basis for a future and more definitive publication. In search of this, then, the cooperation of all users will be very welcome: and anyone noting any omission or error, however small, is earnestly invited to send his correction to: The Director, National Maritime Museum, Greenwich, S.E.10.

21st October, 1954.

[illegible] and the [illegible]

[illegible]

For this reason it is [illegible] to do [illegible] the first [illegible] attempts to [illegible] The former alternative has been chosen, mainly on the grounds that a [illegible] The whole list therefore should be regarded not as a finished model, rather a [illegible] the cooperation of all users will be very welcome [illegible] send his correction to The Director, National Maritime Museum, Greenwich, S.E.10.

ABBOTT, Peter Dupuy
L 25 July 1778
SUP CR 31 Jan 1787
d 16 May 1832 (LT)

ABBS, William
L 7 July 1762
d 20 Sept 1799 (PRO)

ABDY, Anthony
L 7 Feb 1800
CR 29 Apr 1802
CA 21 Oct 1810
d 19 June 1838 (PRO)

ABDY, Sir William
L 1 Feb 1758
CR 19 May 1761
CA 24 June 1766
d 21 July 1803 (NMM)

ABERDOUR, James
L 14 Feb 1799
CR 13 Oct 1807
CA 1 Dec 1812
d 1820 (PRO)

ABLESON, James
L
CA 1654 (PJP)
KIA 3 June 1665 (CH)

ABLESON, Richard
L 1666
d before 1689 (PJP)

ABOLSON, William
L 9 June 1810 (PRO)
Ret CR 6 July 1850 (NMM)
d 1867 (PRO)

ABSON, Samuel
L 22 Feb 1776
d (drowned) 1778 (PJP)

ACKERMAN, Stephen
L
CA 19 Apr 1678

ACKLAND, Charles Dyke
L 1 Jan 1814
CR 29 Jan 1822 (PRO)
CA 30 Jan 1828 (PRO)
d 23 Apr 1833 (PRO)

ACKLAND, Edward
L 17 Feb 1815
d 1849 (PRO)

ACKLAND, Thomas Palmer
L 3 Nov 1790
Ret CR 23 May 1823 (PRO)
d 1844 (PRO)

ACKLOM, George
L 11 Oct 1794
T
CR 24 Dec 1805
CA 8 Jan 1812
d 15 Sept 1837 (PRO)

ACKWORTH, William
L 11 Nov 1729
d 1734 (PRO)

ACLAND, Charles Dyke
See ACKLAND, Charles Dyke

A'COURT, Alexander
L 2 Mar 1734
CR 27 Sept 1740
d 1742 (PRO)

A'COURT, Edward Henry
L 13 Feb 1804 (MB)
CR 10 June 1808
CA 29 Mar 1811
RAB 6 Aug 1847 (PRO)
RAW 15 Sept 1849 (LG)
Ret VA 11 Sept 1854 (PJP)
d 22 Sept 1855 (PJP)

ACTON, Adam
L 1660
d 1746 (PRO)

ACTON, Edward
L
CA 3 Oct 1694
(8 Oct 1694 in C)
KIA 1 May 1707 (CH)

ACTON, John
L 6 Apr 1744
d 1746 (PRO)

ACTON, Richard
L 1661

ACTON, Thomas
L 1672 (P)
CA 24 June 1681
(28 May 1681 in H)
d 5 Aug 1698 (PRO)

ADAIR, Arthur Walter
L 7 Apr 1800
Struck off list 1806 (PRO)

ADAIR, James
L 20 Feb 1815
d 1818 (NMM)

ADAM, Sir Charles
L 8 Feb 1798
CR 16 May 1798
CA 12 June 1799
RAB 27 May 1825 (PRO)
RAW 22 July 1830 (PRO)
KCB 12 Aug 1835 (LG)
VAB 10 Jan 1837 (NMM)
VAW 23 Nov 1841 (PRO)
VAR 8 Nov 1847 (PRO)
AB 8 Jan 1848 (PRO)
AW 29 Apr 1851 (PRO)
d 16 Sept 1852 (PRO)

ADAMS, Charles
L 9 Nov 1803
CR 21 Jan 1824 (PRO)
d 16 Sept 1853 (PRO)

ADAMS, Charles James
L 6 Mar 1815
d 1854 (PRO)

ADAMS, Jacob
L 26 Sept 1777
d 1816 (PRO)

ADAMS, John (1)
L 2 Feb 1815
d 1855 (PRO)

ADAMS, John (2)
L 16 Feb 1815

CR	10 Jan	1837 (PRO)
CA	18 Dec	1843 (PRO)
RAB	6 Feb	1863 (PRO)
RAW	5 Mar	1864 (PRO)
Ret RA	1 Apr	1866 (NMM)
d	17 Dec	1866 (PRO)
ADAMS, Michael		
L	23 Dec	1799
d	Sept	1823 (PRO)
ADAMS, Roger		
L	6 Dec	1739
CR	4 Dec	1744
CA	12 July	1745
d	17 Oct	1749
ADAMS, Thomas (1)		
L		1665
ADAMS, Sir Thomas (2)		
L	8 June	1757
CR	12 Nov	1759
CA	27 Aug	1760
d	3 Oct	1770 (PRO)
ADAMS, William (1)		
L	5 Feb	1747 (PJP)
CR		
CA	12 Mar	1748
d	28 Sept	1748
ADAMS, William (2)		
L	26 Mar	1750
CR	2 Aug	1758
CA	22 Sept	1759
d	3 Feb	1763
ADAMS, William (3)		
L	25 Apr	1797
Ret CR	20 Dec	1830 (PRO)
d		1832 (PRO)
ADAMS, William (4)		
L	9 Dec	1811
d		1818 (PRO)
ADAMSON, Alexander		
L	1 Feb	1796
d		1800 (PRO)
ADAMSON, Charles		
L		
CA	2 Sept	1695
d	27 Feb	1708
ADAMSON, John		
T		
L	6 July	1811
CR	7 Mar	1853 (PRO)
d	25 Sept	1874 (NMM)
ADDAMS, John		
L		1666 (DDA)
ADDEN, John		
L		
CA		1667
ADDERLY, Arden		
L	6 Apr	1804
CR	4 Aug	1806
CA	19 July	1814
Ret CA	1 Oct	1848 (PRO)
Ret RA	2 Sept	1850 (PRO)
Ret VA	14 May	1857 (PRO)
Ret A	16 June	1862 (PRO)
d	15 Jan	1864 (PRO)
ADDERSLY, Joseph		
L		1661
CA	24 Oct	1662 (DDA)
d	before	1689 (PJP)
ADDINGTON, William Sylvester		
L	12 Mar	1807
CR	22 July	1830 (PRO)
Ret CR	1 July	1851 (PRO)
Ret CA	1 Apr	1856 (PRO)
d	28 Jan	1863 (PRO)
ADDIS, Edward Brown		
L	9 Aug	1811
Ret CR	28 July	1851 (PRO)
d	13 Apr	1866 (PRO)
ADDIS, George		
L	9 Mar	1811
CR	28 July	1857 (PRO)
d	13 Apr	1863 (PRO)
ADDISON, James		
L	14 Jan	1780
d	30 Sept	1782 (PMM)
ADLINGTON, James		
L		
CR		
CA	7 Jan	1706
d		1710
ADSTON, James		
L	19 Nov	1757
d		1771 (PRO)
ADY, Henry		
L		1661
d	before	1689 (PJP)
ADYE, John Miller		
L	6 Jan	1797
CR	22 Jan	1806
CA	18 Sept	1815
d	10 Feb	1817 (PRO)
AFFLECK, Sir Edmund		
L	25 July	1746
CR	5 June	1756
CA	23 Mar	1757
MP	4 Mar	1782–
(Colchester)	19 Nov	1788 (MPN)
Cre Bt	10 July	1782 (MPN)
RAB	10 Feb	1784 (PRO)
RAR	24 Sept	1787
d	19 Nov	1788 (MPN)
AFFLECK, Philip		
L	28 May	1755
Seniority adjusted	3 May	1755
CR	1 Aug	1758
CA	20 Aug	1759
RAB	24 Sept	1787
RAW	21 Sept	1790
VAB	1 Feb	1793
COM AD	26 Apr	1793–
	7 Mar	1794 (AO)
VAW	12 Apr	1794
VAR	4 July	1794
AB	1 June	1795
AW	14 Feb	1799
d	21 Dec	1799 (DNB)

AFLECK, Thomas
L 18 June 1781
CR 30 Oct 1793
CA 9 June 1794
Seniority amended 8 Mar 1796 (PRO)
Sentenced by court martial to be incapable of ever commanding a King's ship and to be put at the bottom of the half pay list for life (PRO)
d 1805 (NMM)

AFLECK, William (1)
L 27 Oct 1761
CR 7 Apr 1772
CA 4 June 1774
d 25 Dec 1791 (PRO)

AFLECK, William (2)
L 11 Feb 1788
CR 22 Nov 1790
CA 26 Dec 1791
d 28 Feb 1794 (PRO)

AGAR, William Gapper
T
L 10 Sept 1806
CR 13 July 1824 (NMM)
d 6 Dec 1833 (PRO)

AGASSIZ, James John Charles
L 23 Sept 1795
CR 29 Apr 1802
Ret CA 10 Sept 1840 (NMM)
d Jan 1858 (NMM)

AGNEW, Alexander
L 7 Aug 1761
CR 20 Nov 1777
Dismissed 28 May 1781 (PJP)
d 7 Feb 1792

AIKENHEAD, John
L 14 Apr 1744
d 1763 (NMM)

AIKIN, Alexander
See AITKEN, Alexander

AINSLIE, George
L 1 Mar 1796
d 1797 (NMM)

AIRE, James
L
CA 28 May 1678
Dismissed 6 May 1682 (NMM)

AIRE, John
L 6 June 1794
d 1796 (PRO)

AIRE, Thomas
L 7 Sept 1815
d 1830 (PRO)

AIREY, George Taylor
L 17 Feb 1815
d 20 Apr 1851 (NMM)

AITCHINSON, Robert (1)
L 20 Aug 1779
d 31 Mar 1830 (PRO)

AITCHINSON, Robert (2)
L 6 May 1815
HP June 1815–
May 1816 (MB)
CR 17 July 1819 (PRO)
CA 30 Apr 1827 (PRO)
Ret CA 30 Apr 1847 (PRO)
Ret RA 7 Aug 1854 (NMM)
Ret VA 11 Feb 1861 (PRO)
d 13 Feb 1861 (PRO)

AITKEN, Alexander
L 11 Feb 1815
Ret CR 23 July 1860 (PRO)
d 1874 (PRO)

AKARMAN, Stephen
L
CA 18 Nov 1665

AKERS, Thomas
T
L 16 July 1813
Ret CR 15 Apr 1856 (PRO)
d 1863 (PRO)

ALBERMARLE, George Monck, Duke of
Cre EP 7 July 1660 (DNB)
Captain-General 3 Aug 1660 (DNB)
Joint AF 22 Feb 1665 (RM)
General at Sea Nov 1665 (DNB)
d 3 Jan 1670 (DNB)

ALCOCK, Richard
L 7 Dec 1804
CR 21 Mar 1812
d Oct 1827 (NMM)

ALDEBERGH, Richard
L 4 July 1695

ALDER, William
L 25 Apr 1783
Ret CR 4 Apr 1821 (PRO)
d 1842 (PRO)

ALDERSAY, Joseph
See ADDERSLEY, Joseph

ALDHAM, George
L 27 June 1792
CR 7 May 1802
CA 28 Feb 1805
d 18 Jan 1834 (PJP)

ALDRED, John
L 19 July 1693 (PJP)
CA 11 Feb 1697
d 3 Sept 1740 (M)

ALDRIDGE, John William
L 4 Feb 1815
CR 18 Nov 1833 (NMM)
CA 23 Nov 1841 (NMM)
Ret CA 13 Dec 1855 (PRO)
Ret RA 12 Apr 1862 (NMM)
Ret VA 24 May 1867 (NMM)
d 1875 (PRO)

ALEXANDER, Frederick Fraser
L 14 Feb 1815
d 11 May 1820 (PRO)

ALEXANDER, John (1)
L 17 Mar 1760
d 1785 (PRO)

ALEXANDER, John (2)
L 21 Jan 1783
Ret CR 21 Jan 1820 (PRO)
d Nov 1836 (PRO)

ALEXANDER, John (3)
L 28 Feb 1807

CR 14 Mar 1811
Ret CA 10 Sept 1840 (NMM)
d 23 Dec 1857 (NMM)

ALEXANDER, Nicholas
L 18 May 1806
CR 13 June 1815
Ret CR 1 July 1851 (PRO)
Ret CA 28 July 1851 (PRO)
d 1852 (PRO)

ALEXANDER, Scott
L Jan 1802 (MB)
CR 1809 (MB)
CA 19 Oct 1814 (MB)
CB 1815 (MB)
d 11 Nov 1825 (MB)

ALEXANDER, Thomas (1)
L 19 Nov 1790
CR
CA 27 Dec 1796
CB 4 June 1815 (LG)
RAB 12 Aug 1819 (PRO)
RAW 27 May 1825 (PRO)
VAB 22 July 1830 (PRO)
VAW 10 Jan 1837 (PRO)
AB 23 Nov 1841 (PRO)
d 10 Jan 1843 (LT)

ALEXANDER, Thomas (2)
L 9 Jan 1802
CR 11 Apr 1809 (PRO)
CA 19 Oct 1814
CB 1815 (PJP)
d 10 Jan 1843 (LT)

ALFORD, Thomas
L 30 Aug 1799
d 1801 (PRO)

ALFRAY, William
L 20 Aug 1777
d 1827 (PRO)

ALISON, James
L 3 Mar 1781
d 25 Dec 1791

ALLAN, George
L 23 Dec 1743
d 1757 (PRO)

ALLAN, Grant
L 21 Dec 1793
Ret CR 28 July 1829 (PRO)
d 14 Dec 1843 (PRO)

ALLAN, James (1)
L 14 Jan 1744
CR 24 July 1760
d 1768 (PRO)

ALLAN, James (2)
L 7 Feb 1806
d 14 Feb 1838 (PRO)

ALLAN, Thomas
See ALLEN, Thomas

ALLARDYCE, Titus
L 18 Mar 1795
Ret CR 26 Jan 1831 (PRO)
d 1832 (PRO)

ALLCOT, George
L 25 Mar 1807
d (drowned) 1808 (PJP)

ALLEN, Alexander
L 11 Aug 1776
d 19 Apr 1783 (LG)

ALLEN, Bennett
L 29 July 1697 (PMM)
CA 27 Feb 1699
Dismissed 1706 (PRO)
d Sept 1750

ALLEN, Charles
L 18 June 1799
HP Aug 1807– Sept 1808 (MB)
CR 7 July 1809
Ret CA 10 Sept 1840 (PRO)
d 9 Jan 1853 (PRO)

ALLEN, Charles Arthur
L 6 Mar 1815
d 1822 (PRO)

ALLEN, David (1)
L 18 Apr 1777
d 1798 (PRO)

ALLEN, David (2)
L 25 Oct 1806
d 1826 (PRO)

ALLEN, Edward
L 11 Oct 1712
CR
CA 19 May 1741
d (drowned) 20 Oct 1744 (CH)

ALLEN, Francis
L
CA 1661
d before 1689 (PJP)

ALLEN, George
L 18 Nov 1814
d 30 Apr 1828 (PRO)

ALLEN, George Bennett
L 9 Feb 1796
CR 18 Aug 1809
CA 19 July 1821 (PRO)
d 6 Feb 1830 (PRO)

ALLEN, Henry (1)
L 5 Apr 1727

ALLEN, Henry (2)
L 22 Nov 1790
e 22 Apr 1797 (PJP)

ALLEN, Henry (3)
L 22 Nov 1790
d 1796 (PRO)

ALLEN, James (1)
L 22 Mar 1759
d 1771 (PRO)

ALLEN, James (2)
L 21 Mar 1795
d 1813 (PRO)

ALLEN, James (3)
L 12 Jan 1798
d 1833 (PRO)

ALLEN, James (4)		
L	17 Jan	1810
d		1811 (PRO)
ALLEN, James Rich		
L	22 Feb	1815
Seniority reduced by court martial	23 Oct	1818 (PRO)
d		1833 (PRO)
ALLEN, John (1)		
L	21 Apr	1783
d		1792 (PRO)
ALLEN, John (2)		
L	10 Dec	1793
CR	6 Dec	1796
CA	29 Apr	1802
Ret RA	10 Jan	1837 (NMM)
RAW	17 Aug	1840 (NMM)
RAR	23 Nov	1841 (NMM)
VAB	9 Nov	1846 (NMM)
VAW	26 June	1847 (NMM)
VAR	15 Sept	1849 (NMM)
Ret VA	1 July	1851 (PRO)
Ret A	30 July	1852 (PRO)
d	4 June	1853 (NMM)
ALLEN, John (3)		
L	14 Sept	1807
CR	4 Feb	1814
CA	20 Sept	1815
Ret CA	1 Oct	1846 (PRO)
Ret RA	21 Mar	1851 (NMM)
d	23 Sept	1853 (NMM)
ALLEN, John Carter		
L	14 June	1745
CR	5 June	1757
CA	21 Mar	1758
RAW	24 Sept	1787 (CH)
RAR	21 Sept	1790
VAW	1 Feb	1793
VAR	12 Apr	1794
AB	1 June	1795
AW	14 Feb	1799
d	2 Oct	1800
ALLEN, Nathaniel (1)		
L	16 Sept	1746
d		1771 (NMM)
ALLEN, Nathaniel (2)		
L	16 Jan	1783
d		1795 (NMM)
ALLEN, Richard		
L	13 Apr	1782
CR	12 Nov	1796
d	22 Oct	1799 (PRO)
ALLEN, Robert		
L	28 Apr	1705
CR		
CA	8 May	1740
d	25 June	1751 (PRO)
ALLEN, Robert William		
L	3 Mar	1795
d		1799 (PRO)
ALLEN, Samuel		
L	19 Dec	1807
d		1846 (PRO)
ALLEN, Saunderson		
L	5 Feb	1808
Ret CR	3 Feb	1845 (PRO)
d	19 Aug	1851 (PRO)
ALLEN, Thomas (1)		
L		1673
CA	26 Mar	1678
d	3 May	1690
ALLEN, Thomas (2)		
L	22 Feb	1759
SUP CR	8 Apr	1801 (PMM)
Gone		1881 (PRO)
ALLEN, Thomas (3)		
L	23 Mar	1759
CR	13 Nov	1778
CA	7 June	1780
d		1780(1) (PRO)
ALLEN, Thomas (4)		
L	1 May	1791 (NMM)
Resigned		1798 (PRO)
ALLEN, Thomas (5)		
L	23 Nov	1801
Foundered on cyclone, but exact date not known (PRO)		
ALLEN, Thomas Griffiths		
L	16 May	1794
CR	6 Apr	1813
d	26 Sept	1814 (PJP)
ALLEN, William (1)		
L	1 July	1692
d	24 Oct	1696
ALLEN, William (2)		
L	10 July	1755
SUP L	12 Nov	1794 (PRO)
d		1801 (PMM)
ALLEN, William (3)		
L	17 May	1756
CR	21 Nov	1761
CA	20 June	1765
RAB	1 Feb	1793
RAR	12 Apr	1794
VAR	4 July	1794
VAW	1 June	1795
AB	14 Feb	1799
d	27 Oct	1804 (PRO)
ALLEN, William (4)		
L	2 Mar	1815
CR	20 June	1836 (PRO)
CA	31 Jan	1842 (PRO)
Ret CA	20 Dec	1855 (NMM)
Ret RA	12 Apr	1862 (PRO)
d	23 Jan	1864 (NMM)
ALLEN, William Edward Hughes		
T		
L	25 Mar	1807
CR	28 Aug	1828 (PRO)
CA	15 Aug	1851 (PRO)
d		1856 (PRO)
ALLENBY, Christopher		
L	8 Aug	1695
ALLEYN, Richard Israel		
L	13 Oct	1802
Ret CR	20 Apr	1835 (NMM)
d	Nov	1866 (PRO)

Name / Rank	Date	Year
ALLIN, Edward		
See ALLEN, Edward		
ALLIN, John		
See ALLEN, John		
ALLIN, Thomas		
See ALLEN, Thomas		
ALLIN, Sir Thomas		
L		
CA	29 Feb	1664 (DDA)
VAF		1664
AB		1665
AW	16 Mar	1666 (RM)
CONT	15 Apr	1671–
	28 Jan	1680 (NBO)
Cre Bt	7 Feb	1673 (NBO)
d	Oct	1685 (NMM)
ALLINGTON, Argenton		
L		1668
CA		1669
KIA	3 July	1670 (PJP)
ALLISON, James		
See ALISON, James		
ALLISON, John		
L	17 Dec	1794
CR	4 Oct	1825 (NMM)
d		1839
ALLISON, Thomas		
L	16 July	1740
CR		
CA	9 Feb	1746
SUP RA		1770
d	? 22 Mar	1776
ALLISON, Wenan		
L	16 Nov	1790
d	11 Nov	1795 (PMM)
ALLSOPP, William		
L	12 Mar	1811
d	Apr	1821 (PRO)
ALMES, Benjamin		
L	27 July	1740
d		1746 (PRO)
ALMES, George Pigot		
L	10 Apr	1780
d	12 Apr	1782 (PJP)
ALMES, James (1)		
L	14 May	1749
	(1 May	1749 in C)
CR	10 July	1761
CA	20 June	1765
d	8 June	1791 (NMM)
ALMES, James (2)		
L	26 July	1777
CR	24 Sept	1781
CR	20 Jan	1783
RAB	9 Nov	1805
RAR	28 Apr	1808
VAB	31 July	1810
VAW	12 Aug	1812
VAR	4 June	1814
d	27 June	1816 (PRO)
ALMES, James (3)		
L	28 Apr	1781
d	20 June	1791 (LT)
ALMES, James Edward		
L	23 Dec	1783

Name / Rank	Date	Year
Ret CR	4 Mar	1822 (PRO)
d	16 Jan	1831 (PRO)
ALMS, Benjamin		
See ALMES, Benjamin		
ALNER, William		
L	29 Apr	1797
d	1 June	1821 (PRO)
ALNWICK, William		
L	17 Feb	1778
d		1797 (NMM)
ALSTON, Peter		
L	8 May	1812
d		1817 (PRO)
ALT, Matthew Bowles		
L	31 July	1795
Ret CR	27 Jan	1835 (PRO)
d	13 July	1836 (LT)
AMBROSE, John		
L	20 June	1728
CR		
CA	27 Mar	1734
Dismissed	7 Nov	1745
Restored	12 May	1748 (PJP)
SUP RA	17 Apr	1750
d	25 Mar	1771 (DNB)
AMBROSE, Prosper		
T		
L	10 Feb	1810
d	1 Jan	1848 (PRO)
AMBROSE, William		
L	16 Jan	1741
d		1743 (PRO)
AMBROSS, Henry		
L	25 Mar	1799
Ret CR	26 Nov	1830 (PRO)
d	25 Dec	1839 (PRO)
AMHERST, Jeffrey Reid		
L	3 May	1815
Ret CR	20 Jan	1864 (PRO)
d	Mar	1880 (NMM)
AMHERST, John		
L	24 July	1739
CR		
CA	29 Dec	1744
RAB		1764 (CH)
RAW	18 Oct	1770
VAB	24 Oct	1770
VAW	5 Feb	1776 (CH)
VAR		1777 (C)
AB	29 Jan	1778
d	14 Feb	1778 (CH)
AMIEL, William Eardley		
L	21 Mar	1812
Ret CR	10 Oct	1860 (NMM)
d	2 Apr	1864 (PRO)
AMSINCK, William		
L	24 Aug	1781
d		1782(3) (NMM)
ANCELL, Robert		
L	8 June	1810
d		1843 (NMM)
ANDERSON, Charles		
L	24 Oct	1781
d (drowned)		1782 (PJP)

ANDERSON, David
L 15 Aug 1797
Ret CR 26 Nov 1830 (NMM)
d 31 Jan 1831 (NMM)

ANDERSON, George
L 28 Sept 1811
d 1835 (PRO)

ANDERSON, Henry
L 20 Aug 1794
d 1800 (PRO)

ANDERSON, Hugh
L 14 Aug 1801
CR 11 Feb 1823 (PRO)
d 9 Apr 1827 (PRO)

ANDERSON, James (1)
L 16 Apr 1695

ANDERSON, James (2)
L 20 Mar 1797
CR 22 Jan 1806
CA 1 Feb 1812
d 30 Dec 1835 (DNB)

ANDERSON, James (3)
L 29 Mar 1802
d July 1831 (NMM)

ANDERSON, James (4)
L 24 June 1808
CR 25 Nov 1823 (NMM)
Ret CA 1 Apr 1856 (NMM)
d 1869 (NMM)

ANDERSON, James (5)
L 19 Sept 1815
d 23 Feb 1824 (NMM)

ANDERSON, John (1)
L
CA 1666 (DDA)
CA 24 Sept 1693 (PRO)
SUP 1707 (NMM)
d 15 Apr 1724 (PRO)

ANDERSON, John (2)
L 9 May 1783
CR 18 Sept 1798
d 8 Oct 1815 (LT)

ANDERSON, John (3)
L 7 Jan 1802
Ret CR 13 Aug 1832 (NMM)
d 21 Jan 1843 (NMM)

ANDERSON, John (4)
L 28 Apr 1814
d 1835 (PRO)

ANDERSON, Kenneth
L
CA 19 Feb 1694
KIA 18 Apr 1697 (CH)

ANDERSON, Matthew
L 12 May 1758
d 1776 (NMM)

ANDERSON, Peter
L 3 May 1705
In Russian Service 1735 (PJP)

ANDERSON, Richard
L 21 Jan 1809
CR 13 Dec 1821 (NMM)
d 13 Mar 1831 (PRO)

ANDERSON, Robert
L 1665
CA 1665
d before 1689 (PJP)

ANDERSON, Walter
L 9 Dec 1777
d 1784 (PRO)

ANDERSON, William (1)
L 24 Apr 1782 (PRO)
SUP CR 18 July 1817 (NMM)
d 1849 (PRO)

ANDERSON, William (2)
L 7 Nov 1806
d 1837 (PRO)

ANDOE, James Hilary
L 4 Feb 1815
d 30 Jan 1851 (PRO)

ANDOE, Robert
L 12 Jan 1801
CR 3 Mar 1821 (PRO)
d 1835 (PRO)

ANDREW, George
L 12 Aug 1804
d 1826 (PRO)

ANDREW, John William
L 2 Apr 1806
CR 26 Sept 1811
CA 26 Sept 1812
CB 4 June 1815 (OB)
Ret RA 31 Oct 1846 (LG)
d 5 Jan 1854 (PJP)

ANDREW, William
L 3 Feb 1802 (NMM)
d 3 Feb 1802 (NMM)

ANDREWES, Thomas
See ANDREWS, Thomas

ANDREWES, Benjamin
L 27 May 1814
d 1852 (NMM)

ANDREWS, Edward (1)
L 4 May 1810
d 1826 (NMM)

ANDREWS, Edward (2)
L 20 July 1811
Ret CR 1 Oct 1852 (NMM)
d 12 June 1872 (PRO)

ANDREWS, George (1)
L 1 Dec 1787
CR 9 Nov 1795 (PRO)
CA 9 Apr 1796
d 23 July 1810 (NMM)

ANDREWS, George (2)
L 9 Mar 1797
CR 29 Apr 1802
CA 22 Sept 1809
d 16 June 1840 (NMM)

ANDREWS, George Rich
L 11 Apr 1809
d 1813 (NMM)

ANDREWS, Humphry
L 17 June 1795

ANDREWS, Isaac
L
CA 8 Dec 1694
KIA 28 July 1702 (CH)

ANDREWS, John (1)
L
CA 1664
d before 1665 (PJP)

ANDREWS, John (2)
L 6 Mar 1802
d 1810 (PRO)

ANDREWS, Robert
L 19 May 1747
d 1775(6) (NMM)

ANDREWS, Thomas (1)
L 1670
CA 1672
d before 1689 (PJP)

ANDREWS, Thomas (2)
L 17 Apr 1741
CR 15 July 1745
KIA 20 May 1756 (LG)

ANDREWS, William (1)
L
CA 1666
d before 1689 (PJP)

ANDREWS, William (2)
L 3 Feb 1802
d 20 May 1822 (NMM)

ANDROS, Charles
L 9 Aug 1814
Ret CR 15 Aug 1858 (NMM)
d 25 Jan 1879 (PRO)

ANGEL, Henry
L 25 June 1739
CR 24 July 1755
CA 23 Aug 1756
d 1777

ANGER, Merrick de L'
See L'ANGLE, Merrick de

ANGUISH, William
L 1666
CA 12 Apr 1670 (PRO)
Turned out Nov 1674 (PRO)
L 9 Apr 1677 (PRO)
CA 12 Apr 1678 (PRO)
d before 1689 (PJP)

ANLEY, William
L 13 June 1815
Ret CR 20 Jan 1864 (NMM)
d Mar 1880 (PJP)

ANNESLEY, Abraham
See ANNSLEY, Abraham

ANNESLEY, Charles
See ANSELEY, Charles

ANNESLEY, Hon. Francis Charles (1)
L 30 July 1794
Ret CR 26 Nov 1830 (NMM)
d Sept 1832 (PRO)

ANNESELEY, Francis Charles (2)
L 14 Jan 1808
CR 30 July 1814
d 30 June 1846 (NMM)

ANNESLEY, Henry
L 4 Apr 1720
CR
CA 2 June 1727
d 10 June 1728 (NMM)

ANNESLEY, James
L 11 June 1814
d 4 Nov 1822 (PRO)

ANNINGTON, Joseph
L 22 Aug 1759
SUP CR 22 Aug 1803 (PJP)
d 1817 (NMM)

ANNSLEY, Abraham
L
CA 1664
d Aug 1670 (DDA)

ANNSLEY, Henry
See ANNESLEY, Henry

ANSELL, Henry
L 20 Jan 1815
d 16 July 1829 (LT)

ANSELL, William
L 26 Feb 1745
LGH 1774 (PJP)
d 1782 (NMM)

ANSELEY, Charles
L 9 Mar 1679
d before 1688 (PD)

ANSON, George, Lord
L 19 May 1716 (PMM)
CR June 1722 (DNB)
CA 1 Feb 1724
RAB 23 June 1744
MP (Hendon) 1744 (MPS)
COM AD 27 Dec 1744–22 June 1751 (AO)
RAR 23 Apr 1745 (PRO)
VAB 14 July 1746
VAR 15 July 1747 (PRO)
Cre EP 15 July 1747 (MPS)
AB 12 May 1748
FLA 22 June 1751–17 Nov 1756 (AO)
AW June 1757
FLA 2 July 1757–6 June 1762 (AO)
AF 30 July 1761 (NMM)
d 6 June 1762 (DNB)

ANSRUTHER, Philip
L 3 Nov 1790
d 23 July 1796 (LT)

ANSRUTHER, Philip Charles
L 26 Mar 1796
d 23 Aug 1814 (NMM)

ANTHONY, Charles
L 29 Aug 1800
CR 29 Dec 1817 (PRO)
d 18 Aug 1846 (I)

ANTHONY, Henry
L 30 Apr 1795
Struck off list 1797 (NMM)

ANTHONY, Mark
T
L 22 Apr 1808

Ret CR	6 June	1848 (NMM)
d	June	1867 (PRO)
ANTRAM, Charles Aubrey		
T		
L	9 Nov	1810
d	13 June	1831 (PRO)
ANTRAM, George		
L	14 Dec	1802
d		1846 (NMM)
ANTRAM, Simon Edward		
L	14 July	1811
Ret CR	1 July	1852 (NMM)
d	22 Sept	1862 (PRO)
ANTROBUS, Charles		
L		
CR	15 Nov	1756
CA	17 Feb	1758
d	3 Nov	1769 (PRO)
APLIN, Benjamin		
L	16 May	1811
Ret CR	1 Apr	1852 (NMM)
d	21 Oct	1860 (PRO)
APLIN, Christopher D'Oyley		
L	7 May	1808
d	30 Dec	1820 (PRO)
APLIN, John George		
L	13 Feb	1808
CR	12 Mar	1814
CA	28 July	1826 (NMM)
Ret CA	1 Oct	1846 (PRO)
Ret RA	15 Apr	1854 (NMM)
Ret VA	2 May	1860 (PRO)
d	14 Apr	1861 (PRO)
APLIN, Peter		
L		
CR	23 Apr	1778
CA	23 Nov	1780 (NMM)
RAB	14 Feb	1799
RAW	1 Jan	1801
RAR	23 Apr	1804
VAW	9 Nov	1805
VAR	28 Apr	1808
AB	31 July	1810
AW	4 June	1814
d	17 Apr	1817 (DNB)
APPLEBY, John Frederick		
L	10 Feb	1815
CR	28 Aug	1828 (NMM)
CA	29 Jan	1838 (NMM)
Ret CA	6 Apr	1852 (PRO)
Ret RA	10 Sept	1857 (NMM)
Ret VA	9 Feb	1864 (NMM)
Ret A	10 Sept	1869 (NMM)
d		1878 (NMM)
APPLEBY, Robert Taylor		
L	20 Sept	1777
d (drowned)	30 Sept	1782 (CH)
APPLEBY, Thomas		
L	12 Nov	1761
d	24 July	1790 (PMM)
APPLEBY, Young		
L	4 Dec	1799
Ret CR	7 Jan	1840 (NMM)
d		1849 (PRO)
APREECE, William		
L	22 Jan	1806
Ret CR	10 July	1840 (NMM)
d		1859 (NMM)
APTHORP(E), Charles		
L	25 May	1781
CR	6 Jan	1797
d	3 Nov	1804 (PRO)
ARABIN, Augustus		
L	7 Mar	1815
d	11 Oct	1839 (NMM)
ARABIN, Septimus		
L	4 Aug	1807
CR	27 Aug	1814
CA	20 Mar	1823 (PRO)
Ret CA	1 Oct	1846 (PRO)
Ret RA	17 Dec	1852 (PRO)
d		1855 (PRO)
ARBUTHNOT, Sir Alexander Dundas Young		
T		
L	26 Oct	1809
CR	27 June	1814
Kt (Russia)		1823 (TR)
CA	14 Oct	1824 (NMM)
Kt (Spain)		1837 (TR)
Ret CA	1 Oct	1846 (NMM)
Ret RA	17 Sept	1853 (NMM)
Ret VA	6 Mar	1858 (NMM)
Kt		1859 (TR)
Ret A	30 Nov	1863 (NMM)
d	8 May	1876 (PRO)
ARBUTHNOT, Hon. James		
L	28 Apr	1810
CR	27 Oct	1813
d		1817 (NMM)
ARBUTHNOT, Marriot		
L	21 Aug	1739
CR	29 June	1746 (NMM)
CA	22 June	1747
COMM (Halifax)	July	1775–
	Feb	1778 (PJP)
RAW	23 Jan	1778
VAB	19 Mar	1779
VAW	26 Sept	1780
VAR	24 Sept	1787
AB	1 Feb	1793
d	31 Jan	1794 (CH)
ARCHBOLD, William		
L	9 Dec	1796
Ret CR	27 Aug	1834 (PRO)
d		1843 (NMM)
ARCHBOULD, Ralph		
L	24 Oct	1718
CR	28 Jan	1731
d		1767 (PRO)
ARCHDALL, Edward		
L	1 Jan	1782
SUP CR	12 Sept	1816 (NMM)
d		1822 (NMM)
ARCHER, Anthony		
L		
CA		1660
d		1680 (DDA)

ARCHER, Benjamin
L 15 Mar 1777
CR 31 Jan 1781
CA 18 June 1781
d 26 Oct 1795 (PRO)

ARCHER, Charles Frederick
L 23 Dec 1814
d 1826 (NMM)

ARCHER, John (1)
L
CA 1672
d before 1689 (PJP)

ARCHER, John (2)
L 23 Sept 1745
d 1761 (NMM)

ARCHER, John (3)
L 14 Sept 1809
d 1817 (NMM)

ARCHER, Richard
L 11 Sept 1795
d 1797 (PRO)

ARCHER, Robert Harding
L 25 Apr 1815
d 1826 (PRO)

ARCHER, Thomas
L 27 Dec 1808
CR 28 July 1851 (NMM)
d 24 Mar 1855 (PRO)

ARDEN, George
L 29 Nov 1814
d 1819 (NMM)

ARDEN, Samuel
L 18 July 1780
CR 15 Mar 1782
CA 21 Jan 1783
SUP CA 1805 (NMM)
d 12 Apr 1824 (NMM)

ARDESOIF, John Plummer
L 10 Oct 1759
CR 16 Nov 1779
CA 5 May 1781
d 21 May 1790

ARDESOIF, William Stratford
L 12 Dec 1794
d 1797 (PRO)

ARESKINE, Robert
See ARSKINE, Robert

ARGENT, Benjamin
L 1 Feb 1815
d 8 Feb 1824 (NMM)

ARGELES, George (1)
L 1 Dec 1794
CR 14 Feb 1801
CA 29 Apr 1802
d 2 July 1831 (NMM)

ARGELES, George (2)
L 10 Nov 1810
d 1846 (NMM)

ARGUIMBAU, John
L 20 Apr 1811 (PRO)
d 1818 (PRO)

ARGUIS, Edmond
L 30 Mar 1734

ARMIGER, John
L 19 Jan 1741
CR 28 Jan 1745
d before 1778 (NMM)

ARMIGER, Thomas
L 1666
d before 1689 (PJP)

ARMSTEAD, John
L 4 May 1810
d 1817 (PRO)

ARMSTRONG, John (1)
L 23 Aug 1742
d before 1753 (PRO)

ARMSTRONG, John (2)
L 10 July 1802
Ret CR 9 Mar 1835 (NMM)
d 1838 (NMM)

ARNALL, John
L 11 Feb 1813
d Mar 1825 (NMM)

ARNOLD, James Fearnley
L 4 May 1810
Ret CR 6 Apr 1850 (NMM)
d 24 Feb 1854 (NMM)

ARNOLD, John
L 27 Mar 1807
Ret CR 14 July 1842 (NMM)
d 1850 (PRO)

ARNOLD, Joseph
L 18 July 1810
d 1834 (PRO)

ARNOLD, Robert
L 1 June 1781
SUP CR 1 Jan 1816 (NMM)
d 1831 (NMM)

ARNOLD, Sampson
L 27 Oct 1758
d 3 July 1765 (PMM)

ARNOLD, Thomas
L 23 Oct 1708
CR 18 Oct 1726
CA 19 Sept 1727
d 10 Aug 1732 (NMM)

ARNOLD, William
L 8 Mar 1805
d May 1811 (NMM)

ARNITT, Robert
L 10 Apr 1740
d 1760 (NMM)

ARRIS, Robert
L 25 Feb 1690 (PJP)
CA 28 Apr 1696
COM V 1712 (PJP)
d 7 Jan 1720

ARROW, John Jordan
L 12 Aug 1807
CR 16 May 1814
Ret CA 1 July 1851 (NMM)
d 19 Aug 1853 (NMM)

ARROWSMITH, Joseph
L 6 May 1757
d 1759 (NMM)

ARSCOTT, Amos
L 1664
d before 1689 (PJP)

ARSCOTT, James
T
L 14 Apr 1810
d 27 Sept 1816 (NMM)

ARSCOTT, Thomas
L 18 July 1802
CR 7 June 1814
d 6 Jan 1827 (NMM)

ARKSINE, Robert
L 2 Apr 1729

ARSTON, John
L
CA 7 May 1697

ARTHUR, David
L 11 Oct 1758
d 1789 (NMM)

ARTHUR, Richard
L 28 Feb 1800
CR 1 Nov 1805
CA 11 Jan 1810
CB 28 July 1838 (OB)
RAB 9 Nov 1846 (PRO)
RAW 1 Aug 1848 (PRO)
RAR 29 Apr 1851 (PRO)
VAB 17 Sept 1853 (PRO)
d 26 Oct 1854 (PRO)

ARTHUR, Robert
L
CA 20 Jan 1678
d ? 21 Feb 1693 (PJP)

ARTHUR, Samuel
L 16 Sept 1780
d 13 June 1792

ARTHUR, William
L 10 Sept 1814
d 23 Dec 1815 (NMM)

ARUNDEL, Charles
L
CA 1 Jan 1713
d 8 Nov 1723

ARUNDELL, Francis
L 31 Aug 1739
d 1755(6) (NMM)

ARYMES, George
L 23 June 1794

ASHBURY, Francis
L 27 Dec 1762
d 1766 (NMM)

ASHBY, Arthur (1)
L 1664
CA 7 June 1666 (RM)
d 30 July 1666 (AJ)

ASHBY, Arthur (2)
L 18 June 1690
d 30 Nov 1691

ASHBY, Sir John
L 1665 (P)
CA 8 Apr 1680 (DDA)
RAB 7 June 1689 (PRO)
Kt 1689 (DNB)
VAB 17 Feb 1690
COM N 11 July 1690–
12 June 1694 (NBO)
AB 20 Dec 1691
AF 6 Aug 1690
d 12 July 1693 (DNB)

ASHBY, Nathaniel
L 1673
d 7 Dec 1674 (DDA)

ASHBY, William Richmond
L 18 Feb 1815
CR 1 Jan 1857 (NMM)
d 7 Nov 1867 (NMM)

ASHFORD, Andrew
L
CA 1660
d before 1689 (PJP)

ASHINGTON, Henry
L 14 Dec 1757
SUP CR 1 Dec 1797 (PMM)
d 1797 (NMM)

ASHLEY, Benjamin
L 28 Aug 1807
Ret CR 11 Jan 1849 (NMM)
d 1860 (NMM)

ASHLEY, James
L 25 Feb 1815
d 14 Mar 1818 (NMM)

ASHTON, Herbert
L 20 Sept 1815
Ret CR 14 Apr 1864 (NMM)
d 21 Mar 1876 (PRO)

ASHTON, Thomas
L 21 Mar 1678
CA 22 Apr 1687
d 15 Sept 1688 (DDA)

ASHWORTH, Henry
L 31 Oct 1809
d 25 July 1811 (DNB)

ASKEW, Christopher Crachenthorp(e)
L 27 Nov 1805
CR 26 Nov 1811
CA 19 July 1822 (NMM)
Ret CA 1 Oct 1846 (PRO)
d 7 Dec 1848 (NMM)

ASKEW, Robert
L 4 Mar 1740
CR 12 July 1745 (NMM)
CA 21 Aug 1747
d 1756

ASKEW, William
L 11 Dec 1796
d 11 Dec 1804 (PRO)

ASKEY, James
L 15 July 1806
CR 15 June 1814
d 31 Oct 1824 (NMM)

ASTLE, George
L 14 Jan 1794

Name / Rank	Date	Year (Source)
CR	22 Dec	1796
CA	27 Aug	1798
RAB	27 May	1825 (NMM)
d	21 June	1830 (PRO)
ASTLEY, Sir Edward William Carry		
L	11 Aug	1808
CR	12 Aug	1819 (NMM)
CA	7 Apr	1829 (NMM)
Kt	27 Oct	1830 (MB)
d	20 June	1842 (LT)
ATCHISON, Arthur		
L	8 Sept	1793
T		
CR	24 Dec	1805
CA	12 Aug	1812
d		1818 (TR)
ATHILL, James (1)		
L	8 June	1809
CR	7 June	1814
d	9 Apr	1825 (LT)
ATHILL, James (2)		
L	31 Jan	1812
Ret CR	30 July	1853 (NMM)
d		1863 (PRO)
ATHY, Richard		
L		
CA	31 May	1693
d	12 Jan	1697 (PRO)
ATKIN, James		
L	28 Aug	1780
d		1815 (PRO)
ATKIN, Nicholas		
L	19 Sept	1810
Ret CR	11 Apr	1851 (NMM)
d		1852 (NMM)
ATKINS, Charles		
L		1672
CA	?14 Feb	1676 (NMM)
Dismissed		1675 (PJP)
ATKINS, Christopher		
L	6 Apr	1757
CR	20 Nov	1763
CA	18 Sept	1772
d	21 Jan	1791
ATKINS, David		
L	20 Sept	1784
CR	6 Dec	1796
CA	29 May	1798
d (drowned)	24 Dec	1811 (CH)
ATKINS, George		
L	29 Nov	1775
d		1792 (PRO)
ATKINS, James (1)		
L		
CA	11 Dec	1693
d		1715 (PRO)
ATKINS, James (2)		
L	12 Aug	1809
Ret CR	4 Apr	1848 (PRO)
d		1864 (PRO)
ATKINS, James (3)		
L	4 May	1810
d	4 May	1858 (PRO)
ATKINS, John		
L	3 Oct	1745
d		1777 (PRO)
ATKINS, John Wyatt		
L	28 Oct	1793
d	4 May	1813 (PRO)
ATKINS, Lancelot John		
L	13 Mar	1815
d	Aug	1823 (PRO)
ATKINS, Robert Fendall		
L	15 Nov	1810
d		1826 (PRO)
ATKINS, Samuel		
L		
CR	8 Jan	1718 (PRO)
CA	3 Dec	1718
SUP RA	15 July	1747
d	5 Sept	1765 (PRO)
ATKINS, William		
L	18 Nov	1799
d	4 Dec	1827 (NMM)
ATKINSON, Anthony		
L	28 Nov	1741
d		1771 (PRO)
ATKINSON, Charles		
L	13 Feb	1815
d		1826 (PRO)
ATKINSON, David		
L	23 Sept	1800
Ret CR	26 Nov	1830 (NMM)
d		1839 (NMM)
ATKINSON, Edward		
L	12 May	1759
d		1786 (PRO)
ATKINSON, George (1)		
L	4 May	1796
d		1800 (NMM)
ATKINSON, George (2)		
L	26 Aug	1814
Ret CR	15 Apr	1858 (NMM)
d	14 Mar	1865 (PRO)
ATKINSON, George Augustus		
L	5 Mar	1778
d		1782 (NMM)
ATKINSON, Sir Henry Esch		
L	16 Feb	1815
CR	30 Apr	1827 (NMM)
Kt		1836 (OB)
Ret CR	1 Apr	1856 (NMM)
d	13 May	1857 (PRO)
ATKINSON, John (1)		
L	29 Nov	1745
d		1782 (PRO)
ATKINSON, John (2)		
L	17 Sept	1812
d		1819 (NMM)
ATKINSON, John Anson		
L	18 Apr	1778
d	29 Mar	1791
ATKINSON, John Carr		
L	2 Nov	1815
d		1833 (PRO)

ATKINSON, Jonathan
L 10 Feb 1779 (NMM)
d (drowned) June 1782 (PJP)
ATKINSON, Thomas (1)
L 12 Jan 1796
d 1799 (PRO)
ATKINSON, Thomas (2)
L 28 May 1813
Ret CR 1 Feb 1856 (NMM)
d July 1864 (PRO)
ATKINSON, William Hyndford (1)
L 26 May 1768
Struck off list 1798 (NMM)
ATKINSON, William Hyndford (2)
L 12 Aug 1804
d 1812 (PRO)
ATMAR, William
L 1666
d before 1689 (PJP)
ATWATER, James
L 16 Apr 1802
Ret CR 25 June 1834 (NMM)
d 1847 (NMM)
ATWILL, Henry Russell
L 14 Mar 1815
d 22 Aug 1825 (PRO)
AUBIN, David
L 4 Mar 1705
CR
CA 24 Nov 1731
d 31 Jan 1735 (PRO)
AUCHINLECK, James Richard
L 4 Feb 1815
Ret CR 9 Feb 1860 (NMM)
Name removed from list in 1870, not having drawn half-pay for some years (NMM)
AUCHINLICK, John
L 26 Nov 1776
d 1782(3) (NMM)
AUDELEY, Robert
See AUDLEY, Robert
AUDLEY, John
See AUDLY, John
AUDLEY, Robert
L ?30 Oct 1688
CA 11 Nov 1693
Dismissed ship 28 Feb 1696 (PRO)
Later killed in duel
AUDLY, John
L 7 Mar 1692
AUFRERE, Charles
L 8 Oct 1793
d (drowned) 9 Oct 1799 (PJP)
AUGUSTUS, Edward, Duke of York
See EDWARD AUGUSTUS, Duke of York
AULD, Alexander
L 29 Oct 1778
d 17 Apr 1803
AUSTEN, Charles John
L 13 Dec 1794
CR 10 Sept 1804 (MB)
CA 10 May 1810
CB 1840 (PJP)
RAB 9 Nov 1846 (PRO)
RAW 3 Mar 1849 (PRO)
RAR 9 July 1851 (PRO)
d 7 Oct 1852 (NMM)
AUSTEN, Sir Francis William
L 28 Dec 1792
CR 3 Jan 1799 (NMM)
CA 13 May 1800
HP May 1814 (MB)
CB 4 June 1815 (OB)
CRM 27 May 1825 (LG)
RAB 22 July 1830 (PRO)
RAR 10 Jan 1837 (PRO)
KCB 17 Mar 1837 (LG)
VAB 28 June 1838 (PRO)
VAR 9 Nov 1846 (PRO)
AB 1 Aug 1848 (PRO)
AW 1 July 1851 (PRO)
AR 3 July 1855 (PRO)
GCB May 1860 (DNB)
AF 27 Apr 1863 (DNB)
d 10 Aug 1865 (DNB)
AUSTEN, Nicholas
L 26 May 1768
d 1779 (PRO)
AUSTEN, Sylvester
T
L 24 Dec 1805
d 12 Mar 1816 (PRO)
AUTRIDGE, Charles
L 10 Feb 1815
CR 6 Feb 1857 (NMM)
d 1876 (NMM)
AUTRIDGE, William (1)
L 1800 (MB)
AUTRUDGE, William (2)
L 12 Apr 1802
CR 17 Oct 1804
CA 12 Aug 1812
d 11 Mar 1825 (PRO)
AUVERGNE, Corbet James d'
L 20 Jan 1794
CR 13 Oct 1807
CA 1 Aug 1811
d 18 Sept 1825 (PRO)
AUVERGNE, Philip, d'Prince de Bouillon
L 2 June 1777
CR 18 Aug 1781
CA 22 Jan 1784
RAB 9 Nov 1805
RAW 28 Apr 1808
VAB 31 July 1810
VAW 4 Dec 1813
VAR 4 June 1814
d 18 Sept 1816 (LT)
AVERELL, Adam
L 11 Apr 1794
Ret CR 3 May 1830 (NMM)
d 1833 (PRO)
AVERY, James
L 8 Feb 1815
d 3 Dec 1824 (NMM)

AVERY, William (1)
L | 31 Aug | 1799
d | | 1807 (NMM)

AVERY, William (2)
L | 29 Apr | 1802
d | | 1803 (NMM)

AYERST, Edward
L | 22 Jan | 1806
d | | 1808 (PRO)

AYLETT, John
L
CA | | 1664
d | before | 1689 (PJP)

AYLETT, Thomas
See AYLIFFE, Thomas

AYLIFFE, Thomas
L | 19 Jan | 1672 (DDA)
CA | 8 Oct | 1664 (DDA)
d | before | 1689 (PJP)

AYLING, William
L | 3 Aug | 1815
d | 1 Oct | 1847 (NMM)

AYLMER, Rt. Hon. Frederick William, Lord
L | 17 Dec | 1796
CR | 7 Jan | 1802
CA | 18 May | 1805
CB | | 1816 (PJP)
RAB | 10 Jan | 1837 (NMM)
RAW | 23 Nov | 1841 (NMM)
RAR | 9 Nov | 1846 (NMM)
VAB | 3 Jan | 1848 (NMM)
VAW | 24 Dec | 1849 (NMM)
Cre EP | | 1850 (PJP)
A | 11 Sept | 1854 (NMM)
KCB | | 1855 (PJP)
d | 5 Mar | 1858 (NMM)

AYLMER, George
LF (Buckingham) | 16 Feb | 1673 (EAD)
L | 10 Apr | 1677 (P)
CA | 17 July | 1680
CA | 11 Sept | 1680 (P)
KIA | 1 May | 1689 (EAD)

AYLMER, Henry, Lord
Inh IP | 18 Aug | 1720 (DNB)
L | 14 June | 1735
CR
CA | 18 Sept | 1741
d | 18 Nov | 1766

AYLMER, John (1)
L | 25 Aug | 1777
CR | 18 June | 1781
CA | 28 June | 1782
RAB | 23 Apr | 1804
RAR | 9 Nov | 1805
VAB | 28 Apr | 1808
VAW | 31 July | 1810
VAR | 12 Aug | 1812
AB | 4 June | 1814
AW | 27 May | 1825 (NMM)
AR | 22 July | 1830 (NMM)
d | 19 Apr | 1841 (NMM)

AYLMER, John (2)
L | 9 Oct | 1801
Ret CR | 15 Apr | 1836 (PRO)
d | Dec | 1848 (NMM)

AYLMER, Matthew, Lord
EF (Tangier) | 1 Jan | 1677 (EAD)
L | | 1678 (P)
CA | 9 Jan | 1679 (P)
CA | 5 May | 1679 (C)
| (17 July | 1680 in H)
CAF (Queen Dowager) | 1 June | 1686 (EAD)
RAR | Feb | 1693 (DNB)
VAB | | 1694 (DNB)
COM E | 22 Apr | 1694–
| 17 July | 1702 (NBO)
MP (Dover) | 1697–1713 (MPS)
AF | 20 Dec | 1708
GGH | 1714–1720 (PJP)
MP (Dover) | 1715–18 Aug | 1720 (MPS)
COM AD | 16 Apr | 1717–
| 19 Mar | 1718 (AO)
Cre IP | 1 May | 1718 (EAD)
d | 18 Aug | 1720 (DNB)

AYLMORE, George
See AYLMER, George

AYLMORE, Matthew
See AYLMER, Matthew

AYRE, Charles
L | 2 Nov | 1815
Ret CR | 14 Apr | 1864 (NMM)
d | 8 Apr | 1878 (NMM)

AYRES, Henry
L | 29 Apr | 1797 (NMM)
Ret CR | 29 Dec | 1830 (NMM)
d | Dec | 1831 (NMM)

AYSCOUGH, James (1)
L | 10 Feb | 1757
CR | 10 Jan | 1771
d | | 1789 (PRO)

AYSCOUGH, James (2)
L | 28 Nov | 1796
CR | 21 Nov | 1804
d | 8 Apr | 1808 (PRO)

AYSCOUGH, John
L | 6 Nov | 1793
CR | 12 May | 1797
CA | 18 Apr | 1806
RAB | 23 Nov | 1841 (NMM)
RAW | 9 Nov | 1846 (NMM)
RAR | 13 May | 1847 (NMM)
VAB | 24 Dec | 1849 (NMM)
VAW | 8 July | 1851 (NMM)
VAR | 28 May | 1853 (NMM)
AB | 3 Oct | 1855 (NMM)
AW | 28 Nov | 1857 (NMM)
AR | 11 Feb | 1861 (NMM)
d | 2 Dec | 1863 (NMM)

AYSCOUGH, Richard Maximilian
L | 9 Mar | 1783
d | | 1795 (PRO)

AYSCUE, Sir George
L
CA | | 1664
RAB | | 1664 (DNB)
VAF | | 1664
VAB | | 1665
AB | 16 Mar | 1666 (RM)

AW	30 May	1666 (DNB)
d	Apr	1672 (NJ)
AYSCUE, William		
L		1671
d	before	1689 (PJP)
AYTON, George Henry		
L	4 Mar	1815
Ret CR	10 Jan	1863 (NMM)
d		1865 (PRO)
AYTONE, David		
L	13 Oct	1738
d		1747 (PRO)
AYTOUN, Andrew		
L	28 June	1795
d		1800 (PRO)
BABB, Michael		
L	27 Sept	1810
d	15 Apr	1829 (PRO)
BABB, Samuel		
L	16 Dec	1807
d		1817 (PRO)
BABB, William		
L	2 Aug	1759
d	18 May	1791
BABINGTON, James		
L	8 Oct	1801
d	14 Mar	1808 (PRO)
BABINGTON, James Boyle		
L	13 Apr	1810
CR	16 Sept	1816 (PRO)
d		1826 (PRO)
BABINGTON, William Maitland		
L	24 Nov	1796
d		1798 (PRO)
BACON, Edmund Ker Cranstown		
L	26 Aug	1799
HP	Nov	1814 (OB)
Ret CR	26 Nov	1830 (PRO)
d		1860 (PRO)
BACON, Philemon		
L		1661
CA		1664
KIA	1 June	1666 (DNB)
BACON, William (1)		
L	27 Sept	1740
d	24 June	1741 (PMM)
BACON, William (2)		
L	27 Oct	1757
d	5 Nov	1790
BADCOCK, John		
L	3 Mar	1740
d		?1750 (PRO)
BADCOCK, William Stanhope		
See LOVELL, William Stanhope		
BADGE, John		
L		1666
d	before	1689 (PJP)
BANDINEL, Francis		
L	10 Aug	1761
d		1769 (PRO)
BAGEHOT, Charles		
L	31 Jan	1808
HP		1815–1823 (OB)
d		1857 (PRO)
BAGGE, Arthur		
See WARNER, Arthur Lee		
BAGGOTT, Philip		
L	9 May	1781
d		1784 (PRO)
BAGOT, Hervey		
L	16 Nov	1812
CR	13 June	1815
d	18 Jan	1816 (LT)
BAGOT, Richard		
L	29 Oct	1790
CR	23 June	1794
CA	6 Apr	1795
d	12 June	1798 (PRO)
BAGSTER, John		
L	28 July	1744
CR	14 May	1762
d		1792 (PRO)
BAGUE, George		
L	8 Mar	1805
T	wounded	
Ret CR	13 July	1837 (PRO)
d		1856 (TR)
BAGWELL, Paul Piercy		
L	27 July	1812
CR	15 Feb	1830 (PRO)
d		1836 (PRO)
BAIKIE, Hugh		
L	22 Jan	1761
CR	9 Dec	1777
CA	19 Feb	1780
SUP		1799
d	21 July	1816 (PRO)
BAIKE, John		
L	4 Feb	1807
Ret CR	5 June	1855 (PRO)
d		1875 (PRO)
BAILEY, Henry Williams		
L	26 Oct	1808
d		1817 (PRO)
BAILEY, John		
L	17 Jan	1801
d		1815 (PRO)
BAILEY, John William		
L	23 Aug	1800
Ret CR	3 June	1840 (PRO)
d		1860 (PRO)
BAILEY, Joseph		
L	15 Apr	1813
d	8 May	1842 (PRO)
BAILEY, William		
L	27 June	1814
d		1852 (PRO)
BAILLEY, Thomas		
See BAILLIE, Thomas		
BALLIE, Alexander		
L	9 Nov	1756
d		1766 (PRO)

BALLIE, Alexander Francis		
L	24 Apr	1759
SUP CR	30 Nov	1802
d	29 Apr	1822 (LT)
BAILLIE, Henry		
L	7 Feb	1815
d	21 Nov	1839 (PRO)
BAILLIE, James		
L	20 Feb	1815
d	26 June	1828 (PRO)
BAILLIE, Thomas		
L	29 Mar	1745
CR	10 Nov	1756
CA	30 Mar	1757
LGH		1774–1778 (DNB)
d	15 Dec	1802 (DNB)
BAILY, Edward Seymour		
L	17 July	1780
CR	21 Mar	1782
CA	25 Oct	1809
d		1840 (PRO)
BAILY, Simon		
L		1672
d	before	1689 (PJP)
BAIN, Henderson		
L	22 Jan	1800
CR	29 Mar	1811
CA	6 Apr	1813
Ret RA	1 Oct	1846 (PRO)
Ret VA	28 Dec	1855 (PRO)
Ret A	11 Feb	1861 (PRO)
d	18 Jan	1862 (PRO)
BAINBRIDGE, William		
L	31 Aug	1793 (PRO)
d	17 Mar	1800 (CH)
BAINES, Cuthbert		
L	11 Mar	1761
CR	21 Jan	1771
CA	25 Oct	1809
d		1810 (PRO)
BAIRD, Andrew		
L	19 Sept	1815
CR	20 May	1826 (PRO)
Ret CA	1 Apr	1856 (PRO)
d		1881 (PRO)
BAIRD, Daniel		
L	3 Feb	1815
HP	27 June	1816 (OB)
d		1852 (PRO)
BAIRD, James		
L	15 Jan	1795
d		1806 (PRO)
BAIRD, John		
L	12 Aug	1757
SUP CR	21 Sept	1796 (PMM)
d		1796 (PRO)
BAIRD, Patrick		
L	29 Nov	1738
CR	12 July	1745 (PRO)
CA	`27 May	1747
d		1761
BAIRD, Sir William		
L	15 Feb	1757

CR		
CA	3 Mar	1759
d		1772
BAKE, John Wolland		
L	4 Feb	1815
d		1856 (PRO)
BAKER, Charles (1)		
L	24 Oct	1740
d	19 Oct	1750 (PMM)
BAKER, Charles (2)		
L	5 May	1778
d	24 June	1790
BAKER, Charles Adolphus		
L	11 Nov	1811
CR	15 June	1814
d (drowned)	20 June	1822 (CH)
BAKER, Edward (1)		
L		1672
CR	7June	1695 (PMM)
d		?1696 (PMM)
BAKER, Edward (2)		
L	9 July	1715 (PRO)
CR		
CA	15 Mar	1728 (PRO)
d		1747 (PRO)
BAKER, Francis		
L	1 Feb	1804
T		
CR	27 June	1814
d	Apr	1823 (PRO)
BAKER, George (1)		
L	17 Feb	1798
d		1806 (PRO)
BAKER, George (2)		
L	7 Mar	1815
CR	17 Jan	1822 (PRO)
CA	9 Nov	1846 (PRO)
Ret CA	4 Feb	1857 (PRO)
d	6 Feb	1861 (PRO)
BAKER, Henry (1)		
L	5 July	1746
d		1785 (PRO)
BAKER, Henry (2)		
L	7 Apr	1801
CR	15 June	1814
d	Apr	1823 (MB)
BAKER, Henry (3)		
L	27 Apr	1803
CR	3 Oct	1803
d (drowned)	9 June	1804 (PJP)
BAKER, Henry (4)		
L	31 Oct	1809
CR	15 June	1814
d		1857 (PRO)
BAKER, Henry Edward Reginald		
L	1 July	1794
CR	8 Mar	1797
CA	7 Jan	1802
d	Aug	1820 (PRO)
BAKER, Sir Henry Loraine		
L	18 Oct	1804
CR	8 Apr	1811

CA 13 June 1815
Cre Bt 4 Feb 1820 (OB)
Ret RA 1 Oct 1846 (PRO)
Ret VA 9 July 1857 (PRO)
d 2 Nov 1859 (PRO)

BAKER, Hercules
L 1 July 1708 (PMM)
CR
CA 1 Jan 1713
MP (Hythe) 1722–1 Nov 1744 (MPS)
TGH 1736–1744 (MPS)
d 1 Nov 1744 (MPS)

BAKER, Jacob
L
CA 1666
d 1678

BAKER, James (1)
L 3 Sept 1744
CR 17 Aug 1757
CA 3 Mar 1758
d 31 Mar 1765 (PRO)

BAKER, James (2)
L 6 Oct 1758
d 1780(1) (NMM)

BAKER, James Walker
L 13 Oct 1801
Dismissed 1811 (NMM)

BAKER, John (1)
L 14 Nov 1688 (P)
CA 12 Oct 1691
RAW 17 Jan 1708
RAR 21 Dec 1708
MP (Weymouth and Melcombe Regis) 1713–3 June 1714 (MPS)
MP (Weymouth and Melcombe Regis) 1715–10 Nov 1716 (MPS)
VAW 15 June 1716
d 10 Nov 1716

BAKER, John (2)
L 12 June 1780
d 1784 (NMM)

BAKER, John (3)
L 17 Mar 1781
SUP CR 1 Jan 1816 (NMM)
d 7 Nov 1834 (LT)

BAKER, John (4)
L 9 July 1794
CR 29 Apr 1802
CA 21 Oct 1810
d Mar 1845 (LT)

BAKER, John Eades
L 17 Aug 1795
d (drowned) Mar 1805 (PJP)

BAKER, John Popham
L 18 Oct 1802
CR 29 Jan 1821 (NMM)
d 1859 (NMM)

BAKER, Joseph
L 19 Nov 1790
CR 1 Mar 1799
CA 26 Apr 1802
d June 1817 (PJP)

BAKER, Philip Harman
L 5 Apr 1805
d 1812 (NMM)

BAKER, Richard
L 25 Jan 1725

BAKER, Samuel
L 30 Mar 1756
d 13 Nov 1758 (NMM)

BAKER, Thomas (1)
L 23 May 1738
d ?1753 (NMM)

BAKER, Thomas (2)
L 13 Oct 1792
CR 24 Nov 1795
CA 13 June 1797
CB 4 June 1815 (MB)
CRM 12 Aug 1819 (AL)
RAB 19 July 1821 (PRO)
RAW 27 May 1825 (PRO)
RAR 22 July 1830 (PRO)
KCB 3 Jan 1831 (OB)
VAW 10 Jan 1837 (PRO)
VAR 23 Nov 1841 (PRO)
d 26 Jan 1845 (CH)

BAKER, Thomas (3)
L 6 Feb 1815
CR 29 Mar 1833 (PJP)

BAKER, Thomas (4)
L 20 Sept 1815
Ret CR 9 Feb 1860 (PRO)
d 1887 (PRO)

BAKER, William (1)
L 28 Aug 1711
Gone 1727 (PMM)

BAKER, William (2)
L 1 June 1715
d ?1740 (PMM)

BAKER, William (3)
L 1 May 1738
d ?1753 (PRO)

BAKER, William (4)
L 23 Oct 1806
d 1819 (PRO)

BAKER, William (5)
L 20 Feb 1815
d 1852 (PRO)

BAKER, William Henry
L 18 Feb 1815
CR 1 Jan 1853 (PRO)
Ret CA 1 Aug 1860 (PRO)
d 1879 (PRO)

BALCHEN, George
L 11 Aug 1735
CR
CA 12 Sept 1740
d 18 Dec 1745

BALCHEN, Sir John
L 26 Dec 1695 (PJP)
CA 25 July 1697
RAB 19 July 1728
RAW 4 Mar 1729
RAR 29 June 1732
VAW 26 Feb 1734 (DNB)
VAR 2 Mar 1736

AW	11 Aug	1743 (LG)
GGH	Apr	1744 (DNB)
Kt	May	1744 (PJP)
d (drowned)	4 Oct	1744 (DNB)

BALDERSTON, George (1)

L	16 May	1778
d		1797 (PRO)

BALDERSTON, George (2)

L	11 Jan	1797
d	26 Oct	1799 (LTE)

BALDERSOTON, John Bassett

L	3 Jan	1797
CR	22 Jan	1806
d (murdered)	12 Dec	1808 (PJP)

BALDEY, Robert

L	27 Sept	1809
CR	26 July	1821 (PRO)
d	15 Aug	1849 (PRO)

BALDOCK, Robert

L	10 Jan	1771
d		1777 (PRO)

BALDOCK, Thomas

L	10 Nov	1813
CR	23 Nov	1841 (PRO)
CA	9 Jan	1854 (PRO)
Ret RA	10 Sept	1869 (PRO)
d	11 Mar	1871 (PRO)

BALDWIN, Abraham

L	15 Oct	1800
T		
d		1815 (TR)

BALDWIN, Augustus

L	28 June	1800
CR	19 Sept	1808
CA	1 Jan	1817 (PRO)
Ret RA	16 June	1851 (PRO)
Ret VA	30 July	1857 (PRO)
Ret A	10 Nov	1862 (PRO)
d		1866 (PRO)

BALDWIN, John

L	25 Mar	1803
T		
CR	18 Nov	1811
CA	12 Aug	1819 (PRO)
d	11 Apr	1840 (LT)

BALE, John

L	8 Nov	1746
d		1751 (PRO)

BALEY, Robert

L	14 Nov	1780
d		1810 (PRO)

BALEY, Robert Ashley

L	8 May	1804
Dismissed		1805 (PRO)

BALFOUR, Alexander

L	4 Dec	1745
d (drowned)	14 Apr	1749 (PJP)

BALFOUR, Andrew

L	28 Nov	1811
d		1815 (PRO)

BALFOUR, Charles

L	4 Mar	1740
CR	11 Sept	1747
CA	3 May	1748
d		1750

BALFOUR, David
See BALLFOUR, David

BALFOUR, George

L	5 July	1745
CR	15 Nov	1756
CA	26 July	1758
SUP RA		1787
d	28 June	1794 (PJP)

BALFOUR, James

L	17 Dec	1744
CR	24 May	1748
d		1754 (PRO)

BALFOUR, Robert

L	7 Sept	1796
CR	13 Oct	1807
CA	7 June	1814
d		1816 (PRO)

BALFOUR, William

L	4 Sept	1801
CR	22 Jan	1806
Ret CA	10 Feb	1846 (PRO)
d	10 Sept	1846 (PRO)

BALGONIE, David, Lord
See LEVEN and MELVILLE, David, Earl

BALL, Sir Alexander John

L	7 Aug	1778
CR	14 Apr	1782
CA	20 Mar	1783
Cre Bt	24 June	1801 (PJP)
RAB	9 Nov	1805
RAW	28 Apr	1808
d	20 Oct	1809 (DNB)

BALL, Andrew

L		
CA		1666
d		1668 (LTE)

BALL, George

L	4 Jan	1775
d	21 May	1790

BALL, Henry

L	17 Nov	1774
CR		
CA	25 Jan	1780
d	6 Aug	1792

BALL, Henry Lidgbird

L	23 Aug	1778
CR	28 Apr	1792
CA	9 July	1795
HP		1813 (DUB)
RAB	4 June	1814
d	23 Oct	1818 (PRO)

BALL, John (1)

L		1665
d	before	1689 (PJP)

BALL, John (2)

L	20 July	1745
d		1757 (PRO)

BALL, Nathan Jeremiah

L	5 Nov	1806
d		1822 (NMM)

BALL, Nepthali
L
CA 1665
d before 1689 (PJP)

BALL, Samuel
L 13 May 1778
d 1782(3) (PRO)

BALL, Thomas
L 2 Jan 1809
CR 28 June 1828 (PRO)
d 3 Dec 1852 (PRO)

BALL, William
L 6 Mar 1815
Ret CR 10 Apr 1863 (PRO)
d 1874 (PRO)

BALLANTYNE, John
L 4 June 1807
Ret CR 10 Feb 1843 (PRO)
d 1863 (PRO)

BALLARD, George
L 1673

BALLARD, Samuel James
L 10 Feb 1783
CR 5 July 1794
CA 1 Aug 1795 (MB)
RAB 4 June 1814
RAW 12 Aug 1819 (PRO)
RAR 19 July 1821 (PRO)
VAB 27 May 1825 (PRO)
d 11 Oct 1829 (DNB)

BALLARD, Volant Vashon
L 6 Nov 1795
CR
CA 25 Dec 1798
CB 1815 (PJP)
RAB 27 May 1825 (PRO)
RAW 22 July 1830 (PRO)
d 12 Oct 1832 (DNB)

BALLETT, John
L 11 Aug 1742 (PRO)
CR 18 Jan 1748
d 11 Sept 1749 (LG)

BALLFOUR, David
L 5 Oct 1758
d 1761 (PRO)

BALLVIARD, John
L 16 Feb 1745
d ?1749 (PRO)

BALY, Samuel
L 30 July 1800
Struck off list 17 Feb 1827 (PRO)

BAMBER, William Richard
L 16 July 1796
CR 21 Oct 1810
d 1843 (PRO)

BAMPTON, William
L 16 Mar 1781
d 1797 (PRO)

BANCE, James
L 9 Jan 1809
CR 23 Nov 1841 (PRO)
Ret CR 1 July 1851 (PRO)
Ret CA 24 Dec 1857 (PRO)
d 11 July 1866 (PRO)

BANDINEL, Thomas
L 13 Sept 1759
d 1763 (PRO)

BANFF, Alexander, Lord
L 14 June 1739 (PRO)
CR
CA 19 Feb 1741
d 27 Sept 1748

BANGOR, Viscount
See WARD, Edward Southwell

BANKES, Richard
L 29 Oct 1801 (PRO)
d 21 Apr 1822 (PRO)

BANKS, Francis (1)
L 31 Mar 1756
CR 23 Mar 1757
CA 14 Apr 1760
d 18 June 1777

BANKS, Francis (2)
L 28 Nov 1798
CR 7 Oct 1813
d 1841 (PRO)

BANKS, Sir Jacob
L
CA 26 Aug 1690 (S)
CA 15 Jan 1691 (C)
d 22 Dec 1724

BANKS, James
L 28 Nov 1798 (PRO)
d 25 June 1824 (PRO)

BANKS, John
L 25 Feb 1806
CR 29 May 1812
Ret CA 4 Nov 1845 (PRO)
d 1860 (PRO)

BANKS, Richard
L 20 Apr 1696

BANKS, Thomas
L 23 June 1804
d 1811 (PRO)

BANNATYNE, John
L 8 Feb 1815
HP 27 Oct 1815 (OB)
d 1857 (PRO)

BANNISTER, John William
L 1 July 1814
d 1832 (PRO)

BARADALL, Blumfield
See BARRADALL, Blumfield

BARBER, Charles
L 2 Apr 1805
d 12 Jan 1822 (PRO)

BARBER, Daniel
L 11 Feb 1801
CR 2 May 1810
CA 27 May 1825 (PRO)
d 1837 (PRO)

BARBER, Edward
L 26 July 1727
CR 18 May 1747
CA 15 June 1756
d 4 Apr 1762

Name	Rank	Date	Year
BARBER, Jacob			
	L	5 May	1679
BARBER, James			
	L		1673 (P)
	CA	18 Mar	1689
	d	3 Feb	1692
BARBER, John			
	L		1664
BARBER, Robert			
	L	23 Feb	1756
	CR		
	CA	4 June	1759
	d		1784
BARBER, Stephen			
	L	2 Feb	1678
BARCLAY, Alexander			
	L	6 June	1707
	LGH		1739 (PJP)
	d	6 May	1747 (PMM)
BARCLAY, George Dallas			
	T		
	L	24 Dec	1805
	HP	4 Sept	1815 (OB)
	d	25 Feb	1834 (LT)
BARCLAY, Sir James			
	L	4 Mar	1777
	CR	1 May	1782
	CA	21 Jan	1783
	d	12 June	1793
BARCLAY, John (1)			
	L	3 Feb	1815
	d	2 Jan	1837 (PRO)
BARCLAY, John (2)			
	T		
	L	20 Nov	1805
	Ret CR	12 May	1838 (PRO)
	d		1859 (TR)
BARCLAY, Robert			
	L	14 Dec	1814
	Ret CR	9 Apr	1859 (PRO)
	d	20 Sept	1861 (PRO)
BARCLAY, Robert Heriot			
	L	11 Oct	1805
	T		
	CR	19 Nov	1813 (I)
	CA	14 Oct	1824 (I)
	d	8 May	1837 (I)
BARCLAY, Thomas			
	L	15 Sept	1805
	CR	5 May	1810
	CA	7 June	1814
	d		1838 (PRO)
BARFORD, Francis			
	L	2 Sept	1760
	d		1776 (PRO)
BARGRAVE, Charles			
	L	26 Feb	1708
	CR	28 Apr	1741
	Dismissed	24 Feb	1742
BARGUS, Richard			
	L	24 Sept	1742
	SUP CR	21 Sept	1796 (PMM)
	d		1805 (PRO)
BARHAM, Sir Charles Middleton, Lord			
	L	5 Nov	1745
	CR		
	CA	22 May	1750
	CONT	7 Aug	1778–
		30 Mar	1790 (NBO)
	Cre Bt	23 Oct	1781 (NBO)
	MP (Rochester)		1784–1790 (MPN)
	RAW	24 Sept	1787
	RAR	21 Sept	1790
	VAW	1 Feb	1793
	VAR	12 Apr	1794
	COM AD	12 May	1794–
		20 Nov	1795 (AO)
	AB	1 June	1795
	AW	14 Feb	1799
	Cre EP	1 May	1805 (AO)
	FLA	2 May	1805–
		10 Feb	1806 (AO)
	AR	9 Nov	1805
	d	17 June	1813 (CH)
BARKELEY, Andrew			
See BARKLEY, Andrew			
BARKER, Edward (1)			
	L	18 May	1798
	T		
	CR	24 Dec	1805
	d	25 July	1820 (PRO)
BARKER, Edward (2)			
	L	21 Sept	1801
	d (duel)	18 Feb	1810 (PJP)
BARKER, George (1)			
	L	12 Mar	1782
	CR	19 Dec	1796
	CA	8 June	1799
	Ret RA	6 June	1825 (PRO)
	VAB	12 Nov	1840 (PRO)
	VAW	23 Nov	1841 (PRO)
	VAR	9 Nov	1846 (PRO)
	AB	27 Dec	1847 (PRO)
	AW	21 Mar	1851 (PRO)
	d	25 Dec	1851 (PRO)
BARKER, George (2)			
	T		
	L	23 July	1814
	d		1853 (TR)
BARKER, George Alexander			
	T		
	L	4 Mar	1811
	d		1817 (PRO)
BARKER, James			
	L	13 Apr	1795
	CR	8 Oct	1798
	CA	12 Aug	1812 (DNB)
	d	4 May	1838 (DNB)
BARKER, Jedediah			
	L		
	CA	24 June	1692
		(22 Apr	1691 in C)
	d	31 Mar	1703 (PRO)
BARKER, John (1)			
	L	5 May	1735
	CR	11 June	1744
	CA	19 Sept	1745
	RAW	24 Oct	1770

RAR	31 Mar	1775
d	26 Jan	1776 (CH)
BARKER, John (2)		
L	29 Apr	1802
HP	Dec	1815 (OB)
Ret CR	4 Aug	1848 (PRO)
d		1855 (PRO)
BARKER, Randolph		
L	14 Mar	1709
BARKER, Robert		
L	17 Oct	1809
Ret CR	9 Nov	1848 (PRO)
d		1856 (PRO)
BARKER, Scory		
L	6 Nov	1777
CR	1 Dec	1787
CA	10 Oct	1793
d (drowned)	16 Nov	1797 (CH)
BARKER, Thomas (1)		
L		1672
d	28 May	1672 (M)
BARKER, Thomas (2)		
L	2 June	1744
d		1762 (PRO)
BARKER, Thomas (3)		
L	6 May	1756
CR	22 Apr	1778
d		1779 (PRO)
BARKER, Thomas Dobbins		
L	1 May	1804
T		
d		1807 (PRO)
BARKER, William		
L	2 July	1747
d		1763 (PRO)
BARKER, William Collins		
L	25 Mar	1802
HP	Sept	1821 (OB)
Ret CR	9 Feb	1848 (PRO)
d		1848 (PRO)
BARKLAY, Andrew		
See BARKLEY, Andrew		
BARKLEY, Andrew		
L	27 Oct	1758
CR	31 May	1766
CA	30 May	1770
d	1 Feb	1790
BARLAND, David		
L	17 Apr	1801
d		1812 (PRO)
BARLOW, George		
L	17 July	1761
d	21 Feb	1787 (PMM)
BARLOW, John		
L	17 Sept	1801
Resigned		1805 (NMM)
BARLOW, Sir Robert		
L	6 Nov	1778
CR	22 Nov	1790
CA	24 May	1793
Kt	16 June	1801 (MB)
SUP CA	31 July	1810 (PRO)
KCB	20 May	1820 (MB)
Ret RA	23 Jan	1823 (PRO)
COMM (Chatham)	1823–	1829 (PJP)
AW	12 Nov	1840 (PRO)
AR	23 Nov	1841 (PRO)
d	11 June	1843 (PRO)
BARNABY, –		
L	June	1685 (DDA)
BARNARD, Edward		
T		
L	7 Jan	1806
CR	10 Aug	1814
CA	4 July	1817 (PRO)
Ret RA	1 Oct	1846 (PRO)
Ret VA	8 July	1851 (PRO)
Ret A	22 Nov	1862 (PRO)
d	5 Oct	1863 (PRO)
BARNARD, George		
L	29 May	1797
Ret CR	15 Dec	1830 (PRO)
d	3 June	1864 (PRO)
BARNARD, Isaac		
L	4 Apr	1720
CR	1 Mar	1740
d		1758 (PRO)
BARNARD, Thomas Allen		
L	17 Oct	1808
d		1809 (PRO)
BARNARD, William		
L	14 Feb	1815
Ret CR	18 Jan	1861 (PRO)
d		1887 (PRO)
BARNBY, Joseph		
L	13 Dec	1798 (PRO)
d		1801 (PRO)
BARNES, Botler		
L		1666
CA		1668
BARNES, James Robert		
L	16 Sept	1814
d		1817 (PRO)
BARNES, John (1)		
L		
CA		1668
d	before	1689 (PJP)
BARNES, John (2)		
L	30 Sept	1813
CR	23 Dec	1847 (PRO)
Ret CR	1 July	1851 (PRO)
Ret CA	22 Oct	1861 (PRO)
d		1874 (PRO)
BARNES, John (3)		
L	2 Feb	1815
d		1837 (PRO)
BARNES, Joshua Crew		
L	10 Feb	1797
d (drowned)	9 Oct	1800 (PJP)
BARNES, Nicholas Donnithorne		
L	25 Apr	1809
d	19 Dec	1823 (PRO)
BARNES, Peter		
L	17 Feb	1815
Ret CR	9 Jan	1854 (PRO)
d		1873 (PRO)

BARNES, William (1)
L | 1 Dec | 1787
d | 25 May | 1790

BARNES, William (2)
L | 3 Aug | 1805
Ret CR | 17 Jan | 1838 (PRO)
d | | 1842 (PRO)

BARNESLY, Samuel
L | 13 June | 1758
SUP CR | 1 Aug | 1799

BARNETT, Curtis
L
CR | | 1730 (DNB)
CA | 26 Jan | 1731
d | 2 May | 1746 (DNB)

BARNET, William
See BENNET, William

BARNSLEY, John (1)
L | 15 Oct | 1716
CR
CA | 21 Apr | 1729
d | 7 Aug | 1753 (?1745)

BARNSLEY, John (2)
L | 13 Aug | 1755
d | | 1777 (PRO)

BARNSLEY, John (3)
L | 19 Oct | 1781
d | Oct | 1825 (PRO)

BARNSLEY, Samuel
See BARNESLY, Samuel

BARON, James
L | 9 Nov | 1756
SUP CR | 21 Sept | 1796 (PMM)
d | | 1796 (PRO)

BARR, William Frederick
L | 29 Oct | 1811
HP | 28 Oct | 1815 (OB)
Ret CR | 1 Apr | 1853 (PRO)
d | | 1854 (PRO)

BARRADALL, Blumfield
L | 17 Mar | 1732
CR | 1 Feb | 1743 (PRO)
CA | 18 July | 1744
d | 25 Nov | 1749 (M)

BARRELL, Justinian
L | 19 Dec | 1807
CR | 21 Mar | 1815
Ret CA | 19 Mar | 1852 (PRO)
d | | 1869 (PRO)

BARRETT, John
L | 2 Nov | 1793
CR
CA | 25 Nov | 1795
d (drowned) | 22 Dec | 1810 (CH)

BARRETT, Joseph Fauriel
L | 7 Dec | 1815
Ret CR | 1 July | 1864 (PRO)
d | | 1876 (PRO)

BARRETT, Samuel
L | 25 Mar | 1809
d | | 1836 (PRO)

BARRETTE, George Wilmott
L | 18 May | 1807
CR | 28 Nov | 1812
KIA | 5 Aug | 1813 (CH)

BARRETTE, Henry William
L | 8 Oct | 1798 (PRO)
d | 11 Aug | 1820 (PRO)

BARREY, Henry
L | 17 Aug | 1692

BARRIE, Sir Robert
L | 5 Nov | 1795
CR | 23 Oct | 1801
CA | 29 Apr | 1802
CB | | 1815 (PJP)
KCH | | 1824 (PJP)
RAB | 10 Jan | 1837 (PRO)
RAW | 28 June | 1838 (PRO)
KCB | | 1840 (PRO)
d | 7 June | 1841 (LT)

BARRINGTON, Hon. George
L | 16 May | 1814
CR | 7 Dec | 1818 (PRO)
CA | 27 Mar | 1826 (PRO)
d | 2 June | 1835 (PJP)

BARRINGTON, Hon. Samuel
L | 13 Oct | 1745 (PJP)
CR | 6 Nov | 1746 (PJP)
CA | 29 May | 1747
CRM | 13 Oct | 1770 (AL)
RAW | 23 Jan | 1778
RAR | 29 Jan | 1778
VAB | 29 Mar | 1779 (CH)
VAW | 26 Sept | 1780
LGRM | 26 Jan | 1786 (AL)
AB | 24 Sept | 1787
AW | 12 Apr | 1794
GRM | 20 Aug | 1799 (LG)
d | 16 Aug | 1800 (CH)

BARRON, David
L | 30 Sept | 1799
Ret CR | 1 Dec | 1830 (PRO)
d | | 1839 (PRO)

BARRON, Thomas Charles
L | 9 Sept | 1799
d | | 1834 (PRO)

BARROW, Harris
See HARRIS, Barrow

BARROW, Ralph
L | 8 Jan | 1692

BARROW, Thomas
L | 9 July | 1814
d | | 1834 (PRO)

BARROW, William
L | 31 Oct | 1770
d | | 1772 (PRO)

BARRY, David
L | 10 May | 1797
d | | 1802 (PRO)

BARRY, Garrett
L | 14 Feb | 1815
d | | 1841 (PRO)

BARRY, Hon. Richard
L | 27 Sept | 1740
CR | 1 Apr | 1745 (PRO)
MP (Wigan) | | 1747–1761 (MPN)
d | 23 Nov | 1787 (MPN)

BARRY, William
L 22 Feb 1812
Ret CR 1 Oct 1853 (PRO)
d 1856 (PRO)

BARTER, James
L 2 Apr 1757
d 1758(9) (PRO)

BARTER, John
L
CR 3 Mar 1694 (PJP)
CA 1 May 1705
SUP 1706
d 13 Dec 1708

BARTHOLOMEW, Charles
L 4 July 1777
CR 16 Jan 1783
CA 25 Oct 1809
d 1839 (PRO)

BARTHOLOMEW, David Ewen
L 20 July 1805
CR 21 Mar 1812
HP Mar 1812–
4 Apr 1814 (MB)
CA 13 June 1815
CB 16 Sept 1815 (MB)
d 19 Feb 1821 (DNB)

BARTHOLOMEW, Philip
L 16 Dec 1783
CR 5 Jan 1797
d 1806 (PRO)

BARTHOLOMEW, William
L 10 May 1776
d 1779 (PRO)

BARTLETT, John
L 31 July 1779 (NMM)
d 1800 (NMM)

BARTON, John
L
CA 1660
d before 1689 (PJP)

BARTON, Matthew
L Mar 1739 (DNB)
CR May 1745 (DNB)
CA 7 Feb 1747
RAB 28 Apr 1777
RAW 23 Jan 1778
RAR 29 Jan 1778
VAB 19 Mar 1779
VAW 26 Sept 1780
AB 24 Sept 1787
AW 1 Feb 1793
d 30 Dec 1795 (CH)

BARTON, Richard
L 27 Dec 1808
CR 29 July 1825 (PRO)
CA 2 Jan 1837 (PRO)
Ret CA 1 July 1851 (PRO)
d 1 Aug 1853 (PRO)

BARTON, Robert
L 6 June 1776
CR 6 Nov 1782
CA 2 Apr 1794
RAB 12 Aug 1812
RAR 4 June 1814
VAB 12 Aug 1819 (PRO)
VAW 27 May 1825 (PRO)
VAR 22 July 1830 (PRO)
d 15 Dec 1827 (PRO)

BARTON, Robert Cutts
T
L 5 Apr 1806
CR 12 Aug 1819 (PRO)
d Oct 1827 (PRO)

BARWELL, Henry
L 9 Oct 1780
CR 29 Apr 1802 (PRO)
CA 27 Feb 1812
d 1835 (PRO)

BARWELL, Nathaniel
L 7 Jan 1814
Ret CR 7 Nov 1856 (PRO)
d 1866 (PRO)

BARWICK, Joseph
L 6 Nov 1798
Ret CR 26 Nov 1830 (PRO)
d 23 Oct 1833 (LT)

BAS, Nicholas Le
See LE BAS, Nicholas

BASDEN, Charles
L 2 May 1811
CR 17 Feb 1829 (PRO)
CA 23 Nov 1841 (PRO)
Ret CA 24 Jan 1858 (PRO)
Ret RA 12 Nov 1862 (PRO)
d 17 Apr 1866 (PRO)

BASDEN, Robert
L 3 Dec 1778
d 1810 (PRO)

BASHFORD, James
L 29 Oct 1800
T wounded
CR 25 July 1809
d 1816 (TR)

BASKERVILLE, Peter
L 13 Jan 1758
CR 24 Oct 1779
CA 25 Oct 1814
d 26 Apr 1814 (PJP)

BASS, Edward
L 13 Nov 1790
CR 17 Feb 1798
d 9 Jan 1810 (PRO)

BASSAN, George (1)
L 15 June 1807
d 1811 (PRO)

BASSAN, George (2)
L 9 July 1811
d 31 July 1825 (PRO)

BASSAN, Samuel
L 29 Aug 1799
d May 1811 (PRO)

BASSE, Arthur
L 8 Jan 1695
CR 1710 (PJP)

BASSE, Robert
L 1665

BASSE, William
L
CA 1664

BASSETT, Christopher
L 22 Nov 1745
CR
CA 23 Mar 1757
d 18 May 1765

BASSET(T), John
L 30 July 1794 (PRO)
d 1818 (PRO)

BASTARD, John (1)
L 18 Jan 1744
d 1776 (PRO)

BASTARD, John (2)
L 6 Apr 1804
CR 22 May 1806
CA 12 Oct 1807
MP (Dartmouth) 9 May 1816–1832 (MPT)
d 11 Jan 1835 (MPT)

BASTARD, Richard
L 19 Oct 1807
Ret CR 28 July 1851 (PRO)
d 10 Feb 1867 (PRO)

BASTIN, Robert
L 3 Sept 1803
T
Ret CR 11 May 1836 (PRO)
d 19 Sept 1854 (PRO)

BATE, Elias
L 27 Sept 1740
CR 25 June 1746
CA 13 Dec 1750
d 25 May 1752 (PMM)

BATE, John
L 15 Dec 1800
d 7 Feb 1804 (PJP)

BATE, John Mort
L 1 Mar 1815 (NMM)
CR 15 Jan 1836 (NMM)
d 1845 (NMM)

BATEMAN, Charles Philip Butler
L 31 Oct 1795
CR 29 Apr 1802
CA 25 Sept 1806
RAB 23 Nov 1841 (PRO)
RAW 9 Nov 1846 (PRO)
RAR 27 Dec 1847 (PRO)
VAB 21 Mar 1851 (PRO)
Ret VA 1 July 1851 (PRO)
Ret A 18 June 1857 (PRO)
d 1858 (PRO)

BATEMAN, George
L 20 Nov 1812
d 1833 (PRO)

BATEMAN, Nathaniel
L 5 July 1756
CR 22 Sept 1759
CA 31 Mar 1760
Court martialed and dismissed
after action on 17 Apr 1780 (PRO)
SUP CA 13 Nov 1780 (PRO)

BATEMAN, Samuel
L 27 Mar 1782
CR 27 Apr 1801
d 1803 (PRO)

BATEMAN, Hon. William
L 30 Jan 1744
CR
CA 27 Dec 1745
Quitted 5 May 1751
MP (Gatton) 10 Apr 1752–1754 (MPS)
COM E 14 June 1756–
20 Mar 1761 (NBO)
COM N 20 Mar 1761–
19 June 1783 (NBO)
d 19 June 1783 (MPS)

BATES, Henry Andrew
L 20 Sept 1814
d 1847 (PRO)

BATES, John James
L 31 Aug 1801
KIA 7 Feb 1813 (LG)

BATES, Joseph
L 11 Mar 1815
HP Oct 1815 (OB)
d 1848 (PRO)

BATHURST, Walter
L 15 Nov 1790
CR 22 Aug 1798
CA 24 Oct 1799
KIA 20 Oct 1827 (LG)

BATT, Henry
L 14 Sept 1796
d 1806 (PRO)

BATT, John
L 27 Nov 1793
CR 10 Apr 1805
d Sept 1805 (PRO)

BATT, Joseph Bainbrigg
L 9 Jan 1800
d (drowned) 9 Nov 1810 (CH)

BATT, William
L 15 Mar 1815
CR 1 Jan 1856 (PRO)
d 19 May 1857 (PRO)

BATTEN, Charles
L 14 Feb 1815
HP 14 Feb 1815 (OB)
Ret CR 18 Jan 1861 (PRO)
d 13 Nov 1861 (PRO)

BATTEN, Richard
L 7 Feb 1794
d 1809 (PRO)

BATTERS, Christopher
L
CA 1666

BATTERSBY, Henry Robert
L 26 Apr 1806
CR 16 Sept 1809
CA 7 June 1814
d 28 Nov 1816 (PRO)

BATTIN, William
L
CA 1660
d before 1689 (PJP)

BATTS, George
L

CA 9 June 1666 (RM)
Dismissed 1666 (PD)

BAUGH, Henry
L 19 Feb 1799
CR 19 May 1808
CA 23 Nov 1841 (PRO)
Ret CA 6 June 1854 (PRO)
d 1854 (PRO)

BAUGH, Thomas Folliott
L 2 Nov 1793
CR 29 Apr 1802
CA 21 Oct 1810
Ret CA 1 Oct 1846 (PRO)
d 1857 (PRO)

BAUMGARDT, Charles Augustus
L 26 Feb 1804 (PRO)
d 1813 (PRO)

BAUMGARDT, William Augustus
L 7 Nov 1806
CR 28 Feb 1815
d 6 May 1827 (PRO)

BAWDEN, Charles (1)
L 11 July 1747
d ?1749 (PRO)

BAWDEN, Charles (2)
L 24 Apr 1777
d 1812 (PRO)

BAXTER, Thomas
L 20 Sept 1815
d 1852 (PRO)

BAYFIELD, Henry Wolsay
L 20 Mar 1815 (PRO)
CR 8 Nov 1826 (PRO)
CA 4 June 1834 (PRO)
RAB 21 Oct 1856 (PRO)
RAW 8 Dec 1857 (PRO)
RAR 29 July 1861 (PRO)
VAW 27 Apr 1863 (PRO)
Ret A 18 Oct 1867 (PRO)
d Feb 1885 (PRO)

BAYLEY, John
L 16 July 1793
CR 1 Jan 1801
CA 4 Dec 1813
d 1837 (PRO)

BAYLEY, Paget
See BAYLY, Paget

BAYLEY, Robert Sutton
L 30 July 1810
d 1811 (PRO)

BAYLEY, Thomas
L 20 Nov 1790
CR 3 Oct 1798
CA 15 Mar 1800
d 11 Apr 1819 (PJP)

BAYLIS, Robert
L 15 Oct 1790
d 11 Sept 1798 (PJP)

BAYLY, Charles Booth
L 17 June 1814
d 4 May 1852 (NMM)

BAYLY, George
L 10 Feb 1815
d 1817 (PRO)

BAYLY, James
L 22 Oct 1805
CR 25 Aug 1828 (PRO)
Ret CA 1 Apr 1856 (PRO)
d 1857 (PRO)

BAYLY, John
L 2 Apr 1806
d 1807 (PRO)

BAYLY, John Shoare
L 12 Oct 1807
d 1810 (PRO)

BAYLY, Paget
L 21 June 1776
CR 17 Dec 1782
CA 16 Nov 1789
d 14 Nov 1804

BAYLY, Peter
L 31 Aug 1809
d 1853 (PRO)

BAYLY, Robert Sutton
T
L 4 Nov 1811
d 1832 (PRO)

BAYNE, George
L 3 Oct 1770
CR 5 July 1794
d 1797 (PRO)

BAYNE, William
L 5 Apr 1749
CR 10 Nov 1756
CA 1 July 1760
KIA 9 Apr 1782 (RLB)

BAYNES, Adam
L 13 June 1692

BAYNES, Capel
L 28 Sept 1771
d 19 Mar 1789

BAYNES, Henry
L 4 Oct 1760
d 1813 (PRO)

BAYNES, Robert
L 31 Aug 1739
d 1755 (PRO)

BAYNES, Thomas
L 22 June 1782
CR 1 June 1815
d 14 Feb 1818 (PRO)

BAYNTIN, Walter Pierson
L 8 Mar 1802
Dismissed 1818 (PRO)

BAYNTON, Benjamin
L 2 Jan 1810
HP 1 May 1818 (OB)
CR 23 Nov 1841 (PRO)
d 14 Nov 1854 (PRO)

BAYNTUN, Sir Henry William
L 15 Apr 1783
CR
CA 4 May 1794
T
RAB 12 Aug 1812
RAW 4 June 1814
KCB 2 Jan 1815 (DNB)
RAR 12 Aug 1819 (PRO)

VAB 19 July 1821 (PRO)
VAW 27 May 1825 (PRO)
VAR 22 July 1830 (PRO)
AB 10 Jan 1837 (PRO)
GCB 25 Oct 1839 (DNB)
d 17 Dec 1840 (DNB)

BAZALGETTE, Joseph William
L 12 June 1806
CR 17 May 1814
d 10 Jan 1849 (PRO)

BAZELY, Henry
L 14 Nov 1790
CR 4 Apr 1796
CA 8 Apr 1800
d 13 Apr 1824 (PRO)

BAZELY, John (1)
L 7 Apr 1760
CR 1 Oct 1777
CA 15 Apr 1778
RAW 1 June 1795
VAB 14 Feb 1799
VAW 1 Jan 1801
VAR 23 Apr 1804
AB 9 Nov 1805
d 2 Apr 1809 (PRO)

BAZELY, John (2)
L 19 Apr 1783
CR 5 July 1794
CA 11 Nov 1794
SUP RA 9 June 1814 (MB)
VAB 5 July 1827 (PRO)
d 21 Mar 1828 (PRO)

BEACH, George
L 27 June 1682
d before 1689 (PJP)

BEACH, John
L 24 Aug 1801
d Dec 1828 (PRO)

BEACH, Sir Richard
L
CA 6 July 1666 (RM)
RAD 1670
RAB 1672
COMM (Portsmouth) 1688 (PJP)
COM V 13 May 1690–May 1692 (NBO)
d May 1692 (NBO)

BEAKE, William
L 1665

BEALE, George
L 18 June 1709 (PMM)

BEALE, Jeremiah
L 15 Apr 1779
CR 1 Dec 1787
CA 22 Nov 1790
SUP RA 3 Aug 1810
d 1817 (PRO)

BEALE, Richard
L 29 Nov 1756
d 1787 (PRO)

BEALE, William (1)
L 16 Jan 1687
d before 1689 (PJP)

BEALE, William (2)
L 4 Mar 1740
d 1753 (PRO)

BEALES, Charles
L 26 Nov 1808
Ret CR 13 Apr 1846 (PRO)
d 1860 (PRO)

BEAMISH, William
L 7 Aug 1744
d 1772 (PRO)

BEARD, William
L 26 May 1797
d 1814 (PRO)

BEARE, Amos
L
CA 1664
d before 1689 (PJP)

BEART, Charles James
L 15 Mar 1815
d 18 Feb 1861 (PRO)

BEASANT, Henry
L 11 Dec 1783
d 1807 (PRO)

BEASLEY, Edmund
L 1 Dec 1797
d 1808 (PRO)

BEATSON, Robert
L 7 July 1777
Deprived of two years' seniority in 1780 and 1781
d 18 Apr 1798

BEAUCLERK, Lord Amelius
L 21 Sept 1790
CR
CA 16 Sept 1793
CRM 31 July 1810 (AL)
RAB 1 Aug 1811
RAW 12 Aug 1812
RAR 4 June 1814
KCB 2 Jan 1815 (DNB)
VAB 12 Aug 1819 (PRO)
VAW 19 July 1821 (PRO)
VAR 27 May 1825 (PRO)
AB 22 July 1830
GCH 29 Mar 1831 (DNB)
GCB 4 Aug 1835 (DNB)
AW 10 Jan 1837 (PRO)
AR 23 Nov 1841 (PRO)
d 10 Dec 1846 (DNB)

BEAUCLERK, Lord Aubrey
L
CR
CA 1 Apr 1731
KIA 24 Feb 1741 (LG)

BEAUCLERK, Lord Vere
L 23 Aug 1717 (PMM)
CR
CA 30 May 1721
MP (New Windsor) 31 May 1726–Feb 1738 (MPS)
COM E 24 May 1732–13 Mar 1738 (NBO)
COM AD 13 Mar 1738–19 Mar 1742 (AO)

MP (Plymouth)	1741–28 Mar	1750 (MPS)
COM AD	27 Nov	1744–
	18 Nov	1749 (AO)
RAR	23 Apr	1745
VAB	14 July	1746
VAR	15 July	1747
AB	12 May	1748
d	2 Oct	1781 (PJP)
BEAUCLERK, Lord William		
L	2 Apr	1788
SUP CR	29 July	1822 (PRO)
d	17 July	1825 (PRO)
BEAUFORT, Sir Francis		
L	10 May	1796
CR	13 Nov	1800
CA	30 May	1810
Ret RA	1 Oct	1846 (PRO)
KCB	29 Apr	1848 (DNB)
d	17 Dec	1857 (PRO)
BEAUFOY, Benjamin		
L	29 Apr	1797
d	Dec	1807 (PJP)
BEAUMAN, Francis		
L	26 Oct	1796
CR	4 Mar	1805
CA	13 Oct	1807
RAB	23 Nov	1841 (PRO)
d	22 Dec	1846 (PJP)
BEAUMONT, Basil		
L	28 Oct	1688
CA	21 May	1689
RAB	1 Mar	1703
d (drowned)	27 Nov	1703 (DNB)
BEAUMONT, Francis (1)		
L	12 May	1802
Ret CR	9 July	1834 (PRO)
d	3 Mar	1840 (PRO)
BEAUMONT, Francis (2)		
L	11 Jan	1808
Ret CR	19 Oct	1844 (PRO)
d	28 Sept	1850 (PRO)
BEAUMONT, George		
L	29 Apr	1742
d (drowned)	24 June	1746 (PJP)
BEAVER, Philip		
L	16 Oct	1783
CR	28 June	1800
CA	10 Feb	1801
d	10 Apr	1813 (PRO)
BEAVOR, Edmund		
L	3 Mar	1734
CR	18 Apr	1743
CA	18 Apr	1744
d (drowned)	14 Nov	1745 (DNB)
BEAWES, William		
L		
CA	13 Mar	1694
KIA	25 Oct	1695 (CH)
BEAZELEY, George		
L	18 Apr	1811
Ret CR	1 Mar	1852 (PRO)
d		1875 (PRO)

BECHER, Alexander		
L	9 Aug	1791
CR	26 June	1797
CA	29 Apr	1802
d	17 Feb	1827 (PRO)
BECHER, John		
L	21 Jan	1757
CR	1 Feb	1778
d		1783 (PRO)
BECHER, Michael		
L	3 Jan	1754
d	26 Dec	1760 (PRO)
BECHER, William		
L	25 Sept	1806
d	10 Oct	1810 (PRO)
BECHINOE, Benjamin		
L	29 Mar	1759
CR	30 Apr	1779
d	24 Apr	1791
BECKENHAM, Robert		
L		
CA	6 May	1699
d	Aug	1707
BECKETT, Flowers		
T		
L	24 Dec	1805
d	18 June	1862 (PRO)
BECKETT, John		
L	3 Aug	1809
d	22 Mar	1818 (LT)
BECKETT, Joseph		
L	28 July	1800
d		1808 (PRO)
BECKETT, William (1)		
L	3 Oct	1810
d	May	1820 (PRO)
BECKETT, William (2)		
L	29 May	1813
d	28 Mar	1839 (PRO)
BECKFORD, John Leigh		
L	27 Nov	1810
CR	30 Nov	1821 (PRO)
Ret CR	1 July	1851 (PRO)
Ret CA	1 Apr	1856 (PRO)
d		1858 (PRO)
BECKHAM, Zebedee		
L	20 Nov	1812
d	15 June	1829 (PRO)
BECKWITH, George		
L	3 Sept	1814
d		1819 (PRO)
BECKWITH, Matthew		
L	24 Apr	1720
d	11 Sept	1728 (M)
BEDDINGFIELD, James		
L	10 Jan	1771
d		1775 (PRO)
BEDFORD, Edward		
L	19 Apr	1712 (PMM)
BEDFORD, Frederick		
L	6 Sept	1799
d	14 May	1862 (PRO)

BEDFORD, John
L 2 Sept 1794
T
CR 24 Dec 1805
CA 4 Dec 1814
d 19 Oct 1814 (PRO)

BEDFORD, Thomas
L 15 June 1731
SUP 1748 (PMM)

BEDFORD, William
L 12 Sept 1781
CR 5 July 1794
CA 15 Aug 1794
RAB 12 Aug 1812
RAW 4 June 1814
RAR 12 Aug 1819 (PRO)
VAB 19 July 1821 (PRO)
VAW 27 May 1825 (PRO)
d Oct 1827 (DNB)

BEDINGFIELD, Thomas William
L 11 Dec 1804
d 1854 (PRO)

BEDWELL, Edward Parker
L 28 Feb 1815
d 1854 (PRO)

BEECH, George
L 14 Feb 1705
SUP 20 Mar 1738 (PMM)
d 1749 (PMM)

BEECHEY, Frederick William
L 10 Mar 1815
CR 25 Jan 1822 (DNB)
CA 8 May 1827 (DNB)
RAB 11 Sept 1854 (PRO)
RAW 31 Jan 1856 (PRO)
d 29 Nov 1856 (DNB)

BEECROFT, Charles
L 29 Apr 1802
CR 3 Oct 1809
Struck off list 18 Mar 1825 (PRO)
d 1825 (MB)

BEED, George
L 16 Mar 1742
d ?1749 (PRO)

BEER, Christopher
L 10 Nov 1813
HP Feb 1816 (OB)
Ret CR 18 Aug 1856 (PRO)
d 1872 (PRO)

BEER, John
L
CA 27 Jan 1691
SUP 20 Nov 1694 (PMM)
d 22 Sept 1696

BEER, Thomas
L 4 May 1810
CR 29 July 1825 (PRO)
Ret CA 1 Apr 1856 (PRO)
d 1867 (PRO)

BEERE, John
L
CA 1660

BEESTON, William
L
CA 1671
d before 1689 (PJP)

BEGBIE, James
L 7 Dec 1801
d 11 Oct 1820 (PRO)

BEKENHAM, Robert
See BECKENHAM, Robert

BELBIN, Peter (1)
L 1672
CA 1673
d 1678

BELBIN, Peter (2)
L
CA 1677 (DDA)

BELCHER, John
L
Deserted from HMS CHERUB at Valparaiso while under close arrest 11 Feb 1814

BELCHIER, Nathaniel
L 14 May 1794
CR 21 Oct 1810
d 1838 (PRO)

BELDEN, Nathaniel
L 7 July 1801
Ret CR 15 July 1831 (PRO)
d 1838 (PRO)

BELFOUR, Charles
See BALFOUR, Charles

BELITHIA, Warren
L 25 Apr 1740
CR 19 Mar 1746
d 27 Dec 1758 (PRO)

BELL, Christopher
L 20 Nov 1802
CR 1 Apr 1808
CA 7 Feb 1812
CB 4 July 1840 (OB)
Ret RA 1 Oct 1846 (PRO)
d 16 Oct 1853 (PRO)

BELL, Christopher James
L 1 Mar 1815
d 1837 (PRO)

BELL, George (1)
L 27 Apr 1757
d 1762 (PRO)

BELL, George (2)
L 21 Apr 1781
d 1799 (PRO)

BELL, George (3)
L 6 Dec 1796
CR 12 Oct 1807
CA 31 July 1809
d 3 June 1839 (PRO)

BELL, George (4)
L 16 Jan 1801
Name removed 1811 (PRO)

BELL, John
L 2 July 1800
d 1812 (PRO)

BELL, Michael
L 5 Apr 1801
d 1812 (PRO)

BELL, Nicholas		
L	8 Nov	1799
T		
d	18 Sept	1827 (PRO)
BELL, Richard		
L	1 Aug	1794
d		1796 (PRO)
BELL, Robert		
L		1666
BELL, Robert Benn		
L	4 Sept	1798
d		1817 (PRO)
BELL, Thomas Bush		
L	3 Mar	1810
d	Sept	1829 (PRO)
BELL, William (1)		
L	6 Sept	1760
d	21 Jan	1804
BELL, William (2)		
L	12 Nov	1778
d (drowned)	24 Oct	1782 (PJP)
BELLAIRS, John Henry		
L	30 Sept	1813
Ret CR	23 May	1856 (PRO)
d	29 Nov	1862 (PMM)
BELLAMONT, Lord		
L		1666
KIA	19 June	1667 (DDA)
BELLAMY, John		
L	15 May	1799
CR	21 Jan	1809
d		1818 (PRO)
BELLAMY, Leonard		
L	16 May	1727
CR	13 Feb	1746 (PMM)
d	22 Apr	1746
BELLAMY, William		
L	9 Mar	1799
d		1801 (PRO)
BELLAS, John		
L	15 May	1797
d	July	1800
BELLASYSE, John		
L		
CA	27 July	1666 (RM)
d	before	1689 (PJP)
BELLENDEN, Ker, Lord		
L	6 Nov	1745
d		1753 (PRO)
BELLEW, Henry		
L	23 June	1756
CR	1 Nov	1762
CA	10 Jan	1771
d	18 Apr	1791
BELLEW, William		
L	21 Nov	1793
d		1826 (PRO)
BELLI, George Lawrence		
L	27 Oct	1804
KIA	3 Mar	1807 (CH)
BELLINGHALL, William		
L	10 July	1802
d		1803 (PRO)

BELLOWES, George		
L		1672
BELLWOOD, Roger		
L		
CA	17 Jan	1694
d	11 Aug	1697
BELSEY, Henry		
L	21 Mar	1812
HP	6 July	1833 (OB)
Ret CR	2 Jan	1854 (PRO)
d		1855 (PRO)
BELSON, Henry Fage		
L	7 Mar	1808
Dismissed	22 Feb	1827 (PRO)
Restored		1828 (PRO)
Ret CR	18 Jan	1845 (LT)
d	30 Sept	1849 (LT)
BELT, John		
L		1665
BELTON, Duke of		
See BOLTON, Harry Powlett, Duke of		
BELTON, William		
L	15 Mar	1692
BELVIN, Robert		
L		
CA	21 Jan	1698
BEMBOW, John		
See BENBOW, John		
BENAMOR, Fell		
L	9 Mar	1799
d	4 May	1820 (PRO)
BENBOW, John (1)		
L	1 June	1689 (DNB)
CA	20 Sept	1690 (DNB)
RAB	1 May	1696
RAR	14 Apr	1701
VAB	30 June	1701
VAW	19 Jan	1702
d	4 Nov	1702
BENBOW, John (2)		
L	7 Mar	1700
BENDYSHE, John		
L	11 Nov	1811
Ret CR	1 Apr	1853 (PRO)
d		1856 (PRO)
BENDYSHE, Robert		
L	12 Apr	1806
d		1807
BENETT, Charles Cowper		
L	Apr	1808 (MB)
CR	15 June	1814 (MB)
BENETT, William Wake		
L	7 May	1802
d		1805 (PRO)
BENGAUGH, James		
L	13 May	1778
d		1785 (PRO)
BENGE, Edward		
L	22 Apr	1802
CR	1 Feb	1812
d		1815 (PRO)
BENN, Joseph		
L	2 Dec	1807
d		1811 (PRO)

BENN, Thomas
L 8 Feb 1815
HP 12 July 1815 (OB)
Ret CR 12 Apr 1860 (PRO)
d 1869 (PRO)

BENNET(T), Edmund
L 14 Aug 1801
d 1817 (PRO)

BENNET(T), Edward
L 15 Dec 1708
CR
CA 7 Dec 1731
d 23 Dec 1732

BENNET(T), James
L 27 Aug 1794
KIA 29 Sept 1808 (JH)

BENNET, John (1)
L
CA 1 May 1695
d 30 Jan 1717

BENNET(T), John (2)
L 1 May 1807
d 1808(9) (PRO)

BENNET(T), Hon John Astley
L 2 Aug 1799
CR 14 Apr 1802
CA 12 Jan 1805
d 1812 (PRO)

BENNET, Martin
L 2 Nov 1811
Ret CR 1 Apr 1853 (PRO)
d 1868 (PRO)

BENNET, Richard Henry Alexander
L 5 May 1790
CR 30 Oct 1793
CA 1 Jan 1796
MP (Launceston) 1802–1806 (MPT)
MP (Enniskillen) 1807 (MPT)
MP (Launceston) 17 July 1807–Apr 1812 (MPT)
d 11 Oct 1818 (LT)

BENNET(T), Thomas Pye
L 9 May 1781
d 1809 (PRO)

BENNET, William
L
CR 10 Jan 1759 (PRO)
CA 5 Mar 1760 (PRO)
d 1787 (PRO)

BENNETT, Benjamin
L 21 Dec 1693

BENNETT, Charles
L 21 Dec 1797
T
CR 21 Oct 1810
Ret CA 10 Sept 1840 (PRO)
d Aug 1843 (PRO)

BENNETT, James
L 21 Aug 1815
d 29 Dec 1820 (PRO)

BENNETT, Thomas
L 9 Dec 1803
CR 15 June 1814
CA 16 Sept 1828 (PRO)
RAB 2 May 1855 (PRO)
RAW 12 Nov 1856 (PRO)
RAR 4 Feb 1858 (PRO)
VAB 15 Jan 1862 (PRO)
VAW 1 Apr 1863 (PRO)
VAR 3 Nov 1863 (PRO)
A 12 Sept 1865 (PRO)
d 12 June 1870 (PRO)

BENNETT, Thomas Stanhope
L 21 July 1769
CR 10 Aug 1779
d 25 Sept 1781 (PRO)

BENNETT, William (1)
L 26 Mar 1741
CR 10 Jan 1759
CA 5 Mar 1760 (PRO)
d 1790 (PRO)

BENNETT, William (2)
L 17 Aug 1794
CR 12 Aug 1812
d 1819 (PRO)

BENSELY, John
L 23 Apr 1756
d 1769 (PRO)

BENSELY, William
L 6 Apr 1757
SUP CR 21 Sept 1796 (PMM)
d 1796 (PRO)

BENSON, John Robert
L 27 June 1814 (PRO)
Ret CR 1 Jan 1858 (PRO)
d 1864 (PRO)

BENSON, William
L 19 May 1808
d 10 Sept 1823 (PRO)

BENT, Thomas
L 15 July 1809
d 1815 (PRO)

BENTHAM, Edward Alexander
L 14 Jan 1796
Struck off list 1798 (PRO)

BENTHAM, George
L 24 Dec 1805
CR 14 Oct 1810
CA 16 Sept 1816 (PRO)
Ret CA 1 Oct 1846 (PRO)
Ret RA 11 June 1851 (PRO)
Ret VA 9 July 1857 (PRO)
d 24 Feb 1862 (PRO)

BENTINCK, John Albert
L 21 July 1757
CR 18 May 1758
CA 17 Oct 1758
MP (Rye) 1761–1768 (MPN)
d 23 Sept 1775

BENTINCK, William
L 12 July 1782
CR
CA 15 Sept 1783
RAB 9 Nov 1805

RAW 28 Apr 1808
VAB 31 July 1810
d 21 Feb 1813 (PRO)

BENTLEY, Sir John
L 28 Mar 1734
CR
Kt 1739 (PJP)
CA 1 Aug 1744
COM E 20 Mar 1761–
20 Jan 1764 (NBO)
RAW 28 Dec 1763
VAB 18 Oct 1770
VAW 24 Oct 1770
d 14 Dec 1772

BERANGER, James
L 27 May 1740
d 1744(5) (PRO)

BERESFORD, Sir John Poo
L 4 Nov 1790
CR Nov 1794 (DNB)
CA 25 June 1795
MP 26 June 1809–
(Coleraine) 1812 (MPT)
Kt 22 May 1812 (MPT)
Cre Bt 7 May 1814 (MPT)
RAB 4 June 1814
MP 10 June 1814–
(Coleraine) Jan 1823 (MPT)
RAW 12 Aug 1819 (PRO)
KCB 12 Aug 1819 (MB)
RAR 19 July 1821 (PRO)
MP
(Berwick-on-Tweed) 1823–1826 (MPT)
VAB 27 May 1825 (PRO)
MP (Northallerton) 1826–1832 (MPT)
VAW 22 July 1830 (PRO)
MP
(Coleraine) 1832–May 1833 (MPT)
COM AD 23 Dec 1834–
25 Apr 1835 (AO)
MP
(Chatham) 1835–1837 (MPT)
GCH May 1836 (MPT)
VAR 10 Jan 1837 (PRO)
AB 28 June 1838 (PRO)
AW 23 Nov 1841 (PRO)
d 2 Oct 1844 (PRO)

BERINGTON, Samuel
L 23 Feb 1815
HP 4 July 1815 (OB)
d 1862 (PRO)

BERKELEY, Hon Augustus Fitzharding
L 9 May 1809
Struck off list for having a commission in the army Jan 1814 (PRO)

BERKELEY, Lord Charles
L
CA 2 July 1681
d 6 Mar 1682

BERKELEY, George
L 25 June 1724
CR
CA 27 May 1728
d 15 Jan 1747

BERKELEY, Hon. Sir George Cranfield
L Sept 1772 (DNB)
CR 3 Sept 1778
CA 15 Sept 1780
MP (Gloucestershire) 1783–1810 (MPT)
CRM 1 June 1795 (AL)
RAB 14 Feb 1799
RAW 1 Jan 1801
RAR 23 Apr 1804
VAW 9 Nov 1805
VAR 28 Apr 1808
AB 31 July 1810
Kt 1 Feb 1813 (LG)
AW 4 June 1814
GCB 2 Jan 1815 (MPT)
d 25 Feb 1818 (DNB)

BERKELEY, James, Earl of
L 10 Mar 1699
CR
CA 2 Apr 1701 (DNB)
VAB 12 Jan 1708
(?26 Jan 1708)
AB 19 Dec 1708
AW 21 Dec 1708
AR 14 Nov 1709
Inh EP 24 Sept 1710 (DNB)
FLA 16 May 1717–
2 Aug 1727 (AO)
AF 13 Mar 1719
d 17 Aug 1736

BERKELEY, John, Lord (1)
Inh EP 6 Mar 1682 (DNB)
L 14 Apr 1685
CA 9 July 1686
RAD 14 Dec 1688
RAB 1 May 1689
RAR 12 June 1689
VAB 30 Jan 1693
VAR 22 Aug 1693
AB 12 July 1693 (DNB)
AB 16 Apr 1694
AF 25 May 1696
d 27 Feb 1697

BERKELEY, John (2)
L 5 Apr 1722
d 30 Apr 1727 (PMM)

BERKELEY, Hon. Maurice Frederick
See FITZHARDINGE, Hon. Maurice Frederick, Lord

BERKELEY, Velters Cornewall
L 5 Dec 1773
CR 5 Oct 1782
CA 21 Sept 1790
d 1804 (PRO)

BERKELEY, Sir William (1)
L 1661
CA 1662
Kt 12 Oct 1664 (DNB)
RAR Nov 1664 (DNB)
LGG (Portsmouth) 19 June 1665 (EAD)
VAB 1665
VAW 1666
KIA 1 June 1666 (RM)

BERKELEY, Hon. William (2)
L 10 Mar 1721
CR 22 June 1726
CA 11 Mar 1727
d 25 Mar 1733

BERMINGHAM, Hon. John		
L	31 Aug	1739
CR	16 Nov	1744
CA	14 May	1745
d	8 May	1746
BERNADISTON, Henry		
L		1665
CA		1670
d	before	1689 (PJP)
BERNARD, George		
L		
CA		1661
d	before	1689 (PJP)
BERNARD, Henry Richard		
L	22 May	1809
d	1 Nov	1821 (PRO)
BERNARD, John		
L	29 Mar	1745
SUP	14 Nov	1785 (PRO)
BERNEY, John		
L	27 July	1803
CR	27 June	1814
d		1836 (PRO)
BERNSLEY, Henry		
L	1 Aug	1740
CR	10 Jan	1746
CA	7 May	1748
d (drowned)	25 Sept	1757 (PJP)
BERRELL, Silvester		
L	27 Dec	1808
d		1817 (PRO)
BERRIFF, Robert Cleark		
L	31 Jan	1806 (PRO)
d		1816 (PRO)
BERRIMAN, Daniel		
L	24 May	1704
BERROW, Edward		
L	9 Apr	1760
d		1779 (PRO)
BERRY, Anthony		
L		1666
BERRY, Sir Edward		
L	20 Jan	1794
CR	12 Nov	1796 (PRO)
CA	6 Mar	1797
Kt		1798 (PJP)
T		
Cre Bt	12 Dec	1806 (MB)
KCB	2 Jan	1815 (DNB)
CRM	12 Aug	1819 (AL)
RAB	19 July	1821 (PRO)
RAW	27 Mar	1825 (PRO)
RAR	22 July	1830 (PRO)
d	13 Feb	1831 (DNB)
BERRY, Sir John (1)		
L		1663 (DNB)
CA	17 Sept	1665 (DNB)
Kt		1672 (DNB)
CAMR	1 Oct	1672 (EAD)
CAF (Vane)	18 Aug	1673 (EAD)
COM N	17 Apr	1686–
	12 Oct	1688 (NBO)
RAD	24 Sept	1688 (P)
COM V	12 Oct	1688–
	14 Feb	1690 (NBO)
VAD	13 Dec	1688 (P)
d	14 Feb	1690 (DNB)
BERRY, John (2)		
L	23 Apr	1805
T	wounded	
d		1809 (TR)
BERRY, Joseph (1)		
L		1672 (P)
BERRY, Joseph (2)		
L	26 June	1690 (PMM)
BERRY, Robert (1)		
L	24 Aug	1697
BERRY, Robert (2)		
L	29 Aug	1797
d	9 Feb	1824 (PRO)
BERRY, Thomas		
L		1672 (P)
CA		1673 (P)
Discharged by court martial		1673
L	12 Aug	1678 (PRO)
d	26 Aug	1689 (PRO)
BERRY, William (1)		
L		
CA		1665
BERRY, William (2)		
L	26 May	1795
d	18 Oct	1807 (LT)
BERRY, William (3)		
L	13 Apr	1803
e	19 Oct	1807 (PJP)
BERTIE, Sir Albemarle		
L	20 Dec	1777 (DNB)
CR	3 June	1780
CA	21 Mar	1782
RAW	23 Apr	1804
RAR	9 Nov	1805
VAB	28 Apr	1808
VAR	31 July	1810
Cre Bt	3 Nov	1812 (LG)
AB	4 June	1814
KCB	2 Jan	1815 (DNB)
AW	19 July	1821 (PRO)
d	24 Feb	1824 (DNB)
BERTIE, Hon. Charles		
L		1668
CAF (Coldstream Guards)		1668 (MPH)
MP (Stamford)		1678 (MPH)
MP (Stamford)		1685–
	22 Mar	1711 (MPH)
d	22 Mar	1711 (MPH)
BERTIE, Lord Montague		
L	5 May	1735
CR		
CA	18 July	1740
d	10 Aug	1753
BERTIE, Peregrine		
L	30 July	1697
CR		
CA	3 Mar	1701
KIA	10 Oct	1707 (CH)
BERTIE, Hon. Peregrine Francis		
L	17 Dec	1759

CR	1 Jan	1762
CA	6 Nov	1762
MP (Oxford)	1774–20 Aug	1790 (MPT)
d	20 Aug	1790 (MPT)

BERTIE, Lord Thomas (1)

L		
CR	16 Aug	1743 (PRO)
CA	14 Mar	1744
d	27 July	1749

BERTIE, Sir Thomas (2)

L	21 May	1778
CR	10 Aug	1782
CA	22 Nov	1790
RAB	28 Apr	1808
RAW	31 July	1810
RAR	1 Aug	1811
Kt (Sweden)	June	1813 (MB)
Kt	June	1813 (DNB)
VAB	4 Dec	1813
VAW	4 June	1814
VAR	19 July	1819 (PRO)
AB	27 May	1825 (PRO)
d	13 June	1825 (DNB)

BERTRAM, Allen

L	13 Jan	1815
CR	28 Apr	1827 (PRO)
d		1834 (PRO)

BERTRAM, Charles

L	29 Apr	1802
CR	24 Mar	1808
CA	7 June	1814
Ret CA	1 Oct	1846 (PRO)
Ret RA	9 Oct	1849 (PRO)
d		1854 (PRO)

BESLY, John

L	31 July	1782
d	Jan	1823 (PRO)

BESSON, Charles

L	27 Oct	1758
d	20 Sept	1822 (PRO)

BEST, John (1)

L		
CA		1665
d	before	1689 (PJP)

BEST, John (2)

L	13 Jan	1705
CR	5 May	1735
d	15 May	1751 (PMM)

BEST, Richard

L	17 June	1802
d		1805 (PRO)

BEST, Robert

L		
CA	18 Sept	1677
d (drowned)	25 Feb	1678 (DDA)

BETHELL, Christopher
See CODRINGTON, Christopher q.v.

BETT, William

L	4 Sept	1766
CR	12 Dec	1779
CA	29 July	1781
d	8 Dec	1785 (PMM)

BETTESWORTH, George

L	24 Oct	1801
Ret CR	16 July	1832 (PRO)
d	10 Sept	1832 (LT)

BETTESWORTH, George Edmund Bryon

L	1 May	1804
CR	21 Nov	1804
CA	9 July	1805
KIA	15 May	1808 (CH)

BETTS, William

L		
CA		1674
d	before	1689 (PJP)

BETTY, Christopher William

L	17 Sept	1801
T	wounded	
Ret CR	4 Apr	1832 (PRO)
d		1850 (TR)

BEVAN, Griffith

L	4 May	1809
d		1832 (PRO)

BEVAN, John

L	20 June	1794
d	2 Aug	1831 (PRO)

BEVAN, Rowland

L	28 Oct	1790
CR	6 July	1794
CA	10 June	1808
d		1836 (PRO)

BEVAN, Samuel

L		1664
d	before	1689 (PJP)

BEVERLEY, John (1)

L		1672 (DDA)
d	before	1685 (DDA)

BEVERLEY, John (2)

L		
CA		1673 (P)
SUP	15 Mar	1697 (DDA)
d	12 Feb	1700 (DDA)

BEVERLEY, Thomas

L	20 Mar	1705 (PMM)
CR		
CA	10 June	1709
d	26 June	1722

BEVERSHAM, John

L		1661

BEVES, Thomas

L	13 Sept	1779
d		1796 (PRO)

BEVIANS, William (1)

L	23 Jan	1780
CR	8 Mar	1797
d		1834 (PRO)

BEVIANS, William (2)

L	9 Dec	1780
d (drowned)		1801 (PJP)

BEVIS, Thomas

L	24 Sept	1806
CR	3 Aug	1829 (PRO)
CA	4 Feb	1858 (PRO)
Ret CA	20 Apr	1868 (PRO)
d		1869 (PRO)

BEWICK, George
L 7 Sept 1815
d 1819 (PRO)

BEWICKE, John
L 12 June 1807
d 1814 (PRO)

BIBB, Edward
L
CA 19 Jan 1691
(19 Jan 1692 in C)
d 2 Oct 1701

BICKENSTAFF, Francis
L 16 Mar 1814
d 1863 (PRO)

BICKERTON, Sir Richard
L 8 Feb 1746
CR 2 Aug 1758
CA 21 Aug 1759
Kt 24 June 1773 (MPT)
Cre Bt 29 May 1778 (DNB)
RAB 24 Sept 1787
RAW 21 Sept 1790
MP (Rochester) 1790–25 Feb 1792 (MPT)
d 25 Feb 1792 (DNB)

BICKERTON, Sir Richard Hussey
L 16 Dec 1777
CR 20 Mar 1779
CA 8 Feb 1781
Inh Bt 25 Feb 1792 (DNB)
RAB 14 Feb 1799
RAW 1 Jan 1801
RAR 23 Apr 1804
VAW 9 Nov 1805
COM AD 6 Apr 1807–
25 Mar 1812 (AO)
MP (Poole) 24 Feb 1808-1812 (MPT)
VAR 25 Oct 1809
MGRM 20 Apr 1810 (LG)
AB 31 July 1810
AW 4 June 1814
KCB 2 Jan 1815 (DNB)
LGRM 5 June 1818 (AL)
AR 27 May 1825 (PRO)
GRM 28 June 1830 (AL)
d 9 Feb 1832 (DNB)

BIDDLE, William
L 10 Dec 1718
d 4 Nov 1726 (PMM)

BIDDULPH, Charles
L 16 July 1806
CR 27 Dec 1812
d 22 Apr 1815 (LT)

BIDDULPH, Edward
L 5 Oct 1809
Ret CR 6 Aug 1849 (PRO)
d 1851 (PRO)

BIGANT, Thomas
L
CA 12 Feb 1694
KIA 1 May 1694 (CH)

BIGG, Jeremiah
L 15 Mar 1763
d 1 Aug 1786 (PMM)

BIGGARD, James
L 10 May 1804
d 1808 (PRO)

BIGGLAND, Wilson Braddyll
L 5 Mar 1808
CR 15 June 1814
CA 6 Mar 1821 (PRO)
Ret CA 1 Oct 1846 (PRO)
Ret RA 8 Mar 1852 (PRO)
Ret VA 2 Oct 1857 (PRO)
d 19 Nov 1858 (PRO)

BIGGS, George
L 1660
d before 1689 (PJP)

BIGGS, Robert
L 7 Aug 1761
CR 10 Jan 1771
CA 18 Mar 1778
RAW 1 June 1795
VAB 14 Feb 1799
VAW 1 Jan 1801
d 11 July 1803 (PRO)

BIGGS, William (1)
L 1673
d (drowned) ?1673 (PJP)

BIGGS, William (2)
L 2 Oct 1796 (PRO)
d 1803 (PRO)

BIGNALL, James
L 17 Mar 1780
d 19 Oct 1793

BIGNALL, Samuel
L 6 Sept 1779
d 19 Oct 1780 (PRO)

BIGNELL, George
L 10 Sept 1801
T
CR 19 Sept 1815
CA 1 July 1851 (NMM)
Ret CA 28 July 1851 (PRO)
d 1863 (TR)

BILLINGSLEY, Rupert
L 6 Feb 1694 (PMM)
CA 12 Jan 1699
d 15 Dec 1720

BILLOP, Christopher
CAFMR 20 Nov 1670 (EAD)
L 1671 (P)
CA 7 May 1673

BILLOP, Thomas
L 19 Feb 1702
CR 13 Jan 1728

BILTON, John
L 26 Feb 1703

BINDOSS, Sir Edward
L 27 Aug 1760
d 1789 (PRO)

BINDON, John Read
L 31 July 1799
Ret CR 26 Nov 1830 (PRO)
d 1863 (PRO)

BING, George
See BYNG, George, Viscount Torrington

BINGHAM, Arthur Batt
L 1 May 1804
CR 4 May 1809
CA 7 Feb 1812
d 19 Aug 1830 (PRO)

BINGHAM, Edward
L 31 May 1808
d 30 May 1823 (PRO)

BINGHAM, John
L 5 Feb 1806
Ret CR 9 Apr 1839 (PRO)
d 25 June 1863 (PRO)

BINGHAM, Joseph
L 2 Nov 1790
CR 6 July 1794
CA 20 Apr 1796
RAB 12 Aug 1819 (PRO)
RAW 19 July 1821 (PRO)
RAR 27 May 1825 (PRO)
d 10 Dec 1825 (LT)

BINGHAM, Robert Pollock
L 7 Mar 1815
d 1816 (PRO)

BINKS, William
L 15 Sept 1744
d 1761 (PRO)

BINNEY, John
L 29 Nov 1814
d 1836 (PRO)

BINNING, Thomas
See BYNNING, Thomas

BIRCH, Augustus
See BIRTCH, Augustus

BIRCH, Sir Charles
L
CR
CA 21 Jan 1703
d 17 Oct 1706

BIRCH, Edward
L 18 Mar 1794
d 22 May 1800

BIRCH, Henry
L 16 Feb 1815
d 1819 (PRO)

BIRCH, Joseph
L 20 June 1811
d 1841 (PRO)

BIRCH, William
L 14 Oct 1742
d ?1749

BIRCHALL, Thomas Dorsett
L 13 Nov 1790
d 26 Oct 1836 (LT)

BIRCHALL, Thomas William
L 7 Feb 1799
d 1807 (PRO)

BIRCHALL, William
L 18 June 1793
CR 21 Oct 1797
CA 2 Apr 1801
d 1817 (PRO)

BIRD, Henry
L 4 Aug 1809
Ret CR 12 Aug 1848 (PRO)
d 1853 (PRO)

BIRD, John Gibbs
L 5 Dec 1806
d 1835 (PRO)

BIRD, Joseph
L 13 May 1778
d 1789 (PRO)

BIRD, Mathias
L
CA 1672
d before 1689 (PJP)

BIRD, Timothy (1)
L 2 Feb 1761
d 23 Nov 1793

BIRD, Timothy (2)
L 11 May 1794
d 1826 (PRO)

BIRKHEAD, Henry Hutchings
L 8 Mar 1783
CR 9 Nov 1795
d 12 Feb 1837 (PJP)

BIRKS, Joshua
L 25 Mar 1809
d 1835 (PRO)

BIRMINGHAM, Hon. John
See BERMINGHAM, Hon. John

BIRT, John
L 20 Mar 1756
d 31 Oct 1764 (PRO)

BIRTCH, Augustus
L
CA 1672

BISHOP, Charles
L 19 Apr 1803
d 1807 (PRO)

BISHOP, Francis
L 25 May 1778
d 3 May 1803

BISHOP, George
L 18 Sept 1812
HP 14 Sept 1817 (OB)
Ret CR 3 Sept 1855 (PRO)
d 1878 (PRO)

BISHOP, John
L 16 Jan 1741
d 1743 (PRO)

BISHOP, John Limbrey
L 14 Feb 1815
d 27 June 1824 (PRO)

BISHOP, Sebastian
L 23 Nov 1728
d 1746 (PRO)

BISHOP, Thomas (1)
L 31 Dec 1747
CR 6 Jan 1758
CA 26 May 1768
d about 1790

BISHOP, Thomas (2)
L 6 Feb 1806
d 12 Jan 1829 (PRO)

BISHOP, Thomas Tivitoe
L 14 Sept 1780
d 1 Jan 1800

BISHOP, William
L 1 Oct 1810
HP 1815 (OB)
d 1848 (PRO)

BISSELL, Austin
L 14 Mar 1794
CR 18 Oct 1802
CA 3 Mar 1804
d (drowned) 28 Feb 1807 (PJP)

BISSELL, William
L 22 July 1794
CR 11 Apr 1809 (PRO)
Dismissed 1814 (MB)
d 31 Mar 1826 (MB)

BISSET, Alexander
L 27 Dec 1808 (NMM)
Ret CR 3 Feb 1847 (PRO)
d 12 July 1848 (PRO)

BISSETT, George
L 28 Jan 1811
CR 22 July 1830 (PRO)
d 1843 (PRO)

BISSETT, James
L 17 Feb 1778
CR 22 Nov 1790
CA 24 Oct 1794
RAB 4 Dec 1813
RAW 4 June 1814
RAR 12 Aug 1819 (PRO)
d 20 Jan 1824 (PRO)

BISTON, William
L 22 Nov 1790 (NMM)
d June 1793 (LT)

BIXON, Arthur
L 1666

BLACHFORD, Nathaniel
L 1672

BLACK, Archibald
L 27 May 1807
Ret CR 10 Feb 1843 (PRO)
d 4 Sept 1852 (PRO)

BLACK, James (1)
L 14 Apr 1779
d 1801 (PRO)

BLACK, James (2)
L 20 July 1799
T wounded
CR 8 Sept 1810
CA 29 July 1813
CB 1815 (TR)
d 6 Dec 1835 (LT)

BLACK, John
L 12 Sept 1781
d 1814

BLACK, John Reddie
L 29 Nov 1814
Ret CR 5 Feb 1858 (PRO)
d 1862 (PRO)

BLACK, Matthew
L 10 June 1814
Ret CR 13 Apr 1857 (PRO)
d 1860 (PRO)

BLACK, William
L 13 July 1801
CR 7 Nov 1809
CA 7 June 1814
Ret CA 1 Oct 1846 (PRO)
Ret RA 9 Oct 1849 (PRO)
d 6 Nov 1852 (PRO)

BLACKER, Stewart
T
L 20 Apr 1808
CR 1 Feb 1812
CA 16 Nov 1821 (PRO)
d June 1826 (PJP)

BLACKET, Sir Edward
L
CR
CA 1 Jan 1713
d 1 Mar 1756

BLACKETT, Robert
L 13 Dec 1782
d 1803 (PRO)

BLACKFORD, William
L 4 May 1810
d Sept 1820 (PRO)

BLACKLEACH, Abraham
L 1665 (DDA)
CA 1665 (DDA)
d before 1689 (PJP)

BLACKLER, Robert Tom
L 6 Feb 1800
CR 2 Aug 1811
Ret CA 30 Nov 1842 (PRO)
d 23 July 1844 (PRO)

BLACKMAN, Sir George
L 12 Aug 1813
CR 19 June 1820 (PJP)
Inh Bt 19 Nov 1836 (OB)

BLACKMAN, Thomas
L
CA 1665

BLACKMORE, Nathaniel
L 19 July 1694

BLACKWELL, Charles
L 13 Nov 1790
d 19 June 1791

BLACKWELL, Montagu
L 10 Jan 1779
d 1811 (PRO)

BLACKWOOD, Hon. Sir Henry
L 3 Nov 1790
CR 6 July 1794
CA 2 June 1795
Kt (Two Sicilies) 7 Jan 1801 (MB)
T
RAB 4 June 1814
Cre Bt 1814 (TR)
RAW 12 July 1819 (PRO)
KCB Aug 1819 (DNB)
RAR 19 July 1821 (PRO)
VAB 27 May 1825 (PRO)

VAW	12 Aug	1830 (PRO)
d	Dec	1832 (TR)
BLACKWOOD, Hon Price, Lord Dufferin		
L	10 Mar	1814
CR	4 June	1821 (NMM)
CA	2 Apr	1823 (NMM)
Cre EP	19 Nov	1839 (PRO)
d	21 July	1844 (NMM)
BLADEN, John		
L	1 June	1743
d	11 Jan	1755 (PMM)
BLADWELL, William		
L	6 Oct	1727
CR	29 May	1741
CA	17 Sept	1745
SUP RA		1770
d		1789
BLAGGE, William		
L		1673
CA	22 Feb	1678
d	before	1689 (PJP)
BLAINEY, Thomas Morley		
L	7 Sept	1804
Ret CR	19 May	1837 (PRO)
d		1853 (PRO)
BLAIR, Charles		
L	9 June	1804
CR	30 Sept	1830 (PRO)
d		1836 (PRO)
BLAIR, Duncan		
L	17 May	1814
d		1840 (PRO)
BLAIR, Francis		
L	1 Mar	1815
CR	24 Apr	1828 (PRO)
d		1832 (PRO)
BLAIR, Hamilton		
L	11 June	1814
d		1816 (PRO)
BLAIR, James		
L	3 Nov	1741
d		1770 (PRO)
BLAIR, William		
L	9 Oct	1760
CR	6 Dec	1777
CA	18 Apr	1778
KIA	12 Apr	1782 (RLB)
BLAKE, George		
L	15 Nov	1796
CR	28 Nov	1799
CA	29 Apr	1802
d	4 Apr	1822 (PRO)
BLAKE, George Hans		
L	22 Feb	1815 (PRO)
Ret CR	31 Jan	1862 (PRO)
d	13 Jan	1825 (PRO)
BLAKE, George Charles		
L	7 Apr	1806
CR	11 Oct	1819 (PRO)
CA	28 June	1838 (PRO)
Ret CA	15 Oct	1852 (PRO)
Ret RA	10 Sept	1857 (PRO)
Ret VA	9 Feb	1864 (PRO)
Ret A	10 Sept	1869 (PRO)
d	14 Nov	1872 (PRO)
BLAKE, James (1)		
L		
CA		1665
d	before	1689 (PJP)
BLAKE, James (2)		
L	12 Nov	1784
d		1796 (PRO)
BLAKE, John (1)		
L		1665
CA	27 July	1666 (RM)
d	before	1689 (PJP)
BLAKE, John (2)		
L	1 Dec	1787
CR	2 Jan	1798
d		1804 (PRO)
BLAKE, Joseph		
L	9 July	1780
d		1791 (PRO)
BLAKE, Joseph Andrus		
L	29 May	1807 (PRO)
d		1810 (PRO)
BLAKE, Peter (1)		
L	19 Sept	1757
CR	4 May	1761
d	31 Mar	1764 (PJP)
BLAKE, Peter (2)		
L	27 Nov	1809
d	30 July	1833 (LT)
BLAKE, Thomas (1)		
L		
CA	14 Dec	1693
d (drowned)	27 Nov	1702 (CH)
BLAKE, Thomas (2)		
L	23 Sept	1808
Ret CR	28 Aug	1858 (PRO)
d		1869 (PRO)
BLAKE, Wade		
L	8 July	1814
d		1817 (PRO)
BLAKE, William (1)		
L		
CA		1661
d	before	1689 (PJP)
BLAKE, William (2)		
L	9 Feb	1797
d		1800 (PRO)
BLAKENEY, Robert		
L	1 Sept	1806
d		1810 (PRO)
BLAKEWAY, James		
L	23 Oct	1721
BLAKISTON , Thomas		
L	11 Jan	1810
CR	2 July	1821 (PRO)
Ret CR	1 July	1851 (PRO)
d	30 Apr	1855 (PRO)
BLAKSTON, Peter		
L	29 Jan	1697 (PMM)
In Merchant Service		1699 (PJP)

BLAMEY, George William
L 6 Sept 1794
CR 12 July 1802
CA 21 Oct 1810
d 1832 (PRO)

BLANC, George le
See LE BLANC, George

BLANCHARD, Herbert
L 1672
d before 1689 (PJP)

BLANCKLEY, Edward
L 6 Feb 1815
CR 10 Dec 1825 (PRO)
CA 23 Nov 1841 (PRO)
d 4 May 1845 (PRO)

BLANCKLEY, George
L 18 Mar 1742
CR 8 Mar 1748
d 1759 (NMM)

BLAND, George
L 11 Feb 1815
d 19 Mar 1852 (PRO)

BLAND, Loftus Otway
L 6 Sept 1794
CR 11 Aug 1797
CA 25 Sept 1798
d 7 July 1810 (PRO)

BLANDFORD, James (1)
L 27 Aug 1800
Ret CR 26 Nov 1830 (PRO)
d 26 Mar 1840 (LT)

BLANDFORD, James (2)
T
L 16 Dec 1811
Ret CR 1 Apr 1853 (PRO)
d 1867 (TR)

BLANKETT, John
L 16 Apr 1761
CR 30 Jan 1779
CA 23 Jan 1780
RAW 14 Feb 1799
RAR 1 Jan 1801
d 14 July 1801 (DNB)

BLAQUIERE, Edward
L 20 July 1801
d 1832 (PRO)

BLAQUIERRE, Lewis
L 18 Dec 1798
Name removed 1811 (PRO)

BLAXTON, Henry (1)
L 29 Jan 1777
d 15 Apr 1807 (PJP)

BLAXTON, Henry (2)
L 16 Oct 1805
d 15 Apr 1807 (PJP)

BLEATHMAN, Benjamin
L 25 May 1809
d 1838 (PRO)

BLENKARNE, William
L 20 Mar 1815 (PRO)
Ret CR 29 Jan 1864 (PRO)
d 1872 (PRO)

BLENKINS, James John
T
L 25 Mar 1809
d 26 May 1825 (PRO)

BLENNERHASSETT, Goddard
L 5 Nov 1796
CR 11 Nov 1808
Ret CR 10 Sept 1840 (PRO)
d 1843 (PRO)

BLENNERHASSETT, James Primrose
T
L 29 July 1807
HP Oct 1813 (OB)
Ret CR 3 Sept 1844 (PRO)
d 22 Feb 1868 (PRO)

BLETCHENON, John
L 1665

BLIGH, Francis
L 19 June 1805
d 15 Apr 1825 (PRO)

BLIGH, George Miller
L 6 Mar 1801
T wounded
CR 25 Jan 1806
CA 27 Dec 1808
d 14 Oct 1834 (LT)

BLIGH, John (1)
L 11 Sept 1759
CR 1 Dec 1781
d 19 Jan 1795 (LT)

BLIGH, John (2)
L 25 June 1791
CR 8 Mar 1797 (PRO)
CA 25 Apr 1797
CB 4 June 1815 (LG)
RAB 19 July 1821 (PRO)
RAW 27 May 1825 (PRO)
RAR 22 July 1830 (PRO)
d 19 Jan 1831 (PRO)

BLIGH, Sir Richard Rodney
L 30 Sept 1757
CR 22 Oct 1762
CA 6 Dec 1777
RAB 23 Oct 1794
RAW 1 June 1795
RAR 14 Feb 1799
VAW 1 Jan 1801
AB 23 Apr 1804
AW 28 Apr 1808
AR 4 Dec 1813
GCB 1820 (DNB)
d 30 Apr 1821 (DNB)

BLIGH, William
L 5 Oct 1781
CR
CA 15 Dec 1790
RAB 31 July 1810
Gazetted 1 Aug 1811
RAW 12 Aug 1812
RAR 4 Dec 1813
VAB 4 June 1814
d 7 Dec 1817 (DNB)

BLIGHE, Richard
L 16 July 1740
d 1748 (PRO)

BLIGHT, Emanuel
T

HP 20 Feb 1815 (OB)
Ret CR 15 July 1861 (PRO)
d 10 July 1864 (PRO)

BLIGHT, William
L 15 Apr 1803
T
CR 12 Feb 1821 (DNB)
CA 22 July 1830 (DNB)
Ret CA 1 Oct 1850 (PRO)
Ret RA 27 Sept 1855 (DNB)
d 22 July 1862 (DNB)

BLIMSTONE, William
L 7 June 1695

BLINKERNE, Jo.
L 19 Mar 1694

BLINSTON, Henry (?BLINSTONE)
L
CR
CA 20 Feb 1708
(?28 Feb 1708)
d 28 Sept 1729

BLISSETT, George
L 3 Feb 1812
d 24 July 1834 (PJP)

BLISSETT, Thomas
L 24 Aug 1804
d 1833 (PRO)

BLOIS, Sir John Ralph
L 6 Mar 1815
CR 6 Mar 1821 (PRO)
Ret CR 1 July 1851 (PRO)
d 19 June 1853 (PRO)

BLOMER, Charles
L 12 Mar 1757
d 1770 (PRO)

BLOOD, Charles
L 25 Apr 1815
d 10 June 1839 (PRO)

BLOOM, William
L 15 Nov 1756
d 1777 (PRO)

BLOSS, Thomas
L 27 July 1741
CR 14 May 1745
CA 2 Jan 1746
d 28 Dec 1750 (PMM)

BLOUNT, Caesar
L 22 June 1709
SUP 18 Oct 1743 (PMM)

BLOUNT, William Oakes
L 10 July 1812
d 24 Apr 1831 (LT)

BLOW, John Aitken
L 19 Oct 1797
CR 27 Nov 1826 (PRO)
CA 7 Mar 1842 (PRO)
d Jan 1849 (PRO)

BLOW, Samuel
L 20 June 1777
d 15 Nov 1802 (PRO)

BLOWERS, Humphry
L 20 May 1690 (PJP)
CA 30 July 1679
SUP ?1698 (PJP)
d 14 Sept 1720

BLOYE, Robert
L 2 Oct 1800
CR 4 Aug 1806
CA 23 Sept 1813
CB 4 June 1815 (OB)
d 14 Sept 1847 (PRO)

BLOYS, William
L
CA 27 Aug 1697
d 9 Aug 1720

BLUETT, Buckland Stirling
L 24 Nov 1800
CR 10 Apr 1804
CA 12 Aug 1812
HP Nov 1815 (OB)
d 5 Nov 1845 (PRO)

BLUETT, George Rule
L 22 Sept 1795 (PRO)
d 1795 (PRO)

BLUETT, John
L 1 Apr 1779
d 7 Dec 1793

BLUETT, John Courtnay
L 28 Feb 1815
HP Sept 1815 (OB)
d 1855 (PRO)

BLUETT, Richard
L 7 May 1800
CR 6 Dec 1816 (PRO)
Ret CR 28 July 1851 (PRO)
d 15 Apr 1854 (PRO)

BLUNDEN, Christopher
L 12 June 1800
d June 1822 (PRO)

BLURTON, George
L 7 Feb 1812
HP Apr 1817–1820 (OB)
Ret CR 30 July 1853 (PRO)
d 26 Aug 1854 (PRO)

BLYKE, George
L 22 June 1743 (PRO)
CR 3 Nov 1747
From seniority 9 Mar 1748
d ?1798 (PRO)

BLYTH, Alexander
L 14 Apr 1741
d ?1753

BLYTH, Joseph
L 17 Dec 1798
d 31 Jan 1837 (PRO)

BLYTH. Samuel
L 7 Feb 1806
CR 5 Sept 1811
KIA 5 Sept 1813 (CH)

BLYTHE, John
L 22 Jan 1806
d 1837 (PRO)

BOARDMAN, Robert Ball
L 19 May 1809
Ret CR 3 Mar 1848 (PRO)
d 1868 (PRO)

BOARDMAN, Thomas
L 8 Aug 1811
HP Aug 1814 (OB)
Ret CR 1 Oct 1852 (PRO)
d 1867 (PRO)

BOCKENHAM, Robert
See BOKENHAM, Robert

BOCKENHAM, WIlliam
See BOKENHAM, William

BOCKENHAM, William
L 23 Mar 1728

BODLEDGE, John
L 23 Mar 1757
d 1769 (PRO)

BOGER, Coryndon
L 13 Nov 1794
CR 7 Jan 1801
CA 29 Apr 1802
d 24 May 1804 (PRO)

BOGER, Edmund
L 16 Mar 1795 (NMM)
CR 27 Jan 1803
CA 22 May 1806
RAB 23 Nov 1841 (PRO)
d 19 Dec 1844 (PRO)

BOGER, Richard (1)
L 8 May 1761
CR 2 Apr 1782
CA 6 July 1782
RAB 23 Apr 1804 (PRO)
RAR 9 Nov 1805 (PRO)
VAB 28 Apr 1808 (PRO)
VAW 31 July 1810 (PRO)
VAR 12 Aug 1812 (PRO)
AB 4 June 1814 (PRO)
d 19 Oct 1822 (PRO)

BOGER, Richard (2)
L 23 Mar 1776
CR 20 Sept 1793
d 6 May 1824 (MB)

BOGLE, Vere Warner Hussey
L 2 Sept 1807
Ret CR 11 Jan 1844 (PRO)
d 1876 (PRO)

BOGUE, Joseph Bradby
L 1 Dec 1796 (PRO)
CR ?5 Sept 1806 (PRO)
d 19 July 1806 (PRO)

BOHAM, Jeremiah William
T
L 23 June 1809
d 1840 (TR)

BOILEAU, Lestock Francis
L 22 Jan 1806
d 28 Mar 1849 (PRO)

BOIS, Edward
L 5 July 1686

BOKENHAM, Robert
L 27 June 1694
CA 6 May 1699 (PJP)
d 1707 (PJP)

BOKENHAM, William
L 10 Aug 1681 (P)
CA 7 May 1689
(29 May 1689 in C)
d 9 Nov 1702

BOLD, Edward
L 6 Feb 1815
Ret CR 9 Feb 1860 (PRO)
d Jan 1876 (PRO)

BOLES, John
L 2 Jan 1745
CR 23 May 1748
d 1761 (PRO)

BOLLARD, Robert
L 23 Apr 1742
CR 27 Mar 1756
d 16 Jan 1766 (PMM)

BOLMAN, Henry
L 11 Feb 1813
d 1844 (PRO)

BOLT, Joseph
L 6 June 1806
d 31 Oct 1810 (PRO)

BOLTER, John
L 2 Mar 1815
d 1826 (PRO)

BOLTON, Harry Powlett, Duke of
L 9 Mar 1739 (PJP)
CR
CA 15 July 1740
RAW 4 June 1756 (CH)
RAR 5 Feb 1758
VAW 14 Feb 1759 (CH)
AB 18 Oct 1770
AW 31 Mar 1775
d 25 Dec 1794

BOLTON, David
L 3 Sept 1809
d 14 Jan 1827 (PRO)

BOLTON, Henry
L 14 July 1812 (PRO)
CR 26 Aug 1829 (PRO)
d 1852 (PRO)

BOLTON, William (1)
L 28 Oct 1790
CR 23 Oct 1795
CA 14 Feb 1801
d 1817 (PRO)

BOLTON, Sir William (2)
L 11 Aug 1797
CR 27 Apr 1801
Kt May 1803 (MB)
CA 10 Apr 1805
d Dec 1830 (PRO)

BONAMY, Peter
L
CA 1667
d before 1689 (PJP)

BOND, Charles Wray Camps
L 6 Feb 1815 (PRO)
d 6 May 1828 (PRO)

BOND, Edward
L
CA 1664
d before 1689 (PJP)

BOND, Francis Godolphin
L 14 May 1782
CR 11 Dec 1800
CA 29 Apr 1802
Ret RA 19 Jan 1837 (PRO)
d 26 Oct 1839 (PRO)

BOND, Giles
L
CA 1665

BOND, John Holmes
L 20 Feb 1815
CR 5 Sept 1828 (PRO)
d 1836 (PRO)

BOND, Martin
L 19 May 1702

BOND, Philip
L 19 Sept 1815
Ret CR 14 Apr 1864 (PRO)
d 13 Mar 1868 (PRO)

BOND, Richard
L 21 Apr 1746
d 1748 (PRO)

BOND, Robert
L 13 Mar 1747
CR 7 Feb 1757
CA 13 Jan 1758
d 15 Mar 1772 (PJP)

BOND, Thomas
L 3 Apr 1779
SUP CR 31 Jan 1814
d 1 Apr 1831 (PRO)

BOND, William Francis
L 8 Nov 1814
Ret CR 22 Jan 1859 (PRO)
d 1870 (PRO)

BONE, John
L 28 Nov 1757
d 1762 (PRO)

BONE, William
L 15 Nov 1797
CR 17 Apr 1809
d 1809 (NMM)

BONES, Robert
L 16 Jan 1802
CR 5 Oct 1811
d 1813 (PRO)

BONFOY, Hugh
L 22 Oct 1738
CR 16 Jan 1744
CA 12 Apr 1745
GG 1753–
(Newfoundland) 1754 (DCB)
d 12 Mar 1762

BONIFANT, Bartholomew
L 14 Mar 1809
CR 20 APr 1818 (PRO)
d 2 Jan 1840 (PRO)

BONITHON, John
L 1660

BONN, John
L 1666
d before 1689 (PJP)

BONNAR, John
L 8 Oct 1779
d 1789 (PRO)

BONNAR, William
L
CA 1667
d before 1689 (PJP)

BONNYMAN, Jonas
L 4 Sept 1741
d 1757 (PRO)

BOOG, David
L 3 Apr 1746
SUP CR 21 Sept 1796 (PMM)

BOOKLESS, Thomas
L 3 Dec 1800
Ret CR 26 Nov 1830 (PRO)
d 1832 (PRO)

BOONE, John
L 1673
CA 1666
d before 1689 (PJP)

BOORDER, James
L 12 July 1793
CR 8 Aug 1796
d 1818 (PRO)

BOOTH, Frederick
L 17 Mar 1743
d 31 Oct 1751 (PMM)

BOOTH, James Richard
L 30 Dec 1813
CR 8 Dec 1829 (PRO)
CA 9 Nov 1846 (PRO)
d 21 Aug 1853 (PRO)

BOOTH, Robert
L 14 Mar 1709

BOOTH, Thomas
L 1672
CA 1673
Sentenced to be hanged at Yarmouth for making a riot there and the murder of a night watchman. In view of his position, the King amended the sentence to one of beheading.
e (murder) Sept 1677 (PMM)

BOOTH, Walter
L 1 Nov 1773
CR 29 Nov 1781
CA 14 Dec 1782
SUP 23 Apr 1804
d 1810 (PRO)

BOOTH, Sir William
L
CA June 1673 (DNB)
Kt 12 Nov 1682 (DNB)
CAGA
(Portsmouth) 21 July 1684 (EAD)
CA
(Grenadiers) 28 Feb 1685 (EAD)
LCF 17 June 1687 (EAD)
Resigned (Army) 1688 (EAD)
COM N 20 Feb 1688–
25 Mar 1689 (NBO)
Fled to France 1689 (DNB)
d Feb 1703 (DNB)

BOROUGH, Ralph Blakeney
L 6 Dec 1809
d 1816 (PRO)

BOROUGH, William
L 30 July 1801
Ret CR 12 June 1843 (PRO)
d 1853 (PRO)

BORROW, John
L 27 Oct 1758
d before 1777 (PRO)

BORROWMAN, William
L 1 Feb 1815
d 1861 (PRO)

BORTHWICK, Alexander
L 12 Feb 1802
CR 7 Dec 1818 (PRO)
d 1849 (PRO)

BORTHWICK, Richard
L 18 Sept 1677
CA 1673
d ?before 1689 (PJP)

BORWICK, Hally
L 1 July 1756
d 23 Apr 1770 (PRO)

BOSCAWEN, Hon. Edward
L 14 June 1732
CR 12 Mar 1737 (DNB)
CA May 1742 (DNB)
MP 21 June 1742–
(Truro) 10 Jan 1761 (MPN)
RAB 15 July 1747
RAW 12 May 1749 (DCB)
COM AD 22 June 1751–
10 Jan 1761 (AO)
VAB 6 Feb 1755 (NMM)
VAW 1756
VAR 1757
AB 7 Feb 1758 (NMM)
GRM 10 Nov 1759
d 10 Jan 1761 (DNB)

BOSS, John George
L 14 Sept 1805 (PRO)
CR 26 Nov 1811 (PRO)
CA 14 Nov 1833 (PRO)
d 1 Oct 1837 (PRO)

BOSTOCK, Charles
L 9 Aug 1802
d 1839 (PRO)

BOSTON, Thomas
L 9 June 1762
CR 30 July 1779
CA 19 July 1781
SUP RA 1800 (PRO)
d 5 July 1808 (PRO)

BOSWALL, John Donaldson
L 14 Sept 1805
CR 15 June 1814
CA 26 Dec 1822 (PRO)
Ret CA 1 Oct 1846 (PRO)
d 3 Feb 1847 (PRO)

BOSWALL, Walter
L 20 Mar 1795 (PRO)
CR 15 June 1814 (PRO)
HP 15 June 1814 (OB)
d 1850 (PRO)

BOSWELL, Edward
L
CA 1672

BOSWELL, George
L 8 Oct 1793
d 1799 (PRO)

BOSWELL, Robert
L 5 Sept 1759
d 1777 (PRO)

BOSWELL, Walter
See BOSWALL, Walter

BOTELER, Henry (1)
L 1672
CA 26 Apr 1688
d (duel) 21 Sept 1693 (PRO)

BOTELER, Henry (2)
L 18 Sept 1812
CR 12 Aug 1819 (PRO)
Ret CA 1 Apr 1856 (PRO)
d 22 Aug 1861 (PRO)

BOTELER, John Harvey
L 19 Sept 1815
CR 14 Sept 1830 (PRO)
CA 1 July 1851 (NMM)
Ret CA 1 Apr 1856 (PRO)
d 19 Apr 1885 (PRO)

BOTELER, Philip
L 23 Feb 1756
CR 16 June 1761
CA 26 Mar 1762
Dismissed 7 Mar 1780 (PRO)

BOTELER, William
L 25 June 1718

BOTHAM, John
L 13 Sept 1767
d (drowned) 8 Dec 1778 (PJP)

BOTHAM, William
L 1673 (P)
CA 12 Apr 1678
KIA 30 June 1690 (CH)

BOTHWELL, William
L 30 Jan 1800
d 15 Nov 1851 (PRO)

BOTT, Joseph
L 6 June 1806 (PRO)
CR 31 Aug 1808
d 31 Oct 1810 (PJP)

BOTTERELL, John
L 4 Sept 1742
CR 18 Feb 1760
CA 7 Apr 1762
d 12 Sept 1793 (LT)

BOUCHER, George
L 1661

BOUCHER, James (1)
L 16 Mar 1745
d 1757 (PRO)

BOUCHER, James (2)
L 27 July 1746
d ?1752 (PRO)

BOUILLON, Prince of
See AUVERNGE, Philip D'

BOULDERSON, Leslie
L 3 Sept 1803
Ret CR 4 May 1836 (PRO)
d 1836 (PRO)

BOULER, Robert
See BOWLER, Robert

BOULTBEE, Joseph Bage
L 25 Jan 1813
Ret CR 13 Oct 1855 (PRO)
d 1865 (PRO)

BOULTER, John
L 1665
d June 1666 (PRO)

BOUTLON, John
L 16 June 1807
d 1815 (PRO)

BOUNTON, John
L 4 Aug 1800
KIA 10 Aug 1805 (LG)

BOUNTY, John
L 27 Dec 1673 (P)
CA 15 Dec 1688
KIA 12 July 1691 (CH)

BOURCHIER, Henry
L 1 May 1804
CR 20 Apr 1808
CA 22 Aug 1811
Ret RA 1 Oct 1846 (PRO)
d 14 Oct 1852 (PRO)

BOURCHIER, John
L 13 July 1775
CR 20 Apr 1777
CA 13 Apr 1782 (PRO)
SUP 23 Apr 1804
d 30 Dec 1808 (PRO)

BOURCHIER, Philip
See BOWCHIER, Philip

BOURCHIER, Sir Thomas
L 26 Aug 1808
CR 9 Sept 1822 (PRO)
CA 12 Sept 1827 (PRO)
d 26 Apr 1849 (PRO)

BOURCHIER, William
L 8 Feb 1810
CR 19 Sept 1815
d 22 Jan 1844 (PRO)

BOURKE, William Francis
L 10 June 1758
CR 24 July 1761
d 21 Mar 1802 (PRO)

BOURMASTER, John
L 19 Oct 1759
CR 30 May 1776
CA 9 Sept 1777
RAB 23 Oct 1794
RAR 1 June 1795
VAW 14 Feb 1799
VAR 1 Jan 1801
AB 23 Apr 1804
d 5 Dec 1807 (PRO)

BOURN, George
L 23 Aug 1759
d 29 June 1787 (PMM)

BOURN, George William
L 31 Jan 1801
T
Ret CR 15 Oct 1840 (PRO)
d 1844 (TR)

BOURNE, Corby
L 22 Jan 1806
d 1814 (PRO)

BOURNE, George Hayes
L 20 Mar 1815 (PRO)
d July 1823 (PRO)

BOURNE, George Stanway
L 20 Nov 1812
Ret CR 9 Jan 1854 (PRO)
d 12 Apr 1862 (PRO)

BOURNE, Henry
L 4 Jan 1808
CR 6 Nov 1813
Ret CR 1 July 1851 (PRO)
d 1854 (PRO)

BOURNE, John
L 2 May 1678
d before 1689 (PJP)

BOURNE, Richard
L 4 Aug 1797
HP 14 Oct 1816 (OB)
Ret CR 10 Dec 1840 (PRO)
d 9 Oct 1851 (PRO)

BOURNE, Sampson
L
CR
CA 25 June 1703
Dismissed 1712
d 1719

BOUTFLOWER, Williams
L 20 Jan 1718
CR
CA 23 Dec 1732
d 22 Dec 1733 or 1735 (PJP)

BOUVERIE, Charles
L 19 Sept 1815
d 1825(6) (PRO)

BOUVERIE, Hon Duncombe Pleydell
L 16 Feb 1799
CR 14 Feb 1801
CA 28 Apr 1802
CRM 22 July 1830 (OB)
RAW 10 Jan 1837 (PRO)
RAR 23 Nov 1841 (PRO)
VAB 8 Mar 1847 (PRO)
VAW 24 Jan 1849 (PRO)
VAR 9 Nov 1849 (PRO)
d 5 Nov 1850 (PRO)

BOUZIER, Richard
L 16 Aug 1695 (PJP)
CR
CA 2 Oct 1708
d 11 Jan 1745

BOVER, John (1)
L 19 Sept 1744
CR 23 Mar 1757
CA 12 Mar 1762
d 20 May 1782 (PRO)

BOVER, John (2)
L 3 Apr 1779
d 1782(3) (PRO)

BOVER, Peter Turner
L 3 Jan 1794
CR 14 Feb 1798
CA 11 Aug 1800
d 14 Dec 1802 (PRO)

BOWATER, Edward
L 26 Feb 1776
CR 13 Feb 1781 (PRO)
CA 16 Jan 1783
RAB 23 Apr 1804
RAW 9 Nov 1805
RAR 28 Apr 1808
VAB 31 July 1810
VAW 1 Aug 1811
VAR 4 June 1814
AB 12 Aug 1819 (PRO)
AW 27 May 1825 (PRO)
d 10 Mar 1829 (PRO)

BOWCHIER, Philip
L 10 Feb 1722

BOWDEN, John
L 16 Mar 1814
HP Feb 1840 (OB)
d 1855 (PRO)

BOWDEN, Philip
L 22 Feb 1815
HP Aug 1815 (OB)
d 1852 (PRO)

BOWDEN, Richard Bayly
T
L 9 Feb 1815
Ret CR 16 Apr 1853 (PRO)
d 12 Aug 1861 (PRO)

BOWDEN, Richard Booth
L 29 Apr 1802
CR 5 Aug 1813
Ret CA 14 July 1843 (PRO)
d 7 Mar 1862 (PRO)

BOWDEN, William
L 27 June 1797
d 8 Apr 1827 (PRO)

BOWDICK, James Brown
L 7 May 1804 (PRO)
d 25 May 1829 (PRO)

BOWDLER, John
L 8 Apr 1739
CR
CA 8 Nov 1744
d 16 Apr 1754

BOWEN, Abraham
L 10 Oct 1804
d 1810 (PRO)

BOWEN, Charles (1)
L 6 Mar 1802
d 1810

BOWEN, Charles (2)
L 30 Aug 1807
CR 19 July 1822 (PRO)
CA 27 July 1825 (PRO)
Ret CA 1 Oct 1846 (PRO)
Ret RA 21 Jan 1854 (PRO)
d 29 Sept 1854 (PRO)

BOWEN, Charles Holcombe
L 26 Apr 1806
d 25 Apr 1833 (LT)

BOWEN, Essex
L 28 Feb 1758
SUP CR 11 Aug 1798 (PMM)
d July 1811 (PRO)

BOWEN, George (1)
L 13 Mar 1773
CR 19 Nov 1779
CA 14 Feb 1781
RAB 14 Feb 1799
RAW 1 Jan 1801
RAR 23 Apr 1804
VAB 9 Nov 1805 (PRO)
VAW 28 Apr 1808
VAR 25 Oct 1809
AB 31 July 1810
AW 4 June 1814
d 1 July 1823 (PRO)

BOWEN, George (2)
L 23 Oct 1783 (NMM)
CR 2 Apr 1794
CA 6 Apr 1795
d 25 June 1800 (PJP)

BOWEN, George (3)
L 1 Feb 1796
CR 2 Feb 1797
CA 29 Apr 1802
d 31 Oct 1817 (PJP)

BOWEN, George (4)
L 7 Feb 1806
CR 15 June 1814
Ret CA 1 July 1851 (PRO)
d 1872 (PRO)

BOWEN, James (1)
L 23 June 1794
CR 29 June 1795
CA 2 Sept 1795
COM N 25 Feb 1816–
25 Aug 1825 (NBO)
d 27 Apr 1835 (PRO)

BOWEN, James (2)
L 26 Feb 1801
CR 4 Sept 1804
CA 22 Jan 1806
d 26 Dec 1812 (PRO)

BOWEN, John (1)
L 24 Nov 1762
d 1809 (PRO)

BOWEN, John (2)
L 13 Apr 1802
CR 2 May 1804
CA 22 Jan 1806
d Oct 1827 (PRO)

BOWEN, John (3)
L 5 Feb 1808
CR 4 June 1834 (PRO)
d 1834 (PRO)

BOWEN, Peregrine
T

L	23 Feb	1808
d		1848 (TR)
BOWEN, Peter		
L		
CA	16 Mar	1666 (RM)
d		1673 (PJP)
BOWEN, Richard (1)		
L	21 Sept	1790
CR	20 Mar	1794 (PRO)
CA	23 Apr	1794
KIA	24 July	1798 (LG)
BOWEN, Richard (2)		
L	13 Apr	1815
Ret CR	20 Jan	1864 (PRO)
d		1871 (PRO)
BOWEN, Thomas		
L	29 Sept	1789
CR	8 Nov	1797
CA	24 Dec	1798
d		1809 (PRO)
BOWEN, William (1)		
L	22 Aug	1783
CR	2 July	1796 (PRO)
CA	7 Mar	1797 (PRO)
d	21 Feb	1813 (LT)
BOWEN, William (2)		
L	22 May	1793
d	21 Feb	1813 (PJP)
BOWER, Charles William		
L	1 Feb	1815
d		1817 (PRO)
BOWER, Edmund		
L	14 Oct	1761
d		1811 (PRO)
BOWER, Robert		
L	19 July	1757
d		1770 (PRO)
BOWERBANK, John (1)		
L	14 Apr	1748
CR	19 May	1761
d		1777 (PRO)
BOWERBANK, John (2)		
L	30 June	1812
HP	13 Sept	1815 (PRO)
Ret CR	25 Oct	1854 (PRO)
d		1861 (PRO)
BOWERS, Alexander		
L	27 June	1711
BOWERS, John		
L		
CA		1667
BOWERS, John Hope		
L	2 Sept	1759
CR	15 May	1780
d	26 Sept	1783 (PRO)
BOWERS, William		
L	5 Oct	1810
d	11 Aug	1845 (PRO)
BOWETS, Alexander		
See BOWERS, Alexander		
BOWIE, Adam		
L	21 Dec	1796
d	23 Sept	1824 (PRO)
BOWIE, John		
L	20 July	1812
CR	9 Nov	1846 (PRO)
Ret CA	1 Aug	1860 (PRO)
d		1864 (PRO)
BOWKER, John		
L	10 July	1794
CR	23 Mar	1807
CA	16 Aug	1811
Ret RA	31 Oct	1846 (LG)
d	11 Aug	1847 (PRO)
BOWKER, John Harrison		
L	7 Feb	1815
Dismissed	19 Apr	1827 (PRO)
Restored		1828 (PRO)
CR	17 Jan	1848 (PRO)
d	Jan	1848 (PRO)
BOWLBY, George Henry		
L	27 May	1814
d		1848 (PRO)
BOWLDER, John		
L	8 Apr	1739 (PRO)
CR		
CA	8 Nov	1744 (PRO)
d		?1755 (PRO)
BOWLER, Robert		
L	20 Apr	1695 (PJP)
CR		
CA	28 Jan	1707
GG (Newfoundland)		1724–1726 (DCB)
HP		1728 (DCB)
d	27 July	1734 (DCB)
BOWLER, William Pitt		
L	13 May	1812
d	15 Sept	1823 (PRO)
BOWLES, Archibald		
L	6 Feb	1694
BOWLES, Edward		
L		
CA	18 Oct	1694
d	13 Jan	1695
BOWLES, Phineas		
L		
CA	31 Mar	1692
d	4 Nov	1698
BOWLES, Robert		
L	20 Apr	1695
In Merchant Service		1700 (PJP)
BOWLES, Valentine		
L		
CA	3 Apr	1695
Dismissed	27 Oct	1698 (PJP)
BOWLES, Sir William		
L	30 Aug	1803
CR	22 Jan	1806
CA	13 Oct	1807
CB		1836 (PJP)
RAB	23 Nov	1841 (PRO)
COM AD	22 May	1844–
	13 July	1846 (AO)
RAW	8 Mar	1847 (PRO)
RAR	1 Sept	1849 (PRO)
VAB	3 Mar	1852 (PRO)
VAW	17 Sept	1853 (PRO)
VAR	3 Oct	1855 (PRO)
AB	1 Nov	1860 (PRO)

AW	28 Nov	1860 (PRO)
KCB		1862 (PJP)
AR	27 Apr	1863 (PRO)
AF	15 Jan	1869 (PRO)
d	2 July	1869 (PRO)
BOWLEY, William		
L	7 Nov	1806
d		1810 (PRO)
BOWLING, Edward		
L	27 Mar	1794
d		1797 (PRO)
BOWRY, John		
L		
CA		1660
d	before	1689 (PJP)
BORWRY, Mathias		
L		
CA		1667
d	before	1669 (PJP)
BOWYER, Sir George		
L	13 Feb	1758
CR	4 May	1761
CA	28 Oct	1762
MP (Queensborough)		1784–1790 (MPN)
CRM	24 Sept	1787 (AL)
RAW	1 Feb	1793
RAR	12 Apr	1794
VAB	4 July	1794
Cre Bt	8 Sept	1794 (MPN)
VAR	1 June	1795
AB	14 Feb	1799
d	6 Dec	1799 (MPN)
BOWYER, Henry		
L	30 Oct	1688
BOWYER, Richard Runwa		
L	17 Jan	1780
CR	21 Sept	1790
CA	2 May	1798
d	10 Feb	1823 (PRO)
BOWYER, William (1)		
L	29 June	1711
BOWYER, William (2)		
L	5 Feb	1742
d		1746 (PRO)
BOWYER, William Bohun		
L	4 May	1810
CR	15 Jan	1823 (PRO)
CA	17 Jan	1830 (PRO)
Ret CA	1 June	1850 (PRO)
Ret RA	9 July	1855 (PRO)
d	8 Oct	1859 (PRO)
Box, George		
L	9 Aug	1802
d	30 Jan	1811 (PRO)
BOXER, Edward		
L	8 Jan	1807
CR	1 Mar	1815
CA	23 June	1823 (PRO)
CB	18 Dec	1840 (OB)
RAB	5 Mar	1853 (PRO)
RAW	27 Oct	1854 (PRO)
d	4 June	1855 (PMM)
BOXER, James		
L	14 Nov	1800
CR	13 Oct	1807
CA	19 July	1814
Ret CA	1 Oct	1846 (PRO)
d	5 Oct	1847 (PRO)
BOXER, William		
L	30 Apr	1810
CR	13 Jan	1823 (PRO)
d		1842 (PRO)
BOYACK, Alexander		
L	3 May	1804
Ret CR	6 Dec	1847 (PRO)
d		1858 (PRO)
BOYCE, Crauford		
L	21 July	1761
d		1768 (PRO)
BOYCE, Frederick		
L	10 Feb	1810
CR	10 Aug	1824 (PRO)
d	9 Oct	1824 (PRO)
BOYCE, Henry		
L	27 May	1786
d		1819 (PRO)
BOYCE, Henry William		
L	16 Feb	1815
d		1833 (PRO)
BOYCE, James		
L	31 Jan	1665 (DDA)
BOYCE, John		
L		?1702 (PJP)
CR	4 Oct	1709
Gone		1752
BOYCE, Nathaniel		
L	14 Apr	1697
BOYCE, William Henry		
L	28 May	1805
T		
Ret CR	1 July	1864 (PRO)
d	30 Mar	1866 (PRO)
BOYCE, William Nettleton		
L	15 Feb	1815 (PRO)
Ret CR	18 Jan	1861 (PRO)
d		1867 (PRO)
BOYD, David		
L	30 May	1800
CR	17 Jan	1815
HP	Sept	1815 (OB)
Ret CA	24 Feb	1852 (NMM)
d		1858 (PRO)
BOYD, James		
L	27 Oct	1758
d	19 May	1800
BOYD, James Brown		
L	16 Dec	1801
Ret CR	4 Aug	1832 (PRO)
d		1842 (PRO)
BOYD, John		
L	15 Feb	1756
CR		
CA	5 Nov	1761
d		1762 (PRO)
BOYD, Peter		
L	21 Mar	1812
d		1813 (PRO)

BOYES, Charles
L 8 Nov 1800
d 17 Nov 1809 (LT)

BOYES, Henry
L 14 Jan 1803
CR 11 May 1815
HP May 1814–30 Aug 1815 (OB)
CA 23 Dec 1842 (PRO)
d 10 May 1852 (PRO)

BOYLE, Charles
L 19 Feb 1705 (PMM)
CR
CA 27 Jan 1711
d 28 Mar 1720 (PRO)

BOYLE, Hon. Courtnay
L 22 Nov 1790
CR 6 Apr 1795
CA 30 June 1797
HP July 1797–1798 (MB)
COMM (Sheerness) 1814 (PJP)
Ret CA 1821 (PRO)
COM N 3 July 1823–4 May 1829 (NBO)
Ret RA 26 Feb 1831 (PRO)
KCH 1832 (PJP)
VAW 12 Nov 1840 (PRO)
VAR 23 Nov 1841 (PRO)
d 21 May 1844 (PRO)

BOYLE, Hon. James
L 8 Jan 1814
Ret CR 7 Nov 1856 (PRO)
d 1869 (PRO)

BOYLE, John (1)
L 31 Dec 1765
CR 12 June 1776
CA 1 Dec 1787
SUP RA 8 Oct 1807
d Jan 1811 (PJP)

BOYLE, John (2)
L 24 Dec 1779
d (drowned) 5 Oct 1780 (PJP)

BOYLE, Hon. Robert (1)
L 23 Mar 1756
CR 16 Feb 1757
CA 15 June 1757
CRM 19 Mar 1779 (AL)
d (drowned) 5 Oct 1780 (CH)

BOYLE, Robert (2)
L 18 Dec 1809
CR 7 Dec 1818 (PRO)
d 13 Oct 1825 (PRO)

BOYLE, Charles
L 10 Nov 1777
CR 11 Apr 1783
CA 22 Nov 1790
CRM 28 Apr 1808 (LG)
RAB 25 Oct 1809
RAW 31 July 1810
RAR 12 Aug 1812
VAW 4 June 1814
d 11 Nov 1816 (PRO)

BOYNE, John
L 28 Feb 1806
d 1808 (PRO)

BOYNE, Richard, Lord Viscount
L 2 June 1748
d 30 July 1789 (PJP)

BOYS, Charles Worsley
L 16 June 1795
CR 2 Apr 1801
CA 29 Apr 1802
d 17 Nov 1809 (LT)

BOYS, Edward (1)
L
CA 2 Oct 1689
d (suicide) 24 Sept 1696 (PJP)

BOYS, Edward (2)
L 3 Nov 1790
Ret CR 7 May 1823 (PRO)
d 11 Nov 1827 (PRO)

BOYS, Edward (3)
L 25 May 1809
CR 8 July 1814 (PRO)
HP Sept 1814 (OB)
Ret CA 1 July 1851 (PRO)
d 6 June 1866 (PRO)

BOYS, Henry
L 3 Nov 1790
CR 13 Oct 1807
CA 26 Nov 1811
d 29 Nov 1816 (PRO)

BOYS, John
See BOYCE, John

BOYS, Pearson
L 27 Oct 1758
d 11 June 1793

BOYS, Philip
L 26 Mar 1694 (PJP)
CR 1699 (PJP)
CA 20 Feb 1702
d (suicide) 20 Jan 1727 (PJP)

BOYS, Thomas (1)
L 22 June 1784
CR 13 Oct 1795 (PRO)
CA 3 July 1796
RAB 12 Aug 1819 (PRO)
RAW 19 July 1821 (PRO)
RAR 27 May 1825 (PRO)
VAB 22 July 1830 (PRO)
d 3 Nov 1832 (PMM)

BOYS, Thomas (2)
L 13 Dec 1794
Ret CR 26 Nov 1830 (NMM)
d 1840 (PRO)

BOYS, William (1)
L 5 May 1753
CR 8 June 1741
CA 25 June 1743
LGH 1767 (PJP)
d 4 Mar 1774

BOYS, William (2)
L 14 Sept 1768
d 1779 (PRO)

BOYTER, Alexander
L 18 Feb 1815
d 1858 (PRO)

BRABAZON , Lambert
L 10 Oct 1758
CR
CA 25 Dec 1782
d 4 Apr 1811 (PRO)

BRACE, Sir Edward
L 15 Mar 1792
CR 30 June 1797
CA 22 Apr 1800
CB 4 June 1815 (LG)
CRM 27 May 1825 (AL)
RAW 22 July 1830 (PRO)
KCB 29 Oct 1834 (LG)
RAR 10 Jan 1837 (PRO)
VAB 28 June 1838 (PRO)
VAW 23 Nov 1841 (PRO)
d 26 Dec 1743 (PRO)

BRACE, Francis
L 3 Feb 1813
CR 7 Dec 1818 (PRO)
CA 14 Aug 1827 (PRO)
d 16 May 1850 (PRO)

BRACEY, Jay
L 9 Jan 1760
d 6 Oct 1791

BRACKLEY, Swift
L 2 Apr 1743
d 1746 (PRO)

BRADBY, Bonamy
L 19 Nov 1790
d 1794 (PRO)

BRADBY, Daniel
L 8 Mar 1762
d 1 Mar 1798

BRADBY, James (1)
L 30 Sept 1758 (PMM)
CR 2 July 1778
CA 26 Aug 1780
SUP RA 1799 (PRO)
d 1809 (PJP)

BRADBY, James (2)
L 19 Feb 1782
CR 7 Oct 1794
CA 15 Feb 1797
d 4 June 1801 (PRO)

BRADBY, Matthew Barton
L 14 July 1796
CR 29 Apr 1802
CA 28 June 1810 (PRO)
d 5 May 1831 (PRO)

BRADBY, Thomas
L 7 July 1809
Ret CR 4 Apr 1838 (PRO)
d 8 Mar 1872 (PRO)

BRADDELL, John Tandy
L 16 May 1797
d 1811 (PRO)

BRADFORD, Richard
L 1660
CA 1666
d before 1689 (PJP)

BRADISH, Charles
L 30 Nov 1780
d 1795 (PRO)

BRADISH, Thomas
L 31 Mar 1808
d 1812 (PRO)

BRADLEY, James (1)
L 18 Aug 1810
CR 12 June 1823 (PRO)
d 8 Oct 1829 (PRO)

BRADLEY, James (2)
L 23 July 1814
d 1826 (PRO)

BRADLEY, John
L 15 Oct 1802
CR 28 Nov 1806
CA 1 Jan 1817 (PRO)
d 28 Apr 1808 (PRO)

BRADLEY, Richard Rose
L 9 Feb 1779
d 1815 (PRO)

BRADLEY, Thomas (1)
L 13 May 1720
CR 19 Sept 1727
CA 5 Mar 1734
d 25 Nov 1741 (PMM)

BRADLEY, Thomas (2)
L 6 Dec 1739
d 1742 (PRO)

BRADLEY, William (1)
L 25 Oct 1778
CR 28 Apr 1792
CA 23 June 1794
SUP RA 22 Sept 1812
Struck off list 1814 (PRO)
d 13 Mar 1833 (DUB)

BRADLEY, William (2)
L 12 July 1810
Ret CR 6 July 1850 (PRO)
d 29 Jan 1867 (PRO)

BRADSHAW, James
L 2 Mar 1805
CR 22 Jan 1806
CA 20 Apr 1808
d (suicide) 25 Sept 1833 (LT)

BRADSHAW, John
L 31 Jan 1760
d 1762 (PRO)

BRADSHAW, Peregrine
L 31 Aug 1739
d 1746 (PRO)

BRADSHAW, Thomas
L 9 Nov 1756
COM AD 6 May 1772–
6 Nov 1774 (NBO)
Quitted the Navy 1787 (PRO)

BRADSHAW, William Smith
See William SMITH

BRADSTON, Edward
L 29 Apr 1734
d 1742 (PRO)

BRADY, Charles
L 17 Feb 1800
d 1805 (PRO)

BRADY, James (1)
L 30 Sept 1758
CR 2 July 1778 (PRO)
d 1780 (PRO)

BRADY, James (2)
L 4 Apr 1760
d 1779 (PRO)

BRADY, Matteate
L 8 Feb 1742
d 1772 (PRO)

BRADY, William Hollinshed
L 20 Mar 1815 (PRO)
d 1852 (PRO)

BRAIMER, David
L 3 May 1802
CR 9 Apr 1808
CA 1 Jan 1817 (PRO)
d 1838 (PRO)

BRAITHWAIT(E), Howe
L 24 Sept 1814
d 1826 (PRO)

BRAITHWAITE, James
L
CA 6 Dec 1692
d 1693 (PJP)

BRAITHWAITE, Richard
L 7 May 1755
CR 29 Nov 1756
CA 6 Apr 1761
RAW 21 Sept 1790
VAB 1 Feb 1793
VAW 12 Apr 1794
VAR 1 June 1795
AB 14 Feb 1799
AW 1 Jan 1801
d 28 June 1805 (PRO)

BRAITHWAITE, Robert
L 15 Nov 1790
d 1807 (PRO)

BRAITHWAITE, Samuel
L 2 May 1707 (PMM)
CR
CA 28 Jan 1722
d June 1749

BRAITHWAITE, Thomas Patrickson
L 11 June 1757
d 1794 (PRO)

BRAITHWAITE, William
L 29 Apr 1802
d 1804 (PRO)

BRAKE, William Lenthall
L 2 Nov 1810
Ret CR 11 Apr 1851 (NMM)
d 1858 (NMM)

BRAMWELL, Isaac
L 21 Feb 1815
d 1832 (PRO)

BRAMWELL, Thomas
L 30 Sept 1807
d 1812 (PRO)

BRANCH, Alexander Barc(k)lay
L 8 May 1804
CR 6 June 1814
CA 26 Dec 1822 (PRO)
Ret CA 1 Oct 1846 (PRO)
d 11 Sept 1849 (PRO)

BRAND, Andrew
L 9 Mar 1758
d 1762 (PRO)

BRAND, Comer
L 3 Jan 1778
SUP CR 22 Apr 1813
d 1815 (PRO)

BRAND, Ellis
L
CR
CA 19 Oct 1715
SUP RA 28 July 1747
d 22 Oct 1759

BRAND, George Rowley
L 23 July 1803
KIA 23 Feb 1806 (CH)

BRAND, John (1)
L 7 Apr 1737
d 1753 (PRO)

BRAND, John (2)
L 28 Feb 1783
d 21 Dec 1822 (PRO)

BRAND, Thomas Dickson
L 10 Mar 1815
d 11 Nov 1830 (PRO)

BRAND, William Alexander
L 22 Mar 1813
d 1814 (PRO)

BRAND, William Henry
T
L 30 Dec 1813
CR 9 Nov 1846 (PRO)
CA 27 Oct 1858 (PRO)
d 22 Apr 1867 (TR)

BRANDER, William
L 14 Feb 1811
Ret CR 1 Oct 1851 (PRO)
d 1856 (PRO)

BRANDFORD, John
L 3 Apr 1813
CR 1 Mar 1820 (PRO)
Ret CR 1 July 1851 (PRO)
d 24 Nov 1855 (PRO)

BRANDRETH, William Alston
L 26 July 1762
CR 25 Oct 1809
d 1814 (PRO)

BRASH, Robert
L 25 Oct 1813
d 12 Mar 1841 (LT)

BRASIER, Edward
See BRAZIER, Edward

BRASIER, James
L 10 June 1807
CR 26 Dec 1822 (PRO)
CA 10 Jan 1837 (PRO)
Ret RA 14 May 1847 (PRO)

Ret VA	14 Nov	1863 (PRO)
d	28 July	1864 (PRO)

BRATHWAITE,
See BRAITHWAITE, James
BRAITHWAITE, Richard
BRAITHWAITE, Robert
BRAITHWAITE, Samuel
BRAITHWAITE, Thomas Patrickson
BRAITHWAITE, William

BRATHWELL, Edward

L		1672
d	before	1689 (PJP)

BRAVEL, Palmes

L	16 Nov	1710
d		1727 (PRO)

BRAWN, Ernest

L	17 Aug	1799
CR	13 May	1801
CA	29 Apr	1802
d	23 Jan	1805 (PRO)

BRAY, Benjamin John

L	28 June	1810
d	2 Oct	1846 (LT)

BRAY, Gabriel

L	25 June	1773
d	6 Dec	1823 (LT)

BRAY, James

L	14 Aug	1801
d		1813 (PRO)

BRAY, John (1)

L	10 Mar	1702

BRAY, John (2)

L	16 July	1740
Gone		1752

BRAY, John (3)

L	28 Aug	1743
CR	15 June	1757
CA	6 Jan	1758
d	Dec	1759 (LT)

BRAY, John (4)

L	9 Aug	1794
d		1797 (PRO)

BRAY, John (5)

L	15 Jan	1799
d		1803 (PRO)

BRAY, Josias

L	1 Nov	1800
T	wounded	
HP	16 May	1814 (OB)
CR	27 May	1825 (PRO)
d		1846 (TR)

BRAY, Richard

L	4 May	1697
CR	14 Jan	1699 (PMM)

BRAZIER, Edward

L	29 July	1807
CR	2 Aug	1811
CA	7 June	1814
d		1835 (PRO)

BRAZIER, John
See BRASIER, James

BREAM, William

L	7 Aug	1802
d		1804 (PRO)

BREARY, Arthur

L	1 Feb	1815
d	22 Nov	1820 (PRO)

BREARY, George

L	15 Aug	1806
Ret CR	16 Jan	1840 (PRO)
d		1845 (PRO)

BREDBY, Matthew Barton
See Matthew Barton BRADBY

BREDCOCK, Richard

L		1673
d	before	1689 (PJP)

BREDEN, Abraham

L	27 Mar	1678
d	before	1689 (PJP)

BREDNER, Alexander

L	15 Feb	1746
d		1748(9) (PRO)

BREEDON, Joseph

L	4 Apr	1760
d	18 Feb	1792

BREHOLT, George

L		
CA	22 May	1693
	(25 Sept	1693 in C)
d	24 June	1741

BREMER, James (1)

L	29 Oct	1755
CR	4 June	1762
CA	20 June	1765
d	9 July	1774

BREMER, James (2)

L	5 Apr	1779
d (drowned)	6 Jan	1786 (OB)

BREMER, James (3)

L	22 Nov	1790
CR	1 Aug	1811
d	Feb	1835 (PRO)

BREMER, Sir James John Gordon

L	3 Aug	1805
CR	13 Oct	1807
CA	7 June	1814
CB	4 June	1815 (DNB)
KCH	23 Feb	1836 (OB)
Kt	23 Feb	1836 (OB)
KCB	29 July	1841 (DNB)
RAB	15 Sept	1849 (PRO)
d	14 Feb	1850 (LG)

BRENAN, Alexander

T		
L	16 Mar	1814
Ret CR	19 Jan	1857 (PRO)
d		1862 (TR)

BRENT, Robert

L	18 July	1745
d		1757 (PRO)

BRENTON, Edward Pelham

L	27 May	1795
CR	29 Apr	1802
CA	13 Dec	1808
HP	Nov	1809–
	Apr	1810 (MB)
d	6 Apr	1839 (DNB)

BRENTON, Jahleel (1)
L 6 Apr 1757
CR 23 Aug 1777
CA 3 Sept 1781
RAB 1 Jan 1801
d 30 Jan 1802

BRENTON, Sir Jahleel (2)
L 20 Nov 1790
CR 3 July 1799 (PRO)
CA 25 Apr 1800
Kt (Two Sicilies) 1810 (MB)
Cre Bt 3 Nov 1812 (LG)
COMM (Port Mahon) 1813–1815 (DNB)
KCB 2 Jan 1815 (LG)
CRM 27 May 1825 (LG)
RAB 22 July 1830 (PRO)
LGH 1831 (DNB)
RAR 10 Jan 1837 (PRO)
VAB 1 July 1840 (PRO)
VAW 23 Nov 1841 (PRO)
d 21 Apr 1844 (PRO)

BRENTON, James Wallace
L 21 Jan 1798
d 1800 (PRO)

BRENTON, John
L 5 Sept 1806
CR 20 Nov 1812
CA 26 Dec 1822 (PRO)
Ret CA 1 Oct 1846 (PRO)
Ret RA 17 Dec 1852 (PRO)
Ret VA 5 Jan 1858 (PRO)
d 17 Sept 1859 (PRO)

BRENTON, William
L 29 Aug 1807
d 1808 (PRO)

BRERETON, Godfrey
L 16 Jan 1815
Ret CR 1 Oct 1860 (PRO)
d Oct 1874 (PRO)

BRERETON, Robert Perceval
L 2 Feb 1811
d 1844 (PRO)

BRERETON, William
L 4 July 1755
CR
CA 25 Mar 1758
Lost a year's seniority to 25 Mar 1759
First shown in S.O.L. of 1 July 1760 as L 4 July 1755. The original promotion to CA 25 Mar 1758 may have been made on the East Indies Station, but not confirmed. The loss of a year's seniority is given in Charnock. The S.O.L. dates are 25 Mar 1759 in 1 July 1762 and 25 Mar 1758 in 1 July 1767 and afterwards. (PRO)
SUP CR 1787 (PRO)

BRETON, Francis Le
See LE BRETON, Francis

BRETON, Frederick
L 6 Mar 1745 (PRO)
d 3 May 1747 (PRO)

BRETON, John
L 30 Jan 1759
CR 29 Apr 1778
CA 18 Apr 1782
SUP 23 Apr 1804

BRETT, Henry
L 29 Oct 1810
Ret CR 11 Apr 1851 (PRO)
d 1852 (PRO)

BRETT, John
L 2 Mar 1734
CR 1740 (DNB)
CA 25 Mar 1741
d 1785 (DNB)

BRETT, Sir Piercy (1)
L 6 Dec 1734
CR
CA 30 Sept 1743 (DNB)
Kt 2 Jan 1753 (MPN)
MP (Queensborough) 1754–1774 (MPN)
CRM 10 Nov 1759 (AL)
RAR 21 Oct 1762
COM AD 11 Dec 1766–28 Feb 1770 (AO)
VAB 18 Oct 1770 (CH)
VAW 24 Oct 1770 (CH)
VAR 31 Mar 1775
AB 29 Jan 1778
d 14 Oct 1781 (DNB)

BRETT, Piercy (2)
L 10 Apr 1778
CR 28 June 1781
CA 1 Dec 1787
d 7 June 1791 (LT)

BRETT, Piercy (3)
L 12 Nov 1805
CR 1 Feb 1812
d 16 Feb 1843 (PRO)

BRETT, Thomas
L 28 June 1781
d 1796 (PRO)

BRETT, Timothy
L 26 Dec 1705 (PMM)
CR 24 Apr 1720
CA 4 May 1727
d 3 May 1739 (PJP)

BRETT, William (1)
L 3 Mar 1740
CR 10 Apr 1746
CA 10 July 1747
d 19 Jan 1769

BRETT, William (2)
L 7 Jan 1783
SUP CR 22 Nov 1819 (PRO)
d July 1824 (PRO)

BREWER, Richard
L 26 Sept 1780
d 1805 (PRO)

BREWERTON, Thomas
L 1672

BREWOOD, William
L 21 Jan 1702

BREWSE, Hobart
L 25 May 1749
d 1755(6) (PRO)

BREWSE, John
L 17 Mar 1742
d 1757 (PRO)

BRIARLY, George Alexander		
L	22 June	1814
d		1817 (PRO)
BRICE, Gilbert		
L	6 June	1795
d		1815 (PRO)
BRICE, James,		
L	31 May	1790
Dismissed	13 June	1798 (PJP)
BRICE, Nathaniel		
L	15 Aug	1806
Ret CR	21 Apr	1840 (PRO)
d	Feb	1864 (PRO)
BRICE, Randell		
L	7 Feb	1694
BRICE, Robert		
See KINGSMILL, Sir Robert Brice		
BRICE, Thomas		
L	9 Feb	1815
d		1857 (PRO)
BRICE, William Adair		
L	2 Feb	1780
KIA	12 Apr	1782 (RLB)
BRIDGE, Timothy		
L	26 Feb	1710
CR		
CA	27 May	1728
d	6 Oct	1737
BRIDGEMAN, Hon. Charles Orlando		
L	10 Sept	1810
CR	16 May	1814
CA	2 Sept	1819 (PRO)
Ret CA	1 Oct	1846 (PRO)
Ret RA	19 Jan	1852 (PRO)
Ret VA	10 Sept	1857 (PRO)
d	12 Apr	1860 (PRO)
BRIDGEMAN, Th		
L		1664
CA		1666
BRIDGEMAN, William		
L	10 Dec	1798
d	8 Feb	1801 (PRO)
BRIDGES, Brook George		
L	19 June	1805
d		1808 (PRO)
BRIDGES, Sir Brook William		
L	30 Oct	1790
Inh Bt		1792 (PJP)
Ret CR	1 May	1823 (PRO)
d	23 Apr	1829 (PRO)
BRIDGES, George Francis		
L	1 Aug	1811
CR	9 Sept	1818 (PRO)
Ret CA	1 Apr	1856 (PRO)
d		1872 (PRO)
BRIDGES, Henry Charles		
L	23 May	1776
d	27 Aug	1795 (PMM)
BRIDGES, John (1)		
?L	30 Apr	1678 (P)
?CA	12 Apr	1679 (P)
CA	8 Nov	1689
d	24 May	1694
BRIDGES, John (2)		
?L	30 Apr	1678 (P)
?CA	12 Apr	1679 (P)
CA	17 Sept	1691
d	29 May	1695
BRIDGES, John (3)		
L	12 Aug	1744
d		1755(6) (PRO)
BRIDGES, Philip Henry		
L	4 July	1803
CR	15 Nov	1816 (PRO)
CA	29 Sept	1827 (PRO)
Ret CA	?Oct	1847 (PRO)
d	17 Oct	1848 (PRO)
BRIDGES, Richard		
L	11 Sept	1773
CR	21 Sept	1790
CA	29 Apr	1802
d		1811 (PRO)
BRIDGES, Samuel		
L	5 Sept	1732
d	22 Oct	1739 (PMM)
BRIDGES, Timothy		
L		
CA	2 June	1695
Dismissed	23 July	1708 (CH)
BRIDGES, Walter		
L	7 July	1746
d		1748 (PRO)
BRIDGES, William (1)		
L		
CA	9 May	1690
d	21 Jan	1695
BRIDGES, William (2)		
L	1 Jan	1712
CR	25 Oct	1720
d	16 Jan	1744 (PRO)
BRIDPORT, Rt. Hon. Alexander Hood, Viscount		
L	2 Dec	1746
CR	23 Mar	1756
CA	10 June	1756
TGH		1766 (PJP)
RAW	26 Sept	1780
VAB	24 Sept	1787
Kt		1788 (CH)
VAW	21 Sept	1790
VAR	1 Feb	1793
Cre IP	12 Aug	1794 (DNB)
AB	12 Apr	1794
AW	1 June	1795
IP		
converted to EP	31 May	1796 (DNB)
LGRM	20 Aug	1799 (LG)
AR	9 Nov	1805
d	3 May	1814 (LT)
BRIERLY, George Alexander		
See BRIARLY, George Alexander		
BRIETZEKE, Charles Ware		
L	20 Aug	1794
d	Oct	1795 (LT)
BRIGGS, David		
L	8 July	1814
Ret CR	28 Oct	1857 (PRO)
d		1875 (PRO)

BRIGGS, Francis
L 8 May 1804
SUP CR 25 Jan 1837 (PRO)
d 1853 (PRO)

BRIGGS, Joseph
L 3 May 1798 (PRO)
CR
CA 29 Apr 1802
d 1802 (PRO)

BRIGGS, Stephen
L 20 Oct 1807
SUP CR 30 Apr 1844 (PRO)
d 1850 (PRO)

BRIGGS, Thomas
L 28 Sept 1797
CR 30 Jan 1800
CA 24 May 1801 (PRO)
RAB 27 June 1832 (PRO)
RAW 10 Jan 1837 (PRO)
RAR 28 June 1838 (PRO)
VAB 23 Nov 1841 (PRO)
VAW 9 Nov 1846 (PRO)
VAR 27 Dec 1847 (PRO)
AB 2 Sept 1850 (PRO)
d 16 Dec 1851 (PRO)

BRIGHT, Thomas
L 22 Mar 1799
d (drowned) 28 June 1803 (PJP)

BRIGSTOCKE, Thomas Robert
L 29 Nov 1814
CR 31 Jan 1821 (PRO)
CA 1 July 1851 (NMM)
Ret CA 1 Apr 1856 (PRO)
d 28 Oct 1871 (PRO)

BRINE, Augustus
L 20 Nov 1790
CR 6 Dec 1798
CA 29 Apr 1802
Ret CA 10 Jan 1837 (PRO)
d 29 Jan 1840 (PRO)

BRINE, George
L 15 Apr 1803
CR 13 Aug 1812
CA 7 Dec 1818 (PRO)
Ret CA 1 Oct 1846 (PRO)
Ret RA 17 Aug 1851 (PRO)
Ret VA 10 Sept 1857 (PRO)
Ret A 23 Mar 1863 (PRO)
d 16 Nov 1864 (PRO)

BRINE, Henry
See BRYNE, Henry

BRINE, James
L 1 July 1766
CR 25 Dec 1778
CA 30 Dec 1779
RAW 14 Feb 1799
RAR 1 Jan 1801
VAW 23 Apr 1804
VAR 9 Nov 1805
AB 25 Oct 1809
AW 31 July 1810
d 1814 (PRO)

BRINE, John
L 22 Jan 1806
Ret CR 17 July 1838 (PRO)
d 1856 (PRO)

BRISAC, George
L 10 July 1777
CR 21 Sept 1790
CA 23 May 1793
d 1836 (PRO)

BRISBANE, Sir Charles
L 22 Nov 1790
CR 1 July 1794
CA 22 July 1796
Kt 1807 (PJP)
KCB 2 Jan 1815 (MB)
RAB 12 Aug 1819 (PRO)
RAW 19 July 1821 (PRO)
RAR 27 May 1825 (PRO)
d Dec 1829 (DNB)

BRISBANE, Sir James
L 23 Sept 1794
HP 1797–1801 (MB)
CR 22 May 1797
CA 2 Apr 1801
CB 4 June 1815 (LG)
Kt 2 Oct 1816 (DNB)
d 19 Dec 1826 (DNB)

BRISBANE, John
L 5 Aug 1757
CR
CA 24 Sept 1761
RAB 21 Sept 1790
RAR 1 Feb 1793
VAB 12 Apr 1794
VAW 4 July 1794
VAR 1 June 1795
AB 14 Feb 1799
AW 1 Jan 1801
AR 9 Nov 1805
d 10 Dec 1807

BRISBANE, John Douglas
L 1 Apr 1779
d (drowned) 1782 (PJP)

BRISBANE, John Stuart
L 2 July 1811
d 1819 (PRO)

BRISBANE, Patrick
L 1682
CA 1690 (PJP)

BRISBANE, Stewart
L 24 Jan 1758
d 1762 (PRO)

BRISBANE, William Henry
L 18 June 1781
CR 9 Oct 1794
d 29 Nov 1795 (PRO)

BRISCOE, Edward
L 14 Jan 1695 (PJP)
CR
CA 8 Nov 1698 (PRO)

BRISCOE, John
L
CR
CA 1 Jan 1713
d 1714

BRISTOL, Augustus John Hervey, Earl of		
See HERVEY, Augustus John		
BRISTOW, William		
L	2 Oct	1771
d	27 Oct	1803
BRITTIFF, Charles		
L		?1689 (PJP)
CA	4 June	1692
d		1703
BRITTON, James Suttor		
T		
L	4 Feb	1815
Ret CR	9 Feb	1860 (PRO)
d		1860 (TR)
BROAD, George		
L	9 Apr	1800
d		1812 (PRO)
BROADE, George		
L		1672
CA		1673
d	before	1689 (PJP)
BROADLEY, Henry		
L	21 Jan	1771
d		1775 (PRO)
BROADLEY, Housman		
L	18 May	1745
CR	28 Apr	1755
d	29 Jan	1760 (PRO)
BROADLEY, James		
L	2 Mar	1734
CR	5 May	1741
d		1746(7) (PRO)
BROADWATER, William		
L	24 Oct	1806
d		1847 (PRO)
BROCK, Henry Frederick		
L	24 June	1808
d	9 May	1812 (PJP)
BROCK, John		
L	2 Sept	1745
d		1786 (PRO)
BROCKMAN, James		
L	15 Nov	1800
Ret CR	26 Nov	1830 (PRO)
d	17 Jan	1845 (OB)
BRODERICK, John		
L	29 June	1810
d		1811 (PRO)
BRODERICK, Thomas		
L	11 Jan	1727 (PRO)
CR		1741 (DNB)
CA	25 Mar	1741
RAB	4 June	1756 (CH)
RAW	5 Feb	1758 (CH)
VAB	14 Feb	1759
VAW	21 Oct	1762 (CH)
d	1 Jan	1769
BRODERICK, Thomas James		
See BRODRICK, Thomas James		
BRODIE, Alexander (1)		
L	16 Jan	1741
d	20 Dec	1749 (PMM)
BRODIE, Alexander (2)		
L	3 Mar	1804
HP		1814 (OB)
Ret CR	18 July	1836 (PRO)
d		1848 (PRO)
BRODIE, David		
L	5 Oct	1736
CR	3 May	1743 (DNB)
CA	9 Mar	1748 (DNB)
d		1787 (DNB)
BRODIE, Francis		
L	6 Feb	1815
d	12 Feb	1844 (PRO)
BRODIE, Frederick		
L	30 June	1807
Dismissed		1811 (PRO)
BRODIE, Joseph		
L	16 May	1795
CR	3 Jan	1798
d	7 July	1816 (PRO)
BRODIE, Thomas Charles		
L	7 Feb	1798
CR	14 Feb	1801
CA	29 Apr	1802
d	14 Mar	1811 (PRO)
BRODIE, William		
L	8 Oct	1795
d		1797 (PRO)
BRODRICK, Thomas James		
L	6 Apr	1815
d		1832 (PRO)
BROGRAVE, William		
L	19 Aug	1753
CR	13 Oct	1760 (PRO)
d		1785 (PRO)
BROKE, Sir Philip Bowes Vere		
L	19 Aug	1797
CR	2 Jan	1799
CA	14 Feb	1801
Cre Bt	25 Sept	1813 (DNB)
KCB	3 Jan	1815 (DNB)
RAB	22 July	1830 (PRO)
RAR	10 Jan	1837 (PRO)
d	2 Jan	1841 (DNB)
BROKENSHA, Samuel		
L	16 Mar	1815
Ret CR	31 May	1873 (PRO)
d		1880 (PRO)
BROME, Charles		
L	4 May	1795
d	26 Apr	1830 (PRO)
BROME, Henry		
L	9 Nov	1756
d		1785 (PRO)
BROMEDGE, Hugh		
L	21 Sept	1756
CR	3 Apr	1759
CA	29 Apr	1778
d	18 Aug	1792
BROMEDGE, John		
L	3 Sept	1759
d		1779 (PRO)

BROMFIELD, George
L 26 May 1741
d 1758 (PRO)

BROMFIELD, Philip
L 7 Oct 1794
d 1795 (PRO)

BROMLEY, John
L 1678 (DDA)

BROMLEY, Sir Robert Howe
L 12 Jan 1798
CR 14 Feb 1801
CA 28 Apr 1802
Inh Bt 17 Aug 1808 (MB)
RAW 10 Jan 1837 (PRO)
RAR 23 Nov 1841 (PRO)
VAB 9 Nov 1846 (PRO)
VAW 19 Feb 1847 (PRO)
VAR 1 Aug 1848 (PRO)
AB 17 Aug 1851 (PRO)
AW 21 Jan 1854 (PRO)
d 8 July 1857 (PRO)

BROMLEY, Samuel (1)
L 22 Apr 1800
d 1804 (PRO)

BROMLEY, Samuel (2)
L 6 Sept 1804
d 13 Nov 1845 (OB)

BROMPTON, Alexander Constantine
L 24 Aug 1804
d Oct 1809 (LT)

BROMWICH, Bryan I'anson
L 3 Sept 1794
d 1805 (PRO)

BROOK, Richard
L 19 Feb 1796
d Jan 1808 (PRO)

BROOKBANK, Isaac
L 20 Oct 1800
d 8 May 1824 (PRO)

BROOKE, Edward
L 22 Jan 1702 (PMM)
CR 31 Oct 1720 (PRO)
CA 12 Jan 1728
d 1738

BROOKE, Henry
L 14 Feb 1811
d 15 July 1825 (PRO)

BROOKE, Peter
L 3 Feb 1812
d 1841 (PRO)

BROOKE, William
L 4 Apr 1760
d 29 June 1787 (PMM)

BROOKES, Caesar
L 3 Sept 1697
CR
CA 24 July 1708
d 31 Dec 1711 (PJP)

BROOKES, Edward
See BROOKE, Edward

BROOKES, John
L 9 July 1747
CR 26 May 1758
CA 24 Sept 1762
d 8 July 1791

BROOKES, Martin
L 21 Oct 1790
d 1802 (PRO)

BROOKHOLDING, Thomas William
L 9 Mar 1815
d 19 July 1829 (PRO)

BROOKING, Arthur
L 20 Nov 1812
d 16 May 1838 (LT)

BROOKING, Henry
L 7 Oct 1801
d 1820 (PRO)

BROOKING, Peter Franklin
L 13 Mar 1741
d 1757 (PRO)

BROOKING, Samuel
L 30 May 1779
CR 11 Oct 1779
CA 21 July 1796
SUP RA 31 Aug 1819 (PRO)
d 30 Apr 1837 (PRO)

BROOKING, William
L 1666
d before 1689 (PJP)

BROOKS, Francis
L 21 Aug 1782
d 1791 (PRO)

BROOKS, George
L 17 Mar 1806
HP 4 June 1815 (OB)
Ret CR 25 Aug 1853 (PRO)
d 1856 (PRO)

BROOKS, John (1)
L 1664
d before 1689 (PJP)

BROOKS, John (2)
L 17 Nov 1664 (DDA)
CA 17 May 1678 (DDA)
d before 1689 (PJP)

BROOKS, John (3)
L 7 Aug 1761
d 1790 (PRO)

BROOKS, John
See BROOKES, John

BROOKS, Packington
L 1661
CA 1662

BROOKS, William
L 2 Feb 1815
d Sept 1820 (PRO)

BROOME, Samuel
L 1665
CA 1678
d before 1689 (PJP)

BROOMHEAD, Gilbert
L 24 Sept 1805
d 1826 (PRO)

BROTHERS, James
L 27 Aug 1694 (PMM)

BROTHERS, Richard
L 3 Jan 1783
d Jan 1824 (PRO)

BROUGHTON, Alexander Day
L 24 Feb 1778
d 1809 (PRO)

BROUGHTON, Francis
L 20 Sept 1759
d 1786 (PRO)

BROUGHTON, Hugh
L 19 Jan 1771
CR 10 Mar 1779
CA 30 Dec 1779
d 22 Jan 1780 (PRO)

BROUGHTON, John (1)
L 26 Aug 1789
CR 7 Jan 1795
CA 3 Aug 1801
RAB 22 July 1830 (PRO)
RAW 10 Jan 1837 (PRO)
d Oct 1837 (PRO)

BROUGHTON, John (2)
L 1 Aug 1801 (PRO)
Ret CR 1 Nov 1831 (PRO)
d 1859 (PRO)

BROUGHTON, Richard Delves
L 22 Feb 1804
Dismissed 1822 (PRO)

BROUGHTON, William Robert
L 12 Jan 1782
CR 3 Oct 1793
CA 28 Jan 1797 (DNB)
CB 4 June 1815 (LG)
CRM 12 Aug 1819 (LG)
d 12 Mar 1821 (DNB)

BROUN, Andrew
L 15 July 1794 (PRO)
CR 6 Dec 1799 (PRO)
CA 14 Feb 1801 (PRO)
d 1818 (PRO)

BROWELL, Herbert
L 8 Oct 1779
CR 2 July 1788
CA 22 Nov 1790
d 13 Nov 1790 (PRO)

BROWELL, William
L 10 Nov 1778
CR 30 May 1794
CA 29 Nov 1794 (PRO)
LGH 1809–22 July 1821 (DNB)
SUP CA 1813 (PRO)
d 22 July 1831 (DNB)

BROWN, Adam
L 6 Apr 1811
CR 28 Apr 1814
d 12 Apr 1828 (PRO)

BROWN, Alexander (1)
L 29 Jan 1748
d 1791 (PRO)

BROWN, Alexander (2)
L 1 Apr 1765
d 1800 (PRO)

BROWN, Alexander (3)
L 1 Dec 1796
d 1798 (PRO)

BROWN, Almerick
L 5 Mar 1779
d 1794(5) (PRO)

BROWN, Andrew
L 21 Feb 1815
d 1840 (PRO)

BROWN, Annesley
L 24 July 1760
Dismissed 7 June 1765 (PJP)
d ?1766 (PRO)

BROWN, Charles (1)
L
CR
CA 18 Mar 1709
d 1753 (LTE)

BROWN, Charles (2)
L 2 Mar 1734
COMM (Chatham) 1742–1754 (PJP)
CR 24 Jan 1754
d 23 Mar 1754 (PJP)

BROWN, Charles (3)
L 6 Feb 1815
d 1826 (PRO)

BROWN, Constantine D.
L 16 Mar 1811
d 1815 (PRO)

BROWN, David
L 14 June 1760
d 1774 (PRO)

BROWN, George (1)
L 23 Aug 1797
Ret CR 26 Nov 1830 (PRO)
d 29 June 1837 (LT)

BROWN, George (2)
L 18 Oct 1804
T
CR 7 Mar 1810
Ret CA 28 Sept 1840 (PRO)
d 1856 (TR)

BROWN, George (3)
L 1 Nov 1815
CR 23 Mar 1835 (PRO)
CA 18 Aug 1847 (PRO)
Ret CA 15 Sept 1857 (PRO)
d 29 Aug 1864 (PRO)

BROWN, George Williams
L 29 Apr 1802
Ret CR 25 Feb 1834 (PRO)
d 1854 (PRO)

BROWN, James (1)
L 7 May 1736
CR 1 Oct 1741
d 1742 (PRO)

BROWN, James (2)
L 28 Apr 1756
d 1757 (PRO)

BROWN, James (3)
L 4 Dec 1807
d 23 Feb 1831 (PRO)

BROWN, John (1)
L 31 Aug 1739
d 1755(6) (PRO)

BROWN, John (2)
L 2 May 1755
d 1782(3) (PRO)

BROWN, John (3)
L 6 Apr 1757
d 14 Nov 1793

BROWN, John (4)
L 16 Apr 1757
CR 27 Oct 1761
d 1767 (PRO)

BROWN, John (5)
L 1 Sept 1772
CR 1 Dec 1777
CA 25 Mar 1779
RAB 1 June 1795
RAR 14 Feb 1799
VAB 1 Jan 1801
VAW 23 Apr 1804
VAR 9 Nov 1805
AB 28 Apr 1808
d 2 May 1808 (PRO)

BROWN, John (6)
L 26 Apr 1779
d 1 Dec 1789

BROWN, John (7)
L 25 May 1781
d 1784 (PRO)

BROWN, John (8)
L 20 Apr 1783
d 1810 (PRO)

BROWN, John (9)
L 28 July 1794
d 9 Jan 1809 (PRO)

BROWN, John (10)
L 27 Feb 1800
d 1804(5) (PRO)

BROWN, John (11)
L 22 July 1801
d 1808 (PRO)

BROWN, John (12)
L 10 Apr 1802
d (drowned) 9 Jan 1809 (PJP)

BROWN, John (13)
L 6 Feb 1806
d 1809 (PRO)

BROWN, John Hoskins
T
L 16 Aug 1814
Ret CR 24 Apr 1858 (PRO)
Civil CB 1862 (TR)
Ret CA 20 Mar 1863 (PRO)
d 29 June 1864 (PRO)

BROWN, John William
L 28 Sept 1815
d July 1830 (PRO)

BROWN, Johnson
L 15 June 1785 (PRO)

BROWN, Matthew
L 3 Apr 1779
SUP CR 31 Jan 1814
d Apr 1827 (PRO)

BROWN, Nathaniel
L ?26 Aug 1689 (PJP)
CA 17 Feb 1692
d 28 June 1693

BROWN, Peter
L 26 June 1745
d ?1752 (PRO)

BROWN(E), Philip
L 20 June 1765
CR 4 Mar 1777
d 21 Nov 1779 (PRO)

BROWN, Pulling
L 23 Jan 1779
d 1784 (PRO)

BROWN, Richard (1)
L
CA 4 May 1696
d 12 Nov 1706

BROWN, Richard (2)
L 21 Feb 1741
d Jan 1756 (LTE)

BROWN, Richard (3)
L 9 Jan 1783
CR 18 July 1796
CA 22 Sept 1797
d 1803 (PRO)

BROWN, Richard Cayley
L 1 Apr 1815
d 1842 (PRO)

BROWN, Sir Samuel (1)
L 6 Nov 1801
CR 1 Aug 1811 (PRO)
Ret CA 18 May 1842 (PRO)
d 15 Mar 1852 (PRO)

BROWN, Samuel (2)
L 29 May 1802
d 1806 (PRO)

BROWN, Thomas (1)
L 17 Mar 1780
CR
CA 22 Jan 1806 (MB)
d 1816 (PRO)

BROWN, Thomas (2)
L 23 June 1809
d 1836 (PRO)

BROWN, William (1)
L
CR 2 June 1746
CA 17 June 1755
d 1774

BROWN, William (2)
L 27 Dec 1788
CR 9 Jan 1791
CA 29 Oct 1793
RAB 1 Aug 1811
RAW 12 Aug 1812
RAR 4 June 1814
d 20 Sept 1814 (DNB)

BROWN, William (3)
L 5 Nov 1793

CR 18 Feb 1796
d (murdered) 21 Nov 1798 (PJP)

BROWN, William (4)
L 19 Feb 1800
d 26 Apr 1829 (NMM)

BROWN, William (5)
L 22 Feb 1802
Ret CR 11 Dec 1833 (PRO)
d 1865 (PRO)

BROWN, William (6)
L 2 Mar 1815
d July 1821 (PRO)

BROWN, William
See BROWNE, William

BROWN, Zachary
L
CA 1664

BROWNE, Alexander
L 1666

BROWNE, Arnold
L
CA 1661
Dismissed 1664 (PD)
d before 1688 (PD)

BROWNE, Charles
L 16 Nov 1809
d (drowned) 30 Nov 1812 (CH)

BROWNE, Dodwell
L 13 Nov 1790
d 1820 (PRO)

BROWNE, Edward (1)
L 24 Jan 1783
CR 30 July 1793
CA 13 May 1794
d 1796 (PRO)

BROWNE, Edward (2)
L 15 Apr 1794
d 1806 (PRO)

BROWNE, Edward Walpole
L 9 Nov 1790
CR 25 June 1799
CA 29 Apr 1802
Ret RA 10 Jan 1837 (PRO)
RAW 17 Aug 1840 (PRO)
RAR 23 Nov 1841 (PRO)
d 15 Oct 1846 (PRO)

BROWNE, George Peters
L 26 Apr 1811
d 1819 (PRO)

BROWNE, Henry
L
CA 23 Aug 1666 (RM)

BROWNE, James
L 10 Jan 1800
d 23 Feb 1838 (LT)

BROWNE, Jeremiah (1)
L 21 May 1795
d 1798 (PRO)

BROWNE, Jeremiah (2)
L 27 Feb 1801
T
d 1817 (TR)

BROWNE, John (1)
L
CA 1660
d 1663 (PD)

BROWNE, John (2)
L 2 Oct 1794 (PRO)
Ret CR 9 Dec 1831 (PRO)
d 1844 (PRO)

BROWNE, John (3)
L 14 Sept 1809
d 24 Aug 1828 (PRO)

BROWNE, John Aislie
L 8 Feb 1797
d 1801 (PRO)

BROWNE, John Summers
L 10 May 1775
d 1787 (PRO)

BROWNE, Joseph
L 17 Jan 1762 (PRO)
d 1779 (PRO)

BROWNE, Philip (1)
L 1 May 1691
In Merchant Service 1700 (PJP)

BROWNE, Philip (2)
L 22 Dec 1793
CR 25 Sept 1806
CA 19 June 1810
Dismissed 30 Mar 1814 (MB)
Restored 20 Apr 1815 (MB)
RAB 9 Nov 1846 (PRO)
RAW 19 Nov 1849 (PRO)
Ret RA 1 July 1851 (PRO)
Ret VA 15 Apr 1857 (PRO)
d 25 Jan 1860 (PRO)

BROWNE, Ralph
L 1664

BROWNE, Richard
See BROWN, Richard

BROWNE, Robert
L 1 Nov 1777
d 1808 (PRO)

BROWNE, Robert (2)
L 31 July 1793
d 1810 (PRO)

BROWNE, Roger
L 19 Oct 1694

BROWNE, Thomas (1)
L 11 Feb 1695

BROWNE, Thomas (2)
L 21 Nov 1790
CR 11 Aug 1800
CA 29 Apr 1802
RAB 10 Jan 1837 (PRO)
RAW 28 June 1838 (PRO)
RAR 23 Nov 1841 (PRO)
VAB 10 Dec 1846 (PRO)
VAW 3 Jan 1848 (PRO)
VAR 6 Nov 1850 (PRO)
d 7 Apr 1851 (PRO)

BROWNE, Thomas (3)
L 24 Oct 1794
CR 8 Oct 1802
CA 22 Jan 1806
RAB 28 June 1838 (PRO)

RAW 23 Nov 1841 (PRO)
RAR 22 Jan 1847 (PRO)
VAB 8 June 1849 (PRO)
VAW 16 June 1851 (PRO)
VAR 17 Dec 1852 (PRO)
AB 4 July 1855 (PRO)
d 17 June 1857 (PRO)

BROWNE, Wileman
L 16 Apr 1802
Ret CR 25 Jan 1834 (PRO)
d 1839 (PRO)

BROWNE, William (1)
L 11 Aug 1699

BROWNE, William (2)
L 9 Nov 1756
CR 20 Mar 1779
d 23 Nov 1790

BROWNE, William (3)
L 12 Feb 1783
d 1816 (PRO)

BROWNELL, John
L 9 Dec 1782
d 1786 (PRO)

BROWNING, John
L 19 Jan 1702

BROWNING, Lawrence
L 1664
d 1665 (DDA)

BROWNJOHN, William
L 5 May 1735
d ?1740 (PRO)

BROWNRIGG, William Crosbie
L 24 Mar 1800
CR 29 Apr 1802
d 10 Dec 1805 (PRO)

BRUCE, Alexander (1)
L 27 Sept 1740
d 1748 (PRO)

BRUCE, Alexander (2)
L 18 Apr 1758
d 1 Dec 1765 (PMM)

BRUCE, Charles (1)
L 4 Sept 1800
d 1803 (PRO)

BRUCE, Charles (2)
L 15 Feb 1815
Ret CR 18 Jan 1861 (PRO)
d 1874 (PRO)

BRUCE, George
L 18 Mar 1805
d 1811 (PRO)

BRUCE, Sir Henry William
T
L 5 Jan 1810
CR 27 May 1814
CA 6 Nov 1821
RAB 30 July 1852 (PRO)
RAW 11 Feb 1854 (PRO)
RAR 28 Dec 1855 (PRO)
VAB 2 Oct 1857 (PRO)
VAW 6 Mar 1858 (PRO)
KCB 1861 (TR)
VAR 5 Aug 1861 (PRO)
AB 27 Apr 1863 (PRO)
d 14 Dec 1863 (PRO)

BRUCE, John
L 21 Apr 1794
Ret CR 19 Nov 1830 (PRO)
d 4 June 1831 (PRO)

BRUCE, Laurence Dundas
L 28 Aug 1780
d 1816 (PRO)

BRUCE, Robert
L 7 Nov 1806
CR 9 Nov 1818 (PRO)
d 1834 (PRO)

BRUCE, William Henry
L 23 June 1720
CR 13 Mar 1741
d 12 June 1742 (PMM)

BRUDENEL, John
L 2 Jan 1771
CR 15 Sept 1777
d 1785 (PRO)

BRUDENELL, Richard
L 10 Mar 1757
CR 15 June 1762
d 1762 (PRO)

BRUENE, Richard
L 23 Nov 1777
d 1789 (PRO)

BRUMHALL, John
L 24 Apr 1799
Ret CR 26 Nov 1830 (PRO)
d 1838 (PRO)

BRUNTON, Nathan
L 19 Sept 1777
CR 21 Mar 1782
CA 6 Aug 1783
RAB 9 Nov 1805
RAW 28 Apr 1808
RAR 25 Oct 1809
VAB 31 July 1810
VAW 4 Dec 1813
VAR 4 June 1814
d 19 Nov 1814 (PRO)

BRUSTIS, Paul
L 13 July 1756
SUP CR 21 Sept 1796 (PMM)
d 1798 (PMM)

BRYAN, William
L 27 July 1793
CR 12 Aug 1812
d 1816 (PRO)

BRYANT, Edward
L 7 Sept 1815
Struck off list 6 Nov 1818 (PRO)

BRYANT, George
L 29 Aug 1744
d 1770 (PRO)

BRYANT, John
L 6 July 1795
d 1799 (PRO)

BRYANT, Thomas
See BIGANT, Thomas

BRYANT, William
L 7 Mar 1815
HP 7 Mar 1815 (OB)
d 1852 (PRO)

BRYCE, James
L 21 Nov 1810
d 10 Jan 1822 (PRO)

BRYDGES, Richard (1)
L 18 Aug 1744
d 1754(5) (PRO)

BRYDGES, Richard (2)
L 21 Mar 1812
d 28 Feb 1818 (LT)

BRYER, Wyndham
L 1 Feb 1781
CR 22 Nov 1790
d 23 Oct 1794 (NMM)

BRYETT, Thomas Theophilus
L 3 Oct 1808
d 1812 (PRO)

BRYNE, Henry
L 14 Sept 1762
CR 21 Jan 1771
CA 20 Nov 1775
d (drowned) 11 Oct 1780 (CH)

BUCHAN, David
L 29 Jan 1806
CR 13 Apr 1816 (PRO)
CA 12 June 1823 (PRO)
d 1839 (PRO)

BUCHAN, Edward Wise
L 11 Feb 1800
CR 29 Dec 1813
d 1814 (PRO)

BUCHAN, James
L 31 Dec 1746
d 18 Nov 1750 (PMM)

BUCHAN, Thomas
L 12 June 1804
Gone 1811 (PRO)

BUCHANAN, Alexander
L 24 Aug 1813
d 1850 (PRO)

BUCHANAN, Archibald
L 10 Dec 1810
CR 15 June 1814
d 26 Dec 1822 (PRO)

BUCHANAN, George
L 21 Mar 1812
d 1833 (PRO)

BUCHANAN, James (1)
L 10 Apr 1802
Dismissed 10 Sept 1802 (PJP)
Restored 1805 (PJP)

BUCHANAN, James (2)
L 19 Dec 1804
d 1808 (PRO)

BUCHANAN, John (1)
L 22 Aug 1759
CR 17 July 1780
CA 18 Jan 1783
d 13 Jan 1791

BUCHANAN, John (2)
L 24 Aug 1793
CR 27 Sept 1797
d 1802 (PRO)

BUCHANAN, William
L 18 Dec 1794
CR 31 Oct 1799 (MB)
CA 12 Oct 1809
d 16 Apr 1833 (LT)

BUCHANNAN, William
T
L 24 Dec 1805
CR 18 July 1812
Ret CA 12 Feb 1846 (PRO)
d 1859 (TR)

BUCK, James
L
CA 26 July 1690
d 9 Aug 1691 (PJP)

BUCK, John
L 12 Nov 1666

BUCK, Richard
L 13 Oct 1802
CR 20 Dec 1807
CA 3 Apr 1811
d 7 Aug 1830 (PRO)

BUCKE, John
L 23 Apr 1803
d 1809 (PRO)

BUCKHILL, Thomas
L
CA 1661

BUCKINGHAM, James
L 5 Apr 1757
d 1779 (PRO)

BUCKINGHAMSHIRE, John Sheffield, Earl of Mulgrave
See MULGRAVE, John Sheffield, Earl of

BUCKLE, Mathew
L 31 Jan 1780
d 1837 (PRO)

BUCKLE, Matthew (1)
L 14 June 1739
CR 16 July 1744
CA 29 May 1745
RAW 18 Oct 1770
RAR 24 Oct 1770
VAB 31 Mar 1775
VAW 5 Feb 1776
VAR 29 Jan 1778
AB 26 Sept 1780
d 9 July 1784 (CH)

BUCKLE, Matthew (2)
L 21 Jan 1791
CR 6 Dec 1796
CA 29 Apr 1802
Ret RA 10 Jan 1837 (PRO)
RAW 17 Aug 1840 (PRO)
RAR 23 Nov 1841 (PRO)
VAB 9 Nov 1846 (PRO)
VAW 13 May 1847 (PRO)
VAR 8 June 1849 (PRO)
Ret VA 1 July 1851 (PRO)
Ret A 30 July 1852 (PRO)
d 8 Apr 1855 (PMM)

BUCKLE, William
L 9 Apr 1808
d 1811 (PRO)

BUCKMASTER, William
L 26 Nov 1799
d 1804(5) (PRO)

BUCKNALL, Joseph
L 29 Jan 1743
d 1774 (PRO)

BUCKNER, Charles
L 6 June 1756
CR 26 Sept 1761
CA 17 Feb 1766
RAB 1 Feb 1793
RAW 12 Apr 1794
VAB 4 July 1794
VAW 1 June 1795
AB 14 Feb 1799
AW 9 Nov 1805
AR 28 Apr 1808
d 19 Feb 1811 (PRO)

BUCKNOR, Jacob
L 1 Dec 1808
d 1834 (PRO)

BUCKOLL, Richard
L 14 May 1794
CR 3 Aug 1795
d 23 Apr 1798 (PRO)

BUCKWORTH, Francis
L 27 Oct 1758
d 1759 (PRO)

BUDD, Henry Hayward
L 25 Mar 1807
CR 16 Sept 1842 (PRO)
Ret CR 1 July 1851 (PRO)
d 1859 (PRO)

BUDD, Hopewell Hayward
L 1 May 1804
Ret CR 10 Oct 1836 (PRO)
d 1869 (PRO)

BUDDLE, John Harrison
L 5 Apr 1805
d 1808 (PRO)

BUGDEN, Edmund
L
CA 10 Mar 1697
Dismissed ?1697 (PJP)

BUGDEN, John
L 22 Feb 1815
Ret CR 31 Jan 1862 (PRO)
d 12 Mar 1874 (PRO)

BUGDEN, Richard
L 2 Mar 1815
Ret CR 1 Oct 1860 (PRO)
d 23 Mar 1870 (PRO)

BUGDEN, William
L 27 Mar 1810
d 1813 (PRO)

BUDWORTH, William
L 9 Apr 1762
d 19 June 1791

BULFORD, John
L 27 Jan 1809
Ret CR 16 Aug 1854 (PRO)
d 26 Dec 1859 (PRO)

BULGER, John
L 27 June 1814
d 1833 (PRO)

BULKELEY, James
L 14 Apr 1812
HP 7 Sept 1813 (OB)
Ret CR 7 Feb 1855 (PRO)
d 28 Sept 1865 (PRO)

BULKELEY, Richard
T wounded
L 22 May 1806
Discharged dead from HMS GARLAND at Port Royal 29 Dec 1809 (PRO)
d Dec 1809 (PRO)

BULKELEY, Thomas
L 1 Aug 1682

BULL, John
L 4 Apr 1805
d 1810 (PRO)

BULLEN, Sir Charles
L 9 Aug 1791
CR 2 Jan 1798
CA 29 Apr 1802
T
CB 4 June 1815 (LG)
HP Jan 1817–Dec 1823 (MB)
COMM (Chatham) 1831–1832 (TR)
Kt 1835 (TR)
KCH 13 Jan 1835 (DNB)
KCB 18 Apr 1839 (DNB)
RAW 17 Aug 1840 (LG)
RAR 23 Nov 1841 (PRO)
VAB 9 Nov 1846 (PRO)
VAW 22 Sept 1847 (PRO)
VAR 24 Dec 1849 (PRO)
GCB 7 Apr 1852 (DNB)
AB 30 July 1852 (PRO)
d 2 July 1853 (DNB)

BULLEN, Joseph
L 6 Mar 1781 (PRO)
CR 29 Nov 1793
CA 24 Nov 1796
SUP RA 28 Aug 1819 (PRO)
VAR 12 Nov 1840 (PRO)
AB 23 Nov 1841 (PRO)
AW 10 Dec 1846 (PRO)
AR 12 Nov 1849 (LG)
d 17 July 1857 (PRO)

BULLER, Augustus
L 7 May 1802 (PRO)
d 1805 (PRO)

BULLER, Sir Edward
L 1782 (MPT)
CR 26 Apr 1783
CA 19 July 1790
MP (East Looe) 1802–1820 (MPT)
CRM 9 Nov 1805 (AL)
RAB 28 Apr 1808
Cre Bt 30 Oct 1808 (MPT)
RAW 25 Oct 1809
RAR 31 July 1810
VAB 12 Aug 1812

VAW	4 June	1814
VAR	12 Aug	1819 (PRO)
d	15 Apr	1842 (MPT)
BULLER, George		
L	30 Oct	1793
d		1795 (PRO)
BULLER, John		
L	3 Nov	1790
KIA	17 Oct	1807 (LG)
BULLER, Reginald		
L	12 Oct	1793
d		1796 (PRO)
BULLER, Thomas Wentworth		
L	8 Dec	1812
CR	19 Apr	1817 (PRO)
Ret CR	1 July	1851 (PRO)
d	30 Oct	1852 (PRO)
BULLER, William		
L	24 Dec	1793 (PRO)
d	15 June	1794 (LT)
BULLEY, George		
L	9 Oct	1801
T	wounded	
CR	17 Jan	1814
d	26 Dec	1817 (LT)
BULLEY, John		
L		
CR		
CA	2 Oct	1711
d	2 July	1715
BULLEY, William		
L	4 Sept	1740
CR	17 Oct	1744
CA	12 July	1745
d	7 Oct	1746
BULLOCK, Frederick		
L	22 Jan	1812
CR	26 Aug	1829 (PRO)
CA	28 June	1838 (PRO)
RAB	2 Oct	1857 (PRO)
RAW	1 Nov	1860 (PRO)
RAR	6 Feb	1863 (PRO)
VAB	28 Nov	1864 (PRO)
Ret VA	11 Nov	1865 (PRO)
Ret A	10 Sept	1869 (PRO)
d	Feb	1874 (PRO)
BULLOCK, James		
L	3 Mar	1780
SUP CR	22 Sept	1814
d	18 Mar	1825 (LT)
BULLY, William		
See BULLEY, William		
BULT, James		
L	23 Sept	1801
d		1816 (PRO)
BULTEEL, Rowley		
L	22 July	1778
CR	24 Sept	1782 (PJP)
CA	22 Nov	1790
RAB	25 Oct	1809
RAW	31 July	1810
RAR	12 Aug	1812
VAB	4 June	1814
VAW	12 Aug	1819 (PRO)
d	27 Aug	1820 (PRO)
BULTEELE, James		
L	2 Aug	1748
d		1764 (PRO)
BUMPSTED, John		
L		
CA	14 Dec	1689
d	8 Sept	1691
BUNBURY, Harrison Charles		
L	12 July	1782
Dismissed		1797 (PRO)
BUNCE, James		
L	2 July	1781
SUP CR	1 Jan	1816 (PRO)
d	28 Oct	1829 (PRO)
BUNCE, Joseph Brown		
L	12 Mar	1778
CR	15 Apr	1783
d	9 July	1792 (LT)
BUNDEE, Charles		
L	22 Nov	1688
BUNDOCK, John		
L	15 Feb	1815
d		1839 (PRO)
BUNN, Thomas (1)		
L		
CA		1660
d	before	1689 (PJP)
BUNN, Thomas (2)		
L	4 Feb	1815
HP		1816 (OB)
Ret CR	9 Feb	1860 (PRO)
d		1869 (PRO)
BUNSTER, Grosvenor		
L	8 Feb	1815
d		1851 (PRO)
BUNYAN, William		
L	1 Jan	1749
d		1778 (PRO)
BURBIDGE, William Cave		
L	28 Feb	1815 (PRO)
d	3 Feb	1860 (PRO)
BURCH, Isaac (1)		
L	27 Mar	1800
d	7 June	1829 (PRO)
BURCH, Isaac (2)		
L	11 June	1814
Ret CR	13 Apr	1857 (PRO)
d		1877 (PRO)
BURCHELL, William (1)		
L	28 Jan	1777
d		1778 (PRO)
BURCHELL, William (2)		
L	28 Apr	1809
d	9 Aug	1814 (PRO)
BURCHER, James		
L	27 Dec	1740
d (drowned)	15 Sept	1747 (PJP)
BURDETT, George		
L	24 June	1793
CR	8 Mar	1797

CA 29 Apr 1802
d 1832 (PRO)

BURDICK, John
L
CA 1672

BURDON, Abraham
L 2 Oct 1779
SUP CR 17 Mar 1814
d 1818 (PRO)

BURDON, George (1)
L 12 May 1756
CR 24 Aug 1762
KIA 24 Apr 1778 (CH)

BURDON, George (2)
L 7 June 1776
CR 16 Sept 1783
CA 28 Oct 1793
RAB 1 Aug 1811
RAW 12 Aug 1812
RAR 4 June 1814
d 23 Sept 1815 (PMM)

BURDWOOD, Daniel
L 30 Oct 1782 (PRO)
d 1804 (PRO)

BURDWOOD, Thomas
L 29 Sept 1807 (PRO)
Ret CR 15 Apr 1844 (PRO)
d 31 Jan 1851 (PRO)

BURFORD, Samuel
L 2 May 1759
d 1790 (PRO)

BURGES, John
L 23 Jan 1746
d ?1751 (PRO)

BURGES, Michael
L 27 July 1744
d 1746 (PRO)

BURGES, Richard Rundel
L
CR 7 Dec 1782
CA 21 Sept 1790
KIA 11 Oct 1797 (LG)

BURGESS, Daniel
L 21 July 1780
d 8 May 1824 (PRO)

BURGESS, Isaiah
L 10 Feb 1722

BURGESS, Samuel
L 18 Nov 1799
T
CR 16 Sept 1816 (PRO)
Reduced in seniority in 1831 from
27 Nov 1829 to 27 Nov 1830 (PRO)
Ret CA 26 Dec 1850 (PRO)
d 1 Aug 1851 (PRO)

BURGESS, William
L 22 Oct 1779
CR 5 July 1794
d 18 Dec 1840 (OB)

BURGH, Arthur
L 28 Feb 1812
d 1835 (PRO)

BURGH, John
L 21 Mar 1807
d 1810 (PRO)

BURGH, Thomas
L 3 Jan 1810
d Dec 1829 (PRO)

BURGH, William
L 24 July 1794
d 1798 (PRO)

BURGOYNE, Frederick William
L 7 Mar 1797
CR 22 Oct 1810
CA 20 Sept 1815
Ret CA 1 Oct 1846 (PRO)
d 3 June 1848 (LT)

BURKE, Henry
L 6 July 1796
CR 4 Oct 1800
d (drowned) 31 Dec 1804 (CH)

BURKE, Walter
L 19 May 1800
d Feb 1801 (JH)

BURKE, William
L 1665 (DDA)

BURLEY, John (1)
L 26 Dec 1695

BURLEY, John (2)
L 21 Apr 1780
d 1793 (PRO)

BURLTON, Charles
L 2 Apr 1794
d 5 Apr 1830 (PRO)

BURLTON, Sir George
L 15 Sept 1777
CR 5 July 1794
CRM 5 Dec 1813 (AL)
RAW 4 June 1814
KCB 1815 (PJP)
d 21 Sept 1815 (PJP)

BURMAN, Charles
L 21 June 1804
d 1810 (PRO)

BURN, David
L 24 July 1781
d 1807 (PRO)

BURN, John (1)
L 4 Nov 1790
CR 12 Dec 1799
d 6 Feb 1813 (PRO)

BURN, John (2)
L 3 Sept 1794
d 1802 (PRO)

BURN, John (3)
L 6 Apr 1802
Ret CR 8 Aug 1833 (PRO)
d 1855 (PRO)

BURN, John (4)
L 22 Jan 1806
d 1816 (PRO)

BURN, Lauchlan
L 19 Nov 1811
d 1842 (PRO)

BURN, Miles Brathwait Perry
L 24 Apr 1802
Dismissed 1805(6) (PRO)

BURNABY, Edward Augustus Caesar
L 10 Dec 1780
SUP CR 11 Dec 1815
d 11 Mar 1843 (LT)

BURNABY, Sir William
L 16 Dec 1732
CR 7 Sept 1741
CA 9 Dec 1742
Kt 1754 (PJP)
RAR 21 Oct 1762
Cre Bt 1767 (PJP)
VAW 18 Oct 1770
VAR 24 Oct 1770
d 1776

BURNABY, Sir William Chaloner
L 1 Nov 1763
CR 7 May 1764
Inh Bt ?1776
CA 16 Jan 1777
d 19 Feb 1794 (LT)

BURNABY, Sir William Crisp Hood
Inh Bt 19 Feb 1794 (OB)
L 3 Nov 1809
CR 26 May 1814
Ret CA 1 July 1857 (PRO)
d 1 Aug 1853 (PMM)

BURNABY, William Pitt
L 7 May 1764
d 1782 (PRO)

BURNBY, Thomas
L 4 July 1796 (PRO)
d 1801 (PRO)

BURNET, Thomas
L 20 Aug 1744
CR 12 May 1756
CA 5 May 1757
d 1784

BURNETT, George Stephens
L 27 Dec 1810
d 12 Sept 1820 (PRO)

BURNETT, James
L 12 Mar 1757
d 1779 (PRO)

BURNETT, William
L 5 May 1762
d 1772 (PRO)

BURNEY, James (1)
L 17 Apr 1773
CR 2 Oct 1780
CA 18 June 1782
SUP CA 23 Apr 1804
SUP RA 19 July 1821 (PRO)
d 16 Nov 1821 (PRO)

BURNEY, James (2)
L 4 July 1814
CR 24 Dec 1829 (PRO)
CA 10 Dec 1835 (PRO)
Ret CA 1 July 1851 (PRO)
Ret RA 19 Mar 1857 (PRO)
Ret VA 24 Sept 1863 (PRO)
Ret A 18 Oct 1867 (PRO)
d 1884 (PRO)

BURNEY, John
L 19 Sept 1797
Struck off list 1806 (PRO)
Restored 17 Nov 1821 (PRO)
d 23 June 1830 (PRO)

BURNHAM, Thomas
L 6 Oct 1815
Ret CR 14 Apr 1864 (PRO)
d 1869 (PRO)

BURR, Daniel
L 19 Feb 1756
SUP 21 Feb 1795 (PRO)

BURR, John
L 23 June 1758
CR 13 Sept 1769
CA 15 Oct 1773
d 1776 (H)

BURR, John Davall
L 10 Aug 1775
d 1784 (PRO)

BURR, William
L 21 Feb 1741
d 1767 (PRO)

BURRARD, Sir Charles
L 1 May 1812
Inh Bt 18 Oct 1813 (OB)
CR 7 June 1814
CA 29 Jan 1822 (PRO)
Ret CA 1 Oct 1846 (PRO)
Ret RA 1 Oct 1852 (PRO)
Ret VA 4 Nov 1857 (PRO)
Ret A 27 Apr 1863 (PRO)
d 12 July 1870 (PRO)

BURRARD, Sir Harry
See NEALE, Sir Harry Burrard

BURRELL, Samuel
L 1670 (PMM)
d before 1689 (PJP)

BURRINGTON, Gilbert
L 18 June 1692

BURRISH, George
L 25 Jan 1726
CR
CA 7 May 1733
Dismissed 9 Oct 1745

BURROUGH, Charles
L 11 Apr 1783
CR 2 Jan 1798
d 1810 (PRO)

BURROUGHS, Sackville
L 20 Nov 1812
Ret CR 2 July 1855 (PRO)
d 22 Apr 1857 (PRO)

BURROUGHES, Anthony
L 1660
CA 1664
d before 1689 (PJP)

BURROWES, Alexander Saunderson
L 17 Nov 1794
CR 13 July 1796
CA 22 Jan 1806
KIA 12 Oct 1806 (LG)

BURROWS, John (1)
L 24 May 1762
d 1818 (PRO)

BURROWS, John (2)
L 15 Nov 1790
d 1797 (PRO)

BURROWS, Richard
L 5 Nov 1746
d 1763 (PRO)

BURSELM, Francis
L 17 Sept 1743
CR 24 June 1757
CA 4 Oct 1759
Resigned 1760 (PJP)
d 1787 (PRO)

BURSTALL, John
L 2 Apr 1760
SUP 1807 (PRO)

BURSTALL, William
L 27 Oct 1758
SUP CR 5 Nov 1800
d 1813 (PRO)

BURT, Anthony
L 13 July 1796
d 1803 (PRO)

BURT, Charles
L 18 Mar 1778
d 1782 (PRO)

BURT, Edward
L 28 Dec 1802
CR 1 Apr 1808
Ret CR 1 July 1851 (PRO)
d 18 Nov 1858 (NMM)

BURT, George
T
L 13 Nov 1813
d (drowned) 17 Jan 1815 (TR)

BURT, William
L 1668

BURTON, Casibelan
L 1666
CA 1672
d before 1689 (PJP)

BURTON, George Guy
L 20 Feb 1805
CR 5 Oct 1814
CA 9 Nov 1846 (LG)

BURTON, James
L 9 Aug 1811
d 1832 (PRO)

BURTON, James Ryder
Later RYDER, James
L 15 Feb 1813
CR 27 Nov 1819 (PRO)
CA 23 Feb 1824 (PRO)
Ret RA 28 May 1853 (PRO)
Ret VA 13 Feb 1858 (PRO)
Ret A 14 Nov 1863 (PRO)
d 1876 (PRO)

BURTON, John
L 16 July 1749
d 1755(6) (PRO)

BURTON, Richard
L 4 Sept 1797
T
CR 12 Aug 1812
d 11 Aug 1836 (LT)

BURTON, Robert
L 10 Aug 1802
d 1803(4) (PRO)

BURTON, Thomas
L 1 Jan 1799
CR 3 Dec 1802
CA 21 Oct 1810
d 26 Feb 1843 (LT)

BURVILLE, Peter
L 6 Oct 1722
CR 27 Mar 1742
d 1742 (PRO)

BURY, George
L 11 Jan 1814
d 1849 (PRO)

BURY, Richard Incledon
Formerly INCLEDON, Richard
L 26 May 1778 (PJP)
CR 26 Aug 1789 (PRO)
CA 22 Nov 1790
RAB 31 July 1810
RAW 1 Aug 1811 (PRO)
RAR 12 Aug 1812
VAB 4 June 1814
VAW 12 Aug 1819 (PRO)
d 18 Apr 1825 (LT)

BURY, Thomas (1)
L 2 Mar 1742
CR
CA 3 July 1743
Dismissed 19 Jan 1747

BURY, Thomas (2)
L 12 Mar 1807
CR 15 June 1814
d 1 May 1831 (PRO)

BUSH, George (1)
L 10 Nov 1793
Ret CR 19 Dec 1828 (PRO)
d 1842 (PRO)

BUSH, George (2)
L 25 July 1807
d 17 Feb 1828 (PRO)

BUSH, William
L 11 May 1797
Ret CR 26 Nov 1830 (PRO)
d 1838 (PRO)

BUSHBY, John
L 10 Oct 1795
CR 29 Apr 1802
CA 22 Jan 1806
d 25 Aug 1810 (PRO)

BUSHBY, Thomas
L 16 Aug 1811
CR 26 Dec 1822 (PRO)
CA 3 July 1840 (PRO)
Ret CA 21 Aug 1853 (PRO)
Ret RA 6 Mar 1858 (PRO)
d 25 Mar 1865 (PRO)

BUSHELL, John
L 1666

BUSHELL, Scanderbeg George
L 1666
d before 1689 (PJP)

BUSHELL, William
L 1672
d before 1689 (PJP)

BUSK, William de
L 3 June 1797
d 11 Oct 1803 (PRO)

BUSSELL, William
L 18 Aug 1801
d 1814 (PRO)

BUSTARD, Robert
L 17 Nov 1790
d 1801 (PRO)

BUSTOW, William (1)
L 1664 (DDA)

BUSTOW, William (2)
L
CA 1666 (DDA)
d (drowned) 30 Mar 1675 (PJP)

BUTCHART, John
L 3 Sept 1760
CR 1 Dec 1778
CA 15 June 1779
d 1795 (PRO)

BUTCHER, James Blakeman
L 10 June 1813
d 1818 (PRO)

BUTCHER, John (1)
L 4 Dec 1673

BUTCHER, John (2)
L 20 Feb 1815
Name removed 1821 (PRO)

BUTCHER, Jonathan
L 23 Feb 1815
Ret CR 1 Oct 1860 (PRO)
d 9 May 1871 (PRO)

BUTCHER, Robert (1)
L 14 Aug 1780
d 1790 (PRO)

BUTCHER, Robert (2)
L 3 Mar 1815
d 22 Aug 1851 (PRO)

BUTCHER, Samuel
L 17 July 1794
CR 19 Feb 1801
CA 29 Apr 1802
Ret RA 10 Jan 1837 (PRO)
RAW 17 Aug 1840 (PRO)
RAR 9 Nov 1846 (PRO)
VAB 19 Feb 1847 (PRO)
VAW 23 Mar 1848 (PRO)
d 8 May 1849 (PRO)

BUTCHER, Stephen
L 20 Aug 1811
d 1833 (PRO)

BUTLER, Benjamin (1)
L 11 Sept 1779
d 1784 (PRO)

BUTLER, Benjamin (2)
L 23 Mar 1796
d (drowned) 12 Jan 1799 (PJP)

BUTLER, Daniel
L 3 Mar 1757
d 1768 (PRO)

BUTLER, George
L 19 Nov 1811
Ret CR 1 Apr 1853 (PRO)
d 1871 (PRO)

BUTLER, Henry
L 25 Aug 1672 (DDA)
Dismissed Dec 1685 (DDA)
CA 30 Apr 1688
d (duel) 21 Sept 1693 (DDA)

BUTLER, Jacob
L 31 Aug 1762
d 2 Sept 1768 (PMM)

BUTLER, James
L 25 Feb 1742
CR 11 Nov 1746
d 1754(5) (PRO)

BUTLER, John
L
CA 10 July 1666 (RM)

BUTLER, John Carter
L 11 Apr 1805
d 1807 (PRO)

BUTLER, Sir Roger
L 30 Sept 1718
CR
CA 3 June 1734
d 1747 (H)

BUTLER, Thomas (1)
L
CA 3 Oct 1693
Dismissed 17 June 1711 (WE)
d 24 July 1727

BUTLER, Thomas (2)
L 12 June 1776
d 1782(3) (PRO)

BUTLER, Thomas (3)
L 26 May 1778
CR 22 Apr 1782 (PRO)
d 1788 (PRO)

BUTLER, Thomas, Earl of Ossory
See OSSORY, Thomas Butler, Earl of

BUTLER, Thomas Colelough
L 20 Jan 1796
d 1810 (PRO)

BUTLER, Whitwell
L 27 July 1808
HP 14 July 1809 (OB)
Ret CR 27 Oct 1845 (PRO)
d 1849 (PRO)

BUTT, Henry Samuel
L 8 Jan 1792
CR 8 Aug 1797
d 1838 (PRO)

BUTT, John
L 22 July 1794
d 1799 (PRO)

BUTTANSHAW, Thomas
L 18 Feb 1815
d 1842 (PRO)

BUTTERFIELD, William
- L 11 Apr 1794
- CR 26 Apr 1798
- CA 29 Apr 1802
- Ret RA 10 Jan 1837 (PRO)
- RAW 17 Aug 1840 (PRO)
- RAR 23 Nov 1841 (PRO)
- d 3 Oct 1842 (PRO)

BUTTERWORTH, William
- L 30 Oct 1793
- d 9 Aug 1805 (PMM)

BUTTLER, George
- L 10 Dec 1810
- CR 9 Nov 1846 (PRO)
- d 12 July 1850 (PRO)

BUTTON, John
- L 30 July 1710

BUTTON, Osmond
- L 23 Aug 1800
- Ret CR 26 Nov 1830 (PRO)
- d 1841 (PRO)

BUTTON, William
- L
- CA 1660
- d before 1689 (PJP)

BUTTS, Charles
- L 6 June 1809
- Dismissed 1814 (PRO)

BUXTON, John
- L 18 Mar 1782
- Dismissed 1790 (PRO)
- Restored 29 Apr 1791 (PRO)
- d 1794 (PRO)

BYAM, Edward
- L 26 Oct 1762
- d (drowned) Sept 1784 (PJP)

BYAM, Lawrence
- L 1661

BYAM, William Henry
- L 6 Nov 1795
- CR 4 Sept 1804
- CA 24 Jan 1811
- d 26 Nov 1838 (LT)

BYARD, Sir Thomas
- L 25 June 1773
- CR 15 Nov 1782
- CA 17 Jan 1783
- d 31 Oct 1798 (PRO)

BYNARD, Walter
- L 1672
- CA 24 Oct 1677
- d before 1689 (PJP)

BYNE, Charles
- L 15 Feb 1815
- d June 1831 (PRO)

BYNG, George, Viscount Torrington
- KLB 1678 (DNB)
- L 1683 (MPS)
- LF (Queen's Regiment) Nov 1687 (EAD)
- CAF (Queen's Regiment) Dec 1688 (EAD)
- CA 22 Dec 1688 (DNB)
- RAR 1 Mar 1703 (DNB)
- Kt 22 Oct 1704 (DNB)
- VAB 18 Jan 1705 (DNB)
- MP (Plymouth) 1705–17 Jan 1733 (MPS)
- AB 26 Jan 1708 (DNB)
- AW 21 Dec 1708
- COM AD 8 Nov 1709–19 Jan 1714 (AO)
- COM AD 14 Oct 1715–30 Sept 1721 (AO)
- Cre Bt 17 Nov 1715 (MPS)
- AF 14 Mar 1718 (DNB)
- Cre EP 9 Sept 1721 (DNB)
- FLA 2 Aug 1727–17 Jan 1733 (AO)
- d 17 Jan 1733 (DNB)

BYNG, George, Viscount Torrington
- See TORRINGTON, George Byng, Viscount

BYNG, Henry
- L 17 Apr 1744
- SUP CR 21 Sept 1796
- d 1812 (PMM)

BYNG, Hon. Henry Dilkes
- L 5 May 1804
- CR 12 Dec 1809 (MB)
- CA 9 Mar 1814
- Ret CA 1 Oct 1846 (PRO)
- Ret RA 3 Mar 1849 (PRO)
- Ret VA 31 Jan 1860 (PRO)
- d 23 Sept 1860 (PRO)

BYNG, Hon. John
- L 20 June 1723 (DNB)
- CR
- CA 8 Aug 1727
- GG (Newfoundland) 1742–1744 (BNS)
- RAB 10 Aug 1745 (LG)
- VAB 15 July 1747
- VAR 12 May 1748
- MP (Rochester) 23 Jan 1751–14 Mar 1757 (MPS)
- AB 2 Apr 1756 (PRO)
- e (negligence) 14 Mar 1757 (DNB)

BYNNING, Thomas
- L
- CA 1672
- d before 1689 (PJP)

BYRON, George Anson (1)
- L 31 May 1776
- CR 20 Oct 1778
- CA 3 Apr 1779
- d 11 June 1793 (PRO)

BYRON, Hon. George Anson, Lord (2)
- L 24 Aug 1807
- CR 1 Feb 1812
- CA 7 June 1814
- RAB 24 Dec 1849 (PRO)
- Ret RA 1 July 1851 (PRO)
- Ret VA 19 Mar 1857 (PRO)
- Ret A 20 May 1862 (PRO)
- d 2 Mar 1868 (PRO)

BYRON, Hon. John
- L 22 Mar 1746 (PRO)
- CR 30 Feb 1746 (DNB)
- CA 30 Dec 1746
- GG (Newfoundland) 1769–1772 (BNS)
- RAB 31 Mar 1775
- RAW 28 Apr 1777
- RAR 23 Jan 1778
- VAB 29 Jan 1778

VAW	26 Sept	1780
d	10 Apr	1786 (DNB)
BYRON, Richard (1)		
L		1672
CR	26 May	1701 (PMM)
BYRON, Richard (2)		
L	1 Oct	1792
CR	22 June	1798
CA	29 Apr	1802
CB	4 June	1815 (LG)
Ret RA	10 Jan	1837 (PRO)
d	2 Sept	1837 (PRO)
BYRON, William Lord		
L	27 Mar	1741
d		1743 (PRO)
CABBURN, John Edward		
L	13 Feb	1813
HP	13 Sept	1813–
	26 July	1841 (OB)
Ret CR	1 Oct	1860 (PRO)
d		1861 (PRO)
CABLE, Samuel		
L	23 July	1781
CR	5 May	1795
d		1807 (PRO)
CADENHEAD, Moses		
L	6 Feb	1815
d	Sept	1827 (PRO)
CADMAN, George		
L	9 Oct	1778
CR	24 Apr	1782 (MB)
CA	25 Oct	1809
d		1833 (PRO)
CADMAN, James		
L		
CA		1664
KIA	2 Aug	1665 (ESP)
CADMAN, John		
L	9 Oct	1778
d		1782 (PRO)
CADOGAN, Rt. Hon. George, Earl		
L	12 Apr	1802
CR	4 May	1804
CA	23 Mar	1807
CB	4 June	1815 (LG)
Inh EP	23 Dec	1832 (OB)
RAB	23 Nov	1841 (PRO)
RAW	9 Nov	1846 (PRO)
RAR	5 Sept	1848 (PRO)
VAB	1 July	1851 (PRO)
VAW	22 Apr	1853 (PRO)
VAR	4 July	1855 (PRO)
AB	9 July	1857 (PRO)
AW	25 June	1858 (PRO)
AR	23 Mar	1863 (PRO)
d	16 Sept	1864 (PRO)
CADOGAN, Hon. Thomas		
L	26 July	1770
CR	11 Nov	1776
CA	20 Feb	1779
d (drowned)	30 Sept	1782 (CH)
CADWELL, William		
See CALDWELL, William		

CAESAR, Charles		
L	16 Apr	1756
d		1782 (PRO)
CAIGER, Herbert		
L	13 Dec	1806
CR	11 May	1827 (PRO)
HP		1827 (OB)
Ret CA	1 Apr	1856 (PRO)
d		1868 (PRO)
CAILLOUEL, Isaac		
L	2 Feb	1741
d		1741 (PRO)
CAIRNES, James Webb		
L	2 Dec	1807
CR	16 Aug	1824 (PRO)
d	19 Feb	1831 (LT)
CALDECOT, Charles		
L	23 Dec	1814
Ret CR	9 Apr	1856 (PRO)
d	18 June	1864 (PRO)
CALDECOT, Miller		
L	3 May	1771
CALDER, Francis Anderson		
L	28 Apr	1811
Ret CR	1 Apr	1853 (PRO)
d		1856 (PRO)
CALDER, Patrick		
L	6 Nov	1747
d	16 Nov	1790
CALDER, Sir Robert		
L	31 Aug	1762
CR	27 Aug	1779
CA	27 Aug	1780
Kt	3 Mar	1797 (DNB)
Cre Bt	22 Aug	1798 (DNB)
RAB	14 Feb	1799
RAW	1 Jan	1801
RAR	29 Apr	1802
VAB	23 Apr	1804
VAW	9 Nov	1805
VAR	28 Apr	1808
AB	31 July	1810
AW	4 Dec	1813
KCB	12 Apr	1815 (LG)
d	1 Sept	1818 (LT)
CALDWALL, William		
See CALDWELL, William		
CALDWELL, Sir Benjamin		
L	25 Mar	1760
CR	24 May	1762
CA	1 Apr	1765
IMP		
(Knocktopher)		1776–1783 (DNB)
IMP		
(Harristown)		1783–1790 (DNB)
RAW	1 Feb	1793
RAR	12 Apr	1794
VAB	4 July	1794
VAR	1 June	1795
AB	14 Feb	1799
AW	23 Apr	1804
AR	9 Nov	1805
GCB	May	1820 (DNB)
d	1 Nov	1820 (PRO)

CALDWELL, Charles
L 11 Nov 1756
d 1776 (PRO)

CALDWELL, William
L ?1690 (PJP)
CA 22 Jan 1694
(22 Jan 1693 in C)
RAW 1 Feb 1717
(12 Feb 1716 in C)
RAR 14 Mar 1710
d 17 Oct 1718

CALEY, Richard
L 7 May 1794
d 22 Sept 1799 (PRO)

CALL, Benjamin
L 22 Nov 1777
d 1780(1) (PRO)

CALLAGHER, George
L 14 Feb 1815 (PRO)
d 1819 (PRO)

CALLANAN, George
T
L 12 Oct 1807
KIA 25 July 1809 (TR)

CALLAWAY, Daniel
L 29 May 1801
CR 15 June 1814 (PRO)
d 1816 (PRO)

CALLAWAY, Edmond
L 19 Nov 1812
d (duel) 16 Apr 1813 (LT)

CALLCOTT, Richard
L 23 July 1772
CR 9 Oct 1781
CA 15 Dec 1782
d 19 May 1794 (PMM)

CALLIS, Robert
L 25 June 1705

CALLIS, Smith
L 1 Sept 1731
CR
CA 9 Aug 1742
RAB 1 July 1759 (PJP)
d 22 Oct 1761 (M)

CALMADY, Charles Holmes Everitt
L 20 Oct 1772
CR 11 Nov 1776
CA 7 Sept 1777
RAB 23 Oct 1794
RAR 1 June 1795
VAW 14 Feb 1799
VAR 1 Jan 1801
AB 23 Apr 1804
d Mar 1807 (PRO)

CALMADY, Warwick
L 3 July 1739
CR
CA 30 Sept 1743
Quitted 2 Feb 1757
d 1759

CALTHORPE, Hon. John
L 2 Apr 1814
d 1816 (PRO)

CAM, Joseph
L 22 Jan 1759
d 5 July 1767

CAME, Charles
L 6 Dec 1793
CR 28 Nov 1796
d 2 Nov 1797 (PRO)

CAME, Henry
L 24 May 1811
d Feb 1839 (PRO)

CAMEFORD, Thomas Lord
L 7 Apr 1797
CR 12 Dec 1797
SUP CR Jan 1799 (PJP)
Wounded in a duel 7 Mar 1804 (PJP)
d 10 Mar 1804 (PRO)

CAMERON, Alexander
L 15 Nov 1793
d 1794 (PRO)

CAMERON, Allen
T
L 17 May 1808
d 1812 (PRO)

CAMERON, Charles
L 2 Mar 1795
d 1817 (PRO)

CAMERON, Francis
L 15 Sept 1801
d 1804(5) (PRO)

CAMERON, Hugh
L 5 Dec 1799
CR 5 Sept 1806
KIA 18 Dec 1809 (LG)

CAMERON, James
L 10 Feb 1815
d Nov 1825 (PRO)

CAMERON, John (1)
L 19 Aug 1802
d 1809 (PRO)

CAMERON, John (2)
L 28 Dec 1807
d 1840 (PRO)

CAMERON, John (3)
L 31 Dec 1807
d 1811 (PRO)

CAMERON, Robert
L 27 Apr 1798
d 1807 (PRO)

CAMMILERI, Joseph
L 25 Feb 1815
CR 1 Jan 1829 (PRO)
CA 28 July 1851 (PRO)
d 17 Sept 1860 (PRO)

CAMOCKE, George
L 1690 (DNB)
CR 7 June 1695 (PJP)
CA 6 June 1702
Dismissed 1714
Entered Spanish service and became a Rear-Admiral 1718 (DNB)
d 1722 (DNB)

CAMPBELL, Alexander (1)
L 8 Aug 1740
CR 28 Apr 1747
CA 4 Apr 1757 (PJP)
d 17 Nov 1758

CAMPBELL, Alexander (2)
L 8 Apr 1797
CR 24 July 1801
CA 29 Apr 1802
Deprived of seniority by court-martial.
CA 8 June 1804
d 13 Mar 1825 (PRO)

CAMPBELL, Alexander (3)
L 17 Sept 1806
CR 6 Oct 1815
CA 17 Apr 1828 (PRO)
d 1832 (PRO)

CAMPBELL, Andrew
L 31 July 1761
d ?1766 (PRO)

CAMPBELL, Archibald
Formerly HEWITT, William
L 18 Feb 1815
HP 18 Feb 1815 (OB)
d 10 Feb 1859 (NMM)

CAMPBELL, Charles (1)
L 15 Feb 1720

CAMPBELL, Charles (2)
L 10 Jan 1795
CR 6 Dec 1796
CA 2 Aug 1799
d 18 Apr 1825 (PRO)

CAMPBELL, Colin (1)
L 14 July 1796
CR 27 Oct 1808
CA 7 June 1814
d 1842 (PRO)

CAMPBELL, Colin (2)
L 25 Sept 1804
d 1812 (PRO)

CAMPBELL, Colin (3)
T
L 22 Jan 1806
CR 22 Sept 1809
CA 28 Feb 1812
Ret RA 1 Oct 1846 (PRO)
d 3 Mar 1850 (TR)

CAMPBELL, Donald (1)
L
CR 5 June 1793
CA 26 Oct 1795
RAB 4 June 1814
RAW 19 Aug 1819 (LG)
d 11 Nov 1819 (PRO)

CAMPBELL, Donald (2)
L 4 Jan 1798
CR 4 May 1807
CA 1 Aug 1811
Ret RA 1 Oct 1846 (PRO)
d 16 Dec 1856 (PRO)

CAMPBELL, Duncan (1)
L 2 Dec 1755
SUP CR 21 Sept 1756 (PMM)
d 1801 (PMM)

CAMPBELL, Duncan (2)
L 13 Aug 1778
d 1785 (PRO)

CAMPBELL, Sir George (1)
L 6 June 1778
CR 27 Aug 1780
CA 9 Nov 1781
RAB 1 Jan 1801
RAW 23 Apr 1804
RAR 9 Nov 1805
MP (Carmarthen) 1806–Dec 1813 (MPT)
VAB 13 Dec 1806 (LG)
VAW 25 Oct 1809
VAR 31 July 1810
AB 4 June 1814
KCB 2 Jan 1815 (MPT)
AW 12 Aug 1819 (PRO)
GCB 8 June 1820 (MPT)
d (suicide) 23 Jan 1821 (LT)

CAMPBELL, George (2)
L 5 Apr 1814
HP 30 June 1814 (OB)
Ret CR 19 Jan 1857 (PRO)
d 1862 (PRO)

CAMPBELL, George Henry
L 4 Feb 1808
d 1811 (PRO)

CAMPBELL, Hon. George Pryse
L 15 Mar 1811
CR 16 May 1814
CA 27 Jan 1821 (PRO)
Ret CA 31 Oct 1846 (LG)
Ret RA 8 Mar 1852 (PRO)
d 12 Jan 1852 (PRO)

CAMPBELL, James (1)
L 19 July 1742
CR 4 Sept 1744
CA 26 Jan 1749
Dismissed 16 Aug 1762

CAMPBELL, James (2)
L 12 Aug 1799
d 18 Sept 1818 (PMM)

CAMPBELL, James (3)
L 31 Aug 1807
CR 6 Dec 1813
CA 21 June 1828 (PRO)
d 2 Sept 1847 (PRO)

CAMPBELL, John (1)
L 16 Jan 1693

CAMPBELL, John (2)
L 16 Jan 1745 (PRO)
CR 27 May 1747 (PRO)
CA 23 Nov 1747
RAB 23 Jan 1778
RAW 29 Jan 1778 (CH)
VAB 19 Mar 1779
VAW 26 Sept 1780
GG (Newfoundland) 1782–1786 (DNB)
VAR 24 Sept 1787
d 16 Dec 1790

CAMPBELL, John (3)
L 14 Mar 1794
d 1796 (PRO)

CAMPBELL, John (4)
L 22 Mar 1797
Ret CR 26 Nov 1830 (PRO)
d 1834 (PRO)

CAMPBELL, John (5)
L 12 Sept 1800
CR 20 Dec 1811
d 4 June 1825 (PRO)

CAMPBELL, John (6)
L 6 Oct 1801
CR 6 Dec 1813
HP 6 Dec 1813 (OB)
d 30 Dec 1848 (PRO)

CAMPBELL, John (7)
L 1 Nov 1803
d 15 Mar 1829 (PRO)

CAMPBELL, John (8)
L 6 Sept 1808
d 1814 (PRO)

CAMPBELL, John (9)
L 21 Mar 1812
d 1849 (PRO)

CAMPBELL, John Norman
L 12 June 1807
CR 28 Nov 1820 (PRO)
CA 22 Oct 1827 (PRO)
CB 13 Nov 1827 (LG)
d 12 Jan 1840 (PRO)

CAMPBELL, Joshua
L
CR
CA 1 Jan 1713
d 2 Nov 1718

CAMPBELL, Lewis
L 7 Jan 1802
CR 15 Nov 1816 (PRO)
d 14 Aug 1825 (PRO)

CAMPBELL, Matthew
L
CR 28 Nov 1707 (PJP)
CA 1 Jan 1713
d 27 Apr 1723

CAMPBELL, Patrick (1)
L 8 July 1782
d 1 July 1798

CAMPBELL, Sir Patrick (2)
L 25 Sept 1794
CR 4 Sept 1797
CA 11 July 1800
CB 4 June 1815 (LG)
RAB 22 July 1830 (LG)
KCB 12 Apr 1836 (DNB)
RAR 10 Jan 1837 (NMM)
VAB 28 June 1838 (LG)
d 20 Aug 1841 (LT)

CAMPBELL, Robert (1)
L 18 Nov 1790
CR 8 Mar 1797
CA 30 Oct 1797
d 2 Nov 1815 (LT)

CAMPBELL, Robert (2)
L 5 Nov 1803
CR 12 July 1821 (PRO)
d 1833 (PRO)

CAMPBELL, Robert Bell
L 8 Oct 1793
CR 6 July 1801
CA 16 Aug 1806
d 13 Sept 1808 (PRO)

CAMPBELL, Thomas
L 23 Sept 1779
CR 14 Oct 1794
CA 22 Jan 1806
d 29 Sept 1823 (PRO)

CAMPBELL, William (1)
L 6 Mar 1728
CR 10 Dec 1739 (PRO)
CA 16 Apr 1741 (PRO)
Struck off list 10 Feb 1742 (PRO)

CAMPBELL, William (2)
L 22 Mar 1759
d 1770 (PRO)

CAMPBELL, Lord William (3)
L 5 Dec 1760
CR 28 Jan 1762
CA 20 Aug 1762
MP
(Argyllshire) 17 Jan 1764–
July 1766 (MPN)
d 4 Sept 1778 (MPN)

CAMPBELL, William (4)
L 31 Oct 1794
d 1802 (PRO)

CAMPBELL, William (5)
L 18 July 1810
Ret CR 3 Jan 1851 (PRO)
d 5 Nov 1851 (PRO)

CAMPION, George
L 25 Dec 1798
d 1814 (PRO)

CAMPION, Thomas
L 19 Sept 1692
CR
CA 22 Aug 1703
Dismissed 31 Mar 1704

CANDLER, Bartholomew (1)
L
CR
CA 27 Jan 1806
d 22 Oct 1722

CANDLER, Bartholomew (2)
L 30 June 1733

CANDLER, John
L 15 June 1744
d 1772 (PRO)

CANES, Edward
L 6 July 1814
d 16 May 1848 (PRO)

CANES, Edward Jekyll
L 24 Aug 1780
CR 22 Oct 1799
d (drowned) Nov 1801 (CH)

CANES, Thomas
L 4 Aug 1769
d 1771 (PRO)

CANNADAY, Moses
L 24 July 1794
d 8 Jan 1829 (PRO)

CANNING, George (1)
L 1668
CA 1672
KIA 28 Oct 1677 (CH)
CANNING, George (2)
L 24 Aug 1802
T
CR 15 June 1814
d 9 Nov 1842 (PRO)
CANNING, Richard
L 11 Mar 1691
CR
CA 22 Aug 1702
d Aug 1726
CANNON, Augustus
L 2 Feb 1809
d 22 Sept 1812 (LG)
CANNON, John
L 5 Nov 1771
Dismissed 13 Sept 1790 (PJP)
CANNON, Richard
L 25 Aug 1758
d 1769 (PRO)
CANNON, Roquier
L 26 June 1813
d 1815 (PRO)
CANTY, Dominick
L 7 Mar 1815
d 22 Sept 1830 (PRO)
CAPEL, Bartholomew
See CAPELL, Bartholomew
CAPEL, Hon. Thomas Bladen
L 5 Apr 1797
CR 2 Oct 1798
CA 27 Dec 1798
T
CB 4 June 1815 (LG)
RAB 27 May 1825 (PRO)
RAW 22 July 1830 (PRO)
KCB 22 Feb 1832 (LG)
VAB 10 Jan 1837 (PRO)
VAR 23 Nov 1841 (PRO)
AB 28 Apr 1847 (PRO)
AW 30 Oct 1849 (PRO)
AR 8 July 1851 (PRO)
GCB 7 Apr 1852 (DNB)
d 4 Mar 1853 (DNB)
CAPELL, Bartholomew
L
CA 1661
CARD, Robert
L 6 Mar 1815
d 1826 (PRO)
CARDEN, John Surman
L 24 July 1794
CR 25 Oct 1798
CA 22 Jan 1806 (MB)
Ret RA 28 June 1838 (PRO)
RAB 17 Aug 1840 (PRO)
RAW 23 Nov 1841 (PRO)
RAR 9 Nov 1846 (PRO)
VAB 23 Mar 1848 (PRO)
VAW 6 Nov 1850 (PRO)
VA 1 July 1851 (PRO)
A 3 July 1853 (PRO)
d 22 Apr 1855 (PRO)

CARDEW, Octavius
L 21 Oct 1801
d 1804 (PRO)
CARDINEAUX, Thomas Philip
L 26 May 1795
Struck off list 5 June 1817
Since presumed dead
CAREW, Sir Benjamin Hallowell
L 25 Apr 1783
CR 22 Nov 1790
CA 30 Aug 1793
CRM 31 July 1810 (AL)
RAB 1 Aug 1811
RAW 12 Aug 1812
RAR 4 June 1814
KCB Jan 1815 (DNB)
VAB 12 Aug 1819 (PJP)
VAW 19 July 1821 (PJP)
VAR 27 May 1825 (PJP)
AB 22 July 1830 (PJP)
GCB 6 June 1831 (DNB)
d 2 Sept 1834 (DNB)
CAREW, Henry
L 1 Feb 1779
CR 27 June 1797
d 27 Oct 1840 (PRO)
CAREW, Joseph
L 16 Nov 1743
d 1753 (PRO)
CAREW, Robert
L 4 Mar 1746
d 1754(5) (PRO)
CAREW, Sir Thomas
L 6 July 1805
CR 7 June 1814
CA 1 Mar 1833 (PRO)
d 20 Apr 1840 (PRO)
CAREW, Timothy
L 19 July 1814
Ret CR 15 Feb 1858 (PRO)
d May 1877 (PRO)
CAREY, George
L 1661
CAREY, John
L 6 Mar 1744
CR 14 June 1762
d 1782(3) (PRO)
CAREY, Randell
L 21 Aug 1798
d 1805 (PRO)
CAREY, William (1)
L 10 Dec 1707
d 1742 (PRO)
CAREY, William (2)
L 24 Feb 1741
d 28 June 1741 (PMM)
CARFRAE, James
L 24 Feb 1815
d 2 July 1828 (PRO)
CARKETT, John
L 11 Mar 1742
d 1774 (PRO)
CARKETT, Robert
L 26 Feb 1745

CR
CA 12 Mar 1758
d (drowned) 5 Oct 1780 (DNB)

CARLESS, Thomas
L 4 June 1777
Dismissed 28 July 1780 (PJP)

CARLETON, Henry
L 3 Mar 1815
d Jan 1821 (PRO)

CARLETON, John
L 26 Nov 1779
d 12 Feb 1798

CARLETON, William (1)
L 17 June 1696

CARLETON, William (2)
L 19 Sept 1727

CARLETON, William (3)
T
L 18 July 1810
CR 2 Dec 1826 (PRO)
HP 2 Dec 1826 (PRO)
Ret CA 1 Apr 1856 (PRO)
d 1874 (TR)

CARLILE, Charles
L 18 Apr 1682
CA 18 Nov 1682
d ?1684 (PJP)

CARLTON, James
L ?1692 (PRO)
CR 1 July 1694 (PJP)
CA 6 July 1702
d (duel) 1712 (PJP)

CARLYON, William
L 25 June 1773
CR 6 Aug 1777
CA 9 May 1781
SUP CA 1800 (PRO)
d 1830 (PRO)

CARMAN, John
L
CA 12 Oct 1679

CARMARTHEN, Marquis of, Duke of Leeds
L
CA 2 Jan 1691
RAR 7 July 1693
RAB 28 Oct 1693
RAR 28 Jan 1697
VAB 24 Mar 1702
VAW 8 May 1702
VAR 19 Feb 1703
AR 21 Dec 1708

CARMAST, Thomas
L 14 Jan 1806
d 1836 (PRO)

CARNE, Charles Loder
L 10 Jan 1771
CR 25 Oct 1809
d 1819 (PRO)

CARNE, Thomas William
L 21 Dec 1808
d 1817 (PRO)

CARNEGIE, Hon. George
L 6 Apr 1737

CARNEGIE, George, Earl of Northesk
See NORTHESK, George Carnegie, Earl

CARNEGIE, James
L 27 Oct 1701

CARNEGIE, James Lindsay
L 22 Oct 1805
CR 15 June 1814 (PRO)
d 5 Oct 1814 (LT)

CARNEGIE, Patrick
L 17 July 1780
SUP CR 17 Dec 1814
d 13 Jan 1824 (PRO)

CARNEGIE, William
L 30 Dec 1799
d 1816 (PRO)

CARNEGIE, William, Earl of Northesk
See NORTHESK, William Carnegie, Earl

CARNEGY, James
See CARNEGIE, James

CARNEGY, Patrick
See CARNEGIE, Patrick

CARNELL, Thomas
L 1673

CARPENTER, Hon. Charles (1)
L
CA 6 Dec 1731

CARPENTER, Hon. Charles (2)
L 10 May 1776
CR 23 July 1781
MP
(Berwick-on-Tweed) 1790–1796 (MPT)
CA 12 Aug 1792 (PMM)
d 5 Sept 1803 (PJP)

CARPENTER, Daniel
L 21 Feb 1798
Ret CR 6 July 1835 (PRO)
d Dec 1837 (PRO)

CARPENTER, Edward John
L 1 Aug 1794 (PRO)
CR 11 Apr 1809 (PRO)
Ret CA 2 July 1846 (PRO)
d 1857 (PRO)

CARPENTER, George
L 21 June 1743
d 1746 (PRO)

CARPENTER, James
L 18 Apr 1782
CR 9 Jan 1794 (DNB)
CA 25 Mar 1794
RAB 12 Aug 1812
RAR 4 June 1814
VAB 12 Aug 1819 (PRO)
VAW 27 May 1825 (PRO)
VAR 22 July 1830 (PRO)
AB 10 Jan 1837 (PRO)
AW 23 Nov 1841 (PRO)
d 16 Mar 1845 (DNB)

CARPENTER, John
L 1666

CARPENTER, John Cook
L 1 Aug 1794
CR 11 Apr 1809 (PRO)
CA 19 Jan 1821 (PRO)
Ret CA 1 Oct 1846 (PRO)
d 5 Oct 1850 (PRO)

CARPENTER, Robert
L 28 Apr 1755

CR	9 Feb	1759
CA	3 Jan	1760
d	14 Feb	1773
CARR, Edward James		
L	1 Mar	1800
d		1803 (PRO)
CARR, Henry John		
L	8 Feb	1815
Ret CR	1 Oct	1860 (PRO)
d	26 May	1871 (PRO)
CARR, John (1)		
L	24 Mar	1762
d		1772
CARR, John (2)		
L	8 Nov	1781
d		1810 (PRO)
CARR, Robert (1)		
L	23 June	1748
d		1758 (PRO)
CARR, Robert (2)		
L	15 Aug	1806
d	19 Oct	1811 (PRO)
CARR, William (1)		
L	10 May	1699
LGH		1728 (PJP)
d	14 Oct	1758 (PMM)
CARR, William (2)		
L	18 Oct	1802
d		1808 (PRO)
CARR, William (3)		
L	15 Aug	1806
d		1808 (PRO)
CARRE, Robert		
L		
CR	13 Jan	1758
d		1779 (PRO)
CARRE, Robert Riddell		
See RIDDELL, Robert		
CARROLL, Sir William Fairbrother		
L	15 May	1804
CR	4 Mar	1811
CA	6 Dec	1813
CB	4 June	1815 (LG)
RAB	24 Jan	1849 (PRO)
RAW	11 June	1851 (PRO)
KCB		1852 (CH)
RAR	5 Dec	1853 (PRO)
d	8 Apr	1862 (PRO)
CARSLAKE, John		
T		
L	22 Oct	1805
Ret CR	1 Oct	1852 (PRO)
d	19 Aug	1865 (PRO)
CARSLAKE, Martin		
L		
CA		1665
d	before	1689 (PJP)
CARTER, Benjamin		
L	27 Nov	1793
CR	22 Apr	1800
CA	29 Apr	1802
HP		1812 (MB)
d	1 Nov	1833 (OB)
CARTER, Charles (1)		
L	27 June	1696
CARTER, Charles (2)		
L	22 Nov	1790
CR	15 May	1800
CA	29 Apr	1802
Ret RA	10 Jan	1837 (PRO)
RAW	17 Aug	1840 (PRO)
RAR	23 Nov	1841 (PRO)
VAB	20 Nov	1846 (PRO)
d	20 Dec	1847 (PRO)
CARTER, Charles (3)		
L	23 Sept	1800
d	1 Oct	1845 (OB)
CARTER, Edmund C.L.		
L	15 Sept	1801
CR	16 July	1807
d		1809 (PRO)
CARTER, James (1)		
L	22 Oct	1793
d		1796 (PRO)
CARTER, James (2)		
L	3 Feb	1815 (PRO)
d	5 Jan	1824 (PRO)
CARTER, John (1)		
L	7 Jan	1802
d	19 Nov	1825 (LT)
CARTER, John (2)		
L	4 Sept	1805
T		
CR	22 Aug	1809
CA	7 Dec	1815
RAB	8 Apr	1851 (PRO)
Ret VA	9 July	1857 (PRO)
Ret A	4 Oct	1862 (PRO)
d	2 Apr	1863 (PRO)
CARTER, Nicholas		
L	4 July	1740
d		1741(2) (PRO)
CARTER, Richard (1)		
L		1672 (P)
CR		1673 (P)
CA	29 Aug	1675
DGG		
(Southsea Castle)	3 Feb	1685 (EAD)
CAF		
(Queen's Regiment)	Nov	1687 (EAD)
RAB	20 Jan	1692
KIA	19 May	1692 (DNB)
CARTER, Richard (2)		
L	6 Apr	1815
d		1837 (PRO)
CARTER, Robert (1)		
L	27 Aug	1760
SUP CR	31 Dec	1807 (PRO)
d	23 Apr	1818 (PRO)
CARTER, Robert (2)		
L	14 Aug	1801
T		
d	14 Oct	1845 (OB)
CARTER, Robert (3)		
L	2 Dec	1812
Ret CR	29 Aug	1855 (PRO)
d		1872 (PRO)

CARTER, Samuel Thomas

L	14 Jan	1808
Ret CR	19 Oct	1844 (PRO)
d	22 Dec	1851 (PRO)

CARTER, Thomas

L	6 Apr	1805
T		
d		1810 (PRO)

CARTER, Thomas Gilbert

L	14 Dec	1807
Reduced by court-martial		
L	23 Aug	1808
Ret CR	18 Apr	1854 (PRO)
d		1870 (PRO)

CARTER, Thomas Wren

L	18 Apr	1806
CR	14 July	1815
CA	25 Apr	1831 (PRO)
RAB	31 Jan	1856 (PRO)
RAW	10 Sept	1857 (PRO)
RAR	2 May	1860 (PRO)
VAB	6 Feb	1863 (PRO)
VAW	14 Nov	1866 (PRO)
Ret A	20 Nov	1866 (PRO)
d	8 Feb	1874 (PRO)

CARTER, William (1)

L		
CA	18 Sept	1693
	(5 Dec	1692 in C)
d (drowned)	27 Nov	1703 (CH)

CARTER, William (2)

L	18 Aug	1727
CR	26 Sept	1740
d		1743(4) (PRO)

CARTER, William (3)

L	27 Jan	1809
d		1812 (PRO)

CARTERET,
See CARTERETT, Benjamin
CARTERETT, James
CARTERETT, Philip

CARTERET, James

L	28 Mar	1758
d		1789 (PRO)

CARTERET, Peter

L	20 Apr	1744
CR	5 May	1757
KIA	4 Sept	1777 (CH)

CARTERET, Philip (1)

L	4 Aug	1736
CR		
CA	10 May	1742
d	28 Sept	1748

CARTERET, Philip (2)

L	14 June	1757
CR	1 July	1766
CA	10 Jan	1771
d	21 July	1796 (DNB)

CARTERET, Philip
See SILVESTER, Sir Philip Carteret

CARTERET, Richard

L	15 Nov	1744
CR	18 May	1745
CA	16 Apr	1761
d		1780

CARTERETT, Benjamin

L		1663
CA		1666
Dismissed		?1673 (PJP)

CARTERETT, James

L		1665
CA		1665
d		1682 (DDA)

CARTERETT, Sir Philip

L		1660
Kt		1667 (DDA)
KIA	28 May	1672 (LG)

CARTHEUR, John

L	24 Nov	1815
d		1860 (PRO)

CARTHEW, Alfred

L	13 June	1803
d		1803(4) (PRO)

CARTHEW, Edward

L	20 Mar	1794
d		1800 (PRO)

CARTHEW, Henry

L	16 Aug	1800
d		1810 (PRO)

CARTHEW, James

L	4 Nov	1790
CR	4 June	1798
CA	11 June	1801
RAB	22 July	1830 (PRO)
RAR	10 Jan	1837 (PRO)
VAB	23 Nov	1841 (PRO)
VAW	9 Nov	1841 (PRO)
VAR	6 Aug	1847 (PRO)
AB	14 Jan	1850 (PRO)
AW	15 Mar	1853 (NMM)
d	28 Nov	1855 (PRO)

CARTHEW, William

L	18 Aug	1778
CR	22 Nov	1790
CA	10 May	1794
SUP RA	18 Aug	1812
d	31 July	1827 (PRO)

CARTIER, John Henry

L	25 Aug	1797
CR	10 Feb	1801
d	19 Nov	1825 (LT)

CARTWRIGHT, Charles (1)

L	17 Sept	1665 (DDA)

CARTWRIGHT, Charles (2)

L	1 Feb	1763
d		1807 (PRO)

CARTWRIGHT, John

L	15 Sept	1762
CR	25 Oct	1809
d	23 Sept	1824 (PRO)

CARTWRIGHT, William

L	8 Mar	1815
d	1 Mar	1818 (LT)

CARVERTH, Henry

L		1672
CA		1673
d	16 Sept	1684 (DDA)

CARVERTH, Richard

L	9 Sept	1688

CA 3 May 1691 (PJP)
SUP 1696 (PMM)
d 28 Apr 1728 (PMM)

CARY, Ebenezer
L 7 Nov 1751
d 1756 (PRO)

CARY, Henry
T
L 13 July 1807
Ret CR 10 Apr 1843 (PRO)
d Jan 1847 (OB)

CARY, John
L 24 Oct 1744
d 11 July 1795 (PMM)

CASE, James
L 7 Aug 1761
d 1794(5) (PRO)

CASE, William
L 3 Oct 1797
CR 7 Aug 1812 (PRO)
HP 24 Mar 1814 (OB)
Ret CA 14 May 1846 (PRO)
d 1851 (PRO)

CASEY, David O'Brien
L 11 Oct 1799
d 27 Dec 1848 (PRO)

CASHMAN, William
L 15 Nov 1790
CR 29 Apr 1802
d 3 Nov 1822 (PRO)

CASPAL, William
L 24 Dec 1782
SUP CR 11 Jan 1819 (PRO)
d 1837 (PRO)

CASSELLES, Joseph
L 1666
d Before 1689 (PJP)

CASTLE, Daniel
L 22 Jan 1806
d 19 Dec 1825 (PRO)

CASTLE, George
T
L 20 Aug 1811
d 1826 (PRO)

CASTLE, John
L 1674 (P)
CR
CA 17 Sept 1705
KIA 6 June 1706 (CH)

CASTLE, Joseph
L 1666
d before 1689 (PJP)

CASWELL, George
L 24 Sept 1815
CR 9 Nov 1846 (PRO)
Ret CA 1 Aug 1860 (PRO)
d 1875 (PRO)

CASWELL, Joseph
L 1667
d before 1689 (PJP)

CASWELL, William
L 13 Nov 1813
Ret CR 13 Feb 1857 (PRO)
d 1859 (PRO)

CATER, Charles Joseph
L 28 Feb 1809
d 31 July 1845 (OB)

CATER, John
L 25 Feb 1691

CATFORD, Charles
L 29 July 1727
CR 5 Feb 1742
CA 14 Oct 1743
d 24 Sept 1756

CATHCART, Robert
L 21 Nov 1790
CR 8 Oct 1798 (PRO)
CA 19 June 1808
d 1833 (PRO)

CATHCART, Hon. William
L 2 Sept 1801
CR 14 Apr 1802
CA 1 May 1804
d 5 June 1804 (PRO)

CATOR, Bertie Cornelius
L 3 Mar 1807
CR 13 Feb 1811
CA 7 June 1814
Ret CA 1 Oct 1846 (PRO)
Ret RA 5 Nov 1849 (PRO)
Ret VA 12 Nov 1856 (PRO)
Ret A 12 Apr 1862 (PRO)
d 23 July 1864 (PRO)

CAULDWELL, Edward
L 9 July 1762
CR 20 June 1765
CA 4 Nov 1769
d 1773 (PRO)

CAULFIELD, Edwin Toby
L 3 Mar 1815
HP 3 Mar 1815 (OB)
Ret CR 10 Aug 1872 (PRO)
d 1881 (PRO)

CAULFIELD, James
L 27 Feb 1795
CR 7 May 1804
CA 11 Apr 1809
d 26 Apr 1837 (LT)

CAULFIELD, Robert
L 4 May 1807
CR 4 Nov 1814
d Aug 1820 (PRO)

CAULFIELD, Thomas Gordon
L 9 Sept 1793
CR 5 Dec 1795
CA 13 June 1798
d 23 June 1821 (LT)

CAULFIELD, Toby
L 20 July 1759
CR
CA 6 July 1776
d 31 Jan 1781 (NMM)

CAUSZOR, Robert
L 11 Oct 1778
d 14 June 1798

CAVE, Clempson
L 27 June 1690 (PMM)
CR 18 Jan 1704 (PMM)
CA 24 Jan 1732

CAVE, Clemson
L 21 Jan 1690
CR 3 Oct 1696
CA 18 Nov 1703

CAVE, Joseph
L 10 July 1745
CR 10 Aug 1758
d 1781 (PRO)

CAVELL, Edward Jackman
L 5 Oct 1796
d 1817 (PRO)

CAVENDISH, Philip
L 23 May 1694
CR
CA 17 Jan 1701
TGH 1721–1735 (MPS)
MP (Bare Alston) Apr–6 June 1721 (MPS)
MP (St Germans) 1722–1727 (MPS)
RAB 4 Jan 1728
(9 Jan 1728 in C)
RAW 19 July 1728
RAR 4 Mar 1729
VAB 29 June 1732
VAR 26 Feb 1734
AB 2 Mar 1736
COM AD 19 Mar 1742–
14 July 1743 (AO)
MP (Portsmouth) 1743–14 July 1743 (MPS)
d 14 July 1743 (MPS)

CAWKIT, John Edward
L 7 Jan 1802
d 4 Sept 1823 (PRO)

CAWLEY, John
L 16 Aug 1800
CR 11 May 1825 (PRO)
d 29 Apr 1846 (PRO)

CAWLEY, William
L 7 Sept 1695
CR 2 Feb 1708 (PMM)
CA 11 July 1712
d 1740

CAYLEY, Richard
L 7 May 1794
d 1795 (PRO)

CAYLEY, Tyrwit
See CYLEY, Tyrwit

CAYLEY, William (1)
L 26 July 1762
CR 14 Feb 1781
CA 1 May 1782
d 3 Jan 1801 (PRO)

CAYLEY, William (2)
L 19 Dec 1807
d 1819 (PRO)

CECIL, Thomas Walbeoff
L 19 Dec 1807
CR 7 June 1814 (PRO)
d 15 Oct 1814 (PRO)

CEELEY, William
See SEALY, William

CHADS, Henry
L 7 Mar 1759
CR 18 Sept 1779
CA 14 Apr 1783
d 10 Oct 1799 (PRO)

CHADS, Sir Henry Ducie
L 5 Nov 1806 (DNB)
CR 28 May 1813
CA 25 July 1815
CB 26 Dec 1826 (LG)
RAB 12 Jan 1854 (PRO)
KCB 5 July 1855 (DNB)
RAW 9 July 1855 (PRO)
RAR 18 June 1857 (PRO)
VAB 24 Nov 1858 (PRO)
VAW 29 July 1861 (PRO)
VAR 22 Nov 1862 (PRO)
AB 3 Dec 1863 (PRO)
GCB 28 Mar 1865 (DNB)
d 7 Apr 1868 (PJP)

CHADS, James
L 17 May 1746
CR 18 Oct 1758
CA 2 Apr 1766
d 1781

CHADWICK, Richard
L 20 July 1727
CR 23 Feb 1742
CA 16 Jan 1744
d 9 June 1748 (PJP)

CHADWICK, Robert
L ?1702 (PJP)
CR
CA 23 Feb 1710
d 10 July 1719 (PJP)

CHADWICK, Samuel
L
CR
CA 14 Mar 1718
d 26 Dec 1728 (PJP)

CHAISSANG, Charles Louis
See CHASSAING, Charles Louis

CHALMER, George Constable
L 10 Mar 1814 (PRO)
d 7 July 1831 (PRO)

CHALMERS, Andrew
L 18 July 1780
d 1790 (PRO)

CHALMERS, Sir Charles William
L 2 Nov 1805
CR 15 June 1814
d 1834 (PRO)

CHALONEOR, Thomas
L 16 July 1793 (PRO)
d 1801 (PRO)

CHALONER, Edward
L 22 Apr 1723

CHAMBEPLIN, Clifford
See CHAMBERLIN, Clifford

CHAMBERLAIN, Peter
L 19 May 1694 (PJP)
CR 22 Jan 1703 (PMM)

CA	13 Aug	1703
d (drowned)	18 June	1720 (PJP)

CHAMBERLAIN, William Browne

L	27 Jan	1809
Ret CR	6 Apr	1850 (PRO)
d	10 Mar	1860 (PRO)

CHAMBERLAIN, William Tankerville

L	10 June	1808
d		1809 (PRO)

CHAMBERLAYNE, Charles (1)

L		
CR		
CA	25 Jan	1726
d	16 Apr	1737 (PJP)

CHAMBERLAYNE, Charles (2)

L	25 June	1773
CR	9 May	1777
CA	2 Oct	1778
RAB	1 June	1795 (PRO)
RAW	20 Feb	1797
VAB	14 Feb	1799
VAW	29 Apr	1802
VAR	23 Apr	1804
AB	9 Nov	1805
d		1810 (PRO)

CHAMBERLAYNE, Edwin Henry

L	10 Mar	1802
CR	6 Feb	1805
CA	24 Apr	1807
CB	4 June	1815 (LG)
d	Dec	1821 (PRO)

CHAMBERLAYNE, George

L	6 Nov	1795
CR	15 Jan	1802
d	13 Nov	1802 (PRO)

CHAMBERLAYNE, John

L	11 Jan	1814
CR	28 Aug	1828 (PRO)
Ret CA	1 Apr	1865 (PRO)
d	14 Feb	1861 (PRO)

CHAMBERLAYNE, Thomas

L		
CA		1672
Quitted as being Roman Catholic		1763 (PRO)

CHAMBERLEIN, John

L	18 May	1694

CHAMBERLEIN, Peter

L	19 May	1694

CHAMBERLIN, Clifford

L		
CA	18 Apr	1690
d	6 Nov	1691 (PJP)

CHAMBERLIN, Thomas
See CHAMBERLAYNE, Thomas

CHAMBERS, David

L	11 Oct	1796
Ret CR	23 Jan	1838 (PRO)
d	24 May	1845 (OB)

CHAMBERS, George Rodney

L	3 Mar	1804 (PRO)
d		1805 (PRO)

CHAMBERS, James

L	27 Apr	1807
d	24 Jan	1830 (PRO)

CHAMBERS, King

L	14 Nov	1790
d		1797 (PRO)

CHAMBERS, Samuel

L	24 Sept	1800
CR	6 June	1804
CA	12 Aug	1812
d	29 Oct	1843 (PRO)

CHAMBERS, Thomas (1)

L	4 Nov	1782
d		1812

CHAMBERS, Thomas (2)

L	22 May	1810
d		1818 (PRO)

CHAMBERS, William (1)

L	21 June	1726
CR		
CA	5 Oct	1736
RAW	15 July	1747
RAR	12 May	1748
d	9 Jan	1753 (PJP)

CHAMBERS, William (2)

L	9 May	1771
CR	7 Apr	1780
CA	15 Aug	1783
SUP RA	21 Nov	1805

CHAMIER, Frederick

L	6 July	1815
CR	9 Aug	1826 (PRO)
Ret CA	1 Apr	1856 (PRO)
d	29 Oct	1870 (PRO)

CHAMPAIN, William Burgundy

L	23 Jan	1779
CR	12 July	1797
CA	1 Jan	1801
d	15 Aug	1818 (LT)

CHAMPERNOWNE, Rawlin

L	16 Nov	1756
d		1774 (PRO)

CHAMPION, Charles

L	5 Feb	1799
Ret CR	26 Nov	1830 (PRO)
d	14 Jan	1844 (LT)

CHAMPION, William Brydges

L	29 Oct	1806
KIA	7 Mar	1814 (LTE)

CHANDLER, David

L	20 Mar	1758
d		1789 (PRO)

CHANDLER, Thomas
See CHAUNDLER, Thomas

CHANT, Edward

L		
CA	27 Mar	1691
	(20 Jan	1694 in H)
d		1707 (PJP)

CHANT, William

L		1666 (DDA)
CA	21 Sept	1666 (RM)
d	before	1689 (PJP)

CHANTRELL, William

L	7 Nov	1778
d	July	1801 (PRO)

CHAPELL, Charles
T wounded
L 18 Feb 1808
Ret CR 18 Jan 1845 (PRO)
d 1865 (TR)

CHAPLEN, James
L 8 Nov 1744
CR 9 July 1759
d 4 Feb 1766 (PMM)

CHAPMAN, Henry
L 25 Apr 1800
Ret CR 26 Nov 1830 (PRO)
d 1838 (PRO)

CHAPMAN, Charles
L 1 June 1808
d 1836 (PRO)

CHAPMAN, Charles Matthew
L 19 July 1814
Ret CR 1 Oct 1860 (PRO)
d 1869 (PRO)

CHAPMAN, Edmund Andrew
T wounded
L 4 May 1810
d 1811 (TR)

CHAPMAN, Isaac Fleming
L 11 Feb 1808
CR 31 Aug 1815
CA 29 Dec 1824 (PRO)
Dismissed 1826 (PJP)
Restored 1828 (PJP)
Ret CA 31 Oct 1846 (LG)
d 1852 (PRO)

CHAPMAN, James
L 24 Oct 1814
HP 16 Aug 1815 (OB)
Ret CR 22 Jan 1859 (PRO)
d 20 May 1861 (PRO)

CHAPMAN, John
L 16 Oct 1755
CR 26 May 1768 (PRO)
CA 13 July 1778 (PRO)
d 1778 (PRO)

CHAPMAN, Nicholas
L 31 Dec 1809
d 1837 (PRO)

CHAPMAN, Patrick
L 24 Nov 1794
CR 2 Jan 1798
d 3 Jan 1802 (PRO)

CHAPMAN, Richard
L 6 Mar 1687
(13 July 1687 in P)

CHAPMAN, Richard Edward
L 7 Oct 1794
d 1809 (PRO)

CHAPMAN, Thomas
L 25 Sept 1800
d 1813 (PRO)

CHAPPELL, Edward
L 18 Apr 1811
CR 19 Aug 1826 (PRO)
CA 27 Dec 1838 (PRO)
Ret CA 2 Aug 1853 (PRO)
Ret RA 20 Jan 1858 (PRO)
d 21 Jan 1861 (PRO)

CHAPPELL, George
L
CA 1664
d before 1689 (PJP)

CHAPPELL, John
L 1664
CA 1665
KIA 4 June 1666 (RM)

CHAPPELL, William
L 4 Dec 1779
d 1798 (PRO)

CHAPPELLE, Richard
L 1665

CHAPPELLE, Thomas
L 1674

CHARLES, Alexander
L 25 Mar 1794
d Sept 1823 (PRO)

CHARLES, Claudius
T
L 1 Mar 1811
d Dec 1824 (PRO)

CHARLES, Hornsby
L 7 June 1800
d 1802 (PRO)

CHARLESSON, Dederick
L 30 July 1781
d 1795 (PRO)

CHARLESSON, Lawrence
L 15 Feb 1815
d 17 May 1846 (OB)

CHARLESSON, Richard Williams
L 11 Feb 1815
Ret CR 23 Oct 1860 (PRO)
d Sept 1876 (PRO)

CHARLETON, Thomas William
L 21 Mar 1812 (PRO)
d 9 Feb 1828 (PRO)

CHARLETON, Thomas Williams
L 19 Nov 1811
d 1834 (PRO)

CHARLEY, Isaac
L 6 Apr 1757
d 1784 (PRO)

CHARLTON, St. John
L
CR
CA 10 Nov 1709
MP (Bridgnorth) 8 June 1725–1734 (MPS)
d Sept 1742 (MPS)

CHARLTON, William (1)
L 11 May 1782
CR 22 Jan 1806 (PRO)
CA 15 June 1810 (PRO)
d 7 Aug 1810 (PRO)

CHARLTON, William (2)
L 22 Jan 1806
d (duel) 1808 (PRO)

CHARRINGTON, Nicholas
L 6 June 1773

CR	12 Feb	1781 (PMM)
CA	27 July	1781
SUP RA		1801
d	22 Feb	1803 (PRO)
CHARSLEY, William		
L	10 Mar	1776
d		1792 (PRO)
CHARTRES, Robert William		
L	2 July	1800
Dismissed		1801 (PRO)
CHASE, Robert		
L	19 Mar	1777
d		1794 (PRO)
CHASEMORE, Charles		
L	23 Nov	1742
Gone		1752
CHASMAN, William		
L	22 Oct	1805
CR	29 Jan	1821 (PRO)
d		1848 (PRO)
CHASSAING, Charles Louis		
L	17 Aug	1797
d		1804 (PRO)
CHAUNDLER, Thomas		
L		1665
d	before	1689 (PJP)
CHAVE, Samuel		
L	2 Feb	1815
Ret CR	30 July	1859 (PRO)
d		1862 (PRO)
CHEAP, Andrew		
L	29 June	1796
d	2 July	1829 (PRO)
CHEAP, David		
L	24 Aug	1730
CR		
CA	19 Feb	1741
d	21 July	1752 (PJP)
CHEETHAM, Samuel		
L	19 June	1779
d		1794 (PRO)
CHEGWYN, Joseph		
L	9 Oct	1809
Ret CR	9 Oct	1848 (PRO)
d		1857 (PRO)
CHENOWETH, Michael		
L	31 Mar	1756
d		1761 (PRO)
CHEPMELL, George		
L	1 Nov	1811
d		1817 (PRO)
CHESNAYE, John Christian		
T		
L	17 Mar	1813
d		1854 (TR)
CHESSELL, Richard		
L	17 Aug	1801
d		1819 (PRO)
CHESSHYRE, John		
L	24 July	1781
CR	6 July	1794
CA	26 Dec	1799
Ret RA	22 July	1830 (PRO)
VAB	17 Aug	1840 (PRO)
VAW	23 Nov	1840 (PRO)
d		1843 (PRO)
CHESSMAN, Richard		
L	4 Aug	1793
d	2 Nov	1829 (PRO)
CHESSMIRE, John		
L	12 May	1808 (PRO)
d		1837 (PRO)
CHESTER, Benjamin		
L	20 Feb	1815
d		1833 (PRO)
CHESTER, William		
L	5 Feb	1799
d		1816 (PRO)
CHETHAM, Sir Edward		
See STRODE, Sir Edward Chetham		
CHETWYND, Hon. John Whitmore		
L	19 Mar	1777
CR	27 Jan	1780
CA	3 Feb	1781
d	29 Nov	1788 (PRO)
CHEVALLIER, George		
L	17 Mar	1815 (PRO)
d		1819 (PRO)
CHEYNE, George		
L	25 May	1813
CR	12 Aug	1819 (PRO)
Ret CA	1 Apr	1856 (PRO)
d		1866 (PRO)
CHEYNE, John		
L	3 Jan	1783
d		1797 (PRO)
CHICHELEY, Sir John		
L		1662
CA		1663
Kt		1666 (DNB)
RAR		1672
COM E	26 Nov	1675–
	28 Feb	1680 (NBO)
MP (Newton)		1679–1681 (DNB)
COM AD	20 Jan	1682–
	19 May	1684 (AO)
MP (Newton)		1685–1687 (DNB)
COM AD	8 Mar	1689–
	5 June	1690 (AO)
MP (Newton)		1689–1691 (DNB)
d	May	1691 (DNB)
CHICK, Silvester Evans		
L	24 Feb	1815
d		1834 (PRO)
CHICK, William		
L	11 Mar	1815
d		1833 (PRO)
CHIENE, John		
L	11 Jan	1797
CR	4 Dec	1813
d		1848 (PRO)
CHILCOTT, John		
L	8 Aug	1794

CR	29 Apr	1802
d	15 May	1829 (PRO)
CHILCOTT, Lastly		
L	22 May	1735
d	29 June	1737 (PMM)
CHILCOTT, William		
L	14 Nov	1790
CR	9 July	1798
d	9 Feb	1803 (LT)
CHILD, John		
L	18 Nov	1790
CR	15 Sept	1800
Ret CA	24 Sept	1840 (PRO)
d	9 July	1846 (PMM)
CHILD, Smith		
L	7 Nov	1755
CR	30 Oct	1777
CA	15 May	1780
RAW	14 Feb	1799
RAR	1 Jan	1801
VAB	23 Apr	1804
VAW	9 Nov	1805
VAR	28 Apr	1808
AB	31 July	1810
d	21 Jan	1813 (PRO)
CHILD, William		
L	28 Aug	1801
d		1815 (PRO)
CHILDS, John		
L	25 Sept	1799
d		1807 (PRO)
CHILLEY, John		
L	16 Aug	1689
CR	6 Apr	1703 (PMM)
d	9 July	1706 (PMM)
CHIMLEY, John		
L	13 Feb	1802
CR	1 May	1829 (NMM)
d		1834 (NMM)
CHINNERY, Charles		
L	7 Feb	1815
HP	7 Feb	1815 (OB)
d	10 May	1847 (PRO)
CHINNERY, St. John		
L	19 June	1756
CR	9 Apr	1761
CA	25 June	1773
d	1 Jan	1787 (PMM)
CHIVERS, William (1)		
L	30 June	1795
Ret CR	26 Nov	1830 (PRO)
d	12 May	1837 (PRO)
CHIVERS, William (2)		
L	28 Feb	1815
HP	28 Feb	1815 (OB)
d		1852 (PRO)
CHRISTIAN, Brabazon		
L	18 July	1776
CR	22 Nov	1777
CA	1 Jan	1780
d		1788 (PRO)
CHRISTIAN, Edward		
L	?22 Aug	1744 (PJP)
CR		
CA	28 July	1749
d	15 Jan	1758 (PJP)
CHRISTIAN, Henry		
L	1 Oct	1742
SUP CR	21 Sept	1796 (PMM)
CHRISTIAN, Hood Hanway		
L	25 Jan	1800
CR	21 Mar	1805
CA	30 Jan	1806
RAB	28 June	1838 (PRO)
RAW	23 Nov	1841 (PRO)
RAR	24 Apr	1847 (PRO)
d	28 Aug	1849 (LT)
CHRISTIAN, Sir Hugh Cloberry		
L	21 Jan	1771
CR		1778 (DNB)
CA	8 Dec	1778
RAB	1 June	1795
Kt	17 Feb	1796 (DNB)
RAW	20 Feb	1797
d	23 Nov	1798 (PRO)
CHRISTIAN, Jack		
L	28 Apr	1747
d		1758 (PRO)
CHRISTIAN, Jonathan		
L	9 Dec	1793
CR	1 Feb	1812
d		1834 (PRO)
CHRISTIAN, Thomas		
L	12 Aug	1743
d		1748 (PRO)
CHRISTIE, Alexander		
L	17 Oct	1775
CR	24 Apr	1781
CA	24 Sept	1781
SUP RA	7 Jan	1801
d	12 Aug	1822 (PRO)
CHRISTIE, Andrew		
L	17 Nov	1778
CR	21 Sept	1790
CA	4 Nov	1794
d (drowned)		1801 (PJP)
CHRISTIE, Christopher		
L	17 Dec	1782
d	3 Oct	1806 (PMM)
CHRISTIE, Francis		
L	10 Jan	1741
CHRISTIE, Gabriel		
L	22 Jan	1813
Ret CR	13 Oct	1855 (PRO)
d		1876 (PRO)
CHRISTIE, John		
L	27 Dec	1805
d		1834 (PRO)
CHRYSTIE, Thomas		
T		
L	8 Feb	1809
Ret CR	9 Apr	1847 (PRO)
d		1868 (PRO)
CHUBB, George James		
L	15 Aug	1806
Ret CR	16 Jan	1840 (PRO)
d		1849 (PRO)

CHUBB, John Phoedra
L 27 Aug 1759
d 1786 (PRO)
CHURCH, Charles
L 4 Jan 1806
d 1834 (PRO)
CHURCH, George
L 1665 (DDA)
CHURCH, Henry
L 3 Mar 1815
CR 28 June 1838 (PRO)
d 12 July 1843 (PRO)
CHURCH, James
L 22 Mar 1797
d 1801 (PRO)
CHURCH, John
L 23 June 1815
Ret CR 1 July 1864 (PRO)
d 1870 (PRO)
CHURCH, Richard
L 19 Aug 1704
SUP CR 20 Mar 1738 (PMM)
d 1752 (PMM)
CHURCH, Stephen George
L 15 Aug 1787
CR 22 Nov 1790
CA 8 Oct 1794
d 6 Sept 1801 (PRO)
CHURCHER, Charles
L 16 Feb 1691
CHURCHEY, George
See CHURCH, George
CHURCHFIELD, Thomas
L 30 Apr 1678
CHURCHILL, George
L 1672 (DDA)
EF (Duke of York) 7 June 1676 (EAD)
CA 14 May 1678
MP (St. Albans) 1685–1687 (DNB)
MP (St. Albans) 1689–1708 (DNB)
COM AD 26 Oct 1699–
26 Jan 1702 (AO)
AB 12 Mar 1702
VAR 13 Mar 1702
AB 6 May 1702
MCLHA 22 May 1702–
28 Oct 1708 (AO)
MP (Portsmouth) 1710 (DNB)
d 8 May 1710 (DNB)
CHURCHILL, Jaspar
L 30 Oct 1680
d before 1689 (PJP)
CHURCHILL, Joseph Dixie
T
L 4 May 1810
d 1811 (PRO)
CHURCHILL, Thomas
L 12 Mar 1741
CR 15 Nov 1756
d 1757 (PRO)
CHURCHILL, Winston
L 1672
KIA 28 May 1672 (NJ)
CLACK, Thomas
L 16 June 1808
CR 28 July 1851 (PRO)
d 1872 (PRO)
CLAPHAM, Thomas
L 21 Apr 1797
d 1804 (PRO)
CLAPP, John
L 8 Mar 1745
d 1758(9) (PRO)
CLAPP, Joseph
L 8 Oct 1779
d 1792 (PRO)
CLAPP, Thomas
L
CA 1666
CLAPPERTON, Hugh
L 20 Mar 1815 (PRO)
CR 22 June 1825 (PRO)
d Apr 1827 (PRO)
CLARENCE, H.R.H. William Henry, Duke of
L 17 June 1785
CR
CA 10 Apr 1786
Cre EP 20 May 1789 (DNB)
RAB 3 Dec 1790
RAR 1 Feb 1793
VAB 12 Apr 1794
VAW 4 July 1794
VAR 1 June 1795
AB 14 Feb 1799
AW 1 Jan 1801
AR 9 Nov 1805
AF 24 Dec 1811
MCLHA 2 May 1827–
19 Sept 1828 (AO)
Crowned William IV 26 June 1830 (DNB)
d 20 June 1837 (DNB)
CLARIDGE, Charles
L 11 Sept 1799
CR 22 Sept 1806
Dismissed 10 Aug 1809 (PJP)
d Apr 1823 (PRO)
CLARK, Alexander
L 3 Mar 1795
d 1799 (PRO)
CLARK, Archibald
L 23 Feb 1757
SUP CR 21 Sept 1796 (PMM)
d 1800 (PMM)
CLARK, Arthur (1)
L 21 Nov 1765
CR 25 Oct 1809 (PRO)
d 1817 (PRO)
CLARK, Arthur (2)
L 8 Oct 1793
d 1804 (PRO)
CLARK, Edward
See CLARKE, Edward
CLARK, Edward
L 29 Aug 1744
CR
CA 13 Mar 1758 (PRO)
d (suicide) May 1764 (PJP)
CLARK, Edward Hamilton
L 5 May 1798
Dismissed 11 Sept 1800 (PRO)

CLARK, Fletcher Norton
L 29 Apr 1802
CR 27 Aug 1814
d 1843 (PRO)

CLARK, George Hamilton
L 25 Oct 1800
Dismissed 1804 (PRO)

CLARK, Henry (1)
L 18 Sept 1739
d 1745 (PRO)

CLARK, Henry (2)
L 5 Dec 1760
d 1773 (PRO)

CLARK, Henry (3)
L 6 Mar 1801
Ret CR 12 Nov 1831 (PRO)
d 1842 (PRO)

CLARK, James (1)
L 22 Dec 1776
CR 2 Aug 1780
CA 1782 (PJP)
d (drowned) 1783 (CH)

CLARK, James (2)
L 9 Feb 1811
d 1813 (PRO)

CLARK, James (3)
L 1 Nov 1813
d 1844 (PRO)

CLARK, James Hamilton
L 5 Jan 1760
SUP CR 22 June 1805 (PRO)
d 1816 (PRO)

CLARK, John (1)
L 21 Feb 1741
CR 14 Oct 1755
CA 19 Jan 1758
d 24 Feb 1789 (PJP)

CLARK, John (2)
L 15 Jan 1778
d 1785

CLARK, John (3)
L 1 Apr 1805
T
Ret CR 23 Oct 1837 (PRO)
d 1850 (PRO)

CLARK, Joseph
L 19 Aug 1795
d 1810 (PRO)

CLARK, Richard (1)
L
CA 5 Jan 1691
d 17 Dec 1706 (PJP)

CLARK, Richard (2)
L 2 Nov 1790
Ret CR 13 Mar 1823 (NMM)
d 5 Feb 1845 (PRO)

CLARK, Richard (3)
L 28 Dec 1813
d Jan 1823 (PRO)

CLARK, Thomas
L 11 Oct 1793
d 1796 (PRO)

CLARK, William (1)
L 9 Dec 1755
d 1778 (PRO)

CLARK, William (2)
L 21 Mar 1759
d 1761 (PRO)

CLARK, William (3)
L 28 May 1778
CR
CA 7 July 1782
d 9 Nov 1801 (PRO)

CLARK, William John Stephen
L 24 Apr 1802
Ret CR 25 Jan 1834 (PRO)
d 1861 (PRO)

CLARK, William Nehemish
L 19 Sept 1806
CR 28 Dec 1826 (PRO)
d 1857 (PRO)

CLARKE, Arthur
L 9 Mar 1759
d 1766 (PRO)

CLARKE, Charles
L 30 Apr 1759
d 1798 (PRO)

CLARKE, Edward
L 18 Apr 1735
CR 14 Apr 1744
CA 11 Sept 1747
SUP RA 1778
d 1779

CLARKE, George
L 8 Mar 1794
CR 19 Sept 1796
CA 24 Dec 1798
d 1 Oct 1805 (PRO)

CLARKE, Henry (1)
L 1665
CA 16 Aug 1666 (RM)
d before 1689 (PJP)

CLARKE, Henry (2)
L 14 Feb 1815
d 1818 (PRO)

CLARKE, Hyde John
L 27 Sept 1797
CR 21 Oct 1810
HP 21 Oct 1810 (OB)
Ret CA 10 Sept 1840 (PRO)
d 1857 (PRO)

CLARKE, James (1)
L 7 Nov 1797

CLARKE, James (2)
L 27 Aug 1798
d 1804 (PRO)

CLARKE, James Hamilton
See CLARK, James Hamilton

CLARKE, John (1)
L 1671
CA 1661
d before 1689 (PJP)

CLARKE, John (2)
L 18 Mar 1692

CLARKE, Peter
L 29 July 1757

CR
CA 5 May 1763
d 1776 (PRO)

CLARKE, Richard
L 1666
d before 1689 (PJP)

CLARKE, Richard
See CLARK, Richard

CLARKE, Richard William
L 30 Dec 1796
Ret CR 1 May 1838 (PRO)
d 1842 (PRO)

CLARKE, Robert (1)
L
CA 1660
d before 1688 (PD)

CLARKE, Robert (2)
L
CR 25 June 1706 (PMM)
CA 28 May 1707
KIA 1 Mar 1709 (CH)

CLARKE, Samuel
L 6 Nov 1801
T
CR 2 Apr 1806
d 1834 (TR)

CLARKE, Thomas (1)
L
CA 10 Nov 1673
d before 1689 (PJP)

CLARKE, Thomas (2)
L 15 Nov 1796
d 1798 (PRO)

CLARKE, Thomas Pickering
L 28 Apr 1807
HP 7 Sept 1815 (OB)
Ret CR 17 Jan 1843 (PRO)
d 1862 (PRO)

CLARKE, William (1)
L 21 Apr 1694
CR 14 Dec 1704 (PMM)
CA 8 Mar 1709
d 27 Aug 1727 (PJP)

CLARKE, William (2)
L 16 Jan 1720

CLARKE, William (3)
L 25 Mar 1809
d 20 Jan 1817 (LT)

CLARKSON, John
L 21 Mar 1783
d 1795 (PRO)

CLARRIBUTT, Edward
L 16 Mar 1795
d 1838 (PRO)

CLAUS, Charles
L 25 Apr 1744
d ?1752 (PRO)

CLAVELL, John
L 6 July 1797
T wounded
CR 22 Oct 1805
CA 4 Feb 1808
d 11 Mar 1846 (TR)

CLAVERING, Douglas Charles
L 21 Oct 1814
CR 25 Sept 1821 (PRO)
d (drowned) 1827 (CH)

CLAXTON, Christopher
L 9 Dec 1810
CR 20 June 1842 (PRO)
Ret CA 25 June 1860 (PRO)
d 27 Mar 1868 (PRO)

CLAXTON, Robert
L 4 Apr 1720

CLAY, Edward Sneyd
L 19 Mar 1794
CR 3 Dec 1799
CA 29 Apr 1802
Ret RA 10 Jan 1837 (PRO)
RAW 17 Aug 1840 (PRO)
RAR 23 Nov 1841 (PRO)
d 3 Feb 1846 (PRO)

CLAYSON, Edward
L 27 Apr 1794
d 1810 (PRO)

CLAYSON, John
L 29 Nov 1793
Ret CR 6 Apr 1829 (PRO)
d 1838 (PRO)

CLAYTON, James
L 21 Mar 1812
Ret CR 25 July 1854 (PRO)
d 31 July 1856 (PRO)

CLAYTON, Samuel Writewronge
L 29 Nov 1756
CR 1 Aug 1776
CA 23 Apr 1778
d Oct 1795 (LT)

CLAYTON, Thomas Wittewronge
L 20 Aug 1782
CR 6 July 1794
CA 26 Dec 1799
d 1806 (PRO)

CLEAR, Henry
L 22 May 1758
d 12 Apr 1765 (PMM)

CLEASBY, Thomas
L
CA 26 May 1694
LGH 1718 (PJP)
d 22 May 1718 (PJP)

CLEATHER, Edward
L 17 Mar 1780
CR 29 Apr 1802
d 1802 (PRO)

CLEAVLAND, William
See CLEVLAND, William

CLEILAND, Robert
L 11 Oct 1781
d 1785 (PRO)

CLELAND, John (1)
L 5 Feb 1745
CR 10 June 1756
CA 15 May 1759
SUP RA 1787
d 1795

CLELAND, John (2)
- L 5 Sept 1782
- CR 1 Nov 1797
- CA 2 Jan 1799
- d 9 June 1822 (LT)

CLELAND, John (3)
- L 10 May 1794
- d 1811 (PRO)

CLELAND, Thomas
- L 17 Sept 1735
- CR 20 Feb 1745
- d 1759 (PRO)

CLELAND, William (1)
- L ?13 Jan 1710
- CR
- CA 2 Oct 1739
- d 18 May 1744 (PJP)

CLELAND, William (2)
- L 6 July 1741
- CR 29 Jan 1748
- d 14 July 1749 (LT)

CLEMENT, Benjamin
- L 12 Aug 1801
- T
- CR 18 Apr 1806 (MB)
- CA 1 Aug 1811
- d 5 Nov 1835 (PRO)

CLEMENTS, Bartholomew
- L
- CR
- CA 13 June 1700
- SUP 26 Sept 1707 (PMM)

CLEMENTS, George
- L
- CA 18 July 1694 (PMM)
- KIA 1 May 1707 (CH)

CLEMENTS, Hanbury
- L 15 Mar 1815
- d 1848 (PRO)

CLEMENTS, John (1)
- L
- CA 1 May 1667
- d 10 June 1694 (PRO)

CLEMENTS, John (2)
- L
- LSMR 30 Nov 1691 (EAD)
- CA 13 July 1693
- KIA 11 June 1694 (CH)

CLEMENTS, John (3)
- L 2 Nov 1781
- CR 1 Nov 1793
- CA 24 Oct 1794 (NMM)
- RAB 4 Dec 1813
- RAW 4 June 1814
- RAR 12 Aug 1819 (LG)
- VAW 27 May 1825 (LG)
- d 1 July 1825 (PRO)

CLEMENTS, Michael
- L 4 Dec 1755
- CR 1757 (DNB)
- CA 29 Sept 1757
- SUP RA 1789 (DNB)
- d 1796

CLEMENTS, Nicholas Brent
- L 14 Oct 1797
- CR 11 Apr 1809 (NMM)
- d 1812 (NMM)

CLEMENTS, Peter
- L
- CR 23 Jan 1780
- d 1798 (PRO)

CLEMENTS, Richard
- L 12 Apr 1744
- CR
- CA 29 Sept 1748
- d 1775 (PRO)

CLEMENTS, William
- L 5 Sept 1782
- d 1806 (PRO)

CLEOBURY, Stephen
- L 10 Nov 1781
- d 1784 (PRO)

CLEPHAM, James
- L 31 July 1801
- HP Apr 1802– Mar 1803 (MB)
- T
- CR 20 Apr 1811
- HP 28 Aug 1815 (OB)
- Ret CA 29 Oct 1840 (PRO)
- d 28 Jan 1851 (PRO)

CLEPHANE, Robert
- L 23 May 1793
- CR 24 Dec 1805
- CA 14 Feb 1811
- d Nov 1827 (PRO)

CLERK, James
- L 17 Apr 1794
- d Aug 1796 (LT)

CLERK, John
- L 10 June 1761
- d 1780(1) (PRO)

CLERK, Neil
- L 29 Mar 1815
- d 27 May 1829 (PRO)

CLERKE, Charles
- L 31 July 1771
- CR 26 Aug 1775
- CA 1779 (DNB)
- d 22 Aug 1779 (DNB)

CLERKE, Francis
- L 16 June 1743
- d 1758 (PRO)

CLERKE, Sir John
- L
- CR 9 Mar 1759
- CA 26 May 1761 (PRO)
- Kt 1772 (PJP)
- d 11 Oct 1776 (PRO)

CLEVELAND, Archibald
See CLEVLAND, Archibald

CLEVERLY, James
- L 16 Mar 1791
- d 1807 (PRO)

CLEVLAND, Archibald
- L 28 Apr 1755

CR
CA 5 Nov 1756
d 16 June 1766

CLEVLAND, William
L
CA 12 Feb 1694
(2 May 1692 in C)
(10 Feb 1694 in S)
d 3 June 1735 (M)

CLIFFORD, Sir Augustus William James
L 25 June 1806
CR 12 Feb 1811
CA 23 July 1812
CB 8 Dec 1815 (MPT)
MP
(Bandon Bridge) 1818–1820 (MPT)
MP
(Dungarvan) 1820–Feb 1822 (MPT)
Kt 4 Aug 1830 (MPT)
MP (Bandon Bridge) 1831–1832 (MPT)
Cre Bt 4 Aug 1838 (MPT)
RAB 23 Nov 1848 (PRO)
RAW 11 Nov 1850 (PRO)
RAR 22 Apr 1853 (PRO)
VAB 27 Sept 1855 (PRO)
VAW 10 May 1857 (PRO)
VAR 8 Dec 1857 (PRO)
AB 7 Nov 1860 (PRO)
AW 4 Oct 1862 (PRO)
AR 11 Jan 1864 (PRO)
d 9 Feb 1877 (MPT)

CLIFFORD, Elias
L
CA 1673

CLIFFORD, Herbert John
L 22 Apr 1811
CR 9 Jan 1854 (PRO)
d 1856 (PRO)

CLIFFORD, John
L 1671

CLIFFORD, Nicholas
L 6 Aug 1759
d 1794 (PRO)

CLIFFORD, Thomas
L 1665

CLIFTON, John
L 13 Oct 1692 (PJP)
CR 13 June 1698 (PJP)
CA 2 Feb 1706
d 21 Mar 1723 (PJP)

CLIFTON, William Wilmot
L 3 Apr 1802
d 1833 (PRO)

CLINCH, Timothy
L 23 Aug 1798
CR 22 Mar 1803
CA 12 Aug 1812
d Apr 1843 (PRO)

CLINTON, Hon. George
L
CR
CA 25 June 1716
GG (Newfoundland) 1731–1737 (BNS)
RAR 7 Dec 1743
VAW 23 June 1744 (DAB)
VAR 23 Apr 1745
AW 15 Jan 1747
MP (Saltash) 1754–1761 (MPN)
d 10 July 1761 (DAB)

CLINTON, William
L 1673

CLINTON, Lord William
See CAMPBELL, Lord William

CLITHEROW, James
L 16 Jan 1811
d 29 Mar 1813 (LT)

CLIVE, Benjamin
L 16 Mar 1746
CR 22 July 1756
CA 28 May 1758
d 3 Apr 1764 (PJP)

CLIVERTON, John Budd
L 3 Sept 1801
d 1803 (PRO)

CLOSSON, Josiah
L 3 July 1776
d 1794(5) (PRO)

CLOWES, Thomas Ball
L 26 Dec 1809
CR 23 Mar 1812
CA 16 May 1823 (PRO)
HP 16 May 1823 (OB)
Ret CA 1 Oct 1846 (PRO)
Ret RA 5 Mar 1853 (PRO)
Ret VA 20 Jan 1858 (PRO)
Ret A 24 Sept 1863 (PRO)
d 31 Mar 1864 (PRO)

CLUBLEY, Charles Witty
L 17 Feb 1815
d 1855 (PRO)

CLUGSTON, Alexander Grant
L 1 Mar 1812
CR 2 Sept 1815

CLUTTERBUCK, Christopher Masterman
L 20 July 1782
d 1794 (PRO)

CLYDE, Charles
L 18 Aug 1794
CR 21 Oct 1810
Ret CA 10 Sept 1840 (PRO)
d 1851 (PRO)

COAKLEY, Thomas
T
L 13 Jan 1806
Ret CR 29 Dec 1840 (OB)
d 1851 (TR)

COAL, Thomas
L 24 May 1688 (P)
CA 12 June 1683 (P)
CA 30 Aug 1688
(10 Apr 1689 in C)

COALKE, William
L 29 May 1758
d 11 Sept 1766 (PMM)

COALSEA, William
L 1 Feb 1700

COARD, William
L 20 Feb 1742
d 1756 (NMM)

Name / Rank	Date	Year
COATES, George Lewis		
L	21 Mar	1812
Ret CR	18 Apr	1854 (PRO)
d		1874 (PRO)
COATES, Richard (1)		
L	7 Nov	1806
d		1809 (PRO)
COATES, Richard (2)		
L	14 Mar	1809
Ret CR	9 Apr	1847 (PRO)
d	1 Feb	1850 (PRO)
COATES, Thomas		
See COTES, Thomas		
COBB, Charles (1)		
L	3 Feb	1774
CR	13 Mar	1782
CA	21 Sept	1790
RAB	28 Apr	1808
RAW	25 Oct	1809
d		1809(10) (PRO)
COBB, Charles (2)		
T		
L	1 May	1807
KIA	21 Sept	1811 (TR)
COBB, Smith		
L	21 Apr	1807
CR	15 Oct	1812
d		1833 (PRO)
COBBE, Charles		
L	2 June	1797
d		1798 (PRO)
COBBE, William		
L	18 Nov	1809
CR	7 June	1814
d	8 Apr	1831 (PRO)
COBBY, Thomas		
L	4 Mar	1746
d		1789 (PRO)
COCHET, John		
L	26 Aug	1789
CR	27 May	1795
HP	27 May	1795–
	4 Jan	1796 (MB)
CA	9 Dec	1796
RAB	12 Aug	1819 (PRO)
RAW	19 July	1821 (PRO)
RAR	27 May	1825 (PRO)
VAB	22 July	1830 (PRO)
VAW	10 Jan	1837 (PRO)
VAR	28 June	1838 (PRO)
AB	23 Nov	1841 (PRO)
AW	24 Apr	1847 (PRO)
AR	2 Sept	1850 (PRO)
d	10 June	1851 (PRO)
COCHRAN, Joseph		
L	4 Dec	1798
d		1811 (PRO)
COCHRANE, Hon. Sir Alexander F.I.		
L	19 May	1778
CR	6 Dec	1780
CA	17 Dec	1782
HP		1783–1790 (DNB)
MP		
(Stirling Burghs)		1800–1802 (MPT)
MP		
(Stirling Burghs)		1803–1806 (MPT)
RAB	23 Apr	1804
RAW	9 Nov	1805
Kt	29 Mar	1806 (MPT)
RAR	28 Apr	1808
VAB	25 Oct	1809
VAW	31 July	1810
VAR	4 Dec	1813
GCB	2 Jan	1815 (LG)
AB	12 Aug	1819 (PRO)
AW	27 May	1825 (PRO)
d	26 Jan	1832 (DNB)
COCHRANE, Hon. Archibald		
L	12 Mar	1804
CR		
CA	31 Jan	1806
d		1829 (PRO)
COCHRANE, John		
L	18 Apr	1798
d		1810 (PRO)
COCHRANE, John Dundas		
L	14 Feb	1811
CR	15 Aug	1814
d	12 Aug	1825 (PJP)
COCHRANE, Nathaniel Day		
L	26 Dec	1800
CR	30 July	1805
CA	26 Mar	1806
RAB	23 Nov	1841 (PRO)
d	16 Nov	1844 (PRO)
COCHRANE, Thomas Earl of Dundonald		
L	27 May	1796
CR	28 Mar	1800
CA	8 Aug	1801
MP		
(Honiton)		1806–1807 (MPT)
MP		
(Westminister)		1807–5 July 1814 (MPT)
Kt	24 Apr	1809 (MPT)
HP		1809–1813 (DNB)
Struck off list	25 June	1814 (DNB)
MP		
(Westminister)		July 1816–1818 (MPT)
In Chilean Service	May	1817–
	29 Nov	1822 (DNB)
In Brazilian Service	21 Mar	1823–
	10 Nov	1825 (DNB)
In Greek Service	Mar	1827–
	Dec	1828 (DNB)
Inh EP	1 July	1831 (DNB)
Reinstated	2 May	1832 (DNB)
RAB	2 May	1832 (PRO)
RAW	10 Jan	1837 (PRO)
RAR	28 June	1838 (PRO)
VAB	23 Nov	1841 (PRO)
VAW	9 Nov	1846 (PRO)
GCB	22 May	1847 (MPT)
VAR	3 Jan	1848 (PRO)
AB	21 Mar	1851 (PRO)
AW	2 Apr	1853 (PRO)
AR	8 Dec	1857 (PRO)
d	31 Oct	1860 (DNB)
COCHRANE, Sir Thomas John		
L	14 June	1805
CR	24 Sept	1805

CA 23 Apr 1806
HP 1809–1811 (DNB)
Kt 29 May 1812 (OB)
GG
(Newfoundland) 1825–1834 (BNS)
CB 18 Apr 1839 (OB)
MP
(Ipswich) 1839–1841 (DNB)
RAB 23 Nov 1841 (PRO)
RAW 9 Nov 1846 (PRO)
RAR 26 June 1847 (PRO)
KCB 2 Nov 1847 (PRO)
VAB 14 Jan 1850 (PRO)
VAW 17 Aug 1851 (PRO)
VAR 4 July 1853 (PRO)
AB 31 Jan 1856 (PRO)
AW 8 Dec 1857 (PRO)
GCB 18 May 1860 (DNB)
AR 15 Jan 1862 (PRO)
AF 12 Sept 1865 (DNB)
d 19 Oct 1872 (PRO)

COCK, Horatio Bennet
L 26 Dec 1812
d 23 May 1825 (PRO)

COCK, John George
L 1 Mar 1794
d 1815 (PRO)

COCK, Reginall
See COCKS, Reginall

COCK, Robert
T
L 1 Aug 1811
Ret CR 1 Oct 1852 (PRO)
d 1855 (PRO)

COCK, Samuel
L 25 July 1797
d 1842 (PRO)

COCK, Samuel Strugnell
L 24 Sept 1795
d 1798 (PRO)

COCK, William (1)
L
CR
CA 13 Nov 1699
Dismissed 1715 (PJP)

COCK, William (2)
L 24 Dec 1743
d 1757 (NMM)

COCK, William (3)
L 20 Feb 1746
d 1766 (PRO)

COCKAIN, Samuel
See COCKAYNE, Samuel

COCKAYNE, Samuel
L 1 Mar 1705
CR 10 Oct 1727 (PRO)
CA 19 Sept 1730
d ?1735 (PJP)

COCKBURN, Hon. Sir George
L 21 Jan 1793 (NMM)
CR 11 Oct 1793
CA 20 Feb 1794
CRM 1 Aug 1811 (LG)
RAB 12 Aug 1812
RAW 4 Dec 1813
RAR 4 June 1814
KCB 2 Jan 1815 (LG)
MP
(Portsmouth) 1818–1820 (MPT)
GCB 20 Feb 1818 (DNB)
COM AD 2 Apr 1818–
2 May 1827 (AO)
VAB 12 Aug 1819 (PRO)
MP
(Weobley) 1820–May 1828 (MPT)
MGRM 5 Apr 1821 (OB)
VAW 27 May 1825 (PRO)
MP (Plymouth) 7 June 1828–1832 (MPT)
COM AD 19 Sept 1828–
25 Nov 1830 (AO)
VAR 22 July 1830 (PRO)
AW 10 Jan 1837 (PRO)
MP
(Ripon) 27 Sept 1841–1847 (MPT)
AR 23 Nov 1841 (PRO)
AF 1 July 1851 (DNB)
Inh Bt 26 Feb 1852 (DNB)
d 19 Aug 1853 (DNB)

COCKBURN, John
L 5 Oct 1694
CR
CA 14 Nov 1707
d ?29 Apr 1731 (PJP)

COCKBURN, William
L 19 Sept 1777
d 1798 (PRO)

COCKBURNE, John
See COKBURNE, John

COCKCRAFT, William
L 21 Sept 1790
d 1834 (PRO)

COCKERILL, Green (Hill)
L
CA 1679
d before 1689 (PJP)

COCKFIELD, Samuel
L 9 July 1756
CR 24 Nov 1761
d 1767 (PRO)

COCKS, George
L 2 Sept 1793
CR 29 Apr 1802
CA 13 Oct 1807
d 31 Mar 1829 (PRO)

COCKS, Reginall
L 13 Apr 1741
CR 12 Mar 1758
d 1791 (PRO)

COCKS, Thomas
L 20 July 1759
d 1791 (PRO)

COCKSEDGE, George Edward
T
L 27 Dec 1808
Ret CR 1851 (TR)
d 1860 (TR)

COCKWELL, William
L 2 Jan 1797
d 1802 (PRO)

CODD, John
L 12 July 1796
CR 2 May 1810
CA 19 July 1821 (PRO)
d 1840 (PRO)

CODD, Samuel
L 29 Mar 1783
d 28 June 1815 (PRO)

CODNER, John
L 13 Apr 1696
CR
CA 1 Jan 1713
d 23 Apr 1714 (PJP)

CODRINGTON, Christopher
Later BETHELL, Christopher
L 20 Jan 1755
CR 17 Jan 1757
CA 16 Oct 1758
d 1772 (PRO)

CODRINGTON, Sir Edward
L 28 May 1793
CR 7 Oct 1794 (DNB)
CA 6 Apr 1795
T
CRM 4 Dec 1813 (AL)
RAW 4 June 1814
KCB 2 Jan 1815 (LG)
RAR 12 Aug 1819 (PRO)
MGRM 5 Apr 1821 (AL)
VAB 27 May 1825 (PRO)
Kt
(France) 1827 (DNB)
Kt
(Russia) 1827 (DNB)
Kt
(Greece) 1827 (DNB)
GCB 13 Nov 1827 (LG)
VAW 22 July 1830 (PRO)
MP
(Devonport) 1832–1839 (DNB)
GCMG 1832 (DNB)
AW 23 Nov 1841 (PRO)
AR 9 Nov 1846 (PRO)
d 28 Apr 1851 (DNB)

COE, Fyfield
L 4 May 1727
CR 16 Aug 1743
d 1763 (PRO)

COE, Thomas
L 25 Oct 1800
CR 12 Jan 1805
CA 3 Apr 1811
d 15 Dec 1838 (PRO)

COET, William
L 30 Oct 1793
Ret CR 27 Sept 1828 (PRO)
d 18 Mar 1837 (PRO)

COFFIN, Charles
L 16 Nov 1796
d 1797 (PRO)

COFFIN, Francis Holmes
L 13 July 1791
CR 23 Aug 1797
CA 29 Apr 1802
Ret RA 10 Jan 1837 (PRO)
RAW 17 Jan 1840 (PRO)
RAR 23 Nov 1841 (PRO)
d 10 Apr 1842 (PRO)

COFFIN, Henry Edward
L 20 July 1814
CR 19 Sept 1829 (PRO)
CA 23 Nov 1841 (PRO)
Ret RA 12 Apr 1862 (PRO)
Ret VA 24 May 1867 (PRO)
Ret A 30 July 1875 (PRO)
d 31 Aug 1881 (PRO)

COFFIN, Sir Isaac
L 18 Aug 1776
CR 3 July 1781
CA 13 June 1782
Dismissed 1788 (MPT)
Restored 1789 (MPT)
RAW 23 Apr 1804
Cre Bt 23 May 1804 (DNB)
RAR 9 Nov 1805
VAB 28 Apr 1808
VAW 31 July 1810
(Known as GREENLY from his marriage 3 Apr 1811 to Mar 1813)
VAR 12 Aug 1812
AB 4 June 1814
MP
(I1chester) 1818–1826 (MPT)
AW 19 July 1821 (PRO)
AR 22 July 1830 (PRO)
GCH 1832 (PRO)
d 23 July 1839 (DNB)

COFFIN, John Townsend
L 11 Apr 1808
CR 1 July 1814
CA 26 Dec 1822 (MB)
Ret CA 1 Oct 1846 (PRO)
Ret RA 17 Dec 1852 (PRO)
Ret VA 5 Jan 1858 (PRO)
Ret A 25 June 1863 (PRO)
d May 1883 (PRO)

COGAN, William
L 8 Feb 1810
d 1817 (PRO)

COGGAN, Richard
L 9 Sept 1794
d 1828 (PRO)

COGHILL, Sir Joseph
Formerly CRAMER, John
L 24 Mar 1800 (PRO)
CR 7 May 1802 (PRO)
CA 1 Feb 1806 (PRO)
Inh Bt 21 May 1817 (OB)
RAB 23 Nov 1841 (PRO)
RAW 9 Nov 1846 (PRO)
RAR 28 Apr 1847 (PRO)
VAB 12 Nov 1849 (LG)
d 20 June 1850 (PRO)

COGHLAN, Donkin
L 20 Oct 1790
d 1798 (PRO)

COGHLAN, Francis Rogers
L 18 Apr 1814
CR 2 Sept 1843 (PRO)
d 14 Jan 1856 (PRO)

COGHLAN, Jeremiah
- L 22 Sept 1800
- CR 1 May 1804
- CA 27 Nov 1810
- CB 4 June 1815 (LG)
- d 4 Mar 1844 (LT)

COHAM, William Michael
- L 8 Oct 1793
- d 1810 (PRO)

COKBURNE, Andrew
- L 11 June 1741 (PRO)
- CR
- CA 16 June 1750
- d 13 Nov 1768 (PJP)

COKBURNE, George (1)
- L
- CR
- CA 11 June 1741
- d 20 July 1770 (PJP)

COKBURNE, George (2)
- L 2 Jan 1785 (PRO)
- d 1798 (PRO)

COKBURNE, John
- See COCKBURN, John

COKBURNE, John
- L 2 Mar 1743
- CR
- CA 19 July 1746
- d 8 May 1753 (PJP)

COKER, John
- L 13 Oct 1694

COLBY, Charles
- L
- CR
- CA 12 Jan 1741
- d 9 Feb 1772 (PJP)

COLBY, David
- L 4 Feb 1794
- CR 20 Nov 1798 (PRO)
- CA 29 Apr 1802
- d 21 Oct 1834 (PRO)

COLBY, Stephen
- L 11 Mar 1742
- CR 30 Mar 1746
- CA 20 Aug 1756
- d 1779

COLBY, Thomas
- L 8 Apr 1805
- T
- CR 17 May 1814
- Ret CA 1 July 1864 (PRO)
- d 21 Sept 1864 (PRO)

COLCLOUGH, John
- L 31 Aug 1808
- d 1819 (PRO)

COLE, Ambrose
- L
- CR
- CA 24 Mar 1710
- d 17 Oct 1711 (PJP)

COLE, Sir Christopher
- L 18 Sept 1793
- CR 30 Jan 1800
- CA 20 Apr 1802
- Kt 29 May 1812 (CH)
- KCB 2 Jan 1815 (LG)
- MP (Glamorgan) 6 Sept 1817–1818 (MPT)
- CRM 22 July 1830 (AL)
- d 24 Aug 1836 (PRO)

COLE, Edward (1)
- L
- CA 27 Jan 1697
- died in Bedlam (PJP)

COLE, Edward (2)
- L 23 Sept 1806
- Ret CR 29 Jan 1852 (PRO)
- d 1864 (PRO)

COLE, Francis
- L 30 Apr 1779
- CR 12 Dec 1782
- CA 21 Sept 1790
- d 18 Apr 1798

COLE, George Lewis
- L 19 Feb 1781
- d 1837 (PRO)

COLE, George Ward
- L 29 Mar 1815
- HP 9 Oct 1817 (OB)
- Ret CR 20 Jan 1864 (PRO)
- d 1879 (PRO)

COLE, James
- L 31 Aug 1796
- d 24 July 1824 (PRO)

COLE, John Campbell
- L 28 June 1799
- d July 1803 (PRO)

COLE, John Sutton
- L 23 Aug 1762
- d 1778 (PRO)

COLE, Martin (1)
- L 8 May 1757
- CR 13 May 1778
- d 1804 (PRO)

COLE, Martin (2)
- L 5 Oct 1805
- Ret CR 18 Apr 1838 (PRO)
- d 10 July 1847 (PRO)

COLE, Richard (1)
- L 20 Oct 1795
- d 1807 (PRO)

COLE, Richard (2)
- L 17 Jan 1811
- d 1832 (PRO)

COLE, Robert Martin
- L 17 Jan 1812
- Ret CR 23 Mar 1854 (PRO)
- d 1869 (PRO)

COLE, Samuel (1)
- L 29 Sept 1781
- d 1782 (PRO)

COLE, Samuel (2)
- L 19 Jan 1782
- d 1798 (PRO)

COLE, Sidney
- L 30 May 1702
- SUP 20 Mar 1738 (PMM)

COLE, Thomas (1)
L 21 Nov 1800
CR 12 Jan 1805
d 3 Feb 1822 (LT)

COLE, Thomas (2)
L 7 Feb 1815
d 1826 (PRO)

COLE, Thomas Edmund
L 15 July 1806
CR 19 July 1821 (PRO)
CA 16 Feb 1852 (PRO)
d 1852 (PRO)

COLE, William John
L 18 July 1810
CR 8 Aug 1828 (PRO)
CA 28 July 1833 (PRO)
Ret CA 26 Nov 1852 (PRO)
d 15 May 1856 (PRO)

COLEBROOK, George
L 15 Nov 1809
d 1813 (PRO)

COLEBROOKE, Thomas
L 8 Mar 1815
d 11 Nov 1835 (PJP)

COLEBY, Charles
L 19 June 1727

COLEMAN, James
L
CA 9 June 1665 (PJP)
d before 1689 (PJP)

COLEMAN, John (1)
L 1673
d before 1689 (PJP)

COLEMAN, John (2)
L 2 July 1813
CR 5 June 1856 (PRO)
d 1876 (PRO)

COLEMAN, John (3)
L 5 Oct 1815 (PRO)
Ret CR 14 Apr 1864 (PRO)
d 1870 (PRO)

COLEMAN, Robert (1)
L 16 Nov 1691
CR
CA 25 Sept 1705
d 3 Nov 1739 (LTE)

COLEMAN, Robert (2)
L 5 Feb 1740
CR 7 Feb 1747
Gone 1752

COLEMAN, Thomas (1)
L 4 Sept 1800
T
Resigned 1811 (TR)

COLEMAN, Thomas (2)
T
L 16 Feb 1815
CR 5 Dec 1837 (PRO)
d 28 Apr 1849 (PRO)

COLEMAN, William
L 1665
CA 1666
d before 1689 (PJP)

COLEPEPPER, Francis
L 29 Nov 1738
d 1743(4) (PRO)

COLES, Charles
L 8 Aug 1797
d 1804 (PRO)

COLES, Christopher
L 31 Mar 1744
d 1757 (PRO)

COLES, Richard
L 18 Apr 1810
d 1859 (PRO)

COLINS, Henry
L 2 Nov 1761
CR 23 Aug 1777
CA 20 Mar 1779
d 17 Mar 1791 (PRO)

COLLARD, Sampson Edwards
L 19 Feb 1801
d (drowned) Jan 1804 (PJP)

COLLARD, Valentine
L 17 Nov 1793
CR 8 Mar 1797
CA 13 Oct 1807
RAB 23 Nov 1841 (PRO)
d 18 Mar 1846 (PRO)

COLLAS, John
L 20 Nov 1812
d 1834 (PRO)

COLLER, Richard
L 17 Aug 1779
d 1819 (PRO)

COLLETON, Sir John
L 17 June 1795
d July 1801 (PRO)

COLLETT, Cornelius
L 16 May 1797
d 1831 (PRO)

COLLETT, Isaac Charles Smith
L 9 Sept 1801
d July 1820 (PRO)

COLLEY, William
L 1 Apr 1760
d 1765(6) (PRO)

COLLIER, Sir Edward (1)
L 17 June 1803
CR 25 July 1810
CA 18 Nov 1814
CB 18 Dec 1840 (OB)
RAB 1 Oct 1850 (PRO)
RAW 5 Mar 1853 (PRO)
RAR 3 July 1855 (PRO)
VAB 18 June 1857 (PRO)
A 13 Oct 1862 (PRO)
KCB 1865 (CH)
d 5 Aug 1872 (CH)

COLLIER, Edward (2)
L 28 Feb 1815 (PRO)
CR 1 May 1845 (PRO)
CA 21 Nov 1857 (PRO)
d 1859 (PRO)

COLLIER, Sir Francis Augustus

L	11 Apr	1803
CR	24 Jan	1805 (PRO)
CA	13 Dec	1808
CB	8 Dec	1815 (LG)
Kt	28 July	1830 (OB)
KCH	1 Jan	1833 (OB)
RAB	9 Nov	1846 (PRO)
RAW	23 Mar	1848 (PRO)
d	28 Oct	1849 (PRO)

COLLIER, Sir George

L	3 July	1754
CR	6 Aug	1761
CA	12 July	1762
Kt	27 Jan	1775 (MPN)
MP(Honiton)		1784–1790 (MPN)
RAW	1 Feb	1793
RAR	12 Apr	1794
VAB	4 July	1794
d	6 Apr	1795 (DNB)

COLLIER, Sir George Ralph

L	22 Jan	1796
CR	3 Sept	1799
CA	20 Apr	1802
Kt		1807 (PJP)
Cre Bt	20 Sept	1814 (PMM)
KCB	2 Jan	1815 (LG)
d	24 Mar	1824 (PRO)

COLLIER, Henry

L	8 Aug	1799 (PRO)
d		1800 (PRO)

COLLIER, Henry Theodosus Browne

L	3 June	1807
CR	24 Oct	1812
CA	26 Dec	1822 (OB)
HP	26 Dec	1822 (OB)
Ret RA	17 Dec	1852 (PRO)
Ret VA	5 Jan	1858 (PRO)
Ret A	25 June	1863 (PRO)
d	Sept	1872 (PRO)

COLLIER, James

L	13 Sept	1806
d	30 June	1810 (PRO)

COLLIER, John
 See COLLYER, John

COLLIER, Thomas

L	3 July	1760
d		1761 (PRO)

COLLIER, William

L	6 Aug	1697
CR		
CA	10 May	1710
d	4 Dec	1736 (PRO)

COLLINGWOOD, Cuthbert, Lord

L	17 June	1775
CR	20 June	1779 (PRO)
CA	22 Mar	1780
RAW	14 Feb	1799
RAR	1 Jan	1801
VAB	23 Apr	1804
T		
VAR	9 Nov	1805
Cre EP		1805 (T)
MGRM	4 Jan	1809 (AL)
d	7 Mar	1810 (TR)

COLLINGWOOD, Edward (1)

L	25 June	1773
d		1809 (PRO)

COLLINGWOOD,Edward (2)

L	15 May	1798
d		1800 (PRO)

COLLINGWOOD, Francis (1)

L	20 Sept	1777
CR	22 Apr	1796 (PRO)
CA	21 June	1797
d		1799 (PRO)

COLLINGWOOD, Francis (2)

L	22 Jan	1806
CR	15 Jan	1828 (PRO)
d	15 Nov	1835 (PRO)

COLLINGWOOD, George

L	4 July	1756
d		1796 (PRO)

COLLINGWOOD, John Trevor

L	22 Feb	1759
d		1796 (PRO)

COLLINGWOOD, Thomas

L	28 Oct	1750
CR		
CA	29 Nov	1756
d	2 June	1780 (PJP)

COLLINGWOOD, Wilfred

L	18 Apr	1778
CR	15 Jan	1783
d	20 Apr	1787 (PRO)

COLLINS, Augustus Leveson Rogers

L	5 Dec	1799
d		1810 (PRO)

COLLINS, David

L	15 Nov	1756
CR	15 May	1778
d	12 May	1787 (PRO)

COLLINS, Edward (1)

L	21 Aug	1800
d		1811 (PRO)

COLLINS, Edward (2)

L	1 Dec	1800
CR	15 June	1814
HP	15 June	1814 (OB)
d	12 Jan	1850 (PRO)

COLLINS, Francis

L	26 Oct	1810
d	28 June	1824 (PRO)

COLLINS, George Francis

L	28 Oct	1815
d	18 May	1821 (PRO)

COLLINS, Greenville

L		
CA		1679 (DNB)
d		1693 (DNB)

COLLINS, Griffith

L	11 Apr	1746
d		1751 (PRO)

COLLINS, Henry
 See COLINS, Henry

COLLINS, James

L	30 Jan	1781

CR	6 Oct	1796
CA	21 Oct	1810
d	25 Apr	1828 (PRO)
COLLINS, Sir John (1)		
L	15 June	1757
CR	10 Jan	1771
CA	1 Feb	1778
d	29 Mar	1794 (PRO)
COLLINS, John (2)		
L	17 Jan	1758
d		1759 (PRO)
COLLINS, John (3)		
L	11 Mar	1797
KIA	1 Aug	1798 (LG)
COLLINS, John Bardon		
L	3 July	1799
d	6 Apr	1830 (PMM)
COLLINS, Richard (1)		
L		
CA	17 May	1672
d	before	1689 (PJP)
COLLINS, Richard (2)		
L	11 Nov	1729
CR	27 July	1743 (NMM)
CA	7 July	1744
SUPRA		1762
d		1779
COLLINS, Richard (3)		
L	11 Mar	1755
d	?	1766 (NMM)
COLLINS, Richard (4)		
L	7 Apr	1756
Dismissed	29 Mar	1766 (PJP)
d		1780 (PRO)
COLLYER, John		
L		1672
COLPOYS, Edward Griffith		
L		
CR		
CA	21 May	1794 (MB)
RAB	12 Aug	1812 (MB)
COLPOYS, Sir John		
L	22 Oct	1762
CR		1770 (PMM)
CA	25 Aug	1773
RAB	12 Apr	1794
RAW	4 July	1794
VAB	1 June	1795
Kt		1798 (DNB)
VAR	14 Feb	1799
AB	1 Jan	1801
AW	9 Nov	1805
TGH		1805 (PJP)
AR	25 Oct	1809
GCB	2 Jan	1815 (LG)
GGH	27 Jan	1816 (DNB)
d	4 Apr	1821 (DNB)
COLQUHOUN, Humphrey		
L	20 Mar	1815 (PRO)
Ret CR	20 Jan	1864 (PRO)
d		1873 (PRO)
COLQUHOUN, Sutherland Morrison		
L	10 Nov	1810
CR	12 Sept	1827 (PRO)
d	Feb	1828 (PRO)
COLQUITT, Goodwin		
L	9 Jan	1773
CR	15 Jan	1783
d	2 Jan	1826 (PJP)
COLQUITT, Samuel Martin		
L	15 Feb	1796
CR	29 Apr	1802
CA	21 Oct	1810
Ret RA	1 Oct	1846 (LG)
d	10 July	1847 (PRO)
COLT, George		
L		1663
CA		1666
d (drowned)		1675 (PJP)
COLTHEART, Walter		
L	25 Oct	1758
d		1784 (PRO)
COLTHURST, Nicholas		
T		
L	19 Sept	1806
Ret CR	29 Jan	1841 (PRO)
d	9 Dec	1854 (PRO)
COLTMAN, William		
L	10 Nov	1798
d		1806 (PRO)
COLTON, Caleb		
L	9 Mar	1759
d	13 Jan	1791 (PMM)
COLUMBINE, Edward		
L	2 Apr	1757
d		1788 (PRO)
COLUMBINE, Edward Henry		
L	12 Apr	1782
CR	22 Dec	1796
CA	29 Apr	1802
d	18 June	1811 (PRO)
COLUMBINE, Philip		
L	8 Feb	1740
d	14 June	1745 (PRO)
COLVILL, Alexander, Lord		
KLB		1732 (DCB)
L	31 Aug	1739
CR	5 Mar	1744 (DCB)
CA	24 July	1744 (DCB)
COMM (Halifax)		1760–1762 (DCB)
RAW	21 Oct	1762
d	21 May	1770 (DCB)
COLVILL, Charles		
L	26 June	1765
d		1780(1) (PRO)
COLVILL, Hon. James		
See COLVILLE, Hon. James		
COLVILL, Hon. James John		
L	10 Feb	1781
d		1786 (PRO)
COLVILL, Hon. John, Lord		
L	29 July	1793
CR	28 Aug	1795 (PRO)
CA	6 Dec	1796
Inh EP	8 Mar	1811 (OB)
RAB	12 Aug	1819 (PRO)
RAW	19 July	1821 (PRO)
RAR	27 Mar	1825 (PRO)

VAB	22 July	1820 (PRO)
VAW	10 Jan	1837 (PRO)
VAR	28 June	1838 (PRO)
AB	23 Nov	1841 (PRO)
AW	19 Feb	1847 (PRO)
d	22 Dec	1849 (PRO)
COLVILL, William		
L	6 July	1795
d		1803(4) (PRO)
COLVILLE, Alexander, Lord		
See COLVILL, Alexander, Lord		
COLVILLE, Hon. James		
L		
CR		
CA	17 Oct	1758
d (drowned)	1 Jan	1761 (CH)
COLVILLE, Hon. John		
See COLVILL, Hon. John, Lord		
COMBE, Henry		
L	2 May	1793
CR	8 Aug	1799
d		1803 (PRO)
COMBE, James		
L	7 Mar	1815 (PRO)
d	1 Feb	1818 (PRO)
COMBS, James		
L	23 Nov	1747
d		1785 (NMM)
COMER, Charles		
See CORNER, Charles		
COMERFORD, Michael		
L	17 Nov	1806
Gone		1816 (PRO)
COMPTON, Henry		
L	11 Mar	1796
CR	3 Sept	1799
Ret CA	10 Sept	1840 (PRO)
d		1847 (PRO)
COMPTON, James		
L	7 Sept	1726
CR	9 May	1733 (PRO)
CA	13 Dec	1734
d	?	1746 (PRO)
COMPTON, Richard		
L	13 Feb	1815
d		1856 (PRO)
COMPTON, Thomas		
L	28 Oct	1744
d		1748 (PRO)
COMPTON, William		
L	24 May	1793
CR	?Dec	1802 (PJP)
KIA	15 July	1804 (CH)
COMYN, Maurice Keating		
L	4 May	1810
Struck off list	6 Sept	1819 (PRO)
COMYN, Valens		
L	6 Dec	1793
d	30 June	1810 (PRO)
CONANT, John Edward		
L	18 July	1801 (PRO)
Ret CR	13 July	1831 (PRO)
d		1849 (PRO)
CONAWAY, Thomas		
L		1666 (DDA)
CONDE, Daniel		
L	3 May	1692
CONDON, David		
L		1672 (P)
CA	25 May	1690
KIA	9 June	1692 (CH)
CONEY, William (1)		
L	27 Apr	1695
CR	2 Apr	1703 (PJP)
CA	1 Apr	1704
d (drowned)	22 Oct	1707 (CH)
CONEY, William (2)		
L	18 May	1745
d	24 Mar	1754 (PJP)
CONGALTON, Andrew		
L	4 June	1777
SUP CR	27 Aug	1810
d	May	1823 (PRO)
CONGALTON, Hugh		
L	6 June	1778
d		1800 (PRO)
CONN, Henry		
L	18 Aug	1809
HP	6 Oct	1812 (OB)
Ret CR	4 Apr	1843 (PRO)
d	4 Mar	1860 (PRO)
CONN, John		
L	1 June	1793
CR	11 Aug	1800
CA	29 Aug	1802
T		
d (drowned)	4 May	1810 (PJP)
CONNELL, Thomas		
L	10 Sept	1808
d		1811 (PRO)
CONNER, Richard		
L	13 Nov	1813
d	5 June	1821 (PRO)
CONNER, Samuel		
L	2 Mar	1815
d		1856 (PRO)
CONNER, William Henry		
L	20 Sept	1815
Ret CR	14 Apr	1864 (PRO)
d		1884 (PRO)
CONSBY, Humphry		
L		1660
CA		1662
Dismissed		1665 (PMM)
CONNOLLY, John Bell		
L	3 Dec	1795
Ret CR	24 Mar	1840 (PRO)
d		1849 (PRO)
CONNOLLY, Matthew		
L	22 Aug	1795
HP	13 Jan	1802–
	16 Apr	1804 (MB)
CR	4 Dec	1813
HP	4 Dec	1813 (OB)
Ret CA	9 June	1851 (PRO)
d	14 Feb	1853 (PRO)

CONNOLLY, Richard Lock		
L	29 Jan	1807
Ret CR	21 Feb	1845 (PRO)
d		1869 (PRO)
CONNOR, Richard		
L	5 Jan	1810
CR	19 May	1828 (PRO)
Ret CA	1 Apr	1856 (PRO)
d		1862 (PRO)
CONNOR, Richard		
See CONNER, Richard		
CONNOR, Ross		
L	23 Feb	1807
d		1851 (PRO)
CONOLLY, Matthew		
See CONNOLLY, Matthew		
CONSETT, Christopher		
L		1664
CONSETT, Matthew		
L		
CR		
CA	19 Apr	1721
d		1749
CONSIDINE, John George		
L	26 Oct	1797
d		1803 (PRO)
CONSITT, Thomas		
L	7 Sept	1799
Ret CR	26 Nov	1830 (PRO)
d		1851 (PRO)
CONSTABLE, Charles		
L		
CR		
CA	18 Oct	1708
d		1716 (PJP)
CONSTABLE, John (1)		
L		
CA	14 Oct	1692
	(14 Nov 1692 in C)	
Dismissed	6 Oct	1702 (LG)
Imprisoned		1703 (PRO)
CONSTABLE, John (2)		
L	7 Nov	1696
CONSTABLE, Love		
L	28 Mar	1781
CR	28 Oct	1793
d		1794 (PRO)
CONSTABLE, Thomas		
L	5 Jan	1799
d		1804 (PRO)
CONSTABLE, William		
L		
CA	1 Oct	1688
	(26 Sept 1688 in P)	
Discharged	16 Dec	1688 (PRO)
d		1718 (DDA)
CONWAY, Hon Lord Hugh		
L	10 Aug	1776
CR	18 June	1778
CA	8 Feb	1779
CRM	4 July	1794 (AL)
d	11 Sept	1801 (PRO)
CONWAY, Thomas		
See CONAWAY, Thomas		

CONYERS, John		
L	11 Apr	1809
d	6 Mar	1822 (PRO)
COOBAN, Robert Baron		
L	6 May	1797
d		1811 (PRO)
COODE, Sir John		
L	5 Sept	1799
CR	3 Aug	1802
CA	21 Oct	1810
CB	19 Sept	1816 (OB)
Kt		1828 (PJP)
RAB	26 June	1847 (PRO)
RAW	8 June	1849 (PRO)
RAR	19 June	1852 (PRO)
VAB	26 May	1854 (PRO)
KCB		1855 (CH)
Ret VA	30 Nov	1855 (CH)
d	19 Jan	1858 (PRO)
COODE, Nicholas		
L	27 July	1744
d		1765(6) (PRO)
COOK, Andrew (1)		
L	14 Nov	1746
d		1777 (PRO)
COOK, Andrew (2)		
L	26 Aug	1779
d		1788 (PRO)
COOK, Daniel Molyneux		
L	27 Aug	1745
d		1750(1) (PRO)
COOK, Edward		
See COOKE, Edward		
COOK, Hugh		
L	30 Oct	1793
T		
CR	Oct	1805 (TR)
CA	31 July	1806
d		1834 (TR)
COOK, James (1)		
L	1 Apr	1760
d		1800 (PRO)
COOK, James (2)		
L	25 May	1768
CR	29 Aug	1771
CA	9 Aug	1775
d (murdered)	11 Feb	1779 (DNB)
COOK, James (3)		
L	4 May	1782
CR	24 June	1793
d (drowned)	25 Jan	1794 (DNB)
COOK, James (4)		
L	3 Aug	1801
d		1803 (PRO)
COOK, John		
See COOKE, John		
COOK, John Francis		
T		
L	23 Feb	1815
d		1832 (TR)
COOK, Richard		
L	14 May	1694
COOK, Samuel Edward		
See WIDDRINGTON, Samuel Edward		

COOK, Stephen
L 7 Sept 1801
d 1805 (PRO)

COOK, Theodore
L 17 Sept 1806
d 1808 (PRO)

COOK, Thomas
See COOKE, Thomas Valentine

COOK, William
L 17 Aug 1801
CR 8 May 1804
CA 25 Sept 1806
d (suicide) 1834 (PRO)

COOKE, David Ramsey Kerr
L 24 Sept 1811
d 1834 (PRO)

COOKE, Edward
L 14 Sept 1790
CR
CA 12 Apr 1794
d 25 May 1799 (DNB)

COOKE, Isaac
L 2 Dec 1692
CR 17 Jan 1704 (PMM)
CA 18 Oct 1708
d 18 Dec 1712 (PJP)

COOKE, James (1)
L 1672
CA 1667
d before 1689 (PJP)

COOKE, James (2)
L 2 Feb 1741
Gone 1752

COOKE, James (3)
L 21 Mar 1793
d 1797 (PRO)

COOKE, James (4)
L 25 Nov 1798
Dismissed 1806 (PRO)

COOKE, James (5)
L 17 Apr 1807
d 26 Mar 1831 (PRO)

COOKE, John (1)
L
CA 1673

COOKE, John (2)
L 7 May 1728
CR 8 Nov 1734
d 1762 (PRO)

COOKE, John (3)
L 20 Apr 1776
d (drowned) 5 Oct 1780 (PJP)

COOKE, John (4)
L 21 Jan 1779
CR 21 Feb 1794
CA 23 June 1794
T killed
KIA 21 Oct 1805 (TR)

COOKE, John (5)
L 27 Apr 1781
CR
CA 8 Sept 1795
HP 1810 (MB)
SUP RA 20 June 1814
d 1834 (PRO)

COOKE, John (6)
L 8 Mar 1802
T
d 2 Nov 1813 (LT)

COOKE, John (7)
L 5 Feb 1812
CR 20 Feb 1829 (PRO)
d Feb 1829 (PRO)

COOKE, Thomas
L 29 June 1720

COOKE, Thomas Valentine
T
L 9 Feb 1815
d 1840 (TR)

COOKE, William Henry
L 12 Oct 1812
HP 8 June 1814 (OB)
Ret CR 17 Jan 1855 (PRO)
d 1865 (PRO)

COOKES, Thomas
L 29 Aug 1799
d 1803 (PRO)

COOKESLEY, John
L 16 Dec 1799
CR 11 Apr 1809 (PRO)
CA 7 Dec 1818 (PRO)
Ret CA 1 Oct 1846 (PRO)
Ret RA 8 July 1851 (PRO)
d 26 Nov 1825 (PRO)

COOKNEY, James Thomas
L 19 June 1815
d 4 Dec 1860 (PRO)

COOKSON, Thomas (1)
L 16 Nov 1739
CR 24 Jan 1747
d 18 Nov 1775 (PRO)

COOKSON, Thomas (2)
L 19 Nov 1770
d 1772 (PRO)

COOKLEY, William Roddam
L 3 Feb 1812
d 1838 (PRO)

COOMBE, James
L 7 Mar 1815
d 1 Feb 1818 (NMM)

COOMBE, William
L 21 Oct 1805
CR 23 Apr 1807
KIA 29 Nov 1808 (CH)

COOMBES, Richard
L 25 Apr 1783
d 8 Nov 1806 (PMM)

COOMES, John
L
CA 1 July 1666 (DDA)

COOPER, Francis
L 23 Oct 1706 (PMM)
CR
CA 27 Jan 1711
d 27 Jan 1733 (PJP)

COOPER, James		
L	14 Feb	1745
d		1753 (PRO)
COOPER, John		
L		
CA	29 June	1696
d	10 Sept	1728 (PRO)
COOPER, Joseph		
L	28 Mar	1727
CR	18 July	1740
d		1747 (PRO)
COOPER, Nathaniel		
L	14 Sept	1697
COOPER, Nicholas		
L	31 Aug	1739
Gone		1752
COOPER, Robert Palliser		
L	1 Dec	1766
CR	10 Aug	1775
CA	26 Jan	1778
SUP RA		? 1795 (PRO)
d	23 Oct	1805 (PRO)
COOPER, Thomas		
L	27 Feb	1791
CR	5 May	1735
CA	14 Nov	1738 (PRO)
d	6 Dec	1761 (PJP)
COOPER, William		
L	11 Jan	1740
CR	20 Feb	1746
d		1758(9) (PRO)
COOTE, Charles		
L	29 Dec	1794
CR	29 Apr	1802
CA	7 June	1814
d		1817 (PRO)
COOTE, Richard		
L	6 Mar	1804
CR	7 Mar	1810
CA	7 June	1814
CB	4 June	1815 (LG)
d		1815 (PRO)
COOTE, William		
L	6 Dec	1802
T		
CR	6 May	1807
Ret CA	10 Sept	1840 (PRO)
d	Oct	1857 (PRO)
COPE, Alexander Frederick		
L	16 Feb	1815
Ret CR	18 Jan	1861 (PRO)
d	31 Aug	1867 (PRO)
COPE, James		
L	9 Feb	1745
d		1747 (NMM)
COPE, John		
L	16 Apr	1748
d		1793 (PRO)
COPE, William		
L	Mar	1797
d		1799 (PRO)
COPELAND, Richard		
L	11 Dec	1811
CR	13 June	1815
CA	28 June	1838 (PRO)
d	16 June	1850 (PRO)
COPINGER, John		
L	29 Oct	1797 (PRO)
d		1815 (PRO)
COPOW, William		
L		1665
CA	18 June	1675
d	before	1689 (PJP)
COPPIN, Frederick		
L	11 Feb	1815
Ret CR	1 Oct	1860 (PRO)
d		1869 (PRO)
COPPIN, John		
L		
Ca		1660
KIA	4 June	1666 (RM)
COPPIN, William		
L	24 July	1667 (DDA)
CORBET, Robert		
L	22 Dec	1796
CR	29 Apr	1802
CA	25 May	1806
KIA	13 Sept	1810 (DNB)
CORBETT, Adam		
L	7 Mar	1815
d		1818 (PRO)
CORBETT, Arthur		
L	4 Mar	1815
d		1863 (PRO)
CORBETT, Nathaniel Gordon		
L	12 July	1813
d	26 July	1849 (PRO)
CORBETT, Pelham		
L		1673
d	before	1689 (PJP)
CORBETT, Walter		
L	22 Nov	1757
CR	1 May	1759
d		1778 (PRO)
CORBYN, Joseph		
L	23 Jan	1802
CR	15 June	1814
d	Sept	1850 (PRO)
CORBYN, Major		
L	18 Mar	1815 (PRO)
Ret CR	20 Jan	1864 (PRO)
d		1867 (PRO)
CORDRY, George		
T		
L	11 Mar	1815 (PRO)
HP	15 Oct	1815 (OB)
d		1854 (TR)
CORKE, William		
T		
L	17 July	1811
d		1816 (TR)
CORMACK, John		
L	20 Nov	1744
d		1758(9) (PRO)

CORNE, Richard Carruthers
L 23 Oct 1789
CR 6 Oct 1801
d 1809 (PRO)

CORNELIUS, Gilbert
L 1664

CORNER, Charles
L 15 Oct 1808
d 23 June 1823 (PRO)

CORNER, John
L 6 Oct 1758
CR
CA 20 June 1765
d 1 Nov 1772 (PRO)

CORNER, Robert
L 20 Nov 1779
d 1820 (PRO)

CORNEWALL,
See CORNWALL, Charles
CORNWALL, Frederick
CORNWALL, James
CORNWALL, Thomas

CORNISH, John
L 10 Dec 1807
CR 17 May 1814
d 27 Dec 1816 (PRO)

CORNISH, Sir Samuel (1)
L 12 Nov 1739
CR 25 Feb 1742 (PRO)
CA 12 Mar 1742
RAW 14 Feb 1759 (CH)
RAR 1761
VAB 21 Oct 1762
MP 23 Dec 1765–
(Noe Shoreham) 30 Oct 1770 (MPN)
Cre BT 9 Jan 1766 (DNB)
VAR 18 Oct 1770 (CH)
d 30 Oct 1770 (DNB)

CORNISH, Samuel (2)
Formerly PITCHFORD, Samuel
L 4 Mar 1740
CR
CA 24 Aug 1761
RAB 21 Sept 1790
RAR 1 Feb 1793
VAB 12 Apr 1794 (PRO)
VAW 4 July 1794
VAR 1 June 1795
AB 14 Feb 1799
AW 1 Jan 1801
AR 9 Nov 1805
d 3 Apr 1816 (LT)

CORNWALL, Charles
L
CA 16 Sept 1692 (PMM)
MP 2 Mar 1709–
(Bewdley) 1710 (MPS)
COM N 16 Nov 1714–
8 Aug 1716 (NBO)
MP 1715–
(Weobley) 7 Oct 1718 (MPS)
RAB 16 June 1716 (DNB)
RAR 24 July 1716
VAB 1 Feb 1717
VAW 15 Mar 1718 (C)
d 7 Oct 1718 (DNB)

CORNWALL, Frederick
L 13 Mar 1734
CR
CA 11 Feb 1744
MP 15 June 1771–
(Montgomery) 1774 (MPN)
d 4 Aug 1788 (MPN)

CORNWALL, Jacobs
L 26 Oct 1728

CORNWALL, James
L 9 June 1718 (PMM)
CR
CA 3 Apr 1724
MP
(Weobley) 1732–1734 (DNB)
MP
(Weobley) 1737–1741 (DNB)
KIA 11 Feb 1744 (DNB)

CORNWALL, John
L 13 Apr 1815
CR 22 Nov 1826 (PRO)
CA 28 July 1851 (PRO)
Ret RA 1 Oct 1870 (PRO)
d 1870 (PRO)

CORNWALL, Thomas
L 13 June 1749
CR 6 Aug 1756
CA 7 Feb 1757
SUP CA 1786 (NMM)
d 4 July 1796 (LT)

CORNWALL, Woolfran
EF
(Duke of Monmouth) 1 Jan 1679 (EAD)
L 30 Jan 1682 (P)
LH
(Royal Horse Guards) Feb 1687 (EAD)
CA 23 Aug 1688
CAH
(Royal Horse Guards) 23 Oct 1690 (EAD)
d 21 Jan 1719 (PJP)

CORNWALLIS, Hon James (1)
L 13 May 1720
MP 3 Nov 1722–
(Eye) 28 May 1727 (MPS)
d 28 May 1727 (MPS)

CORNWALLIS, James (2)
L 9 July 1776
CR 9 Dec 1780
CA 14 Sept 1781
d 30 July 1790 (PRO)

CORNWALLIS, John
L 1661
d before 1689 (PJP)

CORNWALLIS, Sir William
L 5 Apr 1761 (DNB)
CR 12 July 1762 (PRO)
CA 20 Apr 1765
MP
(Eye) 1768–Mar 1774 (MPN)
MP
(Eye) 3 Apr 1782–1784 (MPN)
MP
(Portsmouth) 1784–1790 (MPN)
CRM 24 Sept 1787 (AL)
MP
(Eye) 1790–Jan 1807 (MPN)

RAW 1 Feb 1793
RAR 12 Apr 1794
VAB 4 July 1794
VAR 1 June 1795
AB 14 Feb 1799
AW 23 Apr 1804
AR 9 Nov 1805
GCB 2 Jan 1815 (LG)
d 5 July 1819 (DNB)

CORRIE, Francis
L 21 June 1783
d 1809 (PRO)

CORRY, Armar Lowry
L 28 Apr 1812
CR 13 June 1815
CA 23 July 1821 (PRO)
RAB 8 Mar 1852 (PRO)
RAW 21 Jan 1854 (PRO)
d 8 May 1855 (PJP)

CORSBIE, Richard
L 25 Mar 1809
d 14 Jan 1846 (OB)

CORSELLIS, Caesar
L 21 Nov 1790
d (drowned) 14 Feb 1801 (CH)

CORSELLIS, Nicholas Caesar
L 15 May 1780
SUPCR 9 Nov 1814
d 1833 (PRO)

CORY, George Crossley
L 7 Mar 1815
d 1826 (PRO)

CORY, Nicholas
L 4 Mar 1815
CR 20 Aug 1836 (PRO)
CA 1 Aug 1840 (PRO)
RA 24 Nov 1858 (PRO)
d 13 Feb 1864 (PRO)

COSBY, Edward
L 30 July 1793
d 1801 (PRO)

COSBY, Henry
L 22 Mar 1740
CR 29 Dec 1744
CA 26 Aug 1745
d 16 Oct 1753 (PRO)

COSBY, Phillips
L 28 Jan 1755
CR 2 June 1760
CA 19 May 1761
CRM 24 Sept 1787 (AL)
RAW 21 Sept 1790 (PRO)
VAB 1 Feb 1793
VAW 12 Apr 1794 (PRO)
VAR 1 June 1795
AB 14 Feb 1799
AW 1 Jan 1801
AR 9 Nov 1805
d 10 Jan 1808 (DNB)

COSENTINE, Ezekiel
See COZENTINE, Ezekiel

COSNAHAN, Hugh
L 25 Mar 1813
d Dec 1822 (PRO)

COSNAHAN, Michael Finch
L 21 Feb 1815
Ret CR 9 Jan 1872 (PRO)
d 15 Dec 1885 (PRO)

COSTERTON, Samuel
L 4 Nov 1814
Ret CR 22 Jan 1859 (PRO)
d 1872 (PRO)

COSTOBADIE, Henry
L 12 Feb 1746 (PMM)
SUP CR 12 Sept 1796

COSTON, Hugh
L 1 June 1695 (PMM)

COTES, James
L 10 July 1776
CR 14 Jan 1782
CA 27 July 1782
d 1802

COTES, John
L 13 June 1760
d 1772 (PRO)

COTES, Thomas
L 2 Mar 1734
CR 26 July 1738 (PRO)
CA 12 May 1740
RAB May 1755 (CH)
RAW 4 June 1756
RAR Feb 1757
VAB 5 Feb 1758 (CH)
VAW 14 Feb 1759
MP 1761–
(Great Bedwyn) 16 July 1767 (MPN)
VAR 21 Oct 1762
d 16 July 1767 (MPN)

COTESWORTH, Charles
L 10 Oct 1814
d 1858 (PRO)

COTSGRAVE, Edward Stone
L 22 Jan 1806
CR 13 June 1815
Ret CA 7 Feb 1852 (PRO)
d 31 Oct 1868 (PRO)

COTGRAVE, George William
L 8 Mar 1815
d Sept 1824 (PRO)

COTGRAVE, Isaac
L 15 May 1780
CR 2 Jan 1797
CA 29 Apr 1802
d May 1814 (PRO)

COTTEN, Richard
L
CA 22 July 1691
d 28 Jan 1692 (CH)

COTTEREL, Charles
L 7 July 1717 (PMM)
CR 28 Oct 1722
CA 29 June 1726
SUP RA July 1747
d 28 July 1754

COTTEREL, Edward
L
CA 24 July 1664 (DDA)
Dismissed 30 Sept 1665 (PRO)
d before 1689 (PJP)

COTTERELL, Frederick
L 16 Dec 1800
CR 15 Oct 1802
CA 28 May 1803
d 19 Apr 1811 (PRO)

COTTERELL, William
L 18 Oct 1670 (DDA)

COTTON, Andrew
L
CA 20 July 1677
d 13 June 1693 (PJP)

COTTON, Sir Charles
L 29 Apr 1777 (DNB)
CR 3 Apr 1779 (DNB)
CA 10 Aug 1779
Inh Bt 23 Jan 1795 (DNB)
RAB 20 Feb 1797
RAR 14 Feb 1799
VAB 29 Apr 1802
VAW 23 Apr 1804
VAR 9 Nov 1805
AB 28 Apr 1808
AW 31 July 1810
d 23 Feb 1812 (DNB)

COTTON, Richard
L 23 July 1665 (DDA)
CA 1664
d before 1689 (PJP)

COTTON, Rowland (1)
L 28 Mar 1735
d 23 Nov 1739 (PMM)

COTTON, Rowland (2)
L 31 Jan 1760
CR 25 Aug 1762
CA 7 May 1764
RAW 1 Feb 1793
RAR 12 Apr 1794
VAB 4 July 1794
d 30 Nov 1794 (LT)

COTTON, William
L
CA 22 Aug 1673 (DDA)

COUCH, Daniel Little
L 9 Feb 1799
Ret CR 26 Nov 1830 (PRO)
d 31 Oct 1854 (PRO)

COUCH, James
L 6 Sept 1800 (PRO)
T
CR 6 Sept 1817 (PRO)
CA 24 Jan 1824 (PRO)
Ret CA 1 Oct 1846 (PRO)
d 9 Jan 1850 (PRO)

COUCH, John
L 25 July 1799
Ret CR 26 Nov 1830 (PRO)
d 1836 (PRO)

COUCH, Richard
L 10Sept 1797
d 4 Dec 1806 (PRO)

COUCHMAN, John
L 29 Oct 1739
d 1742 (PRO)

COUCHMAN, Samuel
L 31 Oct 1740
e (mutiny) 14 July 1749 (CH)

COUCHMAN, Thomas
L 6 May 1758
d 1776 (PRO)

COULSEA, Christopher
L ?16 May 1695 (PMM)
CR 6 July 1696 (PMM)
CA 10 Dec 1697
d 21 Sept 1698 (CH)

COULSEA, William
See COALSEA, William

COULSON, Robert Lisle
L 5 Sept 1799
CR 15 June 1810
CA 19 July 1821 (PRO)
d 9 June 1822 (PRO)

COULTAS, Jeremiah
L 7 June 1745
d 1756 (PRO)

COUNTESS, George
L 8 July 1774
CR 1 Dec 1787
CA 22 Mar 1790
RAB 25 Oct 1809
RAW 31 July 1810
d 1811 (PRO)

COUNTESS, George Urry
L 11 Apr 1798
d ?1804 (PRO)

COUNTRY, Jeremy
L
CA 1660
d before 1689 (PJP)

COUNTRY, Richard
L 1672
CA 1661
d before 1689 (PJP)

COURCY, Hon Almericus de
L 19 Mar 1806
d 1815 (PRO)

COURCY, Hon Michael de (1)
L 20 Nov 1776
CR 20 Aug 1782
CA 6 Sept 1783
RAB 9 Nov 1805
RAW 28 Apr 1808
RAR 25 Oct 1809
VAB 31 July 1810
VAW 4 Dec 1813
VAR 4 June 1814
AB 19 July 1821 (PRO)
d 22 Feb 1824 (PRO)

COURCY, Hon Michael de (2)
L 10 May 1797
CR 15 Apr 1808
d 22 July 1813 (PRO)

COURCY, Nevinson de
L 29 Jan 1806
CR 26 Jan 1809
CA 7 June 1814
Kt (Portugal) Apr 1825 (MB)
d 1 Nov 1845 (LTE)

COURT, Alexander A.
See A'COURT, Alexander
COURT, Edward Henry
See A'COURT, Edward Henry
COURTENAY, Henry
L 8 Mar 1815
d 24 Sept 1860 (PRO)
COURTENAY, William Major
L 24 Sept 1795 (PRO)
CR 21 Oct 1810
d 1819 (PRO)
COURTNAY, George William Augustus
L 29 July 1781
CR
CA 19 Apr 1782
KIA 1 Aug 1793 (CH)
COURTNAY, George William Conway
L 19 July 1813
CR 26 Dec 1823 (PRO)
CA 14 Apr 1828 (PRO)
RAB 24 Nov 1854 (PRO)
RAW 21 July 1856 (PRO)
RAR 8 Dec 1857 (PRO)
VAB 29 July 1861 (PRO)
VAW 22 Nov 1862 (PRO)
d 31 Mar 1863 (PRO)
COURTNEY, Francis
L
CA 1666
KIA 11 Aug 1673 (CH)
COURTNEY, William Marcus
See COURTENAY, William Major
COURTOYS, George
L 2 May 1804
Struck off list 1814 (PRO)
COUSINS, Stephen
T
L 22 Jan 1806
d 1819 (PRO)
COVELL, Alan
L
CA 1661
d before 1689 (PJP)
COVELL, Charles
L 17 Nov 1795
d 1802 (PRO)
COVEL(L), Isaac
L 3 June 1746
d 1781 (PRO)
COVEY, Edward
L 28 Nov 1784
SUP CR 11 May 1822 (PRO)
d 1832 (PRO)
COVEY, John
L 27 Nov 1778
SUP CR 31 Jan 1814
d 21 June 1824 (PRO)
COW, John
See COWE, John
COWAN, Archibald
L 9 Sept 1795
d 1800 (PRO)
COWAN, James
L 15 Feb 1815
d 1848 (PRO)
COWAN, John Smith
L 8 Apr 1797
CR 19 Dec 1809
d 23 Mar 1821 (PRO)
COWAN, Malcolm
L 15 Nov 1790
CR 23 Oct 1802
d 1833 (PRO)
COWAN, Robert
L 29Apr 1764
d 1780 (PRO)
COWAN, Thomas (1)
L 7 Oct 1794
CR 8 Oct 1798
CA 29 Apr 1802
d 1836 (PRO)
COWAN, Thomas (2)
L 28 Sept 1814
CR 5 May 1827 (PRO)
d 2 Oct 1835 (PJP)
COWAN, William (1)
L 21 Feb 1741
d 10 Dec 1754 (PMM)
COWAN, William (2)
L 17 Jan 1780
d 1808 (PRO)
COWDRY, John
L
CA 1665
d before 1689 (PJP)
COWE, John (1)
L 16 Feb 1692
CR
CA 27 Sept 1703
KIA 13 Aug 1704 (LG)
COWE, John (2)
L 17 June 1757
SUP CR 21 Sept 1796
d 1818 (PRO)
COWE, Peter
L Nov 1739
CR 10 Sept 1756
d 1773 (PRO)
COWEL(L), Henry
L 31 May 1744
CR
CA 1 Feb 1761
d 12 Apr 1765 (LTE)
COWEN, Morrice
L 21 Mar 1812
Ret CR 25 July 1854 (PRO)
d 1869 (PRO)
COWES, Henry
L 1660
d before 1689 (PJP)
COWES, Richard
L
CA 1660
d before 1688 (PD)
COWLEY, George Phillips
L 16 July 1808
d Dec 1827 (PRO)

COWLING, John
L 8 Sept 1758
CR
CA 13 Jan 1780
d 7 Apr 1792 (M)

COWNE, Philip
L
CA 1665 (DDA)

COX, Douglas
L 10 Mar 1809
CR 9 July 1817 (PRO)
CA 23 Nov 1841 (PRO)
Ret CA 21 June 1864 (PRO)
Ret RA 12 Apr 1862 (PRO)
d 10 Feb 1863 (PRO)

COX, Francis
L 22 Nov 1790
Ret CR 15 Feb 1825 (PRO)
d 1856 (PRO)

COX, George (1)
L 18 Mar 1708

COX, George (2)
L 7 May 1800
Dismissed 1804 (PRO)

COX, George (3)
L 1 May 1805
Resigned 1807 (PRO)

COX, George Stackpole
L 13 Apr 1808
d 1810 (PRO)

COX, Henry (1)
L 7 Nov 1758
d 1760 (PRO)

COX, Henry (2)
L 3 Feb 1815
CR 6 Aug 1852 (PRO)
d 1869 (PRO)

COX, James
L 31 May 1782
d 1787 (PRO)

COX, Sir John (1)
L
CA 1665
COMM (Chatham) 1669– 1672 (NJ)
Kt 27 Apr 1672 (NJ)
KIA 28 May 1672 (NJ)

COX, John (2)
L 13 July 1687

COX, John (3)
L 26 Aug 1789
SUP CR 13 Nov 1822 (PRO)
d 1840 (PRO)

COX, Ponsonby
L 17 Sept 1778
d 1786 (PRO)

COX, Richard
L 25 Nov 1799
d 1810 (PRO)

COX, Samuel
L 25 July 1778
CR 21 Mar 1782
d 1800 (PRO)

COX, William (1)
L 20 Apr 1781
d 1793 (PRO)

COX, William (2)
L 13 Nov 1790
d 1795 (PRO)

COXEN, Henry Conyngham
L 8 Nov 1803
T
CR 10 Oct 1809
d 18 July 1836 (LT)

COXWELL, Joseph
L 5 Feb 1798
Ret CR 26 Nov 1830 (PRO)
d 1832 (PRO)

COYLE, Thomas Room
See ROOMCOYLE, Thomas

COYNEY, Walter Hill
L 11 Apr 1785 (PRO)
Resigned 14 Aug 1795 (PRO)

COZENTINE, Ezekiel
L 26 May 1742
d 1770 (PRO)

CRAB, John
L
CA 1665

CRABB, Joseph William
L 16 June 1809
Ret CR 28 July 1851 (CH)
d May 1877 (PRO)

CRACRAFT, William Edward
L 28 Oct 1790
CR 7 June 1794
CA 9 Aug 1794
d 1810 (PRO)

CRAFORD, John
L 3 June 1709
CR 5 May 1735
d 9 Nov 1740 (PRO)

CRAFT, Thomas
L
CA 1665

CRAGG, James
L 1 Mar 1815 (PRO)
d 1835 (PRO)

CRAGG, William
L 7 June 1744
d 1777 (PRO)

CRAGGS, George
L 8 Mar 1815
HP Aug 1815 (OB)
d 25 Jan 1857 (PRO)

CRAIG, Hector
L 8 Oct 1795
d (drowned) Nov 1811 (CH)

CRAIG, Robert
L 27 Feb 1741
CR 23 June 1748
CA 4 Jan 1757
d 1767

CRAISTER, George
L 29 July 1808
d 13 Apr 1842 (PRO)

CRAMER, Ambrose
L 12 Jan 1741
d 1747(8) (PRO)

CRAMER, John
L 13 June 1795
CR 15 Mar 1811 (PRO)
d 1836 (PRO)

CRAMER, John
See COGHILL, Sir Josiah

CRAMER, Lewis
L 11 July 1815
d 1826 (PRO)

CRANBY, John
L
CR 7 July 1694 (PMM)
CA 25 Sept 1696
d 19 Dec 1702 (PJP)

CRANDLEY, Richard
L 1665
d before 1689 (PJP)

CRANE, Poynter
L 12 July 1807 (MB)
Ret CR 6 Apr 1843 (PRO)
d 20 July 1878 (PRO)

CRANE, Thomas
L 18 Sept 1806
Ret CR 13 Oct 1840 (PRO)
d 1851 (PRO)

CRANSTON, James
L 21 Mar 1755
CR 27 Aug 1760
CA 7 Apr 1762
d 23 Nov 1790 (LT)

CRANSTOUN, George Home
L 14 Mar 1794
d 1796 (PRO)

CRANSTOUN, Hon James, Lord
L 19 Oct 1776
CR
CA 31 Jan 1782
d 22 Sept 1796 (DNB)

CRAS, Edward Le
See LECRAS, Edward

CRASKE, John
L 29 Apr 1807
d 17 Apr 1842 (PRO)

CRATCHELEY, Thomas
L 1661
d before 1689 (PJP)

CRAUFURD, Hon Charles
L
CR
CA 6 Sept 1731
d ? 1745 (PJP)

CRAVEN, Charles
L 31 Dec 1778
CR 21 Sept 1790
CA 17 Dec 1793
SUP CA 1811 (PRO)
d Feb 1821 (PRO)

CRAVEN, Thomas
L 20 Nov 1739
CR 14 May 1745 (PRO)
CA 8 Feb 1746
MP 2 Apr 1766–
(Berkshire) 14 Dec 1772 (MPN)
RAB 24 Oct 1770
d 14 Dec 1772 (CH)

CRAWFORD, Abraham
L 25 Nov 1807
CR 23 Mar 1815
CA 5 Jan 1829 (PRO)
Ret CA 5 Jan 1849 (PRO)
Ret RA 3 July 1855 (PRO)
Ret VA 12 Apr 1862 (PRO)
Ret A 12 Sept 1865 (PRO)
d 1869 (PRO)

CRAWFORD, Andrew
L 5 Nov 1802
d 8 May 1821 (PRO)

CRAWFORD, David
L 25 Nov 1778
d 1795 (PRO)

CRAWFORD, Henry
L 1 Mar 1771
d 1783 (PRO)

CRAWFORD, James
L 1 Feb 1815
Ret CR 30 July 1859 (PRO)
d 1862 (PRO)

CRAWFORD, James Coutts
L 10 Aug 1783
CR 14 Feb 1799
CA 29 Apr 1802
d 1828 (PRO)

CRAWFORD, John (1)
L 1667
CA 1667

CRAWFORD, John (2)
L 3 June 1709 (PJP)
CR 5 May 1735 (PJP)
CA 30 Aug 1739
d ? 1740 (PRO)

CRAWFORD, John Campbell
L 19 Oct 1807
d 1818 (PRO)

CRAWFORD, Maurice
L 16 Mar 1814
d 1818 (PRO)

CRAWFORD, Moses
L 14 Sept 1804
d 22 Aug 1828 (PRO)

CRAWFORD, Peter
L 4 Sept 1805
Ret CR 17 Jan 1838 (PRO)
d 1849 (PRO)

CRAWFORD, Richard
L 31 July 1799
d (drowned) 15 Aug 1815 (OB)

CRAWFORD, Thomas (1)
L 14 May 1796
d 1797 (PRO)

CRAWFORD, Thomas (2)
L 17 Dec 1807
Ret CR 21 Dec 1844 (PRO)
d 1849 (PRO)

CRAWFORD, Thomas (3)
L 21 July 1779
d 1809 (PRO)

CRAWLEY, Edmund
L 7 Mar 1778
CR 9 Apr 1783
CA 22 Nov 1790
RAB 25 Oct 1809
RAW 31 July 1810
RAR 12 Aug 1812
VAB 4 June 1814
VAW 12 Aug 1819 (PRO)
VAR 19 July 1821 (PRO)
AW 22 July 1825 (PRO)
d 1834 (PRO)

CRAWLEY, George
L 17 July 1800
CR 22 Jan 1806
d 5 Mar 1810 (PRO)

CRAWLEY, James
L 20 Apr 1799
d 1808 (PRO)

CRAWLEY, Jeremy
L
CA 1667

CRAWLEY, John
L 27 Feb 1782
CR 23 Jan 1797
CA 3 Jan 1799
d 1815 (PRO)

CRAWLEY, Richard
See CRANDLEY, Richard

CRAWLEY, Thomas (1)
L 1 Oct 1688
CA 7 Feb 1690
d 16 Feb 1707 (PJP)

CRAWLEY, Thomas (2)
L 7 Dec 1778
Dismissed 1790 (PJP)
Restored w/srty 23 Dec 1791 (PRO)
SUP CR 31 Dec 1814 (PRO)
d 8 June 1851 (PRO)

CREAK, William
L 3 Feb 1815
CR 5 Feb 1858 (PRO)
d 1858 (PRO)

CREAMER, Henry
See CREMER, Henry

CREASE, Henry
L 31 Jan 1806
CR 12 Feb 1821 (PRO)
d 10 Nov 1862 (PRO)

CREE, David
L 28 Nov 1793
d Dec 1820 (PRO)

CREED, John
L 1673

CREED, Peter
L 6 Mar 1783
d 1833 (PRO)

CREIGHTON, James Augustus Seymour
See CRICHTON, James Augustus Seymour

CRELLIN, William
L 25 Feb 1815 (PRO)
Ret CR 14 Apr 1862 (PRO)
d 1865 (PRO)

CREMER, Henry
L 30 July 1689
CR 16 Jan 1706
d 13 Feb 1707 (PJP)

CRESPIGNY, Augustus
L 1 Nov 1811
CR 30 May 1825 (PRO)
d 24 Oct 1825 (PRO)

CRESPIGNY, Claude
L 8 Aug 1806
CR 31 Mar 1813
d 30 July 1813 (PRO)

CRESPIN, Abraham
L 20 Jan 1762
CR 13 May 1778
CA 17 Jan 1780
d 1786 (PRO)

CRESSLEHAN, John
L 18 Jan 1799 (PRO)
Dismissed 1800 (PRO)

CRESSY, William
L 11 July 1800
d 1808 (PRO)

CREW, John
L 11 Nov 1695

CREW, Samuel
L 1 May 1804
d 1811 (PRO)

CREWS, John
L 13 Nov 1756
d 7 Mar 1811 (PRO)

CREYKE, George Adey
L 9 Jan 1803
CR 15 Aug 1804
d 1811 (PRO)

CREYK(E), Richard (1)
L 23 Mar 1770
CR 17 Oct 1778
CA 17 Dec 1782
SUP CA 1803 (PRO)
d 4 Dec 1826 (PRO)

CREYKE, Richard (2)
L 7 Nov 1806
CR 17 Mar 1812
CA 19 Dec 1814
Ret CA 1 Oct 1846 (PRO)
d 2 Oct 1849 (PRO)

CRIBB, Richard William
L 20 Mar 1794
CR 15 Oct 1801 (PRO)
d 29 June 1805 (PRO)

CRICHLOW, Ralph
L 19 Sept 1815
HP 19 Sept 1815 (OB)
d 1847 (PRO)

CRICHTON, George
L 9 Feb 1808
d 1841 (PRO)

CRICHTON, James Augustus Seymour
L 20 Mar 1799

CR	12 Aug	1812
d		1835 (PRO)
CRICHTON, William		
L	21 Mar	1812
Ret CR	18 Apr	1854 (PRO)
d		1872 (PRO)
CRICKETT, Edward		
L	29 Oct	1740
CR	22 June	1747
d		1769 (PRO)
CRIRIE, John		
L	2 Nov	1809
CR	27 May	1825 (PRO)
d	21 Apr	1847 (PRO)
CRISP, James		
L	3 Mar	1815
Ret CR	13 Nov	1862 (PRO)
d		1870 (PRO)
CRISPE, George		
T		
L	20 Mar	1815 (PRO)
d	26 Dec	1831 (PRO)
CRISPIN, Benjamin		
L	19 Dec	1796
CR	24 Dec	1805
CA	4 Dec	1813
d	7 Mar	1836 (OB)
CRISPO, John (1)		
L	26 Dec	1743
SUP		1777 (PRO)
CRISPO, John (2)		
L	30 Dec	1790
CR	20 Jan	1797
CA	21 Oct	1810
d		1841 (PRO)
CRISPO, John William		
L	8 Mar	1815
d		1857 (PRO)
CRISWICK, Charles		
T		
L	9 Mar	1815
d		1854 (TR)
CRITCH, Lord John		
See CROUTZ, John		
CROAD, William		
L	25 Oct	1796
Dismissed	17 Aug	1801 (PJP)
CROASDAILE, Thomas Pearson		
L	1 Nov	1800
Ret CR	1 Dec	1830 (PRO)
d	12 Sept	1838 (LT)
CROACKATT, George		
L	22 Feb	1815
d	15 June	1821 (PRO)
CROCKER, Arthur		
L	2 Mar	1734
d		1740(1) (PRO)
CROCKER, Henry		
L	7 Feb	1812
Ret CR	1 Oct	1853 (PRO)
d		1866 (PRO)
CROCKER, Thomas		
L	27 Mar	1794
d		1798 (PRO)

CROCKFORD, Thomas Henry		
L	13 Feb	1815
d		1826 (PRO)
CROCOMBE, Richard		
L	25 Nov	1793
d		1810 (PRO)
CROFT, John		
L	2 Feb	1797
T		
CR	24 Dec	1805
d	24 June	1808 (PRO)
CROFT, William		
L	22 Dec	1801
CR	8 May	1804
CA	13 Oct	1807
RAB	23 Nov	1841 (PRO)
RAW	22 Jan	1847 (PRO)
RAR	9 May	1849 (PRO)
Ret VA	8 Mar	1852 (CH)
Ret A	28 Nov	1857 (CH)
d	6 May	1872 (CH)
CROFTON, Ambrose		
L	1 Jan	1778
CR	23 June	1794
d	July	1835 (PRO)
CROFTON, Edward Lowther		
L	19 Mar	1804
CR	12 June	1805
CA	4 Mar	1811
CB	4 June	1815 (PRO)
d	8 Sept	1818 (LT)
CROFTON, Hon. George Alfred		
L	10 Oct	1804
CR	9 Feb	1808
CA	1 Feb	1812
RAB	30 Jan	1848 (PRO)
RAW	21 June	1850 (PRO)
RAR	5 Mar	1853 (PRO)
VAB	9 July	1855 (PRO)
Ret VA	12 Nov	1856 (PRO)
d	23 Feb	1858 (PRO)
CROFTON, Morgan		
L	11 Apr	1814
Ret CR	19 Jan	1857 (PRO)
d		1871 (PRO)
CROFTON, Sir George Morgan		
T		
L	28 Feb	1807
Inh Bt		1834 (TR)
d		1867 (TR)
CROFTS, Henry		
L	6 June	1696 (PMM)
CA	11 Aug	1697
d	16 Dec	1702 (PJP)
CROFTS, John (1)		
L		1673
d	before	1689 (PJP)
CROFTS, John (2)		
L		1673 (P)
CA	23 Mar	1685 (P)
CA	25 Apr	1689
d		?1690 (PJP)
CROKE, John Augustus		
L	24 Feb	1815
d	15 Aug	1840 (PRO)

CROKE, Wentworth Parsons
L 14 Mar 1807
CR 4 Oct 1825 (PJP)
Ret CR 16 Mar 1853 (PRO)
d 16 July 1857 (PRO)

CROKER, Charles
L 17 Dec 1814
CR 4 Oct 1825 (PRO)
Ret CR 1 Apr 1856 (PRO)
d 1878 (PRO)

CROKER, Richard
L 7 Jan 1809
CR 15 June 1814
d 18 Oct 1836 (PRO)

CROKER, Thomas
L 29 Mar 1780
d 1793 (PRO)

CROKER, Walter
L 6 Feb 1806
CR 2 Nov 1814
d 24 June 1840 (PRO)

CROLE, Charles
L 20 Oct 1813
CR 6 May 1822 (PRO)
CA 26 Jan 1828 (PRO)
HP 26 June 1828 (PRO)
d 20 Oct 1850 (PRO)

CROMWELL, Henry
Later FRANKLAND, Henry
L 6 July 1761
CR 10 May 1779
CA 14 Nov 1781
RAB 1 Jan 1801
RAW 23 Apr 1804
RAR 9 Nov 1805
VAB 13 Dec 1806 (LG)
VAW 25 Oct 1809
VAR 31 July 1810
d 1814 (PRO)

CROOK, James
L 21 Mar 1812
d 31 Mar 1825 (LT)

CROOKE, Charles Cunyngham
L 4 Dec 1761
d 1806 (PRO)

CROOKE, Charles Henry
T
L 9 Jan 1809
CR 30 Aug 1815
HP 30 Aug 1815 (OB)
Ret CR 1 July 1851 (PRO)
Ret CA 7 Dec 1854 (PRO)
d 19 Feb 1858 (PRO)

CROOKE, James (1)
L 8 May 1804
d 1815 (PRO)

CROOKE, James (2)
L 15 Oct 1814
d 1848 (PRO)

CROOKE, Peter Thomas
L 9 Nov 1747
d 1760 (PRO)

CROOKE, Thomas Leadley
L 13 Mar 1815
Ret CR 20 July 1863 (PRO)
d 1865 (PRO)

CROOKE, William
L 13 Jan 1794
d 1799 (PRO)

CROOKE, William Boyle
L 7 Mar 1815
Ret CR 10 Apr 1863 (PRO)
d 1875 (PRO)

CROOKS, William
L 11 Apr 1760
d 26 Oct 1768 (PMM)

CROOKSHANKS, John
L 2 Mar 1734
CR
CA 3 July 1742
Dismissed 1747 (DNB)
d 20 Feb 1795 (DNB)

CROSBE, Edward Hawke
L 5 May 1795
d 1809 (PRO)

CROSBE, George Vandeput
L 13 July 1796
d 1826 (PRO)

CROSBE, Robert Boyle
L 5 June 1795
d 1819 (PRO)

CROSBE, William (1)
L 20 Mar 1758
SUP CR 28Sept 1798 (PMM)
d ? 1807 (PRO)

CROSBE, William (2)
L 23 July 1778
Dismissed 1801 (PRO)

CROSBIE, Robert
L 8 July 1805
Seniority amended 10 Mar 1807 (PRO)
CR 3 Aug 1829 (PRO)
d 6 Nov 1841 (LT)

CROSBY, James
L 11 Dec 1807
d 1826 (PRO)

CROSBY, Nathaniel
L 15 Nov 1757
CR 19 Nov 1777
d 1780 (PRO)

CROSBY, Richard
L 1673
d before 1689 (PJP)

CROSBY, Thomas Sackville
L 1 Feb 1815
Struck off list 13 Aug 1821 (PRO)
Restored w/srty 1834 (PRO)
d 1847 (PRO)

CROSBY, William
L 20 June 1756
d 1780(1) (PRO)

CROSBY, William
See CROSBE, William

CROSLEY, Richard
L 1 May 1811
d 1825 (PRO)

Name	Rank	Date	Year
CROSS, George			
	L		
	CA	12 Nov	1688
		(13 Nov 1688 in H)	
CROSS, John			
	L	19 May	1761
	d		1773 (PRO)
CROSS, Lewis			
	L	26 Sept	1804
	d	June	1821 (PRO)
CROSS, Robert			
	L	18 Feb	1815
	d	4 July	1831 (PRO)
CROSS, William			
	L		
	CA	19 Jan	1691
	Dismissed	17 Mar	1704 (CH)
	d	22 Apr	1746 (PMM)
CROSSE, Edward			
	L	14 July	1794
	d		1799 (PRO)
CROSSE, John			
	L	26 Feb	1702
	SUP	20 Mar	1733 (PMM)
	d		1752 (PMM)
CROSSE, Thomas			
	L	10 Jan	1741
	d	29 June	1747 (PMM)
CROSSE, William			
See CROSS, William			
CROSSMAN, Richard			
	L	12 Jan	1805
	d		1818 (PRO)
CROSSMAN, Robert			
	L		
	CA		1664
	d	before	1689 (PJP)
CROTTY, William			
	L	25 Mar	1809
	Ret CR	9 Apr	1847 (PRO)
	d		1848 (PRO)
CROUCH, John			
	L	19 Mar	1694
CROUCH, Edward			
	L	5 Jan	1790
	CR	25 Oct	1843 (PRO)
	d	13 Sept	1847 (PRO)
CROUCH, Edward Thomas			
	L	7 May	1805
	CR	19 July	1821 (PRO)
	d	20 Dec	1846 (PRO)
CROUCH, Isaac			
	L	5 Feb	1747
	d		1789 (PRO)
CROUCH, Joseph			
	L	26 Apr	1780
	SUP CR	9 Nov	1814 (PRO)
	d	Mar	1828 (PRO)
CROUCHER, James			
See CROWCHER, James			
CROUTZ, John			
	L		1673 (DDA)
CROW, Anthony			
	L		
	CA	17 Apr	1685
CROW, George			
	L		1665
	CA		1667
CROW, George			
See CROWE, George			
CROW, Josiah			
	L		
	CA	3 July	1691
	d	24 Sept	1714 (PRO)
CROW, Leonard			
	L		
	CA	11 Jan	1693
	d	9 Sept	1705 (PJP)
CROW, Thomas			
	L		
	CA		1666
	Turned out		1671 (PRO)
CROW, William (1)			
	L	15 Apr	1748
	d		1780 (NMM)
CROW, William (2)			
	L	20 Aug	1801
	d		1834 (PRO)
CROWCHER, James			
	L	14 Aug	1746
	d		1783 (PRO)
CROWDY, Charles			
	L	17 Mar	1806
	CR	25 Mar	1824 (PRO)
	CA	13 Jan	1834 (PRO)
	Ret RA	21 Oct	1856 (PRO)
	Ret VA	27 Apr	1863 (PRO)
	Ret A	18 Oct	1867 (PRO)
	d	17 May	1870 (PRO)
CROWE, George			
	L	1 Mar	1706
CROWLEY, William			
	L	22 May	1758
	d		1768 (PRO)
CROXALL, Scott			
	L	26 June	1799 (PRO)
	d		1800 (PRO)
CRUCHLEY, Evan Jones			
	L	2 Feb	1813
	d	22 Aug	1835 (LT)
CRUSE, Robson			
	T		
	L	17 Feb	1810
	d	3 May	1831 (LT)
CRYMBLE, Murray			
	L	6 Aug	1748
	d		1762 (PRO)
CRYMES, George			
	L	23 June	1794 (PRO)
	d		1796 (PRO)
CRYMES, John			
	L	2 Apr	1779
	SUPCR	31 Jan	1814
	d	12 Aug	1816 (PRO)
CUBITT, Joseph			
	L		

CA		1661
d	? before	1673 (PJP)
CUCKOW, Trevor		
L	21 June	1757
d		1792 (PRO)
CUDD, William		
L	23 Oct	1806
d	24 Feb	1828 (PRO)
CUDLIP, James		
L	11 Feb	1815
d	28 Oct	1844 (PRO)
CUDLIPP, Henry		
L	25 July	1797
CR	8 May	1804
d		1805 (PRO)
CUDLIPP, Richard		
L	28 Sept	1795
d		1800 (PRO)
CULL, Richard (1)		
L	3 Aug	1805
Not seen since		1810 (PRO)
Name removed		1825 (PRO)
CULL, Richard (2)		
L	30 Dec	1808 (PRO)
d		1812 (PRO)
CULL, Thomas (1)		
L	16 Jan	1808
Ret CR	19 Oct	1844 (OB)
d	22 Sept	1846 (OB)
CULL, Thomas (2)		
L	21 Mar	1812
CR	16 Feb	1852 (PRO)
d		1886 (PRO)
CULLEN, Robert		
L	19 Sept	1815
d		1818 (PRO)
CULLIFORD, Richard		
L	15 Feb	1694 (PJP)
CA	9 June	1695
d	7 May	1738 (PMM)
CULLIS, William		
L	29 Nov	1799 (PRO)
Ret CR	26 Nov	1830 (PRO)
d		1842 (PRO)
CULPEPPER, John		
L		1673
CULPEPPER, Joseph		
L		
CA	10 July	1673
CULPEPPER, Thomas		
L	30 Apr	1678
CULVERHOUSE, John		
L	1 Dec	1787
CR	27 Feb	1797
CA	29 Apr	1802
d (drowned)		1809 (PJP)
CUMBERLAND, HRH Henry Frederick, Duke of		
L		
CR		
Cre EP	27 Oct	1766 (DNB)
Cre IP	27 Oct	1766 (DNB)
Kt		1767 (DNB)
CA	28 Oct	1768
RAB		1769 (PRO)
RAW	18 Oct	1770
VAB	24 Oct	1770
VAW	5 Feb	1776
VAR		1776 (PRO)
AB	29 Jan	1778
AW	8 Apr	1782
d	18 Sept	1790 (DNB)
CUMBERLAND, William		
L	26 Feb	1790 (PRO)
CR	3 Oct	1795
CA	8 Nov	1798
RAB	27 May	1825 (PRO)
RAW	22 July	1830 (PRO)
d	15 Nov	1832 (PRO)
CUMBY, Charles		
L	14 Jan	1799
CR	4 Dec	1813
d	28 Sept	1849 (PRO)
CUMBY, David P.		
L	24 Sept	1759
SUP CR	6 May	1805
d	17 Aug	1814 (PRO)
CUMBY, William Pryce		
L	26 Oct	1793
T		
CR		
CA	1 Jan	1806
CB		1831 (TR)
d	27 Sept	1837 (TR)
CUMINE, John		
L	31 Mar	1759
d		1760 (PRO)
CUMING, Penhallow		
L	4 Mar	1740
CR	8 Mar	1748
Dismissed	6 Dec	1758 (PRO)
CUMING, Samuel		
L	7 Feb	1797
Ret CR	15 Oct	1838 (PRO)
d		1845 (PRO)
CUMING, William		
L	7 Dec	1779
CR	28 Dec	1795
CA	13 Oct	1797
CB	4 June	1815 (LG)
RAB	19 July	1821 (PRO)
d	20 June	1824 (PRO)
CUMING, Witter		
L	10 May	1778
d		1784 (PRO)
CUMMERFORD, Nicholas		
L	7 Jan	1783
d		1797 (PRO)
CUMMING, James (1)		
L	7 Apr	1758 (PMM)
CR	20 Apr	1765
CA	30 July	1772
RAB	12 July	1794
RAW	4 July	1794
VAB	1 June	1795
VAR	14 Feb	1799
AB	1 Jan	1801
AW	9 Nov	1805
d		1808 (PRO)

CUMMING, James (2)
L 14 July 1740 (PMM)
d 1766 (PRO)
CUMMING, James (3)
T
L 24 Dec 1805
d 1809 (PRO)
CUMMING, Penhallow
See CUMING, Penhallow
CUMMING, Robert
L 22 Jan 1781
d 1797 (PRO)
CUMMING, William
L 21 Oct 1755
CR 6 Nov 1777
CA 27 Feb 1779
d 1795 (PRO)
CUMMINGS, James
See CUMMING, James (2)
CUMPSTON, George
L 10 Sept 1810
d 1811 (PRO)
CUMYNS, George
L 9 Aug 1797
Dismissed 1803 (PRO)
CUNDALL, George
L 21 July 1756
d 1773 (PRO)
CUNDETT, George
L 27 Oct 1717
CR 2 Apr 1734
d 1741 (PRO)
CUNDETT, John
L
CR
CA 20 Jan 1721
d 26 Apr 1724 (PJP)
CUNINGHAM, Alexander
L 7 Apr 1759
CR 20 Sept 1781
CA 18 Dec 1783
d 12 Dec 1798 (PRO)
CUNINGHAM, Charles
See CUNNINGHAM, Sir Charles
CUNINGHAM, George
L 25 Sept 1800
d 1807 (PRO)
CUNINGHAM, James
See CUNNINGHAM, James
CUNINGHAM, Robert
L 14 July 1741
d 1747 (PRO)
CUNINGHAM, Thomas (1)
L 6 Oct 1744
d 1764 (PRO)
CUNINGHAM, Thomas (2)
L 16 Feb 1747
d 1772 (PRO)
CUNINGHAM, Thomas
See CUNNINGHAM, Thomas
CUNNINGHAM, Alexander
L 22 Oct 1794
CR 24 Dec 1805
CA 12 Aug 1812
d 18 May 1836 (PJP)
CUNNINGHAM, Andrew
L 31 Dec 1799
d 1819 (PRO)
CUNNINGHAM, Sir Charles
L 6 Nov 1782
CR 28 Oct 1790
CA 12 Oct 1793
COMV Sept 1803 (DNB)
COMM (Deptford) 1806–1823 (DNB)
Ret RA May 1829 (DNB)
KCH 24 Oct 1832 (DNB)
d 11 Feb 1834 (LT)
CUNNINGHAM, James
L 22 Feb 1744
CR 19 Nov 1761
d 1780(1) (PRO)
CUNNINGHAM, Thomas
L 13 July 1765
CR 25 Oct 1809 (PRO)
d 5 July 1823 (PRO)
CUNNINGHAM, Thomas
See CUNINGHAM, Thomas
CUNNINGHAM, Henry Montgomery
L 17 June 1815 (PRO)
d 1826 (PRO)
CUNNINGHAM, William (1)
L 15 Mar 1692
CUNNINGHAM, Sir William (2)
L 5 June 1792
CR 25 Oct 1809 (PRO)
d 1812 (PRO)
CUNNINGHAM, William (3)
L 31 Aug 1762
d 1771 (PRO)
CUNNINGS, Henry
L 1661
CUPPAGE, Adam
L 26 May 1814
CR 22 July 1830 (PRO)
Ret CA 1 Apr 1856 (PRO)
d 21 Mar 1860 (PRO)
CUPPAGE, Hugh
L 6 Sept 1779
d 1790 (PRO)
CUPPAGE, William
L 6 Apr 1815
CR 24 Dec 1827 (PJP)
CA 22 July 1830 (PJP)
d 3 Jan 1856 (PRO)
CURGENVEN, Richard
L 7 June 1769
CR 3 Apr 1781
CA 13 Apr 1782
d 30 Aug 1784 (PMM)
CURLE, Edmund
L
CA 1661
d before 1688 (PD)
CURLE, Henry
L 27 Jan 1708
CURLE, Nicholas Wilson
L 8 June 1758
d 1773 (PRO)

CURLEWIS, William Edward
L 28 Nov 1811
CR 23 Nov 1841 (OB)
HP 23 Nov 1841 (OB)
d 4 Jan 1847 (PRO)

CURLING, Alexander
L 29 Apr 1778
d 1787 (PRO)

CURLING, Edward B.
L 10 July 1809
d 1810 (PRO)

CURLING, John
L 18 Mar 1778
d 15 Dec 1778 (PMM)

CURRAN, John Bartholomew Hoar
L 25 June 1806 (PRO)
CR 2 Aug 1811
d 1832 (PRO)

CURRIE, Mark John
L 23 Sept 1814
CR 9 Jan 1823 (PRO)
CA 23 Nov 1841 (PRO)
Ret RA 12 Apr 1862 (PRO)
Ret VA 24 Apr 1862 (PRO)
d 1 May 1874 (PRO)

CURRY, Richard
L 14 Mar 1794
CR 30 Nov 1798
CA 7 Jan 1802
HP 1814 (MB)
CB 1831 (CH)
RAW 10 July 1837 (PRO)
RAR 23 Nov 1841 (PRO)
VAB 9 Nov 1846 (PRO)
VAW 10 Dec 1846 (PRO)
VAR 23 Mar 1848 (PRO)
Ret VA 1 July 1851 (PRO)
Ret A 8 July 1851 (PRO)
d 27 Dec 1855 (PRO)

CURRY, Robert
L 8 Nov 1756
SUP CR 21 Sept 1796
d 8 Nov 1812 (PRO)

CURRY, Roger Carley
L 17 Jan 1810
CR 21 Sept 1832 (PRO)
d 26 Sept 1844 (PRO)

CURSON, Thomas
See CURZON, Hon. Thomas Roper

CURTIS, Clifton
L 17 Oct 1806
d 1811 (PRO)

CURTIS, John (1)
L 16 Mar 1795
d 1817 (PRO)

CURTIS, John (2)
L 30 July 1810
d 1 Jan 1840 (PRO)

CURTIS, Sir Lucius
L 11 Aug 1801
CR 16 Nov 1804
CA 22 Jan 1806
CB 4 June 1814 (OB)
Inh Bt 14 Nov 1816 (MB)
RAB 28 June 1838 (PRO)
RAW 23 Nov 1841 (PRO)
RAR 12 Feb 1847 (PRO)
VAB 15 Sept 1849 (PRO)
VAW 1 July 1851 (PRO)
VAR 5 Nov 1853 (PRO)
AB 9 July 1855 (PRO)
AW 30 July 1857 (PRO)
AR 1 Nov 1864 (PRO)
KCB 1862 (CH)
AF 11 Jan 1864 (PRO)
d 14 Jan 1869 (CH)

CURTIS, Sir Roger (1)
L 19 Jan 1771
CR 11 July 1776
CA 30 Apr 1777
Cre Bt 1794 (CH)
RAB 4 July 1794
RAR 1 June 1795
VAW 14 Feb 1799
VAR 1 Jan 1801
AB 23 Apr 1804
AW 9 Nov 1805
AR 31 July 1810
GCB 2 Jan 1815 (LG)
d 14 Nov 1816 (PRO)

CURTIS, Roger (2)
L 12 Apr 1798
CR 9 Dec 1799
CA 14 Apr 1802
d 12 July 1802 (PRO)

CURTIS, Timothy
L 8 Mar 1815
CR 22 Sept 1821 (PRO)
CA 30 Dec 1826 (PRO)
d 15 Oct 1834 (LT)

CURTISS, Hyde
L 20 June 1758
SUP CR 26 Nov 1799 (PMM)
d 1810 (PRO)

CURZON, Edward
L 14 Mar 1811
CR 29 Mar 1815
CA 8 Mar 1823 (PRO)
Kt (France) 1827 (MB)
Kt (Russia) 1827 (PRO)
CB 13 Nov 1827 (LG)
Ret CA 1 Oct 1846 (PRO)
Ret RA 17 Dec 1852 (PRO)
Ret VA 5 Jan 1858 (PRO)
d 7 Mar 1862 (PRO)

CURZON, Hon. Henry
L 1 Feb 1783
CR 21 Sept 1790 (OB)
CA 22 Nov 1790
CRM 25 Oct 1809 (LG)
RAB 31 July 1810
RAW 1 Aug 1811
RAR 4 Dec 1813
VAB 4 June 1814
VAW 12 Aug 1819 (PRO)
VAR 27 May 1825 (PRO)
AB 22 July 1830 (PRO)
AW 10 Jan 1837 (PRO)
AR 23 Nov 1841 (PRO)
d 2 May 1846 (PRO)

CURZON, Hon. John
L 10 Jan 1783
d 1784 (PRO)

CURZON, Hon Thomas Roper
L 7 Feb 1810
CR 21 Apr 1813
d 15 June 1833 (PRO)

CUSACK, James
L 28 May 1720
CR 3 June 1734
CA 13 Nov 1739
d 19 July 1743 (PJP)

CUST, William
L 26 June 1741
CR 22 Jan 1746 (PRO)
CA 18 July 1747
KIA 8 Mar 1748 (LG)

CUTLIFFE, James
L 18 Nov 1790
SUP CR 16 Feb 1824 (PRO)
d 2 May 1839 (PRO)

CUTFIELD, William
T wounded
L 17 Mar 1806
CR 19 May 1808
d 30 Nov 1823 (TR)

CUTHBERT, Robert
L 8 Oct 1783
CR 7 Oct 1798 (PRO)
CA 28 Nov 1798
d 8 Jan 1821 (PRO)

CUTHBERT, William
L 5 June 1807
d 29 Apr 1810 (PRO)

CUTLER, Frank
L 21 Mar 1812
Ret CR 16 Aug 1854 (PRO)
d 1871 (PRO)

CUTTANCE, –
L 1666

CUTTANCE, Edward
L 1661

CUTTANCE, Henry
L
CA 1660
d Oct 1689 (DDA)

CUTTANCE, Joseph
L 1664
d before 1689 (PJP)

CUTTANCE, Sir Roger
L
CA 1660
Kt 1 July 1665 (DNB)
d 1669 (DNB)

CUTTER, Vincent
L
CA 15 Apr 1695 (20 Jan 1694 in C)
d 10 Apr 1710 (PJP)

CUTTLE, John
L
CA 1664
KIA 3 Sept 1665 (PD)

CYLEY, Tyrwit
L
CR
CA 1 Jan 1713
d 6 Dec 1751 (PJP)

DABINE, Thomas Dymock Jones
L 8 May 1812
HP Oct 1816–Sept 1820 (OB)
d 17 Aug 1848 (PRO)

DACRE, George Hall
L 10 July 1809
Ret CR 4 Apr 1848 (PRO)
d 8 Apr 1851 (PRO)

DACRES, Barrington
L 27 Sept 1796
CR 24 Dec 1798
CA 29 Apr 1802
d Oct 1806 (PRO)

DACRES, James Richard (1)
L 17 Mar 1796
CR 25 Nov 1796
CA 13 Nov 1780
RAB 14 Feb 1799
RAW 1 Jan 1801
RAR 23 Apr 1804
VAW 9 Nov 1805
VAR 28 Apr 1808
d 6 Jan 1810 (NMM)

DACRES, James Richard (2)
L 15 Nov 1804
CR 5 July 1805
CA 14 Jan 1806
RAB 28 June 1838 (NMM)
RAW 23 Nov 1841 (NMM)
RAR 9 Nov 1846 (NMM)
VAB 20 Mar 1848 (NMM)
VAW 2 Sept 1850 (NMM)
VAR 19 Jan 1852 (NMM)
d 4 Dec 1853 (NMM)

DACRES, Sir Richard
L 28 May 1781 (NMM)
CR 10 Mar 1795
CA 31 Oct 1795
SUP RA 29 Mar 1817 (NMM)
RAR 21 Aug 1827 (NMM)
VAW 22 July 1830 (NMM)
GCH 25 Jan 1836 (OB)
VAR 10 Jan 1837 (NMM)
d 22 Jan 1837 (NMM)

DADE, Jonathan
L 4 May 1810 (NMM)
d 1836 (PRO)

DAEL, George
L 26 Sept 1811
d 1818 (PRO)

D'AETH, George William Hughes
T
L 30 Jan 1806
CR 16 Aug 1811
CA 13 June 1815
Ret CA 1 Oct 1846 (NMM)
Ret RA 6 Nov 1850 (NMM)

Ret VA	9 July	1857 (NMM)
Ret A	28 Apr	1862 (NMM)
d	28 Apr	1873 (NMM)
DALBY, George		
L		1672
DALBY, Jacques		
L	28 Oct	1797
d		1803 (NMM)
DALBY, Thomas		
L	31 Dec	1778
CR	5 Dec	1794
Ret CA	10 Sept	1840 (NMM)
d		1844 (NMM)
DALBY, William		
L	26 May	1778
KIA	5 Aug	1781 (LG)
DALE, Alfred		
L	21 Oct	1807
Ret CR	24 July	1844 (NMM)
d		1866 (NMM)
DALE, Harry		
L	3 Mar	1815 (PRO)
d	23 June	1822 (PRO)
DALE, John		
L		1665
d	before	1689 (PJP)
DALE, John Laurence		
L	30 Apr	1802
d		1804(5) (NMM)
DALE, Leonard		
L	25 Feb	1801
d		1811 (NMM)
DALE, William		
L		
CA		1660
d	before	1689 (PJP)
DALGLEISH, James		
L	25 Aug	1794
CR	4 Dec	1813
d	31 Jan	1846 (OB)
DALLING, John Windham		
T		
L	18 Oct	1810
CR	15 June	1815
CA	2 Jan	1828 (PRO)
Ret CA	2 Jan	1848 (NMM)
d	10 Oct	1853 (PRO)
DALMAN, George		
See DOLMAN, George		
DALRYMPLE, Hugh		
L	28 Feb	1756
CR	18 Apr	1759
CA	27 Nov	1763(NMM)
d	26 Dec	1779 (PRO)
DALRYMPLE, James (1)		
L	17 Jan	1762
CR	26 May	1762
d		1773 (NMM)
DALRYMPLE, James (2)		
L	2 June	1794
CR	14 Oct	1799
CA	29 Apr	1802
d	23 Apr	1803
DALRYMPLE, James (3)		
L	17 Nov	1800
Ret CR	15 Dec	1830 (NMM)
d		1863 (NMM)
DALRYMPLE, John		
L	1 Feb	1745 (PRO)
CR	23 Mar	1757
CA	18 Oct	1758
RAW	24 Sept	1787
RAR	21 Sept	1790
VAW	1 Feb	1793
VAR	12 Apr	1794
AB	1 June	1795
d	10 Aug	1798 (PRO)
DALRYMPLE, Primrose		
L	28 Mar	1760
d		1767 (PRO)
DALRYMPLE, Robert		
L	6 Apr	1757
d		1763 (NMM)
DALSTON, Sir George		
L	20 Jan	1742
d		?1743 (NMM)
DALTON, Christopher		
L	25 June	1724
d		1734 (PRO)
DALTON, Edward		
L	9 Oct	1778
d		1795 (PRO)
DALTON, James Robert		
L	26 Nov	1806
CR	30 Apr	1810
Ret CA	10 Sept	1840 (NMM)
d	1 Jan	1860 (NMM)
DALTON, Nathan		
L	27 Jan	1794
d		1799 (PRO)
DALTON, William		
L	5 Oct	1778
d	9 Apr	1801
DALWAY, Noah		
L	8 Oct	1779
IMP (Carickfergus)		1799–1800 (MPT)
MP (Carickfergus)		1801–1802 (MPT)
SUP CR	6 Apr	1814
d	17 July	1820 (MPT)
DALY, Anthony		
L	3 Feb	1815
Struck off list	4 May	1819 (NMM)
DALY, Cuthbert		
L	7 Sept	1814
d	24 May	1824 (NMM)
DALY, Cuthbert Featherstone		
L	30 Sept	1800
CR	10 Apr	1806
CA	18 Aug	1808
CB	20 July	1838 (OB)
RAB	9 Nov	1846 (NMM)
RAW	30 Jan	1848 (NMM)
RAR	11 Nov	1850 (NMM)
d	6 Dec	1851 (NMM)
DALY, James		
L	6 July	1795

SUP CR 26 Nov 1830 (PRO)
d 1839 (PRO)

DALY, Joseph
L 6 Mar 1807
d 1811 (PRO)

DALYELL, Thomas (1)
L 22 Aug 1756
d 1767 (PRO)

DALYELL, Thomas (2)
L 24 July 1797
Dismissed 10 Dec 1800 (PJP)

DALYELL, William Cunningham Cavendish
L 1 Jan 1805
CR 17 Feb 1814
Ret CA 1 July 1864 (NMM)
d 16 Feb 1865 (NMM)

DALZEL, Thomas
L 27 Nov 1727
d 31 Dec 1765 (PMM)

DALZELL, James
L
CR
CA 13 Feb 1712
d 14 Sept 1712

DAMER, Hon. Henry Dawson
See DAWSON, Hon. Henry

DAMERELL, Samuel
See DANERELL, Samuel

DAMPIER, Edward
L 1 Feb 1815 (NMM)
d 1832 (NMM)

DAMPIER, William (1)
L
CR 13 May 1689 (PMM)
CA 26 July 1689
d (drowned) 24 Feb 1701 (CH)

DAMPIER, William (2)
L
CR
CA 25 Mar 1698 (DNB)
d Mar 1719 (DNB)

DAMARESQUE, Edward
L 13 Oct 1696

DANBY, Earl of
See CARMARTHEN, Marquess of

DANCE, William Townsend
L 12 July 1813
CR 23 Oct 1823 (PJP)
CA 5 June 1834 (PJP)
Ret CA 1 July 1851 (PRO)
Ret RA 12 Nov 1857 (NMM)
d Sept 1857 (NMM)

DANCER, George
See DANSER, George

DANCER, John
L 20 Nov 1677
d before 1689 (PJP)

DANDRIDGE, William
L 20 Oct 1709
CR 11 Apr 1738
CA 19 Feb 1741
d 27 Aug 1744 (PRO)

DANERELL, Samuel
L 1655
CA 1665
d before 1689 (PJP)

DANFORD, Richard
L 29 Oct 1806
d 1834 (NMM)

DANIEL, John
L 13 June 1741
d 1746(7) (NMM)

DANIEL, Lionel
L 13 Sept 1739
CR 1745 (PJP)
CA 28 May 1745
d 27 Oct 1752 (PRO)

DANIEL, Robert Savage
L 29 Sept 1783
KIA 1 Aug 1798 (LG)

DANIEL, William
L 27 Oct 1758
CR 14 July 1779
CA 15 Sept 1781
d 21 Feb 1800

DANIEL, William Henry
L 22 Jan 1781
CR 11 Oct 1798
CA 29 Apr 1802
Ret RA 10 July 1837 (NMM)
d 5 May 1838 (NMM)

DANIEL, William Westcott
L 27 Oct 1798
CR 24 Dec 1805
CA 4 Dec 1813
d 1833 (NMM)

DANIELL, Richard
L 18 Feb 1815
Ret CR 1 Nov 1861 (NMM)
d 1868 (NMM)

DANIELL, Thomas
L 3 May 1755
d 27 Aug 1762 (PRO)

DANIELL, Sir William
L 16 Sept 1813
CR 22 Nov 1836 (NMM)
Kt 1836 (OB)
d 15 Sept 1845 (NMM)

DANIELS, Benjamin Simes
L 9 Feb 1814
d 1815 (PRO)

DANSAYS, Francis
L 22 Jan 1708 (PMM)
CR 14 Aug 1721
CA 25 Jan 1726
d 5 Aug 1754

DANSER, George
L 4 Feb 1780
d 1785 (NMM)

DANSER, John
See DANCER, John

DANSEY, Edward Collins
L 17 Aug 1815 (PRO)
d 1842 (PRO)

DANSEY, George
L 8 Mar 1814
d 15 Sept 1823 (NMM)

DANVERS, William		
L	22 Jan	1713
Gone		1729 (PRO)
D'ARAMDA, William		
L	16 Dec	1808
Ret CR	19 Sept	1854 (NMM)
d	10 Oct	1872 (NMM)
DARBY, George		
L	7 Sept	1742
CR		
CA	12 Sept	1747
RAW	23 Jan	1778
RAR	24 Sept	1778 (NMM)
VAB	19 Mar	1779
COMAD	22 Sept	1780–
	1 Apr	1782 (AO)
VAW	26 Sept	1780
MP (Plymouth)		1780–1784 (MPN)
d	26 Nov	1790 (DNB)
DARBY, Sir Henry d'Esterre		
L	13 Nov	1776
CR	1 Jan	1781
CA	15 Jan	1783
RAB	23 Apr	1804
RAW	9 Nov	1805
RAR	28 Apr	1808
VAB	31 July	1810
VAW	1 Aug	1811
VAR	4 June	1814
AB	12 Aug	1819 (CH)
KCB	20 May	1820 (MB)
d	30 Mar	1823 (PMM)
D'ARCY, Gerrard		
L	11 Apr	1778
d		1782 (NMM)
DARCY, John		
L		1677
DARCY, Thomas		
L		1662
CA		1664
d	before	1689 (PJP)
DARE, Jeffrey		
L		
CA		1666
KIA	4 June	1666 (RM)
DARE, Thomas		
L	3 May	1711
d		1743 (PRO)
DARE, William		
L	22 Feb	1759
d		1771 (NMM)
DARELY, Arthur		
L	11 Aug	1813
CR	21 Aug	1827 (NMM)
CA	9 Nov	1848 (NMM)
d		1852 (NMM)
DARRACOTT, Henry Young		
L	3 Dec	1779
d		1807 (NMM)
DARRACOTT, Henry Young Man		
L	3 Feb	1815
HP		1816 (OB)
Ret CR	9 Feb	1860 (NMM)
d		1864 (NMM)
DARRACOTT, Thomas		
L	8 July	1795
d		1832 (NMM)
DARROCK, Archibald		
L	9 Sept	1741
d (drowned)	15 Feb	1760 (PJP)
DARTMOUTH, George Legge, Earl of		
See LEGGE, George, Earl of Dartmouth		
DASHWOOD, Sir Charles		
L	20 June	1794
CR	3 Aug	1799
CA	2 Nov	1801
Kt		1825 (CH)
RAB	22 July	1830 (NMM)
RAW	10 Jan	1837 (NMM)
RAR	28 June	1838 (NMM)
KCB	4 July	1840 (OB)
VAB	23 Nov	1841 (NMM)
VAW	20 Nov	1846 (NMM)
d	21 Sept	1847 (NMM)
DASHWOOD, Joseph		
L	7 Aug	1746 (NMM)
d	17 Oct	1747 (NMM)
DASHWOOD, William Bateman		
L	28 Jan	1808
CR	19 May	1812
CA	24 Oct	1818 (NMM)
Ret CA	1 Oct	1846 (LG)
Ret RA	8 July	1851 (NMM)
Ret VA	22 Nov	1857 (NMM)
Ret A	22 Nov	1862 (NMM)
d		1869 (NMM)
DATHAN, James Hartley		
L	2 July	1798
Ret CR	22 Oct	1841 (PRO)
d	2 Mar	1856 (PRO)
D'AUVERGNE, Corbet James		
See AUVERGNE, Corbet James d'		
D'AUVERGNE, Philip, Prince of Bouillon		
See AUVERGNE, Philip d'		
DAVENHILL, Matthew		
L	22 Jan	1806
Ret CR	2 Jan	1842 (NMM)
d		1856 (PRO)
DAVENPORT, Sir Salusbury Pryce		
L	27 Jan	1797 (NMM)
CR	29 Apr	1802 (NMM)
CA	8 May	1804 (NMM)
HP		1808 (MB)
CB	26 Sept	1831 (OB)
Ret RA	10 Jan	1837 (NMM)
KCH	21 Feb	1840 (OB)
RAB	17 Aug	1840 (NMM)
RAW	23 Nov	1841 (NMM)
d	17 Nov	1845 (LT)
DAVERS, Charles Sydney		
L	4 Nov	1790
CR	13 May	1794 (NMM)
CA	4 July	1795
d	6 Jan	1804 (NMM)
DAVERS, Henry		
L	2 June	1756
d		1760 (NMM)
DAVERS, Thomas		
L		

CR		
CA	1 June	1713
RAR	10 Dec	1743 (LG)
VAW	23 June	1744
VAR	23 Apr	1745
d	17 Sept	1746 (PRO)
DAVEY, George		
L	25 May	1780
CR	18 Jan	1796
d		1829 (MB)
DAVEY, Thomas		
See SPRY, Thomas		
DAVEY, William		
L	5 Mar	1782
d		1813 (NMM)
DAVIDS, Charles		
L	14 Aug	1739
SUP		1754 (PMM)
d		1754(5) (NMM)
DAVIDS, John		
L	7 Dec	1778
d	23 Oct	1789 (M)
DAVIDSON, Alexander (1)		
L	7 June	1800
T		
d	Nov	1821 (PRO)
DAVIDSON, Alexander (2)		
L	25 Mar	1809
d		1834 (NMM)
DAVIDSON, Anthony		
L	1 Dec	1782
d		1786 (NMM)
DAVIDSON, Henry		
L	14 Nov	1739
d		1743(4) (NMM)
DAVIDSON, Peter		
L	13 July	1801
d		1814 (NMM)
DAVIDSON, William (1)		
L	16 Oct	1762
d		1785 (PRO)
DAVIDSON, William (2)		
L	7 May	1802
d		1810 (PRO)
DAVIE, John		
L	2 Sept	1793
CR	6 Sept	1800
CA	22 Aug	1809
d	13 Feb	1825 (MB)
DAVIE, William James		
L	19 Nov	1801
Dismissed		1802 (PRO)
DAVIES, Arthur		
L	27 Dec	1808
Ret CR	3 Nov	1846 (NMM)
d	13 July	1853 (NMM)
DAVIES, Arthur		
See DAVYS, Arthur		
DAVIES, David		
L	27 June	1809
d		1810 (NMM)
DAVIES, David Gam		
L	1 Mar	1815 (NMM)
d		1853 (NMM)
DAVIES, Edward (1)		
L	9 Sept	1793
d		1810 (PRO)
DAVIES, Edward (2)		
L	30 July	1804
d	Dec	1828 (NMM)
DAVIES, Francis Edisbury		
L	29 Apr	1778
d	25 July	1823 (PRO)
DAVIES, George		
L	1 Jan	1784
CR	5 Feb	1798
CA	21 Oct	1810
d		1819 (PRO)
DAVIES, Hamilton		
T		
L	20 Nov	1812
Ret CR	28 May	1855 (PRO)
d	3 Oct	1859 (NMM)
DAVIES, Henry Thomas		
L	24 Dec	1800
CR	28 July	1806
CA	19 Feb	1814
Ret CA	1 Oct	1846 (NMM)
Ret RA	12 Mar	1849 (LG)
d		1869 (PRO)
DAVIES, James (1)		
L	19 Jan	1797
d		1798 (NMM)
DAVIES, James (2)		
L	11 Dec	1807
CR	16 Sept	1816 (PRO)
d		1825 (NMM)
DAVIES, John (1)		
L	26 July	1727
Gone		1744 (PRO)
DAVIES, John (2)		
L	17 Nov	1790
CR	16 Aug	1796
d	29 Jan	1830 (PRO)
DAVIES, John (3)		
L	29 Apr	1797
CR	3 June	1808
d		1815 (NMM)
DAVIES, John (4)		
L	2 Feb	1809
CR	8 Oct	1816 (PRO)
HP	8 Oct	1816 (OB)
Ret CA	1 July	1851 (NMM)
d	21 May	1865 (NMM)
DAVIES, John (5)		
L	7 Mar	1815
d		1851 (NMM)
DAVIES, John George		
L	7 July	1808
HP	Nov	1808 –
	Aug	1810 (OB)
HP	26 Nov	1819 (OB)
Ret CR	19 July	1841 (NMM)
d		1867 (NMM)

DAVIES, Lewis (1)
L 2 Apr 1746
d 1789 (NMM)

DAVIES, Lewis (2)
L 23 Sept 1808
CR 26 Jan 1826 (PRO)
CA 21 Oct 1827 (PRO)
CB 13 Nov 1827 (LG)
d 14 Mar 1843 (NMM)

DAVIES, Peregrine Charles
L 17 Feb 1815
d 1825 (PRO)

DAVIES, Peter
L 24 Aug 1794
d 1803 (NMM)

DAVIES, Richard
L 6 Mar 1802
d 16 Oct 1813 (LT)

DAVIES, Richard Longfield
L 8 June 1799
Ret CR 1 Dec 1830 (PRO)
d 15 May 1846 (OB)

DAVIES, Richard Plummer
L 24 Dec 1805
CR 11 Apr 1809 (NMM)
CA 19 Jan 1812 (NMM)
d Dec 1837 (NMM)

DAVIES, Samuel
L 10 Apr 1802
d 4 Nov 1810

DAVIES, Walter
L 18 July 1744
d 1746 (NMM)

DAVIES, William (1)
L 1664
CA 18 Apr 1665
RAD 13 Dec 1688
VAD 1 May 1689
VAR 12 June 1689

DAVIES, William (2)
L
CA 1665
d before 1689 (PJP)

DAVIES, William (3)
L
CR 26 Feb 1713 (PRO)
CA 30 June 1719
COM V July 1747 (PJP)
COMM (Deptford) Dec 1747 (PJP)
SUP 1753
d 16 Feb 1759

DAVIES, William (4)
L 13 June 1801
d 16 Mar 1830 (NMM)

DAVIES, William (5)
L 29 Aug 1806
d 1818 (PRO)

DAVIS, Arthur
See DAVIES, Arthur

DAVIS, Arthur
See DAVYS, Arthur

DAVIS , Arthur
L
CR
CA 1 Jan 1713
d 10 Apr 1720 (PRO)

DAVIES, Charles
L 26 May 1814
d 1832 (NMM)

DAVIS, Francis
L 1 June 1742
CR 16 May 1758
d 6 Sept 1770 (PRO)

DAVIES, George (1)
L 8 Sept 1781
d 1794 (NMM)

DAVIS, George (2)
L 30 Aug 1806
d 1810 (NMM)

DAVIS, George Evan
L 10 Mar 1815
Ret CR 20 Jan 1842 (NMM)
d 11 May 1850 (NMM)

DAVIS, Henry (1)
L
CA 7 June 1666 (RM)

DAVIS, Henry (2)
L 24 Sept 1756
CR 20 June 1765
CA 26 May 1768
d (drowned) 31 Dec 1776 (CH)

DAVIS, Henry (3)
L 8 May 1759
d 1773 (PRO)

DAVIS, Henry (4)
L 29 Dec 1796
CR 21 Oct 1810
d 1837 (NMM)

DAVIS, Henry (5)
L 31 Mar 1808
d 1818 (NMM)

DAVIS, Henry (6)
L 21 Mar 1812
d 1816 (NMM)

DAVIS, Henry (7)
L 21 Mar 1812
Placed permanently fourth of the junior lieutenants of 1814, allowed to take seniority as of 31 Aug 1816 (PRO)
d 26 Sept 1823 (PRO)

DAVIS, Henry (8)
L 24 Feb 1815
d 1862 (NMM)

DAVIS, James
L 21 Mar 1812
d 1856 (NMM)

DAVIS, John (1)
L
CA 10 July 1666 (RM)

DAVIS, John (2)
L 4 Jan 1799
d 1800 (PRO)

DAVIS, John (3)
L 4 July 1799
d 1804(5) (PRO)

DAVIS, John (4)
L 24 Aug 1804
d 1815 (PRO)

DAVIS, John (5)
L 6 Dec 1805
d 1807 (PRO)

DAVIS, John (6)
L 18 Feb 1815
HP 18 Feb 1815 (OB)
Ret CR 1 Oct 1860 (NMM)
d 1862 (NMM)

DAVIS, John
See DAVIES, John (1)

DAVIS, Joseph William
L 27 Dec 1799
d 1801 (PRO)

DAVIS, Lewis
L 22 Mar 1797
d 1805(6) (NMM)

DAVIS, Matthew (1)
L 1 Mar 1705
d 1727 (PRO)

DAVIS, Matthew (2)
L 22 May 1778
d (drowned) 22 Feb 1782 (CH)

DAVIS, Nathaniel
L 30 May 1744
d 18 May 1765 (PMM)

DAVIS, Philip
L 1666

DAVIS, Richard (1)
L
CR
CA 1 Jan 1713
d 2 Aug 1718

DAVIS, Richard (2)
L 31 Aug 1739
d 1757 (PRO)

DAVIS, Robert
L 3 Feb 1815
Ret CR 19 Oct 1859 (PRO)
d 20 Nov 1865 (PRO)

DAVIS, Roger
L 30 Apr 1678
d before 1689 (PJP)

DAVIS, Thomas
L 26 Feb 1802
d 1804 (NMM)

DAVIS, Thomas John James William
L 2 Feb 1809
d 27 Aug 1831 (PRO)

DAVIS, William (1)
L
CA 26 Aug 1674

DAVIS, William (2)
L 29 Sept 1795
Dismissed 1799 (PRO)

DAVIS, William (3)
L 9 Aug 1797
d 1800 (PRO)

DAVIS, William (4)
L 15 Aug 1799
d 1812 (PRO)

DAVIS, William (5)
L 13 Feb 1802
d 1805(6) (PRO)

DAVIS, William Rees
L 15 Feb 1815
HP 15 Feb 1815 (OB)
Ret CR 22 Oct 1853 (PRO)
d 8 Feb 1860 (PRO)

DAVIS, William Robert
L 18 Mar 1778
d 1 July 1795 (PRO)

DAVISON, Edward Baker
L 25 Apr 1807
d 1847 (PRO)

DAVISON, Gaire
L 30 Mar 1779
d 1780(1) (PRO)

DAVISON, James
L
CA 17 June 1690
(7 July 1692 in C)

DAVISON, John
L
CA 7 July 1690
SUP 1702
d 12 July 1709

DAVISON, Kilgour
L 17 July 1811
Ret CR 1 July 1852 (PRO)
d 1863 (PRO)

DAVY, John
L 5 Jan 1810
CR 15 July 1814
Ret CA 1 July 1851 (PRO)
d Aug 1876 (PRO)

DAVYS, Arthur
L 4 Apr 1720 (NMM)
CR
CA 11 Nov 1729
d 2 May 1743

DAWBNEY, John
L 30 Jan 1702
SUP 20 Mar 1738 (PMM)
d 1741 (PMM)

DAWE, Harry
L 27 Nov 1782
SUP CR 28 Oct 1818 (NMM)
d 2 Dec 1841 (PRO)

DAWES, Henry
L
CA 1665
KIA 17 May 1667 (CH)

DAWES, John (1)
L 27 Oct 1688

DAWES, John (2)
L 1 Dec 1797
d 1 Sept 1807 (NMM)

DAWES, Philip
L
CA 1 June 1693
(13 Sept 1693 in C)
Dismissed 27 June 1710 (PRO)

DAWES, Richard
L 1 Mar 1782
d 6 June 1794 (PRO)

DAWES, William
L 2 Aug 1806
d 1819 (PRO)

DAWKINS, Jeremiah
L 22 Nov 1790
d 1800 (PRO)

DAWKINS, William Robert
L 2 July 1810
CR 1 Sept 1815

DAWNAY, Hon. George
L 11 Jan 1720
CR
CA 8 Jan 1742
d 16 Nov 1766

DAWS, John
L 17 June 1757
d 4 June 1763 (PMM)

DAWS, Philip
See DAWES, Philip

DAWS, Thomas
L 25 Mar 1809
d 1838 (NMM)

DAWSON, George (1)
L 9 Aug 1762
CR 13 May 1776
CA 9 Sept 1777
Dismissed 20 Nov 1788 (PRO)

DAWSON, George (2)
L 26 Sept 1793
d 1796 (PRO)

DAWSON, Hon. Henry
L 16 Feb 1805
CR 25 Sept 1806
CA 1 Aug 1811
d 26 May 1841 (NMM)

DAWSON, Hutton
L 9 May 1809
CR 20 Oct 1812
d 11 Feb 1813 (PRO)

DAWSON, John (1)
L 1666
CA 1670
d 1675 (DDA)

DAWSON, John (2)
L 1672
d before 1689 (PJP)

DAWSON, John (3)
L 10 Mar 1781
CR 1 June 1794
CA 3 Apr 1795
SUP RA 28 June 1814
d June 1836 (PRO)

DAWSON, John (4)
L 27 Aug 1811
Ret CR 1 Oct 1852 (NMM)
d 1853 (PRO)

DAWSON, John Francis
L 21 Mar 1812
d 2 Dec 1825 (PRO)

DAWSON, Lucius Henry
L 28 Oct 1790
CR 10 June 1795
d 11 Oct 1795 (PRO)

DAWSON, Matthew
L
CA 1672

DAWSON, Robert
L 1673

DAWSON, William (1)
L 1664

DAWSON, William (2)
L 20 Mar 1802
CR 8 Mar 1808
CA 9 Mar 1809
d 29 Sept 1811 (PRO)

DAY, Bartholomew George Smith
T
L 1 Feb 1815
Ret CR 23 July 1860 (PRO)
d 1868 (NMM)

DAY, Bunbury
L 23 June 1760
d 10 Mar 1762 (LG)

DAY, Charles Escourt
L 27 Dec 1808
Ret CR 3 Nov 1846 (PRO)
d Aug 1860 (PRO)

DAY, Christopher
L 7 Oct 1762
d 4 Nov 1800

DAY, George
L 9 July 1762
CR 31 Dec 1779
d 3 Feb 1791

DAY, George Major
L 22 July 1794
d 1796 (PRO)

DAY, John (1)
L 1664
CA 4 July 1666 (RM)
d before 1689 (PJP)

DAY, John (2)
L 21 Dec 1808
Ret CR 3 Nov 1846 (PRO)
d 10 Dec 1854 (PRO)

DAY, John Jackson
L 3 Nov 1790
d 1800 (PRO)

DAY, Richard
L 1664
CA 1671
d before 1689 (PJP)

DAY, Robert
L 1666
d before 1689 (PJP)

DAY, Thomas (1)
L 4 Oct 1688
CA 5 Aug 1695
d 20 June 1703

DAY, Thomas (2)
L 16 Nov 1757
d 8 Mar 1762 (PRO)

DAY, Thomas (3)
L 5 Sept 1810
d 1819 (PRO)

DAY, William
L 8 Oct 1794
CR 27 June 1797
CA 29 Apr 1802
d 1806 (PRO)

DAYRELL, Henry
L 24 Apr 1782
SUP CR 23 June 1817 (PRO)
d Feb 1823 (PRO)

DEACON, Henry
L 28 Oct 1777
CR 1 Dec 1787 (MB)
d 13 Apr 1836 (PRO)

DEACON, Henry Collins
L 24 Feb 1808
CR 7 June 1814
CA 2 Apr 1817 (PRO)
Ret CA 1 Oct 1846 (PRO)
Ret RA 16 June 1851 (PRO)
Ret VA 30 July 1857 (PRO)
Ret A 10 Nov 1862 (PRO)
d 9 Nov 1869 (PRO)

DEACON, James
L 31 Mar 1779
CR 15 Apr 1782
CA 25 Oct 1809
d 27 Feb 1813 (PRO)

DEACON, John
L 24 July 1778
d 1819 (PRO)

DEACON, Richard
L 31 Mar 1759
KIA 17 Apr 1780 (LG)

DEACON, Sabine
L 2 Jan 1746
CR 27 Sept 1758
d 27 July 1759 (PRO)

DEAN, John Edward
L 15 Feb 1815
d 1841 (PRO)

DEAN, Joseph
See DEANE, Joseph

DEAN, William (1)
L 15 Apr 1799
Dismissed 1804 (PRO)
Restored 1821 (PRO)
d 1826 (PRO)

DEAN, William (2)
L 22 Jan 1806
CR 15 June 1814
d 1819 (PRO)

DEAN, William (3)
L 9 Nov 1807
d 1820 (PRO)

DEANE, Anthony
L 1664
d before 1689 (PJP)

DEANE, Edward
L 22 Oct 1755
d 1760 (NMM)

DEANE, Joseph
L 29 Apr 1755
CR 23 Apr 1758
CA 17 Oct 1758
d 12 Jan 1780 (NMM)

DEANE, Richard
L 28 Aug 1695
Gone 1719 (PRO)

DEANE, Robert
L
CA 1 Apr 1690 (PRO)
d 6 Jan 1700 (PRO)

DEANS, James
Later DUNDAS, Sir James Whitley Deans
L 28 May 1805
CR 8 Oct 1806
CA 13 Oct 1807
MP (Greenwich) 1832–1834 (DNB)
MP (Devizes) 1836–1838 (DNB)
CB 25 Oct 1839 (OB)
MP (Greenwich) 1841–1852 (DNB)
COM AD 25 June–8 Sept 1841 (AO)
RAB 23 Nov 1841 (NMM)
COM AD 13 July 1846–
13 Feb 1852 (AO)
RAW 13 May 1847 (NMM)
RAR 18 Oct 1849 (NMM)
VAB 17 Dec 1852 (NMM)
VAW 15 Apr 1854 (NMM)
GCB 5 July 1855 (DNB)
VAR 21 Oct 1856 (NMM)
AB 8 Dec 1857 (NMM)
AW 11 Feb 1861 (NMM)
d 3 Oct 1862 (DNB)

DEANS, Robert (1)
L 20 June 1765
CR 7 Sept 1778
CA 9 Mar 1780
RAW 14 Feb 1799
RAR 1 Jan 1801
VAB 23 Apr 1804
VAR 9 Nov 1805
AB 31 July 1810
AW 12 Aug 1812
d Jan 1815 (PRO)

DEANS, Robert (2)
L 15 June 1811
CR 9 Sept 1818 (NMM)
CA 28 June 1838 (NMM)
Ret CA 6 July 1852 (NMM)
Ret RA 10 Sept 1857 (NMM)
Ret VA 9 Feb 1864 (NMM)
d 15 July 1867 (NMM)

DEARDS, John
L 3 July 1746
d 1754(5) (NMM)

DEARING, Griffith
See DERING, Griffith

DEBAT, Peter
L 10 Mar 1759
d 1761 (NMM)

DEBENHAM, John
L 12 Sept 1796
CR 27 Aug 1814
d 15 June 1847 (NMM)

DECHAMP, Richard

L	12 Sept	1783
SUP CR	18 Oct	1821 (NMM)
d		1840 (NMM)

DECKAR, Samuel
See DEECKER, Samuel Bartlett

DECOUERDOUX, George James

L	11 Oct	1793
Ret CR	24 Nov	1827 (NMM)
d	Sept	1831 (PRO)

DECOUERDOUX, George Lacey

L	16 Apr	1802
T		
Ret CR	15 June	1844 (NMM)
d	10 Mar	1850 (PRO)

DE COURCY, Hon. Almericus
See COURCY, Hon. Almericus de

DE COURCY, Hon. Michael
See COURCY, Hon. Michael de

DE COURCY, Nevinson
See COURCY, Nevinson de

DE CRESPIGNY, Augustus
See CRESPIGNY, Augustus

DEEBLE, John

L	7 May	1777
d		1794 (PRO)

DEECKER, Samuel Bartlett
Formerly DECKAR, Samuel

L	24 May	1805
CR	17 Apr	1810
CA	7 June	1814
d	23 Dec	1835 (PRO)

DEERING, Daniel (1)

L	27 Nov	1679
CA	16 July	1681
d	5 Apr	1690

DEERING, Daniel (2)

L	26 Jan	1757
CR	17 Apr	1758
CA	18 Nov	1758
d	20 May	1760 (PRO)

DEERING, Henry

L		
CR		
CA	4 Nov	1703
d	16 Nov	1706

DEERING, Unton

L	7 Jan	1692
?CR	17 Sept	1700 (PRO)
?CA	4 May	1703 (PRO)
d	16 Nov	1706 (PRO)

DE GEUS, John
See GEUS, John de

DE HAVILLAND, James

L	12 Jan	1759
d		1785 (PRO)

DELAFONS, John

L	16 May	1794
CR	27 Apr	1801
HP	Dec	1815 (OB)

DELAFONS, Thomas

L	25 Sept	1794
CR	28 Apr	1814
d	?28 Dec	1848 (NMM)

DELAFONS, William Philip

L	3 Sept	1810
HP	Nov	1815 (OB)
Ret CR	3 Jan	1851 (NMM)
d		1854 (PRO)

DELAFOSSE, Edward Hollingworth

L	9 Apr	1808
CR	16 Sept	1816 (NMM)
CA	28 July	1851 (NMM)
Ret RA	1 Apr	1870 (NMM)
d	27 Apr	1870 (NMM)

DELAMOTTE, Philip

L	10 Feb	1800
d		1803 (PRO)

DELANCEY, Charles Stephenworth

L	16 Apr	1808
d	6 May	1840 (PRO)

DELANEY, Oliver

L	18 Jan	1771
d		1790 (PRO)

DE L'ANGLE, Merrick
See L'ANGLE, Merrick de

DELANOE, George Augustus

L	8 Oct	1793
CR	16 June	1797
d		1802 (PRO)

DELAP, Robert

L	11 Feb	1795
HP	12 Aug	1815 (OB)
d		1849 (NMM)

DELAP, William

L	3 Mar	1779
d (drowned)	5 Oct	1780 (PJP)

DE LA TOUCHE, John
See LA TOUCHE, John de

DELAVAL(L), Francis Blake

L	25 July	1711 (PRO)
CR		
CA	26 Mar	1719
d	11 Dec	1752

DELAVAL(L), George

L		
CA	28 Oct	1695
MP (West Looe)		1715–
	22 June	1723 (MPS)
RAB	28 Mar	1718
RAW	28 Mar	1718 (C)
RAR	10 Mar	1719
VAW	16 Feb	1723
d	22 June	1723 (MPS)

DELAVAL(L), Sir Ralph

L		1666 (P)
CA	6 Jan	1673 (DNB)
CAF		
(First Foot Guards)	9 Feb	1685 (EAD)
LCF		
(First Foot Guards)	4 June	1687 (EAD)
RAR	13 Feb	1689 (PRO)
Kt	31 May	1690 (DNB)
VAB	31 May	1690 (DNB)
VAR	1 Jan	1692
COMAD	15 Apr	1693–
	2 May	1694 (AO)
AB	1 July	1693

MP
(Great Bedwin) 1695–1698 (DNB)
SUP 30 Mar 1701 (DNB)
d 23 Jan 1707 (DNB)

DELGARNO, Arthur
L
CR
CA 18 Dec 1714
d 18 May 1729 (PRO)

DELGARNO, Maurice
L 24 Mar 1777
CR 1 Dec 1787
CA 5 Mar 1790
d 31 July 1796 (LT)

DE LISLE, Peter
L 8 June 1811
d 1812 (PRO)

DELME, George
L 19 Sept 1815
CR 21 Feb 1828 (NMM)
Ret CA 1 Apr 1856 (NMM)
d 18 June 1872 (NMM)

DELORAINE, Hon. Henry Scott, Earl of
See SCOTT, Henry (2)

DEMBRY, John
L 13 Dec 1799 (NMM)
d 1880 (NMM)

DENBY, Earl of
See CARMARTHEN, Marquess of

DENCH, Thomas
L 23 Jan 1801
CR 24 Apr 1808
CA 4 June 1828 (MB)
Ret CA 4 June 1848 (PRO)
d 4 May 1853 (NMM)

DENEW, John
L 27 Apr 1703
SUP 20 Mar 1738 (PMM)
d 19 July 1738 (PMM)

DENIS, Sir Peter
L 12 Nov 1739
CR 25 June 1744
CA 9 Feb 1745
MP
(Hedon) 1754–1768 (MPN)
Cre Bt 19 Sept 1767 (DNB)
RAB 18 Oct 1770
RAW 24 Oct 1770
VAB 31 Mar 1775 (CH)
VAW 5 Feb 1776 (CH)
VAR 29 Jan 1778 (CH)
d 12 June 1778 (DNB)

DENISON, Charles
L 24 Mar 1807
d 5 Mar 1844 (PRO)

DENISON, Charles
See DENNISON, Charles

DENMAN, Benjamin
L 23 Dec 1793
d 31 Jan 1803

DENMAN, Edward
L 14 June 1796
CR 17 Feb 1810
CA 27 May 1825 (OB)
d 6 July 1848 (OB)

DENN, Jonathan
L 19 Jan 1691
CR
CA 12 Jan 1703 (PRO)
d 26 Mar 1703 (PRO)

DENNE, William
L 31 May 1756
CR 16 Sept 1777
CA 20 Oct 1779
d 28 Dec 1791

DENNETT, Thomas
L
CR 25 Aug 1696 (PJP)
CA 1 Jan 1713
Gone 1737 (PRO)

DENNIS, Edward
L 21 Feb 1815
d 7 Dec 1828 (PRO)

DENNIS, Gabriel
L 11 Jan 1802
d 1807 (PRO)

DENNIS, Henry (1)
L 29 July 1727
CR 12 Jan 1741
CA 6 June 1741
SUP RA 29 Sept 1757
d 12 Aug 1767 (PRO)

DENNIS, Henry (2)
L 1 Feb 1815
d 27 June 1825 (PRO)

DENNIS, James Sam Aked
L 24 Sept 1811
CR 22 Jan 1841 (NMM)
CA 18 July 1857 (NMM)
Ret RA 20 Apr 1875 (NMM)
Ret VA 2 Aug 1879 (NMM)
d 1881 (NMM)

DENNIS, John
L 21 Apr 1741
d 1755(6) (PRO)

DENNIS, Peter
See DENIS, Sir Peter

DENNISON, Charles
L 22 Mar 1725
CR
CA 26 Apr 1737
d 28 Oct 1741 (PRO)

DENNYS, Lardner
T
L 6 Feb 1812
Ret CR 30 July 1853 (NMM)
d 18 Nov 1864 (NMM)

DENSTER, Thomas
L 15 June 1812
d 1853 (PRO)

DENT, Charles
L 11 Jan 1798
d 1799 (PRO)

DENT, Cotton
L 18 May 1735
CR 28 Dec 1743 (NMM)
CA 23 Dec 1746
d 28 Jan 1761

DENT, Digby (1)
L 12 Apr 1703 (PRO)
CR 25 Aug 1709 (PRO)
CA 5 Oct 1715
d 7 Aug 1737 (PRO)

DENT, Digby (2)
L 2 Mar 1734
CR 6 Aug 1737
CA 5 June 1738
COM E 3 Apr–24 June 1756 (NBO)
CONT 24 June–29 Dec 1756 (NBO)
COM E 29 Dec 1756–
7 June 1761 (NBO)
d 7 June 1761 (NBO)

DENT, Sir Digby (3)
L
CR
CA 7 July 1758
Kt 1778 (PJP)
SUP RA 5 May 1788
d 15 Mar 1817 (PRO)

DENT, Digby (4)
L 9 May 1781
CR 2 Oct 1797
d 14 Nov 1798 (PRO)

DENT, Digby (5)
T
L 6 Feb 1812
CR 30 Oct 1820 (NMM)
Ret CA 1 Apr 1856 (NMM)
d 15 Apr 1861 (NMM)

DENYER, James Richard
L 20 Sept 1815
Ret CR 1 July 1864 (NMM)
d 1874 (PRO)

DERBY, John
L 7 Dec 1796
d 25 Apr 1831 (PRO)

DERBY, Joseph
L 17 Mar 1807
d Apr 1810 (PRO)

DERING, Griffith
L 10 June 1717
CR 5 Oct 1736 (PRO)
CA 28 July 1738 (PRO)
d Jan 1741

DERING, Robert Charles
L 20 Nov 1790
d 1794 (PRO)

DERINZY, Matthew
L 30 June 1814
d 1817 (PRO)

DE RIPPE, James
See RIPPE, James de

DE ROVERA, Frederick
See ROVERA, Frederick de

DERRIMAN, James
L 26 Jan 1814
d 1837 (PRO)

DERRY, John
L 22 Aug 1794
Ret CR 26 Nov 1830 (PRO)
d 28 Dec 1847 (PRO)

DESBOROUGH, Robert
L 8 Jan 1692

DESBOROW, Charles
L
CR 7 July 1693 (PRO)
CA 24 Aug 1696 (PRO)
d 8 Mar 1723

DESERAT, Samuel Thomas
L 3 Aug 1799
d 1834 (NMM)

DESPARD, Green
L 19 Jan 1779
d 7 Dec 1786 (PMM)

DESPOURRINS, Peter
L 27 Dec 1797
Ret CR 1 Dec 1830 (NMM)
d 1857 (NMM)

DE STARCK, Mauritius Adolphus Newton
See STARCK, Mauritius Adolphus Newton de

DES TOMBE, Pet Jac
See TOMBE, Peter Jacob

DEUCHAR, Patrick
T
L 29 Nov 1813
Ret CR 15 July 1856 (NMM)
d 1869 (TR)

DEVERUEX, Peirce
L 1671
d 11 Aug 1673

DE VITRE, John Denis
L 3 Mar 1781
d 29 Dec 1846 (LT)

DEVON, Sir Thomas Barker
L 8 May 1804
CR 4 May 1813
CA 27 May 1825 (NMM)
KCH 7 Dec 1838 (OB)
d 12 May 1846 (OB)

DEVONSHIRE, Henry
L 10 June 1797

DEVONSHIRE, Sir John Ferris
L 27 Aug 1795
CR 14 Dec 1796
CA 27 Apr 1801
Ret RA 23 July 1830 (NMM)
d 19 Feb 1839 (NMM)

DEVONSHIRE, Richard
L 11 May 1804
CR 27 Aug 1814
CA 28 June 1838 (NMM)
Ret CA 13 Apr 1852 (PRO)
Ret RA 10 Sept 1857 (NMM)
d 19 Mar 1860 (NMM)

DEVONSHIRE, William Ney
L 15 Oct 1812
d 25 Aug 1820 (NMM)

DEW, Anthony
L 1664

DEW, George
L 8 Mar 1815
d 4 Jan 1861 (NMM)

DEWER, John
L 21 Mar 1812

Ret CR	2 Jan	1854 (NMM)
d		1865 (NMM)
DEWEY, Thomas		
L	27 Sept	1759
CR	26 Apr	1789
d		1810 (PRO)
DEWSHIP, Joseph		
L	8 Aug	1799
d	27 Oct	1837 (NMM)
DIAMOND, Thomas		
L		
CA		1660
d	before	1689 (PJP)
DICK, John		
L	4 Aug	1794
CR	28 June	1796
CA	29 Apr	1802
HP		1812 (MB)
RAW	10 Jan	1837 (NMM)
RAR	23 Nov	1841 (NMM)
VAB	9 Nov	1846 (NMM)
VAW	24 Apr	1847 (NMM)
VAR	4 May	1849 (NMM)
AB	16 Jan	1852 (NMM)
d	12 Feb	1862 (NMM)
DICK, Thomas		
L	11 Mar	1799
CR	21 Oct	1810
CA	7 June	1814
Ret CA	1 Oct	1846 (NMM)
Ret RA	30 Oct	1849 (NMM)
Ret VA	21 Oct	1856 (NMM)
Ret A	15 Jan	1862 (NMM)
d	12 Feb	1862 (NMM)
DICK, William		
L	7 Oct	1795
d		1810 (NMM)
DICKEN, Henry Perry		
L	7 Mar	1815
CR	5 Feb	1858 (NMM)
d	30 May	1883 (PRO)
DICKENS, William		
L	16 Nov	1756
d		1794 (NMM)
DICKENSON, Charles		
L	21 Mar	1812
KIA	4 Sept	1814 (JH)
DICKENSON, Richard		
L		1665
CA	13 June	1667
DICKINS, Francis George		
L	21 Apr	1803
CR	6 Aug	1807
CA	1 Aug	1811
d		1818 (NMM)
DICKINS, George		
L	13 July	1807
CR	13 Nov	1813
d (drowned)	17 Jan	1815 (CH)
DICKINS, Samuel Trevor		
L	4 Aug	1806
CR	5 Apr	1814
HP	17 Dec	1814 (OB)
Ret CA	1 July	1851 (NMM)
d		1869 (NMM)
DICKINSON, David Aikmount		
L	28 May	1806 (PRO)
d		1811 (PRO)
DICKINSON, Francis		
L	23 Sept	1797
CR	22 Jan	1806
d	23 Apr	1812 (PRO)
DICKINSON, Frederick		
L	14 May	1810
d		1833 (PRO)
DICKINSON, James (1)		
L	24 Aug	1759
CR	19 June	1779
CA	21 Sept	1790
d	23 Jan	1794 (LT)
DICKINSON, James (2)		
L	14 Aug	1794
CR	21 Oct	1810
d	23 Oct	1813 (PJP)
DICKINSON, James (3)		
L	19 Dec	1807
CR	13 Mar	1811
KIA	23 Jan	1815 (JH)
DICKINSON, John		
L	30 Apr	1678
DICKINSON, Richard		
L	29 Aug	1806
CR	29 Jan	1821 (PRO)
CB	31 Nov	1827 (LG)
CA	13 May	1828 (NMM)
d	1 Jan	1849 (NMM)
DICKINSON, Samuel		
L		
CA		1665
d	before	1689 (PJP)
DICKINSON, Thomas (1)		
L	25 Jan	1778
CR	5 Dec	1796
d	24 May	1828 (LTE)
DICKINSON, Thomas (2)		
T	wounded	
L	15 Aug	1806
Cr	15 June	1814
CA	29 Nov	1832 (NMM)
Ret CA		1847 (NMM)
DICKONSON, Lacy		
L	31 May	1809
Ret CR	5 Oct	1847 (PRO)
d		1861 (NMM)
DICKSEY, William		
See DIXEY, William		
DICKSON, Sir Archibald (1)		
L	19 Sept	1759
CR	10 Jan	1771
CA	31 Jan	1774
RAB	12 Apr	1794
RAW	4 July	1794
VAB	1 June	1795
AB	1 Jan	1801
Cre Bt	4 Sept	1802 (LG)
d	30 May	1803 (LT)

DICKSON, Archibald (2)
L 24 July 1794
CR 1 Jan 1801
CA 29 Apr 1802

DICKSON, Sir Archibald Collingwood
L 31 May 1791
CR 15 Aug 1795 (NMM)
CA 12 Dec 1796
Inh Bt 1803 (PJP)
RAB 12 Aug 1819 (NMM)
RAW 19 July 1821 (NMM)
RAR 27 May 1825 (NMM)
d 18 June 1827 (NMM)

DICKSON, David John
L 8 Nov 1809
CR 29 Sept 1827 (NMM)
Ret CA 1 Apr 1856 (NMM)
d 25 Nov 1870 (NMM)

DICKSON, Edward Stirling
L 9 July 1780
CR 7 July 1796
CA 11 Aug 1800
RAB 22 July 1830 (NMM)
RAR 10 Jan 1837 (NMM)
VAW 23 Nov 1841 (NMM)
d 28 Jan 1844 (LT)

DICKSON, James
L 8 Dec 1779
d 1795 (NMM)

DICKSON, Michael
L 27 Dec 1808 (NMM)
CR 29 July 1825 (NMM)
d 10 Dec 1827 (NMM)

DICKSON, William (1)
L 31 Dec 1755
CR 10 May 1765 (NMM)
CA 2 May 1766
RAB 1 Feb 1793
RAW 12 Apr 1794
VAB 4 July 1794
VAW 1 June 1795
AB 14 Feb 1799
d 17 May 1803 (PRO)

DICKSON, William (2)
L 15 Nov 1762
d 1796 (NMM)

DICKSON, William (3)
L 21 Aug 1812
HP 6 Feb 1816 (OB)
d 1854 (NMM)

DICKSON, William Henry
L 16 Jan 1806
CR 21 Aug 1815
d 30 Nov 1850 (NMM)

DIDHAM, Philemon
L 19 Jan 1795
Dismissed 1801 (NMM)

DIEAS, Thomas
L 17 Nov 1694

DIGBY, Everard
L 10 Feb 1815
HP Dec 1846 (OB)
Ret CR 23 July 1860 (NMM)
d 25 Feb 1873 (NMM)

DIGBY, Francis
L 1666
CA 7 June 1666 (RM)
KIA 28 May 1672 (LG)

DIGBY, George
L 13 Oct 1800
CR 19 Apr 1802
CA 2 Jan 1806
d 15 Jan 1829 (NMM)

DIGBY, Sir Henry
L 20 Oct 1790
CR 11 Aug 1795 (PRO)
CA 16 Dec 1796
T
CB 2 Jan 1815 (LG)
RAB 12 Aug 1819 (NMM)
RAR 27 May 1825 (NMM)
VAB 22 July 1830 (NMM)
KCB 16 Mar 1831 (LG)
VAW 10 Jan 1837 (NMM)
AB 23 Nov 1841 (NMM)
GCB 1842 (TR)
d 13 Aug 1842 (NMM)

DIGBY, Joseph
L 11 Dec 1807
CR 8 Feb 1812
CA 8 Sept 1815
Ret CA 1 Oct 1846 (NMM)
Ret RA 21 Mar 1851 (NMM)
Ret VA 9 July 1857 (NMM)
d 5 Mar 1860 (NMM)

DIGBY, Martin
L 23 Dec 1776
SUP CR 21 Feb 1810
d 1820 (NMM)

DIGBY, Hon. Robert
L 29 Oct 1752
CR
CA 9 Aug 1755
MP (Wells) 15 Dec 1757–1761 (MPN)
CRM 3 Apr 1775 (AL)
RAB 29 Mar 1779
RAR 26 Sept 1780
VAB 24 Sept 1787
VAW 21 Sept 1790 (CH)
VAR 1 Feb 1793
AB 12 Apr 1794
AW 1 June 1795
AR 9 Nov 1805
d 25 Feb 1814 (DNB)

DIGBY, Stephen Thomas
L 6 May 1796
CR 22 Apr 1800
CA 14 Apr 1802
d 8 Apr 1820 (NMM)

DIGGES, Dudley
L 13 July 1745
CR
CA 18 Dec 1753
d 14 Oct 1779 (LTE)

DIGGIN, Samuel
L 13 Mar 1815
d 1822 (PRO)

DIGGS, Dudley
See DIGGES, Dudley

DILKE, William
L 23 May 1717
CR 26 July 1738 (PRO)
CA 16 Jan 1741
Dismissed 11 Feb 1744
Restored ?1753 (PRO)
d 30 May 1756

DILKES, Charles
L 6 Jan 1797
CR 20 Mar 1805
CA 18 Jan 1809
CB 4 July 1840 (OB)
d 5 Oct 1846 (NMM)

DILKES, John
L 31 July 1762 (PRO)
CR 1 Aug 1782
CA 21 Sept 1790
RAB 28 Apr 1808
RAW 25 Oct 1809
RAR 3 July 1810 (NMM)
VAB 12 Aug 1812
VAW 4 June 1814
VAR 12 Aug 1819 (NMM)
AB 27 May 1825 (NMM)
d 25 Feb 1827 (PRO)

DILKES, Sir Thomas
L 29 Apr 1687 (P)
CA 8 Apr 1689
IMP (Castle Matyr) 1703–1707 (DNB)
RAW 1 Mar 1703
Kt 22 Oct 1704 (DNB)
RAR 13 Jan 1705 (PJP)
d 12 Dec 1707 (DNB)

DILLON, Edward
L 7 Aug 1809
Struck off list 1825 (NMM)

DILLON, James
L 22 Apr 1800
d 1811 (NMM)

DILLON, Stephen
T
L 15 Sept 1813
d Feb 1821 (NMM)

DILLON, Thomas
L 18 Sept 1742
d 1744 (NMM)

DILLON, Sir William Henry
L 29 Apr 1797
CR 8 Apr 1805
CA 21 Mar 1808
KCH 13 Jan 1835 (DNB)
KCB 24 June 1835 (DNB)
RAB 9 Nov 1846 (NMM)
RAW 22 Sept 1847 (NMM)
RAR 27 Mar 1850 (NMM)
VAB 5 Mar 1853 (NMM)
VAW 26 May 1854 (NMM)
VAR 12 May 1857 (NMM)
d 9 Sept 1857 (DNB)

DISHER, James
L 31 Aug 1757
d 1795 (NMM)

DISHINGTON, Andrew
L 5 Nov 1745
d 1780(1) (NMM)

DISNEY, Daniel
L 11 Oct 1760
d 11 Mar 1792

DITTY, John
L 1665
CA 1665
d before 1689 (PJP)

DITZWORTH, Edward
L 1673

DIVE, Henry
See DYVE, Henry

DIX, Edward
L 28 Aug 1797
CR 26 Sept 1807
CA 18 Dec 1809
d 1837 (NMM)

DIXEY, William
L
CA 1673 (PMM)

DIXIE, Alexander
L 17 Oct 1804
T
CR 7 June 1814
Ret CA 1 July 1851 (NMM)
d Dec 1857 (NMM)

DIXON, Benjamin
See DIXSON, Benjamin

DIXON, Charles
L 16 Oct 1778
CR 5 Dec 1781
CA 22 Nov 1790
d 13 Feb 1804

DIXON, Edward
L 15 Mar 1695

DIXON, James Thomas Taylor
L 4 Mar 1813
Ret CR 1 Feb 1846 (NMM)
d 26 May 1861 (PRO)

DIXON, John
L 10 Sept 1781
Dismissed 22 Aug 1801 (PJP)
d 11 Feb 1803

DIXON, John Steward
L 1 July 1814
Ret CR 28 Oct 1857 (NMM)
d 1871 (NMM)

DIXON, John William Taylor
L 25 May 1793
CR 27 Feb 1796
CA 24 Dec 1798
d (drowned) 2 Apr 1804 (CH)

DIXON, Sir Manley
L 7 Sept 1777
CR 15 Aug 1780
CA 22 Nov 1790
RAB 28 Apr 1808
RAW 31 July 1810
RAR 1 Aug 1811
VAB 4 Dec 1813
VAW 4 June 1814
KCB 12 Aug 1819 (MB)
VAR 19 July 1821 (NMM)
AB 27 May 1825 (NMM)
AW 22 July 1830 (NMM)
AR 10 Jan 1837 (NMM)
d 8 Feb 1837 (LT)

DIXON, Manley Hall
L 10 Apr 1802
HP Nov 1806–
4 June 1807 (MB)
CR 10 Feb 1809
CA 28 June 1811
RAB 27 Dec 1847 (NMM)
RAW 20 Dec 1849 (NMM)
RAR 8 Oct 1852 (NMM)
VAB 7 Feb 1855 (NMM)
VA 28 Dec 1855 (NMM)
A 1 Nov 1860 (NMM)
d .4 Mar 1864 (NMM)

DIXON, Robert
L 3 Aug 1802
d 1837 (PRO)

DIXON, William Henry
L 25 May 1807
Ret CR 23 Dec 1855 (NMM)
d 1872 (PRO)

DIXSON, Benjamin
L 11 Mar 1815
Ret CR 1 Oct 1860 (NMM)
d 1879 (NMM)

DOAKE, James
L 24 Nov 1747
CR 12 Oct 1756
CA 18 Oct 1758
d 23 Sept 1761 (PRO)

DOBBIE, William Hugh
L 9 Nov 1798
CR 16 Jan 1806
CA 6 May 1806
d 10 June 1830 (LT)

DOBBIN, Robert
L 21 Apr 1782
d 1810 (PRO)

DOBBS, Alexander
L 9 Nov 1804
CR 14 Feb 1814
CA 12 Aug 1819 (NMM)
d 1828 (NMM)

DOBBS, William
L 8 Oct 1771
d 1778 (PRO)

DOBREE,Daniel
L 23 Aug 1778
CR 2 Feb 1796
CA 29 Apr 1802
d 26 Sept 1814 (LT)

DOBREE, Nicholas Charles
L 10 May 1810
CR 20 Nov 1812
d 9 Mar 1818 (NMM)

DOBSON, Charles
L 30 July 1758
d 2 June 1798

DOBSON, James Clarke
L 6 Aug 1802
d 1812 (NMM)

DOBSON, Man
L 23 Sept 1782
CR 9 Nov 1795 (PRO)
CA 28 June 1796
SUP RA 24 Aug 1819 (NMM)
RAR 5 July 1827 (NMM)
VAB 22 July 1830 (NMM)
VAR 10 Jan 1837 (NMM)
AB 23 Nov 1841 (NMM)
AW 9 Nov 1846 (NMM)
d 13 Apr 1847 (NMM)

DOBSON, Robert
L 12 Aug 1690 (PMM)
CR 22 May 1705 (PMM)
SUP 10 Sept 1712 (PMM)

DOBSON, Thomas James
L 9 Nov 1798 (NMM)

DOBSON, William Burdett
L 3 Jan 1814
CR 25 July 1821 (NMM)
CA 23 Nov 1841 (NMM)
HP 23 Nov 1841 (OB)
RA 12 Apr 1863 (NMM)
d 22 Mar 1872 (NMM)

DOBSON, William Henry
L 14 Mar 1815
d 1817 (NMM)

DOCKING, Abraham
L 15 Feb 1815
d 1837 (NMM)

DOD, Edmund
L 26 Feb 1760
CR 12 Nov 1778
CA 18 May 1779
RAB 20 Feb 1797
RAR 14 Feb 1799
VAB 1 Jan 1801
VAW 23 Apr 1804
VAR 9 Nov 1805
AB 28 Apr 1808
AW 31 July 1810
d 18 Dec 1815 (NMM)

DOD, Michael
L 7 Aug 1793
CR 29 Apr 1802
CA 21 Oct 1810
d 1814 (NMM)

DOD, Thomas
L 9 Aug 1745
d 1777 (NMM)

DODD, Edmund
See DOD, Edmund

DODD, Edward
L 4 Apr 1720
CR
CA 25 Jan 1743
d 1763

DODD, Henry
L 22 May 1758
d 1797 (NMM)

DODD, Henry Winship
L 20 Jan 1814 (NMM)
Ret CR 30 July 1859 (NMM)
d 1860 (NMM)

DODD, John
L 1673

DODD, Joseph
L 27 June 1809

HP Dec 1813 (OB)
Ret CR 4 Apr 1848 (NMM)
d 1854 (NMM)

DODDERIDGE, William
L 19 Sept 1780
d 10 June 1787 (PMM)

DODGSON, Percy Currer
L 16 Dec 1801
d 4 Mar 1807 (NMM)

DODS, Stephen Henry
L 10 Jan 1798
Not heard of since Mar 1808 (PRO)
Name removed 1811 (PRO)

DODSON, Henry
L 19 Aug 1704
Gone 1737

DOHERTY, John
L 10 May 1757 (NMM)
d 1788 (NMM)

DOILY, George
See DOYLEY, George

DOILY, Edward
See DOYLEY, Edmund

DOLBIN, Rowland
L 1665

DOLING, John (1)
L 9 Oct 1695 (PRO)
d ? 1719 (NMM)

DOLLING, John (2)
L 24 Nov 1778
CR 21 Sept 1790
CA 4 May 1795
d 24 June 1795 (PRO)

DOLLING, William Brooking
L 26 Apr 1797
CR 6 Aug 1805
CA 1 Aug 1811 (MB)
d 1834 (NMM)

DOLMAN, George
L 11 Mar 1691
CR 19 Jan 1703 (PMM)
CA 2 Feb 1703 (PRO)
d 23 Mar 1706

DOMAN, Edward
L 1 Aug 1794
d 1796 (PRO)

DOMBRAIN, James
L 9 Mar 1815
Resigned 6 Dec 1820 (NMM)

DOMETT, George
L 27 Apr 1812
CR 7 June 1816 (PRO)
Seniority reduced by two years (PRO)
Resigned 17 Apr 1827 (NMM)

DOMETT, Sir William (1)
L 27 Dec 1778
CR
CA 9 Sept 1782
CRM 1 Jan 1801 (AL)
RAB 23 Apr 1804
RAW 9 Nov 1805
RAR 28 Apr 1808
COM AD 9 May 1808–
23 Oct 1813 (AO)
VAW 25 Oct 1809
VAR 4 Dec 1813
KCB 2 Jan 1815 (LG)
AB 12 Aug 1819 (NMM)
GCB 16 May 1820 (DNB)
AW 27 May 1825 (NMM)
d 19 May 1828 (DNB)

DOMETT, William (2)
L 9 Dec 1802
d (drowned) 9 Feb 1804 (DNB)

DON, William
L 2 Aug 1758
CR 25 Dec 1782
CA 25 Oct 1809
d 1816 (NMM)

DONADIEU, Anthony
L 9 Oct 1777
SUP CR 24 Aug 1812
d 31 Mar 1829 (NMM)

DONALDSON, Augustus
L 20 Nov 1812
CR 1 June 1825 (NMM)
d 30 Oct 1826 (LT)

DONALDSON, James
L 2 Sept 1740
d 1765(6) (NMM)

DONALDSON, John
See BOSWALL, John Donaldson

DONALDSON, William
L 22 Dec 1778
d 1787 (NMM)

DONCLIFT, John
L 17 June 1795
d 24 Nov 1830 (NMM)

DONELLAN, Malachi
L 1 Feb 1808
CR 14 June 1844 (OB)
HP 14 June 1844 (OB)
CA 25 Oct 1858 (NMM)
d 21 July 1865 (NMM)

DONELLY, Ross
See DONNELLY, Sir Ross

DONKLEY, John
L 12 Oct 1739
CR 5 July 1745
CA 27 Mar 1756
d 17 Mar 1758

DONNALLY, Ross
See DONNELLY, Sir Ross

DONNELLAN, John Macnamara
L 8 May 1807
d 1816 (NMM)

DONNELLY, Sir Ross
L 27 Sept 1781
CR 6 July 1794
CA 24 June 1795 (MB)
RAB 4 June 1814
RAW 12 Aug 1819 (NMM)
RAR 19 July 1821 (NMM)
VAB 27 May 1825 (NMM)
VAW 22 July 1830 (NMM)
VAR 10 Jan 1837 (NMM)
KCB 17 Mar 1837 (LG)
AB 28 June 1838 (NMM)
d 30 Sept 1840 (NMM)

DONNITHORNE, Thomas
L 17 Oct 1801
CR 25 Apr 1809
d 6 Oct 1810 (PRO)

DONNOR, James
L 17 July 1804
CR 27 Dec 1808
CA 30 Apr 1810
d 1814 (PRO)

DONOVAN, Alexander
L 7 Nov 1806
Ret CR 3 Dec 1841 (NMM)
d 1850 (NMM)

DONOVAN, Edward
L 24 Nov 1801
d 1812 (NMM)

DONOVAN, Philip
L 22 Apr 1783
d 1811 (NMM)

DONOVAN, Richard
L 24 Sept 1801
d 9 Feb 1825 (NMM)

DONOVAN, Stephen
L 28 Apr 1792
SUP CR 5 Sept 1825 (NMM)
d 1832 (NMM)

DOORNE, Thomas
L 18 Apr 1811
d 1839 (NMM)

DORE, Thomas
L 14 Jan 1673
d before 1689 (PJP)

DORE, William Henry
L 2 Aug 1806
d June 1839 (PRO)

DORNFORD, Francis
L 2 Feb 1815
HP 9 Sept 1815 (OB)
Ret CR 17 Oct 1859 (NMM)
d Aug 1878 (PRO)

DORNFORD, Josiah
L 29 Apr 1802
d 2 Mar 1855 (PRO)

DORRELL, Robert
L
CA 20 Feb 1690
d ? before 1699 (PJP)

DORRILL, Richard (1)
L 12 Sept 1739
CR 2 Mar 1747
CA 11 Feb 1755
GG (Newfoundland) 1755–1756 (BNS)
HP 1757 (DCB)
d 1 Jan 1762 (DCB)

DORRILL, Richard (2)
L 20 May 1779
SUP CR 31 Jan 1814
d 4 Dec 1839 (LT)

DORSETT, John
L 23 Aug 1797
d 1804 (PRO)

DOSSY, Thomas
L
CA 1661
d before 1689 (PJP)

DOUCE, Charles B.
T
L 14 Apr 1809
d 1812 (PRO)

DOUGAL, George
L 9 June 1808
CR 13 June 1815
HP 13 June 1815 (OB)
CA 1 July 1851 (NMM)
Ret CA 31 Dec 1853 (NMM)
d 29 Apr 1855 (PRO)

DOUGLAS, Alexander (1)
L 28 June 1777
CR 22 Nov 1790
d 7 June 1793

DOUGLAS, Alexander (2)
L 17 Mar 1780
d 1787 (NMM)

DOUGLAS, Andrew (1)
L
CA 30 Aug 1691 (DNB)
Dismissed 16 Nov 1704
Restored 24 Sept 1709 (DNB)
d 26 June 1725

DOUGLAS, Andrew (2)
L 6 Apr 1779 (NMM)
d 1789 (NMM)

DOUGLAS, Sir Andrew Snape
L 23 Apr 1778
CR 16 Feb 1780
CA 15 May 1797
d 4 June 1797 (NMM)

DOUGLAS, Billy
L 10Aug 1776
CR 18 July 1778
CA 15 Aug 1781
RAB 1 Jan 1801
RAW 23 Apr 1804
VAB 9 Nov 1805
VAW 28 Apr 1808
VAR 31 July 1810
AB 4 Dec 1813
d 2 Dec 1817 (LT)

DOUGLAS, Sir Charles (1)
L 4 Dec 1753
CR 24 Feb 1759 (DNB)
CA 13 Mar 1761
Cre Bt 23 Jan 1777 (DNB)
RAB 24 Sept 1787
d 10 Mar 1789 (CH)

DOUGLAS, Charles (2)
L 1 Oct 1794
d 1797 (NMM)

DOUGLAS, Hon. Dunbar
L 15 Nov 1790
CR 4 Dec 1795 (NMM)
d 30 Oct 1796 (NMM)

DOUGLAS, Francis
L 5 Apr 1794
CR 2 June 1800

CA	21 Oct	1810
d	Oct	1842 (NMM)
DOUGLAS, Hon. George		
L	8 Aug	1807
CR	8 Aug	1809
CA	28 Feb	1812
d	30 Aug	1838 (PMM)
DOUGLAS, George Robert		
L	7 Feb	1811
CR	19 Aug	1815
d	27 Dec	1817 (PRO)
DOUGLAS, Henry		
T		
L	4 Feb	1815
HP	Nov	1816 (OB)
Ret CR	9 Feb	1860 (NMM)
d		1885 (TR)
DOUGLAS, Hugh Cameron		
L	11 Jan	1814
CR	28 Aug	1827 (PRO)
d	17 Nov	1843 (NMM)
DOUGLAS, Sir James (1)		
L	1 July	1732
CR	5 May	1741 (NMM)
CA	19 Mar	1744
GG (Newfoundland)		1746–1748 (BNS)
MP (Shetland)		1754–1764 (MPN)
Kt	16 Oct	1759 (MPN)
RAW	21 Oct	1762
MP (Orkney)		1764–1768 (MPN)
VAB	18 Oct	1770
VAW	24 Oct	1770
VAR	5 Feb	1776
AB	29 Jan	1778
AW	8 Apr	1782 (CH)
Cre Bt	27 June	1786 (MPN)
d	2 Nov	1787 (CH)
DOUGLAS, James (2)		
L	6 Sept	1775
CR	9 Sept	1778
CA	20 Oct	1780
RAB	14 Feb	1799
RAW	1 Jan	1801
RAR	23 Apr	1804
VAW	9 Nov	1805
VAR	28 Apr	1808
AB	31 July	1810
AW	4 June	1814
AR	27 May	1825 (NMM)
d	8 June	1839 (NMM)
DOUGLAS, James (3)		
L	2 Apr	1798
d		1805 (NMM)
DOUGLAS, James Stoddard		
L	15 Jan	1815 (NMM)
Ret CR	14 Apr	1864 (NMM)
d		1875 (NMM)
DOUGLAS, John (1)		
L	13 Jan	1692 (PJP)
CA	21 Dec	1694
d	16 Nov	1697
DOUGLAS, John (2)		
L	16 June	1730
CR		? 1745 (PMM)
CA	22 Apr	1746
d		1787
DOUGLAS, John (3)		
L	25 June	1773
CR	14 June	1782
d	12 July	1782 (PRO)
DOUGLAS, John (4)		
L	1 Oct	1778
CR	24 May	1794
d		1795 (PRO)
DOUGLAS, John (5)		
L	21 Apr	1780
SUP CR	5 Nov	1814
d	26 Apr	1818 (LT)
DOUGLAS, John (6)		
L	19 Dec	1794
CR	29 Apr	1802
Ret CR	10 Sept	1840 (NMM)
d	28 Jan	1842 (NMM)
DOUGLAS, John		
See DOUGLAS, John Leigh		
DOUGLAS, John Alexander (1)		
L	27 May	1800
Dismissed	18 July	1801 (PJP)
DOUGLAS, John Alexander (2)		
L	5 Oct	1802
d		1809 (NMM)
DOUGLAS, John Erskine		
L	21 Apr	1778
CR	24 May	1794
CA	10 June	1795
RAB	4 June	1814
RAW	12 Aug	1819 (NMM)
RAR	19 July	1821 (NMM)
VAB	27 May	1825 (NMM)
VAW	22 July	1830 (NMM)
VAR	10 Jan	1837 (NMM)
AB	28 June	1838 (NMM)
AW	23 Nov	1841 (NMM)
AR	10 Dec	1846 (NMM)
d	25 July	1847 (LT)
DOUGLAS, John Graham		
L	2 Mar	1780
d		1809 (PRO)
DOUGLAS, John Leigh		
L	17 June	1760
CR	19 Sept	1777
CA	5 Apr	1779
RAB	1 June	1795
RAR	14 Feb	1799
VAB	1 Jan	1801
VAW	23 Apr	1804
VAR	9 Nov	1805
AB	28 Apr	1808
AW	31 July	1810
d	13 Nov	1810 (PRO)
DOUGLAS, Patrick		
L	11 Sept	1777
d		1780(1) (PRO)
DOUGLAS, Peter John		
L	11 June	1804
CR	17 Feb	1807
CA	26 Nov	1811
RAB	7 Jan	1848 (NMM)
RAW	14 Jan	1850 (NMM)

RAR 26 Oct 1852 (NMM)
VAB 3 July 1855 (NMM)
d 10 Dec 1858 (NMM)

DOUGLAS, Pringle Home
L 9 Oct 1801
CR 28 May 1814
HP 28 May 1814 (OB)
Ret CA 1 July 1851 (PRO)
d 1859 (PRO)

DOUGLAS, Richard (1)
L 27 Nov 1760
d 1804 (PRO)

DOUGLAS, Richard (2)
T
L 18 Sept 1809
CR 5 Sept 1823 (NMM)
Ret CR 1 July 1851 (PRO)
d 1867 (NMM)

DOUGLAS, Roddam Thomas
L 21 June 1798
CR 9 Aug 1810
d 4 Aug 1813 (PRO)

DOUGLAS, Stair (1)
L 13 Dec 1756
CR 7 July 1761
CA 29 June 1762
d 8 Apr 1789 (PJP)

DOUGLAS, Stair (2)
L 24 Dec 1780
CR 12 Nov 1795
CA 13 Sept 1797
RAB 19 July 1821 (NMM)
RAW 27 May 1825 (NMM)
d 22 Nov 1826 (PJP)

DOUGLAS, Thomas
L 20 Sept 1782
d 3 Oct 1792

DOUGLAS, Townly Ward
L 9 Mar 1815
d 1817 (NMM)

DOUGLAS, William (1)
L
CR 4 Jan 1728 (PRO)
CA 31 Dec 1729
d 20 May 1741 (PRO)

DOUGLAS, William (2)
L 19 Sept 1815
d 1840 (NMM)

DOUGLAS, Sir William Henry (1)
L 28 Sept 1778
CR 13 Mar 1782
CA 15 Apr 1782
RAW 23 Apr 1804
RAR 9 Nov 1805
VAB 28 Apr 1808
d 24 May 1809 (NMM)

DOUGLAS, William Henry (2)
L 11 Jan 1797
CR 4 Dec 1813
d 26 Apr 1826 (NMM)

DOUGLASS, Andrew
See DOUGLAS, Andrew

DOUGLASS, John
See DOUGLAS, John (2)

DOUSE, Nat
L 16 Aug 1697 (PMM)

DOUTHWAITE, George
L 23 Nov 1747
CR 2 June 1760
d 1765(6) (NMM)

DOVE, Francis
L
CA 7 Jan 1693
COMM (Plymouth) July 1716–1725 (PJP)
d 12 Feb 1725

DOVE, George
L 28 Apr 1802
d Jan 1830 (NMM)

DOVE, John (1)
L 1 Mar 1713
Gone 1743 (PRO)

DOVE, John (2)
L 8 May 1812
d 1837 (PRO)

DOVE, Jonathan
L 31 Aug 1761
d 1809 (NMM)

DOVE, Percy
L 24 Apr 1797
Ret CR 26 Nov 1830 (NMM)
d 1835 (NMM)

DOVE, Richard
L 18 Jan 1709
d 1734 (PRO)

DOVE, Thomas
L 16 Dec 1727
CR 18 May 1745
d 1767 (PRO)

DOVER, Edward
L
CA 1 Sept 1688
(9 Sept 1688 in P)
d 16 Nov 1695 (PRO)

DOVER, Robert
L 1667

DOVEY, Edward
L 16 Jan 1728
Gone 1732 (PRO)

DOW, Archibald
L 26 Jan 1762
CR 25 Oct 1809
d 1814 (NMM)

DOW, Charles Kerr
L 21 Mar 1812
d 15 Nov 1833 (LT)

DOW, William
L 17 June 1814
Ret CR 13 Apr 1857 (NMM)
d 14 July 1866 (NMM)

DOWDEN, William Gibbs
L 16 June 1812
HP 12 July 1816 (OB)
Ret CR 25 Oct 1854 (NMM)
d Oct 1879 (PRO)

DOWELL, Thomas
L 13 Oct 1801
d 1819 (NMM)

DOWERS, Purser
L 21 Aug 1779
SUP CR 1 Jan 1816 (NMM)
d 30 Oct 1837 (NMM)

DOWERS, William
L 30 Jan 1802
CR 4 Nov 1808
CA 24 Sept 1814
d 26 Dec 1816 (NMM)

DOWGLAS, John
See DOUGLAS, John

DOWGLASSE, Andrew
See DOUGLAS, Andrew

DOWGLASSE, William
L 10 Mar 1712
d ? 1728 (PRO)

DOWKER, William
L 11 Aug 1800
d 7 Nov 1800

DOWN, Edward
L 12 Oct 1761
d 23 June 1806 (PMM)

DOWN, Edward Augustus
L 26 Dec 1798
CR 12 Jan 1805
CA 12 Aug 1812
Ret RA 31 Oct 1846 (NMM)
d 22 Jan 1855 (PRO)

DOWNES, Henry
L 1 June 1814
CR 2 May 1829 (PRO)
d 3 Apr 1852 (NMM)

DOWNES, William
L 1688

DOWNEY, John
L 1 Feb 1815
d 1823 (NMM)

DOWNEY, William
L 3 Oct 1812
d 12 Feb 1741 (LT)

DOWNIE, George
L 23 Mar 1802
CR 6 July 1808
CA 1 Jan 1813
KIA 11 Sept 1814 (I)

DOWNIE, John
L 2 Feb 1815
d 1821 (PRO)

DOWNING, Dennis
L 16 Jan 1745
CR 18 Oct 1758
d 1763 (PRO)

DOWNING, Joseph
L 7 May 1803
d 1813 (PRO)

DOWNING, Theophilus
L 1673
d before 1689 (PJP)

DOWNMAN, Hugh
L 5 Mar 1790 (MB)
CR 26 July 1797
CA 26 Dec 1798
RAB 27 May 1825 (NMM)
RAW 22 July 1830 (NMM)
VAB 10 Jan 1837 (NMM)
VAR 23 Nov 1841 (NMM)
AB 24 Apr 1847 (NMM)
AW 9 Oct 1849 (NMM)
A 1 July 1851 (NMM)
d 4 Jan 1858 (NMM)

DOWNMAN, William
L 11 Apr 1727
d 1734 (NMM)

DOWNS, Jonathan
L 5 Feb 1759
d 1761 (NMM)

DOWSE, Stephen
L 9 Apr 1709
Gone 1729 (PRO)

DOWSING, Jackson
L 15 Nov 1790
d 1802 (PRO)

DOWSON, Charles
L 28 Apr 1759
d 1775 (PRO)

DOWSON, John
L 28 Aug 1777
d 15 Dec 1803

DOYEL, George
L 15 Mar 1779
SUP CR 31 Jan 1815
d 10 Sept 1820 (NMM)

DOYLE, Sir Bentinck Cavendish
L 29 Aug 1799
CR 18 Sept 1805
CA 3 Apr 1811
Kt 20 Apr 1825 (MB)
d 21 May 1843 (NMM)

DOYLE, Charles
L 19 Nov 1764
d 1776 (NMM)

DOYLEY, Edmund
L
CA 15 Jan 1695
(6 Feb 1695 in S)
d 10 May 1703 (LTE)

DOYLEY, George
L
CR
CA 10 July 1706
d (drowned) 30 Aug 1707 (CH)

DRAFFEN, Frederick
L 7 Mar 1809
Reduced to Jr Lt
Reinstated w/srty of 27 Nov 1810
HP May 1816 (OB)
Ret CR 14 July 1851 (NMM)
d 6 Dec 1854 (NMM)

DRAKE, Duncomb
L 19 Dec 1716
CR 14 Aug 1724
CA 11 Jan 1728
d 22 May 1734 (PRO)

DRAKE, Endimion
L 1667

DRAKE, Sir Francis
L 11 Dec 1693

CR
CA 21 Aug 1709

d 1726

DRAKE, Sir Francis Samuel
L 21 Aug 1749
CR 20 Mar 1756
CA 15 Nov 1756
RAB 26 Sept 1780
Cre Bt 28 May 1782 (DNB)
RAR 24 Sept 1787
MP 1789 (DNB)
(Plymouth)
COM AD 12 Aug–18 Nov 1789 (AO)
d 18 Nov 1789 (AO)

DRAKE, Francis Thomas
L 6 June 1776
CR 15 May 1780
d (drowned) 30 Sept 1781 (CH)

DRAKE, Francis William
L
CR
CA 29 Jan 1748
GG
(Newfoundland) 1750–1753 (BNS)
MP
(Bere Alston) 1771–1774 (MPN)
RAB 23 Jan 1778
RAR 19 Mar 1779
VAB 26 Sept 1780
VAR 24 Sept 1787
d 18 Dec 1787 (MPN)

DRAKE, Hugh
L 26 May 1783
d 1801 (PRO)

DRAKE, John (1)
L
CA 15 Jan 1696
d 22 Nov 1697

DRAKE, John (2)
T
L 1 Aug 1811
CR 2 Oct 1827 (PRO)
CA 12 Mar 1835 (NMM)
Ret CA 1 July 1851 (NMM)
Ret RA 14 Feb 1857 (NMM)
Ret VA 12 Sept 1863 (NMM)
d 8 Aug 1864 (NMM)

DRAKE, Robert Hacche
L 15 Aug 1806
Ret CR 21 Apr 1840 (NMM)
d 26 June 1854 (NMM)

DRAKE, Sir Samuel Francis
See DRAKE, Sir Francis Samuel

DRAKE, Thomas
L 18 May 1809
d 1815 (PRO)

DRAKE, William (1)
L 19 Sept 1727 (NMM)
CR 18 Oct 1743
d 1758 (PRO)

DRAKE, William (2)
L 20 Apr 1807
d 1808 (PRO)

DRAKE, William Edmund
L 14 Nov 1797
Ret CR 15 Dec 1830 (NMM)
d 1861 (PRO)

DRANE, Robert
L Apr 1778
d 1810 (PRO)

DRANE, Thomas
L 22 Aug 1809
HP Oct 1809–28 June 1812 (OB)
Ret CR 4 Apr 1848 (NMM)
d 20 Apr 1850 (PRO)

DRAPER, John (1)
L
CA 18 June 1695
d (drowned) 10 Dec 1697 (CH)

DRAPER, John (2)
L 27 Oct 1726
CR
CA 8 Sept 1741
d 27 Nov 1743 (PRO)

DRAPER, John (3)
L 26 Mar 1780
CR 4 July 1794
CA 2 June 1795
d 23 Feb 1813 (PMM)

DRAPER, John Gray
L 2 Mar 1815
Seniority altered 1817 (NMM)
d 1834 (PRO)

DRAPER, Thomas (1)
L 1672
CA 17 May 1678
d before 1689 (PJP)

DRAPER, Thomas (2)
L 15 Feb 1815
d Oct 1830 (NMM)

DREDGE, William
L 9 Nov 1798
d 1832 (PRO)

DREW, Andrew
L 4 Mar 1814
CR 19 Oct 1824 (PRO)
CA 16 June 1843 (NMM)
RA 30 Jan 1863 (NMM)
VA 16 May 1869 (NMM)
A 30 July 1875 (NMM)
d 19 Dec 1876 (NMM)

DREW, Edward
L 1 Mar 1815 (NMM)
Ret CR 1 Oct 1860 (NMM)
d 23 Mar 1870 (NMM)

DREW, George
L 8 May 1812
CR 11 Jan 1843 (NMM)
Ret CA 1 Aug 1860 (NMM)
d 1872 (PRO)

DREW, James
L 29 July 1775
CR 1 Dec 1787
d (drowned) 23 May 1798 (CH)

DREW, James Rogers
L 16 Mar 1811
CR 26 Aug 1820 (NMM)
d 20 Sept 1834 (LT)

DREW, John (1)
L 19 Sept 1777
CR
CA 6 Feb 1783
d 11 Jan 1798 (NMM)

DREW, John (2)
L 29 Mar 1796
d 16 Oct 1804 (PRO)

DREW, Josias
L 22 Feb 1815
Ret CR 1 Oct 1860 (NMM)
d 1869 (PRO)

DREW, William
L 31 Dec 1813
d 23 Jan 1830 (PRO)

DREWITT, James
L 7 May 1805
CR 13 Oct 1812
d 1822 (PRO)

DRING, Robert
L 24 Sept 1757
CR 3 Aug 1768
d 1789 (PRO)

DRING, Stephen
L 1665
d before 1689 (PJP)

DRING, William
L 11 Oct 1695
Gone 1719 (PRO)

DRINKWATER, Anthony
L 12 Aug 1693
Gone 1719 (PRO)

DRISCOLL, James
L 30 May 1814
d 18 Apr 1828 (PRO)

DRIVER, William
L 26 Nov 1744
d 1745 (NMM)

DROWND, Robert
L 11 Mar 1691

DRUMMOND, Sir Adam
L 13 Oct 1795
CR 29 May 1798
CA 30 Oct 1799
RAW 22 July 1830 (NMM)
VAB 10 Jan 1837 (NMM)
Kt 1 Mar 1837 (OB)
KCH 1 June 1837 (OB)
VAW 23 Nov 1841 (NMM)
VAR 9 Nov 1846 (NMM)
AB 20 Mar 1848 (NMM)
d 3 May 1849 (NMM)

DRUMMOND, Charles
L 23 May 1711
CR 2 Nov 1732 (PRO)
CA 12 Jan 1736
SUP RA July 1747
d 15 Nov 1771 (M)

DRUMMOND, James Francis Edward
L 21 June 1771
Dismissed 30 May 1774 (PJP)

DRUMMOND, John (1)
L 5 Jan 1757
d 1763 (PRO)

DRUMMOND, John (2)
L 24 July 1779
d 1793 (PRO)

DRUMMOND, John Auriol
L 21 June 1774
CR 25 Aug 1777
d (drowned) 11 Oct 1780 (CH)

DRUMMOND, Sir John Forbes
L 19 July 1771 (NMM)
CR 8 Aug 1797 (NMM)
Cre Bt Feb 1828 (MB)
d 23 May 1828 (MB)

DRUMMOND, Patrick (1)
L 4 Sept 1744
CR
CA 22 Oct 1762
d 31 Aug 1792

DRUMMOND, Patrick (2)
L 6 Apr 1815
d 1845 (NMM)

DRUMMOND, Peter
L 7 Mar 1815
d 6 Apr 1824 (NMM)

DRUMMOND, Robert
L 14 Oct 1808
d 17 June 1811 (NMM)

DRUMMOND, William
L 10 Apr 1794
d Oct 1796 (LT)

DRURY, Augustus Vere
L 29 Sept 1799
CR 2 May 1810
CA 7 June 1814
HP 7 June 1814 (OB)
d 9 Feb 1845 (NMM)

DRURY, Edward O'Brien
L 1 Aug 1801
CR 9 Oct 1807
CA 1 Jan 1817 (NMM)
d 10 May 1823 (NMM)

DRURY, Henry
L 14 Sept 1807
CR 10 Sept 1811
CA 23 Nov 1841 (OB)
HP 23 Nov 1841 (OB)
d 1847 (PRO)

DRURY, John Sheppey
L 20 Oct 1806
d (drowned) 1808 (PJP)

DRURY, Joseph
L 30 July 1808
CR 7 Feb 1812
CA 4 Feb 1814
d 1835 (PRO)

DRURY, Thomas
L 18 Mar 1773
CR 1 Mar 1779
CA 21 Oct 1782
RAW 23 Apr 1804
RAR 9 Nov 1805
VAB 28 Apr 1808
VAR 31 July 1810
AB 4 June 1814

AW	19 July	1821 (NMM)
AR	22 July	1830 (NMM)
d	5 Sept	1832 (NMM)

DRURY, William Hamilton

L	30 Sept	1790
CR	6 Aug	1803
d	31 Oct	1805 (NMM)

DRURY, William O'Bryen

L	28 Nov	1778
CR		
CA	18 Jan	1783
RAB	23 Apr	1804
RAW	9 Nov	1805
RAR	28 Apr	1808
VAB	31 July	1810
VAW	1 Aug	1811
Gazetted before news of death was received. (NMM)		
d	6 Mar	1811 (NMM)

DRYCE, Henry
See DYVE, Henry

DUANE, Abraham

L	26 Nov	1756
CR	19 Aug	1766
d	23 Jan	1767 (PRO)

DUBOIS, Henry Richard

L	7 July	1744
CR	2 May	1757
d	Dec	1792

DU CANE, Charles

L	2 Dec	1809
CR	30 Aug	1815
d	17 Nov	1850 (NMM)

DUCIE, Lord
See REYNOLDS, Francis, Lord Ducie

DUCK, Robert

L		
CA		1660

DUCKITT, Peter

L	21 May	1760
d		1767

DUCKWORTH, Sir John Thomas

L	14 Nov	1771
CR	21 July	1779
CA	16 June	1780
CRM	8 June	1797 (AL)
RAW	14 Feb	1799
RAR	1 Jan	1801
Kt	6 June	1801 (DNB)
VAB	23 Apr	1804
VAW	9 Nov	1805
VAR	28 Apr	1808
GG (Newfoundland)		1810–1813 (BNS)
AB	31 July	1810
MP (New Romney)	1812–Feb	1813 (MPT)
MP (New Romney)	12 Feb 1813– 31 Aug	1817 (MPT)
Cre Bt	2 Nov	1813 (DNB)
AW	4 Dec	1813
GCB	2 Jan	1815 (MPT)
d	31 Aug	1817 (DNB)

DUDDINGTON, William
See DUDINGTON, William

DUDINGTON, William

L	10 Oct	1759
CR	28 Aug	1772
CA	19 Sept	1777
SUP RA	12 Nov	1794 (NMM)
d		1817 (NMM)

DUDLEY, O'Brien

L	1 Nov	1741 (NMM)
CR	1 Mar	1745 (PMM)
CA	11 Aug	1746
d	26 Aug	1759

DUELL, Thomas

L	28 Sept	1809
Forfeited 6 months srty in		1813
L	28 Mar	1810
d	30 Mar	1843 (NMM)

DUER, John

L	10Mar	1802
CR	6 Mar	1802
CA	30 Mar	1806
d	17 Nov	1814 (PRO)

DUFF, Archibald

L	8 Dec	1794
CR	29 Apr	1802
CA	22 Jan	1806
Ret RA	28 June	1838 (NMM)
RAB	17 Aug	1840 (NMM)
RAW	23 Nov	1841 (NMM)
RAR	20 Nov	1846 (NMM)
VAB	3 Mar	1849 (NMM)
VAW	29 Apr	1851 (NMM)
A	4 July	1855 (NMM)
d	9 Feb	1858 (NMM)

DUFF, George

L	15 Sept	1779
CR	21 Sept	1790
CA	9 Feb	1793
T	killed	
KIA	21 Oct	1805 (TR)

DUFF, Norwich

T		
L	14 Nov	1811
CR	15 June	1814
CA	23 Apr	1822 (OB)
HP	23 Apr	1822 (OB)
RA	8 Oct	1852 (NMM)
VA	28 Nov	1857 (NMM)
d	20 Apr	1862 (NMM)

DUFF, Robert

L	9 Mar	1739 (NMM)
CR	4 Dec	1744 (DNB)
CA	23 Oct	1746
GG (Newfoundland)		1775–1776 (BNS)
RAB	31 Mar	1775
RAR	5 Feb	1776
VAB	29 Jan	1778
VAR	26 Sept	1780
d	6 June	1787 (DNB)

DUFF, William

L	16 Apr	1756
d		1762 (PRO)

DUFFERIN, Lord
See BLACKWOOD, Hon. Price

DUFFT, Robert

L		
CR	4 Dec	1744

DUFFUS, James
L | 11 Feb | 1815
d | | 1833 (NMM)

DUFFUS, Kenneth, Lord
L | 5 Nov | 1705 (PMM)
CR | 17 Oct | 1706 (PMM)
CA | 7 Apr | 1707
Dismissed | | 1715
Went into Czar's service | | 1715

DUFFY, James John
L | 22 Apr | 1795
d | | 1809 (NMM)

DUFTY, William
L | 14 Aug | 1807
Ret CR | 19 Oct | 1843 (NMM)
d | | 1848 (NMM)

DUGFDALE, Robert
L | 21 Apr | 1747
Cashiered by Court Martial | Nov | 1763 (PJP)
d | 4 Sept | 1791

DUKE, William
L | 24 Feb | 1802
KIA | 20 Nov | 1806 (CH)

DUMARESQ, George
L | 17 Dec | 1761
d | | 1783 (NMM)

DUMARESQ, John
L | 10 Dec | 1719
CR | 2 Jan | 1729
d | | 1733 (NMM)

DUMARESQ, Perry
L | 14 Apr | 1810
d | 13 Mar | 1839 (NMM)

DUMARESQ, Thomas
L | 23 Oct | 1755
CR | 2 Nov | 1772
CA | 23 Jan | 1775
RAB | 12 Apr | 1794
RAW | 4 July | 1794
VAB | 1 June | 1795
VAR | 14 Feb | 1799
AB | 1 Jan | 1801
d | 18 Jan | 1802

DUMARESQ, William
Formerly DUMARESQUE, William
L | 29 Mar | 1744
SUP CR | 21 Sept | 1796
d | 22 Sept | 1813 (NMM)

DUMARESQUE, Philip (1)
L | 31 Jan | 1706 (PRO)
SUP | | 1741 (PRO)

DUMARESQUE, Philip (2)
L | 7 Sept | 1798 (PRO)
d | | 1811 (NMM)

DUMARESQUE, Philip (3)
Later DUMARESQUIN, Philip
L | 7 Mar | 1799
CR | 3 Aug | 1801
CA | 25 Sept | 1806
d | | 1819 (NMM)

DUMARESQUE, William
See DUMARESQ, William

DUMBRECK, William
T
L | 27 Sept | 1810
HP | Aug | 1814 (OB)
d | | 1862 (TR)

DUMERISQUE, John
See DUMARESQ, John

DUNBAR, Charles Duff
L | 9 Aug | 1802
d | | 1805(6) (NMM)

DUNBAR, James (1)
L | | 1672
CA | 29 Sept | 1677
d | 7 Apr | 1682 (DDA)

DUNBAR, Sir James (2)
L | 3 Nov | 1790
CR | 15 Apr | 1798
CA | 29 Apr | 1802
Kt | | 1809 (MB)
Cre Bt | 30 July | 1814 (MB)
d | 5 Jan | 1836 (PRO)

DUNBAR, Robert
L
CA | 28 June | 1698 (PMM)

DUNBAR, William
L | 12 July | 1796
d | | 1802 (NMM)

DUNCAN, Adam, Viscount
L | 10 Jan | 1755
CR | 21 Sept | 1759
CA | 21 Feb | 1761
RAB | 24 Sept | 1787
RAW | 21 Sept | 1790
VAB | 1 Feb | 1793
VAW | 12 Apr | 1794 (CH)
AB | 1 June | 1795
Cre EP | 21 Oct | 1797 (DNB)
AW | 14 Feb | 1799
d | 4 Aug | 1804 (DNB)

DUNCAN, Andrew
L | 5 Nov | 1806
Dismissed | | 1812 (PJP)

DUNCAN, Arthur French
L | 4 July | 1782
d | | 1790 (NMM)

DUNCAN, Henry (1)
L | 21 Sept | 1759
CR | 26 May | 1768
CA | 7 Feb | 1776
CONT | 21 June | 1801–
 | 20 June | 1806 (NBO)
SUP CA | | 1811 (NMM)
d | 7 Oct | 1814 (PJP)

DUNCAN, Henry (2)
L | 4 Apr | 1791
CR | 26 May | 1797
CA | 29 Apr | 1802
d (drowned) | | 1802 (CH)

DUNCAN, Hon. Henry (3)
L | 21 Apr | 1803
CR | 6 Nov | 1804
CA | 18 Jan | 1806
CB | June | 1815 (MB)
d | 1 Nov | 1835 (NMM)

DUNCAN, James (1)
L | 1 Dec | 1778
d | 3 Oct | 1803

DUNCAN, James (2)
L 7 May 1805
Ret CR 9 June 1838 (NMM)
d 24 Mar 1841 (PRO)

DUNCAN, John
L 29 Apr 1807
d 23 Apr 1839 (PRO)

DUNCAN, Samuel
L 19 Dec 1809
d 1832 (PRO)

DUNCAN, Thomas
L 5 Sept 1801
Ret CR 30 Mar 1832 (NMM)
d Dec 1848 (NMM)

DUNCOMB, Abraham
L 13 May 1720
CR 11 Mar 1742
d 1778 (PRO)

DUNCUMB, William
L 16 Nov 1790
d 1798 (PRO)

DUNDAS, Adam
L 25 Nov 1761
d 1773 (PRO)

DUNDAS, Charles
L 31 Mar 1758
d 1772 (NMM)

DUNDAS, George (1)
L 10 Apr 1723
CR 2 Apr 1729
d 20 Apr 1733 (PRO)

DUNDAS, George (2)
L 8 Mar 1779
CR 3 Nov 1790
CA 3 Oct 1795
RAB 4 June 1814
d 6 Aug 1814 (LT)

DUNDAS, George
See DUNDASS, George

DUNDAS, Hon. George Heneage Lawrence
L 23 Mar 1797
CR 26 Dec 1800
CA 9 Aug 1801 (NMM)
CB 2 Jan 1815 (LG)
RAB 22 July 1830 (NMM)
COM AD 25 Nov 1830–
7 Aug 1834 (AO)
CONT 2 Nov 1831–
9 June 1832 (NBO)
d 7 Aug 1834 (AO)

DUNDAS, James
L 15 Nov 1776
CR 12 June 1782
CA 21 Sept 1790
SUP RA 12 May 1808 (NMM)
d 2 June 1811 (NMM)

DUNDAS, John Burnett
L 25 Apr 1815
CR 20 Mar 1823 (NMM)
CA 8 July 1828 (NMM)
RA 7 Feb 1855 (NMM)
VA 5 Aug 1861 (NMM)
A 5 May 1865 (NMM)
d 2 Sept 1868 (NMM)

DUNDAS, James Whitley Deans
See DEANS, Sir James Whitley

DUNDAS, Ralph
L 1 Nov 1757
CR 3 Apr 1779
d 11 June 1787 (PMM)

DUNDAS, Robert
L 14 May 1744
CR 14 June 1757
d 1760 (NMM)

DUNDAS, Sir Thomas (1)
L 15 July 1793
CR 2 Sept 1795
CA 9 July 1798
T
RAB 27 May 1825 (NMM)
RAR 22 July 1830 (NMM)
KCB 13 Sept 1835 (LG)
VAB 10 Jan 1837 (NMM)
VAW 28 June 1838 (NMM)
d 29 Mar 1841 (LT)

DUNDAS, Thomas (2)
L 18 July 1810
d 1845 (NMM)

DUNDASS, George
L 1 Jan 1783
d 1814 (NMM)

DUNDEE, Samuel
L 7 July 1745
d 10 Oct 1750 (PMM)

DUNDERDALE, James Francis
L 3 June 1812
d 18 Mar 1822 (PRO)

DUNDONALD, Thomas Cochrane, Earl
See COCHRANE, Thomas Earl of Dundonald

DUNGAN, John
L 23 Aug 1680
d before 1689 (PJP)

DUNGAN, Thomas
L 1671
d before 1689 (PJP)

DUNHAM, Robert (1)
L 11 Jan 1782
d 1790 (PRO)

DUNHAM, Robert (2)
L 31 Dec 1795
d 1806 (PRO)

DUNJOY, Thomas
L 1685

DUNKLEY, John
L 2 July 1742
d 10 Feb 1765 (PMM)

DUNKIN, Roberts
L 15 Oct 1773
d 1778 (PRO)

DUNLAP, Thomas
L 27 Mar 1797
d 1813 (NMM)

DUNLOP, Robert Graham
L 7 Feb 1812
CR 20 July 1822 (NMM)
d 28 Feb 1841 (NMM)

DUNLOP, Robert Wallace

L	8 May	1795
Ret CR	12 June	1833 (NMM)
d	18 July	1843 (PRO)

DUNN, Sir David

L	12 July	1808
CR	13 Mar	1811
CA	7 June	1814
Kt	12 Aug	1835 (OB)
KCH	1 June	1837 (OB)
RAB	5 Nov	1849 (NMM)
RAW	1 Oct	1852 (NMM)
RAR	29 Oct	1852 (NMM)
VA	16 Nov	1856 (NMM)
d	16 June	1859 (NMM)

DUNN, George (1)

L	30 Apr	1746
d		1755(6) (NMM)

DUNN, George (2)

L	25 June	1773
d		1819 (PRO)

DUNN, James

L	29 Nov	1809
d	4 Mar	1824 (NMM)

DUNN, Nicholas James Cuthbert

L	22 Jan	1806
CR	9 Mar	1814
Ret CA	1 July	1851 (NMM)
d	27 Feb	1858 (NMM)

DUNN, Pascoe

L	7 Jan	1809
CR	15 June	1814
d	28 May	1826 (PJP)

DUNN, Richard Dalling

L	17 Nov	1790
CR	24 Dec	1798
CA	29 Oct	1801
d	11 June	1813 (NMM)

DUNN, Robert

L	28 Mar	1810
d		1812 (NMM)

DUNNITHORNE, Thomas
See DONNITHORNE, Thomas

DUNSFORD, George

T		
L	19 Jan	1809
d		1839 (NMM)

DUNSTAN, Octavious

L	7 Feb	1815
d		1850 (NMM)

DUPRE, Michael

L	1 May	1759
d	2 Aug	1768 (PMM)

D'URBAN, William

L	28 Oct	1790
CR	22 Dec	1796
CA	17 Jan	1804
RAB	10 Jan	1837 (NMM)
d	16 Feb	1837 (NMM)

DURELL, George

L	17 Sept	1720
CR	4 Mar	1743 (NMM)
CA	13 Feb	1745
d	15 May	1745

DURELL, John

L	5 July	1720
CR	28 Nov	1726 (PRO)
CA	8 Nov	1734
d		1748

DURELL, Philip (1)

L	30 June	1731
CR		
CA	6 Feb	1742
RAB	8 July	1758 (CH)
RAR	14 Feb	1759
VAB	21 Oct	1762
d	23 Sept	1766 (PRO)

DURELL, Philip (2)

L	18 June	1757
CR	20 June	1778
CA	14 Mar	1769
d	27 Mar	1772 (PRO)

DURELL, Thomas (1)

L	15 Mar	1706 (PMM)
CR	14 May	1716 (PRO)
CA	9 Feb	1720
d	23 Aug	1741 (PRO)

DURELL, Thomas (2)

L	27 Sept	1757
CR	28 Oct	1778
CA	3 May	1782
d	29 Jan	1804

DURELL, Thomas Philip

L	17 Apr	1778
CR	12 June	1797
CA	29 Apr	1802
d	23 Nov	1836 (LT)

DURLEY, Edward

L		
CA	25 Mar	1695
d	30 July	1702 (PRO)

DURHAM, Sir Philip Charles H.C.

L	26 Dec	1782
CR	12 Nov	1790
CA	24 June	1793
T	wounded	
RAB	31 July	1810
RAW	12 Aug	1812
RAR	4 June	1814
KCB	2 Jan	1815 (LG)
Kt (France)		1815 (TR)
VAB	12 Aug	1819 (NMM)
VAW	19 July	1821 (NMM)
VAR	27 May	1825 (NMM)
MP (Queenborough)		1830 (DNB)
AB	22 July	1830 (NMM)
GCB	1 Dec	1830 (LG)
MP (Devizes)		1834–1836 (DNB)
AW	10 Jan	1837 (NMM)
AR	23 Nov	1841 (NMM)
d	2 Apr	1845 (DNB)

DURSLEY, James, Lord
See BERKELEY, James, Earl

DUTCH, John

L	20 Feb	1796 (NMM)
d		1826 (NMM)

DU TIEL, John
L
CA 1665
d 1675 (DDA)

DUTTON, Benjamin
L 19 Nov 1811
Ret CR 1 Apr 1853 (NMM)
d 15 July 1853 (PRO)

DUTTON, John Peake
L 21 July 1810
d 1839 (PRO)

DUTTON, Richard
L 29 Apr 1796
KIA 4 Feb 1798 (LG)

DUTTON, Thomas (1)
L 10 Nov 1800
CR 1 Feb 1812
d 26 Apr 1837 (NMM)

DUTTON, Thomas (2)
L 13 June 1815 (NMM)
HP Nov 1815 (OB)
Ret CR 1 July 1865 (NMM)
d 1872 (NMM)

DUVAL, Francis
L 26 Nov 1807
CR 15 June 1814
Ret CA 1 July 1851 (NMM)
d 1868 (PRO)

DUVAL, John
L 27 June 1803
d 2 June 1831 (NMM)

DUVALL, Thomas
L 27 Oct 1795
CR 4 May 1799
d (drowned) 27 Dec 1802 (CH)

DWYER, Edward Furman
L 31 Oct 1815
d 31 July 1821 (NMM)

DWYER, Michael
L 21 Mar 1812
CR 21 Sept 1842 (PRO)
d 23 Aug 1857 (PRO)

DWYER, Robert
L 26 Apr 1808
d 1840 (PRO)

DYBALL, Thomas Cooke
L 22 Feb 1815
d 1840 (PRO)

DYER, George (1)
L 23 Oct 1779
d 16 Sept 1798

DYER, George (2)
L 17 Feb 1813
d 1826 (PRO)

DYER, John Parry
L 6 Oct 1781
CR 15 Mar 1783
d 27 Dec 1803

DYER, John Widdicombe (1)
L 15 Oct 1795
d 1796 (PRO)

DYER, John Widdicombe (2)
L 3 Mar 1812
d (drowned) 2 Jan 1818 (PJP)

DYER, Nicholas
L
CA 10 Dec 1696
d 4 June 1697

DYER, Robert Nathaniel
L 26 Feb 1801
d 1802 (NMM)

DYER, Sir Thomas Swinnerton
L 29 June 1793 (NMM)
CR 12 Jan 1810 (NMM)
Cre Bt Apr 1838 (NMM)
d 27 Mar 1854 (NMM)

DYM, Robert
L 1672
d before 1689 (PJP)

DRYCE, Henry
See DYVE, Henry

DYSON, Thomas
L 24 Sept 1759
CR 25 Mar 1782
d 18 Apr 1798

DYVE, Henry
L 12 May 1734
CR 10 Aug 1741
CA 2 Sept 1745
SUP RA 1770(1)
d 1779

EAGER, John
L 10 Oct 1805
CR 27 May 1825 (PRO)
HP 27 May 1825 (OB)
Ret CA 1 Apr 1856 (PRO)
d 19 July 1865 (PRO)

EAGER, Thomas
L 25 Apr 1801
d 1808 (PRO)

EAGLE, James William
T
L 24 Dec 1805
d 1 Dec 1821 (PRO)

EAGLESFEILD, Ralph
L 20 Jan 1692 (PRO)
CR 16 Mar 1708 (PRO)
d ?1733 (PRO)

EAGLESTONE, Thomas
L 31 Dec 1807
CR 17 Mar 1812
Promoted before news of death was received (PRO)
d 6 Feb 1812 (PRO)

EALES, John
L 13 Dec 1793
Resigned 1798 (NMM)

EALES, Robert
L 23 Sept 1695
Gone 1719 (PRO)

EARLE, Edward Charles
L 10 Sept 1813

CR	22 July	1844 (NMM)
d	12 Apr	1845 (PRO)
EARLE, John		
L		1664
CA		1665
d	before	1689 (PJP)
EARNSHAW, William		
L	1 Dec	1793
KIA	24 July	1797 (LG)
EAST, William		
L	21 Jan	1673
CA	17 May	1678
EASTERBROOK, Joseph		
L	19 Sept	1815
d		1823 (PRO)
EASTLEY, Charles		
L	5 Oct	1778 (NMM)
d		1790 (PRO)
EASTLEY, Yard		
L	1 Mar	1815 (NMM)
d	22 Nov	1830 (NMM)
EASTLY, Yard		
L	7 Sept	1697
d		1737 (NMM)
EASTMAN, James Edward		
L	20 Aug	1794
d		1810 (PRO)
EASTWOOD, Henry Nevil		
L	21 Mar	1812
CR	15 June	1827 (NMM)
d		1834 (NMM)
EASTWOOD, Jennings		
L	14 Feb	1755
d		1760 (NMM)
EASTWOOD, Joseph (1)		
L	16 May	1743
CR	1 Nov	1757
d		1760 (PRO)
EASTWOOD, Joseph (2)		
L	26 June	1777
d		1798 (PRO)
EASTWOOD, Joseph (3)		
L	21 Jan	1809
CR	23 June	1815
d		1833 (PRO)
EASTWOOD, Joseph Novil		
L	24 Aug	1781
SUP CR	1 Jan	1816 (NMM)
Struck off list	10 Jan	1828 (NMM)
EASTWOOD, New Hill		
L	5 July	1776
CR	21 Sept	1790
d		1797 (NMM)
EASTWOOD, Thomas		
L	9 Nov	1756
CR	19 Feb	1776
d (drowned)	7 Sept	1776 (CH)
EATON, James		
T		
L	13 Jan	1806
Ret CR	26 May	1842 (NMM)
d		1857 (PRO)
EATON, John		
L	22 Nov	1790 (NMM)
CR	6 July	1794 (PRO)
d		1797 (PRO)
EATON, Nicholas		
L		?1702 (PJP)
CR		
CA	11 Mar	1709
d	5 Apr	1729 (PJP)
EBBON, John Miller		
L	23 Jan	1794
d		1801 (PRO)
EBORALL, Samuel		
L	24 Feb	1815
HP	24 Feb	1815 (OB)
d	30 Nov	1853 (PRO)
EBORALL, Thomas		
L	24 Nov	1808
d	7 June	1823 (PRO)
ECKEN, Mark		
L	12 Mar	1807
d		1826 (PRO)
EDE, Robert		
L	13 Apr	1808
d	24 Apr	1834 (PJP)
EDEN, John		
L		1664
EDEVAIN, John (1)		
L	28 Oct	1809
d		1814 (PRO)
EDEVAIN, John (2)		
L	15 Mar	1815
d	20 Apr	1827 (NMM)
EDGAR, Alexander		
L	20 Dec	1757
CR	27 Aug	1778
CA	30 Nov	1780
SUP RA	20 Feb	1799
d	17 Feb	1817 (NMM)
EDGAR, George		
L	6 May	1807
d		1815 (PRO)
EDGAR, Thomas		
L	30 July	1781
d		1801 (NMM)
EDGAR, William		
L	29 Sept	1781
SUPCR	1 Jan	1816 (NMM)
d		1822 (NMM)
EDGCOMBE, Robert		
L	18 May	1747
d		1781 (NMM)
EDGCUMBE, Hon. George, Earl of Mount		
L	5 Oct	1739
CR		1742 (DNB)
CA	19 Aug	1744
MP (Fowey)	30 July	1746–
	10 May	1761 (MPS)
Inh EP	10 May	1761 (DNB)
RAB	21 Oct	1762
RAR	18 Oct	1770
VAB	24 Oct	1770
VAW	25 June	1773 (C)

VAR	5 Feb	1776 (CH)
AB	29 Jan	1778
Cre EP	17 Feb	1781 (DNB)
AW	8 Apr	1782
d	4 Feb	1795 (DNB)
EDGCUMBE, John		
L	1 Oct	1795
CR	29 Apr	1802
CA	11 May	1807
d	22 Jan	1837 (LT)
EDGCUMBE, Richard		
L	7 May	1777
d		1778 (NMM)
EDGCUMBE, Robert		
L	8 July	1758
d		1763 (NMM)
EDGE, William		
L	26 May	1776
CR	17 Sept	1793
CA	29 June	1795
LGH	Jan	1809 (MB)
SUP RA		1814 (NMM)
d	21 July	1843 (PRO)
EDGECOMBE, James		
L	1 Aug	1811
d		1826 (PRO)
EDGELL, Henry Folkes		
L	16 Nov	1790
CR	5 Mar	1798
CA	29 Apr	1802
HP	Sept	1812 (OB)
Ret RA	10 Jan	1837 (NMM)
RAW	17 Aug	1840 (NMM)
RAR	23 Nov	1841 (NMM)
d	14 June	1846 (PRO)
EDGELL, John		
L	13 Feb	1798
d		1802 (PRO)
EDMONDS, Joseph		
L	30 May	1796
CR	29 May	1798
CA	6 Feb	1807
d	12 June	1818 (LT)
EDMONDS, Thomas (1)		
L	21 Nov	1790
d		1797 (PRO)
EDMONDS, Thomas (2)		
L	28 Apr	1807
Ret CR	17 Jan	1843 (NMM)
d	23 May	1854 (NMM)
EDMONSTONS, Henry		
L	16 May	1778
d		1793 (NMM)
EDRIDGE, John		
Formerly LUCAS, John (4)		
L	23 Oct	1810 (NMM)
HP	23 Oct	1810 (OB)
Ret CR	11 Apr	1851 (NMM)
d		1856 (NMM)
EDWARD, Augustus, H.R.H., Duke of York		
L		
CR		
CA	14 June	1759
RAB	8 Apr	1761
VAB	21 Oct	1762
AB		1766
d	14 Sept	1767 (CH)
EDWARDS, Adams		
L	13 Mar	1815
Ret CR	1 Oct	1860 (NMM)
d		1862 (NMM)
EDWARDS, Arthur		
L	13 June	1759
d	30 Mar	1805 (LT)
EDWARDS, Charles		
L	28 Sept	1761
d		1762 (NMM)
EDWARDS, Charles Turner		
L	6 June	1745
d		1756 (NMM)
EDWARDS, David (1)		
L	2 Feb	1741
CR	29 Aug	1746
CA	24 Sept	1756
d		1781
EDWARDS, David (2)		
L	5 Sept	1803
CR	11 May	1827 (NMM)
Ret CR	1 Apr	1856 (NMM)
d	25 Apr	1857 (PRO)
EDWARDS, Edward		
L	7 Sept	1759
CR	22 Apr	1778
CA	25 Apr	1781
RAB	14 Feb	1799
RAW	1 Jan	1801
RAR	23 Apr	1804
VAB	9 Nov	1805
VAW	28 Apr	1808
AB	31 July	1810
AW	4 June	1814
d	13 Apr	1815 (PRO)
EDWARDS, George		
L	15 Mar	1777
CR	21 Sept	1790
d		1797 (PRO)
EDWARDS, Henry		
L	22 Nov	1802
CR	29 Sept	1813
CA	2 Aug	1826 (NMM)
HP	2 Aug	1826 (OB)
RA	15 Apr	1854 (NMM)
VA	9 June	1860 (NMM)
A	9 Feb	1864 (NMM)
d	21 Oct	1864 (PRO)
EDWARDS, Jeremiah		
L	16 Nov	1790
CR	30 Oct	1795
d		1819 (PRO)
EDWARDS, John (1)		
L	13 Feb	1691 (PJP)
CA	24 Apr	1695
d	12 Feb	1727 (PRO)
EDWARDS, John (2)		
L	14 May	1703
CR	31 Mar	1726

CA 9 Nov 1727
d 28 Aug 1731 (PRO)

EDWARDS, John (3)
L 13 Oct 1781
CR 1 Dec 1787
d 15 Jan 1823 (MB)

EDWARDS, John (4)
L 21 Oct 1790
CR 22 June 1795
d Jan 1823 (PRO)

EDWARDS, John (5)
L 6 Nov 1798
CR 4 Dec 1813
d 25 Feb 1825 (PRO)

EDWARDS, John Browning
L 26 June 1795
CR 29 Dec 1800
CA 29 Apr 1802
d 22 Apr 1813 (PRO)

EDWARDS, Osborne
L 8 Dec 1778
d 1782(3) (NMM)

EDWARDS, Owen
L 14 Mar 1744
CR 6 Apr 1757
d 1762 (NMM)

EDWARDS, Peter
L 1665
CA 21 Dec 1672 (DDA)
d before 1689 (PJP)

EDWARDS, Rice
L 6 Feb 1729
d 1747 (PRO)

EDWARDS, Richard (1)
L 3 Sept 1688 (P)
CA 10 Mar 1690
COMM (Plymouth) 19 June 1711–
21 Nov 1714 (QAN)
d 2 Mar 1724 (PRO)

EDWARDS, Richard (2)
L 19 Oct 1727
CR
CA 4 Nov 1740
SUP RA June 1757
d 16 June 1773

EDWARDS, Richard (3)
L 30 Nov 1740
GG (Newfoundland) 1745–1746 (BNS)
CR 3 Aug 1747
CA 27 Dec 1753
GG (Newfoundland) 1757–1760 (BNS)
RAB 19 Mar 1779
GG (Newfoundland) 1779–1782 (BNS)
RAR 26 Sept 1780
VAW 24 Sept 1787
VAR 1 Feb 1793
AB 12 Apr 1794
d 3 Feb 1795 (NMM)

EDWARDS, Richard (4)
L 4 July 1812
CR 26 Aug 1828 (NMM)
Ret CR 1 Apr 1856 (NMM)
d 1877 (NMM)

EDWARDS, Richard Flanigan
L 10 May 1804
CR 27 Aug 1814
d 23 May 1844 (PRO)

EDWARDS, Richard Venn
L 15 Sept 1814
HP Aug 1815 (OB)
Ret CR 18 Oct 1858 (NMM)
d Aug 1859 (PRO)

EDWARDS, Robert (1)
L 24 Dec 1805
d 1808 (NMM)

EDWARDS, Robert (2)
L 25 Mar 1814
d 1818 (NMM)

EDWARDS, Roger
L 7 Mar 1746
d 1749 (NMM)

EDWARDS, Sampson
L 2 Aug 1774
CR 25 Dec 1778
CA 16 Oct 1781
RAB 1 Jan 1801
RAW 23 Apr 1804
RAR 9 Nov 1805
VAB 13 Dec 1806 (LG)
VAW 25 Oct 1809
VAR 31 July 1810
AB 4 June 1814
AW 12 Aug 1819 (NMM)
AR 22 July 1830 (NMM)
d 14 Sept 1840 (LT)

EDWARDS, Samuel (1)
L 1 Oct 1695
Gone 1719 (PRO)

EDWARDS, Samuel (2)
L 29 Apr 1777
Dismissed 1790 (PJP)

EDWARDS, Thomas (1)
L 19 Sept 1759
d 1804 (PRO)

EDWARDS, Thomas (2)
L 24 Sept 1778
SUP CR 11 Sept 1820 (NMM)
d 4 Nov 1827 (NMM)

EDWARDS, Thomas Ambrose
L 10 June 1809
CR 19 July 1814
d 30 Oct 1826 (PRO)

EDWARDS, Timothy
L 6 Feb 1755
CR 16 Nov 1757
CA 5 Aug 1759
d 30 June 1780 (PRO)

EDWARDS, Valentine
L
CR 22 Oct 1781
CA 1 Dec 1787
d (drowned) 5 Dec 1799 (CH)

EDWARDS, Wakeman
L 4 May 1810
d 1842 (NMM)

EDWARDS, William (1)
L 8 Mar 1796
CR 15 Feb 1805
d 1807 (PRO)

EDWARDS, William (2)
L 14 June 1806
d 14 Feb 1825 (PRO)

EDWARDS, William (3)
L 15 Aug 1806
Ret CR 16 Jan 1840 (NMM)
d 1859 (NMM)

EDWARDS, William (4)
L 8 Feb 1815
d 1816 (PRO)

EDWARDS, William Chichester
L 12 June 1807
d 1826 (PRO)

EDWARDS, William Embury
L 20 Mar 1806
d 1810 (PRO)

EDWARDS, William Jeffrey
L 2 July 1807
d 1843 (PRO)

EDWIN, John
L 1664
d before 1689 (PJP)

EELES, John
Formerly ECLES, John
L 14 Aug 1739
SUP 1754 (PMM)
d 1755(6) (NMM)

EGAN, Charles
L 23 June 1775
d 19 Apr 1783 (LG)

EGAN, Francis
L 22 Oct 1782
d 1798 (PRO)

EGERTON, Francis
L 23 Nov 1796
d 1800 (NMM)

EICKE, James
L 5 May 1810
d 16 Oct 1828 (LT)

EKINES, Thomas
L
CA 15 Apr 1695
Dismissed 26 June 1712 (PJP)

EKINS, Alexander
L 1 June 1691

EKINS, Sir Charles
L 20 Oct 1790
CR 18 June 1795
CA 22 Dec 1796
Kt (Netherlands) 1816 (DNB)
CB 1816 (DNB)
RAB 12 Aug 1819 (NMM)
RAW 27 May 1825 (NMM)
VAB 22 July 1830 (NMM)
KCB 15 June 1831 (LG)
VAW 10 Jan 1837 (NMM)
AB 23 Nov 1841 (NMM)
AW 28 Apr 1847 (NMM)
AR 29 Apr 1851 (NMM)
GCB 7 Apr 1852 (DNB)
d 2 July 1855 (DNB)

ELCOCK, Henry
L 26 Aug 1789
d 1796 (NMM)

ELDER, Charles
L 26 Nov 1778
SUP CR 31 Jan 1814
d 16 May 1823 (NMM)

ELDRIDGE, William
L 5 Sept 1803
d 14 Apr 1844 (LT)

ELERS, Edward
L 12 Feb 1801
T
d 23 Jan 1815 (NMM)

ELFORD, Matthew
L 8 Jan 1708 (PMM)
CR
CA 5 Mar 1711
d 20 Sept 1733 (PRO)

ELFORD, William
See ELLFORD, William

ELFRITH, Robert
L
CA 1673

ELIAS, Joseph
L 15 Aug 1806
Ret CR 7 May 1840 (NMM)
d 1843 (NMM)

ELIBANK, George Murray, Lord
See MURRAY, George, Lord Eilbank

ELIOT, Henry Algernon
L 8 June 1810
CR 2 Sept 1819 (NMM)
CA 22 July 1830 (NMM)
RA 27 Sept 1835 (NMM)
d 17 Aug 1857 (NMM)

ELIOT, John
L
CR 4 Sept 1759
CA 25 Apr 1760
d 12 June 1769 (PJP)

ELIOT, William
L 11 Feb 1795
d 1800 (PRO)

ELIOTT, Eliot
See ELLIOTT, Elliott

ELKEN, Richard
L 10 Oct 1793
d 1794 (PRO)

ELKINGTON, Thomas
L 1 June 1794
d 1818 (PRO)

ELLARY, Robert
L 10 Oct 1801
d 1826 (PRO)

ELLERBY, George (1)
L 9 Feb 1808

ELLERBY, George (2)
L 9 Feb 1810
d 1834 (NMM)

ELLERKER, William
L 26 Oct 1714
SUP 1750 (PMM)
d ?1751 (PRO)

ELLERY, George
L 11 Sept 1747
d May 1781 (LG)
ELLETON, William
L 20 Aug 1759
SUP CR 11 Aug 1803
d 15 Aug 1818 (PRO)
ELLFORD, Matthew
See ELFORD, Matthew
ELLFORD, William
L 4 Aug 1710
CR
CA 10 Oct 1710
d 31 Mar 1732 (PRO)
ELLICE, Alexander
L 30 Oct 1813
CR 19 Feb 1831 (NMM)
CA 20 Dec 1832 (NMM)
d 8 Oct 1853 (PRO)
ELLICOTT, Edward
L 22 June 1794
CR 12 June 1797
CA 12 Aug 1812
Ret RA 1 Oct 1846 (NMM)
d 24 Jan 1847 (PRO)
ELLIOT, Benjamin
L 19 Aug 1757
d 10 Sept 1759 (PJP)
ELLIOT(T), Edward
L 1685 (P)
CA 28 Apr 1685
Dismissed 22 Apr 1689 (PRO)
d 21 Sept 1725 (PRO)
ELLIOT, Hon. George
See ELLIOTT, Hon. Sir George
ELLIOT, John (1)
L 14 Dec 1715
Gone 1734 (PRO)
ELLIOT, John (2)
L 30 Apr 1756 (NMM)
CR
CA 5 Apr 1757
MP
(Cockermouth) 9 Jan 1767–1768 (MPN)
CRM 19 Mar 1779 (AL)
GG
(Newfoundland) 1786–1789 (BNS)
RAR 24 Sept 1787
VAB 21 Sept 1790
VAW 1 Feb 1793
VAR 12 Apr 1794
AB 16 Apr 1795 (NMM)
AW 14 Feb 1799
AR 9 Nov 1805
d 20 Sept 1808 (DNB)
ELLIOT, John (3)
L 20 Sept 1779
SUP CR 17 Mar 1814
d 13 Sept 1834 (NMM)
ELLIOT, John
See ELLIOTT, John
ELLIOT, Stephen
See ELLIOTT, Stephen
ELLIOT(T), Thomas
L 17 Jan 1718 (NMM)
CR 25 June 1742
d 1744(5) (NMM)
ELLIOT, Thomas
See ELLIOTT, Thomas
ELLIOT, William (1)
L 12 May 1781
d July 1795 (PMM)
ELLIOT, William (2)
L 13 Mar 1782
d 1799 (PRO)
ELLIOT, William (3)
L 1 Dec 1787
CR 22 Nov 1790 (NMM)
d 21 July 1792 (PRO)
ELLIOT, William
See ELLIOTT, William
ELLIOT(T), Christopher
L 20 Feb 1695 (PMM)
CR ?1 July 1703 (PMM)
CA 21 July 1703
d 27 Dec 1704 (PRO)
ELLIOTT, Cyrus
L 15 Sept 1806
d 7 Aug 1831 (NMM)
ELLIOTT, Elliott
L 30 Apr 1736
CR
CA 5 Oct 1744
(5 Sept 1744 in H)
d 26 June 1745 (PRO)
ELLIOTT, George (1)
L 20 Oct 1740
CR
CA 12 May 1744
SUP RA 1762
d 5 Aug 1795
ELLIOTT, Hon. Sir George (2)
L 12 Aug 1800
CR 14 Apr 1802
CA 2 Jan 1804
CB Sept 1830 (DNB)
MP
(Roxburghshire) 1832–1835 (DNB)
COM AD 25 Apr 1835–
22 July 1837 (AO)
RAB 10 Jan 1837 (NMM)
RAW 28 June 1838 (NMM)
RAR 9 Nov 1846 (NMM)
VAB 13 May 1847 (NMM)
VAW 3 Mar 1849 (NMM)
VAR 11 June 1851 (NMM)
AB 5 Mar 1853 (NMM)
AW 4 July 1855 (NMM)
A 27 Sept 1855 (NMM)
HP 1855 (DNB)
KCB Nov 1862 (DNB)
d 24 June 1863 (DNB)
ELLIOTT, George (3)
L 12 Jan 1802
CR 8 May 1812
d 27 Feb 1814 (PRO)
ELLIOTT, James
L 17 July 1682
d 31 July 1682 (DDA)

ELLIOTT, James Burnett
T
L 2 Feb 1815
CR 30 July 1859 (NMM)
d 1872 (TR)

ELLIOTT, John (1)
L
CA 21 Sept 1666 (DDA)
Dismissed ?1679 (PRO)

ELLIOTT, John (2)
L 30 Apr 1756
d 1757 (NMM)

ELLIOTT, John
See ELLIOT, John

ELLIOTT, Robert
L 13 July 1793
CR 14 Feb 1801
CA 27 June 1808
RAB 9 Nov 1846 (NMM)
RAW 8 Jan 1848 (NMM)
RAR 6 Nov 1850 (NMM)
VA 22 Apr 1853 (NMM)
d 20 Jan 1854 (NMM)

ELLIOTT, Robert James
L 5 Aug 1805 (NMM)
CR 27 Aug 1814
d 30 Apr 1859 (PRO)

ELLIOTT, Stephen
L
CA 14 Jan 1695
(14 June 1694 C)
d 6 Dec 1704 (PRO)

ELLIOTT, Thomas (1)
L 1673
CA 18 Sept 1673 (DDA)
d before 1689 (PJP)

ELLIOTT, Thomas (2)
L 14 Dec 1814 (NMM)
d 21 Oct 1822 (NMM)

ELLIOTT, Thomas
See ELLIOT, Thomas

ELLIOTT, William (1)
L 17 Mar 1802
CR 16 Oct 1809 (NMM)
CA 16 Oct 1810 (NMM)
CB 1815 (PJP)
Kt (Portugal) 1823 (MB)
d 15 Sept 1839 (NMM)

ELLIOTT, William (2)
L 24 June 1808
d Feb 1810 (PRO)

ELLIOTT, William (3)
L 5 Jan 1810
d 5 June 1811 (NMM)

ELLIOTT, William
See ELLIOT, William

ELLIS, Alexander
L 14 Mar 1763
d 1779 (NMM)

ELLIS, Charles
See ELLYS, Charles

ELLIS, Francis Wilson
L 15 Oct 1812
Ret CR 28 May 1855 (NMM)
d 17 June 1858 (PRO)

ELLIS, Henry
L 19 Mar 1805
CR 19 July 1821 (NMM)
Ret CA 1 Apr 1856 (NMM)
d 15 Nov 1857 (NMM)

ELLIS, James
L 10 Jan 1771
CR 19 Nov 1778
d 7 Sept 1824 (MB)

ELLIS, John (1)
L 14 May 1779
d 1798

ELLIS, John (2)
L 20 Nov 1795
CR 22 Jan 1806
CA 7 June 1814
d 1840 (PRO)

ELLIS, John (3)
L 29 Apr 1797
Ret CR 26 Nov 1830 (NMM)
d 11 May 1848 (PRO)

ELLIS, Peter
L 1673

ELLIS, Thomas
L 13 Nov 1756
d 1764 (NMM)

ELLIS, William
L 17 May 1727
CR
CA 9 Feb 1741
d 13 June 1742 (PJP)

ELLISON, Charles Pole Hardcastle
L 30 Aug 1806
d 22 Mar 1816 (PRO)

ELLISON, Cuthbert Waldegrave
L 12 Jan 1796
d 8 Jan 1801 (PRO)

ELLISON, Joseph
L 29 July 1778
CR 6 June 1782
CA 21 Jan 1783
d 1 Oct 1816 (NMM)

ELLISON, Peter
L 23 Oct 1800
d 1809 (PRO)

ELLISON, William (1)
L 23 Apr 1793
CR 22 Jan 1806
d 12 Feb 1817 (PRO)

ELLISON, William (2)
L 20 Feb 1811
d June 1822 (PRO)

ELLISTON, Edmund
L 30 Mar 1759
SUP CR 29 May 1807 (PMM)
d 1807 (PMM)

ELLWES, Gerrard
L 26 Nov 1688 (P)
CA 19 Jan 1691

ELLYS, Charles
L 1 Mar 1753
CR 21 Nov 1760
CA 10 May 1762
d 3 Mar 1794 (LT)

ELMHURST, Philip James
T wounded
L 27 May 1814
Ret CR 13 May 1857 (NMM)
d 1866 (PRO)

ELMY, Benjamin
L 6 Oct 1741
d 1770 (NMM)

ELPHICK, James
L 15 Jan 1802
CR 19 July 1821 (NMM)
d 1862 (NMM)

ELPHINSTON, George Keith
See KEITH, George, Viscount

ELPHINSTON, John (1)
L 23 Aug 1746
CR 5 May 1757
CA 1 Feb 1759
In Russian service 1769–1771 (DNB)
d 28 Apr 1785 (DNB)

ELPHINSTON, John (2)
L 11 July 1776
CR 21 Sept 1790
CA 16 May 1793
d 17 Jan 1802 (PRO)

ELPHINSTON, Samuel William
L 6 Nov 1778
Entered Russian service 1783 (PMM)
d 1787 (PRO)

ELPHINSTON, Thomas
See ELPHINSTONE, Thomas

ELPHINSTONE, Alexander Francis
L 9 June 1807
CR 15 June 1814
HP 15 June 1814 (OB)
Ret CA 1 July 1851 (NMM)
d 1865 (NMM)

ELPHINSTONE, Charles
L 7 Aug 1799 (NMM)
CR 14 Aug 1799
CA 27 Feb 1801
d 2 Feb 1807 (CH)

ELPHINSTONE, Hon. Charles
See FLEEMING, Hon. Charles Elphinstone

ELPHINSTONE, George Keith
See KEITH, George, Viscount

ELPHINSTONE, Robert Philip Randolph
L 6 July 1809
d 22 June 1823 (PRO)

ELPHINSTONE, Thomas
L 26 Mar 1780
CR 18 Jan 1796 (NMM)
CA 3 June 1797
d Mar 1821 (PRO)

ELRINGTON, George
L 30 Aug 1806
HP 1813 (OB)
Ret CR 1 July 1844 (NMM)
d 22 Nov 1847 (PRO)

ELSE, John
L 17 Feb 1815
d 1837 (PRO)

ELSMERE, Hans Sloane
L 3 Oct 1794
Ret CR 26 Nov 1830 (PRO)
d 20 Jan 1845 (PRO)

ELSMORE, Charles
L 23 Jan 1797
Ret CR 20 Dec 1830 (PRO)
d 23 Sept 1852 (PRO)

ELSTON, John Torry
L 27 Feb 1815
d 1818 (NMM)

ELTON, Henry
L 6 Mar 1807
CR 7 June 1814
HP 7 June 1814 (OB)
Ret CA 1 July 1851 (PRO)
d 10 Nov 1858 (NMM)

ELTON, Jacob
L 28 July 1738
CR
CA 28 Dec 1741
KIA 28 Mar 1745 (CH)

ELVY, George
L 4 Mar 1815
Ret CR 10 Jan 1863 (NMM)
d 8 May 1863 (NMM)

ELWALL, Eber
L 23 June 1740
d 1746 (NMM)

ELWIN, John
L 17 Jan 1811
d 11 Nov 1829 (NMM)

ELWIN, Joseph
L 2 Aug 1814
d July 1849 (PRO)

EMERTON, James
L 9 July 1802
HP 1815 (OB)
Ret CR 30 July 1840 (NMM)
d 9 June 1846 (LT)

EMERY, Charles
L 3 Dec 1761
d 1780(1) (NMM)

EMERY, James
T
L 2 Mar 1808
d 1810 (PRO)

EMES, Fleetwood
L
CA 13 Jan 1692
d (drowned) 26 Nov 1703 (CH)

EMMERSON, Otto William
L 7 Feb 1801
d 1803 (PRO)

EMMES, Fleetwood
See EMES, Fleetwood

ENERY, Edward Augustus
L 16 Nov 1811
d 1814 (PRO)

ENGLAND, Robert
L 29 July 1783
CR 2 Jan 1798
d 29 Jan 1821 (NMM)

ENGLAND, Samuel
L 2 Mar 1815
d 1816 (NMM)

ENGLAND, Thomas
L 23 June 1795
CR 8 Mar 1813
d 1818 (PRO)

ENGLISH, Charles
L 21 Mar 1812
CR 17 Apr 1827 (NMM)
d 10 Oct 1846 (LT)

ENGLISH, Richard
L 10 Feb 1815
d 1818 (NMM)

ENSOM, Robert
L
CA 1663
d before 1689 (PJP)

ENSOR, John
L 11 Jan 1808
Dismissed 1808 (NMM)

ENTWISTLE, Hugh Robert
T
L 28 Jan 1806
HP 20 Aug 1816 (OB)
Ret CR 7 Jan 1839 (NMM)
d 1867 (TR)

ENYS, Samuel
L 1666

EPWORTH, Farmery
L 24 Dec 1762
CR
CA 13 May 1778
SUP RA 1794 (NMM)
d 18 Mar 1804 (PRO)

EPWORTH, Farmery Predam
L 31 Dec 1782
CR 6 Dec 1796
CA 29 Apr 1802
d 18 Aug 1826 (PRO)

EPWORTH, William
L 11 Feb 1796 (NMM)
d 1796 (NMM)

ERICKS, James
L 27 Mar 1741
d 1755(6) (PRO)

ERLSIMAN, Richard
L
CA 1664
d before 1689 (PJP)

ERNLE, Sir John
L 1664
CA 1672
CAH (Barbados Dragoons) 1673 (MPH)
MP (Calne) 1685–25 Oct 1686 (MPH)
d 25 Oct 1686 (MPH)

ERNLE, William
L 11 Jan 1746
d 1758 (NMM)

ERRINGTON, Thomas
L 16 Dec 1797
d 1809 (PRO)

ERSKINE, James
L 16 Mar 1795
d (drowned) 17 Mar 1800 (CH)

ERSKINE, Robert
L 2 Apr 1729
CR 3 Mar 1737
CA 13 Nov 1742
SUP RA ?1762
d 7 Nov 1766

ERWIN, George
L
CR 1664
d before 1689 (PJP)

ESMONDE, James
L 16 Mar 1815
d 1843 (PRO)

ESSINGTON, Claphamson
L 8 Apr 1748
d 1755(6) (PRO)

ESSINGTON, Sir William
L 28 Feb 1777
CR 30 Mar 1781
CA 18 Jan 1783
RAB 23 Apr 1804
RAW 9 Nov 1805
RAR 28 Apr 1808
VAB 31 July 1810
VAW 1 Aug 1811
VAR 4 June 1814
KCB 2 Jan 1815 (LG)
d 12 July 1816 (PRO)

ETOUGH, Henry Gladwell
L 9 July 1813
CR 28 July 1851 (NMM)
d 24 Oct 1854 (NMM)

EUATT, Philip
L 1665 (DDA)
CA 1667 (DDA)
d before 1689 (PJP)

EVANCE, William Devereux
L 3 Sept 1814
CR 15 Aug 1818 (NMM)
d 1860 (PRO)

EVANS, Andrew Fitzherbert
L 1 Dec 1787
CR 12 Sept 1795
CA 15 Apr 1798
RAB 27 May 1825 (NMM)
d 6 June 1826 (PRO)

EVANS, Augustus Benjamin
L 16 Oct 1809
d 6 June 1822 (NMM)

EVANS, Gustavus
L 18 Apr 1811 (NMM)
CR 23 Nov 1841 (NMM)
Ret CA 8 Feb 1858 (NMM)
d 30 Jan 1862 (NMM)

EVANS, Henry
L 13 Mar 1782
CR 2 Oct 1794
CA 20 June 1797
MP (Wexford) 1 Mar 1819–1820 (MPT)
SUP RA 26 July 1821 (NMM)
MP(Wexford) 1826–13 May 1829 (MPT)

VAW 12 Nov 1840 (NMM)
VAR 23 Nov 1841 (NMM)
d 16 Sept 1842 (MPT)

EVANS, Henry Francis
L 27 Sept 1762
CR 12 Nov 1777
CA 29 Apr 1778
KIA 21 July 1781 (CH)

EVANS, John (1)
L
CA 10 July 1691
d 15 Mar 1724 (PRO)

EVANS, John (2)
L 16 Sept 1740
CR 20 Aug 1746
CA 20 Apr 1748
RAW 19 Mar 1779
VAB 26 Sept 1780
VAW 24 Sept 1787
VAR 21 Sept 1790
AB 1 Feb 1793
d 15 July 1794 (CH)

EVANS, John (3)
L 14 Apr 1746
d 1763 (PRO)

EVANS, John (4)
L 16 Aug 1781
d 1795 (PRO)

EVANS, John (5)
L 29 Sept 1797
CR 22 Jan 1806
d 1816 (NMM)

EVANS, John (6)
L 16 Nov 1811
Ret CR 1 Apr 1853 (NMM)
d 26 Oct 1854 (PRO)

EVANS, Raymond
L 13 Feb 1815
CR 8 Feb 1858 (NMM)
d 1863 (PRO)

EVANS, Robert (1)
L 11 Jan 1760
d 1777 (PRO)

EVANS, Robert (2)
L 21 Nov 1790
CR 29 Apr 1802
CA 21 Oct 1810
d 19 July 1828 (LT)

EVANS, Robert William
L 14 July 1813
d 1814 (PRO)

EVANS, Roger
L 29 Dec 1796
Ret CR 1 Dec 1830 (NMM)
d 27 Apr 1852 (NMM)

EVANS, Thomas (1)
L 25 Sept 1743
CR 12 July 1757
CA 30 Jan 1758
d 9 Feb 1775 (PJP)

EVANS, Thomas (2)
L 12 Apr 1805
Ret CR 23 Oct 1837 (NMM)
d 1849 (PRO)

EVANS, Thomas (3)
L 23 Apr 1810
d 1814 (PRO)

EVANS, Thomas (4)
L 13 Dec 1814
d 1816 (PRO)

EVANS, Thomas (5)
L 2 Feb 1815
d 1854 (PRO)

EVANS, Thomas James Cotton
L 29 Mar 1815
CR 10 Feb 1824 (NMM)
d 1826 (PRO)

EVANS, Thomas Pearce
L 5 May 1810
Ret CR 12 Jan 1850 (NMM)
d 19 June 1867 (PRO)

EVANS, Ward
L 28 May 1813
d 1848 (PRO)

EVANS, Watkin
L 4 Sept 1801
CR 2 Aug 1811
CA 7 June 1814
d 1817 (PRO)

EVANS, William
L 9 Aug 1806
d 1811 (PRO)

EVANSON, Alleyn
L 13 June 1815
Ret CR 1 Oct 1860 (NMM)
d 1862 (PRO)

EVE, Thomas
L 14 Feb 1815
d 1843 (PRO)

EVELEIGH, John (1)
L 23 Sept 1795
CR 29 Mar 1810
CA 11 Aug 1812
KIA 23 Jan 1814 (CH)

EVELEIGH, John (2)
L 16 May 1809
CR 4 Mar 1819 (NMM)
d 26 July 1835 (PJP)

EVELYN, Christopher
L
CA 1665

EVELYN, George James
L 30 Aug 1804
Ret CR 24 Jan 1851 (NMM)
d 1866 (NMM)

EVELYN, William
L 2 Sept 1799
d (drowned) Dec 1809 (CH)

EVERARD, Thomas
L 13 Apr 1802
CR 22 Oct 1810
CA 7 June 1814 (NMM)
d 19 June 1814 (PRO)

EVERARD, William		
L	17 Jan	1811
d		1834 (PRO)
EVERITT, Charles Holmes		
See CALMADY, Charles Holmes Everitt		
EVERITT, Michael		
L	15 June	1744
CR		
CA	23 Dec	1747
d	13 Sept	1776 (PRO)
EVERITT, Michael John		
L	5 Sept	1772
CR	7 Sept	1777
KIA	7 June	1779 (LG)
EVERY, Dennis		
L	2 Sept	1741
CR	31 Aug	1762
Dismissed	7 Nov	1763 (PJP)
EVERY, John		
L	6 July	1686 (P)
CA	4 June	1689
LSMR	20 June	1694 (EAD)
d		1729 (DDA)
EVOY, Robert M.		
See M'EVOY, Robert		
EWBANK, Thomas		
L	13 Nov	1745
d		1753 (PRO)
EWENS, Thomas		
L		
CA		1664
EWERS, Philipp		
L		
CA		1666
EXMOUTH, Edward Pellew, Viscount		
L	9 Jan	1778
CR	1 July	1780
CA	25 May	1782
HP		1791–1793 (DNB)
Kt	29 June	1793 (DNB)
Cre Bt	5 Mar	1796 (DNB)
CRM	1 Jan	1801 (AL)
MP (Barnstaple)		1802–1814 (DNB)
RAW	23 Apr	1804
RAR	9 Nov	1805
VAB	28 Apr	1808
VAR	31 July	1810
Cre EP	14 May	1814 (DNB)
AB	4 June	1814
KCB	2 Jan	1815 (DNB)
GCB		1815 (DNB)
Kt (Spain)		1816 (DNB)
Kt (Two Sicilies)		1816 (DNB)
AW	19 July	1821 (NMM)
AR	22 July	1830 (NMM)
d	23 Jan	1833 (DNB)
EXTON, Brudenell		
L	20 Aug	1796
d		1800 (NMM)
EXTON, Francis		
L	17 May	1758
d		1785 (PRO)
EYLES, Sir Joseph		
L	26 July	1780
CR	6 July	1794
CA	26 Dec	1799
d	17 Nov	1806 (PMM)
EYLES, Thomas		
L	22 Nov	1790
CR		
CA	13 July	1795
RAB	4 June	1814
RAW	12 Aug	1819 (NMM)
RAR	19 July	1821 (NMM)
VAB	27 May	1825 (NMM)
VAW	22 July	1830 (NMM)
d	29 Sept	1835 (PRO)
EYRE, Sir George		
L	28 Oct	1790
CR	20 Feb	1794
CA	6 Feb	1796
Kt		1812 (MB)
CRM	4 June	1814 (AL)
KCB	2 Jan	1815 (LG)
RAB	12 Aug	1819 (NMM)
RAW	19 July	1821 (NMM)
RAR	27 May	1825 (NMM)
VAB	22 July	1830 (NMM)
VAR	10 Jan	1837 (NMM)
d	15 Feb	1839 (LT)
EYRE, George Pettiward		
L	19 July	1814
d		1832 (PRO)
EYRE, Thomas		
L	2 Dec	1800
CR	25 July	1812
Ret CA	14 May	1846 (OB)
d	8 Mar	1853 (NMM)
EYTON, William		
L		
CA	23 Feb	1694
d	11 Oct	1698 (PRO)
EYTON, William Wynne		
T		
L	29 July	1814
CR	6 Oct	1852 (NMM)
d		1857 (TR)
FABIAN, Charles Montagu		
L	31 Mar	1795
CR	29 Apr	1802
CA	21 Oct	1810
d	28 Oct	1826 (MB)
FABIAN, George Johnson		
L	20 Mar	1815 (NMM)
d		1843 (NMM)
FABIAN, Lewis		
L	17 July	1771
CR	23 Aug	1781
CA	15 Jan	1783
d	13 Mar	1791
FABIAN, William		
L	10 Feb	1757
d		1762 (PRO)
FABIAN, William Backhouse		
L	20 Mar	1815 (NMM)
d		1841 (NMM)

FACEY, Degory
L 8 Mar 1782
CR 19 Sept 1795
d 4 July 1798

FACEY, John
L 10 Nov 1741
d 1768 (NMM)

FACEY, Philip
L 15 Aug 1793 (NMM)
CR 26 July 1799
d 1800 (PRO)

FADDY, William
L 14 June 1804
d 1811 (PRO)

FAHIE, Sir William Charles
L 13 Jan 1783
CR 5 Aug 1793 (DNB)
CA 2 Feb 1796
CRM 4 June 1814 (AL)
CB 2 Jan 1815 (LG)
Kt (Two Sicilies) 1815 (DNB)
RAB 12 Aug 1819 (NMM)
RAW 19 July 1821 (NMM)
KCB Oct 1824 (DNB)
RAR 27 May 1825 (NMM)
VAB 22 July 1830 (NMM)
d 11 Jan 1833 (DNB)

FAIR, Robert
L 1 July 1809
CR 6 Sept 1823 (NMM)
CA 10 Jan 1837 (NMM)
d Jan 1844 (NMM)

FAIRBAIRN, Alexander
L 22 Jan 1802
Ret CR 19 Dec 1832 (NMM)
d 1836 (NMM)

FAIRBAIRN, John
L 1 June 1798
d ?1809 (NMM)

FAIRBORNE, Sir Stafford
EF
(Earl of Inchiquin) 1 Aug 1678 (EAD)
LF
(Queen Dowager's) 16 Mar 1685 (EAD)
L June 1685 (DNB)
CA 12 July 1686 (DNB)
RAB 30June 1701 (DNB)
Kt 3 Nov 1701 (EAD)
RAW 8 May 1702
RAR 9 Dec 1702
VAR 6 May 1703
MP
(Rochester) 1705–1708 (DNB)
MCLHA 8 Feb 1706–
20 June 1708 (AO)
AW 7 Jan 1708 (DNB)
AF 21 Dec 1708 (DNB)
d 11 Nov 1742 (DNB)

FAIRBORNE, William
L 13 Feb 1693
CR ?26 June 1701 (PRO)
CA 10 Mar 1703
d 5 Oct 1708

FAIRBRIDGE, Charles
L 4 Mar 1815
d 1818 (NMM)

FAIRCHILD, Roger
L 10 Oct 1694

FAIRFAX, Charles
L 1671

FAIRFAX, Robert
L
CA 15 Sept 1690
(15 Nov 1690 in C)
RA 1708 (DNB)
MCLHA 20 June–28 Oct 1708 (AO)
MP(York) 1713–1715 (DNB)
d 17 Oct 1725 (DNB)

FAIRFAX, Sir William George
L 20 Dec 1757
HP June 1769–
Sept 1776 (DNB)
CR 13 May 1778
CA 12 Jan 1782
Kt 1797 (DNB)
CRM 14 Feb 1799 (AL)
RAB 1 Jan 1801
RAW 23 Apr 1804
RAR 9 Nov 1805
VAB 13 Dec 1806 (LG)
VAW 25 Oct 1809
VAR 31 July 1810
d 7 Nov 1813 (DNB)

FAIRGRIEVE, Richard
L 7 Feb 1815
d 1833 (NMM)

FAIRHOLM, Adam
L 7 Oct 1805
Resigned 1807 (PRO)

FAIRLESS, George
L 18 July 1807
HP 21 Apr 1817 (OB)
Ret CR 10 Apr 1843 (NMM)
d 10 Apr 1856 (PRO)

FAIRLIE, Gilbert
L 18 June 1759
d 1797 (PRO)

FAIRLY, George
L
CR
CA 27 Aug 1709 (PRO)
Dismissed 17 Dec 1714 (PRO)
Employed Again 10 Mar 1716
(1715 in H)
Dismissed 30 Aug 1724

FAIRWEATHER, John
L 8 June 1797
HP 7 June 1814 (OB)
Ret CR 26 Nov 1830 (OB)
d 1853 (PRO)

FALCON, Gordon
L 15 May 1800 (NMM)
CR 8 Mar 1811
CA 29 Oct 1813
RAB 1 Aug 1848 (NMM)
RAW 8 Apr 1851 (NMM)
RAR 17 Sept 1853 (NMM)
d 11 Jan 1854 (NMM)

FALCONAR, Hon. George
L 12 Feb 1745
CR 10 Nov 1756
CA 27 Apr 1762
d 3 May 1780 (PRO)

FALCONER, George
L 28 Oct 1794
Ret CR 22 Apr 1839 (NMM)
d 23 Sept 1841 (LT)
FALCONER, James
L 4 May 1725
Gone 1741
FALCONER, John Richard
L 20 Nov 1779
d 1784 (NMM)
FALCONER, Navin Lindsay
L 8 Dec 1782
d 1790 (NMM)
FALKINER, Charles Leslie
L 4 Jan 1810
CR 9 July 1813
HP 9 July 1813 (OB)
Ret CA 5 Apr 1848 (NMM)
d 7 Feb 1858 (NMM)
FALKINGHAM, Edward (1)
L
CR
CA 26 Feb 1713
d 3 May 1780 (PRO)
FALKINGHAM, Edward (2)
L 7 June 1734
CR 2 May 1743 (PRO)
CA 26 May 1746
COM E 23 June 1746–
28 Feb 1755 (NBO)
CONT 28 Feb–13 Nov 1755 (NBO)
SUP RA 1770
d 1783
FALKINGHAM, John
L 20 Feb 1743
CR 5 Apr 1747
CA 18 Oct 1758
d 2 Dec 1777 (PJP)
FALKLAND, Hon. Lord Viscount
L 30 Mar 1797
CR 19 Jan 1801
CA 29 Apr 1802
d (duel) 4 Mar 1809 (PRO)
FALKLAND, Richard
L 14 Nov 1790
SUP CR 25 July 1823 (NMM)
d Dec 1824 (NMM)
FALL, Richard
L 19 Mar 1694
FANCOURT, Robert Devereux
L 29 Jan 1777
CR 17 Dec 1782
CA 2 Dec 1789
RAB 28 Apr 1808
RAW 25 Oct 1809
RAR 31 July 1810
VAB 12 Aug 1812
VAW 4 June 1814
VAR 12 Aug 1819 (NMM)
AB 27 May 1825 (LG)
d July 1826 (NMM)
FANE, Francis William
L 30 May 1801
CR 29 Apr 1802
CA 30 Aug 1803
RAB 10 Jan 1837 (NMM)
RAW 28 June 1838 (NMM)
d 28 Mar 1844 (LT)
FANE, George
L 5 Jan 1698
CR
CA 14 July 1704
d 8 Apr 1709
FANSHAW, Charles
L 27 June 1720
CR
CA 11 Jan 1733
SUP RA July 1747
d 16 Feb 1757 (NMM)
FANSHAWE, Sir Arthur
L 22 Apr 1813
CR 2 Oct 1815
CA 17 Oct 1816 (NMM)
CB 18 Dec 1840 (OB)
RAB 11 June 1851 (NMM)
RAW 4 July 1853 (NMM)
RAR 4 July 1855 (NMM)
VAB 9 July 1857 (NMM)
VAW 5 Jan 1858 (NMM)
KCB 1860 (CH)
VAR 1 Nov 1860 (NMM)
AB 4 Oct 1862 (NMM)
AW 24 Sept 1863 (NMM)
d 14 June 1864 (NMM)
FANSHAWE, Henry
L 25 May 1805
CR 2 May 1808
CA 7 June 1814
Ret CA 1 Oct 1846 (LG)
Ret RA 9 Oct 1849 (NMM)
d 9 Aug 1856 (NMM)
FANSHAWE, Robert (1)
L 11 Sept 1759
CR 23 Aug 1762
CA 25 May 1768
MP (Plymouth) 1784–Jan 1790 (MPN)
COMM (Plymouth) 1797–4 Feb 1823 (OB)
d 4 Feb 1823 (MPN)
FANSHAWE, Robert (2)
L 13 Dec 1799
CR 4 June 1801
CA 3 Nov 1801
d 3 June 1804 (PJP)
FAREBY, William
L
CA 24 Jan 1690 (PMM)
SUP 27 Mar 1700 (PMM)
d 11 Sept 1711
FARER, Robert
L
CA 1664
FAREWELL, Francis George
L 28 Feb 1815 (NMM)
d 1829 (NMM)
FARINGTON, Henry
L 30 Dec 1783
d 1790 (NMM)
FARINGTON, William
L 14 Oct 1799
CR 7 May 1808

CA	18 Sept	1815
Ret CA	1 Oct	1846 (NMM)
Ret RA	2 Mar	1851 (NMM)
Ret VA	9 July	1857 (NMM)
Ret A	4 Oct	1862 (NMM)
d	4 May	1868 (NMM)
FARIS, John		
L	8 Feb	1805
d		?1809 (NMM)
FARISH, Richard		
L	27 Sept	1740
CR	19 June	1745
Gone		1752
FARMAR, Robert		
L	2 Apr	1744
d		1758(9) (NMM)
FARMER, George (1)		
L	23 May	1759
CR	26 May	1768
CA	10 Jan	1771
KIA	6 Oct	1779 (DNB)
FARMER, George (2)		
L	23 Mar	1782
d		1814 (NMM)
FARMER, Robert		
See FARMAR, Robert		
FARMER, William		
L		
CA	16 Jan	1678
FARMOR, Hon. William		
L	16 Aug	1742
CR		
CA	12 Jan	1745
d		1748 (NMM)
FARNALL, Henry		
L	3 Dec	1793
CR		
CA	14 May	1801
d		1806 (NMM)
FARNDALE, Francis		
L	1 May	1705
SUP	20 Mar	1738 (PMM)
Gone		1739 (PRO)
FARNHAM, Thomas		
L	3 Oct	1771
CR	3 Apr	1780
CA	27 Mar	1782
d	1 Dec	1793 (LT)
FARQUHAR, Sir Arthur		
L	26 Apr	1798
CR	29 Apr	1802
CA	8 Apr	1805
HP	Apr–Aug	1809 (MB)
CB		1815 (DNB)
HP	3 Apr	1816 (MB)
KCB		1831 (CH)
KCH		1832 (DNB)
RAB	10 Jan	1837 (NMM)
Kt (Sweden)	23 May	1839 (LG)
RAW	23 Nov	1841 (NMM)
d	2 Oct	1843 (DNB)
FARQUHARSON, Charles		
L	20 Sept	1815
d	10 Feb	1862 (PRO)
FARQUHARSON, Edward Riou Owen		
T		
L	19 Dec	1810
HP	27 Apr	1815 (OB)
d	21 Dec	1846 (OB)
FARQUHARSON, Richard Spencer Godwin		
L	15 July	1809 (NMM)
d (drowned)	20 Dec	1810 (PJP)
FARQUHARSON, William		
L	12 Sept	1814
d		1849 (NMM)
FARR, Charles		
L		
CA		1667
d	before	1689 (PJP)
FARR, Richard		
L	12 Oct	1812
d		1842 (PRO)
FARR, Walker		
L	28 Nov	1747
CR	5 Apr	1756
d		1757 (PRO)
FARRANT, John		
T	wounded	
L	30 Nov	1808
Ret CR	3 Nov	1846 (PRO)
d	15 Apr	1849 (PRO)
FARRANT, William		
L	3 Dec	1810
Ret CR	3 Nov	1862 (NMM)
d	22 Sept	1868 (NMM)
FARRE,		
L		
CA		1669
FARRER, Francis		
L	18 Nov	1776
d	22 Sept	1777 (PRO)
FARRIS, John		
See FARIS, John		
FARRIS, Robert		
L	21 Nov	1796
d	21 Apr	1800 (PRO)
FARRISH, Richard		
See FARISH, Richard		
FARWELL, Charles		
L	30 Apr	1807
CR	17 Mar	1812
d	4 Oct	1836 (PJP)
FAUCONBERGH, Sir John		
L		1666
FAULCONER, James		
See FALCONER, James		
FAULKNER, Jonathan		
See FAULKNOR, Jonathan		
FAULKNER, Samuel (1)		
L	1 Sept	1716
CR	18 Apr	1735
CA	26 May	1736
d (drowned)	5 Oct	1744 (CH)
FAULKNER, Samuel (2)		
L	30 June	1740
CR	2 Sept	1745 (PRO)
CA	21 Apr	1746
d	28 May	1759

FAULKNER, Samuel Churchill
L 27 Jan 1797
d 14 Feb 1827 (NMM)
FAULKNER, William
L 21 Apr 1695
CR
CA 17 Mar 1707
d 28 Feb 1725 (PRO)
FAULKNOR, John
L 28 Aug 1743
d 1748 (NMM)
FAULKNOR, Jonathan (1)
L 24 Aug 1753
CR 28 Sept 1758
CA 9 July 1759
RAW 24 Sept 1787
RAR 21 Sept 1790
VAB 1 Feb 1793
VAW 12 Apr 1794
VAR 4 July 1794
AB 1 June 1795
d 23 June 1795 (PJP)
FAULKNOR, Jonathan (2)
L 24 June 1777
CR 10 Feb 1780
CA 12 Aug 1782
RAB 23 Apr 1804
RAW 9 Nov 1805
RAR 28 Apr 1808 (NMM)
d Jan 1809 (NMM)
FAULKNOR, Jonathan (3)
L 25 Mar 1813
CR 4 May 1827 (NMM)
d 18 May 1829 (PRO)
FAULKNOR, Richard
L 18 July 1780
d 1784 (PRO)
FAULKNOR, Roach
L 20 Oct 1720
Gone 1 Jan 1764
FAULKNOR, Robert (1)
L 5 Oct 1741
CR 5 Nov 1756
CA 19 Jan 1757
d 9 May 1769
FAULKNOR, Robert (2)
L 20 Dec 1780
CR 22 Nov 1790
CA 20 Mar 1794 (PRO)
KIA 5 Jan 1795 (DNB)
FAULKNOR, Samuel
See FAULKNER, Samuel
FAULKNOR, William Humphry
L 30 Dec 1796
CR 29 Apr 1802
d 1812 (NMM)
FAUNCE, Thomas
L 10 July 1794
d 1802 (PRO)
FAUSSETT, Robert
L 16 Oct 1809
d 1818 (NMM)
FAVELL, Thomas
L 9 Dec 1809
CR 29 Sept 1827 (NMM)
d 1835 (NMM)
FAWCETT, Henry Augustus
L 17 Jan 1811
Ret CR 1 Oct 1851 (NMM)
d 3 Mar 1882 (NMM)
FAWLER, John
L 13 Mar 1734
CR 23 Aug 1742
CA 2 Dec 1745
d 17 Aug 1766 (H)
FAWLKNOR, Jonathan
See FAULKNOR, Jonathan
FAYERMAN, Charles
L 17 Feb 1815
d 1818 (PRO)
FAYERMAN, Edward
L 9 Mar 1815
d 29 Jan 1822 (PRO)
FAYERMAN, Francis
L 30 May 1777
CR 20 May 1781
CA 24 Apr 1793
RAB 31 July 1810
RAW 12 Aug 1812
RAR 4 June 1814
VAB 12 Aug 1815 (NMM)
d 18 Dec 1822 (PRO)
FAYERMAN, Robert John
L 19 Dec 1808
HP Aug 1814 (OB)
Ret CR 12 Aug 1848 (NMM)
d 1869 (PRO)
FAZEBY, William
L
CA 1661
FEAD, Francis
L 30 Dec 1806
CR 4 Oct 1814 (NMM)
CA 1 Nov 1826 (NMM)
Ret CA 1 Oct 1846 (LG)
d 31 Jan 1847 (NMM)
FEAKES, Tobias
L 1666
CA 1667
d before 1689 (PJP)
FEATHERSTONE, John
L 31 Jan 1812
d 1840 (NMM)
FEATHERSTONE, Samuel (1)
L 10 Nov 1778
CR 21 Sept 1790
d 1835 (PRO)
FEATHERSTONE, Samuel (2)
L 2 Feb 1815
Ret CR 30 July 1859 (NMM)
d 16 Feb 1871 (PRO)
FEATHERSTONE, William
L 26 Dec 1795
d 1810 (PRO)
FEATTUS, James
L 23 Mar 1757
CR 7 July 1761
d 1784 (PRO)

FEGEN, James
L 25 Sept 1757
d Feb 1821 (PRO)

FEGEN, Richard
L 8 Nov 1806
CR 1 July 1851 (NMM)
Ret CA 1 Apr 1856 (NMM)
d 16 Feb 1859 (NMM)

FEILD, Arthur
L
CR
CA 22 Oct 1711
d 24 Oct 1726

FEILD, Gregory
L 1672
d before 1689 (PJP)

FEILD, John
L 27 Oct 1758
d 1767 (NMM)

FEILD, Thomas
L 27 Oct 1758
d 1766 (PRO)

FEILDING, Bassill
See FEILDING, Basil

FEILDING, Charles (1)
L 19 May 1757
CR 14 Aug 1760
CA 26 Aug 1760
d 11 Jan 1783 (PRO)

FEILDING, Charles (2)
L 27 Nov 1779 (PRO)
CR 28 July 1801 (PRO)
CA 15 Jan 1802 (PRO)
Ret RA 10 Jan 1837 (NMM)
d 2 Sept 1837 (PRO)

FEILDING, George
L 4 May 1725
d 1729 (PRO)

FEILDING, George
See FIELDING, George

FELIX, Robert Rochford
L 20 Sept 1806
CR 10 June 1817 (NMM)
d 30 Aug 1844 (NMM)

FELLOW, James
L 7 June 1709 (PMM)
CR 11 Sept 1735
d 26 Nov 1742 (PMM)

FELLOWES, Bennett
L 20 Jan 1796
Ret CR 26 Nov 1830 (NMM)
d 1845 (PRO)

FELLOWES, Richard
L 22 Apr 1793
CR 7 Apr 1795
CA 7 Dec 1795
RAB 4 June 1814
CB 2 Jan 1815 (LG)
RAW 12 Aug 1819 (NMM)
RAR 27 May 1825 (NMM)
VAW 22 July 1830 (NMM)
VAR 10 Jan 1837 (NMM)
d 28 Aug 1841 (LT)

FELLOWES, Sir Thomas
L 29 June 1807
CR 16 Sept 1809
CA 4 Mar 1811
CB 2 Jan 1815 (LG)
Kt (Spain) 22 Feb 1822 (DNB)
Kt (France) 1827 (DNB)
Kt (Russia) 1827 (DNB)
Kt (Greece) 1827 (DNB)
Kt 13 Feb 1828 (OB)
d 12 Apr 1853 (DNB)

FELLOWES, Thomas Bourdon
L 7 Oct 1794
Ret CR 26 Nov 1830 (NMM)
d 1833 (NMM)

FELTON, Comptom
L 1673 (PMM)
CA 12 Apr 1678
d 1719 (DDA)

FELTON, John
T
L 30 Aug 1806
Dismissed 11 Mar 1809 (PRO)
Restored June 1861 (PRO)
Ret CR 1 July 1861 (PRO)
d 1866 (NMM)

FENN, Henry
L
CA 1660
d before 1689 (PJP)

FENNELL, George
L 19 Nov 1795
d 31 Aug 1805 (PRO)

FENNELL, John (1)
L 21 Nov 1793
d May 1796 (LT)

FENNELL, John (2)
L 7 Oct 1794
CR 15 June 1814
d 1843 (PRO)

FENNELL, Thomas
L 23 June 1794
d 1798 (PRO)

FENTON, John
L 17 Dec 1779
d Jan 1815 (PRO)

FENWICK, Barnabas
L 23 Feb 1757
d 1795 (PRO)

FENWICK, Benjamin
L 10 Jan 1706
CR 1 Mar 1740
CA 8 June 1741
d 14 Mar 1757

FENWICK, John
L 13 May 1720
CR 6 Mar 1741
d 1744 (PRO)

FENWICK, Robert Bissett
L 3 June 1813
d 14 Aug 1821 (PRO)

FERGUISON, John
See FERGUSSONE, John

FERGUSON, George
L 30 Mar 1805
CR 27 Dec 1808
CA 6 June 1814
RAB 4 May 1849 (NMM)
d 15 Mar 1867 (NMM)

FERGUSON, James
L 15 Nov 1756
CR
CA 6 June 1763
LGH 1784 (PJP)
d 14 Feb 1793 (LT)

FERGUSON, John Macpherson
L 13 Jan 1804
CR 13 July 1808
CA 1 Jan 1817 (NMM)
Ret CA 1 Oct 1846 (NMM)
Ret RA 16 June 1851 (NMM)
d 1855 (NMM)

FERGUSON, John
See FERGUSSONE, John

FERGUSON, Pat
L 27 Oct 1758
d 1761 (NMM)

FERGUSSON, John
L 17 Sept 1756
CR 5 Sept 1777
CA 21 Mar 1781
RAB 14 Feb 1799
RAW 1 Jan 1801
RAR 23 Apr 1804
VAB 9 Nov 1805
VAW 28 Apr 1808
AB 31 July 1810
AW 4 June 1814
d 1818 (NMM)

FERGUSSONE, John (1)
L 2 Oct 1739
CR 12 Nov 1745 (NMM)
CA 6 Oct 1746
d 13 June 1767

FERGUSSONE, John (2)
L 15 Jan 1782
CR 21 May 1795
d 3 Dec 1802 (NMM)

FERMOR, Hon William
See FARMOR, Hon. William

FERNANDES, Donald
L 9 Feb 1797
HP 5 Aug 1806 (OB)
Ret CR 21 Dec 1838 (NMM)
d 24 Jan 1851 (NMM)

FERNDALE, Francis
See FARNDALE, Francis

FERNLY, Edmund
L 1666

FERRAND, Benjamin
L 14 Mar 1740
d 19 Feb 1743 (PJP)

FERRERS, Hon. Washington, Earl
L 6 Jan 1742
CR
CA 19 Apr 1746
RAW 31 Mar 1775 (CH)
VAB 5 Feb 1776
VAW 29 Jan 1778
d 1 Oct 1778 (CH)

FERRETT, Francis
L 4 June 1797
KIA 11 Oct 1797 (JH)

FERRIE, William
L 16 Sept 1800
T wounded
CR 18 Jan 1809
d 8 Apr 1816 (PRO)

FERRIER, John
L 16 Dec 1777
CR 26 Aug 1789
CA 22 Nov 1790
RAB 31 July 1810
RAW 1 Aug 1811
RAR 12 Aug 1812
VAB 4 June 1814
VAW 12 Aug 1819 (NMM)
VAR 19 July 1821 (NMM)
AB 22 July 1830 (LG)
d 27 Jan 1836 (LT)

FERRIERES, Isaac
L 13 Dec 1793
CR 29 Apr 1802
CA 21 Oct 1810
d 1820 (PRO)

FERRINES, Henry
L
CA 1665

FERRIOR, John
L 7 Dec 1805
d 1814 (NMM)

FERRIOR, Samuel
L 2 Aug 1758
d 1774 (PRO)

FERRIS, Abel
L 22 Apr 1799
T
CR 10 Oct 1807
CA 18 Apr 1811
Ret RA 1 Oct 1846 (NMM)
Ret VA 1854 (TR)
d 15 Aug 1859 (PRO)

FERRIS, Solomon
L 9 Sept 1778
CR 22 Nov 1790
CA 14 Oct 1793
d 27 May 1803 (PRO)

FERRIS, Thomas
L 19 Oct 1807
CR 20 Sept 1815
CA 20 Aug 1851 (NMM)
d 1862 (PRO)

FERRIS, William
L 7 Sept 1801
CR 29 Oct 1801
CA 21 June 1804
CB 8 Dec 1815 (LG)
d 18 May 1822 (PJP)

FERRITOR, Edward
L 16 Aug 1782
d 1794 (PRO)

FESTING, Benjamin Morton
T
L 19 Feb 1812
CR 22 Dec 1826 (OB)
HP 22 Dec 1826 (OB)
CA 27 Sept 1851 (NMM)
d 10 May 1865 (PRO)

FESTING, Colson
L 10 Mar 1815 (NMM)
CR 15 Jan 1838 (NMM)
CA 7 Mar 1853 (NMM)
Ret CA 17 Mar 1869 (NMM)
d 12 Oct 1870 (NMM)

FESTING, Henry
L 8 Dec 1777
CR 10 Mar 1797
d 1807

FESTING, Robert Morgan
L 14 Aug 1806
CR 14 Aug 1808
CA 9 Oct 1811
CB 20 July 1838 (OB)
Ret RA 1 Oct 1846 (NMM)
Ret VA 4 July 1855 (NMM)
Ret A 1 Nov 1860 (NMM)
d 16 July 1862 (NMM)

FESTING, Thomas Colson
L 23 Nov 1810
Ret CR 14 July 1851 (NMM)
d 10 Aug 1857 (PRO)

FETTIPLACE, Thomas
L 5 Feb 1694
Gone 1719 (PRO)

FEUVRE, John le
See LE FEUVRE, John

FIDGE, William
L 1672
d before 1689 (PJP)

FIDGES, Hugh
L 1672

FIELD, Allen George
L 25 Mar 1809
Ret CR 9 Apr 1847 (NMM)
d 1856 (PRO)

FIELD, Arthur
See FEILD, Arthur

FIELD, Francis Ventris
L 26 Feb 1783
CR 22 June 1795
d (drowned) 31 Dec 1796 (CH)

FIELD, George
L 9 Apr 1781
SUP CR 1 Jan 1816 (NMM)
d Jan 1826 (NMM)

FIELD, John
See FEILD, John

FIELD, John Connor
L 27 May 1796
Ret CR 26 Nov 1830 (NMM)
d 1831 (NMM)

FIELD, Thomas
See FEILD, Thomas

FIELD, William
L 18 Feb 1796
CR 19 June 1828 (NMM)
d 26 Mar 1832 (LT)

FIELDING, Basil
L 28 Aug 1754
CR 19 Nov 1759
d Aug 1777

FIELDING, Charles
See FEILDING, Charles

FIELDING, George
L 1663

FIELDING, Hon. George
See FEILDING, Hon. George

FIELDING, James
L 27 Apr 1727
Gone 1734 (PRO)

FIELDING, Victor
L 24 Feb 1806
d 1810 (NMM)

FIELDING, William
L 3 Dec 1724
CR
CA 11 Jan 1743
SUP RA 1762
d 23 Sept 1773

FIELDING, William Carr
L 11 June 1761
d 1765(6) (NMM)

FIFE, John
L 6 Apr 1779
d Oct 1823 (NMM)

FIFE, John
See FYFFE, John

FIFE, Thomas
L 12 Aug 1800
T
CR 24 Dec 1805
CA 4 Dec 1813
d 5 July 1829 (NMM)

FIGG, James
L 11 June 1814
d 1828 (PRO)

FIGG, William
L 30 Aug 1806
Ret CR 21 Apr 1840 (NMM)
d 11 Aug 1858 (PRO)

FILKIN, Richard
L 24 Mar 1780
d 1783 (PRO)

FILMORE, John
T
L 16 Jan 1808
CR 18 June 1811
CA 20 Aug 1824 (NMM)
d 18 May 1839 (PRO)

FINCH, Hon. Henry
L 28 Dec 1814
d 6 Sept 1820 (NMM)

FINCH, John
L 22 Jan 1806
d 1808(9) (NMM)

FINCH, Richard
L
CA 1 May 1691
d 19 May 1695

FINCH, Hon. Seymour
L 30 Aug 1777
CR 21 Sept 1779
CA 13 Feb 1781
d 1794

FINCH, William (1)
L
CA 1661
Cashiered 3 Nov 1666 (PRO)
Employed again 1671 (PRO)
KIA 28 May 1673 (CH)

FINCH, William (2)
L 1 May 1804
d 7 Feb 1827 (NMM)

FINCH, Hon. William Clement
L 7 July 1772
CR 10 Apr 1776
CA 18 Mar 1777
MP (Surrey) 1790–30 Sept 1794 (MPT)
RAB 4 July 1794
d 30 Sept 1794 (MPT)

FINCHAM, Augustus N.
L 1672

FINCHER, Thomas
L 2 Feb 1741
CR
CA 6 Dec 1745
d 13 Apr 1749

FINCHLEY, John
L 30 Jan 1806
d 1811 (PRO)

FINDLAY, John
L 16 Feb 1815
d 1820 (PRO)

FINEY, Thomas Dixey
L 20 Nov 1799
Dismissed 1801 (PRO)

FINLAISON, William
L 8 Apr 1811
CR 9 Sept 1820 (PRO)
d 19 Dec 1852 (PRO)

FINLAYSON, John
L 9 Apr 1808
Ret CR 18 Jan 1845 (NMM)
d 1857 (NMM)

FINLEY, Justice
L 26 Dec 1796
CR 15 Dec 1808
CA 7 June 1814
d 1838 (PRO)

FINNEMORE, John
L 17 Feb 1815
d 1861 (PRO)

FINNEY, William
L 5 Oct 1807
d 1825 (NMM)

FINNIMORE, Thomas
L 14 Sept 1809
d 1811 (PRO)

FINNIS, Robert
L 9 Nov 1803
KIA 10 Sept 1813 (I)

FINUCANE, Patrick
L 4 May 1810
d 1819 (NMM)

FIOLTT, William Edward
L 29 Apr 1810 (PRO)
d 1849 (PRO)

FIRMAN, William
L 4 May 1810
d 3 Aug 1820 (NMM)

FISH, Gregory
L
CA 1683
d before 1689 (PJP)

FISH, John
L
CR 27 Feb 1781
CA 23 Aug 1781
RAB 1 Jan 1801
RAW 23 Apr 1804
VAB 9 Nov 1805
VAW 28 Apr 1808
VAR 31 July 1810
MP (Wexford) 13 Feb 1813–July 1814 (MPT)
AB 4 Dec 1813
AW 12 Aug 1819 (NMM)
AR 22 July 1830 (NMM)
d 10 Sept 1834 (MPT)

FISH, Nathaniel
L 21 Dec 1801
"Adjusted" to 18 Sept 1805 (NMM)
d 11 Feb 1828 (NMM)

FISHER, Ebenezer
L 13 Nov 1790
d 1814 (PRO)

FISHER, George (1)
L 13 Feb 1691 (PJP)
CR
CA 18 Jan 1705
d 18 Aug 1705

FISHER, George (2)
L 1 Sept 1796
Ret CR 26 Nov 1830 (NMM)
d 1841 (PRO)

FISHER, Henry
L 28 Feb 1815 (NMM)
d 1858 (NMM)

FISHER, John (1)
L 6 Aug 1805
CR 7 June 1814
Ret CR 1 July 1851 (NMM)
d 22 July 1851 (NMM)

FISHER, John (2)
L 21 July 1814
d 1841 (PRO)

FISHER, Peter
L 11 Feb 1800
CR 27 Dec 1808
CA 19 Feb 1814
d 28 Aug 1844 (LT)

FISHER, Richard
L 24 Oct 1778
CR 20 Aug 1779

CA	22 Apr	1782
Insane	22 May	1786 (PMM)
d	23 May	1795 (PRO)
FISHER, Samuel James		
L	29 Apr	1801
d		1802 (PRO)
FISHER, Thomas (1)		
L		
CA		1665
FISHER, Thomas (2)		
L		
CA	24 Apr	1696
d	7 Mar	1697
FISHER, William		
L	3 Sept	1801
CR	25 Sept	1806
CA	18 Apr	1811
RAB	2 Dec	1847 (NMM)
RAW	18 Oct	1849 (NMM)
RAR	4 June	1852 (NMM)
d	30 Sept	1852 (DNB)
FITTON, Henry		
L		
CA		1673
FITTON, Michael		
L	9 Mar	1804
d	31 Dec	1852 (DNB)
FITZGERALD, Hon. Charles Lord		
L	13 May	1778
CR		
CA	23 May	1780
RAW	14 Feb	1799
RAR	1 Jan	1801
VAB	23 Apr	1804
VAW	9 Nov	1805
VAR	28 Apr	1808
d	17 Feb	1810 (PRO)
FITZ-GERALD, Edward		
L		
CA		1672
FITZGERALD, Hamilton		
L	20 July	1801
HP	27 Apr	1809 (OB)
Ret CR	12 July	1831 (NMM)
d	2 Oct	1856 (PRO)
FITZGERALD, Henry		
L	26 Aug	1814
Ret CR	15 Apr	1858 (NMM)
d		1862 (PRO)
FITZGERALD, John (1)		
L	2 Nov	1779
d		1788 (PRO)
FITZGERALD, John (2)		
L	2 Nov	1798
CR	16 June	1802 (OB)
Ret CR	1 June	1842 (NMM)
d		1851 (NMM)
FITZGERALD, Michael		
L	27 Feb	1801
Ret CR	29 Dec	1830 (NMM)
d	17 Sept	1845 (NMM)
FITZGERALD, Richard		
L	4 Mar	1740
d		1742 (3) (NMM)
FITZGERALD, Sir Robert Lewis		
L	21 Feb	1794
CR	13 Feb	1797
CA	24 Dec	1798
SUPRA	2 June	1825 (NMM)
KCH	18 Jan	1835 (LT)
VAB	12 Nov	1840 (NMM)
VAR	23 Nov	1841 (NMM)
d	17 Jan	1844 (LT)
FITZGERALD, Thomas		
L	5 Feb	1795
d (drowned)	25 Feb	1810 (PJP)
FITZGERALD, William (1)		
L	12 Oct	1795
d		1798 (PRO)
FITZGERALD, William (2)		
L	10 June	1800
d		1807 (NMM)
FITZGERALD, William Robert		
L	7 Feb	1815
d	May	1857 (PRO)
FITZ-GIBBON, Philip		
L	31 July	1809 (NMM)
d		1826 (NMM)
FITZHARDINGE, Hon. Frederick, Lord		
L	9 July	1808
CR	19 Dec	1810
CA	7 June	1814
CB		1814 (PJP)
RAB	30 Oct	1849 (PRO)
RAW	30 July	1852 (PRO)
RAR	15 Apr	1854 (PRO)
KCB	5 July	1855 (DNB)
VAB	21 Oct	1856 (PRO)
VAW	10 Sept	1857 (PRO)
VAR	6 Mar	1858 (PRO)
GCB	28 June	1861 (DNB)
Cre EP	5 Aug	1861 (DNB)
AB	15 Jan	1862 (PRO)
AW	27 Apr	1863 (PRO)
d	17 Oct	1867 (DNB)
FITZHERBERT, Thomas		
L	20 Feb	1753
CR	14 Mar	1760
CA	10 July	1761
RAB	21 Sept	1790
RAR	1 Feb	1793
VAB	12 Apr	1794
VAW	4 July	1794
d		1794 (PRO)
FITZHERBERT, Thomas Woodhouse		
L	24 Oct	1778
d		1804 (PRO)
FITZMAURICE, Edward Howe		
L	28 May	1813
HP	14 Jan	1813 (OB)
d		1852 (NMM)
FITZMAURICE, Gamaliel		
L	7 May	1802
CR	1 Feb	1812
d	5 Feb	1836 (LT)
FITZMAURICE, James		
L	18 Nov	1807
Ret CR	28 July	1844 (NMM)
d	10 Sept	1879 (NMM)

FITZMAURICE, William
L 15 Jan 1802
HP Oct 1815–
19 Apr 1825 (OB)
d 7 Jan 1848 (NMM)

FITZPATRICK, James (1)
L 10 July 1782
d 1790 (PRO)

FITZPATRICK, James (2)
L 22 Oct 1789
SUP CR 17 Feb 1823 (NMM)
d Mar 1824 (NMM)

FITZPATRICK, James (3)
L 16 Aug 1806
d 7 Nov 1827 (NMM)

FITZPATRICK, Richard, Lord Gouran
L 14 May 1687 (P)
CA 11 Jan 1690
d 9 June 1727

FITZROY, Lord Augustus (1)
L by 1734 (MPS)
CR
CA 2 Nov 1736
MP (Thetford) 10 Feb 1739–
28 May 1741 (MPS)
d 28 May 1741 (MPS)

FITZROY, Lord Augustus (2)
L 17 Mar 1790
CR 13 Dec 1792
CA 29 Mar 1794
d 28 Sept 1801 (NMM)

FITZROY, Hon. Augustus William
L 23 Nov 1780
d 1786 (PRO)

FITZROY, Lord William
L 13 May 1800
CR 7 Jan 1802
CA 3 Mar 1804
MP (Thetford) 1806–1812 (MPT)
Dismissed 7 Mar 1811 (PRO)
Reinstated 22 Aug 1811 (PRO)
CB 4 June 1815 (MPT)
RAB 10 Jan 1837 (NMM)
KCB 4 July 1840 (MPT)
RAW 23 Nov 1841 (NMM)
RAR 9 Nov 1846 (NMM)
VAB 26 June 1847 (NMM)
VAW 4 May 1849 (NMM)
VAR 1 July 1851 (NMM)
AB 2 Apr 1853 (NMM)
AW 9 July 1855 (NMM)
d 13 May 1857 (NMM)

FITZSIMMONS, Henry
L 28 Feb 1805
d 1808 (PRO)

FLATCHER, John
L 1669
CA 1660
CA 1672
Lost his ship to Dutch 5 May 1672 (PRO)
Fled from trial 1672 (PRO)

FLATT, Nicholas
L 31 Dec 1782
d 1814 (PRO)

FLAWES, John
L 11 Mar 1691

FLAWES, William
L 1670
CA 1665
d before 1689 (PJP)

FLEEMING, Hon. Charles Elphinstone
L 22 Apr 1793
CR 8 Mar 1794 (NMM)
CA 7 Oct 1794
MP (Stirlingshire) 1802–1812 (MPT)
CRM 12 Aug 1812 (MB)
RAB 4 Dec 1813
RAW 4 June 1814
VAB 19 July 1821 (NMM)
VAW 27 May 1825 (NMM)
VAR 22 July 1830 (NMM)
MP (Stirlingshire) 1832–1834 (MPT)
AB 10 Jan 1837 (NMM)
GGH 1839–1840 (MPT)
d 30 Oct 1840 (NMM)

FLEETWOOD, Gerrard
L 26 Jan 1798
d 1811 (PRO)

FLEMING, Hon. Charles Elphinstone
See FLEEMING, Hon. Charles Elphinstone

FLEMING, Humphry
L
CA 1669
d before 1689 (PJP)

FLEMING, John (1)
L 5 Mar 1782
d 25 Jan 1823 (NMM)

FLEMING, John (2)
L 2 Oct 1800
CR 2 Nov 1814
HP May 1816 (OB)
d 1847 (PRO)

FLEMING, Richard Howell
L 26 Sept 1809 (PRO)
CR 17 Sept 1816 (OB)
HP 17 Sept 1816–
21 June 1842 (OB)
CA 28 July 1851 (NMM)
d 16 Mar 1856 (PRO)

FLEMING, William
L 21 Oct 1757
d 1780 (PRO)

FLEMING, William Henry
L 26 Aug 1709
CR
CA 26 July 1728
d 18 May 1771

FLETCHER, James S.
L 11 Feb 1812
d 30 Apr 1814

FLETCHER, John (1)
L
CA 1 Feb 1692
(?1 Feb 1691)
LSMR 21 Aug 1693 (EAD)
Retired Dec 1695 (EAD)
d 23 Jan 1705 (CH)

FLETCHER, John (2)
L

CA	24 May	1695
KIA	26 Aug	1697 (DCB)
FLETCHER, John (3)		
L	23 Dec	1707 (PMM)
CR		
CA	7 Mar	1711
d	May	1750
FLETCHER, John (4)		
L	21 Aug	1809
CR	11 May	1827 (PRO)
d	10 Nov	1827 (PRO)
FLETCHER, John		
See FLATCHER, John		
FLETCHER, Lowther		
L	23 Apr	1748
d		1758(9) (PRO)
FLETCHER, Philip		
L	16 Jan	1761
d		1763 (PRO)
FLETCHER, William		
L	31 Oct	1809
CR	30 Nov	1820 (NMM)
CA	4 Mar	1829 (OB)
HP	4 Mar	1829 (OB)
d	23 May	1846 (NMM)
FLIN, Edward		
L	16 Nov	1804
CR	2 May	1810
CA	7 June	1814
d	May	1820 (LT)
FLINDERS, Matthew		
L	31 Jan	1798
CR	16 Feb	1801
CA	7 May	1810
d	19 July	1814 (DUB)
FLINDERS, Samuel Ward		
L	6 Mar	1801
Reduced by Court Martial to		
L	6 Mar	1804 (NMM)
d		1835 (NMM)
FLINN, Edward		
See FLIN, Edward		
FLINN, John		
L	11 Jan	1783
d	22 Oct	1793 (NMM)
FLINN, John Turner		
L	26 Sept	1811 (NMM)
d		1840 (NMM)
FLINN, Thomas		
L	15 Mar	1802
d		1820 (NMM)
FLINN, William		
L	11 Sept	1813
d		1832 (NMM)
FLINT, Edward		
L	15 Oct	1781
d		1786 (NMM)
FLINT, James		
L	24 Nov	1801
d		1806 (NMM)
FLINT, Thomas		
L	3 Mar	1691
FLINT, William		
L	5 Apr	1802
CR	9 Mar	1809
CA	1 Mar	1811
d	Oct	1818 (PRO)
FLINTOFF, Archibald		
L	19 Nov	1811
d		1816 (PRO)
FLOYD, Thomas (1)		
L	21 May	1777
d		1780(1) (NMM)
FLOYD, Thomas (2)		
L	2 July	1778
d		1785 (PRO)
FLYNN, Edward		
See FLIN, Edward		
FOARD, John		
L	5 Feb	1694
Gone		1719 (PRO)
FOGG , Christopher		
L		
CA	24 Feb	1693
	(8 Sept	1692 in C)
	(24 Jan	1693 in H)
d	24 Nov	1708
FOGG, Nathaniel		
L	25 Feb	1690
FOGGE, John		
L		1672
FOLDS, Thomas John		
L	11 Aug	1797
d	16 July	1818 (PRO)
FOLEY, Edward Kingston		
L	3 Oct	1803
d	18 July	1834 (PRO)
FOLEY, Richard		
L	24 Apr	1807
CR	11 May	1812
CA	7 June	1814
d	23 Dec	1828 (PRO)
FOLEY, Thomas (1)		
L	19 Feb	1741
CR	3 May	1748
CA	2 Apr	1754
d	2 May	1755
FOLEY, Thomas (2)		
L	18 June	1741
CR	6 Aug	1756
d		1772 (PRO)
FOLEY, Sir Thomas (3)		
L	25 May	1778
CR	1 Dec	1782
CA	21 Sept	1790
CRM	2 Oct	1807 (AL)
RAB	28 Apr	1808
RAR	31 July	1810
VAB	12 Aug	1812
VAW	4 June	1814
KCB	12 Apr	1815 (LG)
VAR	12 Aug	1819 (NMM)
GCB	6 May	1820 (DNB)
AB	27 May	1825 (NMM)
AW	22 July	1830 (LG)
d	9 Jan	1833 (DNB)

FOLJAMBE, John
L
CA 20 July 1692
KIA 20 Oct 1705 (CH)

FOLLIOTT, Daniel
L 30 Apr 1778
CR 21 Sept 1790
d 1819 (PRO)

FOLLIOTT, Robert
L 11 June 1807
d 1836 (PRO)

FOLVIL, Stephen
L 22 Jan 1795
CR 12 Dec 1800
CA 29 Apr 1802
d 1833 (PRO)

FOOKS, William
L 20 June 1765
CR 17 July 1776
CA 14 May 1779
RAB 20 Feb 1797
d 2 Oct 1798

FOORD, James John
L 25 Feb 1815
Ret CR 14 Apr 1862 (NMM)
d 1875 (NMM)

FOOT, Charles
L 3 Feb 1813
d 1818 (NMM)

FOOT, Edward James
See FOOTE, Sir Edward James

FOOTE, Charles
L 18 July 1797
CR 22 Oct 1802
CA 5 Sept 1806
d 5 Sept 1811 (NMM)

FOOTE, Sir Edward James
L 12 Aug 1785
CR 1 Oct 1791
CA 7 June 1794
RAB 12 Aug 1812
RAW 4 June 1814
RAR 12 Aug 1819 (NMM)
VAB 19 July 1821 (NMM)
VAW 27 May 1825 (NMM)
VAR 22 July 1830 (PRO)
KCB 25 May 1831 (LFG)
d 23 May 1833 (PRO)

FOOTE, John
L 10 May 1804
CR 29 Sept 1813
CA 29 Sept 1827 (NMM)
Ret CA 3 May 1849 (NMM)
d 28 Oct 1853 (PRO)

FOOTE, Peter
L
CA 1664
d before 1689 (PJP)

FOOTE, William
L 11 Oct 1794
CR 18 Dec 1799
CA 21 Oct 1810
d 5 July 1844 (LT)

FORBES, Alexander William
L 4 Mar 1815
HP 4 Mar 1815 (OB)
Ret CR 1 Oct 1860 (NMM)
d 25 Dec 1864 (PRO)

FORBES, Andrew
L 17 Feb 1815
CR 16 June 1823 (NMM)
CA 27 Aug 1834 (NMM)
d 24 Oct 1847 (PRO)

FORBES, Duncan
L 7 Nov 1727
Gone 1734 (PRO)

FORBES, George, Earl of Grannard (1)
Inh IP 1704 (DNB)
LMR (Holt) 25 June 1704 (EAD)
L 1705 (DNB)
CR
CA 16 July 1706
LH 6 Mar 1707 (DNB)
(Horse Guards)
CAH 18 Nov 1708 (EAD)
(Life Guards)
Resigned (Marines) 16 May 1711 (EAD)
MP 1723–1727 (MPS)
(Queensborough)
RAW 4 May 1734
VAR 16 Dec 1734
VAB 2 Mar 1736
(2 Mar 1735 in H)
MP (Ayr Burghs) 1741–1747 (MPS)
d 19 June 1765 (MPS)

FORBES, George (2)
L 15 Oct 1793
d 24 Oct 1816 (NMM)

FORBES, George (3)
L 16 Aug 1794
d 1800 (PRO)

FORBES, Hay
L 1 Oct 1781
d 1805 (PRO)

FORBES, Henry
T
L 9 Apr 1806
CR 1 Feb 1812
CA 30 May 1819 (NMM)
Ret CA 1 Oct 1846 (NMM)
Ret RA 19 Jan 1852 (NMM)
d 13 Jan 1855 (PRO)

FORBES, Hugh
L 13 Mar 1734
CR 30 May 1745 (NMM)
CA 5 July 1745
S.O.L. shows him still as L as late as Sept 1747 (NMM)
Gone 6 Apr 1748 (NMM)
d 8 Jan 1749 (NMM)

FORBES, James
L 28 Aug 1782
d 1789 (NMM)

FORBES, James Hodder
L 1 Mar 1815 (PRO)
Ret CR 24 July 1862 (PRO)
d 1867 (PRO)

FORBES, Hon. John (1)
L 16 Mar 1731
CR 7 Mar 1737 (PJP)
CA 24 Oct 1737 (PJP)
RAB 15 July 1747
RAW 12 May 1748
IMP (St. Johnstown) 1751 (DNB)
VAB 6 Jan 1755 (CH)
COM AD 13 Dec 1756–
6 Apr 1757 (AO)
VAR Feb 1757
Com AD 2 July 1757–
20 Apr 1763 (AO)
AB 5 Feb 1758 (CH)
IMP (Mullingar) 1761 (DNB)
GRM 1 May 1763 (AL)
AW 18 Oct 1770
AF 24 Oct 1781
d 10 Mar 1796 (DNB)

FORBES, John (2)
L 18 Feb 1800
d 2 Mar 1825 (PRO)

FORBES, John (3)
L 25 Dec 1800
CR 17 Mar 1812
Ret CA 26 Mar 1844 (PRO)
d 16 Jan 1866 (PRO)

FORBES, John
See DRUMMOND, Sir John Forbes

FORBES, Peter
L 4 Apr 1757
CR 2 June 1760
d 1800 (PRO)

FORBES, Hon. Robert (1)
L 28 June 1782
CR 26 Aug 1789
CA 22 Nov 1790
d 7 Dec 1795 (PRO)

FORBES, Robert (2)
L 13 July 1796
CR 29 Apr 1802
CA 21 Oct 1810
d 1819 (PRO)

FORBES, Robert (3)
L 13 July 1797 (NMM)
Ret CR 17 Aug 1839 (NMM)
d 8 Feb 1842 (NMM)

FORBES, Hon William (1)
L 15 Nov 1790
d 1 Feb 1792 (NMM)

FORBES, William (2)
L 16 June 1814
d Oct 1820 (PRO)

FORD, Francis
L 16 July 1759
d 24 May 1787 (PMM)

FORD, George Arnaud
L 4 May 1797
d 1798 (PRO)

FORD, John
L 7 Apr 1761
CR 28 Oct 1772
CA 25 June 1773
RAW 12 Apr 1794
RAR 4 July 1794 (NMM)
VAW 1 June 1795
d 1796 (PRO)

FORD, Samuel
L 1667 (DDA)

FORD, Thomas
L 5 Apr 1757
d 1757 (PRO)

FORD, Thomas
See FORD, Samuel

FORD, William
L 17 July 1797
d 1800 (PRO)

FORDER, George
L 2 June 1810
d 11 Nov 1846 (LT)

FORDER, Robert
L 18 Oct 1804
CR 19 July 1821 (NMM)
d 1864 (PRO)

FORDER, Samuel
L 8 Dec 1800
d 1811 (PRO)

FORDYCE, Alexander
L 30 Mar 1761
d 1783 (PRO)

FOREMAN, Henry
L 4 Feb 1815
d 1842 (PRO)

FOREMAN, John
L Nov 1807
d 24 June 1822 (PRO)

FOREMAN, Richard
L 23 June 1801
Name removed 1811 (PRO)

FORFAR, John Bentinck
L 17 Apr 1794
d 1813 (NMM)

FORMAN, Walter
L 10 Oct 1801 (NMM)
CR 1 Dec 1813 (NMM)
d 1835 (PRO)

FORORD, William
L 29 Jan 1748 (NMM)
d 1772 (PRO)

FORREST, Alexander Austin
L 17 Sept 1799
Dismissed 1808 (PJP)

FORREST, Arthur
L 1741 (DNB)
CR 25 May 1741
CA 9 Mar 1745
d 26 May 1770 (DNB)

FORREST, Digory
L 27 Sept 1759
d 12 Apr 1766 (PMM)

FORREST, John Rocheid
L 23 Dec 1814
HP 29 May 1815 (OB)
d 16 Feb 1850 (PRO)

FORREST, Thomas (1)
L 27 Sept 1775
KIA 16 Jan 1780 (LG)

FORREST, THOMAS (2)
L 29 Apr 1802
CR 22 Jan 1806
CA 25 July 1809
d 8 Sept 1814 (PRO)

FORRESTER, Hon. George, Lord
L 9 Dec 1735
CR
CA 24 Sept 1740
Cashiered 28 Mar 1746 (PRO)
d 26 July 1748

FORRESTER, John
L 30 July 1720
CR
CA 6 Mar 1728
d 12 July 1737

FORRESTER, Hon. William
L 2 Apr 1756 (NMM)
d 1764 (NMM)

FORSTER, Gawen
L 7 Sept 1807

FORSTER, George
L 16 Jan 1802

FORSTER, George Brookes
L 27 Dec 1812
Ret CR 2 July 1855 (NMM)
d Sept 1874 (NMM)

FORSTER, John (1)
L 30 Oct 1761
d 1784 (PRO)

FORSTER, John (2)
L 2 Feb 1808
CR 2 Jan 1829 (NMM)
CA 28 June 1838 (NMM)
d 19 June 1841 (NMM)

FORSTER, Matthew
L 13 Nov 1790
CR 7 May 1802
CA 22 Jan 1806
d 12 Jan 1824 (MB)

FORSTER, Robert
L 20 July 1802
CR 13 June 1815
Struck off list for being in service of Spanish insurgents 1819 (PRO)
Restored 1832 (PRO)
d 1 Mar 1852 (PRO)

FORSTER, Samuel Peter
L 8 Oct 1793
CR 4 July 1797
CA 17 Aug 1798
SUP RA 9 June 1825 (NMM)
d 7 Feb 1840 (NMM)

FORSTER, Stephen
L 10 June 1704
Gone 1727 (PRO)

FORSTER, Thomas
L 18 July 1807
CR 16 Feb 1814
d 14 Dec 1827 (MB)

FORSTER, William
L 26 Apr 1745
CR 24 May 1762
CA 26 May 1768
d 13 Aug 1780 (PRO)

FORSYTH, Alexander
L 27 June 1803
Junior Lieutenant 1803
L 18 June 1804
d 1805(6) (NMM)

FORT, Thomas
L 14 Sept 1727
d 1734 (PRO)

FORTEN, Matthew
L 25 Mar 1809
d 1813 (PRO)

FORTEN, William
L 8 Oct 1801
d 1808(9) (NMM)

FORTESCUE, Bodley Spettigue
L 26 May 1795
d 1797 (PRO)

FORTESCUE, Sir Chichester
L 26 June 1773
CR 23 Oct 1779
CA 2 Nov 1780
SUP RA 5 Mar 1799
d 29 Mar 1820 (NMM)

FORTESCUE, Faithful Adrian
L 24 May 1762
d 1774 (PRO)

FORTESCUE, George
L 7 Oct 1811
Seniority reduced 11 Jan 1819 (NMM)
Original seniority restored 1821 (NMM)
d 15 June 1838 (PRO)

FORTESCUE, Hugh (1)
L 4 Nov 1734
d 1740 (PRO)

FORTESCUE, Hugh (2)
L 9 Feb 1815
d 1826 (PRO)

FORTESCUE, John (1)
L
CA 1661
d before 1689 (PJP)

FORTESCUE, John (2)
L 1665

FORTESCUE, John (3)
L 24 Nov 1744
CR 30 June 1756
CA 4 Sept 1759
d 1787 (PRO)

FORTESCUE, John Faithful
L 11 June 1778
CR 15 Nov 1781
CA 6 Aug 1783
SUP RA 21 Nov 1805
d Dec 1819 (PRO)

FORTESCUE, Matthew (1)
L 4 Apr 1720
d 1748(9) (NMM)

FORTESCUE, Hon. Matthew (2)
L 3 Sept 1775
CR 22 June 1781
CA 24 May 1782
SUP 23 Apr 1804
d 19 Nov 1842 (PMM)

FORTESCUE, Robert
L 1666
FORTESCUE, Thomas
L 14 June 1813
d 12 Jan 1821 (PRO)
FORTESCUE, William
L 5 Nov 1740 (NMM)
CR 8 Feb 1746
CA 4 Jan 1757
d 1775
FORTESQUE, Matthew
See FORTESCUE, Matthew
FORTH, John (1)
L 5 Aug 1759
d 22 Mar 1790
FORTH, John (2)
L 29 Feb 1795
Struck off list 1799 (NMM)
FORTUNE, Adam
L 22 Oct 1795
Name removed 1811 (PRO)
FORTYE, Anthony
L 6 June 1744
LGH 1778 (PJP)
d 16 Mar 1803 (LT)
FORWOOD, Thomas
L 20 Dec 1776
d 1787(8) (NMM)
FOSERBY, Godfrey
L 16 Mar 1815
CR 14 Oct 1865 (NMM)
d 9 Apr 1866 (PRO)
FOSS, Joseph
L 7 Feb 1746
d 1776 (PRO)
FOSSE, William
L 6 Oct 1809
d 1848 (PRO)
FOSTER, Edward Perry
T
L 5 Feb 1806
d 1844 (TR)
FOSTER, Henry
L 13 June 1815
CR 30 Nov 1827 (NMM)
d 5 Feb 1831 (PRO)
FOSTER, Humphrey
L 2 Jan 1695
FOSTER, James
L 1672
FOSTER, William (1) or FORSTER
L 26 Apr 1745 (PRO)
d 13 Aug 1780 (PRO)
FOSTER, William (2)
L 7 May 1800
d 1803 (NMM)
FOTHERBY, Charles
L 5 June 1697
CR
CA 24 Oct 1702
d 1 Aug 1720
FOTHERGILL, William
L 3 June 1800
CR 26 Apr 1802
CA 1 May 1804
d 18 July 1817 (LT)
FOTHERINGHAM, Patrick
L 13 Dec 1760
CR 1 Apr 1765
CA 9 Oct 1773
d 20 May 1781 (PRO)
FOULER, John
L 1 Aug 1809
d 28 Dec 1809 (PRO)
FOULER, Thomas
L 1760
CR
CA 1763
d ? Sept 1768 (PJP)
FOULERTON, John
L 9 Jan 1783
d 1795 (PRO)
FOULERTON, Thomas
L 11 May 1799
Ret CR 1 Dec 1830 (NMM)
d 1842 (PRO)
FOULIS, Thomas (1)
L 1666
CA 27 July 1666 (RM)
KIA 28 May 1672 (SJ)
FOULIS, Thomas (2)
L 23 Aug 1688
FOULKES, John Davy
L 5 Aug 1813
d 1843 (PRO)
FOULKES, Peter
L 29 Mar 1745
CR 15 Dec 1777
d 1782 (PRO)
FOULKS, Simon
L 23 Dec 1680
CA 22 Dec 1688
d 2 Dec 1702
FOWELL, Edward
L 12 Oct 1727 (PRO)
d 22 July 1736 (PRO)
FOWELL, Samuel
L 29 Aug 1794
CR 4 Jan 1808
d 30 Mar 1823 (MB)
FOWELL, William
L 14 Oct 1795
Ret CR 26 Nov 1830 (PRO)
d 1837 (PRO)
FOWKE, George
L 14 Nov 1790
CR 29 Sept 1795
CA 9 July 1798
RAB 27 May 1825 (NMM)
RAR 22 July 1830 (NMM)
d 9 Mar 1822 (PRO)
FOWKE, Henry
L 14 Dec 1711
CR 29 July 1727 (PRO)
CA 4 Jan 1728 (PRO)
d 1 Dec 1729 (PRO)

FOWKE, Thorpe
L 20 Sept 1730
CR
CA 24 May 1742
SUP RA 1759
d 14 Mar 1784

FOWKES, Simon
See FOULKS, Simon

FOWLE, Thomas
L 30 July 1812
d Sept 1821 (PRO)

FOWLER, Andrew
L 15 Aug 1759
d 1770 (PRO)

FOWLER, John
See FOULER, John

FOWLER, Richard
L 29 Sept 1762
d 1797 (PRO)

FOWLER, Robert Merrick
L 27 Feb 1800
CR 4 Feb 1806
CA 20 Apr 1811
Ret CA 31 Oct 1846 (LG)
d 28 May 1860 (PRO)

FOWLER, Samuel
L 1 Mar 1803
d 1804 (PRO)

FOWLER, Thomas
L 11 Feb 1815
d 1860 (PRO)

FOWLER, Thomas
See FOWLE, Thomas

FOWLES, Henry
L 12 Jan 1691 (PJP)
CA 28 Oct 1697
d 24 Apr 1704

FOWLIS, Thomas
L
CA 12 Apr 1690
d 21 July 1703

FOWNES, Henry George
L 30 Oct 1790
d 1796 (PRO)

FOWNES, Jeremiah
L 7 Mar 1696

FOX, Edward
L 8 Feb 1679

FOX, George
L 23 Aug 1801
Ret CR 28 Jan 1847 (NMM)
d Feb 1853 (NMM)

FOX, James
L 6 Feb 1815
d 3 Apr 1840 (PRO)

FOX, John (1)
L
CA 1673

FOX, John (2)
L 5 Apr 1783
Ret CR 1 Mar 1821 (NMM)
d 1822 (NMM)

FOX, Peter
L 8 Nov 1734
d ?1737 (NMM)

FOX, Ralph
L 1661

FOX, Samuel
L 26 Dec 1782
SUP CR 10 Mar 1819 (NMM)
d 1837 (PRO)

FOX, Thomas
L 4 June 1728
CR 30 Dec 1734
CA 6 Aug 1737
Dismissed ship 22 Dec 1747 (NMM)
SUP RA July 1749
d 7 Feb 1763 (NMM)

FOX, William (1)
L 22 Aug 1759
CR
CA 15 Feb 1780
SUP RA 21 Feb 1799

FOX, William (2)
L 6 Nov 1778
d 1782(3) (NMM)

FOXLEY, John
L 22 Aug 1693

FRAINE, Joseph
L 2 Dec 1745
CR 13 Jan 1758
CA 11 Dec 1759
d 1802

FRANCE, Nathaniel
L 27 Apr 1795
Ret CR 26 Nov 1830 (NMM)
d 27 June 1835 (LT)

FRANCE, Nathaniel Cranstoun
L 26 Aug 1814
d 3 Mar 1849 (NMM)

FRANCILLON, John George
L 1 Mar 1815
Ret CR 27 July 1862 (NMM)
d 1881 (PRO)

FRANCILLON, Thomas
L 5 Oct 1814
Ret CR 18 Oct 1858 (NMM)
d 1861 (NMM)

FRANCIS, John
L 12 Mar 1807
d 1842 (PRO)

FRANCIS, Thomas
L 27 Aug 1745
CR 1 Nov 1757
CA 12 Nov 1759
d 21 Oct 1762

FRANKLAND, Edward Augustus
L 16 Mar 1814
CR 19 May 1820 (NMM)
CA 28 May 1835 (NMM)
Ret CA 1 July 1851 (NMM)
Ret RA 14 Feb 1857 (NMM)
d 2 Jan 1862 (NMM)

FRANKLAND, Gilbert
L 11 Jan 1692
KIA 30 May 1702 (CH)

FRANKLAND, Henry
See CROMWELL, Henry

FRANKLAND, Robert

L	18 May	1745
CR	7 Apr	1756
CA	15 Nov	1756
d	26 Dec	1757 (PRO)

FRANKLAND, Sir Thomas

L	23 Feb	1738 (NMM)
CR		
COMAD	13 May	1730–
	19 Mar	1742 (AO)
CA	15 July	1740
MP (Thirsk)	12 May	1747–1780 (MPN)
RAB	May	1755 (CH)
RAW	4 June	1756 (CH)
RAR	Feb	1757 (CH)
VAW	14 Feb	1759
VAR	21 Oct	1762
Inh Bt	11 Jan	1767 (MPN)
AB	18 Oct	1770
AW	31 Mar	1775 (CH)
MP (Thirsk)	3 Nov–21 Nov	1784 (MPN)
d	21 Nov	1784 (DNB)

FRANKLIN, George

L	11 Feb	1808

FRANKLIN, Henry

L	18 Oct	1693
	(?14 Oct	1693)

FRANKLIN, Sir John

T		
L	25 Feb	1815
CR	1 Jan	1821 (DNB)
CA	20 Nov	1822 (DNB)
Kt	29 Apr	1829 (LG)
Kt (Greece)		1836 (TR)
KCH	25 Jan	1836 (OB)
RAB	26 Oct	1852 (NMM)
His death was not known when he was promoted RAB. His name was removed	1 Apr	1854 (NMM)
d	11 June	1847 (DNB)

FRANKLIN, Peter

L	10 Apr	1703
d	25 Jan	1736 (PRO)

FRANKLING, Felix

L	1 Mar	1800
Ret CR	7 Jan	1833 (NMM)
d		1859 (NMM)

FRANKLYN, George

L	7 Nov	1804
d	2 Apr	1855 (NMM)

FRANKLYN, William

L	3 Mar	1804
d	22 Apr	1825 (NMM)

FRANKS, Frederick

L	29 Sept	1813
d		1844 (PRO)

FRANKS, Jacob

L	19 Feb	1756
d		1758(9) (NMM)

FRARY, Ralph

L		
CA		1661
d		before 1689 (PJP)

FRASER, Alexander (1)

L	18 July	1777
CR	1 Dec	1787
CA	1 July	1793
RAB	1 Aug	1811
RAW	12 Aug	1812
RAR	4 June	1814
VAB	12 Aug	1819 (PRO)
VAW	19 July	1821 (NMM)
VAR	27 May	1825 (NMM)
d	24 Dec	1829 (PMM)

FRASER, Alexander (2)

L	10 Oct	1804
CR	2 June	1809
CA	7 June	1814
d		1819 (PRO)

FRASER, Charles

L	11 Mar	1808
CR	29 Sept	1823 (NMM)
CA	7 Mar	1853 (NMM)
d	17 Mar	1861 (PRO)

FRASER, Francis

L	12 June	1795
d	27 Apr	1824 (PRO)

FRASER, Henry Tillieux

L	29 Mar	1805
CR	8 June	1809
d	29 Aug	1816 (NMM)

FRASER, Hugh

L	10 Mar	1778
d		1780(1) PRO

FRASER, James

L	10 Mar	1815
d		1826 (PRO)

FRASER, John (1)

L	13 Apr	1741
d		1747(8) (PRO)

FRASER, John (2)

L	3 Aug	1748
d		1779 (PRO)

FRASER, John (3)

L	12 June	1807
d		1816 (PRO)

FRASER, John (4)

L	29 July	1808 (NMM)
d		1813 (NMM)

FRASER, John (5)

L	1 Jan	1813 (NMM)
CR	22 Feb	1831 (NMM)
CA	23 Nov	1841 (NMM)
d	21 Mar	1861 (NMM)

FRASER, Percy

L	15 Nov	1789
CR	27 May	1794 (NMM)
CA	27 Mar	1795
COM N	21 Dec	1813–
	3 July	1823 (NBO)
SUP RA	12 June	1823 (NMM)
d	Dec	1827 (NMM)

FRASER, Richard

L	1 Nov	1794
d		1808(9) (NMM)

FRASER, Thomas
L 6 Mar 1741
CR 29 June 1762
d 30 Oct 1775
FRAWLEY, Thomas
L 18 June 1815 (NMM)
d Oct 1823 (NMM)
FRAZER, Henry Tillieux
See FRASER, Henry Tillieux
FRAZER, Hiram
L 25 May 1805 (NMM)
d 9 Nov 1836 (PRO)
FRAZIER, John
L 13 Sept 1799
d 13 Jan 1830 (PRO)
FREDERICK, H.R.H. Prince
See CUMBERLAND, Henry Frederick, Duke
FREDERICK, Thomas
L 1 May 1804
d 1818 (NMM)
FREDERICK, Thomas Lenox
L 12 Mar 1770
CR 11 Oct 1776
CA 14 July 1779
RAB 20 Feb 1797
RAW 14 Feb 1799
d 7 Nov 1799 (NMM)
FREEMAN, Frederick
L 19 Sept 1815
d 1829 (PRO)
FREEMAN, John
L 1664
CA 1666
d before 1689 (PJP)
FREEMAN, William Peere Williams
See WILLIAMS, William Peere
FREESTUN, Humphry May
L 2 Jan 1812 (OB)
HP 28 Feb 1816 (OB)
Ret CR 30 July 1853 (PRO)
d 30 July 1863 (PRO)
FREMANTLE, Sir Thomas Francis
L 13 Mar 1782
CR 3 Nov 1790
CA 16 May 1793
T
COM AD 23 Oct 1806–
6 Apr 1807 (AO)
MP 1806–1807 (MPT)
(Sandwich)
RAB 31 July 1810
RAW 12 Aug 1812
RAR 4 June 1814
Kt 1815 (DNB)
(Austria)
KCB 12 Apr 1815 (LG)
GCH 1818 (MPT)
GCB 20 Feb 1818 (MPT)
VAB 12 Aug 1819 (NMM)
GCMG 26 Oct 1819 (MPT)
d 19 Dec 1819 (DNB)
FRENCH, George (1)
L 9 Nov 1756
d 29 Aug 1767
FRENCH, George (2)
L 24 Oct 1807
CR 22 May 1813
CA 20 July 1822 (NMM)
HP 23 Apr 1823 (MB)
d 1838 (NMM)
FRENCH, Wildy
L 18 Oct 1744
d 13 Oct 1791 (LT)
FRENCHARD, George
L
CA 14 Feb 1694
d 21 Apr 1696
FRENO, Zachariah
L 27 Mar 1748
d 1765(6) (NMM)
FRETWELD, John
L 11 Feb 1815
d 1843 (NMM)
FREW, John
L 19 Nov 1790
d 1796 (NMM)
FRICKER, Robert
L 13 May 1795
Ret CR 26 Nov 1830 (OB)
d 12 Aug 1845 (OB)
FRICKER, William
L 15 Oct 1795
d 1796 (PRO)
FRIED, James
L 14 Feb 1815
d 1826 (PRO)
FRIEND, Bravil
L 21 Apr 1760
d 1795 (PRO)
FRIEND, Charles
L 12 June 1812
CR 28 July 1851 (NMM)
d 7 Sept 1867 (PRO)
FRIEND, Matthew Curling
L 16 Feb 1815
Ret CR 18 Jan 1861 (NMM)
FRIEND, Richard
L
CA 1671
d before 1689 (PJP)
FRISSELL, William
L 25 Aug 1797
d 1819 (NMM)
FROAD, John Edmonstune
L 3 Nov 1797
d 1804 (NMM)
FRODSHAM, John
L 11 Oct 1758
CR 30 July 1779
CA 10 Oct 1782
d 28 May 1791
FROGMORE, Rowland
L 13 May 1720
CR
CA 18 July 1740
d 8 Nov 1744 (CH)

FROMOW, William Cady
L 23 Sept 1799
d 1810 (PRO)
FROUDE, Frederick
L 1671 (P)
CA 11 July 1686
FROUDE, James
L 14 May 1746
d 1770 (PRO)
FROWD, Frederick
See FROUDE, Frederick
FROWD, Philip
L 21 May 1800
d 1804 (PRO)
FRY, John Dillon
L 16 May 1814
d 1832 (PRO)
FRY, Henry
L 1 Feb 1805
d 1805(6) (PRO)
FRY, William
L 28 Oct 1778
d 1801 (PRO)
FRYER, Henry
L 17 Aug 1801
d 9 June 1836 (PJP)
FUDGER, Edward
L 27 Sept 1777
d 2 June 1792
FULLARTON, John
L 17 Dec 1798
d 1803 (PRO)
FULLER, James (1)
L 6 Nov 1797
Ret CR 26 Nov 1830 (NMM)
d 1833 (NMM)
FULLER, James (2)
L 22 Aug 1801
Struck off list 1807 (NMM)
FULLER, John
L 27 Feb 1815
d 19 Feb 1823 (PRO)
FULLER, Ross Henry
L 21 Mar 1812
CR 15 June 1814
HP 15 June 1815 (OB)
CA 18 Mar 1851 (NMM)
Ret CA 1 July 1851 (PMM)
d 27 Oct 1860 (PRO)
FULLER, Thomas
L
CA 1667
FULLER, William Stephen
L 8 Nov 1808
CR 13 June 1815
CA 19 May 1825 (NMM)
d 8 Oct 1835 (PJP)
FULLTON, John
L 22 May 1800
Ret CR 26 Nov 1830 (NMM)
d 1843 (PRO)
FUNNEL, Nicholas
L 30 Apr 1678

FURBER, Thomas
L 7 Oct 1801
CR 1 Sept 1824 (PRO)
CA 28 July 1851 (PRO)
RA 1 Apr 1870 (PRO)
VA 29 May 1873 (PRO)
d 23 Oct 1875 (PRO)
FURLONG, Edward
L 1672
CA 17 May 1678
FURMIDGE, William
L 28 Apr 1802
d 1805 (PRO)
FURNEAUX, Abraham
L 2 Aug 1758
d 1776 (PRO)
FURNEAUX, James
L 15 Oct 1744
d 1783 (PRO)
FURNEAUX, John
L 13 June 1812
CR 19 July 1814
CA 16 Mar 1829 (NMM)
RA 3 July 1855 (NMM)
VA 12 Apr 1862 (NMM)
d 14 Feb 1865 (NMM)
FURNEAUX, Tobias
L 10 Oct 1759
CR 28 Nov 1771
CA 10 Aug 1775
d 19 Sept 1781 (DNB)
FURNIVALL, William
L 31 July 1778
d 7 July 1810 (NMM)
FURZE, William Pearce
L 14 Dec 1811
d 22 Oct 1839 (NMM)
FURZER, John
L
CR
CA 16 Mar 1710 (NMM)
d (drowned) 7 Dec 1721 (CH)
FUTTER, Robert
L 16 Aug 1814
d 1839 (NMM)
FUZZER, John
See FURZER, John
FYFFE, John
L 24 Apr 1782
CR 2 Jan 1798
CA 13 Oct 1807
d 28 Mar 1835 (PJP)
FYFFE, John
See FIFE, John
FYTCHE, Robert
L 27 Apr 1727
CR ?24 June 1730 (NMM)
CA 10 May 1731 (NMM)
d (suicide) 6 Oct 1740 (NMM)

GABORIAN, James
L 27 Feb 1759

SUP CR	26 Aug	1801
d		1813 (PMM)
GABORIAN, Thomas		
L	4 Jan	1759
CR	17 Sept	1777
CA	13 May	1778
d		1794 (PRO)
GABRIEL, James Wallace		
L	17 Mar	1800
CR	21 Mar	1812
CA	2 July	1831 (MB)
KH	1 Jan	1837 (OB)
d	8 Aug	1849 (NMM)
GABRIEL, John		
L	9 Feb	1815
d	June	1837 (NMM)
GABRIEL, Vere		
L	3 Oct	1808
d	7 Mar	1824 (NMM)
GACHES, John James		
L	21 Jan	1702
CR	6 June	1741
d		1748 (NMM)
GADSDEN, Thomas		
L	5 Dec	1711
d		?1742 (NMM)
GAGE, John		
L	2 Mar	1734
CR	27 Sept	1740
CA	24 Feb	1743 (PJP)
d	2 Aug	1743 (PJP)
GAGE, Joseph		
L	22 June	1743
d	1 Aug	1755 (PRO)
GAGE, Sir William Hall		
L	11 Mar	1796
CR	13 June	1797
CA	26 July	1797
HP	1802–20 July	1805 (MB)
HP	14 Sept	1814 (MB)
RAB	19 July	1821 (LG)
RAW	27 May	1825 (LG)
RAR	22 July	1830 (LG)
Kt		1834 (CH)
KCB		1834 (PJP)
GCH	19 Apr	1834 (OB)
VAW	10 Jan	1837 (LG)
VAR	23 Nov	1841 (LG)
COM AD	3 Feb	1842–1846 (OB)
AB	9 Nov	1846 (NMM)
AW	27 Dec	1847 (NMM)
AR	1 July	1851 (NMM)
GCB		1860 (CH)
AF	20 May	1862 (CH)
d	5 Jan	1864 (PJP)
GAHAGAN, Thomas		
L	12 June	1807
d	Nov	1828 (NMM)
GAHAN, George		
L	5 Oct	1815 (OB)
d	7 Dec	1851 (NMM)
GAHAN, Robert		
L	8 July	1795
d		1797 (NMM)
GAINES, Francis		
L	31 Oct	1741
CR	10 Feb	1755
d		1767 (NMM)
GAIRDNER, Henry Shettlewood		
L	2 Dec	1814
d		1815 (NMM)
GALBRAITH, James		
L	22 Dec	1740
CR	13 Mar	1745
CA	6 Feb	1756
SUP RA	May	1799 (PRO)
GALBRAITH, John		
L	21 Sept	1758
d	24 Dec	1789
GALE, Charles E.		
L	18 Feb	1815
d (before promotion)		1815 (NMM)
GALE, George		
L	8 Dec	1693 (PMM)
GALLAGHER, George		
L	14 Feb	1815
d		1819 (NMM)
GALLAWAY, Alexander		
T	wounded	
L	21 Mar	1812
Ret CR	2 Jan	1854 (NMM)
d		1873 (TR)
GALLICHAN, James		
L	4 May	1810
HP	4 May	1810 (OB)
Ret CR	12 Oct	1849 (NMM)
d		1863 (NMM)
GALLOPP, George		
L		1664
CA		1672
d	before	1689 (PJP)
GALLOWAY, Alexander		
See GALLAWAY, Alexander		
GALLOWAY, Daniel		
See CALLAWAY, Daniel		
GALLOWAY, George, Earl of		
L	8 Aug	1789
CR	19 Nov	1790
CA	30 Apr	1793
Inh EP	Nov	1806 (MB)
RAB	31 July	1810
RAW	12 Aug	1812
RAR	4 June	1814
VAB	12 Aug	1819 (CH)
VAW	19 July	1821 (CH)
VAR	27 May	1825 (CH)
AB	22 July	1830 (LG)
d	27 Mar	1834 (CH)
GALLOWAY, James		
L	24 July	1799
CR	22 Jan	1806
d	12 Aug	1846 (OB)
GALLOWAY, William		
L	2 Mar	1734
d		1769 (NMM)
GALLWAY, Richard		
L	9 May	1797 (NMM)
d		1803 (NMM)

GALLWEY, James
L 15 Oct 1802
d 1804 (NMM)
GALLWEY, Thomas
L 22 Sept 1807
CR 17 Mar 1812
CA 27 Aug 1844 (NMM)
d 1859 (NMM)
GALTON, William
L 16 Mar 1791
d 1806 (NMM)
GALWAY, Edward
L 24 June 1793
CR 8 Oct 1798
CA 29 Apr 1802 (MB)
RAW 10 Jan 1837 (LG)
RAR 23 Nov 1841 (LG)
d 9 Aug 1844 (NMM)
GALWAY, Montyford Westropp
L 30 Aug 1800
d 1806 (NMM)
GALWAY, Thomas
L 1694 (PJP)
GALWAY, Thomas
See GALLWEY, Thomas
GALWEY, Richard
L 9 May 1797
CR
CA 29 Apr 1802
GAMAGE, Richard Stewart
L 25 Aug 1808 (PJP)
e 23 Nov 1812 (PJP)
GAMBIER, George Cornish
L 6 Mar 1815
CR 7 Dec 1819 (NMM)
CA 4 June 1821 (NMM)
HP Dec 1823 (OB)
Ret CA 1 Oct 1846 (LG)
Ret RA 8 Mar 1852 (NMM)
Ret VA 2 Oct 1857 (NMM)
Ret A 27 Apr 1863 (NMM)
d 18 June 1879 (NMM)
GAMBIER, James (1)
L 6 Mar 1744 (NMM)
CR 3 Apr 1746 (NMM)
CA 5 Dec 1747
COMV 16 July–2 Sept 1773 (NBO)
COMM Aug 1773–
(Portsmouth) Jan 1778 (PJP)
RAB 23 Jan 1778
RAR 23 Mar 1779 (CH)
VAB 26 Sept 1780
VAR 24 Sept 1787
d 8 Jan 1789 (DNB)
GAMBIER, James, Lord (2)
L 12 Feb 1777
CR 9 Mar 1778
CA 9 Oct 1778
CRM 4 July 1794 (AL)
COMAD 7 Mar 1795–
19 Feb 1801 (AO)
RAW 1 June 1795
VAB 14 Feb 1799
VAW 1 Jan 1801
GG (Newfoundland) 1802–1804 (BNS)
VAR 23 Apr 1804
COMAD 15 May 1804–
10 Feb 1806 (AO)
AB 9 Nov 1805
COMAD 6 Apr 1807–
9 May 1808 (AO)
Cre EP 3 Nov 1807 (LG)
AW 31 July 1810
AR 4 June 1814
KCB 2 Jan 1815 (LG)
GCB 7 June 1815 (DNB)
AF 22 July 1830 (DNB)
d 19 Apr 1833 (DNB)
GAMBIER, Robert
L 5 Sept 1810
CR 30 Sept 1812
CA 6 June 1814
Ret CA 31 Oct 1846 (LG)
Ret RA 6 Sept 1849 (LG)
Ret VA 21 Oct 1856 (NMM)
Ret A 15 Jan 1862 (NMM)
d 26 Jan 1872 (NMM)
GAMBIER, Samuel John
L 15 Nov 1783
d 8 Oct 1789
GAME, Aaron
L 16 Mar 1815
d 27 Aug 1842 (PRO)
GAMMON, Henry
L 29 Oct 1778
d 1779 (NMM)
GAMMON, William Snuggs
L 5 Apr 1805
CR 27 May 1825 (PJP)
d 1835 (NMM)
GAPE, Joseph
T
L 19 Mar 1811
CR 16 Feb 1814
CA 23 Nov 1841 (LG)
RA 12 Apr 1862 (NMM)
VA 24 May 1867 (NMM)
A 30 July 1875 (NMM)
d 2 Mar 1876 (PRO)
GAPPER, William Southby
L 26 Sept 1814
d Mar 1833 (NMM)
GARBETT, William
L 29 Oct 1806
d 1834 (NMM)
GARDINER, Allen Francis
L 13 Dec 1814 (MB)
CR 13 Sept 1826 (MB)
d 1852 (PMM)
GARDINER, Arthur
L 4 July 1738
CR 6 June 1744
CA 27 May 1745
KIA 28 Feb 1758 (LG)
GARDINER, Francis Geary
L 16 Dec 1777
CR Feb 1780
d 19 Sept 1780 (PRO)

Name	Rank	Date	Year
GARDINER, James Anthony See GARDNER, James Anthony			
GARDINER, John (1)			
	L	29 May	1742
	d		1778 (PRO)
GARDINER, John (2)			
	L	8 Sept	1777
	SUP CR	19 June	1811
	d	12 May	1831 (NMM)
GARDINER, Martin (1)			
	L		1693 (PMM)
	CA	27 May	1697
	d		1698 (PJP)
GARDINER, Martin (2)			
	L		1778 (PJP)
GARDINER, Thomas (1)			
	L		1666
	CA		1672
	d		1679 (PJP)
GARDINER, Thomas (2)			
	L	19 Mar	1747
	d		1754 (NMM)
GARDINER, Thomas (3)			
	L	9 Apr	1805
	d		1808 (NMM)
GARDINER, Thomas (4)			
	L	19 Mar	1808
	d		1835 (NMM)
GARDINER, Thomas See GARDNER, Thomas			
GARDINER, William			
	L	16 Feb	1815
	HP	16 Feb	1815 (OB)
	Ret CR	18 Jan	1861 (NMM)
	d		1883 (NMM)
GARDNER, Alan, Lord			
	L	7 Mar	1760
	CR	12 Apr	1762
	CA	19 May	1766
	COMAD	19 Jan	1790–
		7 Mar	1795 (AO)
	MP (Plymouth)		1790–1796 (MPN)
	RAB	1 Feb	1793
	RAW	12 Apr	1794
	MGRM	28 June	1794
	VAB	4 July	1794
	Kt	9Sept	1794 (MB)
	VAW	1 June	1795
	MP (Westminster)		1796–1806 (MPN)
	AB	14 Feb	1799
	Cre IP	Dec	1800 (DNB)
	AW	9 Nov	1805
	Cre EP	15 Nov	1806 (LG)
	AR	28 Apr	1808
	d	1 Jan	1809 (DNB)
GARDNER, Alan Hyde, Lord			
	L		
	CR	1 Dec	1788
	CA	12 Nov	1790
	RAB	28 Apr	1808
	Inh EP		1809 (CH)
	RAW	31 July	1810
	RAR	1 Aug	1811
	VAB	4 Dec	1813
	VAW	4 June	1814
	KCB	2 Jan	1815 (LG)
	d	27 Dec	1815 (LT)
GARDNER, Hon.			
	L	7 July	1745 (PJP)
GARDNER, Hon. Francis Farington			
	L	19 June	1791
	CR		
	CA	7 May	1794
	RAB	12 Aug	1812
	RAW	4 June	1814
	RAR	12 Aug	1819 (CH)
	d	7 July	1821 (PJP)
GARDNER, George Johnson			
	L	10 Mar	1815
	Ret CR	1 Oct	1860 (NMM)
	d		1867 (NMM)
GARDNER, H.S.			
	L		1815 (PJP)
	d		1815 (PJP)
GARDNER, James			
	L	8 June	1744
	d		1755 (NMM)
GARDNER, James Anthony			
	L	12 Jan	1795
	HP	7 Dec	1814 (OB)
	Ret CR	26 Nov	1830 (OB)
	d	24 Sept	1846 (OB)
GARDNER, James Baynton			
	L	15 Aug	1803
	CR	13 June	1815
	d	18 Jan	1828 (PJP)
GARDNER, John (1)			
	L	1 Dec	1787
	CR	5 Feb	1798
	d		1813 (NMM)
GARDNER, John (2)			
	L	13 June	1801
	d		1816 (NMM)
GARDNER, John (3)			
	L	15 Feb	1808
	d		1811 (NMM)
GARDNER, John See GARDINER, John			
GARDNER, Martin See GARDINER, Martin			
GARDNER, Savage			
	L	20 Aug	1779
	d		1785 (NMM)
GARDNER, Thomas (1)			
	L	29 Apr	1678
	CA	23 May	1689
			(23 Mar 1690 in C)
	d	29 June	1699
GARDNER, Thomas (2)			
	L	5 Sept	1688
	CA		1680
GARDNER, Thomas (3)			
	L	8 Jan	1806
	d	Feb–Mar	1821 (NMM)
GARDNER, Thomas See GARDINER, Thomas			

GARDNER, Hon. Valentine
L 20 May 1807
CR 30 Apr 1810
CA 10 Aug 1812
d 28 Nov 1820 (PRO)

GARENCIERES, Charles
L 12 Oct 1741
d 1770 (NMM)

GARENCIERES, Theophilus
L 21 Jan 1794
d 1797 (NMM)

GARFORTH, William
L 25 Oct 1813
Ret CR 15 Apr 1856 (PRO)
d 1871 (NMM)

GARLAND, Abraham
L 12 Jan 1805
d 13 Aug 1829 (NMM)

GARLAND, James
L 4 Jan 1808
CR 26 Aug 1815
CA 15 Oct 1828 (MB)
d 18 May 1830 (NMM)

GARLAND, John
L 1813 (PJP)
KIA 10 Sept 1813 (I)

GARLAND, Joseph Gulston
L 2 May 1801
CR 22 Jan 1806
CA 19 Aug 1815
Ret CA 31 Oct 1846 (LG)
Ret RA 11 Nov 1850 (NMM)
d 1854 (NMM)

GARLAND, William
L 17 Feb 1815
Ret CR 20 Apr 1861 (NMM)
d 22 Nov 1873 (NMM)

GARLIES, George, Lord Viscount
See GALLOWAY, George, Earl of

GARNER, Edward
L 25 June 1773
CR 17 July 1776 (NMM)
CA 1 Oct 1779
d 23 Aug 1781 (PRO)

GARNER, George
L 10 Apr 1780
d 1789 (NMM)

GARNER, William
L 23 Sept 1757 (NMM)
CR 1 Feb 1763
CA 3 Aug 1768
d 20 Mar 1787 (PJP)

GARNHAM, John
L 18 Feb 1815
Ret CR 20 Apr 1861 (NMM)
d 26 Nov 1872 (PRO)

GARNIER,Charles
L 19 Nov 1790
CR 1 Aug 1794
CA 6 Apr 1795
d 16 Dec 1796 (NMM)

GARNIER, Daniel
L 1760 (PJP)
d 15 Feb 1760 (PJP)

GARNIER, John Miller
L 9 Nov 1795
CR 27 Aug 1800
CA 3 Aug 1801
d 28 Oct 1801 (PRO)

GARRARD, Charles
See GERRARD, Charles

GARRATT, Walter
L 17 Sept 1813
Struck off list 1814 (NMM)

GARRETT, Cheney Hunt
L 11 Oct 1776
d 1796 (NMM)

GARRETT, Edward (1)
L 3 Jan 1797
d 1836 (NMM)

GARRETT, Edward (2)
L 16 Feb 1815
Ret CR 18 Jan 1861 (NMM)
d 5 Feb 1882 (NMM)

GARRETT, Edward William
L 19 Sept 1801
T wounded
CR 16 Jan 1809
HP 14 July 1813 (MB)
d 2 Sept 1860 (PRO)

GARRETT, Henry (1)
L 24 June 1793
CR 27 Dec 1798
CA 16 Sept 1799
Ret CA 1830 (NMM)
Ret RA 16 Oct 1833 (NMM)
VAB 12 Nov 1840 (NMM)
VAW 23 Nov 1841 (LG)
d 11 Apr 1846 (NMM)

GARRETT, Henry (2)
T
L 21 Aug 1809
CR 28 July 1851 (NMM)
d 14 Jan 1865 (NMM)

GARRETT, William (1)
L 22 Oct 1796
d 1805 (NMM)

GARRETT, William (2)
L 6 July 1805
d 1809 (NMM)

GARRETY, James Henry
L 23 May 1801
CR 3 May 1811
d 1827 (MB)

GARRICK, William
L 17 Nov 1800
Ret CR 26 Nov 1830 (NMM)
d 22 Apr 1846 (OB)

GARRIS, William
L
CA 1666
d before 1689 (PJP)

GARROW, Joseph
L 19 June 1761
d 1800 (NMM)

GARSTIN, Edward
L 18 Mar 1778
d 1779

GARTH, Thomas
L 10 June 1801
CR 3 Mar 1804
CA 4 Jan 1808
d 10 Nov 1842 (PRO)

GARTHSHORE, Alexander
L 14 Oct 1796
d 1805 (NMM)

GASCOIGNE, Edward
L 30 Mar 1742
CR 11 Oct 1755
CA 18 Feb 1760
d 30 Dec 1764 (M)

GASCOIGNE, James (1)
L 16 Dec 1727
CR 26 Sept 1735
d 1763 (NMM)

GASCOIGNE, James (2)
L 25 Mar 1757
d 1765 (NMM)

GASCOIGNE, Joel
L 1667
KIA 28 May 1672 (NJ)

GASCOIGNE, John
L 21 Nov 1714
CR 15 Feb 1727
CA 5 Dec 1727
SUP RA July 1747 (PJP)
d 29 May 1753

GASCOYNE, James
See GASCOIGNE, James

GASCOYNE, John
L 17 Nov 1790
CR 27 Mar 1797
Ret RA 14 Sept 1840 (NMM)
d 16 Jan 1845 (NMM)

GASCOYNE, John
See GASCOIGNE, John

GASCOYNE, Sabine
L 1782 (PJP)

GASPEY, William
L 18 Oct 1759
d 15 Sept 1791

GATEHOUSE, William
L 25 Oct 1793
d 11 Oct 1811 (NMM)

GAUDY, John
L 1716 (PJP)
d 3 Oct 1717 (PMM)

GAUNTLETT, John
L 10 Mar 1757
CR Aug 1767 (PJP)
d 1783 (PRO)

GAUNTLETT, Peter
L 11 July 1797
d 1800 (NMM)

GAVEN, William
L 6 Apr 1757
d 1777 (PRO)

GAWEN, Jeffery
L 2 Sept 1793
Ret CR 26 May 1827 (NMM)
d 1837 (NMM)

GAWEN, William Hamilton
L 11 Nov 1807
CR 30 Apr 1810
CA 4 Dec 1811
CB 4 June 1815 (LG)
d 17 Aug 1834 (NMM)

GAYDON, John
L 7 Aug 1761
d 1805 (NMM)

GAYLER, –
L 1803 (PJP)
d 1803 (PJP)

GAYTON, Clark
L 11 Mar 1742
CR
CA 12 Aug 1744 (DNB)
HP 1747–May 1755 (DNB)
RAW 24 Oct 1770
RAR 31 Mar 1775 (CH)
VAW 5 Feb 1776
VAR 29 Jan 1778
AB 8 Apr 1782
d 1787 (CH)

GAYTON, George
L 6 Mar 1744
CR 11 Dec 1759
CA 26 May 1768
RAW 12 Apr 1794
RAR 4 July 1794
VAW 1 June 1795
d 23 Sept 1797

GEALE, Daniel
L 6 Mar 1815
HP 6 Mar 1815 (OB)
CR 10 Apr 1863 (NMM)
d 16 Aug 1866 (NMM)

GEALE, Ebenezer
L 30 Jan 1800
T killed
KIA 21 Oct 1805 (TR)

GEARY, Sir Francis (1)
L 19 Mar 1734
CR
CA 30 June 1742
RAW 5 June 1759 (NMM)
VAB 21 Oct 1762 (CH)
VAR 18 Oct 1770
AB 31 Mar 1775 (CH)
AW 29 Jan 1778
Cre Bt 1782 (CH)
d 7 Feb 1796 (CH)

GEARY, Francis (2)
L
CR 2 Oct 1755 (PJP)

GEARY, John
T wounded
L 29 May 1810 (OB)
Dismissed 1819 (MB)
Restored 1819 (MB)
CR 17 Feb 1831 (MB)
Ret CA 4 May 1863 (NMM)
d 10 Nov 1874 (PRO)

GEARY, Joseph Vincent
L 15 Feb 1815
d 1844 (PRO)

GEARY, Thomas
L 12 June 1760
CR 26 Aug 1780
d 5 Feb 1805 (NMM)

GED, Dougaldus
L 21 May 1760
d 25 Mar 1765 (PMM)

GEDDES, Alexander
L 11 Oct 1705
CR
CA 15 Nov 1714
COM E 15 Apr 1743–
27 May 1749 (NBO)
d 24 Jan 1751 (H)

GEDDES, John
L 26 June 1809
d 25 June 1813 (PRO)

GEDGE, John
L 10 July 1798
CR 15 Nov 1811
CA 19 July 1821 (NMM)
Ret CA 31 Oct 1846 (LG)
Ret RA 8 Mar 1852 (NMM)
d 1855 (NMM)

GELDING, Isaac
L
CA 1672
d before 1689 (PJP)

GELL, John
L 6 Jan 1760
CR 14 Oct 1762
CA 4 Mar 1766
RAB 1 Feb 1793
RAW 12 Apr 1794 (CH)
VAB 4 July 1794
VAW 1 June 1795
AB 14 Feb 1799
AW 9 Nov 1805
d 28 Sept 1806 (PMM)

GELL, John Sherbrooke
L 14 Jan 1814
d 1837 (NMM)

GELLIE, Lewis
L 9 Nov 1756
SUP CR 21 Sept 1796
d 31 July 1812 (NMM)

GENTIL, George
L 12 May 1745
d 1770 (NMM)

GEORGE, George
L 26 Nov 1799
HP 1816 (OB)
Ret CR 31 May 1844 (NMM)
d 1855 (NMM)

GEORGE, James (1)
L 24 June 1761
d 1809 (NMM)

GEORGE, James (2)
L 8 May 1812
Ret CR 25 Oct 1854 (NMM)
d 1864 (NMM)

GEORGE, John
L 1672
CR 17 Dec 1683
CA 20 Mar 1684 (H)
d 4 May 1690 (PRO)

GEORGE, Reginalds
L 1673

GEORGE, Sir Rupert
L 25 Apr 1769 (NMM)
CR 1781 (PJP)
CA 29 Nov 1781
SUP CA 1801 (NMM)
Kt 1803 (MB)
Cre Bt 18 Sept 1809 (MB)
d 25 Jan 1823 (MB)

GEORGES, W.P.
L 1784 (PJP)

GERRARD, Charles
?GARRARD, Charles
L 27 June 1711

GEST, James
L 27 Dec 1762
d 1772 (NMM)

GETHINGS, John
L
CA 1664
KIA 4 June 1666 (RM)

GETHINGS, William
L 16 Jan 1696 (PJP)

GETTINGS, Henry
See GITTINGS, Henry

GEUS, John de
L
CA 1660

GEYT, George Matthew Le
See LE GEYT, George Matthew

GIBBEE, Humphrey
L 1747 (PJP)

GIBBES, Anthony
L 2 June 1759 (NMM)
CR 11 July 1782
d 1814 (NMM)

GIBBES, Francis Blower
L 15 Jan 1802
T
CR 1841 (TR)
Ret CR 8 Apr 1841 (NMM)
d 23 Nov 1842 (TR)

GIBBES, Robert
L 28 Sept 1814
d 14 May 1825 (PRO)

GIBBON, Francis
See GYBBON, Francis

GIBBON, Nicholas
L 14 Dec 1694
Gone 1719 (PRO)

GIBBONS, Anderson
L
CA 1667
Dismissed 18 Nov 1667 (LG)

GIBBONS, Gerald
L 26 June 1775
d 1806 (NMM)

GIBBONS, John
L 1666

GIBBONS, Owen
L 1666

GIBBONS, Thomas (1)
L 1672
d before 1689 (PJP)
GIBBONS, Thomas (2)
L 1672
GIBBONS, William
L 9 Feb 1796
Ret CR 5 Apr 1831 (MB)
d 21 Oct 1860 (NMM)
GIBBONS, William Henry
L 8 May 1812
d 1835 (NMM)
GIBBS, Anthony (1)
L 1760 (PJP)
Dismissed 26 July 1777 (PJP)
Restored 1781 (PJP)
GIBBS, Anthony (2)
L 2 Feb 1815
d Feb 1824 (NMM)
GIBBS, Edward
L 1702 (PJP)
GIBBS, Henry
L 7 Feb 1812
Struck off list 1814 (NMM)
GIBBS, John (1)
L 23 Sept 1782
d Dec 1788 (PMM)
GIBBS, John (2)
L 13 Nov 1790
d 1798 (NMM)
GIBBS, John (3)
L 25 Mar 1794
d 1796 (NMM)
GIBBS, Samuel
L 12 May 1794 (PJP)
GIBBS, T. B.
L 1802 (PJP)
GIBBS, Thomas
L 7 Nov 1793
d 1796 (NMM)
GIBSON, Daniel
L 1800 (PJP)
GIBSON, Henry
L 23 Jan 1678
GIBSON, James (1)
L 30 Apr 1678
GIBSON, James (2)
L 13 Mar 1811
d 21 Apr 1839 (LT)
GIBSON, John (1)
L 19 Nov 1694 (PJP)
GIBSON, John (2)
L 10 Dec 1760
CR 21 Mar 1782
CA 23 Dec 1782
SUP 23 Apr 1804
d 30 June 1824 (NMM)
GIB(B)SON, John Sanderson
L 6 June 1796
CR 2 Apr 1806
d 17 Sept 1831 (PRO)
GIBSON, Nicholas
L 14 Dec 1694 (PJP)

GIB(B)SON, Robert
L 6 Aug 1807
d 1841 (NMM)
GIBSON, Robert Shelmerdine
L 28 Aug 1807
d 26 Apr 1825 (NMM)
GIBSON, William
L 14 Dec 1798
d 1800 (NMM)
GIDDY, Charles
L 30 Sept 1801
T
CR 10 Sept 1814 (MB)
d 20 Sept 1839 (NMM)
GIDEON, Henry
L 21 Dec 1778
d 1785 (NMM)
GIDEON, Robert
L 7 Mar 1745
d 1785 (NMM)
GIDEON, Solomon
L 17 Sept 1706
CR
CA 6 Sept 1740
SUP RA 1755
d 3 Sept 1756
GIDNEY, Thomas
L 24 Mar 1807
d 1839 (PRO)
GIDOIN, John Lewis
L 19 Jan 1755
CR 9 Mar 1759
CA 26 May 1768
RAW 12 Apr 1794
RAR 4 July 1794
VAW 1 June 1795
d 10 Feb 1796 (PMM)
GIEKIE, William
L 10 Sept 1811
d 1813 (PRO)
GIFFARD, Harry
L 5 Jan 1797
d 1817 (NMM)
GIFFARD, James
L 6 July 1814
d Jan 1847 (OB)
GIFFARD, John
L 20 Oct 1790 (CH)
CR 1 Feb 1796 (CH)
CA 19 Oct 1796
RAB 12 Aug 1819 (CH)
RAW 19 July 1821 (LG)
RAR 27 May 1825 (CH)
VAB 22 July 1830 (LG)
VAR 10 Jan 1837 (LG)
AB 23 Nov 1841 (NMM)
AW 9 Nov 1846 (NMM)
AR 1 June 1848 (NMM)
Ret A 1 July 1851 (CH)
d 25 Sept 1855 (NMM)
GIFFORD, Henry
L 13 July 1696
In Merchant Service Sept 1700 (PJP)

GIFFORD, James		
L	22 Oct	1793 (MB)
CR	29 Apr	1802 (MB)
CA	12 Aug	1812
Ret RA	31 Oct	1846 (LG)
d	20 Aug	1853 (DNB)
GIFFORD, Lucius Henry		
L	6 Dec	1806
d		1812 (PRO)
GIFFORD, Robert		
L	24 Jan	1692
In Merchant Service		1700 (PJP)
GIFFORD, Sir William		
L	2 Nov	1676 (P)
CA	11 Apr	1682 (P)
Kt		1702 (PJP)
COMM (Portsmouth)	18 June	1702–
	13 Jan	1706 (QAN)
COM E	23 Feb	1706–
	16 Nov	1714 (NBO)
GGH		1708 (PJP)
d		1714 (PJP)
GILBERT, Edmund Williams		
L	29 Sept	1808
CR	26 Dec	1822 (NMM)
d	26 Feb	1849 (NMM)
GILBERT, George		
L	26 Nov	1781
d	2 Apr	1786 (M)
GILBERT, Henry Garnett		
L	6 Sept	1799
d (drowned)	May	1805 (OB)
GILBERT, Richard		
L	4 Nov	1790
Removed from Lieutenants list on 20 June 1795 because his private affairs prevented him from going to sea. (See PRO Adm 2/779)		
GILBERT, Thomas		
L	21 Sept	1790
d	26 Jan	1803 (LT)
GILBY, Robert		
L		1644
CA		1666
d	before	1689 (PJP)
GILCHRIST, Archibald (1)		
L	11 Apr	1794
d		1802 (NMM)
GILCHRIST, Archibald (2)		
L	24 Feb	1802
d		1817 (NMM)
GILCHRIST, James		
L	28 Aug	1741
CR	16 Jan	1750
CA	18 July	1755
d	11 June	1777 (M)
GILCHRIST, William		
L	22 June	1799
HP		1813 (OB)
Ret CR	26 Nov	1830 (NMM)
d		1864 (NMM)
GILES, Edward		
L	30 Mar	1799
Ret CR	15 Dec	1830 (NMM)
d		1843 (NMM)
GILES, John		
L	29 May	1795
d		1801 (PRO)
GILES, Robert		
L	29 Apr	1799
CR	12 Mar	1812
d	6 Feb	1824 (MB)
GILES, William		
L	3 Feb	1815
Ret CR	17 Oct	1859 (NMM)
d		1866 (NMM)
GILL, Charles		
L	5 Apr	1797
CR	2 Apr	1806
CA	16 Jan	1809
d	27 June	1842 (NMM)
GILL, Elias Thomas		
L	21 Mar	1812
d	22 Feb	1828 (NMM)
GILL, James		
L	19 Oct	1805
d		1811 (NMM)
GILL, John		
L		
CA		1666
d	before	1689 (PJP)
GILL, Joseph Collings		
T		
L	21 Mar	1812
CR	19 Aug	1842 (NMM)
HP	19 Aug	1842 (OB)
CA	12 Feb	1858 (NMM)
d	24 Oct	1858 (NMM)
GILL, Robert (1)		
L	15 Dec	1780
d		1790 (NMM)
GILL, Robert (2)		
L	16 Sept	1801
d	22 Sept	1829 (PRO)
GILL, Thomas (1)		
L	8 May	1804
CR	15 June	1814
CA	10 Jan	1837 (NMM)
Ret CA	1 July	1851 (NMM)
Ret RA	14 May	1857 (NMM)
Ret VA	14 Nov	1863 (NMM)
Ret A	8 Apr	1868 (NMM)
d		1874 (NMM)
GILL, Thomas (2)		
L	26 Sept	1805
Ret CR	18 Apr	1838 (NMM)
d	18 July	1841 (PRO)
GILLBEE, Humphrey		
L	24 June	1745
d		1754 (NMM)
GILLERY, James		
L		
CA	12 Oct	1679

GILLESPIE, John
L 9 Oct 1800
d 1804 (NMM)

GILLESPIE, Thomas
L 5 Dec 1794
Dismissed 19 Aug 1795 (NMM)
Restored 4 Aug 1800 (NMM)
d 13 Nov 1801 (NMM)

GILLIAM, Thomas (1)
L 6 Sept 1688 (P)
CA 25 Mar 1689
d (drowned) 9 Dec 1693 (CH)

GILLIAM, Thomas (2)
L 5 Dec 1749
d 21 Mar 1758 (PJP)

GILLILAND, Bryce
L 10 Apr 1802
T killed
KIA 21 Oct 1805 (TR)

GILLING, Thomas
L
CA 1666

GILLINGHAM, Robert
L 4 Apr 1760
SUPCR 6 Nov 1807

GILLIS, John
L 19 Dec 1744
d 1773 (NMM)

GILLMOR, Clotworthy
L 13 Feb 1801
Ret CR 1 Dec 1830 (NMM)
d 1855 (NMM)

GILMAN, Samuel
L 8 July 1693

GILMORE, John
L 28 Feb 1815
HP 4 June 1815 (OB)
Ret CR 14 Apr 1862 (NMM)
d 7 July 1862 (NMM)

GILMOUR, Alexander
L 4 Dec 1795
Ret CR 26 Nov 1830 (NMM)
d 21 Mar 1853 (PRO)

GILMOUR, David
L 27 Feb 1794
CR 28 Sept 1799
d 9 Aug 1829 (NMM)

GILMOUR, G.
L 1810 (PJP)

GILMOUR, John
L 21 Sept 1801
CR 1 July 1811
d Sept 1823 (NMM)

GILPIN, Bernard
L
CA 1660
d Apr 1665

GILPIN, Richard
L 16 Feb 1815
d 1825 (PRO)

GILPIN, William
L 20 Nov 1812
d 15 Oct 1821 (NMM)

GILSON, Daniel
L 6 July 1795
d 1811 (NMM)

GIPPS, George
L 20 Mar 1678

GIRLING, John
L 30 Nov 1759
d 1794 (NMM)

GIRLINGTON, Richard Thomas
L 25 Nov 1702 (PMM)
CR
CA 1 Jan 1713
d 14 Dec 1743

GISLING, Woodhouse
L 1664

GITTINGS, Henry
L 29 Apr 1802 (PRO)
d 1833 (PRO)

GITTINS, Richard
L 5 Nov 1804
Ret CR 8 May 1838 (NMM)
d 1843 (NMM)

GLAIRE, Thomas
L 7 Feb 1815
d 1847 (NMM)

GLANVILL, William
L 11 Dec 1798
d 1805 (NMM)

GLANVILLE, George
L 13 July 1799
Ret CR 26 Nov 1830 (OB)
d Oct 1856 (NMM)

GLANVILLE, Henry
L 1704 (PJP)

GLASFORD, James
L 1 Oct 1758
CR 25 Dec 1782
CA 22 Nov 1790
d 1796

GLASGOW, Hon. James, Earl
L 8 Jan 1814 (OB)
HP 11 July 1818 (OB)
Inh EP July 1843 (OB)

GLASSCOCK, William Nugent
L 8 Nov 1808
CR 31 Dec 1818 (MB)
CA 3 June 1833 (DNB)
HP Jan 1847 (OB)
d 8 Oct 1847 (DNB)

GLASSFORD, John
L 30 May 1801
d 1811 (NMM)

GLEN, Nisbet
L 29 Apr 1799
CR 4 Dec 1813
d 13 Feb 1824 (NMM)

GLENDONING, Robert
L 20 Oct 1696
Gone 1719 (PRO)

GLENHAM, Henry
L 1672

GLENNY, Robert
L 1 Aug 1806 (NMM)
d 10 May 1822 (LT)

GLINN, Richard
L 17 Dec 1794 (NMM)
d 21 May 1838 (NMM)

GLOSTER, William Barnett
L 12 Dec 1810
d 1818 (NMM)

GLOVER, Bonovrier
L 8 Dec 1760
CR 6 Aug 1762
CA 20 June 1765
d 23 Apr 1780 (LG)

GLOVER, John (1)
L 20 June 1757
d 1778 (PRO)

GLOVER, John (2)
L 13 June 1781
d 1798 (NMM)

GLOVER, John (3)
L 1 June 1801
d 1809 (NMM)

GLYNN, Edmund
L
CR
CA 1727 (PJP)

GLYNN, Sir Henry Richard
L 28 Oct 1790 (CH)
CR 29 June 1795
CA 10 Apr 1797
RAB 19 July 1821 (LG)
RAW 27 May 1825 (LG)
RAR 22 July 1830 (LG)
VAW 10 Jan 1837 (LG)
VAR 23 Nov 1841 (LG)
AB 9 Nov 1846 (NMM)
AW 13 May 1847 (NMM)
AR 11 June 1851 (NMM)
Ret A 1 July 1851 (NMM)
Cre Bt 1851 (PJP)
d 20 July 1856 (NMM)

GLYNN, Richard
L 17 Dec 1794
d 27 May 1839 (PRO)

GOARD, John
L 16 Jan 1745
d 1755 (NMM)

GOARD, William
L 5 Feb 1697 (PMM)

GOARMAN, –
L 1801 (PJP)
Dismissed 1802 (PJP)

GOATE, William
L 17 Nov 1790
CR 16 Sept 1799
CA 15 Aug 1809
d 1844 (NMM)

GOBLE, Thomas
L 24 Dec 1805
CR 9 Sept 1828 (NMM)
KIA 5 July 1833 (LT)

GODBY, John Hardy
L 15 Oct 1800
CR 25 Sept 1806
CA 27 June 1814
Ret CA 31 Oct 1846 (LG)
Ret RA 21 June 1850 (NMM)
d 25 Feb 1856 (NMM)

GODBY, John Packer
L 24 Sept 1795
d 1798 (NMM)

GODBY, Paul
L 3 Nov 1790
d 1798 (NMM)

GODDALL, John
L 1706 (PJP)

GODDARD, George
L 3 Sept 1810
Ret CR 3 Jan 1851 (NMM)
d 16 Nov 1859 (NMM)

GODDARD, Magnus
L 14 Aug 1739
d 1745 (PRO)

GODDARD, Richard
L 13 Jan 1791
CR 5 July 1794
CA 29 Apr 1802
d 1835 (PRO)

GODDARD, Samuel
L 23 Dec 1727 (PJP)
CR 22 Jan 1741 (PJP)
CA 1 Feb 1743 (PJP)
Dismissed as insane 1746 (PJP)
d 5 Nov 1762 (PJP)

GODDARD, Thomas
L 30 July 1794
d 1796 (NMM)

GODDEN, Joseph Shaw
L 3 Feb 1815
Ret CR 1 Oct 1860 (NMM)
d 1866 (NMM)

GODENCH, Francis
L 23 Mar 1809
CR 7 Mar 1853 (NMM)
d 1864 (NMM)

GODENCH, James
L 3 Sept 1779
CR 9 May 1796
d 6 Jan 1825 (MB)

GODERE, Samuel
See GOODERE, Samuel

GODFREY, Andrew
L 24 June 1761
d 27 Apr 1793 (M)

GODFREY, George Robert
L 24 Apr 1806
HP 30 Apr 1816 (OB)
d 10 Apr 1845 (OB)

GODFREY, H.A.
L 1794 (PJP)

GODFREY, John
L 15 Mar 1757
d 1767 (NMM)

GODFREY, John Race
L 15 Mar 1815
HP 1832 (OB)
Ret CR 20 July 1863 (NMM)
d 8 Nov 1864 (NMM)

GODFREY, Robert
L 17 Jan 1718
Gone 1727 (PRO)

GODFREY, Thomas
L July 1800 (PJP)

GODFREY, William (1)
L 1673
CA 4 July 1666 (RM)
d before 1689 (PJP)

GODFREY, William (2)
L 1665

GODFREY, William (3)
L 7 Mar 1795
T
CR 24 Dec 1805
CA 11 Apr 1809
CB 2 Jan 1815 (LG)
d 14 Dec 1834 (PJP)

GODFREY, William Mackenzie
L 8 Jan 1810
CR 2 Feb 1813
CA 19 July 1822 (MB)
d 6 Dec 1830 (NMM)

GODSLAVE, Henry
L 23 May 1738
CR 4 Apr 1740
CA 17 May 1741
SUP RA 1756
d 1 Dec 1765

GODWIN, James
L 7 Oct 1762
d 14 Dec 1811 (PRO)

GODWIN, Sir John
L 1665
COMM (Chatham) 1679–1685 (MPH)
Kt 1680 (MPH)
MP (Queenborough) 1685 (MPH)
d Mar 1688 (MPH)

GODWIN, Matthew
L 1 Aug 1794
CR 15 Jan 1802
CA 8 May 1804
Ret RA 10 Jan 1837 (NMM)
RAB 17 Aug 1840 (NMM)
RAW 23 Nov 1841 (NMM)
RAR 9 Nov 1846 (NMM)
VAB 26 July 1847 (LG)
VAW 9 May 1849 (LG)
d 17 Oct 1849 (NMM)

GODWIN, Thomas Fry
L 28 Aug 1812
d 1813 (NMM)

GOLBY, Robert
L
CA 9 June 1666 (RM)

GOFFIN, Thomas
L 15 May 1807
d 1809 (PRO)

GOLD, John
L 26 Nov 1776
Dismissed insane 26 July 1791 (PJP)
d 1813 (NMM)

GOLDEN, Stephen
?GOLTON, Stephen
L 1665

GOLDESBOROUGH, Thomas
L
CR 25 Jan 1780
CA 1 Dec 1787
SUP RA 10 Oct 1807 (NMM)
d 24 Dec 1828 (NMM)

GOLDFINCH, William
L 4 Mar 1800
d 1813 (NMM)

GOLDIE, John (1)
L 7 Jan 1802
d 10 Apr 1837 (NMM)

GOLDIE, John (2)
L 8 July 1814
d 1849 (NMM)

GOLDING, John (1)
L
CA 1661
KIA 13 Apr 1665 (NMM)

GOLDING, John (2)
L 1673
d before 1689 (PJP)

GOLDING, John (3)
L
CA 1681
d before 1689 (PJP)

GOLDING, John (4)
L 16 Feb 1814
d 26 July 1825 (NMM)

GOLDING, J.G.
L 1814 (PJP)

GOLDSMITH, Hugh Colville
L 27 Jan 1809
d 8 Oct 1841 (NMM)

GOLDSMITH, Timothy
L 1780 (PJP)

GOLTON, Stephen
?GOLDEN, Stephen q.v.
L 19 Mar 1694
Gone 1719 (PRO)

GOMM, James
L 13 Apr 1782
SUP CR 1 Mar 1817 (NMM)
d 1838 (NMM)

GOMM, Richard
L 6 June 1778
d 1780 (NMM)

GOMM, William Wykes
L 21 Nov 1797
d 28 Feb 1800

GOOCH, Samuel
L 11 Nov 1791
d 17 Apr 1806 (PRO)

GOOCH, William
L 1691 (PJP)

GOOD, Edward (1)
L
CA 6 June 1689
SUP CA 1703 (PJP)
d 9 Feb 1710

GOOD, Edward (2)
L
CA 1689 (PJP)

GOOD, John (1)
L 7 July 1762
d 8 Oct 1769 (NMM)

GOOD, John (2)
L 6 May 1796
Ret CR 26 Nov 1830 (NMM)
d 26 Aug 1838 (NMM)

GOODALL, John (1)
L
CR
CA 25 Sept 1708
d 31 Jan 1729 (NMM)

GOODALL, John (2)
L 4 Mar 1740
d 1746 (PRO)

GOODALL, Samuel Granston
L 1 Sept 1756
CR 2 June 1760
CA 13 Jan 1762
RAB 21 Sept 1790
RAR 1 Feb 1793
VAB 12 Apr 1794
VAW 4 July 1794
VAR 1 June 1795
AB 14 Feb 1799
AW 1 Jan 1801
d 21 Apr 1801

GOODALL, William
L 1797 (PJP)
d (drowned) 1797 (PJP)

GOODCHILD, George Pigot
L 9 Mar 1796
d 1798 (NMM)

GOODE, Sephas
L 16 Feb 1815
Ret CR 19 Feb 1861 (NMM)
d 1872 (NMM)

GOODENCH, James
L 1793 (PJP)

GOODERE, Samuel
L 10 Dec 1712 (PMM)
CR 13 Nov 1733
e (murder) 15 Apr 1741 (DNB)

GOODHEART, Abraham
L
CA 1666
d before 1689 (PJP)

GOODING, James Glassford
L 20 Nov 1805
Ret CR 18 Apr 1838 (NMM)
d 1857 (NMM)

GOODING, John
L 11 Apr 1760
d 1762 (PRO)

GOODING, Nathaniel
L 23 Nov 1759
SUP CR 18 June 1805
d 2 Apr 1811 (NMM)

GOODLAD, Edward
T
L 22 Jan 1814 (OB)
HP 1814–1823 (OB)
d 1849 (TR)

GOODLAD, Richard
L
CA 1665
d before 1689 (PJP)

GOODLAD, William
L 1664
d before 1689 (PJP)

GOODRIDGE, John
L 27 Dec 1775
d 12 July 1776 (PRO)

GOODRIDGE, Nicholas
L 1691 (PJP)

GOODRIDGE, Thomas Bowen
L 8 Oct 1801
d 1802 (NMM)

GOODSON, Samuel
L 16 Oct 1779
d 16 Sept 1801

GOODWIN, James
L 4 Mar 1740
d 1741 (NMM)

GOODWIN, Richard Merrish
T
L 4 Apr 1810
d 1813 (PRO)

GOODWIN, Samuel
L 7 Nov 1806
d 1813 (NMM)

GOODWIN, Uriah
L 14 Aug 1807
d 1810 (NMM)

GOOKIN, Thomas
L 1666
d before 1689 (PJP)

GOOLD, Hugh
L 16 June 1808
CR 22 July 1830 (MB)
Ret CA 1 Apr 1855 (PRO)
d 29 Mar 1866 (NMM)

GOOSE, George
L 18 June 1811
d 1840 (NMM)

GOOSE, William
L 8 Feb 1815
Ret CR 1 Oct 1860 (NMM)
d 16 Aug 1871 (NMM)

GOOSTREY, William
L 5 June 1744
CR 12 Dec 1757
CA 23 Jan 1759
KIA 1 July 1762 (LG)

GORDON, Hon. Adam, Viscount Kenmure
T
L 1 July 1815 (OB)
HP Aug 1816 (OB)
Inh EP 21 Sept 1840 (OB)
d 1 Sept 1847 (PMM)

GORDON, Alexander (1)
L 11 May 1704 (PMM)

GORDON, Alexander (2)
L 13 Jan 1728
CR 10 Feb 1742
d 1743 (PRO)

GORDON, Alexander (3)
L 2 Mar 1734
CR 10 Feb 1742
d 14 Jan 1742 (PRO)

GORDON, Alexander (4)
L 25 Feb 1742
d 1783 (NMM)

GORDON, Alexander (4)
L 2 Mar 1782
d 1795 (NMM)

GORDON, Alexander (5)
L 29 Dec 1796
CR 22 Jan 1806
CA 10 Feb 1814
RA 1837 (PJP)
d 14 Oct 1842 (PRO)

GORDON, Charles
L 11 Mar 1802
CR 20 May 1806
CA 21 Dec 1807
HP 10 Dec 1810 (OB)
CB 4 July 1840 (OB)
RAB 23 Nov 1841 (CH)
RAW 26 July 1847 (LG)
RAR 24 Dec 1849 (LG)
Ret RA 1851 (CH)
VA 5 Mar 1853 (CH)
A 20 Jan 1858 (NMM)
d 3 Oct 1860 (NMM)

GORDON, Charles Rumbold
L 13 Dec 1813
d 1848 (NMM)

GORDON, Edward
L 30 June 1813
CR 3 June 1826 (PRO)
d (drowned) 14 Apr 1828 (CH)

GORDON, Francis Grant
Formerly GRANT, Francis
L 29 June 1753
CR 24 Sept 1762
CA 11 July 1765
d 1793 (NMM)

GORDON, George (1)
L
CR 15 Mar 1708 (PMM)
CA 9 Apr 1709
d 12 July 1732

GORDON, George, Lord (2)
L 5 June 1772
Resigned 1773 (PJP)
MP (Ludgershall) 1774–1780 (MPN)
d 1 Nov 1793 (MB)

GORDON, George (3)
L 5 Aug 1793
d 1800 (NMM)

GORDON, George (4)
L 26 Nov 1810 (MB)
CR 9 Jan 1815
d 1840 (NMM)

GORDON, Henry
L 13 July 1798
CR 29 Apr 1802
CA 8 Apr 1805
Ret RA 10 Jan 1837 (CH)
RAB 17 Aug 1840 (CH)
RAW 23 Nov 1841 (NMM)
RAR 9 Nov 1846 (NMM)
VAB 27 Dec 1847 (CH)
VAW 30 Oct 1849 (NMM)
VAR 1 July 1851 (NMM)
Ret A 21 Jan 1854 (CH)
d 14 Sept 1855 (NMM)

GORDON, Henry Cranmer
L 4 Feb 1815
HP 4 Feb 1815 (OB)
d 25 Feb 1848 (PRO)

GORDON, James (1)
L 19 Feb 1756
d 1776 (NMM)

GORDON, James (2)
L 24 Jan 1758
d 20 Oct 1781 (M)

GORDON, James (3)
L 25 Mar 1802
d 1808 (NMM)

GORDON, James (4)
L 12 Dec 1808
CR 29 Jan 1821 (NMM)
d 1856 (NMM)

GORDON, James (5)
L 3 Mar 1815
HP Jan 1816 (OB)
d 1863 (PRO)

GORDON, Sir James Alexander (1)
L 27 Jan 1800
CR 3 Mar 1804
CA 16 May 1805
KCB 2 Jan 1815 (DNB)
RAB 10 Jan 1837 (LG)
LGH 1 July 1840 (OB)
RAW 23 Nov 1841 (NMM)
RAR 9 Nov 1847 (NMM)
VAB 8 Jan 1846 (DNB)
VAR 26 Oct 1853 (NMM)
GGH 1853 (DNB)
AB 21 Jan 1854 (DNB)
GCB 5 July 1855 (DNB)
Ret AF 30 Jan 1868 (DNB)
d 8 Jan 1869 (DNB)

GORDON, James Alexander (2)
L 26 May 1814
HP Sept 1815 (OB)
CR 13 Apr 1857 (NMM)
d 1877 (NMM)

GORDON, James Edward
L 17 May 1811
HP 23 Apr 1815 (OB)
Ret CR 17 Nov 1863 (NMM)
d 30 Apr 1864 (NMM)

GORDON, James Gabriel
L 3 Oct 1810
CR 20 July 1815
HP 1830–1846 (OB)
CA 28 July 1851 (NMM)
Ret RA 1 July 1867 (NMM)
d 1871 (NMM)

GORDON, James Joseph
L 21 Feb 1815
d 18 July 1824 (PRO)

GORDON, James Murray
L 25 Feb 1803
CR 1 Feb 1806
CA 15 Feb 1808
RAB 9 Nov 1846 (CH)
RAW 6 Aug 1847 (LG)
RAR 14 Jan 1850 (LG)
d 28 Dec 1850 (NMM)

GORDON, John (1)
L 1702 (PMM)

GORDON, John (2)
L 14 Aug 1739
d 1744 (PRO)

GORDON, John (3)
L 6 Oct 1744
d 1762 (NMM)

GORDON, John (4)
L 29 Apr 1803
d 1806 (NMM)

GORDON, John (5)
L 21 Apr 1810
d 31 Dec 1813 (PRO)

GORDON, Hon. John (6)
L 21 Mar 1812
CR 15 June 1814
CA 31 Dec 1818 (MB)
Ret CA 31 Oct 1846 (LG)
Ret RA 27 Aug 1851 (NMM)
Ret VA 10 Sept 1857 (NMM)
Ret A 23 Mar 1863 (NMM)
d 11 Nov 1869 (NMM)

GORDON, Lewis
L 15 June 1757
d May 1758 (PJP)

GORDON, Robert
L 1 Mar 1745
d 1781 (NMM)

GORDON, Robert James
L 11 Dec 1807
CR 6 June 1814
d 27 Sept 1822 (MB)

GORDON, Samuel
L 17 July 1801
CR 19 July 1821 (NMM)
d 1826 (NMM)

GORDON, Thomas (1)
L 19 Nov 1694
CR
CA 7 Nov 1705
Dismissed 1715
Became an Admiral in the Czar's service
d 18 Mar 1741 (CH)

GORDON, Thomas (2)
L 26 Dec 1743
CR 23 May 1757
CA 10 Sept 1761
d 30 Dec 1761

GORDON, Sir William (1)
L 26 Dec 1735
CR 22 May 1742
CA 4 Aug 1744
RAW 21 Oct 1762 (CH)
d 25 Apr 1768

GORDON, Hon. William (2)
L 2 July 1804
CR 14 Apr 1807
CA 12 Mar 1810
COM AD 8 Sept 1841–
17 Feb 1846 (AO)
RAB 9 Nov 1846 (LG)
RAW 24 Jan 1849 (LG)
RAR 16 June 1851 (NMM)
VAB 11 Feb 1854 (NMM)
VAW 3 Oct 1855 (NMM)
VAR 10 Sept 1857 (NMM)
d 3 Feb 1858 (NMM)

GORDON, William (3)
L 21 Mar 1812
CR 13 June 1815
CA 23 Nov 1841 (LG)
Ret CA 2 May 1854 (NMM)
Ret RA 12 Apr 1862 (NMM)
Ret VA 24 May 1867 (NMM)
d 23 Nov 1873 (NMM)

GORE, Hamilton
L 2 Apr 1743
CR 20 June 1765
d 31 Oct 1777 (NMM)

GORE, Henry
L
CR
CA 29 Oct 1703
d 14 Apr 1726 (M)

GORE, John (1)
L 20 July 1768
CR
CA 2 Oct 1780
d 10 Aug 1790 (M)

GORE, Sir John (2)
L 26 Oct 1789 (NMM)
CR 24 May 1794
CA 12 Nov 1794
Kt 21 Feb 1805 (DNB)
RAB 4 Dec 1813
RAW 4 June 1814
KCB 12 Apr 1815 (LG)
RAR 12 Aug 1819 (CH)
VAB 27 May 1825 (CH)
VAR 22 July 1830 (CH)
d 21 Aug 1836 (DNB)

GORE, John (3)
L 19 Aug 1795
CR 23 June 1808
CA 19 July 1821 (MB)
Ret CA 1 Oct 1846 (NMM)
Ret RA 8 Mar 1852 (NMM)
d 1853 (NMM)

GORE, John (4)
L 28 May 1804
CR 10 Oct 1812
CA 27 July 1825 (MB)
Ret CA 31 Oct 1846 (LG)
Ret RA 21 Jan 1854 (NMM)
Ret VA 18 Dec 1858 (NMM)
Ret A 15 Dec 1863 (NMM)
d 1870 (NMM)

GORE, Hon. John (5)
L 2 Jan 1807

CR	2 May	1810
d		1812 (PRO)
GORE, Ralph		
L	15 Oct	1802
Ret CR	15 Apr	1835 (NMM)
d		1859 (NMM)
GORE, Hon. Robert		
L	6 Dec	1813
CR	23 July	1821 (NMM)
CA	9 Nov	1846 (LG)
Ret CA	1 Apr	1856 (NMM)
d		1867 (NMM)
GORGON, Henry		
See GORDON, Henry		
GORGON, Sir James Alexander		
See GORDON, Sir James Alexander		
GOSHAM, –		
L		1780 (PJP)
KIA	8 Dec	1780 (PJP)
GOSLING, George (1)		
L	19 Mar	1734
CR	8 Oct	1741
d		1746 (PRO)
GOSLING, George (2)		
L	27 Sept	1809
CR	24 Apr	1815
CA	16 Aug	1825 (MB)
d	20 Feb	1841 (NMM)
GOSSART, George		
L	15 Oct	1776
d		1778 (PRO)
GOSSELIN, Corbet		
L	22 Oct	1798
d		1803 (NMM)
GOSSELIN, Joshua Carteret		
L	22 Sept	1810
Ret CR	11 Apr	1851 (NMM)
d		1879 (NMM)
GOSSELIN, Thomas Le Marchant		
L	1 Dec	1787
CR	20 Apr	1793
CA	23 July	1795
RAB	4 June	1814
RAW	12 Aug	1819 (CH)
RAR	19 July	1821 (CH)
VAB	27 May	1825 (CH)
VAW	22 July	1830 (CH)
VAR	10 Jan	1837 (CH)
AW	23 Nov	1841 (CH)
AR	24 Apr	1847 (CH)
d	27 Nov	1857 (NMM)
GOSSETT, Abraham		
L	24 Mar	1794
Ret CR	4 Dec	1829 (NMM)
d		1840 (NMM)
GOSTLING, Francis		
L	30 Mar	1811
d	20 Nov	1813 (PJP)
GOSTLING, Philip		
L	25 Apr	1815
CR	2 Mar	1828 (NMM)
CA	23 Nov	1841 (LG)
Ret CA	14 Jan	1855 (PRO)
d	2 June	1861 (NMM)
GOSTLING, Thomas		
L	4 Nov	1790
d		1809 (NMM)
GOTHER, George		
L	14 May	1703
d		1737 (PRO)
GOTHER, James		
L	26 Sept	1688 (P)
CA	3 May	1689
d	9 Nov	1696 (PJP)
GOTT, Thomas		
L	21 Nov	1790
KIA	24 Dec	1796 (CH)
GOUGH, John		
L	27 Sept	1762
d		1771 (NMM)
GOUGH, William		
L	10 July	1744
CR		
CA	26 June	1756
d	2 July	1760 (NMM)
GOULD, Abraham		
L	18 Jan	1728
CR	17 Dec	1740
d		1764 (NMM)
GOULD, Sir Davidge		
L	7 May	1779
CR	13 June	1782
HP		1785–1789 (OB)
CA	25 Mar	1789
RAB	2 Oct	1807
RAW	25 Oct	1809
RAR	31 July	1810
VAB	1 Aug	1811
VAW	4 June	1814
KCB	7 June	1815 (MB)
VAR	12 Aug	1819 (CH)
AB	27 May	1825 (CH)
AW	22 July	1830 (CH)
GCB	7 Feb	1833 (LG)
AR	10 Jan	1837 (CH)
d	23 Apr	1847 (CH)
GOULD, Nicholas		
L	22 Apr	1808
d		1839 (NMM)
GOULD, William		
L	11 Feb	1815
Ret CR	1 Oct	1860 (NMM)
d	11 Jan	1866 (NMM)
GOULETT, Charles		
L	29 Sept	1814
CR	15 Feb	1852 (NMM)
d	12 Aug	1862 (NMM)
GOURAN, Richard Fitzpatrick, Lord		
See FITZPATRICK, Richard		
GOURLEY, John		
L	16 Mar	1814
d (drowned)	18 Dec	1814 (PJP)
GOURLY, John		
L	13 Sept	1793
CR	14 Sept	1808
HP	June	1810–
	Feb	1812 (OB)
CA	1 Jan	1817 (NMM)

Ret CA	31 Oct	1846 (LG)
Ret RA	16 June	1851 (NMM)
d	Sept	1854 (NMM)
GOVETT, James		
L	23 Mar	1815
HP	23 Mar	1815 (OB)
d		1852 (NMM)
GOWDE, John		
L	2 Feb	1815
d		1817 (NMM)
GOWER, Augustus Leveson		
L	11 Jan	1800
CR	20 Oct	1801
CA	28 Apr	1802
d	22 Aug	1802 (PJP)
GOWER, Edward Leveson		
L	19 Mar	1793
CR	8 Oct	1794 (NMM)
CA	1 June	1795
RAB	4 June	1814
RAW	12 Aug	1819 (CH)
Resigned	13 July	1821 (NMM)
GOWER, Sir Erasmus		
L	9 July	1762 (DNB)
CR		
CA	9 Jan	1780
Kt		1794 (MB)
RAW	14 Feb	1799
RAR	1 Jan	1801
VAW	23 Apr	1804
GG (Newfoundland)		1804–1807 (BNS)
VAR	9 Nov	1805
AB	25 Oct	1809
AW	31 July	1810
d	31 May	1814 (PJP)
GOWER, Hon. John Leveson		
L	18 Nov	1758
CR	July	1759 (PJP)
CA	30 June	1760
COM AD	30 Jan–10 Apr	1783 (AO)
COM AD	31 Dec	1783–
	12 Aug	1789 (AO)
RAB	24 Sept	1787
RAW	21 Sept	1790
d	15 Aug	1792 (CH)
GRABRIX, G.		
L		1798 (PJP)
GRACE, Percy		
L	28 Feb	1809
CR	15 June	1814
CA	1 Feb	1825 (MB)
RA	17 Nov	1853 (NMM)
VA	6 Mar	1858 (NMM)
d	11 May	1859 (NMM)
GRAEME, Alexander		
L	24 Aug	1760 (NMM)
CR	14 Nov	1775 (NMM)
CA	24 Jan	1778
RAW	1 June	1795
RAR	20 Feb	1797
VAW	14 Feb	1799
VAR	29 Apr	1802
AB	23 Apr	1804
AW	28 Apr	1808
AR	4 Dec	1813
d		1818 (CH)
GRAEME, Robert		
L	1 Aug	1782
Dismissed	30 July	1793 (PRO)
d		1793 (NMM)
GRAFTON, Henry Fitzroy, Duke of		
L		
Cre EP	Sept	1675 (DNB)
Kt	30 Sept	1680 (DNB)
CA		1683
AD	24 Apr	1683
CAF (1st Foot Guards)	9 Feb	1685 (EAD)
d	9 Oct	1690 (EAD)
GRAHAM, Charles		
L	30 Mar	1741
d		1745 (PRO)
GRAHAM, Edmund		
L	23 Mar	1756
d		1762 (NMM)
GRAHAM, Edwards Lloyd		
L	17 Feb	1797
CR	29 Apr	1802
CA	8 May	1804
d	1 June	1820 (PRO)
GRAHAM, Rt Hon. Lord George		
L	13 Apr	1734
CR		
CA	15 Mar	1740
GG (Newfoundland)		1740–1741 (BNS)
d	2 Jan	1747
GRAHAM, James		
L		
d		1742 (NMM)
GRAHAM, John		
L	23 July	1814
d	31 Oct	1821 (NMM)
GRAHAM, John George		
L	20 Sept	1815
CR	16 June	1823 (MB)
CA	3 Oct	1825 (MB)
Ret CA	31 Oct	1846 (LG)
Ret RA	27 Jan	1854 (NMM)
d	3 June	1854 (NMM)
GRAHAM, Matthew		
L	22 Oct	1795
d	25 Dec	1829 (NMM)
GRAHAM, Mitchell		
L	26 Apr	1753
CR	9 Feb	1759
CA	21 Nov	1760
d		1795
GRAHAM, Philip		
L	14 Apr	1810
HP	Jan–July	1813 (MB)
CR	29 July	1825 (MB)
d		1849 (NMM)
GRAHAM, Robert		
L		1796 (PJP)
d (drowned)	31 Dec	1796 (PJP)
GRAHAM, Thomas		
L	27 Aug	1799
CR	12 Oct	1809
CA	24 Apr	1811
d	9 Apr	1822 (NMM)

GRAHAM, William
L 16 Nov 1702 (PMM)
CR 21 Jan 1705 (PJP)
CA 1 Jan 1713
d 9 Jan 1718
GRAINGER, James
L 9 July 1690
In Merchant Service 1699 (PJP)
CR 6 Feb 1711 (PRO)
Gone 1727 (PRO)
GRAINGER, William
L 3 Nov 1790
d 1793 (NMM)
GRAMSHAW, Joseph George Hutzen
L 22 Jan 1806
Ret CR 5 Jan 1839 (NMM)
d 6 Jan 1865 (PRO)
GRANDIDIER, John Paul
L 2 Feb 1815
d 23 Apr 1842 (NMM)
GRANDY, Samuel
L 25 Mar 1809
CR 2 Jan 1837 (NMM)
HP 1846 (OB)
Ret CA 1 Apr 1856 (NMM)
d 1856 (NMM)
GRANGER, William
L 3 Nov 1790
CR 10 May 1797
CA 22 July 1799
RAW 22 July 1830 (LG)
VAB 10 Jan 1837 (LG)
VAW 23 Nov 1841 (LG)
VAR 9 Nov 1846 (LG)
d 3 Jan 1848 (NMM)
GRANGER, James
See GRAINGER, James
GRANNARD, George, Lord Forbes,Earl
See FORBES, George, Lord (1)
GRANT, Arthur
L 1666
GRANT, Charles
L 28 Oct 1790 (MB)
CR 29 Nov 1797
CA 6 Sept 1800
CB 2 June 1815 (LG)
d 25 July 1824 (NMM)
GRANT, Charles Cathcart
L 12 Jan 1744
CR 23 Mar 1757
CA 17 Jan 1761
d 24 Apr 1769
GRANT, David M'Dowell
L 29 July 1781 (NMM)
SUP CR 1 Jan 1816 (NMM)
d 1841 (NMM)
GRANT, Edward
L 29 Mar 1815
d 1857 (NMM)
GRANT, Francis
See GORDON, Francis Grant
GRANT, George (1)
L 2 Mar 1734
Gone 1737 (NMM)
GRANT, George (2)
L 16 Nov 1781
SUP CR 8 Apr 1816 (PRO)
d June 1823 (NMM)
GRANT, George (3)
L 22 Apr 1800
d 1811 (NMM)
GRANT, Gregory
L 4 Nov 1795
CR 21 Oct 1810
Ret CA 10 Sept 1840 (NMM)
d 1844 (NMM)
GRANT, J.
L 1814 (PJP)
GRANT, James (1)
L 2 Feb 1741
d 1742 (PRO)
GRANT, James (2)
L 14 May 1793
d 1797 (NMM)
GRANT, James (3)
L 31 Jan 1800
CR 12 Jan 1805
d 11 Nov 1833 (DCB)
GRANT, James Lodovick
L 25 Nov 1785 (PMM)
Quit 25 Sept 1786 (PMM)
d 10 Jan 1827 (PMM)
GRANT, Jasper
L
CA 1665
Dismissed 16 Oct 1673 (PRO)
GRANT, John (1)
L 1690 (PMM)
GRANT, John (2)
L 25 June 1812
CR 10 Dec 1835 (NMM)
HP 1840 (OB)
Ret CA 1 Apr 1856 (NMM)
d 1874 (NMM)
GRANT, Lachlan
L 1 Mar 1815
d 1844 (NMM)
GRANT, Lewis
T
L 19 Feb 1811
d 8 Dec 1822 (NMM)
GRANT, Ludovick
L 18 Feb 1815
d 21 Dec 1836 (PJP)
GRANT, Mardo
L 29 Jan 1748
d 1759 (NMM)
GRANT, Sir Richard
L 5 Oct 1805
HP Nov 1814–Apr 1815 (OB)
CR 7 Nov 1818 (MB)
Kt 1820 (MB)
CA 17 May 1828 (MB)
HP 1846 (OB)
RA 7 Feb 1855 (NMM)
d 3 Mar 1859 (NMM)

GRANT, Robert
L 13 Apr 1741
CR 3 July 1746
CA 27 Jan 1758
d 22 Feb 1759 (NMM)

GRANT, Samuel
L 15 Mar 1815
d 17 Apr 1817 (PJP)

GRANT, Walter Edward
L 21 Mar 1812
d 7 Apr 1831 (PRO)

GRANT, William (1)
L 9 Nov 1756
CR 24 Oct 1777
CA 18 May 1781
d 27 Dec 1789 (M)

GRANT, William (2)
L 13 Apr 1761
d 1764 (NMM)

GRANT, William (3)
L 11 Feb 1815
HP Sept 1815 (OB)
d 1 Dec 1845 (OB)

GRANTHAM, Caleb
L
CA 13 Jan 1692 (PJP)
d 1698

GRANTHAM, Charles
L 23 Oct 1809
HP Mar 1811 (OB)
Ret CR 9 Oct 1848 (NMM)
d 1860 (NMM)

GRANTHAM, Nathaniel
L 1689 (PMM)
CA 13 Aug 1694
In Merchant Service 1700 (PJP)
d 17 Nov 1723

GRANVILL, Hon. John
L 24 May 1688 (P)
CA 12 Mar 1689
(22 Dec 1688 in H)
Cre EP 1703 (PJP)
d 27 Jan 1703

GRAPE, Samuel
L 24 Oct 1746
d 1775 (NMM)

GRATRIX, George
L 14 Aug 1801 (NMM)
Ret CR 25 Feb 1832 (NMM)
d 1834 (NMM)

GRAVES, Alexander
L 4 Feb 1814 (NMM)
d 1817 (NMM)

GRAVES, David
L 21 Sept 1770
CR 25 Jan 1778
CA 9 Sept 1779
SUP RA 21 Feb 1799
d 1822 (PRO)

GRAVES, John (1)
L 13 July 1762
d 1806 (NMM)

GRAVES, John (2)
L 4 Nov 1769
CR 6 June 1777 (NMM)
CA 21 Jan 1783 (NMM)
SUP RA 30 Dec 1805 (NMM)
d 1812 (NMM)

GRAVES, John (3)
L 10 Apr 1798
d 30 July 1827 (PRO)

GRAVES, Richard
L 24 Dec 1775
CR
CA 29 Aug 1781
SUP RA 18 June 1804
d 5 Mar 1836 (NMM)

GRAVES, Richard Wilcox
L 27 Dec 1808
d 1838 (PRO)

GRAVES, Samuel (1)
L 3 Mar 1740 (MB)
CR
CA 11 Sept 1744
RAB 21 Oct 1762
RAR 18 Oct 1770
VAB 24 Oct 1770
VAW 31 Mar 1775
VAR 5 Feb 1776
AB 29 Jan 1778 (CH)
AW 8 Apr 1782
SUP A 1783 (MB)
d 8 Mar 1787 (CH)

GRAVES, Samuel (2)
L 7 Apr 1772
CR 15 Nov 1775
CA 15 Sept 1777
d Nov 1802 (PRO)

GRAVES, Samuel (3)
L 4 Nov 1790
Dismissed 21 Sept 1806 (PRO)

GRAVES, Thomas (1)
L
CR 1709 (PJP)
CA 1 Jan 1713
SUP RA 15 July 1747
d 23 Dec 1755 (NMM)

GRAVES, Thomas, Baron (2)
L 25 June 1743
CR 12 Mar 1754
CA 8 July 1755
GG 1761–
(Newfoundland) 1764 (BNS)
MP 2 Jan 1755–
(East Loos) May 1775 (MPN)
CRM 31 Mar 1775 (AL)
RAB 19 Mar 1779 (PJP)
RAR 26 Sept 1780 (CH)
VAB 24 Sept 1787 (CH)
VAW 21 Sept 1790 (CH)
VAR 1 Feb 1793 (CH)
AB 12 Apr 1794 (DNB)
CRE IP 24 Oct 1794 (MPN)
AW 1 June 1795 (CH)
d 9 Feb 1802 (CH)

GRAVES, Thomas Lord (3)
L 30 Oct 1765
CR 15 Mar 1779

CA	19 Mar	1779
RAB	26 Sept	1780
RAR	5 May	1781
VAB	24 Sept	1787
VAW	21 Sept	1790
VAR	1 Feb	1793
AB	12 Apr	1794
AW	1 June	1795
d	1 Feb	1802

GRAVES, Sir Thomas (4)

L	31 Mar	1782
CR	22 Nov	1790
CA	19 Mar	1794
RAW	1 Jan	1801
KCB		1801 (CH)
RAR	23 Apr	1804
VAB	9 Nov	1805
VAW	28 Apr	1808 (CH)
VAR	31 July	1810
AB	12 Aug	1812
d	29 Mar	1814 (NMM)

GRAVES, Thomas (5)

L	19 Mar	1794
CR	8 July	1809
CA	8 Aug	1810
d	29 Mar	1834 (PRO)

GRAY, Charles

L		
CR		
CA	1 Jan	1713
d		1714 (PJP)

GRAY, Francis

T		
L	26 Aug	1814
d	7 Dec	1851 (NMM)

GRAY, George (1)

L	4 Mar	1691
In Merchant Service		1700 (PJP)

GRAY, George (2)

L	14 May	1795
KIA	2 Apr	1801 (JH)

GRAY, George (3)

L	27 Feb	1815
d	3 July	1829 (NMM)

GRAY, Henry
See GREY, Henry

GRAY, James

L	12 Feb	1781
d		1811 (NMM)

GRAY, John (1)

L		
CR	1 June	1708 (PMM)
CA	26 Jan	1711
d		1736 (PJP)

GRAY, John (2)

L	22 Oct	1795
d		1826 (NMM)

GRAY, Matthew

L	9 Feb	1815
HP	Aug	1816 (OB)
d		1851 (NMM)

GRAY, Richard

L	30 Oct	1800
d	May	1801 (NMM)

GRAY, Thomas (1)

L	28 Feb	1805
d	31 Jan	1825 (NMM)

GRAY, Thomas (2)

L	10 Feb	1815
HP	May	1815 (OB)
d	18 Sept	1845 (OB)

GRAY, William (1)

L	5 Mar	1697
Gone		1719 (PRO)

GRAY, William (2)

L	21 June	1810
d		1837 (NMM)

GRAYDON, George

L		1697 (PJP)

GRAYDON, Henry

L	5 Aug	1696
Gone		1719 (PRO)

GRAYDON, James Newenham

L	13 Mar	1815
HP	13 Mar	1815 (OB)
Ret CR	20 July	1863 (NMM)
d		1869 (NMM)

GRAYDON, John

L	17 June	1685 (P)
EH (Herbert)	25 May	1686 (EAD)
CA	6 Sept	1689 (DCB)
GG (Newfoundland)		1701–1702 (DCB)
RAB	12 June	1702
RAW	9 Dec	1702
VAW	1 Mar	1703
VAR	6 May	1703
Dismissed	17 Mar	1704 (CH)
d	12 Mar	1726 (EAD)

GREATWOOD, William

T		
L	22 Feb	1810
d	Nov	1827 (NMM)

GREAVES, Alexander

L	4 Feb	1814

GREEME, Alexander

L	24 Aug	1760 (NMM)
d		1775 (NMM)

GREEN, Sir Andrew Pellet

L	8 Aug	1800
T		
HP	Dec	1805–
	23 Mar	1807 (OB)
CR	1 Feb	1812
KH		1814 (MB)
Kt (Sweden)		1814 (MB)
CA	12 Apr	1814
Kt		1832 (CH)
KCH		1832 (OB)
RAB	3 Mar	1849 (LG)
RAW	16 June	1851 (NMM)
RA	1 July	1851 (NMM)
Ret VA	31 Jan	1856 (CH)
d	26 Dec	1858 (NMM)

GREEN, Benjamin

L	28 July	1794
d		1796 (NMM)

GREEN, Charles

L	4 May	1810
CR	23 July	1814

GREEN, George (1)
L 23 July 1805
d 19 Jan 1815 (NMM)
GREEN, George (2)
L 5 May 1812
d 1843 (NMM)
GREEN, James
L 7 Oct 1799
T
CR 24 Dec 1805
CA 1 Feb 1812 (MB)
d 17 Nov 1836 (NMM)
GREEN, John (1)
L 3 July 1739
CR 4 Dec 1744
Dismissed 17 June 1745 (PMM)
d 1745 (NMM)
GREEN, John (2)
L 27 July 1745
d 1752 (NMM)
GREEN, John (3)
L 9 Mar 1759
d 1768 (PRO)
GREEN, John (4)
L 8 Apr 1805
d 14 June 1806 (PMM)
GREEN, John (5)
L 11 Aug 1809
d 30 Jan 1861 (NMM)
GREEN, John William
L 2 June 1808
d 1837 (NMM)
GREEN, Joseph
L 20 Mar 1815 (NMM)
d 1844 (NMM)
GREEN, Levi
See GREENE, Levi
GREEN, William (1)
L 22 Nov 1790
CR 7 May 1802
CA 22 Jan 1806
d 1811 (NMM)
GREEN, William (2)
L 14 Feb 1815
d 17 Sept 1821 (PRO)
GREEN, William Pringle
T
L 8 Jan 1806 (LTE)
d 18 Oct 1846 (NMM)
GREEN, Young
L 26 Dec 1800
d 1805 (PJP)
GREENAWAY, James
L 24 May 1688 (P)
CA 19 Jan 1691
d (drowned) 26 Nov 1703 (CH)
GREENAWAY, John
L 9 Jan 1779
d 1780 (NMM)
GREENAWAY, Richard
L 13 Dec 1809
CR 26 May 1814
d 20 Mar 1849 (PRO)
GREENE, Alexander
See GREEME, Alexander
GREENE, Charles (1)
L
CA 1667
d before 1689 (PJP)
GREENE, Charles (2)
L 4 May 1810
CR 23 July 1814 (NMM)
Ret CR 1 July 1851 (NMM)
d 3 Dec 1865 (NMM)
GREENE, Levi
L 1665
CA 9 June 1666 (RM)
Dismissed 1672 (PD)
d before 1689 (PJP)
GREENE, Pitt Burnaby
L 16 Nov 1790
CR 8 May 1804
CA 7 Mar 1811
d 24 Apr 1837 (LT)
GREENE, Richard
L
CA 1660
d before 1689 (PJP)
GREENE, William
L
CA 1672
d 1682 (DDA)
GREENFIELD, John
L 3 July 1757 (NMM)
d 1774 (NMM)
GREENHILL, David
L
CA 5 Mar 1689
d 1716
GREENING, Richard
L 20 Sept 1815
GREENLAW, John Potenger
L 4 May 1804
CR 15 June 1814
d 1837 (NMM)
GREENLY, Sir Isaac Coffin
See COFFIN, Sir Isaac
GREENSHIELDS, –
L 1801 (PJP)
KIA 25 Sept 1801 (PJP)
GREENSILL, George
L 21 Sept 1803
CR 1 Feb 1812
d Sept 1821 (NMM)
GREENSWORD, Edward Nathaniel
L 8 Oct 1798
Ret CR 26 Nov 1830 (NMM)
d 17 June 1845 (OB)
GREENWAY, George Courtenay
L 11 Oct 1814
Ret CR 17 Sept 1860 (NMM)
d 26 May 1866 (NMM)
GREENWAY, James
See GREENAWAY, James

GREENWAY, John
L 2 Oct 1800
Ret CR 26 Nov 1830 (NMM)
d Jan 1838 (NMM)

GREENWAY, Joseph
L 19 June 1812
d 1815 (PRO)

GREENWAY, Richard Croft
L 8 Mar 1805
Ret CR 10 Oct 1851 (NMM)
d 8 May 1853 (NMM)

GREENWAY, Samuel
L 15 June 1802
d 13 Apr 1830 (NMM)

GREENWOOD, Charles
L 4 Mar 1740
d 1749 (PRO)

GREENWOOD, John
See GREENFIELD, John

GREENWOOD, Thomas
L 8 Nov 1804
d 1815 (NMM)

GREENWOOD, William
L 7 Sept 1745
CR 15 Nov 1756
CA 26 May 1768
d 1796

GREER, John Miers
L 20 Sept 1799
Ret CR 14 Mar 1840 (NMM)
d 20 Dec 1861 (PRO)

GREGORY, Arthur Thomas
L 4 Aug 1794
Ret CR 26 Nov 1830 (NMM)
d 1848 (NMM)

GREGORY, Cave
L 8 Feb 1815
Ret CR 12 Apr 1860 (NMM)
d 1871 (NMM)

GREGORY, Charles Marshall
L 20 Feb 1797
CR 13 May 1801
KIA 3 Oct 1808 (CH)

GREGORY, Edward (1)
L 29 June 1697
Gone 1719 (PRO)

GREGORY, Edward (2)
L 25 Sept 1711
CR 19 Nov 1712 (PRO)
CA 11 Mar 1719
d 12 Aug 1743

GREGORY, Francis
L 13 Jan 1691 (PMM)
CR 9 Mar 1702 (PMM)

GREGORY, George (1)
L 10 May 1777
CR 26 Aug 1789
CA 22 Nov 1790
RAB 31 July 1810
RAW 1 Aug 1811
RAR 12 Aug 1812
d 24 Jan 1814 (CH)

GREGORY, George (2)
L 13 July 1801
d Dec 1807 (PJP)

GREGORY, John (1)
L 28 Aug 1718

GREGORY, John (2)
L 7 June 1800
d (drowned) 22 Dec 1809 (CH)

GREGORY, John (3)
L 16 Apr 1808
Ret CR 18 Jan 1845 (NMM)
d 1850 (NMM)

GREGORY, Matthew
L 13 Feb 1697
Gone 1719 (PRO)

GREGORY, Richard
L 6 July 1811
d 16 Dec 1827 (NMM)

GREGORY, Robert (1)
L 31 Mar 1709 (PMM)
CR 3 Apr 1721
d 3 Sept 1726 (NMM)

GREGORY, Robert (2)
L 2 Mar 1734
d 1737 (NMM)

GREGORY, Robert (3)
L 19 Feb 1756
CR
CA 27 Apr 1763
d 18 Feb 1774

GREGORY, Thomas (1)
L 25 Jan 1726
CR 29 Aug 1740
CA 7 Sept 1741
Dismissed 17 Sept 1743 (CH)
Restored w/srty 12 Nov 1745
KIA 25 Jan 1747 (PJP)

GREGORY, Thomas (2)
L 20 July 1810
CR 7 Jan 1833 (NMM)
Ret CA 1 Apr 1856 (NMM)
d 1871 (NMM)

GREGORY, William (1)
L
CA 1664
d before 1689 (PJP)

GREGORY, William (2)
L 1665
CA 1672
d before 1689 (PJP)

GREGORY, William (3)
L 4 Oct 1802
CR 18 Apr 1811
Ret CA 24 Sept 1840 (NMM)
d 1844 (NMM)

GREIG, Samuel
L 4 Feb 1762
Went into the Czar's service 1764 (PMM)
d 26 Oct 1788 (M)

GRENFELL, William
L 1759 (PJP)

GRENVILLE, Thomas
L 2 May 1740

CR
CA 6 Apr 1742
MP (Bridport) 12 Dec 1746–
3 May 1747 (LG)
KIA 3 May 1747 (LG)

GRESLEY, Nigel
L 22 Apr 1748
d 1753 (NMM)

GREVILLE, Hon. Henry
L
CR
CA 31 Mar 1703
d 28 Apr 1720 (NMM)

GREVILLE, Henry Francis
L 4 Jan 1814
CR 19 July 1822 (CH)
CA 27 Aug 1832 (CH)
CB 1855 (CH)
RAB 19 May 1856 (NMM)
RAW 4 Nov 1857 (NMM)
RAR 7 Nov 1860 (NMM)
VAB 1 Apr 1863 (NMM)
VA 3 Apr 1863 (NMM)
Ret VA 7 Apr 1863 (NMM)
Ret A 20 Mar 1867 (PJP)
d 21 May 1887 (PJP)

GREVILLE, Hon. Robert Leveson
L 12 Apr 1802
d 1802 (PRO)

GREVILLE, William Fulke
L 11 Jan 1775
CR 18 Apr 1782
CA 16 Jan 1783
SUP 23 Apr 1804
d 14 Jan 1837 (LT)

GREY, Charles
L 25 Aug 1781
SUP CR 1 Jan 1816 (NMM)
d 1826 (NMM)

GREY, Edward
L 29 Sept 1793
CR 29 Apr 1802
CA 4 Dec 1813
d 1 Nov 1825 (PJP)

GREY, Hon. Sir George
L 2 Jan 1781
CR
CA 1 Nov 1793
SUP CA 1811 (NMM)
Inh Bt June 1814 (MB)
KCB 20 May 1820 (MB)
d 3 Oct 1828 (NMM)

GREY, Henry (1)
L 27 Oct 1758
d 1759 (NMM)

GREY, Henry (2)
L 6 June 1796
CR 2 Feb 1798
d (drowned) 12 Jan 1799 (CH)

GREY, Ralph
L 16 Sept 1779
d 1789 (NMM)

GREY, William
L

CR
CA 29 Apr 1705
Gone 1718 (PRO)

GRIBBLE, Samuel
L 1757 (PJP)
Dismissed 5 Dec 1758 (PJP)

GRIERSON, James (1)
L 19 June 1760
SUP CR Dec 1807 (PRO)
d 1 Apr 1810 (PRO)

GRIERSON, James (2)
L 9 Mar 1805
KIA 1808 (PJP)

GRIERSON, James (3)
L 20 Sept 1805
HP 22 Oct 1814 (OB)
Ret CR 10 Aug 1838 (OB)
d 1857 (NMM)

GRIERSON, John
L 29 Nov 1810
HP 9 May 1814 (OB)
d 1851 (PRO)

GRIEVE, Adam
T
L 30 June 1807
HP 4 June 1814 (OB)
Ret CR 10 Aug 1838 (NMM)
d Sept 1845 (OB)

GRIEVE, William
L 18 Mar 1762
CR 25 Oct 1809 (NMM)
d 1810 (NMM)

GRIFFIES, Samuel
L 11 June 1746
d 1757 (NMM)

GRIFFIN, Charles James
L 2 May 1808
d 7 Apr 1819 (LT)

GRIFFIN, Charles William Griffith
L 16 Aug 1814
CR 28 June 1843 (NMM)
d 1844 (NMM)

GRIFFIN, J.
L 1783 (PJP)
d 1785 (PJP)

GRIFFIN, Philip
L 6 June 1798
Dismissed 25 Mar 1800 (PJP)

GRIFFIN, Thomas (1)
L 28 Oct 1718
CR
CA 1 Apr 1731
RAR 15 July 1747 (CH)
VAB 12 May 1748 (C)
Dismissed 3 Dec 1750 (PJP)
Restored 1752 (MPN)
MP (Arundel) 1754–1761 (MPN)
VAW 6 Feb 1755 (NMM)
AB Feb 1757
AW 21 Oct 1762 (CH)
d 23 Dec 1771 (NMM)

GRIFFIN, Thomas (2)
L 26 Apr 1737
CR

CA 25 Feb 1745
d 11 Sept 1748 (PRO)

GRIFFINHOOFE, Thomas Saville
L 26 Mar 1808
CR 20 June 1813
d 9 Feb 1830 (PRO)

GRIFFITH, Edward
See COLPOYS, Sir Edward Griffith

GRIFFITH, John (1)
L 27 Aug 1801

GRIFFITH. John (2)
L 17 Nov 1804 (NMM)
CR 31 May 1809 (MB)
CA 13 Oct 1812 (MB)
d 1826 (MB)

GRIFFITH, Richard
L
CA 27 Apr 1692
d 7 Aug 1719 (DNB)

GRIFFITH, Walter (1)
L 7 May 1755
CR 4 June 1759
CA 11 Dec 1759
KIA 18 Dec 1779 (DNB)

GRIFFITH, Walter (2)
See BOOTH, Walter

GRIFFITH, William (1)
L 1690 (PMM)

GRIFFITH, William (2)
L 22 Mar 1715

GRIFFITH, William (3)
L 5 Feb 1741
d ?1746 (NMM)

GRIFFITH, William Slater
L 6 Apr 1708
Entered Russian Service 1735 (PJP)
d 1738 (PJP)

GRIFFITHS, Anselm John
L 22 Nov 1790
CR 8 Mar 1797
CA 29 Apr 1802
RAW 10 Jan 1837 (LG)
RAR 23 Nov 1841 (LG)
d 14 June 1842 (NMM)

GRIFFITHS, Delanoy
L 24 May 1762
d 1765 (NMM)

GRIFFITHS, Edward
L 2 Feb 1815
CR 11 Nov 1854 (NMM)
d Jan 1884 (NMM)

GRIFFITHS, John
See GRIFFITH, John

GRIFFITHS, Joseph (1)
L 6 Feb 1755
d 1775 (PRO)

GRIFFITHS, Joseph (2)
L 19 Aug 1795 (NMM)
CR 12 Aug 1819 (NMM)
Ret CA 1 Apr 1856 (NMM)
d 1858 (NMM)

GRIFFITHS, Samuel
See GRIFFIES, Samuel

GRIFFITHS, William
L 17 Nov 1815
HP 17 Nov 1815 (OB)
d 1862 (PRO)

GRIFT, William
L
CA 1672
d before 1869 (PJP)

GRIGG, Arthur
L 20 Mar 1746
d 1756 (PRO)

GRIGG, John
L 24 Oct 1783
SUPCR 31 Dec 1821 (NMM)
d 16 May 1829 (NMM)

GRIGG, Joseph Collings
L 16 Feb 1815
d 1835 (PRO)

GRIMES, Edward
L 19 May 1808
d 1833 (PRO)

GRIMSDITCH, John
L 14 Apr 1685 (P)
CA 27 Apr 1688 (P)
Resigned 12 Dec 1688 (PRO)

GRIMSTON, Thomas
L 17 Aug 1694
Gone 1719 (PRO)

GRINDALL, Festing Horatio
T
L 18 July 1809
d 1812 (TR)

GRINDALL, Sir Richard
L 29 Nov 1776
CR 21 Dec 1781
CA 13 Mar 1783
T
RAB 9 Nov 1805
RAW 28 Apr 1808
RAR 25 Oct 1809
VAB 31 July 1810
VAW 12 Aug 1812
VAR 4 June 1814
KCB 2 Jan 1815 (LG)
d 23 May 1820 (CH)

GRINDRED, John
L 28 Sept 1815
d 1851 (NMM)

GRINT, William
T wounded
L 27 July 1807
CR 7 Dec 1818 (NMM)
CA 28 July 1851 (NMM)
d 24 Aug 1851 (NMM)

GRISDALE, Charles
L 30 June 1812
d 1815 (NMM)

GROAT, Archibald
L 19 Sept 1777
d 16 June 1791

GROAT, Robert
L 10 May 1758
d 1773 (NMM)

GROINGE, John
L 11 Mar 1691 (PJP)
CA 27 Dec 1695
d 14 Aug 1696

GROOME, Robert
L 9 Oct 1694
In Merchant Service 1700 (PJP)
Gone 1719 (PRO)

GROS, John Le
See LE GROS, John

GROSE, Arthur
L 27 Feb 1815
CR 9 Feb 1859 (NMM)
d 11 Jan 1867 (NMM)

GROSSETT, Walter
L 25 Oct 1794
CR 6 Oct 1801
CA 21 Oct 1810
Ret RA 31 Oct 1846 (LG)
d 21 Sept 1847 (PRO)

GROSVENOR, William
L 2 Feb 1770
CR 21 Sept 1790
CA 26 Dec 1799
d 1809 (PRO)

GROUBE, Thomas
L 31 Aug 1799 (MB)
CR 31 July 1809
CA 7 June 1814
Ret CA 31 Oct 1846 (LG)
Ret RA 9 Oct 1849 (LG)
d Jan 1850 (NMM)

GROVE, Edward
L
CA 1661
Dismissed 1665 (PD)
d before 1688 (PD)

GROVE, Henry Leslie
L 1 Aug 1801
Ret CR 19 Oct 1831 (PRO)
d 6 May 1866 (PRO)

GROVE, John (1)
L
CA 1659
d before 1689 (PJP)

GROVE, John (2)
L
CA 1673
d before 1689 (PJP)

GROVE, Samuel
L 9 Dec 1795
CR 27 Sept 1809
d 1817 (NMM)

GROVE, Thomas Saunders (1)
L 21 Nov 1762
CR 25 Oct 1809
d Jan 1821 (NMM)

GROVE, Thomas Saunders (2)
L 28 Oct 1796
CR 2 June 1810
d 31 Oct 1814 (NMM)

GROVE, William (1)
L 20 June 1807
d 1811 (PRO)

GROVE, William (2)
L 4 Mar 1812
HP 24 June 1815 (OB)
Ret CR 1 Oct 1853 (PRO)
d 1856 (PRO)

GROVES, James
L 1 June 1802
CR 14 Feb 1814
d 1844 (NMM)

GROVES, Thomas
L 15 Mar 1678
d before 1689 (PJP)

GRUMLY, Arthur
L 12 Sept 1781
CR 29 Apr 1802
d 1825 (PRO)

GRUMLY, William Maynard
L 19 May 1782
d 1796 (PRO)

GRUNSDITCH, John
See GRIMSDITCH, John

GUERIN, Daniel (1)
L 8 Jan 1783
CR 11 Sept 1794
d (drowned) 15 July 1796 (CH)

GUERIN, Daniel (2)
T
L 27 Dec 1808
d 1825 (TR)

GUGELMAN, Charles
L 25 May 1742
d 1761 (PRO)

GUILFORD, John
L 8 May 1705

GUILLAUME, Peter
L 18 June 1762
d 1764 (PRO)

GUILLIARD, John
L 4 Mar 1743
d 1772 (NMM)

GUION, Daniel Oliver
L 18 Apr 1794
CR 22 Dec 1796
CA 21 May 1802
d (drowned) 24 Dec 1811 (PJP)

GUION, Gardiner Henry
L 17 Apr 1794
CR 17 May 1810
CA 26 Sept 1811
d 27 Sept 1832 (PRO)

GUION, John
See GUYON, John

GUISE, Martin George
L 6 Mar 1801
CR 29 Mar 1815
Struck off list 1819 (NMM)

GULLEN, John
L 9 Mar 1696
Gone 1719 (PRO)

GULLETT, Christopher
L 26 July 1793
d 1794 (NMM)

GULLIFER, James Bulkeley
L 27 Feb 1815
d 1831 (NMM)
GUNMORE, John
L 8 Sept 1801
d 8 July 1827 (NMM)
GUNMAN, Christopher
L
CA 1666
Dismissed 1682 (PJP)
Restored 23 June 1682 (NMM)
d before 1689 (PJP)
GUNMAN, George
L 21 Sept 1696 (PJP)
GUNMAN, James
L 4 June 1696
CR
CA 20 Dec 1708
TGH 1742–1754 (PJP)
d 30 June 1756
GUNMAN, William
L 1 Apr 1682
d before 1689 (PJP)
GUNTER, Henry
L 25 Nov 1777
CR 10 Apr 1795
d 1806 (NMM)
GUNTER, Robert
L 10 Aug 1778
d 1779 (NMM)
GURLING, Thomas
L
CA 1666
d before 1689 (PJP)
GURNEY, Edward
L
CA 15 Jan 1691
d 29 Jan 1695
GUTHRIE, James
L 12 Nov 1790
d 1794 (NMM)
GUTHRIE, William
L 9 Aug 1802
d 1826 (NMM)
GUTTERY, James
L 23 Feb 1815
d 1833 (PRO)
GUY, Charles
L
CR
CA 23 Mar 1709
d 1712 (PJP)
GUY, Edward
L 16 May 1720
CR 1 Mar 1740
d 12 Sept 1741 (PRO)
GUY, Henry
L 25 Feb 1815
d 26 May 1820 (PRO)
GUY, John (1)
L 13 Sept 1688 (P)
CA 21 Mar 1690 (PMM)
d 7 Dec 1697 (PMM)

GUY, John (2)
L 22 Mar 1708
d 30 Jan 1730 (M)
GUY, Leonard
L
CA 22 Dec 1664 (DDA)
d before 1689 (PJP)
GUY, Thomas
L
CA 9 June 1666 (RM)
d before 1690 (PJP)
GUYON, John
L 1792 (PJP)
Dismissed 15 Nov 1792 (PJP)
Restored 12 Feb 1794 (PJP)
Ret CR 28 July 1829 (NMM)
d 15 Jan 1844 (NMM)
GUYOT, Abraham
L 13 Aug 1767
CR 22 May 1782
CA 22 Sept 1790
SUP RA 30 Apr 1808 (PJP)
d 4 Mar 1822 (LT)
GWATKIN, John
L 9 Oct 1782
KIA 12 Apr 1782 (RLB)
GWAVAS, Anthony
L 21 Feb 1705 (PMM)
GWENNAP, Walter
L 6 Sept 1760 (PJP)
CR 26 Apr 1782 (PJP)
CA 21 Sept 1790 (PJP)
d 27 May 1798 (PJP)
GWILLIM, Thomas
L 17 Nov 1790
d 1809 (NMM)
GWYN, Richard
L 27 Sept 1711
d 2 Dec 1766 (M)
GWYN, Richard
See GWYNN, Richard
GWYN, William
L 6 Mar 1815
d 28 June 1880 (PRO)
GWYNN, Edmund
L 11 Apr 1727
Gone 1734 (PRO)
GWYNN, Richard
L 14 Aug 1739
CR Dec 1745 (PJP)
CA 27 May 1747
d 10 Dec 1766 (PJP)
GWYNN, Richard
See GWYN, Richard
GWYNNE, Lawrence
L 30 Oct 1795
Ret CR 26 Nov 1830 (OB)
d 1856 (PRO)
GWYNNE, Thomas
L 1727 (PRO)
GYANS, George
L 25 Mar 1782
d 13 Feb 1787 (PMM)

GYBBON, Francis
L 19 Mar 1794
d 1805 (PRO)
GYDE, James
L 12 May 1756
CR 1 Nov 1762
d 1766 (PRO)

HABERFIELD, Isaac
L 11 Mar 1815
d 1838 (NMM)
HACKETT, John
L 11 May 1811
CR 2 Sept 1828 (NMM)
CA 28 June 1838 (NMM)
RA 2 Oct 1857 (NMM)
VA 28 Mar 1864 (NMM)
d 29 Mar 1865 (NMM)
HACKETT, Robert
L 1710 (PJP)
HACKMAN, James
L 21 Feb 1741
CR 9 July 1747
CA 18 Oct 1758
d 1764
HACKMAN, William (1)
L 18 Feb 1740
d 1754 (PRO)
HACKMAN, William (2)
L 2 Apr 1741
Dismissed 1745 (PRO)
HACKNEY, John
L 16 Mar 1814
d 1841 (NMM)
HADAWAY, John
L 21 Nov 1790
d 4 Aug 1805 (NMM)
HADDOCK, Charles
L 16 Sept 1696 (PJP)
HADDOCK, Edward
L 4 June 1778
d 1819 (PRO)
HADDOCK, John
L 9 Feb 1693 (PJP)
HADDOCK, Joseph
L 1672
CA 12 Apr 1678
HADDOCK, Nicholas
L June 1704 (DNB)
CR
CA 6 Apr 1707
RAB 4 May 1734
MP (Rochester) 1734–
26 Sept 1746 (MPS)
RAW 16 Dec 1734
RAR 2 Mar 1736
VAB 13 Mar 1742 (LG)
VAW 11 Aug 1743 (LG)
VAR 7 Dec 1743
AB 23 June 1744 (LG)
d 26 Sept 1746
HADDOCK, Sir Richard (1)
L
CA 9 June 1666 (RM)
COM E 18 Aug 1673–
2 Feb 1682 (NBO)
Kt 3 July 1675 (NBO)
CONT 2 Feb 1682–
17 Apr 1686 (NBO)
COM V 1683 (PJP)
COM N 17 Apr 1686–
12 Oct 1688 (NBO)
CONT 12 Oct 1688–
29 Jan 1715 (NBO)
AF 6 Aug 1690
d 29 Jan 1715 (NBO)
HADDOCK, Richard (2)
L
CA 1672
d 1678
HADDOCK, Richard (3)
L 6 July 1692 (PJP)
CA 20 Dec 1695
CONT 27 Apr 1734–
25 Mar 1749 (NBO)
SUP CA 25 Mar 1749 (NBO)
d 6 Jan 1750 (DNB)
HADDOCK, Richard (4)
L 25 Oct 1740
CR 30 Mar 1744 (PRO)
CA 7 Nov 1744
d 13 June 1749
HADDOCK, William
L
CR
CA 1 Jan 1713
d 21 Oct 1746 (NMM)
HADDON, Boyce Fairclough
L 9 Jan 1802
d 26 Jan 1805 (NMM)
HAGER, John
L 15 Oct 1697
CR 1706 (PJP)
CA 12 June 1707
RAB 16 Dec 1734
RAW 2 Mar 1736
d 27 Feb 1748 (PRO)
HAGGIT, William
L 18 June 1791
CR 22 Oct 1795
d (drowned) 5 Nov 1799 (CH)
HAIG, John
L 25 Mar 1783
d 3 Sept 1792
HAILES, George
L 30 Dec 1782
SUP CR 24 Mar 1819 (PMM)
d 22 Aug 1827 (NMM)
HAILES, John
L 17 June 1685 (P)
CA 1 May 1690
d (drowned) 9 Dec 1693 (PJP)
HAINES, John
L 2 Feb 1815
CR 1 Jan 1849 (NMM)
CA 1 Aug 1860 (NMM)
d 1863 (NMM)

HAINS, William		
L	3 Feb	1815
d		1837 (NMM)
HAKE, John		
L	6 Dec	1813
d	8 May	1829 (PRO)
HALAHAN, Thomas		
L	27 Feb	1815
Ret CR	14 Apr	1862 (NMM)
d		1878 (NMM)
HALBERT, Samuel		
L		
CA	23 Dec	1695
Gone		1718 (PRO)
HALDANE, James		
L	29 Oct	1747
d		1758 (PRO)
HALDANE, Robert		
L	25 May	1741
CR		
CA	24 Feb	1748
d	22 Aug	1761 (NMM)
HALE, Bernard		
L	21 Sept	1790
CR	4 July	1794
CA	6 Dec	1796
d		1802 (PRO)
HALE, John		
L	26 May	1741
CR	27 May	1747
CA	7 Oct	1755
SUP RA		1779
d	Jan	1792 (NMM)
HALES, John		
See HAILES, John		
HALES, Sir Samuel		
L	22 June	1802
d	26 Dec	1805 (PJP)
HALFORD, Charles		
L	21 Mar	1812
d	15 Sept	1849 (NMM)
HALFORD, Richard		
L	7 Mar	1696 (PJP)
HALKETT, Sir Peter		
L	8 Oct	1789
CR	10 Apr	1793
CA	13 Aug	1794
RAB	12 Aug	1812
RAW	4 June	1814
RAR	12 Aug	1819 (CH)
VAB	19 July	1821 (CH)
VAW	27 May	1825 (NMM)
VAR	22 July	1830 (NMM)
AB	10 Jan	1837 (CH)
Kt		1837 (CH)
d	12 Dec	1839 (LT)
HALL, Basil		
L	10 June	1808
CR	22 Feb	1814
CA	5 Nov	1817 (DNB)
d	11 Sept	1844 (DNB)
HALL, Charles		
T		
L	7 Feb	1815
CR	23 Nov	1841 (NMM)
CA	7 Mar	1853 (NMM)
d	Jan	1864 (NMM)
HALL, David		
L	12 Jan	1741
d	14 Apr	1741 (PMM)
HALL, Edward (1)		
L	10 June	1797
CR	12 Aug	1812
Ret CA	5 Nov	1846 (NMM)
d		1862 (NMM)
HALL, Edward (2)		
L	15 Dec	1813
HP	25 Jan	1815 (OB)
Ret CR	15 July	1856 (NMM)
d		1875 (NMM)
HALL, George		
L	29 Oct	1806
Ret CR	3 Aug	1841 (NMM)
d		1857 (NMM)
HALL, Henry John		
L	21 Mar	1812
Ret CR	18 Apr	1854 (NMM)
d		1857 (NMM)
HALL, Henry Watson (1)		
L	11 Apr	1783
d		1796 (NMM)
HALL, Henry Watson (2)		
L	16 Aug	1814
HP	11 Jan	1815 (OB)
Ret CR	1 Oct	1860 (NMM)
d		1873 (NMM)
HALL, James		
L	12 Aug	1801
T		
CR	15 Nov	1809 (PRO)
d		1810 (TR)
HALL, John (1)		
L	26 Jan	1746
d		1787 (NMM)
HALL, John (2)		
L	9 Sept	1793
CR	24 Apr	1797
d		1819 (NMM)
HALL, John (3)		
L	10 Oct	1801
d	1 Jan	1806 (PRO)
HALL, John (4)		
L	26 Sept	1811
d	Jan	1877 (PRO)
HALL, John Netherton O'Brien		
L	9 May	1809
Took Holy Orders		1828 (NMM)
HALL, John Stevens		
L	2 Oct	1777
CR	10 July	1782
CA	21 Sept	1790
RAB	28 Apr	1808
RAW	25 Oct	1809
RAR	31 July	1810
VAB	12 Aug	1812
d	16 Feb	1814 (CH)

HALL, Robert (1)
L
CA 1661
d before 1688 (PD)

HALL, Robert (2)
L 23 Feb 1782
CR 22 Jan 1796
CA 18 Nov 1799
CB 4 June 1815 (LG)
HP July 1815 (MB)
d 7 Feb 1818 (CH)

HALL, Robert (3)
L 14 June 1800
CR 27 June 1808
CA 4 Mar 1811
Kt (Two Sicilies) 11 Mar 1813 (LG)
RAW 22 July 1830 (LG)
VAB 10 Jan 1837 (LG)
VAW 23 Nov 1841 (LG)
d 11 May 1842 (NMM)

HALL, Roger
L 26 Sept 1811
CR 10 Nov 1819 (NMM)
HP 1821 (OB)
Ret CR 1 Apr 1856 (NMM)
d 1861 (NMM)

HALL, Samuel
L 1664

HALL, Thomas
L 3 Nov 1790
d 1812 (NMM)

HALL, Thomas Salkeld
L 9 Oct 1802
d 1876 (NMM)

HALL, William (1)
L 21 Apr 1746
SUP CR 21 Sept 1796 (PMM)
d 23 June 1798 (PMM)

HALL, William (2)
L 1 May 1807
CR 29 July 1814
d 9 Nov 1849 (NMM)

HALL, William Sumner
L 14 Oct 1801
CR 18 May 1806
CA 1 Jan 1817 (NMM)
d Mar 1823 (NMM)

HALLAM, John
L 26 Feb 1745
d 25 Nov 1794 (LT)

HALLETT, John
L 22 Nov 1790
d 25 Nov 1794 (LT)

HALLEY, Edmund
L
CR 4 June 1696 (PMM)
CA 19 Aug 1698 (PJP)
d 14 Jan 1742 (PJP)

HALLIDAY, Christopher
L 23 Jan 1778
CR
CA 9 Oct 1782
d 16 Oct 1790

HALLIDAY, Francis Alexander
L 12 May 1801
CR 29 Aug 1808
d 25 July 1830 (MB)

HALLIDAY, John
See TOLLEMACHE, John Richard

HALLIDAY, Michael
L 26 Oct 1793
CR 9 July 1798
CA 29 June 1799
d 10 June 1829 (NMM)

HALLOWELL, Sir Benjamin
See CAREW, Sir Benjamin Hallowell

HALLOWES, Francis
L 14 June 1813
HP Aug 1815 (OB)
Ret CR 1 Feb 1856 (NMM)
d 1870 (NMM)

HALLOWES, John
L 22 Jan 1814
CR 10 Jan 1837 (NMM)
CA 5 Dec 1842 (NMM)
HP 5 Dec 1842 (OB)
RA 20 May 1862 (NMM)
VA 18 Oct 1867 (NMM)
A 30 July 1875 (NMM)
d 11 Jan 1883 (NMM)

HALLOWES, Thomas
L 3 Aug 1815
d 6 Feb 1864 (NMM)

HALLUM, Edward
L 29 Apr 1783
d 1837 (NMM)

HALLUM, John
L 7 July 1762
d 1780 (NMM)

HALLUM, Thomas
L 6 Jan 1742
CR 10 Aug 1759
CA 24 May 1762
SUP RA 1793
d 1804 (PJP)

HALLYBURTON, Hon. Hamilton Douglas
L 19 Feb 1781
d 1784 (NMM)

HALSTEAD, George
See HALSTED, George

HALSTEAD, John
L 20 Sept 1793
CR 22 June 1798
CA 21 Nov 1808
d Nov 1830 (NMM)

HALSTEAD, John Micklam
L 19 Nov 1790
d 1 Aug 1797

HALSTEAD, Sir Lawrence William
L 8 Dec 1781
CR 22 Nov 1790
CA 31 May 1791
RAB 31 July 1810
RAW 12 Aug 1812
RAR 4 Dec 1813
VAB 4 June 1814
KCB 2 Jan 1815 (LG)

VAW	12 Aug	1819 (CH)
VAR	27 May	1825 (CH)
AB	22 July	1830 (CH)
AW	10 Jan	1837 (CH)
GCB	17 Mar	1837 (LG)
d	22 Apr	1841 (CH)

HALSTEAD, William Anthony

L	20 May	1756
CR	25 June	1773
d	16 May	1778 (PRO)

HALSTED, George

L	27 May	1796
CR	21 Jan	1809
Ret CR	10 Sept	1840 (OB)
d	25 Mar	1846 (OB)

HALTON, Thomas

L	5 Nov	1793
CR	2 Jan	1798 (NMM)
d	16 Feb	1837 (NMM)

HALY, Richard Standish

L	5 Apr	1802
d	2 Oct	1835 (LT)

HAM, Edward

L	21 Apr	1744
d		1748 (NMM)

HAM, William

L	20 Mar	1815 (NMM)
d	Feb	1849 (NMM)

HAMAR, Joseph

L	5 May	1735
CR	10 June	1740
CA	22 Oct	1741
SUP RA		1758
d	14 Jan	1773 (NMM)

HAMBLY, Peter Sampson

T		
L	24 Dec	1805
CR	12 Aug	1819 (NMM)
CA	23 Nov	1841 (LG)
HP	23 Nov	1841 (OB)
d	19 Dec	1847 (NMM)

HAMBLY, Richard

T		
L	19 Jan	1811
d		1832 (TR)

HAMBY, Thomas

L	27June	1814
HP	13 Nov	1818 (OB)
Ret CR	13 Apr	1857 (NMM)
d		1866 (NMM)

HAMES, John

L	28 Dec	1810
d		1814 (PRO)

HAMILTON, Andrew

L	22 Mar	1720
d	9 Nov	1724 (M)

HAMILTON, Lord Archibald (1)

L		1690 (MPS)
CA	11 Sept	1693
MP (Lanarkshire)		1708–1710 (MPS)
MP (Lanarkshire)		1718–1734 (MPS)
COM AD	19 May	1729–
	13 Mar	1738 (AO)
MP (Queensborough)		1735–1741 (MPS)
COMAD	19 Mar	1742–
	25 Feb	1746 (AO)
MP (Dartmouth)		1742–1747 (MPS)
GGH		1744 (PJP)
d	5 Apr	1754

HAMILTON, Archibald (2)

L		
CR		
CA	7 Jan	1707
d		1738 (PMM)

HAMILTON, Archibald (3)

L	8 Dec	1808
d		1809 (NMM)

HAMILTON, Arthur Philip

L	28 Apr	1807
CR	21 Oct	1810
CA	31 May	1816 (NMM)
Ret CA	1 Oct	1846 (NMM)
Ret RA	11 June	1851 (NMM)
Ret VA	9 July	1857 (NMM)
Ret A	4 Oct	1862 (NMM)
d		1877 (NMM)

HAMILTON, Augustus Barrington Price Powell

L	8 Oct	1802
d	8 Sept	1849 (PRO)

HAMILTON, Sir Charles

L	20 Oct	1781
Inh Bt	24 Jan	1784 (MPN)
CR	Dec	1789 (OB)
CA	22 Nov	1790
MP (Dungannon)		1801–1807 (MPN)
MP (Honiton)		1807–1812 (MPN)
CRM	25 Oct	1809 (LG)
RAB	31 July	1810
RAW	1 Aug	1811
RAR	4 Dec	1813
VAB	4 June	1814
GG (Newfoundland)		1818–1825 (BNS)
VAW	12 Aug	1819 (CH)
VAR	27 May	1825 (CH)
AB	22 July	1830 (CH)
KCB	7 Feb	1833 (LG)
AW	10 Jan	1837 (CH)
AR	23 Nov	1841 (CH)
d	14 Sept	1849 (DNB)

HAMILTON, Charles Powell

L	12 Dec	1769
CR	11 June	1778
CA	18 May	1779
RAB	20 Feb	1797
RAR	14 Feb	1799
VAB	1 Jan	1801
VAW	23 Apr	1804
VAR	9 Nov	1805
AB	28 Apr	1808
AW	31 July	1810
AR	12 Aug	1819 (CH)
d	12 Mar	1825 (CH)

HAMILTON, Sir Edward
L 9 June 1793 (DNB)
CR 11 Feb 1796 (CH)
CA 3 June 1797
Kt 1 Feb 1800 (LG)
Dismissed 22 Jan 1802 (CH)
Restored June 1802 (CH)
KCB 2 Jan 1815 (LG)
Cre Bt 20 Oct 1818 (DNB)
RAB 19 July 1821 (LG)
RAW 27 May 1825 (LG)
RAR 22 July 1830 (LG)
VAW 10 Jan 1837 (LG)
VAR 23 Nov 1841 (LG)
AB 9 Nov 1846 (LG)
AW 26 June 1847 (LG)
d 20 Mar 1851 (CH)

HAMILTON, Gawen William
See GAWEN, William Hamilton

HAMILTON, George (1)
L 13 Oct 1741
d 1745 (PRO)

HAMILTON, George (2)
L 25 Oct 1746
CR 21 Aug 1758
CA 9 Mar 1759 (PJP)
d 1760 (NMM)

HAMILTON, Henry
L 25 July 1801
d 1808 (NMM)

HAMILTON, James (1)
L
CR
CA 26 Dec 1707 (PJP)
d 22 Dec 1708 (PJP)

HAMILTON, James (2)
L 11 Mar 1709
d 1743 (NMM)

HAMILTON, Hon. James (3)
L 3 Sept 1741
d 1745 (PRO)

HAMILTON, James (4)
L 3 Apr 1742
CR 2 Dec 1745 (NMM)
CA 29 Dec 1745 (NMM)
KIA 8 Oct 1747 (CH)

HAMILTON, James (5)
L 5 June 1760 (NMM)
d 1776 (NMM)

HAMILTON, James (6)
L 25 June 1760
d 24 Sept 1806 (PMM)

HAMILTON, John (1)
See HAMILTON, James (1)

HAMILTON, Hon. John (2)
L 4 Mar 1736
CR
CA 19 Feb 1741
d (drowned) 18 Dec 1755 (CH)

HAMILTON, Sir John (3)
L 11 Jan 1747
CR 7 Apr 1762
CA 26 May 1768
Cre Bt 6 July 1776 (OB)
d 7 Jan 1784 (PRO)

HAMILTON, John (4)
L 17 Feb 1815
CR 22 Oct 1827 (PRO)
Ret CR 20 Apr 1861 (NMM)
d 1871 (NMM)

HAMILTON, Richard
See BOYNE, Richard, Lord Viscount

HAMILTON, Hon. Richard Somerville
L 14 Apr 1798
d 1807 (NMM)

HAMILTON, Robert
L 23 Sept 1800
Ret CR 26 Nov 1830 (NMM)
d 1837 (NMM)

HAMILTON, Thomas (1)
L 1666
CA 1668
d 9 May 1687 (DDA)

HAMILTON, Thomas (2)
L 29 Apr 1778
CR 29 Nov 1785
CA 22 Nov 1790
COM N 20 June 1806–
31 Dec 1813 (NBO)
RAB 25 Oct 1809
RAW 31 July 1810
RAR 12 Aug 1812
VAB 4 June 1814
d 27 June 1815 (LT)

HAMILTON, Thomas James
L 3 May 1815
d 1817 (PRO)

HAMILTON, William (1)
L 27 May 1692

HAMILTON, William (2)
L 26 Nov 1694
Gone 1719 (PRO)

HAMILTON, Hon. William (3)
L 16 Aug 1742
d 1744 (NMM)

HAMILTON, William (4)
L 6 Feb 1744
CR 17 Jan 1757
CA 10 Jan 1771
d 10 Apr 1790

HAMILTON, Sir William (5)
L 2 July 1781
SUP CR 1 Jan 1816 (NMM)
d 1822 (NMM)

HAMILTON, William (6)
L 20 Jan 1810
HP June 1816 (OB)
Ret CR 27 Dec 1849 (NMM)
d 14 May 1872 (PRO)

HAMILTON, William
See GAWEN, William Hamilton

HAMLEY, William
L 20 Jan 1807
CR 15 June 1814
CA 20 Oct 1834 (NMM)
Ret CA 1 July 1851 (NMM)
Ret RA 1 Dec 1856 (NMM)
Ret VA 12 Sept 1863 (NMM)
d 1866 (NMM)

HAMLINE, David		
L	2 Apr	1794
d		1809 (NMM)
HAMLYN, Charles		
See WILLIAMS, Charles Hamlyn		
HAMMETT, John		
L	29 Sept	1757
d		1785 (NMM)
HAMMICK, John Love		
L	5 May	1805
d	11 July	1810 (LT)
HAMMICK, Stephen		
L	25 Oct	1745
CR	30 Oct	1761
d		1782 (NMM)
HAMMOND, Charles		
L	23 Mar	1805
d		1858 (PRO)
HAMMOND, Edward		
L	15 Sept	1688
HAMMOND, Frederick		
L	7 Nov	1815
HAMMOND, Nicholas		
L	10 Nov	1809
d		1814 (NMM)
HAMMOND, Thomas (1)		
L		
CA		1666
HAMMOND, Thomas (2)		
L	4 Sept	1744
CR	11 May	1748
d		1759 (PMM)
HAMMOND, William (1)		
L		1662
CA	4 July	1666 (RM)
d	8 Oct	1667 (PRO)
HAMMOND, William (2)		
L	21 Apr	1747
d		1779 (NMM)
HAMOND, Sir Andrew Snape		
L	18 June	1759
CR	20 June	1765
CA	7 Dec	1770
Kt		1778 (DNB)
COMM (Halifax)		1780–1784 (PJP)
Cre Bt	10 Dec	1783 (DNB)
COM E	11 Feb	1793–
	7 Mar	1794 (NBO)
CONT	25 Sept	1794–
	3 Mar	1806 (NBO)
MP (Ipswich)		1796–1806 (MPT)
SUP CA		1806 (MB)
d	12 Sept	1828 (PRO)
HAMOND, Sir Graham Eden		
L	19 Oct	1796 (DNB)
CR	20 Oct	1797
CA	30 Nov	1798
CB	4 June	1815 (LG)
RAB	27 May	1825 (LG)
Inh Bt	12 Sept	1828 (DNB)
RAW	22 July	1830 (LG)
KCB	13 Sept	1831 (DNB)
VAB	10 Jan	1837 (LG)
VAR	23 Nov	1841 (LG)
AB	22 Jan	1847 (LG)
AW	15 Sept	1849 (NMM)
AR	1 July	1851 (NMM)
GCB	5 July	1855 (DNB)
AF	10 Nov	1862 (DNB)
d	20 Dec	1862 (DNB)
HAMPTON, Charles Fraser		
L	21 Oct	1778
d		1784 (PRO)
HAMSTEAD, John		
L	28 Oct	1790
CR	6 Feb	1796
CA	13 June	1798
d	14 May	1813 (LT)
HANBURY, Thomas		
L	28 Aug	1743
CR	23 Oct	1747
Dismissed		1754 (NMM)
d		1779 (NMM)
HANBY, Joseph		
L	14 May	1756
SUP CR	21 Sept	1796 (PMM)
d	26 May	1797 (PMM)
HANCE, John		
L	20 Feb	1778
SUP CR	5 June	1813 (NMM)
d	16 Nov	1836 (NMM)
HANCHETT, John Martin		
L	1 May	1804
CR	22 Sept	1807
CA	18 Oct	1809
CB	4 June	1815 (LG)
Struck off list		1819 (NMM)
d		1819 (NMM)
HANCOCK, John (1)		
L	18 Oct	1794
CR	2 Apr	1801
CA	22 Jan	1806
CB	4 June	1815 (LG)
RAB	28 June	1838 (LG)
d	12 Oct	1839 (CH)
HANCOCK, John (2)		
L	24 Apr	1811
HP		1830 (OB)
Ret CR	1 Apr	1852 (NMM)
d		1858 (NMM)
HANCOCK, Richard Turner		
L	26 Aug	1789
CR	4 Sept	1800
CA	25 Sept	1806
RAB	23 Nov	1841 (PRO)
d	5 Mar	1846 (PRO)
HANCOCK, Robert		
L		
CA	6 Feb	1691
d (drowned)	22 Oct	1707 (CH)
HANCOCK, William		
L	1 July	1814
d	7 Apr	1816 (LT)
HANCORN, Richard		
L	15 Feb	1783
d	14 July	1792
HANCORNE, Philip		
L	3 Mar	1779

Entered Portuguese service 1787 (PJP)
d 17 Aug 1807 (PRO)

HAND, Thomas
L 6 Nov 1778
CR 14 Oct 1796
CA 29 Apr 1802
d 12 Jan 1829 (NMM)

HANDBY, William
L 20 Nov 1812
d 23 Feb 1824 (NMM)

HANDFIELD, Edward
L 1 Aug 1811
CR 2 Aug 1826 (PRO)
d 12 Feb 1839 (PRO)

HANDFIELD, Phillips Cosby
L 17 Jan 1798
CR 22 Jan 1806
d (drowned) 30 Jan 1808 (CH)

HANDLEY, John William Henry
L 7 Feb 1815
HP 7 Feb 1815 (OB)
d 1861 (NMM)

HANDY, Thomas
L 26 Aug 1801
d 1808 (NMM)

HANHAM, Edward
L 2 Nov 1793
d 1797 (NMM)

HANKERSON, Thomas
L 21 Feb 1741
CR 26 Aug 1748
CA 11 Mar 1755
SUP RA 1779
d 1779

HANMER, David
L 7 Apr 1813
Ret CR 1 Feb 1856 (PRO)
d 1861 (PRO)

HANMER, Job
L 8 Dec 1772
CR 25 Oct 1809
d 1814 (NMM)

HANMER, Thomas Job Syer
L 4 Jan 1808
CR 6 June 1814
CA 19 July 1822 (MB)
d 1842 (NMM)

HANNAM, Edward
See HANHAM, Edward

HANNAM, Thomas
T
L 27 Dec 1808
d 2 Sept 1830 (NMM)

HANNAM, Willoughby
L
CA 1660
KIA 28 May 1672 (NJ)

HANNAN, William
L 22 July 1799
d 2 Sept 1830 (PRO)

HANNAY, Peter
T
L 14 Mar 1815
d 1819 (TR)

HANNS, James Robert
L 20 Feb 1815
d 1843 (NMM)

HANOVER, William Henry
See CLARENCE, William Henry, Duke of

HANSFORD, William
L 6 Jan 1760
SUP CR 23 Sept 1796 (PMM)
d 1796 (NMM)

HANSON, James
L 17 Nov 1790
CR 24 July 1795
d (drowned) 26 Jan 1800 (CH)

HANWAY, James
L
CR 17 Aug 1709
d 1727 (PRO)

HANWAY, Jonas
L 1 Sept 1692
CR
CA 29 July 1703
d 11 May 1737

HANWAY, Thomas (1)
L
CR 8 Jan 1703 (PMM)

HANWAY, Thomas (2)
L 14 Aug 1739
CR 20 Feb 1742
CA 5 Apr 1744
COMM (Chatham) Jan 1761–1771 (PJP)
COM V 21 Dec 1771–
1 Oct 1772 (NBO)
d 1 Oct 1772 (NBO)

HANWELL, Joseph
L 8 Feb 1781
CR 21 Oct 1790
CA 5 Apr 1794
RAB 12 Aug 1812
RAW 4 June 1814
RAR 12 Aug 1819 (CH)
VAB 19 July 1821 (CH)
VAW 27 May 1825 (CH)
VAR 22 July 1830 (CH)
AB 10 Jan 1837 (CH)
d 2 Nov 1839 (PRO)

HANWELL, William
L 22 Oct 1793
CR
CA 29 Dec 1798
RAB 27 May 1825 (LG)
d 14 June 1830 (NMM)

HANWORTH, Lord
See BEAUCLERK, Lord Vere, q.v.

HARBIN, Henry
L 27 Dec 1808
d 1813 (NMM)

HARBOARD, Sir Charles
L 1672
KIA 28 May 1672 (LG)

HARCOURT, Frederick Edward Vernon
L 29 Apr 1809
CR 29 Apr 1811

CA 7 June 1814
Ret CA 1 Oct 1860 (NMM)
Ret RA 24 Dec 1849 (NMM)
Ret VA 19 Mar 1857 (NMM)
Ret A 20May 1862 (NMM)
d 30 Apr 1883 (NMM)

HARCOURT, Octavius H.C.V.
L 11 Jan 1814 (DNB)
HP 1816–1818 (DNB)
CR 3 Feb 1820 (NMM)
CA 7 Aug 1827 (NMM)
HP 27 Oct 1836 (OB)
RA 26 Oct 1854 (NMM)
VA 4 June 1861 (NMM)
d 14 Aug 1863 (DNB)

HARDACRE, Henry Thomas
L 20 June 1796
d 30 Apr 1822 (NMM)

HARDIMAN, Henry Pocock
L 5 Oct 1815
d 14 Feb 1825 (NMM)

HARDING, George
L 20 Mar 1815 (NMM)
d 1853 (NMM)

HARDING, James
L 27 July 1802
T
Ret CR 7 Jan 1835 (NMM)
d 1839 (TR)

HARDING, John
L 11 Feb 1815
HP 1836–1842 (OB)
CR 9 Nov 1846 (LG)
HP 9 Nov 1846 (OB)
Ret CA 1 Aug 1860 (NMM)
d 1878 (NMM)

HARDING, William
L
CR
CA 23 Mar 1702
Gone 1719 (PRO)

HARDINGE, George Nicholas
L 15 Oct 1800
CR 29 Apr 1802
CA 10 Apr 1804
KIA 8 Mar 1808 (DNB)

HARDINGE, John
L 9 July 1814
d 1815 (PRO)

HARDWICK, John
L 8 Mar 1815
d 8 Mar 1846 (OB)

HARDWICKE, Charles Browne
L 1814 (DNB)
Resigned 1826 (DNB)
d 27 Sept 1880 (DNB)

HARDY, Andrew
L 3 June 1799
d 5 Mar 1816 (PRO)

HARDY, Charles (1)
L 7 Oct 1697
CR
CA 13 Jan 1707
Dismissed 11 June 1748
d 10 June 1749 (M)

HARDY, Sir Charles (2)
L 23 Dec 1702 (PMM)
CR
CA 28 June 1709
Kt 26 Sept 1732 (MPS)
RAB 10 Apr 1742 (LG)
VAB 7 Dec 1743
COM AD 13 Dec 1743–
27 Nov 1744 (AO)
MP (Portsmouth) 14 Dec 1743–
27 Nov 1744 (MPS)
VAR 23 June 1744 (LG)
d 27 Nov 1744

HARDY, Sir Charles (3)
L 26 Mar 1737 (DNB)
CR 9 June 1741
CA 10 Aug 1741
GG
(Newfoundland) 1744–1745 (BNS)
Kt 20 Apr 1755 (MPN)
RAB 4 June 1756
RAW 5 Feb 1758
VAB 14 Feb 1759
VAW 21 Oct 1762
MP
(Rochester) 1764–1768 (MPN)
AB 18 Oct 1770
MP
(Plymouth) 10 Aug 1771–
19 May 1780 (MPN)
GGH 1771 (PJP)
AW 29 Jan 1778
d 19 May 1780 (MPN)

HARDY, Charles (4)
L 16 Oct 1742
Gone 1750 (NMM)

HARDY, Clement
L 6 Feb 1705 (PMM)

HARDY, Edward
L 10 Oct 1723

HARDY, James
L 19 Nov 1778
CR 21 Sept 1790
CA 6 Dec 1796
d 1812 (NMM)

HARDY, John
L 4 Mar 1740
CR 14 Mar 1744 (NMM)
CA 17 Oct 1744
SUP RA 1762
d Apr 1796 (NMM)

HARDY, John Madock
L 11 Oct 1796
d 1798 (NMM)

HARDY, John Oakes
L 10 May 1777
CR 5 Apr 1783
CA 22 Nov 1790
Dismissed Sept 1806
Restored w/srty 24 June 1807
SUP CA Nov 1809 (MB)
d Dec 1832 (NMM)

HARDY, Robert William Hale
L 20 Feb 1815

Ret CR 21 Oct 1861 (NMM)
d 1871 (NMM)

HARDY, Temple
L 4 Nov 1790
CR 1 June 1794
CA 24 Nov 1795
d 29 Mar 1814 (LT)

HARDY, Sir Thomas (1)
L
CA 6 Jan 1693
Kt 1702 (DNB)
RAB 27 Jan 1711
MP (Weymouth) Apr 1711 (DNB)
d 16 Aug 1732

HARDY, Thomas (2)
L 20 Mar 1777
SUP CR 20 Apr 1810
d 1815 (NMM)

HARDY, Sir Thomas Masterman
L 10 Nov 1793
CR 10 July 1797
CA 2 Oct 1798
T
Cre Bt 4 Feb 1806 (DNB)
KCB 2 Jan 1815 (LG)
CRM 19 July 1821 (LG)
RAB 27 May 1825 (LG)
RAW 22 July 1830 (LG)
FSL Nov 1830 (DNB)
GCB 10 Sept 1831 (DNB)
GGH Apr 1834 (DNB)
VAB 10 Jan 1837 (LG)
d 20 Sept 1839 (DNB)

HARDYMAN, Lucius
L 5 Mar 1795
CR 8 Aug 1799 (NMM)
CA 27 Jan 1800
CB 8 Dec 1815 (LG)
CRM 27 May 1825 (LG)
RAW 22 July 1830 (LG)
d 17 Apr 1834 (DNB)

HARE, Charles (1)
L 19 Apr 1782
CR 13 Sept 1793
CA 2 Mar 1794
d 14 July 1801 (NMM)

HARE, Charles (2)
L 8 June 1810
d 14 July 1859 (PRO)

HARE, Daniel
L
CR
CA 10 Apr 1741
SUP RA 1756
d 25 June 1762

HARE, George
L 2 Sept 1814 (NMM)
d Oct 1824 (NMM)

HARE, John
L 2 Aug 1694
CR 18 Dec 1707 (PMM)
Gone 1719 (PRO)

HARE, John Edward
L 2 Feb 1801
d 1812 (NMM)

HARE, Josias
L
CA 1667

HARE, Marcus Theodore
L 20 Sept 1815
d 1846 (PRO)

HARE, Richard
L 16 Sept 1814
HP Mar 1815 (OB)
Ret CR 18 Oct 1858 (NMM)
d 1876 (NMM)

HARE, Thomas
L 4 Feb 1815
d 20 Dec 1847 (NMM)

HARE, William
L 29 Apr 1801
d 1808 (PRO)

HARFORD, Charles
L 8 Mar 1799
d 19 Oct 1808 (NMM)

HARFORD, Henry
L 27 Sept 1800
d 1818 (NMM)

HARFORD, John
L 15 Oct 1790
Dismissed 1800 (NMM)

HARGOOD, Sir William
L 13 Jan 1780
CR 24 June 1789
CA 22 Nov 1790
T
CRM 28 Apr 1808 (LG)
RAB 31 July 1810
RAW 1 Aug 1811
RAR 12 Aug 1812
VAB 4 June 1814
KCB 2 Jan 1815 (LG)
VAW 12 Aug 1819 (CH)
VAR 19 July 1821 (CH)
AB 22 July 1830 (CH)
GCB 13 Sept 1831 (LG)
AW 10 Jan 1837 (CH)
d 12 Dec 1839 (CH)

HARGRAVE, Henry John Smith
L 3 Mar 1804
T
CR 21 Mar 1812
d 18 Mar 1814 (TR)

HARGRAVE, William Henry
L 27 Dec 1782
d 1794 (NMM)

HARLAND, Robert (1)
L
CR
CA 24 Mar 1704
d Feb 1751 (PRO)

HARLAND, Sir Robert (2)
L 11 July 1735 (DNB)
CR 4 Jan 1746 (NMM)
CA 19 Mar 1746
RAB 18 Oct 1770
Kt 5 Mar 1771 (DNB)
RAR 31 Mar 1775
VAB 5 Feb 1776
VAW 1777

VAR 1778
COM AD 1 Apr 1782–
30 Jan 1783 (AO)
AB 8 Apr 1782
d 28 Feb 1783 (CH)

HARLEY, Edward
L 8 Oct 1796
HP July 1814 (OB)
Ret CR 26 Nov 1830 (PRO)
d Aug 1846 (OB)

HARLEY, James
L 17 Dec 1795
d 1817 (NMM)

HARLEY, John
See HARLY, John

HARLOW, Thomas (1)
L
CA 19 Mar 1690
COM V 7 Feb 1705–
16 Sept 1707 (QAN)
d 1741

HARLOW, Thomas (2)
L 14 Dec 1801
d 1804 (NMM)

HARLY, John
L
CA 1667
d before 1689 (PJP)

HARMAN, George
L 25 July 1697
Gone 1719 (PRO)

HARMAN, Sir John (1)
L 1665
CA 1664
Kt 1665 (PD)
RAB 1665
RAW 29 May 1666 (RM)
RAD 1669
RAR 8 Apr 1672 (NJ)
VAB 1672
COM E Nov 1672–
11 Oct 1673 (NBO)
VAR 1673
AD 1666
AB 14 Aug 1673 (NJ)
d 11 Oct 1673 (NBO)

HARMAN, John (2)
L 1672
d before 1689 (PJP)

HARMAN, Thomas
L 1671
CA 1672
KIA 10 Sept 1677 (CH)

HARMAN, William (1)
L 1672 (P)
CA 1673 (P)
d 13 Dec 1677 (PRO)

HARMAN, William (2)
L 26 Sept 1688
CA 10 May 1689 (NMM)
d 6 Oct 1694 (NMM)

HARMAN, William (3)
L 3 Feb 1741 (PJP)
CR
CA 26 Jan 1746
d 19 Jan 1766

HARMAN, William (4)
L 24 Mar 1807
KIA 18 Dec 1812 (CH)

HARMER, Burward
L 17 June 1762
d 1767 (NMM)

HARMER, Jeremiah
L 25 Apr 1743
d 1757 (NMM)

HARMER, Samuel Fielding
L 6 Aug 1814
CR 10 Jan 1837 (NMM)
d 29 May 1843 (PRO)

HARMOOD, Harry
L 19 Feb 1759
CR 16 Feb 1777
CA 17 Oct 1778
COM E 25 Sept 1794–
2 May 1795 (NBO)
COMM (Sheerness) 1796 (PJP)
COM N 3 Aug 1796–
20 June 1806 (NBO)
COMM (Chatham) Jan 1801 (PJP)

HARMOOD, James
L 9 Sept 1747
CR 15 May 1760
d 1773 (PRO)

HARNAGE, George
See BLACKMAN, Sir George

HARNAGE, Richard
L 30 July 1705 (PMM)

HARNESS, Richard Stephens
L 18 Feb 1812
CR 27 Aug 1814
HP 27 Aug 1814 (OB)
Ret CA 1 July 1851 (NMM)
d 6 Jan 1856 (NMM)

HARNETT, Henry
L 11 May 1808
d 1840 (NMM)

HARPER, Benjamin
L 13 Oct 1795
d (drowned) 9 Oct 1799 (PJP)

HARPER, James
L 1 Feb 1815
d 1855 (NMM)

HARPER, John
L 21 Feb 1794
CR 17 Apr 1810
CA 7 June 1814
CB 4 June 1815 (LG)
HP Dec 1818 (OB)
Ret CA 31 Oct 1846 (LG)
Ret RA 18 Oct 1849 (NMM)
d 2 July 1855 (NMM)

HARRIGATE, William
L 1666

HARRINGTON, Daniel
T
L 24 Dec 1805
d 19 Apr 1837 (NMM)

HARRINGTON, Edward Musgrave
L 22 Jan 1806

CR 10 Oct 1822 (NMM)
d 7 July 1842 (NMM)

HARRINGTON, Gilbert
L 1665

HARRINGTON, James Gastrell
L 28 Feb 1809
d 7 July 1842 (PRO)

HARRINGTON, Joseph
L 12 May 1761
d 1781 (NMM)

HARRINGTON, William
L 22 June 1796
d 1804 (NMM)

HARRIOTT, Thomas
L 28 Feb 1815 (OB)
HP 28 Feb 1815 (OB)

HARRIS, Barrow
L 10 Mar 1693 (PJP)
CA 13 Aug 1697
d 24 Mar 1726 (PMM)

HARRIS, Charles Poyntz
L 22 Aug 1811
d 1813 (PRO)

HARRIS, Christopher
L 24 Dec 1706 (PMM)

HARRIS, Edward
L 5 May 1794
d 29 May 1830 (NMM)

HARRIS, Edwin Charlton
L 6 Nov 1795
d 1816 (NMM)

HARRIS, Francis
T
L 1 Mar 1815
Ret CR 1 Oct 1860 (NMM)
d 1883 (NMM)

HARRIS, George (1)
L 22 May 1758
d 1761 (NMM)

HARRIS, George (2)
L 29 Mar 1802
d 1826 (NMM)

HARRIS, George (3)
L 7 May 1805
CR 25 Sept 1806
CA 21 Dec 1807
CB 4 June 1815 (LG)
d 19 Oct 1836 (PRO)

HARRIS, George Samuel
L 3 Nov 1790
Deserted 1804 (NMM)

HARRIS, Henry
L 16 Aug 1808
HP 18 Feb 1814 (OB)
Ret CR 6 Nov 1845 (PRO)
d 1862 (PRO)

HARRIS, Isaac
L 5 June 1808
HP 1813 (OB)
Ret CR 30 Apr 1845 (NMM)
d 1848 (PRO)

HARRIS, James (1)
L 5 June 1805
d 1849 (PRO)

HARRIS, James (2)
L 26 Feb 1810
CR 23 June 1815
Ret CA 16 July 1854 (NMM)
d 2 Jan 1870 (NMM)

HARRIS, John (1)
L 12 Dec 1673
CA 1673

HARRIS, John (2)
L 11 Mar 1703 (PMM)

HARRIS, John (3)
L 3 July 1754
d 26 Sept 1791

HARRIS, John (4)
L 30Mar 1794
d (drowned) 29 Dec 1807 (PJP)

HARRIS, John Wilkinson
L 20 June 1794
d 1795 (PRO)

HARRIS, Joseph (1)
L 1671
CA 1666
Condemned to death by court–martial for suffering dishonour, but pardoned 1675 (NMM)
d before 1689 (PJP)

HARRIS, Joseph (2)
L 9 July 1766
d 1776 (NMM)

HARRIS, Leonard
L
CA 1666 (P)
CA 22 Nov 1673
d before 1689 (PJP)

HARRIS, Mark
L 16 June 1697 (PMM)

HARRIS, Robert
L 22 Jan 1813
d June 1823 (PRO)

HARRIS, Stephen
L 18 Mar 1761
d 1790 (NMM)

HARRIS, Thomas (1)
L 31 Aug 1795
d 1802 (NMM)

HARRIS, Thomas (2)
L 19 July 1800
Ret CR 1 Dec 1830 (NMM)
d 1837 (NMM)

HARRIS, Thomas (3)
L 23 Apr 1808
d 1809 (PRO)

HARRIS, Walter
L 23 Feb 1774
d 2 July 1790

HARRIS, William (1)
L
CA 6 July 1666 (RM)

HARRIS, William (2)
L 2 Feb 1744
CR 6 Apr 1756
CA 30 July 1759
d 14 Nov 1766

Name / Rank	Date	Year
HARRIS, William Clark(e)		
L	18 Apr	1811
d	Aug	1850 (PRO)
HARRISON, Edward (1)		
L	9 Jan	1673
d	before	1689 (PJP)
HARRISON, Edward (2)		
L	16 Feb	1691
In Merchant Service		1700 (PJP)
HARRISON, George		
L	13 Nov	1793
CR	23 June	1796
d	17 Aug	1831 (PJP)
HARRISON, Henry (1)		
L	19 Jan	1706
CR	26 July	1738 (NMM)
CA	28 Feb	1740
RAB	June	1756
RAW		1756
VAB	7 Feb	1758 (NMM)
VAR		1759
d	13 Mar	1759
HARRISON, Henry (2)		
L	7 Apr	1813
d		1818 (NMM)
HARRISON, James (1)		
L	9 July	1762
d		1767 (PRO)
HARRISON, James (2)		
L	7 Sept	1783
SUP CR	18 Sept	1821 (NMM)
d	Feb	1824 (NMM)
HARRISON, John (1)		
L	2 Feb	1741
CR	17 Feb	1755
CA	4 July	1755
SUP RA		1779
d	15 Oct	1791 (LT)
HARRISON, John (2)		
L	27 June	1814
Ret CR	13 Apr	1857 (NMM)
d	24 Nov	1870 (NMM)
HARRISON, John Bayby		
L	22 June	1797 (NMM)
d		1834 (NMM)
HARRISON, Joseph		
L	10 May	1807
CR	14 Sept	1818 (NMM)
CA	9 Oct	1832 (NMM)
Ret CA	1 July	1851 (NMM)
Ret RA	21 July	1856 (NMM)
d	7 Oct	1857 (NMM)
HARRISON, Lancelot		
L	15 Sept	1678 (DDA)
d	before	1689 (PJP)
HARRISON, Mark (1)		
L		
CA		1660
d	before	1689 (PJP)
HARRISON, Mark (2)		
L	4 Nov	1688
HARRISON, Parker Innes		
L	18 Nov	1779
d	13 Oct	1793

Name / Rank	Date	Year
HARRISON, Richard (1)		
L	29 July	1781
d		1811 (PRO)
HARRISON, Richard (2)		
L	25 Aug	1806
d	Oct	1816 (LT)
HARRISON, Robert (1)		
L	10 Nov	1708
CR		
CA	10 July	1733
d	July	1745 (M)
HARRISON, Robert (2)		
L	9 May	1778
d	22 May	1790
HARRISON, Thomas (1)		
L	15 Feb	1723
CR	12 Oct	1741
CA	5 June	1744
d	17 Aug	1752
HARRISON, Thomas (2)		
L	3 Dec	1747
CR	1 Nov	1756
CA	17 Jan	1757
d	1 Feb	1768
HARRISON, Thomas (3)		
L	26 Jan	1780
d		1782 (NMM)
HARRISON, Thomas (4)		
L	16 Sept	1783
CR	29 June	1795
d	23 Apr	1803
HARRISON, Thomas (5)		
L	9 Nov	1795
Dismissed	28 Dec	1796 (NMM)
HARROP, David		
L	1 May	1815
d		1855 (PRO)
HARROW, Henry		
L	27 June	1814
HP	Aug	1815 (OB)
Ret CR	26 Aug	1857 (NMM)
d	Feb	1882 (NMM)
HART, Benjamin		
L	6 Mar	1815
HP	6 Mar	1815 (OB)
Ret CR	10 Jan	1863 (NMM)
d	3 Aug	1867 (NMM)
HART, George (1)		
L	10 Apr	1703
HART, George (2)		
L	9 May	1778
CR	27 June	1782
CA	22 Nov	1790
RAB	28 Apr	1808
RAW	31 July	1810
RAR	1 Aug	1811
d	28 Apr	1812 (CH)
HART, Sir Henry		
L	12 June	1802
CR	12 Oct	1807
CA	1 Aug	1811
Kt	25 Jan	1836 (OB)
KCH	23 Feb	1836 (OB)

Ret RA	31 Oct	1846 (LG)
d	22 Dec	1856 (NMM)
HART, Henry Chichester		
L	29 May	1807
d		1813 (PRO)
HART, Henry Hare		
L	13 Nov	1756
d	26 Feb	1793
HART, John (1)		
L		
CA		1664
d	before	1688 (PD)
HART, John (2)		
L		1664
d	before	1689 (PJP)
HART, John (3)		
L	9 Jan	1691 (PMM)
HART, John (4)		
L	22 Oct	1794
d		1797 (NMM)
HART, William Cole		
L	8 June	1805
d		1817 (NMM)
HART, William Henry		
L	7 Feb	1815
d		1817 (NMM)
HARTLEY, Edward		
T	wounded	
L	24 Dec	1805
d		1813 (NMM)
HARTLEY, Mark		
L		1668
CA	12 July	1667
d	before	1689 (PJP)
HARTNOLL, John		
L		
CA	3 Dec	1694 (PJP)
d		1723 (PJP)
HARTWELL, Broderick		
L	12 June	1741
CR	13 May	1757
CA	18 Oct	1758
LGH		1781 (PJP)
d	20 Mar	1784 (PRO)
HARTWELL, Sir Francis John		
L	7 July	1775
CR	25 Jan	1779
CA	9 Dec	1779
COM V		1794–1796 (PJP)
COMM (Sheerness)	Sept	1796 (PJP)
COMM (Chatham)		1799–1801 (PJP)
COM N	21 Jan	1801–
	3 Dec	1808 (NBO)
Kt	4 May	1803 (NBO)
Cre Bt	26 Oct	1805 (NBO)
SUP CA		1814 (MB)
d	28 June	1831 (NBO)
HARTWELL, George		
L	21 Apr	1783
d	15 Nov	1806 (PMM)
HARTY, Joseph		
L	2 Mar	1805
d		1832 (NMM)
HARVEY, Booty		
L	27 May	1794
CR	20 May	1806
CA	31 Mar	1812
CB	8 Dec	1815 (LG)
d		1833 (PRO)
HARVEY, Charles Bernhard		
L	13 Jan	1803
CR	13 Feb	1814 (OB)
HP	13 Feb	1814 (OB)
d	4 Oct	1847 (NMM)
HARVEY, Sir Edward		
L	24 July	1801
CR	7 Jan	1808
CA	18 Apr	1811
RAB	17 Dec	1847 (LG)
RAW	30 Oct	1849 (NMM)
RAR	30 July	1852 (NMM)
VAB	11 Sept	1854 (NMM)
VAW	21 Oct	1856 (NMM)
VAR	2 Oct	1857 (NMM)
AB	9 June	1860 (NMM)
KCB	28 June	1861 (DNB)
AW	20 May	1862 (NMM)
AR	3 Dec	1863 (NMM)
GCB	28 Mar	1865 (DNB)
d	4 May	1865 (CH)
HARVEY, Edward		
See HARVY, Edward		
HARVEY, Sir Eliab		
L	25 Feb	1779
MP		
(Malden)		1780–1781 (DNB)
CR	21 Mar	1782
CA	20 Jan	1783
MP		
(Essex)		1802–1812 (DNB)
T		
RAB	9 Nov	1805
RAR	28 Apr	1808
Dismissed	23 May	1809 (DNB)
Restored	21 Mar	1810 (DNB)
VAB	31 July	1810
VAW	12 Aug	1812
VAR	4 June	1814
KCB	2 Jan	1815 (LG)
AB	12 Aug	1819 (CH)
MP		
(Essex)		1820–1830 (MPT)
GCB	17 Jan	1825 (MPT)
d	20 Feb	1830 (DNB)
HARVEY, George		
L	15 Feb	1815
d	25 Sept	1820 (NMM)
HARVEY, Sir Henry		
L	10 Mar	1757
HP		1771–1773 (DNB)
CR	15 Oct	1773
CA	9 May	1777
RAB	1 June	1795 (PJP)
VAW	14 Feb	1799
Kt	Jan	1800 (DNB)
VAR	1 Jan	1801
AB	23 Apr	1804
AW	9 Nov	1805
d	28 Dec	1810 (DNB)

HARVEY, James
L 30 July 1801
d 25 Sept 1836 (PRO)

HARVEY, James Watson
T
L 29 Oct 1812
CR 9 Sept 1815
d (drowned) 25 Mar 1816 (LT)

HARVEY, John (1)
L 18 Sept 1759
HP 1766–1768 (DNB)
CR 26 May 1766 (DNB)
CA 16 Sept 1777
KIA 1 June 1794 (LG)

HARVEY, Sir John (2)
L 3 Nov 1790
CR
CA 16 Dec 1794
RAB 4 Dec 1813
RAW 4 June 1814
RAR 12 Aug 1819 (CH)
VAB 27 May 1825 (CH)
VAR 22 July 1830 (CH)
KCB 12 June 1833 (LG)
AB 10 Jan 1837 (CH)
d 17 Feb 1837 (DNB)

HARVEY, John (3)
L 24 July 1812
d 1814 (PRO)

HARVEY, John (4)
L 13 Nov 1813
CR 2 Apr 1819 (OB)
HP 2 Apr 1819 (OB)
Ret CA 1 Apr 1856 (NMM)
d 1882 (NMM)

HARVEY, John (5)
L 26 Oct 1814
d 1834 (NMM)

HARVEY, Philip
L 2 Mar 1815
d 2 Mar 1824 (PRO)

HARVEY, Richard (1)
L 22 May 1793
d 1794 (PMM)

HARVEY, Richard (2)
L 11 Jan 1798
d 1798 (NMM)

HARVEY, Robert
T
L 2 Apr 1806
KIA 9 Aug 1808 (TR)

HARVEY, Robert Savory
L 30 June 1810
d 1820 (PRO)

HARVEY, Thomas (1)
L 18 Aug 1705 (PMM)

HARVEY, Sir Thomas (2)
L 8 Oct 1794
CR 3 July 1796 (CH)
CA 27 Mar 1797
HP 1802–1805 (MB)
CB 4 June 1815 (LG)
RAB 19 July 1821 (LG)
RAW 27 May 1825 (LG)
RAR 22 July 1830 (LG)
KCB 1 May 1833 (LG)
VAW 10 Jan 1837 (LG)
d 28 May 1841 (DNB)

HARVEY, Hon. William (1)
L 31 Dec 1718
CR 1 Feb 1726
d Apr 1729 (NMM)

HARVEY, William (2)
L 15 Dec 1779
CR 21 Oct 1790
d 1807 (NMM)

HARVIE, John
L 20 Mar 1815 (NMM)
d 1837 (NMM)

HARVY, Edward
L
CA 1673

HARWAR, George
L 27 June 1696 (PJP)

HARWARD, Charles
See HAWARD, Charles

HARWARD, John
L 22 July 1794
CR 25 May 1799
d 1817 (PRO)

HARWARD, Richard
L 3 Sept 1801
CR 2 Apr 1806
CA 31 July 1809
d 2 May 1845 (NMM)

HARWARD, Robert
L 5 Sept 1693
CR 1 Jan 1713
d 25 Jan 1748 (M)

HARWARD, Thomas
See HAWARD, Thomas

HARWELL, Robert
L 1665

HARWOOD, James
L 1691 (PMM)

HARWOOD, John
L 16 Feb 1815
d 1826 (NMM)

HARWOOD, Robert
See HARWARD, Robert

HARWOOD, Thomas
L 1664
CA 1665
d before 1689 (PJP)

HASELGRAVE, John
L
CA 1661

HASELWOOD, John
L 1667

HASLEDEN, Thomas
L 19 June 1760
d 1763 (NMM)

HASSARD, Robert Fitzhugh
L 30 May 1778
d 1783 (NMM)

HASSETT, Thomas
L 8 Feb 1815
d 1818 (PRO)

HASTINGS, Anthony		
L		1666 (P)
CA		1676 (P)
CA	1 Oct	1688
d	16 May	1692
HASTINGS, Francis		
See HUNTINGDON, Hans Francis, Earl		
HASTINGS, Frank		
T		
L	16 Mar	1814
CR	27 Apr	1819 (NMM)
Struck off list	19 Aug	1819 (NMM)
d		1819 (TR)
HASTINGS, Sir Thomas		
L	17 Jan	1810
CR	9 May	1825 (CH)
CA	22 July	1830 (CH)
Kt	5 June	1839 (OB)
RAB	27 Sept	1855 (NMM)
RAW	18 June	1857 (NMM)
RAR	24 Nov	1858 (NMM)
KCB		1859 (CH)
VAB	4 Oct	1862 (NMM)
VAW	12 Sept	1863 (NMM)
VAR	5 Mar	1864 (NMM)
Ret A	2 Apr	1866 (CH)
d	3 Jan	1870 (NMM)
HASTY, Peter		
L	20 Mar	1799
d		1804 (PRO)
HASWELL, Charles Henry		
L	9 Aug	1794
d		1799 (NMM)
HASWELL, Edward		
L	10 Feb	1815
HP		1816 (OB)
Ret CR	23 July	1860 (NMM)
d		1866 (NMM)
HASWELL, James Crosby		
L	22 Jan	1783
d		1788 (PRO)
HASWELL, John		
L	7 July	1803
CR	15 Aug	1806
d	28 July	1811 (LT)
HASWELL, John Dawes		
T		
L	10 Feb	1815
HP	10 Feb	1815 (OB)
d	7 July	1848 (NMM)
HASWELL, Robert (1)		
L	13 Apr	1695 (PMM)
HASWELL, Robert (2)		
L	8 July	1744
CR	26 Mar	1762
CA	17 June	1780
SUP		1799
d		1801
HASWELL, William		
L	1 Dec	1756
SUP CR	21 Sept	1796 (PMM)
d		1796 (NMM)
HASWELL, William Henry		
T		
L	28 Feb	1809
CR	22 July	1830 (NMM)
d	27 Jan	1848 (NMM)
HATCH, John		
L	21 Feb	1741
CR	14 June	1757
d	4 Jan	1792
HATFIELD, David		
L		1693 (PMM)
HATHERILL, Richard		
L	18 Oct	1794
CR	13 Jan	1801
CA	29 Apr	1802
d		1805 (NMM)
HATHORN, Robert		
L	1 July	1745
CR	18 Jan	1758
CA	27 Oct	1759
d		1789
HATHWAITE, William		
L	17 Sept	1806
d		1815 (PRO)
HATLEY, John		
L	4 Sept	1782
CR	3 Aug	1797
CA	29 Apr	1802
d	12 Dec	1832 (PRO)
HATTON, Edward Finch		
L	9 July	1812
d		1813 (NMM)
HATTON, George Burrow		
L	24 Feb	1811
d	14 Feb	1812 (NMM)
HATTON, Henry John		
L	3 Nov	1809
CR	30 Aug	1815
d		1832 (NMM)
HATTON, John		
L	6 Feb	1815
d		1828 (NMM)
HATTON, Villiers Francis		
L	31 Jan	1806
CR	19 June	1808
CA	7 Feb	1812
RAB	14 Feb	1848 (LG)
RAW	2 Sept	1850 (NMM)
RA	1 July	1851 (NMM)
VA	27 Sept	1855 (NMM)
d	8 Feb	1859 (NMM)
HATUBB, Robert		
L		
CA		1664
d	before	1689 (PJP)
HAUGHTON, Edward Archer		
L	16 Aug	1814
d	May	1820 (NMM)
HAUGHTON, Henry		
L	4 July	1686
CA	3 July	1685 (DDA)
d		1703 (PJP)
HAUGHTON, John		
L	30 Apr	1670
HAULTAIN, Charles		
L	26 Apr	1806

CR	15 June	1814
KH	1 Jan	1833 (OB)
d	4 June	1845 (OB)
HAVEN, Arthur		
L	14 Apr	1744
d		1755 (NMM)
HAVEN, John		
L	18 Apr	1758
d		1773 (NMM)
HAVERFIELD, Robert		
L	10 May	1804
CR	27 Aug	1814
d		1838 (NMM)
HAWARD, Charles		
L		1672
CA		1665
d	before	1689 (PJP)
HAWARD, Thomas		
L		1664
CA		1665
KIA	2 Aug	1665 (ESP)
HAWES, Andrew		
L	5 Oct	1726
d		1739 (NMM)
HAWES, George		
L	11 May	1691
In Merchant Service	Mar	1700 (PJP)
CR	24 Feb	1703 (PMM)
d (drowned)	18 Sept	1707 (CH)
HAWES, Henry		
L	14 Feb	1797
d		1840 (NMM)
HAWES, James		
L	14 Aug	1794
CR	7 Jan	1802
d (drowned)		1807 (PJP)
HAWFORD, Callis		
L	28 Feb	1778
d		1800 (NMM)
HAWFORD, John		
L	28 Jan	1746
d		1760 (NMM)
HAWFORD, Richard		
L	26 Oct	1776
CR	11 Feb	1781
d (drowned)	29 Oct	1781 (PJP)
HAWFORD, William		
L	29 July	1779
d	2 May	1807 (NMM)
HAWKE, Britisse		
L	22 Jan	1806
d	Sept	1828 (NMM)
HAWKE, Edward, Baron		
L	11 Apr	1729
HP	22 Dec	1729–
	19 May	1731 (DNB)
CR	13 Apr	1733 (PRO)
CA	20 Mar	1734
HP	5 Sept	1735–
	30 July	1739 (CH)
RAW	15 July	1747
Kt	15 Nov	1747 (MPN)
MP (Portsmouth)	28 Dec	1747–
	20 May	1776 (MPN)
VAB	12 May	1748 (CH)
VAW	6 Jan	1755 (CH)
AB	24 Feb	1757 (CH)
AW	21 Oct	1762
FLA	11 Dec	1766–
	12 Jan	1771 (AO)
AF	15 Jan	1768 (CH)
Cre EP	20 May	1776 (DNB)
d	17 Oct	1781 (CH)
HAWKER, Edmund		
L	12 Oct	1759
Quit		1778 (PRO)
HAWKER, Edward		
L	14 July	1796
CR	29 Aug	1803 (PJP)
CA	6 June	1804
HP	30 Apr	1830 (OB)
RAB	10 Jan	1837 (PRO)
RAW	23 Nov	1841 (PRO)
RAR	9 Nov	1846 (PRO)
VAB	22 Sept	1847 (PRO)
VAW	15 Sept	1849 (PRO)
VAR	8 July	1851 (PRO)
AB	17 Sept	1853 (PRO)
AW	3 Oct	1855 (PRO)
A	6 Mar	1858 (PRO)
d	8 June	1860 (PRO)
HAWKER, James		
L	31 Dec	1755
CR	6 Aug	1761
CA	26 May	1768
d		1787
HAWKER, Thomas (1)		
L	11 Apr	1759
CR	14 July	1779
CA	21 Sept	1790
d	29 Oct	1807 (PJP)
HAWKER, Thomas (2)		
L	4 Apr	1783
CR	9 Nov	1795
d	29 Oct	1807 (SPB)
HAWKES, Edward		
L	23 Oct	1744 (PJP)
HAWKES, Richard		
L	23 Aug	1800
d		1810 (PRO)
HAWKES, Thomas		
L	5 July	1805
d	28 May	1823 (NMM)
HAWKES, Thomas Joseph		
L	16 Jan	1806
d (drowned)	28 Nov	1807 (PJP)
HAWKEY, Charles		
L	6 Oct	1809
CR	31 July	1812
d	Sept	1820 (NMM)
HAWKEY, John		
L	5 May	1804
d		1816 (NMM)
HAWKEY, Joseph		
L	24 Mar	1807
KIA	7 July	1809 (CH)

HAWKEY, William
L 6 Sept 1775
d 1778 (PRO)

HAWKINS, Abel
L 3 May 1799
KIA 9 Oct 1814 (JH)

HAWKINS, Abraham Mills
L 11 June 1807
CR 12 Dec 1812
CA 6 Feb 1836 (NMM)
Ret CA 1 July 1851 (NMM)
Ret RA 14 Feb 1857 (NMM)
d 8 Nov 1857 (PRO)

HAWKINS, Charles (1)
L 10 May 1687 (P)
CA 19 Mar 1690
d (drowned) 19 Feb 1694 (CH)

HAWKINS, Charles (2)
L 17 Sept 1743
d (drowned) 15 Sept 1747 (PJP)

HAWKINS, Charles (3)
L 11 May 1804
d Oct 1807 (PMM)

HAWKINS, Charles (4)
T
L 7 Jan 1807
Ret CR 22 Feb 1851 (NMM)
d 22 Dec 1854 (NMM)

HAWKINS, Edward
L 13 Nov 1790
CR 13 Aug 1798
CA 25 Sept 1806
d 30 Apr 1839 (PRO)

HAWKINS, George (1)
L 8 Sept 1806
d 1814 (NMM)

HAWKINS, George (2)
L 5 June 1811
d 1844 (NMM)

HAWKINS, Henry
L 26 May 1814
d 14 June 1821 (LT)

HAWKINS, James
See WHITSHED, Sir James Hawkins

HAWKINS, John (1)
L 10 May 1757
d (drowned) 1 Jan 1761 (PJP)

HAWKINS, John (2)
L 6 Aug 1800
Ret CR 26 Nov 1830 (NMM)
d 1833 (NMM)

HAWKINS, John (3)
L 23 Aug 1801
d 1802 (PRO)

HAWKINS, John (4)
L 11 Dec 1807
d 9 May 1818 (NMM)

HAWKINS, Joseph
L 4 Apr 1760
d 1775 (NMM)

HAWKINS, Richard
L 1 July 1794
CR 8 Oct 1798
CA 29 Apr 1802
HP 1814 (MB)
d Nov 1826 (NMM)

HAWKS, Solomon
L 30 July 1746
d 1751 (NMM)

HAWKSHAW, Richard
L 6 Dec 1806
d 1810 (PRO)

HAWKSHAW, Wallop Brabazon
L 8 Nov 1811
d 1813 (PRO)

HAWORTH, Adrian
L 7 Mar 1815
d 1818 (NMM)

HAWTAYNE, Charles Sibthorp John
L 24 Aug 1799
CR 31 Jan 1806
CA 13 Oct 1807
RAB 23 Nov 1841 (CH)
RAW 28 Apr 1847 (LG)
RAR 9 Oct 1849 (LG)
VAB 30 July 1852 (NMM)
VAW 11 Feb 1854 (NMM)
VAR 31 Jan 1856 (NMM)
d 9 Sept 1857 (NMM)

HAY, Charles (1)
L 13 Mar 1759
CR 19 Jan 1771
d 1773 (PRO)

HAY, Charles (2)
L 1 Dec 1779
d 1811 (NMM)

HAY, Charles (3)
L 27 Dec 1781
CR 26 Dec 1799 (PJP)
d 1796 (NMM)

HAY, David
L 4 Apr 1743
CR 10 Nov 1756
d 1788 (PRO)

HAY, George (1)
L 21 Aug 1695

HAY, George (2)
L 1 Jan 1783
d 27 Dec 1797

HAY, George
See HAYE, George

HAY, George James
L 6 July 1815
CR 18 Sept 1828 (NMM)
CA 11 Jan 1846 (NMM)
CB 27 July 1846 (OB)
HP 1846 (OB)
Ret CA 10 Aug 1856 (NMM)
d 21 Oct 1862 (NMM)

HAY, James
T
L 1 Mar 1806
CR 2 May 1810
CA 12 Aug 1819 (MB)
Ret CA 31 Oct 1846 (LG)

Ret RA	27 Aug	1851 (NMM)
d	3 Feb	1857 (NMM)
HAY, John (1)		
L	13 Feb	1759
CR	4 May	1761
d		1782 (NMM)
HAY, John (2)		
L	31 Oct	1778
d		1802 (PRO)
HAY, Lord John (3)		
Inh EP	9 Aug	1804 (MB)
L	1 Apr	1812
CR	15 June	1814
CA	7 Dec	1818 (MB)
MP (Haddington)		1826–1830 (DNB)
CB		1837 (DNB)
Kt (Spain)		1837 (DNB)
COM AD	13 July	1846–
	9 Feb	1850 (DNB)
MP (Windsor)		1847 (DNB)
RAB	17 Aug	1851 (NMM)
d	9 Sept	1851 (PMM)
HAY, John (4)		
L	1 July	1814
Ret CR	28 Oct	1857 (NMM)
HAY, John Baker		
L	15 Nov	1790
CR	1 Mar	1797
CA	7 Sept	1798
d	13 May	1823 (MB)
HAY, Matthew		
T	wounded	
L	24 Dec	1805
d	19 June	1821 (PRO)
HAY, Patrick Duff Henry		
L	31 July	1812
CR	31 Aug	1815
CA	15 Nov	1833 (NMM)
Ret CA	1 July	1851 (NMM)
d	6 Jan	1854 (NMM)
HAY, Peter		
L	20 Sept	1815
HP	Dec	1839 (OB)
d		1854 (NMM)
HAY, Robert (1)		
L	18 Sept	1739
KIA	Apr	1747 (LG)
HAY, Robert (2)		
L	24 Apr	1747
d	30 Dec	1789
HAY, Robert (3)		
L	13 Aug	1812
CR	16 Sept	1816 (PRO)
d (drowned)	23 Feb	1824 (CH)
HAY, William (1)		
L	5 Aug	1707
d		1728 (NMM)
HAY, William (2)		
L	27 May	1728
d		1740 (NMM)
HAY, William (3)		
L	1 June	1756
CR	21 Nov	1760
CA	12 Apr	1762
d		1801
HAY, William (4)		
L	27 Mar	1781
d	1 Dec	1791
HAYCOCK, Charles		
L	6 Dec	1813
CR	15 July	1856 (NMM)
d	7 Sept	1866 (NMM)
HAYCOCKE, Humphrey		
L	2 Sept	1709
HAYDON, Charles		
L	28 Dec	1810
HP		1821 (OB)
CR	28 July	1851 (NMM)
d	21 Mar	1866 (NMM)
HAYDON, George		
T		
L	9 June	1807
Ret CR	7 Mar	1856 (NMM)
d		1859 (TR)
HAYDON, Richard		
L	12 Sept	1694 (PMM)
HAYDON, William		
L	26 Sept	1799
CR	1 Aug	1811
CA	23 Nov	1841 (LG)
Ret CA	11 Apr	1854 (NMM)
Ret RA	12 Apr	1862 (NMM)
d		1864 (NMM)
HAYDON, William Phippard		
L	8 Dec	1809
Ret CR	11 Apr	1849 (NMM)
d		1860 (NMM)
HAYE, George		
L	9 Aug	1808
CR	19 May	1812
CA	4 Mar	1829 (NMM)
Ret CA	4 Mar	1849 (NMM)
d		1852 (NMM)
HAYES, Frederick		
L	30 Mar	1758
d		1777 (PRO)
HAYES, George (1)		
L	3 May	1688
HAYES, George (2)		
L	25 May	1793
CR	15 June	1814
CA	2 Dec	1829 (NMM)
HP	Feb	1830 (OB)
d	29 Sept	1847 (NMM)
HAYES, John		
L	7 Oct	1793
CR	1 Mar	1799
CA	29 Apr	1802
HP		1802–1812 (MB)
CB	4 June	1815 (LG)
RAW	10 Jan	1837 (LG)
d	7 Apr	1838 (OB)
HAYES, Matthew		
L	26 Mar	1759
d		1762 (NMM)

HAYGARTH, William
L 6 Apr 1757
d 22 Mar 1810 (NMM)

HAYMAN, Atkin
L 25 June 1808
d 1817 (NMM)

HAYMAN, Charles Cherry
L 6 Oct 1801
KIA 15 Aug 1804 (CH)

HAYMAN, Henry
See HEYMAN, Henry

HAYMAN, William
L 26 Aug 1745
d 1753 (PRO)

HAYMES, Philip George
L 20 Nov 1812
CR 13 Mar 1815
CA 9 Nov 1846 (LG)
Ret CA 31 Dec 1856 (NMM)
d 1862 (NMM)

HAYNE, Arthur
L 22 Nov 1757
SUP CR 26 May 1797 (PMM)
d 1797 (PRO)

HAYNES, George Dentaus
L 9 Aug 1794
d 1797 (PRO)

HAYNES, Henry
L 5 Jan 1801
CR 13 Oct 1807
CA 28 Apr 1814
d 17 Jan 1838 (LT)

HAYNES, Joseph
L 8 Oct 1771
CR 25 Oct 1809
d 11 Oct 1828 (PRO)

HAYNES, Thomas
L 1 Nov 1755
CR 9 Apr 1777
CA 30 Jan 1779 (NMM)
d 1789 (NMM)

HAYTER, Samuel
L 28 Aug 1761
d 1800 (PRO)

HAYWARD, John (1)
L
CA 1660
KIA 11 Aug 1673 (NJ)

HAYWARD, John (2)
L 1671
KIA 28 May 1672 (NJ)

HAYWARD, Thomas (1)
L 26 Mar 1758
CR 9 Nov 1761
KIA 23 May 1781 (LG)

HAYWARD, Thomas (2)
L 6 Nov 1762
d 1795 (PRO)

HAYWARD, Thomas (3)
L 26 Oct 1790
CR 22 Dec 1796
d (drowned) 27 Dec 1797 (CH)

HAZELWOOD, Andrew
L 6 Mar 1741
d 1742 (NMM)

HE, Joseph
L 6 Jan 1704 (PMM)

HEA, Robert
L 11 Mar 1815
d 1861 (PRO)

HEACOCK, George
L 13 May 1807
d 1836 (NMM)

HEACOCK, Richard
L 2 Nov 1790
d 1812 (NMM)

HEAD, Hugh Somerville
L 6 Mar 1815
d 29 Mar 1829 (NMM)

HEAD, John
L 3 Nov 1799
d 9 Feb 1804

HEAD, Michael
L 10 Dec 1804
CR 6 Dec 1809
CA 7 June 1814
d 27 June 1844 (NMM)

HEAD, Richard John
L 12 June 1807
CR 15 May 1819 (NMM)
Ret CA 1 Apr 1856 (NMM)
d 1859 (NMM)

HEAL, Charles
L 11 Feb 1815
d 1832 (PRO)

HEAL, Joseph
See HELE, Joseph

HEALEY, George
L 3 July 1746
d 1753 (NMM)

HEALY, John
L 26 Feb 1805
Ret CR 12 Sept 1839 (NMM)
d 27 Apr 1846 (OB)

HEARD, William
L 27 Aug 1794
d 17 June 1823 (NMM)

HEARLE, John
L 13 Apr 1795
d 17 June 1823 (PRO)

HEARLE, Robert
L 9 May 1797
Ret CR 26 Nov 1830 (PRO)
d 1858 (NMM)

HEARNE, John
See HERNE, John

HEASLOP, John Colpoys
L 6 Nov 1813
CR 24 June 1817 (NMM)
Ret CA 4 May 1863 (NMM)
d 26 Dec 1867 (PRO)

HEASTY, George
L 4 May 1810
Ret CR 12 Jan 1850 (NMM)
d 13 Jan 1858 (NMM)

HEASTY, Richard David
L 8 Apr 1797
d 1797 (PRO)

HEATH, John
L 1661
CA 1664
d before 1689 (PJP)

HEATH, Thomas
See HEATHE, Thomas

HEATH, William
L 15 Apr 1774
CR 15 May 1780
CA 1 Dec 1787
SUP RA 2 Nov 1807
d 25 June 1815 (PRO)

HEATHCOCK, John
L
CA 1672

HEATHCOTE, George
L 17 May 1758
d 1771 (PRO)

HEATHCOTE, Gilbert
L 10 Dec 1799
CR 29 Apr 1802
CA 5 Sept 1806
d 22 Apr 1831 (PRO)

HEATHCOTE, Sir Henry
L 19 Sept 1796
CR 11 Aug 1797
CA 5 Feb 1798
Kt 20 July 1819 (OB)
RAB 27 May 1825 (LG)
RAR 22 July 1830 (LG)
Ret RA 1 July 1831 (CH)
VAB 10 Jan 1837 (LG)
VAW 3 July 1838 (LG)
VAR 23 Nov 1841 (LG)
AB 20 Nov 1846 (LG)
AW 8 Jan 1848 (PRO)
A 1 July 1851 (PRO)
d 16 Aug 1851 (PRO)

HEATHE, Thomas
L
CA 2 Apr 1689
d 9 June 1693

HEBDEN, Baker
L 22 Jan 1740
d 1761 (NMM)

HEDDINGTON, Thomas
L 6 Nov 1795
CR 25 Sept 1806 (NMM)
HP Apr 1814 (OB)
Ret CA 1 July 1851 (NMM)
d 1860 (NMM)

HEEMSKIRK, St. Lawrence van
See HEMSKIRK, St. Lawrence van

HEIGHAM, George
L 3 Nov 1790
KIA 29 May 1794 (JH)

HEIGHINGTON, Conway
L 17 June 1782
d 1796 (NMM)

HELE, Joseph
L 6 Jan 1704
SUPCR 20 Mar 1738 (PMM)
d 1743 (PMM)

HELE, William (1)
L 23 Sept 1692 (PMM)

HELE, William (2)
L 16 Mar 1814
d 31 Dec 1824 (NMM)

HELLARD, Joseph
L 5 Sept 1794
Ret CR 26 Nov 1830 (PRO)
d 14 Sept 1844 (NMM)

HELLARD, Samuel
L 29 Oct 1810
CR 22 July 1830 (NMM)
CA 1 Jan 1839 (NMM)
HP 1 Jan 1839 (OB)
d 28 Jan 1848 (NMM)

HELLARD, William
L 3 Jan 1783
T
CR 24 Dec 1805
CA 12 Aug 1812
d 17 July 1837 (NMM)

HELLESON, Richard
L 17 Jan 1697
Gone 1719 (PRO)

HELLING, Daniel
L
CA 7 June 1666 (RM)
d before 1689 (PJP)

HELPMAN, Philip (1)
L 17 Mar 1780
d 1807 (PJP)

HELPMAN, Philip (2)
L 9 Aug 1799
CR 19 July 1821 (NMM)
d 1826 (NMM)

HELPMAN, Robert
L 27 Apr 1808
d 1815 (NMM)

HEMER, Richard
L 16 Feb 1815
d 1826 (PRO)

HEMER, Robert
T
L 9 Feb 1815
Ret CR 18 Feb 1859 (NMM)
d 1862 (TR)

HEMING, Henry
L 26 Mar 1704 (PMM)

HEMING, Samuel Scudamore
L 18 Nov 1790
SUP CR 16 Feb 1824 (NMM)
d 1840 (NMM)

HEMINTON, John
See HEMMINGTON, John

HEMINTON, Gilbert
L 1665

HEMMANS, Samuel Hood
L 5 Feb 1813
d 22 May 1854 (PMM)

HEMMING, Thomas
L 7 May 1735

CR 16 May 1743
d 1748 (NMM)
HEMMINGS, William
L 10 Oct 1759
d 1795 (NMM)
HEMMINGTON, Henry (1)
L 26 May 1704
SUP CR 20 Mar 1738 (PMM)
HEMMINGTON, Henry (2)
L 8 Aug 1740
d 1744 (NMM)
HEMMINGTON, John (or James)
L
CR 16 Mar 1708 (PMM)
CA 12 Nov 1708
SUP RA 3 June 1747
d 26 Dec 1757
HEMSKIRK, St. Lawrence Van
L
CA 1668
d before 1689 (PJP)
HEMSTED, Charles
L 17 Dec 1795
d 1833 (NMM)
HEMSWORTH, William Glassford
L 20 Sept 1815
CR 5 Feb 1858 (NMM)
d Sept 1874 (NMM)
HENDERSON, David
L 3 Mar 1815
d 7 Mar 1860 (NMM)
HENDERSON, George
L 28 Jan 1804
CR 22 Jan 1808
CA 1 Aug 1811
Ret RA 31 Oct 1846 (LG)
Ret VA 3 July 1855 (NMM)
Ret A 1 Nov 1860 (NMM)
d 23 Jan 1864 (NMM)
HENDERSON, James (1)
L 6 Sept 1708
HENDERSON, James (2)
L 11 Mar 1778
KIA 6 Oct 1779 (PJP)
HENDERSON, James (3)
L 19 Aug 1781
d 1799 (NMM)
HENDERSON, James (4)
L 11 Dec 1807
d 14 Feb 1830 (PMM)
HENDERSON, James (5)
L 10 Nov 1810
d Mar 1820 (PRO)
HENDERSON, John (1)
L 8 Aug 1694
Gone 1719 (PRO)
HENDERSON, John (2)
L 5 July 1756
d 1762 (NMM)
HENDERSON, John (3)
L 4 Sept 1807
d (drowned) 16 Oct 1807 (PJP)
HENDERSON, John (4)
L 26 Sept 1811
d 30 Nov 1829 (NMM)
HENDERSON, John (5)
L 10 Mar 1815 (NMM)
Ret CR 20 July 1863 (NMM)
d 1866 (NMM)
HENDERSON, Robert (1)
L 11 Dec 1760
d 1778 (NMM)
HENDERSON, Robert (2)
L 29 May 1799
CR 21 June 1804
CA 22 Jan 1806
RAB 28 June 1838 (LG)
RAW 23 Nov 1841 (LG)
d 14 Jan 1843 (PRO)
HENDERSON, Robert (3)
L 16 Feb 1815
d 1840 (NMM)
HENDERSON, William (1)
L 22 May 1759 (NMM)
d 9 Dec 1797 (PJP)
HENDERSON, William (2)
L 25 July 1799
d Jan 1821 (NMM)
HENDERSON, William Willmot
T
L 11 Apr 1806
CR 13 Mar 1811
CA 9 Oct 1815
KH 13 Jan 1835 (OB)
CB 18 Dec 1840 (OB)
RAB 21 Mar 1851 (NMM)
RAW 22 Apr 1853 (NMM)
d 12 July 1854 (TR)
HENDRA, Thomas
L
CA 1665
d before 1689 (PJP)
HENDRICK, Charles
L 16 May 1694
Entered Swedish Service 1700 (PMM)
HENDRIE, John
L 1 June 1801
CR 16 July 1810
d 9 June 1811 (PRO)
HENDRY, William
L 11 July 1801
CR 27 Apr 1814
CA 19 July 1822 (NMM)
Ret CA 31 Oct 1846 (LG)
Ret RA 8 Oct 1852 (NMM)
d 6 Sept 1857 (NMM)
HENERY, Thomas
L 11 June 1774
CR 1777 (PJP)
d 1779 (NMM)
HENKY, Sir Robert
L 4 Apr 1720
CR 3 July 1739 (NMM)
d 1740 (NMM)

HENLEY, Charles
L 27 July 1745
d 1759 (NMM)

HENLEY, Daniel
L 13 July 1809
d 1811 (NMM)

HENLEY, Francis
L 3 Mar 1815
d 1838 (PRO)

HENN, Richard
L 2 Mar 1815
Ret CR 13 Nov 1862 (NMM)
d 1864 (NMM)

HENNAH, William
L 23 May 1793
CR
T
CA 1 Jan 1806
CB 1815 (TR)
d 22 Feb 1815 (PJP)

HENNIKER, Augustus Bridges
L 1 Feb 1815
Resigned 5 Dec 1820 (NMM)

HENNIKER, Hon. Major Jacob
L 23 July 1799
CR 29 Apr 1802
CA 22 Jan 1806
RAB 17 Aug 1838 (LG)
RAW 23 Nov 1841 (LG)
d 10 June 1845 (PRO)

HENNING, Alexander
L 11 Sept 1815
Ret CR 14 Apr 1864 (NMM)
d 1871 (NMM)

HENRY, Alphonso
L 30 June 1812
CR 1 Jan 1859 (NMM)
d 1862 (NMM)

HENRY, Frederick, Duke of Cumberland
See CUMBERLAND, Henry Frederick, Duke

HENRY, Henry Burnet
L 17 Aug 1801 (NMM)
Dismissed 1808 (NMM)

HENRY, John
L 27 Apr 1757
CR 16 Apr 1777
CA 22 Nov 1777
RAB 23 Oct 1794
RAR 1 June 1795
VAW 14 Feb 1799
VAR 1 Jan 1801
AB 23 Apr 1804
AW 28 Apr 1808
AR 12 Aug 1812
d 6 Aug 1829 (NMM)

HENRY, Thomas
See HENERY, Thomas

HENRY, William
L 13 June 1815
Ret CR 1 Oct 1860 (NMM)
d 1867 (NMM)

HENRYSON, William
L 15 May 1780
CR 1 Jan 1801
CA 29 Apr 1802
d 19 July 1820 (PRO)

HENSHAW, John
L 1 Apr 1758
CR 24 May 1762
d 1780 (NMM)

HENSLEY, Charles
L 20 Oct 1813
Ret CR 15 Apr 1856 (NMM)
d 1875 (NMM)

HENVEY, William
L 3 Mar 1815
CR 17Nov 1826 (NMM)
d 14 Apr 1842 (NMM)

HENVILL, Constantine Phipps
L 22 Dec 1796
d 1802 (PRO)

HEPENSTALL, William
L 17 Sept 1794
T
CR 29 July 1806
d 20 Jan 1809 (PRO)

HEPPEL, William
L 31 Jan 1795 (PRO)
Ret CR 26 Nov 1830 (PRO)
d 1836 (NMM)

HERBERT, Arthur, Earl of Torrington
L 1666
CA 1666
VAD 15 Feb 1678
AD 17 July 1680
COM AD 22 Aug 1683–
19 May 1684 (AO)
MP (Dover) 1685 (MPH)
CF 12 May 1686 (EAD)
In Dutch Service Oct–Nov 1688 (MPH)
MP
(Plymouth) 17 Jan 1689–
29 May 1689 (MPH)
FLA 8 Mar 1689–
20 Jan 1690 (AO)
AF 15 Mar 1689
Cre EP 29 May 1689 (MPH)
CFMR 16 Jan 1690 (EAD)
d 14 Apr 1716 (EAD)

HERBERT, Charles (1)
L 1671
CA 1664
d before 1689 (PJP)

HERBERT, Charles (2)
L 5 Sept 1761
CR 3 July 1765
CA 26 May 1768
MP (Wilton) 1775–1780 (MPT)
Quitted the Navy 1776 (NMM)
MP (Wilton) 1807–5 Sept 1816 (MPT)
d 5 Sept 1816 (MPT)

HERBERT, Hon. Charles (3)
L 15 Apr 1793
CR 24 July 1794
CA 6 Apr 1795
MP (Wilton) 24 Feb 1806–1807 (MPT)
d 12 Sept 1808 (MPT)

HERBERT, Charles (4)
L 4 May 1795

CR	26 Sept	1797
d		1809 (PRO)
HERBERT, Edward (1)		
L		1691 (PMM)
HERBERT, Edward (2)		
L	11 Jan	1728
CR		
CA	5 Mar	1741
d	19 Nov	1752
HERBERT, Edward (3)		
L	22 Sept	1779
CR	14 May	1781
CA	5 Jan	1783
SUP	23 Apr	1804
d	May	1820 (NMM)
HERBERT, George Flower		
T		
L	16 May	1811
HP	Oct	1818–
	Apr	1820 (OB)
CR	7 July	1828 (NMM)
HP	Aug	1840 (OB)
CA	16 Feb	1852 (NMM)
Ret RA	1 July	1867 (NMM)
d	22 Nov	1868 (NMM)
HERBERT, Henry		
L	17 Mar	1718
d		1740 (PRO)
HERBERT, James		
L		
CR		
CA	30 Sept	1709
Gone		1718 (NMM)
HERBERT, Massy Hutchinson		
L	19 Oct	1807
CR	12 Aug	1819 (NMM)
d		1836 (NMM)
HERBERT, Richard		
L	27 Jan	1720
CR	16 May	1729
CA	20 Nov	1733
d	26 Dec	1740
HERBERT, Robert Hutchinson		
L	16 Feb	1815
d		1832 (NMM)
HERBERT, Thomas (1)		
L	21 Feb	1759
d		1785 (NMM)
HERBERT, Thomas (2)		
L	13 July	1765
d	July	1793 (NMM)
HERBERT, Sir Thomas (3)		
L	10 Oct	1809
CR	19 Oct	1814 (PRO)
HP	Feb	1815–
	6 Sept	1821 (OB)
CA	25 Nov	1822 (PRO)
KCB	14 Oct	1841 (OB)
COM AD	2 Mar	1852–
	5 Jan	1853 (DNB)
RAB	26 Oct	1852 (NMM)
MP		
(Dartmouth)		1852–1857 (DNB)
RAW	13 July	1854 (NMM)
RAR	31 Jan	1856 (NMM)
VAB	8 Dec	1858 (NMM)
VAW	18 Dec	1858 (NMM)
d	4 Aug	1861 (NMM)
HERBERT, William		
L	2 Mar	1795
d	June	1798
HERDMAN, Mungo		
L		1705 (PRO)
CR		
CA	1 Jan	1713
d	8 Mar	1728 (H)
HERGEST, Richard		
L	22 Dec	1780
KIA	10 May	1793 (LTE)
HERITAGE, William		
L	5 Dec	1796
Ret CR	26 Nov	1830 (PRO)
d		1844 (NMM)
HERNE, Hanover		
L	3 July	1739
d		1754 (NMM)
HERNE, John		
L		
CA	21 July	1693
d	25 Sept	1705
HERON, Benjamin		
L	3 Oct	1743
d		1771 (NMM)
HERON, Edward		
L	22 Sept	1806
d		1836 (NMM)
HERON, Sir Harry		
L	2 Jan	1762
CR	1 Dec	1777
CA	23 Mar	1782
SUP	23 Apr	1804
d	June	1817 (NMM)
HERON, Patrick		
L	13 Sept	1796
d		1797 (NMM)
HERON, Samuel		
L	24 Mar	1809
d		1840 (NMM)
HERON, William		
L	5 Dec	1760
d		1764 (PRO)
HERRICK, Edward		
T		
L	3 Feb	1815
HP	June	1846 (OB)
CR	5 Mar	1849 (NMM)
CA	16 Apr	1855 (NMM)
Ret CA	1 Aug	1860 (NMM)
d	14 June	1862 (PMM)
HERRICK, William Henry		
L	5 Feb	1806 (PJP)
CR	17 Aug	1813 (PJP)
Ret CA	17 Feb	1849 (NMM)
d		1863 (NMM)
HERRING, John		
L	29 June	1692 (PMM)
HERRING, Samuel Bartholomew		
L	1 Sept	1796

CR 7 May 1802
d 1803 (LT)

HERRINGHAM, William Allan
T wounded
L 2 Nov 1810
CR 16 Jan 1818 (NMM)
CA 10 Jan 1837 (NMM)
Ret CA 1 July 1851 (NMM)
Ret RA 14 May 1857 (NMM)
Ret VA 14 Nov 1862 (NMM)
d 27 Dec 1865 (NMM)

HERRIOTT, William
L 12 Oct 1695
CR
CA 14 Nov 1704
d 1735

HERVEY, Augustus John, Earl of Bristol
L 31 Oct 1740
CR 16 Sept 1746 (NMM)
CA 15 Jan 1747
MP (Bury St. Edmunds) 26 May 1757– Feb 1763 (MPN)
CRM 21 Oct 1762 (AL)
MP (Saltash) 1763–1768 (MPN)
MP (Bury St. Edmunds) 1768– 18 Mar 1775 (MPN)
COM AD 2 Feb 1771– 12 Apr 1775 (AO)
Cre EP 18 Mar 1775 (DNB)
RAB 31 Mar 1775
RAW 28 Apr 1777
RAR 23 Jan 1778
VAB 29 Jan 1778
d 23 Dec 1779 (MPN)

HERVEY, John Augustus, Lord
L
CR
CA 15 Mar 1780
d 10 Jan 1796 (NMM)

HERVEY, Pynsent
L 3 Jan 1749
d 1778 (NMM)

HERVEY, Hon. William (1)
L 31 Dec 1718 (PJP)
CR 1 Feb 1726 (NMM)
CA 2 June 1727
Dismissed 19 Aug 1742
d 6 July 1771 (NMM)

HERVEY, William (2)
L 28 July 1796
d 1810 (NMM)

HESKETH, Robert
L 30 Jan 1781
d 1796 (NMM)

HESKETT, John
L 6 June 1696

HESLEDEN, James
L 28 Apr 1807
d 23 Dec 1825 (NMM)

HESLOP, John
L 25 Jan 1800
d 1811 (NMM)

HESLOPP, Robert
L 10 June 1756
d 1758 (NMM)

HESSEY, George
L 16 Aug 1805
Ret CR 17 Jan 1838 (NMM)
d 3 Nov 1841 (NMM)

HETHERINGTON, Richard
L 8 Nov 1810
HP Aug 1814 (OB)
Ret CR 14 July 1851 (NMM)
d 1859 (NMM)

HEWES, Thomas Oldacres
L 15 Oct 1800
CR 1 Aug 1811
Ret CR 10 Feb 1842 (NMM)
d 14 Jan 1872 (NMM)

HEWETT, James (1)
L 29 Oct 1778
CR 2 Oct 1782
d 1 July 1798

HEWETT, James (2)
L 8 Mar 1805
Ret CR 18 Apr 1843 (NMM)
d 1871 (NMM)

HEWETT, John
L 11 June 1779
SUP CR 31 Jan 1814
d 9 Feb 1827 (PRO)

HEWETT, Matthew Thomas
L 2 Apr 1781
Dismissed 1802 (NMM)
d 1802 (PRO)

HEWETT, Samuel
L 13 Aug 1697 (PMM)

HEWETT, Thomas
L 9 Mar 1815
d 1839 (NMM)

HEWETT, William (1)
L 12 Sept 1695
CR 16 Mar 1708 (PMM)
Gone 1719 (NMM)

HEWETT, William (2)
L 7 Sept 1727
CR July 1740 (PJP)
CA 24 Nov 1740
d 22 May 1749

HEWETT, William (3)
L 17 Dec 1745
CR 25 Feb 1756
CA 10 Jan 1759
d (drowned) 1 Jan 1764 (CH)

HEWETT, William (4)
L 7 Nov 1806
d 1816 (PRO)

HEWETT, William (5)
L 10 Sept 1814
CR 8 Nov 1826 (NMM)
CA 10 Jan 1837 (NMM)
d 16 Feb 1845 (OB)

HEWETT, William (6)
L 1 Apr 1815
d (drowned) 13 Nov 1840 (CH)

HEWETT, William
See HEWITT, William
HEWIT, James
L 19 May 1798
d 1803 (NMM)
HEWITT, Charles
L 8 Oct 1793
CR 1 Feb 1812
CA 7 June 1814
d 1834 (NMM)
HEWITT, John
L
CA 1666 (PMM)
HEWITT, Thomas
L 7 May 1805
d 1807(8) (PJP)
HEWITT, William
See CAMPBELL, Archibald
HEWSON, George
L 16 Mar 1795
T
CR 13 Oct 1807
CA 1 Jan 1817 (NMM)
Ret CA 31 Oct 1846 (LG)
Ret RA 16 June 1851 (NMM)
Ret VA 30 July 1857 (NMM)
d 5 Sept 1870 (PRO)
HEWSON, Maurice
L 11 Apr 1809 (OB)
Ret CR 4 Apr 1848 (NMM)
d 1870 (NMM)
HEWSON, Thomas
L 22 Feb 1771
d 1778 (PRO)
HEXT, George
L 31 Aug 1810
d 23 July 1813 (PRO)
HEXT, William
L 8 Aug 1799
CR 28 Apr 1809
HP Sept 1814 (OB)
CA 23 Nov 1841 (LG)
Ret CA 7 Jan 1854 (NMM)
Ret RA 12 Apr 1862 (NMM)
d 1866 (NMM)
HEXTER, Robert Henry
L 9 May 1797
d 1811 (NMM)
HEYLAND, James
L 19 July 1814
HP 19 July 1814 (OB)
Ret CR 15 Feb 1858 (NMM)
d 1863 (NMM)
HEYMAN, Henry
L 20 Dec 1811
d 1818 (PRO)
HEYWOOD, Charles George
L 13 Feb 1777
CR 8 Oct 1779
d 1780 (NMM)
HEYWOOD, Edmund
L 27 Jan 1797
CR 29 Apr 1802
CA 22 Jan 1806
CB 4 June 1815 (LG)
d 25 Mar 1822 (NMM)
HEYWOOD, Peter (1)
L 13 Oct 1673
CA 12 Apr 1678
d 1725 (DDA)
HEYWOOD, Peter (2)
L 9 Mar 1795 (PJP)
CR Aug 1800 (MB)
CA 5 Apr 1803
d 10 Feb 1831 (NMM)
HIATT, Henry
T
L 4 May 1810
d 1815 (PRO)
HIATT, John
L 29 Apr 1802
Ret CR 25 Jan 1834 (NMM)
d 11 Feb 1853 (NMM)
HIBBS, Robert
L 5 Sept 1777
SUP CR 18 Feb 1811
d 1814 (NMM)
HIBBS, Robert John
L 29 Dec 1796
HP Dec 1813 (OB)
d 1859 (NMM)
HIBBS, William
L 28 Mar 1797
d Nov 1798
HICHENS, Robert Manning
L 28 Sept 1778
CR 13 Feb 1781
CA 25 Oct 1809
d 1812 (PRO)
HICHENS, Thomas Cuthbert
L 22 Feb 1806
CR 26 Aug 1808
CA 7 Nov 1814
d 1825 (MB)
HICKES, Augustus Thomas
T
L 8 Mar 1811
HP Mar 1819 (OB)
Ret CR 1 Oct 1851 (NMM)
d 22 Oct 1857 (NMM)
HICKES, Edward
L
CR
CA 18 Mar 1705
d 25 Sept 1708
HICKES, Jasper
See HICKS, Jasper
HICKES, John
L 10 June 1746
CR 10 Aug 1759
d 1763 (PRO)
HICKES, Zachary
L 26 May 1768
d 26 May 1771 (PMM)
HICKEY, Benjamin
L 24 Nov 1780
d 1816 (PRO)

HICKEY, Frederick
L 30 Oct 1794
CR 22 Jan 1806
CA 19 Feb 1814 (PJP)
d 18 May 1840 (PRO)

HICKMAN, John
L 21 Nov 1812
HP 1846 (OB)
d 1862 (PRO)

HICKMAN, Josiah (or Joseph)
L
CA 14 Dec 1695
d 12 June 1701

HICKMAN, John Collman
L 4 Aug 1806
CR 1 Sept 1817 (NMM)
d 25 Oct 1827 (NMM)

HICKMAN, Stephen William
L 14 Feb 1794
d (suicide) Oct 1799 (PJP)

HICKS, Augustus Thomas
See HICKES, Augustus Thomas

HICKS, Edmund
L 6 Jan 1697
CR
CA 18 Mar 1705 (PJP)
d 25 Sept 1708 (PJP)

HICKS, Edward Buller
L 2 Dec 1812
d 9 Feb 1845 (OB)

HICKS, Henry
L 5 Feb 1780
Dismissed 1802 (NMM)
d 21 Sept 1804 (NMM)

HICKS, Jasper ?HICKS, J.
L
CA 30 May 1689
(30 May 1689 in C)
d 1714

HICKS, John
L 21 Feb 1815
Ret CR 21 Oct 1861 (NMM)
d 13 May 1864 (NMM)

HICKS, Thomas
L 3 May 1758
CR 13 May 1778
CA 10 Nov 1781
RAB 1 Jan 1801
d 9 May 1801

HICKS, Thomas Bickerton Ashton
L 7 Apr 1795
CR 2 Nov 1807
d 5 Dec 1809 (PJP)

HICKS, William (1)
L 27 Mar 1794
d 1798 (NMM)

HICKS, William (2)
L 15 Nov 1798
d 1803 (PRO)

HICKS, William (3)
T wounded
L 30 Jan 1813
Took Holy Orders 1830 (TR)
d 1874 (TR)

HICKS, William (4)
L 15 Mar 1815
d 1848 (NMM)

HICKSON, Thomas
L 20 Feb 1798
d 1798 (NMM)

HICKSON, William
L 28 Dec 1694 (PMM)
d 10 Dec 1695 (PMM)

HIDE, Henry
L 1662
CA 1664
d before 1689 (PJP)

HIDE, Hugh
L
CA 1661
d before 1689 (PJP)

HIDE, James
L 11 Apr 1682
d (drowned) 6 May 1682 (PJP)

HIDE, Jonathan
L
CA 1666

HIGGINS, John
T
L 24 Dec 1805
d 1810 (PRO)

HIGGINS, Thomas
L 3 June 1814
CR 7 Mar 1853 (NMM)
d 1872 (NMM)

HIGGINSON, George Montagu
L 1 Sept 1795
Ret CR 17 Jan 1831 (NMM)
d 1856 (NMM)

HIGGINSON, James
L 5 Aug 1779
d 1813 (PRO)

HIGGINSON, Samuel
L
CA 1660
d before 1689 (PJP)

HIGGS, George
L 11 Nov 1793
d 1809 (NMM)

HIGGS, John
L 22 Jan 1799
d 1799 (PRO)

HIGGS, Richard
L 10 Oct 1743
CR 20 July 1757
d 22 Aug 1782

HIGGS, William Henry
L 7 May 1804
CR 11 Oct 1819 (NMM)
CA 9 Nov 1846 (LG)
Ret CA 9 Jan 1857 (NMM)
d 20 Mar 1863 (NMM)

HIGMAN, Henry
L 3 Sept 1803

CR	23 Feb	1807
CA	1 Jan	1817 (NMM)
Ret CA	31 Oct	1846 (LG)
Ret RA	16 June	1851 (NMM)
Ret VA	30 July	1857 (NMM)
d	19 Aug	1858 (NMM)
HILGROVE, James		
L	5 Apr	1758
SUP CR	2 May	1799
d		1814 (PRO)
HILL, Basil		
L	10 June	1808 (MB)
CR	25 Feb	1814 (MB)
CA	5 Nov	1817 (MB)
HILL, Benjamin		
L	31 Mar	1760
CR	18 Mar	1777
CA	28 Jan	1778
d	9 Sept	1785 (M)
HILL, Caleb		
L	21 June	1780
CR	29 Apr	1802
d		1803 (PRO)
HILL, Charles (1)		
L	27 Jan	1807
d		1813 (NMM)
HILL, Charles (2)		
L	6 Feb	1815
Ret CR	9 Feb	1860 (NMM)
d		1868 (NMM)
HILL, Christopher		
L	17 Mar	1740
CR	29 Jan	1746 (NMM)
CA	5 Dec	1747
RAB	23 Jan	1778
RAW	29 Jan	1778
d	4 July	1778 (CH)
HILL, Edward (1)		
L	5 Mar	1756
SUP CR	21 Sept	1796
d		1814 (PRO)
HILL, Edward (2)		
L	11 Feb	1815
Ret CR	23 July	1860 (NMM)
d		1864 (NMM)
HILL, Frederick Carne		
L	12 Oct	1814
d		1835 (NMM)
HILL, George (1)		
L	25 June	1739
SUP CR		1754 (PMM)
d		1755 (NMM)
HILL, George (2)		
L	26 Apr	1779
d		1794 (PRO)
HILL, George (3)		
L	10 May	1811
d	7 Aug	1830 (PRO)
HILL, Henry (1)		
L	17 Dec	1793
CR	24 July	1795
CA	1 Jan	1801
HP	Mar	1808–
	Sept	1809 (OB)
RAB	22 July	1830 (LG)
RAR	10 Jan	1837 (LG)
VAB	23 Nov	1841 (CH)
VAW	9 Nov	1846 (LG)
VAR	24 Apr	1847 (LG)
d	7 June	1849 (CH)
HILL, Henry (2)		
L	10 May	1797
d		1800 (NMM)
HILL, Henry (3)		
L	28 Feb	1815
d		1834 (PRO)
HILL, James		
L	1 Mar	1759
d		1784 (PRO)
HILL, John (1)		
L	18 Apr	1735
CR	3 Aug	1744
CA	26 Aug	1745
SUP RA		1770
d	8 Mar	1773
HILL, Sir John (2)		
L	28 July	1794
CR	8 Oct	1798
CA	28 Oct	1815
Kt	31 Aug	1831 (OB)
RAB	2 Apr	1851 (NMM)
RAW	28 May	1853 (NMM)
d	20 Jan	1855 (NMM)
HILL, John (3)		
L	14 May	1797
d		1802 (NMM)
HILL, John (4)		
L	4 May	1810
HP	May	1842 (OB)
d		1857 (PRO)
HILL, John (5)		
L	7 Feb	1815
d		1859 (PRO)
HILL, Lionel (1)		
L	31 Jan	1759
Dismissed	6 July	1771 (PJP)
d		1771 (PRO)
HILL, Lionel (2)		
L	1 Sept	1780
d		1800 (NMM)
HILL, Lionel (3)		
L	1 May	1794
d		1798 (PRO)
HILL, Lionel (4)		
L	13 Aug	1798
d	2 Apr	1801 (PRO)
HILL, LITTLETON		
L	9 Nov	1742
d		1753 (NMM)
HILL, Marcus Samuel		
L	17 July	1793
CR	19 Nov	1799
CA	14 Apr	1802
d	2 July	1834 (NMM)
HILL, Mordaunt		
L	19 Oct	1809
d		1838 (PRO)

HILL, Nicholas
L
CA 1665
d before 1689 (PJP)
HILL, Peter
L 27 Dec 1777
SUP CR 12 Apr 1813
d 1819 (PRO)
HILL, Raymond
L 19 Mar 1694 (PMM)
HILL, Richard (1)
L 30 Apr 1678
d before 1689 (PJP)
HILL, Richard (2)
L 14 Aug 1778
CR 15 Aug 1781
CA 21 Oct 1795
d 1799 (PRO)
HILL, Samuel (1)
L 26 Mar 1704
d 1734 (PRO)
HILL, Samuel (2)
L 16 Jan 1741
d 1742 (NMM)
HILL, Samuel (3)
L 20 Nov 1812
HP 1813 (OB)
Ret CR 2 July 1855 (NMM)
d 9 Aug 1864 (NMM)
HILL, Thomas (1)
L 2 Mar 1734
CR 23 Nov 1744
d 1765 (PRO)
HILL, Thomas (2)
L 8 Nov 1760
d 20 Dec 1789
HILL, Thomas (3)
L 2 Jan 1794
CR 15 Jan 1802
d 1837 (NMM)
HILL, Thomas (4)
L 17 June 1811
d 22 Oct 1839 (NMM)
HILL, Thomas (5)
L 13 Mar 1815
d 12 May 1825 (NMM)
HILL, Thomas (6)
L 21 Mar 1815
d 22 Oct 1839 (NMM)
HILL, Walter
See COYNEY, Walter Hill
HILL, William (1)
L
CA 1661
d before 1688 (PD)
HILL, William (2)
L 26 May 1795
Dismissed 8 Apr 1802 (PJP)
HILL, William (3)
L 11 Apr 1803
T
CR 6 Apr 1809
CA 12 Dec 1816 (MB)
d 4 Jan 1840 (NMM)
HILLDRUP, John
L 21 Sept 1815
d 1858 (NMM)
HILLIER, Curry William
L 8 Oct 1801
CR 7 June 1814
Ret CA 1 July 1851 (NMM)
d 28 June 1857 (NMM)
HILLIER, George
L 16 Jan 1798
CR 21 Jan 1821 (PJP)
Ret CA 4 Mar 1863 (NMM)
d 14 June 1865 (NMM)
HILLS, Alexander
T
L 18 Jan 1805
d 1809 (PRO)
HILLS, Archibald Beer
L 15 Nov 1795
d 29 Apr 1804 (PRO)
HILLS, Charles
L 29 Mar 1809
d 14 Feb 1824 (NMM)
HILLS, George
L 17 July 1798
CR 20 Apr 1808
CA 7 June 1814
Ret CA 31 Oct 1846 (LG)
Ret RA 9 Oct 1849 (NMM)
d 4 Apr 1850 (NMM)
HILLS, James
L 23 Nov 1778 (NMM)
CR 14 Feb 1797
d 1804 (NMM)
HILLS, John
L 26 May 1768
CR 4 Oct 1781
CA 1 Dec 1787
d 24 Aug 1794 (NMM)
HILLS, Safry
L 30 May 1777
CR 28 Oct 1781
d 1784 (NMM)
HILLS, Thomas
L 7 Nov 1806
Ret CR 18 Nov 1848 (NMM)
d 1852 (NMM)
HILLS, William (1)
L 21 Sept 1759
d 23 Dec 1777 (NMM)
HILLS, William (2)
L 22 Nov 1790
CR 18 Feb 1797
CA 8 Jan 1798
d 2 Apr 1804
HILLYAR, Sir James
L 8 Mar 1794
CR 16 Apr 1800
CA 29 Feb 1804
CB 4 June 1815 (LG)
KCH 1 Jan 1834 (OB)

RAB	10 Jan	1837 (LG)
RAW	28 June	1838 (LG)
KCB	4 July	1840 (OB)
d	10 July	1843 (CH)
HILLYAR, William		
L	27 Aug	1803
CR	27 Aug	1814
CA	20 Jan	1836 (NMM)
RA	19 Mar	1857 (NMM)
VA	24 Sept	1863 (NMM)
d	11 July	1867 (NMM)
HILSLEY, Francis		
L		
CA	10 Jan	1693
d	2 May	1693
HILSON, George		
L		
CA	6 Sept	1666 (RM)
HILTON, George		
L	29 June	1801
CR	7 June	1814
Ret CA	1 July	1851 (NMM)
d		1877 (NMM)
HILTON, John		
L	15 Aug	1806
Kt (Two Sicilies)	23 Sept	1811 (LG)
CR	15 June	1814
Ret CA	1 July	1851 (NMM)
d	6 Dec	1854 (NMM)
HILTON, Stephen		
T		
L	22 Jan	1806
HP	28 Feb	1817 (OB)
Ret CR	7 Jan	1839 (OB)
d	Mar	1872 (NMM)
HINCKLEY, John		
L	28 Mar	1777
d		1784 (NMM)
HINDE, Benjamin		
L	29 May	1705 (PMM)
HINDE, Richard		
L	14 Jan	1744
d		1760 (NMM)
HINDMAN, Michael		
L	27 Oct	1761
CR		1777 (PJP)
d	1 May	1791
HINDMARSH, Sir John		
L	1 Aug	1803
T		
CR	15 June	1814
CA	3 Sept	1831 (NMM)
KH	4 May	1836 (OB)
Kt		1851 (TR)
RA	31 Jan	1856 (NMM)
d	29 July	1860 (NMM)
HINTON, John		
L	18 Nov	1790
d		1816 (PRO)
HINTON, Martin		
L	28 May	1779
CR	8 Feb	1796
d	28 Oct	1814 (PJP)
HINTON, Richard		
L	19 May	1693 (PMM)
HINTON, Thomas Eyre		
L	8 Jan	1783
d	13 July	1829 (PRO)
HINXMAN, John		
L	6 Feb	1742
CR	30 Jan	1759
d	7 Mar	1764 (M)
HIPPIUS, Thomas		
L	5 Apr	1814
d	19 Nov	1830 (LT)
HIRD, William		
L	13 Jan	1796
CR	29 July	1814
d	3 Oct	1836 (PJP)
HIRE, Frederick		
L	11 Feb	1815
d		1846 (OB)
HIRE, George		
L	14 Apr	1779
d		1804 (PRO)
HIRE, George Augustus		
L	9 Dec	1794
CR	1 Aug	1811
CA	27 May	1825 (PJP)
d	9 Mar	1831 (MB)
HIRE, Henry		
L	16 Oct	1808
d		1853 (PRO)
HITCHCOCK, George		
L	15 Feb	1707 (PMM)
HITCHCOCK, Thomas		
L	30 Mar	1779
d		1786 (PRO)
HITCHENS, Joseph		
L	4 Nov	1803 (OB)
Ret CR	4 May	1836 (OB)
HITCHINS, Charles Benjamin		
L	7 June	1809
d (drowned)	25 Dec	1811 (PJP)
HITCHINS, Joseph		
L	4 Nov	1803
d		1805 (PRO)
HITT, John Dunning		
L	5 Apr	1797
d	3 Mar	1801
HOAD, George		
L	15 Dec	1796
d	2 Aug	1801
HOAR, Balch Nun		
L	15 Apr	1803
HOAR, Thomas q.v. See BERTIE, Thomas		
HOARE, Abraham		
L	30 Apr	1678
HOARE, Edward Wallis		
L	4 Aug	1796
CR	25 Oct	1804
CA	16 Oct	1810
HP	13 Aug	1812 (OB)
RAB	13 May	1847 (LG)
RAW	21 May	1849 (LG)
VA	27 May	1854 (PJP)

HOARE, Nicholas		
L	25 Feb	1780
d	13 Oct	1806 (PMM)
HOARE, Richard		
L	13 Nov	1813
CR	19 July	1822 (NMM)
CA	7 July	1827 (NMM)
Ret CA	July	1847 (NMM)
d	6 Dec	1850 (NMM)
HOARE, Thomas		
See BERTIE, Thomas		
HOBART, Charles		
L	7 Nov	1809
CR	2 Dec	1812
d	20 July	1813 (PRO)
HOBART, Henry		
L	13 Aug	1692
CR		
CA	8 June	1703
d		1711
HOBBLETHWAITE, Edward St. Quinton		
L	4 Nov	1790
d		1797 (NMM)
HOBBS, James		
L	16 Jan	1741
CR		
CA	19 May	1756
d	14 May	1770
HOBBS, John		
T		
L	7 Feb	1806
d	12 May	1826 (LT)
HOBBS, Robert		
L	20 Feb	1693
HOBBS, William (1)		
L		
CA		1671
HOBBS, William (2)		
L	2 Aug	1781
d		1799 (NMM)
HOBBS, William (3)		
L	15 July	1799
KIA	9 May	1801 (PJP)
HOBSON, William		
L	11 Nov	1813
CR	18 Mar	1824 (NMM)
CA	9 July	1828 (NMM)
d	10 Sept	1842 (PMM)
HOCKADAY, William		
L		
CR	20 Feb	1694 (PJP)
CA	20 Feb	1696 (PJP)
d	23 Oct	1724 (PJP)
HOCKIN, Henry		
L	17 Feb	1815
HP		1841 (OB)
Ret CR	20 Apr	1861 (NMM)
d		1869 (NMM)
HOCKINGS, Robert		
L	10 June	1797
CR	11 Apr	1809 (MB)
CA	19 July	1821 (NMM)
Ret CA	31 Oct	1846 (LG)
d	13 Oct	1849 (NMM)
HODDER, Edward (1)		
L	14 Oct	1756
d		1762 (PRO)
HODDER, Edward (2)		
L	5 Feb	1794
CR	27 Apr	1801
CA	27 June	1814
d	27 Jan	1829 (NMM)
HODDER, Michael		
L	18 Feb	1815
Ret CR	15 July	1861 (NMM)
d		1868 (NMM)
HODDER, Peter		
L	21 Mar	1812
HP		1815 (OB)
Ret CR	18 Apr	1854 (NMM)
d		1859 (NMM)
HODDER, Richard		
L		1664
CA	23 Apr	1677
d	10 May	1686 (PRO)
HODGE, Andrew		
L	21 Jan	1800
CR	4 Dec	1807 (NMM)
Ret CA	10 Sept	1840 (NMM)
d		1844 (NMM)
HODGE, Edward		
L	29 Dec	1796
d	26 July	1807 (PMM)
HODGE, James Edward		
L	30 July	1799
d		1808 (PRO)
HODGE, John		
L	4 May	1693 (PMM)
HODGE, Nicholas		
L	27 Aug	1800
d		1814 (NMM)
HODGE, Stephen		
L	16 Feb	1813
CR	5 Jan	1846 (NMM)
HP	5 Jan	1846 (OB)
CA	12 Mar	1859 (NMM)
Ret CA	14 Sept	1871 (NMM)
d	Mar	1876 (NMM)
HODGE, William		
L	2 Sept	1799
d	Dec	1826 (NMM)
HODGES, John		
L	8 Sept	1744
CR	21 Oct	1756
d		1772 (NMM)
HODGES, Richard		
L		
CA		1660
d	before	1689 (PJP)
HODGES, Richard Thomas		
L	22 Jan	1806
HODGES, Samuel		
L	2 May	1678 (PJP)
d	before	1689 (PJP)
HODGES, Thomas		
L	18 July	1812
d (drowned)	May	1832 (CH)

HODGKIN, Joseph Spearman		
L	30 Apr	1810
d		1833 (NMM)
HODGSKIN, John Arundell		
L	27 Nov	1793
d	28 Apr	1827 (NMM)
HODGSKINS, Thomas		
L	25 Sept	1806
Forfeited two years srty		1812
L	25 Sept	1808
HP	25 Apr	1812 (OB)
Ret CR	27 Jan	1846 (OB)
d		1869 (NMM)
HODGSON, Brian		
L	11 Dec	1799
CR	8 Apr	1805
CA	22 Jan	1806
RAB	28 June	1828 (LG)
RAW	23 Nov	1841 (LG)
RAR	8 Mar	1847 (LG)
VAB	19 Oct	1849 (LG)
VAW	1 July	1851 (NMM)
VA	22 Apr	1853 (NMM)
d	6 Feb	1855 (NMM)
HODGSON, Connolly		
L	23 Feb	1757
d		1776 (NMM)
HODGSON, James		
L	11 Apr	1799
Ret CR	8 May	1843 (NMM)
d	4 May	1848 (NMM)
HODGSON, Theophilus		
L		
CA	16 Mar	1695
d	6 May	1695
HODGSON, Thomas		
L		
CA	4 Dec	1694 (PJP)
HODSAL, John		
L	27 July	1697 (PMM)
HODSOLL, James (1)		
L	1 Nov	1697 (PMM)
CR	26 Dec	1707 (PMM)
HODSOLL, James (2)		
L	5 Nov	1723
CR		1741 (PJP)
CA	24 July	1742
d	6 Apr	1754
HOEY, William Parsons		
L	14 Apr	1756
SUP CR	21 Sept	1796
HOFFMAN, Frederick		
L	17 Oct	1799
T	wounded	
CR	22 Feb	1808
Ret CA	12 Sept	1840 (NMM)
d		1849 (TR)
HOGAN, John		
L	17 Dec	1695 (PMM)
HOGG, David		
L	20 Apr	1741
d		1742 (NMM)
HOGG, John		
L	19 Apr	1694 (PMM)
HOGGAN, William		
L	16 June	1781
d		1807 (PRO)
HOGHTON, Henry		
L	4 May	1810
CR	9 Aug	1829 (NMM)
d	15 Nov	1835 (LT)
HOGHTON, William		
L	24 Feb	1815 (OB)
Ret CR	25 Aug	1862 (NMM)
d		1863 (NMM)
HOLBECH, George		
L	16 June	1814
CR	22 July	1830 (NMM)
Ret CA	1 Apr	1856 (NMM)
d	31 Dec	1856 (NMM)
HOLBOURNE, Francis		
See HOLBURNE, Francis		
HOLBOURNE, Thomas William		
See HOLBURNE, Sir Thomas William		
HOLBROOK, Charles		
L	16 Feb	1815
CR	7 Feb	1842 (NMM)
HP	7 Feb	1842 (OB)
d	5 Dec	1852 (NMM)
HOLBROOK, James		
L	15 Feb	1815
Ret CR	18 Jan	1861 (NMM)
d		1866 (NMM)
HOLBROOK, Thomas		
L	23 Sept	1812
CR	6 May	1828 (NMM)
Ret CA	1 Apr	1856 (NMM)
d	1 Apr	1862 (PRO)
HOLBURNE, Sir Alexander		
L	20 July	1757
CR	6 Apr	1761
CA	1 Feb	1763
d	22 Feb	1772 (PJP)
HOLBURNE, Francis		
L	12 Dec	1757
CR		
CA	15 Feb	1740
RAB	5 Feb	1755 (DNB)
RAR	4 June	1756
VAB	24 Feb	1757 (DNB)
VAW	5 Feb	1758 (CH)
VAR	14 Feb	1759
AB	5 Aug	1767 (DNB)
COM AD	28 Feb	1770–
	2 Feb	1771 (AO)
AW	18 Oct	1770 (CH)
GGH	Jan–15 July	1771 (DNB)
d	15 July	1771 (DNB)
HOLBURNE, James		
L	7 July	1745
d		1756 (NMM)
HOLBURNE, Sir Thomas William		
T		
L	5 Feb	1813
Inh Bt	13 Sept	1820 (OB)
d		1874 (TR)
HOBURNE, William		
L	15 Nov	1739
CR	21 Apr	1747

CA	15 Apr	1748
d	1 Apr	1760
HOLCOMBE, Essex		
L	24 May	1730
CR	25 Apr	1740 (NMM)
CA	12 Oct	1740
SUP RA		1755
d	29 Jan	1770
HOLCOMBE, Essex John		
L	7 Jan	1802
T		
d	July	1822 (NMM)
HOLDEN, William (1)		
L		1668
CA		1666
d	20 Sept	1682 (DDA)
HOLDEN, William (2)		
L	25 May	1781
d		1783 (NMM)
HOLDING, William		
L	6 Feb	1694
In Merchant Service	May	1700 (PJP)
HOLDITCH, Abraham		
L		1665
CA		1661
d	before	1689 (PJP)
HOLDSWORTH, Thomas Weston		
L	12 May	1800
d		1808 (NMM)
HOLE, Charles		
L	31 Aug	1807
CR	29 Aug	1812
d	8 Sept	1844 (NMM)
HOLE, Lewis		
L	6 July	1798
T		
CR	24 Dec	1805
CA	4 Dec	1813
Ret RA	31 Oct	1846 (LG)
Ret VA	31 Jan	1856 (NMM)
Ret A	11 Feb	1861 (NMM)
d	16 July	1870 (NMM)
HOLE, Nicholas		
L	2 Sept	1797
d		1801 (NMM)
HOLE, William		
L	3 Feb	1815
CR	7 Mar	1853 (NMM)
d		1875 (NMM)
HOLFORD, John Josiah		
L	7 Nov	1814
d	1 Mar	1831 (NMM)
HOLFORD, Richard		
L	7 Mar	1696
d	16 Sept	1703 (PMM)
HOLGATE, Robert		
T		
L	25 Sept	1806
d		1811 (NMM)
HOLINGBERY, Monins		
L	19 Feb	1777 (PJP)
SUP CR	20 Apr	1810
d	May	1828 (NMM)
HOLL, James		
L	2 July	1760
d		1789 (NMM)
HOLLAMBY, William		
L	31 May	1781
CR	13 Dec	1783
d		1794 (NMM)
HOLLAND, Edward		
L	28 Jan	1696
CR	19 Oct	1704 (PMM)
CA	23 July	1708
d	23 Feb	1725 (M)
HOLLAND, Gilbert		
L		1665
HOLLAND, John		
L		1673
HOLLAND, John Wentworth		
L	19 June	1794
CR	25 Apr	1801
CA	22 Jan	1806
Ret RA	28 June	1838 (NMM)
RAB	17 Aug	1840 (LG)
d	26 Oct	1841 (NMM)
HOLLAND, Ph.		
L		
CA		1666
d	before	1689 (PJP)
HOLLAND, Robert		
L		
CA		1673
HOLLIDAY, Samuel Mark		
L	29 Sept	1795
Ret CR	1 Dec	1830 (PRO)
d	13 Jan	1840 (NMM)
HOLLIMAN, Robert		
L		
CA	8 Feb	1694
KIA	13 Oct	1702 (PJP)
HOLLINGSWORTH, John		
L	27 Aug	1793
KIA	27 Dec	1796 (CH)
HOLLINGWORTH, Thomas		
L	6 Nov	1756
SUP CR	21 Sept	1796 (PMM)
d		1796 (NMM)
HOLLINWORTH, John		
L	10 June	1802
CR	22 Jan	1806
CA	3 Apr	1811
Ret RA	31 Oct	1846 (LG)
Ret VA	11 Sept	1854 (NMM)
Ret A	9 June	1860 (NMM)
d	28 Dec	1861 (NMM)
HOLLIS, Askew Paffard		
L	22 Jan	1781
CR	28 Nov	1796 (CH)
CA	5 Feb	1798
HP		1815–1816 (OB)
CRM	19 July	1821 (LG)
RAB	27 May	1825 (LG)
RAR	22 July	1830 (LG)
VAW	10 Jan	1837 (LG)
VAR	23 Nov	1841 (LG)
d	23 May	1844 (NMM)

HOLLIS, Francis
L 8 Jan 1692
Gone 1719 (PRO)
HOLLIS, Sir Freshville
L
CA 9 June 1666 (RM)
KIA 28 May 1672 (LG)
HOLLOWAY, Henry
L 1 Mar 1695 (PMM)
HOLLOWAY, Hewett
L 6 Feb 1694
Gone 1719 (NMM)
HOLLOWAY, John
L 19 Jan 1771
CR
CA 23 Jan 1780 (MB)
RAW 14 Feb 1799
RAR 1 Jan 1801
VAW 23 Apr 1804
VAR 9 Nov 1805
GG
(Newfoundland) 1807–1810 (BNS)
AB 25 Oct 1809
AW 31 July 1810
AR 12 Aug 1819 (LG)
d 26 June 1826 (PRO)
HOLLOWAY, Richard
L 11 Sept 1793
d 1 Mar 1800
HOLLOWAY, Thomas
L 10 Mar 1812
Ret CR 2 Jan 1854 (NMM)
d 1854 (NMM)
HOLLWALL, John
L 20 Apr 1744
CR 4 Apr 1747
CA 30 June 1753
d 13 July 1775 (PMM)
HOLLWELL, George
L 25 Mar 1794
d 1799 (NMM)
HOLLYMAN, Robert
See HOLLIMAN, Robert
HOLMAN, James
L 27 Apr 1807
d 28 July 1857 (NMM)
HOLMAN, Robert
L 11 Aug 1810
HP 1819 (OB)
Ret CR 13 June 1855 (NMM)
d 1872 (NMM)
HOLMAN, Thomas Holloway
L 6 Feb 1815
CR 15 Jan 1841 (NMM)
Ret CA 1 Apr 1856 (NMM)
d 15 Mar 1866 (NMM)
HOLMAN, William
L 26 Sept 1797
CR 20 Feb 1812
Ret CA 26 Mar 1844 (NMM)
d 19 May 1864 (NMM)
HOLMES, Benjamin
L
CA 14 June 1667 (DDA)

HOLMES, Charles
L 18 June 1734
CR
CA 20 Feb 1742
RAB 6 July 1758 (NMM)
d 21 Nov 1761
HOLMES, James
L 1672
d before 1689 (PJP)
HOLMES, Sir John (1)
L 1665
CA 1664
Kt Apr 1672 (PD)
RAB 14 Aug 1673 (NJ)
CAF 1675 (MPH)
MP
(Newton I.o.W.) 19 Feb 1677–
Mar 1679 (MPH)
RAD 1678
AF 14 Apr 1677
MP
(Newton I.o.W.) Oct 1679–
1681 (MPH)
d 28 May 1683 (MPH)
HOLMES, John (2)
L
CA 1668
d before 1689 (PJP)
HOLMES, John (3)
L 10 Oct 1694 (PMM)
HOLMES, John (4)
L 2 Apr 1781
d 1814 (NMM)
HOLMES, John Henry
L 14 Nov 1794
Ret CR 26 Nov 1830 (PRO)
d 1834 (NMM)
HOLMES, Lancelot
L 26 June 1756
CR 2 June 1760
CA 2 July 1762
d 12 Nov 1785 (PJP)
HOLMES, Meabron
L 14 May 1793
d 1805 (NMM)
HOLMES, Meyrick
L 20 Nov 1790
Resigned 1798 (NMM)
HOLMES, Sir Robert (1)
L
CA July 1660 (MPH)
RAD 1661
Kt 27 Mar 1666 (MPH)
RAR 3 June 1666 (RM)
AD 1667
CAF
(Coldstream Gds) 1667 (EAD)
CAGA
(Isle of Wight) 7 Oct 1669 (EAD)
MP 26 Oct 1669–
(Winchester) Mar 1679 (MPH)
MP
(Newton I.o.W.) Mar 1679–
1685 (MPH)
CAF
(Princess Anne) 1687 (EAD)

MP		
(Yarmouth I.o.W.)		1689 (MPH)
MP		
(Newport I.o.W.)		1690–
	18 Nov	1692 (MPH)
d	18 Nov	1692 (MPH)
HOLMES, Robert (2)		
L		
CA	14 Feb	1694 (PMM)
d	12 July	1697 (PMM)
HOLMES, Smith		
L	18 Mar	1794
d		1805 (NMM)
HOLMES, Thomas		
L	25 Nov	1809
d		1810 (NMM)
HOLMES, Thomas Mills		
L	7 Sept	1795
d		1810 (NMM)
HOLMES, William(1)		
L	16 Mar	1742
CR		
CA	5 Apr	1747
KIA	Sept	1748 (PJP)
HOLMES, William (2)		
L	27 Feb	1812
CR	19 Aug	1815
d (drowned)	12 Dec	1823 (CH)
HOLROYD, Charles		
L	7 Jan	1814
d	Sept	1830 (NMM)
HOLT, William		
L	7 Nov	1810
CR	20 Aug	1824 (NMM)
CA	28 June	1838 (NMM)
RA	10 Sept	1857 (NMM)
d	9 Oct	1859 (NMM)
HOLTON, Frederick		
L	28 June	1756
d		1767
HOLWORTHY, Nicholas Haddock		
L	19 July	1782
SUP CR	2 May	1818 (NMM)
d	4 Feb	1843 (NMM)
HOME, Alexander (1)		
L	18 Dec	1780
SUP CR	22 Dec	1815
d	21 Feb	1823 (NMM)
HOME, Alexander (2)		
L	22 Nov	1790
d		1803 (NMM)
HOME, Alexander Purvis		
L	5 May	1800
d		1808 (NMM)
HOME, George (1)		
L	6 Oct	1758
d		1769 (NMM)
HOME, Sir George (2)		
L	23 Nov	1759
CR	1 Aug	1778 (PJP)
CA	21 July	1779
RAB	20 Feb	1797
RAR	14 Feb	1799
VAB	29 Apr	1802
d	2 May	1803 (CH)
HOME, George (3)		
L	13 Aug	1812
d		1813 (NMM)
HOME, Sir James Everard		
L	14 July	1814 (OB)
CR	28 Jan	1822 (OB)
Inh Bt	31 Aug	1832 (OB)
CA	5 Dec	1837 (OB)
CB	24 Dec	1842 (OB)
HOME, Roddam		
L	21 Nov	1772
CR	19 Apr	1779
CA	6 Nov	1779
RAR	14 Feb	1799
d	13 Feb	1801
HOMER, Robert		
See HEMER, Robert		
HONEY, George John		
See HONY, George John		
HONEYMAN, Robert		
L	21 Oct	1790
CR	13 Aug	1796
CA	10 Dec	1798
MP (Shetland)		1802 (OB)
RAB	27 May	1825 (LG)
RAW	22 July	1830 (LG)
VAB	10 Jan	1837 (LG)
VAR	23 Nov	1841 (LG)
AB	19 Feb	1847 (LG)
d	31 July	1848 (NMM)
HONY, George John		
L	1 May	1804
CR	22 Jan	1806
CA	4 Jan	1808
d		1812 (NMM)
HOOD, Alexander		
L	18 July	1777
CR	17 May	1781
CA	27 July	1781
KIA	21 Apr	1798 (LG)
HOOD, Sir Alexander		
See BRIDPORT, Alexander, Lord		
HOOD, Arthur		
L	3 Aug	1796
d		1799 (NMM)
HOOD, Samuel, Viscount (1)		
L	17 June	1746
HP	Nov	1748 (DNB)
CR	10 May	1754
CA	22 July	1756
COMM		
(Portsmouth)	Jan	1778 (DNB)
Cre Bt	May	1779 (DNB)
RAB	26 Sept	1780
Cre IP	12 Sept	1782 (DNB)
MP		
(Westminster)		1784 (DNB)
VAB	24 Sept	1787
COM AD	16 July	1788–
	7 Mar	1795 (AO)
VAR	1 Feb	1793
AB	12 Apr	1794
Cre EP	1 June	1796 (DNB)

AW	14 Feb	1799
AR	9 Nov	1805
GCB	2 Jan	1815 (LG)
d	27 Jan	1816
HOOD, Sir Samuel (2)		
L	11 Oct	1780
CR	31 Jan	1782
CA	24 May	1788
CRM	15 Aug	1805 (AL)
RAB	2 Oct	1807
Kt		1808 (DNB)
RAW	28 Apr	1808
Cre Bt	1 Apr	1809 (LG)
RAR	31 July	1810
VAB	1 Aug	1811
VAW	4 June	1814
d	27 Dec	1814 (PMM)
HOOD, Silas Thomson		
L	19 Dec	1809
CR	27 Apr	1815
HP	Apr	1816 (OB)
d	26 June	1851 (NMM)
HOOD, William John Thompson		
T		
L	25 Feb	1815
CR	9 Jan	1828 (NMM)
CA	25 Sept	1843 (NMM)
d	18 July	1857 (NMM)
HOOD, William Shaw Arthur See HOOD, Arthur		
HOOKE, Arthur		
L		1672
HOOKE, Edmund		
L	25 Apr	1678 (P)
CR	16 Mar	1707 (PMM)
CA	30 Nov	1711
	(24 June	1712 in H)
d		1733
HOOLEY, Joseph		
L	13 Aug	1761
d		1785 (NMM)
HOOPE, John		
L	13 Mar	1815
d		1841 (NMM)
HOOPER, Benjamin		
L	13 Dec	1809
CR	16 Feb	1853 (NMM)
d		1865 (NMM)
HOOPER, Edward (1)		
L	28 Sept	1745
d		1756 (NMM)
HOOPER, Edward (2)		
L	23 Nov	1757
d		1763 (NMM)
HOOPER, Edward (3)		
L	12 Nov	1778
KIA	17 Apr	1780 (LG)
HOOPER, George William		
L	12 Aug	1800
T		
CR	9 Nov	1808
CA	1 Jan	1817 (NMM)
d	12 July	1839 (NMM)
HOOPER, James		
L		1666

HOOPER, John		
L	11 Mar	1692 (PJP)
CA	17 Dec	1695
d	16 Sept	1705 (PJP)
HOOPER, John Sackett		
L	20 Sept	1815
HP	20 Sept	1815 (OB)
Ret CR	14 Apr	1864 (NMM)
d		1868 (NMM)
HOOPER, Richard		
L	4 July	1810
Ret CR	6 July	1850 (NMM)
d		1867 (NMM)
HOOPER, Robert		
L		1667
CA		1665
HOOPER, Thomas		
L	19 Sept	1777
d	16 Apr	1780 (PJP)
HOOPER, William		
L	8 Feb	1807
d	14 Oct	1838 (NMM)
HOOPER, William Read		
L	29 Apr	1802
d		1808 (NMM)
HOP, John		
L	16 Feb	1794
d		1797 (NMM)
HOPE, Charles		
L	10 June	1767
CR	3 June	1776
CA	29 Nov	1777
COM E	3 June	1794–
	21 Oct	1795 (NBO)
COMM (Chatham)	21 Jan	1801 (NBO)
d	10 Sept	1808 (MB)
HOPE, David		
L	30 Aug	1806
CR	15 June	1814
CA	4 Feb	1830 (OB)
HP	4 Feb	1830 (OB)
d	13 May	1847 (NMM)
HOPE, Sir George Johnstone		
L	29 Feb	1788
CR	22 Nov	1790
CA	13 Sept	1793
T		
CRM	31 July	1810 (LG)
RAB	1 Aug	1811
COM AD	25 Mar	1812–
	18 May	1813 (AO)
RAW	12 Aug	1812
COM AD	23 Oct	1813–
	2 Apr	1818 (AO)
MP (East Grinstead)		
KCB	2 Jan	1815 (LG)
d	2 May	1818 (LT)
HOPE, Sir Henry		
L	3 May	1804
CR	22 Jan	1806
CA	24 May	1808
CB	4 June	1815 (MB)
HP	Sept	1815 (OB)
RAB	9 Nov	1846 (LG)
RAW	21 Dec	1847 (NMM)

RAR	21 June	1850 (LG)
VAB	2 Apr	1853 (NMM)
VAW	11 Sept	1854 (NMM)
VAR	14 May	1857 (NMM)
AB	20 Jan	1858 (NMM)
AW	15 Jan	1862 (NMM)
AR	27 Apr	1863 (NMM)
d	23 Sept	1863 (NMM)
HOPE, John		
L	7 Feb	1812
d	6 Mar	1824 (NMM)
HOPE, Sir William		
L	14 July	1749
d		1756 (NMM)
HOPE, Sir William Johnstone		
L	10 Nov	1782
CR	4 Apr	1791
CA	9 Jan	1794
MP (Dumfries Burghs)		1800–1802 (MPT)
MP (Dumfriesshire)		1804–1830 (MPT)
COM AD	6 Apr	1807–
	30 Mar	1809 (AO)
CRM	1 Aug	1811 (LG)
RAB	12 Aug	1812
RAW	4 Dec	1813
RAR	4 June	1814
KCB	2 Jan	1815 (DNB)
VAB	12 Aug	1819 (CH)
COM AD	13 Mar	1820–
	2 May	1827 (AO)
VAW	27 May	1825 (CH)
GCB		1825 (CH)
VAR	22 July	1830 (CH)
d	2 May	1831 (CH)
HOPKINS, Benjamin		
L	13 Oct	1757
d		1761 (NMM)
HOPKINS, Charles		
L	6 Feb	1815
d		1842 (NMM)
HOPKINS, Edmund		
L	24 Nov	1731
d		1737 (NMM)
HOPKINS, George		
L	7 May	1805
d	Dec	1824 (NMM)
HOPKINS, Harry		
L	4 Dec	1794
CR	22 Jan	1806 (MB)
CA	7 June	1814 (MB)
d		1832 (NMM)
HOPKINS, Humphrey		
L	26 June	1809
d	Dec	1841 (NMM)
HOPKINS, John		
L	12 Mar	1811
d	16 Oct	1836 (PJP)
HOPKINS, Reginald Bean		
L	8 May	1804
d	13 Aug	1811 (NMM)
HOPKINS, Timothy		
L	19 June	1760
d	5 June	1770 (PJP)

HOPKINSON, Simon		
L	18 July	1801
CR	19 July	1821 (NMM)
HP	19 July	1821 (OB)
d	9 Oct	1848 (NMM)
HOPPER, Robert		
L	25 Aug	1694
Gone		1719 (NMM)
HOPPNER, Thomas Parkyns		
L	19 Sept	1815
CR	25 Jan	1822 (MB)
CA	30 Dec	1825 (MB)
d	22 Jan	1834 (PJP)
HOPSON(N), Edward		
L	17 Feb	1691 (PJP)
CA	24 July	1696
RAB	8 May	1719
RAR	16 Feb	1723
VAB	19 Apr	1726
VAW	4 Jan	1728
	(13 Jan	1728 in C)
d	8 May	1728
HOPSON(N), Sir Thomas		
L		1672 (P)
CA	21 Mar	1678 (P)
EGA		
(Portsmouth)	1 Mar	1681 (EAD)
RAR	4 July	1693
RAB	22 Aug	1693
VAD	10 Nov	1693
MP		
(Newton I.o.W.)		1698–1705 (DNB)
VAB	14 Apr	1701
VAR	30 June	1701
Kt		1702 (DNB)
COM E	17 Dec	1702–
	16 Nov	1714 (NBO)
d	12 Oct	1717 (DNB)
HORE, Daniel		
L	29 May	1729
CR		
CA	10 Apr	1741
SUP RA	27 Feb	1762
d	25 June	1762
HORE, Henry Cavendish		
L	29 Mar	1811
Ret CR	1 Jan	1852 (NMM)
d		1867 (NMM)
HORE, Herbert William		
L	21 Nov	1808
CR	11 June	1814
d	10 Jan	1823 (LT)
HORE, James Stopford		
L	7 Mar	1815
CR	28 Aug	1828 (NMM)
d	27 Mar	1848 (NMM)
HORE, Samuel Bradstreet		
L	19 Oct	1807
CR	13 May	1813
HP		1825 (OB)
Ret CA	2 Feb	1848 (NMM)
d		1852 (NMM)
HORN, James		
L	17 Apr	1780
SUP CR	3 Oct	1814
d	25 Nov	1831 (NMM)

HORN, Luke		
L	11 Aug	1800
d	5 Nov	1827 (NMM)
HORN, Philip Thicknesse		
L	7 Oct	1805
CR	16 Sept	1816 (NMM)
d		1826 (NMM)
HORNBY, John		
L	14 Dec	1814
d	2 Jan	1830 (NMM)
HORNBY, Sir Phipps		
L	16 Nov	1804
T		
CR	15 Aug	1806
CA	16 Feb	1810 (MB)
CB	4 June	1815 (MB)
RAB	9 Nov	1846 (LG)
RAW	5 Sept	1848 (LG)
RAR	21 June	1850 (LG)
COM AD	2 Mar	1852–
	5 Jan	1853 (AO)
Kt	7 Apr	1852 (DNB)
VAB	21 Jan	1854 (NMM)
VAW	27 Sept	1855 (NMM)
VAR	22 Aug	1857 (NMM)
AB	25 June	1858 (NMM)
GCB		1861 (DNB)
AW	12 Apr	1862 (NMM)
AR	24 Sept	1863 (NMM)
d	18 Mar	1867 (NMM)
HORNE, Charles		
L	9 Nov	1756
d		1771 (NMM)
HORNE, Edmund		
L	20 Oct	1740 (NMM)
CR	11 Mar	1742
CA	22 Feb	1745
d	23 May	1764
HORNE, Gustavus, Count		
L		1671
CA		1672
d	28 Mar	1686 (DDA)
HORNER, Henry		
L		1673
d	before	1689 (PJP)
HORNSBY, William		
L	26 Sept	1811
HP	Sept	1814 (OB)
d		1854 (NMM)
HORNSEY, John		
L	10 July	1799
CR	22 Apr	1802
d	17 Jan	1803 (NMM)
HORRIE, David		
L	4 July	1802
Ret CR	29 Aug	1834 (NMM)
d	30 Sept	1840 (NMM)
HORRIE, James		
T		
L	26 Oct	1807
d		1826 (TR)
HORROY, Peter		
L	23 Nov	1702

SUP CR	20 Mar	1738 (PMM)
d		1750 (PMM)
HORSEMAN, Andrew		
L	13 Aug	1697
Gone		1719 (NMM)
HORSEMAN, John (1)		
L	22 Aug	1696
Gone		1719 (NMM)
HORSEMAN, John (2)		
L	3 Feb	1697
Gone		1734 (NMM)
HORSENAIL, Samuel		
L	1 Jan	1778
d	16 Apr	1794 (NMM)
HORSELEY, Richard		
L	24 Sept	1795
d	27 Feb	1828 (NMM)
HORSMAN, Richard		
L		
CA	4 July	1666 (RM)
HORTON, Joshua Sydney		
L	12 Oct	1793
CR	25 Nov	1795
CA	18 Feb	1800
RAW	22 July	1830 (LG)
d	24 Nov	1835 (NMM)
HORTON, William		
L	1 Apr	1760
d		1762 (NMM)
HOSHTON, William		
See HOGHTON, William		
HOSIE, William		
T		
L	18 Feb	1808
d		1836 (TR)
HOSIER, Francis		
L		1692 (PJP)
CR	4 Dec	1694 (PMM)
CA	27 June	1697
RAW	8 May	1719
VAB	16 Feb	1723
VAW	9 Mar	1726 (DNB)
d	23 Aug	1727 (CH)
HOSKIN, Henry (1)		
L	5 Mar	1810
d		1813 (NMM)
HOSKIN, Henry (2)		
L	20 Aug	1813
d		1817 (PRO)
HOSKINS, Benjamin		
L		
CA	5 Sept	1688
	(15 Sept	1688 in P)
	(15 Sept	1689 in C)
CAFMR	15 Sept	1694 (EAD)
SUP	21 Jan	1703
d	30 Sept	1712
HOSKINS, Henry		
L	1 Apr	1757
d		1763 (NMM)
HOSKINS, James		
L	21 Aug	1809
d		1811 (NMM)

HOSKINS, Samuel
L 4 Apr 1810
CR 4 July 1814
Ret CA 1 July 1851 (NMM)
d 15 July 1854 (NMM)

HOSTE, Thomas Edward
L 4 July 1814
CR 3 Jan 1825 (NMM)
CA 26 Feb 1830 (NMM)
d 27 July 1834 (LT)

HOSTE, Sir William
L 8 Feb 1798
CR 3 Dec 1798
CA 7 Jan 1802
Kt (Austria) 23 May 1814 (LG)
Cre Bt 23 July 1814 (DNB)
KCB 2 Jan 1815 (LG)
d 6 Dec 1828 (CH)

HOSTE, William
See HOSIE, William

HOTCHKIS, David
L 27 Aug 1779
CR 29 June 1795
d 7 Mar 1801 (PMM)

HOTCHKIS, John
L 17 June 1795
Ret CR 26 Nov 1830 (PRO)
d 1852 (NMM)

HOTCHKYS, Charles
L 12 May 1773
CR 15 June 1779
CA 1 Nov 1780
SUP CA 1799 (NMM)
d 1815 (NMM)

HOTHAM, Hon. Sir Henry
L 6 June 1794
CR
CA 13 Jan 1795
CRM 4 Dec 1813 (AL)
RAW 4 June 1814
KCB 2 Jan 1815 (LG)
COM AD 2 Apr 1818–
23 Mar 1822 (AO)
RAR 12 Aug 1819 (CH)
VAB 27 May 1825 (CH)
COM AD 19 Sept 1828–
25 Nov 1830 (AO)
VAR 22 July 1830 (CH)
GCB 1833 (CH)
d 19 Apr 1833 (CH)

HOTHAM, William, Lord (1)
L 28 Jan 1755
CR 19 Nov 1756
CA 17 Aug 1757
CRM 19 Mar 1779 (AL)
RAR 24 Sept 1787
VAB 21 Sept 1790
VAW 1 Feb 1793
VAR 12 Apr 1794
Cre IP 1797 (DNB)
AW 14 Feb 1799
AR 9 Nov 1805
d 2 May 1813 (CH)

HOTHAM, Sir William (2)
L 27 Oct 1790
CR
CA 7 Oct 1794
HP 1804–1810 (OB)
RAB 4 Dec 1813
HP 4 Dec 1813 (OB)
RAW 4 June 1814
KCB 2 Jan 1815 (LG)
RAR 12 Aug 1819 (CH)
VAB 19 July 1821 (CH)
VAR 22 July 1830 (CH)
AB 10 Jan 1837 (CH)
GCB 4 July 1840 (OB)
AW 23 Nov 1841 (CH)
AR 9 Nov 1846 (CH)
d 31 May 1848 (CH)

HOTHAM, William (3)
L 12 Feb 1812
CR 15 June 1814
CA 4 Apr 1825 (NMM)
Ret CA 1 Oct 1846 (NMM)
Ret RA 5 Dec 1853 (NMM)
Ret VA 25 June 1858 (NMM)
Ret A 30 Nov 1863 (NMM)
d 22 Feb 1873 (NMM)

HOUGH, John James
L 19 Nov 1807
CR 29 Sept 1827 (NMM)
d 16 Feb 1849 (NMM)

HOUGHTON, Charles Evelyn
L 14 Sept 1805
Ret CR 17 Jan 1838 (NMM)
d 1 Jan 1848 (NMM)

HOUGHTON, Frederick
L 22 Jan 1806
Reduced to one of the Junior Lieutenants 1807
Reinstated with seniority 22 Sept 1810
d (drowned) Sept 1812 (OB)

HOUGHTON, Henry
See HAUGHTON, Henry

HOUGHTON, William
L 20 Nov 1807
d 1813 (NMM)

HOULDING, William
L
CR
CA 15 June 1709
d 15 Nov 1731

HOULT, Wheeler
L 21 Feb 1741
d 1749 (NMM)

HOULTON, John
L 28 June 1756
CR 29 Jan 1759
CA 4 Nov 1761 (CH)
RAB 21 Sept 1790
d 16 Jan 1791 (PMM)

HOULTON, Robert
L 18 May 1797
Ret CR 26 Nov 1830 (PRO)
d 1862 (NMM)

HOUSDEN, John
L 22 May 1692 (PMM)

HOUSTON, John
L 11 Jan 1803

Name / Rank	Date	Year
CR	25 Nov	1807
d		1810 (PJP)
HOVELL, James		
L	31 Jan	1745
d		1757 (NMM)
HOW, Henry		
L	6 Nov	1780
d		1783 (NMM)
HOW, James		
L	27 Apr	1725
d		1729 (NMM)
HOW, John (1)		
L		1675
d	before	1689 (PJP)
HOW, John (2)		
L	22 Nov	1745
d		1758 (NMM)
HOW, Samuel		
L	26 Aug	1706 (PMM)
HOWARD, Charles		
L		
CR	25 Sept	1705 (PMM)
d (drowned)	17 Aug	1707 (CH)
HOWARD, Hon. James		
L	17 Mar	1718 (PMM)
HOWARD, Philip		
L	23 Dec	1762
d		1778 (NMM)
HOWARD, Thomas (1)		
L	24 Sept	1664 (DDA)
HOWARD, Thomas (2)		
L		1707 (PJP)
CR		
CA	1 Jan	1713
d	13 Apr	1734 (M)
HOWARD, Thomas (3)		
L	20 Oct	1800
d		1805 (NMM)
HOWARD, Thomas (4)		
L	20 Feb	1805
d		1811 (NMM)
HOWCROFT, Adam		
L	23 Mar	1807
Ret CR	19 July	1842 (NMM)
d		1844 (NMM)
HOWDEN, John		
L	12 Dec	1782
d		1806 (NMM)
HOWDON, Robert		
L	12 Oct	1801
d		1804 (NMM)
HOWE, Alexander Burgoyne		
L	28 May	1803
T		
Ret CR	1 Aug	1849 (NMM)
d		1864 (TR)
HOWE, John		
L	29 May	1779
d		1795 (NMM)
HOWE, Hon. Richard, Earl		
L		1745 (MPN)
CR		
CA	10 Apr	1746
MP	23 May	1757–
(Dartmouth)	20 Apr	1782 (MPN)
Inh IP		1758 (DNB)
CRM	4 Feb	1760 (AL)
COM AD	20Apr	1763–
	31 July	1765 (AO)
RAB	18 Oct	1770
RAW	31 Mar	1775
VAB	5 Feb	1776
VAR		1778
AB	8 Apr	1782
Cre EP	20 Apr	1782 (MPN)
FLA	30 Jan–10 Apr	1783 (AO)
FLA	31 Dec	1783–
	16 July	1788 (AO)
AW	24 Sept	1787
GRM	12 Mar	1796 (LG)
AF	12 Mar	1796
Kt	2 June	1797 (MPN)
d	5 Aug	1799 (DNB)
HOWE, Thomas Harmood		
L	2 Mar	1815
Struck off list	13 Nov	1825 (NMM)
d	14 Feb	1828 (NMM)
HOWE, Tyringham		
L	10 Sept	1765
CR	28 Dec	1770
CA	11 Jan	1775
d		1783 (NMM)
HOWE, William		
L	12 Nov	1756
CR	24 Nov	1759 (PJP)
CA	1 July	1760
d	6 Jan	1765 (NMM)
HOWELL, George		
L	23 Feb	1801
Resigned		1804 (NMM)
HOWELL, Joseph Benjamin		
L	22 Jan	1806
CR	16 Sept	1816 (OB)
HP	16 Sept	1816 (OB)
Ret CA	29 Jan	1856 (NMM)
d	18 Jan	1864 (NMM)
HOWES, George		
L	24 Feb	1815
CR	1 Jan	1847 (NMM)
HP	1 Jan	1847 (OB)
Ret CA	1 Aug	1860 (NMM)
d	19 Apr	1881 (NMM)
HOWES, James		
L	2 Apr	1806
d		1808 (NMM)
HOWE(S), William		
L		
CA		1666

William Howe(s), late commander of the VIRGIN f.s., was court-martialled and sentenced to be shot on 18 Nov 1667 for cowardice against the Dutch Fleet 26 July 1667. Thomas Howe(s), late commander of the VIRGIN f.s., presumably the same person, was, however, reprieved on 14 Nov 1667 (PRO)

Name / Rank	Date	Year
HOWNAM, Joseph Robert		
L	4 May	1809
HP	Jan	1814 (OB)
Ret CR	27 July	1847 (NMM)
d	9 Nov	1859 (NMM)

HOWORTH, Edward
L 21 May 1755
SUP CR 21 Sept 1796 (PMM)
d 1797 (PMM)

HOWORTH, John
L 4 Jan 1757
CR 1 Feb 1777
CA 4 Apr 1781
SUP 1799
d 1801

HOWSE, Stephen Henry Waring
L 1 May 1807
d 5 July 1820 (NMM)

HOY, Isaac
L 6 Oct 1744
d 1783 (NMM)

HOY, Joseph
L 25 Apr 1783
CR 20 Nov 1807
d 1826 (NMM)

HOY, Robert
L 13 Apr 1782
SUPCR 5 Feb 1817 (NMM)
d Feb 1830 (NMM)

HOYLES, Marshall
L 5 July 1813
d 1841 (NMM)

HOZIER, Francis
See HOSIER, Francis

HUBBALD, James
L 19 Jan 1778
Dismissed 20 July 1776 (PJP)
d 1778 (NMM)

HUBBARD, Henry
L 13 Aug 1692 (PMM)

HUBBARD, James
L 2 Mar 1734
d 1737 (NMM)

HUBBARD, John (1)
L
CA 1662
d 19 July 1671 (DDA)

HUBBARD, John (2)
L
CA 6 July 1666 (RM)
KIA Dec 1668 (CH)

HUBBARD, John (3)
L 13 July 1688 (PJP)
CA 18 June 1690 (PJP)
d 1723 (PJP)

HUBBARD, John (4)
L 11 Oct 1703 (PMM)
CR 17 Mar 1718 (NMM)
CA 5 Dec 1718
d 10 Nov 1727 (PMM)

HUBBARD, Nathaniel
L 16 Dec 1690
CR
CA 27 May 1709
d 1 Jan 1732 (M)

HUBBARD, William
L 4 Mar 1815
HP 1833–1837 (OB)

CR 28 June 1838 (NMM)
Ret CA 1 Apr 1856 (NMM)
d 1874 (NMM)

HUBBART, John
L
CA 9 June 1666 (RM)

HUDSON, Charles
L 27 June 1757
CR 24 Aug 1762
CA 20 June 1765
SUP RA 1793
d 3 Mar 1803 (LT)

HUDSON, Christopher
L 1 July 1778
d 1785 (NMM)

HUDSON, George
L 3 Mar 1740
CR 16 Feb 1748
d 1785 (NMM)

HUDSON, James
L 30 Apr 1678
d before 1689 (PJP)

HUDSON, John (1)
L 22 Nov 1790
CR 25 Oct 1800
CA 21 Oct 1810
d 22 Feb 1823 (LT)

HUDSON, John (2)
T
L 31 Mar 1813
d 23 Oct 1848 (NMM)

HUDSON, John (3)
L 8 June 1815
d 7 July 1821 (NMM)

HUDSON, John Thomas
L 6 Oct 1815
d 1841 (NMM)

HUDSON, Richard
L
CA 1673
d before 1689 (PJP)

HUDSON, Samuel
L 13 Sept 1806
d 1811 (NMM)

HUDSON, Thomas (1)
L 1674 (PJP)

HUDSON, Thomas (2)
L
CR 26 June 1699 (PMM)
CA 21 Dec 1701
Was to have been court-martialled for cowardice in action of 24 Aug 1702, but died before it could be held. (PRO)
d 25 Sept 1702 (LG)

HUDSON, Thomas (3)
L 29 Oct 1750
d 2 Feb 1792 (LT)

HUE, Philip
L 22 Sept 1759
CR 17 Apr 1799
d 1812 (NMM)

HUGBONE, Thomas
L 6 Feb 1695
Gone 1719 (NMM)

HUGGATE, Hopkins		
L		
CA		1667
HUGGETT, Gill		
L	17 Mar	1815
d		1838 (NMM)
HUGGETT, William		
L	16 Nov	1790
d (drowned)	27 Dec	1797 (CH)
HUGGINS, James		
L	16 May	1808
d		1811 (NMM)
HUGGINS, James Edward		
L	27 Sept	1810
CR	15 June	1814
Ret CA	1 July	1851 (NMM)
d	30 Apr	1860 (NMM)
HUGGINS, John		
L	8 Dec	1694
Gone		1719 (NMM)
HUGHES, Abraham		
L	24 Apr	1802
d		1832 (NMM)
HUGHES, Charles		
L	7 Nov	1777
CR		
CA	1 Mar	1782
SUP	23 Apr	1804
d	11 Aug	1819 (LT)
HUGHES, Christopher		
L	22 Jan	1702
d		1727 (NMM)
HUGHES, Sir Edward		
L	25 Aug	1740
CR		
CA	6 Feb	1748
RAB	23 Jan	1778
Kt		1778 (CH)
RAR	29 Mar	1779 (CH)
VAB	26 Sept	1780
VAW	24 Sept	1787
VAR	21 Sept	1790
AB	1 Feb	1793
d	17 Feb	1794 (CH)
HUGHES, Gabriel		
L		
CA	5 Aug	1690
d	4 May	1699
HUGHES, George William		
L	30 Jan	1806
d		1808 (NMM)
HUGHES, Henry		
L	24 Feb	1691
In Merchant Service		1700 (PJP)
HUGHES, John (1)		
L	3 Nov	1740
d		1743 (NMM)
HUGHES, John (2)		
L	7 Sept	1741
CR	July	1744 (PJP)
d		1749 (NMM)
HUGHES, John (3)		
L	7 June	1745
CR	15 Nov	1756
CA	21 Nov	1760
d		1787
HUGHES, Mark		
L		1712 (PJP)
HUGHES, Oiysses		
See HUGHES, Ulysses		
HUGHES, Provo Featherstone		
L	10 Oct	1804
d	13 Feb	1833 (NMM)
HUGHES, Richard (1)		
L	4 July	1693
CR		
CA	19 June	1702
COMM		1729–
(Portsmouth)		1754 (PMM)
SUP CA		1754 (LTE)
d	12 Nov	1756
HUGHES, Sir Richard (2)		
L	28 July	1726
CR	3 July	1739
CA	24 Oct	1740
COMM	Feb	1754–
(Portsmouth)	Aug	1773 (PMM)
SUP CA		1773 (LTE)
Cre Bt		1773 (LTE)
d		1782 (NMM)
HUGHES, Sir Richard (3)		
L	2 Apr	1745
CR	6 Feb	1756
CA	10 Nov	1756
COMM	Feb	1778–
(Halifax)	Oct	1780 (PMM)
RAB	26 Sept	1780
RAR	24 Sept	1787
VAB	21 Sept	1790
VAW	1 Feb	1793
VAR	12 Apr	1794
AB	16 Apr	1795 (NMM)
AW	14 Feb	1799
AR	9 Nov	1805
d	4 Jan	1812 (CH)
HUGHES, Richard (4)		
L	16 May	1790
CR	6 Dec	1796
d		1810 (NMM)
HUGHES, Robert (1)		
L	19 Dec	1692 (PJP)
CR		
CA	28 June	1697
	(28 May 1696 in S)	
RAB	21 Apr	1727
RAW	4 Jan	1728
RAR	19 July	1728
	(29 July in C)	
d	14 Mar	1729
HUGHES, Robert (2)		
L		
CR		
CA	24 Oct	1740
Resigned		
HUGHES, Robert (3)		
L	14 July	1738 (NMM)
CR	14 July	1744
CA	2 Apr	1745
RAR	24 Oct	1770 (CH)
d	19 Jan	1774

Name	Rank	Date	Year
HUGHES, Robert (4)			
	L	17 Mar	1780
	d		1780 (NMM)
HUGHES, Robert (5)			
	L	28 Aug	1783
	d		1797 (NMM)
HUGHES, Robert (6)			
	L	12 Oct	1797
	Dismissed		1800 (NMM)
	Restored		1801 (NMM)
	d	29 Nov	1827 (NMM)
HUGHES, Robert (7)			
	L	23 Feb	1807
	HP	Aug	1814 (OB)
	Ret CR	4 Feb	1842 (OB)
	d		1854 (NMM)
HUGHES, Robert Andrew			
	L	2 Mar	1815
	Ret CR	14 Oct	1862 (NMM)
HUGHES, Thomas (1)			
	L		
	CR	7 Dec	1694 (PJP)
	CA	1 Jan	1713
	d	31 Aug	1731
HUGHES, Thomas (2)			
	L	22 Jan	1806
	Ret CR	5 Jan	1839 (OB)
	d	29 Jan	1845 (OB)
HUGHES, Thomas Henry			
	L	10 Mar	1809
	d		1828 (NMM)
HUGHES, Ulysses			
	L	17 Oct	1794
	d		1809 (NMM)
HUGHES, Walter			
	L	25 May	1778
	d		1780 (NMM)
HUGHES, William (1)			
	L		
	CA	1 Apr	1692
	d	4 Apr	1696
HUGHES, William (2)			
	L	23 Oct	1793
	CR	7 May	1804
	d		1819 (NMM)
HUGHES, William			
See HUGHS, William			
HUGHES, William Caesar			
	L	5 Oct	1778
	d		1790 (NMM)
HUGHES, William James			
	L	24 Feb	1802 (NMM)
	CR	25 Sept	1806 (NMM)
	Ret CA	10 Sept	1840 (NMM)
	d	21 Mar	1862 (NMM)
HUGHES, William Rand			
	L	18 Jan	1808
	d	Nov	1828 (NMM)
HUGHS, William			
	L		1666
HUGO, George			
	L	20 Sept	1815
	Ret CR	14 Apr	1864 (NMM)
	d		1874 (NMM)
HUISH, George			
	L	27 Jan	1801
	T		
	d		1809 (NMM)
HUISH, Henry (1)			
	L	15 Oct	1704
	SUP CR	20 Mar	1738 (PMM)
	d		1751 (PMM)
HUISH, Henry (2)			
	L	5 May	1735
	CR	2 Nov	1745 (NMM)
	CA	12 July	1746
	d	26 Feb	1763
HULK, Benjamin			
	L	16 Nov	1756
	d		1757 (NMM)
HULKE, Benjamin			
	L	29 Apr	1778
	CR	29 Oct	1779
	d	31 Aug	1799
HULKE, Thomas Manley			
	L	9 Oct	1777
	d		1788 (NMM)
HULL, Charles John			
	L	13 Feb	1815
	d		1837 (NMM)
HULL, Isaac			
	L	28 Nov	1782
	d	26 Nov	1795 (NMM)
HULL, John			
	L		
	CA		1673
HULL, William Hollamby			
	L	1 May	1811
	HP	May	1814 (OB)
	Ret CR	1 Apr	1852 (NMM)
	d	30 Jan	1862 (NMM)
HUMBLE, William			
	L		
	CA		1666
	d	before	1689 (PJP)
HUME, Francis			
	L		
	CR		
	CA	24 July	1713
	d (suicide)	8 Feb	1753 (PJP)
HUME, George			
	L	13 Sept	1769
	d	6 May	1802
HUME, James (1)			
	L	22 July	1740
	CR	29 Sept	1757
	d		1758 (NMM)
HUME, James (2)			
	L	21 Feb	1741
	d		1757 (NMM)
HUME, John			
	L	7 Feb	1732
	CR	12 Mar	1742
	CA	20 July	1745
	KIA	24 Mar	1759 (LG)

HUME, Joseph
L 22 Jan 1813
d 1849 (NMM)

HUMPHREYS, George
L 14 Feb 1815
d 1834 (NMM)

HUMPHREYS, John
L 1 Oct 1695 (PMM)

HUMPHREYS, Salusbury Pryce
See DAVENPORT, Sir Salusbury Pryce

HUMPHRIES, Harry
See HUMPHRYS, Harry

HUMPHRIS, Thomas (1)
L 20 Jan 1747
d 1761 (NMM)

HUMPHRIS, Thomas (2)
L 13 Nov 1795
d 1 Oct 1811 (NMM)

HUMPHRYS, Harry
L 6 Nov 1795
d 21 Oct 1799

HUMPHRYS, Thomas
L 26 July 1687

HUNGATE, William Anning
L 2 Mar 1815
HP 2 Mar 1815 (OB)
d 18 Feb 1852 (NMM)

HUNGERFORD, Emanuel
L 9 Aug 1791
d 1810 (NMM)

HUNGERFORD, John
L 4 Feb 1815
HP 1815 (OB)
d 1850 (NMM)

HUNLOCK, Henry
L 1661

HUNLOKE, Thomas Windsor
L 1 May 1804
CR 8 Feb 1809
d 5 Dec 1811 (NMM)

HUNN, Frederick
L 5 Apr 1811
CR 27 Aug 1814
CA 26 Dec 1822 (NMM)
Ret CA 31 Oct 1846 (LG)
d 1852 (NMM)

HUNSDON, Edward
L 24 Feb 1815
d 1833 (NMM)

HUNT, Anthony (1)
L 2 Apr 1757
CR 16 Oct 1767
CA 10 Jan 1771
d 1796

HUNT, Anthony (2)
L 26 Aug 1789
CR 22 Nov 1790
CA 22 May 1793
d 3 Dec 1795 (LT)

HUNT, Anthony (3)
L 18 Oct 1799
d 1843 (NMM)

HUNT, Charles (1)
L 5 Jan 1783
d 1803 (NMM)

HUNT, Charles (2)
L 19 July 1798
d Feb 1806 (PRO)

HUNT, Edmund
L 16 Mar 1742
d 1760 (NMM)

HUNT, Henry
L 1672

HUNT, James
L 29 Sept 1795
d 1810 (NMM)

HUNT, John
L 28 May 1813
d Sept 1821 (NMM)

HUNT, John Harmood
L 9 Aug 1802
d 1804 (NMM)

HUNT, Joseph
L 2 June 1756
CR 18 June 1759
CA 21 Nov 1760 (PJP)
KIA 8 Jan 1761 (LG)

HUNT, Peter
L 1 Oct 1793
CR 7 May 1802
CA 29 Dec 1803
d 4 Dec 1824 (MB)

HUNT, Thomas
L 1 July 1814
d 21 May 1841 (NMM)

HUNT, William
L 24 Jan 1799
Ret CR 26 Nov 1830 (PRO)
d 1846 (NMM)

HUNT, William Buckley
L 14 Oct 1793
CR 22 Jan 1806
d 28 Nov 1812 (PRO)

HUNTE, Francis Le
See LE HUNTE, Francis

HUNTER, Charles
L 6 July 1761
d 1803 (NMM)

HUNTER, Charles Newton
L 20 Dec 1806
CR 15 May 1818 (NMM)
d 18 Apr 1828 (NMM)

HUNTER, Collin
L
CR
CA 4 Sept 1698
Dismissed 7 Aug 1700 (PJP)
d 1700

HUNTER, David
T
L 8 Jan 1806
d 1809 (NMM)

HUNTER, Hugh
L 24 Feb 1815
HP Aug 1815 (OB)

Ret CR	24 July	1862 (NMM)
d	16 Apr	1867 (NMM)
HUNTER, James		
L	27 Feb	1815
d	2 July	1853 (NMM)
HUNTER, James Henry		
L	18 Feb	1815
Struck off list for fraud		1818 (NMM)
HUNTER, John (1)		
L	12 July	1780
CR	12 Nov	1782
CA	15 Dec	1786
RAB	2 Oct	1807
RAW	28 Apr	1808
VAB	31 July	1810
VAW	4 Dec	1813
VAR	4 June	1814
d	13 Mar	1821 (LT)
HUNTER, John (2)		
L	4 Sept	1800
Reduced to one of the Junior Lieutenants		1810
d		1811
HUNTER, Lauchlan		
L	21 May	1777
CR	14 Dec	1782
Seniority adjusted to		
CR	25 July	1782
CA	21 Sept	1790
SUP RA	12 May	1808
d	Aug	1830 (NMM)
HUNTER, Robert		
L	26 Sept	1811
Ret CR	13 Jan	1853 (NMM)
d		1862 (NMM)
HUNTER, Robert Edward		
L	9 Apr	1810
d		1833 (NMM)
HUNTER, Valentine Peter		
L	7 Feb	1815
d		1858 (NMM)
HUNTER, William (1)		
L	24 Jan	1760
LGH		1787 (LGH)
d	17 Feb	1810 (NMM)
HUNTER, William (2)		
L	3 Mar	1815
d		1839 (NMM)
HUNTINGDON, Hans Francis, Earl		
L	11 May	1799
HUNTINGDON, James		
L	1 June	1727
d		1728 (NMM)
HUNTINGDON, John		
L		
CA	12 Dec	1693
d		1734 (PMM)
HUNTLEY, William		
L	1 Mar	1815 (NMM)
d	2 Feb	1825 (NMM)
HUPSMAN, William		
L	13 July	1793
Ret CR	1 Dec	1825 (NMM)
d	26 June	1831 (NMM)
HURD, Thomas		
L	30 Jan	1777
CR	18 Aug	1795
CA	29 Apr	1802
d	30 Apr	1823 (MB)
HURDIS, George Clark		
L	16 June	1795
CR	29 Apr	1802
Ret CA	10 Sept	1840 (NMM)
d	1 Jan	1858 (NMM)
HURST, George		
L	4 Dec	1810
d		1859 (NMM)
HURST, John		
L	10 Oct	1793
d	4 Mar	1797 (PRO)
HURT, Cheney		
L	22 July	1742
HURT, Chr Jarvis		
L	14 Nov	1745
d		1751 (NMM)
HUSKISSON, Thomas		
T		
L	15 Nov	1806
CR	18 Jan	1809
CA	14 Mar	1811
d	21 Dec	1844 (OB)
HUSSEY, John		
L	24 Aug	1743
d		1748(9) (NMM)
HUSSEY, John Dennis		
L	11 Jan	1796
Dismissed	June	1811 (PRO)
d		1811 (NMM)
HUSSEY, Philip		
L	4 Mar	1693
In Merchant Service		1700 (PJP)
HUSSEY, Richard Hussey		
See MOUBRAY, Richard Hussey		
HUSSY, Peter		
L	4 Jan	1695
Gone		1719 (NMM)
HUTCHEN, John		
L	18 Feb	1799 (NMM)
d		1799 (NMM)
HUTCHENSON, Thomas Howard		
L	27 Sept	1740
CR	29 May	1745 (NMM)
CA	23 Nov	1747
d		1759 (NMM)
HUTCHINGS, Edward		
L	9 Dec	1747
d		1760 (NMM)
HUTCHINGS, George Bentham		
L	18 Aug	1812
d	May	1829 (NMM)
HUTCHINGS, Stephen		
L		
CR		
CA	25 Apr	1704
d	24 Aug	1709
HUTCHINS, John		
L	1 July	1773
KIA	6 July	1779 (LG)

HUTCHINSON, Charles
L 16 Apr 1807
CR 21 July 1814
Ret CA 1 July 1851 (NMM)
d 28 Sept 1882 (PMM)
HUTCHINSON, Edward
L 30 Dec 1796
CR 14 Oct 1797
Ret CA 10 Sept 1840 (NMM)
d 6 Aug 1851 (NMM)
HUTCHINSON, James
L 20 Sept 1709
CR 21 July 1730
d ?1733 (NMM)
HUTCHINSON, James Verchild
L 21 Mar 1795
d 1807 (NMM)
HUTCHINSON, Thomas
L 26 Mar 1782
d 1811 (NMM)
HUTCHINSON, William (1)
L 5 Feb 1800
Ret CR 15 Dec 1830 (NMM)
d 1841 (NMM)
HUTCHINSON, William (2)
L 9 Feb 1805
CR 1 Dec 1827 (NMM)
HP Oct 1843 (OB)
CA 1 July 1851 (NMM)
d 1855 (NMM)
HUTCHINSON, William (3)
L 12 Dec 1806
CR 26 May 1814
d 1837 (NMM)
HUTCHINSON, Christie Eston
L 3 June 1814
d 1 Mar 1828 (NMM)
HUTCHINSON, George
L 11 Nov 1806
CR 9 Nov 1821 (NMM)
HP 9 Nov 1821 (OB)
Ret CR 1 July 1851 (NMM)
Ret CA 1 Apr 1856 (NMM)
d 3 Feb 1859 (NMM)
HUTCHISON, John Milray
L 20 July 1813
d 30 Sept 1822 (NMM)
HUTCHISON, Robert (1)
L 19 Mar 1813
d 1833 (NMM)
HUTCHISON, Robert (2)
L 20 Mar 1815 (NMM)
d 1841 (NMM)
HUTCHISON, William (1)
L 28 May 1813
d 1853 (NMM)
HUTCHISON, William (2)
L 18 Feb 1815
HP 30 Nov 1816 (OB)
Ret CR 15 July 1861 (NMM)
d 1881 (NMM)
HUTT, John
L 10 Apr 1773
CR 12 Feb 1781
CA 15 Jan 1783
d 30 June 1794 (PRO)
HUTTON, John
L
CA 1666
HUXLEY, William Frederick
L 4 June 1740
d 1744 (NMM)
HYAT, Abraham
L
CA 1673
d before 1689 (PJP)
HYATT, Joseph
L 10 Feb 1815
d 1858 (NMM)
HYDE, Anthony
L 2 Mar 1703
SUP CR 20 Mar 1738 (PMM)
d 1738 (NMM)
HYDE, Benjamin
L 18 Feb 1815
d Aug 1836 (NMM)
HYDE, Boyle
L 19 July 1745
d 1776 (NMM)
HYDE, Frederick
L 3 Feb 1744 (NMM)
CR 5 Mar 1746 (NMM)
CA 11 Nov 1746
d 21 May 1763
HYDE, George
L 20 Sept 1815
HP 1815 (OB)
Ret CR 14 Apr 1864 (NMM)
d 1874 (NMM)
HYDE, John
L 29 Aug 1735
CR 26 Aug 1745
d 1753 (NMM)
HYETT, Joseph
L 10 Feb 1815 (OB)
HYNSON, Joseph
L 23 Dec 1814
HP Sept 1815 (OB)
d 1850 (NMM)

I'ANSON, Henry
See J'ANSON, Henry
I'ANSON, Mark
L 24 Aug 1793
d 1795 (NMM)
IGGULDEN, Edward
L 7 June 1761
CR 5 Dec 1780
CA 18 Jan 1783
SUP CA 23 Apr 1804
d 24 Sept 1819 (LT)
ILLINGWORTH, John
L 1 Aug 1811
Struck off list 13 Aug 1821 (PRO)
IMPEY, John
L 7 Nov 1793

CR	15 Jan	1802
CA	22 Jan	1806
HP	Feb	1806 (OB)
Ret CA	28 June	1838 (PRO)
RAB	17 Aug	1840 (PRO)
RAW	23 Nov	1841 (PRO)
RAR	9 Nov	1846 (PRO)
VAB	1 Aug	1848 (PRO)
VAW	21 Mar	1851 (PRO)
VA	1 July	1851 (PRO)
A	4 July	1855 (PRO)
d	2 Aug	1858 (PRO)
IMRIE, John		
L	10 Sept	1811
d	8 Sept	1847 (NMM)
IMRIE, Thomas		
L	5 July	1745
d		?1752 (NMM)
INCLEDON, Richard (1)		
See BURY, Richard Incledon		
INCLEDON, Richard (2)		
L	17 Apr	1809
CR	14 June	1830 (PRO)
d		1831 (PRO)
INCLEDON, Robert		
L	28 Sept	1807
CR	4 May	1813
Ret CA	22 Jan	1848 (PRO)
d	10 Nov	1849 (PRO)
INFIELD, Caleb		
L	21 Oct	1799
d	10 Apr	1829 (NMM)
INGHAM, George		
L	7 Jan	1802
CR	15 June	1814
d	Dec	1837 (PRO)
INGLEFIELD, John Nicholson		
L	26 May	1768
CR	7 June	1779
CA	11 Oct	1780 (PRO)
COM N		1795–1811 (DNB)
SUP CA	Feb	1799 (MB)
d		1828 (DNB)
INGLEFIELD, Samuel Hood		
L	26 July	1798
CR	29 Apr	1802 (CH)
CA	6 Oct	1807
CB	18 Apr	1839 (OB)
RAB	23 Nov	1841 (LG)
RAW	20 Nov	1846 (NMM)
d	23 Feb	1848 (NMM)
INGLIS, Charles (1)		
L	6 Feb	1755
CR	17 June	1757
CA	15 Dec	1761
RAB	21 Sept	1790
d	10 Oct	1791 (LT)
INGLIS, Charles (2)		
L	16 Nov	1794 (PRO)
CR	13 May	1800
CA	29 Apr	1802
d	27 Feb	1833 (LT)
INGLIS, Charles (3)		
L	14 May	1792 (PRO)
Struck off list		1804 (PRO)
d		1810 (PRO)
INGLIS, Charles (4)		
L	1 July	1814
CR	23 Apr	1829 (NMM)
Ret CA	1 Apr	1856 (NMM)
d	June	1877 (NMM)
INGLIS, George		
L	25 Mar	1813
d	16 Sept	1849 (NMM)
INGLIS, John (1)		
L	7 Aug	1761
CR	11 Apr	1778
CA	28 Mar	1781
d	11 Oct	1789 (M)
INGLIS, John (2)		
L	22 Oct	1761
CR	1 June	1779
CA	23 Aug	1781
RAB	1 Jan	1801
RAW	23 Apr	1804
VAB	9 Nov	1805
d	11 Mar	1807 (NMM)
INGLIS, John (3)		
L	22 Mar	1797
d	28 May	1798
INGLIS, John Dickons		
L	27 Oct	1778
d	26 Oct	1793
INGLISS, Charles		
See INGLIS, Charles		
INGRAM, Alexander		
L	25 Sept	1800
Ret CR	26 Nov	1830 (NMM)
d		1841 (NMM)
INGRAM, Charles		
L	24 Feb	1815
d		1817 (NMM)
INGRAM, Nicholas		
L		1778 (PJP)
CR	4 Apr	1783
CA	3 Nov	1790
SUP RA	21 May	1808
d	1 Jan	1826 (PRO)
INGRAM, Robert		
L	1 Sept	1806
CR	28 Oct	1829 (PRO)
Ret CA	1 Apr	1856 (PRO)
d		1860 (PRO)
INGRAM, William		
L	22 Jan	1806
KIA	28 Mar	1814 (JH)
INGRAM, William Henry		
L	15 Mar	1800
One of the Junior Lieutenants		1802 (PRO)
L	1 Jan	1805 (PRO)
d		1816 (PRO)
INMAN, Henry		
L	14 June	1780
CR	11 Sept	1793
d	15 July	1809 (NMM)
INNES, Alexander (1)		
L	26 July	1739

CR	14 Nov	1752
CA	25 June	1756
RAW	26 Sept	1780
d	21 Jan	1786 (M)
INNES, Alexander (2)		
L	25 July	1794
CR	29 Apr	1802
CA	21 Oct	1810
d	15 Oct	1839 (PRO)
INNES, James		
L	26 Jan	1746
CR	12 May	1759 (PJP)
CA	6 Aug	1761
d		1779
INNES, John		
L	14 Apr	1794
d		1798 (PRO)
INNES, Robert Wintle		
L	6 Dec	1813
HP	Jan	1842 (OB)
d		1850 (NMM)
INNES, Thomas (1)		
L	13 Apr	1738
CR	16 Jan	1744
CA	3 Apr	1746
d	18 Sept	1750
INNES, Thomas (2)		
L	21 Nov	1790
CR	26 Dec	1799
CA	21 Oct	1810
d	15 June	1831 (NMM)
INNES, Thomas (3)		
L	26 Apr	1797
Ret CR	29 Jan	1831 (PRO)
d	26 Jan	1844 (PRO)
INNES, William		
L	22 Jan	1806
d	8 Mar	1837 (LT)
INNES, William John		
L	30 Mar	1808
Ret CR	18 Jan	1845 (PRO)
d	24 Mar	1847 (OB)
INSLIS, Charles		
See INGLIS, Charles		
IRBY, Hon. Charles Leonard		
L	13 Oct	1808
CR	7 June	1814
CA	2 July	1827 (PRO)
d	3 Dec	1845 (OB)
IRBY, Hon. Frederick Paul		
L	6 Jan	1797
CR	22 Apr	1800
CA	14 Apr	1802
HP		1802–1805 (OB)
CRM	22 July	1830 (LG)
CB		1831 (OB)
RAB	10 Jan	1837 (LG)
RAW	23 Nov	1841 (LG)
d	24 Apr	1844 (PRO)
IRELAND, George		
L	25 Feb	1740
Gone		1752
IRELAND, Thomas (1)		
L	25 May	1780
d	15 June	1794 (PRO)
IRELAND, Thomas (2)		
L	1 May	1811
d		1814 (PRO)
IRONS, John		
L	10 Feb	1800
CR	1 Aug	1811
d	Apr	1840 (NMM)
IRVINE, Alexander		
L	14 July	1744
CR	23 Aug	1756
CA	10 Jan	1771
d		1794 (PRO)
IRVINE, Charles Chamberlayne		
L	30 Aug	1799
CR	24 May	1808
Ret CA	10 Sept	1840 (PRO)
d	18 Mar	1856 (PRO)
IRVINE, James		
L	8 Mar	1815
HP	8 Mar	1815 (OB)
Ret CR	10 Apr	1863 (PRO)
d		1867 (PRO)
IRVINE, Lawrence		
L	4 June	1796
d		1801 (NMM)
IRVINE, Thomas Johnson		
L	20 June	1813
d	15 Jan	1848 (PRO)
IRWIN, George		
L	1 Jan	1778
CR	15 Apr	1797
d		1810 (PRO)
IRWIN, James (1)		
L	17 Mar	1781
CR	14 Apr	1802
d	13 Aug	1825 (PRO)
IRWIN, James (2)		
L	8 Jan	1792
CR	12 Jan	1805
d		1809 (NMM)
IRWIN, John (1)		
L	24 Sept	1761
d		1765 (PRO)
IRWIN, John (2)		
L	20 Aug	1779
CR	12 Mar	1795
CA	24 Oct	1796
d	23 Mar	1812 (NMM)
IRWIN, Joseph		
L	1 Sept	1814
Ret CR	1 Oct	1860 (PRO)
d		1890 (PRO)
IRWIN, Samuel Graves		
L	24 Nov	1806 (PRO)
Ret CR	12 Jan	1843 (PRO)
d		1844 (PRO)
IRWIN, Thomas		
L	29 Dec	1796 (PRO)
d		1801 (PRO)
ISHAM, John Edmund		
L	22 Dec	1800
d		1810 (PRO)

ISLES, William		
L		1670
d	before	1689 (PJP)
IVES, Clement		
L	1 May	1804
d		1813 (PRO)
IVEY, Richard		
L	4 Apr	1747
d		?1752 (PRO)
IVIE, Daniel		
L	1 July	1794
d		1816 (NMM)
JACK, James		
L	25 July	1778
SUP CR	31 Jan	1814
d		1816 (NMM)
JACK, Leigh Spark		
L	28 Aug	1806
HP		1816 (OB)
Ret CR	21 Apr	1840 (PRO)
d	5 July	1851 (PRO)
JACKSON, Caleb		
L	11 Dec	1810
CR	12 Aug	1819 (PRO)
Ret CA	1 Apr	1856 (PRO)
d		1875 (PRO)
JACKSON, Charles Scott		
L	7 Dec	1815
HP	Dec	1830 (OB)
Ret CR	1 July	1864 (NMM)
d		1867 (NMM)
JACKSON, Francis		
L	3 June	1807
d		1826 (NMM)
JACKSON, George (1)		
L	14 Dec	1799
CR	4 Jan	1808
CA	1 Aug	1811
d	10 May	1819 (LT)
JACKSON, George (2)		
L	2 July	1810
d		1811 (PRO)
JACKSON, George (3)		
L	8 Mar	1815
d	24 Nov	1845 (OB)
JACKSON, George Vernon		
L	18 Aug	1809
CR	13 July	1824 (PRO)
CA	23 Nov	1841 (PRO)
HP		1841 (OB)
Ret CA	12 Sept	1854 (PRO)
Ret RA	12 Apr	1862 (PRO)
Ret VA	24 May	1867 (PRO)
Ret A	30 July	1875 (PRO)
d	Apr	1876 (PRO)
JACKSON, Henry		
L	28 Dec	1758
d	28 Jan	1794 (LT)
JACKSON, James		
L	20 Sept	1815
d	Apr	1828 (NMM)
JACKSON, John (1)		
L		
CA	3 Aug	1695
d	25 Dec	1724 (M)
JACKSON, John (2)		
L	4 Apr	1720
Gone		1734 (PRO)
JACKSON, John (3)		
L	26 July	1756
CR	22 Jan	1767
CA	29 Oct	1770
d	26 Nov	1777 (PRO)
JACKSON, John (4)		
L	16 June	1808 (NMM)
HP	Oct	1816 (OB)
Ret CR	30 Apr	1845 (NMM)
d		1855 (NMM)
JACKSON, John (5)		
L	19 Oct	1814
d	Jan	1820 (PRO)
JACKSON, John Crawford Barclay		
L	7 Mar	1808
d	16 Apr	1816 (PRO)
JACKSON, Joseph		
L	24 Sept	1757
SUP CR	26 May	1797 (PMM)
d		1797 (PRO)
JACKSON, Launcelot		
L	3 Jan	1810
d		1816 (NMM)
JACKSON, Michael		
L	24 May	1762
d		1794 (PRO)
JACKSON, Ralph		
L		1672
JACKSON, Richard		
L		
CA	6 Feb	1695
d	16 Aug	1695
JACKSON, Robert (1)		
L	3 Nov	1693
CR		1702 (PJP)
CA	11 Feb	1706
Dismissed	14 Feb	1715 (PJP)
d	28 Oct	1726 (M)
JACKSON, Robert (2)		
L	3 Mar	1781
d		1796 (NMM)
JACKSON, Robert (3)		
L	18 Nov	1790
CR	6 Oct	1801 (PRO)
CA	29 Apr	1802
RAB	10 Jan	1837 (LG)
RAW	28 June	1838 (PRO)
RAR	9 Nov	1846 (NMM)
VAB	8 Mar	1847 (PRO)
VAW	1 June	1848 (PRO)
VAR	29 Apr	1851 (PRO)
d	9 June	1852 (PJP)
JACKSON, Robert Aemilius		
L	1 Mar	1815 (PRO)
Ret CR	11 May	1872 (PRO)
d		1886 (PRO)

JACKSON, Robert Milborne
L 26 Nov 1808
CR 31 Mar 1814
d 25 Aug 1835 (LT)

JACKSON, Samuel
L 3 Nov 1796 (NMM)
CR 18 Aug 1801
CA 5 Nov 1807
CB 6 Dec 1817 (OB)
RAB 23 Nov 1841 (NMM)
d 16 Jan 1845 (OB)

JACKSON, Thomas (1)
L 7 Nov 1807
d 1809 (NMM)

JACKSON, Thomas (2)
L 17 May 1808
HP Sept 1818 (OB)
CR 28 July 1851 (PRO)
d 1854 (PRO)

JACKSON, Thomas (3)
L 28 Feb 1815 (PRO)
Ret CR 24 July 1862 (PRO)
d 1868 (PRO)

JACKSON, Thomas Gill
L 13 Dec 1810
d 20 Feb 1825 (PRO)

JACKSON, William (1)
L
CR 8 May 1781
d 25 Apr 1803 (PRO)

JACKSON, William (2)
L 3 Apr 1807
d 1810 (PRO)

JACKSON, William Rush
L 19 Dec 1807
CR 20 Oct 1813
d 1835 (NMM)

JACOB, Edward Hughes
L 31 July 1812
d 1826 (NMM)

JACOB, James Gledstanes
L 12 Dec 1808
d 1826 (NMM)

JACOB, Thomas (1)
L 1665
CA 11 May 1678
d before 1689 (PJP)

JACOB, Thomas (2)
L
CR
CA 26 Apr 1709
d 15 Feb 1749

JACOBS, Chapman
L 6 Apr 1779
d 12 July 1794 (PRO)

JACOBS, Maximilian
L 22 Nov 1752
CR 13 June 1757
CA 4 Jan 1758
d 1780

JACOBS, William (1)
L 13 Apr 1741
d 1758 (PRO)

JACOBS, William (2)
L 6 Oct 1813
d 1854 (PRO)

JACOMB, Robert
L 12 Mar 1807
Ret CR 29 Dec 1842 (PRO)
d 1854 (PRO)

JACQUES, Anthony
L 23 Feb 1801
d 20 Feb 1824 (PRO)

JACQUES, William
See JAQUES, Williem

JAGER, Thomas
L 21 Mar 1807
Ret CR 19 July 1842 (PRO)
d 1858 (PRO)

JAGO, Nathaniel
L 18 Feb 1812
d 1814 (NMM)

JAGO, Richard
L 6 Nov 1762
d 1808 (PRO)

JAGO, Samuel
T
L 3 Feb 1812
d 1819 (PRO)

JAMES, Bartholomew
L 6 May 1779
CR 19 Oct 1796
CA 24 Dec 1798
Ret RA 6 June 1825 (NMM)
d 23 May 1828 (NMM)

JAMES, Edwin
L 18 Dec 1799
CR 17 May 1814 (MB)
d 1829 (PRO)

JAMES, Horatio
L 21 Mar 1812
CR 23 Nov 1841 (PRO)
d 8 Oct 1850 (PRO)

JAMES, Jacob (1)
L 16 June 1784
CR 7 Mar 1797
d 1833 (NMM)

JAMES, Jacob (2)
L 1 Feb 1806
d 1812 (PRO)

JAMES, James
L 16 Nov 1790
CR 1 July 1828 (OB)
HP 1 July 1828 (OB)
d 13 Nov 1845 (OB)

JAMES, John (1)
L 12 May 1758
d 1790 (PRO)

JAMES, John (2)
L 10 Feb 1815
d 27 Apr 1825 (NMM)

JAMES, Joseph
L 16 Nov 1793
CR 29 Apr 1802
CA 21 Aug 1809
d 16 Feb 1837 (PRO)

JAMES, Peter Paumier
L 17 Oct 1804
Ret CR 11 July 1837 (PRO)
d 1844 (PRO)

JAMES, Richard (1)
L 26 Aug 1660 (DDA)
CA 1666
d before 1689 (PJP)

JAMES, Richard (2)
L 3 Mar 1810
d 1834 (NMM)

JAMES, Robert Bastard
L 27 Feb 1815
d 1841 (PRO)

JAMES, Thomas
L 27 Feb 1795
d 1798 (PRO)

JAMES, Thomas Edward
L 20 Feb 1815
HP 1844 (OB)
d 1852 (NMM)

JAMES, William (1)
L 18 Aug 1763
CR 13 Jan 1779
d 1819 (PRO)

JAMES, William (2)
L 9 Aug 1799
d 1804 (PRO)

JAMES, William (3)
L 16 Feb 1815
d 1853 (PRO)

JAMESON, Walter
See JAMIESON, Walter

JAMESON, William
L 23 Oct 1694 (PJP)
CR 15 Feb 1703 (PMM)
CA 13 Jan 1706
Gone 1718 (PRO)

JAMIESON, Walter
L 28 July 1796 (PRO)
Ret CR 26 Nov 1830 (PRO)
d 1848 (PRO)

JANE, Charles
See JAYNE, Charles

JANE, Henry
L 24 Oct 1800
CR 10 May 1810
CA 27 May 1825 (NMM)
d 1840 (NMM)

JANE, John
T
L 10 Feb 1815
d 1835 (TR)

JANEWAY, James
L 29 Apr 1734
Gone 1741 (PRO)

JANNS, Charles
L 24 Mar 1807
Ret CR 19 July 1842 (NMM)
d 1870 (NMM)

J'ANSON, Henry
L 5 May 1755
d 1767 (PRO)

JANVERIN, Richard Gaire
L 15 Dec 1800
CR 7 May 1802
CA 21 Oct 1810
d 1835 (PRO)

JANVERIN, Thomas
L 30 Oct 1800
T
d 1826 (TR)

JAQUES, Anthony
See JACQUES, Anthony

JAQUES, William
L
CA 1667
d before 1689 (PJP)

JARDEN, John
L 6 Apr 1757
d 1775 (NMM)

JARDINE, George (1)
L 6 Apr 1757

JARDINE, George (2)
L 29 Apr 1795 (NMM)
CR 29 June 1799
d 1801 (NMM)

JARDINE, John
L 13 Oct 1795
d 1797 (PRO)

JARVIS, Daniel
L 7 Oct 1743
d 17 June 1777 (M)

JARVIS, James Nibbs
L 24 Nov 1815
d 1842 (PRO)

JARVIS, John
L 3 Sept 1759
d 25 Aug 1789

JASPER, Richard
L 9 Mar 1739
CR Aug 1744 (PJP)
CA 13 Feb 1745
Dismissed in 1753 by court martial for misconduct at Havannah.
Killed (duel) 11 Apr 1761 (PJP)

JAUNCEY, Henry Fyge
L 4 June 1796
CR 1 Feb 1812
CA 19 July 1821 (PRO)
d Aug 1834 (PRO)

JAY, Charles Hawse
L 6 Feb 1815 (NMM)
CR 22 Oct 1841 (NMM)
Ret CA 17 Dec 1857 (NMM)
d 1864 (NMM)

JAYNE, Charles
L 17 Mar 1815
d 1833 (PRO)

JEAFFRESON, Samuel
L 30 Mar 1796
d 1803 (PRO)

JEANS, John
L 2 Apr 1798
d 1842 (PRO)

JEANS, John Thomas
L 28 Nov 1807
d 20 July 1816 (PRO)
JEANS, Robert
See DEANS, Robert (2)
JEBB, William Francis
L 29 Sept 1814
d 6 Apr 1829 (NMM)
JEFF, Thomas
L 22 Oct 1806 (PJP)
d 1815 (PRO)
JEFFERIES, Charles
L 22 May 1809
Ret CR 29 Feb 1848 (PRO)
d 1875 (PRO)
JEFFERIES, John Head
L 8 June 1815 (OB)
JEFFERY, Samuel
L 13 Feb 1805
CR 23 Feb 1807
d 26 Nov 1833 (LT)
JEFFERY, William
L 1672
JEFFERYS, John (1)
L 1664
CA 1664
d before 1689 (PJP)
JEFFERYS, John (2)
L
CA 1666 (DDA)
JEFFERYS, Robert
L 13 Mar 1734
CR 18 July 1744
CA 1 May 1745
SUP RA 1770 (PRO)
After 1745 name is spelt JEFFERIES or JEFFERIS at different dates. Last shown in S.O.L. of 1 Jan 1770.
d 31 Oct 1780 (PRO)
JEFFERYS, Samuel Alexander (1)
L 4 July 1800
d 1801 (NMM)
JEFFERYS, Samuel Alexander (2)
L
Dismissed
Restored 1803 (NMM)
d 31 Jan 1823 (NMM)
JEFFERSON, David
L 25 Apr 1760
d 18 Aug 1789
JEFFERSON, Francis
L 12 June 1807
HP Aug 1810–
24 Nov 1825 (OB)
d 1855 (PRO)
JEFFREYS, Charles
L 8 Mar 1805
d 6 May 1826 (DUB)
JEKYLL, Edward
L 30 Oct 1742 (NMM)
CR 21 Apr 1746
CA 5 Mar 1748
d 19 June 1776

JEKYLL, John
L 2 Dec 1796
CR 21 Mar 1812
d 14 Feb 1839 (LT)
JELFE, Andrews
L 25 Aug 1735
CR 3 Feb 1744
CA 14 Apr 1746
d 14 Mar 1765
JELLICOE, Henry
L 23 Sept 1813
CR 15 Feb 1836 (PRO)
d 6 Dec 1836 (LT)
JELLICOE, Joseph Chitty
L 11 Oct 1814
CR 6 June 1825 (PRO)
d 14 Sept 1825 (PRO)
JELLY, Frederick
L 24 June 1815
d 7 July 1829 (PRO)
JEMMETT, William
L
CA 1673
JENKIN, George Henry
L 6 June 1815
d 1831 (PRO)
JENKINS, Benjamin
L 25 July 1745
d 1756 (NMM)
JENKINS, Edmund
L 15 Aug 1800
KIA 18 Dec 1809 (LG)
JENKINS, Edward
L 14 Mar 1815
d Mar 1831 (PRO)
JENKINS, Henry (1)
L 23 Dec 1780
CR 29 June 1795
CA 28 Sept 1795
d 10 Nov 1813 (PRO)
JENKINS, Henry (2)
L 27 Sept 1810
HP Dec 1845 (OB)
d 1847 (PRO)
JENKINS, John (1)
L 7 Dec 1809
d 1812 (PRO)
JENKINS, John (2)
L 24 Apr 1810
d 1820 (PRO)
JENKINS, John (3)
L 11 Mar 1815
d 25 Sept 1821 (NMM)
JENKINS, Richard
L 2 Oct 1739
d 1743 (PRO)
JENKINS, William (1)
L 6 Aug 1762
d 1769 (PRO)
JENKINS, William (2)
L 18 Mar 1805
d 14 Jan 1828 (PRO)

JENKINSON, Edward
L 1672
KIA 28 May 1672 (NJ)

JENKINSON, Henry
L 11 Dec 1809
CR 13 Aug 1812
CA 7 June 1814
Ret CA 1 Oct 1864 (PRO)
Ret RA 27 Mar 1850 (PRO)
Ret VA 14 May 1857 (PRO)
Ret A 16 June 1862 (PRO)
d 7 Jan 1868 (PRO)

JENKINSON, Robert
L 23 Aug 1693
Gone 1719 (PRO)

JENKINSON, William
L 15 Jan 1695
Gone 1719 (PRO)

JENKS, Robert James
L 16 Jan 1808
d (drowned) 13 Aug 1810 (PJP)

JENNENS, Sir William
L 1661
CA 11 Oct 1664
Kt 1664 (PJP)
Resigned Dec 1688 (CH)
Entered French Service 1690 (CH)
KIA 18 July 1690 (CH)

JENNER, George
L 20 Mar 1815 (OB)
HP 1815 (OB)
Ret CR 20 Jan 1864 (NMM)
d 1873 (NMM)

JENNEY, Richard William
L 30 Aug 1799
d 1811 (PRO)

JENNIFER, James
L 1664
CA 1666
d before 1689 (PJP)

JENNIFER, John
L 1672 (P)
CA 18 Sept 1688
d 2 Feb 1691 (PJP)

JENNINGS, Congreve
L 14 Oct 1801
d 18 July 1828 (NMM)

JENNINGS, Edward
L 27 May 1813
d 12 Apr 1852 (PRO)

JENNINGS, Sir John
L 12 May 1687 (P)
CA 16 Nov 1689
COM V 7 Feb 1701–
8 Sept 1704 (QAN)
Kt 24 Oct 1704 (MPS)
RAB 20 Jan 1705
(24 Jan 1705 in C)
RAW 10 Dec 1707
VAR 8 Jan 1708 (FVT)
AB 17 Dec 1708 (MPS)
AW 14 Nov 1709
MP (Portsmouth) 1710–3 Feb 1711 (MPS)
COM AD 14 Oct 1714–
16 Apr 1717 (AO)
MP (Rochester) 1715–1734 (MPS)
COM AD 19 Mar 1718–
1 June 1727 (AO)
GGH 1720 (PJP)
d 23 Dec 1743 (DNB)

JENNINGS, Robert
L
CR 22 Sept 1709
d 10 July 1742 (NMM)

JENNINGS, Thomas
L 30 Sept 1688 (P)
CA 29 May 1689
COM V 13 May 1703–
8 Sept 1704 (QAN)
COMM (Lisbon) 1707–1709 (QAN)
d 16 Oct 1723 (M)

JENNINGS, Ulick
L 3 Oct 1796
CR 21 Aug 1800
Dismissed 2 Dec 1803 (PJP)
d Mar 1806 (LTE)

JENNINGS, William
L
CA 9 June 1666 (RM)

JENNINGS, Sir William
See JENNENS, Sir William

JENNIS, Thomas
L 24 Jan 1782
d 16 Feb 1805 (PRO)

JEPHCOTT, John
L 26 Jan 1690
Gone 1719 (PRO)

JEPSON, Anthony
L 30 July 1779
d 1809 (PRO)

JERMY, Charles Dayman
L 21 Oct 1807
CR 13 June 1815
d 6 May 1820 (LT)

JERMY, John
L 2 Jan 1742
CR 16 Oct 1745
d 28 Aug 1751

JERMY, Seth
L 26 Jan 1694 (PJP)
CR ?22 Jan 1697 (NMM)
CA 28 Dec 1702 (PRO)
SUP CA 24 May 1710 (PRO)
d 3 Aug 1724

JERRARD, Mathew
L 26 Aug 1779
d 28 Aug 1799

JERRARD, Michael
L 30 Dec 1813
HP July 1814 (OB)
d 1856 (NMM)

JERSEY, William Henry de
L 15 May 1805
d 1809 (PRO)

JERVIS, Sir Henry Meredyth Jervis White
L 26 Aug 1814
Inh Bt 1830 (OB)
Ret CR 15 Apr 1858 (PRO)
d 1869 (PRO)

JERVIS, John, Earl St. Vincent
See ST. VINCENT, John Jervis, Earl
JERVIS, William Henry
See RICKETTS, William Henry
JERVOISE, Sampson
L 24 Dec 1809
CR 26 Apr 1827 (PRO)
Ret CA 1 Apr 1856 (PRO)
d 1 Feb 1857 (PMM)
JERVOISE, William Clarke
T
L 8 Aug 1806
CR 27 Aug 1814
CA 6 Aug 1828 (PRO)
d 1837 (TR)
JESSON, James
L
CA 7 Feb 1694
d 27 Feb 1709 (PJP)
JESSOP, Samuel
T
L 4 May 1810
d 1813 (PRO)
JEWELL, John
L 7 Feb 1805
d 1807 (PRO)
JEWELL, Walter
L 14 Dec 1776
d 1809 (PRO)
JEWELL, William Nunn
T wounded
L 6 Nov 1812
d 30 Sept 1847 (PRO)
JEWERS, Richard
L 13 Mar 1783
SUP CR 28 Dec 1820 (PRO)
d Apr 1823 (PRO)
JEWERS, Richard Francis
L 5 July 1809
HP Feb 1814 (OB)
Ret CR 7 Aug 1861 (PRO)
d 14 Nov 1872 (PRO)
JEWRY, Henry
L 20 May 1807
d 1828 (PRO)
JEYNES, Thomas
L 21 Jan 1779
SUP CR 31 Jan 1814
d Mar 1823 (PRO)
JOACHIM, Richard
L 7 Feb 1815
CR 1 Jan 1855 (NMM)
Ret CA 1 Aug 1860 (NMM)
d 1873 (NMM)
JOASS, John
L 18 Mar 1756
d 1761 (PRO)
JOBSON, Christopher
L 17 Feb 1815
d 1841 (PRO)
JOCELYN, Hon. James Bligh
L 3 Jan 1811
d 10 July 1812 (NMM)
JOCELYN, Robert
L 21 July 1746
CR
CA 9 Feb 1759
SUP 1787 (PRO)
d 7 July 1806 (PRO)
JOHN, Samuel
L 10 Dec 1760
SUP CR 24 Feb 1808 (PRO)
d 1818 (PRO)
JOHNS, Stephen
L 21 Sept 1810
d 1833 (PRO)
JOHNSON, Bryce
See JOHNSTON, Bryce
JOHNSON, Clement
L 30 July 1779
d 19 June 1798
JOHNSON, Edmund
L 6 Feb 1794
KIA 2 Apr 1801 (LG)
JOHNSON, Edward
L 4 Apr 1801
CR 27 Aug 1814
Ret CA 1 July 1851 (NMM)
d 1854 (NMM)
JOHNSON, Edward John
L 28 Feb 1815 (OB)
CR 4 Mar 1829 (OB)
CA 27 Dec 1838 (PRO)
d 1853 (PRO)
JOHNSON, Ewen
L 1665
JOHNSON, Francis (1)
L
CA 1665
JOHNSON, Francis (2)
L 1666
JOHNSON, George Child
L 31 Jan 1809
HP 1815 (OB)
Ret CR 9 Apr 1847 (PRO)
d 15 Jan 1867 (PRO)
JOHNSON, Hendrick
L 5 Oct 1815
d 1832 (PRO)
JOHNSON, Jeremy
L
CA 1667
d before 1689 (PJP)
JOHNSON, John (1)
L
CA 1664
JOHNSON, John (2)
L 1665
CA 1666
JOHNSON, John (3)
L
CA 27 May 1690
d (drowned) 26 Nov 1703 (CH)
JOHNSON, John (4)
L 4 Aug 1780
d 1786 (PRO)

JOHNSON, John (5)
L | 24 Apr | 1786
Not seen for many years; name removed | | 1821 (PRO)

JOHNSON, John (6)
L | 28 June | 1793
d | 24 Sept | 1830 (PRO)

JOHNSON, John (7)
L | 22 Apr | 1811
d | | 1814 (NMM)

JOHNSON, John (8)
L | 25 Feb | 1815
d | | 1858 (NMM)

JOHNSON, John Munnings
L | 16 Aug | 1814
In Holy Orders | 19 Oct | 1831 (PRO)

JOHNSON, John Samuel Willis
L | 18 May | 1814
HP | 1816–13 Sept | 1817 (OB)
CR | 6 Feb | 1821 (PRO)
CA | 9 Nov | 1846 (PRO)
Ret CA | 15 Jan | 1857 (PRO)
d | | 1863 (PRO)

JOHNSON, Joshua
L | 31 Jan | 1798
CR | 27 Apr | 1801
d | 24 Apr | 1830 (NMM)

JOHNSON, Nicholas
L | 5 Dec | 1794
Struck off list | | 1797 (NMM)

JOHNSON, Ralph
L | 20 July | 1697
Gone | | 1719 (PRO)

JOHNSON, Sir Robert
L | 8 July | 1696
In Merchant Service | Aug | 1699–
| Nov | 1700 (PJP)
CR | 3 May | 1705 (PMM)
Kt | | 1719 (PJP)
Dismissed | | 1720 (PJP)
d (drowned) | 5 June | 1723 (PJP)

JOHNSON, Samuel
L | 30 Apr | 1778
d | | 1784 (PRO)

JOHNSON, Thomas (1)
L | 23 June | 1679
CA | 6 Sept | 1688
d | 28 Oct | 1690

JOHNSON, Thomas (2)
L | 8 Apr | 1709
d | | 1734 (PRO)

JOHNSON, Thomas (3)
L | 10 Feb | 1815
d | 21 Apr | 1822 (PRO)

JOHNSON, Thomas (4)
L | 6 Apr | 1815
d | 8 May | 1828 (PRO)

JOHNSON, Urry
L | 9 Jan | 1808
CR | 6 Sept | 1809
d | 17 Feb | 1816 (PRO)

JOHNSON, William (1)
L
CA | 29 Mar | 1697
d | 31 Aug | 1699

JOHNSON, William (2)
L | 18 Aug | 1797
Ret CR | 16 Dec | 1840 (PRO)
d | | 1843 (PRO)

JOHNSON, William (3)
L | 4 May | 1810
HP | Apr | 1813 (OB)
Ret CR | 7 Mar | 1850 (PRO)
d | | 1851 (PRO)

JOHNSON, William Benjamin
T
L | | 1811 (TR)
Ret CR | | 1851 (TR)
d | | 1864 (TR)

JOHNSON, William Ward Perceval
T
L | 18 Oct | 1809
HP | 14 Dec | 1814 (OB)
CR | 19 Sept | 1835 (PRO)
CA | 14 Dec | 1841 (PRO)
Ret RA | 12 Apr | 1862 (PRO)
Ret VA | 24 May | 1867 (PRO)
Ret A | 20 July | 1875 (PRO)
d | 26 Dec | 1880 (TR)

JOHNSTON, Bryce
L | 3 Sept | 1795
d | | 1810 (NMM)

JOHNSTON, Charles
L | 28 Feb | 1795
d | 23 Apr | 1804

JOHNSTON, Charles Alexander
T
L | 8 Feb | 1815
CR | 5 Jan | 1844 (OB)
HP | 5 Jan | 1844 (OB)
Ret CA | 1 Aug | 1860 (PRO)
d | | 1861 (TR)

JOHNSTON, Charles James
L | 26 Feb | 1795
CR | 18 Jan | 1803
CA | 5 Sept | 1806
RAB | 23 Nov | 1841 (LG)
RAW | 9 Nov | 1846 (LG)
RAR | 17 Dec | 1847 (LG)
VAB | 6 Nov | 1850 (PRO)
VAW | 30 July | 1852 (PRO)
VAR | 11 Feb | 1854 (PRO)
Ret VA | 16 Apr | 1854 (PRO)
d | 16 Oct | 1856 (PRO)

JOHNSTON, David
L | 28 June | 1799
d | | 1805 (PRO)

JOHNSTON, George
See JOHNSTONE, George

JOHNSTON, George
L | 19 Dec | 1793
d | | 1809 (PRO)

JOHNSTON, Hendrick
See JOHNSON, Hendrick

JOHNSTON, James
L | 25 July | 1744
CR | 19 Apr | 1758
d (drowned) | 11 Oct | 1780 (CH)

JOHNSTON, James Henry
T
L 16 Feb 1810
HP July 1815 (OB)
Ret CR 8 July 1849 (PRO)
d 5 May 1851 (PRO)

JOHNSTON, John Frederick
L 15 Dec 1813
d 3 Feb 1846 (PRO)

JOHNSTON, Joseph John
L 15 Apr 1815
d June 1824 (PRO)

JOHNSTON, Robert
L 15 Feb 1815
HP Feb 1816
Ret CR 16 Feb 1871 (PRO)
d 1883 (PRO)

JOHNSTON, Robert Ballard
See JOHNSTONE, Robert Ballard

JOHNSTON, Samuel
L 12 Aug 1757
d 1772 (PRO)

JOHNSTON, Sir William (1)
L 25 Feb 1742
d 1772 (PRO)

JOHNSTON, William (2)
L 28 May 1760
d 1779 (PRO)

JOHNSTON, William (3)
L 27 Oct 1778
d 1798 (PRO)

JOHNSTON, William Benjamin
L 18 Apr 1811
d 1822 (PRO)

JOHNSTON, William Henry
L 6 July 1814
d 1822 (PRO)

JOHNSTON, William Irvine
L 22 Feb 1815
d 7 Feb 1823 (PRO)

JOHNSTONE, Brent
L 18 July 1807
d 1808 (PRO)

JOHNSTONE, George
L 9 Oct 1755
CR 6 Feb 1760
CA 11 Aug 1762
MP (Cockermouth) 24 May 1768–1774 (MPN)
MP (Appleby) 1774–1780 (MPN)
MP (Lostwithiel) 1 Dec 1780–22 Feb 1786 (MPN)
MP (Ilchester) 22 Feb 1786–Feb 1787 (MPN)
d 24 May 1787 (MPN)

JOHNSTONE, Gideon
L 26 Dec 1758
CR 23 Mar 1771
CA 2 June 1772
d 1788 (PRO)

JOHNSTONE, James
L 11 June 1793
CR 22 June 1802
CA 22 Jan 1806
d 1 Apr 1823 (PRO)

JOHNSTONE, John
L 8 Jan 1783
d ?1811 (PRO)

JOHNSTONE, John
See JOHNSON, John (2)

JOHNSTONE, Robert
L 7 Nov 1811
d 1813 (PRO)

JOHNSTONE, Robert Ballard
L 27 June 1814
HP 1816 (OB)
Ret CR 28 Oct 1837 (PRO)
d 23 Mar 1863 (PRO)

JOLLEY, Thomas
L 21 Feb 1715
CR
CA 12 May 1740
d 8 May 1741 (PRO)

JOLLIFFE, George
L 29 Nov 1797 (PRO)
KIA 1 Aug 1798 (LG)

JOLLIFFE, Henry
L 8 Dec 1795
Ret CR 26 Nov 1830 (PRO)
d 1837 (PRO)

JOLLIFFE, John
L 23 Dec 1760
d (drowned) 1762 (PJP)

JONES, Hon. Alexander
L 15 May 1800
CR 22 Jan 1806
CA 1 Aug 1811 (PRO)
RAB 3 Jan 1848 (PRO)
RAW 24 Dec 1849 (PRO)
Ret RA 1 July 1851 (PRO)
Ret VA 3 July 1855 (PRO)
Ret A 8 Jan 1860 (PRO)
d 8 Jan 1862 (PJP)

JONES, Anthony
L 1 July 1761
d 1793 (PRO)

JONES, Arthur
L
CR
CA 1 Jan 1713
d 23 Apr 1731 (PJP)

JONES, Benjamin
L 28 July 1802
d 1803 (PRO)

JONES, Hon. Charles, Viscount (1)
L 12 Jan 1782
CR 22 Nov 1790
CA 24 May 1793
Cre EP 1797 (PRO)
d 24 Dec 1800 (PRO)

JONES, Charles (2)
L 18 July 1793
CR 14 Feb 1801

CA	22 Jan	1806
d		1834 (PRO)
JONES, Charles (3)		
L	5 Apr	1805
Struck off list	12 Aug	1829 (PRO)
Restored		1830 (PRO)
Ret CR	23 Oct	1837 (PRO)
d	19 Jan	1847 (PRO)
JONES, Sir Charles Thomas		
L	16 Oct	1798
Kt		1809 (OB)
CR	15 Aug	1810
CA	12 Aug	1819 (PRO)
Ret CA	1 Oct	1846 (PRO)
Ret RA	27 Aug	1851 (PRO)
d	4 Apr	1853 (PRO)
JONES, Christopher Bassett		
L	19 June	1783
CR	27 June	1798
Dismissed	24 Aug	1802 (PRO)
d	Jan	1805 (PJP)
JONES, Daniel		
L		1673
CA	12 Apr	1678
d	12 Feb	1694 (PRO)
JONES, David		
L	10 Oct	1801
d		1810 (PRO)
JONES, Francis		
L	14 Feb	1815
d		1817 (PRO)
JONES, George		
L	12 May	1794
CR	24 Dec	1798
d	2 Jan	1834 (PRO)
JONES, George Matthew		
L	28 Apr	1802
CR	13 Dec	1810
CA	7 Dec	1817 (PJP)
d	29 Apr	1831 (PRO)
JONES, Griffith		
L	20 Nov	1777
d		1809 (PRO)
JONES, Henry		
L	20 Nov	1805
CR	11 Apr	1809 (PJP)
d	20 June	1829 (PJP)
JONES, Henry Paget		
L	26 Sept	1814
d	30 Jan	1854 (PRO)
JONES, Henry Spark		
L	12 Sept	1801
CR	4 May	1809
d	7 July	1809 (PRO)
JONES, Herbert John		
L	23 Nov	1810
CR	9 Nov	1846 (PRO)
HP	9 Nov	1846 (OB)
Ret CA	1 Aug	1860 (PRO)
d	27 Feb	1866 (PRO)
JONES, James (1)		
L	15 Mar	1744
CR	20 June	1765
CA	2 Aug	1777
d (drowned)	Dec	1779 (CH)
JONES, James (2)		
L	24 Feb	1802
d	22 June	1828 (PRO)
JONES, James (3)		
L	21 Feb	1815
HP	Aug	1815 (OB)
d		1855 (PRO)
JONES, James Howell		
L	27 Nov	1760
CR	26 May	1768
d	22 Feb	1791
JONES, Jenkin		
L	18 June	1813
CR	18 May	1816 (PRO)
CA	28 Aug	1828 (PRO)
d	14 July	1843 (PRO)
JONES, John (1)		
L	8 Sept	1741
d		1753 (PRO)
JONES, John (2)		
L	19 May	1761
d		1764 (PRO)
JONES, John (3)		
L	12 July	1782
Struck off list		1801 (PRO)
Restored		1802 (PRO)
SUP CR	30 Mar	1818 (PRO)
d	2 Nov	1828 (PRO)
JONES, John (4)		
L	28 Feb	1783
CR	22 Oct	1793 (PRO)
d	May	1824 (PRO)
JONES, John (5)		
L	14 Oct	1801
Ret CR	2 July	1832 (PRO)
d		1850 (PRO)
JONES, John (6)		
L	27 July	1802
Ret CR	6 July	1835 (PRO)
d		1863 (PRO)
JONES, John William		
L	28 Feb	1809
HP		1834 (OB)
Ret CR	9 Apr	1847 (PRO)
d		1850 (PRO)
JONES, Joseph Kenny		
L	14 Mar	1809
d	29 July	1824 (PRO)
JONES, Morgan (1)		
L		
CA		1660
JONES, Morgan (2)		
L	23 May	1745
Insane		1754 (PMM)
d		1780(1) (PRO)
JONES, Nathaniel Charles		
L	22 Feb	1791
d		1801 (PRO)
JONES, Philip		
L	6 Aug	1779
d	Dec	1828 (PRO)

JONES, Philip Kyrle		
L	16 Feb	1815
Not seen for many years; name removed		1829 (PRO)
JONES, Richard (1)		
L	14 Feb	1794
CR	8 Oct	1798
CA	29 Apr	1802
d	11 Dec	1829 (PRO)
JONES, Richard (2)		
L	27 Mar	1800
CR	22 Oct	1844 (PRO)
Ret CR	5 Nov	1844 (PJP)
d		1848 (PRO)
JONES, Robert (1)		
L		
CA	1667	
JONES, Robert (2)		
L	11 Feb	1812
HP	Aug	1814 (OB)
d		1851 (PRO)
JONES, Robert Lewis		
L	1 Mar	1815
d	29 June	1828 (PRO)
JONES, Robert Parker		
L	30 Aug	1806
Ret CR	9 July	1840 (OB)
d		1866 (PRO)
JONES, Roger (1)		
L		
CA		1665
JONES, Roger (2)		
L	4 Mar	1740
d		1763 (PRO)
JONES, Theobald		
L	8 July	1809
CR	19 July	1814
CA	25 Aug	1828 (PRO)
MP (Londonderry)	1830–1847 (OB)	
Ret CA	25 Aug	1848 (PRO)
Ret RA	2 May	1855 (PRO)
Ret VA	15 Jan	1862 (PRO)
Ret A	12 Sept	1865 (PRO)
d		1868 (PRO)
JONES, Theophilus		
L	18 Sept	1778
CR		
CA	4 Sept	1782
RAB	23 Apr	1804
RAW	9 Nov	1805
RAR	28 Apr	1808
VAB	25 Oct	1809
VAW	31 July	1810
VAR	12 Aug	1812
AB	12 Aug	1819 (CH)
AW	27 May	1825 (CH)
d	8 Nov	1835 (PRO)
JONES, Thomas (1)		
L	20 Apr	1744
d		1769 (PRO)
JONES, Thomas (2)		
L	30 Oct	1777
d		1780 (PRO)
JONES, Thomas (3)		
L	5 Nov	1796
d		1798 (PRO)
JONES, Thomas (4)		
L	30 Jan	1800
d		1814 (PRO)
JONES, Thomas (5)		
L	4 Jan	1808
HP		1813 (OB)
Ret CR	19 Oct	1844 (PRO)
d	27 Sept	1845 (PRO)
JONES, Thomas Parry		
L	28 June	1803
d		1807 (PRO)
JONES, Thomas William		
L	7 Apr	1801
KIA	10 Sept	1813 (JH)
JONES, William (1)		
L		
CA	1 Aug	1666 (DDA)
JONES, William (2)		
L	30 Jan	1694 (PJP)
CR	23 May	1701 (PMM)
CA	15 Feb	1705
d (drowned)	24 Aug	1708
JONES, William (3)		
L	24 Sept	1756
d		1758(9) (PRO)
JONES, William (4)		
L	6 Dec	1757
d	3 Aug	1763 (PRO)
JONES, William (5)		
L	14 Mar	1759
d	27 Nov	1779 (PRO)
JONES, William (6)		
L	28 Nov	1799
d		1841 (PRO)
JONES, William (7)		
L	16 May	1809
Ret CR	27 July	1847 (PRO)
d		1852 (PRO)
JONES, William (8)		
L	24 July	1811
CR	1 May	1826 (PRO)
CA	18 Aug	1828 (PRO)
d	24 May	1846 (PRO)
JONES, William (9)		
L	15 Feb	1815
HP	Nov	1824 (OB)
Ret CR	18 Jan	1861 (PRO)
d		1862 (PRO)
JONES, William (10)		
L	15 Mar	1815 (PRO)
HP	15 Mar	1815 (OB)
Ret CR	20 July	1863 (PRO)
d		1871 (PRO)
JONES, William Charles		
L	11 Feb	1815
d		1854 (PRO)
JORDAN, Charles		
L	26 Nov	1777
d	15 Dec	1779 (PRO)

JORDAN, Sir Joseph (1)
L
CA 1664
RAW 1665
Kt 1665 (PD)
RAR 3 Apr 1672 (NJ)
VAB 8 Apr 1672 (NJ)
VAR 29 May 1666 (RM)
d 1685 (PD)

JORDAN, Joseph (2)
L 16 Sept 1778
d 1782(3) (PRO)

JORDAN, Robert
L 3 Aug 1805
d 1836 (PRO)

JORDAN, Thomas
L 27 Oct 1758
CR 11 Sept 1766
CA 7 July 1772
d 30 Apr 1779 (PRO)

JOWLES, Henry
L 1666

JOWLES, John
L 20 Dec 1711

JOWLES, Valentin
L
CA 1660

JOY, John
L
CA 1673
d before 1689 (PJP)

JOYCE, John (1)
L 13 May 1793
CR 29 Apr 1802
CA 11 Apr 1809
d 24 May 1839 (PRO)

JOYCE, John (2)
L 18 Dec 1794
CR 29 Apr 1802 (PRO)
CA 11 Apr 1809 (PRO)
d 1839 (PRO)

JOYCE, John (3)
L 25 Dec 1800
d 1815 (PRO)

JOYCE, John Barnett
L 19 Dec 1812 (PRO)
d 9 Aug 1822 (PRO)

JUDAS, Joseph
L 3 Aug 1805
d (drowned) Mar 1814 (PJP)

JUDD, Robert Hayley
L 3 Oct 1794
CR 29 Apr 1802
Ret CA 10 Sept 1840 (PRO)
d 29 Dec 1847 (PRO)

JUDD, William
L 20 Feb 1759
CR 13 Mar 1773
CA 7 Sept 1774
d 1783 (PRO)

JULIAN, John
L 27 Dec 1799
T
CR 15 June 1814
d 20 July 1828 (PRO)

JULIAN, Robert
T
L 17 Mar 1815
d 12 Apr 1822 (PRO)

JULIAN, Robert
See JULYAN, Robert

JULIUS, William
L
CA 10 June 1693
d 3 Oct 1698

JULYAN, Robert
L 3 June 1799
CR 7 June 1814
HP 2 Dec 1815 (OB)
Ret CA 1 July 1851 (PRO)
d 1856 (PRO)

JUMP, Robert
L 21 Dec 1782
SUPCR 31 Dec 1818 (PRO)
d 1837 (PRO)

JUMPER, Sir William
L 29 Mar 1688 (P)
CA 17 Feb 1692
Kt 1704 (DNB)
COMM (Plymouth) Nov 1714 (PJP)
d 12 Mar 1715 (DNB)

JURD, William
L 30 Aug 1746
d 1757 (PRO)

JURIN, Francis
L 27 Nov 1692
d 1719 (PRO)

JUSTICE, Philip (1)
L 10 July 1782
SUP CR 11 Dec 1817 (PRO)
d 29 Sept 1827 (PRO)

JUSTICE, Philip (2)
L 5 Aug 1813
CR 5 Dec 1824 (PRO)
CA 2 July 1846 (PRO)
d 1855 (PRO)

JUXON, Charles
L 1662
CA 1665
d before 1689 (PJP)

KAINS, John
L 1 July 1807
CR 8 Jan 1814
CA 9 Nov 1846 (LG)
HP 1848 (OB)
Ret CA 17 Dec 1856 (PRO)
d 1862 (PRO)

KANE, James
L 23 Apr 1798
d 1809 (NMM)

KATON, Edward
L 13 Mar 1759
d 1780 (NMM)

KATON, James
L 18 Feb 1794
CR 11 July 1801
CA 23 Oct 1801
Ret RA 22 July 1830 (PRO)
RAR 17 Aug 1840 (PRO)
VAB 23 Nov 1841 (LG)
d 14 Dec 1845 (PRO)

KAY, John
L 13 Dec 1793
d 20 June 1803

KAY, John
See KEAY, John

KEAN, James
See MEARA, James

KEAN, Thomas
L 10 July 1809
d 1817 (PRO)

KEANE, Edward
L 7 Mar 1815
CR 21 Nov 1858 (NMM)
d 1859 (NMM)

KEANE, Richard
L 6 July 1814
CR 26 Aug 1828 (PRO)
CA 28 June 1838 (PRO)
d 1843 (PRO)

KEARNY, Michael
L 6 Feb 1744
CR 20 Aug 1759
d June 1797

KEATING, Christopher
L 31 Mar 1756
d 1764 (NMM)

KEATS, Sir Richard Goodwin
L 7 Apr 1777
CR 18 Jan 1782
CA 24 June 1789
CRM 9 Nov 1805 (DNB)
Kt 1807 (DNB)
RAB 2 Oct 1807
RAW 25 Oct 1809
RAR 31 July 1810
VAB 1 Aug 1811
GG (Newfoundland) 1813–1818 (BNS)
VAW 4 June 1814
GCB 1815 (PJP)
MGRM 7 May 1818 (DNB)
VAR 12 Aug 1819 (CH)
GGH 1821 (PJP)
AB 27 May 1825 (CH)
AW 22 July 1830 (CH)
d 5 Apr 1834 (CH)

KEATS, William
L 6 Aug 1813
CR 17 Apr 1826 (NMM)
CA 27 Mar 1826 (PJP)
RA 15 Apr 1854 (NMM)
VA 2 May 1860 (NMM)
A 11 Jan 1864 (NMM)
d 2 May 1874 (NMM)

KEAY, James
L 4 May 1810
d 1811 (PRO)

KECK, Lawrence
L
CA 16 Mar 1691
SUP 8 Jan 1705 (PRO)
d 30 Oct 1724

KEEBLE, Henry
L
CA 1667

KEECH, Maximilian
L 1672
d before 1689 (PJP)

KEEFE, William
L 22 Oct 1814
d 1817 (NMM)

KEEK, Lawrence
See KECK, Lawrence

KEELE, Charles
L 24 Sept 1814
CR 22 July 1826 (PRO)
CA 19 July 1843 (PRO)
Ret CA 31 Jan 1856 (PRO)
Ret RA 30 Jan 1863 (PRO)
d 9 Oct 1865 (PRO)

KEELER, Alexander
L 5 June 1794
Ret CR 26 Nov 1830 (PRO)
d 31 Aug 1831 (PRO)

KEELER, Robert
L 26 Aug 1756
CR 4 Sept 1759
CA 19 May 1761
SUP RA 22 Sept 1790
d 1810 (NMM)

KEELING, John James
L 13 May 1812
CR 2 Jan 1854 (NMM)
Ret CA 1 Aug 1860 (NMM)
d 1876 (NMM)

KEEN, Robert
L 6 July 1783
CR 10 Apr 1797
CA 21 Oct 1810
d 1835 (PRO)

KEENAN, John (1)
L 26 Dec 1795
CR 1 June 1812
d 18 Oct 1841 (PRO)

KEENAN, John (2)
L 25 Mar 1809
d 1840 (NMM)

KEENE, John
L 1667 (DDA)
CA 1671 (DDA)
d before 1689 (PJP)

KEENOR, George
L 20 July 1797
Ret CR 24 Nov 1840 (PRO)
d May 1841 (PRO)

KEGWIN, Richard (1)
L 1665 (PRO)
CA 1672 (PRO)
d Apr 1673 (PRO)

KEGWIN, Richard (2)
L

CA 17 May 1689 (PRO)
KIA 21 June 1690 (PJP)

KEILY, Benjamin
L 30 Apr 1811 (NMM)
d 1812 (NMM)

KEILY, Richard
L 21 Aug 1797
CR 10 Oct 1804
d (drowned) Feb 1807 (CH)

KEIR, Francis
L 26 Feb 1760
d 15 Sept 1794 (M)

KEITH, Alexander
L 24 May 1748
d 1786 (NMM)

KEITH, Sir Basil
L 13 Nov 1756
CR 18 Oct 1758
CA 11 Apr 1760
d 15 Nov 1777

KEITH, Charles
L 25 May 1813
d 1818 (PRO)

KEITH, George
L 30 Aug 1779
KIA 16 Apr 1781 (LG)

KEITH, Hon. George, Viscount
MP (Southwark) 1768–1775 (MB)
L 28 June 1770
CR 18 Sept 1772
CA 11 May 1775
MP (Dunbartonshire) 1781–1790 (MPT)
MP (Stirlingshire) 1790–1801 (MPT)
RAB 12 Apr 1794
Kt 30 May 1794 (DNB)
RAW 4 July 1794 (PRO)
VAB 1 June 1795
Cre IP 16 Mar 1797 (MPT)
VAR 14 Feb 1799
AB 1 Jan 1801
Cre Bt 17 Sept 1803 (MPT)
AW 9 Nov 1805
AR 31 July 1810
Cre EP 1 June 1814 (MPT)
GCB 2 Jan 1815 (MPT)
d 20 Mar 1823 (PJP)

KEITH, George Mouat
L 12 Aug 1801
CR 16 Mar 1814
d 22 July 1832 (LT)

KELBURNE, Hon. James, Viscount
See BOYLE, Hon. James

KELBY, Robert
L 1668

KELLAWAY, Christopher Farwell
L 5 Aug 1778
d 1781 (PRO)

KELLER, Edward
L 21 Aug 1741
CR 20 Nov 1744
CA 23 Apr 1748
d 10 Sept 1750 (PRO)

KELLETT, Augustus Henry
L 14 Feb 1815
CR 25 July 1825 (NMM)
d 1828 (NMM)

KELLEY, John
L 24 Sept 1795
d 1814 (PRO)

KELLEY, Peter
L 13 May 1778
d 1811 (NMM)

KELLIE, James
L 27 May 1779
d 1794 (PRO)

KELLING, John
L
CA 3 Mar 1697
d 20 Oct 1698

KELLOCK, Adam
L 25 Mar 1809
d 1837 (NMM)

KELLOCK, James Robert
L 11 Feb 1815
d 1 Jan 1823 (PRO)

KELLY, Benedictus Marward
L 31 Jan 1806
CR 28 Nov 1811
CA 19 July 1821 (NMM)
HP Feb 1822 (OB)
RA 8 Mar 1852 (NMM)
VA 2 Oct 1857 (NMM)
A 27 Apr 1863 (NMM)
d 1867 (NMM)

KELLY, Charles
L 15 Nov 1759
d 20 Oct 1800

KELLY, Edward
L 27 Dec 1808
CR 13 May 1828 (PRO)
d 1837 (PRO)

KELLY, James Francis
L 29 Sept 1799 (NMM)
d 1803 (NMM)

KELLY, John
L 21 Jan 1809
d 1810 (NMM)

KELLY, Magnus Morton
L 2 Feb 1808
d July 1822 (PRO)

KELLY, Montagu
L 18 Sept 1797
Ret CR 20 Dec 1830 (PRO)
d 1838 (PRO)

KELLY, Richard Nugent
L 21 Mar 1812
Ret CR 27 Apr 1854 (PRO)
d 20 Nov 1861 (PRO)

KELLY, Timothy
L 17 July 1762
CR 13 Jan 1780
d 1788 (PRO)

KELLY, William (1)
L 18 Nov 1794
d 1797 (NMM)

KELLY, William (2)
L 4 July 1798
T
CR 23 Aug 1811
HP 23 Aug 1811 (OB)
Ret CR 1 July 1851 (PRO)
d 1859 (TR)

KELLY, William (3)
L 23 Apr 1799
CR 21 Oct 1810
d Oct 1823 (PRO)

KELLY, William (4)
L 8 Mar 1815
CR 25 Apr 1831 (NMM)
CA 5 Apr 1844 (NMM)
Ret CA 26 Feb 1856 (NMM)
Ret RA 23 Mar 1863 (NMM)
Ret VA 3 July 1869 (NMM)
d 1875 (NMM)

KELLY, William Hancock
L 16 May 1776
CR 7 Apr 1782
CA 8 Aug 1783
RAB 9 Nov 1805
RAW 28 Apr 1808
RAR 25 Oct 1809
VAB 31 July 1810
d 2 May 1811 (CH)

KELSALL, Brook
L 27 June 1746
d 1754 (PRO)

KELSEY, John
L
CA 1665
d before 1688 (PD)

KEMBALL, William Henry
L 18 Feb 1815
d Dec 1853 (NMM)

KEMBLE, William Gage
L 18 Nov 1790
d 9 July 1797

KEMP, John
L 17 Feb 1815
d July 1818 (PRO)

KEMP, Richard
L 6 Aug 1759
SUP CR 21 May 1803
d 1820 (NMM)

KEMPE, Arthur
L 10 Jan 1771
CR 10 Aug 1775
CA 10 May 1780
RAW 14 Feb 1799
RAR 1 Jan 1801 (PRO)
VAB 23 Apr 1804
VAW 9 Nov 1805
VAR 28 Apr 1808
AB 31 July 1810
AW 4 Dec 1813
AR 19 July 1821 (CH)
d 1 Jan 1823 (PRO)

KEMPE, Nicholas
L 26 Oct 1780
CR 14 July 1797
d 25 Apr 1829 (PRO)

KEMPENFELT, Richard
L 14 Jan 1741
CR 5 May 1756
CA 17 Jan 1757
RAB 26 Sept 1780
d (drowned) 29 Aug 1782 (CH)

KEMPSTER, Ralph Richard Tomkin
L 1 Feb 1815
d 1859 (NMM)

KEMPT, Francis
L 21 Apr 1783
CR 7 Jan 1802
CA 27 June 1806
d 1815 (PJP)

KEMPTHORN, Charles Henry
L 25 Dec 1813
CR 6 Aug 1852 (NMM)
d 1865 (NMM)

KEMPTHORN, John
See KEMPTHORNE

KEMPTHORN, Thomas
See KEMPTHORNE, Thomas

KEMPTHORNE, James
L 6 Aug 1761
CR
CA 25 Sept 1781
RAB 1 Jan 1801
RAW 23 Apr 1804
RAR 9 Nov 1805
VAB 13 Dec 1806 (LG)
d 1808 (NMM)

KEMPTHORNE, Sir John (1)
L
CA 1664
RAB 9 June 1666 (RM)
Kt 24 Apr 1670 (MPH)
RAR 1672
VAB Aug 1673 (NMM)
COMM (Portsmouth) 1675–Oct 1679 (MPH)
VAD 12 Mar 1678
MP (Portsmouth) Mar–Aug 1679 (MPH)
d 19 Oct 1679 (MPH)

KEMPTHORNE, John (2)
L 1672
CA 1673

KEMPTHORNE, Morgan
L 1671
CA 10 Nov 1673
KIA 22 May 1681 (CH)

KEMPTHORNE, Rupert
L
CA 13 Oct 1690
d (murdered) 28 Oct 1691 (PJP)

KEMPTHORNE, Samuel
L 11 Aug 1778
CR 26 Aug 1789
d 1837 (PRO)

KEMPTHORNE, Thomas
L 19 Jan 1697
CR
CA 31 Mar 1704
GG (Newfoundland) 1715–1717 (DCB)
COMM (Chatham) 1722–1736 (PJP)
d 23 July 1736 (PJP)

KEMPTHORNE, William (1)
L 1664
CA 1665
d before 1689 (PJP)

KEMPTHORNE, William (2)
L 19 Feb 1800
CR 3 Apr 1811
CA 16 Sept 1816 (NMM)
d 1835 (NMM)

KENAH, Richard
L 6 Feb 1806
CR 1 July 1811
KIA 3 Oct 1814 (CH)

KENDAL, Charles
L 24 Aug 1697
CR
CA 26 July 1715
d 19 Jan 1744

KENDALL, Charles
L 1 Feb 1763
d 7 May 1806 (PMM)

KENDALL, Edward
L 29 May 1793
CR 12 Sept 1800
CA 29 Apr 1802
d 1806 (PRO)

KENDALL, John
L 28 Apr 1765
CR
CA 24 Nov 1778
SUP RA 3 July 1795
d 1824 (PRO)

KENDALL, Thomas
L 8 Feb 1815
d 1847 (PRO)

KENDERDINE, John
L 7 Mar 1815
HP 7 Mar 1815 (OB)
Ret CR 10 Apr 1863 (NMM)
d 1867 (NMM)

KENMURE, Hon. Adam Gordon, Viscount
See GORDON, Hon. Adam, Viscount Kenmure

KENNEDY, Alexander (1)
L 2 Apr 1806
CR 2 June 1809
Dismissed Apr 1814 (PJP)
d 1849 (PRO)

KENNEDY, Alexander (2)
L 25 July 1811
CR 9 Oct 1822 (PRO)
HP 9 Oct 1822 (PRO)
Ret CA 1 Apr 1856 (PRO)
d 1864 (PRO)

KENNEDY, Andrew
L 9 Feb 1815
CR 27 May 1842 (PRO)
Ret CR 1 July 1851 (PRO)
d 1854 (NMM)

KENNEDY, Archibald
L 16 Dec 1744
CR 13 Mar 1756
CA 4 Apr 1757
d 29 Dec 1794 (PJP)

KENNEDY, David
L 9 Dec 1800
d 1808 (NMM)

KENNEDY, Richard
L 17 Feb 1815
d 1832 (PRO)

KENNEDY, Silvester
L 30 Apr 1708
CR 28 Apr 1740
d 1755 (PRO)

KENNEDY, Thomas Fortescue
L 5 July 1796
T
CR 24 Dec 1805
CA 4 Dec 1813
d 15 May 1846 (OB)

KENNEDY, Walter
L 24 Nov 1800
d 1811 (PRO)

KENNETT, Henry
L 19 June 1799
Ret CR 15 Dec 1830 (PRO)
d 1839 (PRO)

KENNEY, Thomas (1)
L
CA 9 Aug 1695
KIA 4 Aug 1704 (CH)

KENNEY, Thomas (2)
L 23 June 1815
d 5 Apr 1827 (NMM)

KENNICOTT, Gilbert
T wounded
L 22 Aug 1810
CR 9 Nov 1846 (NMM)
HP 1847 (OB)
CA 9 Feb 1859 (NMM)
Ret CA 19 July 1871 (NMM)
d 1874 (TR)

KENSALL, Brook
See KELSALL, Brook

KENSEY, William
L 2 Sept 1708
d 1744 (NMM)

KENSY, William
See KINSEY, William

KENT, Bartholomew (1)
L 16 June 1801
KIA 9 Dec 1803 (PJP)

KENT, Bartholomew (2)
L 2 May 1804
CR 29 Mar 1815
d Jan 1841 (NMM)

KENT, Henry (1)
L 11 Oct 1793
d 17 June 1801 (PJP)

KENT, Henry (2)
L 14 Mar 1811
CR 26 Dec 1822 (PRO)
HP 26 Dec 1822 (OB)
Ret CA 1 Apr 1856 (PRO)
d 1873 (PRO)

KENT, John (1)
L 31 May 1762
d 1786 (NMM)

KENT, John (2)
L 13 Nov 1809
d 27 Jan 1816 (PJP)

KENT, Joseph
L 7 Aug 1793
Ret CR 14 Sept 1826 (PRO)
d 23 Feb 1839 (PRO)

KENT, Mark
L 3 Oct 1812
d 4 Oct 1828 (PRO)

KENT, Thomas
L 1665

KENT, Thomas Westerly
L 15 Aug 1806
d 24 Sept 1812 (LT)

KENT, William
L 27 Oct 1781
CR 15 Oct 1802 (PRO)
CA 22 Jan 1806
d 29 Aug 1812 (MB)

KENT, William George Carlile
L 17 May 1809
CR 15 June 1814
HP 15 June 1814 (OB)
Ret CA 1 July 1851 (PRO)
d 1871 (PRO)

KENTISH, Samuel
L 22 Sept 1810
d Feb 1827 (NMM)

KENTISH, Thomas
L 5 Nov 1802
d 1809 (PRO)

KEPPEL, Hon. Augustus, Lord Viscount
L 25 Aug 1744 (PMM)
CR 7 Nov 1744 (PMM)
CA 11 Dec 1744
MP (Chichester) 1755–1761 (MPN)
CRM 3 Feb 1760 (AL)
MP (New Windsor) 1761–1780 (MPN)
RAB 21 Oct 1762
COM AD 31 July 1765–
11 Dec 1766 (AO)
RAR 18 Oct 1770
VAB 24 Oct 1770
VAW 31 Mar 1775
VAR 5 Feb 1776
AB 29 Jan 1778
MP (Surrey) 1780–22 Apr 1782 (MPN)
COM AD 1 Apr 1782–
30 Jan 1783 (AO)
AW 8 Apr 1782
Cre EP 22 Apr 1782 (AO)
COM AD 10 Apr–31 Dec 1783 (AO)
d 2 Oct 1786 (CH)

KEPPEL, George (1)
L 14 May 1774
CR 18 Mar 1777
CA 26 Jan 1778
RAW 1 June 1795
RAR 20 Feb 1797
VAW 14 Feb 1799
VAR 29 Apr 1802
AB 23 Apr 1804
d 1805 (NMM)

KEPPEL, George (2)
L 6 Nov 1778
d 1781 (PRO)

KEPPEL, George Augustus
L
CR 14 Feb 1781
CA 22 May 1782
d 1782 (NMM)

KER, William
L 31 Mar 1760
d 1770 (PRO)

KERCHER, Thomas
L
CA 29 Apr 1690
d 17 Oct 1694

KERKE, Charles
L
CA 1678
d before 1689 (PJP)

KERLY, Anthony
L 5 June 1741
CR 8 Feb 1746 (PRO)
CA 2 July 1746
d 28 Apr 1764 (M)

KERLY, Joseph
L 12 Dec 1740
d 1765 (NMM)

KERR, Alexander Robert
L 15 Nov 1790
CR 29 Apr 1802
CA 22 Jan 1806
CB 1815 (PJP)
d 4 Aug 1831 (PRO)

KERR, Charles Julius
L 31 Dec 1805
CR 30 Nov 1808
CA 5 Oct 1814
d 6 July 1833 (PRO)

KERR, George Lewis
L 29 Aug 1799
d 1809 (NMM)

KERR, Hugh
L 3 Feb 1802
d 1815 (NMM)

KERR, James
L 20 Nov 1812
HP 1816 (OB)
Ret CR 2 July 1855 (PRO)
d 1871 (PRO)

KERR, Hon. Lord Mark Robert
L 1 Nov 1794
CR 1 Nov 1796 (NMM)
CA 7 Mar 1797
RAB 19 July 1821 (LG)
RAW 27 May 1825 (LG)
RAR 22 July 1830 (LG)
VAW 10 Jan 1837 (LG)
d 9 Sept 1840 (NMM)

KERR, Robert (1)
L 30 Mar 1734
SUP 22 Dec 1749 (PMM)

KERR, Robert (2)
L 9 Jan 1748
LGH 1766 (PJP)
d 15 Mar 1804

KERR, Robert (3)
L 18 Apr 1783
d 10 Oct 1786 (PMM)

KERR, William
L 13 Sept 1688 (P)
CA 14 May 1690
Dismissed 1708 (CH)
d 1729 (PJP)

KERSTMAN, Lambert
L 20 Sept 1806
d 1809 (NMM)

KERSWELL, Edward
L 7 Dec 1756
d 1782 (NMM)

KERWORTH, Richard
L
CA 3 May 1691
SUP 1696
d 28 Apr 1728

KESTELL or KESTLE, Francis
L 19 Sept 1694
CR 15 Nov 1704 (PMM)
CA 12 Dec 1705
d 16 Sept 1706

KESTELL, John (1)
L 10 Feb 1749
d 1755 (NMM)

KESTELL, John (2)
L 16 Mar 1805
Seniority adjusted to
L 16 Mar 1806
d 15 Oct 1837 (PRO)

KEVELL, John
L 1673

KEVERN, Richard
L 24 Oct 1793
Ret CR 3 Dec 1827 (PRO)
d 1857 (PRO)

KEY, William Strugnel
L 12 Feb 1803
d (drowned) 18 Dec 1812 (CH)

KEYBURN, George
L 11 Dec 1780
d 26 July 1792

KEYS, David
L 21 July 1798
Ret CR 12 Oct 1841 (PRO)
d Dec 1847 (PRO)

KIDD, Dandy (1)
L 23 Apr 1708
CR
CA 26 Dec 1739
d 23 Jan 1741 (PRO)

KIDD, Dandy (2)
L 11 Apr 1759
d 1772 (NMM)

KIDD, Joseph
L 15 Aug 1801
d (drowned) Mar 1808 (CH)

KIDDLE, John
L 29 July 1814
d 29 May 1851 (NMM)

KIDWELL, John
L
CA 10 June 1693
Gone 1718 (PRO)

KIELL, John
L 19 Mar 1794
d 1804 (PRO)

KIEMAR, Thomas
L 5 Dec 1705
d 1737 (NMM)

KIGGENS OR KIGGINS, William
L
CA 19 Nov 1689
d 16 Sept 1698

KIGGINS, Joseph
L 7 Sept 1706
SUP L 1741 (NMM)

KIGWIN, Richard
See KEGWIN, Richard

KILGOUR, Alexander
L 6 May 1796
d 1798 (PRO)

KILLIGREW, Charles
L 19 Feb 1708 (PMM)

KILLIGREW, Henry
L 1666 (P)
CA 9 Jan 1672
GG
(Landguard Point Fort) 20 Jan 1688 (EAD)
VAB 8 June 1689
VAR 17 Feb 1690
AB 3 June 1690
CSMR 1 Jan 1691 (EAD)
COM AD 15 Apr 1693–
2 May 1694 (AO)
Dismissed 1693 (DNB)
d 9 Nov 1712 (PRO)

KILLIGREW, James
L 5 Sept 1688 (P)
CA 11 Apr 1690
LSMR 16 July 1691 (EAD)
CAFMR 10 Dec 1693 (EAD)
KIA 7 Jan 1695 (CH)

KILLINGWORTH, Thomas
L
CA 17 Feb 1692
KIA 18 July 1694 (CH)

KILLWICK, Edward
L 10 Dec 1782
CR 22 July 1796
d 1835 (PRO)

KILLWICK, John Arthur
L 1 Sept 1807
d Jan 1823 (NMM)

KILNER, Christopher
L 9 Oct 1787 (PRO)
CR 13 Apr 1796
d 1816 (PRO)

KILSHA, George
L 4 Nov 1795 (PRO)
d 1797 (PRO)

KING, Andrew
L 11 Aug 1797
T
CR 22 Jan 1806
CA 13 Oct 1807
d 30 June 1835 (PJP)

KING, Charles (1)
L 6 Aug 1779
SUP CR 31 Jan 1814
d 17 Aug 1825 (PRO)

KING, Charles (2)
L 11 Feb 1796
d 21 Sept 1827 (PRO)

KING, Charles (3)
L 27 Mar 1799 (PRO)
Ret CR 7 Apr 1843 (PRO)
d 1858 (PRO)

KING, Christopher
L
CA 12 Oct 1691
Gone 1718 (PRO)

KING, Custis
L 30 Jan 1741
d 1744(5) (PRO)

KING, Desory
L 8 Oct 1793
Ret CR 31 Oct 1827 (PRO)
d 1835 (PRO)

KING, Hon. Edward
L 15 June 1796
CR 29 Apr 1802
MP
(County Roscommon) 1802–1806 (MPT)
CA 8 May 1804
d 25 Sept 1807 (PRO)

KING, Sir Edward Durnford
L 5 Sept 1795
CR 23 June 1796
CA 8 Jan 1801
HP 1808–1811 (OB)
RAB 22 July 1830 (LG)
Kt Jan 1833 (OB)
RAR 10 Jan 1837 (LG)
VAB 23 Nov 1841 (LG)
VAW 9 Nov 1846 (PRO)
VAR 13 May 1847 (PRO)
AB 30 Oct 1849 (PRO)
AW 8 July 1851 (PRO)
AR 9 July 1855 (PRO)
d 16 Jan 1862 (PJP)

KING, George (1)
L 7 May 1782
d 1793 (PRO)

KING, George (2)
L 9 July 1798
d 1800 (PRO)

KING, George (3)
L 12 Mar 1807
d 1844 (PRO)

KING, George (4)
L 12 Jan 1810
CR 19 July 1814
d 17 Aug 1822 (LT)

KING, George (5)
L 3 Sept 1810
CR 15 June 1814
HP 15 June 1814 (OB)
Ret CR 1 July 1851 (PRO)
Ret CA 22 Jan 1852 (PRO)
d 1859 (PRO)

KING, George Morrison
L 22 Oct 1814
CR 14 Dec 1821 (PRO)
Ret CR 1 July 1851 (PRO)
Ret CA 1 Apr 1856 (PRO)
d June 1858 (PRO)

KING, Henry
L 18 Oct 1802
CR 19 Oct 1814
Ret CR 1 July 1851 (PRO)
Ret CA 19 Mar 1852 (PRO)
d 1874 (PRO)

KING, Isaac
L 27 July 1757
d 1759 (PRO)

KING, James (1)
L 10 Jan 1771
CR
CA 3 Oct 1780
d 22 Oct 1784 (PRO)

KING, James (2)
L 24 Nov 1778
d 1794 (PRO)

KING, Hon. James William
L 3 Mar 1804
CR 15 Aug 1806
CA 18 Jan 1809
RAB 9 Nov 1846 (PRO)
d 14 Feb 1848 (PJP)

KING, Jeremy
L 1704 (PJP)

KING, John (1)
L
CA 1661
d before 1689 (PJP)

KING, John (2)
L 26 Jan 1746
d 1747(8) (PRO)

KING, John (3)
L 3 Mar 1815
CR 25 Apr 1825 (OB)
HP 5 July 1843 (OB)
Ret CA 23 Mar 1852 (PRO)
d 9 Nov 1857 (PRO)

KING, Mathew
L 4 Mar 1740
CR 5 Nov 1745 (PRO)
CA 23 Oct 1747
d 7 June 1749

KING, Norfolk
L 12 Mar 1812
d 1839 (PRO)

KING, Philip Gidley
L 25 Dec 1778 (DUB)
CR 2 Mar 1791
CA 5 Dec 1798

Governor of Australia 1802–1806 (DUB)
d 3 Sept 1808 (DUB)

KING, Philip Parker
L 28 Feb 1814
CR 7 July 1821 (PRO)
CA 25 Feb 1830 (PRO)
Ret CA 1 Oct 1850 (PRO)
Ret RA 27 Sept 1855 (PRO)
d 29 Feb 1856 (PRO)

KING, Sir Richard (1)
L 1 Feb 1746
CR 23 July 1756
CA 29 Jan 1759
Kt 2 June 1784 (MPT)
RAW 24 Sept 1787
RAR 21 Sept 1790
GG
(Newfoundland) 1792–1794 (MPT)
Cre Bt 18 July 1792 (MPT)
VAB 1 Feb 1793
VAW 12 Apr 1794
MP
(Rochester) 12 May 1794–1802 (MPT)
VAR 4 July 1794
AB 1 June 1795
AW 14 Feb 1799
T
AR 9 Nov 1805
d 25 Nov 1806 (PRO)

KING, Sir Richard (2)
L 14 Nov 1791
CR 1793 (PMM)
CA 14 May 1794
T
Inh Bt Nov 1806 (DNB)
RAB 12 Aug 1812
RAW 4 June 1814
KCB 2 Jan 1815 (DNB)
RAR 12 Aug 1819 (PRO)
VAB 19 July 1821 (LG)
VAW 27 May 1825 (LG)
VAR 22 July 1830 (LG)
d 4 Aug 1834 (PRO)

KING, Richard Henry
L 12 July 1813
CR 27 Aug 1828 (PRO)
CA 1 May 1839 (PRO)
Ret RA 13 Feb 1858 (PRO)
d 14 Sept 1862 (PRO)

KING, Solomon
L 21 Sept 1795
d 1812 (PRO)

KING, Sydney
L 8 Mar 1815
d 1841 (PRO)

KING, Thomas
L 23 Nov 1799
d 1806 (PRO)

KING, William (1)
L 27 Oct 1718
d 20 Dec 1727 (PMM)

KING, William (2)
L 3 Nov 1790
CR 22 Jan 1806
CA 13 Oct 1807
d 1836 (PRO)

KING, William (3)
L 16 Nov 1790
d 1803 (PRO)

KING, William (4)
L 27 May 1797
CR 21 June 1804
d (drowned) 18 Feb 1807 (CH)

KING, William (5)
L 27 Sept 1809
d 7 Mar 1831 (PRO)

KING, William Elletson
L 22 Mar 1797
d 8 Mar 1829 (PRO)

KINGCOME, John
L 1 July 1815
CR 8 Jan 1828 (PRO)
CA 28 June 1838 (PRO)
RAB 10 Sept 1857 (PRO)
RAW 9 June 1860 (PRO)
RAR 30 Jan 1863 (PRO)
VAB 5 Mar 1864 (PRO)
Ret VA 1 Apr 1866 (PRO)
Ret A 10 Sept 1869 (PRO)
d 1871 (PRO)

KINGDOM, John
L 16 Jan 1813
d 2 Sept 1821 (PRO)

KINGDON, John
T
L 20 Nov 1812
Ret CR 20 Aug 1855 (PRO)
d 1862 (TR)

KINGHORNE, George
L 15 Oct 1800
d 1804 (PRO)

KINGSLEY, Richard
L 3 Mar 1740
d 1742 (PRO)

KINGSMILL, Sir Robert Brice
Formerly BRICE, Robert
L 29 Apr 1756
CR 3 July 1761
CA 26 May 1762
MP
(Yarmouth I.o.W.) 1779–1780 (MPN)
MP
(Tregony) 1784–1790 (MPN)
RAW 1 Feb 1793
RAR 12 Apr 1794
VAW 4 July 1794
VAR 1 June 1795
AB 14 Feb 1799
Cre Bt 4 Nov 1800 (LG)
AW 23 Apr 1804
AR 9 Nov 1805
d 23 Nov 1805 (CH)

KINGSTON, Benjamin
L 5 Feb 1813
d 1 Aug 1827 (PRO)

KINGSTON, Robert
L 17 Sept 1811
HP Sept 1818 (OB)
d 1851 (PRO)

KINGSTON, Thomas		
L	27 Jan	1809
d		1836 (PRO)
KINKAID, James		
L	30 July	1736
d		1750(1) (PRO)
KINLOCH, David		
L	22 May	1758
SUP CR	1 Aug	1799
d		1818 (PRO)
KINNEER, Francis William		
L	22 July	1794
d		1801 (PRO)
KINNEER, James		
L	7 Aug	1759
CR	19 Nov	1778
CA	26 Aug	1789
SUP RA	6 May	1808 (LT)
d	19 Apr	1811 (PRO)
KINNEER, James Jervis		
L	2 Oct	1797
d (drowned)	9 Oct	1799 (PJP)
KINSEY, William		
L	29 May	1741
CR	13 Feb	1745
d	30 May	1755 (M)
KINSMAN, John Knill		
L	7 Jan	1802
CR	17 Sept	1813
d	30 Apr	1831 (PRO)
KIPPEN, George		
L	7 Jan	1802
T		
CR	21 Aug	1812
CA	1 Aug	1814
d	21 Aug	1826 (MB)
KIRBY, Anthony		
L	17 July	1761
d		1770 (PRO)
KIRBY, Mathew		
L	31 Oct	1753
d		1781 (PRO)
KIRBY, Michael		
L		1690 (PJP)
KIRBY, Richard		
L		
CA	7 Feb	1690
e (cowardice)	16 Apr	1703 (LG)
KIRBY, Richard		
See KYRBY, Richard		
KIRBY, Robert		
L		
CA		1660
KIA	3 June	1665 (CH)
KIRBY, Thomas		
L	17 Oct	1811
HP	Dec	1813 (OB)
Ret CR	11 Jan	1853 (PRO)
d	9 Apr	1866 (PRO)
KIRBY, Walter		
L	6 Feb	1811
CR	22 July	1830 (PRO)

Ret CA	1 Apr	1856 (PRO)
d		1860 (PRO)
KIRBY, William		
L	6 Mar	1815
d	30 Jan	1816 (PJP)
KIRCHNER, John G.		
L		1798 (PJP)
KIA	1 Aug	1798 (LG)
KIRCHNER, Thomas		
L		
CA	29 Apr	1690
KIRK, Daniel		
L	14 Feb	1797
d		1805 (PRO)
KIRK, Francis		
L	28 Jan	1712
Gone		1734 (PRO)
KIRK, James		
L	29 Jan	1743
CR	23 June	1748
COM V		1777 (PJP)
SUP CA		1786 (PRO)
d	Oct	1787 (PJP)
KIRK, John		
See KIRKE, John		
KIRK(E), P(i)ercy		
L	19 Dec	1688 (PRO)
CA	8 July	1690
d	22 May	1693
KIRK, Robert		
L		
CR		
CA	1 Oct	1758
SUP CA		1787 (PRO)
d		1798
KIRKBY, Richard		
See KIRBY, Richard		
KIRKE, Francis		
See KIRK, Francis		
KIRKE, James		
See KIRK, James		
KIRKE, John		
L		1667
CA	16 Mar	1675
d	Oct	1678 (DDA)
KIRKE, Percy		
See KIRK(E), P(i)ercy		
KIRKES, Morecroft		
L	22 Jan	1806
d		1808 (PRO)
KIRKLAND, James		
L	23 Feb	1778
CR	26 Sept	1781
d	31 Jan	1787 (PMM)
KIRKLEY, William		
L	15 Mar	1783
d		1794 (PRO)
KIRKPATRICK, James		
L	29 Aug	1744
d		1753 (PRO)
KIRKWOOD, Alexander		
L	26 July	1762
d	29 Dec	1792

KIRKWOOD, Charles
L 14 Aug 1810
HP Nov 1815 (OB)
d 1860 (PRO)

KIRTLEY, John
L 26 Apr 1800
Ret CR 26 Nov 1830 (PRO)
d 1842 (PRO)

KIRTON, Robert
L
CA 23 Nov 1693
d 9 July 1718

KIRWAN, Thomas
L 22 Jan 1806
d (drowned) 6 Dec 1808 (PJP)

KITCHCOCK, George
L
CR 14 Aug 1716 (PRO)
d 31 Jan 1718 (PRO)

KITCHEN, William Hewgill
L 12 May 1808
CR 2 Mar 1827 (PRO)
CA 9 Nov 1846 (PRO)
Ret CA 28 July 1858 (PRO)
Ret RA 15 June 1864 (PRO)
d 30 Sept 1865 (PRO)

KITCHIN, Thomas
L 31 Jan 1706
d 1737 (PRO)

KITE, William
L 7 Mar 1746
CR 4 Mar 1761
d 25 June 1792

KITSON, Francis
L 1 Dec 1672 (DDA)

KITTOE, Edward
L 26 Feb 1794
CR 21 Sept 1797
CA 4 Jan 1810
d 16 Feb 1823 (PRO)

KITTOE, William Hugh
L 23 Dec 1781
CR 22 Nov 1790
d 13 Oct 1820 (PRO)

KITVILL, John
L 30 Apr 1678

KNACKSTON, Thomas
L 15 Dec 1738
CR 12 July 1745
CA 5 Apr 1757
d 1788

KNAPMAN, E.
L 1814 (PJP)

KNAPMAN, Edward
T wounded
L 21 Mar 1812 (PRO)
Ret CR 8 Apr 1858 (PRO)
d 1868 (PRO)

KNAPMAN, John
T
L 14 Sept 1809
HP Dec 1832 (OB)
Ret CR 23 Aug 1852 (PRO)
d 1866 (TR)

KNAPP, John
L ?1689 (PJP)
CA 17 Feb 1692
d 1708 (PJP)

KNATCHBULL, Charles
L 9 Nov 1770
CR 11 Aug 1779
CA 13 May 1781
Resigned

KNATCHBULL, John
L 29 Dec 1810
CR 6 Dec 1813
SUP CR 1815 (DCB)
Struck off list for fraud 1818 (PRO)
e (murder) 13 Feb 1844 (DCB)

KNEESHAW, E.
L 1803 (PJP)

KNEESHAW, Joshua
L 18 Sept 1800
CR 12 Jan 1814
d 1 Nov 1843 (PRO)

KNELL, William
L 21 Aug 1778
CR 16 Mar 1779
CA 22 Nov 1779
d 3 Sept 1798

KNEVETT, Thomas
L
CA 1663
d before 1689 (PJP)

KNEVITT, Thomas Lepard
L 1 Feb 1815
HP Mar 1832 (OB)
d 1848 (PRO)

KNIBLO, Ingram
L 30 Mar 1734
d 1740 (PRO)

KNIGHT, Christopher
L 14 Dec 1814
CR 3 June 1822 (PRO)
KH 1 Jan 1837 (OB)
Ret CA 28 July 1851 (PRO)
d 29 Dec 1862 (PRO)

KNIGHT, George
L 1 Apr 1758
d 2 July 1768 (PMM)

KNIGHT, George William Henry
L 5 Mar 1799
CR 21 Oct 1810
CA 7 June 1814
d 7 Nov 1838 (LT)

KNIGHT, Hood
L 27 May 1807
CR 15 June 1814
d 31 Oct 1823 (MB)

KNIGHT, James (1)
L 9 Jan 1760
d 29 Sept 1765 (PMM)

KNIGHT, James (2)
L 4 Apr 1760
d 1762 (PRO)

KNIGHT, James (3)
L 30 May 1814
d 1841 (PRO)

KNIGHT, John (1)		
L	18 July	1740
CR	3 Apr	1746
CA	8 May	1756
SUP RA		1782 (PJP)
d	29 Jan	1785 (PRO)
KNIGHT, Sir John (2)		
L	25 May	1770
CR		
CA	21 Sept	1781
RAB	1 Jan	1801
RAW	23 Apr	1804
VAB	9 Nov	1805
VAW	28 Apr	1808
VAR	31 July	1810
AB	4 Dec	1813 (CH)
KCB	2 Jan	1815 (MB)
AW	12 Aug	1819 (CH)
AR	22 July	1830 (LG)
d	16 June	1831 (LT)
KNIGHT, John Ellis		
L	1 Mar	1815
CR	1 Jan	1850 (PRO)
Ret CA	1 Aug	1860 (PRO)
d		1867 (PRO)
KNIGHT, Sir Joseph		
L	11 Feb	1740
CR	2 June	1743
CA	31 July	1746
Kt	24 June	1773 (PJP)
RAW	31 Mar	1775
d	8 Sept	1775 (PRO)
KNIGHT, Peter		
L		1691 (PJP)
KNIGHT, Richard		
L		
CR	4 Apr	1745
CA	5 Feb	1756
SUP RA		1780
d		1798 (PRO)
KNIGHT, Samuel (1)		
L	21 May	1800
d		1811 (PRO)
KNIGHT, Samuel (2)		
L	8 Mar	1805
d		1809 (PRO)
KNIGHT, Thomas Edward		
L	15 Apr	1811 (PRO)
d		1832 (PRO)
KNIGHT, William (1)		
L	25 Jan	1726
CR		
CA	12 May	1734
d (drowned)	20 Oct	1744 (CH)
KNIGHT, William (2)		
L	21 July	1798
CR	22 Jan	1806
d	28 Dec	1811 (PRO)
KNIGHT, William (3)		
L	26 Aug	1799
Ret CR	28 Nov	1833 (PRO)
d	6 May	1846 (OB)
KNIGHT, William (4)		
L	25 Jan	1802
d		1818 (PRO)

KNIGHT, William (5)		
L	19 Jan	1811
HP	Apr	1814 (OB)
d		1850 (PRO)
KNIGHTLEY, Thomas		
L		1703 (PJP)
KNIGHTON, Charles		
L	27 Mar	1799
Ret CR	7 Apr	1843 (PRO)
d		1858 (PRO)
KNIGHTON, Francis		
L		
CR	8 Dec	1712 (PRO)
CA	17 Apr	1718
d	16 July	1727
KNIPE, Robert (1)		
L	7 Sept	1801 (PRO)
d		1811 (PRO)
KNIPE, Robert (2)		
L	7 Sept	1801
d	1 Jan	1805 (PRO)
KNITCH, George		
L		1691 (PJP)
d	13 Oct	1694 (PMM)
KNOCKER, John Bedingfield		
L	10 July	1813
Ret CR	15 Apr	1856 (PRO)
d		1862 (PRO)
KNOCKER, William		
L	8 Mar	1815
Ret CR	20 July	1863 (PRO)
d	12 July	1882 (PRO)
KNOLLIS, Cyprian		
L	27 Oct	1758
d	10 Apr	1760 (LG)
KNOWESLEY, John		
L	15 Dec	1802
d		1804 (PRO)
KNOWLER, Charles		
L	30 Mar	1734
CR	2 Apr	1744
CA	23 Jan	1746
SUP RA		1770
d		1789
KNOWLER, George		
L	14 Feb	1705
CR	2 May	1729
d		1743(4) (PRO)
KNOWLER, Thomas		
L	14 Sept	1739
CR	19 Aug	1744 (PRO)
CA	11 Aug	1746
SUP RA	Mar	1775
d		1784 (PRO)
KNOWLES, Sir Charles		
L		1730 (DNB)
CR	24 Nov	1732 (DNB)
CA	4 Feb	1737
RAW	15 July	1747
RAR	12 May	1748
VAB	6 Jan	1755 (CH)
VAW		1756 (C)
VAR	Feb	1757

AB	5 Feb	1758 (CH)
Cre Bt		1765 (DNB)
AW		1770
Entered Russian Service		1770–1774 (PJP)
d	9 Dec	1777 (DNB)
KNOWLES, Sir Charles Henry		
L	28 May	1776
CR		
Inh Bt	9 Dec	1777 (DNB)
CA	2 Feb	1780
RAW	14 Feb	1799
RAR	1 Jan	1801
VAB	23 Apr	1804
VAR	9 Nov	1805
AB	31 July	1810
AW	12 Aug	1812
GCB	20 May	1820 (DNB)
AR	19 July	1821 (LG)
d	28 Nov	1831 (PRO)
KNOWLES, Edward		
L	22 Feb	1759
CR	11 Feb	1761
d (drowned)		1762 (CH)
KNOWLES, James		
L	27 Jan	1696
Gone		1719 (PRO)
KNOWLES, John		
L	19 Jan	1759
CR	29 Sept	1778
CA	1 July	1780
RAB	14 Feb	1799
RAW	1 Jan	1801
d	14 Mar	1801 (CH)
KNOX, David		
L	10 May	1776
CR	13 Mar	1783
CA	10 Feb	1789
d		1795 (PRO)
KNOX, Edmund Sexten Pery		
L	1 Sept	1806
CR	2 June	1809
CA	28 Feb	1812
Ret RA	31 Oct	1846 (LG)
Ret VA	27 Sept	1855 (PRO)
Ret A	7 Nov	1860 (PRO)
d		1867 (PRO)
KOCK, Thomas		
L	6 Feb	1694 (PMM)
KORTRIGHT, Nicholas		
L	15 Jan	1802
Ret CR	28 Aug	1832 (PRO)
d		1841 (PRO)
KRUMPHOLTZ, Lewis		
L	17 Mar	1806
d		1807 (PRO)
KYD, James		
L	3 May	1745
SUP	7 Feb	1793
KYLE, George		
L	7 July	1804
HP	Sept	1815 (OB)
Ret CR	25 Jan	1837 (PRO)
d		1856 (PRO)
KYLE, Samuel		
L	14 Sept	1809
d	27 Dec	1829 (PRO)

KYRBY, Richard		
L	24 May	1744
d		1770
LACEY, John		
L	14 Apr	1741
d		1748(9) (PRO)
LACKEY, John		
L	10 Feb	1800
d	11 Oct	1804 (PRO)
LADD, Charles Pybus		
L	7 Feb	1815
Ret CR	1 Oct	1860 (PRO)
d		1873 (PRO)
LAFFER, Nathaniel		
L	10 May	1809
HP	May	1815 (OB)
Ret CR	27 July	1847 (PRO)
d		1850 (PRO)
LAFITTE, Augustus		
L	9 June	1741
d		1746 (PRO)
LAFOREY, Sir Francis		
L	26 Aug	1789
CR	22 Nov	1790
CA	5 June	1793
Inh Bt	6 June	1796 (DNB)
T		
RAB	31 July	1810
RAW	12 Aug	1812
RAR	4 June	1814
KCB	2 Jan	1815 (MB)
VAB	12 Aug	1819 (CH)
VAW	19 July	1821 (CH)
VAR	27 May	1825 (CH)
AB	22 July	1830 (CH)
d	17 June	1835 (PRO)
LAFOREY, Sir John		
L	12 Apr	1748
CR	24 May	1755
CA	26 July	1758
COMM (Leeward Islands)	Sept	1779 (PMM)
COMM (Plymouth)	Apr	1784 (PMM)
RAW	10 Nov	1789
Cre Bt		1789 (DNB)
VAW	1 Feb	1793
VAR	12 Apr	1794
AB	1 June	1795
d	14 June	1796 (PJP)
LAFOREY, Loftus		
L	11 Apr	1760
d		1770 (PRO)
LAING, Andrew		
L	14 July	1744
d		1748(9) (PRO)
LAING, George		
L	2 June	1800
Ret CR	26 Nov	1830 (PRO)
d	8 Nov	1842 (PRO)
LAIRD, David		
L	2 July	1762

CR	18 May	1778
CA	1 Dec	1787
SUP RA	3 Nov	1807
d	Aug	1812 (PRO)
LAIRD, Francis		
L	21 July	1801
d	20 Oct	1824 (PRO)
LAKE, Francis		
L		1673
LAKE, Henry		
L		1665
LAKE, James		
L	21 Mar	1707
SUP		1742 (PMM)
d		1742(3) (PRO)
LAKE, John		
L	17 Mar	1796
CR	20 July	1805
CA	19 Sept	1809 (PRO)
d		1818 (PRO)
LAKE, Thomas (1)		
L		
CA	26 Sept	1694
Gone		1718 (PRO)
LAKE, Thomas (2)		
L	20 July	1726
CR		
CA	2 Dec	1741
d	18 Apr	1750 (PRO)
LAKE, Hon. Warwick		
L	7 May	1804
CR	22 Jan	1806
CA	23 Sept	1808
Dismissed	6 Feb	1810 (CH)
LAKE, Sir Willougby Thomas		
L	20 Nov	1790
CR	25 Nov	1794
CA	4 Jan	1796
HP		1797–1803 (OB)
CRM	4 June	1814 (MB)
CB	2 Jan	1815 (MB)
RAW	12 Aug	1819 (PRO)
RAR	27 May	1825 (LG)
VAB	22 July	1830 (LG)
KCB	1 Dec	1830 (LG)
VAR	10 Jan	1837 (LG)
AW	23 Nov	1841 (PRO)
d	18 Feb	1847 (PRO)
LAMB, James Thomas		
L	1 Mar	1815
Ret CR	29 Dec	1862 (PRO)
d		1864 (PRO)
LAMB, John		
L	20 June	1808
HP	Aug	1814 (DUB)
Ret CR	7 May	1846 (PRO)
d	17 Jan	1862 (DUB)
LAMB, Lewis		
L	9 Aug	1802
d		1809 (PRO)
LAMB, Philip		
L	9 Sept	1782
CR	29 Apr	1802
d	2 May	1837 (PRO)
LAMB, William		
L	13 Nov	1790
CR	2 Jan	1798
d	22 May	1800
LAMBE, John		
L	4 Mar	1796
d		1813 (PRO)
LAMB(E), Robert Charles		
L	18 Nov	1812
d		1813 (PRO)
LAMBERT, Charles		
T		
L	6 Dec	1813
d	Aug	1856 (PRO)
LAMBERT, David (1)		
L		
CR	20 May	1661 (P)
CA	24 June	1689
SUP	1 Jan	1695 (PRO)
d		1703
LAMBERT, David (2)		
L	10 Feb	1693 (PJP)
LAMBERT, George Robert		
L	5 May	1815
CR	9 Jan	1822 (PRO)
CA	3 Aug	1825 (PRO)
RAB	21 Jan	1854 (PRO)
RAW	9 July	1855 (PRO)
RAR	9 July	1857 (PRO)
VAB	18 Dec	1858 (PRO)
VAW	5 Aug	1861 (PRO)
VAR	23 Mar	1863 (PRO)
AB	15 Dec	1863 (PRO)
Ret A	5 Mar	1864 (PRO)
d	5 June	1869 (PRO)
LAMBERT, Henry (1)		
L	27 Oct	1758
SUP CR	18 July	1800
d		1815 (PRO)
LAMBERT, Henry (2)		
L	15 Apr	1801
CR	5 Apr	1803
CA	10 Apr	1805
d	4 Jan	1813 (LG)
LAMBERT, James (1)		
L		
CA		1661
KIA	Sept	1665 (PJP)
LAMBERT, James (2)		
L	8 Sept	1808
d		1836 (PRO)
LAMBERT, John (1)		
L	28 Sept	1693
LGH		1728 (PJP)
d		1739 (PRO)
LAMBERT, John (2)		
L	11 Feb	1796
CR	15 June	1814
d	23 Oct	1827 (PRO)
LAMBERT, Robert (1)		
L	12 June	1747
d		1767
LAMBERT, Robert (2)		
L	3 July	1754
CR	10 Jan	1759

CA	18 Feb	1760
COMM (Jamaica)		1782–1784 (PMM)
d		1787 (PRO)
LAMBERT, Robert Stuart		
L	1 Aug	1791
CR	4 May	1795
CA	11 Apr	1796
RAB	12 Aug	1819 (LG)
RAW	19 July	1821 (LG)
RAR	27 May	1825 (LG)
VAB	22 July	1830 (LG)
d	16 Sept	1836 (PRO)
LAMBERT, Thomas (1)		
L		
CR	4 Mar	1696 (PJP)
CA	20 Oct	1696
d	16 Feb	1700
LAMBERT, Thomas (2)		
L	29 Oct	1697
In Merchant Service		1700 (PJP)
LAMBERT, William		
L	7 May	1808
Ret CR	30 Apr	1845 (OB)
d	7 Jan	1847 (PRO)
LAMBORN, John		
L	17 Apr	1794
CR	29 Apr	1802
CA	21 Oct	1810
d		1837 (PRO)
LAMBRICK, John		
L	23 May	1796
Ret CR	26 Nov	1830
d	Aug	1848 (PRO)
LAMMING, Thomas		
L		1664
CA	9 June	1666 (RM)
d	before	1689 (PJP)
LAMONT, James		
L	16 Oct	1805
Ret CR	18 Apr	1838 (PRO)
d	31 Dec	1853 (PRO)
LAMPEN, Augustus		
L	15 Feb	1815
d	22 Sept	1827 (PRO)
LAMPEN, John		
L	3 Jan	1782
KIA	20 Oct	1782 (LG)
LANCASTER, Henry		
T		
L	20 Oct	1813
Ret CR	28 July	1851 (PRO)
d	25 Feb	1862 (PRO)
LANCASTER, Robert Daniel		
L	26 Feb	1805
Ret CR	26 May	1837 (PRO)
d	7 Sept	1863 (PRO)
LANCASTER, Samuel		
L	15 Mar	1692
In Merchant Service		1700 (PJP)
LANCE, Samuel		
L		1692 (PJP)
LAND, Henry		
L		
CA		1660
d	before	1689 (PJP)
LANDLESS, William		
L	3 June	1796
T		
CR	15 Aug	1806
d		1826 (MB)
LANE, Charles		
L	8 Dec	1777
d		1782(3) (PRO)
LANE, Charles Henry		
L	6 Sept	1777
CR	23 Sept	1782
CA	22 Nov	1790
d	13 Nov	1807 (PJP)
LANE, David (1)		
L	30 July	1794
d		1797 (PRO)
LANE, David (2)		
L	15 Jan	1798
Struck off list		1798 (PRO)
LANE, John		
L	15 June	1810
d		1816 (PRO)
LANE, John Edward		
L	17 Jan	1811
Ret CR	20 Sept	1860 (PRO)
d		1876 (PRO)
LANE, Lewis		
L	23 Mar	1779
d		1789 (PRO)
LANE, Michael		
L	27 Oct	1777
d		1794 (PRO)
LANE, Odaine Morgan		
L	14 Nov	1790
d		1793 (PRO)
LANE, Richard		
L	16 Jan	1781
CR	22 Nov	1790
CA	24 May	1794
d	28 Feb	1799 (PRO)
LANE, Thomas		
L	4 Oct	1799
d		1805 (PRO)
LANE, William (1)		
L	17 Apr	1795
d		1811 (PRO)
LANE, William (2)		
L	11 Mar	1815
Not seen since 1817		
Name removed		1821 (PRO)
LANE, William (3)		
L	13 Mar	1815
d		1858 (PRO)
LANG, Gustavus		
L	13 Apr	1690
Gone		1719 (PRO)
LANG, Richard		
L	11 Apr	1760
d	5 Jan	1800

LANGDON, George
L 31 Aug 1779
d 1741 (PMM)

LANGDON, John
L 6 Sept 1799
Ret CR 26 Nov 1830 (PRO)
d 1838 (PRO)

LANGDON, Richard
L 21 Mar 1812
d 25 Apr 1839 (PRO)

LANGDON, William (1)
L 31 Sept 1743
CR 18 Dec 1753
CA 5 June 1756
RAW 26 Sept 1780
d 29 June 1785 (PRO)

LANGDON, William (2)
L 20 July 1744
d 1746 (PRO)

LANGDON, William (3)
L 29 Oct 1811
Ret CR 1 Apr 1853 (PRO)
d 23 May 1879 (DUB)

LANGFORD, Frederick
L 25 Apr 1800
CR 29 Apr 1802
CA 28 Nov 1806
d 17 Feb 1815 (PRO)

LANGFORD, George
L 16 Dec 1797
CR 27 Apr 1801
CA 5 Mar 1808
d 5 Oct 1832 (LT)

LANGFORD, John
L 10 Dec 1760
d 1780(1) (PRO)

LANGHAM, John Henry
L 25 Feb 1779
d 1780(1) (PRO)

LANGHORNE, Arthur
L
CA 4 July 1666 (RM)

LANGLANDS, Roger
L 24 July 1812
d 1843 (PRO)

L'ANGLE, Merrick de
L 2 Mar 1734
CR
CA 13 Nov 1742
d 18 May 1753

LANGLEY, George
L 18 Mar 1780
d 1807 (PRO)

LANGLEY, John
L 20 June 1777 (PRO)
d (drowned) 21 Sept 1782 (PJP)

LANGLEY, John Arnold
L 30 June 1720
d 1734 (PRO)

LANGLEY, Samuel
L 10 Feb 1809
d 1 Nov 1836 (PRO)

LANGLEY, Stephen
L 20 May 1804
d 1807 (PRO)

LANGLEY, Thomas
L
CA 1665

LANGLEY, William
L 3 Feb 1815
HP 1815 (OB)
d 1856 (PRO)

LANGREEK, James
L 1665

LANGRIDGE, Thomas
L 6 June 1693 (PJP)

LANGRISH, Henry
L 26 Feb 1703 (PMM)

LANGRISH, Thomas
L 6 Feb 1694
d 10 May 1704 (PRO)

LANGSTAFFE, Thomas
L 25 Feb 1706
CR 1 Mar 1740
d 1742(3) (PRO)

LANGSTON, Anthony
L 1665
CA 9 June 1666 (RM)
d 19 Mar 1679 (DDA)

LANGTON, William
L 1 Feb 1815
d 1817 (PRO)

LANHAM, Joseph
L 15 Aug 1781

LANPHIER, Vernon
T
L 26 Nov 1808
Ret CR 13 Apr 1846 (PRO)
d 1867 (TR)

LANYON, William
L 23 Aug 1779
SUP CR 17 Mar 1814
d 1818 (PRO)

LAPENOTIERE, Frederick
L 6 May 1780
d 1790 (PRO)

LAPENOTIERE, John Richards
L 29 Apr 1794
T
CR 6 Nov 1805
CA 1 Aug 1811
d 1834 (PRO)

LAPIDGE, William Frederick
L 9 Apr 1814
CR 2 Oct 1833 (PRO)
CA 6 Jan 1837 (PRO)
Ret RA 14 May 1857 (PRO)
d 17 July 1860 (PRO)

LAPP, John
L 7 Feb 1811
d 4 May 1824 (PRO)

LAPSLIE, Andrew
l 14 July 1796
Ret CR 26 Nov 1830 (PRO)
d 1837 (PRO)

LAPSLIE, John
L 20 Nov 1812
d 5 Feb 1825 (PRO)

LAPTHORNE, John
L
CA 5 May 1697
Gone 1718 (PRO)

LARCOM, Joseph
L 7 Dec 1782
CR 6 July 1794
CA 24 July 1795
SUP 1814
d 17 Feb 1818 (LT)

LARCOM, Joseph Paffard Dickson
L 26 Sept 1814
CR 8 Aug 1829 (PRO)
CA 23 Nov 1841 (PRO)
d 1 Nov 1850 (PRO)

LARGE, Thomas
L
CA 1660

LARGUE, James
L 10 Oct 1810
d 1816 (PRO)

LARKAN, John
L 4 Feb 1778
CR 6 July 1794
d 1830 (MB)

LARKAN, Robert
L 28 Apr 1780
CR 6 July 1794
CA 16 Sept 1796
SUP CA Aug 1819 (OB)
d 10 June 1841 (PRO)

LARKE, William
L 1 July 1802
Ret CR 7 July 1834 (PRO)
d 1850 (PRO)

LARMOUR, John
L 28 June 1784
CR 8 July 1795
CA 16 Apr 1800
d 16 Jan 1807 (PRO)

LAROCHE, Christopher
L 11 Sept 1793
CR 18 Aug 1798
CA 29 Jan 1800
Ret CA 1830 (PRO)
d 5 June 1850 (PRO)

LAROCHE, Henry
L 22 Nov 1790 (MB)
CR 2 June 1804 (PRO)
CA 22 June 1806 (PRO)
d 14 Feb 1832 (LT)

LASCELLES, Cornelius
L 15 Oct 1808
Dismissed Feb 1812 (PJP)
d 1812 (PRO)

LASCELLES, John Francis
L 28 Apr 1807
CR 27 Aug 1814

LASCELLES, Michael
L 31 Jan 1806
d 1807 (PRO)

LASCELLES, Ralph
See LASSELLS, Ralph

LASH, Joseph
L 20 July 1759
d 1787 (PRO)

LASH, Joseph Henry
L 17 Apr 1778
d 1790 (PRO)

LASH, Robert
L 1690 (PJP)

LASHAM, Richard
L 20 Jan 1801
T
d 1812 (TR)

LASHBROOK, Walter
L 1 Apr 1703 (PMM)

LASHLEY, Edward
L 1702 (PJP)

LASINBY, Louis
L 2 Feb 1741
d 1754(5) (PRO)

LASSELLS, Ralph
L
CA 21 Sept 1666 (RM)
d May 1677 (PRO)

LASTON, Samuel Hornigold
L 15 Feb 1815
Ret CR 1 Oct 1860 (PRO)
d 1878 (PRO)

LATHAM, Thomas
L 10 Aug 1741
CR 15 July 1745
CA 14 Mar 1747
Resigned on the grounds of ill health 2 Mar 1759 (PRO)
d 13 Feb 1762 (PRO)

LATELY, John
L 1673

LATELY, Oliver
L 31 May 1688

LATELY, Philip
L 1668
d before 1689 (PJP)

LATON, Charles
L
CR 27 Apr 1695 (PJP)
CA 2 Mar 1703
d 11 Nov 1704

LATON, John
L 1685
CA 15 June 1688
d 2 Jan 1691 (PRO)

LATON, Sheldrake
L 2 Mar 1734
CR
CA 25 Aug 1741
SUP RA 1756
d 22 Apr 1776 (PRO)

LA TOUCHE, John de
L 6 May 1775
d 26 Oct 1803 (PJP)

LAUDER, George
L 1740 (PJP)

LAUDERDALE, Hon. Anthony, Earl of
See MAITLAND, Hon. Anthony
LAUGA, Thomas Robinson
L 13 Mar 1815
d 1823 (PRO)
LAUGHARNE, Arthur (1)
L 1660
CA 1661
KIA 9 Sept 1665 (DDA)
LAUGHARNE, Arthur (2)
L 22 June 1665 (DDA)
CA 1666 (DDA)
d 24 Mar 1667 (DDA)
LAUGHARNE, John
L 25 June 1776
CR 1 Dec 1787
CA 22 Nov 1790
RAB 31 July 1810
RAW 1 Aug 1811
RAR 12 Aug 1812
VAB 4 June 1814
VAW 12 Aug 1819 (LG)
d 1819 (PRO)
LAUGHARNE, Morgan
L 17 Mar 1777
CR 4 Nov 1780
CA 25 Oct 1809
d 7 June 1810
LAUGHARNE, Thomas (1)
L 7 Nov 1759
CR 14 Sept 1783
CA 3 Nov 1790
d 1797
LAUGHARNE, Thomas (2)
L 25 Mar 1805
d (drowned) Aug 1809 (PJP)
LAUGHARNE, Thomas Lamb Poulden
L 8 Aug 1806
CR 12 Feb 1811
CA 4 Apr 1832 (OB)
HP 4 Apr 1832 (OB)
d 30 Sept 1863 (PRO)
LAUGHARNE, William
L 14 Nov 1806
CR 23 Sept 1814
HP 23 Sept 1814 (OB)
Ret CA 1 July 1851 (PRO)
d 1856 (PRO)
LAUGHORNE, Arthur
See LAUGHARNE, Arthur
LAUGHTON, John
See LOUGHTON, John
LAUNDER, Philip Watson
L 3 Nov 1790
KIA 1 Aug 1798 (LG)
LAUNG, William
L 1666 (DDA)
LAURENCE, P.S.
L 1814 (PJP)
LAURIE, Peter
L 1790 (MB)
CR
CA 17 July 1797 (MB)
RAB 19 July 1821 (MB)
RAW 27 May 1825 (LG)
RAR 22 July 1830 (LG)
VAW 10 Jan 1837 (LG)
VAR 23 Nov 1841 (LG)
LAURIE, Sir Robert
See LAWRIE, Sir Robert
LAURIE, Thomas
L 14 Nov 1761
d 1769 (PRO)
LAUZUN, Francis Daniel
T
L 2 Feb 1811
Ret CR 1 Oct 1851 (PRO)
d 24 Mar 1861 (PRO)
LAVENDER, James Robert
L 18 Feb 1815
d 2 Oct 1825 (PRO)
LAVERS, Richard
L 4 Aug 1806
d 1837 (PRO)
LAVETT, John
See LEVETT, John
LAVIE, Sir Thomas
L 4 Nov 1790
CR 9 Nov 1795
CA 1 Jan 1801
d 1 Feb 1822 (LT)
LAWDER, George
L 14 Aug 1739
d 1746 (PRO)
LAWES, Joseph
L 28 Aug 1711 (PRO)
CR 1 June 1721
CA 28 Oct 1722
d 19 Mar 1734 (PRO)
LAWES, William
L 2 Feb 1757
d 1780(1) (PRO)
LAWES, William
See LAWS, William
LAWFORD, Sir John
L 23 Dec 1777
CR 1 Dec 1787
CA 1 Dec 1793
RAB 1 Aug 1811
RAW 4 Dec 1813
RAR 4 June 1814
VAB 12 Aug 1819 (CH)
VAW 19 July 1821 (CH)
AB 22 July 1830 (CH)
AW 10 Jan 1837 (CH)
KCB 1838 (CH)
AR 23 Nov 1841 (CH)
d 22 Dec 1842 (CH)
LAWLESS, Henry
L 27 Apr 1814
Ret CR 9 Jan 1854 (PRO)
d 1865 (PRO)
LAWLESS, Paul
L 29 Sept 1801
CR 19 Sept 1808
d (drowned) Mar 1814 (PJP)
LAWNCE, James
L
CA 12 Jan 1693
d 15 Sept 1695

LAWRENCE, Daniel
L 19 May 1808
CR 19 May 1810
CA 2 Sept 1816 (PRO)
Ret CA 1 Oct 1846 (PRO)
Ret RA 11 June 1851 (PRO)
d 1855 (PRO)

LAWRENCE, Edwin
L 17 June 1802
d 1809 (PRO)

LAWRENCE, George
L 22 Oct 1795 (PRO)
Ret CR 16 Feb 1836 (PRO)
d 7 Nov 1843 (PRO)

LAWRENCE, George Bell
L 8 Sept 1803
Ret CR 4 May 1836 (PRO)
d 9 Apr 1846 (OB)

LAWRENCE, Henry
L
?CR 20 June 1694
CA 24 May 1699
Ship taken 24 July 1704 (PRO)
To be imprisoned for seven years and forfeit his whole pay by court-martial 5 Jan 1705 (PJP)

LAWRENCE, Humphrey
L
CR
CA 21 Jan 1703
Dismissed 5 Jan 1705 (CH)
d 10 Jan 1738

LAWRENCE, Jacob (1)
L 29 Sept 1795
Dismissed 1797 (PRO)

LAWRENCE, Jacob (2)
L 4 Apr 1798
Ret CR 26 Nov 1830 (PRO)
d 1835 (PRO)

LAWRENCE, James (1)
L 13 Jan 1802
KIA 18 Aug 1808 (CH)

LAWRENCE, James (2)
L 18 Mar 1815 (PRO)
HP 1838 (OB)
d 1847 (PRO)

LAWRENCE, John (1)
L 21 Mar 1692
d 5 Apr 1703 (PRO)

LAWRENCE, John (2)
L 1 Mar 1794
CR 25 Aug 1804
d 1815 (PRO)

LAWRENCE, John (3)
L 28 June 1799
CR 30 Mar 1808
CB 8 Dec 1815 (OB)
CA 1 Jan 1817 (OB)
HP Jan 1842 (OB)
d 19 Mar 1849 (PRO)

LAWRENCE, Joseph
L 1 May 1683
d before 1689 (PJP)

LAWRENCE, Paul Sandby
L 6 May 1801
Ret CR 25 Dec 1845 (PRO)
d 15 Nov 1853 (PRO)

LAWRENCE, Peter
L 11 Feb 1727
CR 23 Dec 1734
CA 16 July 1739
SUP RA 1755
d 23 Nov 1758 (M)

LAWRENCE, R.R.
L 1792 (PJP)

LAWRENCE, Thomas (1)
L 10 Feb 1692
CR
CA 18 Oct 1704
d 9 Dec 1747

LAWRENCE, Thomas (2)
L 29 Dec 1813
HP 1816 (OB)
Ret CR 15 July 1856 (PRO)
d Jan 1876 (PRO)

LAWRENCE, William
L 29 Apr 1802
d 1809 (PRO)

LAWRIE, Sir Robert
L 12 Nov 1790
CR 25 June 1795
CA 17 July 1797
Inh Bt 1804 (OB)
RAB 19 July 1821 (LG)
RAW 27 May 1825 (PRO)
RAR 22 July 1830 (PRO)
KCB 1831 (PJP)
VAW 10 Jan 1837 (PRO)
VAR 23 Nov 1841 (PRO)
AB 9 Nov 1846 (PRO)
AW 26 July 1847 (PRO)
d 7 Jan 1848 (PRO)

LAWRIE, Thomas
L 10 July 1759
d 1802 (PRO)

LAWRIE, Thomas
See LAURIE, Thomas

LAWRY, Mark
L 1666

LAWRY, Richard
L 5 Oct 1793
d 1800 (PRO)

LAWS, Joseph
See LAWES, Joseph

LAWS, William
L 17 Dec 1723
CR
CA 5 Mar 1731
SUP RA before July 1748

LAWSON, Aaron
L 1665
d before 1689 (PJP)

LAWSON, Henry
L 1 July 1703 (PMM)
CR
CA 31 July 1708
d 17 Apr 1734 (PRO)

LAWSON, Hugh
L 6 Nov 1762
CR

CA	16 Jan	1780 (PJP)
d	Jan	1780 (PJP)
LAWSON, James		
L	3 June	1745
SUP CR	21 Sept	1796 (PMM)
d	29 Mar	1798 (PMM)
LAWSON, Sir John (1)		
L		
CA		1660
Kt		1660 (DNB)
VAF		1660
VAR		1664
AD		1662
KIA	3 June	1665 (CH)
LAWSON, John (2)		
L	23 May	1793
CR	26 June	1797
CA	21 Oct	1810
d	Aug	1831 (PRO)
LAWSON, Joseph		
L	8 May	1780
d		1790 (PRO)
LAWSON, Philip		
L		1681
LAWSON, Robert		
L	10 Feb	1807
d		1809 (PRO)
LAWSON, Thomas		
L		
CA		1664 (DDA)
KIA	2 Aug	1665 (ESP)
LAWSON, William		
L	23 Dec	1814
d		1842 (PRO)
LAWSON, William		
See LAWSON, Thomas		
LAYMAN, William		
L	12 Sept	1800
CR	8 May	1804
Srty forfeited to	9 Mar	1805
d (suicide)	22 May	1826 (LT)
LAYTON, Buxton		
L	10 Feb	1815
HP	10 Feb	1815 (OB)
Ret CR	12 Apr	1860 (PRO)
d		1867 (PRO)
LAYTON, Henry		
See LEIGHTON, Henry		
LAYTON, William		
L	29 Dec	1702 (PMM)
LEA, John Robert		
L	3 Oct	1794
CR	22 Sept	1798
d	2 Mar	1824 (PRO)
LEA, William		
L		
CR	17 July	1741
d (drowned)	20 Oct	1744 (CH)
LEACH, James		
L	18 Mar	1797
CR	21 Oct	1810
d	22 Aug	1831 (MB)
LEACH, John		
L	23 Aug	1796
Ret CR	26 Nov	1830 (PRO)
d		1843 (PRO)
LEADER, John		
L		
CA	5 Jan	1691
	(24 Aug 1690 in C)	
d	18 Jan	1702
LEAK, John		
L	23 Oct	1759
d		1764 (PRO)
LEAKE, Sir Andrew		
L		
CR	7 June	1690 (PRO)
CA	25 June	1693 (PRO)
Kt		1702 (DNB)
KIA	13 Aug	1704 (LG)
LEAKE, Henry Martin		
L	14 Oct	1814
d		1840 (PRO)
LEAKE, Sir John		
L		
CA	14 Sept	1689 (DCB)
GG		1702 (DCB)
(Newfoundland)		
RAB	9 Dec	1702
VAB	1 Mar	1703
Kt	Feb	1704 (DCB)
VAW	13 Jan	1705
AW	8 Jan	1708
MCLHA	19 June–28 Oct	1708 (AO)
AF	21 Dec	1708
COM AD	8 Nov	1709–
	14 Oct	1714 (AO)
d	21 Aug	1720
LEAKE, Henry Sebastian		
or LEEK(E)		
L	27 Oct	1758
d	15 Sept	1776 (PRO)
LEAKE, Richard		
L		
CR		
CA	20 Aug	1705
d	24 Feb	1721
LEAKE, William Thomas Martin		
L	22 Apr	1802
KIA	3 Apr	1804 (PJP)
LEAN, James Sedgwick		
L	4 Jan	1810
Ret CR	28 July	1851 (PRO)
d	Jan	1876 (PRO)
LEARY, Daniel		
L	16 Feb	1815
d		1839 (PRO)
LEARY, John		
L	30 Sept	1758
CR		
CA	13 July	1765
d	22 Aug	1787 (PMM)
LEARY, Richard		
L		1762 (PJP)
LEAVER, Charles Tovey		
L	13 Mar	1797
d		1826 (PRO)

LEAVER, Robert
L 16 Dec 1776
d 1786 (PRO)

LEAVER, Robert Giffard
L 4 Apr 1795
d 1804 (PRO)

LEAVER, William
L 29 Aug 1740
CR 10 May 1747
d 4 Feb 1764 (PRO)

LEAVER, William Henry
L 22 Feb 1815
d 1844 (PRO)

LEAVEY, Samuel Price
L 17 July 1794
d 1807 (PRO)

LE BAS, Nicholas
L 30 June 1807
d 1808 (PRO)

LE BLANC, George
L 1 Oct 1806
d 1811 (PRO)

LE BRETON, Francis
L 26 Mar 1795
d 1800 (PRO)

LECALE, Charles Lord
See FITZGERALD, Lord Charles

LECHMERE, Charles
L 11 Dec 1807
CR 18 Sept 1815
d 9 Nov 1822 (PRO)

LECHMERE, Edmund
L 3 Feb 1815
d 30 Jan 1841 (OB)

LECHMERE, Edward
See LETCHMERE, Edward

LECHMERE, John
T
L 3 Feb 1815
Ret CR 9 Feb 1860 (PRO)
d 1867 (PRO)

LECHMERE, William
L 20 Dec 1774
CR 23 Sept 1782
CA 21 Sept 1790
CRM 2 Oct 1807 (AL)
RAB 28 Apr 1808
RAR 31 July 1810
VAB 12 Aug 1812
VAW 4 June 1814
d 12 Dec 1815 (LT)

LECKIE, John
L 20 Sept 1783
SUP CR 31 Dec 1821 (PRO)
d 17 Sept 1828 (PRO)

LECKY, James
L 14 July 1777
CR 22 Nov 1790
CA 8 Dec 1794
SUP 1813
d 1820 (PRO)

LE CRAS, Edward
L 11 Dec 1739
CR 24 Feb 1748
CA 4 Feb 1755
COM E 10 Apr 1778–
11 Feb 1793 (NBO)
d 20 Dec 1793 (NBO)

LEDGER, Edward (1)
L 1666

LEDGER, Edward (2)
L 17 Nov 1790
Originally 22 Nov 1790, but amended in 1794 for administrative reasons.
d 1794 (PRO)

LEDGER, John
L 21 Jan 1702
Gone 1734 (PRO)

LEE, Hon. Fitzroy Henry
L 15 Mar 1722
CR
CA 25 Oct 1728
GG 1735–
(Newfoundland) 1737 (DCB)
RAR 15 July 1747
VAW 12 May 1748
d 14 Apr 1750 (DCB)

LEE, James
L 27 Aug 1795
d 1809 (PRO)

LEE, John
L 3 Apr 1779
CR 6 July 1797
d 23 Nov 1800 (PRO)

LEE, Richard (1)
L 31 Aug 1739
d ?1743 (PRO)

LEE, Sir Richard (2)
L 28 Feb 1782
CR 26 Dec 1791
CA 7 June 1794
RAB 12 Aug 1812
RAW 4 June 1814
KCB 2 Jan 1815 (DNB)
Kt
(Portugal) 31 May 1815 (LG)
RAR 12 Aug 1819 (CH)
VAB 19 July 1821 (CH)
VAW 27 May 1825 (CH)
VAR 22 July 1830 (CH)
AB 10 Jan 1837 (CH)
d 5 Aug 1837 (PRO)

LEE, Thomas (1)
L 12 Apr 1755
CR 21 Nov 1760
CA 14 July 1763
d (drowned) 31 Dec 1769 (PRO)

LEE, Thomas (2)
L 7 Feb 1777
d 1782 (PRO)

LEE, Thomas (3)
L 23 Jan 1782
CR 22 Nov 1790
d 11 Jan 1800

LEE, Thomas (4)
L 19 Feb 1811
d 1835 (PRO)

LEE, William (1)
L
CA 1665
Entered Swedish Service 1676 (PMM)
d (murdered) 1678 (PMM)

LEE, William (2)
L 6 May 1796
d 1816 (PJP)

LEECH, Robert
L 26 July 1811
HP Dec 1814 (OB)
d 4 Dec 1848 (PRO)

LEEDS, Duke of
See CARMARTHEN, Marquis of

LEEF, Thomas
L 12 Aug 1793
CR 29 Nov 1797
d 1815 (PRO)

LEEKE, Sir Henry John
L 24 Nov 1810
CR 15 June 1814
CA 27 May 1825 (MB)
Kt 1 Apr 1835 (OB)
KH 25 Jan 1836 (OB)
Ret RA 15 Apr 1854 (PRO)
KCB 1858 (DNB)
RAR 14 Aug 1858 (PRO)
COM AD 23 Apr–28 June 1859 (AO)
VAB 2 May 1860 (PRO)
VAW 15 Jan 1862 (PRO)
VAR 27 Apr 1863 (PRO)
AB 11 Jan 1864 (PRO)
d 26 Feb 1870 (PRO)

LEEKE, Thomas Samuel
L 7 Nov 1806
KIA 2 Nov 1810 (PJP)

LE FEBVRE, William
L 22 Aug 1741
LGH 1766 (PJP)
d 1778 (PRO)

LE FEUVRE, John
L 31 Mar 1806
HP May–Dec 1807 (OB)
Ret CR 15 July 1839 (PRO)
d 27 Jan 1864 (PRO)

LEFEVRE, Charles Gore
L 15 Oct 1775
d 1778 (PRO)

LEGARD, Sir Thomas
L 19 July 1782
SUP CR 5 May 1818 (PRO)
d 5 July 1830 (PRO)

LEGAT, Sir Thomas
L
CA 1665
d before 1689 (PJP)

LE GEYT, George
L 27 Jan 1797
CR 28 May 1803
CA 12 Aug 1812
CB 4 July 1840 (OB)
Ret RA 31 Oct 1846 (LG)
Ret VA 3 Oct 1855 (PRO)
Ret A 11 Feb 1861 (PRO)
d 23 Sept 1861 (PRO)

LEGEYT, Matthew
L 1 Aug 1758
SUP 27 Dec 1799

LEGG, George
L 19 Feb 1711
d 1727(8) (PRO)

LEGG, Julian
L 16 Feb 1711
d 28 July 1727 (PRO)

LEGG, Thomas
L ?24 May 1688 (P)
CA 26 Nov 1688 (P)
(24 Oct 1688 in H)
CA 11 Apr 1690
(?11 May 1690)
Dismissed 16 Jan 1705 (PRO)

LEGGATT, Richard
L 30 Nov 1778
d 1817 (PRO)

LEGGATT, William
L 23 Jan 1779
d 1783 (PRO)

LEGGE, Hon. Sir Arthur Kaye
L 3 Aug 1789
CR 19 Nov 1790
CA 6 Feb 1793
RAB 31 July 1810
RAW 12 Aug 1812
RAR 4 Dec 1813
VAB 4 June 1814
KCB 2 Jan 1815 (MB)
VAW 12 Aug 1819 (CH)
VAR 27 May 1825 (CH)
AB 22 July 1830 (CH)
d 12 May 1835 (CH)

LEGGE, Hon. Edward
L 2 Mar 1734
CR
CA 26 July 1738
MP
(Portsmouth) 15–19 Dec 1747 (MPS)
d 19 Dec 1747 (MPS)

LEGGE, George, Earl of Dartmouth (1)
L 1665 (DNB)
CA 1667 (P)
LGG
(Portsmouth) 1670 (DNB)
MP
(Ludgershall) 1–6 Feb 1673 (MPH)
MP
(Ludgershall) 12 Feb 1673–
Mar 1674 (MPH)
MP
(Portsmouth) Mar–Oct 1678 (MPH)
CF
(Royal Fusiliers) Nov 1678 (EAD)
MP
(Portsmouth) 1681 (MPH)
Cre EP 2 Dec 1682 (DNB)
AD 2 Aug 1683
AF 24 Sept 1688
d 25 Oct 1691 (DNB)

LEGGE, George (2)
L 6 May 1741
CR 11 Mar 1755
CA 2 Dec 1756
Dismissed Apr 1758

LEGGE, John
L
CR 11 June 1745 (PRO)
CA 6 May 1746
d 29 June 1762

LEGGE, Thomas
L
CR
CA 15 Aug 1704
d 28 Feb 1712

LEGGETT, Benjamin
L 29 Nov 1814
d 1833 (PRO)

LE GROS, John
L 1 Aug 1794
CR 18 June 1803
d June 1807 (PRO)

LE HUNTE, Francis
L 26 Sept 1811
CR 15 June 1814
Ret CA 1 July 1851 (PRO)
d 1860 (PRO)

LEIGH, Benjamin
L 10 Mar 1795
Ret CR 10 Jan 1833 (PRO)
d 22 Feb 1846 (OB)

LEIGH, Edward
L 25 Nov 1697
Gone 1719 (PRO)

LEIGH, Jodrell
L 29 Feb 1808
CR 12 June 1820 (PRO)
CA 2 June 1829 (PRO)
Ret RA 3 July 1855 (PRO)
Ret VA 12 Apr 1862 (PRO)
d 27 Oct 1863 (PRO)

LEIGH, Thomas (1)
L 16 Sept 1741
d 1765(6) (PRO)

LEIGH, Thomas (2)
L 11 Dec 1796
d 26 Feb 1814 (PRO)

LEIGH, Thomas (3)
T
L 26 Jan 1814
CR 23 June 1835 (OB)
HP 23 June 1835 (OB)
d 1846 (TR)

LEIGHTON, Edward
L 10 June 1747
CR
CA 9 Jan 1749
d 27 Mar 1750

LEIGHTON, Henry
L
CA 1673
d before 1689 (PJP)

LEIGHTON, Thomas (1)
?L 10 May 1679 (P)
?CA 11 May 1682 (P)
CA 12 July 1683
d 2 Jan 1691 (PJP)

LEIGHTON, Thomas (2)
L
CA 23 June 1688
d 9 Oct 1690

LEIGHTON, Charles, John and Sheldrake
See LATON, Charles, John and Sheldrake

LEITCH, William
L 18 May 1745
d 1757 (PRO)

LEITH, John
L 10 Oct 1809
CR 13 June 1815
CA 11 Nov 1825 (PRO)
HP Sept 1827–
6 Feb 1837 (OB)
HP Oct 1841 (OB)
RAB 11 Feb 1854 (PRO)
d 25 Oct 1854 (PRO)

LEITH, Lockhart
L 10 Mar 1815 (PRO)
d 1861 (PRO)

LEITH, William Forbes
L 7 May 1804
CR 15 June 1814
HP 15 June 1814 (OB)
CA 11 Nov 1825 (PJP)
RA 11 Feb 1854 (PJP)
d 23 Sept 1861 (PRO)

LEMAGE, Thomas
L 23 Oct 1797
d 1808 (PRO)

LE MAISTRE, Charles
L 9 July 1778
d 1780(1) (PRO)

LEMAN, Daniel R.
L 1764 (PJP)

LE MARCHANT, T.
L 1792 (PJP)

LE MESURIER, Edward
L 24 Mar 1815
d 1855 (PRO)

LE MESURIER, Frederick
L 3 Mar 1804
d 1808 (PRO)

LE MESURIER, William
L 16 Nov 1796
Ret CR 26 Nov 1830 (PRO)
d 29 Jan 1833 (PRO)

LEMOINE, Francis
L 1 Nov 1755
d 1765(6) (PRO)

LEMOYNE, John Thomas
L 25 May 1805
d 5 June 1827 (PRO)

LEMPRIERE, George
L 15 July 1794
d 1803 (PRO)

LEMPRIERE, George Ourry
L 25 Mar 1807
CR 30 Jan 1813
CA 27 May 1825 (PRO)
Ret CA 1 Oct 1846 (PRO)
Ret RA 12 Jan 1854 (PRO)
Ret VA 24 Nov 1858 (PRO)

Ret A 3 Dec 1863 (PRO)
d 16 Jan 1864 (PRO)

LEMPRIERE, John
L 1745 (PJP)

LEMPRIERE, Thomas
L 11 Aug 1741
CR 10 June 1757
CA 26 Dec 1758
d 30 Dec 1763 (M)

LENDRICK, John
L 4 June 1746
CR 30 June 1756
CA 26 Dec 1758
d 1780 (PRO)

LE NEVE, Anselm Peter
L 25 July 1814
Ret CR 19 Feb 1858 (PRO)
d July 1870 (PRO)

LE NEVE, Richard
L 1666
CA 1671
CAMR 1 Oct 1672 (EAD)
KIA 11 Aug 1673 (CH)

LENHAM, James
L 1791 (PJP)

LENNOCK, Charles Adam
L 29 Nov 1800
Ret CR 26 Nov 1830 (PRO)
d 1862 (PRO)

LENNOCK, George Gustavus
L 8 May 1795
CR 6 Aug 1806
CA 4 June 1814
Ret CA 1 Oct 1846 (PRO)
Ret RA 4 May 1849 (PRO)
Ret VA 31 Jan 1856 (PRO)
Ret A 11 Feb 1861 (PRO)
d 12 May 1866 (PRO)

LENOX, James
L 13 June 1760
d 1771 (PRO)

LENOX, Joseph
L 23 June 1796
d (drowned) 1801 (PJP)

LEONARD, Robert
L
CA 3 May 1690
d 15 Apr 1693

LEONARD, Solomon
L
CA 1673
d before 1689 (PJP)

LEPARD, Thomas
L 27 Sept 1799 (PRO)
Broke 1800 (PRO)

LEPINE, George
L 19 Sept 1815
d 1826 (PRO)

LEROUX, Frederick James
L 25 Apr 1800
Ret CR 26 Nov 1830 (PRO)
d 18 Oct 1850 (PRO)

LESCHEN, Christian
L 8 Aug 1797
d 1801 (PRO)

LESINGHAM, Thomas
L 7 Dec 1759
d 16 Jan 1787 (M)

LESLEY, William
L 10 Feb 1815
d 2 June 1838 (PRO)

LESLIE, Andrew
See LESSLY, Andrew

LESLIE, Charles
L 24 May 1757
CR 7 Apr 1762
CA 20 June 1765
d 29 Dec 1775

LESLIE, John
See LESSLY, John

LESLIE, Lachlin
L 14 Apr 1733
CR 14 Oct 1742 (PRO)
CA 8 Sept 1744
d 31 Mar 1762

LESLIE, Patrick
L 23 June 1755
CR 4 Mar 1779
CA 26 Jan 1780
d 1783 (PRO)

LESLIE, Samuel
L 16 Oct 1800
CR 1 Mar 1811
CA 31 July 1812
Ret RA 31 Oct 1846 (LG)
d 3 Sept 1851 (PRO)

LESLIE, Thomas
L 26 Mar 1764 (PRO)
d 1771 (PRO)

LESLIE, Walter
L 24 Aug 1814
Ret CR 15 Apr 1858 (PRO)
d 1863 (PRO)

LESLIE, William
See LESSLY, William

LESLYE, Patrick
See LESLIE, Patrick

LESSLY, Andrew
L 18 Oct 1782
d 14 Jan 1804 (PRO)

LESSLY, John
L 1 Apr 1779
d 4 Apr 1790

LESSLY, William
L 16 July 1756
CR
CA 20 Mar 1763
d 2 Dec 1766

LESTER, William
L 6 July 1808
Ret CR 6 Feb 1846 (OB)

LESTOCK, Gerrard
L 16 Jan 1693 (PJP)

LESTOCK, Richard (1)
L
CA 1667

LESTOCK, Richard (2)
L
CA 5 Jan 1691
SUP 24 Apr 1705 (PRO)
d 18 May 1713

LESTOCK, Richard (3)
L
CR
CA 29 Apr 1706
RAW 13 Mar 1742
RAR 11 Aug 1743 (LG)
VAW 7 Dec 1743
AB 7 June 1746 (LG)
d 13 Dec 1746 (M)

LESTOCK, Thomas
L 1703 (PJP)

L'ESTRANGE, Samuel
L 12 June 1807
d 1811 (PRO)

LETCH, Charles
L 19 Mar 1805
Ret CR 15 July 1837 (PRO)
d 1856 (PRO)

LETCHMERE, Edward
L 6 June 1696 (PJP)
CA 16 Mar 1699
KIA 15 Jan 1704 (CH)

LETHBRIDGE, Robert
L 17 Jan 1811
Ret CR 23 Mar 1854 (PRO)
d 3 June 1864 (PRO)

LETHBRIDGE, Thomas
L 23 July 1780
SUP CR 5 Apr 1815
d 28 Oct 1829 (LT)

LEVELL, Thomas
L 27 Jan 1809
Ret CR 3 Feb 1847 (PRO)
d 1860 (PRO)

LEVEN and MELVILLE, Hon. David, Earl of
Formerly BALGONIE, David, Lord
L 8 Aug 1806
CR 16 Sept 1809
CA 28 Feb 1812
Inh EP 22 Feb 1820 (OB)
Ret RA 31 Oct 1846 (LG)
Ret VA 27 Sept 1855 (NMM)
d 8 Oct 1860 (NMM)

LEVENTHORPE, Edward
L
CA 1664

LEVERICK, James
L 31 Jan 1806
d 1809 (PRO)

LE VESCONTE, Henry
T
L 27 Oct 1800
HP Jan–July 1808 (OB)
CR 5 Jan 1828 (OB)
HP 5 Jan 1828 (OB)
d 7 July 1850 (PRO)

LE VESCONTE, Philip
L 23 May 1801
HP Dec 1815 (OB)
CR 7 Nov 1816 (PRO)
d 16 Jan 1850 (PRO)

LEVESON, Robert
L 27 July 1697
Gone 1719 (PRO)

LEVETT, John (1)
L 10 June 1782
d 27 Jan 1837 (PRO)

LEVETT, John (2)
L 27 Jan 1794
d 1796 (PRO)

LEVETT, John (3)
L 1 Sept 1796
d 1796 (PRO)

LEW, Henry Padon
L 20 May 1812
d 1837 (PRO)

LEW, James
L 22 Jan 1806
One of the Jr. Lts. 1810 (PRO)
L 2 July 1812 (PRO)
d 14 Mar 1827 (PRO)

LEW, John
L 20 Nov 1812
d 18 June 1825 (PRO)

LEWES, Robert Riddell
L 7 Mar 1803
Not heard of since 1804
Name removed 1811 (PRO)

LEWES, Thomas (1)
L 20 Nov 1761 (PRO)
d 1782 (PRO)

LEWES, Thomas (2)
L 20 Nov 1761
CR 10 May 1781
CA 7 June 1782
d 16 July 1796 (PRO)

LEWES, William
See LEWIS, William

LEWIN, Sir Gregory Allnut
L 23 Dec 1814
Kt 1818 (OB)
d 12 Oct 1845 (OB)

LEWIN, Richard John
L 27 Dec 1808
CR 4 Nov 1814
d 22 May 1837 (PRO)

LEWIS, Benjamin
L 19 July 1813
HP Dec 1815 (OB)
Ret CR 15 Apr 1856 (PRO)
d 5 July 1861 (PRO)

LEWIS, Francis James (1)
L 14 May 1798
d 1801 (PRO)

LEWIS, Francis James (2)
L 11 Sept 1805
CR 29 Jan 1821 (PRO)
CA 22 July 1830 (PRO)
d 1849 (PRO)

LEWIS, Frederick
L 29 Jan 1806

Ret CR | 4 Apr | 1829 (PRO)
d | | 1869 (PRO)

LEWIS, Henry (1)
L | 1 Apr | 1758
d | | 1789 (PRO)

LEWIS, Henry (2)
L | 9 Sept | 1806
d | | 1814 (PRO)

LEWIS, Henry (3)
L | 10 Feb | 1810
HP | Sept | 1815 (OB)
Ret CR | 9 July | 1849 (PRO)
d | | 1880 (PRO)

LEWIS, Henry (4)
L | 6 Feb | 1815
HP | 6 Feb | 1815 (OB)
d | | 1850 (PRO)

LEWIS, Henry William
L | 5 Apr | 1814
d | | 1834 (PRO)

LEWIS, Isaac
L | 11 Jan | 1760
d | 8 Apr | 1761 (M)

LEWIS, James Dalton
L | 24 Apr | 1802 (PRO)
d | | 1826 (PRO)

LEWIS, James Edward
L | 26 Aug | 1799
d | | 1801 (PRO)

LEWIS, John
L | 4 May | 1796
Struck off list | | 1801 (PRO)

LEWIS, John Carteret
L | 15 July | 1781
d | 30 Sept | 1790

LEWIS, John Joseph
L | 23 June | 1773
d (drowned) | Dec | 1776 (PJP)

LEWIS, John Mason
L | 2 Nov | 1790
CR | 14 Apr | 1796
CA | 1 Jan | 1801
COM N | 25 Aug | 1825–
 | 8 May | 1829 (NBO)
COMM (Sheerness) | 8 May | 1829 (NBO)
Ret RA | 9 June | 1832 (PRO)
d | 6 May | 1835 (PRO)

LEWIS, Joseph
L | 15 Nov | 1799
d | | 1808 (PRO)

LEWIS, Joshua
L | 30 Mar | 1759
d | | 1773 (PRO)

LEWIS, Robert
L | 20 Mar | 1815 (PRO)
d | | 1840 (PRO)

LEWIS, Theophilus (1)
L | 12 June | 1797
Broke | | 1800 (PRO)

LEWIS, Theophilus (2)
L | 13 June | 1805
d | 25 May | 1813 (PRO)

LEWIS, Theophilus Caractacus
L | 26 July | 1809
KIA | 25 May | 1813 (PJP)

LEWIS, Thomas
L | 20 Nov | 1761
CR | 10 May | 1781 (PJP)
CA | 7 June | 1782 (PJP)
d | | 1782 (PRO)

LEWIS, Thomas
See LEWES, Thomas

LEWIS, William (1)
L | 1 Aug | 1799
d | | 1803 (PRO)

LEWIS, William (2)
L | 23 Mar | 1805 (PRO)
Ret CR | 23 Oct | 1837 (PRO)
d | | 1847 (PRO)

LEY, Andrew
L | 15 Jan | 1693
CR | |
CA | 26 Jan | 1710
SUP | 10 Oct | 1712 (PRO)

LEY, George
L | 6 Dec | 1813
Ret CR | 15 July | 1856 (PRO)
d | 22 Jan | 1864 (PRO)

LEY, George Stephen
L | 29 Dec | 1796
Ret CR | 26 Nov | 1830 (PRO)
d | | 1835 (PRO)

LEY, Thomas (1)
L | 16 Apr | 1678 (P)
CA | 24 Oct | 1688
CASMR | 6 Apr | 1693 (EAD)
d | 19 Sept | 1702 (EAD)

LEY, Thomas (2)
L | 23 June | 1720
d | | 1737 (PRO)

LEY, Thomas Arthur
L | 21 Mar | 1757
CR | 29 June | 1782
d | 27 Sept | 1786 (PMM)

LEY, Thomas John
L | 1 Sept | 1803
d | | 1837 (PRO)

LEY, William
L | | 1777 (PJP)

LEYCESTER, Henry
L | 8 July | 1789
CR | 7 Oct | 1794
d | 26 Feb | 1796 (PRO)

LEYDEN, William
L | 2 Dec | 1797
Ret CR | 20 Dec | 1830 (PRO)
d | | 1839 (PRO)

L'HOSTEIN, Gustavus
L | |
CA | | 1673

LIARDET, William
L | 23 Dec | 1814
Ret CR | 9 Apr | 1859 (PRO)
d | 25 July | 1867 (PRO)

LIBBY, Edward
L | 22 Mar | 1797

Ret CR 26 Nov 1830 (PRO)
d 1839 (PRO)
LICORRIS, John
L
CA 1666
LIDALE, –
L 1666
d before 1689 (PJP)
LIDDALL, William
L 1665
d before 1689 (PJP)
LIDDELL, George
L 1661
CA 1665
d 14 Aug 1672 (DDA)
LIDDLE, David
L 5 Mar 1798
d 1804 (PRO)
LIDDLE, John
L 10 Apr 1802
d 1814 (PRO)
LIDDLE, Stephen
L 4 July 1798
d 1826 (PRO)
LIDDON, Matthew
L 3 May 1811
CR 8 Nov 1821 (PRO)
Ret CR 1 July 1851 (PRO)
Ret CA 1 Apr 1856 (PRO)
d 1869 (PRO)
LIELL, David
See LYELL, David
LIELL, Thomas
See LYELL, Thomas
LIELL, Thomas
L 7 Apr 1761
d 1796 (PRO)
LIENBERGH, James
L 3 Feb 1694
Entered Swedish Service 1700 (PJP)
LIGHTERNESS, Alexander
L 28 June 1798
d 21 Nov 1829 (PRO)
LIGHTERNESS, James
L 28 June 1784
d 10 Mar 1790
LIGHTFOOT, Henry
L 15 Nov 1782
d 24 Dec 1790
LIGHTFOOT, John
L
CA 1665
d before 1689 (PJP)
LIGHTFOOT, Paul
See LIGHTFOOT, Philip
LIGHTFOOT, Philip
L 1666 (DDA)
LIHOU, John
L 29 Oct 1811
CR 12 May 1827 (PRO)
CA 4 Feb 1833 (PRO)
d 1840 (PRO)

LIKE, John
L 24 Apr 1780
d 1810 (PRO)
LILBURNE, James
L 2 July 1798
T
CR 24 Dec 1805
KIA 29 Apr 1812 (TR)
LILBURNE, Richard
L 22 Oct 1795
d 1800 (PRO)
LILLICRAP, James
L 30 Oct 1793
CR 18 Aug 1801
CA 21 Oct 1810
Ret RA 31 Oct 1846 (LG)
d 9 July 1851 (PRO)
LIMBERLY, William
L 28 Apr 1781
SUP CR 1 Jan 1816 (PRO)
d 3 Oct 1840 (PRO)
LIMEBURNER, Thomas
L 13 May 1720
CR
CA 11 July 1740
d 4 Dec 1750 (PRO)
LINCOLNE, James
L 4 Oct 1746
d 1756 (PRO)
LIND, Sir James (1)
L 25 Jan 1778
CR 2 Nov 1796 (PRO)
CA 6 Mar 1804
Kt 1805 (PJP)
KCB 2 Jan 1815 (MB)
d 12 June 1823 (LT)
LIND, James (2)
L 7 Feb 1815
HP 7 Feb 1815 (OB)
d 17 July 1847 (OB)
LIND, John
L 4 Jan 1744
SUP 1778 (PRO)
LIND, Joseph
L 31 May 1777
d 1783 (PRO)
LINDESAY, George
L 9 Nov 1814
d 1829 (PRO)
LINDESAY, John
L 3 Apr 1757
d 1763 (PRO)
LINDSAY, Alexander
L 12 Jan 1799
Ret CR 26 Nov 1830 (PRO)
d 1844 (PRO)
LINDSAY, Sir Charles
L 30 Sept 1793
CR 21 June 1796 (PRO)
CA 6 Mar 1797
d (drowned) 10 Mar 1799 (PJP)
LINDSAY, George
L 20 Aug 1759
CR 22 Apr 1781

CA 6 Mar 1797
d 1798 (PRO)

LINDSAY, James (1)
L 17 May 1711
Struck out; said to be in the land service 1729 (PRO)

LINDSAY, James (2)
L 1806 (PJP)

LINDSAY, James (3)
T wounded
L 13 Feb 1815
d 18 Sept 1845 (OB)

LINDSAY, James (4)
See CARNEGIE, James Lindsay

LINDSAY, Sir John (1)
L 2 Mar 1756
CR 4 Apr 1757
CA 29 Sept 1757
Kt 1771 (PJP)
CRM 21 June 1781 (AL)
COM AD 10 Apr–31 Dec 1783 (AO)
RAR 24 Sept 1787
d 4 June 1788 (CH)

LINDSAY, John (2)
L 23 Dec 1809
d 1840 (PRO)

LINDSAY, John (3)
See LINDSEY, John

LINDSAY, Martin
L 25 Jan 1778
SUP CR 27 May 1813
d 27 Nov 1837 (LT)

LINDSAY, Hon. William
L 26 Oct 1731
Gone 1734 (PRO)

LINDSEY, John
L 1 June 1810
CR 27 Aug 1814
HP 27 Aug 1814 (OB)
Ret CA 1 July 1851 (PRO)
d 23 Aug 1864 (PRO)

LINDSEY, Michael
L 1661
CA 1665
d before 1689 (PJP)

LINDSEY, William
L
CA 29 May 1694
d 16 Oct 1694

LINE, Joseph
L 5 Dec 1696 (PJP)

LINE, Kerry
See LYNE, Kerry

LINGARD, John
L 11 Mar 1815
d 5 Feb 1843 (PRO)

LINGEN, Joseph
L
CR 30 July 1710
CA 26 July 1728
SUP RA before July 1748
d 23 Nov 1752 (PRO)

LINKLATER, Thomas
L 21 Apr 1804
d 6 June 1830 (PRO)

LINTHORNE, Thomas (1)
L 17 May 1779
CR 2 Jan 1798
d 6 June 1830 (PRO)

LINTHORNE, Thomas (2)
L 8 Sept 1809
d 1833 (PRO)

LINTON, James
L 1804 (PJP)

LINTON, John (1)
L 1693 (PJP)

LINTON, John (2)
L 12 Aug 1796
Ret CR 26 Nov 1830 (PRO)
d 1834 (PRO)

LINZEE, Edward
L 14 Jan 1781
d 6 Mar 1792

LINZEE, John
L 13 Oct 1768
CR 19 Jan 1771
CA 16 Feb 1777
Resigned 23 Sept 1791 (PRO)

LINZEE, Richard
L 12 July 1781
d 1782 (PRO)

LINZEE, Robert
L 29 Jan 1761
CR 25 Nov 1768
CA 3 Oct 1770
CRM 1 Feb 1793 (AL)
RAW 12 Apr 1794
RAR 4 July 1794
VAW 1 June 1795
VAR 14 Feb 1799 (PRO)
AB 1 Jan 1801
d 1 Oct 1804 (PRO)

LINZEE, Samuel Hood
L 21 July 1790
CR 5 Nov 1793
CA 8 Mar 1794
CRM 1 Aug 1811 (LG)
RAB 12 Aug 1812
RAW 4 Dec 1813
RAR 4 June 1814
VAB 12 Aug 1819 (LG)
d 2 Sept 1820 (PRO)

LIPSON, Thomas
L 29 June 1809
CR 4 Mar 1819 (PJP)
Ret CR 1 July 1851 (PRO)
Ret CA 1 Apr 1856 (PRO)
d 1863 (PRO)

LISLE, Peter de
See DE LISLE, Peter

LISLE, Toby
L
CR
CA 2 Sept 1709
d (duel) 1719 (PJP)

LISLE, Trevelyan
L 1 Feb 1758
d 1761 (PRO)

LISLE, William (1)
L 16 Jan 1728
In Merchant Service 1729 (PRO)

LISLE, William (2)		
L	16 Jan	1728
CR		
CA	28 May	1740
d	26 Jan	1752
LISTON, Andrew		
L	9 Feb	1815
d	9 Aug	1821 (PRO)
LITCHFIELD, Henry		
L	29 June	1807
CR	12 July	1813
CA	20 Nov	1826 (PRO)
Ret CA	1 Oct	1846 (PRO)
Ret RA	13 July	1854 (PRO)
Ret VA	7 Nov	1860 (PRO)
Ret A	15 June	1864 (PRO)
d	24 Aug	1864 (PRO)
LITCHFIELD, John		
L	25 Aug	1804
d	Sept	1804 (PJP)
LITTLE, Charles		
L	3 May	1759
d		1772 (PRO)
LITTLE, Francis		
L	30 July	1810
d	24 Oct	1841 (PRO)
LITTLE, George		
L	13 Feb	1805
d		1807 (PRO)
LITTLE, James (1)		
L	11 June	1801
d	6 Mar	1835 (PJP)
LITTLE, James (2)		
L	15 Aug	1806
d		1814 (PRO)
LITTLE, John (1)		
L	29 Nov	1793
CR	2 Aug	1799 (PRO)
d	25 May	1801 (PRO)
LITTLE, John (2)		
L	18 Aug	1801
CR	19 July	1821 (PRO)
d	28 Jan	1841 (PRO)
LITTLE, Robert		
L		1715 (PJP)
LITTLE, Watkin William		
L	17 Apr	1812
d		1820 (PRO)
LITTLEFAIRE, William		
L		1666
LITTLEFIELD, John		
L	6 Aug	1759
d	17 Dec	1801
LITTLEHALES, Bendall Robert		
L	21 Sept	1790
CR	27 Sept	1797
CA	15 May	1800
Ret RA	22 July	1830 (PRO)
VAB	17 Aug	1840 (LG)
VAW	23 Nov	1841 (LG)
VAR	20 Nov	1846 (LG)
d	5 Aug	1847 (PRO)

LITTLEJOHN, Adam		
L	31 Mar	1780
CR		
CA		1795 (PJP)
KIA	7 Mar	1795 (CH)
LITTLEJOHN, George		
L	9 Sept	1688
LITTLEJOHN, William Hotham		
T		
L	18 June	1811
d (drowned)	24 Nov	1812 (PJP)
LITTLETON, Edward		
L		
CA	17 Feb	1692
d	2 Jan	1696
LITTLETON, Hugh		
See LYTTLETON, Hugh		
LITTLETON, James		
L		
CA	27 Feb	1693
MP (Weymouth and Melcombe Regis)	1710–17 Nov	1711 (MPS)
MP (Weymouth and Melcombe Regis)		1713–1715 (MPS)
RAR	1 Feb	1717
VAB	14 Mar	1718
	(15 Mar	1718 in C)
VAW	7 Mar	1719
MP (Queensborough)	1722– 3 Feb	1723 (MPS)
d	3 Feb	1723 (MPS)
LITTLETON, William		
L		1673
LITTLEWORT, Richard		
L	9 Sept	1778
d	3 May	1798
LIVESAY, Thomas		
L	7 Mar	1802
d		1804 (PRO)
LIVINGSTONE, Sir Thomas		
L	22 Nov	1790
CR	26 Dec	1796
CA	13 Jan	1800
Inh Bt	12 Jan	1821 (MB)
RAW	22 July	1830 (PRO)
RAR	10 Jan	1837 (LG)
VAB	28 June	1838 (LG)
VAW	23 Nov	1841 (LG)
VAR	9 Nov	1846 (PRO)
AB	1 June	1848 (PRO)
AW	11 June	1851 (PRO)
d	1 Apr	1853 (PRO)
LLEWHELLIN, Richard		
L	7 Dec	1758
d		1768 (PRO)
LLOYD, Alexander Thomas		
L	29 Dec	1796
d		1800 (PRO)
LLOYD, Charles (1)		
L		
CA		1673
LLOYD, Charles (2)		
L	17 Apr	1743
d		1755(6) (PRO)

LLOYD, David (1)
L 1672 (PJP)
CA 18 Sept 1677
Dismissed 1688
d 4 Jan 1723 (DDA)

LLOYD, David (2)
L
CA 15 Sept 1695
d (drowned) 25 July 1699 (PJP)

LLOYD, David (3)
L 4 May 1788
CR 13 June 1796
CA 1 Mar 1799
d 1819 (PRO)

LLOYD, David
See LOYDE, David

LLOYD, Edward
L 14 Jan 1808
CR 8 May 1811
CA 19 July 1821 (OB)
KH 1 Jan 1834 (OB)
Ret RA 8 Mar 1852 (PRO)

LLOYD, Francis (1)
L 19 Aug 1747
d 1759 (PRO)

LLOYD, Francis (2)
L 6 Oct 1793
d 16 Oct 1800 (PJP)

LLOYD, Frederick
L 20 Aug 1811
d Dec 1732 (PRO)

LLOYD, George
L 3 Nov 1812
CR 8 Nov 1815
CA 26 Aug 1828 (OB)
HP 26 Aug 1828 (OB)
Ret CA 26 Aug 1848 (PRO)
Ret RA 2 May 1855 (PRO)
d June 1860 (PRO)

LLOYD, Henry (1)
L 13 Oct 1757
CR 26 May 1768
CA 23 Mar 1771
d 15 Nov 1792

LLOYD, Henry (2)
L 20 May 1758
d 1771 (PRO)

LLOYD, Henry (3)
L 11 Oct 1794
Ret CR 26 Nov 1830 (PRO)
d 1841 (PRO)

LLOYD, Howell
L 2 Nov 1772
CR 2 Oct 1778
CA 15 May 1780
d 15 Sept 1779 (PRO)

LLOYD, Hugh
L 8 July 1760
d 9 May 1789 (M)

LLOYD, James (1)
L 13 May 1720
CR 31 Dec 1729 (PRO)
CA 30 Aug 1739
Dismissed 13 Nov 1746 (PJP)
Restored 4 Nov 1747 (PJP)
LGH 1754 (PJP)
d 8 Feb 1761

LLOYD, James (2)
L 24 Jan 1782
d 1809 (PRO)

LLOYD, James Llewin
L 8 Aug 1799
T wounded
d 1806 (TR)

LLOYD, James Simmons
L 20 Aug 1795
d 1796 (PRO)

LLOYD, John (1)
L
CA 9 June 1666 (RM)

LLOYD, John (2)
L 30 May 1709 (PMM)

LLOYD, John (3)
L 3 Dec 1727
CR 27 July 1744
CA 30 May 1745 (C)
d 21 Sept 1748 (PRO)

LLOYD, John (4)
L 19 Mar 1734 (PRO)
CR 4 July 1745 (PRO)
CA 4 Sept 1746
RAB 31 Mar 1775
RAR 5 Feb 1776
VAB 29 Jan 1778
d 8 Mar 1778

LLOYD, John (5)
L 8 June 1805
CR 29 Aug 1808
d 12 Feb 1813 (PRO)

LLOYD, John (6)
L 1 July 1808
d 18 June 1829 (PRO)

LLOYD, John (7)
L 22 July 1814
Ret CR 14 Sept 1858 (PRO)
d 1869 (PRO)

LLOYD, Richard
L 22 Sept 1810
Ret CR 5 Jan 1852 (PRO)
d 13 Dec 1859 (PRO)

LLOYD, Robert (1)
L 13 Nov 1790
CR 6 Dec 1796
CA 6 Dec 1799
HP Apr 1811–Feb 1812 (OB)
RAW 22 July 1830 (PRO)
VAB 10 Jan 1837 (PRO)
VAW 23 Nov 1841 (LG)
d 17 Jan 1846 (OB)

LLOYD, Robert (2)
L 13 Jan 1797
T killed
KIA 21 Oct 1805 (TR)

LLOYD, Thomas (1)
L 1672 (DDA)
d 19 July 1678 (DDA)

LLOYD, Thomas (2)
L 2 Mar 1756
d 1772 (PRO)

LLOYD, Thomas (3)
L 17 Sept 1764
CR 10 July 1776
CA 24 July 1778
d (drowned) 11 Oct 1780 (CH)

LLOYD, Thomas (4)
L 26 May 1768
CR 17 Apr 1778
CA 30 Oct 1778
d 1794 (PRO)

LLOYD, Thomas Henry
L 22 Jan 1807
d 1810 (PRO)

LLOYD, Vaughan
L 20 Sept 1815
Ret CR 1864 (PRO)
d 13 June 1864 (PRO)

LLOYD, Whitworth
L 6 July 1814
CR 2 Aug 1820 (PRO)
d Aug 1828 (PRO)

LLOYD, William (1)
?L 16 Mar 1699
CR
CA 1 Jan 1713
d (drowned) 22 May 1723 (PJP)

LLOYD, William (2)
L 13 Mar 1744
CR 18 July 1747
CA 12 Jan 1748
RAB 23 Jan 1778
RAR 19 Mar 1779
VAB 26 Sept 1780
VAR 24 Sept 1787
AB 1 Feb 1793
AW 1 June 1795
d 19 July 1796 (LT)

LLOYD, William (3)
L 27 June 1757
d 4 Nov 1758 (PMM)

LLOYD, William (4)
L 13 Nov 1790
SUP CR 1 July 1823 (PRO)
d 1832 (PRO)

LLOYD, William (5)
L 15 Oct 1801
d 1805 (PRO)

LLOYD, William (6)
L 9 June 1806 (OB)
Ret CR 19 Aug 1840 (OB)

LLOYD, William Hynam
L 6 Feb 1815
HP 1844 (OB)
Ret CR 9 Feb 1860 (PRO)
d 1865 (PRO)

L'MONTAIS, Francis
See LEMOINE, Francis

LOADES, Edmund
L
CA 12 July 1693
d (drowned) 22 Oct 1707 (CH)

LOANE, William
L 24 Sept 1794
d 5 Mar 1823 (PRO)

LOBB, Charles
L 1746 (PJP)

LOBB, Jacob
L 9 Jan 1748
CR 23 Dec 1757
d 20 Feb 1773 (PRO)

LOBB, William Granville
L 27 Dec 1777
CR 24 Oct 1794
CA 1 Sept 1795
d 28 July 1814 (PMM)

LOCH, Francis Erskine
L 22 Jan 1806
CR 6 Jan 1813
CA 29 Sept 1814
RAB 2 Sept 1850 (PRO)
RAW 17 Dec 1852 (PRO)
RAR 7 Feb 1855 (PRO)
VAB 14 May 1857 (PRO)
VAW 8 Dec 1857 (PRO)
VAR 9 June 1860 (PRO)
AB 16 June 1862 (PRO)
Ret A 25 June 1863 (PRO)
d 13 Feb 1868 (PRO)

LOCHARD, Anthony
L 21 Dec 1705 (PMM)

LOCHTIE, Robert
L 4 Sept 1782
d 1804 (PRO)

LOCK, Campbell
L 30 May 1814
CR 17 July 1828 (PRO)
Ret CA 1 Apr 1856 (PRO)
d 15 May 1861 (PRO)

LOCK, Charles (1)
L 1691 (PJP)

LOCK, Charles (2)
L 21 Apr 1780
d 1793 (PRO)

LOCK, Charles (3)
L 17 Nov 1790
CR 22 Sept 1796
d 14 Feb 1800 (PRO)

LOCK, James
L
CA 1665

LOCK, James Ferguson
L 30 Mar 1808
d 1808 (PRO)

LOCK, John
L 17 May 1694
Gone 1724 (PRO)

LOCK, Nagle
L 20 Nov 1812
CR 18 Feb 1815
d 25 Sept 1818 (PJP)

LOCK, Richard
L 21 Oct 1772
CR 24 Nov 1778
d 20 Sept 1779 (PRO)

LOCK, Robert
L 1745 (PJP)

LOCK, Thomas
L
CA 1665

LOCK(E), Walter
L 1 Feb 1778
CR 4 July 1794
CA 22 Sept 1795
RAB 4 June 1814
RAW 12 Aug 1819 (CH)
RAR 19 July 1821 (CH)
VAB 27 May 1825 (CH)
VAW 22 July 1830 (CH)
d 9 May 1835 (LT)

LOCKER, William
L 4 July 1756
CR 7 Apr 1762
CA 26 May 1768
LGH 1793 (PJP)
d 26 Dec 1800 (PRO)

LOCKHART, Andrew
L 7 Apr 1777
SUP CR 30 May 1810
d 2 Mar 1831 (PRO)

LOCKHART, Charles
L 14 Mar 1815
d 20 Dec 1829 (PRO)

LOCKHART, John
See ROSS, Sir John Lockhart

LOCKHART, William
L 18 Dec 1760
CR 7 Nov 1777
CA 7 Oct 1779
SUP 1799
d 1800 (PRO)

LOCKWOOD, David
L 21 Dec 1758
Deserted 1778 (PJP)
d 1787 (PRO)

LOCKWOOD, Richard
L 6 Aug 1800
d 1819 (PRO)

LOCKYER, Nicholas
L 17 Dec 1803
CR 25 Sept 1806
CA 29 Mar 1815
CB 4 June 1815 (OB)
d 27 Feb 1847 (OB)

LODDER, Charles
L 6 May 1808
d 1809 (PRO)

LOEFFS, Charles
L 24 Aug 1743
d 1757 (PRO)

LOFTIN, Samuel
L 13 Mar 1734
CR 25 Feb 1742
CA 28 June 1744
Dismissed 16 July 1745
d 14 Dec 1779 (M)

LOFTUS, Arthur
L 14 June 1813
Ret CR 15 Apr 1856 (PRO)
d 1861 (PRO)

LOGAN, Andrew
L 1666
e (cowardice) Sept 1670 (CH)

LOGAN, Paulett
L 3 Aug 1741
d 1745 (PRO)

LOGAN, Randall
L 1707 (PJP)

LOGGAN, George
L 3 Feb 1703 (PMM)
d 8 Mar 1704 (PMM)

LOGGIE, Charles
L 29 Mar 1776
d 1782 (PRO)

LOGGIE, James
See LOGIE, James

LOGIE, Charles
L 13 Feb 1759
SUP 2 Feb 1801
d 1805 (PMM)

LOGIE, Gustavus
L 30 Dec 1775
d 1783 (PRO)

LOGIE, James
L 29 May 1741
CR 23 Mar 1756
CA 20 Apr 1758
d Jan 1779

LOMAX, John
L 30 Apr 1678

LONDON, Richard
L 1665
CA 1670

LONEY, Henry
T
L 24 Dec 1805
d Dec 1828 (PRO)

LONEY, John Jenkins
L 11 Aug 1807
HP 1 Apr 1842 (OB)
d 3 June 1860 (PRO)

LONEY, Robert
L 8 May 1812
CR 10 Jan 1837 (OB)
HP 10 Jan 1837 (OB)
Ret CA 6 Aug 1852 (PRO)
Ret RA 1 Apr 1870 (PRO)
Ret VA 25 Aug 1873 (PRO)
Ret A 15 June 1879 (PRO)
d 22 Feb 1882 (PRO)

LONG, Charles
L 18 May 1735 (PRO)
CR
CA 13 May 1741
Dismissed 16 Sept 1746 (PRO)
d 4 Aug 1761 (PRO)

LONG, George (1)
L 5 Apr 1779
KIA 5 Jan 1782 (PJP)

LONG, George (2)
L 16 July 1794
CR 23 Apr 1799
d 15 Sept 1801 (PRO)

LONG, Henry
L 16 Aug 1697
CR
CA 17 Sept 1706
d 12 Dec 1723

LONG, James
L 7 Nov 1806
Ret CR 11 Feb 1842 (PRO)
d 1864 (PRO)

LONG, John
L 30 Jan 1707 (PMM)

LONG, Lionel
L 1702

LONG, Richard (1)
L
CA 1664

LONG, Richard (2)
L
CA 4 Dec 1697
Dismissed 12 Sept 1705
d 1717

LONG, Richard Eyre
L 26 Aug 1790
d 1792 (PRO)

LONG, Robert (1)
L 1666
CA 1668

LONG, Robert (2)
L 22 May 1709 (PRO)
CR 3 Oct 1719
CA 21 Mar 1727
SUP RA before 1748
d 6 July 1771

LONG, Samuel
L 1745 (PJP)

LONG, Thomas
L
CR 6 Feb 1694 (PJP)
CA 27 Jan 1696
KIA 13 Dec 1710 (CH)

LONG, Walter
L 13 June 1757
CR 30 Aug 1779
d 7 June 1781 (CH)

LONG, William
L 1665
CA 3 Feb 1673

LONG, William (2)
L 4 Mar 1740
CR 15 Nov 1756
CA 22 Feb 1760
d 1779 (PRO)

LONG, William (3)
L 7 Apr 1798
d 1807 (PRO)

LONGCHAMP, John
L 5 Dec 1806
CR 26 Dec 1822 (OB)
HP 1832 (OB)
Ret CA 1 Apr 1856 (PRO)
d Nov 1857 (PRO)

LONGDEN, Sandys
L 20 Apr 1727
Gone 1742 (PRO)

LONGFIELD, William
L 25 May 1805
d 1807 (PRO)

LONGFORD, Edward Michael, Lord
L 12 Aug 1761
CR 20 June 1765
CA 31 May 1766
d 6 June 1792

LONGUEVILLE, Sir Thomas
L 3 June 1709
d 1762 (PRO)

LOPDELL, John
L 7 Feb 1708
Gone 1734 (PRO)

LORD, Anthony Bliss William
L 17 Mar 1806
d May 1821 (PRO)

LORD, William Henry
L 23 May 1797 (PJP)
d 1802 (PRO)

LORING, John
L 3 Dec 1779
CR 16 May 1793
CA 3 Nov 1794 (PRO)
d 9 Nov 1808 (PRO)

LORING, Sir John Wentworth
L 24 May 1794
CR 3 Jan 1799
CA 28 Apr 1802
CB 4 June 1815 (OB)
RAB 10 Jan 1837 (LG)
KCH 30 Apr 1837 (OB)
KCB 4 July 1840 (OB)
RAR 23 Nov 1841 (LG)
VAB 9 Nov 1846 (PRO)
VAW 22 Jan 1847 (PRO)
VAR 1 July 1848 (PRO)
AB 8 July 1851 (PRO)
d 29 July 1852 (PRO)

LORING, Joshua
L 23 May 1745
CR 13 Mar 1756
CA 19 Dec 1757
HP 1763 (DAB)
d Oct 1781 (DAB)

LORING, Joseph Royall
L 17 Feb 1779
d 16 Oct 1792

LORT, George
L 12 Nov 1756
d 1764 (PRO)

LOSACK, George
L 18 Apr 1778
CR 19 July 1781
CA 22 Nov 1790
RAB 28 Apr 1808
RAW 31 July 1810
RAR 1 Aug 1811
VAB 4 Dec 1813
VAW 4 June 1814
VAR 19 July 1821 (PRO)
AB 27 May 1825 (PRO)
d 22 Aug 1829 (PRO)

LOSACK, Woodley
L 23 Dec 1793

CR 31 July 1801
CA 22 Jan 1806
d 30 May 1838 (PRO)

LOTEN, James
L 23 June 1784
d 1803 (PRO)

LOUD, Richard
L 29 Sept 1795
d 1805 (PRO)

LOUDON, William
L 18 Aug 1812
Ret CR 25 Oct 1854 (PRO)
d 16 Jan 1870 (PRO)

LOUGHTEN, John
L 21 Feb 1741
d 1744 (PRO)

LOUIS, Charles Belfield
L 1 Aug 1811
CR 12 Aug 1819 (PRO)
d 1835 (PRO)

LOUIS, Sir John
L 21 Apr 1801
CR 28 Feb 1805
CA 22 Jan 1806
Inh Bt 17 May 1807 (OB)
RAB 28 June 1838 (LG)
RAW 23 Nov 1841 (LG)
RAR 19 Feb 1847 (PRO)
VAB 9 Oct 1849 (PRO)
VAW 1 July 1851 (PRO)
VAR 2 Apr 1853 (PRO)
AB 27 Sept 1855 (PRO)
AW 22 Aug 1857 (PRO)
Ret A 2 May 1860 (PRO)
d 31 Mar 1863 (PJP)

LOUIS, Sir Thomas
L 18 July 1777
CR 9 Apr 1781
CA 20 Jan 1783
Kt (Two Sicilies) 19 Apr 1802 (LG)
RAB 23 Apr 1804
RAW 9 Nov 1805
Cre Bt 29 Mar 1806 (LG)
d 17 May 1807 (LT)

LOUND, Sherard Philip
L 24 Apr 1811
d 1813 (PRO)

LOUTTED, Duncan
L 5 July 1799
d 18 May 1828 (PRO)

LOVE, Henry
L 3 Nov 1812
d 1842 (PRO)

LOVE, Henry Ommanney
L 27 June 1814
CR 10 July 1826 (PRO)
CA 5 Dec 1837 (PRO)
Ret CA 4 Dec 1851 (PRO)
Ret RA 22 Aug 1857 (PRO)
Ret VA 11 Jan 1864 (PRO)
Ret A 3 July 1869 (PRO)
d 16 Sept 1872 (PRO)

LOVE, John
L 1691 (PJP)

LOVE, Richard
L 1689 (PJP)

LOVE, Robert (1)
L 1691 (PJP)
d (drowned) 3 Sept 1691 (PJP)

LOVE, Robert (2)
L 20 Jan 1778
d 13 Mar 1801

LOVE, Tobias
L 30 May 1778
d 1783 (PRO)

LOVE, William
L 16 Apr 1794
CR 13 Feb 1807 (MB)
d 17 Apr 1839 (OB)

LOVEDAY, Edward
L 8 Mar 1815
d 1819 (PRO)

LOVEDAY, Francis
L 16 June 1778
d 1796 (PRO)

LOVELACE, Paul
L 6 Mar 1741
d 1754(5) (PRO)

LOVELESS, Bassett James
L 2 Feb 1811
d 2 Nov 1863 (PRO)

LOVELESS, James
L 8 Feb 1815
Ret CR 1 Oct 1860 (PRO)
d 1870 (PRO)

LOVELL, John
L 11 May 1795
Gone 1811 (PRO)

LOVELL, Matthew
L 15 July 1799
d 1810 (PRO)

LOVELL, Michael
L 15 Feb 1696 (PJP)

LOVELL, Philip Cranmer
L 14 Feb 1815
d 1816 (PRO)

LOVELL, Thomas
L
CA 1672
Discharged from service 1711 (PRO)

LOVELL, William
L 6 July 1781
d 1790 (PRO)

LOVELL, William Stanhope
T
L 29 Jan 1806
CR 13 Aug 1812
CA 21 Aug 1815
KH 25 Jan 1836 (OB)
Ret CA 1 Oct 1846 (PRO)
Ret RA 30 Dec 1850 (PRO)
Ret VA 9 July 1857 (PRO)
d 20 May 1859 (PRO)

LOVESY, Thomas
L 5 Jan 1811
d 13 Feb 1827 (PRO)

LOVETT, John
L 2 Mar 1734

CR 11 June 1741
CA 16 Nov 1741
d 27 Feb 1758 (M)

LOVING, John
L 16 Nov 1739
CR 12 Jan 1745
d 1785 (PRO)

LOVITT, William
L 26 July 1810
d 1842 (PRO)

LOW, John
L 1673
d before 1689 (PJP)

LOW, John M'Arthur
L 4 May 1810
CR 20 Jan 1818 (PRO)
d 18 Feb 1840 (PRO)

LOW, Robert
L 7 Feb 1815
d 29 Feb 1840 (PRO)

LOWCAY, George
L 16 Feb 1815
d 1827 (PRO)

LOWCAY, Henry
L 7 Jan 1799
CR 29 Oct 1813
HP Oct 1813 (OB)
Ret CA 24 May 1849 (PRO)
d 4 Feb 1859 (PRO)

LOWCAY, Loftus
L 7 Oct 1811
d 1814 (PRO)

LOWCAY, Robert
L 7 Feb 1815
HP 20 Oct 1844 (OB)
d 1853 (PRO)

LOWCAY, William
T
L 25 Mar 1809
CR 9 Apr 1847 (OB)
Ret CR 1 July 1851 (PRO)
d 3 Nov 1852 (PRO)

LOWDER, John
L 2 Apr 1760
SUP CR 12 Oct 1807
d 1813 (PRO)

LOWE, Abraham
L 24 Nov 1794
HP 1802–31 Jan 1804 (OB)
CR 13 Oct 1807
CA 7 June 1814
Ret CA 1 Oct 1846 (PRO)
Ret RA 15 Sept 1849 (PRO)
d 10 Apr 1854 (PRO)

LOWE, George
L 23 Mar 1797
d 1799 (PRO)

LOWE, John
L 28 May 1778
d 1 Mar 1824 (PRO)

LOWE, Joseph
L 15 Mar 1815
d 1845 (PRO)

LOWE, Patrick (1)
L 1 Sept 1801
d 1809 (PRO)

LOWE, Patrick (2)
L 9 Mar 1809
d 1817 (PRO)

LOWE, Peter
L 1742 (PJP)

LOWE, Thomas
L 24 Mar 1800
d 1803 (PRO)

LOWEN, John
L 11 Mar 1691 (PJP)
CR 4 Mar 1696 (PJP)
CA 1 Oct 1703
Dismissed 1705
Restored 1710 (PJP)
d 30 Sept 1713 (PJP)

LOWEN, Thomas
L 25 Jan 1796
Dismissed 1798

LOWER, Edward
L 15 Nov 1756
SUP CR 24 Sept 1796 (PMM)
d 29 May 1802 (PMM)

LOWFIELD, William
L 19 June 1745
d 29 Oct 1762 (PRO)

LOWLEY, Miles
L 27 Nov 1778
d 11 Nov 1785 (PRO)

LOWNDES, Richard
L 27 Jan 1748
d 1759 (PRO)

LOWRY, James
L 28 Jan 1802
CR 12 Sept 1822 (PRO)
d 8 Oct 1847 (PRO)

LOWRY, John
L 1728 (PJP)

LOWSAY, William
See LOWCAY, William

LOWTHER, Henry
L 1690 (PJP)

LOWTHIAN, Robert
L 2 Nov 1799
CR 4 Dec 1813
Ret CA 1 July 1851 (PRO)
d 3 Nov 1852 (PRO)

LOYDE, David, James, John and William
See LLOYD

LOYDE, David
L
CA 30 Oct 1694
d 24 July 1697

LUCAS, Charles
L 20 June 1743
CR 15 Nov 1756
CA 18 Oct 1758
d 23 Mar 1773

LUCAS, Francis
L 5 Apr 1769
d 1775 (PRO)

LUCAS, James Owen		
L	25 Sept	1793
d		1826 (PRO)
LUCAS , John (1)		
L		
CA		1673
LUCAS, John (2)		
L	24 Apr	1782
SUP CR	17 June	1817 (PRO)
d		1817 (PRO)
LUCAS, John (3)		
L	28 May	1807
d		1809 (PRO)
LUCAS, John (4)		
See EDRIDGE, John		
LUCAS, Mark Robinson		
L	28 Mar	1799
CR	19 July	1821 (PRO)
d		1834 (PRO)
LUCAS, Richard		
L	19 Nov	1778
CR	Mar	1782 (PJP)
CA	14 Apr	1782
d	7 July	1797 (PRO)
LUCAS, Robert		
L	15 Feb	1815
d	22 Apr	1822 (PRO)
LUCAS, Thomas		
L	5 Sept	1797
d (drowned)	Oct	1800 (PJP)
LUCAS, William		
L	18 Sept	1793
d		1797 (PRO)
LUCE, John (1)		
L	18 Oct	1758
d	11 Dec	1795 (PMM)
LUCE, John (2)		
L	19 Nov	1793
CR	8 Mar	1797
d	27 May	1827 (MB)
LUCE, William		
L	16 Mar	1814
HP	Nov	1841 (OB)
CR	9 Jan	1854 (PRO)
d		1874 (PRO)
LUCK, James		
L		
CR		
CA	29 May	1720
d	22 Dec	1736 (PRO)
LUCK, John		
L	30 Nov	1776
CR	23 Sept	1781
CA	25 Oct	1809
d		1814 (PRO)
LUCKOMB, Philip		
L	14 Mar	1811
d		1818 (PRO)
LUCKRAFT, Alfred		
T	wounded	
L	3 Sept	1810
Kt (Greece)		1828 (TR)
Kt (Russia)		1828 (TR)
CR	28 Oct	1829 (OB)
CA	28 June	1838 (OB)
HP	28 June	1838 (OB)
Ret CA	5 May	1853 (PRO)
Ret RA	4 Nov	1857 (PRO)
Ret VA	15 June	1864 (PRO)
Ret A	10 Sept	1869 (PRO)
d	11 June	1871 (PMM)
LUCKRAFT, John		
L	29 Mar	1802
d		1846 (PRO)
LUCKRAFT, William		
L	11 Dec	1807
CR	27 July	1825 (PRO)
CA	4 Nov	1840 (PRO)
Ret CA	14 Oct	1853 (PRO)
Ret RA	18 Dec	1858 (PRO)
d	5 Jan	1865 (PRO)
LUDMAN, Bernard		
L		1665
CA		1666
d	before	1689 (PJP)
LUFFE, John		
L		1689 (PJP)
LUGCAR, Godfrey		
L		
CR	16 Apr	1695 (PJP)
LUGG, William		
L	8 Nov	1806
Ret CR	10 Mar	1845 (PRO)
d		1849 (PRO)
LUKE, George (1)		
L	21 Sept	1790
CR	3 Nov	1794
d	5 June	1824 (PRO)
LUKE, George (2)		
L	16 Nov	1801
CR	8 July	1814
d		1840 (PRO)
LUKE, William		
L	1 Aug	1777
CR	11 Dec	1782
CA	22 Nov	1790
RAB	25 Oct	1809
RAW	31 July	1810
RAR	12 Aug	1812
VAB	4 June	1814
d		1818 (PRO)
LUKEY, Patherick		
L	25 Nov	1757
d		1768 (PRO)
LUKIN, William		
See WINDHAM, William		
LUMLEY, George		
L	23 May	1694
CR	6 Feb	1706 (PMM)
CA	17 Sept	1706
d	20 Sept	1710 (PRO)
LUMLEY, Henry		
L		
CA	22 Mar	1693
	(3 Mar	1693 in S)
d		1720
LUMLEY, John Richard		
L	13 Aug	1801

CR	12 Jan	1805
CA	14 Sept	1808
d	23 July	1821 (PRO)
LUMLEY, Hon. Thomas		
L	3 July	1778
CR	25 July	1780
CA	?25 Apr	1781
KIA	3 Sept	1782 (LG)
LUMLEY, William		
L	18 Apr	1735
Gone		1741 (PRO)
LUMSDAINE, George		
L	13 July	1776
CR	15 July	1781
CA	1 Dec	1787
RAB	2 Oct	1807
RAW	28 Apr	1808
RAR	31 July	1810
VAB	1 Aug	1811
d	9 Feb	1812 (PRO)
LUNDIN, John		
L	3 Apr	1794
d		1811 (PRO)
LUNN, John		
L	6 Mar	1703
d		1727 (PRO)
LUNN, Thomas		
L	2 Mar	1705 (PMM)
LUNT, Peter		
L		1664
d	before	1689 (PJP)
LURCHEN, John		
L	31 July	1797
d	25 Dec	1828 (PRO)
LURCOCK, William		
L	23 Aug	1759
LGH		1782 (PJP)
d		1786 (PRO)
LUSCOMBE, Edward		
L	3 Dec	1810
Ret CR	14 July	1851 (PRO)
d	16 July	1851 (PRO)
LUSHINGTON, Franklin		
L	16 Jan	1728
CR		
CA	24 June	1739
d	4 Mar	1743 (LG)
LUSK, George		
L	29 Apr	1802
d		1806 (PRO)
LUSK, Joseph		
L	12 Feb	1808
d		1811 (PRO)
LUTHER, William		
L	16 Jan	1728
d	13 May	1735 (PMM)
LUTMAN, Charles William		
L	18 Feb	1815
d		1861 (PRO)
LUTMAN, William		
L	9 Oct	1810
d		1832 (PRO)

LUTTRELL, Hon. James		
L	2 Feb	1770
MP (Stockbridge)	16 Dec	1775–1784 (MPN)
CR	27 Oct	1780 (PRO)
CA	23 Feb	1781
MP (Dover)	1784–23 Dec	1788 (MPN)
d	23 Dec	1788 (MPN)
LUTTRELL, John, Lord Newark		
L	10 Oct	1758
CR	4 Mar	1761
CA	25 Aug	1762
d	17 Mar	1829 (PRO)
LUTWIDGE, Henry Thomas		
L	6 Sept	1800
Ret CR	26 Nov	1830 (PRO)
d	30 Jan	1861 (PRO)
LUTWIDGE, Skeffington		
L	15 Aug	1759
CR	21 Jan	1771
CA	15 Oct	1773
RAB	12 Apr	1794
RAW	4 July	1794
VAB	1 June	1795
VAR	14 Feb	1799
AB	1 Jan	1801
AW	9 Nov	1805
AR	31 July	1810
d	15 Aug	1814 (PRO)
LUX, John		
L	21 Sept	1757
d		1779 (PRO)
LYALL, Haseldine		
L	18 Mar	1815
d		1824 (PRO)
LYALL, William		
L	30 Oct	1793
CR	30 Aug	1803
CA	27 Dec	1804
d		1814 (PRO)
LYDE, George		
L	9 Sept	1814
HP		1814 (OB)
Ret CR	7 July	1858 (PRO)
d		1870 (PRO)
LYDIARD, Charles		
L	25 Nov	1793
CR	22 July	1796
CA	1 Jan	1801
d (drowned)	29 Dec	1807 (PJP)
LYE, William Jones		
L	15 Jan	1802
CR	31 Jan	1806
CA	22 May	1806
RAB	23 Nov	1841 (LG)
d	7 Mar	1846 (CH)
LYELL, David		
L	6 Feb	1746
d		1758 (PRO)
LYELL, Thomas		
L		
CA	19 Aug	1692
In Merchant Service		1700 (PJP)
d	Jan	1736 (M)

LYFORD, Henry James
L 16 Mar 1799
CR 8 May 1804
CA 4 Dec 1813
d 8 Aug 1830 (PRO)

LYNAM, William
L 12 Aug 1695 (PJP)

LYNCH, Stephen
L 17 July 1762
d 1768 (PRO)

LYNDON, Chadwick
L 1 Aug 1776
d 27 Oct 1781 (PRO)

LYNE, Kerry
L 31 Jan 1707
Gone 1719 (PRO)

LYNE, Philip
L 26 July 1794
CR 29 Apr 1802
d 24 Nov 1823 (MB)

LYNE, Thomas
L 12 Oct 1793
CR 29 Apr 1802
Ret CA 10 Sept 1840 (PRO)
d 1848 (PRO)

LYNE, Thomas Jones
L 28 Nov 1794
d 1800 (PRO)

LYNN, Charles Seymour
L 11 Apr 1777
d 6 Oct 1790 (LT)

LYNN, Francis
L 15 Mar 1755
CR 26 Oct 1761
d 1810 (PRO)

LYNN, Thomas
L 20 Jan 1747
CR 6 Apr 1756
CA 10 Nov 1756
Reduced seniority 16 June 1763
Restored 1766
d 19 Mar 1781 (PRO)

LYNNE, Henry
L 11 Mar 1794
CR 18 Apr 1811
d 6 Oct 1835 (LT)

LYNNE, Thomas
L 18 June 1791
d 1826 (PRO)

LYON, Boswell
L 25 Jan 1746
d 1755 (PRO)

LYON, Edward
L 2 Nov 1799
d 1832 (PRO)

LYON, Francis
L 18 Nov 1814
HP July 1815–1837 (OB)
Ret CR 7 Mar 1853 (PRO)
d 1868 (PRO)

LYON, George Francis
L 30 July 1814
CR 3 Jan 1821 (PRO)
CA 13 Nov 1823 (PRO)
In Brazilian Service
d 8 Nov 1832 (LT)

LYON, Scroop
L 17 Sept 1718
d 1757 (PRO)

LYON, Simon
L 31 May 1705
d 25 Apr 1741 (PMM)

LYONS, Edmund, Lord
L 22 Nov 1809
CR 21 Mar 1812
CA 7 June 1814
KCH 1835 (PJP)
Cre Bt 1840 (PJP)
GCB 10 July 1844 (OB)
RAB 14 Jan 1850 (PRO)
RAW 26 Oct 1852 (PRO)
RAR 11 Sept 1854 (PRO)
Cre EP 1856 (PJP)
VAB 19 Mar 1857 (PRO)
VAW 2 Oct 1857 (PRO)
d 23 Nov 1858 (PJP)

LYONS, John
T
L 24 Dec 1805
HP 1813 (OB)
CR 27 June 1814
CA 22 July 1830 (PRO)
HP 1830 (OB)
Ret CA 1 Oct 1850 (PRO)
Ret RA 27 Sept 1855 (PRO)
Ret VA 4 Oct 1862 (PRO)
Ret A 2 Apr 1866 (PRO)
d 15 Dec 1872 (PRO)

LYS, James (1)
L 7 June 1760
CR 29 Apr 1778
d 1814 (PRO)

LYS, James (2)
L 30 Nov 1776
SUP CR 16 Feb 1810
d 6 Dec 1833 (LT)

LYS, James Oades
L 1 Aug 1794
d 19 Oct 1830 (PRO)

LYSAGHT, Arthur
L 3 Aug 1802
CR 22 Jan 1806
CA 25 Sept 1806
RAB 23 Nov 1841 (LG)
RAW 9 Nov 1846 (LG)
RAR 8 Jan 1848 (LG)
VAB 8 Apr 1851 (PRO)
Ret VA 1 July 1851 (PRO)
Ret A 18 June 1857 (CH)
d 19 Mar 1859 (PRO)

LYTCOTT, John
L
CA 23 Jan 1693
d 23 July 1697 (PRO)

LYTTLETON, Hugh
L 5 Dec 1739
CR 7 July 1744
d 1744 (PRO)

MABB, John
L 1673
d before 1689 (PJP)

MABBOT, Thomas
L 9 Feb 1705 (PMM)
d 9 Mar 1712 (PMM)

MABBOT, William
L 15 Apr 1711 (PMM)

M'ARTHUR, Charles
L 21 Mar 1812
d 1828 (PRO)

M'ARTHUR, James
L 12 Sept 1796
d 21 Dec 1814 (PJP)

MACARTHY, Robert, Lord Muskery
See MACCARTHY, Robert, Lord Muskery

MACARTNEY, John
L 20 Jan 1756
CR 22 Sept 1759
CA 4 Sept 1766
KIA 5 Aug 1781 (LG)

MACBEAN, Gillies
L 5 June 1799 (PRO)
Struck off list 1801 (PRO)

M'BREATH, Alexander
L 30 Mar 1794
d 1797 (PRO)

MACBRIDE, John
L 27 Oct 1758
CR 7 Apr 1762
CA 20 June 1756
MP (Plymouth) 1784–1790 (MPN)
RAB 1 Feb 1793
RAR 12 Apr 1794
VAB 4 July 1794
VAW 1 June 1795
AB 14 Feb 1799
d 17 Feb 1800

M'CANDLISH, John
L 15 Oct 1805
CR 22 Jan 1828 (PRO)
d 12 Oct 1830 (PRO)

M'CARTHY, Michael
L 8 Dec 1800
d 31 Dec 1827 (PJP)

MACCARTHY, Robert, Lord Muskery
L 31 May 1718 (PMM)
CR
CA 17 Mar 1722
Went into the Foreign Service and was struck off list 16 July 1747 (?1749)

M'CARTHY, William
L 11 Feb 1795
d (drowned) May 1795 (CH)

M'CARTIE, Alexander
L 27 Apr 1741
d 31 Jan 1761 (M)

MACCAUSLAND, John
L 22 Feb 1811
CR 14 Oct 1824 (PRO)
d 1835 (PRO)

M'CLELLAN, Samuel Wallis
L 9 Feb 1815
d 1836 (PRO)

M'CLEVERTY, George Anson
L 5 Nov 1777
SUP CR 8 Apr 1813
d 1821 (PRO)

M'CLEVERTY, William
L 13 July 1745
CR 21 June 1756
CA 1 Nov 1757
d 1780

MACONOCHIE, Alexander
L 15 Sept 1809 (PRO)
CR 8 Sept 1815
HP Sept 1815 (OB)
KH 4 May 1836 (OB)
Ret CA 17 Feb 1855 (PRO)
d 25 Oct 1860 (DUB)

M'CORMICK, John
L 5 Nov 1793
d 1798 (PRO)

M'CORMICK, Shephard
L 21 June 1813
CR 23 Nov 1841 (OB)
HP 1841 (OB)
d 28 Feb 1852 (PRO)

M'COY, Alexander
L 25 Oct 1777
CR
CA 10 Feb 1779
d 1782 (PRO)

M'COY, Edward Thomas Pye
L 17 Mar 1795
Struck off list 1798 (PRO)
Reinstated 28 June 1798 (PRO)
d 1799 (PRO)

M'COY, Robert
L 3 July 1802
HP Oct 1806–July 1807 (OB)
CR 15 June 1814
HP 1834 (OB)
d 12 Nov 1848 (PRO)

M'CREA, Robert Contart
T
L 20 Nov 1812
CR 4 June 1824 (PRO)
CA 10 Jan 1837 (PRO)
Ret RA 14 May 1857 (PRO)
Ret VA 14 Nov 1863 (PRO)
Ret A 8 Apr 1868 (PRO)
d 14 Jan 1875 (PRO)

M'CERRY, David
L 31 Aug 1810
d 28 Dec 1831 (LT)

M'CULLAGH, Henry
L 22 July 1779
d 1789 (PRO)

M'CULLOCH, Andrew
L 25 Sept 1806
CR 15 June 1814
d 1817 (PRO)

M'CULLOCH, Thomas

L	28 Nov	1796
CR	13 Oct	1812
d	10 Sept	1830 (PRO)

M'CULLOCH, William

L	28 Sept	1807
CR	22 Jan	1810
CA	8 July	1814
d	25 Oct	1825 (PRO)

M'CULLOCK, George

L	8 Feb	1799
d		1800 (PRO)

M'CURDY, John

L	22 Jan	1806
d		1826 (PRO)

M'CURDY, Stephen Cuppage

L	26 Mar	1807 (PJP)
Dismissed	Jan	1809 (PJP)
Restored	6 Oct	1809 (PJP)
d		1816 (PRO)

M'DANIEL, Jeremiah

L	19 Oct	1814
HP	Apr	1815 (OB)
Ret CR	22 Jan	1859 (PRO)
d		1871 (PRO)

M'DERMEIT, James

L	21 Mar	1799 (PRO)
CR	17 July	1800
d	26 Feb	1801 (PRO)

M'DONALD, Alexander

L	5 Jan	1811
d	15 Jan	1822 (PRO)

M'DONALD, Archibald (1)

L	1 May	1804

M'DONALD, Archibald (2)

L	22 Dec	1806
Ret CR	26 Jan	1842 (PRO)
d	June	1852 (PRO)

MACDONALD, Colin

L	3 June	1799
HP	June	1802–
	Jan	1803 (OB)
CR	4 June	1807
CA	7 June	1814
CB	4 June	1815 (OB)
Ret CA	1 Oct	1846 (PRO)
Ret RA	1 Sept	1849 (PRO)
d	15 Nov	1857 (PRO)

MACDONALD, Coll.

L	26 June	1741
CR	11 June	1750
d	8 Sept	1753 (PMM)

M'DONALD, Duncan

L	7 Jan	1802
d		1816 (PRO)

M'DONALD, Francis

L	9 June	1802
CR	6 Feb	1804
d	28 June	1804 (PRO)

M'DONALD, James

L	25 Mar	1809
CR	27 May	1825 (PRO)
d	Dec	1825 (PRO)

M'DONALD, John (1)

L	29 Nov	1793
HP	Oct	1799–
	May	1800 (OB)
Ret CR	14 Feb	1825 (PRO)
d		1845 (PRO)

MACDONALD, John (2)

L	17 Mar	1815
d	9 June	1827 (PRO)

M'DONALD, Randolph
See MACDONELL, Randall

M'DONALD, Terence

L	6 May	1778
d		1789 (PRO)

MAC(K)DONELL, Daniel

L	10 May	1688
d		1734 (DDA)

MACDONELL, Randall

CAF	23 Dec	1673 (EAD)
(Marquis of Worcester)		
L	29 Mar	1678
CA	27 Aug	1681
Dismissed	13 Dec	1688 (PRO)
Followed James II to France		
d		1711 (DDA)

MACDONNELL, Randall

L	22 Oct	1794
CR	5 Aug	1803
CA	5 July	1805
d	13 Jan	1813 (PRO)

M'DONNELL, Sommerled

L	13 Aug	1800
d		1803 (PRO)

M'DONNELL, Thomas

L	18 July	1810
HP		1813 (OB)
Ret CR	14 Jan	1852 (PRO)
d		1865 (PRO)

M'DOUAL, William

L	21 May	1756
d		1770 (PRO)

M'DOUALL, David

L	29 July	1781
d		1795 (PRO)

MCDOUALL, James

L	22 Apr	1802
CR	12 Oct	1814
SUP CR	1 Jan	1816 (PMM)
d	30 Dec	1845 (OB)

M'DOUALL, Robert
See M'DOUGALL, Robert

M'DOUGAL, Sir John

L	3 Jan	1810
HP	Apr	1817–
	June	1818 (OB)
CR	9 Feb	1820 (PRO)
CA	16 Aug	1836 (PRO)
RAB	12 May	1857 (PRO)
RAW	24 Feb	1858 (PRO)
RAR	12 Apr	1862 (PRO)
KCB		1862 (PJP)
VAB	3 Nov	1863 (PRO)
d	12 Apr	1865 (PRO)

M'DOUGALL, Donald
L 28 Apr 1798
d 1815 (PRO)
M'DOUGALL, John (1)
L 30 July 1772
CR 9 Aug 1781
CA 20 Jan 1783
RAB 9 Nov 1805 (PRO)
RAR 28 Apr 1808
VAB 31 July 1810
VAW 12 Aug 1812
VAR 4 June 1814
d 21 Nov 1814 (LT)
M'DOUGALL, John (2)
L 26 Apr 1800
Ret CR 1 Dec 1830 (PRO)
d 1860 (PRO)
M'DOUGALL, John
See M'DOUGAL, Sir John
M'DOUGALL,, Robert
L 7 Sept 1759
CR 23 Mar 1780
CA 24 July 1781
RAB 1 Jan 1801
RAR 23 Apr 1804
VAB 9 Nov 1805 (PRO)
VAW 28 Apr 1808
VAR 31 July 1810
AB 4 Dec 1813
d 16 Feb 1816 (PRO)
M'DOUGALL, William
L 11 Jan 1810
d 1834 (PRO)
M'DOUGALL, William Howard
L 9 May 1807
CR 27 Mar 1826 (PRO)
d 1844 (PRO)
M'DOWALL, James
L 4 Mar 1815
d Apr 1827 (PRO)
M'DOWALL, James
See M'DOUALL, James
M'EVOY, Robert
L 20 Apr 1771
CR 8 July 1780
CA 18 Sept 1782
d 1796 (PRO)
M'FARLAND, James
L 23 June 1794
CR 18 June 1803
Ret CA 10 Sept 1840 (PRO)
d Feb 1852 (PRO)
M'FARLANE, James
L 20 Jan 1812
d 2 Dec 1813 (PRO)
M'FARLANE, John Boucher
L 17 Oct 1793
KIA 9 June 1795 (LG)
MACFARLANE, William
L 24 Feb 1815
d 14 Feb 1846 (OB)
M'GEORGE, John
L 11 June 1803
CR 19 Dec 1809
d 9 Apr 1878 (PJP)
M'GHIE, James
L 9 Apr 1808
M'GIE, David
L 1 Aug 1801
M 'GIE, Francis
L 18 June 1781
d 29 Apr 1800
M'GUIRE, William
L 18 Mar 1793
CR 22 May 1797
Ret CA 10 Sept 1840 (OB)
M'GUIRE, William
See M'GWIRE, William
M'GLADERY, John
L 24 Apr 1811
M'GRATH, Myles Monk
L 4 June 1814
M'GREGOR, Alexander
L 21 Apr 1780
M'GWIRE, William
L 10 Feb 1779
CR
CA 5 Aug 1790
M'GWIRE, William
See M'GUIRE, William
MACHEN, Robert
L 24 Oct 1812
M'INERHENY, John
L 8 May 1795
d (murdered) 1797 (PJP)
M'INTOSH, Joseph
L 8 June 1762
d 22 Oct 1765 (PMM)
M'INTYRE, William
L 26 May 1814
M'IVER, David
L 14 Nov 1790
CR 4 July 1795
MACKAY, Alexander
L 1 June 1779 (PMM)
CR 25 Mar 1783
MACKAY, David
L 21 Mar 1777
CR 14 Sept 1781
d 1823 (MB)
MACKAY, Hon. Donald Hugh
L 27 Mar 1798
CR 29 Apr 1802
CA 22 Jan 1806
RAB 28 June 1838 (LG)
RAW 23 Nov 1841 (LG)
RAR 20 Nov 1846 (LG)
VAB 4 May 1849 (PRO)
d 26 Mar 1850 (PRO)
MACKAY, George
L 6 Apr 1782
d 1808 (PRO)
MACKAY, Hugh
L 2 Jan 1746
d 1765(6) (PRO)
MACKAY, James
L 17 Jan 1801
d 1808 (PRO)
MACKAY, John
L 17 Nov 1801
d 17 Oct 1821 (PRO)

M'KEAN, James
L 4 Mar 1815
d 17 Apr 1841 (PRO)

MACKELLAR, John
L 18 Nov 1790
CR 5 July 1797
CA 27 Apr 1799 (PRO)
Dismissed 1802 (PRO)
Restored 1804 (PRO)
RAB 27 May 1825 (PRO)
RAW 22 July 1830 (PRO)
VAB 10 Jan 1837 (PRO)
VAW 23 Nov 1841 (LG)
VAR 9 Nov 1846 (PRO)
AB 26 July 1847 (PRO)
AW 2 Sept 1850 (PRO)
Ret A 1 July 1851 (PRO)
d 14 Apr 1854 (PRO)

M'KELLAR, Peter
L 9 Dec 1782
CR 4 July 1794
d 4 June 1830 (PRO)

MACKENZIE, Adam
L 13 Mar 1790
CR 22 June 1796
CA 2 Sept 1799
HP 2 Sept 1799–Oct 1801 (MB)
d 13 Nov 1823 (LT)

M'KENZIE, Alexander (1)
L 16 Mar 1796
d 1798 (PRO)

M'KENZIE, Alexander (2)
L 27 Dec 1808
d 1832 (PRO)

MACKENZIE, Alexander (3)
T
L 27 Apr 1811
HP 1815 (OB)
Ret CR 1 Apr 1852 (PRO)
d 29 Jan 1870 (PRO)

MACKENZIE, Alexander Richard
L 16 Mar 1796
CR 28 Dec 1805
CA 9 May 1812
d 27 Oct 1825 (MB)

M'KENZIE, Charles (1)
L 1746 (PJP)
KIA 8 Oct 1747 (PJP)

M'KENZIE, Charles (2)
L 9 Dec 1799 (PRO)
d 10 Sept 1849 (PRO)

M'KENZIE, Duncan Chisholm
L 10 Dec 1803
CR 13 July 1824 (PRO)
d 26 May 1828 (PRO)

MACKENZIE, Evan Francis Gwynn
L 7 Jan 1809
d June 1828 (PRO)

MACKENZIE, Frederick
L 7 Feb 1815
d 1819 (PRO)

MACKENZIE, George (1)
L 2 May 1740
CR 22 Aug 1745 (PRO)
CA 24 Jan 1747
RAB 28 Apr 1777
RAW 23 Jan 1778
RAR 29 Jan 1778
VAB 19 Mar 1779
d 29 July 1780 (PRO)

MACKENZIE, George (2)
L 9 Nov 1756
d 1764 (PRO)

MACKENZIE, George (3)
L 18 May 1758
d 1783 (PRO)

MACKENZIE, George (4)
L 5 Sept 1777
CR Mar 1780 (PJP)
d (drowned) 5 Oct 1780 (CH)

MACKENZIE, George Charles
L 6 June 1796
CR 7 Jan 1802
CA 26 Nov 1808 (PRO)
d Jan 1828 (PRO)

MACKENZIE, James (1)
L 19 Mar 1744
CR 4 Apr 1757
d 1789 (PRO)

MACKENZIE, James (2)
L 22 Jan 1806
CR 22 Jan 1808
d (drowned) 31 Aug 1809 (CH)

MACKENZIE, John (1)
L 24 Dec 1778
d 1801 (PRO)

MACKENZIE, John (2)
L 17 July 1799
d 1817 (PRO)

MACKENZIE, John (3)
L 8 Oct 1802
d 4 Sept 1822 (PRO)

M'KENZIE, Kenneth (1)
L 9 Nov 1795
d 1808 (PRO)

MCKENZIE, Kenneth (2)
L 5 June 1798
CR 29 Apr 1802
CA 6 June 1804
d 5 Nov 1824 (MB)

MACKENZIE, Murdoch
L 5 Aug 1779
SUP CR 31 Jan 1814
d 27 Jan 1829 (PRO)

MACKENZIE, Samuel
L 1 Apr 1779
d 1790 (PRO)

MACKENZIE, Simon
L 5 Nov 1778
CR
CA 13 Dec 1783
d Mar 1804

MACKENZIE, Thomas
L

CR	15 Apr	1771
CA	12 June	1776
RAB	4 July	1794 (PRO)
RAR	1 June	1795
VAW	14 Feb	1799
VAR	1 Jan	1801
AB	23 Apr	1804
AW	9 Nov	1805
AR	31 July	1810 (PRO)
d	20 Sept	1813 (PRO)
MACKENZIE, Thomas Henry		
L	18 Aug	1810
Ret CR	3 Jan	1851 (PRO)
d	13 Aug	1856 (PRO)
MACKENZIE, William (1)		
L	17 July	1746
d		1761 (PRO)
MACKENZIE, William (2)		
L	21 Nov	1799
KIA	6 Jan	1807 (PJP)
MACKERELL, Thomas		
L	24 May	1762
d		1778 (PRO)
M'KERLIE, John		
L	18 Aug	1800
T		
CR	24 Dec	1805
CA	4 Dec	1813
Ret RA	1 Oct	1846 (PRO)
d	12 Sept	1848 (PRO)
M'KEY, John		
L	1 July	1780
d		1814 (PRO)
M'KEY, John		
See MACKAY, John		
MACKEY, Michael		
L	19 June	1797
Dismissed		1800 (PRO)
MACKIE, Charles		
L	30 Sept	1746
d		1754(5) (PRO)
MACKIE, James (1)		
L	30 Mar	1734
KIA	11 Feb	1744 (CH)
MACKIE, James (2)		
L	29 Dec	1743
CR	29 Mar	1759
d		1771 (PRO)
MACKIE, John		
L	27 May	1799
Ret CR	26 Nov	1830 (PRO)
d		1844 (PRO)
MACKIE, Robert		
L	1 Nov	1780
d		1789 (PRO)
MACKIE, Thomas		
L	23 Mar	1761
d	4 Mar	1790
M'KILLOP, Archibald		
T		
L	28 Mar	1809 (PRO)
d		1820 (PRO)
M'KILLOP, David		
L	16 Dec	1762
d		1805(6) (PRO)
M'KILLOP, John (1)		
L	4 Nov	1778
d (drowned)	29 Aug	1782 (PJP)
M'KILLOP, John (2)		
L	8 May	1812
HP	Sept	1813 (OB)
Ret CR	25 Oct	1854 (PRO)
d		1863 (PRO)
M'KILLOP, John Gardner M'Bride		
L	3 Oct	1797
CR	26 May	1814
d	6 Dec	1829 (MB)
M'KILLOP, Richard		
L	14 Jan	1794
d	8 Dec	1812 (PRO)
M'KINKY, John		
See M'KINLEY, John		
M'KINLAY, Daniel		
L	21 Apr	1783
d		1797 (PRO)
M'KINLAY, Patrick		
L	21 Feb	1783
d		1784 (PRO)
M'KINLEY, Archibald		
L	25 May	1825
d		1801 (PRO)
M'KINLEY, George		
L	14 Jan	1782
HP	Dec	1794–
	Mar	1975 (OB)
CR	16 May	1798
CA	20 Oct	1801
RAB	13 Oct	1830 (PRO)
RAW	10 Jan	1837 (PRO)
RAR	28 June	1838 (PRO)
VAB	23 Nov	1841 (PRO)
VAW	9 Nov	1846 (PRO)
VAR	20 Mar	1848 (PRO)
AB	11 June	1851 (PRO)
Ret A	16 Sept	1851 (PRO)
d	18 Jan	1852 (PRO)
M'KINLEY, John		
L	20 July	1779
d		1783 (PRO)
M'KINLEY, Robert		
L	13 Oct	1800
d		1802 (PRO)
MCKINLEY, Samuel		
L	27 Aug	1745
d		1777 (PRO)
M'KINNON, Hugh		
L	1 Aug	1801
d	5 May	1816 (PRO)
MACKINTOSH, Farquharson		
L	26 Nov	1779
d		1783 (PRO)
M'KIRDY, John		
L	8 May	1804

Ret CR | 28 Feb 1837 (PRO)
d | 1853 (PRO)

M'KIRDY, Robert
L | 4 Feb 1814
HP | Aug 1814 (OB)
d | Jan 1847 (OB)

MACKLEY, John
L |
CA | 1673

MACKLIN, John
L | 1672

MACKONOCHIE, Alexander
See MACONOCHIE, Alexander

MACKRELL, John
L | 6 Apr 1812
d | 1815 (PRO)

MACKWORTH, Herbert
L | 29 Apr 1811
d | 1848 (PRO)

M'LAWRIN, John
L | 19 Apr 1779
CR | 1779 (PJP)
CA | 5 June 1780
d | 18 June 1792

M'LEAN, Charles William
L | 31 July 1806
Dismissed | 6 May 1808 (PMM)
d | 1808 (PRO)

M'LEAN, Francis
L | 3 June 1797
Ret CR | 1 Dec 1830 (PRO)
d | 1837 (PRO)

M'LEAN, Hector
L | 22 Oct 1793
d | 6 Mar 1816 (PRO)

M'LEAN, Hector Alexander
L | 22 Oct 1806
d | 1809 (PRO)

M'LEAN, Hugh
L | 12 May 1783
d | 1794 (PRO)

M'LEAN, Neal
L | 20 May 1800
KIA | 29 July 1804 (PJP)

MACLEAN, Rawdon
T | wounded
L | 7 July 1806
CR | 1 July 1823 (PRO)
Ret CA | 1 Apr 1856 (PRO)
d | 8 Nov 1863 (PRO)

MCLEAN, William
L | 1 Apr 1802
d (suicide) | 1804 (PJP)

MACLELLAN, Hon. Dunbar
L | 11 May 1776
CR |
CA | 30 Apr 1782
KIA | 6 July 1782 (LG)

M'LEOD, Alexander (1)
L | 20 Nov 1790
SUP CR | 4 Oct 1824 (PRO)
d | 13 Apr 1848 (PRO)

M'LEOD, Alexander (2)
L | 22 Jan 1806
d | 5 Aug 1828 (PRO)

M'LEOD, Donald
L | 2 Jan 1794
CR | 29 Apr 1802
CA | 22 Jan 1806
CB | 1815 (PJP)
d | 4 Apr 1831 (PRO)

M'LEOD, John
L | 3 Apr 1798
d | 1817 (PRO)

M'LEOD, Roderick
L | 14 May 1806
d | 20 Apr 1810 (PRO)

M'LEOD, William (1)
L | 23 June 1796
d | 1805(6) (PRO)

M'LEOD, William (2)
L | 10 Sept 1811
HP | Sept 1815 (OB)
Ret CR | 1 Oct 1852 (PRO)
d | 1855 (PRO)

M'LEROTH, William Bacon
L | 19 Sept 1815
d | 1841 (PRO)

M'MAHON, John
L | 1 Aug 1800
d | 1810 (PRO)

M'MEEKAN, Arthur
L | 15 Aug 1806
CR | 7 May 1812
d | 1835 (PRO)

M'MILLAN, Allan
L | 31 Oct 1810
d | 7 June 1850 (PRO)

M'MILLAN, George
L | 13 Sept 1809
d | Oct 1810 (LT)

M'MILLAN, William
L | 7 June 1802
d (drowned) | 20 Oct 1806 (PJP)

MACNAMARA, Sir Burton
L | 1 July 1815
CR | 19 July 1822 (PRO)
CA | 16 Nov 1833 (PRO)
Kt | 1839 (OB)
Ret RA | 21 July 1856 (PRO)
Ret VA | 3 Apr 1863 (PRO)
Ret A | 20 Mar 1867 (PRO)
d | 1876 (PRO)

M'NAMARA, James (1)
L | 25 June 1761
CR | 2 May 1779
CA | 5 Feb 1781
SUP RA | ?1799 (PRO)
d | 1 Mar 1802 (PRO)

MACNAMARA, James (2)
L | 1 Dec 1788
CR | 22 Oct 1793
CA | 6 Oct 1795
RAB | 4 June 1814
RAW | 12 Aug 1819 (PRO)

RAR	27 May	1825 (PRO)
d	15 Jan	1826 (LT)
M'NAMARA, Jeremiah		
L	20 Mar	1815
d		1835 (PRO)
MACNAMARA, Michael Nugent		
L	1 Feb	1781
d		1790 (PRO)
M'NEILL, Archibald		
L	17 Jan	1798
d	17 Mar	1808 (PRO)
MACNEVIN, John		
L	31 Aug	1810
d		1856 (PRO)
MACONOCHIE, Alexander		
L	15 Sept	1809 (PJP)
CR	8 Sept	1815
M'PHERSON, George		
L	16 Mar	1808
CR	16 Sept	1816 (PRO)
d	27 May	1824 (PRO)
M'QUHAE, Peter		
L	7 Oct	1809
CR	15 June	1814
CA	10 Dec	1835 (PRO)
d	June	1853 (PRO)
M'RABIE, James		
L	31 May	1798
d		1803 (PRO)
MACRAE, George		
L	27 Aug	1800
T		
d	26 May	1823 (LT)
MACREDIE, John		
L	7 Oct	1793
Ret CR	4 Oct	1827 (PRO)
d		1834 (PRO)
M'TAGGART, John		
L	7 Jan	1783
CR	2 Jan	1798
d	11 May	1799 (PRO)
M'VICAR, Alexander		
L	12 Sept	1798 (PJP)
T		
CR	13 Oct	1807
CA	1 Jan	1817 (PRO)
d	May	1840 (TR)
M'WHINNIE, Hugh		
L	11 Feb	1815 (PRO)
d	14 Mar	1828 (PRO)
MADGE, Robert Pepperel		
L	21 Feb	1815
d		1849 (PRO)
MAESE, George		
L		
CA	6 Apr	1689
MAFFIN, John		
L	6 July	1795
Dismissed		1804 (PRO)
MAGAN, Arthur		
L	16 June	1814
HP	16 June	1814 (OB)
Ret CR	13 Apr	1857 (PRO)
d	3 Feb	1858 (PRO)
MAGIN, Joseph		
L	4 Jan	1808
Ret CR	13 Sep	1844 (PRO)
d	3 Jan	1848 (PRO)
MAGURK, Samuel		
L	6 Feb	1780
d		1806 (PRO)
MAHANY, William		
L	4 Sept	1781
d		1796 (PRO)
MAHONEY, Jeremiah		
L	20 Nov	1812
d	9 Oct	1829 (PRO)
MAIDEN, William		
L		
CA		1666
d	before	1689 (PJP)
MAINE, Covill		
See MAYNE, Covill		
MAINE, Dawson		
See MAYNE, Dawson		
MAIN(E), John		
See MAYNE, John		
MAINE, Perry		
See MAYNE, Perry		
MAINE, Robert		
See MAYNE, Robert		
MAINGAY, Henry		
L	17 Sept	1806
CR	14 Dec	1821 (PRO)
d	22 Aug	1846 (PRO)
MAINGAY, Peter		
L	11 Sept	1807
CR	13 June	1815
Ret CA	20 Aug	1853 (PRO)
d		1869 (PRO)
MAINWARING, Benjamin		
T		
L	19 July	1814
d		1852 (TR)
MAINWARING, Edward Reeves Philip		
L	11 June	1807
CR	27 Mar	1826 (PRO)
CA	23 Nov	1841 (PRO)
Ret CA	27 Nov	1854 (PRO)
Ret RA	12 Apr	1862 (PRO)
d	5 Oct	1865 (PRO)
MAINWARING, George		
L		1665
MAINWARING, Jemmett		
L	24 June	1789
CR	6 Apr	1795
CA	7 July	1796
d (drowned)		1801 (CH)
MAINWARING, Rowland		
L	7 Dec	1801
HP	Jan–Aug	1811 (OB)
CR	13 Aug	1812
CA	22 July	1830 (PRO)
Ret CA	1 Oct	1850 (PRO)
Ret RA	27 Sept	1855 (PRO)
d	11 Apr	1862 (PRO)

MAINWARING, Thomas (1)

L		1673
d		before 1683 (PJP)

MAINWARING, Thomas (2)

L	28 Feb	1766 (PRO)
d		1798 (PRO)

MAINWARING, Thomas Bornford

L	1 June	1756
CR	13 May	1778
d		1780(1) (PRO)

MAINWARING, Thomas Francis Charles

L	11 July	1800
T		
CR	31 Jan	1806
CA	27 Nov	1810
Ret RA	1 Oct	1846 (PRO)
Ret VA	11 Sept	1854 (PRO)
d	20 Sept	1858 (PRO)

MAINWARING, William (1)

L	4 Mar	1740 (PJP)

MAINWARING, William (2)

L	5 Apr	1756
CR	9 Jan	1760 (PJP)
CA	6 Aug	1761 (PJP)
d	26 Oct	1763 (PJP)

MAISTERSON, Samuel

L	20 June	1729
CR	30 May	1744
CA	26 Aug	1745
d	10 Sept	1762

MAISTRE, Charles le
See LE MAISTRE, Charles

MAITLAND, Hon. Sir Anthony, Earl Lauderdale

L	2 Feb	1805
CR	6 May	1806
CA	25 Sept	1806
MP (Haddington Burghs)		1813–1818 (MPT)
CB	19 Sept	1816 (MPT)
KCMG	26 Feb	1820 (MPT)
HP	Mar	1821 (OB)
MP (Berwickshire)		1826–1832 (MPT)
KCB	6 Apr	1832 (MPT)
RAB	23 Nov	1841 (PRO)
RAW	9 Nov	1846 (PRO)
RAR	23 Mar	1848 (PRO)
VAB	11 June	1851 (PRO)
VAW	5 Mar	1853 (PRO)
VAR	11 Sept	1854 (PRO)
AB	18 June	1857 (PRO)
AW	6 Mar	1858 (PRO)
Cre EP	22 Aug	1860 (MPT)
AR	10 Nov	1862 (PRO)
GCB	10 Nov	1862 (MPT)
d	22 Mar	1863 (MPT)

MAITLAND, Benjamin

L	2 Apr	1794
d		1794 (PRO)

MAITLAND, Charles

L	20 Nov	1812
d	6 July	1827 (PRO)

MAITLAND, David

L	19 Oct	1757
d		1779 (PRO)

MAITLAND, Edward

L	13 July	1802
CR	25 May	1805
KIA		1805 (PJP)

MAITLAND, Hon. Frederick

L	11 June	1750
CR	17 Jan	1757
CA	9 Mar	1759
d	16 Dec	1786 (PRO)

MAITLAND, Sir Frederick Lewis

L	3 Apr	1795
CR	14 June	17995
CA	21 Mar	1801
CB		1815 (PJP)
RAB	22 July	1830 (LG)
KCB	23 Feb	1831 (LG)
RAR	10 Jan	1837 (LG)
d	30 Nov	1839 (PRO)

MAITLAND, Henry Topham Harley

L	19 Oct	1793
KIA		1793 (PJP)

MAITLAND, John (1)

L	9 Dec	1776
CR	24 July	1781
CA	20 Jan	1783
d	July	1788 (M)

MAITLAND, John (2)

L	20 July	1794
CR	23 Dec	1796
CA	11 Aug	1797
RAB	19 July	1821 (LG)
RAW	27 May	1825 (LG)
RAR	22 July	1830 (LG)
d	20 Oct	1836 (LT)

MAJOR, Christopher

L	1 Feb	1761
d		1784 (PRO)

MAJOR, James

L		
CA	20 Oct	1677

MAJOR, Timothy

L	11 Aug	1809
d		1838 (PRO)

MAJOR, William

L	12 Sept	1799
d		1802 (PRO)

MALBON, Micajah

L	7 Jan	1783
CR	25 Apr	1795
CA	11 Aug	1800
d		1813 (PRO)

MALBON, Samuel

L	1 May	1804
CR	1 Oct	1814 (PRO)
d	1 Feb	1816 (LT)

MALBOTT, Thomas

L		
CR		
CA	2 Feb	1711
Gone		1718 (PRO)

MALCOLM, Sir Charles

L	12 Jan	1799
CR	28 May	1802 (PJP)
CA	29 Dec	1802

Name	Rank	Date	Year
	HP		1815–1817 (OB)
	Kt		1827 (PJP)
	RAB	10 Jan	1837 (PRO)
	RAW	28 June	1838 (PRO)
	RAR	9 Nov	1846 (PRO)
	VAB	28 Apr	1847 (PRO)
	VAW	24 Jan	1849 (PRO)
	d	14 June	1851 (PRO)
MALCOLM, James			
	L	18 May	1778
	Dismissed	27 Mar	1792 (PJP)
	d		1792 (PRO)
MALCOLM, Sir Pulteney			
	L	3 Mar	1783
	CR	3 Apr	1794
	CA	22 Oct	1794
	CRM	12 Aug	1812 (MB)
	RAB	4 Dec	1813
	RAW	4 June	1814
	KCB	2 Jan	1815 (DNB)
	RAR	12 Aug	1819 (CH)
	VAB	19 July	1821 (CH)
	GCMG		1829 (CH)
	VAR	22 July	1830 (CH)
	GCB	1 May	1833 (LG)
	AB	10 Jan	1837 (CH)
	d	20 July	1838 (CH)
MALE, Thomas			
	L	4 July	1757
	CR	31 Dec	1761
	d	4 Aug	1769 (PMM)
MALING, Thomas James			
	L	6 Oct	1797
	CR	24 Dec	1798
	CA	6 Sept	1800
	HP	Apr–Oct	1801 (OB)
	RAB	22 July	1830 (PRO)
	RAR	10 Jan	1837 (PRO)
	VAB	23 Nov	1841 (PRO)
	VAW	9 Nov	1846 (PRO)
	VAR	10 Dec	1846 (LG)
	d	23 Jan	1849 (PJP)
MALLETT, John			
	L	4 Apr	1720
	Gone		1724 (PRO)
MALLETT, William			
	L	8 July	1795
	Ret CR	18 Nov	1834 (PRO)
	d	9 Mar	1838 (PRO)
MALLON, Thomas			
	L	10 Mar	1708 (PMM)
MALONE, Edmund			
	L	18 Sept	1809
	d		1863 (PRO)
MALONE, William (1)			
	L	18 May	1782
	SUP CR	4 Oct	1817 (PRO)
	d		1819 (PRO)
MALONE, William (2)			
	L	31 Aug	1807
	d		1817 (PRO)
MALPASS, Henry Potter			
	L	26 Dec	1799
	Dismissed		1814 (PRO)
MALTBY, William			
	L	22 Aug	1759
	CR	26 May	1768
	CA	10 Jan	1771
	d	26 Apr	1793
MALTMAN, Robert			
	T		
	L	12 July	1814
	d		1823 (TR)
MAN, Elias			
	L	19 July	1795 (PRO)
	Dismissed		1808 (PRO)
MAN, John			
	T		
	L	24 Dec	1805
	d		1811 (PRO)
MAN, Robert (1)			
	L	26 Aug	1702 (PMM)
	CR		
	CA	22 Dec	1716
	d	15 Dec	1745
MAN, Robert (2)			
	L	17 Sept	1740
	CR		
	CA	22 June	1745
	RAB	18 Oct	1770
	RAR	24 Oct	1770
	VAW	5 Feb	1776
	VAR	29 Jan	1778
	AB	26 Sept	1780
	d	10 Apr	1783 (PRO)
MAN, Robert (3)			
	L	26 May	1768
	CR	24 June	1776
	CA	30 May	1777
	RAB	4 July	1794
	RAR	1 June	1795
	VAW	14 Feb	1799
	VAR	1 Jan	1801
	AB	23 Apr	1804
	AW	28 Apr	1808
	AR	12 Aug	1812
	d	21 Sept	1813 (PRO)
MAN, Robert	See MANN, Robert		
MANBY, Edward			
	L	28 July	1793
	Ret CR	14 Sept	1826 (PRO)
	d		1841 (PRO)
MANBY, Thomas			
	L	27 Oct	1795
	CR	15 Feb	1797
	CA	22 Jan	1799
	RAB	27 May	1825 (PRO)
	RAW	22 July	1830 (PRO)
	d	3 June	1834 (PRO)
MANDERSON, James			
	L	12 Sept	1795
	CR	22 Jan	1806
	d	13 Feb	1837 (PRO)
MANDERSON, John William			
	L	28 Feb	1781
	d		1798 (PRO)
MANDERSON, Patrick			
	L	27 Apr	1794
	d		1815 (PRO)

MANDERSON, Stephen
L 9 May 1795
d 1813 (PRO)

MANDRY, John
L 30 Apr 1678

MANFIELD, Edward
L 20 Feb 1705 (PMM)

MANGIN, Reuben Caillaud
L 3 Dec 1800
CR 8 May 1804
CA 13 Oct 1807
RAB 23 Nov 1841 (PRO)
d 20 Aug 1846 (PJP)

MANGLES, James
L 24 Sept 1806
CR 13 June 1815
Ret CA 8 Feb 1853 (PRO)
d 18 Nov 1867 (PRO)

MANGLES, Robert
L 13 Oct 1781
d 2 Mar 1792 (LT)

MANICO, Peter Smith
L 16 Mar 1814
d 9 Nov 1857 (PRO)

MANISTRE, Fiske
L 9 Apr 1762
d 1785 (PRO)

MANLEY, Francis
L 11 Oct 1688 (P)
CA 19 Jan 1691
KIA 17 June 1693 (CH)

MANLEY, Isaac George
L 7 May 1777
CR 18 Dec 1782
CA 22 Nov 1790
RAB 25 Oct 1809
RAW 31 July 1810
RAR 12 Aug 1812
VAB 4 June 1814
VAW 12 Aug 1819 (CH)
VAR 19 July 1821 (CH)
AW 22 July 1830 (CH)
AR 10 Jan 1837 (CH)
d 29 July 1837 (PJP)

MANLEY, John (1)
L 9 Oct 1770
CR 16 May 1779
CA 9 Oct 1782
RAB 23 Apr 1804
RAW 9 Nov 1805
RAR 28 Apr 1808
VAB 25 Oct 1809
VAW 31 July 1810
VAR 4 Dec 1813
d 24 Sept 1816 (PRO)

MANLEY, John (2)
L 9 Jan 1782
CR 29 Apr 1802
d 28 Aug 1834 (PRO)

MANLEY, John Lampen
L 14 Apr 1802
CR 25 Sept 1806
CA 29 Aug 1812
d 9 June 1817 (PRO)

MANLEY, Richard
L 25 May 1744
d 1758(9) (PRO)

MANN, James
L 19 Aug 1688

MANN, John Hollingbery
L 20 Mar 1756
d 1795 (PRO)

MANN, Robert
L 6 Mar 1747
CR 10 Nov 1756
CA 16 Nov 1757
KIA 7 Mar 1762 (LG)

MANN, Robert
See MAN, Robert

MANN, Samuel
L 17 Oct 1804
d 1809 (PRO)

MANN, Thomas
L 9 Apr 1694
CR
CA 1 Nov 1705
d 19 Apr 1719

MANNERS, Lord Robert
L 13 May 1778
CR
CA 17 Jan 1780
MP 1780–
(Cambridgeshire) 23 Apr 1782 (MPN)
d 23 Apr 1782 (MPN)

MANNERS, William
L 14 Aug 1806
CR 7 Feb 1812
KIA 28 June 1814 (CH)

MANNING, Edward
L 1 May 1690
Gone 1719 (PRO)

MANNING, John
L 9 Aug 1802
d 1802 (PRO)

MANNING, Robert
L 24 July 1790
CR 18 Sept 1793
d Feb 1800 (PRO)

MANNING(S), Thomas
L 4 Feb 1743
CR
CA 4 Feb 1758 (PRO)
d 1771 (PRO)

MANSEL, Christopher
L 1794 (PJP)

MANSEL, Richard
L 3 Nov 1790
d 1793 (PRO)

MANSEL, Robert
L 27 Nov 1793
CR 3 Jan 1798
CA 14 Feb 1801
Ret RA 22 July 1830 (PRO)
d 5 Jan 1838 (PRO)

MANSELL, Anthony
L 1672

MANSELL, Bonamy
L 7 Mar 1809

Ret CR	9 Apr	1847 (PRO)
d	4 Jan	1868 (PRO)
MANSELL, Bushy		
L	2 Jan	1707
Gone		1734 (PRO)
MANSELL, Charles		
L		
CA		1667 (PJP)
MANSELL, Edward		
L		
CR	5 Oct	1709
d	Mar	1736 (PRO)
MANSELL, Edward Wogan		
L	25 Sept	1806
d		1810 (PRO)
MANSELL, Philip		
L		1664
Sentenced by court-martial to be cashiered for insubordination.	6 Apr	1665 (PRO)
MANSEL(L), Richard		
See MANSEL, Richard		
MANSELL, Samuel		
L	11 Aug	1757
d		1758 (PRO)
MANSELL, Sir Thomas (1)		
L	17 Apr	1799
CR	17 Apr	1808
Kt (Sweden)		1812 (OB)
CA	7 June	1814
KCH		1837 (SPB)
Ret CA	1 Oct	1846 (PRO)
Ret RA	9 Oct	1849 (PRO)
d	22 Apr	1858 (PRO)
MANSELL, Thomas (2)		
L	16 Sept	1804 (PRO)
CR	15 June	1814 (PRO)
CA	12 Feb	1834 (PRO)
Ret RA	21 Oct	1856 (PRO)
Ret VA	27 Apr	1863 (PRO)
Ret A	18 Oct	1867 (PRO)
d		1869 (PRO)
MANSELL, William		
L	15 Nov	1790
CR	26 Apr	1802
d		1810 (PRO)
MANSFIELD, Barrington		
L	1 Apr	1780
d		1801 (PRO)
MANSFIELD, Charles John Moore		
L	25 Nov	1778
CR	19 July	1793
CA	4 Oct	1794
T		
d	May	1813 (TR)
MANSFIELD, Michael		
L		
CA		1672
d	before	1689 (PJP)
MANSFIELD, Philip		
L	8 Oct	1777
d		1786 (PRO)
MANSFIELD, William Moreshead		
L	16 Dec	1776
d (drowned)	31 Oct	1777 (PJP)

MANSON, George		
L	18 Oct	1802
d		1816 (PRO)
MANT, Joseph Bingham		
L	6 Sept	1796
Ret CR	26 Dec	1837 (PRO)
d	2 Mar	1845 (OB)
MANTELL, William		
L	12 May	1740
CR	1 Mar	1749 (PRO)
CA	8 June	1749 (PRO)
SUP		1762 (PJP)
d	13 Dec	1765 (PRO)
MANTON, John		
L	17 Mar	1806
Ret CR	15 July	1839 (PRO)
d	JULY	1846 (OB)
MANWARING, George		
See MAINWARING, George		
MANWARING, Thomas		
See MAINWARING, Thomas		
MANWARING, William		
See MAINWARING, William		
MAPLES, John		
L	7 Nov	1806
CR	12 Aug	1819 (PRO)
d	7 Apr	1827 (LT)
MAPLES, John Fordyce		
L	16 May	1795
T		
CR	21 Oct	1810
CA	23 Aug	1813
CB	4 June	1815 (OB)
Ret RA	1 Oct	1846 (OB)
d	12 May	1847 (OB)
MAPLESDEN, Jervis		
L	3 Nov	1739
CR	6 Oct	1746
CA	21 May	1756
LGH		1778 (PJP)
d		1780(1) (PRO)
MAPLETON, David		
L	10 May	1804
CR	17 May	1814
d	22 Mar	1842 (PRO)
MARA, John		
L	22 Aug	1797
d		1802 (PRO)
MARBEUF, Daniel		
L	20 Mar	1761
Dismissed	18 Nov	1761 (PJP)
d		1761 (PRO)
MARCH, Jeremiah		
L	11 Mar	1815
d		1853 (PRO)
MARCH, William		
L	4 Mar	1815 (PRO)
d	28 July	1818 (PRO)
MARGERUM, Matthew		
L		1689 (PJP)
MARJORIBANKS, George		
L	13 Jan	1812
d		1818 (PRO)

MARJORIBANKS, John		
L	14 Feb	1814
d		1833 (PRO)
MARKETT, Augustus		
L	22 Dec	1780
d	15 Apr	1833 (LT)
MARKETT, John		
L	16 Oct	1711
Gone		1752
MARKHAM, John		
L		
CR		
CA	3 Jan	1783
HP		1786–1793 (MPT)
MP (Portsmouth)		1801–1818 (MPT)
COM AD	Feb	1801–
	May	1804 (AO)
RAB	23 Apr	1804
RAW	9 Nov	1805
COM AD	Feb	1806–
	Apr	1807 (AO)
RAR	28 Apr	1808
VAB	25 Oct	1809
VAW	31 July	1810
VAR	4 Dec	1813
AB	12 Aug	1819 (PRO)
MP (Portsmouth)		1820–1826 (MPT)
AW	27 May	1825 (PRO)
d	13 Feb	1827 (MPT)
MARKHAM, Walter		
L		1703 (PJP)
MARKLAND, John Duff		
L	8 June	1801
CR	22 Jan	1806
CA	18 Apr	1811
CB	4 June	1815 (OB)
Kt (Austria)		1816 (OB)
Ret RA	1 Oct	1846 (PRO)
d	28 Aug	1848 (PRO)
MARKS, Richard		
T		
L	2 Nov	1805
Resigned	2 Apr	1814 (PRO)
MARKS, Thomas		
L		
CA	26 Mar	1694 (PJP)
MARLBOROUGH, James Ley, Earl of		
Inh EP	1 Apr	1638 (DNB)
L		
CA		1661
AD		1661
KIA	3 June	1665 (DNB)
MARLEY, Robert Roper		
L	31 Dec	1807 (PJP)
d	25 Oct	1855 (PRO)
MARLOW, Benjamin		
L	25 July	1743
CR		
CA	6 June	1756
RAW	26 Sept	1780
VAB	24 Sept	1787
VAW	21 Sept	1790
VAR	1 Feb	1793
AB	12 Apr	1794
d		1795 (CH)
MARLOW, Thomas		
L	26 July	1697
Gone		1719 (PRO)
MARRETT, Joseph		
L	5 Apr	1799
CR	26 May	1812
Ret CA	20 Oct	1845 (PRO)
d	30 Sept	1857 (PRO)
MARRIOTT, George		
L	17 Feb	1795
d		1803 (PRO)
MARRIOTT, John		
L	16 Dec	1758
d		1800 (PRO)
MARRYAT, Frederick		
L	26 Dec	1812
CR	13 June	1815
CA	25 July	1828 (OB)
CB	26 Dec	1825 (OB)
d	9 Aug	1848 (DNB)
MARSDIN, Henry Tom		
L	25 July	1794
d		1814 (DNB)
MARSH, Digby		
L	24 Dec	1813
CR	5 Jan	1822 (OB)
CA	1 Jan	1842 (OB)
HP	1 Jan	1842 (OB)
Ret RA	12 Apr	1862 (PRO)
d	5 Jan	1863 (PRO)
MARSH, Edward (1)		
L	19 Sept	1777
CR	15 July	1781
d	7 Sept	1786 (PMM)
MARSH, Edward (2)		
L	14 Sept	1780
CR	23 July	1795
CA	6 Mar	1797
d	18 Dec	1812 (PRO)
MARSH, Henry (1)		
L	20 Jan	1740
CR	23 July	1795
CA	6 Mar	1797
d	18 Dec	1812 (PRO)
MARSH, Henry (2)		
L	20 Jan	1740
CR	6 Mar	1744
CA	12 Mar	1748
d		1772 (PRO)
MARSH, Henry (3)		
L	1 Feb	1779
SUP CR	31 Jan	1814
d	14 Sept	1821 (PRO)
MARSH, Isaac		
L	29 Jan	1745
d	4 Nov	1750 (PMM)
MARSH, John (1)		
L	18 Oct	1758
d		1770 (PRO)
MARSH, John (2)		
L	17 Mar	1780
CR	6 July	1794
d	Sept	1819 (PRO)

MARSH, Stephen
L 26 Sept 1795
d 1811 (PRO)

MARSH, William (1)
L 18 Mar 1732
CR 25 May 1741
CA 25 May 1743
SUP RA 1762
d 15 Oct 1765

MARSH, William (2)
L 26 Dec 1778
d 28 July 1818 (PRO)

MARSHALL, Charles
L 10 Sept 1759
d 29 Dec 1803

MARSHALL, Charles Henry
T
L 14 June 1813
d 1835 (TR)

MARSHALL, David
L 8 Oct 1802
d 1804 (PRO)

MARSHALL, Francis
L 22 Jan 1806
One of the four Jr. Lts. Dec 1815
d 1824 (PRO)

MARSHALL, George (1)
L 26 Jan 1707 (PMM)

MARSHALL, George (2)
L 27 Sept 1748
KIA 3 Nov 1758 (LG)

MARSHALL, George (3)
L 7 May 1802
d 1809 (PRO)

MARSHALL, George Edward
L 22 Sept 1807
HP Dec 1809–
June 1810 (OB)
CR 27 May 1825 (PRO)
HP 1835 (OB)
Ret CA 1 Apr 1856 (PRO)
d 29 Aug 1856 (PRO)

MARSHALL, Henry Masterman
L 30 Aug 1803
CR 27 June 1814
HP 27 June 1814 (OB)
Ret CR 1 July 1851 (PRO)
d 1854 (PRO)

MARSHALL, James (1)
L 30 Mar 1783 (PRO)
KIA 18 July 1805 (LT)

MARSHALL, James (2)
L 4 Mar 1815
CR 6 Aug 1827 (PRO)
CA 19 Nov 1832 (PRO)
d 1835 (PRO)

MARSHALL, James Nasmyth
L 15 Nov 1790
CR 18 Mar 1800
d 16 Aug 1830 (PRO)

MARSHALL, John (1)
L
CA 1672

MARSHALL, John (2)
L 17 Feb 1759
d 1771 (PRO)

MARSHALL, John (3)
L 22 Mar 1797
CR 10 June 1804
d 1813 (PRO)

MARSHALL, John (4)
L 18 Feb 1800
CR 10 June 1804 (PJP)
Ret CR 26 Nov 1830 (PRO)
d 1851 (PRO)

MARSHALL, Sir John (5)
L 17 Mar 1806
CR 24 Oct 1812
CA 7 June 1814
CB 4 June 1815 (OB)
Kt (Russia) 1815 (MB)
Kt (Sweden) 1815 (MB)
KCB 1832 (PJP)
KCH June 1832 (OB)
RAB 27 Mar 1850 (PRO)
d 30 Sept 1850 (PRO)

MARSHALL, John (6)
L 25 Jan 1808
d 1812 (PRO)

MARSHALL, John (7)
L 14 Feb 1815
d 22 Feb 1837 (PRO)

MARSHALL, John Houlton
L 30 June 1794
T
CR 21 Oct 1810
d 1837 (TR)

MARSHALL, John Willoughby
L 26 Sept 1796
CR 29 Apr 1802
CA 21 Oct 1810
d 22 Jan 1824 (MB)

MARSHALL, Joseph (1)
L 12 May 1813
d 1841 (PRO)

MARSHALL, Joseph (2)
L 1 July 1813 (PRO)
d May 1824 (PRO)

MARSHALL, Leonard
L 13 Jan 1740
CR 17 Apr 1746
d 1773 (PRO)

MARSHALL, Sampson
L 3 Feb 1812
d 1843 (PRO)

MARSHALL, Samuel (1)
L 26 Aug 1732
CR 12 Sept 1743
CA 17 July 1747
d 17 Apr 1768 (PRO)

MARSHALL, Samuel (2)
L 11 Feb 1760
CR 24 Sept 1762
CA 24 Jan 1771
COM E 4 Dec 1793–
25 Sept 1794 (NBO)
d 2 Oct 1795 (NBO)

MARSHALL, Samuel Edward

L	12 July	1782
In Russian Service		1790 (PMM)
d		1790 (PRO)

MARSHALL, Thomas (1)

L		1665 (P)
CA		1666 (P)
Turned out	Nov	1674 (PRO)
L	4 Nov	1679 (PRO)
d	29 Aug	1690

MARSHALL, Thomas (2)

L	11 May	1760
CR	5 May	1778
d		1809 (PRO)

MARSHALL, Thomas (3)

L	30 July	1810
d	Dec	1827 (PRO)

MARSHALL, Thomas Gaborian

L	15 Aug	1801
Gone		1811 (PRO)

MARSHALL, Thomas Hastings

L	6 Oct	1809
d		1814 (PRO)

MARSHALL, William (1)

L	14 Feb	1757
CR	16 Apr	1761
d		1775 (PRO)

MARSHALL, William (2)

L	10 Feb	1815
HP	May	1815 (OB)
d	6 Oct	1853 (PRO)

MARSHAM, Henry Shovell Jones

L	30 June	1813
CR	21 Apr	1825 (PRO)
CA	24 Dec	1833 (PRO)
HP	July	1834 (OB)
Ret CA	1 July	1851 (PRO)
Ret RA	21 Oct	1856 (PRO)
Ret VA	27 Apr	1863 (PRO)
Ret A	18 Oct	1867 (PRO)
d		1875 (PRO)

MARSHAM, Robert

L	15 June	1709
In Customs Service		1729 (PRO)

MARSINGALL, Samuel

L	20 Aug	1807
Ret CR	1 Nov	1843 (PRO)
d	24 Apr	1859 (PRO)

MARSTON, J

L		1790 (PJP)
d	21 Sept	1813 (PJP)

MARTIN, Alexander

T		
L	29 Oct	1811
Ret CR	1 Apr	1853 (PRO)
d		1868 (TR)

MARTIN, George (1)

L	25 Sept	1695
CR		
CA	8 July	1700 (PJP)
d	22 Oct	1724

MARTIN, George (2)

L		
CR		
CA	24 Sept	1740
SUP RA		

MARTIN, Sir George (3)

L	16 July	1780
CR	9 Mar	1782 (DNB)
CA	17 Mar	1783
HP	Oct	1802–
	May	1803 (OB)
CRM	23 Apr	1804 (LG)
RAB	9 Nov	1805
RAW	28 Apr	1808
RAR	25 Oct	1809
VAB	31 July	1810
Kt (Two Sicilies)	6 July	1811 (LG)
VAW	12 Aug	1812
VAR	4 June	1814
KCB	2 Jan	1815 (DNB)
GCB	20 Feb	1821 (DNB)
AB	19 July	1821 (CH)
AW	22 July	1830 (CH)
GCMG		1836 (DNB)
AR	10 Jan	1837 (CH)
AF	9 Nov	1846 (CH)
d	28 July	1847 (PRO)

MARTIN, Henry (1)

L	19 Dec	1688
CA	16 June	1689
RA		1701
d	19 Feb	1702

MARTIN, Sir Henry (2)

L	18 Dec	1755
CR	21 Jan	1757
CA	19 Dec	1757
COMM (Portsmouth)		1780–1790 (MPT)
CONT	29 Mar	1790–
	1 Aug	1794 (NBO)
MP (Southampton)		1790–
	1 Aug	1794 (MPT)
Cre Bt	28 July	1791 (NBO)
d	1 Aug	1794 (NBO)

MARTIN, Henry (3)

L	11 Dec	1780 (PRO)
CR	17 Feb	1800
d	7 May	1823 (PRO)

MARTIN, Hugh

L	3 Oct	1719
Gone		1727 (PRO)

MARTIN, James

L	21 Nov	1800
d (drowned)	Nov	1801 (PJP)

MARTIN, John (1)

L		
CA		1672

MARTIN, John (2)

L		
CR	23 May	1700 (PMM)

MARTIN, John (3)

L	12 Dec	1744
CR	4 Oct	1759
d		1775 (PRO)

MARTIN, Joseph Winthrop

L	27 May	1814
d		1851 (PRO)

MARTIN, Josiah		
L	11 Mar	1691
Gone		1719 (PRO)
MARTIN, Nathaniel		
L	19 Mar	1807
CR	27 July	1825 (PRO)
d		1847 (PRO)
MARTIN, Philip Clarke		
L	23 Feb	1815
Struck off list	4 July	1822 (PRO)
MARTIN, Richard		
L	13 Apr	1794
Resigned		1798 (PRO)
MARTIN, Robert (1)		
L		
CA		1660
MARTIN, Robert (2)		
L	8 May	1782
d		1797 (PRO)
MARTIN, Roger		
L	1 May	1723
CR	25 July	1734
CA	24 Sept	1740
SUP RA		1756
d		1779
MARTIN, Roger		
See MARTYN, Roger		
MARTIN, Samuel		
L	9 Oct	1694 (PJP)
CA	18 Oct	1697
KIA	20 Oct	1705 (CH)
MARTIN, Stephen		
L	13 Feb	1691 (PJP)
CR	2 Feb	1697 (PJP)
CA	6 Mar	1702
d	Jan	1737
MARTIN, Thomas		
L	22 Jan	1806
CR	10 Aug	1813
CA	2 Aug	1826 (PRO)
Ret RA	15 Apr	1854 (PRO)
Ret VA	9 June	1860 (PRO)
Ret A	9 Feb	1864 (PRO)
d	1 Nov	1868 (PRO)
MARTIN, Sir Thomas Byam		
L	22 Oct	1790
CR		1793 (MPT)
CA	5 Nov	1793
Kt (Sweden)		1808 (OB)
RAB	1 Aug	1811
RAW	12 Aug	1812
Kt		1814 (OB)
RAR	4 June	1814
KCB	2 Jan	1815 (LG)
CONT	24 Feb	1816–
	9 Nov	1831 (NBO)
MP (Plymouth)		1818–1832 (MPT)
VAB	12 Aug	1819 (CH)
VAW	19 July	1821 (CH)
VAR	27 May	1825 (CH)
GCB	3 Mar	1830 (LG)
AB	22 July	1830 (CH)
AW	10 Jan	1837 (CH)
AR	23 Nov	1841 (CH)
AF	30 Oct	1849 (LG)
d	21 Oct	1854 (CH)

MARTIN, William (1)		
L		
CA		1665
KIA	25 July	1666 (PD)
MARTIN, William (2)		
KLB	26 Aug	1708 (DNB)
L	30 July	1710 (DNB)
CR		
CA	9 Oct	1718
RAB	10 Dec	1743 (LG)
VAB	23 June	1744 (LG)
VAW	23 Apr	1745
AB	15 July	1747 (LG)
d	17 Sept	1756
MARTIN, William (3)		
L	29 Aug	1746
CR		
CA	16 Aug	1748
d	27 June	1766
MARTIN, William (4)		
L	2 Apr	1757
d		1780(1) (PRO)
MARTIN, William (5)		
T		
L	1 Aug	1806
CR	19 July	1821 (PRO)
Ret CA	1 Apr	1856 (PRO)
d		1866 (TR)
MARTIN, William		
See MARTYN, William		
MARTIN, William George		
L	28 Mar	1815
CR	2 Apr	1818 (PRO)
d	13 Jan	1822 (PRO)
MARTINE, George		
L		
CR		
CA	8 July	1700
d	22 Nov	1732
MARTYN, Roger		
L	10 June	1756
d		1763 (PRO)
MARTYN, William		
L	21 Feb	1815
d		1835 (PRO)
MARWOOD, Thomas		
L	1 Apr	1703 (PMM)
CR		
CA	1 Jan	1713
d	5 Sept	1731
MARYCHURCH, Isaac		
L		
CA		1661
d	before	1689 (PJP)
MASCLARY, William Henry		
L	3 July	1731
Gone		1752
MASEFIELD, Joseph Ore		
L	17 Apr	1795
CR	27 Apr	1801
d	19 Sept	1808 (PRO)
MASON, Charles (1)		
L	5 Oct	1727
d		1747 (PRO)

MASON, Charles (2)
L 18 June 1791
d 1816 (PRO)

MASON, Christopher (1)
L 1666 (P)
CA 10 June 1672
SUP 8 Jan 1694 (PMM)

MASON, Christopher (2)
L 21 Nov 1762
CR 7 June 1776
CA 22 Apr 1778
RAW 1 June 1795
VAB 14 Feb 1799
VAW 1 Jan 1801
d 20 May 1802 (PRO)

MASON, Sir Francis
L 8 July 1799
CR 29 Apr 1802
CA 22 Jan 1806
HP 1807–1809 (OB)
CB 4 June 1815 (OB)
RAB 28 June 1828 (PRO)
KCB 24 Aug 1841 (OB)
RAW 23 Nov 1841 (PRO)
HP May 1843 (OB)
RAR 10 Dec 1846 (PRO)
VAB 9 May 1849 (PRO)
VAW 11 June 1851 (PRO)
VAR 30 July 1852 (PRO)
d 27 May 1853 (PRO)

MASON, Henry Browne
T
L 2 Feb 1811
HP Jan–June 1813 (OB)
CR 13 June 1815
Ret CA 2 June 1854 (PRO)
d 1859 (TR)

MASON, Holman
L 25 Aug 1762
d 12 June 1798 (PRO)

MASON, John (1)
L 1673

MASON, John (2)
L
CA 1679
d before 1689 (PJP)

MASON, John (3)
L
CA 4 Apr 1690
d 5 Feb 1691 (PJP)

MASON, John (4)
L 19 Nov 1790
SUP CR 20 July 1824 (PRO)
d 1833 (PRO)

MASON, Robert
L 4 Mar 1740
d 1761 (PRO)

MASON, Samuel
L 12 May 1783
d (drowned) 1798 (CH)

MASON, Thomas Monck
L 24 Mar 1807
CR 13 June 1815
CA 12 May 1828 (PRO)
d 21 Oct 1838 (PRO)

MASON, Thomas Tunstall
L 18 Nov 1758
d 1776 (PRO)

MASON, William (1)
L 6 Feb 1702
SUP 20 Mar 1738 (PMM)
d 1742 (PMM)

MASON, William (2)
L 3 Nov 1790
d 1801 (PRO)

MASON, William Henry
L 27 Feb 1815 (OB)
HP 1817 (OB)

MASSAM, William
L 19 Aug 1695
CR
CA 17 May 1708
d 2 Oct 1708

MASSEY, John
L 9 Apr 1810
Ret CR 5 Oct 1840 (PRO)
d 5 Nov 1853 (PRO)

MASSIE, Henry George
L 9 Sept 1806
HP Sept 1813 (OB)
Ret CR 5 Oct 1840 (PRO)
d 18 Mar 1860 (PRO)

MASSINGBERD, Thomas
L 27 Jan 1784
SUP CR 1 Apr 1822 (PRO)
d 1837 (PRO)

MASSY, Walter
L 13 Jan 1692
CR 16 Feb 1708 (PMM)
Gone 1719 (PRO)

MASTER, Harcourt
See MASTERS, Harcourt

MASTER, Henry (1)
L 23 June 1761
d 1790 (PRO)

MASTER, Henry (2)
L 12 Mar 1807
d 1811 (PRO)

MASTER, James
L 14 Jan 1727
d 1747 (PRO)

MASTER, James
See MASTERS, James

MASTER, Somerset
L 13 Aug 1728
In Russian Service 1735–1738 (PMM)
CR 14 Jan 1745 (PRO)
d 1747 (PRO)

MASTER, Streynsham
L 1704 (DNB)
CR 5 July 1709 (DNB)
CA 22 Mar 1710
d 22 June 1724 (DNB)

MASTERMAN, Charles Henry
L 14 July 1815
d 1861 (PRO)

Name / Rank	Date	Year
MASTERMAN, Henry		
L	27 Feb	1801
d		1812 (PRO)
MASTERS, Charles		
L		1666
MASTERS, Elias		
L	25 Dec	1693 (PJP)
MASTERS, Harcourt		
L	27 Sept	1720
CR		
CA	3 Jan	1738
MASTERS, James (1)		
L	11 Apr	1795 (PRO)
CR	29 Apr	1802
CA	8 May	1804
Ret RA	10 Jan	1837 (PRO)
d	18 Aug	1839 (PRO)
MASTERS, James (2)		
L	22 Sept	1806
Ret CR	29 Jan	1841 (PRO)
d	6 Dec	1863 (PRO)
MASTERS, Thomas James Poole		
L	4 Nov	1809
Ret CR	11 Apr	1849 (PRO)
d	13 Dec	1858 (PRO)
MASTERTON, Robert		
L	18 Jan	1692 (PJP)
CR	16 Feb	1697 (PJP)
MASTON, John		
L	27 Feb	1783
d		1813 (PRO)
MATHER, William (1)		
L		
CA		1672
MATHER, William (2)		
L	12 Oct	1799
CR	23 Feb	1807
Ret CA	10 Sept	1840 (PRO)
d	4 Jan	1841 (PRO)
MATHEWES, Thomas		
L	27 Aug	1794
d		1800 (PRO)
MATHEWS, Daniel		
L	14 Oct	1762
d		1772 (PRO)
MATHEWS, Faithful		
L	12 Feb	1783
d		1790 (PRO)
MATHEWS, George		
L	18 May	1746
d (drowned)	31 July	1781 (CH)
MATHEWS, Harry Nuland		
L	11 Sept	1795
d		1798 (PRO)
MAT(T)HEWS, Henry Bathurst		
L	13 June	1815
d		1827 (PRO)
MATHEWS, John (1)		
L	14 May	1759
d	19 July	1800 (PRO)
MATHEWS, John (2)		
L	1 Mar	1783
CR	30 Apr	1793
CA	13 Sept	1793
d	21 Mar	1798 (PRO)
MATHEWS, Robert Bates		
L	4 May	1810
Ret CR	12 Oct	1849 (PRO)
d	6 June	1858 (PRO)
MATHEWS, Thomas		
L	16 Mar	1700
CR		
CA	24 May	1703
VAR	13 Mar	1742 (LG)
AB	11 Aug	1743 (LG)
MP (Glamorgan)	2 Jan	1745–1747 (MPS)
AW	18 Feb	1745
MP (Carmarthan)	2 Oct	1747–1751 (MPS)
Dismissed	13 June	1748
d	2 Oct	1751 (DNB)
MATHIAS, Herbet		
L	4 June	1756
d		1773 (PRO)
MATHIAS, James		
L	13 Feb	1815
d		1841 (PRO)
MATHIAS, John		
L	17 July	1744
SUP CR	21 Sept	1796 (PMM)
d	18 July	1800 (PMM)
MATHISON, John		
L	17 Aug	1745
d	4 Jan	1764 (PMM)
MATSON, George William		
L	1 Feb	1815
CR	22 Oct	1830 (OB)
HP	22 Oct	1830 (OB)
Ret CA	1 Apr	1856 (PRO)
d		1856 (PRO)
MATSON, Henry		
L	21 Apr	1796 (PRO)
CR	22 Mar	1799
CA	15 Dec	1802
HP		1810 (MB)
d	31 May	1827 (PRO)
MATSON, John		
L	10 May	1811
d	6 Apr	1830 (PRO)
MATSON, Richard		
L	15 Oct	1794
CR	22 Sept	1797
CA	22 Mar	1799
HP	Feb	1810 (OB)
RAB	27 May	1825 (PRO)
RAW	22 July	1830 (PRO)
VAB	10 Jan	1837 (LG)
VAW	23 Nov	1841 (PRO)
VAR	9 Nov	1846 (PRO)
AB	26 June	1847 (PRO)
d	19 Mar	1848 (PRO)
MATTERFACE, William		
L	8 July	1807
KIA	26 Sept	1814 (JH)
MATTHEWES, Abednego		
L	22 Mar	1708 (PMM)

MATTHEWS, Alfred
L 11 Feb 1812
CR 19 July 1822 (OB)
HP Apr 1823 (OB)
Ret CA 1 Apr 1856 (PRO)
d 27 Apr 1873 (PRO)

MATTHEWS, James
L 16 Oct 1805
d 1808 (PRO)

MATTHEWS, John
L
CR 21 Oct 1702 (PMM)

MATTHEWS, Michael
L 15 Oct 1806
CR 20 Sept 1815
HP Aug 1816 (OB)
Ret CA 29 Dec 1855 (PRO)
d 1871 (PRO)

MATTHEWS, Richard
L 14 Sept 1739
CR 22 May 1758
d 1759(60) (PRO)

MATTHEWS, Robert Bates
See MATHEWS, Robert Bates

MATTHEWS, William
L 14 Feb 1812
CR 27 Aug 1814
d 1 Sept 1815 (LT)

MAUDE, Hon. Sir James Ashley
L 29 Mar 1805
CR 22 Oct 1810
CA 11 Mar 1814
d 23 Oct 1841 (PRO)

MAUDE, John
L 20 June 1769
CR 28 Aug 1783
CA 22 Nov 1790
d 17 June 1796 (LT)

MAUDE, William
L 26 Sept 1800 (PJP)
CR 11 Dec 1805
CA 26 Sept 1807
RAB 23 Nov 1841 (PRO)
d 18 June 1843 (PMM)

MAUDE, William George
L 24 July 1799
Ret CR 20 Oct 1840 (OB)
d July 1858 (PRO)

MAUGER, Nicholas
L 17 June 1800
Ret CR 15 Dec 1830 (PRO)
d 1851 (PRO)

MAUGHAM, George
L 23 Apr 1693 (PJP)
CA 5 June 1697
KIA 28 Aug 1702 (PJP)

MAUGHAN, John
L 23 Dec 1793
CR 3 Feb 1801
d Aug 1801 (PRO)

MAULE, George
L 30 Aug 1806
Ret CR 9 July 1840 (PRO)
d 1844 (PRO)

MAUND, Christopher
L
CA 29 Jan 1692
d 17 Mar 1692

MAUNDRELL, Richard
L 2 Dec 1795 (PRO)
d 1809 (PRO)

MAUNSELL, Robert
L 7 Mar 1805
CR 15 Feb 1808
CA 7 Feb 1812
CB 20 July 1838 (OB)
d 31 Aug 1845 (OB)

MAUNSELL, Robert
See MANSEL, Robert

MAURICE, Ferdinand Moore
L 29 Dec 1796
CR 21 Oct 1810
d (drowned) Sept 1812 (OB)

MAURICE, James Wilkes
L 3 Apr 1797
CR 7 May 1804
CA 18 Jan 1809
Ret RA 1 Oct 1846 (PRO)
d 4 Sept 1857 (DNB)

MAURICE, John
L 9 Nov 1756
d 1779 (PRO)

MAURICE, Salmon
See MORRICE, Salmon

MAVER, John
L 14 Aug 1794
Ret CR 26 Nov 1830 (PRO)
d 1835 (PRO)

MAW, Richard Stovin
L 8 Oct 1807
HP June 1817 (OB)
Ret CR 3 Oct 1856 (PRO)
d 1862 (PRO)

MAWBEY, John
T
L 8 Feb 1815
d Sept 1852 (PRO)

MAWDESLEY, John
L 25 June 1810
d 1835 (PRO)

MAWDESLEY, Othnel
L 10 June 1809
d 9 Nov 1812 (PRO)

MAWMAN, William
L 2 Feb 1741
Gone 1752

MAX, John George
L 6 Feb 1806
HP Apr 1814 (OB)
d 1852 (PRO)

MAXEY, Edward
L 27 May 1814
HP Oct 1816 (OB)
Ret CR 5 Feb 1858 (PRO)
d 24 Nov 1871 (PRO)

MAXEY, Lewis
L 1 May 1807
d 23 Sept 1828 (PRO)

MAXFIELD, John
L 13 Mar 1802
d June 1823 (PRO)

MAXTONE, Thomas
L 21 Nov 1790
CR 16 Feb 1796
d (drowned) 30 Sept 1796 (PRO)

MAXWELL, Arthur
L 8 Sept 1795
d 1812 (PRO)

MAXWELL, Francis
L 26 Sept 1811
HP June 1814 (OB)
CR 1 Oct 1852 (PRO)
d 1863 (PRO)

MAXWELL, George
L 19 Nov 1777
CR 21 Sept 1790
d 6 Mar 1833 (PRO)

MAXWELL, George Berkeley
L 22 Sept 1807
CR 15 June 1814
CA 20 Nov 1830 (OB)
HP 20 Nov 1830 (OB)
d 1855 (PRO)

MAXWELL, George William
L 14 Jan 1780
d 13 Apr 1791 (PMM)

MAXWELL, John
L 12 May 1800
CR 22 Jan 1806
CA 15 June 1810
d 31 May 1826 (MB)

MAXWELL, John James
L 31 Dec 1810 (PRO)
d 1815 (PRO)

MAXWELL, Keith
L 28 Mar 1794
CR 18 Aug 1801
CA 1 May 1804
d 22 Apr 1823 (MB)

MAXWELL, Sir Murray
L 10 Oct 1796
CR 15 Dec 1802
CA 4 Aug 1803
CB 1815 (DNB)
Kt 27 May 1818 (DNB)
d 26 June 1831 (DNB)

MAY, Christopher
L 22 Nov 1815 (PRO)
d 1863 (PRO)

MAY, James
L 23 July 1778
CR 26 Aug 1789
CA 12 Aug 1794
d 1808 (PRO)

MAY, John
L 20 Feb 1759
SUP CR 8 Apr 1801
d Sept 1825 (PRO)

MAY, Richard
L
CA 1665
d before 1689 (PJP)

MAY, Stephen Yonge
T
L 4 Feb 1815
d July 1828 (PRO)

MAY, William
L 19 Oct 1798
CR 22 July 1809 (PRO)
d 1834 (PRO)

MAYBURY, Stephen William
L 25 Dec 1800
d 1810 (PRO)

MAYER, Charles
L 11 Jan 1803
d 1803 (PRO)

MAYHEW, Ralph
L
CA 1667
Dismissed 26 July 1667 (PMM)
d before 1689 (PJP)

MAYNARD, Francis
L
CA 15 June 1691
d (drowned) 21 Nov 1693 (CH)

MAYNARD, Henry Lord
L 19 May 1695
CR
CA 15 Jan 1702
d 7 Dec 1742 (PJP)

MAYNARD, Joseph
L 4 Mar 1815
CR 4 Oct 1825 (PRO)
Ret CA 1 Apr 1856 (PRO)
d 1859 (PRO)

MAYNARD, Robert
L 14 Jan 1707
CR 3 July 1739
CA 22 Sept 1750
d 1750

MAYNARD, Thomas
L 5 July 1796
CR 12 Jan 1805
Ret CA 17 Oct 1840 (PRO)
d 1857 (PRO)

MAYNE, Coville
L 24 May 1696
CR
CA 16 May 1711
d 25 Aug 1746

MAYNE, Dawson
L 10 Apr 1794
KIA 14 Dec 1798 (CH)

MAYNE, John
L
CR 17 May 1678 (P)
CA 4 Feb 1690
SUP 1703
d 13 Aug 1712

MAYNE, Perry
L 7 July 1720
CR 22 Mar 1725 (DNB)
CA 24 Sept 1725
RAB 23 Apr 1745
VAW 15 July 1747
VAR 12 May 1748

SUP	25 Feb	1757
d	5 Aug	1761
MAYNE, Robert (1)		
L	26 Jan	1759
SUP CR	9 Jan	1801 (PMM)
d	29 Sept	1820 (PRO)
MAYNE, Robert (2)		
L	2 Oct	1804
T		
Ret CR	22 Dec	1842 (PRO)
d	19 Jan	1846 (OB)
MAYO, Charles		
L	21 Aug	1801
d		1804 (PRO)
MAYO, Thomas		
L		1672
CA		1672
d	before	1689 (PJP)
MAYOR, John Hollings		
L	7 Mar	1809
d	1 July	1827 (PRO)
MAYOTT, William		
L	11 Feb	1815
d		1839 (PRO)
MAYRIS, Thomas		
L	1 Dec	1793
d	4 May	1825 (PRO)
MEAD, Joseph		
L	19 Aug	1747
CR	5 Apr	1757
CA	7 July	1761
d		1799
MEAD, Robert		
L	5 Apr	1729
In Merchant Service	21 Jan	1735 (PMM)
d		?1737 (PMM)
MEAD, Samuel		
L	13 Mar	1718
CR	June	1725 (PRO)
CA	29 Aug	1727
SUP	Sept	1742 (PJP)
d	21 Oct	1776
MEADE, John		
L	19 Apr	1803
CR	4 Nov	1812
Ret CA	20 Nov	1847 (PRO)
d	Mar	1851 (PRO)
MEADS, Samuel		
L	3 May	1692
CR		
CA	20 Sept	1708
Dismissed	16 Apr	1709
Reinstated	16 Feb	1714
	(13 Feb in C)	
d		1725
MEADS, Thomas		
L	2 Dec	1690
CR		
CA	3 Jan	1703
d		1740
MEADOWS, Charles		
See MEDOWS, Charles		
MEADOWS, Edward		
See MEDOWS, Edward		
MEADOWS, William		
L	1 Mar	1810
Ret CR	7 July	1849 (PRO)
d	28 Mar	1860 (PRO)
MEADWAY, John Allen		
L	9 Oct	1807
d (drowned)	24 Dec	1811 (CH)
MEAGER, Nicholas		
L	27 July	1793
d		1794 (PRO)
MEARA, James		
L	30 May	1807
CR	7 June	1814
d		1843 (PRO)
MEARES, James		
See MERES, James		
MEARES, John		
L	18 Sept	1778
In Merchant Service		1783–1790 (DNB)
CR	26 Feb	1795
d		1809
MEARES, William		
L	1 Oct	1777
d		1810 (PRO)
MEARNS, George		
L	17 June	1795
d		1798 (PRO)
MEARS, Robert		
L	25 Nov	1796
d (drowned)	25 Dec	1798 (PRO)
MEARS, Roger		
L	21 Oct	1790
CR	6 July	1794
d		1798
MECHI, Henry		
L	23 Feb	1815
d		1817 (PRO)
MEDLEY, Edward (1)		
L	24 Feb	1741
Gone		1752
MEDLEY, Edward (2)		
L	22 Dec	1807
d	11 Apr	1849 (PRO)
MEDLEY, Henry		
L	5 Sept	1710 (DNB)
CR		1720 (DNB)
CA	17 Feb	1721
GG (Newfoundland)		1739 (BNS)
RAW	23 June	1744 (LG)
VAB	23 Apr	1745
VAR	15 July	1747
d	5 Aug	1747 (DNB)
MEDLICOTT, John		
L	7 Jan	1802
T		
CR	4 June	1814
d	19 Apr	1831 (PRO)
MEDLY, Benjamin		
L	20 Feb	1808
d		1811 (PRO)

MEDOWS, Charles, Viscount Newark
L 5 Aug 1755
CR 5 Apr 1757
CA 17 Aug 1757
Resigned 1769
MP 9 Dec 1778–
(Nottinghamshire) 1796 (MPN)
Cre EP 23 July 1796 (MPN)
d 17 June 1816 (MPN)

MEDOWS, Edward
L 9 June 1762
CR 26 May 1768
CA 10 Jan 1771
Quitted 26 Dec 1793

MEE, John
L 9 Feb 1815
HP May 1816 (OB)
Ret CR 12 Apr 1860 (PRO)
d Mar 1872 (PRO)

MEECH, Radford Gundrey
T
L 15 June 1810
d 1849 (TR)

MEEKE, William Ingram
L 15 Jan 1777
d 1780 (PRO)

MEEKESON, John
L 3 Dec 1761
d 4 June 1766 (PMM)

MEES, George
L 7 July 1686 (P)
CA 6 Apr 1689
RAR 3 Feb 1697
d 20 July 1697

MEESE, Harcott
L 14 Sept 1693
Gone 1719 (PRO)

MEGGISON, William Henry
L 16 Mar 1811
d 1853 (PRO)

MEHEUX, Archibald Bryan
L 6 May 1796
d Apr 1808 (PRO)

MEIK, James Lind
L 30 Dec 1802
d 1803 (PJP)

MEIK, John Lind
L 15 Jan 1802
d 1818 (PRO)

MEIK, Thomas
L 6 Apr 1783
d 1790 (PRO)

MEIN, James
L 9 Aug 1794
CR 22 Jan 1806
d (drowned) 22 Jan 1809 (CH)

MEIN, John
L 21 Mar 1812
HP May 1821 (OB)
Ret CR 18 Apr 1854 (PRO)
d 1864 (PRO)

MELCOMBE, John
L 15 Sept 1777
CR 25 Sept 1781
d 1785 (PRO)

MELDRUM, John
L 1665
d before 1689 (PJP)

MELDRUM, William (1)
L 19 Mar 1744
d 1762 (PRO)

MELDRUM, William (2)
L 29 Jan 1759
d 1800 (PRO)

MELHUISH, John
L 11 Sept 1793
CR 8 Apr 1799
d 25 Apr 1804 (PRO)

MENDS, Sir Robert
L 26 Aug 1789
CR 15 Nov 1796
CA 2 May 1800
Kt (Spain) 25 May 1815 (MB)
Kt 25 May 1815 (DNB)
d 4 Sept 1823 (MB)

MENDS, William Bowen
L 9 Apr 1801
HP 26 Feb 1809–
26 Feb 1811 (OB)
CR 26 Feb 1811
CA 26 May 1814
RAB 19 Mar 1849 (PRO)
RAW 17 Aug 1851 (PRO)
RAR 12 Jan 1854 (PRO)
VAB 31 Jan 1856 (PRO)
Ret VA 17 Oct 1856 (PRO)
Ret A 11 Feb 1861 (PRO)
d 7 July 1864 (PJP)

MENNELL, George
L 8 Dec 1759
d 1780(1) (PRO)

MENNES, Henry
L 1664

MENNES, Sir John
Kt 25 Feb 1642 (DNB)
L
CA 1661
VA 1661
CONT 28 Nov 1661–
18 Feb 1671 (NBO)
d 18 Feb 1671 (NBO)

MENZIES, Alexander
L 6 Oct 1780
d 1800 (PRO)

MENZIES, Duncan
L 1 Apr 1781
SUP CR 1 Jan 1816 (PRO)
d 20 Dec 1846 (PRO)

MENZIES, James
L 11 Jan 1796
d 4 Apr 1804

MERCADELL, Alexander
L 14 May 1808
CR 3 Sept 1814
d 1832 (PRO)

MERCER, Henry Courthouse		
L	17 Mar	1810
d		1820 (PRO)
MERCER, John Davis		
L	8 Dec	1809
CR	9 Sept	1824 (PRO)
HP	9 Sept	1824 (OB)
CA	1 July	1851 (PRO)
d	5 July	1855 (PRO)
MERCER, Paul		
L		1672
CA	3 Apr	1680
d	before	1689 (PJP)
MERCER, William		
L	30 Oct	1793
Ret CR	16 May	1828 (PRO)
d		1836 (PRO)
MERCIER, Charles		
L	28 Feb	1812
d		1819 (PRO)
MEREDITH, David		
L	11 Apr	1746
d		1770 (PRO)
MEREDITH, Richard		
T		
L	15 Aug	1806
CR	16 Mar	1824 (PRO)
CA	6 June	1837 (PRO)
d	13 July	1850 (PRO)
MEREDITH, Samuel		
L	24 Nov	1815
CR	7 May	1828 (PRO)
Ret CA	1 Apr	1856 (PRO)
d	13 May	1873 (PRO)
MERES, James		
L	2 Aug	1794
d	7 Mar	1836 (LT)
MERRICK, William Augustus		
L	23 Apr	1774
CR	13 Sept	1779
CA	19 Apr	1782
d	18 Dec	1785 (M)
MERRIMAN, Charles		
L	27 Feb	1815
d	18 June	1859 (PRO)
MERRITON, Henry		
L	18 Oct	1693 (PJP)
MERRYWEATHER, John		
L		1665
d	29 Jan	1673 (NJ)
MESSERVY, Francis		
L	16 Sept	1779
SUP CR	17 Mar	1814
d		1818 (PRO)
MESURIER, Edward, Frederick or William le		
See LE MESURIER, Edward, Frederick or William		
METCALFE, Stephen		
L	14 Oct	1761
d	20 Oct	1790
METCALFE, William		
L	29 Oct	1722
d		1741 (PRO)
METHVEN, Thomas		
L	19 Jan	1798 (PRO)
CR	21 Feb	1812
d	22 Jan	1833 (PRO)
MEYNELL, Henry		
L	8 Nov	1809 (PRO)
CR	24 Aug	1813
CA	10 Apr	1816 (PRO)
HP	28 June	1838 (OB)
RAB	29 Apr	1851 (PRO)
Ret RA	1 July	1851 (PRO)
Ret VA	9 July	1857 (PRO)
Ret A	4 Oct	1862 (PRO)
d	25 Mar	1865 (PRO)
MIALL, George Gover		
L	11 Apr	1808
CR	28 June	1838 (PRO)
CA	7 Mar	1853 (PRO)
d		1868 (PRO)
MICHELL, Alexander		
L	14 June	1731
d		1748(9) (PRO)
MICHELL, Andrew		
L		
CA	12 July	1677
d	before	1689 (PJP)
MICHELL, Sir David		
See MITCHELL, Sir David		
MICHELL, Sir Frederick Thomas		
L	29 May	1807
CR	16 Sept	1816 (PRO)
CA	22 Feb	1830 (PRO)
CB		1855 (PJP)
RAB	9 July	1855 (PRO)
RAW	14 May	1857 (PRO)
RAR	25 June	1858 (PRO)
VAB	16 June	1862 (PRO)
VAW	25 June	1863 (PRO)
VAR	9 Feb	1864 (PRO)
A	2 Apr	1866 (PRO)
KCB		1867 (PJP)
d	14 Jan	1873 (PRO)
MICHELL, John		
L		
CR	7 Jan	1708 (PMM)
CA	31 Mar	1708
d	5 Aug	1746
MICHELL, John Taylor		
L	4 July	1793
CR	6 May	1797
CA	29 Apr	1802
d	6 Jan	1833 (PRO)
MICHELL, Matthew		
See MITCHELL, Matthew		
MICHELL, Reynell		
L	19 July	1759
d		1802 (PRO)
MICHELL, Sampson		
L	5 Aug	1778
d	Jan	1809
MIDDLEHURST, James		
L	18 June	1757
d		1761 (PRO)
MIDDLEMORE, John		
L	1 Dec	1796
d		1798 (PRO)

MIDDLETON, Arthur
L 1665
d before 1689 (PJP)
MIDDLETON, Charles
L 31 July 1782
d 1785 (PRO)
MIDDLETON, Sir Charles
See BARHAM, Hon. Charles, Lord
MIDDLETON, Christopher
L
CR 5 Mar 1741
d 12 Feb 1770 (DNB)
MIDDLETON, Hon. Digby Willoughby, Lord
L 10 Jan 1794 (OB)
CR 7 May 1802 (OB)
Inh EP 19 June 1835 (OB)
Ret CA 10 Sept 1840 (OB)
MIDDLETON, Henry
L
CA 13 Oct 1694
d (drowned) 29 Jan 1703 (CH)
MIDDLETON, Hugh (1)
L
CA 1660
MIDDLETON, Sir Hugh (2)
L
CR
CA 1 Jan 1713
Dismissed 1727
Restored
MIDDLETON, James
L 27 Dec 1808
d 22 July 1822 (PRO)
MIDDLETON, John
L 29 Oct 1811
Ret CR 1 Apr 1853 (PRO)
d 29 Jan 1867 (PRO)
MIDDLETON, Robert
L 13 Apr 1741
d 1753 (PRO)
MIDDLETON, Robert Gambier
L 1 Jan 1793
CR
CA 11 Aug 1794
SUP CA 1812 (PRO)
Ret RA 9 June 1832 (PRO)
d 21 Aug 1837 (LT)
MIDDLETON, Thomas (1)
L 21 Sept 1790
d 1798 (PRO)
MIDDLETON, Thomas (2)
L 18 May 1797
d 16 July 1800
MIDDLETON, William
L 1673
MIDWINTER, John
L 25 June 1743
CR 5 June 1747
d 1753 (PRO)
MIGHELLS, James
L
CA 24 Aug 1694
RAB 18 Mar 1718
RAW 28 Mar 1718
RAR 5 Mar 1719
VAB 7 Mar 1719
(7 Mar 1718 in H)
CONT 9 Feb 1723–
21 Mar 1734 (NBO)
d 21 Mar 1734 (NBO)
MIGHELLS, John
See MICHELL, John
MIGHELLS, Joseph (1)
?L 11 June 1692
CR
CA 30 Mar 1703
d 30 Aug 1707
MIGHELLS, Joseph (2)
L 16 Feb 1706 (PMM)
MIGHELLS, Josiah
See MIGHELLS, Joseph
MIHELL, Best
L 4 Dec 1739
CR 6 Sept 1747
d 1755(6) (PRO)
MIHELL, John
See MICHELL, John
MILBANK, Henry
T wounded
L 16 Mar 1808
d 1808 (PRO)
MILBANK, William
L 1 Apr 1760
d 1766 (PRO)
MILBANK, Mark
L 20 Apr 1744
CR 13 Sept 1746
CA 21 May 1748
HP 1748–1755 (DNB)
HP 1763–1775 (DNB)
RAW 29 Mar 1779 (CH)
VAB 26 Sept 1780
VAW 24 Sept 1787
VAR 21 Sept 1790
AB 1 Feb 1793
AW 1 June 1793
d 10 June 1805 (DNB)
MILBANKE, Ralph (1)
L 14 Nov 1776
CR 12 Sept 1781
CA 20 July 1782
SUP CA 23 Apr 1804 (PRO)
d 21 Nov 1823 (LT)
MILBANKE, Ralph (2)
L 11 Mar 1778 (PRO)
Promotion to CR never confirmed
d (drowned) 5 Oct 1780 (CH)
MILBOURNE, Charles Robert
L 22 Jan 1813
CR 6 Sept 1823 (PRO)
d 29 Jan 1833 (LT)
MILDMAY, Hon. Francis John St. John
L 20 Sept 1815
CR 25 Nov 1821 (PRO)
d 31 Aug 1823 (PRO)
MILDMAY, George William St. John
L 19 May 1812
CR 10 Aug 1822 (OB)
CA 16 Aug 1828 (OB)
d 1851 (PRO)

MILDREDGE, Matthew
L 24 Mar 1808
d 14 Oct 1810 (PJP)

MILES, Edmund
L 8 Feb 1815
HP 8 Feb 1815 (OB)
d 1856 (PRO)

MILES, Jefferson
L 23 July 1807
Ret CR 28 July 1843 (PRO)
d 19 June 1844 (PRO)

MILES, John
L 1666

MILES, John William
L 30 Aug 1800
d 1810 (PRO)

MILES, Thomas (1)
L 12 Feb 1690
Gone 1719 (PRO)

MILES, Thomas (2)
L 29 July 1779
SUP CR 31 Jan 1814
d 1817 (PRO)

MILES, Thomas (3)
L 7 Jan 1783
CR 9 Nov 1795
CA 29 Apr 1802
d 20 Mar 1822 (PRO)

MILLAR, Archibald
L 21 May 1746
CR 29 Sept 1757
CA 16 June 1761
d 14 Sept 1766 (M)

MILLAR, Thomas
L 29 Mar 1802
d 1807 (PRO)

MILLBANK, Mark
See MILBANK, Mark

MILLER, Adlart
L 18 Feb 1815
d 1838 (PRO)

MILLER, Alexander
L 27 July 1812
d 1851 (PRO)

MILLER, Archibald
See MILLAR, Archibald

MILLER, Charles (1)
L 3 May 1705 (PMM)
d 13 June 1707

MILLER, Charles (2)
L 10 May 1810
Struck off list 17 Mar 1821 (PRO)

MILLER, Charles Fitzgerald
L 17 Dec 1779
d 1789 (PRO)

MILLER, Daniel (1)
L 20 Sept 1798
CR 4 Mar 1819 (PRO)
d Dec 1827 (PRO)

MILLER, Daniel (2)
L 2 Aug 1806
d 3 May 1824 (PRO)

MILLER, David (1)
L 18 Oct 1745
d 1755(6) (PRO)

MILLER, David (2)
L 20 Apr 1778
d 1811 (PRO)

MILLER, George (1)
L 1 Mar 1758
d 1760 (PRO)

MILLER, George (2)
L 6 May 1794
CR 18 Nov 1799
CA 29 Apr 1802
d 15 Sept 1812 (PRO)

MILLER, Henry George
L 7 July 1797
d 13 Aug 1825 (PRO)

MILLER, James
L 16 Jan 1692
In Merchant Service 1700 (PJP)

MILLER, John (1)
L 21 Sept 1790
CR 12 Dec 1796
CA 11 Sept 1797
SUP CA 1821 (PRO)
d 26 July 1843 (PRO)

MILLER, John (2)
L 7 Feb 1815
d July 1829 (PRO)

MILLER, John Francis
L 31 Jan 1806
d 1809 (PRO)

MILLER, Joseph
L 8 Dec 1809
d 1833 (PRO)

MILLER, Lewis
L 5 Apr 1797
d 1799 (PRO)

MILLER, Martin
L 21 Mar 1812
d 1826 (PRO)

MILLER, Ralph Willett
L 25 May 1781
CR 1 July 1794
CA 12 Jan 1796
KIA 14 May 1799 (LG)

MILLER, Robert
L 23 Apr 1741
d 1758 (PRO)

MILLER, Roger
L
CA 1666
KIA 4 June 1666 (CH)

MILLER, Simon
L
CR 22 Mar 1783
CA 4 Nov 1794
SUP RA 16 Aug 1814
d May 1825 (PRO)

MILLER, Thomas
L 9 Feb 1802
d 1803 (PRO)

MILLER, Thomas		
See MILLAR, Thomas		
MILLER, William (1)		
L	14 May	1703
CR		
CA	18 Nov	1727
d	17 July	1750 (PMM)
MILLER, William (2)		
L	18 Mar	1778
CR	14 Apr	1782
d		1786 (PRO)
MILLER, William (3)		
L	9 Mar	1780
SUP CR	22 Sept	1814
d	22 Feb	1831 (PRO)
MILLER, William (4)		
L	17 Dec	1782
d		1789 (PRO)
MILLER, William (5)		
L	26 Apr	1797
Ret CR	6 July	1839 (PRO)
d		1844 (PRO)
MILLESON, James		
L	3 Feb	1694
CR	28 Nov	1704 (PRO)
d		1727(8) (PRO)
MILLET, William Smith		
L	25 Jan	1802
T		
d		1804 (PRO)
MILLETT, Henry		
L		1660
CA		1666
d	before	1688 (PD)
MILLETT, John		
L	15 Feb	1815
Ret CR	18 Jan	1861 (PRO)
d		1870 (PRO)
MILLETT, Richard (1)		
L		
CA	9 June	1666 (RM)
MILLETT, Richard (2)		
L	21 Mar	1812
d	18 July	1812 (PRO)
MILLETT, William		
L	4 Dec	1806
d	Jan	1821 (PRO)
MILLETT, William Smith		
See MILLET, William Smith		
MILLIGAN, John		
L	28 June	1746
CR	27 Feb	1761
CA	26 May	1768
d		1788
MILLISON, Gabriel (1)		
L		1673
CA	14 Dec	1688
MILLISON, Gabriel (2)		
L		
CA	9 June	1695 (PJP)
MILLS, Adrian		
L	23 Dec	1695
Gone		1719 (PRO)
MILLS, Brace		
L	1 June	1721
d		1727(8) (PRO)
MILLS, George		
L	20 May	1807
d		1819 (PRO)
MILLS, George Frederick		
L	19 June	1800
d		1805(6) (PRO)
MILLS, John		
L		1670
MILN, James		
L	8 Aug	1793 (PRO)
KIA	10 Mar	1794 (LG)
MILN, Robert		
L	11 Aug	1800
d	Oct	1824 (PRO)
MILNE, Colin		
L	12 Apr	1799
d		1811 (PRO)
MILNE, Sir David		
L	13 Jan	1794
CR	26 Apr	1795
CA	2 Oct	1795
RAB	4 June	1814
KCB	21 Sept	1816 (DNB)
Kt (Netherlands)		1816 (DNB)
Kt (Two Sicilies)		1816 (DNB)
RAW	12 Aug	1819 (CH)
MP (Berwick)		1820 (DNB)
RAR	19 July	1821 (CH)
VAB	27 May	1825 (CH)
VAW	22 July	1830 (CH)
VAR	10 Jan	1837 (CH)
GCB	4 July	1840 (DNB)
AW	23 Nov	1841 (CH)
d	5 May	1845 (DNB)
MILNE, George		
L	26 Dec	1796
KIA	21 Aug	1800 (LG)
MILNE, James		
L	24 Oct	1794
Ret CR	14 May	1832 (PRO)
d	3 Sept	1833 (LT)
MILNE, Robert (1)		
L	5 Aug	1707
Gone		1734 (PRO)
MILNE, Robert (2)		
L	6 Sept	1760
d		1796 (PRO)
MILNE, Robert		
See MILN, Robert		
MILNE, William (1)		
L	18 Nov	1799
d	27 Jan	1825 (PRO)
MILNE, William (2)		
L	19 Nov	1807
Ret CR	24 July	1844 (PRO)
d		1852 (PRO)
MILNER, Alexander		
L	1 Dec	1795

CR	8 July	1797 (PRO)
CA	12 Aug	1812
d	15 Feb	1823 (PRO)
MILNER, Edmund		
L	28 Apr	1802
Ret CR	5 Feb	1834 (PRO)
d		1841 (PRO)
MILNER, Rowland		
L	27 Dec	1808
Struck off list	26 Nov	1822 (PRO)
MILNER, William		
L	7 Dec	1779
d		1802 (PRO)
MILTON, William		
L	10 Feb	1747
d		1766 (PRO)
MILWARD, Clement		
L	8 July	1800
CR	14 June	1809
CA	28 May	1813
Ret RA	1 Oct	1846 (PRO)
d	14 Jan	1857 (PRO)
MILWARD, Thomas		
L	18 Oct	1759
d		1780 (PRO)
MINCHIN, Paul		
L	20 Oct	1779
CR		
CA	18 Dec	1783
RAB	9 Nov	1805
RAW	28 Apr	1808
VAB	31 July	1810
d		1810 (PRO)
MINCHIN, William		
L	27 Dec	1796
CR	19 July	1821 (OB)
d	7 Sept	1845 (OB)
MINGAYE, William James		
L	6 July	1805
CR	2 Oct	1817 (PRO)
CA	29 Jan	1822 (PRO)
RAB	1 Oct	1852 (PRO)
RAW	15 Apr	1854 (PRO)
RAR	31 Jan	1856 (PRO)
VAB	4 Nov	1857 (PRO)
VAW	25 June	1858 (PRO)
Ret VA	18 Dec	1858 (PRO)
Ret A	27 Apr	1863 (PRO)
d	30 Nov	1865 (PRO)
MINGEAM, John		
See MINGEN, John		
MINGEN, John		
L		
CA		1666 (DDA)
d	before	1689 (PJP)
MINGS, Sir Christopher		
See MYNGS, Sir Christopher		
MINISIE, John		
L	22 Jan	1761
d		1772 (PRO)
MINORS, Richard		
L		1665
CA		1661
MINSTER, Peter Ryder		
L	30 Oct	1793
Ret CR	11 Jan	1828 (PRO)
d	7 Feb	1836 (PRO)
MINTERNE, William		
L		1666
CA		1667 (DDA)
MIST, Charles		
L	31 Mar	1779
d		1786 (PRO)
MITCHEL, Cornelius, Henry and John		
See MITCHELL, Cornelius, Henry and John		
MITCHELL, Ambrose		
L	28 Jan	1706 (PMM)
MITCHELL, Sir Andrew (1)		
L	11 Oct	1777 (DNB)
CR	10 Aug	1778 (DNB)
CA	25 Oct	1778
RAB	1 June	1795
RAW	20 Feb	1797
VAB	14 Feb	1799
Kt	9 Jan	1800 (DNB)
VAW	1 Jan	1801
VAR	23 Apr	1804
AB	9 Nov	1805
d	26 Feb	1806 (PRO)
MITCHELL, Andrew (2)		
L	15 Aug	1808
CR	24 Aug	1813
CA	23 Apr	1822 (PRO)
d		1840 (PRO)
MITCHELL, Bowles		
L	18 May	1777
SUP CR	24 Aug	1810
d	18 Jan	1824 (PRO)
MITCHELL, Charles		
L	11 Aug	1806
CR	24 May	1811
CA	8 Apr	1825 (PRO)
d	25 Nov	1834 (PJP)
MITCHELL, Cornelius		
L	22 Dec	1720
CR	20 June	1729 (PRO)
CA	14 June	1731
Dismissed	28 Jan	1748 (DNB)
d		1749
MITCHELL, Sir David		
L	16 Jan	1678 (P)
CA	1 Oct	1683 (DNB)
MFMR	26 Oct	1691 (EAD)
RAB	7 Feb	1693
VAB	4 July	1693
Kt		1694 (DNB)
LCFMR	14 Oct	1695 (EAD)
COM AD	31 May	1699–
	26 Jan	1702 (AO)
VAW	28 Jan	1702
MCLHA	22 May	1702–
	19 Apr	1708 (AO)
d	1 June	1710
MITCHELL, Duncan Forbes		
L	16 Nov	1790
d		1797 (PRO)
MITCHELL, Edward James		
L	9 May	1794

CR	29 Apr	1802
d		1805 (PRO)
MITCHELL, George		
L	3 Mar	1815
d		1857 (PRO)
MITCHELL, Gilbert John		
L	2 Mar	1803
d		1839 (PRO)
MITCHELL, Henry		
L	28 Oct	1703
Gone		1727 (PRO)
MITCHELL, Hercules		
L		
CR	26 Sept	1697 (PRO)
CA	29 June	1701 (PRO)
d (drowned)	11 Aug	1705 (CH)
MITCHELL, James (1)		
L	21 Oct	1756
d		1773 (PRO)
MITCHELL, James (2)		
L	13 Aug	1812
d		1815 (PRO)
MITCHELL, John (1)		
L		
CA	3 Jan	1695
	(14 Feb	1694 in H)
SUP		1712
MITCHELL, John (2)		
L	26 Nov	1779
d		1793 (PRO)
MITCHELL, John (3)		
L	21 Nov	1794
d		1799 (PRO)
MITCHELL, John (4)		
L	26 Feb	1801
Ret CR	20 Dec	1830 (PRO)
d		1832 (PRO)
MITCHELL, John (5)		
L	4 Dec	1801
MITCHELL, John (6)		
L	19 Nov	1811
d	24 Dec	1811 (PRO)
MITCHELL, John Taylor		
See MICHELL, John Taylor		
MITCHELL, Matthew (1)		
L	11 Apr	1728
CR	28 July	1738 (PRO)
CA	30 June	1740 (MPS)
Resigned	Mar	1748 (DNB)
MP	16 Nov	1748–
(Westbury)	29 Apr	1752 (MPS)
d	29 Apr	1752
MITCHELL, Matthew (2)		
L	16 Aug	1814
d		1834 (PRO)
MITCHELL, Nathaniel		
L	22 May	1807
CR	5 Apr	1810
CA	7 June	1814
d	24 Nov	1842 (PRO)
MITCHELL, Peter		
L	12 Aug	1801
T		
d	14 Feb	1807 (TR)
MITCHELL, Richard (1)		
L	20 Dec	1806
d		1816 (PRO)
MITCHELL, Richard (2)		
L	18 Dec	1813 (OB)
MITCHELL, Richard Alexander Slocombe		
L	29 Dec	1808
MITCHELL, Spalding		
L	22 Jan	1806
Ret CR	13 Oct	1848 (PMM)
d	22 Aug	1866 (PRO)
MITCHELL, Thomas (1)		
L		
CA	25 July	1699
SUP		1707
d	23 Feb	1715
MITCHELL, Thomas (2)		
L	7 Nov	1801
d		1810 (PRO)
MITCHELL, Thomas (3)		
L	29 Apr	1802
Ret CR	25 Mar	1834 (PRO)
d	30 July	1861 (PRO)
MITCHELL, Sir William		
L	2 Nov	1781
CR	27 Apr	1782
CA	22 Nov	1790
RAB	28 Apr	1808
RAW	31 July	1810
RAR	1 Aug	1811
VAB	4 Dec	1813
VAW	4 June	1814
KCB		1815 (PJP)
d	7 Mar	1816 (LT)
MITCHENER, George		
T		
L	5 July	1806
CR	27 July	1825 (PRO)
d		1828 (PRO)
MITFORD, Henry		
L	26 Aug	1789
CR		
CA	2 Feb	1796
d (drowned)	21 Jan	1804 (CH)
MITFORD, Robert		
L	13 Jan	1802
CR	16 Feb	1807
CA	31 Mar	1813
Ret RA	1 Oct	1846 (PRO)
Ret VA	28 Dec	1855 (PRO)
Ret A	11 Feb	1861 (PRO)
d	15 June	1870 (PRO)
MITHERELL, Anthony		
L	22 May	1758
d		1778 (PRO)
MITTEN, William		
L	2 Mar	1808
d		1832 (PRO)
MOAT, William		
L	27 Feb	1801
d		1809 (PRO)
MOBERLY, John		
L	14 Oct	1807

CR 29 May 1813
CA 26 Aug 1815
Ret CA 1 Oct 1846 (PRO)
d 15 Jan 1848 (PRO)

MOCKLER, Thomas
T
L 31 Mar 1810
d 1840 (TR)

MOE, Cheeseman
L 12 Oct 1805
d 26 Oct 1838 (PRO)

MOFFATT, John
L 13 Mar 1811
d 29 Apr 1849 (PRO)

MOFFAT(T), Richard
L 14 Feb 1815
d 4 Feb 1822 (PRO)

MOFFAT(T), Thomas
L 20 Apr 1813
d 20 Dec 1831 (PRO)

MOFFETT, Thomas Wiggins
L 23 Dec 1814
d 1838 (PRO)

MOGAN, David
See MORGAN, David

MOGG, Thomas
L 28 July 1726
CR 31 July 1741
CA 16 July 1744
d 22 Oct 1756

MOHUN, Francis
L 23 July 1739
d 1744(5) (PRO)

MOHUN, George
L
CA 5 June 1697 (PJP)
d 28 Aug 1702 (PJP)

MOHUN, Robert
L 1660
CA 1662
d before 1688 (PD)

MOLESWORTH, Bourchier
L 14 Oct 1805
CR 16 May 1814
HP 1814 (OB)
Ret CA 1 July 1851 (PRO)
d 7 Nov 1855 (PRO)

MOLESWORTH, Edward
L 8 Mar 1742
d 1746(7) (PRO)

MOLESWORTH, Francis
T
L 26 Nov 1806
d (suicide) 23 May 1812 (PJP)

MOLESWORTH, John
L 24 Apr 1808
CR 14 Dec 1821 (PRO)
Ret CA 1 Apr 1856 (PRO)
d 14 Aug 1858 (PRO)

MOLINEUX, Charles John
L 27 June 1814
d 1815 (PRO)

MOLINEUX, Henry Moore
L 21 Apr 1813
d 23 Dec 1822 (PRO)

MOLINEUX, James
L 1 Oct 1794
CR 4 May 1810
d 8 Sept 1833 (LT)

MOLINEUX, John
See MOLYNEUX, John

MOLLOY, Anthony James Pye
L 3 Aug 1768
CR 6 July 1776
CA 11 Apr 1778
Dismissed 16 May 1795 (PRO)
d 25 July 1814 (PRO)

MOLLOY, Sir Charles
L 16 Mar 1705 (PRO)
CR 18 Apr 1719
CA 6 Apr 1742
SUP 1753
d 24 Aug 1760

MOLLOY, Michael
L 5 Aug 1813
d 1834 (PRO)

MOLYNEUX, John
L 28 Jan 1794
Struck off list 13 Aug 1798 (PRO)

MOLYNEUX, Charles John, Henry Moore and James
See MOLINEUX, Charles John, Henry Moore and James

MONCK, George, Duke of Albermarle
See ALBEMARLE, George, Duke of

MONCK, Thomas
L 30 Apr 1678 (P)
CA 15 May 1690
d 1715

MONCKTON, John
See MONKTON, John

MONCKTON, Hon. Robert Henry
L 3 Mar 1804
d 1815 (PRO)

MON(C)KTON, William
L 13 Aug 1697
Gone 1719 (PRO)

MONCRIEF(F), Robert
L 15 Mar 1796
d 20 Jan 1798

MONCUR, John
L 20 Sept 1799
CR 22 July 1796
d 5 Apr 1814 (LT)

MONDAY, Edward
L 7 Nov 1806
HP 1814 (OB)
CR 9 Nov 1846 (PRO)
Ret CA 30 July 1863 (PRO)
d 12 Aug 1867 (PRO)

MONDAY, John
L 27 June 1814
CR 22 Oct 1827 (PRO)
CA 27 Dec 1838 (PRO)
HP 27 Dec 1838 (OB)

Ret CA	2 Aug	1853 (PRO)
Ret RA	20 Jan	1858 (PRO)
Ret VA	13 Apr	1865 (PRO)
d	Aug	1867 (PRO)
MONEY, James		
L	27 Feb	1800
Ret CR	25 Feb	1831 (PRO)
d		1832 (PRO)
MONEY, Rowland		
L	12 Jan	1805
CR	9 Nov	1809
CA	29 Mar	1815
Ret CA	1 Oct	1846 (PRO)
Ret RA	6 Nov	1850 (PRO)
Ret VA	9 July	1857 (PRO)
d	21 June	1860 (PRO)
MONEYPENNY, James		
L	16 Apr	1697
CR		
CA	16 Aug	1704
d	23 Oct	1723
MONEYPENNY, James See MONYPENNY, James		
MONILAWS, William		
L	10 Feb	1812
CR	20 Sept	1815
d		1833 (PRO)
MONK, George Mitford		
L	23 Jan	1812
d	11 Mar	1858 (PRO)
MONK, John		
L	13 June	1814
CR	11 Feb	1868 (PRO)
d (suicide)	2 May	1880 (PRO)
MONK, Thomas See MONCK, Thomas		
MONKE, George Paris		
L	17 Nov	1781
CR	11 Mar	1797
CA	12 Jan	1810
d	14 Nov	1828 (PRO)
MONKTON, John		
L	19 Nov	1777
HP		1783–1784 (MB)
CR	6 July	1794
CA	29 June	1795
SUP RA	18 June	1814
d	31 Aug	1826 (PRO)
MONKTON, Robert Henry and William See MONCKTON, Robert Henry and William		
MONTAGU(E), Charles See MOUNTAGUE, Charles		
MONTAGUE, Edward, Earl of Sandwich See SANDWICH, Earl of		
MONTAGU, Edward See MOUNTAGUE, Edward		
MONTAGU, Edward Proudfoot		
L	1 July	1814 (PRO)
Ret CR	28 Oct	1857 (PRO)
d	8 Jan	1862 (PRO)
MONTAGU, Sir George		
L	14 Jan	1771
CR	9 Apr	1773
CA	15 Apr	1774
RAB	12 Apr	1794
RAW	4 July	1794
VAB	1 June	1795
VAR	14 Feb	1799
AB	1 Jan	1801
AW	9 Nov	1805
AR	31 July	1810
GCB	2 Jan	1815 (DNB)
d	24 Dec	1829 (DNB)
MONTAGU, James (1)		
L	18 Oct	1771
CR	11 Sept	1773
CA	14 Nov	1775
KIA	1 June	1794 (LG)
MONTAGU, James (2)		
L	1 May	1795
Gone		1811 (PRO)
MONTAGU, James (3)		
L	17 Aug	1810
CR	7 June	1814
CA	17 July	1824 (PRO)
Ret CA	1 Oct	1846 (PRO)
Ret RA	4 July	1853 (PRO)
Ret VA	24 Feb	1858 (PRO)
Ret A	30 Nov	1863 (PRO)
d	9 Mar	1868 (PRO)
MONTAGU, John		
L	22 Dec	1740
CR	2 Mar	1745 (DNB)
CA	15 Jan	1746
MP (Huntingdon)	10 Nov	1748–1754 (MPS)
RAB	24 Oct	1770
RAR	31 Mar	1775
GG (Newfoundland)		1776–1782 (BNS)
VAB	5 Feb	1776
VAW	18 Apr	1777
VAR	29 Jan	1779
AB	8 Apr	1782
AW	24 Sept	1787
d	7 Sept	1795 (CH)
MONTAGU, John William		
L	9 Oct	1809 (PRO)
CR	31 May	1814
CA	30 Nov	1820 (PRO)
Ret CA	1 Oct	1846 (PRO)
Ret RA	8 Mar	1852 (PRO)
Ret VA	2 Oct	1857 (PRO)
Ret A	27 Apr	1863 (PRO)
d	12 Dec	1882 (PRO)
MONTAGU, Montague See MONTAGUE, Montague		
MONTAGU, Robert		
L	5 Apr	1779
CR		1780 (PJP)
CA	3 Mar	1781
RAB	14 Feb	1799
RAW	1 Jan	1801
RAR	23 Apr	1804
VAB	9 Nov	1805
VAW	28 Apr	1808
AB	31 July	1810
AW	4 June	1814
AR	27 May	1825 (PRO)
d	27 Nov	1830 (PRO)
MONTAGU, Sidney Wortley		
L	17 Mar	1702 (PMM)

MONTAGU, Thomas
See MONTAGUE, Thomas
MONTAGU, Hon. William
See MONTAGUE, Hon. William
MONTAGU, William Augustus

L	14 Nov	1804
CR	31 Oct	1805
CA	12 Oct	1807
CB	8 Dec	1815 (MB)
Kt	Jan	1832 (OB)
KCH	22 Feb	1832 (LG)
RAB	23 Nov	1841 (LG)
RAW	20 Nov	1846 (PRO)
RAR	3 Mar	1849 (LG)
VAB	17 Aug	1851 (PRO)
d	6 Mar	1852 (PRO)

MONTAGUE, George
See MONTAGU, Sir George
MONTAGUE, Montague

L	5 Mar	1806
CR	13 June	1815
HP	13 June	1815 (OB)
Ret CA	10 Jan	1853 (PRO)
d	Aug	1863 (PRO)

MONTAGUE, Thomas

L	19 Feb	1756
d		1786 (PRO)

MONTAGUE, Hon. William

L	20 Sept	1741 (DNB)
CR	23 May	1744 (DNB)
CA	23 May	1745
MP (Huntingdon)		1745–1752 (DNB)
MP (Bossiney)		1752–1757 (DNB)
d	12 Feb	1757 (PRO)

MONTGOMERIE, Alexander

L	4 May	1810
CR	7 June	1814
CA	3 Oct	1820 (PRO)
Ret CA	1 Oct	1846 (PRO)
Ret RA	8 Mar	1852 (PRO)
Ret VA	2 Oct	1857 (PRO)
Ret A	27 Apr	1863 (PRO)
d	26 Dec	1863 (PRO)

MONTGOMERY, Augustus

L		
CR		
CA	24 May	1782
d	6 Feb	1797 (PRO)

MONTGOMERY, Charles

L	8 July	1774
d		1777 (PRO)

MONTGOMERY, Hugh

T		
L	22 Jan	1806
d		1837 (TR)

MONTGOMERY, James

L		1673
CA	10 July	1686
Dismissed	24 Mar	1689

MONTGOMERY, Roger

L	3 June	1797
d	Jan	1798 (PJP)

MONTGOMERY, Thomas

L	1 Oct	1806
HP		1810–1811 (OB)
CR	13 June	1815
Ret CA	9 Apr	1853 (PRO)
d		1869 (PRO)

MONTRESOR, Henry

L	8 July	1796
CR	11 Apr	1809 (PRO)
CB	4 June	1815 (MB)
CA	13 June	1815
d	8 May	1833 (PRO)

MONTRESOR, James

L	15 June	1760
d (drowned)		1770 (PJP)

MONYPENNY, James

L	17 Oct	1735
d	19 Feb	1788 (PMM)

MOODIE, Charles

L	16 Jan	1693 (PJP)

MOODIE, James (1)

L	10 Oct	1688 (P)
CA	14 Apr	1690
d (murdered)	26 Oct	1725 (DNB)

MOODIE, James (2)

L	18 Apr	1811
d		1814 (PRO)

MOODIE, John

L	21 Feb	1741
d		1755(6) (PRO)

MOODIE, Joseph

L	24 Feb	1795
d		1796 (PRO)

MOODIE, Robert

L	8 Oct	1807
d		1840 (PRO)

MOODY, Thomas

L	29 Jan	1748
SUP CR	21 Sept	1796 (PMM)
d	11 Nov	1807 (PJP)

MOON, William

L	6 June	1744
d		1748(9) (PRO)

MOOR, Henry

L	17 Aug	1801
d		1808 (PRO)

MOOR, Joseph
See MOORE, Joseph
MOOR, Philip

L	16 Feb	1815
HP	16 Feb	1815 (OB)
Ret CR	18 Jan	1861 (PRO)
d		1873 (PRO)

MOORE, Adrian

L	17 Sept	1735
d		1742(3) (PRO)

MOORE, Charles (1)

L	7 Jan	1812
d		1835 (PRO)

MOORE, Charles (2)

L	26 Jan	1813
CR	24 June	1817 (PRO)
Ret CA	1 Apr	1856 (PRO)
d	10 Nov	1870 (PRO)

MOORE, Christopher

L	24 Dec	1694 (PJP)

CA 28 June 1695
d 29 Apr 1696

MOORE, Edward (1)
L 1 Dec 1794
d 1824 (PRO)

MOORE, Edward (2)
T
L 13 Mar 1815
HP July 1815 (OB)
d 1857 (TR)

MOORE, Sir Graham
L 8 Mar 1782
CR 22 Nov 1790
CA 2 Apr 1794
RAB 12 Aug 1812
RAR 4 June 1814
KCB 2 Jan 1815 (DNB)
COM AD 24 May 1816–
13 Mar 1820 (AO)
VAB 12 Aug 1819 (CH)
GCMG 28 Sept 1820 (DNB)
VAW 27 May 1825 (CH)
VAR 22 July 1830 (CH)
GCB 23 Mar 1836 (LG)
AB 10 Jan 1837 (CH)
AW 23 Nov 1841 (CH)
d 25 Nov 1843 (DNB)

MOORE, Henry
L 18 Feb 1815
d 10 Aug 1829 (PRO)

MOORE, Henry
See MOOR, Henry

MOORE, Howard
L 27 June 1814
d 1849 (PRO)

MOORE, John (1)
L
CA 1665
d before 1689 (PJP)

MOORE, Sir John (2)
L 6 Apr 1738 (DNB)
CR
CA 24 Dec 1743
RAR 21 Oct 1762
Cre Bt 4 Mar 1766 (DNB)
VAB 18 Oct 1770
VAW 24 Oct 1770
Kt 1772 (DNB)
VAR 31 Mar 1775
AB 29 Jan 1778
d 2 Feb 1779

MOORE, John (3)
?L 12 May 1740
CR 2 May 1757
d 1803 (PRO)

MOORE, John (4)
L 26 July 1762
d 14 Apr 1792

MOORE, John (5)
L 12 Feb 1801
d 1831 (PRO)

MOORE, John (6)
L 24 July 1801
HP Oct 1801–
7 Jan 1804 (OB)
Ret CR 25 July 1831 (PRO)
d 1849 (PRO)

MOORE, John (7)
L 5 May 1812 (PRO)
d 1837 (PRO)

MOORE, John (8)
L 19 Oct 1814
HP 1815 (OB)
Ret CR 23 Feb 1859 (PRO)
d 15 Feb 1871 (PRO)

MOORE, John Alfred
L 7 Feb 1811
d 19 Nov 1831 (LT)

MOORE, John Arthur
L 18 Feb 1815
d 1860 (PRO)

MOORE, John Hartnoll
L 14 Mar 1815
d 8 Jan 1830 (PRO)

MOORE, John James
L 7 Nov 1809
HP 1814 (OB)
Ret CR 22 Jan 1850 (PRO)
d 21 Nov 1866 (PRO)

MOORE, Joseph
L 6 Dec 1692 (PJP)
CA 8 Jan 1697
d 27 Feb 1706

MOORE, Joseph Henry
T
L 13 Feb 1815
HP 13 Feb 1815 (OB)
d 1857 (TR)

MOORE, Matthew
L 15 Aug 1743
CR 15 Jan 1748
CA 20 Aug 1756
RAB 26 Sept 1780
d 4 July 1787 (CH)

MOORE, Ogle
L 16 Nov 1804
d 1817 (PRO)

MOORE, Samuel Hewitt
L 4 Apr 1814
d 1833 (PRO)

MOORE, Thomas
L 6 Mar 1747
d 1768 (PRO)

MOORE, William (1)
L 28 Oct 1779
SUP CR 18 Apr 1814
d 1836 (PRO)

MOORE, William (2)
L 27 Sept 1783
d 17 May 1798

MOORE, William (3)
L 16 Nov 1790
CR 24 Dec 1798
d 18 Feb 1830 (PRO)

MOORE, William (4)
L 12 July 1814

Ret CR	28 Oct	1857 (PRO)
d		1880 (PRO)
MOORE, William Henry		
L	8 Feb	1815
Ret CR	9 Jan	1854 (PRO)
d		1880 (PRO)
MOORHEAD, George		
L	24 Dec	1779
d		1807 (PRO)
MOORHEAD, John		
L	6 Mar	1741
d		1742(3) (PRO)
MOORHOUSE, Benjamin		
L	5 Apr	1810
d		1814 (PRO)
MOORMAN, Richard		
L	14 Apr	1807
Kt (Two Sicilies)	14 Mar	1813 (LG)
CR	15 June	1814
HP	15 June	1814 (OB)
d	5 Sept	1850 (PMM)
MOORSOM, Constantine Richard		
L	6 June	1812
CR	19 July	1814
CA	7 Dec	1818 (PRO)
Ret RA	27 Aug	1851 (PRO)
Ret VA	10 Sept	1857 (PRO)
d	26 May	1861 (PRO)
MOORSOM, Sir Robert		
L	5 Jan	1784
CR		
CA	22 Nov	1790
T	wounded	
CRM	28 Apr	1808 (LG)
COM AD	30 Mar	1809–
	3 July	1810 (AO)
RAB	31 July	1810
RAW	1 Aug	1811
MP (Queensborough)	15 Jan	1812–
		1820 (MPT)
RAR	12 Aug	1812
VAB	4 June	1814
KCB	2 Jan	1815 (MPT)
VAW	12 Aug	1819 (CH)
VAR	27 May	1825 (CH)
AB	22 July	1830 (CH)
d	14 May	1835 (MPT)
MOOTHAM, Peter		
L		
CA		1660
KIA	4 June	1666 (RM)
MORAY, John		
L	13 Mar	1734
d		1737 (PRO)
MORCE, William		
L	4 May	1795
CR	27 Apr	1801
d	11 Dec	1823 (PRO)
MORDAUNT, Butler		
L	7 Mar	1708 (PMM)
MORDAUNT, Charles		
See PETERBOROUGH, Earl of		
MORDAUNT, L'Estrange		
L	31 Jan	1706
CR	1 Mar	1740
Gone		1752
MORDAUNT, Hon. Henry		
L		
CR		
CA	9 Apr	1703
MP (Malmesbury)		1705 (DNB)
d	24 Feb	1710 (DNB)
MORDAUNT, John		
L	14 Feb	1705
Gone		1737 (PRO)
MORE, Leighton		
L	3 July	1742
d		1744(5) (PRO)
MORESBY, Sir Fairfax		
L	10 Apr	1806
CR	18 Apr	1811
Kt (Austria)	23 May	1814 (DNB)
CA	7 June	1814
CB	4 June	1815 (DNB)
RAB	20 Dec	1849 (PRO)
RAW	8 Oct	1852 (PRO)
RAR	26 May	1854 (PRO)
KCB		1855 (PJP)
VAB	12 Nov	1856 (PRO)
VAW	10 Sept	1857 (PRO)
VAR	25 June	1858 (PRO)
AB	12 Apr	1862 (PRO)
AW	27 Apr	1863 (PRO)
GCB	28 Mar	1865 (DNB)
AR	21 Jan	1870 (PRO)
d	21 Jan	1877 (DNB)
MORESBY, Richard		
L	17 Feb	1815
d	Feb	1827 (PRO)
MORETON, Henry		
L	18 Oct	1693
d	8 Apr	1766 (M)
MOREY, George (1)		
L	17 Mar	1781
SUP CR	1 Jan	1816 (PRO)
d		1821 (PRO)
MOREY, George (2)		
T		
L	13 Feb	1815
d	Aug	1842 (TR)
MOREY, John Doling		
T		
L	27 Dec	1808
d	8 Feb	1825 (PRO)
MORGAN, Benjamin		
L	11 Aug	1794
d	9 Jan	1822 (PRO)
MORGAN, Charles		
L	15 June	1781
SUP CR	1 June	1816 (PRO)
d		1817 (PRO)
MORGAN, David		
L	11 Jan	1722
d	29 Dec	1727
MORGAN, James (1)		
L	2 Sept	1793

Ret CR 25 Apr 1827 (PRO)
d 1836 (PRO)

MORGAN, James (2)
L 30 Jan 1806
CR 19 July 1819 (PJP)
CA 15 Jan 1836 (PRO)
Ret CA 1 July 1851 (PRO)
Ret RA 19 Mar 1857 (PRO)
d 22 Sept 1862 (PRO)

MORGAN, James Seymour
L 15 Aug 1806
d 1808 (PRO)

MORGAN, Jeremiah (1)
L 22 Nov 1746
CR 11 Aug 1762
d Feb 1773 (M)

MORGAN, Jeremiah (2)
L 18 Oct 1800
T
d 1817 (TR)

MORGAN, John
L 17 Feb 1815
CR 10 Jan 1837 (PRO)
d 2 June 1849 (PRO)

MORGAN, John Fortescue
L 15 Sept 1806
CR 12 Oct 1814
d 9 Dec 1843 (PRO)

MORGAN, Martin
L 1665

MORGAN, Probert
L 15 Feb 1746
d 1756 (PRO)

MORGAN, Rice
L 30 Aug 1799
d 1818 (PRO)

MORGAN, Richard
L 6 Feb 1815
CR 23 Apr 1834 (OB)
HP 1840 (OB)
Ret CA 1 Apr 1856 (PRO)
d 5 June 1867 (PRO)

MORGAN, Robert (1)
L 9 Feb 1815
HP July 1815 (OB)
d 23 Dec 1854 (PRO)

MORGAN, Robert (2)
L 15 Mar 1815
HP Nov 1815 (OB)
d 23 Aug 1849 (PRO)

MORGAN, Rowland
L 16 Feb 1815
d 1826 (PRO)

MORGAN, Thomas
L 10 May 1809
CR 16 Nov 1814
d 1843 (PRO)

MORGAN, Walter
L
CA 1665

MORGAN, William (1)
L 1689 (PJP)
CA 19 Mar 1693
Gone 1718 (PRO)

MORGAN, William (2)
L 9 Apr 1803
CR 14 May 1828 (PRO)
d 1835 (PRO)

MORGAN, William Thomas
T
L 30 Nov 1809
CR 18 Feb 1815
d (drowned) 21 Apr 1822 (TR)

MORIARTY, Edmund Joshua
L 29 June 1776
CR 11 Aug 1779
CA 25 Oct 1809
d 7 Sept 1833 (PJP)

MORIARTY, Edward
L 18 Nov 1799
d 1809 (PRO)

MORIARTY, James (1)
L 1777 (PRO)

MORIARTY, James (2)
L 24 Dec 1805
Ret CR 7 June 1838 (PRO)
d 1838 (PRO)

MORIARTY, Marion Marshall
L 26 Sept 1814
HP Sept 1815 (OB)
Ret CR 14 Feb 1859 (PRO)
d 1864 (PRO)

MORIARTY, Redmond
L 7 Jan 1812
Ret CR 28 July 1851 (PRO)
d 19 Dec 1851 (PRO)

MORIARTY, Sylverius
L 6 July 1776
CR 11 Nov 1780
CA 20 May 1781
RAW 1 Jan 1801
RAR 23 Apr 1804
VAB 9 Nov 1805
VAW 28 Apr 1808
d 1809 (PRO)

MORIARTY, William
L 23 Oct 1813
CR 1 Nov 1822 (PRO)
d 1850 (PRO)

MORICE, Richard
L 31 Mar 1779
CR 24 Sept 1781
CA 4 Nov 1794 (PRO)
d 15 June 1810 (PJP)

MORICE, Thomas
L 21 June 1756
d 1779 (PRO)

MORIENCOURT, Joseph Salvador
L 12 Sept 1793
HP Dec 1793–July 1794 (OB)
Ret CR 1 Sept 1827 (PRO)
d 10 Mar 1854 (PRO)

MORIER, William
L 4 May 1810
CR 13 June 1815 (PRO)
CA 18 Jan 1830 (PRO)
Ret CA 18 Jan 1850 (PRO)

Ret RA 9 July 1855 (PRO)
Ret VA 16 June 1862 (PRO)
d 29 July 1864 (PRO)

MORISON, George
L 4 Aug 1809
d 22 Sept 1824 (PRO)

MORISON, John
L 12 June 1807
d 17 Jan 1831 (PRO)

MORLAND, Samuel
L 31 Dec 1755
d 1758(9) (PRO)

MORLEN, Richard
L 30 Sept 1706
d 1734 (PRO)

MORLEY, James
L 6 Aug 1794
d 1804 (PRO)

MORLEY, Thomas
L
CA 1666

MORLEY, William
L 6 Feb 1815
d 1861 (PRO)

MORRELL, Arthur
L 28 July 1809
CR 18 Apr 1823 (OB)
HP Jan 1847 (OB)
Ret CA 1 Apr 1856 (PRO)
d 13 Sept 1880 (PRO)

MORRELL, John
L 9 Jan 1799
d 1813 (PRO)

MORRELL, John Arthur
L 4 June 1801
CR 19 July 1821 (PRO)
d 13 Feb 1831 (PRO)

MORRES, Edward
L 16 Dec 1801
d 1815 (PRO)

MORRETT, Benjamin
L 29 Sept 1744
d 1754(5) (PRO)

MORRICE, Humphry
L 1673
d before 1689 (PJP)

MORRICE, Salmon
L
CA 14 May 1697
RAW 21 Apr 1727
RAR 4 Jan 1728
VAB 19 July 1728
VAW 29 June 1732
d 27 Mar 1741

MORRICE, Thomas
L 22 Apr 1760 (PRO)
d 25 May 1793

MORRICE, Wright
L 16 May 1727
Gone 1734 (PRO)

MORRIS, Amherst
L 21 Sept 1790 (PRO)
CR 25 June 1793
d 1802 (PRO)

MORRIS, Andrew
Later MORRIES, Andrew
L 25 Aug 1806
Ret CR 5 May 1841 (PRO)
d 10 Jan 1856 (PRO)

MORRIS, Daniel
L 18 Aug 1709 (PMM)
CR
CA 30 Sept 1720
d 11 July 1728

MORRIS, Edward
L 15 Jan 1800
d (drowned) 18 Feb 1807 (CH)

MORRIS, George (1)
L 19 Sept 1777
SUP CR 6 Jan 1812
d 7 Oct 1814 (PRO)

MORRIS, George (2)
L 2 June 1796
CR 14 Apr 1802
CA 1 Feb 1812
Ret RA 1 Oct 1846 (PRO)
d 29 Sept 1857 (PRO)

MORRIS, Henry Gage
L 2 Apr 1793
CR 8 May 1804
CA 12 Aug 1812
Ret RA 1 Oct 1846 (PRO)
d 1851 (PRO)

MORRIS, Sir James Nicoll
L 14 Sept 1780
CR 21 Sept 1790
CA 7 Oct 1793
T wounded
CRM 31 July 1810 (LG)
RAB 1 Aug 1811
RAW 12 Aug 1812
RAR 4 June 1814
KCB 2 Jan 1815 (DNB)
VAB 12 Aug 1819 (PRO)
VAW 19 July 1821 (PRO)
VAR 27 May 1825 (PRO)
d 15 Apr 1830 (TR)

MORRIS, James
L 1666

MORRIS, John (1)
L 29 June 1695
SUP CR 20 Mar 1738 (PMM)
d 1743 (PMM)

MORRIS, John (2)
L 27 June 1697
Gone 1719 (PRO)

MORRIS, John (3)
L 31 Aug 1739
d 1741 (PMM)

MORRIS, John (4)
L 10 July 1755
CR 7 Jan 1771
CA 15 Oct 1775
d 2 July 1776 (DNB)

MORRIS, John (5)
L 9 Sept 1800
d 1801 (PRO)

MORRIS, John Chafin
L 22 Sept 1807
CR 27 May 1825 (PRO)
d 1835 (PRO)

MORRIS, John Row
L 20 May 1795
CR 15 June 1814
d 5 May 1850 (PRO)

MORRIS, Peter
L 10 Mar 1815
d 1848 (PRO)

MORRIS, Richard
L 18 May 1814
d 1836 (PRO)

MORRIS, Robert
L 14 June 1800
T
d 5 Feb 1823 (PRO)

MORRIS, William (1)
L 1 Nov 1810 (PRO)
d May 1830 (PRO)

MORRIS, William (2)
L 24 Aug 1813
CR 23 Nov 1841 (OB)
HP 23 Nov 1841 (OB)
Ret CA 9 Jan 1854 (PRO)
d 1869 (PRO)

MORRISON, Isaac Hawkins
L 1 May 1804
CR 10 June 1808
CA 7 June 1814
Ret CA 1 Oct 1846 (PRO)
Ret RA 9 Oct 1849 (PRO)
Ret VA 21 Oct 1856 (PRO)
d 16 Aug 1860 (PRO)

MORRISON, John (1)
L 18 Nov 1790
CR 27 May 1797
CA 5 Mar 1806
d (drowned) 1806 (CH)

MORRISON, John (2)
L 31 Mar 1813
d 18 Oct 1827 (PRO)

MORRISON, John
See MORISON, John

MORRISON, Kenneth
L 6 Sept 1800
d 1802 (PRO)

MORRISON, Peter
L 4 Nov 1814
d 1815 (PRO)

MORRISON, Richard James
L 3 Mar 1815
Ret CR 10 Jan 1863 (PRO)
d 1874 (PRO)

MORRISS, Edward John
L 17 Feb 1815
Ret CR 1 Oct 1860 (PRO)
d 7 Aug 1870 (PRO)

MORSE, Robert
L 27 Oct 1703 (PMM)

MORSE, Thomas
L 17 Sept 1745
d 1751(2) (PRO)

MORTIMER, George
L 17 Dec 1813
Ret CR 15 July 1856 (PRO)
d 12 Nov 1864 (PRO)

MORTIMER, John
L 12 June 1779
CR 8 Mar 1797
d 1818 (PRO)

MORTIMER, Robert
L 4 Apr 1746
SUP L 24 Mar 1790 (PMM)
SUP CR 21 Sept 1796 (PMM)
d 2 May 1799 (PMM)

MORTLOCK, Lewis
L 13 May 1794
CR 26 Apr 1798
d 9 Jan 1799 (PRO)

MORTON, Andrew
L 6 Apr 1797
d (suicide) 1803 (PRO)

MORTON, Thomas Constant Paggett
L 15 Oct 1812
HP 1814 (OB)
Ret CR 3 Dec 1855 (PRO)
d 1867 (PRO)

MORTON, Thomas Seaton
L 11 Aug 1800
d 10 May 1804

MOSES, John
L
CA 5 Mar 1694
d 23 Oct 1705

MOSES, William (1)
L
CR 23 Jan 1694
CA 12 Dec 1698
d 3 Feb 1740

MOSES, William (2)
L 16 May 1727
Gone 1729 (PRO)

MOSEY, Leonard
L 17 Feb 1778
d 1793 (PRO)

MOSS, John
See ROSE, John (1)

MOSS, John Ralph
L 3 Nov 1790
CR 9 July 1798
d 9 Aug 1799 (PRO)

MOSSE, James Robert
L 4 Oct 1771
CR 15 June 1782
CA 21 Sept 1790
KIA 2 Apr 1801 (CH)

MOSTYN, Robert
L 23 Sept 1778
CR 9 Mar 1782
CA 15 Nov 1782
d 1784

MOSTYN, Savage
L 2 Mar 1734
CR 3 July 1739 (DNB)
CA 6 Mar 1740 (DNB)

MP (Weobley)	1747–16 Sept	1757 (MPN)
CONT	27 Mar	1749–
	28 Feb	1755 (NBO)
RAB	4 Feb	1755
VAB		1757
COM AD	6 Apr–2 July	1757 (AO)
d	16 Sept	1757

MOTH, John

L		1667

MOTLEY, John

L	4 June	1746
d		1776 (PRO)

MOTLEY, Samuel
See MOTTLEY, Samuel

MOTT, Andrew (1)

L	30 May	1782
CR	27 Apr	1801
CA	12 Aug	1812
d	12 Nov	1819 (PMM)

MOTT, Andrew (2)

L	15 May	1805
CR	18 Sept	1815
d	June	1818 (PRO)

MOTT, Pierce Humphry

L	16 Aug	1814
d		1843 (PRO)

MOTTLEY, Samuel (1)

L	30 May	1782
CR	29 Apr	1799
CA	29 Apr	1802
Ret RA	10 Jan	1837 (PRO)
RAW	17 Aug	1840 (PRO)
d	27 May	1841 (PRO)

MOTTLEY, Samuel (2)

L	20 May	1808
Ret CR	30 Apr	1845 (PRO)
d		1845 (PRO)

MOUAT, Alexander

L	1 Nov	1780
CR	22 Nov	1790
d	11 Oct	1793 (PRO)

MOUAT, Patrick

L	20 Jan	1746
CR	22 May	1758
CA	28 Apr	1765
d	5 May	1790

MOUAT, Stephen Peter

L	6 May	1777 (PRO)
CR	1 Dec	1787
d		1805 (PRO)

MOUATT, George

L	19 Oct	1759
SUP CR	18 June	1805 (PRO)
d	27 Feb	1822 (PRO)

MOUATT, John Alexander

L	11 Feb	1815
HP		1838 (OB)

MOUBRAY, George

L	29 Mar	1760
d		1793 (PRO)

MOUBRAY, George
See MOWBRAY, George

MOUBRAY, Sir Richard Hussey
Later HUSSEY, Sir Richard Hussey

L	29 Dec	1793
CR	9 June	1794
CA	10 Apr	1797
CB	4 June	1814 (MB)
RAB	19 July	1821 (LG)
RAW	27 May	1825 (LG)
RAR	22 July	1830 (LG)
KCB	16 May	1833 (LG)
VAW	10 Jan	1837 (LG)
GCMG		1837 (PJP)
VAR	23 Nov	1841 (LG)
d	6 Nov	1842 (PRO)

MOUBRAY, Robert Toby

L	7 Dec	1801
d		1803 (PRO)

MOUBRAY, Thomas
See MOWBRAY, Thomas

MOULD, James

L	12 Oct	1797
T	wounded	
CR	21 Oct	1810
CA	16 Sept	1816 (PRO)
d		1819 (TR)

MOULD, John Rawe

L	16 Aug	1794
CR	21 Jan	1824 (PRO)
d	6 July	1827 (PRO)

MOULD, Richard Cotton

L	12 May	1807
HP	Sept	1814–
	Apr	1815 (OB)
Ret CR	10 Feb	1843 (PRO)
d	2 Apr	1854 (PRO)

MOULDEN, William (1)

L	4 Mar	1760
d		1779 (PRO)

MOULDEN, William (2)

L	12 Sept	1767
d		1769 (PRO)

MOULDING, Jeffery

L	12 Apr	1797
d		1806 (PRO)

MOULSON, Thomas

L	26 May	1803
d		1817 (PRO)

MOULTON, Robert

L		
CA		1664

MOUNCHER, Andrew

L	6 Apr	1780
d	17 Nov	1789

MOUNIER, John Hallier

L	23 Dec	1779
d		1811 (PRO)

MOUNIER, William

L	31 July	1795
d	6 Oct	1830 (PRO)

MOUNSEY, William

L	22 May	1793
CR	29 Apr	1802
CA	6 July	1809
CB	June	1815 (MB)
d	25 Sept	1830 (PRO)

MOUNSHER, Eyles
L 29 Dec 1796
T
CR 24 Dec 1805
CA 4 Dec 1813
d 1836 (TR)

MOUNTAGU(E), Charles
L
CA 1672
d before 1689 (PJP)

MOUNTAGU, Edward, Earl of Sandwich
See SANDWICH, Earl of

MOUNTAGU(E), Edward
L 1672

MOUNTAGU(E), George
L 1678

MOUNT EDGECUMBE, Earl of
See EDGECUMBE, George, Lord

MOUNTFORD, Edward
L 2 Feb 1741
CR 27 Sept 1758
d 1772 (PRO)

MOURILYAN, Edward
L 31 Jan 1806
Ret CR 6 Apr 1839 (PRO)
d 11 Mar 1855 (PRO)

MOURILYAN, Joseph
L 13 Nov 1790
d 1796 (PRO)

MOUTRAY, James
L 23 Apr 1793
d 1794 (PRO)

MOUTRAY, John
L 12 May 1744
CR 16 Feb 1757
CA 28 Dec 1758
d 22 Nov 1785 (DNB)

MOWAT, Alexander
L 26 Feb 1703 (PMM)

MOWAT, Francis Ritchie
L 1 Mar 1780
d 29 Mar 1788 (M)

MOWAT, John
L 9 Aug 1797
d Oct 1821 (PRO)

MOWATT, Henry
L 22 Jan 1759
CR 2 June 1776 (PRO)
CA 26 Oct 1782
d 14 Apr 1798 (PMM)

MOWATT, William
L 21 Mar 1803
T
d 11 Jan 1833 (PRO)

MOWBRAY, George
L 27 May 1794
T
CR 24 Dec 1805
CA 12 Aug 1812
d 20 Sept 1856 (PRO)

MOWBRAY, John
L 28 Mar 1780
Struck off list 1811 (PRO)

MOWBRAY, Thomas
L 2 Feb 1813
HP 1 Sept 1815 (OB)
Ret CR 13 Oct 1855 (PRO)
d 16 June 1864 (PRO)

MOXEY, Benjamin Soloman
L 9 Aug 1796 (PRO)
Ret CR 26 Nov 1830 (PRO)
d 1837 (PRO)

MOXON, James
L 27 Mar 1813
HP June 1813 (OB)
Ret CR 1 Feb 1856 (PRO)
d 1865 (PRO)

MOYES, David
L 10 Sept 1778
d 25 Oct 1805 (PMM)

MOYLE, Anthony
L 1661

MOYLE, Henry
L 23 Oct 1745
d 1787 (PRO)

MOYLE, Robert
L 24 June 1776
d 1779 (PRO)

MOYSE, Moses
L 26 Dec 1695
Gone 1719 (PRO)

MOYSES, Choyce William
L 11 Mar 1815
d Oct 1853 (PRO)

MOYSEY, Henry George
L 30 Aug 1806
d 12 Aug 1809 (PRO)

MUCKLE, George
L 11 Mar 1783
SUP CR 5 Dec 1820 (PRO)
d 30 Apr 1823 (LT)

MUDDLE, Richard Henry
L 23 July 1803
CR 22 May 1806
CA 1 Jan 1817 (PRO)
d 24 June 1833 (PJP)

MUDGE, George
L 21 Feb 1815
d 27 July 1838 (PRO)

MUDGE, John
L 17 July 1797
d 27 July 1838 (PRO)

MUDGE, John Mills
L 6 July 1797
d 23 May 1820 (PRO)

MUDGE, Robert
L 21 Feb 1815
Ret CR 31 Jan 1862 (PRO)
d 1871 (PRO)

MUDGE, William
L 19 Feb 1815 (DNB)
CR 4 Oct 1825 (DNB)
d 20 July 1837 (DNB)

MUDGE, Zachary
L 24 May 1789

CR	24 Nov	1797
CA	15 Nov	1800
RAB	22 July	1830 (PRO)
RAR	10 Jan	1837 (PRO)
VAB	23 Nov	1841 (PRO)
VAW	9 Nov	1846 (PRO)
VAR	19 Feb	1847 (PRO)
AB	15 Sept	1849 (PRO)
d	26 Oct	1852 (DNB)
MUDIE, David		
L	31 Mar	1782
CR	27 Apr	1801
d	10 Apr	1831 (PRO)
MUIR, Thomas (1)		
L	14 Aug	1794
HP	30 Apr	1814 (OB)
Ret CR	16 Aug	1831 (PRO)
d	Oct	1853 (PRO)
MUIR, Thomas (2)		
L	21 Aug	1806 (PRO)
d		1836 (PRO)
MUIRSON, John		
L	4 Jan	1808
d		1819 (PRO)
MULCASTER, Sir William		
L	31 Jan	1800
CR	13 May	1809 (PRO)
CA	29 Dec	1813
CB		1815 (PJP)
KCH		1831 (I)
Kt	13 Sept	1831 (I)
d	12 Mar	1837 (PRO)
MULES, William		
L	7 Dec	1782
SUP CR	28 Oct	1818 (PRO)
d	May	1821 (PRO)
MULGRAVE, Constantine John Phipps, Earl of		
See PHIPPS, Constantine John		
MULGRAVE, John Sheffield, Earl of		
L		
CA		1672
MULLER, Henry		
L	4 Nov	1803 (PRO)
d	12 July	1852 (PRO)
MULLINS, Thomas		
L	31 May	1809
d	4 July	1821 (PRO)
MULOCK, Joshua		
L	14 Nov	1778
CR	19 Mar	1791
CA	21 Oct	1794 (PRO)
d		1805 (PRO)
MULSO, Charles		
L	6 Mar	1741
d		1741 (PRO)
MULSO, William		
L	8 Oct	1793
CR	22 July	1796 (PRO)
d (drowned)	Jan	1797 (CH)
MUNBEE, Valentine		
L	1 Sept	1814
d	22 Dec	1824 (PRO)
MUNDAY, Richard		
L		
CA	17 Aug	1666 (RM)
MUNDELL, John		
L	10 Jan	1801
CR	1 Nov	1825 (PRO)
d	19 July	1833 (PRO)
MUNDEN, Sir John		
L	30 Nov	1677 (P)
CA	14 Dec	1688 (DNB)
RAB	14 Apr	1701
Kt	1 July	1701 (DNB)
RAW	28 Jan	1702
	(30 June	1701 in C)
RAR	30 June	1701
Dismissed		1702 (DNB)
d	13 Mar	1719 (DNB)
MUNDEN, Sir Richard		
L		
CA		1666
Kt	6 Dec	1673 (DNB)
d	25 June	1680 (DNB)
MUNDEN, Thomas		
L	2 May	1746
d	31 Oct	1765 (PMM)
MUNDY, Sir George		
L	11 Mar	1796
CR	24 Dec	1798
CA	10 Feb	1801
CB	June	1815 (OB)
MP (Boroughbridge)		1818–1820 (MPT)
MP (Boroughbridge)		1820–1830 (MPT)
RAB	22 July	1830 (LG)
RAR	10 Jan	1837 (LG)
KCB	17 Mar	1837 (LG)
VAB	23 Nov	1841 (PRO)
VAW	9 Nov	1846 (PRO)
VAR	26 June	1847 (PRO)
AB	24 Dec	1849 (LG)
AW	19 Jan	1852 (PRO)
AR	28 Nov	1857 (PRO)
d	9 Feb	1861 (PRO)
MUNFORD, Robert		
L	16 Jan	1704 (PMM)
MUNN, Thomas		
L	20 Dec	1695
Gone		1719 (PRO)
MUNN, Thomas Callis		
L	15 Oct	1805
CR	30 Dec	1811
d	7 Apr	1815 (PRO)
MUNRO, Andrew		
L	20 Nov	1812
d	Jan	1839 (LT)
MUNRO, James		
L	8 July	1745
SUP	17 Oct	1786 (PMM)
MUNRO, John		
L	3 Feb	1815
d	9 Jan	1830 (PRO)
MUNRO, Matthew		
L	4 Mar	1815
HP	19 June	1818 (OB)

Ret CR	10 Jan	1863 (PRO)
d	14 Mar	1866 (PRO)
MURCH, William		
L	4 Mar	1815
d		1816 (PRO)
MURCOTT, Abraham		
L	8 Feb	1693
Gone		1719 (PRO)
MURIEL, William		
L	5 Dec	1812
HP		1820 (OB)
Ret CR	2 July	1835 (PRO)
d	Nov	1876 (PRO)
MURLEY, William		
T		
L	29 June	1808
CR	29 Oct	1813 (MB)
HP	Jan	1814 (OB)
Ret CR	11 Nov	1849 (PRO)
d		1870 (TR)
MURPHY, James		
L	11 Apr	1796
Dismissed		1803 (PRO)
MURPHY, John		
L	5 Apr	1806
d		1817 (PRO)
MURRAY, Alexander		
L	5 July	1813
d		1838 (PRO)
MURRAY, Archibald		
L	4 Mar	1740
d		1758(9) (PRO)
MURRAY, Sir David		
L	19 Feb	1769
d	23 Jan	1791 (PMM)
MURRAY, Francis Aberdein		
L	6 July	1815
d		1848 (PRO)
MURRAY, Hon. Lord Frederick		
L	8 Nov	1734
d		1743(4) (PRO)
MURRAY, George, Lord Eilbank (1)		
L	5 May	1727
CR	24 July	1740
CA	3 Nov	1740
SUP RA		1755
d	11 Nov	1785
MURRAY, George (2)		
L	14 Oct	1762
CR	20 June	1765
CA	26 May	1768
CRM	1 Feb	1793 (AL)
RAW	12 Apr	1794
RAR	4 July	1794
VAW	1 June	1795
d	17 Oct	1797
MURRAY, Sir George (3)		
L	31 Dec	1778
CR	9 Oct	1782 (DNB)
CA	12 Oct	1782
RAB	23 Apr	1804
RAW	9 Nov	1805
RAR	28 Apr	1808
VAB	25 Oct	1809
VAW	31 July	1810
VAR	4 Dec	1813
KCB	2 Jan	1815 (DNB)
d	28 Feb	1819 (DNB)
MURRAY, Guy		
L	26 Oct	1794
d		1798 (PRO)
MURRAY, James (1)		
L	15 Mar	1782
d	18 Sept	1790
MURRAY, James (2)		
L	16 Nov	1790
d		1804 (PRO)
MURRAY, James (3)		
L	4 Dec	1802
Ret CR	14 Apr	1849 (PRO)
d		1867 (PRO)
MURRAY, James (4)		
L	27 Mar	1807
CR	14 June	1809 (PRO)
CA	7 Dec	1818 (PRO)
d	29 June	1834 (PJP)
MURRAY, James (5)		
L	1 Feb	1815
Struck off list	6 Jan	1829 (PRO)
MURRAY, James Arthur		
L	25 Sept	1809
CR	6 Dec	1813
CA	15 Nov	1816 (PRO)
Ret CA	1 Oct	1846 (PRO)
Ret RA	16 June	1851 (PRO)
Ret VA	30 July	1857 (PRO)
d	6 Mar	1860 (PRO)
MURRAY, James Copeland		
L	11 July	1797
Ret CR	26 Nov	1830 (PRO)
d		1862 (PRO)
MURRAY, James Hamilton		
L	12 Dec	1812
CR	2 Sept	1828 (PRO)
d	22 Dec	1841 (PRO)
MURRAY, John (1)		
L	13 July	1745
d		1770 (PRO)
MURRAY, John (2)		
L	3 Apr	1783
Gone		1794 (PRO)
MURRAY, Hon. John (3)		
L	3 Nov	1790
CR	24 Sept	1793
CA	25 Nov	1794
d	4 July	1805 (PRO)
MURRAY, John (4)		
L	12 June	1801
d	12 Dec	1804 (PRO)
MURRAY, John (5)		
L	3 July	1807
d		1817 (PRO)
MURRAY, John (6)		
L	5 Oct	1807
d		1817 (PRO)
MURRAY, John (7)		
L	6 Dec	1813

CR 12 Aug 1819 (PRO)
d 13 Mar 1821 (PRO)

MURRAY, John Stevens
L 9 Mar 1815
d 1832 (PRO)

MURRAY, Joseph
L 24 Apr 1779
d 1808 (PRO)

MURRAY, Richard
L 2 Feb 1757
CR 26 Jan 1778
CA 2 July 1781
d 1788 (PRO)

MURRAY, Robert
L 29 Jan 1781
CR 28 Apr 1782
RAB 23 Apr 1804
RAW 9 Nov 1805
RAR 28 Apr 1808
VAB 25 Oct 1809
VAW 31 July 1810
VAR 4 Dec 1813
AB 12 Aug 1819 (PRO)
AW 27 May 1825 (PRO)
d 31 May 1834 (PRO)

MURRAY, Lord William (1)
L 23 May 1688
d 3 Feb 1726 (DDA)

MURRAY, William (2)
L 4 Nov 1790
d ?1 July 1808 (PRO)

MURRAY, William Hamilton
L 4 Feb 1815
d 7 July 1850 (PRO)

MUSKERY, Robert MacCarthy, Lord
See MACCARTHY, Robert

MUSTON, Thomas Goldwire
L 4 July 1804
CR 11 Apr 1809 (PRO)
Ret CA 10 Sept 1840 (PRO)
d 24 Sept 1851 (PRO)

MYNGS, Sir Christopher
L
CA 1662
VAD 1664
VAB 1665
VAW 1665
Kt 27 June 1665 (DNB)
VAR 1666
KIA 4 June 1666 (RM)

MYNGS, Christopher (2)
L 1684
CR 3 Sept 1688 (PRO)
CA 25 June 1689 (PRO)
d 23 Oct 1725 (PJP)

MYNGS, Sir John
See MENNES, Sir John

NAGGS, James
L 1672

NAGLE, Archibald
T
L 14 Mar 1815
HP 1830 (OB)
d 1849 (TR)

NAGLE, Sir Edmund (1)
L 25 Oct 1777
CR 1 Aug 1782
CA 27 Jan 1783
Kt 1794 (DNB)
RAB 9 Nov 1805
RAR 28 Apr 1808
VAB 31 July 1810
VAW 12 Aug 1812
GG
(Newfoundland) 1813–1814 (DNB)
VAR 4 June 1814
KCB 2 Jan 1815 (DNB)
AB 12 Aug 1819 (DNB)
d 14 Mar 1830 (DNB)

NAGLE, Edmund (2)
L 4 July 1804

NAILOUR, Charles
L 7 Apr 1756

NAINBY, Robert
L 3 Nov 1800

NAIRN, James
L 25 Oct 1806

NAIRNE, John
L 20 Mar 1797
CR 7 Sept 1805
d 24 July 1807 (PJP)

NAIRNE, Richard
L 26 Jan 1780

NAISH, Giles
L 22 Mar 1727

NANNY, Lewis
L 20 Aug 1800

NAPIER, Andrew Nathaniel
L 7 Nov 1807

NAPIER, Hon. Charles (1)
L 31 July 1754
CR
CA 17 Aug 1762
d 19 Dec 1807 (OB)

NAPIER, Sir Charles (2)
L 30 Nov 1805
CR 30 Nov 1807
CA 22 May 1809
HP 1809–1811 (DNB)
CB 4 June 1815 (DNB)
Kt (Portugal) 1833 (DNB)
Kt (Austria) 1840 (DNB)
Kt (Prussia) 1840 (DNB)
Kt (Russia) 1840 (DNB)
KCB 4 Dec 1840 (OB)
MP (Marylebone) 1841 (DNB)
RAB 9 Nov 1846 (LG)
RAW 3 Apr 1848 (LG)
VA 28 May 1853 (DNB)
MP (Southwark) 1855 (DNB)
A 6 Mar 1858 (DNB)
d 6 Nov 1860 (DNB)

NAPIER, Charles Frederick
L 24 Dec 1796

NAPIER, Hon. Francis
L 29 Dec 1812
d 1814 (PJP)

NAPIER, Henry Edward
L 4 May 1810

CR 7 June 1814
HP Aug 1815–
Jan 1821 (OB)
CA 31 Dec 1830 (MB)

NAPIER, Hope
L 28 July 1794

NAPIER, Hon. Patrick
L 5 Sept 1777
CR 29 Apr 1782
CA 8 Aug 1783
d 15 June 1801

NAPIER, William
L 5 Sept 1799

NAPIER, Hon. William John, Baron
T
L 6 Oct 1809
CR 1 June 1812
CA 4 June 1814
Inh EP 1 Aug 1823 (DNB)
d 11 Oct 1834 (DNB)

NARBROUGH, Sir John
L 1664
CA 1666
CAMR 1 Oct 1672 (EAD)
RAR 17 Sept 1673
Kt 30 Sept 1673 (DNB)
AD 18 Oct 1674
COM V 29 Apr 1680–
17 Apr 1686 (NBO)
COM N 17 Apr 1686–
27 May 1688 (NBO)
d 27 May 1688 (DNB)

NARES, William Henry
L 17 Apr 1809
CR 1 July 1814
HP Oct 1814 (OB)

NARRACOTT, John
L 26 June 1804

NARRACOTT, William
L 28 May 1813

NASH, Ezekiel
L 2 June 1760
d 16 Apr 1803

NASH, James
L 25 Oct 1793
CR 8 Mar 1797
CA 29 Apr 1802
d 1827 (PJP)

NASH, John
L 16 Aug 1793
CR 16 Sept 1796
CA 29 Apr 1802
d 1824 (PJP)

NASH, Richard
L 16 Jan 1779

NASH, Richard John
L 29 Oct 1813

NASH, William (1)
L 26 Jan 1796

NASH, William (2)
L 1 Feb 1815

NASH, William Graves
L 27 May 1803
T
Gone 1806 (TR)

NASMITH, John Lockhart
L 14 Dec 1762

CR 14 Feb 1779
d 25 Aug 1792

NASON, Arthur Hyde
L 31 Jan 1806
d (suicide) 1807 (PJP)

NASON, Henry
L 28 Oct 1809
HP Nov 1813 (OB)

NASON, Richard
L 21 Mar 1812
HP Aug 1816 (OB)

NASWORTHY, John
L 7 Feb 1811

NAYLOR, Gates
L 2 Feb 1673

NAYLOR, Henry
L 10 Dec 1799

NAYLOR, Thomas Rumsey
L 18 Nov 1809

NAZER, Henry
L 2 May 1808
CR 28 Aug 1828 (OB)
d 1846 (OB)

NAZER, John
L 23 Sept 1796
d 1798 (OB)

NAZER, Kelly
L 11 Nov 1807 (OB)
Ret CR 3 Feb 1847 (PMM)

NAZER, William
L 10 Jan 1794
d 1804 (OB)

NEAGLE, Francis
L 27 Dec 1693

NEAL, James
L 20 Mar 1760

NEALE, Francis
L 8 Sept 1665 (DDA)

NEALE, Sir Harry Burrard
Formerly BURRARD, Sir Harry
L 29 Sept 1787
MP (Lymington) 1790–1802 (MPT)
CR 3 Nov 1790
Inh Bt 12 Apr 1791 (DNB)
CA 1 Feb 1793
COM AD 17 Jan–13 Sept 1804 (AO)
MP (Lymington) 1806–1807 (MPT)
COM AD 10 Feb 1806–
6 Apr 1807 (AO)
RAB 31 July 1810
MP (Lymington) 1812–Mar 1823 (MPT)
RAW 12 Aug 1812
RAR 4 Dec 1813
VAB 4 June 1814
KCB 2 Jan 1815 (DNB)
GCB 14 Sept 1822 (DNB)
MP (Lymington) 1823–1834 (MPT)
GCMG 1823 (DNB)
VAR 27 May 1825 (CH)
AB 22 July 1830 (CH)
AW 10 Jan 1837 (CH)
d 7 Feb 1840 (CH)

NEALE, John (1)
L 3 Mar 1740

NEALE, John (2)
L 8 June 1741

NEALE, John (3)
L 15 Feb 1745
NEALE, John (4)
L 21 Mar 1805
T
Gone 1820 (TR)
NEALE, John (5)
L 22 Sept 1806
Ret CR 27 Oct 1846 (PMM)
NEALE, Richard (1)
L
CA Feb 1665 (DDA)
d before 1689 (PJP)
NEALE, Richard (2)
L Feb 1665 (DDA)
d before 1689 (PJP)
NEAME, William
L 20 June 1808
CR 4 Apr 1832 (PMM)
NEEDHAM, William
L 22 July 1795
NEEVE, Anselm and Richard
See LA NEVE, Anselm and Richard
NEILL, Joseph
L 11 Nov 1806
CR 26 Aug 1815
HP 26 Aug 1815 (OB)
NEILSON, Benjamin
L 16 Oct 1745
NEILSON, Thomas
L 21 July 1741
CR 1 Mar 1760
d (drowned) Mar 1762 (PJP)
NELLY, Francis
L 16 May 1692
NELSON, Charles
L 5 Feb 1812
CR 13 June 1815
CA 9 Oct 1822 (MB)
Ret CA 1 Oct 1846 (OB)
NELSON, Horatio, Viscount
L 10 Apr 1777
CR 8 Dec 1778
CA 11 June 1779
HP 1783–1784 (DNB)
CRM 1 June 1795 (AL)
Kt 1797 (DNB)
RAB 20 Feb 1797
Cre EP 1798 (DNB)
RAR 14 Feb 1799
VAB 1 Jan 1801
VAW 23 Apr 1804
T killed
KIA 21 Oct 1805 (TR)
NELSON, John
L 8 May 1800
NELSON, John Bird
L 7 Dec 1809
NEPEAN, Edmund
L 20 Dec 1781
NEPEAN, Evan
L 13 Feb 1815
CR 22 Oct 1823 (OB)
CA 23 Nov 1841 (OB)
NEPEAN, John
L 25 Sept 1806
NESBIT(T), Alexander
L 12 Nov 1805
CR 18 Jan 1809
d 19 Apr 1824 (LT)
NESBIT, John
L 13 Mar 1781
NESBIT, Matthew
L 1702 (PJP)
NESBIT(T), Thomas
L 18 July 1799
NESBIT, William
L 20 Jan 1728
NESHAM, Christopher John Williams
L 17 Nov 1790
CR 2 Jan 1798
CA 29 Apr 1802
Ret RA 10 Jan 1837 (DNB)
RA 17 Aug 1840 (DNB)
VA 9 Nov 1846 (DNB)
A 30 July 1852 (DNB)
d 4 Nov 1853 (DNB)
NETHERWOOD, William
L 3 Feb 1815
NEVE, Frederick Brownson
L 26 Sept 1811
NEVE, Robert Jenner
L 30 Apr 1796
CR 29 Apr 1802
CA 22 Jan 1806
d 1815 (PJP)
NEVE, Anselm or Richard le
See LE NEVE, Anselm or Richard
NEVILE, Christopher
L 17 Nov 1790
CR 10 Jan 1797
NEVILE, Martin
L
CA 29 Apr 1802
d 27 July 1803 (PRO)
NEVIL(L)E, Samuel
L 5 Oct 1803
d 5 Feb 1804 (PRO)
NEVILL, Edward
L
CA 23 Dec 1690
d 12 Sept 1701
NEVILL, Joseph
L 11 Apr 1759
NEVILLE, Christopher
See NEVILE, Christopher
NEVILLE, James
L 3 Dec 1802
CR 2 Sept 1828 (OB)
HP 2 Sept 1828 (OB)
NEVILLE, John
L 1673 (P)
CA 21 Feb 1681 (P)
RAB 7 July 1693
CASMR 30 Nov 1693 (EAD)
RAR 28 Apr 1696
VA Oct 1696 (C)
d 27 Aug 1697
NEVILLE, Ralph, Viscount
T
L 22 Jan 1806
CR 30 May 1808
CA 16 Feb 1811
d May 1826 (MB)

NEVISON, John
L 25 Jan 1726
NEW, Thomas
L 9 June 1794
CR 10 Aug 1801
CA 27 Feb 1812
d Dec 1824 (MB)
NEW, William
L 1672
d 25 Dec 1678 (DDA)
NEWALL, Adam
L 6 July 1797
NEWARK, Charles Herbert Pierrepont, Viscount
See PIERREPONT, Charles Herbert
NEWARK, Charles Medows, Viscount
See MEDOWS, Charles
NEWARK, John Luttrell, Lord
See LUTTRELL, John
NEWBERRY, Richard
L 1673 (DDA)
NEWBOLT, Charles
L 24 Feb 1815
NEWCOMBE, Francis
L 7 Feb 1794
CR 15 Sept 1801
CA 11 Apr 1809
NEWCOME, Henry
L
CR
CA 19 May 1782
d 1799
NEWELL, Charles
L 1683
NEWELL, John
L 3 Nov 1790
d 1816 (PJP)
NEWELL, Julius James Farmer
L 4 Mar 1815
CR 20 Nov 1828 (PMM)
CA 28 June 1838 (PMM)
HP 28 June 1838 (OB)
RA 2 Oct 1857 (PMM)
d 24 Dec 1862 (PMM)
NEWELL, Obadiah (1)
L 16 Oct 1778
d 2 June 1790 (PMM)
NEWELL, Obadiah (2)
L 4 Sept 1781 (PMM)
d 1 Feb 1837 (PMM)
NEWENHAM, Charles Burton
L 13 Nov 1790
d Sept 1793 (LG)
NEWENHAM, Nathaniel
L 1 Jan 1815
NEWENHAM, William Persse
L 23 July 1810
NEWHOUSE, John
L 23 June 1795
CR 13 June 1798
CA 29 Apr 1802
d 1803 (PJP)
NEWLAND, Robert
L 1666
CA 1667
d before 1689 (PJP)

NEWMAN, Francis
L 8 Feb 1815
NEWMAN, James Newman
L 26 Nov 1789 (PMM)
CR 24 May 1794 (PMM)
CA 1 Aug 1794
d (drowned) 25 Dec 1811 (CH)
NEWNAM, James
L 3 May 1721
CR 29 May 1741
d 7 Jan 1753 (PMM)
NEWNHAM, Thomas
L 6 Dec 1760
CR 24 Mar 1779
CA 30 July 1779
d 16 Aug 1785 (PMM)
NEWSHAM, John
L 25 Aug 1777
NEWSON, William (1)
L 4 Apr 1743
CR 15 June 1757
Dismissed 24 Aug 1762 (PJP)
d 17 Sept 1787 (M)
NEWSON, William (2)
L 16 Sept 1779
NEWTON, George
L 9 May 1746
d 18 Sept 1782
NEWTON, Henry (1)
L 31 Dec 1755
NEWTON, Henry (2)
L 2 Dec 1758
NEWTON, James
L 2 Mar 1815
d 29 July 1845 (OB)
NEWTON, John (1)
L 10 Dec 1760
d 3 Feb 1803
NEWTON, John (2)
L 2 July 1808
NEWTON, Joseph
L 7 Jan 1802
NEWTON, Robert (1)
L 1666
NEWTON, Robert (2)
L 19 Dec 1759
NEWTON, Robert (3)
T
L 3 Feb 1815
HP June 1815 (OB)
d 1856 (TR)
NEWTON, Roger
L
CA 15 May 1690
d 1693 (PJP)
NEWTON, Thomas (1)
L 12 May 1771
NEWTON, Thomas (2)
L 23 May 1795
NEWTON, Vincent
L 12 May 1803
CR 26 May 1814
NEWTON, William (1)
L 15 Nov 1776
NEWTON, William (2)
L 3 July 1777

NEWTON, Witham
L 13 Jan 1758
NICHOLAS, Edward
L 7 Aug 1706
NICHOLAS, James
L 25 June 1759
NICHOLAS, John (1)
L 29 June 1777
NICHOLAS, John (2)
L 6 May 1796
CR 11 Sept 1797
CA 14 Feb 1801
NICHOLAS, John (3)
L 11 Aug 1808
CR 17 May 1814
d Dec 1831 (MB)
NICHOLAS, John (4)
L 15 Feb 1815
HP 1846 (OB)
NICHOLAS, John Harris
See NICOLAS, John Harris
NICHOLAS, John Toup
L 1 May 1805
CR 26 Aug 1809
CB 4 June 1815 (DNB)
CA 26 Aug 1815
Kt (Two Sicilies) 4 Oct 1815 (MB)
KH 1 Jan 1834 (DNB)
RA 30 Dec 1850 (DNB)
d 1 Apr 1851 (DNB)
NICHOLAS, Nicholas Harris
See NICOLAS, Nicholas Harris
NICHOLAS, Robert
L 14 Aug 1801
CR 6 Dec 1805
d (drowned) 8 Aug 1809 (CH)
NICHOLAS, Robert Boyle
L 5 June 1772
CR 15 Jan 1778
CA 19 Apr 1779
d (drowned) 5 Oct 1780 (CH)
NICHOLAS, Thomas
L 29 July 1809
d (drowned) 20 Dec 1810 (PJP)
NICHOLAS, William Keigwin
L 15 Apr 1809
NICHOLL, Edward or James Harvey
See NICKOLL, Edward or James Harvey
NICHOLL, Joseph Axtell
L 1799 (PJP)
d 30 May 1800
NICHOLL, Whitlock
L 12 Feb 1772
NICHOLLS, Francis
L 27 Sept 1740
NICHOL(L)S, George
L 23 Apr 1708 (PMM)
CR
CA 17 Nov 1708
d (drowned) 5 Jan 1709 (CH)
NICHOLLS, Sir Henry
L 20 May 1780
CR 9 Dec 1782
CA 1 Dec 1788
CONT 3 Mar–20 June 1806 (NBO)
RAB 2 Oct 1807
RAW 28 Apr 1808
RAR 31 July 1810
VAB 1 Aug 1811
VAW 4 June 1814
VAR 12 Aug 1819 (PJP)
KCB 20 May 1820 (MB)
AB 27 May 1825 (PJP)
d 1829 (PJP)
NICHOLLS, James
L 25 June 1793
NICHOLLS, James Thomas
L 24 Feb 1815
HP 1844 (OB)
NICHOLLS, Robert
L 19 Mar 1778
NICHOLLS, Thomas
L 1666
NICHOL(L)S, Thomas George
L 2 Jan 1812
NICHOLLS, Thomas Wilcocks
L 13 Aug 1807
Ret CR 19 Oct 1843 (OB)
d 1847 (OB)
NICHOLS, William Henry
L 29 Sept 1814
NICHOLSON, Charles
L 6 Aug 1805
NICHOLSON, John (1)
L 4 Mar 1795
?CR 2 Aug 1805
NICHOLSON, James (2)
L 13 Aug 1796
?CR 2 Aug 1805
NICHOLSON, John
L
CA 21 Jan 1673
NICHOLSON, Richard Adams
L 18 Feb 1815
NICHOLSON, Richard St. Lo
L 23 Nov 1781
NICHOLSON, Robert
L 21 Sept 1810
NICHOLSON, William
L 14 Feb 1803
NICKOLL, Edward
L 27 Feb 1815
HP Aug 1815 (OB)
NICKOLL, James Harvey
L 6 Feb 1815
NICOL, David
L 14 Oct 1801
NICOLAS, John Harris
L 23 Sept 1779
SUP CR 17 Mar 1814
d 12 July 1844 (OB)
NICOLAS, John Toup
See NICHOLAS, John Toup
NICOLAS, Sir Nicholas Harris
L 20 Sept 1815
HP 1816 (OB)
KH Oct 1831 (OB)
KCMG Oct 1831 (OB)
GCMG Oct 1840 (OB)
NICOLLS, James
L 14 Mar 1783
NICOLLS, Jonathan
L 19 Oct 1807
NICOLLS, Robert
L 19 Mar 1778
SUP CR 31 Jan 1814

NICOLLS, Robert Trafford
L 3 Mar 1815
NIGHTINGALE, David Thomas
L 21 Sept 1812
d 22 Dec 1844 (OB)
NIGHTINGALE, Gamaliel
L 8 July 1753
CR 3 Aug 1757
CA 18 Oct 1758
d 1 Jan 1791 (M)
NIGHTINGALE, Henry
L 4 Apr 1797
NIND, Philip Pitt
L 17 Mar 1810
CR 5 Jan 1844 (OB)
NINIS, George
L 12 Mar 1799
CR 15 June 1814
NISBET, Josiah
L
CR 18 Sept 1797
CA 24 Dec 1798
d 14 July 1830 (PMM)
NISBETT, Samuel
L 22 Jan 1806
d (drowned) 14 Aug 1812 (CH)
NIVEN, Charles
L 8 Sept 1796
d 11 Mar 1804
NIVEN, James
L 12 Oct 1808
NIXON, Anderson
L 7 July 1762
d 7 Jan 1800
NIXON, Christopher
L 25 Sept 1800
CR 18 Apr 1809 (MB)
CA 27 May 1825 (MB)
NIXON, Edward
L
CA 1660
e (cowardice) 25 May 1665 (PRO)
NIXON, James
L 3 Jan 1812
HP Aug 1814 (OB)
d 1847 (OB)
NOAKES, Daniel
L 15 Oct 1790
NOBLE, Francis
L 28 June 1808
NOBLE, George (1)
L 11 June 1761
NOBLE, George (2)
L
CR 25 Oct 1809
NOBLE, George (3)
L 16 Mar 1815
d 1847 (OB)
NOBLE, James
L 9 Mar 1796
CR 27 Feb 1797
CA 29 Apr 1802
Ret RA 10 Jan 1837 (DNB)
RA 17 Aug 1840 (DNB)
VA 9 Nov 1846 (DNB)
d 24 Oct 1851 (DNB)

NOBLE, Mark
L
CA 12 July 1697
d 22 Mar 1702
NOBLE, Robert
L 6 Jan 1778
CR 21 Mar 1782
NOBLE, William Blackmore
L 27 Aug 1814
HP Sept 1815 (OB)
NODEN, Hugh
L
CA 1673
NODEN, Thomas
L 16 Jan 1678
d before 1689 (PJP)
NOEL, Hon. Frederic
L 18 July 1811
CR 29 July 1813
CA 12 Aug 1819 (MB)
NOEL, Thomas
L 27 Feb 1740
CR 16 Nov 1744
CA 12 Nov 1745
KIA 20 May 1756 (CH)
NOPS, John George
L 11 Sept 1810
NORBROOKE, John
L
CA 1665
d before 1689 (PJP)
NORBURY, Coningsby (1)
L
CR
CA 12 Jan 1709
d 12 July 1734
NORBURY, Coningsby (2)
L 10 Apr 1734
CR
CA 17 Nov 1744
d 1786
NORBURY, John
L 17 Oct 1709
NORBURY, Richard
L 28 May 1742
CR 10 Jan 1757
CA 4 June 1759
d 1800
NORBURY, Thomas
L 27 Dec 1758
NORCOTT, Edmund
L 10 Feb 1815
CR 28 June 1838 (OB)
NORFORD, James
L 6 Jan 1794
NORIE, Evelyn
L 12 Sept 1806
Ret CR 13 Oct 1840 (OB)
NORMAN, Alfred
L 17 Feb 1805
NORMAN, Charles Rice
L 26 Dec 1809
KIA 26 Sept 1814 (JH)
NORMAN, George Robert Grills
L 15 Sept 1800
KIA 18 Aug 1810 (PJP)

NORMAN, James (1)
L 25 June 1756
CR 27 Aug 1779
CA 21 Sept 1790
Sentenced by court–martial to half–pay for life Mar 1796 (PMM)
d 1806 (PJP)

NORMAN, James (2)
L 9 May 1797

NORMAN, Masters
L 5 Apr 1814

NORMAN, Samuel
L 1 June 1795

NORMAN, William
L 31 May 1799
T
KIA 13 Aug 1810 (TR)

NORMAND, William
L 17 Sept 1806

NORRINGTON, Charles Harvey
L 11 Feb 1812

NORRIS, Edward
L 15 July 1721

NORRIS, Harry
L
CR
CA 26 Sept 1740
RAW 4 June 1756
RAR 31 Jan 1758 (C)
VAW 14 Feb 1759
d 13 June 1764

NORRIS, Henry
L 8 Oct 1801

NORRIS, Hugh
L 6 Aug 1779

NORRIS, James Butler
L 17 Apr 1782

NORRIS, Sir John (1)
L Aug 1689 (DNB)
CA 8 July 1690
Kt 5 Nov 1705 (DNB)
RAB 10 Mar 1707
MP (Rye) 1708–1722 (MPS)
RAW 8 Jan 1708 (C)
VAW 26 Jan 1708 (FVT)
VAR 18 Dec 1708
AB 21 Dec 1708
COM AD 19 Mar 1718–
13 May 1730 (AO)
MP (Portsmouth) 1722–1734 (MPS)
AW 20 Jan 1732
AF 20 Feb 1734 (DNB)
MP (Rye) 1734–13 May 1749 (MPS)
d 19 July 1749 (DNB)

NORRIS, John (2)
L 8 May 1761

NORRIS, John (3)
L 19 Feb 1780

NORRIS, Joseph
L 22 Feb 1812
HP 18 Sept 1815 (OB)

NORRIS, Matthew
L 1718 (PRO)
CR
CA 3 Apr 1724
MP (Rye) 21 Jan 1733–1734 (MPS)
d 15 Dec 1738

NORRIS, Richard (1)
L
CR
CA 17 Oct 1735
Absconded 1744

NORRIS, Richard (2)
L 7 Aug 1794

NORRIS, Stephen
L 22 Oct 1761

NORTH, Abraham
L 24 Feb 1739
CR 6 May 1748
CA 16 Jan 1755
d 1781

NORTH, Fountain
L 10 Jan 1771

NORTH, John
L 1665
CA 16 Aug 1666 (RM)

NORTHESK, George Carnegie, Earl of
L
CR
CA 25 Aug 1741
RAB 4 June 1756
VAB 14 Feb 1759
VAW 21 Oct 1762
AB 18 Oct 1770 (CH)
AW 29 Jan 1772
d 22 Jan 1792

NORTHESK, William Carnegie, Earl of
L 7 Dec 1777
CR 10 Sept 1780
CA 7 Apr 1782
Inh EP 22 Jan 1792 (TR)
RAW 23 Apr 1804
T
Kt 1805 (TR)
RAR 9 Nov 1805
VAB 28 Apr 1808 (MB)
VAR 31 July 1810
AB 4 June 1814
AW 19 July 1821 (CH)
AR 22 July 1830 (CH)
d 28 May 1831 (CH)

NORTHEY, James Murray
L 23 Apr 1783
CR 25 Dec 1800
CA 25 Sept 1806

NORTHON, John
L 1 Dec 1790
d Jan 1792 (LT)

NORTON, George
L 14 Nov 1790
CR 15 June 1814

NORTON, John (1)
L 8 Jan 1799
CR 21 Oct 1810
Ret CR 10 Sept 1840 (OB)
d 26 Sept 1845 (OB)

NORTON, John (2)
L 1 Nov 1805
d 24 Dec 1811 (PMM)

NORTON, John
See NORTHON, John

NORTON, Nathaniel
L 3 June 1808

NORTON, Richard
L 9 Aug 1814
NORTON, William
L 7 Apr 1742
CR 4 Nov 1744
CA 15 Nov 1756
d 1799
NORWAY, John Arthur
L 4 July 1793
CR 29 Apr 1802
Dismissed 1805(6) (PJP)
d 1813(4) (PJP)
NORWOOD, John
L
CA 1673
NORWOOD, Joseph
L 21 Jan 1748
CR 21 Nov 1760
CA 7 June 1763
d 10 May 1793 (LT)
NORWOOD, Matthew
L 1664
NORWOOD, Stephen
L 3 Mar 1781
NORWOOD, Thomas
L 28 Aug 1730
NOTT, Francis
L 7 Aug 1761
NOTT, Francis John
L 12 Jan 1795
CR 14 Nov 1801
CA 21 Oct 1810
d 1840 (PJP)
NOTT, John
L 3 Nov 1790
NOTT, John Neal Pleydell
L 3 July 1756
CR 7 Sept 1759
CA 24 Sept 1761
KIA 29 Apr 1781 (LG)
NOTT, John Thomas
L 18 Oct 1810
CR 9 Nov 1846 (OB)
NOTT, William
L 26 Jan 1814
NOTTER, Edward John
L 12 Oct 1795
NOTTER, William
L 18 May 1795
NOURSE, Edward
See NURSE, Edward
NOURSE, Joseph
L 10 Dec 1799
CR 4 Aug 1803
CA 30 Apr 1804
CB 1815 (PJP)
HP 1815–1821 (MB)
d 4 Sept 1824 (MB)
NOURSE, Robert
L 23 June 1755
NOVELL, John
L 7 Dec 1739
NOVOSIELSKI, Michael
L 19 Dec 1806
NOWELL, Henry Freeman
L 8 Oct 1795
d 17 June 1804

NOWELL, William (1)
L 19 Nov 1776
HP 1783–1787 (MB)
CR 21 Sept 1790
CA 24 Oct 1794
HP 1802–1811 (MB)
RAB 4 Dec 1813
RAW 4 June 1814
RAR 12 Aug 1819 (PJP)
d 1827 (PJP)
NOWELL, William (2)
L 14 Nov 1790
d 12 July 1810 (PJP)
NOWELL, William (3)
L 21 Mar 1812
NOYCE, James
L 18 May 1798
CR 12 Aug 1812
d 24 Mar 1813 (PJP)
NUCELLA, Timothy
L 15 July 1740
CR 17 Dec 1744
CA 12 Apr 1745
d 4 Apr 1756
NUGENT, Sir Charles Edmund
L 3 June 1776
CR 26 May 1778
CA 2 May 1779
MP (Buckingham) 1784–1790 (MPN)
RAB 20 Feb 1797
RAR 14 Feb 1799
VAB 1 Jan 1801
VAW 23 Apr 1804
VAR 9 Nov 1805
AB 28 Apr 1808
AW 31 July 1810
AR 12 Aug 1819
AF 24 Apr 1833
GCH 12 Mar 1834 (DNB)
d 7 Jan 1844 (DNB)
NUGENT, Dominick
L 1665
CA 1671
NUGENT, Frederick
L 7 Feb 1798
NUGENT, John
L 15 Jan 1800
CR 23 Nov 1841 (OB)
NUNN, John
L 14 Apr 1778
NUNN, Joseph
L 23 Dec 1760
CR 12 June 1776
CA 25 Oct 1809
NURSE, Edward
L
CR
CA 1 Jan 1713
NUTT, Justinian
L 21 June 1743
CR
CA 12 Aug 1745
d 11 Dec 1758
NUTTALL, John
L 13 Nov 1746
NUTTON, Michael
L

CA 1660
d before 1689 (PJP)

OAKE, John
L 22 Nov 1697
CA 9 Nov 1698
Gone 1718 (NMM)

OAKE, Josiah
L 2 Mar 1815
CR 28 Apr 1827 (MB)
CA 9 Nov 1846 (OB)
Ret CA 20 Aug 1857 (NMM)
d 1864 (NMM)

OAKELEY, Richard
L 16 July 1810
d 16 Apr 1824 (PRO)

OAKER, Edward
L 8 Sept 1742
d 1745 (PRO)

OAKES, Edmund
L 1 July 1814
d 1841 (NMM)

OAKES, George
L 6 Jan 1776
CR 28 Nov 1781
CA 14 Apr 1783
d 1797 (NMM)

OAKEY, Richard
L 10 July 1778
CR 6 July 1782
CA 25 Oct 1809
d 28 Jan 1815 (PRO)

OAKLEY, Edward
L
CA 22 Oct 1690
d 20 Sept 1693

OAKLEY, John
L 13 Nov 1756
d 4 June 1790

OAKLEY, Thomas
L 4 Apr 1741
d 1769 (NMM)

OAKLEY, William
L 13 Aug 1761
CR 25 Oct 1809
d 1811 (NMM)

OATES, Christopher
L 11 Sept 1706
CR 18 Nov 1729
d 14 Feb 1741 (NMM)

OATES, Samuel (1)
L 4 Mar 1693
Gone 1719 (PRO)

OATES, Samuel (2)
L 12 Apr 1697
d 1706 (PJP)

OBEN , Warwick
L 14 July 1777
d 11 Aug 1787 (NMM)

O'BRIEN, Andew
L 25 Apr 1807
HP May 1815 (OB)
Ret CR 19 Apr 1850 (NMM)
d 1858 (NMM)

O'BRIEN, Hon. Charles
L 8 Jan 1718 (PMM)

O'BRIEN, Christopher (1)
L
CR
CA 11 Apr 1713
Entered Russian service in 1714 and was Rear Admiral. Returned to England and was employed again.
d 11 Feb 1743 (PJP)

O'BRIEN, Christopher (2)
L 28 July 1726
d 1729 (NMM)

O'BRIEN, Christopher (3)
L 2 July 1746
d 1771 (NMM)

O'BRIEN, Donat (Henchy)
L 29 Mar 1809
CR 22 Jan 1813
CA 5 Mar 1821 (DNB)
RA 8 Mar 1852 (DNB)
d 13 May 1857 (DNB)

O'BRIEN, Edward
L 17 Aug 1797
d 1807 (PRO)

O'BRIEN, Edward
See O'BRYEN, Edward

O'BRIEN, George
L 2 Sept 1807
d 1813 (PRO)

O'BRIEN, John James
L 1 Nov 1780
Dismissed 1797 (PRO)

O'BRIEN, Joseph (1)
L 17 Mar 1814
d 1819 (PRO)

O'BRIEN, Joseph (2)
L 1 Oct 1814
CR 3 May 1826 (MB)
CA 8 Aug 1829 (MB)
HP 1829 (OB)
RA 3 July 1855 (NMM)
VA 12 Apr 1862 (NMM)
A 12 Sept 1865 (NMM)
d 17 Nov 1865 (NMM)

O'BRIEN, Lucius (1)
L 14 Feb 1738
In Russian service 1739 (PJP)
CR 31 Mar 1744
CA 3 Dec 1745
RAW 24 Oct 1770
d 17 Dec 1770 (CH)

O'BRIEN, Lucius (2)
L 19 Sept 1761
d 16 Apr 1780 (M)

O'BRIEN, Robert
L 13 Jan 1797
CR 26 Aug 1800
CA 1 May 1804
Dismissed Apr 1816 (PJP)
Restored Mar 1817 (MB)
Ret RA 10 Jan 1837 (NMM)
d 21 Jan 1838 (NMM)

O'BRIEN, Thomas
L 25 Sept 1799
Dismissed 1801 (NMM)
d 7 Apr 1830 (LT)
O'BRYEN, Charles
L 1665
CA 9 June 1666 (RM)
O'BRYEN, Edward (1)
L 11 Apr 1778
CR 17 Mar 1783
CA 14 June 1783
RAB 9 Nov 1805
RAW 28 Apr 1808
d 18 Dec 1808 (DNB)
O'BRYEN, Hon. Edward (2)
L 26 Sept 1793
CR 15 Oct 1800
CA 29 Apr 1802
d 9 Mar 1824 (PRO)
O'BRYEN, Edward
See O'BRIEN, Edward
O'BRYEN, Lord James, Marquess of Thomond
L 19 Nov 1790
CR 5 Dec 1796
CA 14 Dec 1799
Cre IP 10 Feb 1808 (MB)
RAB 27 May 1825 (LG)
RAW 22 July 1830 (LG)
GCH 1831 (PJP)
VAB 10 Jan 1837 (LG)
VAW 23 Nov 1841 (LG)
VAR 9 Nov 1846 (LG)
AB 13 May 1847 (LG)
AW 24 Dec 1849 (LG)
AR 5 Mar 1853 (LG)
d 3 July 1855 (PRO)
O'BRYEN, John (1)
L 27 Sept 1747
d 1789 (PRO)
O'BRYEN, John (2)
L 13 Oct 1777
CR 22 Nov 1790
CA 23 May 1797
d 26 Jan 1804
O'BRYEN, Lucius
See O'BRIEN, Lucius
O'CALLAGHAN, Edward
L 6 June 1807
d 1809 (NMM)
O'CALLAGHAN, Henry John
L 25 Feb 1815
HP 1815 (OB)
Ret CR 14 Apr 1862 (NMM)
d 1863 (NMM)
OCHTERLONY, Alexander
L 15 Oct 1757
d 5 Feb 1760 (M)
OCKMAN, William (1)
L 16 Oct 1694
CR 10 Mar 1707 (PMM)
CA 8 Mar 1709
d 1740
OCKMAN, William (2)
L 1706 (PJP)
d (drowned) 22 Oct 1707 (PJP)

O'CONNELL, Edward
L 23 Oct 1800
d 1808 (NMM)
O'CONNELL, Maurice Fitzgerald
L 14 Feb 1815
d 1856 (NMM)
O'CONNOR, John
L 9 Dec 1795
d 29 Jan 1798
O'CONNOR, Sir Richard
L 1 Feb 1806
CR 17 Aug 1810
CA 16 Aug 1814
KCH 25 Jan 1836 (LG)
Ret CA 31 Oct 1846 (LG)
Ret RA 2 Sept 1850 (NMM)
d 10 Jan 1855 (NMM)
O'CONNOR, Richard James Lawrence
L 6 Dec 1793
CR 3 May 1800
CA 21 Oct 1810
d 1826 (PRO)
ODELL, John
L 21 May 1799
Struck from list 1801 (PRO)
ODGER, Nicholas
L 15 Mar 1810
d 1812 (PRO)
ODLUM, John
L 21 Nov 1790
d 22 Aug 1795 (PMM)
ODWAY, Edward
L 1672
O'DWYER, William Thomas
L 6 Mar 1815
d 17 May 1820 (NMM)
ODY, William
L 21 Dec 1809
d 1842 (NMM)
OGILVIE, David
T
L 25 Aug 1806
d 25 Dec 1821 (PRO)
OGILVIE, Edward
L 3 Oct 1810
d 25 Dec 1821 (PRO)
OGILVIE, George
L 23 May 1745
d 1808 (PJP)
OGILVIE, Henry
L 7 Feb 1812
HP 16 Aug 1817 (OB)
d 1855 (PRO)
OGILVIE, John (1)
L 26 July 1707 (PMM)
OGILVIE, John (2)
L 29 July 1725
CR
CA 13 Jan 1732
d 10 Mar 1734 (PRO)
OGILVIE, John (3)
L 24 Feb 1794
d 1797 (NMM)

OGILVIE, Michael
L 18 Feb 1778
d 1808 (PRO)

OGILVIE, Primrose
L 21 Nov 1790
d 1796 (PRO)

OGILVIE, William
L 27 June 1801
Ret CR 11 Aug 1832 (OB)
d 5 Mar 1859 (NMM)

OGILVY, Sir William
L 8 Jan 1780
CR 6 July 1794
CA 5 July 1797
SUP RA 6 Dec 1821 (MB)
d 29 Aug 1823 (NMM)

OGLE, Sir Chaloner (1)
L 29 Apr 1702 (DNB)
CR 21 Apr 1705 (PMM)
CA 14 May 1708
Kt Apr 1723
RAB 11 July 1739
RAR 13 Mar 1742 (LG)
VAB 11 Aug 1743 (LG)
AB 23 June 1744 (LG)
MP (Rochester) 24 Nov 1746–
11 Apr 1750 (MPS)
AW 15 July 1747
AF 10 July 1749
d 11 Apr 1750 (DNB)

OGLE, Sir Chaloner (2)
?L 19 Nov 1745
CR 17 June 1755
CA 30 June 1756
RAB 26 Sept 1780
VAB 24 Sept 1787
AB 12 Apr 1794
AW 14 Feb 1799
AR 9 Nov 1805
Cre Bt 23 Jan 1816 (LG)
d 28 Aug 1816 (PRO)

OGLE, Sir Chaloner (3)
?L 31 Jan 1748
CR 27 Dec 1759
CA 29 Mar 1762
d 1814 (PRO)

OGLE, Sir Charles
L 15 Nov 1793
CR 21 May 1794
CA 11 Jan 1796
Inh Bt 27 Aug 1816 (DNB)
RAB 12 Aug 1819 (NMM)
RAW 19 July 1821 (NMM)
RAR 27 May 1825 (NMM)
VAB 22 July 1830 (NMM)
VAR 10 Jan 1837 (NMM)
AB 23 Nov 1841 (NMM)
AW 9 Nov 1846 (NMM)
AR 26 June 1847 (NMM)
AF 8 Dec 1851 (NMM)
d 16 June 1858 (NMM)

OGLE, Henry
L 6 Mar 1815
d 22 Apr 1840 (PRO)

OGLETHORPE, Robert
L 17 Aug 1682

O'GRADY, Hayes
L 21 Mar 1807
CR 15 June 1810
CA 7 June 1814
HP 7 June 1814 (OB)
RAB 19 Oct 1849 (LG)
RA 1 July 1851 (PRO)
VA 21 Oct 1856 (PRO)
A 15 Jan 1862 (PRO)
d 8 July 1864 (PRO)

O'HARA, Francis
L 25 May 1756
CR 28 Dec 1763
CA 20 June 1765
d 14 June 1769 (NMM)

O'HARA, James
L 12 Apr 1748
CR 2 June 1756
CA 20 June 1765
d 1790 (PRO)

O'HARA, Patrick
L 16 May 1727
CR 10 Oct 1743 (PRO)
CA 16 Nov 1744
SUP RA 1762
d 18 Sept 1774

O'HARA, Peter
L 27 Nov 1756
d 1761 (PRO)

O'HARA, William Charles
L 4 Feb 1815
d 1843 (PRO)

O'HARA, William Henry King
L 16 Jan 1768
CR 31 July 1778
CA 15 Feb 1780
d 1 Dec 1789 (PRO)

O'HEA, Daniel
L 26 Jan 1805
T
d 21 Dec 1835 (PJP)

O'HEA, Matthew
L 4 Feb 1815
HP 4 Feb 1815 (OB)
Ret CR 9 Feb 1860
d 1861 (PRO)

OKE, John
L 16 Apr 1802
d 1812 (PRO)

OKELY, Battison
L 21 July 1747
d 1753 (PRO)

OKES, Charles
L 18 Feb 1807
d 7 May 1860 (PRO)

OKES, John
L 7 Feb 1760
SUP 1805 (PRO)

OKES, William
L 10 Oct 1809
d 1810 (PRO)

OLDFIELD, William
L 11 Aug 1801
d 18 Dec 1831 (PRO)

OLDMIXON, George
L 1 June 1815
CR 27 Sept 1847 (OB)
Ret CA 1 Aug 1860 (NMM)
d May 1880 (NMM)

OLDMIXON, John William
L 11 Feb 1812
Ret CR 1 Oct 1853 (NMM)
d 1869 (NMM)

OLDMIXON, William Henry
L 24 Feb 1815
Ret CR 1 Oct 1853 (PRO)
d 1869 (PRO)

OLDREY, William
L 7 July 1812
CR 24 Apr 1828 (MB)
CA 28 June 1838 (OB)
d 1852 (NMM)

OLIPHANT, John (1)
L 14 Dec 1709
CR 29 July 1730
CA 28 July 1738
d 28 Mar 1743 (N MM)

OLIPHANT, John (2)
L 28 Apr 1802
d 2 June 1810 (PRO)

OLIVER, George Colin
L 3 Mar 1815
HP Dec 1826 (OB)
Ret CR 13 Nov 1862 (NMM)
d 31 Jan 1870 (NMM)

OLIVER, James
L 8 June 1797
CR 4 Dec 1813
Ret CA 12 June 1851 (NMM)
d 24 Apr 1857 (NMM)

OLIVER, John
L 25 Aug 1794
d 23 Apr 1795 (LT)

OLIVER, Joseph
L 11 May 1799
CR 18 Sept 1805
d 1811 (NMM)

OLIVER, Robert (1)
L 30 Jan 1806
CR 27 Aug 1814
HP 27 Aug 1814 (OB)
d 1851 (NMM)

OLIVER, Sir Robert (2)
L 22 Feb 1810
CR 29 Oct 1827 (MB)
CA 28 Aug 1834 (OB)
Kt 20 Apr 1843 (OB)
d Aug 1848 (NMM)

OLIVER, Robert Dudley
L 21 Sept 1790
CR 21 Oct 1794
CA 30 Apr 1796
RAB 12 Aug 1819 (NMM)
RAW 19 July 1821 (NMM)
RAR 27 May 1825 (NMM)
VAB 22 July 1830 (NMM)
VAR 10 Jan 1837 (NMM)
AB 23 Nov 1841 (NMM)
AW 9 Nov 1846 (NMM)
AR 26 July 1847 (NMM)
d 2 Sept 1850 (PJP)

OLIVER, Thomas
L 31 July 1793
CR 22 Jan 1806
Ret CR 10 Sept 1840 (PRO)
d 1842 (PRO)

OLIVER, William Sandford
L 26 Sept 1799
HP Mar 1812 (OB)
Ret CR 26 Nov 1830 (OB)
d 28 July 1845 (NMM)

OMER, Joseph Robert
L 20 Aug 1801
d 1807 (NMM)

OMMANNEY, Cornthwaite
L 22 Aug 1758
CR 20 June 1765
CA 22 Feb 1772
SUP RA 1794 (PJP)
d 26 Mar 1801 (PJP)

OMMANNEY, Henry Maneton
L 10 Apr 1794
CR 29 Apr 1802
CA 22 Jan 1806
Ret RA 10 Jan 1837 (PRO)
RAB 17 Aug 1840 (PRO)
RAW 23 Nov 1841 (PRO)
RAR 9 Nov 1846 (PRO)
VAB 24 Jan 1849 (PRO)
VAW 8 Apr 1851 (PRO)
VA 1 July 1851 (PRO)
A 4 July 1855 (PRO)
d 22 Mar 1857 (PRO)

OMMANNEY, John
L 11 Mar 1757
d 1760 (PRO)

OMMANEY, Sir John Acworth
L 20 May 1793
CR 6 Dec 1796
CA 16 Oct 1800
CB 13 Nov 1827 (LG)
Kt (Russia) 1827 (DNB)
Kt (Greece) 1827 (DNB)
RAB 22 July 1830 (PRO)
Kt 20 May 1835 (DNB)
RAR 10 Jan 1837 (PRO)
KCB 20 July 1838 (DNB)
VAB 23 Nov 1841 (LG)
VAW 9 Nov 1846 (LG)
VAR 22 Jan 1847 (LG)
AB 4 May 1849 (LG)
AW 1 July 1851 (PRO)
AR 4 July 1855 (PRO)
d 8 July 1855 (PRO)

O'NEILL, Terence
L 16 Mar 1795
CR 24 Apr 1800
d 1832 (PRO)

O'NEIL, William
L 18 June 1801
d 1803 (PRO)

ONLEY, John
L 28 Sept 1708

CR	28 Sept	1727 (NMM)
CA	18 Jan	1729
Dismissed	3 Dec	1738 (PRO)
ONSLOW, Sir Richard		
L	17 Dec	1758
CR	11 Feb	1761
CA	14 Apr	1762
CRM	21 Sept	1790 (AL)
RAW	1 Feb	1793
RAR	12 Apr	1794
VAW	4 July	1794
VAR	1 June	1795
Cre Bt	17 Oct	1797 (LG)
AB	14 Feb	1799
AW	23 Apr	1804
AR	9 Nov	1805
LGRM	7 May	1814 (AL)
GCB	2 Jan	1815 (LG)
d	3 Jan	1818 (PMM)
OPIE, John		
L	21 Feb	1709
CR	25 June	1741
Entered Russian service as CA		1735 (PJP)
d		1758 (PRO)
ORCHARD, Francis		
L	11 Nov	1756
d		1763 (PRO)
ORCHARD, Joel		
L	26 Nov	1799
d		1813 (PRO)
ORCHARD, Richard		
L	11 Jan	1718
d	16 July	1732 (PRO)
ORCHARD, Samuel		
L	15 Oct	1812
d		1813 (PRO)
ORCHARD, William		
L		
CA		1673
ORD, Christopher		
L	14 July	1758
d		1785 (PRO)
ORDE, John (1)		
L	23 Aug	1759
SUP CR	24 Jan	1805
d		1819 (PRO)
ORDE, Sir John (2)		
L	7 Apr	1774
CR	26 Sept	1777
CA	19 May	1778
Cre Bt	7 Aug	1790 (MPT)
RAW	1 June	1795
VAB	14 Feb	1799
VAW	1 Jan	1801
VAR	23 Apr	1804
AB	9 Nov	1805
MP (Yarmouth I.o.W)		1807–1824 (MPT)
AW	25 Oct	1809
AR	4 June	1814
d	19 Feb	1824 (DNB)
ORDE, Thomas (1)		
L	28 Oct	1790
Resigned		1796 (PRO)
ORDE, Thomas (2)		
L	3 July	1799
CR	29 Apr	1802
d	23 Sept	1805 (PRO)
ORE, James		
L	21 May	1746
d		1753 (PRO)
O'REILLY, Dowell		
L	30 May	1807
CR	23 Sept	1813
CA	29 Aug	1815
d	28 May	1816 (PRO)
O'REILLY, John		
L	2 Nov	1815
Ret CR	1 Oct	1860 (PRO)
d		1873 (PRO)
ORFORD, Edward Russel, Earl of		
See RUSSELL, Edward		
ORKNEY, John		
L	1 May	1804
d		1813 (PRO)
ORLEBAR, Orlando		
L	14 May	1811
HP		1814 (OB)
Ret CR	1 Oct	1851 (NMM)
d	30 Dec	1879 (NMM)
ORME, Humphrey		
L	20 Jan	1708 (PMM)
CR	17 Mar	1718
CA	1 June	1720
d	6 Aug	1751 (NMM)
ORME, John		
L	5 Mar	1712
CR		
CA	20 Aug	1745
d	23 Aug	1764
ORMEROD, Charles		
L	25 May	1696 (PJP)
CA	21 Feb	1697
ORMOND, Francis		
L	3 Dec	1810
CR	27 May	1825 (MB)
HP	27 May	1825 (OB)
CA	28 July	1851 (NMM)
d	11 Sept	1851 (NMM)
ORMSBY, Charles Cutts		
L	27 Mar	1794
d	6 Dec	1810 (NMM)
ORMSBY, George		
L	29 Jan	1794
CR	29 Apr	1799
d	28 Jan	1801 (NMM)
ORMSBY, John Boteler		
L	13 Dec	1813
d		1819 (NMM)
ORRIS, Nathaniel		
L	23 June	1720
d	19 Oct	1749 (PMM)
ORROK, Alexander		
L	23 June	1702
SUP	20 Mar	1738 (PMM)
d		1742 (PMM)
ORROK, James		
L	19 June	1745
CR	19 Oct	1757

CA 5 May 1779
d 1785 (NMM)

ORROK, John
L 9 Apr 1781
d 1798 (NMM)

ORROK, Thomas Archibald
L 19 Sept 1777
CR 4 Apr 1779
d 2 Aug 1796 (LT)

ORSBRIDGE, Philip
L 13 Jan 1758
d 1767 (NMM)

ORSEUR, Abdiel
L 26 Feb 1801
d 16 Nov 1815 (PJP)

ORSEUR, William
L 1 Nov 1744

ORSMOND, James
L 4 May 1810
d 1813 (NMM)

ORTON, George Anthony
L 5 Dec 1781
d 8 Feb 1812 (NMM)

ORTON, Isaac
L 30 Oct 1793
d 1801 (NMM)

OSBORN, Edward Oliver
L 6 Nov 1778
CR 22 Nov 1790
CA 1 Oct 1791
RAB 31 July 1810
RAW 12 Aug 1812
RAR 4 Dec 1813
VAB 4 June 1814
VAW 12 Aug 1819 (CH)
d 29 July 1820 (NMM)

OSBORN, George
L 30 Mar 1808
d 28 Nov 1811 (PRO)

OSBORN, Henry
L 7 July 1717 (MPN)
CR
CA 4 Jan 1728
GG (Newfoundland) 1729–1731 (BNS)
RAR 15 July 1747
VAW 12 May 1748 (CH)
VAR 6 Jan 1755 (CH)
AB Feb 1757
MP (Bedfordshire) 13 Dec 1758–1761 (MPN)
AW 21 Oct 1762
d 4 Feb 1771 (MPN)

OSBORN, James
L 26 Dec 1738
CR 9 Aug 1742
CA 28 Sept 1744
d 13 Dec 1754

OSBORN, James
See OSBORNE, James

OSBORN, James Guy
L 16 Aug 1811
d 13 Feb 1836 (NMM)

OSBORN, John (1)
L 22 Feb 1777
CR 15 Jan 1783
CA 22 Nov 1790
RAB 25 Oct 1809
RAW 31 July 1810
RAR 12 Aug 1812
VAB 4 June 1814
VAW 12 Aug 1819 (CH)
d Jan 1820 (PRO)

OSBORN, John (2)
L 22 Jan 1806
Ret CR 13 Oct 1838 (OB)
d 1854 (NMM)

OSBORN, John
See OSBORNE, John

OSBORN, Peter
L 12 Dec 1709
CR
CA 28 July 1740
d 24 Feb 1754 (PRO)

OSBORN, Samuel
L
CR 29 Apr 1779
CA 6 July 1782
RAB 23 Apr 1804
RAR 9 Nov 1805
VAB 28 Apr 1808
VAW 31 July 1810
VAR 12 Aug 1812
AB 4 June 1814
d 10 Oct 1816 (PJP)

OSBORN, William (1)
L 10 Oct 1759
d 1781 (PRO)

OSBORN, William (2)
L 1 Sept 1781
d 1815 (PRO)

OSBORN, William
See OSBORNE, William

OSBORNE, Charles
L 23 Mar 1761
d 14 Oct 1797

OSBORNE, Francis
L 27 Mar 1744
d 1758 (PRO)

OSBORNE, Frederick William
L 23 Apr 1794
d (drowned) 1797 (PJP)

OSBORNE, Henry
L 14 Jan 1803
Dismissed 11 Nov 1806 (PJP)
d 1813 (PRO)

OSBORNE, James
L 1 May 1753
d 1759 (NMM)

OSBORNE, John
L 22 Jan 1745
d 1757 (NMM)

OSBORNE, Peregrine, Duke of Leeds
See CARMARTHEN, Marquis of

OSBORNE, Thomas
L 5 May 1762
d 1762 (NMM)

OSBORNE, Wadham
L 21 Dec 1758
d 1768 (NMM)

OSBORNE, William
L 9 June 1747
CR 1 Mar 1760
d 1781 (NMM)

OSBOURNE, Elias
L
CA 22 Apr 1665 (DDA)

OSBOURNE, Robert
L
CA 1689 (PJP)
KIA 17 Aug 1695 (CH)

OSGOOD, Henry
L
CA 1665

O'SHAUGNESSY, Edward
L 31 Aug 1800
CR 22 May 1813
d 28 Feb 1818 (PRO)

OSMAN, John
L 16 Mar 1815
d 8 June 1820 (PRO)

OSMER, Thomas Spearing
L 26 May 1795
Ret CR 13 Dec 1833 (NMM)
d 1844 (NMM)

OSMOND, William
L 15 Mar 1779
d 7 Apr 1800

OSSORY, Thomas Butler, Earl of
L
IMP (Dublin Univ.) 1661–1662 (DNB)
MP (Bristol) 16 May 1661–14 Sept 1666 (MPH)
Cre IP 22 June 1662 (DNB)
LG in Irish Army 16 Aug 1665 (DNB)
CA 3 June 1666 (RM)
RAB 18 Apr 1673 (NJ)
RAR 14 Aug 1673 (NJ)
AF Sept 1673
COM AD 26 Sept 1677–14 May 1679 (AO)
Commander of Flanders expedition 1678 (EAD)
Commander of Troop of Horse for the Tangier garrison 13 July 1680 (EAD)
d 30 July 1680 (DNB)

OSWALD, James
L 28 Aug 1795
CR 3 Jan 1798
CA 3 Sept 1799
d 19 July 1822 (NMM)

OTTER, Charles
L 16 Nov 1790
CR 29 June 1795
CA 29 Apr 1802
d 2 Jan 1831 (PRO)

OTTLEY, Edward
L 30 Apr 1795
d 1807 (PRO)

OTTLEY, John
L 3 Dec 1802
d 1817 (PRO)

OTTLEY, Richard
L 1795 (PJP)

OTTY, Allen
L 14 Apr 1810
CR 1 July 1815
HP 1817 (OB)
Ret CR 13 Aug 1854 (NMM)
d 1859 (NMM)

OTWAY, Robert
L 14 May 1812
CR 6 Jan 1837 (OB)
HP 6 Jan 1837 (OB)
d 1855 (NMM)

OTWAY, Sir Robert Waller
L 8 Aug 1793
CR 7 Aug 1795 (PMM)
CA 30 Oct 1795
RAB 4 June 1814
RAW 12 Aug 1819 (PRO)
RAR 27 May 1825 (PRO)
KCB 8 June 1826 (DNB)
VAW 22 July 1830 (PRO)
Cre Bt 15 Sept 1831 (DNB)
VAR 10 Jan 1837 (PRO)
AW 23 Nov 1841 (PRO)
GCB 8 May 1845 (DNB)
d 12 May 1846 (PRO)

OTWAY, William Albany
L 25 Aug 1773
CR 29 Mar 1781
CA 1 Dec 1781
RAB 2 Oct 1807
RAW 28 Apr 1808
RAR 31 July 1810
VAB 1 Aug 1811
VAW 4 June 1814
d 30 July 1815 (CH)

OUDE, Thomas (1)
See ORDE, Thomas (1)

OUGHTON, James
L 30 Sept 1783
CR 29 June 1795
CA 15 May 1799
Ret RA 7 June 1825 (PRO)
d 1832 (PRO)

OURRY, George
L 9 July 1755
CR
CA 10 Nov 1762
SUP RA 1793
d Feb 1800 (NMM)

OURRY, Isaac Florimond
L 14 Feb 1745
CR
CA 6 June 1761
d 24 Aug 1773 (NMM)

OURRY, Paul Henry
L 13 Nov 1742
CR 27 Apr 1756
CA 3 Feb 1757
MP (Plympton Erle) 25 Nov 1763–Jan 1775 (MPN)

COMM 1775–
(Plymouth) 31 Jan 1783 (MPN)
d 31 Jan 1783 (MPN)

OVEREND, Henry
L 9 Jan 1808
HP Aug 1812 (OB)
Ret CR 19 Oct 1844 (OB)
d 1870 (NMM)

OWEN, Bagnard
L 1728 (PJP)

OWEN, Bell Robert
L 1 Aug 1811
Ret CR 31 Mar 1856
d 3 Dec 1861 (NMM)

OWEN, Charles Cunliffe
L 13 Feb 1808
CR 28 Feb 1815
HP 1815 (OB)
Ret CA 24 Feb 1852 (NMM)
d 20 Feb 1872 (NMM)

OWEN, Edward (1)
L
CA Sept 1694
(7 Aug 1694 in H)
d 17 Oct 1708

OWEN, Edward (2)
L 19 Sept 1815
HP 19 Sept 1815 (OB)
d 7 Jan 1849 (NMM)

OWEN, Sir Edward William Campbell Rich
L 6 Nov 1793
CR 19 Sept 1796
CA 23 Apr 1798
KCB 14 May 1816 (LG)
CRM 20 July 1820 (LG)
RAB 27 May 1825 (LG)
MP 1826–1827 (MB)
(Sandwich)
MCLHA 12 Mar–19 Sept 1828 (AO)
RAR 22 July 1830 (LG)
GCH 24 Oct 1832 (DNB)
VAB 10 Jan 1837 (PRO)
VAW 28 June 1838 (PRO)
VAR 23 Nov 1841 (PRO)
GCB 8 May 1845 (DNB)
AB 10 Dec 1846 (PRO)
AW 1 June 1848 (PRO)
d 8 Oct 1849 (PRO)

OWEN, Humphrey
L 25 June 1708 (PMM)

OWEN, John
L 16 June 1756
d 1780(1) (PRO)

OWEN, Owen
L 7 May 1802
d 1837 (PRO)

OWEN, Thomas (1)
L 2 Oct 1743
CR 28 Apr 1755
CA 28 Sept 1758
d 8 Apr 1797 (LT)

OWEN, Thomas (2)
L 18 Oct 1793
d ?1811 (NMM)

OWEN, William (1)
L 3 May 1697
CR
CA 1 Jan 1713
d 14 Aug 1722

OWEN, William (2)
L 25 Mar 1758
CR 7 Nov 1777
d 24 Oct 1778 (NMM)

OWEN, William (3)
L 22 June 1759
d 15 July 1768 (PMM)

OWEN, William (4)
L 4 Aug 1809
d 1811 (NMM)

OWEN, William Fitzwilliam
L 25 Oct 1794
Dismissed 26 June 1795
Restored 12 June 1797
CR 20 May 1809
CA 2 May 1811
RAB 21 Dec 1847 (NMM)
RAW 5 Nov 1849 (NMM)
RAR 1 Oct 1852 (NMM)
VAB 27 Oct 1854 (NMM)
Ret VA 6 Feb 1855 (CH)
d 3 Nov 1857 (NMM)

OXBROUGH, William
L 23 May 1796
Ret CR 17 May 1837 (OB)
d 1842 (NMM)

OXLEY, John
L 25 Nov 1807
d 25 May 1828 (DNB)

OZARD, Thomas
L 18 Nov 1779
d 21 May 1794 (NMM)

PACE, George
L 9 Jan 1797
d 1 Oct 1822 (LT)

PACE, John
L 2 June 1695
CR
CA 27 Feb 1713

PACEY, Thomas Samuel ?PACY
L 26 Oct 1798
d (drowned) May 1805 (CH)

PACK, John
L 16 Feb 1815

PACKER, Joseph
L 16 May 1800

PACKMAN, Robert Charles
L 1 Feb 1815

PACKWOOD, Joseph
L 28 Sept 1796
CR 22 Jan 1806
CA 14 Feb 1811

PADDON, George
L 18 Jan 1693
CR
CA 17 Jan 1705
Dismissed 1714

Went into the Russian Service 1717 (PMM)
d 31 Dec 1718 (PJP)

PADDON, Silas Hiscutt
L 20 Apr 1804
CR 27 Mar 1826 (OB)
HP 1831 (OB)

PADESON, Edmund
L 3 Oct 1761
d 1806 (PJP)

PADGET, Henry
L 24 Sept 1759
d 21 Feb 1773 (M)

PADNALL, Thomas
L 1664

PAGE, Benjamin William
L 20 Nov 1784
CR 12 Apr 1796 (PRO)
CA 22 Dec 1796
RAB 12 Aug 1819 (MB)
RAW 27 May 1825 (PRO)
VAB 22 July 1830 (PRO)
VAW 10 Jan 1837 (PRO)
AB 23 Nov 1841 (LG)
d 3 Oct 1845 (DNB)

PAGE, Henry
L 25 June 1735
SUP ?1753
d 1777 (PRO)

PAGE, James
L 1665
CA 1672

PAGE, John
See PACE, John

PAGE, John Henry St. John
L 11 Oct 1794

PAGE, Thomas
L 1668
CA 12 Jan 1670 (AJ)

PAGE, William (1)
L 3 Feb 1780
d 1826 (PRO)

PAGE, William (2)
L 4 Feb 1808
d 1809 (PRO)

PAGET, Hon. Sir Charles
L 12 Dec 1796
CR 27 June 1797
CA 17 Oct 1797
MP (Milborne Port) 1804–1806 (MPT)
MP (Caernarvon Boroughs) 1806–1826 (MPT)
KCH Oct 1819 (DNB)
RAB 9 Apr 1823 (MB)
RAW 27 May 1825 (PRO)
RAR 22 July 1830 (PRO)
MP (Caernarvon Boroughs) 1831–1833 (MPT)
GCH Mar 1832 (DNB)
MP (Caernarvon Boroughs) 1833–1834 (MPT)
VAW 10 Jan 1837 (PRO)
d 29 Jan 1839 (PJP)

PAGET, John
L 20 Dec 1806
CR 1 Apr 1837 (OB)
HP 1843 (OB)
Ret CA 1 Apr 1856 (PRO)
d 16 Jan 1857 (PRO)

PAGET, Hon. William
L
MP (Anglesey) 1790–Sept 1794 (MPT)
CR 19 Nov 1790
CA 6 Feb 1793
d 15 Sept 1794 (PRO)

PAIN, Martin
L 7 Feb 1815
CR 12 May 1837 (OB)
Ret CR 9 Feb 1860 (PRO)
d 1867 (PRO)

PAIN, Stephen
L 23 Oct 1806
d 1840 (PRO)

PAINE, John (1)
L 10 Oct 1745

PAINE, John (2)
L 4 Feb 1761
SUP CR 24 Feb 1809

PAINE, Joseph
L
CA 1665
Dismissed 18 Nov 1667 (CH)

PAINE, Joshua
L 23 Mar 1703
SUP 20 Mar 1738 (PMM)
d 1748 (PMM)

PAINE, Rheuben
L 19 Jan 1809
CR 19 June 1828 (PRO)
d 2 Nov 1838 (PRO)

PAINE, William
L 30 Oct 1703 (PMM)

PAINTER, Richard
L
CA 1673
d before 1689 (PJP)

PAKENHAM, Edward
L 17 July 1777
CR 9 Apr 1783
CA 22 Nov 1790
d 24 July 1798 (SPB)

PAKENHAM, Hon. Edward Michael, Lord Longford
L 12 Aug 1761
CR 29 June 1765
CA 31 May 1766
d 3 June 1792 (PRO)

PAKENHAM, John (1)
L 17 June 1769
CR 1 Apr 1779
CA 1 Jan 1780
RAW 14 Feb 1799
RAR 1 Jan 1801
VAW 23 Apr 1804
VAR 9 Nov 1805
d 2 Dec 1807 (CH)

PAKENHAM, John (2)
L 16 July 1811
CR 15 June 1814
CA 26 Aug 1826 (MB)
Ret CA 31 Oct 1846 (LG)

PAKENHAM, Hon. Sir Thomas
L 16 May 1776

CR	21 Sept	1779
CA	2 Mar	1780
CRM	1 June	1795 (AL)
RAW	14 Feb	1799
RAR	1 Jan	1801
VAB	23 Apr	1804
VAR	9 Nov	1805
AB	31 July	1810
AW	12 Aug	1812
GCB	20 May	1820 (DNB)
AR	19 July	1821 (PRO)
d	2 Feb	1836 (DNB)
PAKENHAM, Hon. William		
L	29 June	1803
CR	18 Feb	1805
CA	9 May	1807
d (drowned)	4 Dec	1811 (JH)
PALK, Robert		
L	23 June	1801
CR	1 Apr	1812
HP	5 Sept	1814 (OB)
Ret CR	22 Apr	1831 (OB)
d	12 May	1845 (OB)
PALLISER, Sir Hugh		
L	18 Sept	1741
CR	3 July	1747 (PRO)
CA	25 Nov	1746
GG (Newfoundland)		1764–1769 (BNS)
CONT	6 Aug	1770–
	4 Apr	1775 (NBO)
Cre Bt	6 Aug	1773 (DNB)
MP (Scarborough)	1774–Feb	1779 (MPN)
RAB	31 Mar	1775
LGRM	8 Dec	1775 (AL)
COM AD	12 Apr	1775–
	23 Apr	1779 (AO)
RAW	5 Feb	1776
RAR	23 Jan	1778
VAB	29 Jan	1778
GGH		1780 (PJP)
VAW	26 Sept	1780
MP (Huntingdon)	28 Nov	1780–1784 (MPN)
AB	24 Sept	1787
AW	1 Feb	1793
d	19 Mar	1796 (DNB)
PALMER, Abraham		
L	27 June	1679 (DDA)
PALMER, Arthur		
L	8 Nov	1808
d		1836 (PRO)
PALMER, Edmund		
L	3 Apr	1801
CR	8 May	1804
CA	10 Oct	1807
CB	4 June	1815 (LG)
d	19 Sept	1834 (PRO)
PALMER, Edward (1)		
L	27 Oct	1758
d		1796 (PRO)
PALMER, Edward (2)		
L	12 May	1800
CR	22 Jan	1805
d (drowned)	8 Jan	1807 (PJP)
PALMER, Edward Gascoigne		
L	19 Oct	1809
Ret CR	15 June	1849 (PRO)
d	29 June	1849 (PRO)
PALMER, George (1)		
L	23 Apr	1778
CR	1 Dec	1780
CA	18 Jan	1783
RAB	23 Apr	1804
RAW	9 Nov	1805
RAR	28 Apr	1808
VAB	31 July	1810
VAW	1 Aug	1811
VAR	4 June	1814
AB	12 Aug	1819 (CH)
AW	27 May	1825 (CH)
d	8 Sept	1834 (CH)
PALMER, George (2)		
L	20 Nov	1812
CR	1 Jan	1840 (OB)
Ret CA	1 Jan	1856 (PRO)
d	8 Sept	1864 (PRO)
PALMER, George Henry		
L	18 Nov	1813
d		1814 (PRO)
PALMER, James		
L	18 Nov	1778
d		1786 (PRO)
PALMER, John		
L	8 Sept	1793
CR	22 Jan	1806
CA	9 Oct	1814
d	5 July	1828 (PRO)
PALMER, Nisbet		
L	30 Oct	1790
T		
CR	24 Dec	1805
d	June	1811 (TR)
PALMER, Richard		
L	24 Feb	1684
PALMER, Thomas		
L	21 Sept	1790
CR	23 June	1796
d (suicide)	3 May	1800 (PJP)
PALMER, William (1)		
L	8 Oct	1758
d		1782 (PRO)
PALMER, William (2)		
L	26 Aug	1800
KIA	3 Jan	1801 (CH)
PALMER, William (3)		
L	17 Aug	1813
Dismissed	30 Sept	1822 (MB)
Restored		1824 (MB)
Ret CR	15 Apr	1856 (PRO)
PALMER, William (4)		
L	25 Apr	1815
d		1823 (PRO)
PAMFLET, James		
L	14 Oct	1702
d		1727 (PRO)
PAMP, Thomas		
L	18 Dec	1793
d		1805 (PRO)
PANIWELL, Thomas		
L		1709 (PJP)

PANTIN, Charles
L 12 Feb 1808
d 1810 (PRO)

PANTON, Henry Gibson
L 8 Dec 1759
KIA Apr 1769 (PJP)

PANTON, John Alexander
L 4 Nov 1762
CR 22 Feb 1776
CA 26 June 1777
d 1781 (PRO)

PANTON, Paul Griffith
L 7 Feb 1812
Ret CR 1 Oct 1853 (PRO)
d 1872 (PRO)

PARDOE, Charles
L 24 Dec 1802
d 1808 (PRO)

PARDOE, William
L 12 Apr 1761
HP June 1810 (OB)
Ret CR 24 Dec 1830 (OB)
d 1861 (PRO)

PARISH, John
L 1 Feb 1802
CR 28 Nov 1806
CA 1 Jan 1817 (MB)
d 1837 (PRO)

PARK, John Steele
L 16 Feb 1815
HP 16 Feb 1815 (OB)
Ret CR 16 Jan 1861 (PRO)
d 1862 (PRO)

PARKE, Henry
L 8 Oct 1777
d 4 Nov 1824 (PRO)

PARKE, Thomas (1)
L 7 Oct 1746
d 1777 (PRO)

PARKE, Thomas (2)
L 4 July 1777
d 1805 (PRO)

PARKER, Abel
L 1664
CA 1665
KIA 27 July 1665 (LG)

PARKER, Charles
L 21 Mar 1812
HP Sept 1815 (OB)
Ret CR 19 Aug 1865 (PRO)
d 3 Feb 1872 (PRO)

PARKER, Charles Christopher
L 17 June 1811
CR 5 Apr 1815
CA 23 Apr 1822 (OB)
HP 23 Apr 1822 (OB)
Ret RA 7 Oct 1852 (DNB)
Ret VA 28 Nov 1857 (DNB)
Ret A 27 Apr 1863 (DNB)
d 13 Mar 1869 (DNB)

PARKER, Christopher (1)
L 1 July 1702 (PMM)
CR 17 Aug 1708 (PMM)
CA 1 Jan 1713
SUP RA 1 Sept 1747
d 1 Feb 1765

PARKER, Christopher (2)
L
CR 7 Dec 1778 (PMM)
CA 7 Mar 1779
RAB 14 Feb 1799
VAB 1 Jan 1801
VAR 23 Apr 1804
d 26 May 1804 (LT)

PARKER, Christopher (3)
L 19 July 1794
CR 17 Nov 1795
d 22 Jan 1798 (PRO)

PARKER, Edward
L 2 Feb 1741
CR 28 Jan 1746
d 1762 (PRO)

PARKER, Edward Thornbrough
L 6 July 1796
CR 25 Oct 1799
d 26 Aug 1801 (PJP)

PARKER, Frederick
L 17 Aug 1801
CR 22 Jan 1806
d (drowned) 7 July 1809 (PJP)

PARKER, Frederick Augustus Hargood
L 22 Jan 1806
CR 15 June 1814
HP 15 June 1814 (OB)
d 1849 (PRO)

PARKER, Sir George
L 13 Mar 1782
CR 4 Nov 1793
CA 7 Apr 1795
RAB 4 June 1814
RAW 12 Aug 1819 (PRO)
RAR 19 July 1821 (PRO)
VAB 27 May 1825 (PRO)
VAW 22 July 1830 (LG)
KCB 12 June 1833 (LG)
AB 10 Jan 1837 (PRO)
AW 23 Nov 1841 (PRO)
AR 9 Nov 1846 (PRO)
d 24 Dec 1847 (PRO)

PARKER, Henry
T
L 28 Apr 1808
CR 27 June 1814
Ret CA 1 July 1864 (PRO)
d 7 Apr 1873 (TR)

PARKER, Henry Dickson
L 11 Apr 1803
Ret CR 23 Jan 1836 (OB)
d 22 Jan 1855 (PRO)

PARKER, Henry Harding
L 30 May 1786
CR 20 Aug 1796
d (drowned) 2 Jan 1797 (CH)

PARKER, Humphrey
L 11 Apr 1689

PARKER, Sir Hyde (1)
L 16 Jan 1745

CR 1747
CA 24 Mar 1748
RAB 23 Jan 1778
RAR 26 Mar 1779 (CH)
VAB 26 Sept 1780
Cre Bt 1782 (CH)
d (drowned) 1783 (CH)

PARKER, Sir Hyde (2)
L 25 Jan 1758
CR 16 Dec 1762
CA 18 July 1763
Kt 1779 (PJP)
Inh Bt 1783 (PJP)
CRM 1790 (DNB)
RAW 1 Feb 1793
RAR 12 Apr 1794
VAB 4 July 1794
VAR 1 June 1795
AB 14 Feb 1799
AW 23 Apr 1804
AR 9 Nov 1805
d 16 Mar 1807 (PRO)

PARKER, Sir Hyde (3)
L 24 Sept 1804
CR 22 Jan 1806
CA 13 Oct 1807
CB 1839 (PJP)
RAB 23 Nov 1841 (PRO)
RAW 24 Apr 1847 (PRO)
RAR 15 Sept 1849 (PRO)
VAB 4 June 1852 (PRO)
FSL 1853 (DNB)
VAW 21 Jan 1854 (PRO)
d 25 May 1854 (PRO)

PARKER, John (1)
L
CA 9 June 1666 (RM)
KIA 25 July 1666 (RM)

PARKER, John (2)
L 27 Feb 1783
CR 21 Oct 1790
d 4 Aug 1794 (PRO)

PARKER, John (3)
L 29 Nov 1814
CR 26 Feb 1829 (OB)
CA 28 June 1838 (OB)
HP 1842 (OB)
d 2 Sept 1867 (PRO)

PARKER, John Frederick
L 24 June 1807
d 1809 (PRO)

PARKER, Nicholas
L
CA 1661
d Sept 1669 (AJ)

PARKER, Sir Peter (1)
L
CR 17 Mar 1735 (PRO)
CA 6 May 1747
Kt 1772 (MPN)
RAB 20 May 1777 (CH)
RAW 23 Jan 1778
RAR 29 Jan 1778 (CH)
GRM 1779 (DNB)
VAB 29 Mar 1779 (CH)
VAW 26 Sept 1780
Cre Bt 13 Jan 1783 (MPN)
MP (Seaford) 1784–1786 (MPN)
MP (Maldon) 1787–1790 (MPN)
AB 24 Sept 1787
AW 12 Apr 1794
AF 16 Sept 1799
d 21 Dec 1811 (DNB)

PARKER, Sir Peter (2)
L 21 Oct 1801
CR 8 May 1804
CA 22 Oct 1805
MP (Wexford) 3 Mar 1810–
June 1811 (MPT)
Inh Bt 21 Dec 1811 (MPT)
KIA 30 Aug 1814 (LG)

PARKER, Richard William
L 28 Feb 1798
CR 15 Aug 1806
d Apr 1824 (MB)

PARKER, Robert (1)
L 3 Feb 1777
CR 1 Dec 1787
CA 22 Nov 1790
d (drowned) 23 Nov 1797 (PJP)

PARKER, Robert (2)
L 20 Sept 1815
Ret CR 1 Oct 1860 (PRO)
d 22 Mar 1861 (PRO)

PARKER, Samuel
L 6 Feb 1758
d 1775 (PRO)

PARKER, Samuel Roberts
L 20 Nov 1812
d 1820 (PRO)

PARKER, Stephen
L 13 Feb 1764
d 1808 (PRO)

PARKER, Thomas (1)
L 26 Sept 1705
SUP 1737 (PRO)
d 1752 (PMM)

PARKER, Thomas (2)
L 6 Feb 1801
CR 1 Aug 1811
d (drowned) 1 Jan 1813 (JH)

PARKER, Walter Turner
L 17 Mar 1815
d 1852 (PRO)

PARKER, Sir William (1)
L 29 Nov 1766
CR 25 June 1773
CA 28 Aug 1777
RAB 4 July 1794
RAR 1 June 1795
Cre Bt 24 June 1797 (DNB)
VAW 14 Feb 1799
VAR 1 Jan 1801
d 31 Oct 1802 (PJP)

PARKER, Sir William (2)
L 5 Sept 1799
CR 10 Oct 1799
CA 9 Oct 1801
CB 4 June 1815 (LG)
RAB 22 July 1830 (PRO)

KCB	16 July	1834 (DNB)
COM AD	1 Aug–23 Dec	1834 (AO)
COM AD	25 Apr	1835–
	25 June	1841 (AO)
RAW	10 Jan	1837 (PRO)
RAR	28 June	1838 (PRO)
VAB	23 Nov	1841 (PRO)
GCB	18 May	1843 (DNB)
Cre Bt	18 Dec	1844 (DNB)
COM AD	13–24 July	1846 (AO)
VAW	9 Nov	1846 (PRO)
VAR	8 Jan	1848 (PRO)
AB	29 Apr	1851 (PRO)
AW	17 Sept	1853 (PRO)
AR	25 June	1858 (PRO)
AF	27 Apr	1863 (PRO)
d	13 Nov	1866 (PRO)

PARKER, William (3)

L	16 Mar	1801
d	24 July	1862 (PRO)

PARKER, William Frederick

L	3 Mar	1815
HP		1824 (OB)
Ret CR	10 Jan	1863 (PRO)
d		1866 (PRO)

PARKER, Sir William George

L	2 Feb	1803
CR	29 Nov	1810
CA	6 June	1814
Ret CA	31 Oct	1846 (LG)
d	24 Mar	1848 (OB)

PARKES, John (1)

L	17 Oct	1759
d		1764 (PRO)

PARKES, John (2)

L	1 Feb	1815
d		1837 (PRO)

PARKES, Robert

L		1666

PARKIN, Henry

L	17 Apr	1746
d		1769 (PRO)

PARKIN, John Pengelly

T		
L	15 Sept	1814
CR	12 Dec	1816 (MB)
CA	28 Aug	1841 (OB)
HP		1842 (OB)
Ret CA	31 Dec	1853 (PRO)
d	1 May	1854 (TR)

PARKINSON, Thomas (1)

L	19 June	1759
d		1778 (PRO)

PARKINSON, Thomas (2)

L	25 Dec	1781

PARKINSON, William

L	12 July	1720
CR	18 Jan	1742
d	26 June	1747 (PMM)

PARKINSON, William Standway

L	14 May	1794
CR	12 Aug	1799
CA	9 Feb	1808
d	19 May	1838 (PRO)

PARKMAN, John

L	20 Nov	1812
Ret CR	28 May	1855 (PRO)
d		1856 (PRO)

PARKS, Abraham

L	15 Mar	1815
d	1 Oct	1863 (PRO)

PARKYNS, Augustus

L	14 Dec	1805
d		1811 (PRO)

PARKYNS, George

L	16 Nov	1811
d		1844 (PRO)

PARNELL, John

L	8 June	1762
d		1765(6) (PRO)

PARR, Alexander Forsyth

T		
L	2 Apr	1806
d	12 Nov	1856 (TR)

PARR, John

L	25 July	1695 (PJP)
CR	8 Jan	1706 (PJP)
CA	1 Jan	1713
d	23 May	1742

PARR, John Seppins

L	14 June	1809

PARR, Thomas

L	20 Jan	1777
CR	3 Mar	1781
CA	21 Sept	1790
d	17 June	1800 (PRO)

PARR, William

L	8 May	1812
d	10 May	1816 (PRO)

PARREY, John

L	6 Nov	1778
d		1790 (PRO)

PARREY, Robert (1)

L	22 Feb	1759
CR	17 Jan	1783
CA	22 Nov	1790
d	24 Aug	1808 (LT)

PARREY, Robert (2)

L	2 Nov	1790
CR	26 Aug	1808
d		1832 (OB)

PARRY, Andrew

L	18 Sept	1809
d	10 Dec	1813 (PJP)

PARRY, Charles Spencer

L	16 May	1778
d		1797 (PRO)

PARRY, Francis (1)

L	24 July	1735
CR	25 Mar	1741
CA	10 Feb	1742
d	17 Apr	1742

PARRY, Francis (2)

L	20 Aug	1759
CR	11 Jan	1775
CA	7 Apr	1778

RAW 1 June 1795
VAB 14 Feb 1799
VAW 1 Jan 1801
d 18 Dec 1803

PARRY, Henry
L 16 Aug 1811
CR 28 July 1851 (PRO)
d 1861 (PRO)

PARRY, Howard Lewis
L 10 Mar 1815
CR 10 Feb 1832 (OB)
HP 10 Feb 1832 (OB)
Ret CA 1 Apr 1856 (PRO)
d 1869 (PRO)

PARRY, Hugh
L 21 May 1746
d 1746(7) (PRO)

PARRY, Paul
L 13 May 1778
d 12 Feb 1803

PARRY, Thomas Parry Jones
L 28 Jan 1803 (OB)
CR 27 Dec 1808
HP Nov 1814 (OB)
Ret CA 10 Sept 1840 (OB)
d 26 May 1845 (OB)

PARRY, William (1)
L 10 Sept 1708
Dismissed 13 Dec 1708 (FVT)
Restored
CR
CA 18 Apr 1732
d 7 Feb 1753 (PRO)

PARRY, William (2)
L 22 July 1738
CR 29 Dec 1743 (PRO)
CA 2 Oct 1744
RAB 1763 (CH)
RAR 18 Oct 1770
VAB 24 Oct 1770
VAW 31 Mar 1775
VAR 5 Feb 1776
AB 29 Jan 1778 (CH)
d 29 Apr 1779 (CH)

PARRY, William Bowen
L 22 Nov 1776
KIA 6 July 1779 (LG)

PARRY, Sir William Edward
L 6 Jan 1810
CR 4 Dec 1820 (MB)
CA 8 Nov 1821 (OB)
Kt 29 Apr 1829 (LG)
RAB 4 June 1852 (PRO)
RAW 27 Jan 1854 (PRO)
d 7 July 1855 (PRO)

PARRY, William Henry Webly
Formerly WEBLY, William
L 28 Sept 1790
CR 8 Oct 1798
CA 29 Apr 1802
CB 4 June 1815 (LG)
RAW 10 Jan 1837 (PRO)
d 31 May 1837 (PMM)

PARSON, John
L 1 Nov 1807
CR 16 Sept 1816 (PRO)
CA 10 Jan 1837 (PRO)
d 29 Nov 1847 (LT)

PARSONS, Charles
L 1701 (PRO)
CR
CA 6 Apr 1704
KIA 11 Apr 1706 (PJP)

PARSONS, Daniel
L
CA 14 June 1679
d 22 Dec 1702 (PRO)

PARSONS, George Samuel
L 25 Mar 1802
HP Dec 1810–1841 (OB)
Ret CR 15 Feb 1850 (PRO)
d 20 Jan 1854 (PRO)

PARSONS, John
T
L 3 Feb 1815
CR 9 Jan 1854 (PRO)
d 1864 (TR)

PARSONS, Robert White
L 11 Apr 1806
CR 7 Nov 1816 (MB)
CA 11 Nov 1828 (MB)
HP 1829 (OB)
Ret CA 11 Nov 1848 (OB)
Ret RA 3 July 1855 (PRO)
d 20 Jan 1861 (PRO)

PARSONS, Thomas (1)
L 28 Oct 1694 (PJP)

PARSONS, Thomas (2)
L 24 July 1797

PARSONS, Thomas (3)
L 30 Nov 1799
d (drowned) 1803 (PJP)

PARSONS, Timothy
L 2 Mar 1815

PARSONS, William (1)
L 18 Feb 1796
Ret CR 26 Nov 1830 (OB)
d 1846 (OB)

PARSONS, William (2)
L 21 Feb 1815

PARTINGTON, Henry
L 13 Mar 1693
CR
CA 20 Oct 1703
d 30 Jan 1737 (PJP)

PARTINGTON, John
L 17 May 1746

PARTRIDGE, Richard
L
CA 1666

PARTRIDGE, Robert
L
CA 28 May 1691
KIA 9 July 1692 (CH)

PASCAL, Michael Henry
L 9 Dec 1745
CR 21 Aug 1759
In Portuguese Service 1761 (PJP)
CA 20 June 1765
d 1787

PASCO, John
L 15 July 1795
T wounded
CR 24 Dec 1805
CA 3 Apr 1811
RAB 22 Sept 1847 (OB)
RAW 9 Oct 1849 (LG)
RAR 1852 (PMM)
d Nov 1853 (TR)

PASCOE, John Eyre
L 7 Mar 1815
HP 7 Mar 1815 (OB)
Ret CR 10 Apr 1863 (PRO)
d 1865 (PRO)

PASCOE, Richard
L 23 May 1744
d 1762 (PRO)

PASCOE, William Beard
L 5 Dec 1796
d 1806 (PRO)

PASCOE, William Richard
L 1 Feb 1805
KIA 7 Feb 1813 (LG)

PASLEY, James
L 20 July 1800
Ret CR 26 Nov 1830 (OB)
d 1860 (PRO)

PASLEY, James Thomas
L 28 May 1813
CR 13 June 1815
d 7 July 1818 (PRO)

PASLEY, Sir Thomas
L 10 Oct 1757
CR 9 Aug 1762
CA 21 Jan 1771
Cre Bt 1794 (OB)
RAB 12 Apr 1794
RAR 4 July 1794
VAW 1 June 1795
VAR 14 Feb 1799
AB 1 Jan 1801 (PRO)
AW 9 Nov 1805
d 29 Nov 1808 (DNB)

PASMORE, James
L 28 Oct 1778
d 1790 (PRO)

PASSENGER, Charles
L 1709 (PJP)

PASSENGER, William
L
CA 20 May 1695
d 10 May 1728 (LTE)

PASSMORE, John
L 30 Dec 1808
d 21 Jan 1830 (PRO)

PASSMORE, Robert
L 18 Mar 1794
d 1798 (PRO)

PASTON, Robert
L 8 Sept 1706 (PMM)
CR
CA 3 June 1709
d (drowned) 7 Oct 1711 (CH)

PASTON, William
L 19 Sept 1755
CR 8 Mar 1757
CA 3 Aug 1757
d 1774

PATCH, Zachariah
L 23 Feb 1782
d 1795 (PRO)

PATER, Charles Dudley
L 8 Oct 1779
CR 7 Oct 1794
CA 16 Mar 1795
RAW 4 June 1814
d 5 Feb 1818 (PRO)

PATERSON, Charles William
L 3 Feb 1777
CR 8 Apr 1782
CA 20 Jan 1794
RAB 12 Aug 1812
RAW 4 Dec 1813
RAR 4 June 1814
VAB 12 Aug 1819 (CH)
VAW 27 May 1825 (CH)
VAR 22 July 1830 (CH)
AW 10 Jan 1837 (CH)
d 10 Mar 1841 (CH)

PATERSON, David
L 26 Nov 1802
CR 16 Oct 1810
d 9 Sept 1813 (PJP)

PATERSON, James
L 10 May 1745
d 1761 (PRO)

PATERSON, William
L 18 Feb 1805
CR 9 Apr 1808
CA 16 July 1810
CB 19 Sept 1816 (LG)
d 18 May 1838 (PRO)

PATERSON, William Love
L 6 Sept 1806
Became Junior Lt 20 Jan 1807
L 20 Jan 1809
Ret CR 3 Feb 1847 (OB)
d 16 Mar 1856 (PRO)

PATESHALL, Nicholas Lechmere
L 20 Nov 1801
CR 24 July 1811
CA 18 Feb 1815
Ret CA 31 Oct 1846 (LG)

PATEY, Benjamin
L 4 July 1801
T
d 1806 (PRO)

PATEY, Charles
L 22 Nov 1790
Ret CR 20 July 1825 (MB)
d 3 Nov 1854 (PRO)

PATEY, George
L 21 Apr 1780
d 1782(3) (PRO)

PATEY, George Edward
L 20 July 1813
Ret CR 15 Apr 1856 (PRO)
d 1865 (PRO)

PATEY, John
L 22 July 1797
d 1807 (PRO)

PATEY, Joseph
L 6 Sept 1802
CR 19 July 1815
HP Sept 1835 (OB)
Ret CR 1 July 1851 (PRO)
d 11 July 1852 (PRO)

PATEY, William
L 15 Jan 1782
d 1811 (PRO)

PATFULL, William
L 7 May 1804
d 1809 (PRO)

PATRIARCH, Charles
L 26 Nov 1799
HP June 1813 (OB)
Ret CR 26 Nov 1830 (OB)
d 16 Jan 1850 (PRO)

PATTE, Joseph
L 22 Jan 1806
Dismissed 1814 (PRO)

PATTERSON, Benjamin
L 8 Feb 1805

PATTERSON, Forbes
L 17 Nov 1746
d 1777 (PRO)

PATTERSON, John
L 30 Jan 1741
d 10 Mar 1744 (PMM)

PATTERSON, William
L 21 Feb 1815
Ret CR 21 Oct 1861 (PRO)
d 1874 (PRO)

PATTISON, George
L 11 Apr 1778
d 19 Mar 1803

PATTISON, Henry
L
CA 1666
KIA 3 May 1673 (NJ)

PATTISON, Mark
L 15 Jan 1759
CR 14 Oct 1762
CA 21 Aug 1765
d 1793 (PRO)

PATTON, Charles
L 17 Feb 1780
CR 25 Sept 1781
CA 30 May 1795
SUP 1816

PATTON, Hugh
T
L 1 Feb 1811
CR 6 Dec 1813
CA 12 Aug 1819 (MB)
Ret CA 31 Oct 1846 (LG)
Ret RA 19 Jan 1852 (PRO)
Ret VA 10 Sept 1857 (PRO)
Ret A 27 Apr 1863 (PRO)
d 18 Mar 1864 (TR)

PATTON, Philip
L 3 July 1763
CR 9 May 1778
CA 22 Mar 1779
RAB 1 June 1795
RAR 14 Feb 1799
VAB 1 Jan 1801
VAR 23 Apr 1804
COM AD 15 May 1804–
10 Feb 1806 (AO)
AB 9 Nov 1805
AW 31 July 1810
AR 4 June 1814
d 31 Dec 1815 (DNB)

PATTON, Robert
T
L 13 Nov 1810
CR 13 June 1815
CA 30 Apr 1827 (MB)
Ret CA 30 Apr 1847 (PRO)
Ret RA 1854 (TR)
Ret VA 1861 (TR)
Ret A 1864 (TR)
d 1883 (TR)

PATTON, Thomas
L 21 Mar 1812

PATTY, Robert
L 17 Apr 1809

PAUL, Christmas
L 26 May 1768
CR 27 July 1781
CA 11 Nov 1794
d 12 Dec 1816 (PJP)

PAUL, Edward
L 9 Nov 1806

PAUL, George
L 3 Mar 1783

PAUL, John
L 4 Jan 1695
CR 13 Aug 1703 (PMM)
CA 12 Sept 1706
d 3 Apr 1720 (PJP)

PAUL, Richard
L
CA 23 Jan 1694
d 17 Mar 1703 (PJP)

PAUL, Robert
L 10 May 1794
CR 29 Apr 1802
d 1804 (PJP)

PAULET, Lord Henry
See POWLETT, Lord Henry

PAWLE, Christopher
L 12 Jan 1796

PAWLE, Richard
L 3 Nov 1807

PAWLETT, Edmund
L 29 Mar 1757

PAXTON, Wentworth
L
CA 22 Jan 1694
Quitted 1699
d 1736

PAYNE, Charles
L 4 May 1810

PAYNE, Charles Frederick
L 18 Apr 1799
CR 26 Dec 1806

CA	7 June	1814
Ret CA	31 Oct	1846 (LG)
Ret RA	6 Sept	1849 (LG)
PAYNE, Christopher Wyvil		
L	16 May	1814
PAYNE, John Willett		
L	9 Mar	1777
CR	6 Nov	1779
CA	8 July	1780
MP (Huntingdon)	9 May 1787–	1796 (MPN)
TGH		1799 (PJP)
RAB	14 Feb	1799
RAW	1 Jan	1801
RAR	29 Apr	1802
d	17 Nov	1803 (MPN)
PAYNE, Richard (1)		
L	9 Dec	1796
d	5 Aug	1802 (PJP)
PAYNE, Richard (2)		
L	13 Feb	1815
HP	13 Feb	1815 (OB)
PAYNE, Robert		
L	11 May	1804
d (drowned)		1805 (PJP)
PAYNE, Samuel J.		
L		1815 (PJP)
PAYNE, Thomas		
L	16 June	1781
d	13 Sept	1790 (PRO)
PAYNE, William		
L	9 Oct	1795
Ret CR	26 Nov	1830 (OB)
PAYNTER, Charles		
L	27 June	1814
PAYNTER, John		
L	1 Aug	1810
CR	7 Nov	1816 (OB)
HP	7 Nov	1816 (OB)
PAYNTER, John Meyrick		
L	11 Oct	1814
PAYNTER, William		
L	18 Apr	1778
d	1 May	1789
PEACE, Richard		
L	22 Apr	1811
PEACH, Henry		
L		1665
PEACH, Joseph (1)		
L	13 Sept	1704 (PMM)
PEACH, Joseph (2)		
L		1706 (PJP)
PEACH, William (1)		
L		
CA		1665
PEACH, William (2)		
L		1711 (PJP)
PEACH, –		
L		1666
PEACHEY, Hon. Henry John		
L	5 Jan	1807
CR	11 July	1811
CA	7 Aug	1812
PEACOCK, James		
L		1690 (PJP)
CA		1693 (PJP)
PEACOCK, Samuel Blackshaw		
L	2 Mar	1815
PEACOCK, Thomas		
L	6 Feb	1694
PEACOCK, William		
L	12 June	1776
CR	30 Jan	1778
	(22 July	1778?)
CA	27 Jan	1780
PEACOCKE, Richard		
L	22 Jan	1796
CR	28 Jan	1801
CA	4 June	1801
Ret RA	22 July	1830 (OB)
RAR	17 Aug	1840 (LG)
VAB	23 Nov	1841 (LG)
d	24 Apr	1846 (OB)
PEADLE, Moses		
L	29 Jan	1737
PEAKE, Charles		
L	1 July	1814
HP	Aug	1821 (OB)
d	2 Jan	1847 (OB)
PEAKE, Daniel		
L	18 Nov	1814
PEAKE, Thomas Ladd		
L	8 May	1805
CR	8 May	1812
CA	1 Mar	1822 (MB)
Ret CA	31 Oct	1846 (LG)
PEAKE, William		
L	21 July	1797
CR	22 Jan	1806
KIA	24 Jan	1813 (CH)
PEALLY, William		
L		
CR		
CA	22 Jan	1703
PEAR, Gilbert		
L	28 Jan	1708 (PMM)
PEARCE, Edward		
L		
CA		1671 (PJP)
d (drowned)	16 Jan	1674 (PJP)
PEARCE, John (1)		
L		1666 (DDA)
CA		1664
e (cowardice)	Sept	1671 (CH)
PEARCE, John (2)		
L		1665
CA		1667 (DDA)
d	before	1689(PJP)
PEARCE, John Jones		
L	9 July	1814
PEARCE, John Street		
L	5 Nov	1802
T		
Gone		1809 (TR)
PEARCE, Joseph		
L	18 Nov	1799
CR	2 Apr	1804
CA	7 June	1814
PEARCE, Marle		
L		
CA		1665
PEARCE, Robert (1)		
L	29 June	1797
PEARCE, Robert (2)		
L	25 Feb	1812

PEARCE, Robert (3)
L 5 Apr 1814
PEARCE, Vincent (1)
or PEARSE, Vincent?
L 1664
CA 1665
KIA 2 Aug 1665 (ESP)
PEARCE, Vincent (2)
or PEARSE, Vincent?
L
CR
CA 5 Oct 1715
d 28 May 1745
PEARCE, Vincent (3)
or PEARSE, Vincent?
L 19 Feb 1741
CR 11 Sept 1747
CA 4 Nov 1748
d Dec 1759
PEARCE, William
L 19 Dec 1804
CR 21 July 1837 (PMM)
d 12 Feb 1843 (PMM)
PEARCE, William
See PEARSE, William
PEARCE, William Isaac
L 21 Nov 1799
PEARD, George (1)
L 15 June 1744
CR 23 Aug 1759
PEARD, George (2)
L 5 July 1815
CR 7 May 1827 (PJP)
d 16 Feb 1837 (LT)
PEARD, Gilbert
L 1709 (PJP)
PEARD, Shuldham
L 26 Apr 1780
CR
CA 30 Nov 1795
SUP RA 5 July 1814
RAR 5 July 1827 (CH)
VAW 22 July 1830 (CH)
d 21 Jan 1833 (CH)
PEARKERS, John
L 21 Mar 1801
PEARL, Sir James
T
L 21 Dec 1808
CR 29 Sept 1827 (CH)
KH 1836 (TR)
Kt 1838 (TR)
d 1839 (TR)
PEARS, J.C.
L 1797 (PJP)
PEARSALL, Andrew
See PERSALL, Andrew
PEARSE, Alexander
L 8 Mar 1783
PEARSE, Henry Whitmarsh
or PEARSE, William Whitmarsh
L 29 Sept 1796
CR 8 May 1804
CA 23 Dec 1809
CB 4 June 1815 (LG)
PEARSE, Jeffrey
L 1664
CA 1664
KIA 28 May 1672 (LG)
PEARSE, John (1)
L 1665
PEARSE, John (2)
L 29 Dec 1800
CR 27 May 1825 (OB)
HP 27 May 1825 (OB)
PEARSE, Joseph
L 22 July 1813
CR 8 June 1841 (OB)
HP Mar 1843 (OB)
CA 8 Jan 1846 (OB)
PEARSE, Philip
L 23 Feb 1782
d 19 Sept 1800
PEARSE, Thomas (1)
L
CA 1667
PEARSE, Thomas (2)
L
CR 1 Sept 1794
CA 6 Dec 1796
SUP CA 24 Aug 1819 (OB)
d 10 Apr 1830 (PMM)
PEARSE, Thomas (3)
L 1 Aug 1807
d 16 July 1846 (OB)
PEARSE, Thomas (4)
L 16 June 1812
PEARSE, Vincent
See PEARCE, Vincent
PEARSE, William (1)
L 6 July 1805
PEARSE, William (2)
L 6 May 1808
PEARSE, William Whitmarsh
See PEARSE, Henry Whitmarsh
PEARSON, Alexander Stevenson
L 14 Dec 1814
CR 3 Oct 1820 (MB)
HP 1839 (OB)
PEARSON, Charles (1)
L 8 Nov 1808
CR 29 July 1814
CA 3 Apr 1837 (OB)
HP 3 Apr 1837 (OB)
PEARSON, Charles (2)
L 8 Nov 1808
HP 1815 (OB)
Ret CR 27 Jan 1846 (OB)
PEARSON, George
T wounded
L 21 Sept 1811
d 1816 (TR)
PEARSON, Hugh
L 11 Dec 1799
CR 7 June 1814
PEARSON, James
L 20 Sept 1814
PEARSON, Sir Richard
L 16 Dec 1755
CR 29 Oct 1770
CA 25 Jan 1773
Kt 1779 (PJP)
LGH Dec 1800 (PJP)
d 26 Jan 1808 (PJP)

PEARSON, Richard Harrison
L 11 May 1793
CR 5 Dec 1796
CA 7 Aug 1798
RAB 27 May 1825 (LG)
RAR 22 July 1830 (LG)
VAB 10 Jan 1837 (LG)
d 9 Jan 1838 (CH)

PEARSON, Robert (1)
L
CR
CA 25 Dec 1710
d 30 Aug 1723

PEARSON, Robert (2)
L 1 Jan 1781
CR 6 Dec 1796
SUP CR Sept 1806
d Mar 1827 (MB)

PEARSON, Thomas (1)
L 5 Feb 1694

PEARSON, Thomas (2)
L 27 Feb 1815

PEAT, George
L 22 Mar 1762

PEAT, John Green
L 17 Mar 1815
HP 17 Mar 1815 (OB)

PECHELL, George Richard
L 25 June 1810
CR 30 May 1814
CA 22 Dec 1822 (OB)
HP 22 Dec 1822 (OB)
Ret RA 17 Dec 1852 (DNB)
Ret VA 5 Jan 1858 (DNB)
d 29 June 1860 (DNB)

PECHELL, Samuel George
T
L 6 Feb 1806
CR 25 Apr 1809
CA 30 Apr 1810
d 1840 (TR)

PECHELL, Sir Samuel John
L 1 Apr 1803
CR 23 Mar 1807
CA 16 June 1808
CB 4 June 1815 (LG)
Cre Bt 18 June 1826 (DNB)
KCH 6 Jan 1833 (DNB)
RAB 9 Nov 1846 (LG)
RAW 7 Jan 1848 (LG)
d 3 Nov 1849 (DNB)

PECHELL, Thomas John
See PESHALL, Thomas John

PECK, Andrew
L 1689 (PJP)

PECK, George
L 19 Apr 1754

PECK, Robert
L 21 Jan 1690 (PJP)

PECKETT, Nathaniel
L 1669
d Feb 1692 (M)

PECKOVER, John
L 1692 (PJP)

PEDDER, Andrew
L
CA 27 Feb 1693 (PJP)

PEDDER, George Murray M'Kinley
L 3 Mar 1808
d 26 Aug 1847 (OB)

PEDDIE, John
L
CR 24 Nov 1740
d Aug 1742

PEDING, John
L 1 Feb 1806

PEDLAR, George
L 7 Jan 1802
CR 12 Oct 1814

PEED, James
L 6 June 1801
d 1812 (PJP)

PEELE, Peter
L 4 Nov 1801

PEERMAN, John
L 28 Aug 1743
d June 1758 (PJP)

PEERS, James
L 3 Dec 1727
CR
CA 2 Feb 1741
d 26 Nov 1746

PEERS, John Consett
L 2 Nov 1778 (PJP)
CR 20 July 1797

PEEVEY, William
L 7 Mar 1746

PEEVOR, Richard Tattersall
L 7 Nov 1806
d (drowned) 24 Dec 1811 (PJP)

PEIGHIN, John
L 2 June 1745
CR 4 Jan 1758
CA 1 Dec 1761
d 1787

PEIRSON, George
L 11 Oct 1814

PEIRSON, Thomas
L 1665

PELL, Thomas
L 29 July 1757

PELL, Sir Watkin Owen
L 11 Nov 1806
CR 29 Mar 1810
CA 1 Nov 1813
KCH Apr 1837 (OB)
RAB 5 Sept 1848 (LG)
Ret VA 28 Dec 1855 (CH)
Ret A 11 Feb 1861 (CH)
d 29 Dec 1869 (DNB)

PELLATT, Thomas
L 20 Apr 1727
CR 29 July 1740

PELLEW, Edward, Viscount Exmouth
See EXMOUTH, Edward Pellew, Viscount

PELLEW, Sir Fleetwood Broughton Reynolds
L 8 Sept 1805
CR 12 Oct 1807
CA 14 Oct 1808
CB 4 June 1815 (LG)
KCH Jan 1836 (DNB)
RAB 9 Nov 1846 (OB)

RAW 20 Mar 1848 (LG)
VA 22 Apr 1853 (DNB)
A 13 Feb 1858 (DNB)
d 28 July 1861 (DNB)

PELLEW, Sir Israel
L 1 Apr 1779
CR 22 Nov 1790
CA 25 June 1793
T
RAB 31 July 1810
RAW 12 Aug 1812
RAR 4 June 1814
KCB 1 July 1816 (LG)
VAB 12 Aug 1819 (CH)
VAW 19 July 1821 (CH)
VAR 27 May 1825 (CH)
AB 22 July 1830 (CH)
d 19 July 1832 (CH)

PELLEW, Hon. Pownoll Bastard
L 9 Apr 1802
CR 1 May 1804
CA 22 Jan 1806
MP (Launceston) 1812–Mar 1829 (MPT)
d 2 Dec 1833 (OB)

PELLOWE, Richard
L 14 Nov 1790
CR 11 May 1796
CA 29 Apr 1802

PELLY, Augustus
L 8 May 1812

PELLY, Charles
L 26 Nov 1799
CR 7 May 1802
CA 10 Apr 1804
d Nov 1811 (LT)

PELTMAN, William Robert Ashley
L 28 July 1804

PELTON, John
L 1689

PEMBLE, Thomas
L 15 Feb 1745
CR 20 June 1765

PEMBERTON, Henry
L 16 Mar 1761
CR 1 Apr 1778

PEMBERTON, Henry Charles
L 25 Jan 1813
CR 20 Jan 1818

PEMBERTON, William
L 9 Jan 1779

PEMBRIDGE, Richard
L 1672
d before 1689 (PJP)

PENBERTHY, Thomas
L 18 July 1810

PENDER, Francis
L 2 June 1772
CR 20 June 1780
CA 1 Dec 1787
RAB 2 Oct 1807
RAW 28 Apr 1808
RAR 31 July 1810
VAB 1 Aug 1811
VAW 4 June 1814
VAR 12 Aug 1819 (CH)
d Sept 1820 (PRO)

PENETEER, Edward
L 1692 (PJP)

PENFOLD, Charles
L 1783 (PJP)
Dismissed 31 July 1783 (PJP)

PENGELLEY, Charles
L 16 Feb 1805
CR 20 Sept 1814
d 30 Dec 1853 (PMM)

PENGELLY, Henry
L 21 Mar 1812
HP May 1815 (OB)

PENGELLY, James
L 25 Oct 1793

PENGELLY, John (1)
L 24 Aug 1780
CR 18 Feb 1800
d 1810 (PJP)

PENGELLY, John (2)
L 8 Feb 1815
HP 8 Feb 1815 (OB)

PENHALLOW, Thomas
L 27 Dec 1707 (PMM)

PENN, Sir William (1)
L
MP
(Weymouth and Melcome Regis)
1660,1661–16 Sept 1670 (MPH)
COM E 4 July 1660–
16 Jan 1667 (NBO)
CA 1664
AW 24 Mar 1665
COM V 16 Jan 1667
17 June 1669 (NBO)
d 16 Sept 1670 (DNB)

PENN, William (2)
L 30 Apr 1678

PENN, William (3)
L 30 Aug 1688

PENNICHICK, Henry
L 1692 (PJP)

PENNIE, John Cobham
L 29 Apr 1802

PENNINGTON, Joseph
L 10 Aug 1766
d (duel) 18 Jan 1776 (PMM)

PENNINGTON, Thomas
L 4 May 1814

PENNY, George
L 1690 (PJP)

PENNY, Taylor
L 6 Aug 1745
CR 31 Dec 1755
CA 1 Nov 1757
d 1786

PENROSE, Sir Charles Vinicombe
L 17 Aug 1779
CR 1794 (PMM)
CA 7 Oct 1794
RAB 4 Dec 1813
RAW 4 June 1814
KCB 3 Jan 1816 (MB)
RAR 12 Aug 1819 (CH)
Kt (Two Sicilies) 27 Aug 1819 (LG)
VAB 19 July 1821 (CH)
VAW 27 May 1825 (CH)
d 1 Jan 1830

PENROSE, Mathias
L 1666

PENROSE, Thomas (1)
L
CA 1665
PENROSE, Thomas (2)
L 14 July 1744
PENRUDOCK, George
L 28 July 1807
CR 15 June 1814
HP 15 June 1814
PEPPER, William Barker
L 10 Oct 1777
SUP CR 19 Nov 1812
PEPWELL, John
L 1689 (PJP)
PEPWELL, Thomas
L 19 Oct 1797
PEPYS, John
L 3 May 1690
CR 25 Mar 1704 (PMM)
PERCEVAL, Hon. George James, Earl of Egmont
T
L 7 June 1813
CR 13 June 1815
CA 7 Dec 1818 (PJP)
MP (West Sussex) 1837–1840 (TR)
Inh EP 1840 (PMM)
RA 17 Aug 1851 (PMM)
VA 10 Sept 1857 (PMM)
A 23 Mar 1863 (PMM)
d 2 Aug 1874 (PMM)
PERCEVAL, Hon. Philip Tufton
L
CR 5 Sept 1759
CA 21 July 1760
d 21 Apr 1795 (PMM)
PERCEVAL, Richard
L 6 Apr 1815
PERCEVAL, Westby
L 17 Oct 1800
CR 14 Sept 1808
CA 16 Oct 1815
Kt (Austria) 5 Mar 1816 (LG)
d 1835 (PJP)
PERCHARD, Robert
L 7 Oct 1737
PERCIVAL, Crean
L 16 Dec 1757
PERCIVAL, Francis
L 22 Jan 1719
PERCIVAL, Samuel
L 21 July 1706 (PMM)
PERCIVAL, Thomas
L 11 Mar 1802
CR Aug 1811 (PJP)
PERCIVAL, Westby
See PERCEVAL, Westby
PERCY, Lord Algernon, Duke of Northumberland
L 16 Dec 1811
CR 8 Mar 1814
CA 19 Aug 1815
HP 19 Aug 1815 (OB)
Inh EP 1847 (OB)
RAB 11 Nov 1850 (LG)
FLA 2 Mar 1852–
5 Jan 1853 (AO)
Ret VA 9 July 1857 (CH)
Ret A 4 Oct 1859 (CH)
d 12 Feb 1865 (DNB)

PERC(E)Y, Francis
L 1702 (PJP)
CR 18 Dec 1704 (PMM)
CA 12 Feb 1708
d 16 Feb 1742 (PMM)
PERCY, Hon. Jocelyn
L 30 Apr 1804
CR 22 Jan 1806
CA 25 Sept 1806
MP (Bere Alston) 1806–1820 (MPT)
CB 26 Sept 1831 (DNB)
RAB 23 Nov 1841 (LG)
RAW 9 Nov 1846 (LG)
RAR 20 Mar 1848 (LG)
RAR 29 Apr 1851 (DNB)
d 19 Oct 1856 (DNB)
PERCY, Philip
L 20 Mar 1808
PERCY, Robert
L 19 Apr 1783
PERCY, Hon. William Henry
L 6 July 1807
CR 2 May 1810
CA 21 Mar 1812
MP (Stamford) 1818–1826 (MPT)
Ret RA 1 Oct 1846 (LG)
d 5 Oct 1855 (MPT)
PERDRIEAU, Stephen
L 20 Dec 1796
PERDU, John
L 1665
CA 1667
PEREGRINE, Thomas
L 1807 (PJP)
PERKINS, Charles James
L 16 Feb 1801
PERKINS, George
L 1665
PERKINS, Henry Augustus
L 16 Mar 1814
PERKINS, John (1)
L 25 Feb 1782
CR 21 June 1797
CA 6 Sept 1800
d 27 Jan 1812 (PJP)
PERKINS, John (2)
L 27 Dec 1808
d July 1811 (LT)
PERKINS, Robert
L 21 Nov 1790
PERKINS, Thomas Paul
L 22 Mar 1797
T
CR 21 Oct 1810
d 1815 (TR)
PERKINS, William (1)
L 29 Jan 1745
d June 1793 (M)
PERKINS, William (2)
L 27 May 1795
d 1812 (PJP)
PERKINS, William (3)
L 2 Aug 1799
PERREAU, Samuel
L 1756
KIA 24 Mar 1757 (LG)

PERROT, Henry Dundas
L 23 June 1809
PERRY, John (1)
L
CA 17 Feb 1692
Dismissed Sept 1693 (PJP)
d 1733 (CH)
PERRY, John (2)
L 11 Mar 1760
PERRY, John Cardew
L 14 May 1798
PERRY, Joseph (1)
L 1673
CA 1673
PERRY, Joseph (2)
L 26 Nov 1697 (PJP)
PERRY, Michael
L 1689 (PJP)
PERRY, Swift
L 1797 (PJP)
PERRY, Walter
L 1672 (CH)
CA 1667
KIA 28 May 1672 (CH)
PERRYMAN, John
L
CA 1665
PERRYMAN, Joseph
L
CA 1673
PERSALL, Andrew
L 1672
PESHALL, Thomas John
L 3 Mar 1804
PESTELL, William
L
CA 1661
PETCH, William Tatton
L 27 June 1814
HP 1827 (OB)
PETER, Robert
L 27 Aug 1804
PETER, William Franklin
T
L 30 Nov 1809
d 1830 (TR)
PETERBOROUGH, Charles Mordaunt, Earl of
CA 1687 (DNB)
CF 10 Nov 1688 (EAD)
CH 15 June 1689 (EAD)
Inh EP 19 June 1697 (HBC)
Commander of Allied Forces in Spain
31 Mar 1705 (DNB)
Joint Admiral with Sir Cloudesley Shovell
1 May 1705
d 25 Oct 1735 (DNB)
PETERS, Daniel
L 1692 (PJP)
PETERS, James
L 5 May 1735
PETERS, Lewis Charles
L 29 Aug 1812
PETERS, Peter
L 26 Mar 1710
d 1754 (PMM)
PETERS, William Ostwicke
L 27 Aug 1814

PETERSON, Charles
L 28 Sept 1795
d (duel) 13 Jan 1798 (PJP)
PETERSON, Matthew
L
CA 1662
PETERSON, Moses
L 10 Jan 1710 (PMM)
PETLEY, Horrace
L 4 Sept 1801
PETT, Phineas (1)
L
CA 1661
KIA 2 May 1666 (CH)
PETT, Phineas (2)
L 1689 (PJP)
PETT, Robert
L 19 Sept 1727
CR
CA 15 July 1740
COM V 1775 (PJP)
d 19 Oct 1776 (M)
PETTET, James
L 6 Mar 1802
d 22 July 1813 (PJP)
PETTET, John Bentinck
L 19 May 1797
PETTET, Robert
L 6 Oct 1794
CR 2 Jan 1804
d 13 Nov 1833 (LT)
PETTET, Samuel
L 8 Feb 1794
PETTIGREW, William
L
CR 30 Apr 1746
CA 18 July 1755
d 24 Nov 1756
PETTILLO, William
L 1703 (PJP)
PETTIT, Mark
L 29 Mar 1815
PETTMAN, Richard
L 15 Aug 1810
PETTMAN, Thomas
L 19 Mar 1805
CR 15 June 1814
CA 5 Sept 1823 (MB)
d 1828 (MB)
PETTMAN, William Robert Ashley
L 18 Nov 1800
Jr Lt 1803
CR 7 June 1814
PEWTRISS, Thomas
L 23 Aug 1777 (PJP)
PEYTON, Edward
L 30 Apr 1727
CR 24 June 1739
CA 4 Apr 1740
d 4 Apr 1749 (PJP)
PEYTON, George (1)
L 20 Apr 1694
PEYTON, George (2)
L
CR

CA 18 Nov 1790
d 1801

PEYTON, John (1)
L 10 Feb 1772
CR 27 Mar 1782
CA 21 Jan 1783
RAB 9 Nov 1805
RAR 29 Apr 1808
d 2 Aug 1809 (CH)

PEYTON, John (2)
L 27 June 1814

PEYTON, Sir John Strutt
L 7 Oct 1805
CR 1 Dec 1807
CA 26 Sept 1811
KCH 25 June 1836 (OB)
d 20 May 1838 (OB)

PEYTON, Joseph (1)
L 4 June 1743
CR 23 Mar 1756
CA 2 Dec 1757
RAW 24 Sept 1787
VAB 21 Sept 1790
VAW 1 Feb 1793
VAR 12 Apr 1794
AB 1 June 1795
AW 14 Feb 1799
d 22 Sept 1804 (CH)

PEYTON, Joseph (2)
L 2 Sept 1772
CR 14 Dec 1778
CA 26 Sept 1788
SUP RA 12 Oct 1807
d 1816 (PJP)

PEYTON, Joseph (3)
L 22 Jan 1802
d (drowned) 26 Dec 1803 (PJP)

PEYTON, Joseph Lyddell
L 11 Oct 1806

PEYTON, Thomas
L 19 Sept 1777
d 1801 (PJP)

PEYTON, Sir Yelverton
L 22 Jan 1704 (PMM)
CR 9 Apr 1723
CA 22 Mar 1725
Dismissed 11 June 1742 (LG)
d 17 Oct 1749 (M)

PHELIPS, John
L 11 July 1776

PHELP, Cecil Tufton
L 6 Mar 1815

PHENNEY, John
L
CA 17 Aug 1666 (RM)

PHEPOE, John
T
L 13 June 1809
Ret CR 5 Jan 1848 (OB)
d 1862 (TR)

PHIBBS, Matthew
L 9 Feb 1815

PHILIP, Arthur
L 7 June 1761
CR 2 Sept 1779
CA 30 Nov 1781
RAB 1 Jan 1801
RAW 23 Apr 1804
RAR 9 Nov 1805
VAB 13 Dec 1806 (PMM)
VAW 25 Oct 1809
VAR 31 July 1810
AB 4 June 1814
d 31 Aug 1814 (CH)

PHIL(L)IPS, Bernard
L 1664

PHILIPS, George
L 10 Jan 1771

PHILIPS, Griffin
L 1696 (PJP)

PHILIPS, Henry
L 16 May 1746
CR 26 May 1768

PHILIPS, Henry John
See PHILLIPS, Henry John

PHILIPS, James Robert
L 10 Dec 1795
CR 15 Mar 1805
CA 13 Oct 1807
RAB 23 Nov 1841 (LG)
RAW 12 Feb 1847 (LG)
RAR 8 June 1849 (LG)
Ret VA 1851 (CH)

PHILIPS, John (1)
L 21 Apr 1785
CR 18 Oct 1797
CA 13 Nov 1797
d 18 Mar 1813 (PJP)

PHILIPS, John (2)
L 6 Mar 1815
d 2 June 1835 (LT)

PHILIPS, John
See PHELIPS, John

PHILIP(P)S, John Philipps
L 4 Mar 1815

PHILIPPS, Rowland (1)
L 1703 (PJP)

PHILIP(P)S, Rowland (2)
L 2 Oct 1778

PHILIPS, William
L 26 June 1745
CR 24 Mar 1760 (PJP)

PHILIPS, William
See PHILLIPS, William

PHILLIMORE, George
L 20 Oct 1803
d (duel) 20 Dec 1807 (LT)

PHILLIMORE, Sir John
L 4 Apr 1801
CR 10 May 1804
CA 13 Oct 1807
CB 4 June 1815 (LG)
Kt 1820 (PJP)
d 21 Mar 1840 (OB)

PHILLIP, Arthur
See PHILIP, Arthur

PHILLIPS, Baker
L 5 Feb 1741
e (cowardice) 19 Apr 1745 (PMM)

PHILLIPS, Charles
L 17 Sept 1806

CR 6 Oct 1812
CA 15 May 1823 (MB)
d 21 Oct 1839 (LT)

PHILLIPS, Edward
L 20 Nov 1812

PHILLIPS, Edward Seward
L 21 Dec 1808

PHILLIPS, Erasmus
L 15 May 1702
CR
CA 23 Dec 1715
d (drowned) 28 Mar 1719 (CH)

PHILLIPS, Frederick
L 7 Feb 1815

PHILLIPS, George (1)
L 11 Mar 1755

PHILLIP(P)S, George (2)
L 4 Feb 1815

PHILLIPS, Henry Cranmer March
L 10 Mar 1814
HP 1815 (OB)

PHILLIPS, Henry John
later TOWRY, Henry John Phillips
L 6 Aug 1742
CR 27 Apr 1756
CA 17 Jan 1757
d 3 Sept 1762

PHILLIPS, James Robert
See PHILIPS, James Robert

PHILLIPS, John George
L 8 Feb 1805
CR 22 Oct 1814
HP 22 Oct 1841 (OB)

PHILLIPS, John William
L 20 Sept 1813 (PRO)
d 29 Nov 1832 (LT)

PHILLIPS, Morgan
L
CA 1673

PHILLIPS, Nathaniel
L 5 June 1761
d 17 June 1784 (M)

PHILLIPS, Richard Charles
L 26 Nov 1808

PHILLIPS, Thomas
L 1673 (PJP)

PHILLIPS, William (1)
L 27 Oct 1746

PHILLIPS, William (2)
L 21 June 1756
CR 24 Mar 1760
d 5 Mar 1771 (M)

PHILLIPS, William (3)
L 6 Mar 1815
HP Nov 1815 (OB)

PHILLIPS, William
See PHILIPS, William

PHILLIPSON, John
L 7 Jan 1740
CR
CA 17 Feb 1744
d 30 Mar 1745

PHILLOT(T), Charles George Rodney
L 1 July 1801
CR 27 Aug 1809
CA 7 Dec 1818 (OB)
Ret CA 31 Oct 1846 (LG)
Ret RA 8 July 1851 (PMM)
Ret VA 22 Aug 1857 (PMM)
d 11 Mar 1863 (PMM)

PHILPOT, Edward
L 1689 (PJP)

PHILPOT, George
L 9 Dec 1757

PHILPOT, George Stannard
L 1 Aug 1809

PHILPOT, Robert
L 18 Nov 1790
CR
CA 1 July 1800
d 1826 (PJP)

PHILPOT, Stephen Dawson
L 14 Jan 1808

PHIL(L)POT, Thomas
L 12 Sept 1732
CR
CA 5 Mar 1741
d 13 May 1742

PHIPPS, Hon. Charles
L 19 Jan 1771
CR
CA 1 Aug 1776
MP 27 Feb 1779–
(Scarborough) 1784 (MPN)
MP 19 June 1784–
(Minehead) 20 Oct 1786 (MPN)
d 20 Oct 1786 (MPN)

PHIPPS, Constantine John, Earl of Mulgrave
L 17 Mar 1762
CR 24 Nov 1763
CA 20 June 1765
MP (Lincoln) 1768–1774 (MPN)
MP (Huntingdon) 1776–1784 (MPN)
COM AD 15 Dec 1777–
1 Apr 1782 (AO)
MP (Newark) 1784–1790 (MPN)
Cre EP 7 July 1790 (MPN)
d 10 Oct 1792 (MPN)

PHIPPS, David
See PHIPS, David

PHIPPS, Francis
L 18 Mar 1778
d June 1794 (LT)

PHIPPS, James
L 15 Aug 1806

PHIPPS, Keston
L 4 Aug 1806
CR 30 Apr 1810
CA 7 June 1814
Ret CA 31 Oct 1846 (LG)
d 1847 (OB)

PHIPPS, Spencer
See PHIPS, Spencer

PHIPPS, Thomas
L 11 Dec 1807
d 22 Nov 1827 (LT)

PHIPPS, William
L 11 Sept 1810
HP 1814 (OB)

PHIPS, David
L 24 Nov 1750
CR 1 May 1779

CA 25 Oct 1809
d 1811 (PJP)
PHIPS, Spencer
L 1 Dec 1782
d 26 Sept 1796 (LT)
PIBUS, John
L
CA 1666
d before 1689 (PJP)
PICKARD, James
L 11 Oct 1805
CR 7 June 1814
PICKARD, Peter
L
CA 3 Apr 1680
d 10 Mar 1702
PICKERING, Gilbert
L 16 Apr 1678
PICKERING, Thomas Woolley
L 8 May 1740
d 21 Apr 1792 (M)
PICKERNELL, Peter Giles
L 5 July 1800
T
CR 4 July 1810
d 1859 (TR)
PICKERNELL, Thomas
L 1 Aug 1811
PICKERSGILL, Richard
L 29 Aug 1771
d (drowned) 1816 (PJP)
PICKFORD, Charles
L 21 Jan 1794
CR 27 Apr 1805 (CH)
PICKING, William
L 10 Oct 1807
CR 18 Sept 1828 (PJP)
PICKMORE, Francis
L 18 Dec 1777
CR 27 June 1782
CA 21 Sept 1790
RAB 28 Apr 1808
RAW 25 Oct 1809
RAR 31 July 1810
VAB 12 Aug 1812
VAW 4 June 1814
GG (Newfoundland) 1816–1818 (BNS)
d 24 Feb 1818 (CH)
PICKMORE, Francis John
L 9 Dec 1811
d 1837 (PJP)
PICKTHORNE, John
L 3 Mar 1808
PIDDLE, John
L 2 Oct 1763
PIDGELY, Andrew Bowden
L 7 May 1804
T
Gone 1821 (TR)
PIERCE, George
L 21 Mar 1812
CR 5 Sept 1823 (MB)
PIERCE, Thomas (1)
L 27 Feb 1795
KIA 18 May 1804 (PJP)
PIERCE, Thomas (2)
L 1 Sept 1807
HP Jan 1816 (OB)
PIERCY, Richard
L 28 Aug 1779
CR 7 May 1794
CA 25 Sept 1806
d 1815 (PJP)
PIERCY, Thomas
L 14 Feb 1757
CR 18 Apr 1778
CA 19 Apr 1780
d 22 Sept 1793 (M)
PIERIE, John (1)
L 9 Oct 1778
SUP CR 31 Jan 1814
PIERIE, John (2)
L 2 Apr 1803
PIERREPONT, Charles Herbert, Viscount Newark
L 10 Mar 1797
CR 11 Aug 1797
CA 24 Dec 1798
MP (Nottinghamshire) 1801–1816 (MPT)
HP 1803 (MPT)
Inh EP 17 June 1816 (MB)
d 27 Oct 1860 (MPT)
PIERREPONT, William
L 2 Dec 1789
CR 19 May 1794
CA 4 Aug 1794
RAB 12 Aug 1812
d 7 Aug 1813 (PRO)
PIERSON, Robert
L 6 Aug 1697
PIERSON, Sir William Henry
T wounded
L 24 Dec 1805
CR 27 Mar 1826 (MB)
Kt 11 June 1836 (OB)
CA 28 June 1836 (OB)
Ret CA 1852 (TR)
Ret RA 1857 (TR)
d 1858 (TR)
PIGGOT, Walter
See PIGOT, Walter
PIGOT, George (1)
L 26 Nov 1802
CR 15 Aug 1806
CA 17 Sept 1808
d (drowned) 2 Feb 1807 (CH)
PIGOT, George (2)
L 15 July 1811
PIGOT(T), Henry
L 27 Sept 1809
PIGOT, Hugh (1)
L 9 Feb 1742
CR
CA 22 Apr 1746
MP (Penryn) 1768–1774 (MPN)
CRM 12 Mar 1770 (AL)
RAW 31 Mar 1775
VAB 5 Feb 1776
VAW 29 Jan 1778
MP (Bridgnorth) 16 Feb 1778–1784 (MPN)
VAR 26 Sept 1780

COM AD 1 Apr 1782–
31 Dec 1783 (AO)
AB 24 Apr 1782
AW 24 Sept 1787
d 15 Dec 1792 (MPN)

PIGOT, Hugh (2)
L 21 Sept 1790
CR 10 Feb 1794
CA 1 Sept 1794
d (murdered) 21 Sept 1797 (DNB)

PIGOT, Sir Hugh (3)
L 12 Nov 1794
CR 29 Apr 1802
CA 8 May 1804
CB 26 Sept 1831 (OB)
KCH 1834 (OB)
RAB 10 Jan 1837 (LG)
RAW 23 Nov 1841 (LG)
RAR 9 Nov 1846 (LG)
KCB 10 July 1847 (OB)
VAB 6 Aug 1847 (LG)
VAW 8 June 1849 (LG)
A 4 July 1853 (CH)
d 30 July 1857 (CH)

PIGOT(T), James
L 28 Mar 1771
CR 25 Aug 1773
CA 22 Feb 1776
RAB 4 July 1794
VAB 1 June 1795
VAR 14 Feb 1799
AB 29 Apr 1802
AW 9 Nov 1805
AR 31 July 1810
d 1822 (CH)

PIGOT(T), John
L 24 Feb 1815

PIGOT(T), Joseph
L 1689 (PJP)

PIGOT, Richard (Henry Hollis)
L 22 Oct 1806
CR 31 May 1814
HP 31 May 1814 (OB)

PIGOT, Robert
L 27 Sept 1796

PIGOT(T), Rowland
L 26 Mar 1759

PIGOT(T), Thomas
L 31 Dec 1747
d 29 Sept 1754

PIGOT, Walter
L 8 Oct 1694
CR
CA 13 Nov 1707
d 19 May 1754

PIKE, Abraham
L 15 May 1807

PIKE, Edward
L 30 July 1746

PIKE, James
L 1691 (PJP)
d 1766 (M)

PIKE, John (1)
L
CA 19 Sept 1673

PIKE, John (2)
L 16 Aug 1800

PIKE, Richard
L 18 Dec 1774
KIA 28 June 1776 (LG)

PIKE, Thomas
L 25 Mar 1807
Ret CR 14 Jan 1847 (OB)

PIKE, Walter
L 20 Feb 1805
T
Ret CR 12 Aug 1840 (OB)
d 1850 (TR)

PILCH, Robert
L 22 Dec 1795
CR 4 Dec 1813
d 1846 (OB)

PILCH, William
T
L 24 Sept 1814
d 1863 (TR)

PILES, Thomas
L 1664
CA 1672
d before 1689 (PJP)

PILFORD, John
L 9 Mar 1795
CR
T
CA 25 Dec 1805
CB 4 June 1815 (LG)
d 1834 (TR)

PILLOW, Edward
L 20 Dec 1808

PILOT, Henry Digby
L 8 Oct 1800

PINDAR, Thomas
L
CA 11 Apr 1696
d (drowned) 5 Jan 1699 (CH)

PINE, Horace
L 22 Aug 1783
CR 22 Mar 1793
d (drowned) 1798 (PJP)

PINFOLD, Richard
L 23 Feb 1757
d 4 Mar 1793

PINN, Edward
L 1666
CA 1672
d before 1689 (PJP)

PINTO, Thomas
L 20 Feb 1805
T
CR 9 Feb 1808
Ret CA 10 Sept 1840 (OB)
d 1851 (TR)

PIPER, Edmund John
L 21 Nov 1812
HP May 1813 (OB)

PIPON, Philip
L 8 Oct 1794
CR 29 Apr 1802
CA 17 Sept 1808
d 7 Dec 1829 (PMM)

PITCAIRN, Robert
L 1 Mar 1760
PITCHFORD, Samuel (1)
L 4 Mar 1740 (PJP)
PITCHFORD, Samuel (2)
L 6 Aug 1759
PITCHFORD, Samuel
See CORNISH, Samuel
PITFIELD, Joseph Edward Chilcott
L 9 Jan 1815
PITFORD, John
See PILFORD, John
PITMAN, John (1)
?L 5 Aug 1727
?CR 2 Dec 1741
CA 8 Feb 1743
d 13 May 1752 (M)
PITMAN, John (2)
?L 2 Mar 1734
CR 5 Sept 1745 (PJP)
d (drowned) 24 June 1746 (PJP)
PITMAN, John (3)
L 6 July 1783
d 1796 (PJP)
PITMAN, Samuel
L 7 Oct 1709 (PMM)
CR 15 Aug 1721
CA 9 Nov 1727
d 5 Oct 1728
PITMAN, William
L 31 Jan 1806
HP June 1816
PITT, Charles
T
L 25 Mar 1809
Gone 1821 (TR)
PITT, Edward William
L 11 Mar 1809
HP 1815–22 Dec 1836 (OB)
PITT, Hon. James Charles
L 18 Feb 1778
PITT, John
L 7 Feb 1812
PITT, William (1)
L 10 Apr 1806
PITT, William (2)
L 29 Jan 1814
HP Feb 1816 (OB)
PITTS, Edward
L 7 Mar 1805
CR 22 July 1830 (OB)
PLACE, Copeland
L 20 Apr 1801
d (drowned) 24 Dec 1811 (PJP)
PLAGGENBORG, Edward
L 15 Mar 1815
d (drowned) 14 Apr 1828 (CH)
PLAINE, John
L 3 Sept 1795
PLAISTER, Thomas
L 12 Apr 1697
PLAMPIN, Robert
L 3 Dec 1781
CR 30 Aug 1793
CA 21 Apr 1795
RAB 4 June 1814
RAW 12 Aug 1819 (LG)
RAR 19 July 1821 (LG)
VAB 27 May 1825 (LG)
VAW 22 July 1830 (LG)
d 14 Feb 1834 (OB)
PLANNER, John
L 23 Feb 1802
PLATT, J.
L 1795 (PJP)
PLAYER, William Hopson
L 7 Jan 1778
d 16 Mar 1790
PLAYSTOWE, Philip
L 8 June 1757
PLAYTERS, John
L 19 Feb 1741
PLINT, Thomas
L 9 Nov 1756
d 31 July 1776 (PRO)
PLOWDEN, James Chichley
L 19 July 1762
KIA 29 Apr 1781 (LG)
PLOWMAN, George
L 25 May 1798
PLUCKNETT, Thomas Adolphus
L 4 June 1814
PLUMRIDGE, Sir James Hanway
T
L 20 Aug 1806
CR 7 June 1814
CA 9 Oct 1822 (MB)
MP (Falmouth) 1841–1847 (TR)
RA 7 Oct 1852 (CH)
KCB 5 July 1855 (CH)
VA 28 Nov 1857 (CH)
A 27 Apr 1863 (CH)
d 29 Nov 1863 (TR)
PLUNKET, John
L 18 May 1780
PLYMSELL, Amos
L 18 Feb 1813
POAD, Thomas
L 21 Jan 1797
POATE, James
L 22 Dec 1800
Ret CR 25 Sept 1845 (OB)
POCKLINGTON, Christopher
L 3 July 1716
CR
CA 14 Nov 1727
SUP RA
POCOCK, Sir George
L 7 Dec 1726
CR 26 Feb 1734
CA 1 Aug 1738
RAW 6 Jan 1755
RAR 4 June 1756
VAW Feb 1757
VAR 5 Feb 1758
MP (Plymouth) 20 Jan 1760–1768 (MPN)
Kt 23 Mar 1761 (MPN)
AB 21 Oct 1762
SUP A 11 Sept 1766
d 3 Apr 1792 (DNB)
POCOCK, Richard (1)
L 16 Jan 1728

Name / Rank	Date	Year
POCOCK(E), Richard (2)		
L	7 June	1808
POCOCK, William Innes		
L	1 Aug	1811
PODMORE, John George King		
L	14 Mar	1815
POGSON, Henry Freeman Young		
L	28 Apr	1798
CR	4 May	1819 (MB)
POINGDESTER, John		
L	1 Dec	1782
POINTER, Jasper		
See POYNTER, Jasper		
POINTON, Samuel		
L	13 Mar	1815
POINTZ, John		
L		
CA		1660
POINTZ, Newdigate or Stephen		
See POYNTZ, Newdigate or Stephen		
POLE, Sir Charles Morice		
L	26 June	1777
CR		
CA	22 Mar	1779
RAB	1 June	1795
RAR	14 Feb	1799
GG (Newfoundland)		1800–1802 (BNS)
VAB	1 Jan	1801
MP (Newark)		1802–1806 (MPT)
VAR	23 Apr	1804
AB	9 Nov	1805
MP (Plymouth)		1806–1818 (MPT)
COM AD	10 Feb–23 Oct	1806 (AO)
AW	31 July	1810
AR	4 June	1814
KCB	12 Apr	1815 (LG)
GCB	17 Apr	1818 (LG)
AF	22 July	1830 (LG)
d	6 Sept	1830 (LG)
POLE, Hon. William Wesley		
L	22 Nov	1782
d	22 Feb	1845 (OB)
POLKINGHORNE, Charles		
L	9 Feb	1709
CR	29 Aug	1740
POLKINGHORNE, James		
See PUCKINGHORN, James		
POLKINGHORNE, John		
L	1 Aug	1772
POLLAND, John		
L		1665
POLLARD, Charles		
L	9 Dec	1809
POLLARD, Christopher		
L		
CA	18 Feb	1696 (PJP)
POLLARD, George		
L	7 May	1761
d	1 July	1797
POLLARD, John		
T	wounded	
L	14 Nov	1806
Ret CR		1864 (TR)
d		1868 (TR)
POLLARD, William		
L		1748 (PJP)
POLLEA, John		
L		1665
CA		1672
d	2 Oct	1678 (DDA)
POLLEXFEN, John		
L	3 Mar	1795
d (drowned)	Nov	1798 (CH)
POLLINGTON, Stephen		
L	31 Aug	1739
POLLOCK, Carlisle		
L	7 May	1802
POLWHELE, Edward		
T		
L	10 Nov	1807
d		1810 (TR)
POMEROY, George (1)		
L	1 Dec	1688 (P)
CA	21 June	1690
KIA	18 July	1691 (LG)
POMEROY, George (2)		
L		
CR	8 Jan	1718
POMEROY, Thomas		
L	4 Aug	1761
d	27 July	1768 (PMM)
POMEROY, William		
L		
CA		1661
d	10 July	1690 (CH)
POND, James		
T		
L	24 Aug	1812
Ret CR		1855 (TR)
d		1858 (TR)
PONSONBY, Anthony		
L	15 July	1782
d	29 Aug	1800
PONSONBY, John		
L	8 Aug	1801
PONSONBY, Miles		
L	25 Sept	1806
PONSONBY, Milham		
L	25 Feb	1777
CR	15 Jan	1781
CA	25 Oct	1809
d		1815 (PJP)
POOK, Henry		
L	9 Apr	1800
POOLE, Benjamin		
L	27 Mar	1677
CA	20 Dec	1680
d	12 Jan	1714 (M)
POOLE, Charles (1)		
L		
CR		
CA	1 Jan	1739
d	26 Jan	1739
POOLE, Charles (2)		
L	25 Apr	1800
POOLE, Edward		
L		1691 (PJP)
POOLE, Jonas		
L		
CA		1665
Dismissed		1665 (PD)
d		1666 (PD)

POOLE, Nicholas
L 30 Apr 1678
POOLE, Richard
L
CA 1665

d 1678 (DDA)
POOLE, Robert
L 9 Dec 1755
POOLE, Sir William (1)
L
CA 9 June 1666 (RM)
Kt 1675 (PD)

d before 1689 (PJP)
POOLE, William (2)
L 9 Apr 1677
CA 1672 (PJP)
POOLEY, William
L 21 Jan 1708 (PMM)
POORE, John
L 25 Feb 1815
HP 28 Feb 1815 (OB)
POORE, William
L 2 Mar 1809
Ret CR 9 Apr 1847 (OB)
POPE, Daniel
L 21 Sept 1795
POPE, John
L 29 Aug 1803

KIA 7 Feb 1813 (LG)
POPE, Walter
L 12 Jan 1703 (PMM)
POPHAM, Sir Home Riggs
L 16 June 1783
CR 26 Nov 1794
CA 4 Apr 1795
MP 1804–1806 (MPT)
(Yarmouth I.o.W.)
MP 1806–1807 (MPT)
(Shaftesbury)
MP 1807–1812 (MPT)
(Ipswich)
RAW 4 June 1814
KCB 12 Apr 1815 (LG)
RAR 12 Aug 1819 (LG)

d 11 Sept 1820 (OB)
POPHAM, Joseph Lamb
L 15 Aug 1794
CR 8 Mar 1797
CA 22 Jan 1806

d 1833 (PJP)
POPHAM, Stephen
L 7 Oct 1801
CR 1 Aug 1811
CA 19 Sept 1815

d 25 Feb 1842 (I)
POPHAM, William
L 14 Feb 1812
CR 23 Dec 1814
CA 19 May 1819 (MB)
Ret CA 31 Oct 1846 (LG)
POPKINS, John
L 1 Feb 1744
POPLEWELL, Matthew Jones
L 22 Jan 1806
CR 6 Nov 1813
HP 6 Nov 1813 (OB)

PORTEN, Robert
L 1672
CA 1673
PORTEUS, John
L 22 Jan 1806
CR 3 Mar 1808
CA 7 June 1814

d 1833 (PJP)
PORTER, George
L 18 Nov 1799
PORTER, Jervis Henry
L 31 Aug 1739
CR 16 Nov 1744
CA 3 Apr 1746

d 31 Mar 1763
PORTER, John Fitzroy
L 23 Sept 1796
PORTER, Jonathan
L 15 Feb 1815
PORTER, Peter
L 23 July 1756

KIA 5 Oct 1761 (LG)
PORTER, Stephen
L 1666
PORTER, Thomas (1)
L 10 Mar 1757
CR 3 Oct 1770

d 29 Jan 1792 (M)
PORTER, Thomas (2)
L 27 July 1814
CR 26 Aug 1822 (MB)
PORTER, William
L 10 Aug 1814
PORTLOCK, Nathaniel
L 14 Sept 1780
CR 4 Nov 1793
CA 28 Sept 1799

d 12 Sept 1817 (MB)
POSTLETHWAITE, Edward
L 2 Mar 1815
POTTER, Abraham
L 26 Jan 1678 (P)
CA 9 Sept 1688

d 6 Jan 1695
POTTER, Donald
L 6 Oct 1800
POTTER, Richard
L 2 Jan 1812
POTTINGER, Edward
L
CA 19 Mar 1690

d (drowned) 9 Oct 1690 (CH)
POTTS, John
T
L 7 May 1808
HP July 1814 (OB)

d 1847 (TR)
POTTS, Joseph
L 22 Feb 1759
POTTS, Robert
L 9 Dec 1760
POTTS, Thomas
L 1666
POULDEN, Richard
L 12 Feb 1783
CR 29 June 1795

CA	29 Apr	1802
Ret RA	10 Jan	1837 (OB)
RAW	17 Aug	1840 (LG)
RAR	23 Nov	1841 (LG)
d	16 Mar	1845 (OB)
POULDEN, William		
L	8 Mar	1796
POULETT, Hon. George		
L	3 Apr	1804
CR	12 Oct	1805
CA	31 July	1806
RAB	23 Nov	1841 (LG)
RAW	9 Nov	1846 (LG)
RAR	6 Aug	1847 (LG)
VAB	24 June	1850 (LG)
d	10 Feb	1854 (CH)
POULSON, Edward		
L		
CA	5 Sept	1688
d	22 Sept	1695 (LTE)
POULTON, Edward		
L		
CA	7 Sept	1688
d	22 Dec	1695
POULTON, Thomas		
L		
CA	14 Jan	1695 (PJP)
d (duel)	20 June	1699 (PJP)
POUND, Thomas		
L		
CA	5 Aug	1691
Dismissed		1699 (DAB)
d		1703 (DAB)
POWELL, Edward		
L		
CA		1666
KIA	17 Oct	1667 (LG)
POWELL, George Eyre		
L	22 Jan	1813
CR	23 Nov	1841 (OB)
POWELL, Herbert (Brace)		
L	26 Jan	1805
CR	15 June	1814
HP	Feb	1819 (OB)
CA	26 Dec	1822 (OB)
POWELL, Samuel		
L	13 Apr	1741
POWEL(L), Stewart		
L	15 Mar	1745
POWELL, Walter		
L		
CA		1673
POWER, Benjamin		
L		1800 (PJP)
POWER, Henry (1)		
L	14 Dec	1708
LGH		1724 (PJP)
POWER, Henry (2)		
L	13 Aug	1793
POWER, Isaac		
L	1 Aug	1712
LGH		1743 (PJP)
POWER, John		
L	7 Aug	1692
POWER, Pierce		
L		1673
d	before	1689 (PJP)

POWER, Richard		
L	18 Nov	1790
POWER, William		
L		
CA	17 Jan	1701 (PJP)
d		1703
POWIS, Joseph		
L	31 July	1693 (PJP)
POWLETT, Charles		
L	4 Apr	1735
CR	22 Oct	1741
CA	10 Oct	1743
d	4 Apr	1762
POWLETT, Edmund		
L		1757 (PJP)
POWLETT, Francis Lascoe		
L	1 Dec	1757
SUP	5 Sept	1797
d	27 Dec	1799 (PMM)
POWLET(T), Lord Harry		
See BOLTON, Harry Powlet, Duke of		
POWLETT, Lord Henry or PAULET		
L	12 Mar	1789
CR	20 Feb	1793
CA	9 Jan	1794
CRM	1 Aug	1811 (LG)
RAB	12 Aug	1812
COM AD	18 May	1813–
	24 May	1816 (AO)
RAW	4 Dec	1813
RAR	4 June	1814
KCB	12 Apr	1815 (LG)
VAB	12 Aug	1819 (CH)
VAW	27 May	1825 (CH)
VAR	22 July	1830 (CH)
d	28 Jan	1832 (CH)
POWLETT, Percy		
L	23 Mar	1756
POWLETT, William		
L	12 July	1739
POWNELL, Philip		
L	16 Aug	1697
POWNEY, Sir John		
L	13 Sept	1806
Became Jr Lt		1807
L	8 May	1808
CR	26 June	1827 (OB)
KH	1 Jan	1837 (OB)
POWNOLL, Philemon (1)		
L	6 Aug	1697
POWNOLL, Philemon (2)		
L	7 Oct	1755
CR	6 Aug	1759
CA	10 Jan	1771
KIA	15 June	1780 (CH)
POWSON, Edward		
L		1689 (PJP)
POWYS, Hon. Charles		
L	12 Apr	1802
CR	3 Mar	1804
d	13 Aug	1804 (PJP)
POYNTER, Jasper		
L	8 Jan	1695
POYNTON, Jonathan		
L		1691 (PJP)
CA		1694 (PJP)

POYNTZ, Newdigate
L 11 Sept 1807
CR 19 Sept 1815
HP 19 Sept 1815 (OB)

POYNTZ, Stephen
L 17 Apr 1791
CR 31 Oct 1795
CA 5 Oct 1796
RAB 12 Aug 1819 (LG)
RAW 19 July 1821 (LG)
RAR 27 May 1825 (LG)
VAB 22 July 1830 (LG)
VAW 10 Jan 1837 (LG)
VAR 28 June 1838 (LG)
AB 23 Nov 1841 (LG)
AW 22 Jan 1847 (LG)
d 12 May 1847 (OB)

PRAED, Buckley Macworth
L 1 Sept 1793
CR 21 Apr 1799
CA 29 Apr 1802
Ret RA 10 Jan 1837 (OB)
RAW 17 Aug 1840 (LG)
RAR 23 Nov 1841 (LG)
VAB 9 Nov 1846 (LG)
VAW 27 Dec 1847 (LG)

PRANNALL, Frederick
L 6 Mar 1815
d 18 Oct 1842 (LT)

PRASHWAITE, Edward
L 1672

PRATER, Richard
L 4 Nov 1790
CR 8 Mar 1797

PRATT, George (1)
L 18 July 1807
?CR 15 June 1814
KIA 14 Dec 1814 (JH)

PRATT, George (2)
L 14 Mar 1810
?CR 15 June 1814

PRATT, Matthew
L
CA 17 Dec 1673

PRATT, William
L 20 Aug 1745
CR 8 Apr 1757

PRATTEN, Edward
L 6 Dec 1739
CR
CA 2 June 1743
d 22 Oct 1763

PRATTENT, John
L 10 Mar 1815

PREENE, Jacob
L 26 Nov 1688

PREISTMAN, Henry
See PRIESTMAN, Henry

PRENDERGAST, John
L 15 Aug 1809 (PRO)
d 8 Sept 1814 (PJP)

PRESCOTT, Christopher
L 1705 (PJP)

PRESCOTT, Sir Henry
L 28 Apr 1802
CR 4 Feb 1808
CA 25 July 1810
CB 4 June 1815 (DNB)
GG (Newfoundland) 1834–1841 (BNS)
RAB 24 Apr 1847 (OB)
COM AD 20 July–23 Dec 1847 (AO)
RAW 4 May 1849 (LG)
VA 15 Apr 1854 (CH)
KCB 1856 (PJP)
A 2 May 1860 (CH)
Ret A 9 June 1860 (CH)
GCB 1869 (PJP)
d 18 Nov 1874 (DNB)

PRESCOTT, Isaac
L 22 May 1758
CR 28 Nov 1777
CA 8 Apr 1778
RAW 1 June 1795
VAB 14 Feb 1799
VAW 1 Jan 1801
VAR 23 Apr 1804
AB 9 Nov 1805
AW 25 Oct 1809
AR 4 June 1814
d 1830 (MB)

PRESCOTT, Thomas
L 3 June 1743
CR 22 July 1761
d 12 Nov 1808 (PMM)

PRESCOTT, Thomas Lennox
L 12 July 1797
Ret CR 27 Apr 1839 (OB)

PRESSLAND, Thomas
L 6 Sept 1779
CR 3 May 1797
CA 7 Jan 1802

PRESTICK, Edward
L
CA 1672

PRESTON, D'Arcy
L 4 Nov 1790
CR 4 Apr 1794
CA 13 June 1796
SUP RA 24 Aug 1819 (MB)
VAR 12 Nov 1840 (LG)
AB 23 Nov 1841 (LG)
AW 9 Nov 1846 (LG)
d 21 Jan 1847 (OB)

PRESTON, Edward
L 20 Sept 1815
d 17 Mar 1830 (LT)

PRESTON, Henry
L 18 Nov 1809
CR 22 July 1830 (OB)
HP 22 July 1830 (OB)

PRESTON, James (1)
L 27 Oct 1758
SUP CR 1 Aug 1800 (PMM)

PRESTON, James (2)
L 24 July 1778
In Russian Service 1788 (PMM)

PRESTON, Robert
L 17 Oct 1805
CR 29 Sept 1808
CA 22 Jan 1810
d 16 Apr 1817 (PJP)

PRESTON, Thomas
L 28 Feb 1815 (OB)

Name / Rank	Date	Year
PRESTON, William		
L	10 Nov	1740
CR	20 Oct	1746
CA	1 Mar	1749
d	11 Mar	1756
PRETTIE, Henry		
L	28 Sept	1741
PRETTY, Saxey		
L		1666
PRETYMAN, George		
L	17 Feb	1815
HP		1831 (OB)
PREVOST, James		
L	19 June	1793
CR	8 Oct	1801
CA	13 Mar	1809
Ret CA	31 Oct	1846 (LG)
PREVOST, Thomas L.		
L		1798 (PJP)
PRICE, Charles Papps		
L	13 May	1778
CR	11 May	1798
CA	29 Apr	1802
d	Jan	1813
PRICE, David (1)		
L	28 Sept	1809
CR	6 Dec	1813
CA	13 June	1815
RA	6 Nov	1850 (PRO)
d (suicide)	30 Aug	1854 (DNB)
PRICE, David (2)		
L	23 Feb	1815
d		1834 (PJP)
PRICE, David See PRYCE, David		
PRICE, Edward (1)		
L		1673
PRICE, Edward (2)		
L	9 Nov	1756
KIA	20 Nov	1759 (PJP)
PRICE, Francis Swaine		
T	wounded	
L	30 Jan	1806
Ret CR	6 Apr	1839 (OB)
d		1854 (TR)
PRICE, Frederick		
L	7 Nov	1806
PRICE, George		
L	14 Sept	1805
CR	10 July	1808
CA	7 Jan	1812
d	13 Nov	1840 (OB)
PRICE, Henry See PRYCE, Henry		
PRICE, Herbert		
L		1673
d	before	1689 (PJP)
PRICE, Hugh		
L	28 Feb	1815
HP	Dec	1815 (OB)
PRICE, James		
L	21 July	1703 (PMM)
d	19 Jan	1704 (PMM)
PRICE, James Hervey		
L	17 July	1805
Ret CR	17 Jan	1838 (OB)

Name / Rank	Date	Year
PRICE, John (1)		
L		
CA	30 July	1688
SUP CA		1705 (PJP)
d	1 Apr	1709
PRICE, John (2)		
L		1691 (PJP)
PRICE, John (3)		
L	19 Jan	1707
CR		
CA	2 June	1727
d	27 Dec	1727 (PJP)
PRICE, John (4)		
L	31 July	1795
CR	28 Apr	1812
d	Jan	1828 (MB)
PRICE, John (5)		
L	16 Jan	1802
PRICE, Joseph		
L	11 Sept	1777
SUP CR	19 June	1811
PRICE, Marmaduke		
L		1782 (PJP)
Dismissed	Dec	1782 (PJP)
PRICE, Richard		
L	22 Feb	1759
PRICE, Samuel (1)		
L	2 Jan	1771
PRICE, Samuel (2)		
L	3 July	1812
CR	18 Sept	1815
CA	25 June	1831 (MB)
PRICE, Thomas (1)		
L	13 Nov	1790
PRICE, Thomas (2)		
L	1 Nov	1803
d (drowned)	17 Nov	1807 (CH)
PRICE, William		
L	4 Jan	1799
CR	19 July	1821 (PJP)
d	12 Sept	1835 (PJP)
PRICKETT, John		
L	25 Apr	1799
CR	12 Aug	1812
d		1823 (MB)
PRICKETT, John David		
L	24 Aug	1804
PRICKETT, Thomas		
L	28 Apr	1805
CR	30 Jan	1813
CA	20 Aug	1824 (MB)
Ret CA	31 Oct	1846 (LG)
PRIDEAUX, Bayntun		
L	4 Aug	1744
PRIDEAUX, Humphrey		
L	23 Nov	1780
PRIDEAUX, John		
L		
CA		1667
PRIDHAM, Richard		
L	2 Jan	1798
CR	15 June	1814
CA	22 July	1830 (MB)
RA	27 Sept	1855 (PMM)
VA	4 Oct	1862 (PMM)
d	3 May	1864 (PMM)

PRIDHAM, William
L 1 July 1815
PRIEST, John
L 27 Dec 1808
PRIEST, Joseph
L 9 Dec 1793
PRIESTMAN, Henry
L 1672
CA 23 Aug 1673
CONT 7 Nov 1689 (AO)
COM AD 5 June 1690–
31 May 1699 (AO)
d 20 Aug 1712 (M)
PRIESTWOOD, Richard
L 29 Mar 1745
PRIEUR, Peter Stephen
L 1 May 1804
d (drowned) Jan 1806 (PJP)
PRIME, Philip
L 1691 (PJP)
PRINCE, Charles
L 25 July 1757
SUP CR 21 Sept 1796 (PMM)
d 17 Aug 1799 (LT)
PRINCE, John
L 7 Nov 1807
Ret CR 16 Oct 1841 (OB)
PRINCE, Lawrence
L 1671
PRINCE, Thomas
L 1760 (PJP)
PRINCE, William
L 1666
PRING, Daniel
L 12 May 1808
CR 13 Nov 1813
CA 19 Sept 1815
d 29 Nov 1847 (I)
PRING, William
L 2 Feb 1809
PRINGLE, David
L 23 Sept 1800
PRINGLE, Edward
L 22 May 1778
d 19 Apr 1783 (LG)
PRINGLE, George
L 17 Nov 1801
CR 27 Dec 1808
CA 7 June 1814
PRINGLE, James
L 6 Mar 1804
CR 9 Oct 1805
CA 1 June 1812
Ret RA 31 Oct 1846 (LG)
PRINGLE, Robert
L 12 July 1784
PRINGLE, Thomas
L 30 Nov 1760
CR 1776 (PJP)
CA 25 Nov 1776
RAB 4 July 1794
RAR 1 June 1795
VAW 14 Feb 1799
VAR 1 Jan 1801
d 9 Dec 1803
PRINGLE, William
L 3 Sept 1794

PRIOR, Henry
T
L 5 Feb 1808
d 1825 (TR)
PRIOR, Joseph
L 20 Mar 1805
CR 11 July 1811
CA 27 Dec 1812
d 13 Sept 1818 (LT)
PRIOR, Richard Samuel
L 10 Nov 1793
PRIOR, William
L 9 Nov 1796
PRISSICK, Christopher
L 15 Apr 1756
PRITCHARD, John
L 9 Apr 1723
CR 27 Sept 1740
CA 5 Feb 1742
SUP RA 1758
d 1777
(?1779)
PRITCHARD, John White
T
L 22 Sept 1808
CR 24 Jan 1828 (MB)
d 1851 (TR)
PRITCHARD, Richard Davison
T
L 26 Oct 1807
CR 22 Aug 1841 (OB)
HP 22 Aug 1841 (OB)
d 1849 (TR)
PRITCHARD, Robert
L 9 Sept 1801
PRITCHARD, Samuel Perkins
L 4 Mar 1815
CR 27 Aug 1834 (OB)
CA 8 June 1841 (OB)
HP 8 June 1841 (OB)
PROBY, Charles
L
CR 1745 (PJP)
CA 17 Sept 1746
COM V 22 July– 22 Dec 1771 (NBO)
COMM 1771–1779 (PJP)
(Chatham)
d 31 Mar 1799 (PMM)
PROBY, Hon. Granville Leveson
L 24 Oct 1804
CR 15 Aug 1806
CA 28 Nov 1806
MP 1816–1829 (MPT)
(Wicklow)
RAB 23 Nov 1841 (LG)
RAW 9 Nov 1846 (LG)
RAR 1 June 1848 (LG)
VA 16 June 1851 (DNB)
Inh EP 1855 (PJP)
A 9 July 1857 (DNB)
d 3 Nov 1868 (DNB)
PROBY, Henry Joshua Philadolphus
L 23 Feb 1808
Ret CR 18 Jan 1845 (OB)
PROBY, William Allen
L 1 Mar 1796

CR	23 Dec	1796
CA	17 Dec	1798
MP		1802–
(Buckingham)	6 Aug	1804 (MPT)
d	6 Aug	1804 (MPT)
PROBY, William Henry Baptist		
L	9 Jan	1814
CR	19 Mar	1829 (PJP)
PROBYN, Henry		
L	2 Feb	1791
CR	18 Aug	1796
Ret CA	10 Sept	1840 (OB)
d	31 Jan	1845 (OB)
PROBYN, William		
L	8 Sept	1705 (PMM)
PROCTER, James		
L	6 Mar	1805
d (drowned)	18 June	1809 (PJP)
PROCTER, Peter		
L	12 Nov	1798
CR	2 June	1810
d	Mar	1826 (MB)
PROCTER, George		
L	4 Feb	1706 (PMM)
CR	21 Nov	1721
CA	31 Mar	1726
d	4 Oct	1736 (PMM)
PROCTOR, Salkeld John		
L	29 Apr	1741
PROCTOR, Sir William Beauchamp		
L	25 Feb	1801
CR	29 Apr	1801
CA	5 Sept	1806
Inh Bt	29 June	1837 (OB)
RAB	23 Nov	1841 (LG)
RAW	9 Nov	1846 (LG)
RAR	22 Sept	1847 (LG)
Ret VA	2 Sept	1850 (CH)
Ret A	18 June	1857 (CH)
d	14 Mar	1861 (CH)
PROLE, Henry		
L	31 July	1748
PROSSER, Robert		
L	9 Jan	1706
PROSSER, William		
L	11 Feb	1772
PROTHEROE, George		
L		1702 (PJP)
CR		
CA	4 Dec	1718
PROWER, John		
L	14 Nov	1692 (PJP)
PROWER, William		
? See PROWTHER, William		
L		
CA	21 May	1691
PROWETT, Charles		
L	10 June	1801
d	18 Feb	1852 (PRO)
PROWSE, James Edgar		
L	9 Apr	1801
PROWSE, John		
L	1 Mar	1779
d	16 Sept	1781 (PMM)
PROWSE, Thomas		
L	25 June	1801
T		
CR	22 Jan	1806
d (drowned)	Sept	1806 (TR)
PROWSE, William (1)		
L	6 Dec	1782
CR		1796 (TR)
CA	6 Mar	1797
T		
CB	4 June	1815 (LG)
CRM	12 Aug	1819 (MB)
RAB	19 July	1821 (LG)
RAW	27 May	1825 (LG)
d		1826 (TR)
PROWSE, William (2)		
L	16 Aug	1814
CR	11 Jan	1843 (OB)
PROWSE, William Jones		
L	23 May	1809
CR	27 Mar	1826 (OB)
HP	June	1830 (OB)
CA	23 Nov	1841 (OB)
PROWTHER, William		
? PROWTHER, William		
L		
CA	21 May	1691
d	17 Apr	1703
PRYCE, David		
L	30 Sept	1745
CR	11 Jan	1758
PRYCE, Henry		
L	15 Apr	1805
CR	19 July	1821 (MB)
PRYNN, Parkins		
L	10 Oct	1800
T	wounded	
Ret CR		1830 (TR)
d		1838 (TR)
PUCKINGHORN, James (1)		
L	2 Aug	1755
PUCKINGHORN, James (2)		
L	1 Dec	1808 (PRO)
CR	27 June	1814 (PJP)
CA	25 Aug	1828 (MB)
d	9 Jan	1839 (PJP)
PUDDICOMBE, James		
L	15 Apr	1745
PUDDICOMBE, Stephen		
L	2 Feb	1758
SUP CR	23 June	1798
PUDNER, Humphrey		
L		
CR		
CA	10 July	1703
d	30 Nov	1753
PUGET, Peter		
L	15 Nov	1790
CR		1795 (PJP)
CA	29 Apr	1797
CB		1819 (SPB)
RAB	19 July	1821 (LG)
d		1822 (PRO)
PUGH, John		
L	17 Mar	1815
PUGH, Richard		
L	9 Sept	1688
CA	26 May	1691
d (drowned)	6 Oct	1692 (CH)

PULHAM, John
L
CA 1667
PULHAM, Joseph
L 17 Nov 1790
PULLEN, Henry
L 13 May 1778
d 3 Nov 1798
PULLEN, Robert
L 18 Dec 1777
PULLEN, Samuel George
L 16 Mar 1815
PULLEN, William
L 25 Mar 1809
PULLESTON, John
L 1 July 1809
HP 30 Sept 1815 (OB)
PULLEY, John
L
CR
CA 2 Oct 1711
d 2 July 1715 (PJP)
PULLEYN, George
L 1694 (PJP)
PULLIBANK, Abraham
L 18 Dec 1782
d (drowned) 16 Dec 1793 (CH)
PULLING, Arthur
L 20 June 1794
PULLING, George Christopher
L 28 Oct 1790
CR 27 Oct 1798
CA 29 Oct 1802
PULLING, James
L 23 Feb 1815
CR 8 Sept 1829 (OB)
CA 16 Jan 1845 (OB)
HP 16 Jan 1845 (OB)
PULLING, John King
L 25 Jan 1794
CR 2 Dec 1795
CA 1797 (PJP)
d (drowned) 11 Jan 1798 (PJP)
PULLMAN, John
L 18 Sept 1810
PULTENEY, George Ann
L 1 May 1775
CR 1 Feb 1779
CA Mar/Apr 1779
PULTON, Richard
L 14 Feb 1815
PURCELL, Edward
L 4 Dec 1811
CR June 1820 (PJP)
CA 25 Aug 1828 (MB)
PURCELL, James John
L 21 Feb 1741
PURCELL, John
L 4 Apr 1747
SUP CR 21 Sept 1796 (PMM)
d 12 Oct 1801 (PMM)
PURCHAS, Francis
L 15 Mar 1815
PURCHAS, William
L 6 Feb 1812
Resigned 4 Feb 1841 (OB)
PURCHAS, William Jardine
L 9 Dec 1809
CR 7 Dec 1818 (MB)
CA 16 May 1828 (OB)
HP 16 May 1828 (OB)
d 2 July 1848 (LT)
PURCHES, James Uzuld
L 26 July 1804
T
HP 1821 (OB)
Ret CR 1851 (TR)
d 1869 (TR)
PURDUE, Simon Smith
L 9 Oct 1801
PURKIS, Robert
L 19 May 1812
PURVIS, Charles Wager
L 19 June 1735
CR
CA 18 July 1740
SUP RA 1756
d 15 Jan 1772
PURVIS, George
L
CR
CA 22 May 1709
MP 21 Jan 1732–
(Aldeburgh) 8 Mar 1741 (MPS)
COM N 1735–8 Mar 1741 (MPS)
d 8 Mar 1741 (MPS)
PURVIS, John Brett
L 1 May 1805
CR 9 Aug 1808
CA 16 Sept 1809
RAB 9 Nov 1846 (LG)
HP 1847 (OB)
RAW 1 June 1848 (LG)
VA 4 July 1853 (CH)
d 1857 (CH)
PURVIS, John Child
L 11 Feb 1778
CR 9 Apr 1781
CA 1 Sept 1782
RAB 23 Apr 1804
RAW 9 Nov 1805
RAR 28 Apr 1808
VAB 25 Oct 1809
VAW 31 July 1810
VAR 12 Aug 1812
AB 12 Aug 1819 (MB)
PURVIS, Richard
L 10 June 1779
CR 1 Dec 1787
CA 22 Nov 1790
d 3 May 1802 (LT)
PURVIS, Richard Oadham
L 5 Apr 1802
PURVIS, William (1)
L 9 Apr 1808
PURVIS, William (2)
L 16 Feb 1815
d 15 May 1842 (LT)
PUTLAND, John
L 4 Feb 1799
d 1807 (PJP)
PYBUS, John
See PIBUS, John
PYE, John
L 26 Mar 1703

PYE, Sir Thomas
L 18 Apr 1735
CR
CA 13 Apr 1741
RAB 8 July 1758 (CH)
RAR 14 Mar 1759 (CH)
VAB 21 Oct 1762
VAR 18 Oct 1770 (CH)
MP 9 Mar 1771–
(Rochester) 1774 (MPN)
Kt 24 June 1773 (MPN)
AB 24 June 1773
AW 29 Jan 1778
LGRM 26 Sept 1780 (AL)
d 26 Dec 1785 (M)

PYE, Tobias
L 31 Aug 1739

PYE, William (1)
L 29 Apr 1799
Became Jr Lt 27 Jan 1801
T
L 28 Aug 1808
d 1876 (TR)

PYE, William (2)
L 28 Dec 1810 (OB)

PYEND, Stephen
L 1664
CA 27 July 1666 (RM)
d before 1689 (PJP)

PYEND, Valentine
L
CA 1662

PYKE, Foot
L 24 Nov 1706

PYM, Richard Ellsworthy
L 1 Aug 1815

PYM, Robert
L 1665

PYM, Sir Samuel
L 7 Mar 1795
CR 10 Feb 1801
CA 29 Apr 1802
CB 4 June 1815 (DNB)
RAB 10 Jan 1837 (LG)
RAW 28 June 1838 (LG)
KCB 25 Oct 1839 (DNB)
RAR 23 Nov 1841 (LG)
VAB 12 Feb 1847 (LG)
VAW 20 Mar 1848 (LG)
d 2 Oct 1855 (DNB)

PYNE, Henry
L 22 Jan 1806
CR 19 July 1814

PYNE, William (1)
L 1702 (PJP)

PYNE, William (2)
T
L 21 Mar 1812
d 1836 (TR)

PYNSENT, Christopher Alexander Martin
L 16 Mar 1815

PYOT, Charles
L 22 June 1726

PYSING, Robert
L 28 Feb 1713

PYWELL, Elmer
L 17 Nov 1790

QUARME, William
L 19 Mar 1761

QUARRY, Michael
L 17 May 1809

QUASH, Charles Kempthorne
L 10 Jan 1801
T
CR 21 Sept 1806
CA 1 Aug 1811
d 5 Aug 1817 (LT)

QUELCH, John
L 11 Feb 1797

QUELCH, Thomas
L 8 Feb 1815

QUICK, William
L 1660

QUILL, Richard
L 7 Feb 1812

QUILLIAM, John
L 6 Oct 1798
T
CR
CA 24 Dec 1805
d 1839 (TR)

QUIN, Michael
L 16 July 1812
CR 5 Oct 1824 (OB)
CA 10 Jan 1837 (OB)
HP Dec 1844 (OB)
RA 14 May 1857 (PJP)
VA 14 Apr 1863 (PJP)
A 8 Apr 1868 (PJP)
d 1870 (PJP)

QUIN, Robert
L 8 May 1752

QUIN, William Henry
L 9 Jan 1813

QUINTON, Cornelius
L 26 Mar 1794
CR 23 Mar 1798
CA 29 Apr 1802

RABAN, Robert Bruce
L 29 Nov 1814
HP Jan 1815 (OB)

RADCLIFFE, Copleston
T
L 13 May 1807
KIA 12 Aug 1814 (TR)

RADFORD, Arthur
L 7 May 1697 (PJP)

RADFORD, RICHARD
L 1689 (PJP)

RADFORD, Samuel
L 18 Aug 1806
CR 22 Jan 1814
CA 31 May 1832 (OB)
KH 25 Jan 1836 (OB)

RADFORD, William
L 22 Feb 1815

RADSTOCK, William Waldegrave, Lord
See WALDEGRAVE, William

RAGGETT, Richard
L 15 Dec 1778
CR 7 Oct 1793
CA 21 Apr 1799
RAB 27 May 1825 (LG)

RAIGERSFELD, Jeffrey, Baron von

L	31 Aug	1793
CR	21 Sept	1797
CA	29 Apr	1802
Ret RA	10 Jan	1837 (CH)
RAW	17 Aug	1840 (LG)
RAR	23 Nov	1841 (LG)
d	7 Sept	1844 (PMM)

RAINES, Thomas

L		
CA	10 May	1689
d	5 May	1702

RAINEY, Edward

L	23 Aug	1694
CR		
CA	14 Sept	1702
d (drowned)	12 Oct	1702 (CH)

RAINEY, Thomas
See RAINY, Thomas

RAINIER, Daniel

L	25 May	1745

RAINIER, John Sprat

L	11 May	1794
CR		
CA	22 Dec	1796
MP (Sandwich)	22 Apr	1808–1812 (MPT)
RAB	12 Aug	1819 (LG)
d	13 Nov	1822 (MPT)

RAINIER, Peter (1)

L	26 May	1768
CR	3 May	1777
CA	29 Oct	1778
RAB	1 June	1795
RAW	20 Feb	1797
VAB	14 Feb	1799
VAW	29 Apr	1802
VAR	23 Apr	1804
AB	9 Nov	1805
MP (Sandwich)	May	1807–
	7 Apr	1808 (DNB)
d	7 Apr	1808 (DNB)

RANIER, Peter (2)

L		
CR		
CA	17 Jan	1806
CB	4 June	1815 (LG)
d	13 Apr	1836 (OB)

RAINS, James

L	2 Dec	1793
HP	Apr–July	1796 (OB)
Ret CR	25 Apr	1829 (OB)

RAINS, John

L	2 Dec	1793
d		1832 (OB)

RAINS, Stephen (1)

L	29 June	1760
CR	12 Aug	1779
Dismissed	28 May	1781 (PJP)

RAINS, Stephen (2)

L	14 Oct	1779
CR	6 Oct	1796
CA	29 Apr	1802
d	1 Feb	1824 (MB)

RAINTON, John

L		
CA		1665

RAINY, Thomas

L	28 Feb	1783

RAITT, William

L	6 Nov	1800
CR	22 Jan	1806
CA	16 Sept	1809

RALEIGH, Brud

L	6 Feb	1694 (PJP)

RALPH, Robert

L	18 Mar	1815 (OB)

RAM, James George

L	7 Jan	1806
d (drowned)		1808 (PJP)

RAM, William Alexander

L		1805 (TR)
T	killed	
KIA	21 Oct	1805 (TR)

RAMAGE, Edward

L	23 Oct	1790
CR		1795 (PJP)
CA	22 Dec	1796
d	23 July	1806 (PJP)

RAMAGE, William

L	14 Mar	1799
CR	23 Mar	1807
CA	1 Jan	1817 (MB)
d	Jan	1828 (MB)

RAMSAY, David

L	25 June	1773
CR	21 Sept	1790
CA	22 Jan	1806
d	18 Nov	1818 (LT)

RAMSAY, Edward William

L	13 Sept	1814

RAMSAY, George

L		
CR	5 Mar	1694 (PJP)
CA	11 Oct	1708
d	11 Aug	1717

RAMSAY, J.

L		1800 (PJP)

RAMSAY, John

L	25 Apr	1807

RAMSAY, Robert (1)

L	8 June	1799
CR	1 Feb	1812
CB	4 June	1815 (LG)
CA	13 June	1815
Ret CA	31 Oct	1846 (LG)

RAMSAY, Robert (2)

L	21 Feb	1815

RAMSAY, Thomas
See RAMSEY, Thomas

RAMSDEN, Freschvile

L	11 Feb	1673

RAMSDEN, William

L	30 Dec	1808
CR	14 June	1813
CA	26 Dec	1822 (MB)
Ret CA	31 Oct	1846 (LG)

RAMSEY, David

L	2 June	1812

RAMSEY, Edward

L	4 May	1810
d	21 Feb	1871 (PRO)

RAMSEY, Frederick

L	12 Nov	1799

RAMSEY, Jacob
L | 21 Oct | 1693 (PJP)
RAMSEY, Joseph
L | 21 Dec | 1808 (PRO)
HP | Sept | 1814 (OB)
Ret CR | 12 Feb | 1848 (OB)
RAMSEY, Samuel
L | 11 July | 1811
CR | 22 Aug | 1828 (MB)
RAMSEY, Samuel Smith
L | 13 Mar | 1815
RAMSEY, Thomas
L | 11 Mar | 1815
HP | Mar | 1815 (OB)
RAMSHAY, George
L | 29 Aug | 1807
Ret CR | 11 Jan | 1844 (OB)
RAND, Nordash
L | | 1672
d | 11 Feb | 1715 (PMM)
RAND, Thomas
L
CA | | 1666
RANDALL, Daniel White
L | 22 Jan | 1806
RANDALL, Edward
L | 20 May | 1682
CA | 23 Jan | 1681
RANDALL, Francis
L | 16 May | 1778
d | 5 Aug | 1781 (PMM)
RANDALL, Henry
L | 22 Feb | 1815
CR | 5 Jan | 1846 (OB)
HP | | 1848 (OB)
RANDALL, Nicholas
L | 31 Mar | 1697
In Merchant Service | | 1700 (PJP)
RANDALL, William
T
L | 10 Dec | 1810 (TR)
RANDELL, James
L | 21 Jan | 1741
CR | 10 Oct | 1758
CA | 12 Mar | 1762
d | | 1765
RANDELL, John
L | 6 Apr | 1748
RANDLE, Charles
L | 22 Jan | 1783
RANDLE, Henry Richard Pye
L | 21 Nov | 1790
RANDOLPH, Charles Granville
L | 14 Aug | 1812
CR | 13 June | 1815
CA | 20 Apr | 1827 (OB)
RANELAGH, Viscount
See JONES, Hon Charles, Viscount
RANKIN, John
L | 27 Sept | 1740
RANWELL, William
L | 21 Mar | 1812
HP | July | 1814 (OB)
RAPER, Christopher
L | 13 Sept | 1756
RAPER, George
L | 27 June | 1794
d | | 1797 (DUB)

RAPER, Henry
L | 14 Nov | 1790
CR | 4 July | 1794
CA | 1 Feb | 1796
RAB | 12 Aug | 1819 (LG)
RAW | 19 July | 1821 (LG)
RAR | 27 May | 1825 (LG)
VAB | 22 July | 1830 (LG)
VAR | 10 Jan | 1837 (LG)
AB | 23 Nov | 1841 (OB)
d | 5 Apr | 1845 (DNB)
RASHER, Henry
L | 19 Nov | 1790
RATFORD, Richard
L
CA | | 1666
RATHBORNE, Wilson
L | 18 Mar | 1780
CR | 9 Nov | 1795
CA | 18 Oct | 1802
CB | 4 June | 1815 (LG)
d | | 1831 (MB)
RATSEY, Edward
L | 9 Apr | 1795
CR | 4 Feb | 1806
CA | 5 Sept | 1806
HP | Oct | 1807 (OB)
RAB | 23 Nov | 1841 (LG)
RAW | 9 Nov | 1846 (LG)
RAR | 21 Dec | 1847 (LG)
Ret VA | 11 Nov | 1850 (CH)
Ret A | 18 June | 1857 (CH)
d | | 1868 (CH)
RATSEY, John
L | 8 Dec | 1800
RATSEY, Nathaniel
L | 22 Jan | 1806
Ret CR | 27 July | 1847 (OB)
RATSEY, Restell
L | 7 Aug | 1794
d | | 1796 (PJP)
RATSEY, Robert (1)
L | 23 Apr | 1781
RATSEY, Robert (2)
L | 28 July | 1794
d | | 1813 (PJP)
RATSEY, Thomas
L | 10 Feb | 1797 (OB)
Ret CR | 31 Dec | 1838 (OB)
RATTENBURY, Peter
L | 21 July | 1743
d (drowned) | 14 Nov | 1745 (PJP)
RATTRAY, James
T
L | 24 Mar | 1807
CR | 1 Feb | 1812
CA | 20 Sept | 1815
Ret CA | 31 Oct | 1846 (LG)
Ret RA | | 1851 (TR)
Ret VA | | 1857 (TR)
d | 25 Oct | 1862 (PMM)
RAVEN, Mitchell
L | 28 May | 1808
Ret CR | 30 Apr | 1845 (OB)
RAVEN, William
L | 20 Apr | 1797

RAVENSCROFT, George
L 24 Mar 1796
RAVENSHAW, George
L 2 Aug 1796
CR 2 Apr 1806
RAWE, Richard
L 5 Mar 1778
RAWE, Thomas
L 7 Aug 1761
CR 9 Sept 1779
CA 16 Jan 1783
SUP 1 June 1804
RAWLANCE, Roger Randall
L 17 Nov 1790
KIA 29 May 1794 (LG)
RAWLE, Richard
L 20 Apr 1809
Ret CR 9 Apr 1847 (OB)
RAWLIN, William
L 8 June 1762
RAWLING, John
L
CR 26 May 1737
CA 11 Mar 1755
KIA 30 Apr 1757 (LG)
RAWLINGS, Humphrey
L 28 May 1740
RAWLINGS, James
L 10 Mar 1758
d (drowned) 1 Jan 1761 (PJP)
RAWLINGS, John
L 22 Oct 1777
d 13 Apr 1790
RAWLINGS, Peter
L 29 May 1741
RAWLINS, George
L 6 Nov 1705
RAWLINS, John
L 29 May 1750
RAWLINS, Robert Dicklegg
L 1 Feb 1815
Dismissed 1827 (OB)
Restored 1827 (OB)
RAWLINS, Thomas
T
L 26 Sept 1811
Ret CR 1853 (TR)
d 1860 (TR)
RAWLINS, William
T
L 24 Mar 1807
CR 26 May 1814
d 1818 (TR)
RAWLINSON, Charles James
L 15 Mar 1810
HP 1815 (OB)
RAWLINSON, John
L 26 Jan 1746
Dismissed 21 July 1755 (PJP)
RAWSTORNE, James
L 3 Mar 1815
CR 9 Nov 1846 (OB)
Dismissed 21 July 1855 (PJP)
RAYE, Henry
L 23 Mar 1794

RAYER, William
L 1672
RAYLEY, Charles
L 17 Nov 1800
CR 1 Dec 1813
RAYMENT, Thomas
L 22 Jan 1759
CR 26 Aug 1789
d 30 Dec 1791 (M)
RAYMOND, Baymont
L 31 Dec 1692
CR
CA 21 Jan 1703
d May 1718 (CH)
RAYMOND, George
L 17 Feb 1815
RAYMOND, Hugh
L 5 June 1694
d 10 July 1737 (M)
RAYNER, Edmund
L 25 July 1794
Ret CR 22 Apr 1831 (OB)
d 12 Jan 1846 (OB)
RAYNES, Thomas
See RAINES, Thomas
RAYNHAM, Mark
L 26 Oct 1809
Deserted 3 June 1815 (PMM)
RAYNOR, John (1)
L 26 Feb 1757
CR 1 July 1766
CA 26 July 1775
d 1784
RAYNOR, John (2)
L 29 June 1791
CR 27 Oct 1796
d (drowned) 17 May 1800 (CH)
RAYNSFORD, Robert
L 12 Jan 1798
CR 29 Apr 1802
CA 21 Sept 1806
d (drowned) 27 Oct 1806 (JH)
RAYSON, James
L 28 Mar 1807
READ, Francis
L 1666
CA 1672
d before 1689 (PJP)
READ, George (1)
L 22 Sept 1807
READ, George (2)
L 27 Feb 1815
READ, Jacob
L 2 Feb 1741
READ, James
See READE, James
READ, John (1)
L 5 Oct 1758
d 15 Feb 1799 (PJP)
READ, John (2)
L 5 Apr 1797
READ, John (3)
L 3 Mar 1815
READ, Roddam Augustus
L 1 Sept 1794
d 1805 (PJP)

READ, Samuel
L 1797 (PJP)
d (murdered) 22 Sept 1797 (PJP)

READ, Thomas
L 20 Feb 1805
T
CR 7 Feb 1829 (OB)
d 1850 (TR)

READ, William (1)
L 6 Nov 1778
d 24 July 1790 (PMM)

READ, William (2)
L 18 Mar 1782

READE, James
L 1665

READGROVE, Thomas
L
CA 1667

READY, Henry
T wounded
L 8 July 1807
CR 13 Aug 1812
KIA 19 Aug 1812 (TR)

REBOTIER, Anthony Richard
See ROBOTIER, Anthony Richard

REDDALL, Ambrose
L 8 July 1762
CR 23 Aug 1777
CA 20 Feb 1779
d 16 Dec 1790 (M)

REDDIE, Andrew
L 16 Jan 1805

REDDIE, Peter
L 13 May 1812

REDDISH, Edward (1)
L 7 June 1709 (PMM)
CR
CA 28 Sept 1720
d 19 Aug 1736

REDDISH, Edward (2)
L 14 Apr 1756
SUP CR 11 Sept 1795 (PMM)
d 17 Oct 1800 (LT)

REDDISH, Henry
L 11 Sept 1705
CR
CA 11 Jan 1728
d 1742

REDDY, James
L 22 July 1793

REDE, T.W.
L 1802 (PJP)

REDE, Thomas Rede
L 7 Mar 1794

REDING, Edward
L 17 Aug 1801

REDMAN, Charles (1)
L 2 Feb 1711 (PMM)

REDMAN, Charles (2)
L 1756 (PJP)

REDMAN, John (1)
L
CR 3 Oct 1694
SUP 1707
d 29 Feb 1728

REDMAN, John (2)
L 20 Apr 1703

REDMAN, William
L 1707 (PJP)

REDMILL, Robert
L 24 Dec 1783
CR 1795
CA 16 Dec 1796
T
CB 4 June 1815 (LG)
d Mar 1819 (TR)

REDMON, William
L 11 July 1759
CR 16 Oct 1779

REEBKOMP, Augustus
See MONTGOMERY, Augustus

REED, Anthony
L 15 June 1810

REED, Francis
L 8 Feb 1706 (PMM)

REED, Nehemia John
L 11 Mar 1815
HP Oct 1815 (OB)

REED, Richard Bowen
L 19 Nov 1811

REED, Thomas
L 27 Oct 1781

REED, William
L 16 Jan 1728
d 24 July 1790

REEKIE, William
L 8 Mar 1800

REES, Arthur
L 17 Dec 1782

REES, James
L 2 Aug 1806

REES, Thomas Gwynne
T wounded
L 7 Jan 1806
KIA 26 May 1811 (TR)

REES, William Lee
L 15 Sept 1813

REES, William Sherring
L 1 Aug 1811

REEVE, John
L 22 Feb 1808
CR 2 Feb 1830 (OB)
d 1836 (PJP)

REEVE, Samuel
L 4 Jan 1757
CR
CA 1 Feb 1778
RAW 1 June 1795
RAR 20 Feb 1797
VAW 14 Feb 1799
d 5 June 1803 (PMM)

REEVE, William
L 26 June 1810

REEVES, Daniel
L
CA 8 June 1695 (PMM)
d 23 Sept 1702

REEVES, John
L 12 Aug 1757

REEVES, John Andrews
L 14 Feb 1815

REEVES, Thomas
L
CA 21 May 1666 (RM)

REEVES, Sir William (1)		
K		1664
CA		1664
CL to Prince Rupert	27 Nov	1668 (EAD)
CAMR	1 Oct	1672 (EAD)
KIA	11 Aug	1673 (CH)
REEVES, William (2)		
L		
CA	16 June	1665
KIA	4 June	1666 (RM)
REEVES, William (3)		
L		
CA	7 Aug	1694
d	29 Oct	1694
REID, Charles		
L	10 Feb	1810
REID, Charles Hope		
L	22 Jan	1806
CR	2 June	1812
CA	26 Dec	1822 (MB)
Ret CA	31 Oct	1846 (LG)
REID, Curtis		
L	10 Oct	1809
REID, David		
L	27 June	1794
REID, Henry		
L	24 Feb	1815
HP	24 Feb	1815 (OB)
REID, James (1)		
L	16 Sept	1755
CR	25 June	1773
CA	5 July	1776
d	29 June	1798 (LT)
REID, James (2)		
L	25 Apr	1809
REID, James (3)		
L	6 July	1814
d	17 Jan	1836 (LT)
REID, James (4)		
L	13 Feb	1815
REID, John (1)		
L	21 Dec	1758
REID, John (2)		
L	22 Mar	1779
Entered the American service		?1780 (DAB)
REID, Sir John (3)		
L	12 Mar	1781
d	28 May	1804 (PJP)
REID, Thomas Livingstone		
L	5 Mar	1812
REIKIE, William		
L	8 Mar	1800
HP	Mar–22 Dec	1807 (OB)
SUP CR	31 Dec	1807 (OB)
RELPH, Thomas		
L	23 Jan	1783
REMER, Thomas		
L	5 Dec	1705 (PMM)
REMINGTON, Robert		
L	30 Nov	1782
d	24 July	1791 (PMM)
RENEAU, Henry		
L	16 Feb	1815
RENNIE, George (1)		
L	8 Nov	1799
KIA	12 Aug	1809 (LG)
RENNIE, George (2)		
L	22 July	1807
CR	18 Apr	1811
CA	7 June	1814
Dismissed	14 July	1821 (PJP)
Restored		1822 (PJP)
d	11 Feb	1834 (LT)
RENNIE, James		
L	13 Mar	1811
RENNIE, John		
L	28 N ov	1793
CR	14 Aug	1796
CA	3 Sept	1799
d	17 Mar	1801 (PMM)
RENNIE, William		
L	1 July	1815
d	2 Dec	1818 (LT)
RENNY, Alexander		
L	23 June	1796
CR	13 Oct	1807
CA	1 Jan	1817 (PJP)
d	13 June	1825 (PJP)
RENOU, Adrian		
L	9 May	1777
CR	5 July	1794
CA	26 Dec	1799
d		1805 (OB)
RENOU, Timothy		
T		
L	2 Jan	1812
d		1849 (TR)
RENTON, William		
L	2 Aug	1793
CR	2 Jan	1798
d (suicide)	Feb	1799 (PJP)
RENTONE, James		
L		
CR	22 Dec	1739 (PJP)
CA	17 Apr	1740
KIA	8 Mar	1748 (LG)
RENWICK, Henry		
L	5 Nov	1795
RENWICK, Thomas		
L	17 Nov	1795
CR	25 Sept	1806
CA	1 Jan	1817 (MB)
Ret CA	31 Oct	1846 (LG)
RENWICK, William		
L	13 Apr	1795
d	1 Oct	1839 (LT)
REPINGTON, Henry		
L	13 Feb	1804
CR	10 June	1808
CA	29 Mar	1811
RAB	6 Aug	1847 (CH)
RAW	15 Sept	1849 (CH)
RAR	1 July	1851 (CH)
VA	11 Sept	1854 (NMM)
d	22 Sept	1855 (CH)
RETALICK, James		
L	5 Nov	1793
d	Dec	1803 (PJP)
RETALICK, Richard		
L	6 Sept	1779

CR	12 Aug	1794
CA	24 Dec	1798
REVANS, Thomas		
L	4 Aug	1806
CR	16 Sept	1816 (OB)
HP	16 Sept	1816 (OB)
REWCASTLE, Richard		
L		1664
REYNELL, Carew		
L	18 Mar	1778
REYNOLDS, Sir Barrington		
L	18 Sept	1801
CR	3 Oct	1810
CA	22 Jan	1812
CB	20 July	1838 (OB)
RAB	8 Jan	1848 (OB)
RAW	27 Mar	1850 (LG)
VA	4 July	1855 (DNB)
KCB	4 Feb	1856 (DNB)
A	1 Nov	1860 (DNB)
GCB	28 June	1861 (DNB)
d	3 Aug	1861 (DNB)
REYNOLDS, Francis, Lord Ducie		
L	28 Apr	1758
CR	21 Nov	1760
CA	12 Apr	1762
MP		1784–
(Lancaster)	11 Sept	1785 (MPN)
SUP CA		1785 (PJP)
Inh EP	11 Sept	1785 (MPN)
d	20 Aug	1808 (MPN)
REYNOLDS, George (1)		
L	21 Sept	1790
CR	2 Aug	1797
CA	29 Apr	1802
d	25 Dec	1822 (MB)
REYNOLDS, George (2)		
L	10 July	1794
Ret CR	30 Mar	1831 (OB)
REYNOLDS, Henry		
L	7 May	1776
CR	16 Jan	1781
CA	Jan	1782
KIA	17 Feb	1782 (LG)
REYNOLDS, Jacob		
L		
CA		1664
d		1688 (PD)
REYNOLDS, James		
L	1 Mar	1815
REYNOLDS, John (1)		
L	14 Oct	1736
CR	Feb	1745 (PJP)
d	19 Dec	1765 (PMM)
REYNOLDS, John (2)		
L	27 June	1741
CR	23 Apr	1745
CA	30 Oct	1746
RAB	31 Mar	1775
RAW	5 Feb	1776
RAR	23 Jan	1778
VAB	29 Jan	1779
VAW	26 Sept	1780
AB	24 Sept	1787
d	3 Feb	1788 (DNB)
REYNOLDS, John (3)		
L	19 May	1758
CR	14 May	1778
CA	10 July	1782
d	19 June	1793
REYNOLDS, John (4)		
L	26 Sept	1804
CR	20 Nov	1815
CA	22 July	1830
REYNOLDS, John (5)		
L	13 May	1807
REYNOLDS, Mark		
L	1 May	1716
REYNOLDS, Robert		
L	23 Apr	1677
CA	10 Apr	1689
REYNOLDS, Robert Carthew (1)		
L	26 Feb	1777
CR	14 Apr	1783
CA	24 Sept	1790
RAB	28 Apr	1808
RAR	31 July	1810
d (drowned)	24 Dec	1811 (DNB)
REYNOLDS, Robert Carthew (2)		
L	16 Aug	1799
CR	1 May	1804
d	13 Sept	1804 (PRO)
REYNOLDS, Thomas		
L		
CR		
CA	21 Sept	1709
d	19 Mar	1720
REYNOLDS, Vesey John		
L	16 Mar	1815
REYNOLDS, William (1)		
L	24 Aug	1759
REYNOLDS, William (2)		
L	16 Apr	1812
HP		1813 (OB)
RHODES, Alexander		
L	27 Feb	1811
RHODES, John Henry		
L	11 Feb	1808
CR	15 June	1814
HP		1815 (OB)
RHIND, William Graeme		
L	24 Feb	1815
RHYND, Joseph		
L	25 Oct	1780
RIBOULEAU, John		
L	16 May	1797
RIBOULEAU, Peter		
L	31 Aug	1793
CR	25 July	1796
CA	29 Apr	1802
Ret RA	10 Jan	1837 (OB)
RAW	17 Aug	1840 (LG)
RAR	23 Nov	1841 (LG)
VAB	9 Nov	1846 (LG)
VAW	28 Apr	1847 (LG)
d	16 Dec	1847 (OB)
RICE, Charles		
L	7 Aug	1799
RICE, David		
L	2 Feb	1813
RICE, George		
L	2 Oct	1777
CR	6 July	1794
RICE, Henry (1)		
L	16 June	1709 (PMM)

RICE, Henry (2)
L 22 July 1736
RICE, Henry (3)
L 26 Feb 1794
d 17 Oct 1808 (LT)
RICE, Henry (4)
L 9 Nov 1808
Ret CR 13 Apr 1846 (OB)
RICE, John
L
CA 1672
KIA 11 Aug 1673 (CH)
RICE, John Ap.
L 25 Nov 1695
RICE, William M'Pherson
L 1 Nov 1793
d 27 Nov 1800
RICH, Sir Charles (1)
L 9 Jan 1697
CR
Cre Bt 1698 (PJP)
CA 12 Jan 1703 (PJP)
d 17 Oct 1706 (PJP)
RICH, Charles (2)
L 28 July 1810
CR 27 Jan 1816 (MB)
CA 28 Jan 1838 (OB)
RICH, Edward
L 12 Mar 1740
CR 25 June 1743
CA 28 Jan 1745
d 4 July 1750 (PMM)
RICH, Edward Ludlow
L 15 Oct 1812
CR 24 Sept 1822 (MB)
CA 23 Nov 1841 (OB)
RICH, George Frederick
L 30 Dec 1805
CR 26 Oct 1813
CA 1 July 1823 (MB)
RA 2 Apr 1853 (CH)
VA 20 Jan 1858 (CH)
Ret VA 17 June 1859 (CH)
d 1863 (CH)
RICH, Henry
T
L 26 Nov 1808
HP Dec 1815 (OB)
Ret CR 3 Nov 1846 (OB)
d 1864 (TR)
RICH, T.W.
L 1794 (PJP)
d (drowned) Feb 1794 (CH)
RICH, Sir Thomas
L 25 Mar 1758
Inh Bt 17 July 1762 (MPN)
CR 1 Mar 1769
CA 14 Feb 1771
MP 1784–
(Great Marlow) 1790 (MPN)
RAB 12 Apr 1794
RAR 4 July 1794
VAB 1 June 1795
VAR 14 Feb 1799
AB 1 Jan 1801
d 6 Apr 1803

RICHAN, William
L 9 June 1781
CR 29 Apr 1802
d 1829 (MB)
RICHARDS, Charles
L 3 Mar 1691 (PJP)
CA 4 Dec 1694
d 23 Mar 1704
RICHARDS, Edward (1)
L 17 Sept 1761
d 14 Apr 1765 (PMM)
RICHARDS, Edward (2)
L 12 June 1807
RICHARDS, Edwin
L 26 Apr 1811
CR 28 Apr 1827 (MB)
RICHARDS, Francis
L 8 June 1744
CR 27 Sept 1758
RICHARDS, G.
L 1806 (PJP)
RICHARDS, George
L 7 May 1804
RICHARDS, George Spencer
L 1806 (PJP)
RICHARDS, Gregory Gard
L 13 June 1794
RICHARDS, Harry Brown
T
L 12 Dec 1812
CR 1834 (TR)
d 1839 (TR)
RICHARDS, Harry Lord
L 12 Nov 1809
CR 20 Aug 1828 (OB)
HP 28 Aug 1828 (OB)
RICHARDS, Henry
L 12 Nov 1807
RICHARDS, Isaac
L 19 July 1814
RICHARDS, James (1)
L 6 Nov 1704
SUP 20 Mar 1738 (PMM)
d 1743 (PMM)
RICHARDS, James (2)
L 3 Mar 1795
CR 23 Aug 1814
RICHARDS, John (1)
L 14 Nov 1790
CR 26 Dec 1799
CA 2 June 1809
d 1830 (PJP)
RICHARDS, John (2)
L 3 Aug 1815
RICHARDS, Morgan
L 13 Aug 1770
RICHARDS, Sir Peter
L 12 Dec 1807
CR 16 Sept 1816 (MB)
CA 17 Sept 1828 (OB)
CB 24 Dec 1842 (OB)
RA 6 June 1855 (CH)
Ret VA 12 Apr 1862 (CH)
KCB 1865 (PJP)
Ret A 12 Sept 1865 (CH)

RICHARDS, Thomas
L 28 Feb 1693
In Merchant Service Feb 1700 (PJP)
RICHARDS, Thomas Salmon
L 12 Nov 1777
d 21 Apr 1801
RICHARDS, William (1)
L 6 Apr 1757
d 7 Nov 1784 (M)
RICHARDS, William (2)
L 21 Sept 1806
CR 5 June 1814 (MB)
RICHARDS, William (3)
L 19 Oct 1807
Dismissed July 1809 (PJP)
RICHARDS, William (4)
L 10 Dec 1813
RICHARDS, William (5)
L 7 Feb 1815
HP May 1815 (OB)
RICHARDSON, Alexander (1)
L 10 Oct 1798
RICHARDSON, Alexander (2)
L 1 June 1801
RICHARDSON, Caesar William
L 22 Nov 1809
RICHARDSON, Charles (1)
L 3 Mar 1691 (PJP)
RICHARDSON, Sir Charles (2)
L 4 Aug 1794
CR 9 Oct 1802
CA 27 Sept 1804
CB 4 June 1815 (LG)
RAB 10 Jan 1837 (LG)
KCB 29 June 1841 (OB)
RAW 23 Nov 1841 (LG)
RAR 9 Nov 1846 (LG)
VAB 17 Dec 1847 (LG)
VAW 9 Oct 1849 (LG)
RICHARDSON, Clement (1)
L 28 Oct 1780
RICHARDSON, Clement (2)
L 15 Aug 1801
RICHARDSON, David
L 6 Sept 1782
d 1835 (PJP)
RICHARDSON, Felix
L 15 Jan 1802
RICHARDSON, Francis
L 18 May 1796
RICHARDSON, George
L 4 Feb 1815
RICHARDSON, Henry (1)
L 2 Aug 1794
RICHARDSON, Henry (2)
L 2 Oct 1795
CR 6 Aug 1801
CA 29 Apr 1802
RICHARDSON, Henry James
L 3 Aug 1793
RICHARDSON, John (1)
L 6 Apr 1757
RICHARDSON, John (2)
L 3 Nov 1790
CR 29 Apr 1802
d Jan 1815 (OB)
RICHARDSON, John (3)
L 13 Aug 1800

RICHARDSON, John (4)
L 3 Feb 1805
RICHARDSON, Sir John Charles
L 26 Aug 1806
CR 28 May 1813
RICHARDSON, Luke
L 13 Mar 1703
RICHARDSON, Philip
L 16 Aug 1799
RICHARDSON, Thomas
L 23 Dec 1760
d 14 Aug 1793
RICHARDSON, William (1)
L 27 Nov 1782
CR 8 Oct 1798 (PRO)
RICHARDSON, William (2)
L 7 Feb 1797
CR 8 May 1804
d 19 Aug 1818 (LT)
RICHARDSON, William (3)
L 30 Apr 1804
CR 7 Dec 1818 (MB)
CA 28 June 1838 (OB)
RA 10 Sept 1857 (PMM)
d 1864 (PMM)
RICHARDSON, William (4)
L 12 Oct 1808
RICHBELL, Thomas
L 14 Jan 1780
CR 26 Dec 1799
CA 29 Apr 1802
d 24 Apr 1833 (LT)
RICHES, Robert Watson
L 24 Jan 1810
RICHES, Watson Thomas
L 22 Jan 1814
RICHIE, William
L 11 Feb 1815
HP 11 Feb 1815 (OB)
RICHMAND, Edward
L 10 Sept 1800
RICHMOND, James
L 19 May 1691 (PJP)
RICHMOND, Thomas Foord
L 31 Aug 1793
RICKARD, Jose Langman
L 17 Mar 1815
RICKARDS, John
L 13 Nov 1807
RICKETTS, Charles Spencer
L 14 Dec 1809
HP 1815 (OB)
RICKETTS, George
L 12 Aug 1809
RICKETTS, James Otto
L 18 May 1815
RICKETTS, Sir Tristram Roberts
L 23 July 1793
CR 1 Jan 1801
CA 9 Oct 1801
Cre Bt 1828 (OB)
RAB 22 July 1830 (CH)
RAW 10 Jan 1837 (LG)
RAR 28 June 1838 (LG)
VAB 23 Nov 1841 (LG)
d 18 Aug 1842 (CH)

RICKETTS, William (1)
L
CA 1672

RICKETTS, William (2)
L 9 Jan 1794
CR 23 Sept 1799
CA 29 Apr 1802

RICKETTS, William Henry
L 5 Sept 1782
CR 17 Mar 1783
CA 22 Nov 1790
d 18 May 1840 (LT)

RICKIE, William
L 1804 (PJP)

RICKMAN, John
L 8 Feb 1776

RIDDALL, Finch
L 25 Sept 1693
?CA 21 Dec 1703

RIDDELL, Joseph
L 12 Jan 1796

RIDDELL, Robert
L 5 Oct 1805
CR 1 Feb 1812
CA 12 Aug 1819 (PJP)
RA 27 Aug 1857 (PMM)
VA 10 Sept 1857 (PMM)
d 1860 (PMM)

RIDEOUT, Samuel
L 21 Sept 1807
CR 11 May 1827 (PJP)

RIDER, John
L 2 Feb 1815

RIDER, William Barnham
L 9 Mar 1796
CR 22 Jan 1806
Dismissed 20 Nov 1810 (MB)
Restored Mar 1811 (MB)
HP Mar 1811 (OB)
d 11 Nov 1849 (LT)

RIDGE, John James
L 7 May 1802
T
CR 13 Jan 1809
d Mar 1809 (TR)

RIDGE, Thomas Roger
L 14 June 1799
d 1809 (JH)

RIDGEWAY, William
L 22 May 1813

RIDLEY, Hugh
L
CA 12 June 1667

RIDLEY, Ralph
L 28 Aug 1783

RIGBY, Christopher
L 28 Mar 1758
CR 25 Oct 1777
d 11 Jan 1795 (LT)

RIGBY, Edward
L
LFMR 20 Dec 1692 (EAD)
CA 13 Jan 1693
CAF (Gibson) 10 Mar 1707 (EAD)

RIGBY, Peter
L 18 Aug 1801

RIGBY, Robert Preston
L 29 Aug 1807

RIGBY, William
L 1672
d before 1689 (PJP)

RIGGS, Thomas
L
CR 23 Oct 1746

RIGHTLEY, Thomas
L 19 Nov 1702 (PMM)

RIGMAIDEN, James
L 21 Mar 1812
HP 1816 (OB)

RILEY, Charles
L 1665
CA 1665

RIOU, Edward
L 28 Oct 1780
CR 21 Sept 1790 (PRO)
CA 4 June 1791
KIA 2 Apr 1801 (DNB)

RIPLEY, Horatio
L 26 Feb 1756
d 4 Oct 1789

RIPLEY, Langdale
L 1665

RIPLEY, Lionel
L
CA 26 Jan 1693
SUP
d 1 Apr 1725

RIPLEY, Thomas
L 8 Jan 1806 (PMM)

RIPLEY, William
L
CA 11 Dec 1695
d (drowned) Aug 1697 (PJP)

RIPPE, James de
L 8 May 1807
CR 18 Apr 1811
d Nov 1828 (PRO)

RISBY, Joe
L 14 Oct 1694

RITCHIE, James
L 15 July 1794

RITCHIE, Robert
L 21 Nov 1744

RITCHIE, Thomas
L 10 July 1812
d 9 Feb 1851 (DUB)

RITCHIE, William
L 8 June 1807

RIVERS, William
T wounded
L 8 Jan 1806
d 1856 (TR)

RIVETT, Peter
L 26 Oct 1777
CR 23 Aug 1781
d Aug 1782 (PJP)

RIX, George Albert
L 18 Nov 1799

ROACH, Charles
L 1702 (PJP)

ROACH, George		
L	18 Nov	1799
ROACH, Henry		
L		1702 (PJP)
d	5 Sept	1787 (M)
ROACH, Jeremiah		
L		1665 (P)
CA	4 Apr	1689
d	6 June	1690
ROACH, John		
See ROCHE, John		
ROACH, William		
L		1664
ROAPE, Anthony		
L	30 Apr	1678
ROBARTS, Joseph		
L	8 May	1740
Gone	1 Jan	1764
ROBARTS, Richard		
L	3 Feb	1744
ROBARTS, Samuel		
L	26 Oct	1776
ROBB, Charles		
L	3 Oct	1804
CR	12 Nov	1810
d (drowned)		1813 (PJP)
ROBB, Joseph		
L	19 Nov	1793
ROBBIN, George		
L	8 Sept	1803
CR	14 Apr	1810
d		1814 (PJP)
ROBBINS, George		
L	11 Mar	1755
ROBBINS, Henry		
L	9 Jan	1695
ROBERTS, Bartholomew		
L	9 July	1782
CR	24 Apr	1794
CA	8 Aug	1796
d		1797 (LT)
ROBERTS, Benjamin		
L	24 Oct	1812
ROBERTS, Charles Fowler		
L	10 June	1794
ROBERTS, Christopher (1)		
L	7 July	1762
d		1815 (PJP)
ROBERTS, Christopher (2)		
L		
CR	25 Oct	1809
ROBERTS, Daniel		
L	12 July	1809
CR	16 May	1812
Ret CA	25 June	1845 (OB)
ROBERTS, Duncan		
L	15 Feb	1815
HP	15 Feb	1815 (OB)
ROBERTS, Edward (1)		
L	18 Jan	1759
SUP CR	9 Jan	1801 (PMM)
ROBERTS, Edward (2)		
L	7 Mar	1795 (OB)
ROBERTS, Edward (3)		
L	5 Apr	1797
ROBERTS, Edward (4)		
L	10 Nov	1810
ROBERTS, Eldred		
L	2 Feb	1815
ROBERTS, Francis (1)		
L	21 June	1768 (PRO)
CR	4 Feb	1780
CA	25 Mar	1782
ROBERTS, Francis (2)		
L	3 May	1811
HP	July	1839 (OB)
ROBERTS, Francis Cateby		
L	14 Feb	1797
ROBERTS, Frederick		
L		1800 (PJP)
ROBERTS, George		
L		
CA		1665
ROBERTS, Henry (1)		
L	2 July	1696 (PJP)
ROBERTS, Henry (2)		
L	28 Oct	1780
CR	1 Jan	1790
CA	28 Aug	1794
d	25 Aug	1796 (PMM)
ROBERTS, James Wolf		
L	1 Dec	1778
Ret CR	9 July	1840 (OB)
ROBERTS, John (1)		
L	6 Feb	1706 (PMM)
ROBERTS, John (2)		
L		
CR		
CA	19 Apr	1706
d	11 Feb	1745 (PMM)
ROBERTS, John (3)		
L	20 Mar	1741
SUP CR	22 Dec	1768 (PMM)
d	19 Aug	1815 (PMM)
ROBERTS, John (4)		
L	27 Mar	1795
CR	12 Apr	1833 (PMM)
d		1837 (PMM)
ROBERTS, John (5)		
L	24 Aug	1799
CR	26 Nov	1830 (PMM)
d	2 June	1837 (LT)
ROBERTS, John (6)		
L	20 Feb	1805
ROBERTS, John Charles Gawen		
L	12 Oct	1805
CR	23 July	1812
CA	13 June	1815
Ret CA	31 Oct	1846 (LG)
ROBERTS, John Walter		
L	6 Mar	1812
CR	26 Aug	1814
CA	16 June	1823 (MB)
d	2 Oct	1845 (OB)
ROBERTS, Lazarus		
L	15 Oct	1815
ROBERTS, Mitchell		
L	15 Aug	1800 (PMM)
CR	24 Sept	1814
HP	24 Sept	1814 (OB)
ROBERTS, Owen		
L	12 July	1778
ROBERTS, Richard		
L		1747 (PJP)

Name	Rank	Date	Year
ROBERTS, Robert (1)			
	L		1665
ROBERTS, Robert (2)			
	L	6 Mar	1808
ROBERTS, Sir Samuel			
	L	22 May	1806
	CR	6 Dec	1813
	CB	4 June	1815 (LG)
	CA	13 June	1815 (PJP)
	Kt		1833 (LG)
	Ret CA	31 Oct	1846 (LG)
ROBERTS, Thomas (1)			
	L		
	?CA	23 Aug	1696
ROBERTS, Thomas (2)			
	L	24 Dec	1796
	CR	23 July	1798
	Ret CA	10 Sept	1840 (OB)
ROBERTS, William (1)			
	L		1747 (PJP)
ROBERTS, William (2)			
	L	11 Jan	1779
	d	7 July	1791
ROBERTS, William (3)			
	L	23 Dec	1793
	CR	14 Feb	1801
	CA	24 Aug	1804
	d	19 Feb	1811 (LT)
ROBERTS, William (4)			
	L	12 July	1810
	CR	5 Aug	1816 (MB)
ROBERTS, William (5)			
	L	2 Feb	1815
ROBERTS, William Gilbert			
	L	3 Mar	1810
	CR	20 Sept	1815
	d	4 Oct	1843 (OB)
ROBERTS, William Pender			
	L	5 Feb	1806
	CR	21 Mar	1812
	Ret CA	27 Mar	1845 (OB)
ROBERTSON, Adam			
	L	21 Mar	1812
	d		1835 (PJP)
ROBERTSON, Alexander			
	L	7 June	1814
ROBERTSON, Bowen Robert			
	L	6 July	1811
	HP	Aug	1815 (OB)
ROBERTSON, George (1)			
	L	5 Mar	1762
	d	27 Sept	1799 (PJP)
ROBERTSON, George (2)			
	L	15 Dec	1768
	CR	4 Nov	1778 (PJP)
	CA	15 Aug	1781 (PJP)
	d	23 Nov	1791 (LT)
ROBERTSON, George (3)			
	L	19 June	1802
ROBERTSON, Hugh			
	L	10 Apr	1747
ROBERTSON, J.B.			
	L		1814 (PJP)
ROBERTSON, James (1)			
	L	3 Aug	1759
	CR	26 May	1768
	CA	25 Oct	1809
ROBERTSON, James (2)			
	L	18 Jan	1806
ROBERTSON, James (3)			
	L	17 Mar	1815
	HP	17 Mar	1815 (OB)
ROBERTSON, John (1)			
	L		1709 (PJP)
ROBERTSON, John (2)			
	L	26 Jan	1805
	CR	9 Dec	1816 (OB)
	CA	28 June	1838 (OB)
	HP	28 June	1838 (OB)
ROBERTSON, John (3)			
	L	8 Mar	1815
ROBERTSON, Lewis			
	L	22 June	1773
	CR	9 Feb	1778
	CA	30 Dec	1782
	KIA	2 July	1795 (LG)
ROBERTSON, Peter			
	L	29 May	1741
	CR	3 Apr	1746
	d	1 Aug	1747
ROBERTSON, Robert ?ROBINSON			
	L	5 May	1735
ROBERTSON, William (1)			
	L	12 Mar	1760
	SUP CR	20 Apr	1807
	d		1813 (PMM)
ROBERTSON, William (2)			
	L	26 Sept	1793
ROBERTSON, William (3)			
	L	19 Nov	1798
ROBERTSON, William (4)			
	L	28 Oct	1800
ROBERTSON, William (5)			
	T		
	L	26 Feb	1810
	CR	12 Nov	1827 (MB)
	CA	10 Jan	1837 (OB)
	Ret RA		1857 (TR)
	d		1861 (TR)
ROBILLIARD, William			
	L	13 July	1799
	CR	24 Nov	1808
	CA	14 Dec	1812
ROBINETT, Roger			
	L	1 Feb	1806
	CR	12 Oct	1814
ROBINS, Henry			
	L	4 Jan	1695 (PJP)
ROBINS, Thomas			
	L	3 Sept	1810
ROBINS, Thomas Lowton (1)			
	L	24 June	1793
	CR	19 July	1821 (PJP)
	d	17 May	1836 (PJP)
ROBINS, Thomas Lowton (2)			
	T		
	L	22 Oct	1805
	CR	21 July	1819 (OB)
	CA		1851 (TR)
	d		1852 (TR)
ROBINS, William			
	L	17 Mar	1815
ROBINSON, Abraham			
	L	7 Feb	1815

ROBINSON, Alfred Samuel
L 2 Jan 1810
HP June 1846 (OB)

ROBINSON, Charles (1)
L 12 Feb 1780
CR 5 Apr 1794

ROBINSON, Charles (2)
L 13 Nov 1809

ROBINSON, Charles (3)
L 21 Feb 1815
d 20 Oct 1816 (LT)

ROBINSON, Charles C.
T
L 21 Mar 1812
d 1850 (TR)

ROBINSON, Christopher
L 1667

ROBINSON, Edward (1)
L
CA 1672

ROBINSON, Edward (2)
L 4 Dec 1739

ROBINSON, Edward (3)
L 15 Apr 1813
HP 1845 (OB)

ROBINSON, Francis
L 4 June 1709

ROBINSON, George (1)
L 4 Nov 1790
CR 23 June 1795

ROBINSON, George (2)
L 7 May 1807

ROBINSON, George (3)
L 16 Feb 1815
HP 16 Feb 1815 (OB)

ROBINSON, Henry (1)
L
CA 17 June 1689
d 11 July 1701 (PJP)

ROBINSON, Henry (2)
L 4 Sept 1717 (PMM)
CR 2 Jan 1724

ROBINSON, Hercules
T
L 25 Apr 1807
CR 30 Aug 1809
CA 7 June 1814
Ret CA 31 Oct 1846 (LG)
Ret RA 9 Oct 1849 (LG)
Ret VA 21 Oct 1856 (CH)
Ret A 15 Jan 1862 (CH)
d 15 May 1864 (DNB)

ROBINSON, Hugh
L 5 Aug 1761
CR 10 Jan 1771
CA 8 May 1777
SUP RA

ROBINSON, James (1)
L 11 Jan 1710
CR 29 Aug 1727

ROBINSON, James (2)
L 1760 (PJP)

ROBINSON, James (3)
L 11 Aug 1808

ROBINSON, James (4)
L 12 Feb 1810

ROBINSON, John (1)
L
CA 1667

ROBINSON, John (2)
L 1676

ROBINSON, John (3)
L
CR 27 Mar 1690
CA
d 5 Sept 1736 (M)

ROBINSON, John (4)
L 2 Mar 1734

ROBINSON, John (5)
L 30 Jan 1758
CR 20 June 1765
CA 26 Jan 1774
SUP RA 1794
d 19 Sept 1807 (PJP)

ROBINSON, John (6)
L 4 Sept 1759

ROBINSON, John (7)
L 5 July 1797
d (drowned) 9 Nov 1799 (PJP)

ROBINSON, John Parker
L 23 Sept 1777
CR 24 Oct 1796
d (drowned) 17 May 1800 (CH)

ROBINSON, Joseph (1)
L 15 Apr 1813

ROBINSON, Joseph (2)
L 9 Feb 1815

ROBINSON, Louis A.
L 7 Feb 1812
CR 10 Jan 1837 (OB)
HP 10 Jan 1837 (OB)

ROBINSON, Mark (1)
L 30 Mar 1746
CR 27 Sept 1758
CA 13 Aug 1760
SUP RA
d 23 Nov 1799 (PJP)

ROBINSON, Mark (2)
L 5 Oct 1776
CR 23 Aug 1781
CA 21 Sept 1790
RAB 28 Apr 1808
RAW 25 Oct 1809
RAR 31 July 1810
VAB 12 Aug 1812
VAW 4 June 1814
VAR 12 Aug 1819 (CH)
AB 27 May 1825 (CH)
AW 22 July 1830 (CH)
d 21 Feb 1834 (CH)

ROBINSON, Nicholas
L 16 Feb 1727
CR
MP (Wootton Bassett) 1734–1741 (MPS)
CA 8 May 1735
d 1 Feb 1753 (MPS)

ROBINSON, Peter
L 25 July 1781

ROBINSON, Sir Robert (1)
L
CA 1661
Kt 1675 (DCB)
d 1705 (DCB)

ROBINSON, Robert (2)		
?L	12 Apr	1678
CA	8 Aug	1692 (PJP)
LGH		1705 (PJP)
d	16 Mar	1719
ROBINSON, Robert (3)		
L	8 July	1696
CR	1 Apr	1708
CA	22 Feb	1744
SUP RA		1762
d	10 Sept	1785 (M)
ROBINSON, Robert (4)		
L	7 Mar	1815
ROBINSON, Samuel		
L	28 Feb	1690 (PJP)
ROBINSON, Sir Tancred		
L	19 Dec	1705 (PMM)
CR	27 Mar	1707 (PMM)
CA	8 Jan	1708
RAB	2 Mar	1736
	(2 Mar	1735 in C)
RAW	11 July	1739
Resigned		1741
d	3 Sept	1754 (M)
ROBINSON, Thomas (1)		
L		
CA	8 Dec	1688 (DDA)
ROBINSON, Thomas (2)		
L		
CA	5 Feb	1690 (PJP)
ROBINSON, Thomas (3)		
L		
CR	15 June	1705 (PMM)
ROBINSON, Thomas (4)		
L	7 Nov	1778
ROBINSON, Thomas (5)		
L	11 June	1807
ROBINSON, Thomas Pitt		
T		
L	21 Mar	1812
CR	26 Aug	1828 (OB)
CA		1851 (TR)
d		1861 (TR)
ROBINSON, William (1)		
L	18 July	1747
d	?Oct	1782 (M)
ROBINSON, William (2)		
L	6 June	1766
d	?Sept	1781 (M)
ROBINSON, William (3)		
L	21 May	1782
d	29 Sept	1806 (PMM)
ROBINSON, William (4)		
L	20 Apr	1793
CR	27 Aug	1799
d	6 Aug	1801
ROBINSON, William (5)		
L	18 Feb	1798
ROBINSON, William M'Dowall		
L	23 Sept	1795
ROBISON, Samuel		
L	24 Mar	1807
ROBOTIER, Anthony Richard		
L	19 Mar	1794
KIA	29 June	1798 (LG)
ROBSON, Christopher		
L		1668
ROBSON, James		
L		1745 (PJP)
ROBSON, John		
L	21 Aug	1758
ROBSON, John Martin		
L	2 June	1808
ROBY, Fasham		
L	13 Aug	1794
CR	29 Apr	1802
ROCH, Hugh		
L	30 June	1756
ROCH, Mark		
L	6 July	1797
ROCH, William		
L	22 May	1758
ROCHE, Charles		
L	31 May	1755
CR	7 Apr	1762
ROCHE, Henry		
L		
CR	4 June	1705 (PMM)
ROCHE, John		
L	23 Oct	1806
Ret CR	16 Sept	1841 (OB)
ROCHE, Joseph		
L	4 May	1814
CR	28 June	1838 (OB)
HP	Aug	1838 (OB)
ROCHFORT, John Prime Iron		
L	30 Dec	1775
CR	25 Oct	1809
ROCHFORT, Robert		
L	26 Apr	1811
CR	10 Mar	1828 (OB)
HP	10 Mar	1828 (OB)
Ret CA	31 Oct	1846 (LG)
ROCHFORT, Thomas		
L		1702 (PJP)
ROCHFORT, William		
L	2 May	1810
CR	15 June	1814
CA	27 Mar	1826 (OB)
Ret CA	1 Oct	1846 (OB)
d	21 Dec	1847 (OB)
RODD, Sir John Tremayne		
L	4 Nov	1790
CR	19 Mar	1795
CA	7 Sept	1798
CB	4 June	1815 (LG)
RAB	27 May	1825 (LG)
RAW	22 July	1830 (LG)
KCB	22 Feb	1832 (OB)
VAB	10 Jan	1837 (LG)
VAW	28 June	1838 (LG)
d	4 Oct	1838 (OB)
RODD, Thomas		
L	24 Mar	1747
RODDAM, Robert		
L	2 Nov	1741
CR	7 June	1746
CA	9 July	1747
RAW	23 Jan	1778
VAB	29 Mar	1779
VAW	26 Sept	1780
VAR	24 Sept	1787
AB	1 Feb	1793
AW	12 Apr	1794

AR 9 Nov 1805
d 31 Mar 1808 (DNB)
RODDAM, William
L 17 Aug 1812
HP Oct 1816 (OB)
RODERICK, George
L 23 Mar 1807
RODGER, William
L 27 Feb 1815
HP 27 Feb 1815 (OB)
RODNEY, Hon. Edward
L 29 Aug 1799
CR 8 Apr 1805
CA 22 Jan 1806
d 12 Nov 1828 (OB)
RODNEY, George Brydges, Lord (1)
KLB July 1732 (DNB)
L 15 Feb 1740
CR Skipped to CA
CA 9 Nov 1742
GG
(Newfoundland) 1749–1750 (BNS)
MP (Saltash) 13 May 1751–1754 (MPS)
RAB 19 May 1759 (CH)
MP
(Okehampton) 24 Nov 1759–1761 (MPS)
MP (Penryn) 1761–1768 (MPS)
VAB 21 Oct 1762
GGH 1765–1770 (PJP)
MP (Northampton) 1768–1774 (MPS)
VAW 18 Oct 1770
VAR 24 Oct 1770
AW 29 Jan 1778
MP (Westminster) 1780–June 1782 (MPS)
Cre EP 19 June 1782 (DNB)
d 23 May 1792 (DNB)
RODNEY, George Brydges (2)
L 12 Mar 1811
RODNEY, James
L 27 Aug 1771
CR 7 Sept 1774
d (drowned) Aug 1776 (CH)
RODNEY, Hon. John
L 3 Feb 1780 (PMM)
CR 14 Oct 1780
CA 14 Oct 1780 (OB)
MP (Launceston) 1790–1796 (MPT)
d 9 Apr 1847 (DNB)
RODNEY, Hon. Robert
T
L 15 Aug 1806
CR 2 Aug 1811
CA 22 Feb 1813
d 20 July 1826 (MB)
RODSDELL, Richard
L 6 June 1777
ROE, Edward
L 14 July 1777
CR 22 Nov 1790
CA 6 Dec 1796
ROE, Robert Bradley
L 10 May 1810
ROE, Samuel William
L 26 Apr 1797
ROE, William
L 1692 (PJP)

ROEBUCK, Henry
L 10 Mar 1815
ROEPEL, Juste Peter
L 10 Aug 1814
CR 23 Nov 1841 (OB)
CA 6 Nov 1846 (OB)
d 1847 (OB)
ROFFEY, Kerryll ?Kerritt
L
CA 23 Jan 1694
d 11 Sept 1716
ROGERS, Benjamin
L 23 July 1795
ROGERS, Edward
L 10 Feb 1815
HP 10 Feb 1815 (OB)
ROGERS, Francis
L 3 Sept 1810
ROGERS, Sir Frederick (1)
L
CR 15 May 1741
CA 2 Dec 1741
COMM (Plymouth) 1753–1775 (PJP)
Inh Bt 1773 (PJP)
d 9 June 1777 (PJP)
ROGERS, Frederick (2)
L 8 Mar 1815
CR 3 June 1831 (OB)
ROGERS, George (1)
L 6 June 1697
CR
CA 8 July 1703
d 24 Oct 1729
ROGERS, George (2)
L 1 Aug 1803
ROGERS, Jacob
L 4 Apr 1757
ROGERS, James (1)
L 5 Sept 1779
ROGERS, James (2)
L 19 July 1793
CR 22 Jan 1806
ROGERS, James (3)
L 22 Oct 1808
d (drowned) 24 Dec 1811 (PJP)
ROGERS, James (4)
L 10 Dec 1811
HP Sept 1814 (OB)
ROGERS, John (1)
L
CA 1673
ROGERS, John (2)
L 29 Aug 1745
ROGERS, John (3)
L 1756 (PJP)
ROGERS, John (4)
L 8 July 1797
ROGERS, John (5)
L 6 Oct 1803
ROGERS, Josias
L 19 Oct 1778
CR 2 Dec 1780
CA 1 Dec 1787
d 24 Apr 1795 (DNB)
ROGERS, Nathaniel
L 20 July 1726

ROGERS, Philip
L 19 Sept 1809
ROGERS, Robert
L 30 Apr 1678
ROGERS, Robert Henley
L 4 Feb 1803
CR 1 Feb 1812
CA 2 Sept 1816 (MB)
Ret CA 31 Oct 1846 (LG)
ROGERS, Samuel
L 26 May 1768
ROGERS, Thomas (1)
L 26 Aug 1789
CR 25 Mar 1794
CA 10 Aug 1795
RAB 4 June 1814
d 29 Sept 1814 (CH)
ROGERS, Thomas (2)
L 6 Mar 1815
HP 3 Sept 1816 (OB)
ROGERS, Timothy
L 21 Jan 1794
ROGERS, William (1)
L 1689 (PJP)
ROGERS, William (2)
L 21 Nov 1696 (PJP)
ROGERS, William (3)
L 26 Sept 1793
CR 22 Jan 1806
Ret CA 10 Sept 1840 (OB)
d 29 Jan 1848 (OB)
ROGIER, Richard
L 16 Aug 1695
ROKEBY, Henry Ralph
L 27 Jan 1809
CR 13 June 1815
ROKENHAM, William
See BOKENHAM, William
ROLFE, William
L 5 July 1813
ROLLES, Robert
L 26 Mar 1782
CR 10 May 1793
CA 12 Aug 1795
RAB 4 June 1814 (CH)
RAW 12 Aug 1819 (CH)
RAR 19 July 1821 (CH)
VAB 27 May 1825 (CH)
VAW 22 July 1830 (CH)
VAR 10 Jan 1837 (CH)
d 18 Nov 1839 (CH)
ROLLESTON, James
L 8 June 1811
HP Feb 1816 (OB)
ROLLS, Hon. James
L 21 Jan 1800
d 21 Nov 1802 (PJP)
ROMNEY, Francis Darby
L 25 Mar 1809
Ret CR 9 Apr 1847 (OB)
RONTREE, John
L 22 June 1697 (PJP)
ROOKE, Frederick William
L 15 Nov 1805
CR 21 Mar 1812
Ret CA 25 Mar 1845 (OB)
ROOKE, Sir George
L 1672
CA 13 Sept 1673
(?13 Nov 1673)
LF (Duke of York) 1 Jan 1676 (EAD)
CL in Prince George of Denmark's Regiment 1 June 1686 (EAD)
CA in Prince George of Denmark's Regiment 10 May 1687 (EAD)
RAB 6 May 1690
RAR 3 June 1690
VAB 20 Jan 1692
(15 May in C)
COM E 22 Jan 1692–
22 Apr 1694 (NBO)
Kt 1693 (DNB)
VAW Spring 1693 (C)
VAR 26 Jan 1693
(Feb 1694 in C)
AB 2 July 1693
COM AD 2 May 1694–
26 Jan 1702 (AO)
AW 2 Aug 1695
AF 28 Apr 1696
MP (Portsmouth) 1689–1709 (DNB)
MCLHA 22 May 1702–
11 June 1705 (AO)
d 24 Jan 1709 (DNB)
ROOKE, James
L 1704 (PJP)
ROOKE, Nicholas
L 23 Mar 1757
SUP CR 21 Sept 1796 (PMM)
d 1805 (PMM)
ROOKE, Thomas (1)
L 11 May 1681
CA 4 Mar 1691
d 20 May 1701
ROOKE, Thomas (2)
L 19 Aug 1697 (PJP)
ROOKE, William Ley
L 14 Jan 1744
ROOMCOYLE, Thomas
L 1664
CA 25 Mar 1665 (PRO)
KIA 12 May 1689 (CH)
ROOME, Charles
L 13 July 1745
ROOPE, Anthony
L
CA 19 Nov 1689
d 25 June 1692
ROOSE, John
L 11 June 1705
ROOTES, John (1)
L 3 July 1806
ROOTES, John (2)
L 3 Feb 1810
HP Mar 1814 (OB)
ROOTH, Sir Richard
L 1672
CA 1660 (PJP)
Kt 1675 (PJP)
d before 1688 (PD)
ROOTS, James
L 8 Apr 1740
ROPER, Bryant
L 14 Oct 1702
SUP 20 Mar 1738 (PMM)
ROPER, Cadwallader Blaney
L 9 Nov 1786

ROPER, George B.
T
L 26 Dec 1809
d 1815 (TR)
ROPER, William
L 29 Oct 1794
RORIE, George
L 25 Mar 1809
Ret CR 9 Apr 1847 (OB)
d 8 Dec 1847 (OB)
RORIE, John James
L 4 Dec 1798
Ret CR 26 Nov 1830 (OB)
ROSBEE, George
L 2 Mar 1734
d 1741 (PMM)
ROSCO, James
L 24 Sept 1759
ROSCOW, Samuel (1)
L 25 Jan 1796
ROSCOW, Samuel (2)
L 4 May 1809
Ret CR 27 July 1847 (OB)
ROSE, Abraham
L 2 Mar 1780
ROSE, Alexander
L 13 Oct 1797
CR 21 Oct 1810
d 1826 (MB)
ROSE, C.
L 1806 (PJP)
ROSE, Charles
L 10 Mar 1815 (OB)
ROSE, Henry
L 11 Oct 1742
ROSE, James (1)
L 1665
ROSE, James (2)
L 18 Sept 1796
CR 7 Oct 1813
Kt (Sweden) 16 Feb 1815 (LG)
ROSE, John (1) ?ROSS
L 15 Sept 1695
In Merchant Service 1699 (PJP)
CA 14 Sept 1716
d 27 Mar 1731
ROSE, John (2)
L 6 Aug 1801
Ret CR 16 Dec 1831 (OB)
ROSE, Jonas
L 9 Oct 1779
CR 1 Aug 1795
CA 1 Jan 1801
ROSE, S.W.
L 1797 (PJP)
ROSE, Thomas Barton
L 20 May 1812
ROSENHAGEN, Philip Lewis J.
L 7 Sept 1795
CR 29 Apr 1802
CA 22 Jan 1806
d 13 Apr 1813 (LT)
ROSENHOLME, Peter
L 1672
ROSEWELL, Henry
L 19 Jan 1740
CR
CA 21 July 1745
d 9 May 1771
ROSHER, Henry
L 1791 (PJP)
ROSKRUGE, Francis
L 18 Jan 1796
T killed
KIA 21 Oct 1805 (TR)
ROSS, Alexander (1)
L 5 Mar 1778
ROSS, Alexander (2)
L 21 Feb 1815
ROSS, Charles
L 19 Mar 1815
ROSS, Charles Alexander
L 24 Feb 1815
ROSS, Charles Bayntun Hodgson
L 14 July 1796
CR 11 June 1800
CA 15 Oct 1802
CB 8 Dec 1815 (LG)
COM N July 1822 (OB)
COMM (Plymouth) 1829–1837 (PJP)
RAB 10 Jan 1837 (LG)
RAW 28 June 1838 (LG)
RAR 9 Nov 1846 (LG)
VAB 24 Apr 1847 (LG)
VAW 1 Aug 1848 (LG)
d 2 Mar 1849 (CH)
ROSS, Charles Henry
L 13 Mar 1810
ROSS, Daniel
L 12 May 1799
CR 7 Aug 1810
CA 9 Feb 1816 (MB)
d 1827 (MB)
ROSS, Edward
L 12 Mar 1807
Dismissed Apr 1811 (PJP)
ROSS, George (1)
L 21 Oct 1755
ROSS, George (2)
L 3 Jan 1784
CR 19 Aug 1799
d 1 Nov 1812 (PJP)
ROSS, George Adam
L 28 Sept 1799
ROSS, George Davis
L 6 Feb 1815
ROSS, Francis
L 28 Aug 1779
KIA 1 June 1794 (LG)
ROSS, Hugh
L 26 Apr 1802
d (drowned) May 1805 (PJP)
ROSS, James (1)
L 21 Oct 1790
CR
CA 4 July 1794
ROSS, James (2)
L 22 Oct 1795
ROSS, John (1)
L 14 Feb 1798
ROSS, Sir John (2)
L 13 Mar 1805
CR 1 Feb 1812

Kt (Sweden) 4 Dec 1813 (LG)
CA 7 Dec 1818 (DNB)
CB 24 Dec 1834 (DNB)
Kt 24 Dec 1834 (DNB)
d 30 Aug 1856 (DNB)

ROSS, John
See ROSE, John

ROSS, Sir John Lockhart
Formerly LOCKHART, John
L 21 Oct 1743
CR 22 Apr 1755
CA 23 Mar 1756
Cre Bt 28 Oct 1758 (MPN)
MP
(Linlithgow Burghs) 1761–1768 (MPN)
MP (Lanarkshire) 1768–1774 (MPN)
RAB 29 Mar 1779 (CH)
RAR 26 Sept 1780
VAB 24 Sept 1787
d 9 June 1790 (DNB)

ROSS, Richard Colmer
L 20 Nov 1812

ROSS, Robert
L 10 Mar 1815 (OB)

ROSS, Simon
L 1711 (PRO)

ROSS, Walter
L 14 Feb 1705 (PMM)
CR
CA 2 Feb 1711

ROSS, William (1)
L 24 Dec 1779

ROSS, William (2)
L 30 Jan 1781

ROSS, William (3)
L 28 Apr 1796
d 1801 (PJP)

ROSSE, James
L 29 June 1709 (PMM)

ROSSINGTON, Henry
L 17 Aug 1709
SUP 18 Oct 1743 (PMM)

ROSSON, William
L 21 Apr 1795

ROTHE, Peter
L 24 Sept 1771
CR 18 May 1779
d 14 Mar 1798

ROTHERAM, Edward
L 14 Apr 1793
CR 6 July 1794
CA 27 Aug 1800
T
CB 4 June 1815 (LG)
d 2 Nov 1830 (LT)

ROTHERY, John
L 8 Feb 1815

ROTHERY, John Carpenter
L 4 Apr 1780
Dismissed 26 June 1800 (CH)

ROTHERY, Thomas
L 7 Feb 1815

ROTHERY, Thomas Henry
L 4 Feb 1814

ROTTON, Edward
T
L 16 June 1814
d 1839 (TR)

ROUETT, John Smollett
L 23 Jan 1794
CR 28 Aug 1799
CA 29 Apr 1802
Ret RA 1837 (PJP)
RA 17 Aug 1840 (PJP)
d 1842 (PJP)

ROUNTREE, Robert
L 1735 (PJP)

ROUS, Hon. Henry John
L 18 May 1814
CR 2 Aug 1817 (DNB)
CA Apr 1823 (DNB)
MP (Westminster) 1841–1846 (DNB)
COM AD 1846 (DNB)
RAB 17 Dec 1852 (DNB)
RAW 11 Sept 1854 (DNB)
VAR 12 Apr 1862 (DNB)
AB 25 Jan 1863 (DNB)
AW 15 June 1864 (DNB)
d 19 June 1877 (DNB)

ROUS, John
L 22 June 1745
CR
CA 24 Sept 1745
d 3 Apr 1760

ROUSE, Augustus
L 29 Apr 1702 (PMM)
CR
CA 27 June 1711
d 5 Oct 1714

ROUSE, Edward
L 1691 (PJP)

ROUSE, James
L 1707 (PJP)

ROUSE, John Wood
L 24 Aug 1807

ROUSE, Richard (1)
L 12 June 1779

ROUSE, Richard (2)
L 23 Feb 1815

ROUTH, Robert
L 7 Aug 1746
CR
CA 19 Jan 1755
d 3 Oct 1760 (PMM)

ROUTLEDGE, W.H.
L 1815 (PJP)

ROUZIER, John
L 1747 (PRO)

ROVERA, Frederick de
L 24 Feb 1815
d Jan 1847 (OB)

ROWAN, Edward
L 19 Oct 1807
Ret CR 15 Apr 1844 (OB)

ROWE, Henry
L 21 Dec 1808

ROWE, Henry Nathaniel
L 19 Mar 1805
T
CR 2 May 1810
Ret CA 10 Sept 1840 (OB)
d 1860 (TR)

ROWE, James (1)
L 16 Aug 1814
HP 1814 (OB)

ROWE, James (2)		
L		1815 (PJP)
ROWE, John		
L	25 Mar	1795
KIA	12 Oct	1799 (CH)
ROWE, Joshua Latimer		
L	10 Jan	1797
ROWE, Lisle		
L		1739 (PJP)
ROWE, Simon		
L	17 Apr	1683
CA	14 July	1686
ROWE, Thomas		
L	3 Mar	1804
CR	26 Dec	1810
ROWE, William		
L	3 Nov	1794
ROWED, Henry		
L	30 Nov	1794
CR	15 June	1814
d	6 Jan	1831 (MB)
ROWLAND, James		
L	9 Feb	1815
ROWLANDS, John Samuel		
L	29 Mar	1813
HP	Dec	1815 (OB)
ROWLANDSON, Francis		
L		
CA		1671
ROWLESTON, Henry		
L	15 Feb	1815
ROWLEY, Bartholomew Samuel		
L		
CR		
CA	31 Jan	1781
RAB	14 Feb	1799
RAW	1 Jan	1801
RAR	23 Apr	1804
VAW	9 Nov	1805
VAR	25 Oct	1809
AB	31 July	1810
d	7 Oct	1811 (DNB)
ROWLEY, Sir Charles		
L	8 Oct	1789
CR	20 Apr	1795
CA	1 Aug	1795
Kt (Austria)	23 May	1814 (LG)
RAB	4 June	1814
RAW	12 Aug	1819 (CH)
RAR	19 July	1821 (CH)
VAB	27 May	1825 (CH)
VAW	22 July	1830 (CH)
COM AD	23 Dec	1834–
	25 Apr	1835 (AO)
GCH	7 Oct	1835 (DNB)
Cre Bt	22 Feb	1836 (DNB)
VAR	10 Jan	1837 (CH)
GCB	4 July	1840 (DNB)
AW	23 Nov	1841 (OB)
d	10 Oct	1845 (DNB)
ROWLEY, Edward		
T		
L	28 July	1810
CR	28 Feb	1815
d		1817 (TR)
ROWLEY, Sir Joshua		
L	2 July	1747
CR		
CA	14 Dec	1753 (CH)
CRM		1777 (PJP)
RAB	29 Mar	1779 (CH)
RAR	26 Sept	1780
Inh Bt	10 June	1786 (DNB)
VAW	24 Sept	1787
d	26 Feb	1790 (DNB)
ROWLEY, Sir Joshua Ricketts		
L	9 Apr	1808
CR	8 Aug	1810
CA	30 Sept	1812
Inh Bt	20 Oct	1832 (OB)
RAB	3 Apr	1848 (OB)
VA	3 Oct	1855 (CH)
d	18 Mar	1857 (CH)
ROWLEY, Sir Josias		
L	24 Dec	1783
CR	14 Mar	1794
CA	6 Apr	1795
CRM	4 Dec	1813 (LG)
RAW	4 June	1814
KCB	2 Jan	1815 (DNB)
RAR	12 Aug	1819 (LG)
VAB	27 May	1825 (CH)
VAW	22 July	1830 (CH)
GCMG	22 Feb	1834 (DNB)
AB	10 Jan	1837 (CH)
GCB	4 July	1840 (DNB)
AW	23 Nov	1841 (CH)
d	10 Jan	1842 (CH)
ROWLEY, Robert		
L	29 Aug	1803
CR	21 Mar	1812
CA	21 Aug	1815
ROWLEY, Samuel		
L	8 May	1691
In Merchant Service		1700 (PJP)
ROWLEY, Samuel Campbell		
L	30 Jan	1794
CR	6 Apr	1799
MP (Downpatrick)	10 Mar	1801–1802 (MPT)
CA	29 Apr	1802
MP (Kinsale)	1802–Apr	1806 (MPT)
RAB	10 Jan	1837 (LG)
RAW	28 June	1838 (LG)
RAR	23 Nov	1841 (LG)
d	28 Jan	1846 (OB)
ROWLEY, Sir William		
L	Dec	1708
CR		
CA	26 June	1716
RAW	10 Dec	1743 (LG)
VAB	23 June	1744 (LG)
VAW	23 Apr	1745 (LG)
AB	15 July	1747
AW	12 May	1748
MP (Taunton)	27 Feb	1750–1754 (MPS)
COM AD	22 June	1751–
	17 Nov	1756 (AO)
MP (Portsmouth)		1754–1761 (MPS)
Kt	12 Dec	1753 (DNB)
COM AD	6 Apr–2 July	1757 (AO)
AF	17 Dec	1762
d	1 Jan	1768 (DNB)
ROWLING, John Ford		
L	7 Feb	1812

ROWLINSON, William Henry
L 18 July 1810
ROWZIER, John
L 31 Aug 1739
CR 27 Dec 1745
CA 9 Oct 1748
d 25 July 1752
ROWZIER, Richard
L 16 Aug 1695 (PMM)
CR
CA 2 Oct 1708 (PMM)
d 11 Jan 1745 (PMM)
ROY, James
L 27 Oct 1814
ROY, St. Alban
L 29 May 1759
CR 11 Apr 1778
ROYDEN, Charles
L 1664
CA 1672
Dismissed 1678 (AJ)
d 1687 (DDA)
ROYDHOUSE, Josiah
L 21 Aug 1695 (PJP)
CR 23 Nov 1705 (PMM)
CA 14 June 1708
ROYER, Charles
L 19 Nov 1804
Ret CR 22 Feb 1838 (OB)
ROXBURGH, William
L 1 Dec 1760
In Russian Service 1764–1777 (PMM)
RUBIDGE, Charles
L 29 Oct 1806
Ret CR 12 Oct 1841 (OB)
RUBIDGE, Robert Henry
L 2 June 1808
HP 18 May 1814 (OB)
Ret CR 1 Nov 1845 (OB)
RUDALL, John
T
L 21 Sept 1806
d (drowned) 26 Nov 1809 (TR)
RUDALL, William
L 10 May 1809
RUDDACH, Alexander
L 25 Dec 1781
CR 30 Apr 1796
RUDE, John
L 15 Apr 1803
RUDSDELL, Richard
L
CR 4 July 1794
RUE, Thomas
L 8 Jan 1706
CR 12 Sept 1739
RUFFIN, John
L 6 Feb 1694
In Merchant Service Oct 1699 (PJP)
RUFFIN, Thomas (1)
L 1703 (PJP)
RUFFIN, Thomas (2)
L 2 Apr 1739
SUP
d 1754 (PMM)
RULE, James
L 4 Apr 1760
RULE, John
L 25 Sept 1779
CR 11 June 1783
RULE, William
T
L 4 Feb 1815
HP June 1815 (OB)
d 19 Apr 1850 (LT)
RUMBALL, George
L 23 Sept 1695
In Merchant Service Aug 1700 (PJP)
RUMFORD, William
L 17 Dec 1812
RUMLEY, James
L 23 Feb 1815
RUMSEY, Edward
L 6 Feb 1694 (PJP)
CA 1 Sept 1699
KIA 29 Dec 1709 (CH)
RUMSEY, Edy
L 29 Nov 1707
d 1735 (PMM)
RUMSEY, Henry
L 3 Apr 1678
RUMSEY, Nathaniel
L 1704 (PJP)
d 1711 (PMM)
RUMSEY, Thomas
L 10 Apr 1705
d 1726 (PMM)
RUNDELL, Benjamin
L 14 Oct 1795
RUNSIMAN, William
L 7 July 1744
RUNWA, Benjamin
L 13 June 1757
CR 13 Jan 1779
RUNWA, John
L 22 July 1755
RUNWA, William
L 22 July 1755
RUPERT, Prince
Cre EP 26 Jan 1644 (HBC)
L
CA Aug 1664 (DNB)
AD Aug 1664 (DNB)
AW Apr 1665 (DNB)
AF 1666
CMR 29 Aug 1672 (EAD)
Commander of the expedition to the United Provinces 4 July 1673 (EAD)
COM AD 9 July 1673–14 May 1679 (AO)
CH (Dragoons) 15 Feb 1678 (EAD)
d 29 Nov 1682 (DNB)
RUSDEN, James
L 4 Sept 1807
d 23 Apr 1836 (PJP)
RUSH, Abraham
L 1691 (PJP)
RUSH, William Beaumaris
L 30 May 1777
RUSHWORTH, Edward
L 7 July 1804
CR 29 Mar 1806
CA 13 Sept 1808
d 14 June 1812 (PJP)

Name / Rank	Date	Year
RUSHWORTH, John		
L	12 May	1741
CR	5 May	1757
CA	7 Dec	1758
d	30 Aug	1780 (M)
RUSSELL, Edward, Earl of Orford		
L		1671 (P)
CA	10 June	1672
CAF (Guards)	22 Apr	1679 (EAD)
Resigned from Army	Sept	1682 (EAD)
MP (Launceston)		1689 (MPH)
AB	22 July	1689
MP (Portsmouth)		1690 (MPH)
AF	30 May	1690
COM AD	5 June	1690–
	23 Jan	1691 (AO)
MP (Cambridgeshire)		1695–
	7 May	1697 (MPH)
Cre EP	7 May	1697 (DNB)
d	26 Nov	1727 (DNB)
RUSSELL, Francis		
L	23 May	1793
RUSSELL, George (1)		
L	24 Aug	1807
Dismissed	2 Dec	1809 (PMM)
RUSSEL(L), George (2)		
L	13 Aug	1814
RUSSELL, James (1)		
L	5 Dec	1768
RUSSELL, James (2)		
L	24 Aug	1794
CR	21 Mar	1801
d	26 Dec	1801 (LT)
RUSSELL, James (3)		
L	24 Apr	1802
RUSSELL, John (1)		
L		1673
KIA	20 Mar	1678 (DDA)
RUSSELL, John (2)		
L		1705 (PJP)
RUSSELL, John (3)		
L	31 Dec	1721
CR	6 June	1735
CA	22 July	1736
d	11 Feb	1744 (CH)
RUSSELL, John (4)		
L	24 June	1741
COM E	27 July	1747–
	27 May	1749 (NBO)
CR	27 Nov	1748
CA		
d	21 Dec	1752 (PMM)
RUSSEL(L), John (5)		
L	20 Nov	1790
CR	14 Feb	1797
CA	29 Apr	1802
RUSSELL, John (6)		
L	7 June	1798
RUSSELL, John (7)		
L	25 Nov	1808
RUSSELL, John (8)		
L	26 July	1815
CR	29 Jan	1822 (MB)
RUSSEL(L), Jonathan		
L	14 Aug	1739
CR	27 Dec	1745
RUSSELL, Patrick		
L	25 Mar	1807
RUSSELL, Robert (1)		
L	28 Nov	1707 (PMM)
RUSSELL, Robert (2)		
L	6 June	1798
RUSSELL, Robert (3)		
L	24 Nov	1801
CR	21 June	1814
RUSSELL, Robert (4)		
L	1 Mar	1805
CR	3 Jan	1811
RUSSELL, Thomas (1)		
L	16 Sept	1695 (PMM)
SUP	20 Mar	1738 (PMM)
RUSSELL, Thomas (2)		
L	16 Jan	1779
d	19 Apr	1798
RUSSELL, Thomas (3)		
L	27 Aug	1794
RUSSELL, Thomas Macnamara		
L	2 June	1776
CR	11 May	1780 (DNB)
CA	7 May	1781
RAW	1 Jan	1801
RAR	23 Apr	1804
VAB	9 Nov	1805
VAW	28 Apr	1808
VAR	31 July	1810
AB	12 Aug	1812
AW	12 Aug	1819 (CH)
d	22 July	1824 (DNB)
RUSSEL(L), William (1)		
L		
CA	19 Aug	1695
d	30 June	1703
RUSSEL(L), William (2)		
L	14 Sept	1728
RUSSELL, William (3)		
L	27 Jan	1778
d	16 Oct	1791
RUSSELL, William (4)		
L	30 Oct	1793
CR	10 Oct	1808
d	16 May	1828 (MB)
RUSSELL, William (5)		
L	10 Nov	1813
RUST, Robert		
L	6 Dec	1813
d	21 Oct	1845 (OB)
RUTHERFORD, Charles		
L	12 June	1802
RUTHERFORD, David, Lord		
L	12 Nov	1757
d	15 Oct	1785 (M)
RUTHERFORD, George		
L	2 Apr	1798
RUTHERFORD, Henry		
L	3 June	1796
KIA	19 Jan	1798 (JH)
RUTHERFORD, Richard		
L	31 Dec	1778
CR	28 Oct	1790
d	7 Dec	1795 (PMM)

RUTHERFORD, William Gordon		
L	9 Jan	1794
CR	4 July	1794
CA	15 Nov	1796
T		
CB	4 June	1815 (LG)
d	14 Jan	1818 (PJP)
RUTHVEN, Hon. John		
L	23 Dec	1760
CR		
CA	24 May	1762
d	14 Dec	1771 (M)
RYALL, George		
L	31 Aug	1739
Deserted		1748 (PJP)
RYALL, Maltis Lucullus		
L	30 Apr	
d	28 Apr	1749 (M)
RYAN, Charles		
L	30 Aug	1800
RYAN, James		
L		1794 (PJP)
RYAN, Thomas		
L	12 Mar	1811
RYCAULT, James ?RYCAUT		
L	4 Feb	1708
CR	28 Aug	1730
CA	10 Aug	1739
d	5 June	1758
RYDDALL, Samuel		
L	28 May	1694
RYDER, Charles		
L	26 Aug	1789
CR	2 Jan	1798
CA	29 Apr	1802
RYDER, James (1)		
L	27 July	1745
d	27 Nov	1776 (M)
RYDER, James (2)		
L	10 Jan	1794
RYE, Edward		
L	22 July	1778
RYE, George Herbert		
L	8 Mar	1809
Ret CR	9 Apr	1847 (OB)
RYE, Peter		
L	16 Mar	1791
CR	1 Jan	1801
CA	12 Aug	1812
Ret RA	31 Oct	1846 (LG)
RYLAND, Henry		
L	17 Oct	1810
RYVES, George Frederick (1)		
L	4 July	1779
CR	Oct	1775
CA	29 May	1798
RAB	27 May	1825 (LG)
d	20 May	1826 (DNB)
RYVES, George Frederick (2)		
L	24 Nov	1810
CR	22 Oct	1823 (MB)
CB	26 Dec	1826 (DNB)
CA	22 July	1830 (OB)
HP	22 July	1830 (OB)
d		1858 (DNB)
RYVES, Thomas		
L	2 Mar	1734

SABBEN, James		
T	wounded	
L	10 Sept	1810
HP		1821 (OB)
d		1849 (TR)
SACKLER, Tobias		
L		
CA		1660
SACKVILLE, Ralph		
L		1666
SADD, Simon		
L		1660
CA		1665
SADLER, John Thomas		
T		
L	24 Dec	1805
Gone		1807 (TR)
SADLINGTON, Richard		
L		1666
CA		1672
KIA	4 June	1673 (HJ)
ST. ALBANS, William, Duke of		
See BEAUCLERK, Lord William		
ST. AUBYN, John		
L	8 Mar	1796
ST. BARB, Henry		
L		1672 (DDA)
ST. BARBE, John		
L	21 Jan	1761
SUP CR	22 Aug	1808
ST. CLAIR, David Latimer		
L	17 Apr	1802
CR	20 Nov	1812
Ret CA	20 Nov	1847 (OB)
ST. CLAIR, Matthew		
L	8 Oct	1793
CR	14 Jan	1797
d (drowned)	Oct	1800 (PJP)
ST. CYR, Peter		
L	19 Dec	1807
ST. GEORGE, Henry		
L		1748 (PJP)
ST. GEORGE, William Molyneux		
L	21 Jan	1805
T	killed	
KIA	21 Oct	1805 (TR)
SAINTHILL, Humphrey		
L	1 Jan	1746
SAINTHILL, Richard		
L	15 June	1779
SUP CR	31 Jan	1814
SAINTHILL, Richard Tillidge		
L	23 Apr	1812
ST. JOHN, Hon. Henry (1)		
L	15 Sept	1760
CR	28 Jan	1762
CA	31 Aug	1762
KIA	17 Apr	1780 (LG)
ST. JOHN, Henry (2)		
L	26 Aug	1789
d	6 Mar	1834 (PJP)
ST. JOHN, James		
L	20 Sept	1808
HP	Feb	1837 (OB)
CR	7 Mar	1842 (OB)
ST. JOHN, William		
L		1690 (PJP)

ST. JOHN, William Oliver
L 21 July 1810
ST. JOHN, William St. Andrew
L 17 Apr 1811
d 24 May 1822 (LT)
ST. LO(E), Edward (1)
L 1702 (DNB)
CR
CA 9 Sept 1703
RAB 4 Mar 1729 (DNB)
d 22 Apr 1729 (CH)
ST. LO(E), Edward (2)
L 14 Oct 1755
KIA May 1760 (PJP)
ST. LOE, Edward (3)
L 21 Dec 1758 (PMM)
CR 31 Jan 1760 (PMM)
ST. LO(E), George (1)
L 16 Jan 1678 (PJP)
CA 17 Apr 1682
COM E 28 Sept 1693–
25 Apr 1695 (NBO)
COMM (Portsmouth) 26 Mar 1695–
29 Apr 1703 (NBO)
COMM (Chatham) 30 Apr 1703–
16 Nov 1714 (QAN)
d 1714 (M)
ST. LO(E), George (2)
L 28 Dec 1708 (PMM)
d 1718 (M)
ST. LO(E), John
L
CR
CA 1 Jan 1713
SUP RA 15 July 1747
d 21 Dec 1757 (M)
ST. MICHELL, Balthazar
L
CA 1677
COMM (Deptford) Oct 1688 (PMM)
ST. PRIX, Martin
L 11 Mar 1806
ST. QUINTIN, James
T
L 7 Jan 1814
Ret CR 1856 (TR)
d 1865 (TR)
ST. VINCENT, John Jervis, Earl
L 19 Feb 1755
CR 15 May 1759
CA 13 Oct 1760
MP (Launceston) Jan 1783–1784 (MPT)
MP (Great Yarmouth) 1784–1790 (MPT)
RAB 24 Sept 1787
RAW 21 Sept 1790
MP (Chipping Wycombe) 1790–1794 (MPT)
VAB 1 Feb 1793
VAW 12 Apr 1794
AB 1 June 1795
Cre EP 23 June 1797 (MPT)
AW 14 Feb 1799
LGRM 26 Aug 1800 (AL)
FLA 19 Feb 1801–
15 May 1804 (AO)
AR 9 Nov 1805
GRM 11 May 1814 (AL)
GCB 2 Jan 1815 (LG)
AF 19 July 1821 (LG)
d 13 Mar 1823 (MPT)
SALISBURY, John
L 3 Dec 1777
CR 14 Apr 1783
CA 26 Aug 1789
SALISBURY, T.
L 1798 (PJP)
SALKELD, Ralph
L 1666
SALKELD, Thomas
L 4 Feb 1815
SALL, Joseph
L 13 Mar 1779
d 7 Jan 1790
SALLORY, George
L 3 June 1697 (PJP)
SALMON, James (1)
L 1689 (PJP)
SALMON, James (2)
L 1797 (PJP)
SALMON, John (1)
L 29 Apr 1802
d (drowned) Dec 1806 (JH)
SALMON, John (2)
L 24 June 1807
Ret CR 10 Apr 1843 (OB)
d 7 Sept 1854 (PMM)
SALMON, Joseph
L 13 July 1745
d 14 Apr 1790 (M)
SALMON, Robert (1)
L
CA 1664 (DDA)
SALMON, Robert (2)
L
CA 1668 (DDA)
SALMON, William
L 29 Dec 1793
SALMOND, Peter
L 1 July 1789
SALT, George Burgoyne
L 1 July 1789
CR 4 July 1797
CA 13 Oct 1807
SALT, Sampson
L 16 Nov 1739
CR 13 July 1748
d 27 July 1792 (M)
SALTER, Daniel
T
L 26 Nov 1809
d 1843 (TR)
SALTER, Elliott
L 3 July 1765
CR 4 Nov 1769
CA 21 Mar 1776
d 1 Feb 1790 (M)
SALTER, George Elliott
L 29 Apr 1801
KIA 14 July 1803 (LT)
SALTER, John (1)
L 14 Aug 1801
d (drowned) 20 Oct 1806 (PJP)

SALTER, John (2)
L 26 Oct 1813

SALTER, William
L 31 July 1812

SALTERLEY, George
L 6 Aug 1697

SAWLEY, Theophilus
L 25 June 1796

SAMBER, James
L 9 Apr 1760
CR 1 Feb 1780
CA 26 Mar 1782
SUP 23 Apr 1804
Living 1816

SAMPSON, Michael
L
CR
CA 14 Jan 1708
d 3 Nov 1711

SAMPSON, William
L 1702 (PJP)

SAMWELL, Peter
L 6 Feb 1798
Ret CR 26 Nov 1830 (OB)

SAMWELL, William (1)
L 19 Sept 1777
SUP CR 18 Sept 1811
d 8 Sept 1816 (PJP)

SAMWELL, William (2)
L 17 Mar 1795
Ret CR 26 Nov 1830 (OB)
d 22 Dec 1846 (OB)

SANDAY, Samuel
L 20 Jan 1792

SANDBY, Edward
L 1681 (PJP)

SANDEMAN, Peter
L 30 Apr 1800

SANDERS, Francis
L
CA 1665
d before 1688 (PD)

SANDERS, Gabriel
L
CA 1660

SANDERS, Sir George (1)
L 5 Dec 1694
CR
CA 11 Jan 1705
Kt 1720 (DNB)
COM V 1721 (PJP)
MP (Queensborough) 1728 (DNB)
COM E 18 Jan 1728–
15 Jan 1729 (NBO)
RAB 9 June 1732 (DNB)
RAR 26 Feb 1734
d 5 Dec 1734 (DNB)

SANDERS, George (2)
L 11 Jan 1794
CR 29 Apr 1802
CA 2 June 1809

SANDERS, Humphrey
L
CA 25 July 1690
SUP 1707
d 4 Jan 1726

SANDERS, James (1)
L 25 Oct 1794
CR 26 Sept 1798
CA 29 Apr 1802

SANDERS, James (2)
L 28 Oct 1812

SANDERS, James (3)
L 1815 (PJP)

SANDERS, John
L 6 Apr 1815
CR 7 Mar 1853 (PMM)

SANDERS, John Harry
T
L 23 Sept 1806
Ret CR 29 Jan 1841 (OB)

SANDERS, Joseph
L
CA 1665
KIA 25 July 1666 (CH)

SANDERS, Robert
L
CA 1665
KIA 5 Feb 1667 (CH)

SANDERS, Thomas
L 19 Sept 1806
CR 16 Sept 1816 (PRO)
HP June 1834 (OB)
CA 23 Nov 1841 (OB)

SANDERS, William (1)
L 12 May 1798
CR 2 Apr 1806

SANDERS, William (2)
L 7 Jan 1809

SANDERSON, Edward
L 27 Apr 1709 (PMM)

SANDERSON, James (1)
L 1797 (PJP)

SANDERSON, James (2)
L 1815 (PJP)

SANDERSON, John Proctor
L 26 July 1815 (OB)

SANDERSON, P.
L 1800 (PJP)

SANDERSON, Ralph
L
CR
CA 17 Oct 1709
d 30 Apr 1718 (PJP)

SANDERSON, Robert
L 1705 (PJP)

SANDERSON, Sir William (1)
See SAUNDERSON, Sir William

SANDERSON, William (2)
L 23 Apr 1796
CR 10 Nov 1797
CA 1 Mar 1799

SANDEY, William
L 25 Sept 1801
T
d 1832 (TR)

SANDFORD, George
L 12 June 1811

SANDFORD, Jacob
L
CA 1667

SANDHAM, Edward Mullins
L 23 Dec 1800

SANDILANDS, Alexander
L 3 July 1807

SANDILANDS, James		
L	19 Aug	1747
SANDIVER, Philip		
L	20 Nov	1758
SANDOM, William		
L	30 Apr	1808
CR	26 Dec	1822 (MB)
CA	23 Mar	1828 (MB)
HP	Sept	1843 (OB)
RA	27 Oct	1854 (CH)
SANDRY, Hugh		
L	1 Feb	1779
SANDS, Edwin		
L		1672
SANDS, Jordan		
See SANDYS, Jordan		
SANDSBURY, Thomas		
L	29 Aug	1794
SANDWELL, William		
L		1664
SANDWICH, Edward Montagu, Earl of		
L		
General of the Fleet	23 Feb	1660 (DNB)
MP (Dover)	23 Apr–24 July	1660 (MPH)
Cre EP	12 July	1660 (DNB)
CA		1661
AD	19 June	1661 (DNB)
AB	13 Nov	1664 (DNB)
AF	2 July	1665 (DNB)
KIA	28 May	1672 (DNB)
SANDYS, Charles		
L	7 Jan	1773
CR	7 Feb	1782
CA	21 Jan	1783
SUP RA	21 Nov	1805
d		1814 (PJP)
SANDYS, George		
L	12 Feb	1811
d (drowned)		1812 (PJP)
SANDYS, John		
L	18 Apr	1811
SANDYS, Jordan		
L	12 June	1697 (PJP)
CR		
CA	12 Mar	1703
d		1734
SANDYS, Richard Erwin		
L	18 Apr	1794
KIA	2 Apr	1801 (LG)
SANDYS, Stephen		
L	21 Aug	1762
SANDYS, Thomas		
L		1700 (PJP)
SANDYS, William		
L	4 Apr	1794
SANGSTER, Robert		
L	31 May	1800
Ret CR	26 Nov	1830 (OB)
SANHAM, Henry		
L	9 Feb	1759 (PRO)
Dismissed	2 Mar	1762 (PJP)
SANKEY, Henry		
L	21 Mar	1812
d	1 June	1840 (LT)
SANSOM, Michael		
L		1702 (PRO)
CR	9 Mar	1705 (PMM)
CA		1709 (PRO)
SANSOME, Robert		
L	1 Aug	1683
SANSUM, Robert		
L		
CA		1664
RAD		1664
RAW		1665
KIA	3 June	1665 (LG)
SAPSFORD, John (1)		
L	16 Dec	1691 (PJP)
CR		
CA	18 Mar	1709
SAPSFORD, John (2)		
L	18 Sept	1809
d (drowned)	22 Dec	1810 (PJP)
SARGENT, Francis		
L	11 May	1794
SARGENT, Stephen		
L	30 Mar	1747
SARGENT, William		
L	24 Oct	1799
CR	4 Dec	1813
CA	12 Aug	1819 (MB)
d	26 Aug	1835 (LT)
SARMON, George Woods		
L	20 Sept	1808
CR	13 June	1815
SARRADINE, George		
L	29 Oct	1794
CR	8 Oct	1798
d		1805 (PJP)
SARRATT, George		
L	1 July	1815
d		1837 (PJP)
SARSFIELD, Dominick		
L	14 Feb	1815
HP	14 Feb	1815 (OB)
SARTAINE, Stephen		
L		
CA		1664
d	8 Oct	1670 (DDA)
SARTORIUS, Sir George Rose		
T		
L	5 Mar	1808
CR	1 Feb	1812
CA	6 June	1814
Kt	21 Aug	1841 (DNB)
RAB	9 May	1849 (LG)
VA	31 Jan	1856 (DNB)
A	11 Feb	1861 (DNB)
KCB	28 Mar	1865 (DNB)
AF	3 July	1869 (DNB)
GCB	23 Apr	1880 (DNB)
d	13 Apr	1885 (DNB)
SATTERTHWAITE, Edward		
L	14 June	1811
SATTERTHWAITE, Thomas		
L	9 Feb	1815
SAUCE, Robert		
L	21 Apr	1783
CR	3 Aug	1795
CA	29 Apr	1802
d	13 June	1827 (MB)

SAUL, Nicholas
L 27 Oct 1701 (PMM)
d (drowned) 22 Oct 1707 (PMM)

SAUMAREZ, James (1)
L 7 Sept 1776

SAUMAREZ, James, Lord de (2)
L 25 Jan 1778
CR 23 Aug 1781
CA 7 Feb 1782
Kt 1793 (PJP)
CRM 14 Feb 1799 (AL)
RAB 1 Jan 1801
Cre Bt 13 June 1801 (DNB)
RAW 23 Apr 1804
RAR 9 Nov 1805
VAB 13 Dec 1806 (LG)
VAR 31 July 1810
Kt (Sweden) 4 May 1813 (LG)
AB 3 June 1814
GCB 2 Jan 1815 (LG)
AW 12 Aug 1819 (CH)
AR 22 July 1830 (LG)
Cre EP 15 Sept 1831 (DNB)
GRM 13 Feb 1832 (LG)
d 9 Oct 1836 (DNB)

SAUMAREZ, Philip
L 6 Aug 1737
CR
CA 21 June 1743
KIA 14 Oct 1747 (SPB)

SAUMAREZ, Richard
L 5 Dec 1812
CR 19 May 1819 (MB)
Kt (Austria) 28 Apr 1821 (LG)
CA 17 Apr 1824 (MB)
Ret CA 31 Oct 1846 (LG)

SAUMAREZ, Thomas (1)
L 15 Dec 1744
CR 23 Nov 1747
CA 27 Nov 1748
d 21 Sept 1766

SAUMAREZ, Thomas (2)
L 4 Mar 1815
d 21 May 1823 (LT)

SAUNDER, Charles
L 17 Sept 1806

SAUNDERS, Ambrose
L 16 Jan 1706 (PMM)
CR
CA 24 July 1720
d 6 Mar 1731 (PMM)

SAUNDERS, Andrew
L 20 Aug 1771
CR 25 Oct 1809

SAUNDERS, Charles (1)
L 8 Nov 1734
CR
CA 1 Oct 1741

SAUNDERS, Sir Charles (2)
L 8 Nov 1734 (DNB)
CR 19 Feb 1743 (PJP)
CA 26 Sept 1741
MP (Plymouth) 6 Apr 1750–1754 (MPS)
TGH 1754–1756 (PJP)
MP (Hedon) 1754–7 Dec 1775 (MPS)
CONT 25 Nov 1755–
24 June 1756 (AO)
RAB 4 June 1756 (CH)
RAW 1758
VAB 14 Feb 1759
LGRM 10 Nov 1759 (AL)
Kt 26 May 1761 (DNB)
VAW 21 Oct 1762
FLA 31 July 1765–
11 Dec 1766 (AO)
AB 18 Oct 1770
d 7 Dec 1775 (DNB)

SAUNDERS, Charles (3)
L 1741 (PJP)

SAUNDERS, Francis
L 2 Feb 1741

SAUNDERS, Sir George
See SANDERS, Sir George

SAUNDERS, George
L 29 Nov 1775
d (drowned) 29 Aug 1782 (PJP)

SAUNDERS, George Lawrence
L 26 Dec 1802
T
CR 1814
d 1834 (TR)

SAUNDERS, Jacob
L 1702 (PJP)
CR 15 June 1705 (PMM)
CA 1705 (PRO)

SAUNDERS, Jeffry (or Jeffery) Thomas
L 3 Nov 1708

SAUNDERS, John (1)
L 9 Aug 1705 (PMM)

SAUNDERS, John (2)
L 19 Nov 1740

SAUNDERS, Ralph
L 1708 (PJP)

SAUNDERS, Richard
L 16 Oct 1759
SUP CR 18 June 1805

SAUNDERS, Thomas (1)
L 1671

SAUNDERS, Thomas (2)
L 1705 (PJP)
CR 30 Apr 1708 (PMM)

SAUNDERS, Thomas (3)
L 25 Nov 1809

SAUNDERS, Thomas (4)
L 24 May 1812

SAUNDERSON, Charles William
L 4 Mar 1815

SAUNDERSON, James
L 25 Apr 1815
HP 30 Dec 1815 (OB)

SAUNDERSON, Ralph
L 1666
CA 17 Nov 1667
d 1699 (DDA)

SAUNDERSON, Sir William
L
CA 16 Nov 1688
Kt 1714 (PJP)
Cre Bt 1720 (PJP)
d 17 May 1727 (PJP)

SAURIN, Edward
L 2 May 1810
CR 12 Dec 1812
CA 7 June 1814

Ret CA	31 Oct	1846 (LG)
Ret RA	24 June	1850 (LG)
d	28 Feb	1878 (DNB)
SAUTEL, George		
L	2 June	1761
SAUVAIRE, Thomas		
L	7 July	1756
SAVAGE, Henry		
L	20 July	1758
CR	June	1780 (PJP)
CA	31 Jan	1781
RAB	14 Feb	1799
RAW	1 Jan	1801
RAR	23 Apr	1804
VAW	9 Nov	1805
VAR	25 Oct	1809
AB	31 July	1810
AF	4 June	1814
d	16 Mar	1820 (MB)
SAVAGE, Roger Hall		
L	25 Dec	1800
CR	29 Apr	1802
CA	1 Feb	1806
SAVAGE, Thomas		
L	14 Feb	1705 (PMM)
SAVAGE, William		
L	17 Sept	1806
CR	31 Dec	1830 (MB)
SAVAGE, William Henry		
L	13 Dec	1813
d		1847 (OB)
SAVILLE, George Augustus		
L	13 Nov	1802
HP	14 Dec	1815 (OB)
Ret CR	21 Apr	1835 (OB)
SAVILLE, John Griffin		
L	3 Nov	1790
CR	1 Nov	1793
CA	7 Jan	1802
d	18 Aug	1804 (LT)
SAWYER, Charles		
L	8 July	1785
CR	1 Nov	1793
CA	25 Mar	1794
SAWYER, Herbert (1)		
L	4 Mar	1756
CR	19 May	1758
CA	26 Dec	1758
RAW	24 Sept	1787
RAR	21 Sept	1790
VAB	1 Feb	1793
VAW	12 Apr	1794
VAR	4 July	1794
AB	1 June	1795
d	4 June	1798 (CH)
SAWYER, Sir Herbert (2)		
L	9 Dec	1780
CR	14 Jan	1783
CA	3 Feb	1789
RAB	2 Oct	1807
RAW	28 Apr	1808
RAR	31 July	1810
VAB	1 Aug	1811
VAW	4 June	1814
KCB	4 Dec	1815 (LG)
VAR	12 Aug	1819 (CH)
AB	27 May	1825 (CH)
AW	22 July	1830 (CH)
d	13 Nov	1833 (CH)
SAWYER, John		
L		1705 (PJP)
SAWYER, Samuel		
L	10 Aug	1793
SAX, Robert		
L	20 Jan	1755
SAXTON, Sir Charles		
L	2 Jan	1757
CR	11 Oct	1760
CA	28 Jan	1762
COMM (Portsmouth)		1791 (PJP)
Cre Bt	19 July	1794 (DNB)
d	Nov	1808 (DNB)
SAYER, George (1)		
L	23 Aug	1790
CR	10 Nov	1798 (PJP)
CA	21 Oct	1810 (PJP)
d		1846 (OB)
SAYER, George (2)		
L	24 Aug	1793
CR	11 May	1796 (PJP)
CA	14 Feb	1801 (PJP)
CB	4 June	1815 (LG)
RAB	22 July	1830 (LG)
d		1831 (PMM)
SAYER, George (3)		
L	11 Nov	1809
HP	Apr	1825 (OB)
SAYER, James		
L	19 Dec	1743
CR		
CA	22 Mar	1746
RAB	24 Oct	1770
RAR	31 Mar	1775 (CH)
VAB	5 Feb	1776
d	15 Oct	1777 (CH)
SAYER, Joshua		
L	27 Sept	1759
SAYER, Nathaniel		
L	25 June	1773
SAYER, Robert		
L	17 Nov	1790
SAYER, Robert Richard		
L	8 June	1815
SAYER, Saffery		
L	13 Aug	1781
d	5 June	1798
SAYER, William Frederick		
L	6 Dec	1813
SBIREL, John		
L	30 Sept	1739
d	5 Feb	1770 (M)
SCAIFE, John		
L	19 Dec	1747
CR	10 May	1755
CA	22 Feb	1759
d		1773
SCALLEY, William		
L	25 Feb	1694 (PJP)
CA	26 June	1699
d	26 Sept	1703
SCALLON, Robert		
L	23 June	1798

CR	15 May	1823 (MB)
d	26 Mar	1848 (OB)
SCAMBLER, Jasper		
L	17 Nov	1799
SCANDERBERG, George		
L		1666
SCANLAN, Richard		
L	8 Feb	1815
SCANLAN, Thomas		
L	20 Nov	1812
SCANTLEBURY, Jehu Caudle Bend		
L	4 Oct	1814
SCARDON, George Briscoe		
L	4 Feb	1814
SCARLETT, Nathaniel		
L	7 June	1746
SCHABNER, John James		
L	13 Mar	1815
d	1 Dec	1816 (PJP)
SCHANK, John		
L	2 Jan	1776
CR	8 Apr	1780
CA	15 Aug	1783
RAB	9 Nov	1805
RAW	28 Apr	1808
RAR	25 Oct	1809
VAB	31 July	1810
VAW	4 Dec	1813
VAR	4 June	1814
AB	19 July	1821 (MB)
d		1823 (MB)
SCHAW, Frederick David		
L	8 Feb	1800
HP	Oct	1804
Ret CR	26 Nov	1830 (OB)
d	23 July	1850 (LT)
SCHOMBERG, Sir Alexander		
L	11 Dec	1747
CR		
CA	5 Apr	1757
Kt		1777 (DNB)
d	19 Mar	1804 (DNB)
SCHOMBERG, Alexander Wilmot		
L	26 July	1793
CR	2 Apr	1798
CA	1 Jan	1801
RAB	22 July	1830 (LG)
RAR	10 Jan	1837 (LG)
VAB	23 Nov	1841 (LG)
VAW	9 Nov	1846 (LG)
VAR	28 Apr	1847 (LG)
AB	9 Oct	1849 (LG)
d	Jan	1850 (LG)
SCHOMBERG, Sir Charles Marsh		
L	30 Apr	1795
CR	29 Apr	1802
CA	6 Aug	1803
CB	4 June	1815 (DNB)
KCH	21 Sept	1832 (DNB)
d	2 Jan	1835 (DNB)
SCHOMBERG, Isaac		
L	21 Aug	1777
CR	3 Mar	1790
CA	22 Nov	1790
COM N	3 Dec	1808–
	21 Jan	1813 (NBO)
d	21 Jan	1813 (NBO)
SCHULTZ, George Augustus		
L	22 Jan	1806
Ret CR	5 Jan	1839 (OB)
SCHUYLER, Adoniah		
L	10 Apr	1778
SUP CR	31 Jan	1814
SCLATER, George		
L	26 Sept	1716 (PMM)
CR	9 Apr	1723
CA	25 July	1734
d		1750
SCOBELL, Edward		
L	13 Aug	1801
CR	29 Sept	1808
CA	3 Apr	1811
d	17 Apr	1825 (MB)
SCOBELL, George		
L	29 Mar	1805
CR	1 Feb	1812
Ret CA	14 Aug	1843 (OB)
SCOFFIN, John		
L	24 Dec	1780
CR	10 May	1794
d	11 May	1801
SCOFFIN, T.H.		
L		1794 (PJP)
SCOT, Anthony		
L	30 Apr	1706 (PMM)
SCOTLAND, Thomas C.		
L	21 Mar	1812
d	Dec	1812 (LT)
SCOTT, Adam		
L	9 Feb	1747
SCOTT, Alexander (1)		
L	14 Mar	1770 (PMM)
CR	15 Mar	1770
CA	25 Apr	1776
SUP RA	9 July	1794
d	25 Apr	1811 (PJP)
SCOTT, Alexander (2)		
L	30 Apr	1778
CR	1 Aug	1782
d	12 Feb	1804
SCOTT, Arthur		
L	20 Dec	1739
CR		
CA	4 Aug	1743
COMM (Chatham)	26 Jan	1754–
	13 Nov	1755 (PMM)
COM E	25 Nov	1755–
	27 Feb	1756 (NBO)
d	27 Feb	1756 (NBO)
SCOTT, Cecil		
L	9 Nov	1756
SCOTT, David		
L	4 Mar	1800
T	wounded	
CR	2 Aug	1811
CA	22 Oct	1814
Ret CA	31 Oct	1846 (LG)
Ret RA		1850 (TR)
d		1852 (TR)
SCOTT, Edmund		
L	4 May	1810
SCOTT, Edward		
L	19 Dec	1695

SCOTT, Edward Forlow
L 16 Mar 1808
CR 20 Sept 1815
HP 20 Sept 1815 (OB)
Ret CA 7 Jan 1856 (PMM)
d 10 July 1857 (PMM)

SCOTT, Edward Hinton
L 12 June 1807
CR 18 July 1823 (MB)
CA 15 Jan 1838 (OB)

SCOTT, Edward William
L 15 Feb 1815
d 1834 (PJP)

SCOTT, Francis
L 4 Apr 1720

SCOTT, George (1)
L 12 May 1776

SCOTT, George (2)
L 10 Apr 1780

SCOTT, George (3)
L 4 Nov 1790

SCOTT, Sir George (4)
L 19 Feb 1791
CR 20 Jan 1796
CA 15 June 1798
CB 4 June 1815 (LG)
CRM 19 July 1821 (AL)
RAB 27 May 1825 (LG)
RAR 22 July 1830 (CH)
KCB 13 Sept 1831 (LG)
VAB 10 Jan 1837 (CH)
VAW 28 June 1838 (CH)
VAR 23 Nov 1841 (CH)
d 21 Dec 1841 (CH)

SCOTT, George (5)
L 12 Sept 1805
CR 24 Mar 1812
CA 12 Feb 1830 (MB)

SCOTT, Henry (1)
L 1703 (PJP)

SCOTT, Henry (2)
Afterwards Lord DELORAINE
Inh EP 25 Dec 1730 (HBC)
L 25 Jan 1732
CR
CA 31 Mar 1737
d 19 Apr 1740

SCOTT, Henry (3)
L 20 Feb 1745
CR 23 May 1757

SCOTT, Henry William
L 26 May 1807
CR 13 June 1815
HP 13 June 1815 (OB)

SCOTT, James (1)
L 11 July 1712

SCOTT, James (2)
L
CR 13 June 1738

SCOTT, James (3)
L 17 July 1762

SCOTT, James (4)
L 11 Sept 1793

SCOTT, Sir James (5)
L 16 Nov 1809
CR 19 Oct 1814
CA 8 Jan 1828 (DNB)
CB 29 June 1841 (DNB)
RA 26 Dec 1854 (DNB)
VA 4 June 1861 (DNB)
A 10 Feb 1865 (DNB)
KCB 24 Mar 1866 (DNB)
Ret A 2 Apr 1866 (DNB)
d 2 Mar 1872 (DNB)

SCOTT, James Woodward
L 6 Nov 1795
d 21 Sept 1803 (LG)

SCOTT, John (1)
L 6 Feb 1694

SCOTT, John (2)
L 9 July 1762
d 27 Feb 1790 (M)

SCOTT, John (3)
L 4 Nov 1790

SCOTT, John (4)
L 27 Aug 1794

SCOTT, John (5)
L 2 Oct 1795

SCOTT, John (6)
L 31 May 1805
CR 13 June 1815
HP 13 June 1815 (OB)

SCOTT, John (7)
L 24 Aug 1814

SCOTT, John Philip
L 28 Sept 1795

SCOTT, Joshua
L 4 Mar 1746

SCOTT, Matthew Henry
L 1 Dec 1787
CR
CA 4 Apr 1794
RAB 12 Aug 1812
RAR 4 June 1814
VAB 12 Aug 1819 (CH)
VAW 27 May 1825 (CH)
VAR 22 July 1830 (CH)
d 31 Oct 1836 (CH)

SCOTT, Richard (1)
L 18 Apr 1695
In Merchant Service 1700 (PJP)

SCOTT, Richard (2)
L 7 Sept 1795

SCOTT, Robert (1)
L 15 Sept 1760
d 19 Dec 1770 (PMM)

SCOTT, Robert (2)
L 28 July 1796
CR 29 Apr 1802
CA 22 Jan 1806
d (drowned) 28 Nov 1807 (PJP)

SCOTT, Robert (3)
L 1810 (PJP)

SCOTT, Samuel (1)
L 4 Nov 1740
CR July 1745 (PJP)
CA 29 Jan 1748
d 28 Aug 1774

SCOTT, Samuel (2)
L 5 Oct 1761

SCOTT, Theophilus
L
CA 1666

SCOTT, Thomas (1)
L 1665
CA 1666

SCOTT, Thomas (2)
L 14 Dec 1695
CR
CA 2 Mar 1704
d 13 Sept 1725

SCOTT, Thomas (3)
L 13 May 1720

SCOTT, Thomas (4)
L 6 Feb 1771

SCOTT, Thomas (5)
L 6 Dec 1809

SCOTT, Tufton Charles
L 13 Aug 1782

SCOTT, Walter
L 13 Sept 1781
d 10 June 1806 (PMM)

SCOTT, William (1)
L 10 July 1761
CR
CA 25 Sept 1781

SCOTT, William (2)
L 12 Nov 1776

SCOTT, William (3)
L 21 Aug 1798
d (drowned) Aug 1805 (CH)

SCOTT, William Isaac
L 10 May 1799
CR 21 Oct 1810
CA 7 June 1814
Ret CA 1 Oct 1846 (OB)
Ret RA 12 Nov 1849 (LG)

SCREECH, James
L 25 Jan 1758
SUP 29 Mar 1798

SCRIVEN, John Barclay
L 4 Jan 1810

SCRIVEN, Timothy
L 28 Mar 1803
CR 7 Oct 1813
CB 4 June 1815 (LG)
CA 12 Aug 1819 (PJP)
d 25 Mar 1824 (MB)

SCRODER, Christopher
L 6 Nov 1802

SCROPE, Adrian
L 1672
CA 15 July 1682

SCROPE, Carr
L 19 Nov 1740
CR 11 Aug 1746
CA 14 Nov 1752
d 1762

SCRYMGOUR, William
L 15 Mar 1815

SCUDAMORE, William James
L 30 Apr 1812

SCURRY, Joseph
L 15 Mar 1692 (PJP)

SEAGER, John
L 20 Apr 1799
CR 15 June 1814
d 7 June 1846 (OB)

SEAGROVE, James
L 29 Oct 1810

SEALE, Charles Henry
L 15 July 1809
CR 8 June 1826 (MB)
CA 23 Nov 1841 (OB)

SEALE, Thomas
L 1663
CA 24 Aug 1660 (DDA)
KIA 2 Aug 1665 (ESP)

SEALE, William
See SEALY, William

SEALY, George Francis
L 16 June 1811

SEALY, Uriah
L 4 Apr 1810

SEALY, William
L
CA 1665
Dismissed Feb 1667 (CH)
e (cowardice) 5 Mar 1667 (CH)

SEAMAN, Edmund
L
CA 1665

SEAMAN, Francis Reynolds
L 23 Feb 1808

SEAMAN, Lawrence
L 1689 (PJP)

SEARLE, Henry
L
CA 5 June 1697
d 12 Nov 1699 (CH)

SEARLE, Henry Holland
L 9 Nov 1778
d 14 Nov 1813 (PJP)

SEARLE, John Clarke
L
CR 17 Mar 1795
CA 13 July 1796
SUP RA 8 Feb 1822 (MB)
d 19 Dec 1824 (PMM)

SEARLE, Thomas
L 19 Aug 1796
CR 22 Nov 1799
CA 25 Apr 1808
CB 4 June 1815 (LG)
RAB 9 Nov 1846 (LG)
RAW 17 Dec 1847 (LG)
d 18 Mar 1849 (DNB)

SEATER, John (or James)
L 23 May 1793
CR 20 Jan 1796
CA 2 Nov 1798

SEATON, Andrew
L 11 Mar 1691 (PJP)

SEATON, Archibald
L 22 Apr 1745

SEATON, George
L 20 Jan 1794

SEATON, John
L 9 Mar 1815

SEATON, R.H.
L 1797 (PJP)

SEAVER, Jeremiah
L 26 Mar 1794

SECCOMBE, Ambrose
L 2 Mar 1734
CR 23 Jan 1746
d 5 Dec 1758 (M)

SECCOMBE, Thomas
L 8 Jan 1782

CR	26 Sept	1793
CA	13 July	1795
KIA	30 Jan	1808 (CH)
SEDLEY, Davenport		
L	10 Sept	1808
SEEDS, Arthur Freemantle		
L	20 Oct	1813
SELBIE, John		
L	15 Mar	1815
d	29 July	1846 (OB)
SELBY, George		
L	20 May	1811
HP	June	1816 (OB)
SELBY, Jerrard		
L	31 Jan	1759
SELBY, Ralph		
L		1672
SELBY, Samuel		
L	27 Feb	1815
HP	27 Feb	1815 (OB)
SELBY, William		
L	18 July	1793
CR	1 Oct	1798
CA	25 Dec	1800
d	28 Mar	1811 (PJP)
SELDEN, John		
L	13 Apr	1741
SELKRIG, James		
L	30 Apr	1800
SELLERS, George		
L	7 June	1744
SELLERS, John		
L	7 Feb	1696 (PJP)
SELSEY, Lord Henry John		
L	5 Jan	1807
CR		
CA	7 Aug	1812
Inh EP	27 Jan	1816 (MB)
SELWYN, Charles William		
L	20 Aug	1806
CR	15 June	1814
SENHOUSE, Edward Hooper		
L	22 May	1807
CR	20 Jan	1843 (OB)
CA	28 Oct	1860 (PMM)
d	22 May	1863 (PMM)
SENHOUSE, George Septimus		
L	12 Mar	1807
SENHOUSE, Sir Humphrey Fleming		
L	9 Apr	1802
T		
CR	2 June	1809
CA	12 Oct	1814
KCH		1832 (DNB)
Kt	5 June	1834 (TR)
d	14 June	1841 (DNB)
SENHOUSE, William		
L	2 Jan	1769
SENHOUSE, William Wood		
L	19 Oct	1795
CR	14 Oct	1799 (PRO)
SENIOR, Abraham		
L	16 Nov	1757
SENIOR, Christopher		
L	25 June	1810
d	26 June	1816 (PJP)
SENIOR, James		
L	4 Mar	1815
SEPPINGS, John Milligen		
L	14 Oct	1793
SEPPINGS, Robert		
L		1704 (PJP)
SERLE, John		
L		1697 (PRO)
SERLE, Owen		
L	16 Feb	1691
In Merchant Service		1700 (PJP)
SEROCOLD, Walter		
L	11 Apr	1779
CR		1794 (PJP)
KIA	8 July	1794 (LG)
SERRELL, Henry		
L	19 Dec	1809
SERRELL, John		
L	22 July	1793
CR	31 Jan	1800
CA	27 Jan	1803
d	4 Apr	1830 (PMM)
SERRES, John Edmund Dominick		
L	20 Oct	1813
SERVANTE, John		
L	26 Feb	1782
d	14 July	1801
SERVANTE, John Henry		
L	5 Aug	1809
d	22 Apr	1837 (PMM)
SETFORD, James		
L	24 Mar	1807
SETON, David		
L	1 Apr	1778
SETON, George		
L	28 Oct	1741
d		1758 (PMM)
SETON, James Grant		
L	18 May	1815
HP	June	1816 (OB)
SETON, Peter		
L	19 July	1793
SEVERNE, Roger		
L		1672
SEWARD, Abraham		
L	15 July	1782
SEWARD, Charles (1)		
L	28 Apr	1782
CR	15 Nov	1814 (OB)
SEWARD, Charles (2)		
L	31 Aug	1801
CR	15 Nov	1814
SEWARD, George (1)		
L	16 Nov	1805
SEWARD, George (2)		
L	16 Nov	1807
SEWARD, James		
L	30 July	1779
CR	15 Apr	1797
CA	29 Apr	1802
SEWARD, John		
L	23 Dec	1747 (PJP)
SEWELL, Henry Frederick		
L	10 Dec	1810
SEWELL, John Edmund Pyke		
L	24 Feb	1766
SEYMER, William		
L	24 Feb	1684

SEYMORS, John
L 17 May 1779
SUP CR 31 Jan 1814

SEYMOUR, Berkeley
L 11 June 1741
d Dec 1777 (M)

SEYMOUR, Bowles
L 18 Sept 1739

SEYMOUR, Edward
L 24 June 1741
d 1741 (PMM)

SEYMOUR, Edward William
L 16 Feb 1815

SEYMOUR, Francis Edward
L 3 Oct 1808
CR 16 May 1814
d 26 July 1866 (LTE)

SEYMOUR, Sir George Francis
L 12 Oct 1804
CR 22 Jan 1806
CA 29 July 1806
CB 4 June 1815 (DNB)
GCH 9 Dec 1834 (DNB)
COM AD 8 Sept 1841–22 May 1844 (AO)
RAB 23 Nov 1841 (LG)
RAW 9 Nov 1846 (LG)
RAR 26 July 1847 (LG)
VAB 27 Mar 1850 (LG)
KCB 7 Apr 1852 (DNB)
A 14 May 1857 (DNB)
GCB 1860 (PJP)
AF 30 Nov 1866 (DNB)
d 20 Jan 1870 (DNB)

SEYMOUR, Horace Beauchamp Seymour
L 16 June 1809

SEYMOUR, Hugh (1)
L 1663
CA 1665
KIA 25 July 1666 (RM)

SEYMOUR, Hon. Hugh (2)
L 10 Aug 1776
CR 18 June 1778
CA 8 Feb 1779
MP (Newport I.o.W.) 1784–Apr 1786 (MPN)
MP (Tregony) 16 June 1788–1790 (MPN)
MP (Wendover) 1790–1796 (MPN)
CRM 1794 (PJP)
RAB 1 June 1795
MP (Portsmouth) 1796–11 Sept 1801 (MPN)
RAW 20 Feb 1797
VAB 14 Feb 1799
d 11 Sept 1801 (MPN)

SEYMOUR, John
L 18 Mar 1734
d 1 Jan 1738 (PMM)

SEYMOUR, John Crossley
L 16 July 1813
HP Aug 1815 (OB)

SEYMOUR, Matthew Cassan
L 8 Mar 1815
HP 8 Mar 1815 (OB)

SEYMOUR, Sir Michael
L 28 Oct 1790
CR 20 Aug 1795
CA 11 Aug 1800
Cre Bt 1809 (PJP)
KCB 20 Apr 1816 (LG)
Ret RA 1829 (PJP)
COMM (Portsmouth) 1829–1832 (PJP)
RAB 27 June 1832 (DNB)
d 9 July 1834 (DNB)

SEYMOUR, Phineas
L 4 Nov 1741
SUP CR 21 Sept 1796 (PMM)

SEYMOUR, Richard
L 7 Aug 1794
KIA 13 Mar 1806 (LG)

SEYMOUR, Stephen
L 26 Dec 1791
CR 6 Apr 1795
CA 1796
d (drowned) 10 June 1796 (OB)

SEYMOUR, William (1)
L 1685 (PJP)

SEYMOUR, William (2)
L 1795 (PJP)

SHACKERLY, William
L 26 June 1744
CR 4 Nov 1744

SHACKETON, Charles
L 11 Mar 1801

SHADFORTH, John
L 24 Aug 1757

SHAFTO, William
L 1666 (DDA)

SHAIRP, Alexander
L 9 Mar 1815
CR 30 Apr 1827 (OB)

SHAIRP, John (1)
L 22 July 1757
CR 10 Apr 1783
d 15 May 1795 (PMM)

SHAIRP, John (2)
L 17 Dec 1796

SHAKESPEAR, Arthur
T
L 3 Apr 1810
d 1847 (TR)

SHALES, John
L
CR 23 Nov 1703 (PMM)
CA 21 Nov 1707
d 24 Apr 1720

SHAMBLER, James
L 6 Feb 1815

SHAMMON, William
L 5 Oct 1758
d 23 Nov 1795 (PMM)

SHANCK, John
See SCHANK, John

SHANK, Joseph
L 29 Jan 1759

SHANNAN, George
L 21 Feb 1815

SHANNON, Hector James
L 6 Dec 1813
d 4 Sept 1815 (PRO)

SHANNON, Hugh
L 19 Sept 1815

SHANNON, Rodney
L 15 June 1810
CR 13 June 1815
CA 3 Aug 1826 (MB)
SHAPCOTE, Edward
L 18 Mar 1782
SHAPCOTE, John
L 12 Jan 1778
SHAPCOTE, Thomas
L 19 Mar 1811
SHARE, James
L 27 June 1782
SHARLAND, James
L
CA 1660
SHARNE, John
L 21 Dec 1696 (PJP)
SHARP, Thomas
L 16 July 1798
CR 30 Jan 1806
SHARP, William
L 2 May 1794
d 7 Sept 1844 (LT)
SHARPE, Alexander Renton
L 8 Dec 1806
CR 25 Mar 1809
CA 22 Jan 1813
CB 8 Dec 1815 (MB)
RAB 1 June 1848 (OB)
VA 30 Oct 1855 (CH)
Ret A 21 Jan 1858 (CH)
d 1 May 1860 (CH)
SHARPE, Bartholomew
L
CA 30 Nov 1682
SHARPE, Isaac
L 23 Apr 1762
CR 10 Jan 1771
SHARPE, Robert (1)
L 16 Nov 1711 (PMM)
SHARPE, Robert (2)
L 13 Mar 1815 (MB)
CR 24 Nov 1826 (MB)
CA 31 Jan 1848 (OB)
SHARPE, Sutton
L 16 Mar 1815
d 18 Dec 1821 (LT)
SHARPE, Thomas
L 6 Nov 1756
SHARPE, William
L 31 Dec 1690
SHARVELL, Benden
L 26 Feb 1815
SHAUGHNESSY, Edward
L 1811 (PJP)
SHAUGHNESSY, William
L 10 May 1757
SHAW, Charles (1)
L 1799 (PJP)
SHAW, Charles (2)
L 8 Apr 1805
CR 26 Sept 1811
CA 1 July 1814
d 2 May 1829 (MB)
SHAW, Charles (3)
L 1 Feb 1815
SHAW, George (1)
L 30 Aug 1806
SHAW, George (2)
L 20 Mar 1815 (OB)
SHAW, Harding
L 11 May 1797
SHAW, Isaac
L 25 June 1801
T
CR 9 Aug 1813
d 1848 (TR)
SHAW, James
L 30 Apr 1802
KIA 2 May 1813 (LG)
SHAW, John (1)
L 1673
SHAW, John (2)
L 8 Sept 1798
d 1805 (PJP)
SHAW, Theophilus
L 23 Oct 1807
SHAW, Thomas Bernard
L 10 Feb 1815
SHAW, Thomas Gibbon
L 30 Sept 1806
SHAW, William
L 1673
SHAW, William John
L 27 July 1795
SHEA, James
L 18 Mar 1805
KIA 7 Aug 1808 (PJP)
SHEALL, John
L 12 Feb 1800
SHEALL, Robert
L 23 Mar 1757
SHEBALD, George Charles
See SIEUBLADH, George
SHEBBEARE, Robert
L 30 Nov 1813
SHED, Robert
L 18 Dec 1799
CR 15 June 1814
HP 15 June 1814 (OB)
SHEERMAN, Richard
L
CA 26 Oct 1695 (PJP)
d 15 June 1704 (PJP)
SHEFFIELD, John, Earl of Mulgrave
See MULGRAVE, Earl of
SHEILS, James Waldegrave Ludlow
L 1 July 1814
d 1845 (OB)
SHELDON, Edison
L 1702 (PJP)
SHELDON, Edward
L
CA 1667
SHELDON, Slingsby
L 2 Jan 1781
SHELDRAKE, Robert William
L 25 Apr 1800
SHELLEY, Giles
L
CA 1664
SHELLEY, John
L 1664
CA 1667
d 5 Apr 1690 (PJP)

SHELVOCKE, George
L 25 Apr 1704
Dismissed 1713
d 1728 (DNB)
SHEPHARD, James Keith
L 19 Sept 1777
CR 28 May 1781
CA 12 July 1798
Ret RA 1825 (CH)
VAW 12 Nov 1840 (LG)
VAR 23 Nov 1841 (LG)
d 1843 (CH)
SHEPHARD, William
L 8 Feb 1815
HP 8 Feb 1815 (OB)
SHEPHEARD, Joseph Walwyn
L 18 Oct 1809
SHEPHEARD, Lewis
L 5 Jan 1797
CR 7 Jan 1802
CA 21 Oct 1810
d 18 Apr 1838 (LT)
SHEPHEARD, William (1)
L 8 Sept 1793
CR 15 Aug 1806
CA 1 Feb 1812
SHEPHEARD, William (2)
T
L 24 Feb 1815
CR 30 Sept 1831 (MB)
CA 26 Oct 1840 (OB)
HP 26 Oct 1840 (OB)
Ret CA 1853 (TR)
Ret RA 1858 (TR)
Ret VA 1865 (TR)
d 1870 (TR)
SHEPHERD, Benjamin
T
L 29 May 1811
d 1850 (TR)
SHEPHERD, Edward
L 7 Apr 1778
CR 30 May 1781
CA 15 Apr 1783
d 3 June 1791
SHEPHERD, John (1)
L 10 May 1799
CR 12 Aug 1812
CA 20 Nov 1847 (OB)
SHEPHARD, John (2)
L 2 Feb 1813
CR 28 Aug 1828 (MB)
CA 26 Oct 1840 (OB)
SHEPHERD, Thomas
L 21 Mar 1812
SHEPPARD, Ponsonby
L 4 Feb 1814
SHEPPARD, Richard
L 1666
SHEPPARD, Robert
L
CA 1664
SHEPPARD, William
L 1 May 1804
SHEPPARD, William Domett
L 23 July 1808

SHEPTON, Henry Barmfylde
L 16 June 1814
SHERBORNE, Richard
L 27 Sept 1687 (PJP)
SHERIDAN, Henry
L 11 Sept 1811
SHERIDAN, John
L 21 Dec 1801
CR 27 Nov 1810
CA 13 June 1815
Ret CA 31 Oct 1846 (LG)
SHERIVE, James
L
CA 1672
SHERMAN, Thomas
L
CA 19 Jan 1691
d 15 June 1699
SHERMER, William
L 28 Feb 1795
d (drowned) 1799 (PJP)
SHERRARD, Hon. Daniel
L 10 Feb 1742
d 29 Jan 1744 (PMM)
SHERRIFF, John
L 9 Dec 1795
CR 22 Jan 1806
KIA 3 Dec 1807 (JH)
SHERRIFF, Patrick
L 9 Feb 1815
SHERWIN, Thomas Cowper
L 22 July 1796
CR 27 May 1825 (MB)
SHERWIN, William
L
CA 1673
SHERWOOD, William
L 9 Nov 1756
CR 25 Aug 1762
SHERWOOD, William Tuttle
L 19 Sept 1806
SHEWARD, Ridgway
L 4 Dec 1745
SHEWEN, Daniel
L 19 Aug 1799
Ret CR 22 Jan 1844 (OB)
d 7 Dec 1845 (OB)
SHEWEN, Henry Thomas
L 8 Jan 1800
SHEWEN, Richard Phillips
L 17 June 1757
SUP CR 21 Sept 1796 (PMM)
d 1805 (PMM)
SHIELD, William
L 30 Dec 1779
CR
CA 7 Oct 1794
COMM (Plymouth) 1815–1829 (NBO)
SUP RA 1821 (TBM)
AB 12 Nov 1840 (CH)
AW 23 Nov 1841 (CH)
SHIELDS, William
L 15 Jan 1802
SHIELS, Daniel
L 1 Dec 1778
SHIELS, Ludlow
L 24 Dec 1780
KIA 1 Oct 1793 (LG)

SHIFFNER, Sir Henry
L 10 Feb 1809
CR 22 Feb 1814
CA 10 Nov 1819 (MB)
HP 12 Jan 1838 (OB)
Cre Bt 3 Feb 1842 (OB)
Ret CA 31 Oct 1846 (LG)
d 18 Mar 1859 (LTE)

SHILLINGFORD, Alexander
L 28 Feb 1815

SHINE, David
L 17 Oct 1804

SHIPLEY, Conway
L 11 Jan 1800
CR 19 Aug 1803
CA 4 May 1804
KIA 23 Apr 1808 (CH)

SHIPLEY, James
L 17 Apr 1810
HP Sept 1814 (OB)

SHIPMAN, Robert
L 27 Apr 1763

SHIPPARD, Alexander
L 28 Oct 1793
CR 3 Mar 1804
CA 22 Jan 1806
RAB 28 June 1838 (LG)
d 4 Apr 1841 (CH)

SHIPPARD, William
L 10 May 1794
CR 12 Aug 1812 (MB)
CA 2 Sept 1846 (OB)

SHIPPERSON, Ralph
L 4 Aug 1806

SHIPTON, James Maurice
L 25 June 1810
Ret CR 6 July 1850 (PMM)
d 1886 (PMM)

SHIPTON, Philip
L 1690 (PJP)

SHIRLEY, George James
L 20 Nov 1790
CR 11 Sept 1797
CA 26 Apr 1798
HP 2 June 1825 (OB)
Ret RA 2 June 1825 (OB)
VAW 12 Nov 1840 (LG)
VAR 23 Nov 1841 (LG)
d 2 Aug 1845 (OB)

SHIRLEY, James (1)
L 9 Oct 1746
CR 15 Oct 1759
CA 27 Apr 1762
d 3 Apr 1774 (M)

SHIRLEY, James (2)
L 20 Dec 1757
CR 26 May 1768
CA 10 Feb 1772
d (drowned) Dec 1777 (CH)

SHIRLEY, Thomas (1)
L 11 Oct 1755
CR 22 Feb 1759
CA 19 Nov 1759
SUP RA 1 Jan 1791
d 7 Apr 1814 (LTE)

SHIRLEY, Thomas (2)
L 18 Nov 1790

SHIRLEY, Hon. Washington
L 6 Jan 1742
CR
CA 19 Apr 1746
d 1778 (PJP)

SHIRLEY, William Warden
L 7 Nov 1793

SHIRREFF, James William
L 31 May 1809

SHIRREFF, Patrick
L 9 Feb 1815
HP 9 Feb 1815 (OB)

SHIRREFF, William Henry
L 3 Mar 1804
CR 5 Mar 1806
CA 15 Nov 1809 (MB)
RAB 9 Nov 1846 (OB)
d 1 Dec 1847 (OB)

SHIRRER, James
L 3 Sept 1781

SHIVERS, Thomas Revell
L 9 May 1777
CR 24 Jan 1782
CA 21 Sept 1790
RAB 28 Apr 1808
RAW 25 Oct 1809
RAR 31 July 1810
VAB 12 Aug 1812
VAW 4 June 1814
VAR 12 Aug 1819 (LG)
AB 27 May 1825 (LG)

SHOREDICHE, Richard
L 17 May 1760
d Sept 1786 (PMM)

SHORT, Arthur
L 1 July 1815
d 4 Nov 1844 (OB)

SHORT, Henry Middleton
L 3 Aug 1815

SHORT, James Ides
L 27 Nov 1780
SUP CR 11 Nov 1815

SHORT, John Ides
L 21 Sept 1757

SHORT, Joseph (1)
L 5 May 1705

SHORT, Joseph (2)
L 4 Apr 1783
CR 15 Sept 1793

SHORT, Joseph (3)
L 29 Sept 1813

SHORT, Joseph (4)
L 13 Mar 1815 (OB)

SHORT, Richard
L 30 Apr 1678
CA 16 Mar 1691 (LTE)
d 23 May 1702 (LTE)

SHORT, Samuel
L 21 Nov 1747
SUP CR 21 Sept 1796 (PMM)
d 17 May 1803 (PMM)

SHORT, Thomas
L 1666

SHORTEN, Robert
L
CA 1672

SHORTER, Daniel
L 7 Oct 1793

SHORTER, John
L 22 Oct 1703 (LTE)
CR 30 Aug 1710 (LTE)
CA 1 Jan 1713
d 2 May 1723

SHORTING, Robert
L 5 Apr 1727
CR
CA 2 Mar 1734
d 8 Aug 1734 (M)

SHORTLAND, John (1)
L 12 Dec 1763
CR 21 Sept 1790
d 17 Jan 1804

SHORTLAND, John (2)
L 10 Oct 1793
CR 1 Jan 1801
CA 6 Aug 1805
d 21 Jan 1810 (DNB)

SHORTLAND, John Thomas
L 3 Feb 1812
d 15 Oct 1816 (PJP)

SHORTLAND, Thomas George
L 19 Nov 1790
CR 20 Apr 1799
CA 1 Mar 1802
d 1827 (MB)

SHOUT, William
L 11 Feb 1800

SHOVELL, Sir Cloudisley
L 25 Sept 1673
CA 17 Sept 1677
Kt 1 May 1689 (EAD)
RAB 3 June 1690
MFMR 17 Feb 1691 (EAD)
LCSMR 14 Sept 1691 (EAD)
RAR 20 Jan 1692
Joint Admiral with Killegrew and Delaval 24 Jan 1693
COM E 27 Apr 1693–
1 Mar 1699 (NBO)
VAR 16 Apr 1694
AB 3 July 1693
CSMR 1 Mar 1697 (EAD)
COM V 1 Mar 1699–
25 Dec 1704 (NBO)
AW 6 May 1702
MCLHA 26 Dec 1704–
22 Oct 1707 (AO)
Joint Admiral with Earl of Peterborough 1 May 1705
d (drowned) 22 Oct 1707 (CH)

SHOVELL, John
L
CA 12 Sept 1692

SHOWELL, Edward Waldron
L 3 Apr 1813

SHRAPNELL, Edward
L 11 May 1797

SHRAPNELL, James
L 14 Nov 1810

SHREWSBURY, William
L 31 Aug 1797

SHUCKBURGH, Richard
L 8 Mar 1779

SHUCKBURGH, Thomas Stewkley
L 30 July 1813

SHUCKFORTH, David
L 7 June 1753
SUP CR 21 Sept 1796
d 1813 (PMM)

SHULDHAM, John George Evelyn
L 28 Apr 1797

SHULDHAM, Lemuel
L 29 Mar 1757
CR 26 Mar 1762
d 9 Mar 1766 (PMM)

SHULDHAM, Molyneux, Lord (1)
L 31 Aug 1739
CR
CA 12 May 1746
GG (Newfoundland) 1772–1775 (BNS)
MP (Fowey) 1774–1784 (MPN)
RAW 31 Mar 1775
VAB 5 Feb 1776
Cre IP 31 July 1776 (DNB)
VAW 29 Jan 1778
VAR 26 Sept 1780
AB 24 Sept 1787
AW 1 Feb 1793
d 30 Sept 1798 (MPN)

SHULDHAM, Molyneux (2)
L 15 Apr 1799
CR 8 June 1841 (OB)
Ret CR 10 June 1843 (OB)

SHURMUR, William
L 23 Jan 1746
CR
CA 12 Mar 1757
d 13 Feb 1777

SHUTTLEWORTH, Peter
L 21 Feb 1815

SIBBALD, James
T
L 19 Dec 1807
CR 15 June 1814
d 1843 (TR)

SIBBALD, Thomas
L 18 Apr 1811

SIBLY, Edward Reynolds
L 23 June 1794
CR 4 Aug 1806
CA 8 Mar 1814
d 19 Sept 1842 (LT)

SIBRELL, John
L 3 Jan 1797
d 10 June 1811 (PJP)

SIBTHORP, Henry Walter
L 12 Nov 1805
d (drowned) 14 Feb 1807 (PJP)

SIDDALL, John
L 15 Jan 1756

SIDDY, Charles
L
CR 10 Sept 1814

SIDNAM, John
L 19 Feb 1678

SIEUBLADH, Errick
L 1666

CA		1672
d	31 May	1725 (DDA)
SIEUBLADH, George		
L		1666
CA		1672
Went into Swedish Service		1676 (SJ)
SILBURNE, James		
L		1800 (PJP)
SILLY, John		
L	20 July	1808
SILLY, John Samuel		
L	22 Nov	1776
SILVER, Jacob		
L	17 Jan	1781
SILVER, John		
L		1665
CA	7 June	1666 (RM)
SILVER, William		
L	4 Sept	1797
SILVESTER, Sir Philip Carteret		
L	8 Oct	1795 (DNB)
CR	29 Apr	1802 (DNB)
CA	22 Jan	1806 (DNB)
CB	4 June	1815 (DNB)
Cre Bt	30 Mar	1822 (DNB)
d	24 Aug	1828 (DNB)
SIMCOE, John		
L	7 Aug	1739
CR		
CA	28 Dec	1743
d	14 May	1759
SIMEON, Charles		
L	2 June	1812
CR	13 June	1815
CA	10 Mar	1827 (MB)
Ret CA		1847 (OB)
d	12 Nov	1858 (LTE)
SIMES, Gustavus Adolphus		
L	6 Dec	1800
SIMKIN, John		
L	28 Feb	1815
HP		1815 (OB)
SIMKIN, Thomas Allen		
L	7 Nov	1806
Ret CR	12 Oct	1841 (OB)
SIMKIN, William		
L	14 July	1813
SIMMONDS, George		
L	17 Apr	1809
SIMMONDS, Joseph		
L	7 Oct	1805
T		
CR	7 Mar	1810
d		1838 (TR)
SIMMONDS, Richard		
L	18 July	1781
SIMMONDS, Richard S.		
See SIMONDS, Richard S.		
SIMMONDS, Richard William		
L	15 Sept	1795
SIMMONDS, Thomas		
L	6 June	1813
SIMMONS, Edward		
T		
L	14 May	1811
d		1849 (TR)
SIMMONS, George Valentine		
L	10 Mar	1815 (OB)
SIMMONS, Richard		
L	16 May	1801
SIMMS, Benjamin Symes		
L	22 Feb	1815
SIMONDS, Richard S.		
T		
L	20 Nov	1812
Ret CR		1855 (TR)
d		1865 (TR)
SIMONS, Christopher		
L	17 May	1709
SIMONS, Thomas (1)		
L	14 Mar	1763
d	3 Mar	1765 (PMM)
SIMONS, Thomas (2)		
L	3 Oct	1800
T	killed	
KIA	21 Oct	1805 (TR)
SIMONTON, Robert		
L	27 June	1759
CR	5 May	1778
CA	9 July	1778
SIMPKINS, Phil.		
L	29 Nov	1694
SIMPSON, Aemilius		
L	2 Mar	1815
SIMPSON, Benjamin		
L	4 Jan	1798
SIMPSON, Edward		
L		1664
SIMPSON, George		
L	5 Sept	1803
KIA	3 Sept	1807 (PJP)
SIMPSON, James (1)		
L	30 May	1741
d	12 Sept	1750 (PMM)
SIMPSON, James (2)		
L	18 Feb	1815
SIMPSON, John (1)		
L	26 Aug	1779
SUP CR	17 Mar	1814
SIMPSON, John (2)		
L	31 May	1798
Ret CR	1 Dec	1830 (OB)
SIMPSON, John (3)		
L	7 Dec	1793
CR	19 Apr	1803
CA	12 Dec	1809
d	20 Feb	1849 (LT)
SIMPSON, John (4)		
L	28 July	1808
SIMPSON, John (5)		
L	14 Dec	1811
CR	3 July	1840 (OB)
CA	9 Nov	1846 (OB)
SIMPSON, Robert (1)		
L	21 May	1778
SIMPSON, Robert (2)		
L	17 Nov	1798
CR	27 Dec	1804
CA	22 Sept	1806
d	June	1808 (MB)
SIMPSON, Samuel Ash		
L	4 May	1804

Ret CR	25 Jan	1837 (OB)
d	22 Nov	1845 (OB)
SIMPSON, Thomas (1)		
L	6 July	1797
CR	1 Aug	1811
Ret CA	1 Mar	1841 (OB)
d	28 Mar	1848 (OB)
SIMPSON, Thomas (2)		
L	3 Nov	1801
CR	20 Oct	1813
SIMPSON, Thomas (3)		
L	21 May	1807
Ret CR	10 Feb	1843 (OB)
SIMPSON, Thomas (4)		
L	13 June	1815
d	1 May	1818 (LT)
SIMPSON, William (1)		
L	26 Oct	1778
SIMPSON, William (2)		
L	26 Nov	1807
CR	22 Apr	1811
CA	14 Oct	1824 (MB)
SIMS, Andrew		
L	15 Feb	1815
SIMSON, John		
L	9 Apr	1803
SINCLAIR, Alexander		
L	29 Dec	1796
d (drowned)	24 Dec	1811 (JH)
SINCLAIR, Sir John Gordon		
Inh Bt	4 Aug	1795 (OB)
L	7 July	1809
HP	Oct	1811–
	11 Feb	1812 (OB)
CR	13 Aug	1812
CA	6 June	1814
RAB	8 June	1849 (LG)
VA	17 Oct	1856 (CH)
A	5 Aug	1861 (CH)
d	13 Nov	1863 (CH)
SINCLAIR, Patrick		
L	29 Jan	1771
CR	3 Sept	1781
CA	16 Jan	1783
d	5 May	1794 (M)
SINCOCK, Robert		
L		
CA	27 June	1689
d	12 Oct	1702 (CH)
SINGLETON, William		
L		1691 (PJP)
SINTES, Anthony		
L	15 Nov	1809
SIRR, William Whiteway		
L	9 May	1796
d	Aug	1797
SISON, Samuel		
L	20 Aug	1807
Ret CR	11 Jan	1844 (OB)
SISSON, John		
L	1 Aug	1811
SISSON, Robert		
L	18 May	1740
CR	2 May	1746 (PJP)
d (drowned)	27 Feb	1748 (PJP)

SKARDON, George		
L	4 Feb	1814 (OB)
SKEAD, Thomas		
T		
L	21 Dec	1808
d		1841 (TR)
SKEKEL, John		
L	21 Feb	1804
CR	28 June	1811
CA	27 May	1825 (OB)
Ret CA	31 Oct	1846 (LG)
SKELLY, Gordon		
L	1 Oct	1762
SKELTON, Charles (1)		
L		1672
CA	5 Feb	1673
SKELTON, Charles (2)		
L		
CA	1 May	1688
d (drowned)	3 Sept	1691(CH)
SKELTON, Charles Cornwallis		
L	19 Feb	1799
SKELTON, Jeremiah		
L	27 Aug	1799
SKELTON, John (1)		
L		
CA		1665
SKELTON, John (2)		
L		1739 (PJP)
SKELTON, William		
L	23 Apr	1800
d	12 Dec	1808 (PJP)
SKENE, Alexander (1)		
L	12 Apr	1744
d	28 Dec	1768 (PMM)
SKENE, Alexander (2)		
L	28 Nov	1793
CR	18 Nov	1799
CA	29 Apr	1802
d	14 Sept	1823 (MB)
SKENE, James		
L	25 Apr	1815
HP	Apr	1824 (OB)
SKILL, Seth		
L	24 Mar	1794
SKINNER, Andrew Johnstoke		
L	9 Dec	1782
SKINNER, Augustus		
L		1665
SKINNER, Fitzowen George		
L	1 Feb	1802
CR	12 Jan	1805
d	23 May	1810 (LT)
SKINNER, George		
L	15 Sept	1756
SKINNER, George Augustus Elliott		
L	26 Mar	1803
SKINNER, Jeremiah		
L	23 Feb	1734
SKINNER, John (1)		
L	10 June	1746
SKINNER, John (2)		
L	12 June	1782
SKINNER, John Watson		
L	27 Mar	1794
KIA	4 June	1808 (CH)

SKINNER, Lancelot
See SKYNNER, Lancelot

SKINNER, Stephan
L 21 Nov 1790
d June 1806 (PMM)

SKINNER, William
L 1667

SKIPSEY, Robert
L 14 Nov 1790
CR 28 Aug 1815

SKIPSEY, William
L 7 Apr 1778
CR 6 Dec 1796
CA 18 Mar 1802
CRM 22 July 1830 (LG)
RAW 10 Jan 1837 (LG)
RAR 23 Nov 1841 (LG)
d 18 Mar 1846 (OB)

SKONE, Thomas
L 21 July 1745
CR 15 Oct 1756

SKOTTOWE, George
L 9 Dec 1798
d 1817 (PJP)

SKUES, Thomas
L 1685

SKYES, William
L 9 June 1746

SKYNNER, John
L 8 Mar 1802
Ret CR 10 Apr 1838 (OB)
d 1846 (OB)

SKYNNER, Lancelot (1)
L 23 Apr 1748
CR 15 Nov 1756
CA 7 Feb 1758
KIA 4 Apr 1760 (LG)

SKYNNER, Lancelot (2)
L 12 Nov 1790
CR 1 Nov 1794
CA 16 Sept 1795
d (drowned) 9 Oct 1799 (DNB)

SKYRME, Charles
L 14 Sept 1782

SKYRME, Francis
L 21 Oct 1790

SKYRME, John
L 3 Nov 1743

SKYRMSHER, Richard
L 28 Feb 1782
d 1805 (PJP)

SLADE, Frederick
L 26 Sept 1811

SLADE, Henry (1)
L 27 Sept 1740

SLADE, Henry (2)
L 12 Nov 1808
CR 27 May 1825 (OB)
HP 27 May 1825 (OB)

SLADE, James
L 8 Apr 1793
CR 2 Sept 1799
CA 21 Oct 1810
Ret RA 1 Oct 1846 (PMM)
d 26 Oct 1846 (OB)

SLADE, John
L 29 Dec 1760

SLADE, Thomas
L 5 Aug 1703

SLANNING, William
L 2 Oct 1741
d 12 May 1744 (PMM)

SLATER, George
See SCLATER, George

SLATER, William Gill
L 11 Mar 1815

SLAUGHTER, Sir William
L 18 Sept 1806
CR 21 Nov 1810
KH 1 Jan 1837 (OB)
CA 10 Jan 1837(OB)

SLEATH, Henry
L 16 Sept 1813

SLEIGH, Francis
L 27 Oct 1800

SLEIGH, John (1)
L 23 Sept 1715

SLEIGH, John (2)
L 2 Nov 1815
d Jan 1848 (OB)

SLEORGIN, John
L 17 Jan 1794

SLESSOR, Henry Thomas
L 3 Mar 1803

SLIFORD, Thomas
L 17 Apr 1742

SLINGSBY, Joseph
L 3 Feb 1815

SLOAN, David
L 9 July 1802
CR 8 Feb 1809
d (drowned) 24 Nov 1812 (JH)

SLOAN, George
L 30 Dec 1812
HP Aug 1814 (OB)

SLOASS, James
L 24 Sept 1759
d 23 July 1765 (PMM)

SLOLY, James
L 13 Mar 1815
HP 13 Mar 1815 (OB)

SLOPER, Richard
L 28 Oct 1745

SLORACH, James
L 30 May 1745

SLOUT, Samuel
L 24 Feb 1807
KIA 2 Aug 1811 (JH)

SLYMAN, Daniel
L 16 Mar 1815

SMAIL, John
L 21 May 1802
d 1804 (OB)

SMAIL, William Archibald
L 17 Dec 1812

SMALL, Francis
L 1 Dec 1800

SMART, Alexander
L
CA 1673

SMART, Benjamin
L 31 July 1811

SMART, John Norval
L 25 Nov 1815
d 8 Feb 1846 (OB)
SMART, Thomas
L 4 May 1702 (PMM)
CR
CA 26 July 1715
d 8 Nov 1727 (PMM)
SMART, William
L 23 Feb 1815
SMELT, Cornelius
L 21 Feb 1741
CR 9 Apr 1748
d 2 June 1755 (M)
SMILLIE, George
L 5 Oct 1801
SMITH, Abel
L 19 Feb 1741
CR
CA 22 Jan 1746
d 12 May 1756
SMITH, Alexander
L 31 Dec 1729
SMITH, Andrew (1)
L 23 Aug 1790
CR 29 June 1795
CA 6 Jan 1797
RAB 19 July 1821 (MB)
RAW 27 May 1825 (LG)
RAR 22 July 1830 (LG)
d 29 Sept 1831 (OB)
SMITH, Andrew (2)
L 28 Aug 1815
SMITH, Anthony
L
CA 1666
SMITH, Benjamin
L 6 Nov 1795
Ret CR 1 Dec 1830 (OB)
d Jan 1848 (OB)
SMITH, Charles (1)
L 1693 (PJP)
CR
CA 12 Oct 1702
LGH 1740 (PJP)
d 2 Aug 1750 (PJP)
SMITH, Charles (2)
L 24 June 1727
SMITH, Charles (3)
L 1733 (PJP)
SMITH, Charles (4)
L 1790 (PJP)
SMITH, Charles (5)
L 13 May 1813
CR 22 July 1830 (OB)
CA 23 Nov 1841 (OB)
HP 11 May 1842 (OB)
SMITH, Charles Thurlow
L 14 Oct 1806
CR 3 Oct 1809
CA 28 Feb 1812
Dismissed
Entered Mexican Service 1823 (PJP)
d Nov 1826 (MB)
SMITH, Charles Wood
L 29 Nov 1811

SMITH, Cornelius
L 16 Feb 1796
SMITH, David
L 7 Dec 1793
SMITH, Edward (1)
L 6 Oct 1719
CR 4 May 1727
CA 16 Nov 1739
d 18 Apr 1743
SMITH, Edward (2)
L 26 Feb 1812
CR 30 Aug 1828 (MB)
SMITH, Edward Tyrrel
L 27 May 1778
CR
CA 2 May 1781
RAW 1 Jan 1801
RAR 23 Apr 1804
VAB 9 Nov 1805
VAW 28 Apr 1808
VAR 31 July 1810
AB 12 Aug 1812
AW 12 Aug 1819 (CH)
d 15 Oct 1824 (PRO)
SMITH, Elliott
L 18 Sept 1726
CR 10 Aug 1739
CA 25 Feb 1742
d 31 Mar 1769
SMITH, Francis (1)
L 1 June 1801
SMITH, Francis (2)
L 22 Jan 1806
SMITH, George (1)
L 1 July 1690 (PJP)
CR 21 Nov 1698
d 2 Nov 1704
SMITH, George (2)
L 5 Nov 1742
d 24 Sept 1751 (M)
SMITH, George (3)
L 18 Jan 1771
SMITH, George (4)
L 24 May 1794
SMITH, George (5)
L 20 Sept 1815
CR 8 Sept 1829 (OB)
CA 13 Apr 1832 (OB)
HP 13 Apr 1832 (OB)
d 6 Apr 1850 (PRO)
SMITH, George Barlow
L 25 Apr 1783
d 2 Nov 1799
SMITH, George Sidney
L 21 Jan 1814
CR 12 Mar 1827 (MB)
CA Aug 1828 (MB)
d 13 Sept 1832 (LT)
SMITH, Godfrey
L 1694 (PJP)
SMITH, Harris
L 21 Sept 1790
SMITH, Henry (1)
L 2 Nov 1745
CR 4 July 1755 (PJP)
CA 24 Aug 1756 (PJP)

SMITH, Henry (2)		
L		1756 (PJP)
SMITH, Henry (3)		
L	27 Aug	1760
d		1801 (PJP)
SMITH, Henry (4)		
L	11 July	1781
SMITH, Horatio Sharp		
L	27 Jan	1809
SMITH, Hugh William		
L	24 Nov	1801
SMITH, Isaac		
L	19 Aug	1775
CR	13 May	1781
CA	1 Dec	1787
SUP RA	8 Oct	1807
d		1831 (PMM)
SMITH, James (1)		
L		
CA		1661
d		1664 (AJ)
SMITH, James (2)		
L	8 Jan	1709
SMITH, James (3)		
L	22 July	1729
CR	2 July	1740
d		1740 (PJP)
SMITH, James (4)		
L	1 Feb	1745
SMITH, James (5)		
L	17 Feb	1748
CR	10 Nov	1756 (PMM)
CA	28 Oct	1758 (PMM)
d		1786 (PMM)
SMITH, James (6)		
L	2 Oct	1779
d	17 Nov	1798 (M)
SMITH, James (7)		
L	22 Sept	1781
d	Mar	1783 (PMM)
SMITH, James (8)		
L	20 May	1782
SMITH, James (9)		
L	3 Mar	1795
Ret CR	26 Nov	1830 (OB)
d	5 Jan	1848 (OB)
SMITH, James (10)		
L	12 Feb	1805
SMITH, James Edward		
L	26 Nov	1799
d	1 May	1804 (LG)
SMITH, James George		
L	25 Jan	1798
SMITH, Sir Jeremy		
L		
CA		1664
AD		1665
Kt	22 June	1665 (EAD)
AB	7 June	1666 (RM)
COM V	17 June	1669–
	3 Nov	1675 (NBO)
Adjutant General to Duke of York in the Dutch expedition	May	1673 (EAD)
d	3 Nov	1675 (NBO)
SMITH, John (1)		
L		
CA	23 Jan	1694
d	15 June	1722
SMITH, John (2)		
L	15 Oct	1694
SMITH, John (3)		
L	15 Nov	1708
SMITH, John (4)		
L		
CR	14 June	1727
CA	13 Jan	1728
d	19 Aug	1729 (M)
SMITH, John (5)		
L	3 Apr	1742
SMITH, John (6)		
L	18 June	1746
SMITH, John (7)		
L	23 Jan	1759
d	25 June	1762 (PMM)
SMITH, John (8)		
L	5 June	1779
CR	15 Jan	1783
CA	22 Nov	1790
d	6 May	1808 (LT)
SMITH, John (9)		
L	4 Dec	1779
SUP CR	30 May	1814
SMITH, John (10)		
L	1 Dec	1780
SMITH, John (11)		
L	30 Mar	1781
SMITH, John (12)		
L	29 Aug	1793
SMITH, John (13)		
L	17 Apr	1794
SMITH, John (14) Later SKENE, John		
L	25 July	1794
T		
CB		1815 (TR)
d		1833 (TR)
SMITH, John (15)		
L	8 May	1798
CR	24 Dec	1805
CA	27 Oct	1813
CB	8 Dec	1815 (MB)
SMITH, John (16)		
L	25 Oct	1800
SMITH, John (17)		
L	24 Nov	1800
SMITH, John (18)		
L	14 Aug	1801
Ret CR	28 Jan	1847 (OB)
SMITH, John (19)		
L	10 July	1802
d	Jan	1848 (OB)
SMITH, John (20)		
L	27 Apr	1804
SMITH, John (21)		
L	26 Mar	1805
CR	3 July	1812
CA	22 Dec	1822 (MB)
d		1836 (PJP)
SMITH, John (22)		
L	21 May	1807
HP	Jan	1813 (OB)

Name / Event	Date	Year
SMITH, John (23)		
L	11 Sept	1811
SMITH, John Bernhard		
L	8 Sept	1807 (PJP)
CR	1 Dec	1812
d	11 Jan	1844 (LT)
SMITH, John Broadsly		
L	8 Sept	1808
SMITH, John Langdale		
L	3 Nov	1790
CR	14 Jan	1806
d	30 Oct	1827 (MB)
SMITH, John Samuel (1)		
L	7 Aug	1778
CR	23 July	1781
CA	29 July	1782
SMITH, John Samuel (2)		
T	wounded	
L	8 Aug	1806
Became fourth of the four Junior Lieutenants	June/July	1807
Became second of the three Junior Lieutenants		1809
Became first of the four Junior Lieutenants		1810
Became first of the three Junior Lieutenants		1812
L	16 June	1813
d		1840 (TR)
SMITH, John Sparhawke		
L	11 Mar	1815
SMITH, John William		
T		
L	13 Mar	1815
HP	13 Mar	1815 (OB)
d		1860 (TR)
SMITH, John Wynter		
L	12 July	1810
d		1846 (OB)
SMITH, Joseph (1)		
L		1703 (PJP)
d	May	1738 (M)
SMITH, Joseph (2)		
L	2 May	1810
SMITH, Lawrence		
L	15 Aug	1801
SMITH, Marmaduke		
L	27 Dec	1808
SMITH, Mathew		
L	4 Dec	1779
CR	18 Apr	1782
CA	18 Apr	1783
Dismissed		1796 (PJP)
Restored		1798 (PJP)
d	21 Sept	1844 (LT)
SMITH, Matthew		
L	6 Oct	1794
CR	16 Feb	1801
CA	24 Apr	1808
d	30 May	1840 (LT)
SMITH, Michael		
L	8 Oct	1802
SMITH, Nicholas		
L	4 Sept	1692
CR	18 Dec	1704 (PMM)
CA	8 Mar	1709
d	7 July	1721
SMITH, Peter		
L	27 Dec	1782
SMITH, Richard (1)		
L		1664
CA	10 July	1666 (RM)
SMITH, Richard (2)		
L	10 Mar	1712
SMITH, Richard (3)		
L	12 June	1760
CR	4 May	1761
CA	1 Nov	1762
d	July	1811 (MB)
SMITH, Richard (4)		
L	25 June	1761
SMITH, Richard (5)		
L	16 Feb	1794
SMITH, Richard (6)		
L	27 June	1801
CR	24 Feb	1806
SMITH, Robert (1)		
L		
CA		1679
d (drowned)	26 Nov	1703 (LG)
SMITH, Robert (2)		
L	5 Dec	1800
SMITH, Robert (3)		
L	17 May	1802
SMITH, Robert (4)		
L	24 Aug	1807
CR	4 Mar	1814
HP	4 Mar	1814 (OB)
d		1849 (CH)
SMITH, Thomas (1)		
L		
CA		1661
SMITH, Thomas (2)		
L	5 Apr	1678
CA	11 July	1688
SMITH, Thomas (3)		
L		
CA	1 Apr	1688
Dismissed	1 Sept	1703 (DNB)
Entered French Service as a privateer		1705 (CH)
Captured	30 Dec	1707 (LG)
e (treason)	18 June	1708 (CH)
SMITH, Thomas (4)		
L		
CA	26 Nov	1696
d	2 June	1722
SMITH, Thomas (5)		
L	6 Feb	1727 (DNB)
Dismissed	27 Mar	1729
CR		
CA	5 May	1730
GG (Newfoundland)		1741–1742 (BNS)
GG (Newfoundland)		1743–1744 (BNS)
RAR	15 July	1747
VAW	12 May	1748
AB		1757
d	28 Aug	1762 (DNB)
SMITH, Thomas (6)		
L	2 Sept	1740

SMITH, Thomas (7)
L 6 June 1746
CR 18 Oct 1758
d 2 June 1765 (PMM)

SMITH, Thomas (8)
L 5 June 1780

SMITH, Thomas (9)
L 19 Oct 1797

SMITH, Thomas (10)
L 5 Sept 1800
Ret CR 26 Nov 1830 (OB)
d 14 Nov 1849 (LT)

SMITH, Thomas (11)
L 12 June 1807

SMITH, Thomas (12)
L 1 Sept 1807
CR 15 June 1814
CA 16 Aug 1825 (MB)
d 19 Sept 1847 (OB)

SMITH, Thomas (13)
L 13 June 1808

SMITH, Thomas (14)
L 29 Nov 1808
CR 22 Oct 1827 (MB)
CA 23 Nov 1841 (OB)
d 9 Jan 1846 (OB)

SMITH, Thomas (15)
L 3 Apr 1810

SMITH, Thomas (16)
L 3 Mar 1815
CR 22 Oct 1844 (OB)

SMITH, Titus
L 29 Jan 1702 (PMM)

SMITH, William (1)
L 1667
CA 1673

SMITH, William (2)
L
CA 25 June 1694
d 31 Dec 1695

SMITH, William (3)
L 26 June 1695 (PJP)
CR 22 June 1708 (PMM)
CA 10 May 1716
d 23 Feb 1756

SMITH, William (4)
L 11 Jan 1718
CR
CA 13 June 1728
SUP A 21 July 1747 (PJP)
d 23 Feb 1756 (PJP)

SMITH, William (5)
L 10 Dec 1741

SMITH, William (6)
L 17 Jan 1758
SUP CR 13 Mar 1798 (PMM)
d 8 Apr 1801 (PMM)

SMITH, William (7)
L 31 Dec 1762
CR 2 Apr 1781
CA 25 Oct 1809

SMITH, William (8)
L 16 Oct 1778
CR 25 Oct 1783

SMITH, William (9)
Formerly BRADSHAW, William Smith
L 4 Nov 1780
CR 23 Dec 1782
CA 21 Sept 1790
Dismissed Jan 1795 (CH)

SMITH, William (10)
L 1 May 1782

SMITH, William (11)
L 10 July 1782

SMITH, William (12)
L 19 Mar 1798
CR 27 Mar 1826 (MB)

SMITH, William (13)
L 4 July 1801
CR 27 Mar 1826 (OB)
HP 27 Mar 1826 (OB)

SMITH, William (14)
L 17 Feb 1802

SMITH, William (15)
L 17 Apr 1808

SMITH, William (16)
L 22 Dec 1807
Ret CR 24 July 1844 (OB)

SMITH, William (17)
L 27 May 1808

SMITH, William (18)
L 4 May 1810

SMITH, William (19)
L 18 Apr 1811

SMITH, William (20)
L 12 June 1811

SMITH, William (21)
L 14 July 1813
CR 22 July 1826 (MB)
CA 13 Mar 1846 (OB)
d 1862 (PMM)

SMITH, William Harris
L 10 Aug 1801
Ret CR 30 Dec 1831 (OB)
d 1846 (OB)

SMITH, William Henry (1)
L 3 Dec 1799
CR 2 May 1810
d 9 Feb 1825 (LT)

SMITH, William Henry (2)
L 8 Feb 1809
Ret CR 9 Apr 1847 (OB)

SMITH, William Murray
L 22 Jan 1806

SMITH, William Richard
L 2 Mar 1804
CR 15 Dec 1808
CA 1 Jan 1817 (MB)

SMITH, William Robert
L 14 Aug 1799
CR 11 Apr 1809 (MB)
Ret CA 19 Sept 1840 (OB)

SMITH, Sir William Sidney
L 25 Sept 1780
CR 6 May 1782
CA 7 May 1783
In Swedish Service 1790–1793
MP (Rochester) 1802–1806 (MPT)
CRM 23 Apr 1804 (LG)
RAB 9 Nov 1805
Kt (Two Sicilies) 25 Aug 1807 (LG)
RAW 28 Apr 1808

RAR 25 Oct 1809
VAB 31 July 1810
VAR 4 June 1814
KCB 2 Jan 1815 (LG)
AB 19 July 1821 (MB)
LGRM 28 June 1830 (OB)
AW 22 July 1830 (CH)
AR 10 Jan 1837 (CH)
GCB 4 July 1838 (DNB)
d 26 May 1840 (DNB)

SMITHERS, George
L 23 Aug 1811
HP 1832 (OB)

SMITHETT, William
L 7 Aug 1761

SMITHIES, Thomas
L 16 Aug 1793

SMITHSON, James
L 25 Aug 1796

SMITHWICK, Henry
L 28 Nov 1812

SMOLLETT, John Rovett
L 1794
CR 28 Aug 1799
CA 29 Apr 1802 (MB)
Ret RA 10 Jan 1837 (CH)
RAW 17 Aug 1840 (LG)
RAR 23 Nov 1841 (LG)
d 1842 (CH)

SMYTH, Charles
L 2 Sept 1780
CR 26 Oct 1793

SMYTH, George Thomas
L 23 Nov 1814

SMYTH, Henry
L 25 May 1755

SMYTH, James (1)
L 18 June 1778
CR 16 Sept 1780
KIA 28 May 1781 (CH)

SMYTH, James (2)
L 17 Nov 1781
KIA 16 Aug 1791 (PJP)

SMYTH, John
L 24 Nov 1800
CR 4 May 1804

SMYTH, Spenser
T
L 2 June 1812
CR 22 Oct 1827 (MB)
CA 28 July 1851 (PMM)
Ret RA 1 Apr 1870 (PMM)
Ret VA 29 May 1873 (PMM)
Ret A 26 Sept 1878 (PMM)
d 1879 (TR)

SMYTH, Thomas
L 15 Oct 1802
CR 8 May 1804
CA 22 Jan 1806
d 1810 (PMM)

SMYTH, Thomas William Anthony
L 16 Mar 1808

SMYTH, William Henry
L 25 Mar 1813
CR 18 Sept 1815
Kt (Two Sicilies) 16 Mar 1816 (LG)

Ret CA 31 Oct 1846 (LG)
Ret RA 28 May 1853 (DNB)
Ret VA 13 Feb 1858 (DNB)
Ret A 14 Nov 1863 (DNB)
d 9 Sept 1865 (DNB)

SMYTHE, Thomas Purnell
L 11 Dec 1807

SMYTHIES, Charleton
L 1785 (PJP)
Dismissed 1 Aug 1785 (PJP)

SNAIL, John
L 21 May 1802

SNELGAR, Giles
L 8 Oct 1799

SNELL, Francis Johnson
L 29 Aug 1799
CR 29 Apr 1802
CA 22 Jan 1806
d 17 Feb 1818 (LT)

SNELL, John Coxetter
T wounded
L 17 Oct 1808
d 1838 (TR)

SNELL, Robert (1)
L 7 Nov 1806

SNELL, Robert (2)
L 26 Sept 1812

SNELL, William
T
L 4 Dec 1811
Ret CR 1853 (TR)
d 1860 (TR)

SNELLGROVE, Henry
T wounded
L 1 Aug 1811
d Mar 1848 (TR)

SNEYD, Clement
L 14 Oct 1793
CR 25 Sept 1806
CA 3 Apr 1811
Ret RA 31 Oct 1846 (LG)

SNEYD, Edward
L 19 Sept 1775
d (drowned) Nov 1776 (PJP)

SNEYD, Ralph
L 29 June 1793
d 7 Mar 1805 (OB)

SNODGRASS, Peter
L 29 June 1782
d 10 May 1792

SNOW, Nicholas
L 2 Aug 1692 (PJP)

SNOW, Robert
L 21 Feb 1815
d 1848 (OB)

SNOW, Thomas Rolls
L 9 Mar 1815

SNOW, William
L 5 Apr 1779
SUP CR 31 Jan 1814
d 1 Jan 1819 (LT)

SNOW, William John
T wounded
L 4 June 1814
d 1827 (TR)

SNOWEY, William
T
L 4 June 1814
d 1837 (TR)
SOADY, Joseph
L 17 Aug 1807
CR 26 Dec 1822 (MB)
SOANES, Joseph (1)
L
CA 23 Feb 1691
d 12 Sept 1737
SOANES, Joseph (2)
L 2 Mar 1734
CR 3 Dec 1745
SOLEY, Philip
L 29 July 1799
SOLGARD, Peter
L 13 Jan 1703 (PMM)
CR
CA 2 July 1722
d 19 Mar 1739 (PMM)
SOMERS, Thomas
L 24 Feb 1743
CR
CA 4 Sept 1744
Dismissed 1748
SOMERSET, John Stukley
L
CR
CA 2 Mar 1758
d 2 Sept 1805 (PMM)
SOMERVELL, James
L 23 Dec 1779
SUP CR 15 July 1814
SOMERVILL, Mark
L 26 Feb 1757
KIA 11 Sept 1758 (LG)
SOMERVILLE, Charles
L 18 Oct 1809
SOMERVILLE, George Field
L 7 May 1805
Ret CR 16 Sept 1841 (OB)
SOMERVILLE, James
See SOMERVELL, James
SOMERVILLE, James Bowen
L 27 May 1814
HP 1842 (OB)
SOMERVILLE, John (1)
L 21 Nov 1782
SOMERVILLE, John (2)
L 26 Oct 1795
SOMERVILLE, John (3)
L 3 Jan 1814
SOMERVILLE, Hon. Sir Kenelm
L 11 Nov 1807
CR 1 Feb 1812
CA 7 June 1814
Inh Bt 3 June 1842 (OB)
Ret CA 31 Oct 1846 (LG)
SOMERVILLE, Philip
L 4 Sept 1782
CR 9 Apr 1796
CA 29 Apr 1802
SOMERVILLE, William (1)
L 23 June 1779
SOMERVILLE, William (2)
L 17 Dec 1798
Ret CR 1 Oct 1840 (OB)
SOMERVILLE, William (3)
L 10 July 1815
SOMERVILLE, Hon. William (4)
L 18 Nov 1808
SOMERVILLE, William Hugh
L 24 Apr 1802
SOMMERVILLE, George
L 14 Mar 1811
d 11 Jan 1816 (LT)
SOPER, Richard
L 13 July 1808
SORREL, Paul
L 28 Sept 1695
In Merchant Service 1700 (PJP)
SORRELL, John
L 31 July 1695
SOTHEBY, Charles
L 25 Jan 1802 (MB)
CR 8 Jan 1810
CA 28 Feb 1812
RAB 20 Mar 1848 (OB)
SOTHEBY, Thomas
L
CR
CA 11 June 1783
RAB 9 Nov 1805
RAW 28 Apr 1808
RAR 25 Oct 1809
VAB 31 July 1810
VAW 12 Aug 1812
VAR 4 June 1814
AB 19 July 1821 (CH)
AW 22 July 1830 (LG)
d 16 July 1831 (LT)
SOTHERON, Frank
L 1782 (MB)
CR
CA 11 Dec 1793
RAB 1 Aug 1811
RAW 4 Dec 1813
RAR 4 June 1814
MP
(Nottinghamshire) 1814–1831 (MPT)
VAB 12 Aug 1819 (CH)
VAW 19 July 1821 (CH)
AB 22 July 1830 (CH)
AW 10 Jan 1837 (CH)
d 7 Feb 1839 (CH)
SOULE, John
L
CA 19 Oct 1694
d 1 Oct 1695 (CH)
SOUTH, William Wilson
L 13 June 1809 (OB)
SOUTHACK, Cyprian
L 1673
CA 1696
d 27 Mar 1745 (DCB)
SOUTHCOTT, Edward
L 1799
d 1802 (PJP)
SOUTHCOTT, John
L 26 Mar 1802 (PJP)
d 1837 (PJP)
SOUTHEY, Thomas
L
CR 1 Aug 1811 (MB)

Name / Rank	Date	Year
SOUTHEY, William		
L	17 Sept	1814
CR	14 Aug	1844 (OB)
HP	14 Aug	1844 (OB)
SOUTHWELL, Daniel		
L	11 Feb	1794
d	21 Aug	1797 (DUB)
SOUTHWICK, Cyprian		
See SOUTHACK, Cyprian		
SOUTHWOOD, Henry		
L		
CA		1666
SOUTTED, Daniel		
L		1804 (PJP)
SOWERBY, John		
L	7 Sept	1796
SOWTON, George		
L	14 Oct	1801
SOWTON, James (1)		
L	2 Apr	1798
SOWTON, James (2)		
L	15 Aug	1799
SPANN, Jonathan		
L	4 May	1694 (PJP)
CA	13 Aug	1697 (PJP)
d	30 Aug	1712
SPARGO, Sampson Jones		
L	2 Mar	1811
SPARKE, Henry		
L	22 Mar	1757
SPARKE, Thomas		
L	Oct	1778 (PJP)
CR	15 Apr	1782
CA	3 Dec	1799
SPARKES, George		
L	30 Apr	1678
SPARKES, Isaac		
L		1713 (PRO)
SPARKES, James		
L		1706 (PRO)
SPARKES, John Hindes		
L	16 Feb	1794
d	5 Jan	1835 (PJP)
SPARKES, Israel		
L	13 Oct	1702
CR		
CA	9 Nov	1729
d	13 June	1753 (PMM)
SPARKS, Thomas		
L	15 Oct	1812
CR	23 Apr	1846 (OB)
SPARLING, Thomas		
L		
CA		1660
d	before	1688 (PD)
SPARROW, Charles		
L	14 Nov	1790
SPARROW, Francis (1)		
L		
CA		1661
SPARROW, Francis (2)		
L	26 June	1807
SPARROW, John		
L		1665
SPARROW, Meyrick Bodychen		
L	21 Apr	1813
d	Jan	1848 (OB)
SPARSHOTT, Edward		
L	28 Apr	1809
CR	29 Jan	1821 (OB)
CA	22 July	1830 (OB)
KH	19 Apr	1831 (OB)
SPARSHOTT, Samuel		
L	31 Aug	1809
CR	16 Oct	1818 (OB)
SPEAR, Joseph		
L	15 Oct	1790
CR	23 Oct	1799
CA	13 Apr	1809
d	14 Dec	1836 (PJP)
SPEAR, Richard		
L	29 Jan	1800
T		
CR	24 Dec	1805
CA	3 May	1813
d		1825 (TR)
SPEARING, George		
L	8 Sept	1757
d	24 Oct	1824 (PRO)
SPEARING, George Augustus		
L	6 Jan	1802
KIA	3 July	1808 (CH)
SPECIALL, Abraham		
L		1689 (PJP)
SPECK, William		
L	28 Feb	1809
CR	11 Jan	1843 (OB)
SPEKE, Henry		
L	2 Nov	1745
CR	8 June	1749
CA	20 Jan	1754
d	17 Nov	1760
SPELMAN, James		
L	22 May	1709 (PMM)
SPENCE, Charles		
L	7 June	1802
SPENCE, David		
L	7 Aug	1794
SPENCE, George		
L	3 Mar	1804
SPENCE, Henry Francis		
T		
L	21 Mar	1812
CR		1854 (TR)
d		1856 (TR)
SPENCE, Henry Hume		
L	1 Nov	1797
CR	28 May	1806
CA	24 Aug	1809
d	26 Jan	1842 (LT)
SPENCE, John		
L	21 June	1744
SPENCE, Thomas		
L	6 June	1794
SPENCE, William		
L	1 Feb	1802
SPENCER, Christopher		
L	21 Sept	1795
SPENCER, George Allen		
L	19 June	1794
SPENCER, Henry		
L	6 Apr	1778
SPENCER, Michael		
L	10 Apr	1802

SPENCER, Sir Richard
L 8 Jan 1801
CR 20 Apr 1808
CA 7 Feb 1812
CB 8 Dec 1815 (LG)
KH 1833 (DUB)
d 24 July 1839 (DUB)

SPENCER, Hon. Sir Robert Cavendish
L 13 Dec 1810
CR 22 Jan 1813
CA 4 June 1814
KCH 24 Nov 1828 (DNB)
d 4 Nov 1830 (DNB)

SPENCER, Samuel (1)
L 21 Jan 1742
CR 15 Oct 1756
CA 3 June 1757
d 1795

SPENCER, Samuel (2)
T
L 18 Oct 1806
d 1850 (TR)

SPENDELOW, Charles
L 1 May 1752

SPENDER, Richard
L 1666
d before 1689 (PJP)

SPENDLOVE, Samuel
L 28 May 1747
d 12 Dec 1787 (M)

SPEPRARD, John
L 2 Feb 1813

SPICER, John
L 9 Apr 1760

SPICER, Peter
L 7 Mar 1794
CR 8 Mar 1797
CA 29 Apr 1802
d 21 Oct 1830 (PMM)

SPICER, Robert
L 3 Nov 1790
d July 1794 (LT)

SPICER, William
L 13 Jan 1758

SPIEKER, Gustavus Joachim
L 16 Jan 1796

SPIERS, William
L 3 Jan 1811
HP Apr 1814 (OB)

SPILLER, James
L 10 May 1812

SPILLER, John
L 11 Jan 1746

SPILSBURY, Francis Brockell
L 27 Dec 1805
CR 8 Mar 1813
CA 19 Sept 1815

SPILSBY, George
L
CA 1672

SPINKS, James
L 16 Apr 1806

SPLAINE, Timothy
L 1 May 1694
CR 13 Mar 1711

SPOONER, Henry
L 1702 (PJP)

SPRAGG, Sir Edward
L
CA 1661
CAGA (Portsmouth) 1661 (EAD)
Kt 24 June 1665
VAB 8 June 1666 (RM)
VAD 1669
VAR 3 Apr 1672 (NJ)
AB 8 Apr 1672 (NJ)
AD 1670
MP (Dover) 1–6 Feb 1673 (MPH)
MP (Dover) 11 Feb–11 Aug 1673 (MPH)
KIA 11 Aug 1673 (DNB)

SPRAGG, John
L 20 Nov 1677

SPRAGG, Thomas
L 22 Jan 1678
CA 17 Sept 1683

SPRAGGE, Edward
L 12 Nov 1729
CR 28 Aug 1742
CA 11 June 1744
d 29 Jan 1757 (M)

SPRAGGE, Thomas
L
CA 3 Apr 1685

SPRALVE, J.
L 1736 (PRO)

SPRANGER, John William
L 23 Aug 1790
CR 7 June 1794
CA 24 Nov 1795 (CH)
RAB 4 June 1814
RAW 12 Aug 1819 (CH)

SPRANGER, Robert Walter
L
CR
CA 24 Nov 1795

SPRATT, James
T wounded
L 24 Dec 1805
Ret CR 17 July 1838 (OB)
d 15 June 1853 (DNB)

SPREAD, John Mathias
L 3 Nov 1790
CR 21 June 1798
d 1847 (OB)

SPRENT, George
L 17 Dec 1812
d 2 Mar 1816 (PJP)

SPRIDDLE, Henry
L 26 Dec 1782
d 15 Mar 1790

SPRIGGS, John
L 10 Apr 1778

SPRINGTHORPE, William
L 20 Dec 1776

SPROTT, James Walter
L 29 May 1810
d 22 Dec 1810 (PJP)

SPROULE, Andrew
L 13 Apr 1782

CR	22 May	1797
CA	28 Apr	1802
SPROULE, Benjamin		
L	7 Apr	1801
SPROULE, Thomas		
L	30 Aug	1780
SUP CR	3 Nov	1815
SPRY, John Tooker		
L	17 July	1813
SPRY, Sir Richard		
L	27 Sept	1740
CR	21 Sept	1744 (DNB)
CA	23 Sept	1745
RAB	18 Oct	1770
RAW	24 Oct	1770 (CH)
Kt	24 June	1773 (DNB)
RAR	31 Mar	1775
d	1 Dec	1775 (M)
SPRY, Thomas (1)		
L	1 Dec	1777
SUP CR	12 Apr	1813
SPRY, Thomas (2)		
Formerly DAVEY, Thomas		
L	16 May	1769
CR	29 July	1772
CA	5 May	1778
RAW	1 June	1795
VAB	14 Feb	1799
VAW	1 Jan	1801
VAR	23 Apr	1804
AB	9 Nov	1805
AW	25 Oct	1809
AR	4 June	1814
d	27 Nov	1828 (CH)
SPURIN, John		
L	10 Oct	1815 (OB)
SPURLING, Thomas		
L	1 Apr	1748
SPURWAY, John		
L	8 July	1814
HP	1 June	1815 (OB)
SQUAREY, Charles		
L	27 Nov	1801
T		
d		1820 (TR)
SQUIBB, Charles		
L	5 Feb	1695
SQUIRE, Charles		
L	26 Nov	1802
CR	4 Dec	1811
Ret CA	9 Aug	1843 (OB)
d	Oct	1855 (PMM)
SQUIRE, George		
L	19 Mar	1694
SQUIRE, Henry		
L	26 Apr	1797
SQUIRE, Matthew (1)		
L	12 Jan	1741
CR	June	1745 (PJP)
SQUIRE, Matthew (2)		
L	20 Sept	1765
CR	21 Jan	1771
CA	6 Nov	1779
RAB	1 June	1795
RAR	14 Feb	1799
d	22 Jan	1800
STACE, Thomas		
L	10 Nov	1760
STACEY, Tuson		
L	10 June	1735
STACY, Gabriel		
L		
CA		1667
STACKPOOLE, Edmund		
L	22 Jan	1806
STACKPOOLE, Hassard		
L	8 Feb	1795
CR	12 Mar	1800
CA	29 Apr	1802
d (duel)	28 Apr	1814 (LT)
STACKPOOLE, Michael		
L	23 Jan	1812
CR	7 Dec	1818 (MB)
d	Jan	1847 (OB)
STAFFORD, Israel		
L	22 Sept	1709
SUP	18 Oct	1743 (PMM)
d		1756 (PMM)
STAGG, William		
L	24 Aug	1780
d	9 Jan	1815 (PJP)
STAGGINS, Charles		
L	1 Aug	1682
CA	22 Feb	1690
KIA	12 July	1691 (CH)
STAINES, Sir Thomas		
L	3 July	1796
CR	26 July	1802
CA	22 Jan	1806
Kt (Two Sicilies)	21 Nov	1809 (LG)
Kt	6 Dec	1809 (DNB)
KCB	2 Jan	1815 (DNB)
d	13 July	1830 (DNB)
STAINFORTH, George		
L	11 Sept	1761
CR	25 Oct	1809
d		1810 (PJP)
STAINS, Robert		
L	17 Feb	1757
STAINSBY, John		
L		
CR		1664
STALLARD, Barrow		
L	13 Mar	1734
STAMP, Thomas		
L	24 Dec	1796
CR	23 Dec	1809
CA	7 June	1814
STANBURY, Philip		
L	17 Feb	1815
STANBURY, William		
L	4 Feb	1815
STANCOMBE, George		
L	25 July	1745
CR	17 Nov	1747
STANDISH, Edward		
L		1667
STANDISH, George		
L	20 Aug	1697
STANDISH, Ralph		
L	9 Jan	1802
STANDLY, Robert		
L	29 Apr	1807
CR	6 Dec	1813
d (drowned)	30 Sept	1814 (JH)

STANDSBURY, T.		
L		1799 (PJP)
STANFELL, Francis		
L	31 July	1795
CR	4 Feb	1803
CA	19 Mar	1810
STANFORD, William		
L	28 Aug	1759
STANHOPE, Alexander		
L		1693 (PJP)
STANHOPE, Arthur		
L	21 July	1773
STANHOPE, Charles		
L		1705 (PJP)
STANHOPE, Sir Edwyn Francis		
L	9 Oct	1811
CR	27 Aug	1814
HP	27 Aug	1814 (OB)
Inh Bt		1821 (MB)
STANHOPE, Henry		
L	30 Dec	1811
CR	27 June	1814
CA	26 Dec	1822 (MB)
Ret CA	31 Oct	1846 (LG)
STANHOPE, Hon. Sir Henry Edwyn		
L	10 Mar	1777
CR	6 Aug	1779
CA	16 June	1781
RAB	1 Jan	1801
RAR	23 Apr	1804
VAB	9 Nov	1805
Cre Bt	3 Nov	1807 (LG)
VAW	28 Apr	1808
AB	12 Aug	1812
d	20 Dec	1814 (OB)
STANHOPE, John		
L	15 Oct	1762
CR	4 June	1774
CA	5 Mar	1779
RAB	1 June	1795
RAR	14 Feb	1799
d	1 Dec	1800 (LT)
STANHOPE, Michael		
L	25 Jan	1778
Dismissed	Aug	1783 (PJP)
STANHOPE, Philip		
L		
CR		
CA	7 Nov	1704
KIA	17 Oct	1708 (CH)
STANHOPE, Sir Thomas		
L	26 Aug	1740
CR		
CA	12 July	1745
Kt	5 Oct	1759 (LG)
CRM	21 Oct	1762 (AL)
d	7 Mar	1770
STANHOPE, William Spencer		
L	17 Aug	1812
STANLEY, Edward (1)		
L		1681
CA	2 Mar	1683
STANLEY, Edward (2)		
L		
CA	1 Sept	1688
d	19 Mar	1693
STANLEY, Henry		
L	6 Nov	1793
STANLEY, John		
L	15 May	1705
CR		
CA	26 July	1728
d	29 June	1740 (M)
STANLEY, Peter		
L		1671 (PJP)
STANLEY, William Pearce		
L	15 Aug	1806
CR	19 July	1821 (MB)
CA	28 June	1838 (OB)
STANNIS, James		
L	6 Feb	1815
STANSBURY, Thomas		
L	14 Aug	1795
STANTON, Anthony Collins		
L	11 Jan	1802
CR	27 Aug	1814
d	18 May	1831 (LT)
STANTON, James		
L	5 Oct	1802
Ret CR	18 Apr	1835 (OB)
d	Jan	1848 (OB)
STANTON, John		
L	14 Feb	1746
CR		
CA	4 Mar	1758
d	24 Aug	1796 (LT)
STAP, William		
L	25 Apr	1783
CR	10 Apr	1794
CA	21 June	1797
STAPLEDON, Arthur		
L	25 Dec	1795
d		1833 (PJP)
STAPLES, John		
L		1694 (PMM)
STAPLES, William		
L	3 Nov	1790
STAPLES, William Conolly		
L	3 Nov	1790
CR	30 July	1795
STAPLETON, John		
L		
CA	26 Sept	1694
d (drowned)	20 Dec	1694 (CH)
STAPLETON, Miles		
L	4 Apr	1720
CR		1725 (PRO)
CA	20 June	1728
SUP RA	July	
d		1750
STAPLETON, Robert		
L		
CA	13 Jan	1693
d	20 Dec	1702
STAPLETON, William		
L		1754 (PJP)
STARCK, Mauritius Adolphus Newton de		
L	20 Nov	1790
CR	1 May	1804
CA	25 Sept	1806
RAB	23 Nov	1841 (LG)
RAW	9 Nov	1846 (LG)
RAR	3 Jan	1848 (LG)
d	4 Sept	1848 (LG)

STARK, John
L 22 June 1776
d 13 Mar 1793
STARK, Peter
L 6 July 1814
STARR, John
L 5 May 1762
d 24 July 1801
STAUNTON, John
See STANTON, John
STAYNER, Sir Richard
L
CA 1660
RAF 16 Apr 1660
Kt 24 Sept 1660 (DNB)
RAD 1661
VAF Apr 1662
d 15 Oct 1662 (AJ)
STEAD, Thomas Fisher
L 27 Feb 1815
STEANE, John
L 18 Feb 1815
CR 22 Nov 1841 (OB)
HP 22 Nov 1841 (OB)
STEDMAN, George William
L 10 Dec 1802
d 24 Nov 1803 (PJP)
STEDDY, John
L 25 Oct 1815
STEEDMAN, William
L 30 July 1762
STEEL, John
L 8 Apr 1784 (PRO)
STEEL, Robert
L 5 Apr 1760
STEELE, Elmes
L 26 Mar 1805
Ret CR 25 Apr 1838 (OB)
STEELE, George (1)
L 27 Feb 1794
d (drowned) Feb 1806 (CH)
STEELE, George (2)
L 21 Apr 1794
STEELE, Henry Perin
L 22 Nov 1815
HP 12 Mar 1816 (OB)
STEELE, John
L
CA 1670
STEELE, Joseph
L 24 Jan 1811
d 1848 (OB)
STEENBERGEN, James
L 8 May 1807
STEEVENS, Charles
L 12 Mar 1729
CR 25 Mar 1741 (DNB)
CA 11 Jan 1742
RAB 6 July 1758 (DNB)
RAR 1759
d 17 May 1761 (DNB)
STENHOUSE, William
L 7 Jan 1802
STENT, Thomas Payne
L 3 July 1781

STEPHEN, John
L 23 Feb 1815
CR 9 Nov 1846 (OB)
HP 1846 (OB)
STEPHENS, Daniel
L
CA 1666
STEPHENS, Edward
L 11 Mar 1796
CR 11 Apr 1817 (MB)
STEPHENS, George Hopewell
L 17 Apr 1778
CR 7 Feb 1794
CA 11 Oct 1794
RAB 4 Dec 1813
RAW 4 June 1814
RAR 12 Aug 1819 (CH)
d 25 Dec 1819 (CH)
STEPHENS, John (1)
L
CA 1661
STEPHENS, John (2)
L 12 Dec 1694
d (drowned) 22 Oct 1707 (PJP)
STEPHENS, John (3)
L 5 Feb 1695
d (drowned) 26 Nov 1703 (PJP)
STEPHENS, Nathaniel
L 17 Aug 1742
CR 21 July 1745
CA 1 Feb 1746
d 23 Mar 1748
STEPHENS, Philip
Formerly WILKINSON
L Oct 1790
CR 30 Mar 1794
CA 5 Sept 1794
RAB 4 Dec 1813
RAW 4 June 1814
RAR 12 Aug 1819 (LG)
VAB 19 July 1821 (LG)
VAW 27 May 1825 (LG)
VAR 22 July 1830 (LG)
AB 10 Jan 1837 (LG)
AW 23 Nov 1841 (LG)
AR 9 Nov 1846 (LG)
d 1846 (OB)
STEPHENS, Robert
L 25 June 1695 (PJP)
STEPHENS, Stephen
L 20 June 1762
CR 25 Oct 1809
STEPHENS, William
L 25 Apr 1800
CR 4 Jan 1808
CA 7 Oct 1813
STEPHENS, William James
L 12 June 1779
d 14 Aug 1779
STEPHENSON, Edward
L 22 Dec 1706 (PMM)
STEPHENSON, John (1)
L 9 Jan 1697 (PJP)
STEPHENSON, John (2)
L 19 Feb 1800

STEPHENSON, Thomas (1)
L 21 Apr 1778
CR 7 Mar 1798
CA 24 Dec 1798
d 23 Jan 1809 (PMM)

STEPHENSON, Thomas (2)
L 24 Aug 1814

STEPHENSON, William
L 6 Mar 1703 (PMM)
CR 25 Feb 1712

STEPNEY, George
L 25 Oct 1728
CR
CA 11 June 1743
d 24 May 1753

STEPNEY, John
L 25 July 1711

STEPNEY, Rowland
L 1665
CA 1672
d before 1689 (PJP)

STEPNEY, Thomas
L
CA 10 Jan 1693 (PJP)
d 1738 (PJP)

STEPPING, Isaac
L 2 Sept 1710 (PMM)

STERLING, Charles
L 15 Oct 1812

STERLING, Christopher Carleton
L 16 Mar 1801
CR 21 June 1804
KIA 7 July 1809 (LG)

STERLING, James
L 20 May 1811

STERLING, Samuel
L 10 May 1678

STERLING, Walter
See STIRLING, Sir Walter

STERNE, William
L 23 Aug 1813

STEUART, Hew
L 28 June 1799
CR 22 Jan 1806
Kt (Russia) 1812 (SPB)
CA 20 Nov 1812
Dismissed Dec 1816 (PJP)
d 15 June 1837 (LT)

STEUART, James (1)
L
CA 17 Feb 1692
d 27 Feb 1705

STEUART, James (2)
L
CR
CA 14 Jan 1709
MP 1741–
(Weymouth and Melcombe Regis) 1747 (MPS)
RAB 10 Apr 1742 (LG)
RAW 11 Aug 1743 (LG)
VAR 23 June 1744 (LG)
AW 15 July 1747 (LG)
AF 1750
d 30 Mar 1757 (MPS)

STEUART, James (3)
L 23 Dec 1814
d 12 Apr 1820 (PJP)

STEVEN, John
L 1 Dec 1787
CR 22 Oct 1798
d Dec 1802 (PJP)

STEVENS, Andrew
L 11 Jan 1728

STEVENS, Charles
See STEEVENS, Charles

STEVENS, Charles
L 13 Mar 1815

STEVENS, Daniel
L 9 June 1796

STEVENS, James
L 24 June 1745
Quit 3 July 1754 (PMM)

STEVENS, James Agnew
L 7 July 1812
CR 4 May 1842 (OB)

STEVENS, John (1)
L 14 Apr 1707 (PMM)

STEVENS, John (2)
L
CR
CA 10 Aug 1716
d 3 Nov 1731

STEVENS, John (3)
L 10 June 1779
SUP CR 31 Jan 1814

STEVENS, Richard (1)
L 12 Apr 1720

STEVENS, Richard (2)
L 12 Feb 1759
d (drowned) 5 Oct 1780 (PJP)

STEVENS, Robert
L
CA 13 Aug 1694
d 24 Feb 1704 (PMM)

STEVENS, Thomas (1)
L 9 Jan 1697

STEVENS, Thomas (2)
L 21 Oct 1795

STEVENS, William
L 11 May 1757
CR 25 Jan 1780
CA 2 Jan 1782
d 1 Mar 1782 (PRO)

STEVENSON, Charles Goude
L 27 Oct 1808
HP Nov 1809 (OB)
Ret CR 20 Apr 1846 (OB)

STEVENSON, Edward
L 22 Jan 1806

STEVENSON, Henry
L 10 Apr 1778
d (drowned) 1779 (PJP)

STEVENSON, James (1)
L 16 Nov 1790
CR 7 Sept 1795
CA 15 Feb 1797
d 10 May 1818 (PJP)

STEVENSON, James (2)
L 11 June 1798
CR 22 Jan 1806

CA 27 Feb 1812
Ret RA 31 Oct 1846 (LG)
STEVENSON, John
L 23 Sept 1777
SUP CR 5 May 1812
STEVENSON, Joseph
L 15 June 1757
SUP CR 21 Sept 1796 (PMM)
d 26 Nov 1799 (PMM)
STEVENSON, Neal
L 7 July 1783
STEVENSON, Thomas
L 1701 (PJP)
STEVENSON, William (1)
L 29 Jan 1807
STEVENSON, William (2)
L 13 Sept 1813
STEVENSON, William Perryman
L 5 Aug 1807
STEVENTON, Robert
L 1807 (PJP)
STEVENTON, Thomas
L 31 May 1799
STEWARD, Alexander
L 19 Nov 1694 (PJP)
STEWARD, Hon. Archibald
See STUART, Hon. Archibald
STEWARD, Hon. Charles
L 1698 (PMM)
d 5 Feb 1741 (PJP)
STEWARD, Francis
L
CA 1665
STEWARD, James Pattison
L 7 June 1808
STEWARD, John (1)
L 1664
CA 1665
STEWARD, John (2)
L 24 Mar 1696
STEWARD, John (3)
See SEWARD, John
STEWARD, Samuel
L 18 Oct 1758
d 13 Feb 1795 (M)
STEWART, Allan
L 29 Aug 1799
CR 15 June 1814
STEWART, Alexander
L 30 Jan 1731
CR 30 June 1742
d (drowned) 10 Oct 1742 (PJP)
STEWART, Alexander George
L 9 Apr 1814
STEWART, Hon. Charles (1)
L 9 Jan 1703 (PMM)
CR
CA 1 Dec 1704
RAB 9 Dec 1729
RAW 29 June 1732
VAB 26 Feb 1734
VAW 2 Mar 1736
d 13 Aug 1740
STEWART, Charles (2)
L 7 Sept 1798
d 1833 (PJP)

STEWART, Edward
L 16 Mar 1805
CR 7 June 1814
d (drowned) 23 Dec 1823 (PJP)
STEWART, Edward Brenton
L 1 Sept 1814
CR 18 June 1844 (OB)
HP 1844 (OB)
STEWART, Francis
L 22 Sept 1740
STEWART, Frederick Augustus
L 25 Apr 1815
STEWART, Sir George (1)
L
CR 8 Nov 1710
d 3 Nov 1759 (M)
STEWART, George (2)
L 24 Mar 1807
d 1815 (PJP)
STEWART, Gordon
L 2 July 1807
STEWART, H.
L 1803 (PJP)
STEWART, Henry
L 24 Sept 1731
CR
CA 16 Apr 1743
d 7 Nov 1746
STEWART, Sir Houston
L 1 Aug 1811
CR 13 Aug 1814
CA 10 June 1817 (DNB)
CB 8 Dec 1840 (DNB)
MP 1850–
(Greenwich) 1852 (DNB)
COM AD 9 Feb 1850–
2 Mar 1852 (AO)
RA 16 June 1851 (DNB)
KCB 5 July 1855 (DNB)
VA 30 July 1857 (DNB)
A 10 Nov 1862 (DNB)
GCB 28 Mar 1865 (DNB)
AF 20 Oct 1872 (DNB)
d 10 Dec 1875 (DNB)
STEWART, James (1)
L
CA 31 May 1691 (PJP)
d 17 Feb 1705 (PJP)
STEWART, James (2)
L 1702 (PJP)
CR
CA 14 Jan 1709
RAB 6 Apr 1742
RAW 9 Aug 1743
VAB 7 Dec 1743
VAR 19 June 1744
AW 15 July 1747
AF 22 Nov 1751
d 30 Mar 1757
STEWART, James (3)
L 9 Nov 1756
STEWART, James (4)
L 27 May 1795
STEWART, James (5)
L 4 Mar 1797
CR 29 Apr 1802

STEWART, James (6)
L 1801 (PJP)
STEWART, James (7)
L 2 June 1809
STEWART, James (8)
L 14 May 1811
d 1836 (PJP)
STEWART, James (9)
L 4 Mar 1815
STEWART, James Pattison
L 21 Mar 1805
CR 15 Feb 1808
CA 1 Feb 1812
CB 8 Dec 1815
Ret RA 31 Oct 1846 (LG)
STEWART, John (1)
L 13 Oct 1720
STEWART, John (2)
L 20 Oct 1757
STEWART, John (3)
L 1 Apr 1760
STEWART, John (4)
L 22 Nov 1790
d 31 May 1794 (M)
STEWART, John (5)
L 1792 (PJP)
STEWART, John (6)
L 3 Nov 1795 (PMM)
CR 25 Dec 1800
CA 6 Aug 1801
d 25 Oct 1811 (LT)
STEWART, Hon. Keith
L 2 Jan 1759
CR 11 Feb 1761
MP (Wigtownburghs) 19 Feb 1762–Mar 1762 (MPN)
CA 7 Apr 1762
MP (Wigtownshire) 1768–July 1784 (MPN)
RAB 21 Sept 1790
RAR 1 Feb 1793
VAB 12 Apr 1794
VAW 4 July 1794
d 3 Mar 1795 (MPN)
STEWART, Levison Stewart
L 9 Sept 1806
STEWART, Peter
L 26 Feb 1805
CR 13 Oct 1807
STEWART, Robert (1)
L 8 Jan 1706 (PMM)
STEWART, Robert (2)
L 2 Apr 1746
STEWART, Thomas (1)
L 1704 (PJP)
STEWART, Thomas (2)
L 2 Apr 1804
STEWART, Thomas Dilnot
L 19 Sept 1815
CR 19 July 1843 (OB)
HP 19 July 1843 (OB)
STEWART, William (1)
L 1672 (PJP)
d before 1674 (PJP)
STEWART, William (2)
L 1 Jan 1712
d 9 Mar 1712 (PMM)
STEWART, William (3)
L 17 Mar 1741
d ? Feb 1759 (PMM)
STEWART, William (4)
L 22 Aug 1746
d ? Feb 1759 (PMM)
STEWART, William (5)
L 7 Feb 1764
STEWART, William (6)
L 15 May 1797
CR 30 May 1810
CA 23 July 1812
d 24 July 1814 (PRO)
STIDSON, George
L
CR 13 Oct 1705 (PMM)
STIDSON, William
L 13 Feb 1694 (PJP)
STIGANT, John
L 22 Sept 1709 (PMM)
STILES, John (1)
L 12 Sept 1781
CR 10 Apr 1797
CA 14 June 1799
RAW 22 July 1830 (LG)
d 6 Dec 1830 (LT)
STILES, John (2)
L 21 Mar 1812
STILES, John (3)
L 1815 (PJP)
STILES, Robert
L 8 Oct 1694
d 18 June 1739 (M)
STILES, Samuel C.
L 7 Feb 1812
STILES, Thomas
L 15 Nov 1692 (PJP)
STILL, William
L 7 Sept 1815
STILLING, Samuel
L 5 Nov 1793
d 16 Feb 1796 (LT)
STIMPSON, Philip
L 7 June 1808
STIRLING, Alexander
L 14 Oct 1796
Ret CR 26 Nov 1830 (OB)
STIRLING, Charles
L 12 June 1778
CR 15 May 1780
CA 15 Jan 1783
RAW 9 Nov 1805
RAR 28 Apr 1808
VAW 31 July 1810
Court Martialled and sentenced to remain on Half Pay list, and not to be included in any future promotions 9 May 1814
d 7 Nov 1833 (DNB)
STIRLING, James (1)
L 20 May 1812
CR 15 June 1814
CA 7 Dec 1818 (PJP)
STIRLING, Sir James (2)
L 12 Aug 1809
CR 15 June 1814

CA	7 Dec	1818 (DNB)
RA	8 July	1851 (DNB)
COM AD	13 Feb–2 Mar	1852 (AO)
VA	22 Aug	1857 (DNB)
A	22 Nov	1862 (DNB)
d	22 Apr	1865 (DNB)
STIRLING, Thomas		
L	20 Sept	1815
STIRLING, Sir Walter		
L	18 Feb	1746
CR	9 Dec	1756
CA	10 Jan	1759
Kt		1781 (DNB)
d	24 Nov	1786 (DNB)
STOAKES, John		
L		
CA		1660
d	11 Feb	1665 (DDA)
STOAKS, John		
L	20 Mar	1705
SUP	20 Mar	1738 (PMM)
STOCK, William		
L	7 July	1807
STOCKDALE, Charles Roddam		
L	8 May	1812
STOCKER, Charles Maurice		
L	8 May	1783
KIA	23 June	1795 (LG)
STOCKER, Stephen		
L	1 Feb	1815
HP	10 Aug	1846 (OB)
STOCKHAM, John		
L	29 Apr	1797
CR		
T		
CA	24 Dec	1805
d	6 Feb	1814 (PMM)
STODDART, George		
L	28 Mar	1777
STODDART, James Douglas		
L	15 June	1815
STODDART, John (1)		
L	30 July	1763
d	17 July	1803
STODDART, John (2)		
L	14 May	1804
CR	3 July	1812
CA	27 May	1825 (OB)
Ret CA	31 Oct	1846 (LG)
STODDART, Pringle		
In Russian Service		1786–1790 (PJP)
L	16 Apr	1796
CR	22 Jan	1806
CA	13 Oct	1807
RAB	23 Nov	1841 (LG)
RAW	19 Feb	1847 (LG)
d	29 Jan	1848 (OB)
STOKES, Edward		
L		1692 (PJP)
STOKES, Henry		
L	26 Apr	1808
d (drowned)	6 Dec	1808 (PJP)
STOKES, Humphrey		
L	27 Nov	1778
SUP CR	31 Jan	1814
STOKES, James		
L	19 Feb	1800
STOKES, John (1)		
L	19 June	1795
STOKES, John (2)		
L	31 Mar	1810
Becames second of the three Junior Lieutenants		1813
L	29 Oct	1814
STOKES, Pringle		
L	2 Mar	1815
CR		1825 (PJP)
d	Aug	1828 (PJP)
STOKES, Robert		
L		1689 (PMM)
STOKES, William Smith		
T		
L	1 Nov	1811
d		1826 (TR)
STOKOE, John		
L	5 Dec	1712
STOKOE, Thomas		
L	26 May	1804
KIA	10 Sept	1813 (PJP)
STOLLARD, Thomas		
L		
CA		1666
STOLY, James		
L	14 Mar	1815
STOMLEY, John		
L		1728 (PJP)
STONE, Charles		
L		1709 (PJP)
STONE, George (1)		
L	2 Feb	1741
STONE, George (2)		
L	16 Aug	1799
T		
Gone		1810 (TR)
STONE, James (1)		
L	31 Mar	1800
STONE, James (2)		
L	17 Mar	1806
STONE, James (3)		
L	26 Dec	1806
STONE, James (4)		
L	15 Feb	1815
STONE, John		
L	12 Dec	1776
CR	22 June	1781
CA	23 Aug	1781
d	29 June	1786 (M)
STONE, Thomas (1)		
L	17 Apr	1781
STONE, Thomas (2)		
L	23 Feb	1807
STONE, Thomas (3)		
L	29 Jan	1811
STONE, Valentine		
L	1 Feb	1815
STONE, William (1)		
L		
CA	16 July	1677
STONE, William (2)		
L		
CA	10 Sept	1688
d	29 Nov	1689
STONE, William (3)		
L	29 May	1801

STONE, William (4)
L 16 May 1812
STONEY, George
L 13 Apr 1761
CR 19 Nov 1778
CA 27 Feb 1781
d 1784
STOPFORD, Edward
L 1 May 1804
CR 28 Apr 1809
CA 18 Dec 1811
d 19 Apr 1837 (PJP)
STOPFORD, Hon. Philip
L 20 June 1765
STOPFORD, Sir Robert
L 15 July 1785
CR 2 June 1789
CA 12 Aug 1790
CRM 9 Nov 1805 (OB)
MP (Ipswich) 1806–1807 (MPT)
RAB 28 Apr 1808
RAW 25 Oct 1809
RAR 31 July 1810
VAB 12 Aug 1812
VAW 4 June 1814
KCB 12 Apr 1815 (LG)
VAR 12 Aug 1819 (LG)
AB 27 May 1825 (CH)
AW 22 July 1830 (CH)
GCB 6 June 1831 (DNB)
AR 10 Jan 1837 (LG)
GCMG 10 May 1837 (DNB)
GGH 1840–25 June 1847 (LT)
d 25 June 1847 (DNB)
STOPFORD, Thomas
L 20 Oct 1811
STOPFORD, William
L 25 Sept 1806
STORCK, Robert Henry
T
L 20 May 1812
d 4 Dec 1816 (PJP)
STORER, John
L 30 Oct 1739
STOREY, Edward
L
CR
CA 17 June 1709
d 14 June 1727
STOREY, James (1)
L 1665
CA 1667
LMR 10 Oct 1672 (EAD)
d before 1689 (PJP)
STOREY, James (2)
L 28 Apr 1810
HP Sept 1815 (OB)
STOREY, James (3)
L 1815 (PJP)
STOREY, Richard
L 15 Oct 1779
STOREY, Thomas
L 1707 (PJP)
STORR, John (1)
L
CR
CA
KIA 28 Feb 1758 (LG)
STORR, John (2)
L
CR 3 July 1746
CA 1 Nov 1748
RAW 19 Mar 1779
RAR 26 Sept 1780
d Jan 1783 (CH)
STORY, Edward
See STOREY, Edward
STORY, Francis
L 16 Jan 1802
STORY, John Fairfax
L 13 Apr 1782
STOTHER, John Meyrick
L 9 Nov 1808
Ret CR 27 Jan 1846 (OB)
STOTT, John
L 17 Feb 1757
CR 5 June 1757
CA 3 Aug 1758
KIA 22 Aug 1778 (CH)
STOUT, Joseph
L 29 Jan 1748
In Merchant Service 31 Aug 1749 (PMM)
STOUT, Robert
L 1665
CA 1668
d before 1689 (PJP)
STOUT, William
L 1689 (PJP)
STOVIN, George Charles
L 30 July 1810
STOVIN, George Samuel
L 21 Dec 1796
CR June 1800 (PJP)
d (drowned) 9 Oct 1800 (CH)
STOW, Arthur
L 27 June 1800
CR 7 Jan 1812
CA 17 May 1814
d 26 Sept 1820 (PMM)
STOW, Benjamin
L 13 Jan 1815
STOW, Charles Robert
L 31 Oct 1798
d (drowned) 26 Sept 1800 (PJP)
STOW, Daniel George
L 27 Nov 1809
STOW, David
L 16 Sept 1778
CR 10 Feb 1781
CA 1 Dec 1787
SUP RA 9 Oct 1807
Living 1816
STOYLE, John
L 23 Sept 1795
STRACHAN, James (1)
L 4 Mar 1740
STRACHAN, James (2)
L 5 Feb 1747
STRACHAN, Sir John
L Jan 1746 (DNB)
CR
CA 9 Sept 1756

Cre Bt 1765 (DNB)
d 26 Dec 1777 (DNB)

STRACHAN, Patrick
L 6 Apr 1757

STRACHAN, Sir Richard John
Inh Bt 1777 (PJP)
L 5 Apr 1779
CR Jan 1783
CA 26 Apr 1783
CRM 23 Apr 1804 (LG)
RAB 9 Nov 1805
KCB 29 Jan 1806 (DNB)
RAW 28 Apr 1808
RAR 25 Oct 1809
VAB 31 July 1810
VAW 12 Aug 1812
VAR 4 June 1814
GCB 2 Jan 1815 (LG)
AB 19 July 1821 (MB)
d 3 Feb 1828 (DNB)

STRACHEY, Christopher
L 15 Mar 1798
CR 29 Apr 1802
CA 28 June 1814
Kt (Russia) 20 Mar 1820 (LG)
Ret CA 31 Oct 1846 (LG)
Ret RA 24 June 1850 (LG)

STRACHEY, Thomas
L 13 Mar 1734
d 20 May 1740 (PMM)

STRANGE, Edmund
L 22 Mar 1727
CR
CA 14 Feb 1739
SUP RA 1755
d 10 Dec 1756

STRANGE, Thomas
L 15 Feb 1815
HP 15 Feb 1815 (OB)

STRANGUAGE, Edward
L 1666

STRANGWAYS, Charles
L 28 Oct 1809
CR 14 July 1815
CA 20 Apr 1827 (MB)

STRANGWAYS, George
L 16 Mar 1791
CR
CA 1827 (PJP)
d 1836 (PJP)

STRATFORD, Hon. Robert
L 25 Jan 1766
CR 27 Oct 1774

STRATFORD, William Samuel
L 14 Mar 1815
HP 14 Mar 1815 (OB)
d 29 Mar 1853 (DNB)

STRATON, Francis Richard (1)
L 15 Oct 1790

STRATON, Francis Richard (2)
L 26 Dec 1795
CR 11 June 1800
d 1800 (PJP)

STRATTON, Thomas
See STURTON, Thomas

STRAUGHAN, George
L
CA 1666

STREATFIELD, Richard
L 19 July 1809
CR 26 May 1814

STREATFIELD, Robert
L 27 Jan 1806
CR 13 June 1815

STREATE, Richard
L
CA 1660

STREET, Benjamin
L 16 July 1800
CR 4 Mar 1811

STREET, John (1)
L 14 May 1756
d 8 Aug 1767 (M)

STREET, John (2)
L 7 Mar 1803

STREET, Joseph
L 11 Apr 1794
d 1835 (PJP)

STRENGTHFIELD, Edmund
L 1715 (PJP)

STRETELL, Francis
L 1 Aug 1692 (PJP)

STRETTELL, William Thomas
L 24 Feb 1815

STREVINS, John Harris
L 11 Feb 1815

STRICKLAND, Charles
L 15 Jan 1694 (PJP)
CA 7 Aug 1696
RAW 16 Feb 1722 (C)
VAW 5 Feb 1723
d 11 Nov 1724

STRICKLAND, Robert
L 4 May 1810

STRICKLAND, Sir Roger
L 1661
CA 1666
CAMR 1 Oct 1672 (EAD)
Kt 1673
CAF 12 Oct 1673 (EAD)
(Widdrington)
RAD 19 Feb 1678
MP 1685 (MPH)
(Aldborough)
VAD 4 July 1687
VAF 24 Sept 1688
Resigned 13 Dec 1688 (EAD)
d 8 Aug 1717 (DNB)

STRINGER, John
L 23 Feb 1734
CR 13 May 1742
CA 16 Sept 1745
Dismissed 12 Jan 1748

STRINGER, Thomas
L 1702 (PJP)

STRODDER, George
L
CA 31 Oct 1682

STRODE, Sir Edward
Formerly CHEATHAM
L 18 Aug 1794
CR 7 Nov 1800
CA 17 Apr 1807

CB	8 Dec	1815 (LG)
KH	1 Jan	1837 (OB)
RAB	23 Nov	1841 (LG)
HP	23 Nov	1841 (OB)
KCB	8 Mar	1845 (OB)
RAW	10 Dec	1846 (LG)
RAR	4 May	1849 (LG)
VAB	19 Jan	1852 (CH)
A	22 Aug	1857 (CH)
d	11 Apr	1862 (CH)
STRONG, Charles Burrough		
L	25 Feb	1801
CR	14 Mar	1811
CA	12 Aug	1819 (MB)
d	8 Apr	1846 (OB)
STRONG, Samuel		
L	19 Dec	1807
STRONG, Thomas		
L	5 Feb	1806
STRONG, William		
L	18 July	1810
STRONGE, Charles		
L	9 Feb	1815
d		1835 (PJP)
STRONGFIELD, Edmund		
L		1710 (PJP)
STROUD, Henry		
L	9 Mar	1815
CR	28 June	1838 (OB)
CA	30 Oct	1841 (OB)
HP		1841 (OB)
STROVER, Samuel		
L	5 Feb	1814
STROVER, Thomas		
L	7 Aug	1812
STRUDWICK, William		
L	15 Nov	1776
CR	31 Dec	1779
STRUGNELL, James Alabaster		
L	29 Apr	1802
STRUGNELL, William Baker		
L	18 July	1814
STRUTT, Isaac		
L	18 May	1796
STRUTT, John		
L	24 Dec	1708
CR	1 Mar	1740
STUART, Hon. Archibald (1)		
L	20 Jan	1741
CR	5 Apr	1744 (PJP)
CA	20 Feb	1745
d		1795
STUART, Archibald (2)		
L	24 Sept	1761
KIA	16 Nov	1761 (LG)
STUART, Charles (1)		
L		1703 (PRO)
STUART, Charles (2)		
L	11 Jan	1746
STUART, Charles (3)		
L	31 Oct	1781
CR	2 Nov	1795
CA	19 Sept	1796
d	27 Apr	1814 (PJP)
STUART, Charles Francis		
L	4 May	1810
STUART, Hon. David		
L	15 Apr	1761
STUART, Sir George (1)		
L		1704 (PRO)
STUART, Lord George (2)		
L	21 Mar	1801
CR	22 Apr	1802
CA	3 Mar	1804
CB		1815 (PJP)
RAB	10 Jan	1837 (LG)
d	19 Feb	1841 (CH)
STUART, Henry (1)		
L		1779 (PJP)
STUART, Henry (2)		
L	30 Oct	1793
CR		
CA	16 Oct	1800
RAB	22 July	1830 (LG)
RAW	10 Jan	1837 (LG)
d	9 Apr	1840 (CH)
STUART, James, Duke of York (1) Later James II of England		
Cre EP	27 Jan	1644 (HBC)
COM AD	29 Jan	1661–
	15 June	1673 (AO)
AF		1665
Crowned King	6 Feb	1685 (HBC)
Deposed	11 Dec	1688 (HBC)
d	6 Sept	1701 (DNB)
STUART, James (2)		
L		1703 (PRO)
STUART, James (3)		
L	22 Aug	1797
T		
CR	24 Dec	1805
CA	4 Dec	1813
d		1838 (TR)
STUART, James (4)		
L	11 Oct	1814
CR	5 Jan	1846 (OB)
d	Aug	1847 (OB)
STUART, James (5)		
L	23 Dec	1814
STUART, James (6)		
L	23 Feb	1815
STUART, James Grant		
L	12 Sept	1806
STUART, John, Viscount (1)		
L	10 Dec	1759
STUART, John (2)		
L	12 Aug	1800
CR	18 Mar	1802
CA	6 Aug	1803
d	19 Mar	1811 (PJP)
STUART, Nathaniel (1)		
L	19 May	1745
KIA	19 Nov	1759 (PJP)
STUART, Nathaniel (2)		
L	3 Nov	1778
d		1798 (PJP)
STUART, Patrick		
L	25 Aug	1758
d	4 Dec	1797

STUART, Peter		
L	2 May	1793
d		1796 (LT)
STUART, Richard		
L	14 June	1809
CR	12 Mar	1827 (MB)
STUART, Robert		
L	21 Mar	1812
CR	17 July	1824 (MB)
CA	23 Nov	1841 (OB)
STUART, William (1)		
L		1672
Dismissed	16 Oct	1673 (PRO)
d		1675 (PMM)
STUART, Lord William (2)		
L	11 Oct	1797
CR	24 Dec	1798
CA	9 Nov	1799
MP		1802–
(Cardiff Boroughs)		1814 (MPT)
CB	4 June	1815 (LG)
d	25 July	1814 (MPT)
STUBBIN, John		
L	23 Feb	1815
STUDDERT, John Fitzgerald		
L	26 Jan	1811 (MB)
CR	12 Aug	1814
CA	10 Jan	1828 (MB)
HP	Aug	1828 (OB)
Ret CA		1848 (OB)
STUDDERT, Thomas		
L	1 Apr	1807
STUDLEY, James		
L		
CA	23 May	1696
d	28 May	1697 (CH)
STUDLEY, Robert		
L	24 Oct	1692
CR	1 July	1702 (PMM)
CA	11 Feb	1708
SUP		1716
d	23 Aug	1717
STUKELY, Charles		
L	8 Aug	1696
CR		
CA	1 July	1703
d	3 Apr	1720
STUPART, Gustavus		
L	12 Sept	1796
CR	29 Apr	1802
CA	21 Oct	1810
Ret RA	31 Oct	1846 (LG)
STUPART, Robert (1)		
L	8 Apr	1780
STUPART, Robert (2)		
L	8 Nov	1791
STURGESS, William		
L	20 Oct	1808
STURT, Henry Evelyn Pitfield		
L	20 Feb	1800
CR	29 Apr	1802
CA	21 Oct	1810
STURTON, Thomas		
L	2 July	1739
CR	15 Oct	1741 (PMM)
CA	28 Mar	1743
d	22 May	1754
STUTEVILLE, Charles		
L	12 Apr	1744
d	27 July	1773 (M)
STYLE, Thomas		
L	6 Oct	1809
CR	20 Sept	1815
STYLE, William		
L	15 Aug	1806
CR	1 Feb	1812
Ret CA	7 Feb	1844 (OB)
STYLES, John		
L	11 Sept	1793
STYLES, William		
L	5 Jan	1796
SUCKLING, Maurice		
L	8 Mar	1745
CR	3 Jan	1754
CA	2 Dec	1755
CONT	12 Apr	1775–
	14 July	1778 (NBO)
MP	18 May	1776–
(Portsmouth)	14 July	1778 (MPN)
d	14 July	1778 (MPN)
SUCKLING, Maurice William		
L	8 Mar	1794
SUCKLING, William Benjamin		
L	23 Oct	1809
CR	1 July	1814
HP		1829 (OB)
CA	23 Nov	1841 (OB)
SUDBURY, John		
L	17 Feb	1815
SULIVAN, Daniel Hunt		
T		
L	3 Feb	1815
d		1836 (TR)
SULIVAN, James Inglefield		
L	25 Feb	1815
SULIVAN, James Reading		
L	6 Apr	1815
SULIVAN, Samuel Hood		
T		
L	24 Nov	1808
d		1836 (TR)
SULIVAN, Thomas Ball		
L	26 Apr	1797
Jr Lt		1798
L	30 May	1800
CR	23 Feb	1807
CA	19 Oct	1814
CB	4 June	1815 (LG)
Ret CA	31 Oct	1846 (LG)
d	17 Nov	1857 (DNB)
SULLIVAN, Sir Charles		
L	25 Apr	1808
CR	24 Mar	1812
Cre Bt		1814 (CH)
CA	7 June	1814
RAB	15 Feb	1850 (LG)
VA	12 May	1857 (CH)
A	20 May	1862 (CH)
d	21 Nov	1862 (CH)
SULLOCK, George		
L	21 Mar	1812
SUMERS, John		
L	30 Apr	1678
CA		1673

SUMMERS, James
L 20 Sept 1796
SUMMERS, John
L 1689 (PJP)
SUMMERS, Thomas
L 1745 (PJP)
SUMPTER, Nicholas
L 28 Feb 1815 (OB)
SUMPTER, Robert (1)
L 1672
CA 1667
SUMPTER, Robert (2)
L 1689 (PJP)
SUNN, Isaac
L 22 Apr 1723
SUPPLE, Charles
L 1666
SURRIDGE, Thomas
L 9 June 1779
CR 19 Dec 1793
CA 1 Mar 1794
RAB 12 Aug 1812
RAW 4 Dec 1813
RAR 4 June 1814
VAB 12 Aug 1819 (CH)
SURTEES, George
L 17 Mar 1762
d ?7 Jan 1800
SUSSEX, Joseph
L 1750 (PJP)
SUTHERLAND, Andrew
L 28 Dec 1770
CR
CA 5 Dec 1780
d 18 July 1795 (LT)
SUTHERLAND, Donald
L 16 Nov 1776
SUTHERLAND, George Martin
L 3 July 1805
SUTHERLAND, Henry Erskine (1)
L 2 Feb 1801
SUTHERLAND, Henry Erskine (2)
L 31 Oct 1803
d 18 June 1806 (PJP)
SUTHERLAND, James
L 15 June 1757
d 1793 (PMM)
SUTHERLAND, John
L 13 Aug 1806
SUTHERLAND, Robert
L 22 Nov 1802
HP 1807 (OB)
SUTHERLAND, Thomas
L 7 July 1800
SUTTIE, Robert
L 11 May 1748
SUTTON, Charles
L 30 Apr 1678
SUTTON, Charles T.
L 27 May 1813
SUTTON, Evelyn
L 17 Nov 1765
CR 26 May 1768
CA 10 Jan 1771
SUP RA 17 Apr 1794
Living 1816
SUTTON, George Manners
L Aug 1803 (MB)
CR 22 Jan 1806
d 13 Jan 1836 (LT)
SUTTON, John (1)
L 2 Mar 1734
SUTTON, Sir John (2)
L 21 May 1778
CR 1781 (PJP)
CA 28 Nov 1782
RAB 23 Apr 1804
RAR 28 Apr 1808
VAB 25 Oct 1809
VAW 31 July 1810
VAR 4 Dec 1813
KCB 12 Apr 1815 (LG)
AB 12 Aug 1819 (MB)
AW 27 May 1825 (LG)
d 1825 (PJP)
SUTTON, Robert (1)
L 7 June 1776
KIA 8 Dec 1780 (LG)
SUTTON, Robert (2)
L 28 Oct 1803
SUTTON, Robert (3)
L 1 Aug 1811
SUTTON, Robert Manners
L
CR
CA 25 Aug 1779
d (drowned) Apr 1794 (JH)
SUTTON, Samuel
L 21 Apr 1783
CR July 1795 (PJP)
CA 27 June 1797
RAB 19 July 1821 (MB)
RAW 27 May 1825 (LG)
RAR 22 July 1830 (LG)
d 1832 (CH)
SUTTON, William
L 2 Nov 1815
d 1848 (OB)
SWAFFIELD, William
L 4 Mar 1780
CR 18 Nov 1790
CA 1 Nov 1793
KIA 22 Sept 1796 (JH)
SWAIN, Thomas
L 22 Apr 1802
Ret CR 26 May 1845 (OB)
SWAINE, Spelman
L 27 Oct 1795
CR 29 Apr 1802
CA 17 May 1810
Ret RA 31 Oct 1846 (LG)
d 14 Jan 1848 (OB)
SWAINE, Thomas
L 1672
CA 10 Oct 1688
d 4 June 1696
SWAINSON, William
L 13 June 1815
d 6 July 1850 (LT)
SWAINSTON, Francis
L 21 Aug 1745
SWALE, William
L 11 Mar 1719

CR 8 Feb 1731
CA 1 Sept 1731
d 8 Nov 1736

SWAN, J.A.
L 1796 (PJP)

SWAN, Nathaniel
L 24 July 1799

SWAN, Oliver
L 11 Feb 1815
HP Oct 1815 (OB)

SWANLEY, John
L
CA 1664

SWANLEY, Richard
L 1666
CA 1680

SWANLY, George
L
CA 1664

SWANN, John
L Apr 1688 (DDA)

SWANN, John Beardmore
L 20 Aug 1779

SWANTON, Robert
L 17 Jan 1735
CR
CA 27 Aug 1744
RAB 21 Oct 1762
d 1 Aug 1765 (CH)

SWANTON, Thomas (1)
L 1690 (MPS)
CA 8 May 1695
COMM 16 Apr 1715–
(Plymouth) 8 Aug 1716 (NBO)
CONT 23 Apr 1718–
17 Jan 1723 (NBO)
MP 1722–17 Jan 1723 (MPS)
(Saltash)
d 17 Jan 1723 (NBO)

SWANTON, Thomas (2)
L 9 May 1728
CR
CA 19 Feb 1741
d 12 Aug 1744 (PJP)

SWAYNE, Edward
L 1666

SWAYNE, John
L
CA 1667

SWAYNE, Thomas
See SWAINE, Thomas

SWAYSLAND, Henry
L 27 Apr 1718
CR
CA 22 Jan 1741
SUP RA 1756
d 19 Nov 1757 (M)

SWEEDLAND, Henry Johnson
L 25 Jan 1808
KIA 11 Dec 1813 (PJP)

SWEETLAND, Henry
L 8 Feb 1815
HP 8 Feb 1815 (OB)

SWENY, Mark Halpen
T wounded
L 22 Jan 1806

CR 19 July 1821 (MB)
HP June 1836 (OB)
CA 28 June 1838 (OB)
d 1865 (TR)

SWIFT, Thomas
L 15 May 1795

SWINBURN, William
L 18 Nov 1806

SWINBURNE, Thomas
L 16 May 1797
d (drowned) 20 Oct 1806 (PJP)

SWINEY, Noel
L 27 Nov 1793
d 1805 (PJP)

SWINEY, William (1)
L 10 Jan 1771
CR
CA 2 May 1779
RAB 20 Feb 1797
RAR 14 Feb 1799
VAB 1 Jan 1801
VAW 23 Apr 1804
VAR 9 Nov 1805
AB 28 Apr 1808
AW 31 July 1810
AR 12 Aug 1819 (LG)

SWINEY, William (2)
L 10 Sept 1799
Ret CR 1830 (CH)
d 1841 (CH)

SWINLEY, William
L
CR 30 May 1777

SWINTON, Samuel
L 29 Jan 1748
SUP CR 21 Sept 1796 (PMM)
d 1 Dec 1797 (PMM)

SYDDENHAM, Philip
L 16 May 1727

SYER, Dey Richard
T
L 2 Nov 1809
HP Dec 1815 (OB)
CR 1849 (TR)
d 1867 (TR)

SYFRETT, George James
L 1 Apr 1797

SYFRETT, William
L 4 Dec 1811

SYKES, Edmund
L 25 Sept 1806

SYKES, John (1)
L 6 Nov 1795
CR 18 June 1800
CA 22 Jan 1806
RAB 28 June 1838 (LG)
RAW 23 Nov 1841 (LG)
RAR 9 Nov 1846 (LG)
VAB 1 June 1848 (LG)
A 3 July 1855 (CH)
d 12 Feb 1858 (CH)

SYKES, John (2)
L July 1796 (MB)
CR 2 Nov 1814

SYKES, Thomas
L 14 Mar 1799 (PJP)

T
CR 9 Nov 1813
Ret CA 1851 (TR)

d 1855 (TR)

SYME, George
L 26 Oct 1813

SYME, William
L 6 Oct 1794
CR 16 Sept 1799

SYMES, Benjamin
L 5 Sept 1799

d 1804 (PJP)

SYMES, Joseph
T
L 13 Mar 1808
CR 13 Mar 1810
CA 21 Mar 1812
Ret RA 31 Oct 1846 (LG)

d 1856 (TR)

SYMES, Robert
L 28 June 1800

SYMES, Samuel
L 3 May 1777

SYMES, Thomas (1)
L 28 Apr 1757

d 8 Feb 1795 (LT)

SYMES, Thomas (2)
L 6 Feb 1815

SYMES, William Charles
L 21 Nov 1783

d 14 May 1790

SYMMERS, Thomas
L 21 June 1743

SYMMONDS, Thomas Edward
L 8 Oct 1802
CR 22 Jan 1806
CA 29 Sept 1813
Ret RA 31 Oct 1846 (LG)

SYMONDS, Benjamin
L 1666
CA 27 July 1666 (RM)

SYMONDS, C.
L 1803 (PJP)

SYMONDS, George
L
CA 19 Aug 1693
Dismissed 14 Feb 1698 (CH)

d 1704 (CH)

SYMONDS, James
L 25 Aug 1709

SYMONDS, Jermyn John
L 15 July 1780
CR 29 June 1795

d (drowned) 3 Nov 1796 (CH)

SYMONDS, John (1)
L
CA 11 Nov 1695 (PJP)

d 19 Jan 1707

SYMONDS, John (2)
L 30 Aug 1709

SYMONDS, John (3)
L 1779 (PJP)

SYMONDS, John Charles
L 11 Aug 1807
CR 16 Aug 1814

d 16 Dec 1840 (LT)

SYMONDS, Joseph
L
CA 1673 (PJP)

SYMONDS, Richard
L 2 Sept 1706
CR
CA 22 Feb 1729

d 23 Oct 1740 (PJP)

SYMONDS, Thomas (1)
L
CA 31 Aug 1690

d 26 Oct 1694

SYMONDS, Thomas (2)
L 22 Jan 1755
CR 18 Feb 1762
CA 18 Jan 1771

d 1793 (DNB)

SYMONDS, Thomas Edward
See SYMMONDS, Thomas Edward

SYMONDS, William (1)
L 1702 (PJP)

SYMONDS, Sir William (2)
L 14 Oct 1801
CR 4 Oct 1825 (DNB)
CA 5 Dec 1827 (DNB)
Kt 15 June 1836 (DNB)
Ret CA Oct 1847 (DNB)
Civil CB 1 May 1848 (DNB)
Ret RA 1854 (DNB)

d 30 Mar 1856 (DNB)

SYMONDS, William Ley
L 6 Oct 1801
Ret CR May 1832 (OB)

SYMONS, Christopher
L 20 Mar 1800

SYMONS, James (1)
L 26 Aug 1780

SYMONS, James (2)
L 16 Feb 1808
Dismissed 27 Oct 1811 (MB)
Restored 1813 (MB)
CR 17 Sept 1816 (MB)

d 1829 (MB)

SYMONS, John
L 24 Apr 1755
CR 15 Jan 1761
CA 28 Jan 1771
RAB 12 Apr 1794
RAR 4 July 1794
VAB 1 June 1795
VAR 14 Feb 1799

d 16 Dec 1799 (LT)

SYMONS, Nathaniel
L 13 Feb 1690 (PJP)
CA 4 May 1695 (PJP)

SYMONS, Thomas
L 26 Mar 1782

SYMONS, William Henry
T
L 22 Oct 1805
HP Sept 1834 (OB)
CR 1842 (TR)

d Nov 1851 (TR)

SYMONS, William Joseph
L 23 June 1796

Name / Rank	Date	Year
Ret CR	30 Aug	1837 (OB)
d	22 Jan	1845 (OB)
SYMPSON, William		
L	17 June	1779
d	5 Aug	1798
TAAFF, John		
L	23 Nov	1744
d	19 Sept	1773 (M)
TAASE, John		
L	16 Aug	1748
TACKLE, Charles Solomon		
L	28 Nov	1806
TAHOURDIN, William		
L	20 Nov	1776
CR	27 July	1781
CA	20 Jan	1783
d	1 May	1804
TAILOUR, John		
See also TAYLEURE, John		
L	8 July	1797
CR	1 Nov	1809
CA	26 Oct	1813
TAIT, Alexander		
L	1 June	1814
CR	9 July	1825 (MB)
TAIT, Dalhousie		
L	28 Jan	1806
KIA	1 Nov	1809 (LG)
TAIT, George		
L	5 Aug	1800
TAIT, James		
L	31 July	1802
TAIT, James Haldane		
L	6 July	1796
CR	29 Apr	1802
CA	5 Sept	1806
RAB	23 Nov	1841 (LG)
d	7 Aug	1845 (OB)
TAIT, Peter		
L	27 Oct	1758
SUP CR	18 July	1800 (PMM)
d	27 Mar	1830 (PMM)
TAIT, Robert		
L	13 Dec	1813
CR	7 Dec	1819 (MB)
CA	17 Apr	1827 (MB)
Ret CA		1847 (OB)
TALBOT(T), Charles		
L		1661
CA		1664
d	before	1688 (PD)
TALBOT, Francis		
L	14 Oct	1795
TALBOT, George		
L	19 Feb	1756
CR	19 May	1761
CA	26 May	1768
d		1787
TALBOT, Gilbert		
L	1 Feb	1697
TALBOT, James Hugh		
L	4 Apr	1796
d		1817 (PJP)
TALBOT, Sir John		
L	3 Nov	1790
CR	17 Apr	1795
CA	27 Aug	1796
CRM	4 June	1814 (MB)
KCB	12 Apr	1815 (LG)
RAB	12 Aug	1819 (LG)
RAW	19 July	1821 (LG)
RAR	27 May	1825 (LG)
VAB	22 July	1830 (LG)
VAR	10 Jan	1837 (LG)
AB	23 Nov	1841 (LG)
GCB	23 Feb	1842 (DNB)
AW	9 Nov	1846 (LG)
d	7 July	1851 (DNB)
TALBOT, Sherington		
L	17 Sept	1688
TALMACH, William		
See TOLLEMACHE, William		
TALMARSH, William		
L		
CA	13 Dec	1688
d	25 Mar	1691
TAMM, Charles		
L	11 Feb	1812
TAMPLIN, William		
L	15 Feb	1803
TANCOCK, John (1)		
L		1666
TANCOCK, John (2)		
L	9 Mar	1799
CR	15 Aug	1806
CA	1 Feb	1812
Ret RA	31 Oct	1846 (LG)
TANCOCK, Samuel		
L	15 Mar	1815
TANCRED, Charles		
L		1800 (PJP)
d (drowned)	16 Jan	1800 (PJP)
TANCRED, John		
L		1690 (PJP)
TANDY, Daniel		
L	22 Nov	1790
Ret CR	13 Apr	1825 (OB)
d	26 Jan	1848 (OB)
TANDY, James		
L	2 Feb	1815
d		1835 (PJP)
TANES, C.		
L		1808 (PJP)
KIA	15 Mar	1808 (PJP)
TANNER, John		
L		
CA	23 Aug	1666 (RM)
TAPLEN, Thomas		
L	18 Oct	1802
TAPLIN, John		
L	15 Feb	1815
TAPP, William		
L	14 May	1794
Ret CR	3 Mar	1831 (PMM)
d	7 Dec	1834 (PMM)
TAPPEN, Samuel		
L	4 Dec	1806
d	28 Feb	1811 (PJP)

Name / Rank	Date	Year
TAPPER, William		
L	20 Sept	1806
TAPSON, George		
L	20 Mar	1738 (PMM)
In Merchant Service		1700 (PJP)
d		1750 (PMM)
TAPSON, Richard (1)		
L		1672
CA	9 Aug	1673
d	before	1689 (PJP)
TAPSON, Richard (2)		
L	15 Sept	1678
d	before	1689 (PJP)
TARDREW, George		
T		
L	26 Apr	1811
Ret CR		1852 (TR)
d		1871 (TR)
TARPLEY, John		
See TORPLEY, John		
TATAM, William		
L	27 Nov	1800
TATERSELL, Nicholas		
L		
CA		1660
d	26 July	1674 (DDA)
TATE, Matthew		
L	13 Feb	1691
CR	8 July	1702 (PMM)
CA	21 Apr	1704
SUP		1711
d	20 Mar	1712
TATHAM, Sandford		
L	6 Dec	1776
CR	21 Sept	1790
CA	4 Nov	1794
SUP RA	7 Dec	1813
d	24 Jan	1840 (LT)
TATHAM, Thomas		
L	10 Sept	1759
TATHAM, William		
L	27 June	1793
TATHWELL, Joseph		
L	19 June	1756
CR	25 June	1773
TATLOCK, James Thomas		
L	21 Mar	1812
HP	July	1815 (OB)
TATNELL, Valentine		
L		
CA		1660
TATON, Bellew		
L	21 Feb	1744
TATTERSALL, Edmund		
L	7 Nov	1806
TATTERSALL, Nicholas		
See TATERSELL, Nicholas		
TATTNALL, James Barnwell		
L	18 Apr	1811
CR	14 Apr	1819 (MB)
TATTUM, John		
L	20 Oct	1757
TAUNTON, John Joseph		
L	1 Apr	1779
d	23 Jan	1787 (PMM)
TAUSE, Charles		
L	26 Feb	1806
TAVENER, David		
L		1702 (PMM)
TAYLER, George Robert		
L	20 Feb	1815
HP		1827 (OB)
TAYLER, Joseph		
L	17 Feb	1815
TAYLER, Joseph Needham		
L	29 Apr	1802
CR	27 Aug	1810
CA	16 Aug	1813
CB	8 Dec	1815 (LG)
Ret RA	10 Oct	1846 (DNB)
d	18 Mar	1864 (DNB)
TAYLEURE, John		
See also TAILOUR, John		
L	30 July	1778
SUP CR	31 Jan	1814
TAYLOR, Andrew Bracey		
L	5 Apr	1782
d	22 Jan	1800
TAYLOR, Bridges Watkinson		
L	23 Jan	1799
CR	17 Oct	1799
CA	31 Aug	1802
d (drowned)		1814 (CH)
TAYLOR, Charles (1)		
L	28 Nov	1810
TAYLOR, Charles (2)		
L	28 Feb	1815
HP	28 Feb	1815 (OB)
TAYLOR, Hon. Clotworthy		
L	21 Sept	1790
TAYLOR, Edward Samuel		
L	18 Feb	1815
TAYLOR, Fletcher le Fleming		
L	15 Aug	1800
TAYLOR, George		
L	21 May	1798
TAYLOR, Henry (1)		
L		1672
TAYLOR, Henry (2)		
L	17 Mar	1806
CR	15 June	1814
TAYLOR, Henry Packhurst		
L	6 Feb	1815
d	July	1819 (LT)
TAYLOR, James		
L	3 Dec	1783
TAYLOR, John (1)		
L		
CA		1660 (PJP)
TAYLOR, John (2)		
L	2 May	1759
TAYLOR, John (3)		
L	5 Jan	1799
CR	13 Oct	1807
Dismissed		1814 (PJP)
Restored		1818 (PJP)
d		1843 (PMM)
TAYLOR, John (4)		
L	2 Apr	1806
Ret CR	23 July	1839 (OB)
TAYLOR, John (5)		
L	25 Mar	1809

TAYLOR, John (6)
L 21 Mar 1812
TAYLOR, Joseph (1)
L 27 Aug 1694 (PJP)
CR
CA 15 Feb 1703
d 23 May 1734 (DCB)
TAYLOR, Joseph (2)
L 30 Sept 1795
KIA 23 Mar 1801 (JH)
TAYLOR, Joseph Needham
See TAYLER, Joseph Needham
TAYLOR, Michael
L 10 Jan 1741
d 30 Oct 1758 (PMM)
TAYLOR, Nathaniel
L 17 Sept 1695
CR 13 Sept 1707
TAYLOR, Polycarpus
L 4 May 1733
CR 21 June 1739
CA 2 May 1743
SUP RA 1762
d 1780 (M)
TAYLOR, Robert (1)
L
CA 1664
TAYLOR, Robert (2)
L 13 Mar 1740
CR 21 Sept 1759
TAYLOR, Samuel
L 7 July 1745
CR 2 Mar 1759
d 6 June 1790 (LT)
TAYLOR, Thomas (1)
L
CA 25 Nov 1693
KIA 4 Jan 1695 (CH)
TAYLOR, Thomas (2)
L 29 Nov 1745
CR 17 Aug 1756
CA 3 Mar 1757
d 1797
TAYLOR, Thomas (3)
L 9 July 1778
CR 18 Apr 1780 (PMM)
CA 27 May 1780
RAW 14 Feb 1799
RAR 1 Jan 1801
VAB 23 Apr 1804
VAW 9 Nov 1805
VAR 28 Apr 1808
AB 31 July 1810
TAYLOR, William (1)
L 28 Oct 1780
CR 21 Jan 1783
CA 24 Sept 1793
RAB 1 Aug 1811
RAW 12 Aug 1812
RAR 4 June 1814
VAB 12 Aug 1819 (CH)
VAW 19 July 1821 (CH)
VAR 27 May 1825 (CH)
AB 22 July 1830 (CH)
AW 10 Jan 1837 (CH)
AR 23 Nov 1841 (CH)
d 1842 (CH)

TAYLOR, William (2)
L 1744 (PJP)
TAYLOR, William (3)
L 24 July 1794
d 1835 (OB)
TAYLOR, Wittewronge
L 7 Sept 1741
CR 1 Nov 1748
CA 16 Dec 1755
d (drowned) 15 Feb 1760 (CH)
TAYNTON, Robert
L 20 June 1765
TEAGUE, William
L 26 Apr 1759
TEALE, Andrew
L 1690 (PJP)
TEALE, Richard
L 7 Dec 1743
CR 5 Mar 1760
d 4 Nov 1798
TEAPE, James
L 12 Feb 1746
TEATE, John
L 30 Apr 1678
TEATE, Matthew
See TATE, Matthew
TEATE, Richard
L
CA 1661
TEDDEMAN, Henry (1)
L
CA 1664
TEDDEMAN, Henry (2)
L 1665
TEDDEMAN, Sir Thomas (1)
L
CA 1660
RAD 1664
Kt 1 July 1665 (DNB)
RAB 1665
RAW 1665
RAR 1665
VAB 29 May 1666 (RM)
VAW 8 June 1666 (RM)
d May 1668 (PJP)
TEDDEMAN, Thomas (2)
L 1666
TEDDEMAN, Thomas (3)
L 3 Sept 1697
SUP 20 Mar 1738 (PMM)
TEED, Richard Manston
L 23 July 1800
Ret CR 9 Nov 1848 (OB)
TEED, Roger Bidgood
L 4 Mar 1815
TEER, George
L 18 Apr 1767
CR 23 Aug 1781
CA 17 Jan 1783
TELFER, Archibald
L 24 Nov 1800
TELLEY, Joseph Swabey
L 27 Dec 1795
TEMPEST, John
L 1665
CA 1672
KIA 28 May 1673 (SJ)

TEMPEST, Robert
L 29 Jan 1707 (PMM)
TEMPLAR, Richard
L 6 Dec 1796
TEMPLE, Francis
L 8 Oct 1793
CR 4 July 1803
CA 12 Mar 1805
Ret RA 10 Jan 1837 (OB)
RAB 17 Aug 1840 (LG)
RAW 23 Nov 1841 (LG)
RAR 9 Nov 1846 (LG)
VAB 21 Dec 1847 (OB)
VAW 19 Oct 1849 (LG)
Ret A 21 Jan 1854 (CH)
d 19 Jan 1863 (CH)
TEMPLE, Henry
L 14 June 1762
TEMPLE, Henry Edward
L 26 Sept 1814
TEMPLE, John (1)
L 1660 (P)
Dismissed 1666 (RM)
CA 1671 (P)
d July 1687 (PJP)
TEMPLE, John (2)
L 21 Sept 1703 (PMM)
CR 12 Sept 1705 (PMM)
CA 24 Mar 1712
d 1734
TEMPLE, John (3)
L 21 Sept 1790
CR 11 Jan 1796
CA 1 Jan 1801
d (drowned) 6 Dec 1808 (CH)
TEMPLE, Sands
L 1665
d before 1688 (PJP)
TEMPLE, William
L 1720 (PJP)
d 15 July 1768 (M)
TEMPLEMAN, John Weare
L 4 Nov 1809
HP 1819 (OB)
TEMPLER, William
L 6 Mar 1802
CR 3 Mar 1804
d (drowned) 1805 (PJP)
TENNANT, Matthew
L 3 Feb 1673 (P)
CR 1 Sept 1678 (P)
CA 20 Oct 1683 (DDA)
d 12 Oct 1690 (CH)
TENNANT, William
L 1677 (PJP)
TERMING, C.
L 1801 (PJP)
TERNAN, Austin
L 23 Sept 1783
TERNE, Henry
L
CA 1661
KIA 4 June 1666 (RM)
TERRY, John
L 20 Apr 1695

TERRY, Thomas Harding
L 10 Apr 1802
TETLEY, Joseph Swabey
L Dec 1795
CR 31 Aug 1809 (CH)
CA 7 Jan 1812
d 29 Nov 1828 (MB)
TEWART, William
L 11 May 1795
THACKER, Thomas
L 1689 (PJP)
THACKERAY, Charles
L 18 June 1791
d 20 Aug 1794 (M)
THACKSTONE, Henry
L 9 Aug 1802
THANE, James
L 1 June 1775
THANE, John
L 1 Oct 1745
THATCHER, Thomas
L
CA 19 Oct 1695
d 20 Aug 1697
THEED, John
L 25 Apr 1812
CR 15 June 1814
THEWALL, Bevis
L 25 Aug 1807
Ret CR 11 Jan 1844 (OB)
THESIGER, Frederick
In Russian Service 1788–1797 (DNB)
L 7 Oct 1799
CR 14 Feb 1801
CA 29 Apr 1802
Kt (Russia) 27 Oct 1803 (LG)
d 26 Aug 1805 (DNB)
THEW, George
L 26 Apr 1811
THICKNESSE, John
L 26 May 1795 (OB)
CR 29 Jan 1800
Ret CA 10 Sept 1840 (OB)
d 5 Aug 1846 (OB)
THOM, John
L 8 Dec 1781
THOMAS, Abel Watner
L 18 Oct 1802
CR 15 June 1814
HP 15 June 1814 (OB)
THOMAS, David
T
L 26 Aug 1806
Gone 1811 (TR)
THOMAS, Dolby
L 4 Dec 1706 (PMM)
THOMAS, Edmund
L 1664
THOMAS, Edmund Fanning
L 30 Aug 1798
T
CR 1830 (TR)
d 28 Apr 1842 (TR)
THOMAS, Fisher
L 26 May 1768
THOMAS, Frederick Augustus
L 2 May 1771

THOMAS, Frederick Jennings
T
L 14 Feb 1806
CR 4 Mar 1811
CA 8 Dec 1813
Ret CA 31 Oct 1846 (LG)
d 19 Dec 1855 (DNB)

THOMAS, George (1)
L 26 Sept 1799
Ret CR 26 Nov 1830 (OB)
d 10 Feb 1850 (LT)

THOMAS, George (2)
L 8 May 1812

THOMAS, Henry
L 8 May 1708

THOMAS, Herbert
L 13 July 1765
d 25 July 1793

THOMAS, James (1)
L 12 May 1759

THOMAS, James (2)
L 21 July 1794

THOMAS, James (3)
L 2 Feb 1808
d 20 Feb 1827 (LT)

THOMAS, John (1)
L 9 Feb 1702

THOMAS, John (2)
L 29 July 1728
d 7 Aug 1735 (PMM)

THOMAS, John (3)
L 10 Sept 1777
CR 9 Apr 1779
CA 11 Dec 1779
RAR 14 Feb 1799
VAW 23 Apr 1804
VAR 9 Nov 1805
AB 25 Oct 1809
AW 31 July 1810
d 11 Oct 1810 (CH)

THOMAS, John (4)
L 22 Aug 1799

THOMAS, Joseph Rawlins
L 21 Oct 1811
d 30 May 1839 (LT)

THOMAS, Richard (1)
L 20 Jan 1709
CR 11 Jan 1728
d 5 Sept 1758 (PMM)

THOMAS, Richard (2)
L 1 Oct 1756

THOMAS, Richard (3)
L 13 May 1778

THOMAS, Richard (4)
L 1 Dec 1784

THOMAS, Richard (5)
L 15 Jan 1797
CR 18 Jan 1803
CA 22 Oct 1805
RAB 10 Jan 1837 (LG)
RAW 23 Nov 1841 (LG)
RAR 9 Nov 1846 (LG)
VAB 8 Jan 1848 (OB)
VAW 14 Jan 1850 (LG)
A 11 Sept 1854 (CH)
d 1857 (CH)

THOMAS, Robert (1)
L 1707 (PJP)

THOMAS, Robert (2)
L 11 Aug 1800

THOMAS, Robert (3)
L 8 Feb 1815
HP Dec 1815 (OB)

THOMAS, Robert Strickland
L 11 Mar 1815

THOMAS, Robinson
L 17 Mar 1815

THOMAS, Samuel
L 21 Aug 1794
KIA 24 May 1810 (CH)

THOMAS, Thomas
L 5 Jan 1799
Ret CR 26 Nov 1830 (OB)

THOMAS, William (1)
L 11 Mar 1690 (PMM)

THOMAS, William (2)
L 9 Dec 1729
CR 13 Oct 1744

THOMAS, William (3)
L 2 Feb 1761
CR 8 Mar 1780
d 2 Oct 1800

THOMAS, William (4)
L 29 Mar 1805

THOMAS, William George
L 13 May 1812
HP Aug 1815 (OB)

THOMPSON, Adolphus Frederick
L 11 May 1815

THOMPSON, Albion
L 25 Apr 1678
d 10 Jan 1682 (DDA)

THOMPSON, Andrew (1)
L 21 Mar 1812

THOMPSON, Andrew (2)
L 18 Mar 1815
HP 1847 (OB)

THOMPSON, Anthony
L 21 Nov 1790

THOMPSON, Bradshaw
L 22 June 1728
CR
CA 15 Feb 1740
d 15 Feb 1756

THOMPSON, Sir Charles (1)
L 16 Jan 1761
CR 14 Feb 1771
CA 7 Mar 1772
RAB 12 Apr 1794
RAW 4 July 1794
VAB 1 June 1795
MP 1796–
(Monmouth) 17 Mar 1799 (MPT)
Cre Bt 1797 (PJP)
VAR 14 Feb 1799
d 17 Mar 1799 (DNB)

THOMPSON, Charles (2)
L 15 Mar 1787
Ret CR 30 Apr 1840 (OB)

THOMPSON, Edward (1)
L 4 May 1696 (PJP)

THOMPSON, Edward (2)
L 16 Nov 1757

HP 1763–1771 (DNB)
CR 10 Jan 1771
CA 2 Apr 1772
HP 1772–1778 (DNB)
d 17 Jan 1786 (DNB)

THOMPSON, Edward (3)
L 13 Aug 1762

THOMPSON, Francis
L 1 July 1794
d 19 June 1815 (PJP)

THOMPSON, Frederick
L 3 Feb 1815
d 22 July 1833 (PJP)

THOMPSON, George
L 8 Jan 1777

THOMPSON, Godbold
L 2 Mar 1734

THOMPSON, Granville
L 13 Oct 1809

THOMPSON, Henry Clements
L 14 Sept 1802
CR 19 Sept 1808
Kt (Sweden) 7 Jan 1809 (LG)
d 22 May 1824 (MB)

THOMPSON, James (1)
L 1705 (PJP)

THOMPSON, James (2)
L 1782 (PJP)
d 1783 (PJP)

THOMPSON, James (3)
L 1 Aug 1811

THOMPSON, John (1)
L 1702 (PRO)

THOMPSON, John (2)
L 20 Nov 1790 (PJP)
CR 24 Dec 1805
CA 12 Aug 1812 (MB)

THOMPSON, John (3)
L 18 Dec 1794
CR 28 Apr 1802
CA 21 Oct 1810
Ret RA 20 Nov 1846 (LG)
Ret VA 27 May 1854 (DNB)
Ret A 9 June 1860 (DNB)
d 30 Jan 1864 (DNB)

THOMPSON, John (4)
L 11 Feb 1796
d 1804 (CH)

THOMPSON, John (5)
L 7 June 1809
CR 5 Jan 1848 (OB)

THOMPSON, John (6)
L 23 Feb 1815
HP 23 Feb 1815 (OB)

THOMPSON, John Last
L 17 Dec 1810

THOMPSON, John Thorp
L 31 Jan 1806

THOMPSON, Joseph (1)
L 21 July 1795

THOMPSON, Joseph (2)
L 28 May 1805

THOMPSON, Joseph George
L 22 Jan 1806

THOMPSON, Josiah
L 31 Jan 1806
CR 28 June 1838 (OB)

THOMPSON, Kershever
L 19 Sept 1777
d 28 Mar 1791 (M)

THOMPSON, Lenox
L 19 Feb 1780
CR 30 Mar 1799
CA 15 Jan 1802

THOMPSON, Norborn (1)
L 4 Nov 1790
CR 23 Mar 1795
CA 11 Aug 1800
RAB 22 July 1830 (LG)
RAR 10 Jan 1837 (LG)
VAW 23 Nov 1841 (LG)
d 28 May 1844 (LT)

THOMPSON, Sir Norborn(e) (2)
L 6 Mar 1801

THOMPSON, Norris
L 5 Dec 1777

THOMPSON, Peter
L 24 July 1690 (PJP)
CA 18 Sept 1696 (PJP)

THOMPSON, Richard
L 21 Sept 1795

THOMPSON, Robert (1)
L 1692 (PJP)
CA 19 July 1694 (PJP)
SUP 1703
d 30 Jan 1729

THOMPSON, Robert (2)
L 1689 (PJP)
CR
CA 26 Sept 1702
SUP 1714 (PJP)
d 20 Jan 1736 (PMM)

THOMPSON, Robert (3)
L 10 May 1804

THOMPSON, Samuel (1)
L 25 July 1744
CR 14 Feb 1757
CA 4 Nov 1760
SUP RA 23 May 1788
d 13 Aug 1818 (PJP)

THOMPSON, Samuel (2)
L 2 Aug 1776
d 28 Oct 1782 (PJP)

THOMPSON, Thomas (1)
L
CA 1672

THOMPSON, Thomas (2)
L 13 Oct 1794

THOMPSON, Sir Thomas Boulden
L 14 Jan 1782
CR 27 Mar 1786
HP 1787 (MPT)
CA 22 Nov 1790
CONT 20 June 1806–
24 Feb 1816 (NBO)
Cre Bt 11 Nov 1806 (MPT)
MP 1807–
(Rochester) 12 June 1816 (MPT)
RAB 25 Oct 1809
RAW 31 July 1810
RAR 12 Aug 1812

VAB 4 June 1814
KCB 2 Jan 1815 (DNB)
VAW 12 Aug 1819 (CH)
GCB 14 Sept 1822 (DNB)
VAR 19 July 1821 (CH)
TGH 1828 (PJP)
d 3 Mar 1828 (DNB)

THOMPSON, Thomas Browne
L 23 Nov 1799

THOMPSON, William (1)
L 12 Mar 1742

THOMPSON, William (2)
L 20 Aug 1800
KIA 4 July 1806 (PJP)

THOMPSON, William Ayton
L 27 Oct 1781

THOMSON, Andrew
L 21 Sept 1790 (PJP)
CR
CA 17 Oct 1801
d 1828 (PJP)

THOMSON, Andrew James
L 17 Dec 1794
CR 17 Oct 1801
d 1828 (MB)

THOMSON, Henry
L 29 Mar 1802
CR 6 June 1810
d 23 Jan 1827 (MB)

THOMSON, John (1)
L 9 Jan 1777
d May 1809 (PJP)

THOMSON, John (2)
L 3 July 1793
CR 20 Jan 1797 (PJP)
d 12 Nov 1803 (PJP)

THOMSON, John (3)
L 23 Sept 1797 (PJP)
CR 12 June 1809 (PJP)
CA 11 Sept 1815 (PJP)

THOMSON, William Augustus
L 20 Oct 1806
CR 15 Feb 1832 (MB)
HP 15 Feb 1832 (OB)

THORESBY, Richard
L 16 Oct 1779

THORLEY, Robert (1)
L 8 Apr 1805

THORLEY, Robert (2)
L 18 Feb 1815
HP 18 Feb 1815 (OB)

THORN, John
L 1783 (PJP)

THORNBROUGH, Edward (1)
L 6 June 1744
CR 15 Apr 1774
d 1784

THORNBROUGH, Sir Edward (2)
L 16 Apr 1773
CR 14 Sept 1780
CA 24 Sept 1782
CRM 14 Feb 1799 (AL)
RAB 1 Jan 1801
RAW 23 Apr 1804
VAB 9 Nov 1805
VAW 28 Apr 1808
VAR 31 July 1810
AB 4 Dec 1813
KCB 12 Apr 1815 (LG)
AW 12 Aug 1819 (LG)
GCB 11 Jan 1825 (DNB)
AR 22 July 1830 (LG)
d 3 Apr 1834 (DNB)

THORNBROUGH, Edward le Cras
L 12 Dec 1814
CR 25 May 1818 (MB)
CA 17 Apr 1827 (MB)
HP 17 Apr 1827 (OB)

THORNBROUGH, William Henry
L 26 Dec 1800
d Jan 1801 (PJP)

THORNE, John Coham
L 20 Jan 1800

THORNHILL, Henry
L 1 Mar 1695 (PJP)
CA 4 Feb 1696 (PJP)

THORNHILL, John
L 1698
d 1699 (PRO)

THORNLOW, James
L 1704 (PRO)

THORNTON, Henry Alexander Daniel
L 4 Feb 1815
HP 4 Feb 1815 (OB)

THORNTON, Richard
L 26 Aug 1808
Ret CR 1 Nov 1845 (OB)

THOROWGOOD, Charles
L 1672
d before 1689 (PJP)

THOROWGOOD, Dynes
L 18 Oct 1759

THOROWGOOD, Selby
L 30 Jan 1759

THORP, George
L 7 May 1796
KIA 25 July 1797 (LG)

THORP, Henry
L 3 May 1777

THORP, James
L 15 Jan 1747
CR 26 Aug 1762
d 22 Jan 1798

THORP, Solomon
L 2 Feb 1741

THORPE, Jacob
L 19 May 1744

THORROLL, Anthony
L 1672

THORY, William
L 21 Jan 1708 (PMM)

THRACKSTON, Edwin
L 25 July 1801
Ret CR 24 Mar 1840 (OB)

THRASHER, Thomas
L 1666
d before 1689 (PJP)

THRESHER, James
L 30 Oct 1790
CR 29 Oct 1793

THRUSH, Thomas
L 16 June 1797
CR 29 Apr 1802
CA 8 June 1809 (MB)
Resigned 14 Jan 1825 (MB)

THRUSTON, Charles Thomas
L 15 Nov 1806
CR 7 Feb 1812
Ret CA 11 Mar 1844 (OB)

THURGOOD, Charles
L 10 Mar 1815

THURSTON, Charles
L 1694 (PJP)

THURSTON, Charles Thomas
See THRUSTON, Charles Thomas

THURSTON, Seth
L 1665 (P)
CA 17 Apr 1689
d 24 Oct 1689

THURTELL, Edward
L 3 Feb 1815

THWAITS, Richard
L 18 June 1791
CR 27 June 1800

TICKELL, Richard
L 30 Dec 1813

TICKELL, Richard Brinsley
L 13 July 1801

TICKLE, William
L 1659
CA 1664
d before 1689 (PJP)

TIDDEMAN, Mark
L 27 Mar 1741
d 1770 (PJP)

TIDDEMAN, Richard
L 21 July 1732
CR
CA 9 Mar 1745
d 6 Oct 1761 (LG)

TIDDEMON, Thomas
L 3 Sept 1697

TIDY, Thomas Holmes
L 3 Nov 1790
CR 8 July 1800
d 1807 (PJP)

TIEL, Sir John du
See DU TIEL, Sir John

TILDESLEY, Daniel
L 9 June 1695 (PJP)

TILDESLEY, John
L 18 Jan 1804

TILDESLEY, Thomas
L 9 Mar 1696 (PJP)

TILLARD, James
L 23 Jan 1794
CR 28 Feb 1805
CA 11 Dec 1811
d 9 Jan 1814 (LT)

TILLARD, Robert
L 1745 (PJP)

TILLEDGE, Richard
L 8 Dec 1777
CR 12 Sept 1781

TILLER, Jonah
L 13 June 1783

TILLER, William
L 9 Jan 1802

TILLEY, James
L 21 Mar 1812
HP Dec 1826 (OB)

TILLEY, J.S.
L 1797 (PJP)

TILLEY, Samuel (1)
L 20 June 1689
CR 2 Apr 1702 (PMM)

TILLEY, Samuel (2)
L 31 Mar 1705 (PMM)

TILLEY, Samuel (3)
L 16 Nov 1744

TILLIARD, Robert
L 21 Apr 1744
d 23 Jan 1753 (PMM)

TILLY, Charles
L 7 Oct 1805
HP Sept 1814 (OB)
Ret CR 15 Apr 1844 (OB)
d 8 June 1845 (OB)

TILLY, Thomas
L 29 Aug 1759

TILSON, George
L 19 Nov 1790
d 18 Mar 1795 (LT)

TIMINS, Charles Sheldon
L 18 Oct 1799
d 13 Apr 1838 (LT)

TIMINS, George
L 2 May 1797
Ret CR 26 Nov 1830 (OB)
d Jan 1848 (OB)

TINCKLER, Robert
See TINKLER, Robert

TINCOMBE, George
L 4 May 1810
CR 19 Aug 1825 (OB)
HP 19 Aug 1825 (OB)

TINDAL(L), Charles
L 7 Nov 1806
CR 19 Aug 1825 (PJP)
Ret CR 4 Feb 1842 (OB)

TINDAL(L), George
L 23 Apr 1741
CR 11 Apr 1745
CA 18 Oct 1758
d 17 Oct 1777 (M)

TINDAL(L), John
L 29 Dec 1779
d 22 Jan 1780

TINDAL(L), Thomas
L
CA 1665
d before 1689 (PJP)

TINDAL(L), William
L 24 Oct 1795

TINDALE, Joseph
L 5 Sept 1800

TINGEY, Thomas
L
CR 31 July 1771 (DAB)
Resigned 1772 (DAB)

Went into the American Service 1798 (DAB)
d 23 Feb 1829 (DAB)

TINKER, John
L
CA 1661
d before 1688 (PD)

TINKER, John Bladen
L 25 Dec 1748
CR
CA 4 July 1756
d 18 July 1767 (M)

TINKLER, Robert
L 26 Sept 1793
CR 27 Apr 1801

TINLING, Charles
L 27 July 1793
CR 7 Sept 1798
CA 14 Feb 1801
Ret RA 22 July 1830 (CH)
RAR 17 Aug 1840 (LG)
d 27 Nov 1840 (CH)

TINSLEY, Francis
L 27 Aug 1764
CR 1 Mar 1779

TIPPET(T), George
L 12 June 1800

TIPPET, James (1)
L 27 Sept 1794
CR 29 Apr 1802
d (drowned) May 1805 (CH)

TIPPET(T), James (2)
L 8 Nov 1809
d (drowned) 24 Dec 1811 (PJP)

TIPPET, Stephen
L 18 Apr 1745

TIPPING, William
L 1 May 1782
d 30 Sept 1786 (PMM)

TIREMAN, Thomas
L 28 Jan 1777
CR 1 Aug 1795

TISDALE, Archibald
See TISDALL, Archibald

TISDALE, Thomas
L 14 Aug 1739

TISDALL, Archibald
L 7 Oct 1806
CR 16 Feb 1813
CA 14 July 1815
Ret CA 31 Oct 1846 (LG)

TITCHBORNE, William
L
CA 16 July 1689
d (drowned) 9 Feb 1692 (CH)

TITCHER, William
L 21 Jan 1777
CR 15 Jan 1783

TITSELL, Samuel
L
CA 1660
d (drowned) Aug 1664 (PJP)

TOBIN, Edward
L 11 July 1800

TOBIN, George
L 14 Nov 1790
CR 12 July 1798
CA 29 Apr 1802
CB 8 Dec 1815 (LG)
RAW 10 Jan 1837 (LG)
d 10 Apr 1838 (DNB)

TOBY, Richard
L 23 July 1748
CR 11 Mar 1756
d Mar 1773 (M)

TOBY, Richard James Walter
L 16 Nov 1790

TOCKETTS, George
L 13 May 1720
CR 21 Nov 1740

TOD, George
L 17 Jan 1781

TOD, John
L 1 Mar 1815 (OB)

TODD, Alexander
L 6 Oct 1758
SUP CR 1 Feb 1800 (PMM)

TODD, Andrew
L 22 Apr 1783
CR
CA 22 Dec 1796
d 17 Mar 1800 (CH)

TODD, James
L 1703 (PJP)

TODD, Robert
L 9 June 1811

TODMAN, William
L 8 July 1795

TOFT, Samuel
L 7 June 1704

TOKELY, Joseph
L 27 Mar 1794

TOKER, Thomas Richard
L 20 Dec 1800
T
CR 24 Dec 1805
CA 4 Dec 1813
d 27 June 1846 (OB)

TOLESON, Edward
L 27 Nov 1692 (PJP)

TOLL, Edmund
L 24 May 1734
CR
CA 14 June 1744
SUP RA 1762
d 1 Aug 1767 (M)

TOLLAT, Anthony
L
CA 23 Mar 1695 (PJP)
d 2 Mar 1711 (PJP)

TOLLEMACHE, Hon. John
L 9 Oct 1770
CR 29 Oct 1775
d 25 Sept 1777 (PMM)

TOLLEMACHE, John Richard
Formerly HALLIDAY, John Richard
L 1795 (MB)
CR
CA 19 Sept 1796
RAB 12 Aug 1819 (LG)
RAW 19 July 1821 (LG)

RAR 27 May 1825 (LG)
VAB 22 July 1830 (LG)
VAR 10 Jan 1837 (LG)
d 16 July 1837 (CH)

TOLLEMACHE, William (1)
L 5 Oct 1688
CA 13 Dec 1688
d 15 May 1691 (PMM)

TOLLEMACHE, Hon. William (2)
L 21 Oct 1772
d (drowned) Dec 1776 (PJP)

TOLLER, John
L 27 Oct 1703 (PMM)
CR 18 May 1719
CA 20 Nov 1728
d (suicide) 8 May 1747 (PJP)

TOLLET(T), Anthony
See TOLLAT, Anthony

TOLMACH, William
See TOLLEMACHE, William

TOM, Philip
L 10 Jan 1732
CR 19 June 1745

TOM, Robert Brown
L 10 Nov 1793
CR 19 June 1801
CA 21 Oct 1810 (MB)

TOMBE, Peter Jacob
L 11 May 1727
Gone 1741 (PRO)

TOMKIN, John
L 17 June 1696
CR 21 Jan 1703 (PMM)

TOMKINS, Christopher
L 18 Oct 1757
d 1759 (PMM)

TOMKINS, Thomas
L 27 June 1696 (PJP)

TOMKINSON, James
L 19 Sept 1805
CR 12 Mar 1810
CA 12 Aug 1819 (MB)

TOMKYS, Hope
L 23 Dec 1760

TOMLINSON, George
L 3 Mar 1815

TOMLINSON, Nicholas (1)
L 23 Mar 1782
In Russian service 1790–1793 (DNB)
CR July 1794
CA 12 Dec 1796
Dismissed 20 Nov 1798
Restored w/srity 22 Sept 1801
Ret RA 22 July 1830
RAR 17 Aug 1840 (LG)
VAB 23 Nov 1841 (LG)
VAW 9 Nov 1846 (LG)
d 6 Mar 1847 (DNB)

TOMLINSON, Nicholas (2)
L 16 Jan 1810

TOMLINSON, Philip
L 10 Dec 1782
d 1839 (OB)

TOMLINSON, Robert (1)
L 19 Feb 1758
CR 15 Nov 1782
SUP CA 25 Oct 1809 (PJP)
d 29 Nov 1813 (PJP)

TOMLINSON, Robert (2)
L 26 Apr 1782
CR 15 June 1814
d 9 June 1844 (OB)

TOMLINSON, Robert C.
L 14 July 1813

TOMM, William
L 14 Jan 1695 (PMM)
In Merchant Service 1700 (PJP)

TOMS, Peter
L 5 Oct 1727
CR 27 July 1741
CA 12 Feb 1743
SUP RA 1762
d 17 Nov 1763

TOMS, Philip
See TOM, Philip

TOMSON, Ormond
L 14 Oct 1727
CR 10 June 1741
CA 26 July 1744
d 17 Nov 1753

TOMSON, William
L 1664
d before 1689 (PJP)

TONGE, Hern William
L 3 Aug 1759

TONGE, William Norris
L 2 Sept 1794

TONKEN, Hugh
L 24 Nov 1777
d 16 Dec 1793

TONKEN, Thomas (1)
L 6 Apr 1757
CR 25 Dec 1778
CA 15 May 1780
d 5 Sept 1790 (PMM)

TONKEN, Thomas (2)
L 2 Apr 1779

TONKIN, John
L
CR 21 Jan 1703

TONKIN, Renatus
L 23 July 1741

TONSON, Hon. Francis
L 31 Aug 1798

TONYN, George Anthony
L 13 Jan 1756
CR 2 Dec 1757
CA 14 Nov 1758
d 17 Oct 1770

TONYN, Patrick
L 15 Nov 1790
CR 11 July 1797
CA 29 Apr 1802
d 22 Jan 1810 (PRO)

TOOKEY, Ranceford
L 25 July 1782
CR 6 Dec 1796
d 1837 (PJP)

TOOLEY, John
L 1673

TOOLEY, Richard
L 29 Apr 1802
d (drowned) 20 Nov 1808 (PJP)

TOONE, John
L 29 July 1812

TOPPER, George Alfred
L 6 Nov 1810
d 27 Mar 1829 (LT)

TOPPIN, Jeremiah
L 1 June 1695 (PJP)

TOPPING, Charles
L 7 Nov 1806

TOPPING, William
L 29 Jan 1761

TOPSHAM, George
See TAPSON, George

TORLESSE, Henry Bowden
L 11 May 1815
HP 11 May 1815 (OB)

TORPLEY, John
L
CA 1666 (P)
CA 15 Feb 1690
(27 Jan 1691 in C)
SUP 18 Apr 1693 (PMM)
d 29 Oct 1699

TORRINGTON, Arthur Herbert, Earl of
See HERBERT, Arthur

TORRINGTON, George Byng, Viscount
L Sept 1790 (MB)
CR Oct 1794 (MB)
CA 18 June 1795
Inh EP 8 Jan 1813 (MB)
RAB 4 June 1814
RAW 12 Aug 1819 (CH)
RAR 19 July 1821 (CH)
VAB 27 May 1825 (CH)
VAW 22 July 1830 (CH)
d 18 June 1831 (CH)

TORRINGTON, George Byng, Viscount
See BYNG, George

TORWAY, John
L 17 Sept 1706 (PMM)

TOTHILL, Christopher
L 20 July 1809

TOSYER, John
See TOZIER, John

TOTTENDALE, Henry
L 1695 (PJP)

TOTTY, John
L
CA 1665
d before 1689 (PJP)

TOTTY, Thomas
L 30 Apr 1775
CR 17 Feb 1778
CA 31 Jan 1782
RAB 1 Jan 1801
d 2 June 1802 (PMM)

TOUCHE, John de la
L 6 May 1775
d 26 Oct 1803

TOUCHKIN, Anthony
L 1665
d before 1689 (PJP)

TOULMIN, John
L 4 Nov 1762
d 17 Feb 1780 (M)

TOUZEAU, Charles
L 22 July 1794
d 1814 (PJP)

TOUZELL, Edward
L 1709 (PJP)

TOVEY, Nicholas
L
CA 1666

TOWER, John
L 15 July 1797
CR 29 Apr 1802
CA 8 May 1804
CB 1831 (PJP)
RAB 10 Jan 1837 (LG)
d 13 Dec 1837 (LT)

TOWERS, George
L 28 Oct 1758
d 5 June 1767 (M)

TOWERS, Robert
L 21 Feb 1815
d May 1847 (OB)

TOWERS, Thomas
L 21 Dec 1758

TOWLE, Edward
L 24 Mar 1808
d 1812 (PJP)

TOWNE, John
L 17 Sept 1812
HP 25 Apr 1813 (OB)

TOWNES, Jeremy
L 2 Mar 1696 (PMM)

TOWNING, William Sidney Smith
L 25 Sept 1806

TOWNLEY, Charles Haswell
L 16 Nov 1739
CR 26 Aug 1745
CA 21 June 1756
d 1759

TOWNLEY, Poyntz Stepney
L 24 June 1809
KIA 4 May 1810 (LG)

TOWNLEY, Thomas (1)
L 25 Aug 1757
SUP CR 21 Sept 1796 (PMM)
d 15 Aug 1803 (PMM)

TOWNLEY, Thomas (2)
L 1 June 1801

TOWNSEND, Bryant
L
CA 7 Aug 1689
d 14 Jan 1692

TOWNSEND, Edward
L 19 Aug 1800

TOWNSEND, Henry
L 30 Nov 1756

TOWNSEND, Horatio
L
CA 12 July 1693
d 12 Mar 1699

TOWNS(H)END, Sir Isaac (1)
L 11 May 1687
CA 11 Apr 1690
COMM 14 Jan 1706–
(Portsmouth) 17 May 1713 (QAN)
COM E 15 Apr 1713–
16 Nov 1714 (NBO)
COMM 16 Nov 1714–
(Portsmouth) 19 May 1729 (NBO)
Kt 31 Aug 1722 (NBO)
SUP 1729
d 26 May 1731 (NBO)
TOWN(S)HEND, Isaac (2)
L 24 July 1706 (PMM)
CR
CA 9 Feb 1720
RAR 23 June 1744 (LG)
MP 1744–
(Portsmouth) 1754 (MPS)
VAB 23 Apr 1745 (LG)
VAW 14 July 1746 (C)
AB 15 July 1747
GGH 1754 (PJP)
AW Feb 1757
MP 1757–
(Rochester) 1765 (MPS)
d 22 Nov 1765 (CH)
TOWNSEND, Jacob
L 24 Nov 1688
TOWNSEND, James (1)
L 4 Mar 1746
d (drowned) 25 Sept 1757 (PJP)
TOWNSEND, James (2)
L 19 Dec 1800
CR 27 June 1814
HP 29 June 1819 (OB)
TOWNSEND, Joseph Cuthbert
L 2 Feb 1815
HP 2 Feb 1815 (OB)
TOWNSHEND, Bryant
See TOWNSEND, Bryant
TOWNSHEND, Hon. George
L
CR
CA 30 Jan 1739
RAW 6 Jan 1755 (CH)
RAR 4 June 1756
VAB Feb 1757
VAW 5 Feb 1758
VAR 14 Feb 1759
AB 1765 (C)
d Aug 1769 (DNB)
TOWNSHEND, Lord James
L 31 Jan 1806
CR 14 Nov 1806
CA 2 June 1809
MP 1818–
(Helston) 1832 (MPT)
MP 1835–
(Helston) 1837 (MPT)
d 28 June 1842 (OB)
TOWNSEND, Thomas (1)
L 4 Mar 1759
SUP CR 12 Oct 1801
TOWNSEND, Thomas (2)
L 27 June 1809
Ret CR 5 Jan 1848 (OB)

TOWNSHEND, William James
L 15 Aug 1813
HP May 1814 (OB)
TOWRY, Charles George
L 23 Oct 1790
TOWRY, George Henry
L 23 Oct 1790 (DNB)
CR 14 Sept 1793
CA 18 June 1794
d 6 Apr 1809 (PRO)
TOWRY, George Phillips
L 10 Feb 1757
d 1817 (PJP)
TOWRY, Henry John Phillips
See PHILLIPS, Henry John
TOWRY, John
L 9 Oct 1718
CR
CA 7 Nov 1732
COMM 9 Jan 1748–
(Port Mahon) 6 June 1749 (NBO)
d 20 Mar 1757 (NBO)
TOWSELL, Edward
L 30 May 1709
TOZER, Aaron
L 11 Aug 1807
CR 15 June 1814
CA 14 Jan 1830 (OB)
HP 14 Jan 1830 (OB)
TOZIER, John
L 31 Jan 1673 (PJP)
CA 21 Jan 1674 (PMM)
TRACEY, John
L 6 Oct 1800
CR 11 June 1814
TRACY, Francis M'Mahon
L 12 Dec 1800
TRAFFORD, Thomas
L 1660
CA 1666
TRAGENT, Richard Jenkins
L 2 May 1811
d 19 Dec 1812 (PJP)
TRAHERNE, Griffith Rice
L 13 Dec 1810
TRAIL, Thomas
L 26 Dec 1782
d Mar 1795 (PMM)
TRAILL, Gilbert
L 21 Jan 1809
HP 1835 (OB)
TRAILL, William
L 2 May 1759
TRAIN, John
L 8 Nov 1815
TRANT, Henry
L 20 Apr 1742
TRANT, Philip Henry
L 10 Feb 1809
TRANTUN, John
L 7 Oct 1779
TRAPPS, George
L 1673 (DDA)
TRASHER, William
L 1679
TRAVERS, Sir Stannard Eaton
L 23 Sept 1804

CR	18 June	1814
CA	19 Nov	1829 (OB)
HP		1829 (OB)
KH	5 Mar	1834 (DNB)
Ret RA	9 July	1855 (DNB)
d	4 Mar	1858 (DNB)
TRAVERS, Robert		
L		1783 (PJP)
KIA	20 June	1783 (LG)
TREACHER, Samuel Sharpe		
L	29 Mar	1806
d (drowned)	29 Jan	1814 (CH)
TREACY, Joshua		
L	13 Dec	1797
CR	21 Mar	1812
SUP CA	13 Sept	1814
d	15 Apr	1845 (OB)
TREACY, William		
L	7 Nov	1806
TREBY, George		
L	12 Apr	1748
TREDENHAM, Daniel		
L	8 Dec	1692 (PJP)
TREDENHAM, George		
L		1701 (PMM)
TREDENHAM, Walter		
L		1703 (PJP)
TREDWIN, Hugh		
L	20 Oct	1798
TREEVE, John		
T		
L	20 July	1809
Ret CR	4 Apr	1848 (OB)
TREEVE, Richard		
L	9 Dec	1772
TREFUSIS, Hon. George Rolle Walpole		
L	10 Dec	1813
CR	2 May	1816 (MB)
CA	24 June	1824 (MB)
Ret CA	1 Oct	1846 (OB)
d	28 May	1849 (LT)
TREFUSIS, Thomas		
L	18 Oct	1711
CR		
CA	25 Dec	1736
MP (Grampound)		1739–1741 (MPS)
COMM (Port Mahon)	29 June – 23 July	1744– 1748 (NBO)
HP	July	1748 (MPS)
SUP RA	July	1748
d	21 Apr	1754 (MPS)
TREGURTHA, Edward Primrose		
L	2 Dec	1799
TREHEARN, John		
L	21 Nov	1691
d		1704 (PJP)
TREHEARNE, John		
L	17 Sept	1744
TREHEARNE, William		
L		1660
CA		1666
d	before	1689 (PJP)
TREHOLM, John		
L		1803 (PJP)
TRELAUNY, Reynald		
L		1663
d	before	1689 (PJP)
TRELAUNY, William		
L		1665 (DDA)
CA	26 Jan	1678 (DDA)
d	before	1689 (PJP)
TRELAWNEY, John		
L	10 Jan	1799
TRELAWNEY, Sir William		
L		1743
CR	10 May	1754
CA	9 Apr	1756
MP (West Looe)	16 May – June	1757– 1762 (MPN)
Inh Bt	7 Apr	1762 (MPN)
d	11 Dec	1762 (MPN)
TRELIVING, Thomas		
L	11 Oct	1781
TREMLETT, George		
L	7 Feb	1815
d (suicide)	30 May	1816 (PJP)
TREMLETT, George Neat		
L	1 Aug	1794
Ret CR	1 Dec	1830 (OB)
d		1865 (PJP)
TREMLETT, Richard Stiles		
L	12 May	1797
d (duel)		1798 (PJP)
TREMLETT, William Henry Brown		
L	21 Sept	1795
CR	1 Jan	1801
CA	29 Apr	1802
Ret RA	10 Jan	1837 (CH)
RAW	17 Aug	1840 (LG)
RAR	23 Nov	1841 (LG)
VAB	22 Jan	1847 (LG)
VAW	8 Jan	1848 (LG)
Ret A	17 Dec	1852 (CH)
TRENCH, Hon. William Le Poer		
L	16 June	1793
CR	19 Nov	1799
CA	29 Apr	1802
Ret RA	10 Jan	1837 (OB)
RAW	17 Aug	1840 (OB)
RAR	23 Nov	1841 (LG)
d	16 Aug	1846 (OB)
TRENCHARD, George		
L	12 Apr	1696 (PJP)
CA	14 Feb	1695 (PJP)
d	21 Apr	1696 (PMM)
TRENCHARD, Joseph		
L	5 June	1793
TRENHOLM, John		
L	18 Feb	1800
TRENT, George		
L	14 Feb	1815
HP	14 Feb	1815 (OB)
TRENWITH, Thomas		
L	15 Feb	1740
SUP CR	21 Sept	1796 (PMM)
d		1798 (PMM)
TRESAHAR, Thomas		
L	19 Aug	1793

Ret CR	28 Feb	1827 (OB)
d	29 Dec	1844 (OB)
TRESILLIAN, Nicholas		
L	28 Mar	1743
d	13 Sept	1767
TREVANION, Sir Nicholas		
L	30 Oct	1688 (P)
CA	25 May	1696
Kt		1714 (PJP)
COMM	5 May	1726–
(Plymouth)	22 Dec	1737 (NBO)
d	22 Dec	1737 (NBO)
TREVANION, Richard		
L		1665 (P)
CR	July	1666
CA	29 Apr	1675
TREVE, John		
L	20 July	1809
TREVENEN, James		
L	28 Oct	1780
Resigned	Dec	1787 (DNB)
Entered Russian Service		1788 (DNB)
KIA	9 July	1790 (DNB)
TREVETHICK, Thomas		
L	27 Feb	1742
CR	15 Apr	1748
TREVETHICK, William		
L	1 June	1812
d	5 Jan	1816 (PJP)
TREVOR, Arthur		
L	28 Feb	1709
Entered Russian Service		1735 (PJP)
d	22 Jan	1759 (M)
TREVOR, John		
L		
CR	17 Feb	1721
CA	15 Nov	1726
	(Feb 1727 in H)	
d		1741 (PJP)
TREVOR, Robert		
L		
CR		
CA	2 Mar	1709
d		1740
TREVOR, Thomas		
L	11 Oct	1711
CR		
CA	26 Feb	1732
d	3 July	1745 (M)
TREVOR, Tudor		
L	17 May	1695 (PJP)
CA	3 Oct	1697
LGH		1737 (PJP)
d	28 Jan	1740
TREW, J.		
L		1793 (PJP)
TREWMARD, Joseph		
L		1723 (PMM)
d	11 July	1723 (PMM)
TREWREN, William		
L	15 June	1808
d	24 Dec	1812 (PJP)
TRIBE, William		
L	19 Sept	1815

TRIGG(E), John		
L	28 May	1766
CR	1 Dec	1787
CA	1 Oct	1790
SUP RA	4 May	1808
TRIGGS, John		
L	19 Mar	1694
TRIMMER, Thomas		
L	4 Mar	1805
CR	27 Aug	1814
TRINDER, John		
L	17 Oct	1806
d	29 Jan	1834 (LT)
TRIPP, Charles		
L		1702 (PJP)
TRIPP, George		
L	6 Dec	1776
CR	18 Oct	1782
CA	27 Mar	1786
Dismissed		1800
TRIPP, John Upton		
L	7 June	1809
Ret CR	5 Oct	1847 (OB)
TRIST, Robert		
L	24 Mar	1808
d		1847 (OB)
TRISTAM, Lawrence		
L	3 Mar	1759
TRISTAM, Samuel Barrington		
L	19 Dec	1809
d (drowned)	24 Dec	1811 (PJP)
TRITTON, Ewell		
L	16 Dec	1800
CR	21 Jan	1809
d	28 Sept	1819 (LT)
TRITTON, John (1)		
L		1709 (PJP)
TRITTON, John (2)		
L		1803 (PJP)
TROKE, George		
L	22 Jan	1806
TROKES, John		
L	15 Dec	1777
d	18 Nov	1786 (PMM)
TROLLOPE, George Barne		
L	13 Dec	1796
CR	1 May	1804
CA	7 June	1814
CB	8 Dec	1815 (MB)
Ret CA	31 Oct	1846 (LG)
Ret RA	9 Oct	1849 (LG)
d	31 May	1850 (DNB)
TROLLOPE, Sir Henry		
L	25 Apr	1777
CR	16 Apr	1779
CA	4 June	1781
Kt		1796 (PJP)
RAW	1 Jan	1801
RAR	23 Apr	1804
VAB	9 Nov	1805
VAW	28 Apr	1808
VAR	31 July	1810
AB	12 Aug	1812
AW	12 Aug	1819 (CH)
KCB	19 July	1820 (LG)
AR	27 May	1825 (LG)

GCB	8 June	1831 (LG)
d (suicide)	2 Nov	1839 (DNB)
TROLLOPE, William		
L	13 Dec	1794
TROTH, William		
L	16 Dec	1793
TROTTEN, Richard		
L	8 Apr	1757
CR	16 May	1778
TROTTER, David		
L		1665
CA		1672
d		1682 (PJP)
TROTTER, Edward		
L	26 Dec	1797
TROTTER, George		
L	17 Mar	1708 (PMM)
d		1746 (PJP)
TROTTER, John		
L	8 May	1695 (PMM)
CR		
CA	7 Feb	1704 (PMM)
d	12 Nov	1747 (PMM)
TROTTER, Robert		
L	15 Nov	1799
Ret CR	30 Nov	1841 (OB)
TROTTER, Savage		
L	15 Nov	1756
TROTTER, William		
L	19 Aug	1813
TROUBRIDGE, Sir Edward Thomas		
L	22 Feb	1806
CR	5 Sept	1806
Inh Bt	1 Feb	1807 (DNB)
CA	28 Nov	1807
MP		1831–
(Sandwich)		1847 (DNB)
COM AD	25 Apr	1835–
	8 Sept	1841 (AO)
CB	20 July	1838 (DNB)
RAB	23 Nov	1841 (LG)
HP	23 Nov	1841 (OB)
RAW	26 June	1847 (LG)
RAR	12 Nov	1849 (LG)
d	7 Oct	1852 (DNB)
TROUBRIDGE, Sir Thomas		
L	1 Jan	1781
CR	11 Oct	1782
CA	1 Jan	1783
Cre Bt	23 Nov	1799 (LG)
COM AD	19 Feb	1801–
	15 May	1804 (AO)
CRM	1 Jan	1801 (AL)
MP		1802–1806 (MPT)
(Great Yarmouth)		
RAB	23 Apr	1804
RAW	9 Nov	1805
d (drowned)	1 Feb	1807 (DNB)
TROUGHTON, Ellis		
L	25 July	1762
TROUGHTON, Joseph		
L	7 Feb	1815
HP	28 Jan	1818 (OB)
TROUGHTON, Miles		
L		1690 (PJP)
TROUGHTON, Nicholas		
L	4 Mar	1815
d		1845 (OB)
TROUGHTON, Thomas Lion		
L	7 Sept	1807
TROUNCE, Peter		
L	25 June	1810
TROUNCE, Roger		
L	16 June	1778
d	20 June	1787 (PMM)
TROUNSELL, George Patey		
L	20 Feb	1815
TRUPPO, Peter		
T		
L	5 Nov	1805
d		1822 (TR)
TRUSCOTT, Francis		
L	28 Feb	1805
CR	22 Oct	1814
d	29 Dec	1827 (MB)
TRUSCOTT, George		
L	28 Feb	1805
CR	21 Mar	1812
Ret CA	1 Feb	1845 (OB)
TRUSCOTT, William (1)		
L	8 Feb	1757
CR	17 Aug	1762
CA	14 Dec	1778
RAB	1 June	1795
RAW	20 Feb	1797
d	31 Jan	1798
TRUSCOTT, William (2)		
L	9 July	1794
d		1811 (PJP)
TRUSS, William		
L	25 July	1809
d	3 Feb	1837 (PJP)
TRUSSELL, George		
L	22 Dec	1761
d	30 Dec	1798
TRYON, Henry		
L	18 Mar	1815 (OB)
TRYON, Robert		
L	24 May	1810
d	16 Jan	1811 (PMM)
TUBERVILLE, Edmund		
L	15 Aug	1810 (PJP)
CR	15 June	1814
TUBLAY, Roger		
L	19 Nov	1705
TUBMAN, John		
L	12 Oct	1740
TUCKER, Sir Edward		
L	21 May	1799
CR	22 Jan	1806
CA	23 Mar	1807
Kt	6 May	1813 (OB)
KCB	2 Jan	1815 (MB)
RAB	23 Nov	1841 (LG)
RAW	9 Nov	1846 (LG)
RAR	24 Jan	1849 (LG)
VA	8 July	1851 (CH)
A	30 July	1857 (CH)
Ret A	28 Jan	1858 (CH)
d		1864 (CH)

TUCKER, Francis
L 5 May 1746
TUCKER, Henry
L 17 Aug 1812
d 1836 (PJP)
TUCKER, James
L 6 Oct 1800
TUCKER, John (1)
L 30 Mar 1691 (PMM)
TUCKER, John (2)
L 20 Nov 1790
TUCKER, John Coates
L 14 Mar 1808
TUCKER, Nathaniel
L 13 Apr 1710
CR 21 Apr 1740
TUCKER, Nicholas
L 16 May 1797
TUCKER, Robert (1)
L 31 Mar 1795
CR 21 Mar 1804
Ret CA 10 Sept 1840 (OB)
d 12 Jan 1846 (OB)
TUCKER, Robert (2)
L 3 Feb 1815
TUCKER, Thomas
L 4 Apr 1720
CR 8 Aug 1740
CA 17 July 1741
SUP RA 1756
d 8 Aug 1756
TUCKER, Thomas Tudor
L 20 May 1800
CR 15 Feb 1808
CA 1 Aug 1811
CB 4 July 1840 (OB)
Ret RA 31 Oct 1846 (OB)
d 20 July 1852 (DNB)
TUCKER, Tudor
L 22 Apr 1783
CR 18 Feb 1796
TUCKER, William (1)
L 15 Apr 1678
d before 1689 (PJP)
TUCKER, William (2)
L 11 May 1754
CR 18 Feb 1769
d 31 Jan 1772
TUCKER, William (3)
L 2 June 1779
d 26 Nov 1786 (PMM)
TUCKER, William (4)
L 18 Sept 1798
Ret CR 25 Nov 1830 (OB)
d 26 Oct 1850 (LT)
TUCKER, William Ley
L 23 Feb 1815
TUCKEY, James Hingston
L 3 Oct 1800 (PJP)
CR 27 Aug 1814
d 4 Oct 1816 (PJP)
TUCKEY, John
L 17 June 1689 (PMM)
CA 1 Jan 1694
d 24 Sept 1696

TUDD, William
L 1760 (PJP)
TUDOR, Abraham
L 27 June 1696
CR
CA 5 Aug 1707
KIA 6 Mar 1709 (LG)
TUDOR, John Kelly
L 15 Oct 1808
d 4 May 1845 (OB)
TUDWAY, Robert
L 21 Oct 1790
d 30 Dec 1795 (PMM)
TUGWELL, William
L 19 Feb 1691
TUITE, Henry
L 15 Dec 1761
d 26 Aug 1805 (PMM)
TULL, Henry
L 14 Dec 1814
TULLIDGE, Joseph
L 17 Oct 1800
CR 1 Aug 1811
Ret CA 7 Feb 1842 (OB)
d 19 Mar 1845 (OB)
TULLIS, William
L 7 June 1814
d 1848 (OB)
TULLOCK, Andrew
L 25 Jan 1802
TULLOH, Charles
L 15 Aug 1808
Ret CR 27 Oct 1845 (OB)
TULLOH, John (1)
L 20 Sept 1779
TULLOH, John (2)
L 12 Mar 1811
TULLOH, William Izod
L 16 Oct 1808
Ret CR 27 Jan 1846 (OB)
TULLY, John
L 11 Mar 1815
HP 3 Feb 1817 (OB)
TULLY, Keevy
L 10 Nov 1813
TUNSTALL, Mathew
L 13 Aug 1761
d Oct 1771 (PRO)
TUPLEY, John
L
CA 27 July 1666 (RM)
TUPMAN, George
L 19 Mar 1805
CR 9 Oct 1815
d 22 Apr 1847 (OB)
TUPPE, Peter
L 1806 (PJP)
TUPPER, Cary
L 28 Feb 1782
KIA 24 Apr 1794 (LG)
TURBERVILLE, Edmund
L 15 Aug 1810
CR 15 June 1814 (OB)
HP 15 June 1814 (OB)

TURNBULL, Cornelius
L 14 Mar 1815
TURNBULL, George
L 13 May 1774
CR 25 Oct 1809
d Jan 1826 (MB)
TURNBULL, Robert
L 13 May 1774
HP Jan 1813 (OB)
TURNER, Barnard
T
L 6 Feb 1809
d 1830 (TR)
TURNER, Charles (1)
L 26 Mar 1796
KIA 1808 (PJP)
TURNER, Charles (2)
L 16 June 1807
TURNER, Charles (3)
L 20 Sept 1815
TURNER, Charles Fox
L 17 Oct 1811
TURNER, Charles Pye
L 2 Oct 1795
TURNER, Edmund
L 21 Aug 1741
TURNER, Ethelbert
L 22 Jan 1806
d June 1815 (PJP)
TURNER, Francis
L
CA 1672
TURNER, Francis John
L 19 Dec 1807
HP 1811–1813 (OB)
TURNER, Henry
L 1691 (PJP)
TURNER, James
L 15 July 1779
TURNER, Jellicoe
L 30 Aug 1806
TURNER, John (1)
L 1665
CA 29 Aug 1666 (RM)
d 16 July 1672 (NJ)
TURNER, John (2)
L
CA 1667
d 2 Jan 1731 (M)
TURNER, John (3)
L 15 Mar 1763
TURNER, John (4)
L 18 Nov 1790
d 16 Nov 1801
TURNER, John (5)
L 13 Feb 1801
TURNER, John (6)
L 13 Feb 1802
Ret CR 23 Mar 1833 (OB)
TURNER, Joseph (1)
L 1691 (PJP)
TURNER, Joseph (2)
L 5 Mar 1778
CR 7 Oct 1794
d May 1816 (PJP)

TURNER, Robert (1)
L 1664
CA 1665
d before 1689 (PJP)
TURNER, Robert (2)
L 17 Dec 1798
d 1837 (PJP)
TURNER, Simon
L 1 Mar 1745
TURNER, Thomas
L 17 Feb 1815
TURNER, William
L 6 Sept 1779
TURNOR, John
L 22 Nov 1790 (PJP)
CR Jan 1796 (PJP)
CA 26 Dec 1796
d 1801 (PJP)
TURNOUR, Hon. Arthur (1)
L 12 June 1781
HP Nov 1816 (OB)
TURNOUR, Hon. Arthur (2)
L 28 Aug 1807
CR 20 Sept 1815
TURNOUR, Hon. Gerard
L 15 Aug 1806
TURNOUR, Hon. Henry
L 1 July 1795
d 1805 (PJP)
TURQUAND, William James
L 3 Nov 1790
CR 22 Oct 1798
d (drowned) 26 Sept 1800 (CH)
TURRELL, Charles
L 13 Feb 1815
d 13 Jan 1846 (OB)
TURVILLE, Henry
L
CR 29 Sept 1699 (PMM)
d 5 June 1719
TUSON, Augustine
L 20 Oct 1795
TWEED, John Powell
L 26 May 1814
CR 22 July 1830 (MB)
HP 22 July 1830 (OB)
d 17 Mar 1848 (OB)
TWEED, Robert
L 10 May 1809
Ret CR 27 July 1847 (OB)
TWIGG, Richard Elliot
L 19 Dec 1807
Ret CR 24 July 1844 (OB)
TWINER, C.P.
L 1796 (PJP)
TWISDEN, John (1)
L 1705 (PJP)
d (drowned) 22 Oct 1707 (PJP)
TWISDEN, John (2)
L 28 Oct 1790
SUP CR 27 Mar 1823 (OB)
d 1853 (PJP)
TWISDEN, William
L 4 Apr 1760

TWYCROSS, Robert
L 26 June 1778
d 21 Apr 1783 (PRO)

TWYMAN, Arthur
L 27 Sept 1759
CR 17 May 1778

TWYSDEN, Henry Duncan
L 9 June 1815
CR 28 June 1838
HP July 1845 (OB)

TWYSDEN, Thomas
L 8 Dec 1781
CR 9 June 1794
CA 4 Dec 1794
d 4 Sept 1801 (PRO)

TYETE, George
L 1672
CA 1667
d before 1689 (PJP)

TYHURST, Philip
L 7 July 1740

TYLER, Charles (1)
L 26 Sept 1757

TYLER, Sir Charles (2)
L 5 Apr 1779
CR 31 Dec 1782
CA 21 Sept 1790
T
RAB 28 Apr 1808
RAR 31 July 1810
VAB 4 Dec 1813
VAW 4 June 1814
KCB 20 Apr 1816 (LG)
VAR 19 July 1821 (LG)
AB 27 May 1825 (CH)
AW 22 July 1830 (CH)
GCB 1 May 1833 (LG)
d 28 Sept 1835 (DNB)

TYLER, Charles (3)
L 9 Oct 1801
CR 7 Feb 1812
Ret CA 5 Mar 1844 (OB)
d 16 Aug 1846 (OB)

TYLER, Sir George
L 6 Feb 1813
CR 7 Feb 1815
CA 10 Oct 1822 (MB)
HP 10 Oct 1822 (OB)
KH 4 Mar 1833 (DNB)
Kt Nov 1838 (DNB)
RA 1852 (DNB)
VA 1857 (DNB)
d 1862 (DNB)

TYLER, John
L 6 Apr 1813

TYLER, Robert
L 1742 (PJP)

TYLER, Thomas William
L 20 Sept 1815

TYRE, Theophilus
L 22 Sept 1781

TYRHWITT, John
See TYRWHIT(T), John

TYRREL, Edward
L 21 Apr 1783
CR 8 Feb 1794
d 31 May 1798

TYRRELL, George
L 9 Jan 1812

TYRRELL, John
L 1665
CA 16 Jan 1678
CAFMR 23 Nov 1690 (EAD)
d 1692 (DDA)

TYRRELL, Joseph
L
CA 3 Apr 1680

TYRRELL, Richard
L 29 Nov 1740
CR 5 Mar 1743
CA 26 Dec 1743
RAW 21 Oct 1762
d 27 June 1766 (M)

TYRWHIT, Henry
L 1665
d before 1689 (PJP)

TYRWHIT, John (1)
L
CA 20 Sept 1660

TYRWHIT(T), John (2)
L
CA 11 July 1686

TYRWHIT(T), John (3)
L 24 Sept 1759
SUP CR 6 May 1805
d 1813 (PMM)

TYRWHIT, Strickland
L 15 Sept 1688 (P)

TYRWHIT, Willoughby
L 1693 (PJP)

TYTCHE, Robert
L
CR
CA 10 May 1731
d 1 Oct 1740

TYTE, George
See TYETE, George

TYTE, Robert
L 22 Apr 1802
Ret CR 30 June 1840 (OB)

UMFREVILLE, John Brand
L 16 Jan 1806
CR 6 Dec 1813

UMFREVILLE, Samuel Charles
L 25 Mar 1813
CR 29 Jan 1838 (OB)

UNDERDOWN, John
L
CR 4 Jan 1695 (PJP)
CA 25 Aug 1696
d 4 Nov 1728

UNDERDOWN, Thomas
L 30 Sept 1758

UNDERDOWN, William
L 24 Apr 1744

UNDERWOOD, Coope John
L 1703 (PRO)

UNDERWOOD, Thomas
L 17 Nov 1763
CR 10 Feb 1772

UNDRELL, John
L 13 Sept 1806
CR 13 June 1815
UPJOHN, John
L 11 Dec 1807
UPPLEBY, Samuel
L 9 Nov 1756
CR 2 June 1772
CA 8 Apr 1776
d (drowned) 11 Oct 1780 (CH)
UPTON, Arthur
L 13 Mar 1734
CR 1 Sept 1741
d (drowned) 24 Sept 1757 (CH)
UPTON, Charles
L 3 July 1739
CR 30 Aug 1745
d 17 Aug 1749 (M)
UPTON, Clotworthy
L 16 Sept 1795
CR 1 Jan 1801
CA 29 Apr 1802
UPTON, Francis (1)
L 21 June 1748
CR 15 June 1756
UPTON, Francis (2)
L 1 Dec 1782
d 7 Aug 1793 (PMM)
UPTON, Jonathan
L 23 Feb 1778
UREDALE, Samuel
See UVEDALE, Samuel
URMSTON, George Constantine
L 7 July 1809
CR 5 Oct 1814
URQUHART, Arthur
L 1703 (PJP)
URRY, David
L
CR 5 Oct 1709
URRY, John
L 12 Nov 1755
CR 6 Aug 1761
CA 26 May 1768
d Jan 1801 (PJP)
URRY, Thomas
L
CA 13 Apr 1690
d 18 Nov 1699
URRY, William
L
CA 5 Sept 1695
Dismissed 1703
USHER, Arthur
L 1 Dec 1745
CR 22 Jan 1761
CA 17 Jan 1763
d 6 May 1763
USHER, Ignatius
L 13 Oct 1683
USHER, Sir Thomas
See USSHER, Sir Thomas
USHER, William Armstrong
L 30 May 1815
HP 1838 (OB)

USHERWOOD, William
L 23 Dec 1809
CR 22 July 1830 (MB)
d 18 Dec 1844 (OB)
USSHER, Sir Thomas
L 17 July 1797
CR 18 Oct 1806
CA 24 May 1808
CB 4 June 1815 (DNB)
KCH 1831 (DNB)
RAB 9 Nov 1846 (OB)
RAW 27 Dec 1847 (LG)
d 6 Jan 1848 (CH)
UTBER, John
L 1663
CA 1665
KIA 2 Aug 1665 (ESP)
UTBER, Richard
L
CA 1661
RAW 29 May 1666 (RM)
d 1669 (AJ)
UTLAY, John Taylor
L 1 Aug 1811
HP Aug 1814 (OB)
UTTING, Ashby
L 4 Nov 1729
CR 27 Sept 1740 (PMM)
CA 25 Mar 1741
d 7 Jan 1746 (PMM)
UVEDALE, Samuel
L 5 May 1747
CR 16 Jan 1758
CA 18 Feb 1760
d 14 Dec 1808 (PJP)
UZULD, Azariah
L 13 Aug 1779
CR 9 May 1795
d 1798 (PJP)

VACHELL, George
L 10 Jan 1741
CR 9 July 1747
d (drowned) 31 Dec 1747 (PJP)
VAILLANT, Isaac
L 25 Nov 1761
CR 8 Oct 1777
CA 23 Nov 1780
d 25 Oct 1804 (PJP)
VAILLANT, Paul Henry
L 7 Oct 1794
d 24 Dec 1803
VAIR, John
L 15 Oct 1781
VALE, William (1)
L 14 May 1808
VALE, William (2)
L 21 Feb 1815
d 18 Oct 1842 (LT)
VALENTINE, David
L 3 July 1795
CR 22 Jan 1806

VALENTINE, John
L 6 Dec 1757
d (drowned) 1 Jan 1761 (PJP)

VALLACK, Benjamin
L 11 Aug 1801
T
d 1811 (PJP)

VALLACK, George
L 7 May 1808
d 1844 (PJP)

VALLACK, Richard Glynn
L 17 May 1807
HP 1826 (OB)
Ret CR 17 Nov 1855 (PJP)
d 1867 (PJP)

VALLIANT, Isaac
See VAILLANT, Isaac

VALOBRA, James
L 31 Aug 1799
Ret CR 10 Feb 1831 (OB)
d 1861 (PJP)

VALPY, Anthony Blagrave
L 11 Oct 1811
CR 19 July 1814
HP 2 Aug 1814 (OB)

VANBRUGH, Charles
L
CR 4 Apr 1707 (PMM)
CA 21 Feb 1709
MP
(Plymouth) 17 Jan 1740–
2 Nov 1740 (MPS)
d 2 Nov 1740 (MPS)

VANBRUGH, Giles Richard
L 29 Aug 1740
CR Aug 1743 (PJP)
CA 13 Jan 1744
d (drowned) 6 Feb 1746 (PJP)

VANBRUGH, Philip
L
CR
CA 27 Nov 1710
GG
(Newfoundland) 1738–1739 (BNS)
COMM
(Portsmouth) 1 Feb 1739–
22 July 1753 (NBO)
d 22 July 1753 (NBO)

VAN COURT, Peter
L 25 Dec 1747
d 24 Sept 1807 (LT)

VANCOUVER, George
L 9 Dec 1780
CR 15 Dec 1790
CA 28 Aug 1794
d 12 May 1798 (DNB)

VANDEPUT, George
L 24 Sept 1759
CR 17 Apr 1764
CA 20 June 1765
RAB 1 Feb 1793
RAR 12 Apr 1794
VAB 4 July 1794
VAW 1 June 1795
AB 14 Feb 1799
d 14 Mar 1800 (DNB)

VANE, Hon. Raby
L 1758 (PJP)
MP
(Durham Co.) 22 Mar 1758–1761 (MPN)
CR 14 Jan 1759
CA 4 Sept 1759
MP
(Carlisle) 1761–1768 (MPN)
d 23 Oct 1769 (MPN)

VANS, Randall
L 18 Apr 1811

VANS, Samuel
L 1 Apr 1780

VANSITTART, Henry
L 21 Feb 1795
CR 30 May 1798
CA 3 Feb 1801
RAB 22 July 1830 (LG)
RAR 10 Jan 1837 (LG)
VAB 23 Nov 1841 (LG)
d 21 Mar 1843 (DNB)

VANTHUYSEN, Thomas
L 13 Apr 1797
Dismissed Jan 1800 (PJP)

VARLO, Weston
L 16 May 1743
CR
CA 12 May 1759
SUP RA 1787
d 22 Dec 1789 (M)

VASHON, James
L 1 June 1774
CR 5 Aug 1779
CA 12 Apr 1782
RAW 23 Apr 1804
RAR 9 Nov 1805
VAB 28 Apr 1808
VAR 31 July 1810
AB 4 June 1814
AW 19 July 1821 (CH)
d 20 Oct 1827 (DNB)

VASHON, James Giles
L 13 Jan 1794
CR
CA 26 May 1802 (PJP)

VASSALL, Nathaniel
L 4 Nov 1790
CR 15 June 1814
d 8 Sept 1832 (MB)

VASSMER, Henry
L 7 Feb 1760

VAUGHAN, Arthur
L 1 Mar 1740

VAUGHAN, Charles
L 7 Dec 1778
d 25 Nov 1790 (M)

VAUGHAN, Edward
L 1702 (PMM)

VAUGHAN, Francis
L 28 May 1694
CR 29 May 1705
d (drowned) 9 Feb 1707 (CH)

VAUGHAN, George
L 22 Feb 1778
CR 23 Apr 1794
CA 24 Nov 1795
VAUGHAN, Henry
L 3 Oct 1780
CR 6 July 1794
CA 22 Jan 1806
d 6 Aug 1833 (PJP)
VAUGHAN, Hugh
L 31 Dec 1755
VAUGHAN, James
L 25 Mar 1780
VAUGHAN, John
L 17 Apr 1740
CR
CA 11 Aug 1746
RAW 31 Mar 1775
RAR 5 Feb 1776
VAW 29 Jan 1778
VAR 26 Sept 1780
AB 24 Sept 1787
d 7 Nov 1789 (M)
VAUGHAN, Roger (1)
L 1665
CA 1672
KIA 28 May 1672 (NJ)
VAUGHAN, Roger (2)
L 6 Sept 1688
CA 23 Oct 1690
KIA 4 Feb 1695 (CH)
VAUGHAN, Samuel
L 1710 (PRO)
VAUTIER, David
L 17 Nov 1790
VAVASOR, Richard
L 30 Jan 1746
SUP CR 21 Sept 1796 (PMM)
d 21 May 1803 (PMM)
VAVASOUR, Henry
L 1760 (PJP)
VEALE, John
L 1779 (PJP)
KIA 6 July 1779 (PJP)
VEALE, Joseph
L
CR 30 Aug 1746
VEITCH, James
L 11 Apr 1793
CR 1 Jan 1801
CA 12 Aug 1812
d 17 Oct 1839 (OB)
VENNER, John
L
CA 17 June 1689
VENOUR, William
L 17 Sept 1794
CR 29 Apr 1802
d (drowned) 30 July 1803 (PJP)
VENUS, William
T
L 14 Dec 1814
d Dec 1846 (TR)
VERE, Lord
See BEAUCLERK, Lord Vere

VERNON, Edward (1)
L 16 Sept 1702 (DNB)
CR
CA 22 Jan 1706
HP 1721–1726 (DNB)
MP
(Penrym) 1722–1734 (MPS)
VAB 9 July 1739
MP
(Portsmouth) 21 Feb 1741–
27 Apr 1741 (MPS)
MP
(Ipswich) 1741–1757 (MPS)
VAW 13 Mar 1742 (LG)
VAR 11 Aug 1743 (LG)
AW 23 Apr 1745 (LG)
Dismissed 11 Apr 1746 (DNB)
d 30 Oct 1757 (DNB)
VERNON, Sir Edward (2)
L 4 Apr 1743
CR 5 Dec 1747
CA 3 Apr 1753
Kt 24 June 1773 (PJP)
RAW 29 Mar 1779 (CH)
RAR 26 Sept 1780
VAW 24 Sept 1787
VAR 1 Feb 1793
AB 12 Apr 1794
d 16 June 1794 (DNB)
VERNON, Francis Venables
L 25 Sept 1793
d 1795 (PMM)
VERNON, Frederick
See HARCOURT, Frederick Edward Vernon
VERNON, Octavius
L 11 Jan 1814
CR 3 Feb 1820 (MB)
CA 7 Aug 1827 (MB)
VESCONTE, Henry or Philip le
See LE VESCONTE, Henry or Philip
VESEY, Francis
L 8 Sept 1793
CR 1 Sept 1797
CA 16 Sept 1799
VEVERS, George
L 7 Feb 1815
HP Nov 1818 (OB)
VEYSEY, John
L 28 Feb 1760
SUP CR 28 Jan 1806
d 1813 (PMM)
VIALL, John
L
CA 22 Mar 1693
d 14 Mar 1702
VIBART, James
L 1 Jan 1814
HP July 1814 (OB)
VICARS, George
L 19 Sept 1815
VICARY, William
T
L 8 Feb 1815
Ret CR 1852 (TR)
d 1882 (TR)

VICKERS, Lewis
L 14 Feb 1778
KIA May 1781 (PJP)

VICKERS, William
L
CA 31 Mar 1690
d 25 Nov 1694

VICKERY, Robert Caryer
L 25 Mar 1809

VICTOR, John George
L 28 Apr 1807
d 16 Mar 1844 (PRO)

VIDAL, Alexander T. E.
L 6 Feb 1815
CR 15 May 1823 (MB)
CA 4 Oct 1825 (MB)
RA 27 Jan 1854 (CH)
VA 17 June 1859 (CH)
d 5 Feb 1863 (CH)

VIDAL, Richard
L 10 July 1809
CR 22 July 1830 (MB)

VIGNOLES, John
L 17 Sept 1812
d 29 Apr 1815 (PJP)

VILLIERS, Francis
L 1740 (PJP)

VILLIERS, Henry
L 17 Apr 1683
d 18 Aug 1707 (M)

VINCENT, Sir Andrew
L 22 Jan 1806
CR 6 Feb 1816 (MB)
KCH 26 Apr 1831 (OB)
CA 9 May 1832 (OB)
HP 9 May 1832 (OB)

VINCENT, Francis
L 1666

VINCENT, John (1)
L 1 Aug 1709 (PMM)

VINCENT, John (2)
L 16 June 1756

VINCENT, Nathaniel
L 28 July 1757
d 1779 (M)

VINCENT, Nicholas
L 3 Feb 1744
CR
CA 5 July 1748
Dismissed ship 8 June 1758
No half pay until 1763.
RAW 19 Mar 1779
RAR 27 Sept 1780
VAW 24 Sept 1787
VAR 1 Feb 1793
AB 12 Apr 1794
AW 1 June 1795
AR 9 Nov 1805
d 1809 (CH)

VINCENT, Philip
L 13 May 1720
CR
CA 18 July 1729
d 11 Dec 1746

VINCENT, P.L.
L 1801 (PJP)

VINCENT, Richard Budd
L 3 Nov 1790
CR 29 Apr 1802
CA 8 Apr 1805
CB 4 June 1815 (LG)
d 18 Aug 1831 (MB)

VINCENT, Samuel
L
CA 1 June 1692
d 27 Sept 1729 (M)

VINCENT, William
L 17 June 1695 (PJP)
In Merchant Service 1700 (PJP)

VINE, George Ballard
L 1 Feb 1798

VINE, William
L 21 Mar 1812

VIOLETT, James
L 4 Aug 1802

VIRTUE, Benjamin
L 19 Jan 1811
d (drowned) 29 Dec 1811 (PJP)

VITRE, John Denis de
See DE VITRE, John Denis

VITTLES, Richard
L
CA 22 May 1678

VITU, John
L 16 June 1756

VIVIAN, Thomas
L 15 Oct 1712

VIVION, Thomas
L 10 Nov 1794
CR 21 Oct 1810

VOL, Thomas
L 8 May 1804

VOLLER, Frederick
L 24 May 1809

VOSE, James
L 13 Dec 1780
d 5 Aug 1803

VOSPER, William
L 6 Apr 1796

VOTIER, Cornelius
L 29 Apr 1702 (PMM)

VOTIER(E), John (1)
L
CA 16 June 1667
SUP 3 Apr 1693 (PMM)

VOTIER, John (2)
L 1702 (PJP)

VOWELLS, John
L 7 Oct 1780

VYOLL, John
See VIALL, John

WADDELL, William
L 11 Nov 1776
SUP CR 11 Jan 1810
d 1815 (PJP)

WADDON, Richard
L 23 June 1720

WADDY, Bellingham
L 9 Aug 1794

WADE, Cales
L
CR 1 Mar 1706 (PMM)
CA 18 Nov 1709
d 5 July 1735 (PMM)

WADE, Cooper
L
CA 24 May 1693
e (cowardice) 16 Apr 1703 (LG)

WADE, George
T
L 15 Dec 1813
d 1825 (TR)

WADE, Thomas
L 19 June 1782
Dismissed 13 Apr 1791 (PMM)

WADE, Walter Peter
L 23 Jan 1808

WADE, William John
L 21 Sept 1812

WADESON, Charles
L 28 Feb 1815

WADHAM, Robert Adams
L 31 Aug 1805
CR 17 Jan 1838 (PRO)
d 20 Sept 1840 (PRO)

WADMAN, John
L 6 Aug 1759
d 9 Dec 1793 (PJP)

WAFFE, Elias
L 1 May 1690

WAGER, Charles (1)
L
CA 1660
d 24 Feb 1665 (PJP)

WAGER, Sir Charles (2)
L 1690 (MPS)
CA 7 June 1692
RAB 15 Apr 1708
RAW 21 Dec 1708
RAR 14 Nov 1709
Kt 18 Dec 1709 (DNB)
MP 23 Jan 1710–
(Portsmouth) 3 Feb 1711 (MPS)
MP 1713–1715 (MPS)
(West Looe)
CONT 16 Mar 1715–1718 (NBO)
MP 1715–1734 (MPS)
(Portsmouth)
VAB 15 June 1716
VAR 14 Mar 1718
(15 Mar 1717 in C)
COM AD 19 Mar 1718–
21 June 1733 (AO)
AB 10 July 1731
FLA 1733–1742 (DNB)
MP 1734–1741 (MPS)
(Westminster)
AW 26 Feb 1734
MP 1741–
(West Looe) 24 May 1743 (MPS)
d 24 May 1743 (DNB)

WAGER, James
L 21 Apr 1740

WAGHORN, Martin
L 16 Dec 1762
CR 15 Aug 1781
CA 6 Apr 1782
HP July 1782 (DNB)
d 17 Dec 1787 (DNB)

WAGMAN, John
L 1 May 1804

WAID, Andrew
L 7 Dec 1778

WAINWRIGHT, John (1)
L 19 June 1760
CR 16 Oct 1778
CA 28 Nov 1782
SUP 23 Apr 1804
d 22 July 1810 (PJP)

WAINWRIGHT, John (2)
L 22 Nov 1790
CR 12 July 1798
CA 29 Apr 1802
CB 4 June 1815 (LG)

WAKELEY, Charles
L 8 Aug 1696 (PJP)

WAKELIN, William
?WAKELYN, William
L
CA 11 June 1692
In Merchant Service 1700 (PJP)
d 1 Oct 1705

WAKEMAN, Francis
L 10 Sept 1728
CR 2 May 1740

WAKEN, Nicholas
L 20 Mar 1815 (OB)
HP 1816 (OB)

WALBEOFF, Thomas
L 17 Dec 1776
CR 24 June 1782

WALCONBERGH, Anthony St John Van
L 1666

WALCOTT, John Edward
L 26 Nov 1808
CR 6 June 1815
CA 6 May 1822 (MB)
RA 7 Oct 1852 (PRO)
VA 28 Nov 1857 (PRO)
d 1868 (PRO)

WALDEGRAVE, Hon. George Granville
L 20 July 1804
CR 22 Feb 1806
CA 16 Feb 1807
CB 4 June 1815 (DNB)
Inh IP 20 Aug 1825 (DNB)
RAB 23 Nov 1841 (LG)
RAW 9 Nov 1846 (LG)
RAR 1 Aug 1848 (LG)
VA 1 July 1851 (DNB)
d 11 May 1857 (DNB)

WALDEGRAVE, William, Lord Radstock (1)
L 1 Aug 1772
CR 23 June 1775 (DNB)
CA 30 May 1776
RAB 4 July 1794
VAB 1 June 1795
GG 1797–
(Newfoundland) 1800 (BNS)
Cre IP 29 Dec 1800 (DNB)

VAR 1 Jan 1801
AB 29 Apr 1802
AW 9 Nov 1805
AR 31 July 1810
GCB 2 Jan 1815 (DNB)
d 20 Aug 1825 (DNB)

WALDEGRAVE, Hon. William, Earl (2)
L 29 July 1806
CR 2 Dec 1809
CA 8 Mar 1811
MP (Bedford) 17 July 1815–1818 (MPT)
CB 18 Dec 1840 (OB)
Inh IP 11 Sept 1846 (MPT)
Ret RA 31 Oct 1846 (LG)
d 24 Oct 1859 (MPT)

WALDEN, Richard
L 27 Sept 1740
d 11 Mar 1743 (PMM)

WALDRON, Beaumont
L
CR 11 Mar 1706 (PMM)
CA 14 Dec 1709
d 20 Mar 1720

WALDRON, John (1)
L 1691 (PJP)

WALDRON, John (2)
L 19 May 1716 (PMM)
CR
CA 13 Apr 1719
KIA 19 Apr 1722 (PJP)

WALDRON, Joseph
L 20 Aug 1812
d 1818 (PJP)

WALE, George
L 9 Feb 1815

WALES, Richard Waller
L 13 July 1799
CR 16 June 1808
CA 1 Jan 1817 (MB)

WALFORD, John
L
CA 21 July 1690 (PJP)
d 29 Aug 1690 (PJP)

WALFORD, Michael
L 2 Mar 1694

WALFORD, William
T
L 1 June 1810
Ret CR 1850 (TR)
d 1859 (TR)

WALKER, Benjamin (1)
L 13 Dec 1796
CR 15 Jan 1802
CA 15 June 1810

WALKER, Benjamin (2)
L 20 May 1811

WALKER, Bethune James
L 24 Apr 1815
HP 1830 (OB)

WALKER,Charles
L 17 Mar 1796

WALKER, Charles Montagu
L 11 Jan 1803
CR 1 Feb 1812
CA 27 Mar 1825 (MB)

WALKER, Edward Barnaby
L 3 Mar 1815

WALKER, Frederick
L 22 Aug 1783
d 5 June 1790

WALKER, George
L 29 Apr 1802
Ret CR 25 Mar 1834 (OB)

WALKER, Harry
L 31 Jan 1806
KIA 21 Jan 1807 (JH)

WALKER, Henry (1)
T
L 3 Oct 1810
HP 26 Aug 1815 (OB)
d 1849 (TR)

WALKER, Henry (2)
T
L 28 May 1813
HP 26 Aug 1815 (OB)
d 1854 (TR)

WALKER, Sir Hovenden
L 30 Oct 1688
CA 17 Feb 1692 (PJP)
RAB 1709
RAW 3 Apr 1711
HP 1713 (WE)
Dismissed July 1715 (WE)
d 6 Jan 1728 (WE)

WALKER, James (1)
L 11 Oct 1756
CR 4 May 1761
KIA 13 June 1762 (LG)

WALKER, James (2)
L 18 June 1781 (DNB)
CR 6 July 1794
Dismissed 1796 (CH)
Restored 1797 (CH)
CA 17 Oct 1797
CB 4 June 1815 (LG)
Kt (Portugal) 30 Apr 1816 (LG)
RAB 19 July 1821 (MB)
RAW 27 May 1825 (LG)
RAR 22 July 1830 (LG)
d 13 July 1831 (DNB)

WALKER, James (3)
L 29 Apr 1802

WALKER, James Robertson
T
L 21 July 1809
CR 29 Aug 1815
Ret CA 28 July 1851 (DNB)
d 26 Oct 1858 (DNB)

WALKER, John (1)
L 1672

WALKER, John (2)
L 13 June 1794

WALKER, John (3)
L 17 Dec 1795

WALKER, John (4)
L 17 Feb 1815
HP 17 Feb 1815 (OB)

WALKER, J.L.
L 1779 (PJP)

Name	Rank/Event	Date	Year
WALKER, Joseph			
	L	20 Sept	1815
	d (drowned)	13 Jan	1836 (PJP)
WALKER, Nehemiah			
	L		1672
WALKER, Norris			
	T		
	L	14 Nov	1809
	Gone		1813 (TR)
WALKER, Robert			
	L	30 Dec	1808
	CR	8 Dec	1813
WALKER, Russell			
	L	13 May	1720
WALKER, Samuel Hood			
	L		
	CR	22 Mar	1780
	CA	26 Aug	1780
	d (drowned)	5 Oct	1780 (CH)
WALKER, Thomas			
	L	25 Nov	1794
WALKER, William (1)			
	L		1746
	d (drowned)	15 June	1746 (PJP)
WALKER, William (2)			
	L	3 Aug	1793
WALKER, William (3)			
	L	1 Aug	1811
	CR	25 Aug	1828 (MB)
	HP	25 Aug	1828 (OB)
WALKER, William Hovendon			
	L	29 Oct	1806
WALKIE, John			
	L	20 May	1812
	HP	July	1832 (OB)
	CR	23 Nov	1841 (OB)
	d	Jan	1848 (OB)
WALKINS, Thomas Vernon			
See WATKINS, Thomas Vernon			
WALL, Allen			
	L	7 Sept	1815 (OB)
WALL, Andrew			
	L		1664
WALL, J.			
	L		1790 (PJP)
WALL, James (1)			
	L	30 July	1758
WALL, James (2)			
	L	20 May	1781
WALL, J. Ellis			
	L		1802 (PJP)
WALL, John Howell			
	L	25 Feb	1815
WALL, Robert			
	L	24 Feb	1815
WALL, William (1)			
	L	9 July	1778
WALL, William (2)			
	L	16 Jan	1779
	SUP CR	31 Jan	1814
WALLAC, James			
	L	31 Dec	1813
WALLACE, Sir James (1)			
	L	11 Mar	1755
	CR	1 Nov	1762
	CA	10 Jan	1771
	Kt	13 Feb	1777 (DNB)
	CRM	1 Feb	1793 (AL)
	RAW	12 Apr	1794
	RAR	4 July	1794
	VAW	1 June	1795
	GG (Newfoundland)		1796–1797 (BNS)
	VAR	14 Feb	1799
	AB	1 Jan	1801 (CH)
	d	6 Mar	1803 (PJP)
WALLACE, James (2)			
	L	14 Apr	1798
WALLACE, James (3)			
	L	24 Oct	1807
	Ret CR	24 July	1844 (OB)
WALLACE, John (1)			
	L		
	CR	18 May	1779 (PJP)
	d (drowned)	July	1781 (PJP)
WALLACE, John (2)			
	L	9 May	1797
	T		
	Gone		1809 (TR)
WALLACE, Thomas			
	L	8 Feb	1815
	d		1847 (OB)
WALLACE, William Richard			
	L	20 Nov	1790
WALLER, Edmund			
	L	27 May	1797
	CR	20 July	1808
	CA	1 Jan	1817 (MB)
	d	15 July	1845 (OB)
WALLER, George			
	L	11 Feb	1815
WALLER, Jacob			
	L	4 Sept	1766
	CR	23 Aug	1781
	CA	16 Jan	1783
	d	Oct	1798 (PJP)
WALLER, John (1)			
	L	19 Feb	1781
WALLER, John (2)			
	L	8 Jan	1794
	CR	29 Apr	1802
	d (drowned)	Sept	1806 (CH)
WALLER, John (3)			
	L	22 Jan	1806
WALLER, Richard			
	L	16 Feb	1815
WALLER, Thomas Moutray			
	L	10 Jan	1791
	CR		
	CA	7 Mar	1797
	d	2 June	1818 (PRO)
WALLER, William			
	L	8 Aug	1793
	CR	12 June	1797
	CA	7 Mar	1799
WALLINGTON, Charles			
	L	19 Nov	1808
WALLINGTON, Edmund			
	L	13 Jan	1796
WALLIS, Gilbert			
	L	21 Oct	1703
	CR	26 Feb	1734

CA	30 June	1738
d	Oct	1739 (M)
WALLIS, James (1)		
L	31 Mar	1779
CR	20 Jan	1794
CA	4 May	1797 (PJP)
d		1808 (PJP)
WALLIS, James (2)		
L	2 June	1797
CR	3 Nov	1813
CA	26 Nov	1817 (MB)
Ret CA	31 Oct	1846 (LG)
WALLIS, James (3)		
L	10 Feb	1815
HP	10 Feb	1815 (OB)
WALLIS, Matthew		
L	16 Mar	1744
d	29 May	1788 (M)
WALLIS, Patrick		
L	15 Dec	1812
WALLIS, Sir Provo William Parry		
L	30 Nov	1808 (DNB)
CR	9 July	1813
CA	12 Aug	1819 (MB)
GCB	24 May	1823 (DNB)
RA	27 Aug	1851 (DNB)
VA	10 Sept	1857 (DNB)
KCB	24 May	1860 (DNB)
A	2 Mar	1863 (DNB)
AF	11 Dec	1877 (DNB)
d	13 Feb	1892 (DNB)
WALLIS, Samuel		
L	19 Oct	1746
CR	30 June	1756
CA	8 Apr	1757
COM E	29 Dec	1780–
	13 Dec	1784 (NBO)
COM E	29 Oct	1787–
	21 Jan	1795 (NBO)
d	21 Jan	1795 (NBO)
WALLIS, William		
L	21 Sept	1790
WALLOP, Thomas		
L		1665
WALPOLE, Galfridus		
L	14 Feb	1705 (PMM)
CR		
CA	17 Oct	1706
TGH		1714–1715 (PJP)
MP		1715–
(Lostwithiel)	21 Mar	1721 (MPS)
d	7 Aug	1726
WALPOLE, George		
L	15 Sept	1801
WALPOLE, Hon, William (1)		
L	11 Oct	1802
CR	22 Jan	1806
CA	9 Nov	1809
d	29 June	1814 (LT)
WALPOLE, William (2)		
T		
L	8 Aug	1808
CR	15 June	1814
CA	7 Dec	1819 (MB)
RA	19 Jan	1852 (CH)
VA	10 Sept	1857 (CH)
Ret VA	26 Feb	1858 (CH)
Ret A	27 Apr	1863 (CH)
d		1875 (TR)
WALSH, Archibald		
L	24 June	1796
WALSH, John (1)		
L	23 Nov	1744
SUP CR	21 Sept	1796 (PMM)
d	15 Dec	1798 (PJP)
WALSH, John (2)		
L	24 Sept	1782
WALSH, John (3)		
L	28 May	1782
WALSH, Lucas		
L		1660
CA		1672
d		before 1689 (PJP)
WALSH, Maurice		
L	19 Jan	1797
d	4 Dec	1799
WALSH, Philip		
L	16 June	1760
CR	18 May	1778
d	Sept	1789 (M)
WALSH, Stephen Russell		
L	6 Feb	1815
HP	6 Feb	1815 (OB)
d	24 Apr	1845 (OB)
WALSH, Thomas (1)		
L	6 June	1740
WALSH, Thomas (2)		
L	4 Sept	1796
WALSINGHAM, Hon. Robert		
See BOYLE, Hon. Robert q.v.		
WALTER, Arthur		
L	4 Aug	1774
CR	25 Aug	1779
CA	25 Oct	1809
WALTER, Jacob		
L		1768 (PJP)
WALTER, John		
L		1665
WALTER, Robert		
L	4 Nov	1755
CR	10 May	1781
WALTER, William		
L	8 Feb	1782
d	16 June	1787 (PMM)
WALTERS, Benjamin		
L		1672 (P)
CA	2 Sept	1687 (P)
CA	14 May	1688
SUP	18 Apr	1693 (PMM)
d	26 Feb	1698
WALTERS, Joseph		
L	2 May	1678
CA	19 May	1689
WALTERS, George Robinson		
L	27 Dec	1762
CR		
CA	2 Sept	1773
d	9 Dec	1789 (M)
WALTERS, Samuel		
L	8 Mar	1805
d	1 June	1812 (LG)

WALTON, Sir George
L 22 Feb 1690 (PJP)
CA 19 Jan 1697
Kt 1722 (DNB)
RAB 16 Feb 1723
RAR 21 Apr 1727
VAB 4 Jan 1728
VAR 29 June 1732
AB 26 Feb 1734
SUP A 1735 (PJP)
d 21 Nov 1739 (DNB)

WALTON, Jacob
L 11 Oct 1793
CR 2 Nov 1798
CA 29 Apr 1802
Ret RA 10 Jan 1837 (CH)
RAW 17 Aug 1840 (LG)
RAR 23 Nov 1841 (LG)

WALTON, Jeremiah
L 18 July 1744

WALTON, John Bently
L 31 July 1781

WALTON, Pierpont
L 27 Mar 1741

WALTON, Samuel
L 18 May 1756

WALTON, Thomas
L 9 Jan 1777

WALTON, William
L 31 Aug 1739
d 16 July 1787 (M)

WANLY, Nicholas
L 1795 (PJP)

WAPLE, Edward
L 2 July 1762

WARBURTON, Benjamin
L 12 Sept 1800
CR 16 Dec 1807

WARBURTON, Charles
L 5 Mar 1762

WARBURTON, Robert
L 11 Jan 1786
CR 22 Nov 1790
CA 21 Apr 1795
d Dec 1807 (PJP)

WARCUP, George
L 17 June 1808
d 22 Nov 1811 (PJP)

WARCUP, Henry
L 1665

WARD, Edward Southwell, Lord Bangor
L 22 May 1809
d 1837 (PJP)

WARD, Edward Willis
L 18 Mar 1815

WARD, Henry (1)
L 12 Sept 1694

WARD, Henry (2)
L 26 Mar 1737
CR
CA 25 May 1741
SUP RA 1 June 1757
d 4 Dec 1766

WARD, James (1)
L 1665 (P)
CA 17 Dec 1689
KIA 31 May 1693 (PJP)

WARD, James (2)
L 5 Mar 1778

WARD, James (3)
L 22 Aug 1782
d 28 Sept 1806 (PMM)

WARD, James (4)
L 25 Dec 1812

WARD, John (1)
L
CA 1667 (P)
CA 25 Mar 1692 (PJP
d 1703

WARD, John (2)
L 8 Dec 1695

WARD, John (3)
L
CA 27 May 1695
SUP 1705
d 19 Jan 1717

WARD, John (4)
L 2 Nov 1796

WARD, Richard (1)
L 8 Feb 1706

WARD, Richard (2)
L 18 Dec 1810

WARD, Thomas (1)
L
CA 1667

WARD, Thomas (2)
L 25 May 1696 (PMM)

WARD, Thomas (3)
L 14 July 1740
CR 15 Jan 1747
CA 22 July 1756
d 1774 (PJP)

WARD, Thomas (4)
L 23 June 1781

WARD, William (1)
L 21 Nov 1762
d 4 July 1806 (PMM)

WARD, William (2)
L 11 Apr 1783
d 29 Aug 1801

WARD, William (3)
L 10 Jan 1800
CR 23 July 1806
CA 10 June 1808
HP Jan 1810 (OB)
RAB 9 Nov 1846 (LG)
RAW 3 Jan 1848 (LG)
Ret RA 1851 (CH)
Ret VA 22 Apr 1853 (CH)

WARD, William Robert (1)
L 27 June 1814

WARD, William Robert (2)
L 3 Aug 1814

WARDE, Charles (1)
L 23 Mar 1771

WARDE, Sir Charles (2)
L 13 Feb 1805
CR 29 Apr 1808
CA 18 Sept 1815
KH 1 Jan 1837 (OB)
Ret RA 31 Oct 1846 (LG)

WARDE, Henry
L 26 Sept 1811
WARDEN, James
L 27 Aug 1760
d 28 Apr 1792
WARDEN, John (1)
L 28 Oct 1726
SUP CR 5 Sept 1749 (PMM)
WARDEN, John (2)
L 18 Oct 1744
WARDEN, William (1)
L 22 Feb 1796
CR 12 Oct 1807
Ret CR 26 Nov 1830 (OB)
WARDEN, William (2)
L 24 Jan 1800
d 5 June 1807 (PJP)
WARDLAW, William
L 26 Mar 1767
CR 26 Mar 1779
WARDLE, John
L 10 Sept 1814
HP July 1814 (OB)
WARDROBE, Robert
L 5 May 1795
WARE, Thomas
L 25 May 1696
WARFFE, George
L 19 Oct 1797
d 2 Feb 1801
WARHAM, Ambrose
L 9 Jan 1778
WARHAM, John
L 7 Apr 1761
WARING, Henry
L 3 Oct 1794
CR 29 Apr 1802
WARING, James
T
L 11 Apr 1808
KIA 20 Sept 1813 (PJP)
WARING, Rupert
L 20 Oct 1714
CR 26 Oct 1739
CA 8 Sept 1741
(?16 Sept 1741)
d 13 Feb 1753
WARNER, Arthur Lee
Formerly BAGGE, Arthur
L 6 Dec 1813
CR 22 Nov 1821 (MB)
HP 1824 (OB)
d 1848 (OB)
WARNER, John
L
CA 5 May 1694 (PJP)
WARNER, Patrick
L 17 May 1804
WARNER, Samuel George
L 4 Dec 1781
CR 29 June 1795
WARNER, William
L 3 Jan 1794
d 20 June 1794 (M)
WARR, George
L 11 Mar 1815
WARRAND, Thomas
L 19 Feb 1800
CR 27 July 1812
CA 27 July 1825 (MB)
Ret CA 31 Oct 1846 (LG)
d 17 May 1848 (OB)
WARRE, Charles
L 15 Nov 1771
CR 26 June 1777
d (drowned) 1778 (CH)
WARRE, Henry
L 23 July 1781
CR 1 Dec 1787
CA 22 Nov 1790
SUP RA 31 Aug 1810
WARRE, William Archibald
L 13 Aug 1812
WARREN, Charles Gayton
L 10 July 1797
Ret CR 26 Nov 1830 (OB)
WARREN, David
L 17 Oct 1708
WARREN, Frederick
L 24 Oct 1794
CR 10 Aug 1797 (DNB)
CA 12 May 1801
RAB 22 July 1830 (LG)
RAR 10 Jan 1837 (LG)
VAB 23 Nov 1841 (LG)
VAW 9 Nov 1846 (LG)
VAR 26 July 1847 (LG)
d 22 Mar 1848 (DNB)
WARREN, George (1)
L
CA 19 Oct 1691
d 28 Apr 1693
WARREN, George (2)
L 1703 (PJP)
WARREN, George Baker
L 15 Mar 1815
WARREN, James Ferris
L 16 Feb 1809
One of four Jr. Lts. Dec 1815
L 15 May 1817 (OB)
WARREN, John
L 6 Nov 1793
WARREN, Sir John Borlase
MP 1774–1784 (MPN)
(Great Marlow)
Cre Bt 1 June 1775 (MPN)
L 19 July 1778
CR 5 Aug 1779
CA 25 Sept 1781
Kt 30 May 1794 (MPN)
MP 11 Nov 1797–
(Nottingham) 1806 (MPT)
RAB 14 Feb 1799
RAW 1 Jan 1801
RAR 23 Apr 1804
VAB 9 Nov 1805
MP 23 Mar 1807–
(Buckingham) 29 Apr 1807 (MPN)
VAW 28 Feb 1808
AB 31 July 1810
AW 4 June 1814
GCB 2 Jan 1815 (LG)
GCH 1819 (MPT)
d 27 Feb 1822 (DNB)

WARREN, John Talbot
L 17 Feb 1815
CR 1 Mar 1833 (OB)
CA 6 Aug 1852 (PRO)
d 6 Feb 1861 (PRO)

WARREN, Oliver
L 21 July 1719
d 1724 (M)

WARREN, Sir Peter
L 23 July 1723
CR 28 May 1727
CA 19 June 1727
RAB 10 Aug 1745 (LG)
RAW 14 July 1746
Kt 1747 (DNB)
MP 1 July 1747–
(Westminster) 29 July 1752 (MPS)
VAW 15 July 1747
VAR 12 May 1748
d 29 July 1752 (DNB)

WARREN, Robert
L 26 May 1814

WARREN, Samuel (1)
L 25 Aug 1759
CR 25 June 1773
CA 5 Sept 1777
d 1 June 1792

WARREN, Sir Samuel (2)
L 3 Nov 1790
CR 1 Mar 1797
CA 29 Apr 1802
CB 4 June 1815 (LG)
KCH 3 Aug 1835 (DNB)
RAW 10 Jan 1837 (LG)
KCB 18 Apr 1839 (DNB)
d 15 Oct 1839 (DNB)

WARREN, Thomas (1)
L
CA 28 May 1689
d 12 Nov 1699

WARREN, Thomas (2)
L 11 Aug 1691 (PJP)
CA 25 May 1696 (PJP)

WARREN, Thomas Hills
L 22 Jan 1806
Dismissed Nov 1807 (PJP)

WARREN, William Smith
T wounded
L 8 Feb 1815
d 1838 (TR)

WARRINER, George
L 24 Feb 1745

WARTON, Joseph
L 3 Mar 1804
HP Jan 1811 (OB)
Ret CR 18 July 1836 (OB)

WARWICK, Thomas
?WARRICK, Thomas
L 18 May 1745
CR 4 Jan 1758 (PJP)
CA 1 Dec 1758
d 1775

WASHBORNE, Robert
L 1668
CA 1672
d before 1689 (PJP)

WASHBURN, Edward
L 1669
d before 1689 (PJP)

WASHINGTON, Richard
L 1672
d before 1689 (PJP)

WASTELL, James
L 9 Nov 1756
CR 16 Jan 1768

WATERFALL, Mathew
L 13 Sept 1748

WATERHOUSE, Bartholomew George
L 10 Aug 1814
HP Oct 1821 (OB)

WATERHOUSE, Henry
L May 1792
CR 17 July 1794
CA 25 Oct 1800
d 27 July 1812 (DNB)

WATERHOUSE, John Wilmot
L 10 Oct 1793

WATERHOUSE, Thomas
L 12 Aug 1703 (PMM)
CR
CA 26 Mar 1720 (PRO)
d 1 Apr 1743 (M)

WATERMAN, John
T
L 15 July 1809
Ret CR 4 Apr 1848 (OB)
d 1859 (TR)

WATERMOUTH, John
L
CA 9 June 1666 (RM)

WATERS, Benjamin
See WALTERS, Benjamin

WATERS, Dominick Creagh
L 13 Feb 1815

WATERS, Francis
L 20 Jan 1779

WATERS, John Lawes
L 20 Sept 1796

WATERS, Joseph
L
CA 29 May 1689
d 15 Jan 1694

WATERS, William
L 13 Apr 1741

WATERWORTH, John
L 1662
CA 1665
KIA 28 May 1672 (NJ)

WATFORD, John
L
CA 21 July 1690
d 29 Aug 1690

WATHAM, Jonathan
L 1672
CA 1671
d before 1689 (PJP)

WATHERSON, Alexander
L 8 May 1761

WATHERSON, John (1)
L 13 May 1778

WATHERSON, John (2)
L | 29 Apr 1802
WATKINS, Benjamin
L | 24 Nov 1801
WATKINS, Frederick
L | 20 Nov 1790
CR
CA | 26 Apr 1795
SUP RA | 11 June 1814
AB | 12 Nov 1840 (LG)
AW | 23 Nov 1841 (LG)
AR | 20 Nov 1846 (LG)
d | 1856 (CH)
WATKINS, James
L
CA | 1665
WATKINS, John (1)
L
CA | 14 Aug 1696
KIA | 10 Oct 1707 (CH)
WATKINS, John (2)
L | 7 Sept 1727
CR | 14 Aug 1742
CA | 4 Aug 1743
d | 24 Apr 1757
WATKINS, Philip
L | 11 Mar 1691 (PJP)
WATKINS, Richard
L
CR | 19 Feb 1741
CA | 24 Feb 1743
Dismissed | Jan 1757 (PJP)
SUP RA | 15 Mar 1763
d | 4 Apr 1770 (M)
WATKINS, Robert (1)
L | 20 Jan 1691 (PMM)
CA | 13 Feb 1692 (PMM)
d | 1732
WATKINS, Robert (2)
L | 14 Sept 1739
d | 29 July 1746 (PMM)
WATKINS, Thomas Vernon
L | 29 Mar 1815
CR | 10 Jan 1837 (PMM)
CA | 29 Apr 1847 (PMM)
WATKINS, Timothy
L | 9 Dec 1782
d | 30 Mar 1793
WATKINS, Walter
L | 28 Feb 1815
WATKINSON, William
L | 21 Feb 1741
WATLING, John Wyatt
L | 22 Sept 1808
CR | 1 Dec 1813
CA | 22 July 1830 (MB)
HP | 22 July 1830 (OB)
WATLY, John
L
CA | 1665
d | before 1689 (PJP)
WATSON, Anthony
L | 7 Sept 1807
WATSON, Charles
L | 2 Aug 1734
CR
CA | 14 Feb 1738
RAB | 12 May 1748
GG (Newfoundland) | 1748–1749 (BNS)
RAR | 4 Feb 1755
VAB | June 1756
VAW | 1757
d | 16 Aug 1757 (DNB)
WATSON, Charles Hope
T
L | 10 June 1807
CR | 13 Aug 1812
CA | 6 June 1814
d | 1836 (TR)
WATSON, Christopher
L | 9 July 1782
CR | 2 Jan 1798
CA | 21 Oct 1810
d | Nov 1823 (MB)
WATSON, David George
L | 23 Oct 1778
WATSON, Edward
L | 7 Nov 1806
KIA | 1 Mar 1807 (JH)
WATSON, Edward Barnes
L | 16 Nov 1808
WATSON, George (1)
L | 1660
CA | 1665
d | before 1689 (PJP)
WATSON, George (2)
L | 22 Feb 1690 (PJP)
WATSON, George (3)
L | 6 Aug 1755
CR | 23 Dec 1758
CA | 11 Dec 1759
d | 16 June 1774
WATSON, George (4)
L | 7 May 1802
WATSON, James (1)
L | 13 July 1745
WATSON, James (2)
L | 23 Jan 1794
d | 5 Jan 1800 (JH)
WATSON, James (3)
L | 29 May 1782
CR | 1 Jan 1801
CA | 22 Jan 1806
WATSON, James (4)
L | 5 July 1801
Ret CR | 5 July 1831 (PMM)
d | 1834 (PMM)
WATSON, John (1)
L | 2 Mar 1734
Gone | 1752
WATSON, John (2)
L | 30 Apr 1794
WATSON, John (3)
L | 11 Aug 1794
CR | 15 June 1814
HP | Aug 1814 (OB)
WATSON, Joshua Rowley
L | 10 Aug 1793
CR | 16 May 1795
CA | 23 Mar 1798
d | 26 May 1818 (PJP)

WATSON, Nathaniel
L 19 May 1731
CR
CA 16 Jan 1741
d 17 Feb 1766

WATSON, Robert (1)
L 24 Nov 1778
CR 1 Dec 1787
CA 25 Oct 1790
RAB 28 Apr 1808
RAW 31 July 1810
RAR 1 Aug 1811
VAB 4 Dec 1813
VAW 4 June 1814

WATSON, Robert (2)
L 29 Apr 1802

WATSON, Robert (3)
L 23 Nov 1809
KIA 1 June 1812 (PJP)

WATSON, T.
L 1799 (PJP)

WATSON, Thomas (1)
L 22 Apr 1723
CR
CA 7 Oct 1739
KIA 8 May 1744 (LG)

WATSON, Thomas (2)
L 6 Sept 1759
CR
CA 17 Jan 1780
KIA 19 May 1780 (LG)

WATSON, Thomas William
L 29 Oct 1806

WATSON, William (1)
L
CA 5 Jan 1673

WATSON, William (2)
L 4 Aug 1798
Ret CR 23 Dec 1840 (OB)
d 1846 (OB)

WATT, George Topham Lawrye
L 20 Jan 1806
KIA 1 June 1813 (LG)

WATT, James
L 24 June 1762
CR 23 Nov 1777
CA 9 May 1781
KIA 3 Sept 1782 (LG)

WATT, John Ellis
L 3 Aug 1801
CR 1806
d Sept 1813 (LT)

WATT, Thomas Alexander
L 26 Sept 1809
d 4 Feb 1834 (LT)

WATT, William
L 22 Dec 1813

WATTON, Peter
L
CA 30 May 1678 (PJP)
SUP 1704 (PJP)
d 1717

WATTON, Thomas
L 6 Nov 1696

WATTS, George (1)
L 1702 (PJP)

WATTS, George (2)
L 1 May 1804

WATTS, George Edward
L 1 May 1804 (OB)
CR 17 Sept 1807
CA 7 June 1814
RAB 6 Sept 1849 (LG)
Ret RA 1851 (CH)
Ret VA 21 Oct 1856 (CH)
d 2 Jan 1860 (CH)

WATTS, James (1)
L 1666
CA 30 Sept 1673

WATTS, James (2)
L
CA 11 July 1686 (MB)

WATTS, John
L 14 Dec 1781
CR 22 Dec 1796 (PMM)
d 4 Mar 1801 (PMM)

WATTS, Jonathan
L 14 June 1689 (PJP)
CA 29 Oct 1696
d 25 July 1698

WATTS, Joseph
L 1691 (PJP)

WATTS, Robert
L 30 Jan 1801

WATTS, Walter
L 3 July 1760
SUP CR 30 Nov 1807
d 24 May 1814 (PJP)

WATTS, William Butler
L 20 June 1808
CR 22 July 1830 (MB)
d 1836 (PJP)

WAUCHOPE, Robert
L 21 Dec 1808
CR 21 Mar 1812
CA 6 June 1814
HP 6 June 1838
RAB 21 May 1849 (LG)
VA 21 July 1856 (CH)
A 29 July 1861 (GH)
d 14 June 1862 (CH)

WAUD, Edward
L 9 Nov 1746

WAUDBY, Daniel
L 18 Aug 1747

WAUDBY, William Daniel
L 9 Oct 1778

WAUGH, John Middleton
L 16 Mar 1814
d 1 Mar 1844 (LT)

WAVELL, David
L
CA 26 Jan 1694 (PJP)
d (drowned) 16 Jan 1704 (CH)

WAY, William
L 27 Feb 1812
d 14 Aug 1814 (LT)

WAYMAN, John
L 27 Feb 1760

WAYMAN, William
L
CA 1667

WAYNE, Gabriel Williams
L 13 Aug 1795
WEALE, Edward Taylor
L 1 Jan 1806
CR 27 Oct 1827 (MB)
WEARG, John
L 29 May 1720
WEATHERHEAD, John
L 1797 (PJP)
KIA 24 July 1797 (LG)
WEAVER, Robert
L 4 June 1813
WEAVER, William
T
L 20 Feb 1815
HP 20 Feb 1815 (OB)
Ret CR 1861 (TR)
d 1864 (TR)
WEBB, Alexander
L 16 Feb 1815
d Jan 1847 (OB)
WEBB, Charles (1)
L 3 Nov 1790
CR 26 Apr 1798
CA 16 Mar 1811
WEBB, Charles (2)
L 20 July 1805
WEBB, Edward (1)
L 1666
WEBB, Edward (2)
L 6 Dec 1777
Struck off List 13 Apr 1791 (PMM)
WEBB, Edward (3)
L 14 June 1813
CR 29 Sept 1827 (MB)
WEBB, James
L
CR July 1744 (PJP)
CA 25 June 1746
GG (Newfoundland) 1760–1761 (BNS)
d 14 May 1761
WEBB, John
L 18 Jan 1761
d 8 Nov 1786 (PMM)
WEBB, Joseph Richard Raggett
L 17 Mar 1806
CR 1 May 1828 (MB)
WEBB, Nicholas
L 19 July 1814
WEBB, Noah
L 8 Oct 1779
WEBB, Robert Rose
L 7 Oct 1811
WEBB, Sackvill
L 6 Apr 1690 (PJP)
WEBB, Vincent
L 1798 (PJP)
WEBB, William (1)
L 30 Dec 1795
WEBB, William (2)
L 12 Mar 1801
WEBB, William (3)
L 1 Sept 1806
WEBB, William (4)
L 29 Mar 1815
CR 17 July 1824 (MB)
CA 2 Dec 1826 (MB)
Ret CA 31 Oct 1846 (LG)
WEBBER, Arthur
L 26 Dec 1781
d 3 Apr 1793 (PRO)
WEBBER, Charles
L 23 Jan 1744
CR
CA 5 Apr 1756
RAW 26 Sept 1780 (CH)
d 23 May 1783 (M)
WEBBER, John (1)
L 15 Mar 1779
WEBBER, John (2)
L 31 May 1782
WEBBER, John Incledon
L 6 May 1780
WEBBER, Peter
L 12 Jan 1782
WEBBER, Philip
L 3 Mar 1795
WEBLING, Thomas
L 1703 (PJP)
WEBLY, William Henry
See PARRY, William Henry q.v.
WEBSTER, Henry
L 1666
WEBSTER, Robert
L 1797 (PJP)
KIA 11 Oct 1797 (LG)
WEBSTER, William (1)
L 15 Feb 1757
CR 14 Oct 1762
d Feb 1777 (M)
WEBSTER, William (2)
L 23 July 1807
d ?8 Feb 1844 (LT)
WEBSTER, William (3)
L 22 Aug 1808
d ?8 Feb 1844 (LT)
WEDDLE, Samuel
L 8 Oct 1813
WEEDON, Thomas
L 1703 (PJP)
WEEKES, Henry
T
L 24 Dec 1805
Gone 1814 (TR)
WEEKES, William Burt
L 21 Mar 1812
HP Aug 1840 (OB)
WEEKS, John
L 14 Dec 1798
CR 29 Mar 1812
d 24 Oct 1824 (LT)
WEIGHMAN, Frederick
L
CA 5 Apr 1690
d 16 Feb 1697
WEIGHMAN, William
L 17 June 1695
WEIGHT, George
L 1746 (PJP)
WEIR, Benjamin
L 4 Sept 1799
KIA 14 May 1807 (CH)

Name / Rank	Date	Year
WEIR, Henry		
L	12 May	1794
CR	28 June	1810
CA	22 July	1812
WEIR, John		
L	29 Apr	1811
HP	Aug	1811 (OB)
WEISS, William		
L	17 July	1811
WELBEY, W.H.		
L		1791 (PJP)
WELBY, Joseph		
L		
CA	26 Feb	1695
d (drowned)	31 May	1696 (CH)
WELBY, Richard		
L	22 Jan	1806
WELCH, Charles (1)		
L	15 Nov	1790
WELCH, Charles (2)		
L	26 Sept	1807
d (drowned)	Aug	1809 (PJP)
WELCH, David		
L	3 Feb	1812
CR	9 Nov	1846 (OB)
d		1847 (OB)
WELCH, Pierce		
L	4 July	1694
WELCH, Richard		
L	26 July	1800
WELCH, Robert		
L	17 Nov	1803
Ret CR	18 July	1836 (OB)
WELD, Charles		
L		
CA	4 July	1666 (RM)
WELD, Daniel		
L	10 Sept	1803
CR	17 May	1825 (MB)
HP	June	1827 (OB)
WELDE, Joseph		
L	30 Sept	1706 (PMM)
WELD, Richard		
L	29 Sept	1814
WELDON, John		
L	22 June	1726
WELDON, Joshua		
L	9 Aug	1745
WELLAND, Richard		
L	6 Apr	1779
WELLAND, Walter Palk		
L	23 Oct	1782
WELLARD, John		
L	12 Mar	1740
CR		
CA	31 May	1746
d	18 Apr	1776 (M)
WELLER, John (1)		
L	26 Mar	1710 (PMM)
CR		
CA	7 Apr	1721
d	29 Dec	1752 (PJP)
WELLER, John (2)		
L	15 Sept	1739
CR		
CA	29 Nov	1745
SUP RA		1770
d	7 Sept	1772
WELLING, David		
L	25 Jan	1796
WELLS, Andrew		
L	29 Apr	1802
SUP CR	25 Mar	1824 (OB)
WELLS, Benjamin		
L	31 May	1743
WELLS, Edward		
L	15 Jan	1718
WELLS, James		
L		1702 (PJP)
WELLS, John (1)		
L		1760 (PJP)
WELLS, Sir John (2)		
L	22 July	1779
CR	1 June	1782
CA	1 Mar	1783
RAB	9 Nov	1805
RAW	28 Apr	1808
RAR	25 Oct	1809
VAB	31 July	1810
VAW	12 Aug	1812
VAR	4 June	1814
KCB	29 May	1820 (LG)
AB	19 July	1821 (MB)
AW	22 July	1830 (CH)
GCB	29 Oct	1834 (LG)
AR	10 Jan	1837 (CH)
d	19 Nov	1841 (CH)
WELLS, John (3)		
T		
L	28 Apr	1812
Resigned		1816 (TR)
d		1841 (TR)
WELLS, Samuel		
L		1691 (PJP)
WELLS, Thomas (1)		
L	3 Mar	1740
CR	27 Sept	1745
WELLS, Thomas (2)		
L	14 Jan	1780
CR	7 Feb	1781
CA	30 Apr	1782
RAW	23 Apr	1804
RAR	9 Nov	1805
VAB	28 Apr	1808
VAR	31 July	1810
d	31 July	1811 (CH)
WELLS, Thomas (3)		
L	6 July	1795
CR	26 Nov	1808
d		1825 (MB)
WELLS, William (1)		
L	23 Mar	1794
WELLS, William (2)		
L	17 July	1805
CR	28 Dec	1807
CA	28 Apr	1809
d	3 Aug	1826 (MB)
WELSFORD, John		
L	28 Feb	1795
WELSH, George		
L	21 Sept	1807
d	14 Feb	1822 (PRO)

WELSH, James
L 3 May 1799
CR 29 Apr 1802
d 8 Nov 1809 (PJP)

WELSH, Thomas
L 2 Feb 1809

WELSTED, Frederick
L 17 Nov 1802
Ret CR 14 July 1835 (OB)
d 14 June 1848 (LT)

WEMYSS, Andrew
L 8 Dec 1778
d July 1794 (LT)

WEMYSS, Charles
L 17 Nov 1790
CR 2 Apr 1794
CA 19 Mar 1795
d 4 June 1802 (LT)

WEMYSS, Francis
L 23 July 1812
CR 20 Sept 1815
d 1816 (PJP)

WEMYS(S), Hon. James (1)
L 26 Sept 1745
Resigned 12 Jan 1757 (MPN)
MP (Fifeshire) 7 Jan 1763–1768 (MPN)
MP (Sutherland) 1768–1784 (MPN)
d 10 May 1786 (MPN)

WEMYSS, James (2)
L 30 Dec 1808
CR 1 Feb 1812
CA 1 July 1814
HP Dec 1814 (OB)
MP (Fife) 1820–1831 (OB)
MP (Fife) 1832–1849 (OB)
RAB 21 June 1850 (LG)
Ret RA 1851 (CH)
d 3 Apr 1854 (CH)

WEMYSS, Robert
L 5 Nov 1814
d May 1846 (OB)

WENLOCK, James
L 10 Sept 1741

WENTWORTH, Mark
L 28 Feb 1780

WENTWORTH, Samuel
L 1671
CA 1665
d before 1689 (PJP)

WENTWORTH, Thomas
L 30 May 1741

WENTWORTH, William Fitzwilliam
L 13 Apr 1813

WERDEN, Robert
L 1663
CA 1665
KIA 28 May 1673 (SJ)

WERGE, Thomas
L 14 June 1813

WESCOTT, John
L 30 Apr 1678

WESKETT, John
L 6 June 1696 (PJP)

WEST, Christopher
T
L 9 Feb 1808
CR 4 June 1814
HP 4 June 1814 (OB)
Ret CR 1851 (TR)
d 12 Aug 1854 (TR)

WEST, G.
L 1794 (PJP)

WEST, George
L 16 Mar 1815

WEST, Henry (1)
L 26 Nov 1793
CR
CA 22 Apr 1800
d 11 Feb 1803

WEST, Henry (2)
L 16 Aug 1808
CR 25 June 1832 (PJP)

WEST, Humphrey
L 10 July 1777
CR 19 Nov 1796

WEST, John (1)
L 1678 (DDA)

WEST, John (2)
L 18 May 1745
d 14 Jan 1759 (PMM)

WEST, John (3)
L 21 May 1761

WEST, John (4)
L 5 Aug 1778

WEST, Sir John (5)
L 27 July 1793
CR 7 Sept 1795
CA 15 Nov 1796
RAB 12 Aug 1819 (LG)
RAW 19 July 1821 (LG)
RAR 27 May 1825 (LG)
VAB 22 July 1830 (LG)
VAW 10 Jan 1837 (LG)
VAR 28 June 1838 (LG)
KCB 4 July 1840 (DNB)
AB 23 Nov 1841 (LG)
AW 20 Nov 1846 (LG)
AR 15 Sept 1849 (LG)
AF 25 June 1858 (DNB)
GCB 18 May 1860 (DNB)
d 14 Apr 1862 (PJP)

WEST, Joseph
See WEST, John

WEST, Joseph
L 6 July 1814
CR 23 Nov 1841 (OB)

WEST, Matthew Thomas
L 1 Oct 1814
d 1841 (OB)

WEST, Richard
L 10 June 1730

WEST, Temple
L 23 Feb 1734
CR 4 Apr 1737 (DNB)
CA 13 June 1738
Dismissed 11 Feb 1744
Restored 1746 (MPS)
MP (Buckingham) 17 Jan 1753–1754 (MPS)

RAR	6 Feb	1755
COM AD	17 Nov	1756–
	6 Apr	1757 (AO)
VAB	8 Dec	1756
VAW		1757
COM AD	2 July–9 Aug	1757 (AO)
d	9 Aug	1757 (AO)
WEST, Thomas (1)		
L	22 Feb	1759
WEST, Thomas (2)		
L	11 Apr	1769
CR	30 May	1777
CA	19 Oct	1780
RAB	14 Feb	1799
RAW	1 Jan	1801
RAR	23 Apr	1804
VAW	9 Nov	1805
VAR	23 Apr	1808
AB	31 July	1810
AW	4 June	1814
WEST, William (1)		
L	12 Oct	1802
WEST, William (2)		
L	18 July	1812
WEST, William Wade		
L	11 Apr	1810
HP		1819 (OB)
WESTBEACH, Joseph (1)		
L	27 May	1793
CR	16 Nov	1796
d		1811 (PMM)
WESTBEACH, Joseph (2)		
L		1811 (PJP)
WESTBROOK, Edmund Barford		
L	6 July	1815
CR	1 Jan	1839 (OB)
WESTCOMB, James		
L	20 May	1695
WESTCOTT, George Blagden		
L	6 Aug	1777
CR	1 Dec	1787
CA	1 Oct	1790
KIA	2 Aug	1798 (LG)
WESTCOTT, John		
L	6 Aug	1798
WESTERN, Thomas		
L	10 Sept	1780
CR	24 Apr	1793
CA	12 Nov	1795
RAB	4 June	1814
Kt (Portugal)	26 Aug	1814 (LG)
d	26 Dec	1814 (CH)
WESTFIELD, Crosby		
L	30 Mar	1734
WESTLAKE, Bernard		
L	10 Aug	1759
WESTLAKE, William Hole		
L	20 Nov	1812
WESTLEY, George		
L	30 July	1742
WESTON, Francis		
L	7 Feb	1704 (PMM)
WESTON, George		
L	17 Dec	1714
WESTON, James		
L	17 Sept	1740
WESTON, John		
L	22 Nov	1790
KIA	21 Mar	1793 (LT)
WESTPHAL, Philip		
L	4 Apr	1808 (DNB)
CR	13 June	1815
CA	22 July	1855 (DNB)
Ret RA	27 Sept	1855 (DNB)
Ret VA	4 Oct	1862 (DNB)
Ret A	2 Apr	1866 (DNB)
d	16 Mar	1880 (DNB)
WESTPHAL, Sir George Augustus		
T	wounded	
L	15 Aug	1806
CR	8 July	1813
CA	12 Aug	1819 (MB)
Kt	7 Apr	1824 (DNB)
RA	17 Aug	1851 (DNB)
VA	10 Sept	1857 (DNB)
A	23 Mar	1863 (DNB)
d	11 Jan	1875 (DNB)
WESTROPP, Amos Freeman		
L	21 Dec	1797
T		
CR	12 Aug	1812
CA	7 Dec	1818 (MB)
d		1844 (TR)
WETENHALL, Thomas		
L	28 Feb	1766
WETHERALL, Frederick Augustus		
L	24 Feb	1807
CR	15 June	1814
CA	13 Nov	1826 (MB)
Ret CA	31 Oct	1846 (LG)
d	21 Dec	1856 (PMM)
WETWANG, Sir John		
L		
CA		1665
Kt	20 Nov	1680 (DNB)
d		1684 (DNB)
WETWANG, Joseph		
L		1678
WETWORTH, Michael		
L		1780 (PJP)
WEYMOUTH, Richard		
L	9 Feb	1801
CR	13 Dec	1814
d	Aug	1832 (OB)
WEYMYS, John		
L		
CA		1673
WHALEY, Thomas		
L	26 Dec	1809
d	27 Oct	1820 (LT)
WHARAM, James		
L	8 Nov	1794
WHARTON, George		
L		1709 (PJP)
WHARTON, John Francis		
L	26 Dec	1798
Ret CR	10 May	1838 (OB)
d	Oct	1848 (OB)
WHARTON, Thomas		
L	31 Jan	1806

WHATLEY, John
L
CA 1665 (DDA)
WHATLEY, Thomas
L
CA 1665
d before 1689 (PJP)
WHATLING, Henry
L 12 Sept 1810
WHEADEN, H.
L 1790 (PJP)
WHEATE, Sir Jacob
L 20 June 1765
CR 15 Nov 1779
CA 2 Apr 1782
WHEATLEY, Francis
L 8 Nov 1781
WHEATLEY, John Hood
L 9 Feb 1815
WHEELER, Daniel
L 5 Dec 1695 (PJP)
WHEELER, Edward
L 23 Jan 1742
CR
CA 5 July 1748
KIA 1 Apr 1761 (CH)
WHE(E)LER, Sir Francis (1)
CAGA (Windsor) 22 Oct 1674 (EAD)
L 30 Apr 1678
CA 11 Sept 1680
CAF
(1st Foot Guards) 26 Jan 1683 (EAD)
Kt Aug 1683 (DNB)
LCF 12 June 1687 (EAD)
RAB Oct 1692 (PMM)
RAR 1693
d (drowned) 19 Feb 1694 (DNB)
WHEELER, Francis (2)
L
CA 28 July 1683
d 19 Feb 1693
WHEELER, John
L 25 Feb 1815
HP Dec 1825 (OB)
WHEELER, Samuel
L 6 July 1814
WHEELOCK, John
L 26 June 1741
CR 19 Feb 1756
CA 21 Dec 1757
d 1779 (M)
WHELON, John
L 12 July 1800
WHETSTONE, Sir William
L
CA 30 July 1689
RAB 8 Jan 1704
RAW 13 Jan 1705
(18 Jan in C)
Kt 22 Feb 1705 (DNB)
Dismissed 1707 (PJP)
d May 1711 (DNB)
WHILLEY, John
L 19 July 1802
WHIMPER, William
L 20 Apr 1802

WHINFIELD, Philip
L 12 July 1809
WHINGATES, George B.
See WHINYATES, George B.
WHINGATES, Thomas
See WHINYATES, Thomas
WHINYATES, George B.
L 11 Aug 1804
CR 2 Jan 1806
d 5 Aug 1808 (DNB)
WHINYATES, Thomas
L 7 Sept 1799
CR 16 May 1805
CA 12 Aug 1812
Ret RA 31 Oct 1846 (LG)
d 15 Mar 1857 (DNB)
WHIPPLE, John
L 28 Aug 1794
CR 8 Oct 1798
WHISTON, John (1)
L 1673
CA 20 Oct 1677
WHISTON, John (2)
L 19 June 1760
WHISTON, John (3)
L 31 Mar 1794
WHITACRE, Samuel
See WHITAKER, Samuel
WHITAKER, Sir Edward
L 6 Oct 1688
CA 15 May 1690
RAB Dec 1705 (DNB)
Kt 1706 (DNB)
RAR 17 Jan 1708
AB 20 Dec 1708
VAB 21 Dec 1708
VAW 14 Nov 1709
(12 Nov in C)
Dismissed 1715 (PJP)
d 20 Nov 1735 (DNB)
WHITAKER, John (1)
L 4 Mar 1782
WHITAKER, John (2)
L 15 Feb 1815
WHITAKER, Samuel
L 21 June 1694 (PJP)
CA 15 June 1695
In Merchant Service 1700 (PJP)
d (drowned) 22 Oct 1707 (CH)
WHITAKER, Thomas (1)
L 19 Jan 1705
SUP 20 Mar 1738 (PMM)
WHITAKER, Thomas (2)
L 22 Dec 1809
CR 13 June 1815
WHITAKER, Thomas W.
L 24 Nov 1801
d 1 Jan 1839 (LT)
WHITBY, Henry
L 4 June 1799
d 6 May 1812 (PJP)
WHITBY, J.
L 1802 (PJP)
WHITBY, John
L Apr 1780 (PJP)
CR

CA	20 Apr	1793 (PJP)
d	7 Apr	1806 (PJP)
WHITCOMB, Robert		
L	8 Feb	1815
WHITCOMBE, Samuel Richard		
L	6 Mar	1815
HP		1825 (OB)
WHITE, Abraham Harcourt		
L	20 Jan	1808
KIA	19 June	1808 (CH)
WHITE, Charles		
L	2 May	1782
CR	24 Mar	1794
CA	13 July	1795
d	12 Apr	1810 (PMM)
WHITE, Charles Samuel		
L	13 June	1808
CR	24 Sept	1814
CA	26 Dec	1822 (MB)
d	23 May	1823 (MB)
WHITE, David		
L	27 Oct	1758
WHITE, Edward		
L	6 Nov	1801
WHITE, Frederick Lea		
T	wounded	
L	10 Feb	1812
CR	9 Nov	1846 (OB)
d		1859 (TR)
WHITE, George (1)		
L	16 July	1759
WHITE, George (2)		
L	1 Aug	1793
CR	26 Apr	1798
CA	30 Aug	1799
WHITE, George (3)		
T		
L	2 Nov	1809
Ret CR	2 Mar	1849 (OB)
d		1852 (TR)
WHITE, Gerard		
L		1661
CA		1665
d	before	1689 (PJP)
WHITE, Hugh Brice		
L	15 Jan	1802
T		
d		1847 (TR)
WHITE, Isaac		
L		
CA		1668
KIA	28 May	1673 (LG)
WHITE, James (1)		
L		1690 (PMM)
WHITE, James (2)		
L	27 Oct	1758
d		1790 (PJP)
WHITE, James (3)		
L	31 Jan	1806
WHITE, James Kearney		
L		
CR	10 June	1811
CA	7 Dec	1818 (MB)
d	2 Mar	1828 (MB)
WHITE, John (1)		
L	26 Apr	1800
Ret CR	23 Jan	1832 (OB)
WHITE, John (2)		
L	12 Sept	1807
Ret CR	15 Apr	1844 (OB)
WHITE, Sir John Chambers		
L	22 Nov	1790
CR	28 Aug	1795
CA	2 Aug	1799
RAW	22 July	1830 (LG)
VAB	10 Jan	1837 (LG)
KCB	29 June	1841 (OB)
VAW	23 Nov	1841 (LG)
d	4 Apr	1845 (OB)
WHITE, Joseph (1)		
L	2 Apr	1798
WHITE, Joseph (2)		
L	6 Feb	1815
WHITE, Mark		
T		
L	13 Aug	1810
CR	10 Oct	1815
HP	10 Oct	1815 (OB)
d		1850 (TR)
WHITE, Martin		
L	12 Dec	1800
CR	25 Sept	1806
CA	7 Dec	1818 (MB)
Ret CA	31 Oct	1846 (LG)
RA	8 July	1851 (PMM)
VA	22 Aug	1857 (PMM)
WHITE, Oliver		
L	7 July	1756
WHITE, Peter		
L	16 July	1812
WHITE, Richard (1)		
L		1664
CA		1665
KIA	4 June	1673 (HJ)
WHITE, Richard (2)		
L	13 Nov	1692 (PJP)
WHITE, Richard (3)		
L		
CA	28 Apr	1696
d	27 Apr	1701 (LTE)
WHITE, Richard (4)		
L	20 Feb	1815
WHITE, Thomas (1)		
L		
CA		1673
d	before	1689 (PJP)
WHITE, Thomas (2)		
L		1689 (PJP)
WHITE, Thomas (3)		
L	4 Mar	1783
CR	8 Oct	1798
CA	21 Oct	1810
d		1833 (PJP)
WHITE, Thomas (4)		
L	19 July	1790
CR	17 Aug	1798
CA	7 Aug	1810
HP	4 May	1839 (OB)
Ret RA	31 Oct	1846 (LG)
d	31 Dec	1846 (OB)

Name	Rank	Date	Year
WHITE, Thomas (5)			
	L	20 Nov	1799
WHITE, William (1)			
	L		1665
WHITE, William (2)			
	L	29 Aug	1772
	CR	17 July	1780
	CA	28 Aug	1783
	d	26 Jan	1801
WHITE, William (3)			
	L	20 Aug	1794
	Ret CR	26 Nov	1830 (OB)
	d		1846 (OB)
WHITE, William (4)			
	L	7 Apr	1795
	d	14 Feb	1801
WHITE, William (5)			
	L	29 Apr	1796
WHITE, William (6)			
	L	12 June	1807
	d	Feb	1809 (PJP)
WHITE, William (7)			
	L	24 Feb	1815
	HP	24 Feb	1815 (OB)
	d		1847 (OB)
WHITE, William Grove			
	L	29 Mar	1815
WHITEHEAD, Abraham			
	L	20 Mar	1815 (OB)
	HP		1825 (OB)
WHITEHEAD, Richard			
	L	3 Feb	1797
	d	25 Mar	1837 (PJP)
WHITEHEAD, Robert Ellis			
	L	8 Mar	1804
WHITEHEAD, William			
	L	4 Mar	1815
WHITEHOUSE, John			
	L	10 Aug	1775
WHITEHURST, Frederick John			
	L	20 Nov	1812
WHITEHURST, Thomas			
	L	11 Oct	1759
	d (duel)		1765 (PMM)
WHITEING, John			
	L		1703 (PJP)
WHITEING, Richard			
	L		
	CA		1660
	d	26 May	1662 (DDA)
WHITEING, William			
	L		
	CA		1672
WHITELOCK, James Bulstrode			
	L	21 Mar	1812
WHITELOCK, William			
	L	21 Oct	1793
WHITEMAN, William			
	L		1757 (PJP)
WHITEWAY, Samuel			
	L	21 Dec	1808
	Ret CR	3 Nov	1846 (OB)
WHITEWOOD, Edward			
	L	31 May	1746
WHITEWOOD, Thomas			
	L	18 Apr	1811
WHITEY, John			
See WHITTY, Thomas			
WHITLEY, Peter			
	L		1668
WHITLEY, Robert			
	L	11 Mar	1719
WHITLOCK, Bulstrode			
	L	?28 Mar	1667
	d	28 July	1675 (M)
WHITLY, John			
	L	3 Sept	1779
	CR	20 July	1795
	d	20 Jan	1803
WHITLY, Joseph			
	L	11 Dec	1797
WHITMORE, Nathaniel Courtenay			
	L	11 Feb	1815
WHITMORE, Roger			
	L		1738 (PJP)
WHITMORE, William			
	L	19 Jan	1771
WHITNEY, Thomas			
	L		
	CR		
	CA	13 Oct	1716
	d	9 Dec	1741
WHITSHED, Sir James Hawkins			
Formerly HAWKINS, James			
	L	4 Sept	1778
	CR	10 Feb	1780
	CA	18 Apr	1780
	RAW	14 Feb	1799
	RAR	1 Jan	1801
	VAB	23 Apr	1804
	VAW	9 Nov	1805
	VAR	28 Apr	1808
	AB	31 July	1810
	AW	12 Aug	1812
	KCB	12 Apr	1815 (LG)
	AR	19 July	1821 (LG)
	GCB	1 Dec	1830 (LG)
	Cre Bt	16 May	1834 (DNB)
	AF	8 Jan	1844 (DNB)
	d	28 Oct	1849 (DNB)
WHITSTRONG, James			
	L	17 May	1708 (PMM)
WHITTAKER, Edward			
See WHITAKER, Sir Edward			
WHITTAKER, Samuel			
See WHITAKER, Samuel			
WHITTER, Header			
	L	8 Feb	1794
	CR	1 Jan	1801
	CA	22 Nov	1806
WHITTER, Tristam			
	L	30 Oct	1790
	CR	24 Aug	1795
	d	22 Jan	1801
WHITTHORN, James			
	L	5 July	1811
WHITTINGTON, Charles			
	L		1672
WHITTLE, D.			
	L		1798 (PJP)
WHITTLE, Henry			
	L	16 Mar	1809

Name / Rank	Date	Year
WHITTLE, Price Warren		
L	5 Jan	1762
d (drowned)		1798 (CH)
WHITTOLL, John		
L		
CR	29 May	1696 (PJP)
WHITTON, Thomas		
L	3 May	1746
WHITTY, Thomas		
L		
CA		1665
KIA	4 June	1666 (RM)
WHITWELL, Matthew		
L	10 Jan	1741
CR	5 Dec	1747
CA	6 May	1748
SUP RA		1779
d	15 Feb	1789
WHITWORTH, William		
L		
CR		
CA	2 June	1715
d	28 Apr	1721 (M)
WHORWOOD, Thomas		
L		
CR		
CA	1 Jan	1713
COMM (Deptford)	15 June 30 Jan	1744– 1745 (NBO)
d	13 Feb	1746 (NBO)
WHORWOOD, William Henry		
L	8 Dec	1798
CR	27 Dec	1808
WHYMPER, William		
L	29 Apr	1802 (OB)
Ret CR	21 Dec	1841 (OB)
WHYTE, Adam		
L	22 Sept	1806
WHYTE, Edward		
L	2 May	1804
CR	6 Dec	1813
d		1837 (PJP)
WHYTE, John		
L	4 Aug	1794
CR	24 Apr	1799
CA	19 Apr	1802
WHYTE, Mark		
L	24 Jan	1756
WHYTE, Nicholas Charles		
L	25 Sept	1806
WICKEY, John		
L	25 Nov	1778
CR	16 Apr	1781
CA	22 Aug	1781
RAB	1 Jan	1801
RAW	23 Apr	1804
VAB	9 Nov	1805
VAW	28 Apr	1808
VAR	31 July	1810
AB	4 Dec	1813
AW	12 Aug	1819 (LG)
AR	22 July	1830 (LG)
d	9 July	1833 (CH)
WICKHAM, Francis		
L	28 July	1794
WICKHAM, George		
L	21 Jan	1771
WICKHAM, Henry		
L	17 June	1685
CA	May	1689 (PJP)
Dismissed	21 Sept	1693
Given life in prison.		
WICKHAM, John		
L	24 Nov	1731
CR		
CA	1 Nov	1742
SUP RA		1759
d	21 Oct	1763
WICKHAM, Power		
L	17 Jan	1718
WICKHAM, Samuel (1)		
L	5 May	1780
Dismissed	25 July	1781 (PJP)
WICKHAM, Samuel (2)		
L	4 Dec	1782
WICKHAM, William		
L	11 Aug	1797
WIDDRINGTON, Samuel Edward		
L	10 June	1809
CR	3 June	1824 (MB)
Ret CR	1 July	1851 (PRO)
d	11 Jan	1856 (PRO)
WIGHT, John		
L	8 Sept	1796
CR	3 Jan	1798
CA	29 Apr	1802
Ret RA	10 Jan	1837 (OB)
RAW	17 Aug	1840 (LG)
RAR	23 Nov	1841 (LG)
VAB	9 Nov	1846 (LG)
VAW	17 Dec	1847 (LG)
VAR	14 Jan	1850 (LG)
Ret A	17 Dec	1852 (CH)
WIGHTMAN, Thomas		
L	20 Nov	1782
WIGHTMAN, William		
L	8 Oct	1756
WIGLEY, John Gwyn		
L	30 Aug	1806
CR	23 Nov	1841 (OB)
WIGMORE, Edmund Thomas		
L	9 July	1778
KIA	17 Apr	1780 (LG)
WIGONER, John		
L		
CA		1667
WIGSTON, James		
L	13 June	1811
CR	14 Jan	1822 (MB)
CA	22 July	1830 (MB)
WILBRAHAM, James		
L	12 Feb	1801
WILBRAHAM, Richard		
L	8 Oct	1801
CR	15 June	1814
HP	15 June	1814 (OB)
d	29 Nov	1824 (PJP)
WILBRAHAM, William		
L	24 Feb	1801
CR	12 Aug	1807
CA	13 Jan	1809
WILBY, John		
L	26 Nov	1776

WILCOCKS, Thomas
L 14 May 1703
SUP 20 Mar 1738 (PMM)
d 1741 (PMM)
WILCOX, James
L 23 June 1806
d (drowned) 25 Dec 1811 (PJP)
WILCOX, Robert
See WILLCOX, Robert
WILD, Barron
L 2 Jan 1683
CA 25 Feb 1694
WILD, Daniel
L 1803 (PJP)
WILD, John
L 1673 (PJP)
WILDE, Charles
See WYLDE, Charles
WILDE, Charles
L 1678 (PMM)
WILDE, Henry
L
CA 1 May 1696
d 1706
WILDE, Thomas
See WYLDE, Thomas
WILDEY, Henry
L 3 Nov 1797
CR 3 May 1810
Ret CA 10 Sept 1840 (OB)
WILDING, Alexander
See WILLDING, Alexander
WILDING, Peter Mainwaring
L 17 Jan 1749
d 2 May 1766 (PMM)
WILES, Habback
L
CA 1667 (DDA)
WILEY, John (1)
L 3 Oct 1798
WILEY, John (2)
L 21 June 1800
WILFORD, Robert
L 1672
CA 19 Dec 1678
d before 1689 (PJP)
WILGRESS, John
L
CA 1660
d before 1689 (PJP)
WILKES, Anthony
L 24 June 1708 (PMM)
WILKES, Thomas
L 12 Dec 1796
WILKIE, Alexander
L 16 Feb 1742
d 26 Jan 1759 (PMM)
WILKIE, James (1)
L 9 Dec 1748
WILKIE, James (2)
T
L 19 Oct 1807
d 1821 (TR)
WILKIE, John
L 4 June 1814
d 26 Aug 1835 (PJP)

WILKINS, John (1)
L 4 Mar 1794
WILKINS, John (2)
L 13 July 1809
d 8 June 1815 (PJP)
WILKINS, Michael
L
CA 23 Feb 1694
d 16 Aug 1694
WILKINS, Thomas (1)
L 29 Apr 1795
WILKINS, Thomas (2)
L 27 Jan 1809
WILKINS, William
L 3 Dec 1751
WILKINSON, Andrew
L 22 Aug 1747
CR 2 Aug 1756
CA 23 Mar 1757
d 24 May 1787 (M)
WILKINSON, Benjamin
L 9 Apr 1796
WILKINSON, George
L 9 Jan 1760
CR 27 May 1780
CA 14 May 1781
d (drowned) Sept 1782 (CH)
WILKINSON, James
L 26 Oct 1814
CR 31 Jan 1828 (MB)
In Portuguese Service 1833 (PJP)
CA 3 July 1840 (OB)
WILKINSON, John
L 14 Aug 1811
WILKINSON, Mathew
L 2 Jan 1759
WILKINSON, Philip
L 22 Oct 1790
CR 30 Mar 1794
CA 5 Sept 1794
RAB 4 Dec 1813
RAW 4 June 1814
RAR 12 Aug 1819 (CH)
VAB 19 July 1821 (CH)
VAW 27 May 1825 (CH)
VAR 22 July 1830 (CH)
AB 10 Jan 1837 (CH)
AW 23 Nov 1841 (CH)
AR 9 Nov 1846 (CH)
d 1846 (CH)
WILKINSON, Richard
L 21 Jan 1692 (PJP)
WILKINSON, Robert
L 1672
CA 1665
WILKINSON, Stephen
L 19 Sept 1815
WILKINSON, Thomas
L 22 Aug 1759
CR 4 Sept 1766
CA 10 June 1771
d 1776
WILKINSON, Thomas L.
L 10 Dec 1810
WILKINSON, William (1)
L 29 Apr 1797
CR 27 Apr 1801

CA	21 Oct	1810
d	28 Feb	1816 (PJP)
WILKINSON, William (2)		
L	1 May	1798
WILKINSON, William (3)		
L	23 Feb	1815
WILKINSON, William (4)		
L	15 June	1815
WILKS, Anthony		
L	24 June	1708
WILKS, Thomas		
L		1797 (PJP)
WILKSHAW, Francis		
L		1665
CA	9 June	1666 (RM)
d		1686 (DDA)
WILKSHAW, Thomas		
L		
CA	23 Aug	1666 (RM)
WILLBRAHAM, William		
See WILBRAHAM, William		
WILLCOX, Robert		
L	16 May	1809
CR	6 Sept	1823 (MB)
HP		1846 (OB)
WILLDING, Alexander		
L	25 Feb	1815
WILLES, Cornelius		
L	16 Aug	1806
d	10 July	1810 (OB)
WILLES, George Wickins		
L	6 Nov	1801
CR	2 June	1810
CA	7 June	1814
d	26 Oct	1814 (OB)
WILLES, John (1)		
L	1 Mar	1749
SUP CR	21 Sept	1796 (PMM)
WILLES, John (2)		
L	30 May	1778
d		1804 (PJP)
WILLETT, William Saltern		
L	23 July	1741
CR	Dec	1745 (PJP)
CA	1 Oct	1747 (PJP)
d	Dec	1769 (M)
WILLETTS, Moses de		
L		1808 (PJP)
KIA	3 Sept	1808 (PJP)
WILLEY, Edmund		
L		
CA	16 Apr	1695 (PJP)
William Henry, Duke of Clarence		
See CLARENCE, Duke of		
WILLIAMS, Augustus Aldborough Lloyd		
L	18 Jan	1813
HP	Jan	1815 (OB)
WILLIAMS, Bosville		
L	27 July	1736
SUP		1750 (PMM)
d		1757 (PMM)
WILLIAMS, Charles (1)		
L	22 Feb	1797
d		1810 (PJP)
WILLIAMS, Charles (2)		
L	9 Apr	1808
KIA	5 June	1813 (CH)
WILLIAMS, Charles David		
L	27 Oct	1797
WILLIAMS, Charles Hamlyn		
L	24 Apr	1811 (OB)
CR	27 Aug	1814 (OB)
CA	4 July	1832 (OB)
RA	19 May	1856 (NMM)
d		1858 (NMM)
WILLIAMS, Cornelius		
L		1712 (PJP)
WILLIAMS, Courtenay		
L	8 Apr	1760
WILLIAMS, David (1)		
L	1 Sept	1794
WILLIAMS, David (2)		
L	7 Jan	1799
WILLIAMS, Edmund (1)		
L	8 Nov	1708
CR		
CA	2 Apr	1734
Dismissed	17 Oct	1745
Restored		1745 (CH)
HP		1745 (CH)
SUP RA	3 May	1750 (PMM)
d	1 Mar	1752 (M)
WILLIAMS, Edmund (2)		
L	2 Nov	1734
d	27 Apr	1741 (PMM)
WILLIAMS, Edward (1)		
L		1664
WILLIAMS, Edward (2)		
L		1735 (PJP)
WILLIAMS, Edward (3)		
L	26 May	1795
WILLIAMS, Edward (4)		
L	3 Sept	1795
T		
CR	24 Dec	1805
d		1843 (TR)
WILLIAMS, Edward (5)		
L		1779
CR	Mar	1797
d	21 Jan	1839 (LT)
WILLIAMS, Edward Richard		
L	14 Dec	1813
CR	15 Dec	1815
CA	28 Apr	1827 (OB)
HP	Apr	1836 (OB)
WILLIAMS, Henry (1)		
L		
CA		1667
d	23 Dec	1667 (M)
WILLIAMS, Henry (2)		
L		
CA	7 Jan	1677
WILLIAMS, Henry (3)		
L	13 Feb	1800
WILLIAMS, Henry More		
L	4 Apr	1812
WILLIAMS, Henry Peter		
L	26 Nov	1808
WILLIAMS, James (1)		
L	22 Apr	1769

CR	12 June	1780
CA	1 Jan	1781
d	2 Apr	1792 (LT)
WILLIAMS, James (2)		
L	16 Mar	1814
WILLIAMS, John (1)		
L	28 Mar	1693
CR		
CA	25 Sept	1706
d	6 Nov	1711
WILLIAMS, John (2)		
L	14 Sept	1732
CR	18 July	1740
d	Feb	1779 (PMM)
WILLIAMS, John (3)		
L	4 Mar	1740
WILLIAMS, John (4)		
L		1776 (PJP)
WILLIAMS, John (5)		
L	23 Jan	1783
WILLIAMS, John (6)		
L	22 Oct	1797
CR	13 Oct	1807
CA	4 Mar	1811
d	12 Apr	1824 (MB)
WILLIAMS, John (7)		
L	8 Feb	1815
WILLIAMS, John (8)		
L	20 Mar	1815 (OB)
WILLIAMS, John Poulton		
L	29 Apr	1802
T		
KIA	30 July	1809 (TR)
WILLIAMS, John Sutton		
L	9 Feb	1815
WILLIAMS, Jonathan		
L	29 Nov	1738
SUP		1754 (PMM)
d	6 June	1763 (PMM)
WILLIAMS, Joseph (1)		
L		1677
WILLIAMS, Joseph (2)		
L	17 Nov	1807
d		1848 (OB)
WILLIAMS, Owen (1)		
L	7 Dec	1782
WILLIAMS, Owen (2)		
L	1 June	1797
WILLIAMS, Peter		
L	27 Feb	1801
CR	27 Aug	1814
d		1839 (PMM)
WILLIAMS, Richard (1)		
L	15 Aug	1746
CR	5 May	1781
CA	27 June	1799
WILLIAMS, Richard (2)		
L	26 Feb	1800
WILLIAMS, Richard (3)		
L	13 Dec	1804
CR	Sept	1828 (MB)
WILLIAMS, Richard (4)		
L	4 May	1810
WILLIAMS, Richard Nicholls		
L	3 Nov	1813
WILLIAMS, Robert (1)		
L	25 Feb	1778
SUP CR	14 Sept	1813
d	15 Oct	1827 (LT)
WILLIAMS, Robert (2)		
L	15 Aug	1781
CR	5 May	1800
d	7 Mar	1831 (MB)
WILLIAMS, Robert (3)		
L	12 Feb	1783
CR	8 Mar	1797
CA	10 Nov	1797
RAB	9 Apr	1823 (DNB)
RAW	27 May	1825 (LG)
d	1 Mar	1827 (DNB)
WILLIAMS, Roger		
L	7 Oct	1756
CR	27 Aug	1760
WILLIAMS, Samuel		
L	4 Mar	1796
WILLIAMS, Thomas		
See WILLYAMS, Thomas		
WILLIAMS, Thomas (1)		
L	2 Mar	1734
CR	27 Feb	1741
CA	23 Apr	1744
d	11 May	1754
WILLIAMS, Thomas (2)		
L	10 Aug	1746
WILLIAMS, Sir Thomas (3)		
L	8 Dec	1779
CR	15 Apr	1783
CA	22 Nov	1790
Kt		1796 (DNB)
CRM	28 Apr	1808 (MB)
RAB	25 Oct	1809
RAW	31 July	1810
RAR	12 Aug	1812
VAB	4 June	1814
KCB	2 Jan	1815 (LG)
VAW	12 Aug	1819 (LG)
VAR	19 July	1821 (LG)
AB	22 July	1830 (CH)
GCB	13 Sept	1831 (LG)
AW	10 Jan	1837 (CH)
d	10 Oct	1841 (PJP)
WILLIAMS, Thomas (4)		
L	15 May	1780
d	2 Sept	1781 (MB)
WILLIAMS, Thomas (5)		
L	25 Dec	1800
CR	27 June	1814
HP	Nov	1815 (OB)
d	Jan	1849 (OB)
WILLIAMS, Thomas (6)		
L	14 Feb	1815
WILLIAMS, Thomas (7)		
L	16 Feb	1815
WILLIAMS, Thomas Mark		
L	20 Feb	1815 (PMM)
WILLIAMS, Vincent		
L	22 Oct	1751
WILLIAMS, William (1)		
L	25 May	1741
Gone		1752

WILLIAMS, William (2)
L 25 Sept 1742
WILLIAMS, William (3)
L 10 Feb 1757
CR 2 Mar 1759
CA 10 Jan 1771
d Sept 1778 (CH)
WILLIAMS, William (4)
L 17 Nov 1778
WILLIAMS, William (5)
L 4 Jan 1783
WILLIAMS, William John
L 6 Mar 1815
HP 6 Mar 1815 (OB)
WILLIAMS, William Paul
L 2 Feb 1815
WILLIAMS, William Peere
L 18 Sept 1764
CR 26 May 1768
CA 10 Jan 1771
RAW 12 Apr 1794
RAR 4 July 1794
VAW 11 June 1795
AB 14 Feb 1799
AW 9 Nov 1805
AR 25 Oct 1809
AF 28 June 1830 (DNB)
d 11 Feb 1832 (DNB)
WILLIAMS, Woodford
L 6 Feb 1806
KIA 14 May 1807 (CH)
WILLIAMSON, Allan Martin
L 13 June 1815
d 1833 (PJP)
WILLIAMSON, George
L 10 Apr 1807
WILLIAMSON, Innocent
L 21 Jan 1783
WILLIAMSON, John
L 8 Mar 1774
CR 3 Oct 1780
CA 11 June 1782
Court–martialed after action of
11 Oct 1797. Not employed again (PRO)
d 1799 (PJP)
WILLIAMSON, Neilson
L 17 Jan 1810
d 1846 (OB)
WILLIAMSON, Robert
L
CA 1660
d before 1688 (PD)
WILLIAMSON, Thomas
L 25 Mar 1809
WILLIAMSON, William (1)
L 1707 (PJP)
WILLIAMSON, William (2)
L 6 Oct 1744
CR 15 Nov 1756 (PJP)
CA 18 Oct 1758
d 13 June 1771
WILLIAMSON, William (3)
L 24 Apr 1780
WILLIAMSON, William (4)
L 9 Aug 1793

WILLIS, Francis
L
CR
CA 20 Sept 1714
d (drowned) 10 Nov 1729 (CH)
WILLIS, Harry Bulkeley
L 11 Mar 1815
WILLIS, James W.
L 13 Dec 1809
HP 24 Aug 1809 (OB)
WILLIS, John (1)
L 1672
d before 1689 (PJP)
WILLIS, John (2)
L 21 May 1800
WILLIS, Joseph
L 13 Apr 1741
d 25 Nov 1749 (PMM)
WILLIS, Richard (1)
L 1 Jan 1698
In Merchant Service 1700 (PJP)
WILLIS, Richard (2)
L 23 Oct 1778
CR
CA 3 Nov 1790
SUP RA May 1808 (LT)
d 29 Jan 1829 (LT)
WILLIS, Thomas (1)
L 11 July 1747
CR 5 June 1759
CA 4 Apr 1761
d 1766
WILLIS, Thomas (2)
L 11 Feb 1778
WILLISON, John
L 17 Jan 1811
d 1847 (OB)
WILLMORE, Cornelius (1)
?WILMOT, Cornelius
L 1690 (PJP)
CA 1693 (PJP)
d (drowned) 22 Aug 1695 (CH)
WILLMORE, Cornelius (2)
L 1712 (PJP)
WILLMOTT, David
L 3 Aug 1793
CR 7 Sept 1798
KIA 8 Apr 1799 (LG)
WILLMOTT, William
L 1660
WILLOCK, Francis Gore
L 12 June 1807
CR 4 Mar 1811
CA 24 Nov 1815
d 18 Jan 1834 (LT)
WILLOUGHBY, Hon. Digby, Lord
See MIDDLETON, Hon. Digby, Lord
WILLOUGHBY, Henry Frere
L 13 Mar 1815
WILLOUGHBY, Sir Josiah Nesbit
L 13 Jan 1798
Dismissed 23 June 1801 (PJP)
Restored 26 Oct 1803 (PJP)
CR 9 Apr 1808
CA 5 Sept 1810
In Russian Army 1812–1814 (DNB)

CB	4 Jan	1815 (DNB)
Kt	30 June	1827 (DNB)
KCH	21 Aug	1832 (DNB)
RAB	28 Apr	1847 (LG)
RAW	9 May	1849 (LG)
d	19 May	1849 (DNB)
WILLOUGHBY, Thomas		
L		
CA		1665
KIA	25 June	1667 (CH)
WILLOUGHBY, William		
L	13 Nov	1810
WILLS, Abraham		
L	7 Jan	1783
WILLS, Austin		
L	1 Apr	1697
WILLS, Francis		
L	9 Jan	1801
T		
Gone		1811 (TR)
WILLS, George		
L	15 June	1808
KIA	7 Feb	1813 (LG)
WILLS, John (1)		
L	23 Feb	1757
d	8 Apr	1804
WILLS, John (2)		
L	25 Sept	1806
WILLS, John (3)		
L	7 Sept	1815
HP	7 Sept	1815 (OB)
WILLS, Methuselah		
T		
L	25 May	1811
d		1842 (TR)
WILLS, Michael		
L	11 Feb	1801
d		1802 (PJP)
WILLS, Roger		
L	12 Oct	1745
CR	25 June	1775
WILLS, Thomas		
L	20 Oct	1779
d	20 Oct	1792
WILLS, Thomas George		
L	22 Jan	1806
CR	27 May	1820 (MB)
CA	7 Jan	1835 (OB)
d	11 May	1847 (OB)
WIL(L)SHAW, Thomas		
COMM (Portsmouth)		1690 (PJP)
L	1 Sept	1693
CA	15 May	1696
d	23 Sept	1702 (NBO)
WILLSON, George		
L	7 May	1804
WILLSON, James		
L	23 May	1694
WILLSON, John (1)		
L	2 Mar	1734
CR		
CA	13 Aug	1744
d	18 Oct	1750 (PMM)
WILLSON, John (2)		
L	16 May	1809
CR	6 June	1815
d	17 July	1820 (LT)
WILLSON, John (3)		
L	8 Feb	1815
CR	23 Nov	1841 (OB)
HP	25 Apr	1842 (OB)
WILLSON, Jonathan		
L	7 Mar	1697
WILLSON, Richard		
L		1745 (PJP)
WILLSON, Robert		
L	17 July	1778
WILLSON, Senhouse		
L	4 Dec	1807
WILLSON, William		
L	11 Jan	1696
WILLYAMS, John		
See WILLIAMS, John		
WILLYAMS, Thomas		
L	11 Mar	1691 (PJP)
CR	21 Oct	1695 (PJP)
CA	9 July	1715
d	21 July	1752
WILMOT, Robert		
L		
CR	Mar	1690 (PJP)
CA		1692
d	15 Sept	1695 (DNB)
WILMOT, William		
L	22 Oct	1802
WILMOTT, Charles More		
L	26 July	1799
WILSFORD, Christopher		
L	5 Dec	1718
WILSHAW, Benjamin		
L		1702 (PJP)
WILSHAW, Francis		
See WILKSHAW, Francis		
WILSHAW, Thomas		
See WILKSHAW, Thomas		
WILSHAW, Thomas		
See WIL(L)SHAW, Thomas		
WILSON, Albany Howard		
L	27 May	1813
WILSON, Alexander (1)		
L	1 Dec	1787
WILSON, Alexander (2)		
L	1 June	1794
CR	29 June	1795
CA	2 Sept	1795
SUP CA	18 July	1814
d		1834 (OB)
WILSON, Alexander (3)		
L	1 Feb	1815
WILSON, Andrew		
L	20 Feb	1800
CR	17 Sept	1812
WILSON, Charles (1)		
L	15 Feb	1780
WILSON, Charles (2)		
L	10 Aug	1801
d (drowned)	2 Apr	1804 (PJP)
WILSON, David		
L	17 Apr	1802

WILSON, Edward Hughes
L 8 Dec 1794
WILSON, George (1)
L 28 Jan 1776
CR
CA 1 Feb 1780
RAW 14 Feb 1799
RAR 1 Jan 1801
VAB 23 Apr 1804
VAR 9 Nov 1805
AB 25 Oct 1809
AW 31 July 1810
AR 12 Aug 1819 (LG)
d 6 Mar 1826 (LT)
WILSON, George (2)
L 20 Aug 1794
Ret CR 9 Oct 1834 (OB)
WILSON, George (3)
L 15 Feb 1815
HP 15 Feb 1815 (OB)
WILSON, Harry
L 26 Apr 1811
WILSON, Henry Smith
L 9 Sept 1799
CR 19 July 1821 (MB)
d 22 Dec 1844 (OB)
WILSON, James (1)
L 10 Nov 1745
d 18 Dec 1750 (PMM)
WILSON, James (2)
L 5 Feb 1798
WILSON, James (3)
L 22 Jan 1806
CR 18 Sept 1828 (MB)
HP 18 Sept 1828 (OB)
WILSON, John (1)
L 13 Apr 1752
CR 15 Nov 1756
d 1796
WILSON, John (2)
L 1755 (PJP)
WILSON, John (3)
L 13 Nov 1796
CR 27 Dec 1808
CA 7 June 1814
WILSON, John (4)
L 16 May 1809
CR 6 June 1815
CA 22 Oct 1830 (MB)
WILSON, John (5)
L 23 Feb 1815
WILSON, John (6)
L 14 Mar 1815
WILSON, John Smith
L 9 Feb 1815
WILSON, Orlando Hart
L 1 Mar 1815 (OB)
d 3 Jan 1845 (OB)
WILSON, Ralph
L 5 Apr 1780
WILSON, Richard
L 3 July 1719
WILSON, Robert (1)
L 31 Aug 1739
CR 21 Sept 1747
d (drowned) 14 Apr 1749 (PJP)

WILSON, Robert (2)
L 6 Apr 1758
d 14 June 1787 (PMM)
WILSON, Robert (3)
L 17 July 1778
d 29 Mar 1798
WILSON, Robert (4)
L 14 May 1784
d Dec 1797
WILSON, Thomas (1)
L 10 May 1779
CR 20 Jan 1783
d 19 Apr 1783 (LG)
WILSON, Thomas (2)
L 11 Jan 1808
WILSON, Thomas (3)
L 6 July 1811
CR 26 Aug 1814
WILSON, Thomas Henry
L 11 Feb 1794
CR 15 June 1814
WILSON, William (1)
L 23 Dec 1702
SUP 20 Mar 1738 (PMM)
WILSON, William (2)
L 10 Aug 1759
WILSON, William (3)
L 27 Aug 1779
WILSON, William (4)
L 3 Sept 1802
WILWARD, Thomas
L 1760 (PJP)
WIMBLETON, Charles
L 24 Dec 1732
CR 23 Apr 1741
WIMBLETON, Richard
L 28 June 1777
KIA 12 Apr 1782 (RLB)
WINDEYER, Walter
L 21 Oct 1806
CR 13 June 1815
d 19 Aug 1837 (LT)
WINDER, Joseph
L 19 Jan 1694
CR
CA 1 Dec 1706
d 18 Mar 1738
WINDHAM, Charles
See WYNDHAM, Charles
WINDHAM, James
L 9 Feb 1709 (PMM)
CR
CA 30 May 1721
d 3 Jan 1725 (PJP)
WINDHAM, William
L 1793
CR 1795
CA 28 Nov 1795
RAB 4 June 1814
RAR 27 May 1825 (LG)
VAW 22 July 1830 (LG)
d Jan 1833 (LT)
WINDSOR, Edward
L 31 July 1693 (PJP)
CR 30 Oct 1695 (PJP)

CA 12 Feb 1703
Dismissed 23 July 1708 (LG)
d 23 July 1709

WINDSOR, Hon. James
L
CR 14 Feb 1777

WINDSOR, Hon. Thomas
L 27 Mar 1772
CR 14 Feb 1777 (PJP)
CA 7 Feb 1778
Resigned 1795

WING, Thomas
L 7 Nov 1804
d 29 Sept 1838 (LT)

WINGATE, George Thomas
L 10 Aug 1798
CR 15 June 1814

WINGATE, John
L 10 Nov 1722
CR
CA 6 Apr 1732
d 18 May 1760 (M)

WINGATE, Robert
L 5 Apr 1704 (PMM)

WINGFIELD, David
L 20 Mar 1815
HP 20 Mar 1815 (OB)

WINGFIELD, George
L 1689 (PJP)

WINGRAVE, John
L 21 Mar 1812

WINKWORTH, Grosvenor
L 21 Aug 1778
CR 7 June 1793
CA 6 Dec 1796
d 14 Aug 1802 (LT)

WINLACK, George Bryon
T
L 17 Mar 1806
Gone 1810 (TR)

WINLACK, William
L 17 Dec 1807

WINN, Pelham
L 6 Aug 1709

WINN, Robert
See WYNN, Robert

WINNE, John
L 19 Nov 1790
CR 21 Apr 1799
CA 28 Apr 1802

WINNEL, John
L
CR
CA 14 June 1739
d June 1750

WINNIETT, Edward
L 15 Dec 1761

WINTER, John
L 19 Apr 1774

WINTER, Robert
L 27 Dec 1808

WINTER, Thomas
L 17 Apr 1742

WINTERBOTTOM, John
L 16 Feb 1815
HP 16 Feb 1815 (OB)

WINTERBOTTOM, Richard
L 1782 (PJP)
KIA 12 Apr 1782 (PJP)

WINTHROP, Robert
L 3 Nov 1790
CR
CA 16 Dec 1796 (MB)
RAB 12 Aug 1819 (LG)
RAW 19 July 1821 (LG)
RAR 27 May 1825 (LG)
VAB 22 July 1830 (OB)
d 10 May 1832 (PJP)

WINTLE, Fred Broughton
L 5 Sept 1810
d 5 Sept 1817 (PJP)

WINTON, Ebenezer
L 6 May 1809
d 9 Apr 1818 (PJP)

WINTON, Henry
L 23 Feb 1815

WINTOUR, C.F.
L 1778 (PJP)

WINTOUR, Charles Forth
L 1 Mar 1794
d 5 Aug 1817 (PJP)

WINTOUR, George Stevenson
L 19 Nov 1790
CR 24 Feb 1824 (PMM)
d 16 June 1839 (LT)

WINZAR, David
L 14 Feb 1757

WISCARD, Benjamin
L 13 Sept 1707 (PMM)

WISE, Abraham
L
CA 1689 (PJP)
d (drowned) 18 Mar 1690 (CH)

WISE, Chapman
L 29 Mar 1815

WISE, George Samuel
L 20 Aug 1800

WISE, Henry
L 20 Apr 1811

WISE, John
L 10 Feb 1815

WISE, William Furlong
L 1 May 1804
CR 1 Nov 1805
CA 18 May 1806
CB 21 Sept 1816 (DNB)
RAB 23 Nov 1841 (LG)
d 29 Apr 1844 (DNB)

WISEMAN, Robert
L 1673
CA 25 Sept 1688
SUP 3 Apr 1693 (PJP)
d 10 Jan 1694 (PJP)

WISEMAN, Sir William Saltonstall
L 30 Apr 1807
Cre Bt 30 Jan 1810 (LT)
CR 24 Sept 1811
CA 22 Nov 1820 (MB)
d 1 July 1845 (OB)

WISHART, Sir James
L

CA 4 July 1689
RAB 8 Jan 1704
Kt 8 Jan 1704 (DNB)
MCLHA 20 June–28 Oct 1708 (AO)
AB 20 Dec 1708
COM AD 20 Dec 1710–
14 Oct 1714 (AO)
MP
(Portsmouth) 1711–1715 (DNB)
AW 8 Dec 1713
Dismissed 1715
d 31 May 1723 (DNB)

WITHERS, Francis
L 6 Apr 1727

WITHERS, George
L 4 Apr 1720

WITHERS, James
L 1799 (PJP)

WITHERS, John
L
CA 1664
d before 1689 (PJP)

WITHERS, Joseph
L 19 Nov 1790
d 1802 (PJP)

WITHERS, Thomas
L 22 Mar 1797
CR 11 Apr 1803
CA 13 May 1809
d 4 July 1843 (DNB)

WITHERSPOON, David
L 20 Mar 1761

WITHERSPOON, John
L 24 Oct 1777
SUP CR 30 Mar 1814

WITHY, John
L 12 Oct 1759

WITTERONG, James
L 17 May 1708

WITTERONG, Thomas
L 1704 (PJP)

WITTMAN, Josiah
L 17 Mar 1781
CR 12 Dec 1796
d 13 Jan 1810 (PJP)

WITTS, Thomas
L 3 Feb 1696 (LTE)

WIVELL, Francis
See WYVELL, Francis

WODEHOUSE, J.
L 1801 (PJP)

WODEHOUSE, Hon. Philip
L 6 Jan 1794
CR 1796 (PJP)
CA 23 Dec 1796
COMM
(Halifax) 1811–1819 (PJP)
RAB 12 Aug 1819 (MB)
RAW 27 May 1825 (LG)
VAB 22 July 1830 (LG)
VAW 10 Jan 1837 (LG)
d 21 Jan 1838 (OB)

WOLFE, George
L 24 Dec 1794
CR 1 Sept 1797
CA 10 Dec 1800
CB 4 June 1815 (LG)
d 1825 (PJP)

WOLFE, William
L 23 Aug 1759

WOLGER, John
L 1660

WOLLASTON, Charles
L 25 Oct 1790 (OB)
CR 6 Dec 1796
CA 1 Jan 1801
Ret RA 22 July 1830 (OB)
RAR 17 Aug 1840 (LG)
VAB 23 Nov 1841 (LG)
d 19 Feb 1845 (OB)

WOLLASTON, Robert
L 23 Oct 1758

WOLLEY, Isaac
L 16 Oct 1793
CR 3 Jan 1795
CA 1 Sept 1797
COMM
(Port Mahon) 1813–1818 (PJP)

WOLLEY, Thomas
L 31 Oct 1777
CR Nov 1793 (PJP)
CA 19 Dec 1793
RAB 1 Aug 1811
RAW 4 Dec 1813
RAR 4 June 1814
VAB 12 Aug 1819 (CH)
VAW 19 July 1821 (CH)

WOLRIGE, Charles
T
L 5 Jan 1808
Ret CR 3 Mar 1857 (PMM)
d 1874 (TR)

WOLRIGE, Thomas
L 29 Mar 1802
CR 24 Jan 1811
CA 19 July 1822 (MB)
d 1 Dec 1845 (OB)

WOLRIGE, William
L 23 Mar 1807 (OB)
CR 13 Mar 1811
CA 7 Dec 1818 (MB)
Ret CA 31 Oct 1846 (LG)
RA 8 July 1851 (PMM)
VA 22 Aug 1857 (PMM)
A 22 Nov 1862 (PMM)
d 19 June 1863 (PMM)

WOLSELEY, Charles
L
CR 17 Nov 1760
CA 4 Nov 1761 (CH)
MP
(Milborne Port) 1775–1780 (MPN)
RAB 21 Sept 1790
RAR 1 Feb 1793
VAB 12 Apr 1794
VAW 4 July 1794
VAR 1 June 1795
AB 14 Feb 1799
AW 1 Jan 1801
AR 9 Nov 1805
d 10 Apr 1808 (MPN)

WOLSELEY, William
L 11 June 1778
CR 3 Sept 1782

CA 14 Sept 1782
RAB 23 Apr 1804
RAW 9 Nov 1805
RAR 28 Apr 1808
VAB 25 Oct 1809
VAW 31 July 1810
VAR 4 Dec 1813
AB 12 Aug 1819 (CH)
AW 27 May 1825 (CH)
AR 10 Jan 1837 (CH)
d 7 June 1842 (DNB)

WOLSTONECRAFT, James
L 7 Feb 1805

WOOD, Andrew (1)
L 1665

WOOD, Andrew (2)
L 11 Feb 1780
Struck off list 13 Apr 1791 (PMM)

WOOD, Basil
L 4 Apr 1720

WOOD, Charles (1)
L 15 Oct 1756
CR 4 June 1779
CA 23 July 1781
KIA 3 Sept 1782 (PJP)

WOOD, Charles (2)
L 11 May 1804
T
d 1820 (TR)

WOOD, George (1)
L 20 Jan 1746

WOOD, George (2)
L 16 Oct 1798
Ret CR 24 Dec 1830 (OB)
d 30 Aug 1846 (OB)

WOOD, George Francis
L 6 Dec 1813
d 9 Aug 1827 (LT)

WOOD, George Herbert
L 30 July 1793

WOOD, Giles
L 1672
d 1673 (PMM)

WOOD, Jacob
L 27 Jan 1801

WOOD, James (1)
L 1782 (PJP)

WOOD, James (2)
L 2 Aug 1794

WOOD, James (3)
L 19 Dec 1808

WOOD, James (4)
L 11 Feb 1815
HP 11 Feb 1815 (OB)

WOOD, James (5)
L 13 Feb 1815

WOOD, Sir James Athol
L 18 Oct 1778
CR 8 July 1795
CA 27 Mar 1797
MP
(Gatton) 1806–1807 (MPT)
Kt 1810 (PJP)
KCB 4 June 1815 (LG)
RAB 19 July 1821 (MB)
RAW 27 May 1825 (LG)
d July 1829 (DNB)

WOOD, James Moneypenny
L 23 Feb 1815

WOOD, John (1)
L 1671
CA 1660
d before 1689 (PJP)

WOOD, John (2)
L 1673 (DDA)
CA 1673 (DDA)

WOOD, John (3)
L 15 Mar 1692 (PMM)
CR 20 Jan 1707 (PMM)
CA 1 Jan 1713 (PMM)
d 8 Nov 1725 (PMM)

WOOD, John (4)
L 22 May 1704
SUP 20 Mar 1738

WOOD, John (5)
L 30 Mar 1758

WOOD, John (6)
L 6 Dec 1787
CR 4 Apr 1796
CA 13 May 1800
d 24 June 1820 (LT)

WOOD, John (7)
L 6 Sept 1796

WOOD, John (8)
L 23 Sept 1812
HP 1827 (OB)

WOOD, John (9)
L 3 Feb 1815

WOOD, Joseph
L 30 Oct 1790

WOOD, Lambert
L
CA 1665

WOOD, Ralph
L 1691 (PJP)

WOOD, Robert (1)
L 1666 (PJP)
CA 1666
d 9 Apr 1685 (M)

WOOD(D), Robert (2)
L 31 Jan 1800
Ret CR 26 Nov 1830 (OB)
d 1847 (OB)

WOOD, Stephen
L 1746 (PJP)

WOOD, Thomas
L 14 Feb 1778

WOOD, Wagden
L 13 Jan 1740

WOOD, Walter
L
CA 1660
KIA 4 June 1666 (RM)

WOOD, William (1)
L 1 Aug 1801
Ret CR 3 Oct 1831 (OB)
d 28 Aug 1849 (LT)

WOOD, William (2)
L 25 Aug 1801

WOOD, William (3)
L 27 Aug 1814

WOODALL, Thomas
L 1664

WOODBURN, William
L 30 Jan 1742
WOODCOCK, Francis Henry
L 25 May 1811
d 11 Nov 1845 (OB)
WOODCOCK, William (1)
L 15 Oct 1790
WOODCOCK, William (2)
L 1814 (PJP)
WOODEN, John (1)
L
CA 5 Apr 1693 (PJP)
d 20 May 1703 (PJP)
WOODEN, John (2)
L 30 Sept 1705
WOODFORD, James
L 14 Nov 1805
KIA 23 Aug 1807 (LG)
WOODGER, Charles
L 28 Oct 1782
WOODHAM, William Henry
L 15 Feb 1815
WOODHOUSE, Henry Bowman
L 7 Nov 1812
d 2 July 1821 (LT)
WOODIN, John
L 17 Oct 1804
T killed
KIA 21 Oct 1805 (TR)
WOODIN, William Henry
L 31 May 1813
HP 1834 (OB)
WOODLEY, John
L 8 July 1785
CR 12 Nov 1790
CA 9 Feb 1793
d (drowned) 11 Feb 1796 (CH)
WOODLEY, William
L 25 June 1812
CR 11 Mar 1816 (OB)
HP 11 Mar 1816 (OB)
WOODMAN, Henry Frederick
L 25 July 1794
WOODMAN, James
L 1748 (PJP)
WOODMAN, William Ingle
L 3 May 1804
HP Dec 1813 (OB)
WOODNOTT, Edward
L 22 Nov 1778
WOODON, Thomas
L 1702 (PJP)
WOODRIDGE, James
L
CR 13 Oct 1807
WOODRIFF, Daniel
L 1 Apr 1783
CR 18 Sept 1795
CA 28 Apr 1802
CB 26 Sept 1832 (OB)
d 24 Feb 1842 (OB)
WOODRIFF, Daniel James
T
L 11 Dec 1807
CR 22 Sept 1822 (PJP)
HP 22 Sept 1822 (OB)
d 1860 (TR)

WOODRIFF, John Robert
L 26 Apr 1811
CR 1 Jan 1848 (OB)
WOODRIFF, Robert M.
L 1 Aug 1811
d 1 Mar 1820 (LT)
WOODS, David
L 20 Sept 1800
WOODWARD, Augustine
L 21 Mar 1812
WOODWARD, James
L 28 Nov 1800
WOODWARD, John
L 25 Apr 1746
WOODWARD, Richard
L 1667
WOODYATT, Thomas
T
L 7 Feb 1811
d 1841 (TR)
WOODYEAR, Thomas
L 30 Jan 1778
d 2 Aug 1792
WOOLCOCK, William (1)
L 25 Mar 1809
WOOLCOCK, William (2)
L 28 Dec 1810
d 1846 (OB)
WOOLCOMBE, Edward
L 22 Apr 1802
CR 6 June 1804
CA 29 Sept 1808
d Dec 1824 (MB)
WOOLCOMBE, John Charles
L 14 Nov 1801
CR 1 May 1804
CA 17 Oct 1804
WOOLDRIGE, James
L 27 May 1794
CR
CA 11 Apr 1809
d 3 Sept 1814 (LT)
WOOLFE, John
L 1748 (PJP)
WOOLGATE, Stephen
L
CA 21 July 1690
d 1690
WOOLLAMS, Francis
L 28 Feb 1815
d Jan 1847 (OB)
WOOLLARD, William
T
L 26 Sept 1809
Gone 1810 (TR)
WOOLLCOMBE, George
L 23 Feb 1815
CR Apr 1824 (MB)
CA 22 July 1830 (MB)
WOOLLETT, Thomas Spencer
L 13 June 1815
WOOLNOUGH, Sir Joseph Chappell
T
L 19 Jan 1811
Kt (Russian) 1814 (TR)
CR 8 May 1828 (MB)

Kt		1834 (TR)
d	17 Apr	1839 (LT)
WOOLRIDGE, Francis		
L	24 Jan	1760
CR	29 June	1782
d		1805 (PJP)
WOOLRIDGE, Francis William		
L	9 May	1783
WOOLRIDGE, James		
See WOOLRIGE, James		
WOOLRIDGE, William		
L	25 Dec	1774
CR	22 Jan	1802
CA	10 June	1807
d		1820 (PJP)
WOOLS, John		
L	31 Jan	1797
WOOLSEY, William		
L	9 May	1801
CR	14 Mar	1805
d (drowned)	June	1806 (CH)
WOOLSTONCRAFT, J.		
L		1794 (PJP)
WOOLVER, Richard James		
L	8 Feb	1815
HP	Dec	1842 (OB)
WOOLWARD, John		
L	10 Feb	1802
d	16 Feb	1836 (LT)
WOOTTON, Peter		
See WATTON, Peter		
WORLEDGE, Joseph		
L		1702 (PMM)
WORLOCK, John		
L	13 Dec	1777
WORMELEY, Ralph Randolph		
L	22 Jan	1806
CR	16 Feb	1810
CA	7 June	1814
RAB	9 Oct	1849 (LG)
d		1852 (CH)
WORRALL, John		
L	17 June	1795
d	30 June	1831 (LT)
WORRELL, John		
L		
CA	23 Dec	1693 (PJP)
d	16 Dec	1706
WORSLEY, Miller		
T		
L	12 July	1813
CR	13 July	1815
d		1835 (TR)
WORSLEY, Richard		
L	4 Nov	1790
CR	24 June	1794
CA	29 Nov	1797
RAB	9 Apr	1823 (MB)
RAW	27 May	1825 (LG)
RAR	22 July	1830 (LG)
VAW	10 Jan	1837 (LG)
d	25 Jan	1838 (LT)
WORTH, Charles Oliver		
L	30 Nov	1779
d	12 Apr	1800
WORTH, James		
L	20 Apr	1744
CR	1 July	1760 (PJP)
CA	2 Nov	1772
SUP RA		1795
WORTH, James Andrew		
L	22 Oct	1794
CR	29 Mar	1799
CA	21 Oct	1810
WORTH, John		
L	26 May	1798
CR	21 Aug	1809
WORTH, Joseph		
L	7 May	1804
d (drowned)	5 Jan	1807 (PJP)
WORTH, Philip		
L	3 Sept	1745
WORTHINGTON, Benjamin		
L	2 Feb	1813
HP	23 Nov	1814 (OB)
WORTHINGTON, James		
L		
CA	28 Dec	1695
d (drowned)	6 Oct	1697 (PJP)
WORTHY, John Dewdney		
L	7 Feb	1812
WOTTON, Peter		
See WATTON, Peter		
WRAY, Charles		
L	24 June	1739
CR		
CA	9 Dec	1746
d		1773
WRAY, Henry		
L	5 June	1780
CR	22 June	1795
d		1825 (MB)
WRAY, Luke Henry		
L	14 Apr	1805
CR	29 Dec	1824 (MB)
HP	Dec	1825 (OB)
WRAY, Nicholas		
L	2 Apr	1794
WRAYFORD, Michael		
L	10 Nov	1795
Ret CR	28 Apr	1836 (OB)
d	Jan	1847 (OB)
WREN, John		
L	5 Feb	1780
WRENCH, Matthew		
L	14 Nov	1790
CR	27 Mar	1797
d	7 June	1831 (MB)
WRENN, Ralph		
L	23 Feb	1675
CA	10 July	1677
d	26 Mar	1692 (CH)
WRENTMORE, John		
L	4 May	1810
WRIFORD, Samuel		
L	22 Nov	1805
CR	10 Oct	1815
WRIGHT, David		
L	9 July	1798
WRIGHT, Ezekiel		
L	3 Nov	1703 (PMM)
CR		

CA 1 Jan 1713
d 1736

WRIGHT, Frederick Augustus
L 13 June 1807

WRIGHT, Henry
L 28 Oct 1673

WRIGHT, Jacob
L 1690 (PJP)

WRIGHT, John (1)
L
CA 29 June 1691
d 17 Oct 1691

WRIGHT, John (2)
L 1693 (PJP)

WRIGHT, John (3)
L 13 July 1765
CR 31 May 1780
CA 18 Jan 1783
d 1804 (LT)

WRIGHT, John (4)
L 18 Sept 1797
CR 21 June 1800
CA 29 Apr 1802 (PJP)
Ret RA 1837 (PJP)
RA 17 Aug 1840 (PJP)
VA 9 Nov 1846 (PJP)
A 17 Dec 1852 (PJP)

WRIGHT, John (5)
L 6 July 1814
d 18 Dec 1848 (OB)

WRIGHT, John Allan
L 2 Feb 1813

WRIGHT, John Elworthy Fortunatus
L 6 Dec 1777
d 18 Dec 1798

WRIGHT, John Rogerson Tomkyns
L 14 May 1811
CR 27 Aug 1814

WRIGHT, John Wesley
L 29 Mar 1800
CR 7 May 1802
d (suicide) 28 Oct 1805 (PJP)

WRIGHT, Joseph (1)
L 14 Mar 1802

WRIGHT, Joseph (2)
L 13 June 1815

WRIGHT, Lawrence
L 1665
CA 1672
COMM (Kinsale) 14 May 1702–
8 May 1713 (QAN)
COM E 9 May 1713–
27 Nov 1713 (NBO)
d 27 Nov 1713 (NBO)

WRIGHT, Mayson
L 1 May 1794
CR 7 Oct 1813

WRIGHT, Patrick
L 26 June 1813

WRIGHT, Peter Watson
L 12 June 1804
d (suicide) 23 July 1807 (PJP)

WRIGHT, Philip
L 9 Aug 1806
Ret CR 16 Jan 1840 (OB)

WRIGHT, Robert (1)
L 9 May 1781

WRIGHT, Robert (2)
L 15 Apr 1783

WRIGHT, Thomas (1)
L 1 Oct 1794

WRIGHT, Thomas (2)
L 17 Feb 1815

WRIGHT, William (1)
L
CA 1666

WRIGHT, William (2)
L 13 Oct 1688 (PJP)
CA 12 Nov 1689 (PJP)
COM V 3 Feb 1702–
13 May 1703 (QAN)
COMM (Plymouth) 30 Apr 1703–
9 Feb 1705 (QAN)
COMM (Lisbon) 1705–1707 (QAN)
COMM (Plymouth) 1 July 1708–
25 Dec 1710 (QAN)
d 22 Oct 1735

WRIGHT, William (3)
L
CA 30 Sept 1689
d 9 Nov 1689

WRIGHT, William (4)
L 27 Nov 1779
d 13 Aug 1786 (PMM)

WRIGHT, William (5)
L 6 July 1795

WRIGHT, William (6)
L 8 Feb 1800

WRIGHT, William (7)
L 3 Sept 1802
T
Gone 1809 (TR)

WRIGHT, William Elliott
L 11 Dec 1807
CR 20 Aug 1817 (MB)
Dismissed 1817 (MB)
Restored 1819 (MB)

WROOT, Michael Milson
L 21 Nov 1807
CR 11 May 1827 (MB)
HP May 1828 (OB)

WROTH, Philip
L 5 Aug 1691 (PJP)

WROTH, William
L 1689 (PJP)

WROTTESLEY, Edward
L 10 June 1807
CR 7 Jan 1812
d 28 July 1814 (PJP)

WYARD, Robert
L
CA 1661
d before 1689 (PJP)

WYATT, Francis
L 4 Apr 1740
CR 7 Mar 1748
CA 17 Aug 1756
d 1777

WYATT, Henry Benjamin
L 3 July 1809
CR 18 Sept 1815
HP 18 Sept 1815 (OB)
d 11 June 1863 (PMM)

WYATT, John
L 14 Feb 1696

WYATT, Richard
L
CA 6 Mar 1693
d 14 Dec 1703

WYATT, William Madox
L 24 Mar 1808

WYBERGH, Hilton Cris
L 29 Aug 1745

WYBERGH, Peter
L 18 May 1814
CR 31 Mar 1824 (MB)
d Jan 1849 (OB)

WYBORN, Hercules
L 30 July 1762
CR 19 Nov 1777
CA 29 Jan 1781

WYBORN, John
L 19 Nov 1801
CR 18 Dec 1809
Ret CA 10 Sept 1840 (OB)
d 1846 (OB)

WYBORNE, John
L
CA 1666

WYBOURNE, Joshua
L 30 June 1741

WYDOWN, James Lewis
L 11 Sept 1794

WYE, Edward (1)
L
CA 1661
d before 1689 (PJP)

WYE, Edward (2)
L 3 May 1711

WYE, Richard
L
CA 1673
d before 1689 (PJP)

WYE, Thomas
L 25 June 1744

WYKE, William
L 11 June 1793

WYLD, Henry
L
CA 1 May 1696

WYLDE, Baron
L
CA 24 Dec 1694
Dismissed Oct 1707 (PRO)
Restored with seniority
as CA 8 Oct 1707
Original seniority restored 1724
d 25 Sept 1739 (PJP)

WYLDE, Charles
L
CA 1665
d 17 Mar 1684 (PJP)

WYLDE, Edward
L 16 Mar 1814

WYLDE, Thomas
L 1665
CA 3 Aug 1678

WYLEY, Habbkuk
L 19 Jan 1702

WYLEY, John
L 27 Nov 1702 (PMM)

WYLIE, Hugh
L 10 Apr 1802

WYLLY, William Cunningham
L 29 Dec 1814

WYNCH, Robert
L 30 July 1773

WYNDHAM, Charles
L
CR
CA 12 Jan 1733
d 6 May 1747 (M)

WYNDHAM, George
L 7 July 1806
CR 30 Apr 1810
CA 3 July 1812

WYNELL, John Salt
L 26 May 1768

WYNN, Robert
L 14 Dec 1688 (PJP)
CA 17 Feb 1692

WYNNE, John
L 1 Sept 1741
CR 20 Jan 1747

WYNNELL, John
L 16 Mar 1720
CR 30 Mar 1727
CA 14 June 1739
d 1759

WYNTER, Delamore
L 3 June 1797
CR 22 Jan 1806
d 10 Apr 1810 (PJP)

WYSE, Thomas
L 16 May 1727

WYVELL, Francis
L 22 Mar 1682
CA 28 Sept 1688
d 22 Dec 1729 (M)

WYVILL, Christopher
L 5 July 1813
CR 29 July 1824 (DNB)
CA 22 Feb 1832 (DNB)
RA 31 Jan 1856 (DNB)
d 29 Jan 1863 (DNB)

YALDWYN, Richard
L 29 July 1813

YARD, Eastly
L 7 Sept 1697

YARD, William
L 8 Mar 1778

YARKER, Robert
L 23 Aug 1794
CR 10 Apr 1805
CA 29 Apr 1808

YATES, Edward Vernon
L 29 Oct 1755
CR 2 June 1760

YATES, Ezekiel
L 16 Jan 1692 (PMM)

YATES, James Thomas
L 27 June 1814
HP 27 June 1814 (OB)

YATES, Lenox M'Bean
L 31 Aug 1809
d 17 Sept 1812 (PJP)

YATES, Richard Augustus
L 10 May 1809
CR 7 June 1814
CA 12 Mar 1827 (MB)

YATES, Robert B.
L 5 Sept 1800
CR 15 Nov 1814
HP 15 Nov 1814 (OB)

YATES, Robert Winthrop
L 14 Feb 1810

YATES, Thomas
L 24 June 1782
d 1794 (PMM)

YATES, Vernon Gambier
L 12 Nov 1801
d 26 Sept 1802 (PJP)

YEAMAN, Alexander
L 10 Feb 1815

YEAMANS, Sherwood
L 1755 (PJP)

YEATES, Edward Vernon
L
CR 2 June 1760
d 20 Apr 1801

YEATS, John Samuel
L 2 Feb 1815
HP 2 Feb 1815 (OB)

YELLAND, Edward (1)
L 27 Oct 1778

YELLAND, Edward (2)
L 25 Feb 1815

YELLAND, James
L 1800 (PJP)

YELLAND, John
L 13 Mar 1783
CR 27 Apr 1801
CA 22 Jan 1806

YENNIS, Ezekiel
L 1665
CA 1672
KIA 28 May 1672 (CH)

YENNIS, John
L 14 Feb 1705 (PMM)

YEO, George Colby
L 9 June 1815

YEO, Sir James Lucas
L 20 Feb 1797
CR 21 June 1805
CA 19 Dec 1807
Kt
(Portugal) 17 Mar 1810 (LG)
Kt 21 June 1810 (LG)
KCB 2 Jan 1815 (DNB)
d 21 Aug 1818 (DNB)

YEO, John
L
CR
CA 27 June 1718
SUP RA 25 July 1747
d 1 Dec 1756 (M)

YEO, William
L 20 June 1776
CR 10 Oct 1778
CA 21 Dec 1782
d 15 June 1808 (LT)

YEOMAN, A.
L 1815 (PJP)

YEOMAN, Bernard
L 6 Feb 1812
CR 15 June 1815 (MB)
CA 22 July 1830 (MB)
d 1836 (PJP)

YEOMANS, Sherwood
L 6 Feb 1755

YETTS, John
L 19 Jan 1761

YETTS, Robert
L 31 Mar 1796

YONGE, Charles Brown
L 10 Nov 1804

YONGE, Edward
L 6 Mar 1815
CR 10 Feb 1830 (MB)
CA 23 Nov 1841 (OB)
HP 26 Jan 1842 (OB)

YONGE, William
L 8 July 1748
CR 5 Aug 1755

YORK, Edward Augustus, Duke of
See Edward Augustus, Duke of York

YORKE, Sir Joseph Sidney
L 16 June 1789
MP
(Reigate) 1790–1806 (MPT)
CR 19 Nov 1790
CA 4 Feb 1793
Kt 21 Apr 1805 (MPT)
MP
(St. Germans) 1806–Apr 1810 (MPT)
COM AD 3 July 1810–
2 Apr 1818 (AO)
RAB 31 July 1810
MP
(West Looe) 1812 (MPT)
RAW 12 Aug 1812
MP
(Sandwich) 1812–1818 (MPT)
RAR 4 Dec 1813
VAB 4 June 1814
KCB 2 Jan 1815 (LG)
MP
(Reigate) 1818–May 1831 (MPT)
VAW 12 Aug 1819 (CH)
VAR 27 May 1825 (CH)
AB 22 July 1830 (CH)
d 5 May 1831 (CH)

YOUEL, Edward
L 21 Nov 1812 (OB)
HP 1839 (OB)

YOUNG, Alexander
L 30 Aug 1806
Ret CR 9 July 1840 (OB)

YOUNG, Andrew
L 22 Jan 1806

YOUNG, Anthony
L 1673

CA	9 July	1679
KIA	9 Dec	1703 (LG)
YOUNG, Archibald (1)		
L	20 Nov	1782
YOUNG, Archibald (2)		
L	10 June	1795
YOUNG, Benjamin (1)		
L		
CA	26 July	1666 (RM)
KIA	July	1670 (CH)
YOUNG, Benjamin (2)		
L	9 Sept	1709
CR	20 June	1728
CA	27 Sept	1740
d		1754 (PJP)
YOUNG, Benjamin (3)		
L	20 Nov	1741
YOUNG, Charles		
L	30 Aug	1800
d	20 Feb	1816 (PJP)
YOUNG, David		
L	7 Jan	1747
YOUNG, Sir George (1)		
L	16 Nov	1761
CR	29 Sept	1768
CA	7 Nov	1777
Kt	24 Aug	1781 (DNB)
RAB	23 Oct	1794
RAR	1 June	1795
VAW	14 Feb	1799
VAR	1 Jan	1801
AB	23 Apr	1804
AW	28 Apr	1808
d	28 June	1810 (DNB)
YOUNG, George (2)		
L	27 Nov	1805
YOUNG, George (3)		
L	22 Sept	1808
Ret CR	27 Jan	1846 (OB)
YOUNG, George (4)		
L	3 May	1810
CR	30 Nov	1817 (MB)
YOUNG, George Forbes Freeman		
L	20 Nov	1790
d		1799 (PJP)
YOUNG, Gilbert		
L	25 July	1740
CR	3 July	1746
d	5 Apr	1755 (M)
YOUNG, Harry		
L		1666
CA		1666
d	before	1689 (PJP)
YOUNG, Isaac		
L	28 Oct	1695
In Merchant Service		1700 (PJP)
d	3 May	1763 (M)
YOUNG, Jacob Ley		
L	7 Apr	1813
CR	12 Oct	1847 (OB)
YOUNG, James (1)		
L	9 Mar	1739
CR		1742 (CH)
CA	16 May	1743
RAR	21 Oct	1762 (CH)
VAW	28 Oct	1770 (CH)
VAR	31 Mar	1775
AW	29 Jan	1778 (CH)
d	24 Jan	1789 (CH)
YOUNG, James (2)		
L	10 Oct	1782
CR	17 Apr	1794
CA	5 Oct	1795
RAB	4 June	1814
RAW	12 Aug	1819 (LG)
RAR	19 July	1821 (LG)
VAB	27 May	1825 (LG)
VAW	22 July	1830 (LG)
d	8 Mar	1833 (OB)
YOUNG, James (3)		
L	10 Feb	1801
YOUNG, James (4)		
L	2 Feb	1813
YOUNG, John (1)		
L		
CA		1672
YOUNG, John (2)		
L	11 Feb	1744
YOUNG, John (3)		
L	17 Oct	1745
YOUNG, John (4)		
L	2 Sept	1762
CR	9 Dec	1780
CA	3 Oct	1796
d	25 Nov	1797 (LT)
YOUNG, John James		
L	14 July	1796
YOUNG, John T.		
L	11 Apr	1803
HP	29 Dec	1813 (OB)
Ret CR	23 Jan	1836 (OB)
d		1848 (OB)
YOUNG, John Wilmot		
L	2 Nov	1815
YOUNG, Matthew		
L	13 Feb	1806
Ret CR	15 July	1839 (OB)
YOUNG, Michael		
L		
CA		1665
d	Oct	1675 (M)
YOUNG, Patrick (1)		
L		1704 (PJP)
YOUNG, Patrick (2)		
L	14 Apr	1746
YOUNG, Philip		
L	21 Jan	1704 (PMM)
YOUNG, Richard (1)		
L	27 Sept	1740
d	7 May	1741 (PMM)
YOUNG, Richard (2)		
L	28 June	1796
YOUNG, Robert (1)		
L	12 Apr	1719 (PJP)
CR	13 Apr	1741
CA	1 Oct	1741
d	9 Nov	1750 (PMM)
YOUNG, Robert (2)		
L	28 Aug	1760
YOUNG, Robert (3)		
L	22 Jan	1783

YOUNG, Robert (4)		
L	2 Nov	1797
d		1815 (PJP)
YOUNG, Robert Benjamin		
L	26 Jan	1796
T		
CR	21 Oct	1810
d		1846 (TR)
YOUNG, Robert Parry		
L	18 Oct	1777
d		1798 (TR)
YOUNG, Stewart		
L	6 Feb	1755
YOUNG, Thomas		
L	8 Oct	1801
CR	5 Nov	1806
CA	1 Jan	1817 (MB)
d	5 May	1831 (LT)
YOUNG, Thomas Bristow		
L	18 Apr	1794
CR	24 Nov	1813
d	27 Feb	1846 (OB)
YOUNG, Tobias		
L	20 Oct	1812
YOUNG, Walter		
L	1 Nov	1765
CR	22 Feb	1779
CA	1 Oct	1779
d	2 May	1780 (PMM)
YOUNG, William (1)		
L		1694 (PJP)
YOUNG, William (2)		
L	13 May	1720
YOUNG, Sir William (3)		
L	12 Nov	1770
CR	10 May	1777
CA	23 Sept	1778
CRM	4 July	1794 (AL)
RAW	1 June	1795
COM AD	20 Nov	1795–
	19 Feb	1801 (AO)
VAB	14 Feb	1799
VAW	1 Jan	1801
VAR	23 Apr	1804
AB	9 Nov	1805
AW	31 July	1810
Kt	28 July	1814 (LG)
GCB	2 Jan	1815 (LG)
d	25 Oct	1821 (CH)
YOUNG, William (4)		
L		1781 (LT)
CR	3 July	1798
CA	29 Apr	1802
Ret RA	10 Jan	1837 (OB)
RAW	17 Aug	1840 (LG)
RAR	23 Nov	1841 (LG)
VAB	9 Nov	1846 (LG)
d	11 Feb	1847 (OB)
YOUNGER, Thomas		
L	10 Sept	1800
YOUNGER, William		
L		
CA		1665
YOUNGHUSBAND, George (1)		
L	17 June	1761
d	20 Aug	1792 (M)
YOUNGHUSBAND, George (2)		
L	11 Nov	1794
CR	6 Sept	1800
CA	6 Sept	1804
d	28 July	1806 (PMM)
YOWELL, Edward		
L	21 Nov	1812
YULE, John		
L	11 Mar	1797
T		
CR	24 Dec	1805
d		1840 (TR)
YULE, Robert		
L	2 Oct	1802
Ret CR	12 Feb	1840 (OB)
d	10 Feb	1849 (OB)

Navy Records Society
Works in Print

This list includes all volumes of which stock remains; very few copies are left of that volume (No 46), marked with an asterisk. Members wishing to order any books should write to Mrs Annette Gould, 5 Goodwood Close, Midhurst, West Sussex GU29 9JG, United Kingdom. For orders of a single volume please add £3.15 for postage and packing (to addresses in the British Isles), £9.65 (Europe), £10.65 (elsewhere by sea) or £11.50 (elsewhere by air). For cost of postage and packing of more than one volume, please contact Mrs Gould. No discounts are available from the prices quoted. Any member wishing to purchase large numbers of volumes should write in the first instance to the Hon Secretary.

Titles marked 'TS' and 'SP' are published for the Society by Temple Smith and Scolar Press, and are available to non-members from the Ashgate Publishing Group, Gower House, Croft Road, Aldershot, Hampshire GU11 3HR. Those marked 'A & U' are published by George Allen & Unwin, and are available to non-members only through bookshops.

Vols. 1 and 2. *State papers relating to the Defeat of the Spanish Armada, Anno 1588* Vols. I & II, ed. Professor J.K. Laughton. (£12.00 ea.)

Vol. 11. *Papers relating to the Spanish War, 1585–87*, ed. Julian S. Corbett. (£15.00)

Vol. 16. *Logs of the Great Sea Fights, 1794–1805*, Vol. I, ed. Vice-Admiral Sir T. Sturges Jackson. (£12.00)

Vol. 18. *Logs of the Great Sea Fights, 1794–1805*, Vol. II, ed. Vice-Admiral Sir T. Sturges Jackson . (£12.00)

Vol. 20. *The Naval Miscellany*, Vol. I, ed. Professor J.K. Laughton. (£15.00)

Vol. 31. *The Recollections of Commander James Anthony Gardner, 1775–1814*, ed. Admiral Sir R. Vesey Hamilton and Professor J.K. Laughton. (£15.00)

Vol. 32. *Letters and Papers of Charles, Lord Barham, 1758–1813*, Vol. I, ed. Sir J.K. Laughton (£15.00)

Vol. 38. *Letters and Papers of Charles, Lord Barham, 1758–1813*, Vol. II, ed. Sir J.K. Laughton (£15.00)

Vol. 39. *Letters and Papers of Charles, Lord Barham, 1758–1813*, Vol. III, ed. Sir J.K. Laughton. (£15.00)

Vol. 40. *The Naval Miscellany*, Vol. II, ed. Sir J.K. Laughton. (£15.00)

Vol. 41. *Papers relating to the First Dutch War, 1652–54*, Vol. V, ed. C.T. Atkinson (£10.00)

Vol. 42. *Papers relating to the Loss of Minorca in 1756*, ed. Captain H.W. Richmond. (£15.00)

Vol. 43. *The Naval Tracts of Sir William Monson*, Vol. III, ed. M. Oppenheim. (£10.00)

Vol. 45. *The Naval Tracts of Sir William Monson*, Vol. IV, ed. M. Oppenheim. (£10.00)

Vol. 46.* *The Private Papers of George, Second Earl Spencer*, Vol. I, ed. Julian S. Corbett. (£15.00)

Vol. 47. *The Naval Tracts of Sir William Monson*, Vol. V, ed. M. Oppenheim. (£10.00)

Vol. 49. *Documents relating to Law and Custom of the Sea*, Vol. I, ed. R.G. Marsden. (£15.00)

Vol. 50. *Documents relating to Law and Custom of the Sea*, Vol. II, ed. R.G. Marsden. (£10.00)

Vol. 52. *The Life of Admiral Sir John Leake*, Vol. I, ed. G.A.R. Callender. (£10.00)

Vol. 53. *The Life of Admiral Sir John Leake*, Vol. II, ed. G.A.R. Callender. (£10.00)

Vol. 54. *The Life and Works of Sir Henry Mainwaring*, Vol. I, ed. G.E. Manwaring. (£10.00)

Vol. 60. *Samuel Pepys's Naval Minutes*, ed. Dr. J.R. Tanner. (£15.00)

Vol. 65. *Boteler's Dialogues*, ed. W.G. Perrin. (£10.00)

Vol. 66. *Papers relating to the First Dutch War, 1652–54*, Vol. VI, ed. C.T. Atkinson. (£10.00)

Vol. 67. *The Byng Papers*, Vol. I, ed. W.C.B. Tunstall. (£15.00)

Vol. 68. *The Byng Papers*, Vol. II, ed. W.C.B. Tunstall. (£15.00)

Corrigenda to *Papers relating to the First Dutch War, 1652–54*, ed. Captain A.C. Dewar. (free)

Vol. 70. *The Byng Papers*, Vol. III, ed. W.C.B. Tunstall. (£10.00)

Vol. 73. *The Tangier Papers of Samuel Pepys*, ed. Edwin Chappell. (£15.00)

Vol. 74. *The Tomlinson Papers*, ed. J.G. Bullocke. (£10.00)

Vol. 77. *Letters and Papers of Admiral The Hon. Samuel Barrington*, Vol. I. ed. D. Bonner-Smith. (£10.00)

Vol. 79. *The Journals of Sir Thomas Allin, 1660–1678*, Vol. I, ed. R.C. Anderson. (£10.00)

Vol. 80. *The Journals of Sir Thomas Allin, 1660–1678*, Vol. II, ed. R.C. Anderson. (£10.00)

Vol. 89. *The Sergison Papers, 1688–1702*, ed. Cdr R.D. Merriman. (£10.00)

Vol. 96. *The Keith Papers*, Vol. III, ed. C.C. Lloyd. (£10.00)

Vol. 104. *The Navy and South America, 1807–1823*, ed. Professor G.S. Graham and Professor R.A. Humphreys. (£10.00)

Vol. 107. *The Health of Seamen*, ed. Professor C.C. Lloyd. (£10.00)

Vol. 108. *The Jellicoe Papers*, Vol. I, ed. A. Temple Patterson. (£8.00)

Vol. 111. *The Jellicoe Papers*, Vol. II, ed. A. Temple Patterson. (£10.00)

Vol. 112. *The Rupert and Monck Letterbook, 1666*, ed. Rev. J.R. Powell and E.K. Timings. (£10.00)

Vol. 113. *Documents relating to the Royal Naval Air Service*, Vol. I, ed. Captain S.W. Roskill. (£10.00)

Vol. 114. *The Siege and Capture of Havana, 1762*, ed. Professor David Syrett. (£10.00)

Vol. 116. *The Jacobean Commissions of Enquiry, 1608 and 1618*, ed. Dr. A.P. McGowan. (£10.00)

Vol. 117. *The Keyes Papers*, Vol. I, ed. Dr. Paul G. Halpern. (£10.00)

Vol. 119. *The Manning of the Royal Navy: Selected Public Pamphlets 1693–1873*, ed. Professor J.S. Bromley. (£8.00)

Vol. 120. *Naval Administration, 1715–1750*, ed. Professor D.A. Baugh. (£8.00)

Vol. 121. *The Keyes Papers*, Vol. II, ed. Dr. Paul G. Halpern. (£8.00)

Vol. 122. *The Keyes Papers*, Vol. III, ed. Dr. Paul G . Halpern. (£8.00)

Vol. 123. *The Navy of the Lancastrian Kings: Accounts and Inventories of William Soper, Keeper of the King's Ships 1422–1427*, ed. Dr. Susan Rose. (£10.00)

Vol. 124. *The Pollen Papers: The Privately Circulated Printed Works of Arthur Hungerford Pollen, 1901–1916*, ed. Dr. Jon. T. Sumida. *A&U*. (£10.00)

Vol. 125. *The Naval Miscellany*, Vol. V, ed. N.A.M. Rodger. *A&U*. (£8.00)

Vol. 126. *The Royal Navy in the Mediterranean, 1915–1918*, ed. Professor Paul G. Halpern. *TS*. (£10.00)

Vol. 127. *The Expedition of Sir John Norris and Sir Francis Drake to Spain and Portugal, 1589*, ed. Professor R.B. Wernhan. *TS*. (£10.00)

Vol. 128. *The Beatty Papers, Vol. I, 1902–1918*, ed. Professor B.McL. Ranft. *SP*. (£10.00)

Vol. 129. *The Hawke Papers, A Selection: 1743–1771*, ed. Dr. Ruddock F. Mackay. *SP*. (£15.00)

Vol. 130. *Anglo-American Naval Relations 1917–1919*, ed. Dr. Michael Simpson. *SP*. (£15.00)

Vol. 131. *British Naval Documents 1204–1960*, ed. Professor J.B. Hattendorf, Dr. R.J.B. Knight, A.W.H. Pearsall, Dr. N.A.M. Rodger, and Professor G. Till. *SP*. (£25.00)

Vol. 132. *The Beatty Papers, Vol. II, 1919–1936*, ed. Professor B.McL. Ranft. *SP*. (£25.00)